CRIMINAL LAW

AND

ITS ADMINISTRATION

By

FRED E. INBAU
John Henry Wigmore Professor of Law Emeritus,
Northwestern University

JAMES R. THOMPSON
Attorney-at-Law, Winston and Strawn, Chicago;
Former Governor of Illinois;
Former United States Attorney, Northern District of Illinois;
Former Associate Professor of Law, Northwestern University

JAMES B. ZAGEL
District Judge, United States District Court,
Northern District of Illinois, Eastern Division;
Former Director, Illinois Department of Law Enforcement;
Former Chief, Criminal Division,
Office of Attorney General of Illinois

JAMES P. MANAK
Senior Counsel, Northwestern University
Traffic Institute;
Adjunct Professor of Law, John Marshall Law School,
Chicago, Illinois

SIXTH EDITION

Westbury, New York
THE FOUNDATION PRESS, INC.
1997

615 Merrick Ave.
Westbury, N.Y. 11590–6607
(516) 832–6950

Printed in the United States of America

ISBN 1–56662–402–9

PREFACE

This book is designed, as were its earlier editions, for police officers enrolled in college courses, and for other college students interested in careers in law enforcement. It utilizes the casebook method of instruction rather than a textual treatment. This is precisely the method law school professors employ in the instruction of their students.

The advantages of the casebook method are primarily two-fold: (a) it provides information as to what the law is; and (b) it affords a means for obtaining an insight into why and how appellate courts arrive at their decisions. Such a book also affords an opportunity for the interchange of viewpoints between students and instructor as to the wisdom of the law as it now exists and the direction into which it may, or should be, headed.

The present sixth edition, updated, enlarged, and revised in format, is presented in three parts: (1) Substantive Criminal Law ("The Law of Crimes"); (2) Basic Concepts Regarding Proof of Guilt; and (3) Legal Limitations Upon Law Enforcement Practices. Chapters 12 and 14 have undergone extensive reorganization.

The authors gratefully acknowledge the assistance of Bernard J. Farber, Adjunct Professor of Law at IIT Chicago-Kent College of Law, in revising and updating Chapter 2 of this book.

In addition to reproducing carefully selected case opinions of the Supreme Court of the United States and of other appellate courts, *Criminal Law and Its Administration* contains introductory textual material as well as many notes which implement the objectives underlying the presentations of the main case reports. Also included is a reproduction of those portions of the Constitution of the United States and its Amendments which are relevant to the general problems raised and discussed in the reported cases.

Although the casebook was prepared primarily for the above stated purpose, the authors suggest that its Part 3 is very suitable for a separate law school course on law enforcement practices.

Many of the court opinions in the cases which comprise this casebook have been condensed, and footnotes were either omitted completely or reduced in number. Otherwise this book would be of unmanageable size.

In our textual and note material, whenever "he" and other masculine pronouns are used, they should, in appropriate instances, be considered to mean both females as well as males.

F. E. I.
J. R. T.
J. B. Z.
J. P. M.

October, 1996

*

SUMMARY OF CONTENTS

*

TABLE OF CONTENTS

*

TABLE OF CASES

Principal cases are in bold type. Non-principal cases are in roman type. References are to Pages.

CRIMINAL LAW
AND
ITS ADMINISTRATION

*

PART 1

SUBSTANTIVE CRIMINAL LAW

Chapter 1

OUTLINE OF CRIMINAL PROCEDURE

An outline of criminal procedure is here presented for the purpose of familiarizing the student with the basic procedures that are involved or referred to in the case reports and notes he will be encountering throughout the casebook.

The procedure followed in a criminal case is not the same for all states, but the differences are rather slight as regards basic concepts and principles. In essential respects there is also very little difference between the procedure of the state courts and that which exists in the federal courts.

The following outline of criminal procedure is here presented for the purpose of familiarizing the law student with the basic procedures that are involved or referred to in the case reports he will be encountering in subsequent chapters.

A. PROCEDURE BETWEEN ARREST AND TRIAL

In most states there is a statutory provision to the effect that an arrested person must be taken without unnecessary delay before the nearest judge or magistrate. What happens after presentation to the judge or magistrate will depend upon whether the arrested person is accused of a felony or a misdemeanor. If the charge is a misdemeanor, the judge or magistrate will sometimes have the power and authority to hear the case himself, and he may proceed with the trial unless the accused demands trial by jury or a continuance is requested or ordered for some reason. If the offense charged is a felony, the judge or magistrate before whom the accused is brought will ordinarily lack the constitutional or legislative authority to conduct trials for crimes of that degree of seriousness, and in such instances he only conducts what is known as a "preliminary hearing," which will be subsequently described.

The Right to Bail

After arrest, the first decision made by a court is, frequently, whether the accused is entitled to release on bail. Subject to some exceptions for persons charged with death penalty offenses, persons on parole and others, an accused is entitled to have the court set bail. Bail is fixed at a specific dollar amount. If the accused places cash or property worth that amount with the clerk of court, he will be at liberty pending his trial. If the accused appears at the required proceedings, bail is refunded but failure to appear results in forfeiture of bail. In some states, professional bail bondsmen will, in effect, deposit bail in exchange for a non-refundable fee from the defendant. In other states, a defendant is allowed to deposit a portion of his bail (usually equivalent to the bondsman's fee, i.e., 10%), most of which is refunded if the defendant honors his obligation to appear. Moreover, courts generally have the power to allow release without any deposit—merely accepting the defendant's signature on a bond that makes him liable for the amount of bail if he fails to appear. Such defendants, usually those thought to be highly likely to appear for trial, are said to be released on "recognizance," "signature," or "individual bond." An accused has no right to have bail set at an amount he can meet. A number of defendants will fail to "make" bail and remain in jail pending trial.

Although the U.S. Supreme Court at first declined to consider the issue of preventive detention for adults in Murphy v. Hunt, 455 U.S. 478, 102 S.Ct. 1181 (1982), a 6–3 majority of the Court in Schall v. Martin, 467 U.S. 253, 104 S.Ct. 2403 (1984), had no difficulty resolving the issue for juveniles. In an opinion written by Mr. Justice Rehnquist the Court held that New York's statute providing for the detention of an accused juvenile delinquent on the basis of a finding of a "serious risk" that he may, before his case is adjudicated, commit a criminal act does not violate the Due Process Clause of the Fourteenth Amendment. The Court found a legitimate state interest for such statutes, stating that, "the combined interest in protecting both the community and the juvenile himself from the consequences of future criminal conduct is sufficient to justify such detention." Thus, while the juvenile may have a substantial interest in his freedom, under appropriate circumstances the state's parens patriae interest in promoting his welfare may be paramount. The statute was not used or intended as punishment; the detention was strictly limited in time, and conditions of confinement reflected proper regulatory purposes. The Court also found sufficient procedural protections in the statute to satisfy the Fourteenth Amendment: notice, a hearing, and a statement of facts and reasons were afforded a juvenile prior to any detention; additionally, a formal probable cause hearing was provided shortly thereafter. The Court noted that such statutes have gained universal acceptance among the states:

The traditional purpose of bail is to assure the trial court that the defendant will appear for trial. In 1984 Congress enacted the Bail Reform Act of 1984, 18 U.S.C.A. § 3141 *et seq.,* which provided that bail could be denied in the federal system if (1) there is no reasonable assurance that the person will appear as required, or (2) release will endanger the safety of any other person or the community. The latter provision is in the nature of preventive detention and its constitutionality was at first in doubt.

Doubts about the constitutionality of the preventive detention aspects of the Act, however, were resolved by the U.S. Supreme Court in United States v. Salerno, 481 U.S. 739, 107 S.Ct. 2095 (1987), when the Court approved the key provisions of the Act authorizing pre-trial detention of arrestees facing serious felony charges where the trial court finds that no combination of release conditions can reasonably assure the safety of individuals or the community. The Court rejected a two-prong attack on the statute, due process and the Eighth Amendment Bail Clause. These factors led to a finding of no violation of due process: (1) there is an adversary hearing where the defendant has full procedural rights, including the right to counsel; (2) a finding in favor of pre-trial detention must be based upon "clear and convincing evidence"; (3) the nature and seriousness of the charge must be considered; (4) the defendant's background and characteristics must be considered; (5) the nature and seriousness of the danger posed by the defendant's release must be weighed; and (6) the prosecution's evidence must be weighed. The statute does not "punish" a defendant before trial, it merely prevents danger to the public and individuals, which the Court identified as a "legitimate goal," one that is "regulatory" in nature rather than "punitive." "When the government proves by clear and convincing evidence that an arrestee presents an identified and articulable threat to an individual or the community, we believe that, consistent with the Due Process Clause, a court may disable the arrestee from executing that threat." The Eighth Amendment issue was dispatched with relative ease; the Court noted that the Excessive Bail Clause of the federal constitution does not constitute a general direction that *all* defendants have a constitutional right to bail. On similar grounds, the Court held in Hilton v. Braunskill, 481 U.S. 770, 107 S.Ct. 2113 (1987), that the dangerousness of a successful federal habeas corpus petitioner may be considered by a federal district court in deciding the issue of bail for the petitioner pending appeal by the state.

Probable Cause to Detain and the Habeas Corpus Writ

After a person has been arrested as a suspect by the police or upon authorization of a prosecutor, and remains deprived of his liberty, he is entitled, as a constitutional right, to a prompt, though limited judicial hearing on the question of probable cause to detain. At this kind of hearing (prior to the filing of formal charges), the normal rules of evidence are not applicable and counsel for the accused is not required. This procedure is akin to that used when, prior to arrest, the prosecutor seeks an arrest warrant from a court.

In the event an arrested person is not formally charged with an offense and is not taken before a judge or other magistrate without unnecessary delay he, or rather someone on his behalf, may petition a judge for a "writ of habeas corpus" and thereby attempt to secure his release or at least compel the police to file a specific charge against him. In the latter event he may then seek his release on bond. If the court issues the writ, the police or other custodians of the arrested person are required, either immediately or at an early designated time, to bring him into court (that is, "you have the body," which is the literal meaning of the term habeas corpus), and to explain to the court the reason or justification for holding the accused person in custody. In the federal system habeas corpus can also be used to review various aspects of a state defendant's trial after his conviction, such as whether his *Miranda* rights were violated. Thompson v. Keohane, ___ U.S. ___, 116 S.Ct. 457 (1995).

Upon the police showing adequate cause, a court may continue the hearing in order to give the police a little more time to conduct a further investigation before making the formal charge against the arrestee. Many times, however, the police are required to file their charges immediately or release the prisoner. In some jurisdictions the prosecutor makes the decision as to whether the initial charge shall be filed.

Preliminary Hearing

Following the *filing in court* of a police accusation against a person, or after an accusation has been filed by a prosecuting attorney in the form of an "information" detailing the charge, the accused is entitled to a preliminary hearing. This is a relatively informal judicial proceeding during which a determination is made as to whether there are reasonable grounds for believing the accused person committed the offense—as to whether it is fair, under the circumstances, to require him to stand trial. If after such a hearing the judge or magistrate decides that the accusation is without probable cause, the accused will be discharged. This discharge, however, will not bar a grand jury indictment if subsequently developed evidence (or the same evidence presented on the preliminary hearing) satisfies the grand jury that the accusation is well founded.

If the preliminary hearing judge or magistrate decides that the accusation is a reasonable one, the accused will be "bound over" to the grand jury—that is, held in jail until the charge against him is presented for grand jury consideration. If the offense is a bailable one, however, the accused may be released after a bond of a certain amount is given to ensure his presence until the grand jury has acted in the matter. (The nature and composition of a grand jury and the difference between it and a petit or trial jury is described later in this chapter.)

In some jurisdictions, as subsequently detailed, once the magistrate has found probable cause, the prosecutor may bypass the grand jury and file a felony "information" upon which the accused will be tried.

The Right to an Attorney

The Sixth Amendment to the Constitution of the United States provides that "in all criminal prosecutions, the accused shall enjoy the right ... to have the assistance of Counsel for his defense." And the Supreme Court of the United States has held that where incarceration may be a consequence of the prosecution, the defendant is entitled to appointed counsel in the event he cannot afford one. A preliminary hearing, of course, is a part of the "criminal prosecution."

Coroner's Inquest

At this point in a discussion of criminal procedure, mention should be made of a proceeding peculiar to homicide cases, which comes into operation soon after a killing or discovered death. This is the "coroner's inquest."

The coroner's inquest is a very old proceeding and its function was and still is to determine the cause of death. The verdict of the coroner's jury, which is made up, in some states, of six laymen selected by the coroner or one of his deputies, is not binding on the prosecuting attorney, grand jury or court. In effect, it is merely an advisory finding which can be either accepted or completely ignored. For instance, even though a coroner's jury returns a verdict of accidental death, a grand jury, either upon its own initiative or upon evidence presented by the prosecutor, may find that death resulted because of someone's criminal act and charge that person with the offense.

In some jurisdictions the office of coroner has been replaced by what is known as a medical examiner system. Whereas the coroner is usually an elected official (who may or may not be a physician), a medical examiner must be a physician appointed by a state or county officer or agency; moreover, in many jurisdictions he must be a forensic pathologist, specially trained for the position. He, in turn, has the power of appointing assistants who are physicians already trained for the purpose or at least in the process of receiving such training.

The Grand Jury

Misdemeanors are usually prosecuted upon an information filed by the prosecuting attorney after he has received and considered the sworn complaint of the victim or of some other person with knowledge of the facts. For felonies, however, many states require that the matter must first be submitted to a "grand jury." Then, after hearing the alleged facts related by the victim or other persons, the grand jury determines whether there are reasonable grounds for proceeding to an actual trial of the person charged.

A grand jury is usually composed of 23 citizen-voters, 16 of whom constitute a quorum. The votes of 12 members are necessary to the return of an "indictment." This indictment is also known as a "true bill."

The Constitution of the United States does not require that state prosecutors use a grand jury to charge felony offenses, and there is an increasing tendency to enact statutes that permit the prosecution to charge felonies by filing an "information." Ordinarily a person charged by information must have a preliminary hearing before he can be tried for the charge. A defendant charged by a grand jury, however, may not have a right to a preliminary hearing because it is thought that his rights are adequately safeguarded by his fellow citizens who serve on the grand jury.

One highly significant and increasing modern purpose of the grand jury is to investigate complex crimes. The grand jury has the right to subpoena witnesses, to ask them questions, and to require the production of books and records. It may exercise these rights before any charge is filed and before the specific crime or its perpetrator is known. Police agencies usually do not possess this authority to compel the production of evidence and it is generally conceded that such a right is required for effective investigation of much financial crime, official corruption, and organized crime.

The consideration of a felony charge by a grand jury is in no sense a trial. Only the state's evidence is presented and considered; the suspected offender is usually not even heard nor is his lawyer present to offer evidence in his behalf. Some state laws, however, now provide that the suspect has a right to appear before the grand jury if he elects to do so, but very few suspects exercise that option. Other laws provide that a "target" of the grand jury investigation has the right to have counsel with him if he is summoned to appear before the grand jury.

The Arraignment and Plea

Following an indictment, the next step in felony cases is the appearance of the accused person before a judge who is empowered to try felony cases. The indictment is read to the defendant or the essence of its contents is made known to him; in other words, he is advised of the criminal charges made against him. If he pleads guilty, the judge can sentence him immediately or take the matter under advisement for a decision at an early date. If the accused pleads not guilty, a date is then set for his actual trial.

In some states, and in the federal system, the defendant may enter a plea of "nolo contendere," a plea which has the same effect as a plea of guilty, except that the admission thereby made cannot be used as evidence in any judicial action (although such a plea might be considered in a non-judicial setting, such as the administrative discipline of a law enforcement officer. See County of Los Angeles v. Civil Serv. Com'n, 46 Cal.Rptr.2d 256 (Cal.App. 2 Dist.1995)).

Pre-trial Motions

After the formal charge has been made against the accused, he may, in advance of trial, seek to terminate the prosecution's case, or at least seek to prepare a better defense, by utilizing a procedure known as making or filing a *motion*. A motion is merely a request for a court ruling or order that will afford the defendant the assistance or remedy he is thereby seeking. Some of the more frequently used motions are the following:

Motion to Quash the Indictment. With this motion the defendant may question the legal sufficiency of the indictment. If the court decides that the indictment adequately charges a criminal offense, and that it was obtained in accordance with the prescribed legal procedures, the motion will be overruled; otherwise the indictment will be considered invalid and "quashed." Even after an indictment has been thus rejected and set aside, the prosecutor may proceed to obtain another and proper indictment. Moreover, the prosecution is entitled to appeal from a court order quashing an indictment; at this stage of the proceedings the defendant has not been placed in jeopardy, and consequently a subsequent indictment and trial would not constitute a violation of his constitutional privilege against double jeopardy.

Motion for a Bill of Particulars. Although the indictment, if valid, will ordinarily contain all the allegations of fact necessary for the defendant to prepare his defense, he may, by a motion for a "bill of particulars," obtain further details respecting the accusation.

Motion for Discovery. In addition to the motion for a bill of particulars, there now exists an expanded right, accorded to both the prosecution and the defense, to learn what evidence the other side intends to use. It is known as a motion for discovery, whereby both parties seek to learn not only the details of the crime but also the names of the other side's witnesses and what they are expected to say.

Motion for a Change of Venue. A defendant may attempt to avoid trial before a particular judge or in the city, county, or district where the crime occurred by seeking a "change of venue." In instances where this appears to be necessary in order that the defendant may receive a fair trial, the motion for a change of venue will be granted.

Motion to Suppress Evidence. A defendant has the privilege of filing with the court, normally in advance of trial, a "motion to suppress" evidence that he contends has been obtained from him in an unconstitutional manner. The evidence in question may be, on the one hand, a tangible item such as a gun, narcotics, or stolen property or, on the other hand, an intangible item such as a confession or the testimony of eyewitnesses who are expected to identify the accused as the offender. If the court is satisfied that the evidence has been illegally obtained, it will order the evidence suppressed, which means that it cannot be used at the trial. In some cases, as will be discussed in Chapter 15 of this book, if the evidence was illegally obtained, but the police acted in good faith, the evidence will not be suppressed. If the court decides that the evidence was lawfully obtained, it is usable against the defendant at the trial.

B. THE TRIAL

In all states, and in the federal system, the accused is entitled to a "speedy trial." This right to an early trial is guaranteed by the various state and federal constitutions, and the constitutional provisions are generally supplemented by legislative enactments that particularize and specifically limit the pre-trial detention period. In many states, for instance, once a person is jailed upon a criminal charge, he must be tried within a certain number of days, unless the delay has been occasioned by him, or is necessitated by a hearing to determine his mental competency to stand trial. If the accused is out on bail, he can demand trial within a certain number of days. In either instance, however, if the court determines that the prosecution has exercised, without success, due diligence to obtain evidence material to the case, and that there are reasonable grounds to believe that such evidence will be forthcoming, the time for trial may be extended. Such time limits vary from state to state, but the consistent rule is that unless the accused person is tried within the specified period of time he must be released and is thereafter immune from prosecution for that offense.

The federal courts are governed by a statutory scheme that provides specific time periods within which federal trials must begin. Even under the federal act, however, some circumstances permit the accused to waive his right to a trial within the statutory period.

Jury Trial—Trial by Judge Alone

A person accused of a "serious crime", which is considered to be one for which there may be incarceration beyond six months, is entitled to trial by jury, as a matter of constitutional right. However, he may waive this right and elect to be tried by a judge alone. In some jurisdictions the defendant has an absolute right to this waiver; in others (e.g., the federal system) it is conditioned upon the concurrence of the judge and the prosecution.

If the case is tried without a jury, the judge hears the evidence and decides for himself whether the defendant is guilty or not guilty. Where the trial is by a jury, the jury determines the facts and the judge serves more or less as an umpire or referee; it is his function to determine what testimony or evidence is legally "admissible," that is, to decide what should be heard or considered by the jury. But the ultimate decision as to whether the defendant is guilty is one to be made by the jury alone.

Jury Selection

In the selection of the jurors, usually twelve in number, who hear the defendant's case, most states permit his attorney as well as the prosecuting attorney to question a larger number of citizens who have been chosen for jury service from the list of registered voters. In the federal system and a growing number of states, however, most trial judges will do practically all of the questioning, with very little opportunity for questioning accorded the prosecutor and defense counsel. Nevertheless, each lawyer has a certain number of "peremptory challenges" which means that he can arbitrarily refuse to accept as jurors a certain number of those who appear as prospective jurors. In some states, by statutory provision, the defendant in larceny cases has ten such challenges and the state has an equal number; in a murder case the defendant and the state each have twenty peremptory challenges; and in minor criminal cases, such as petit larceny, the challenges are five in number for each side.

The prosecutor, however, cannot exercise his "peremptory challenges" in a racially discriminatory manner. In Swain v. Alabama, 380 U.S. 202, 85 S.Ct. 824 (1965), the U.S. Supreme Court ruled that exclusion by the prosecution of prospective jury members solely on racial grounds violated the Equal Protection Clause of the U.S. Constitution, but that a defendant would have to show a prosecutorial pattern of discriminatory use of peremptory challenges in order to prevail with this argument, a procedure that few defendants were able to comply with. In Batson v. Kentucky, 476 U.S. 79, 106 S.Ct. 1712 (1986), the *Swain* procedure was overruled. Now, in order to establish a prima facie case of discrimination, a defendant only needs to show that he is a member of a cognizable racial group, that the prosecutor used peremptory challenges to keep members of that group off the jury panel, and "... that these facts and any other relevant circumstances raise an inference that the prosecutor used that practice to exclude the veniremen from the petit jury on account of their race." The burden then shifts to the prosecutor to explain the exclusion on a "neutral" basis, which does *not* include a simple assumption that members of the defendant's race would be partial to him simply because of race. In Purkett v. Elem, ___ U.S. ___, 115 S.Ct. 1769 (1995), the Court held that a prosecutor's explanation for a peremptory challenge of a black male that the juror had long, unkempt hair, a moustache and a beard, was race-neutral and satisfied the prosecution's burden of articulating a nondiscriminatory reason for the strike.

In all cases, if any prospective juror's answers to the questions of either attorney reveal a prejudice or bias that prevents him from being a fair and impartial juror, the judge, either on his own initiative or at the suggestion of either counsel, will dismiss that person from jury service. Although the desired result is not always achieved, the avowed purpose of this practice of permitting lawyers to question prospective jurors is to obtain twelve jurors who will be fair to both sides of the case.

As a safeguard against a juror becoming ill or disabled for some other reason, in many states, and within the federal system, provision is made for alternate jurors (usually two) who will hear all the evidence but not participate in the deliberation of the jury unless there is a replacement of one of the original jurors.

Opening Statements

After the jury is selected, both the prosecuting attorney and the defense lawyer are entitled to make "opening statements" in which each outlines what he intends to prove. The purpose of this is to acquaint the jurors with each side of the case, so that it will be easier for them to follow the evidence as it is presented.

The Prosecution's Evidence

After the opening statements the prosecuting attorney produces the prosecution's testimony and evidence. He has the burden of proving the state's case "beyond a reasonable doubt." If at the close of the prosecution's case the judge is of the opinion that reasonable jurors could not conclude that the charge against the defendant has been proved, he will "direct a verdict" of acquittal. That ends the matter and the defendant goes free—forever immune from further prosecution for the crime, just the same as if a jury had heard all the evidence and found him not guilty.

The Defendant's Evidence

If at the close of the prosecution's case the court does not direct the jury to find the defendant not guilty, the defendant may, if he wishes, present evidence in refutation. He himself may or may not testify, and if he chooses not to appear as a witness, the prosecuting attorney is not permitted to comment upon that fact to the jury. The basis for this principle whereby the defendant is not obligated to speak in his own behalf is the constitutional privilege that protects a person from self-incrimination.

The prosecution is given an opportunity to rebut the defendant's evidence, if any, and the presentation of testimony usually ends at that point. Then, once more, defense counsel will try to persuade the court to "direct a verdict" in favor of the defendant. If the court decides to let the case go to the jury, the prosecuting attorney and defense counsel make their closing arguments.

The defense and the prosecution have the right to subpoena witnesses and require them to testify at trial or to produce records if such evidence would be of value at trial. It is possible in certain case situations to enforce subpoenas against out-of-state witnesses and, in some instances, against witnesses in foreign countries.

The prosecution has the obligation in most, if not all, cases to notify the defense of any evidence that would be of significance in exculpating the accused or in mitigating his sentence. This obligation includes the duty to personally be aware of the existence of exculpatory material. Kyles v. Whitley, ___ U.S. ___, 115 S.Ct. 1555 (1995).

Closing Arguments

In their closing arguments the prosecutor and defense counsel review and analyze the evidence and attempt to persuade the jury to render a favorable verdict.

Instructions of the Court to the Jury

After the closing arguments are completed, the judge in most jurisdictions will read and give to the jury certain written instructions as to the legal principles that should be applied to the facts of the case as determined by the jury. The judge also gives the jury certain written forms of possible verdicts. The jury then retires to the jury room where they are given an adequate opportunity to deliberate upon the matter, away from everyone, including the judge himself.

The Verdict of the Jury

When the jurors have reached a decision, they advise the bailiff that they have reached a verdict and then return to the courtroom. The foreman, usually selected by the jurors themselves to serve as their leader and spokesman, announces the verdict of the jury. Jury participation in the case is then at an end.

If the defendant is acquitted, he is free forever from any further prosecution by that particular state or jurisdiction for the crime for which he was tried. He is not, however, free from potential civil liability based on the same facts. If he is found guilty, then, in most types of cases and in most jurisdictions, it becomes the function of the trial judge to fix the sentence within the legislatively prescribed limitations.

In the event the jurors are unable to agree upon a verdict—and it must be unanimous in most states—the jury, commonly referred to as a "hung jury," is discharged, and a new trial date may be set for a retrial of the case before another jury. The retrial does not constitute a violation of the constitutional protection against double jeopardy—trying a person twice for the same offense—because there actually has not been a first trial; in other words, it has been terminated by the failure of the jury to agree upon a verdict.

The Motion for a New Trial

After a verdict of guilty there are still certain opportunities provided the defendant to obtain his freedom. He may file a "motion for a new trial," in which he alleges certain "errors" committed in the course of his trial; if the trial judge agrees, the conviction is set aside and the defendant may be tried again by a new jury and usually before a different judge. Where this motion for a new trial is "overruled" or "denied," the judge will then proceed to sentence the defendant.

The defendant may also seek a new trial on the grounds of newly discovered evidence favorable to him. Such motions are rarely granted. The defendant must establish that he was not aware of the evidence, that he could not have discovered the evidence by exercising due diligence, and that the evidence would probably change the result of the trial.

The Sentence

In cases tried without a jury, the judge, of course, will determine the sentence to be imposed. In jury cases the practice varies among the states, with most of them following the practice of confining the jury function to a determination of guilt or innocence and permitting the judge to fix the penalty. For the crimes of murder and rape, however, most of the states place both responsibilities upon the jury.

In some states there are statutory provisions that prescribe that upon conviction of a felony, the defendant must be sentenced for a specified minimum-maximum term in the penitentiary—for example, one year to ten years for burglary. In many states a judge is permitted to set a minimum-maximum period anywhere within the minimum-maximum term prescribed by the legislature. In other words, the sentence given for grand larceny may be one to ten years, the statutory range, or one to two, nine to ten, or any other combination between one and ten. The minimum-maximum term means that the defendant cannot be released before serving the minimum period, less "time off for good behavior," nor can he be kept in the penitentiary longer than the maximum period, less "time off for good behavior." In between this minimum-maximum period the convict is eligible for "parole." The determination of the appropriate time of his release within that period is to be made by a "parole board," whose judgment in that respect is based upon the extent of the convict's rehabilitation, the security risk involved, and similar factors.

In instances where imprisonment is fixed at a specified number of years, rather than for an indeterminate period, the law usually provides that the convicted person must serve one-third of the sentence before becoming eligible for parole.

In recent years there has been an increase in new forms of incarceration and alternatives to incarceration. "Work release" allows an inmate to work at a job and return to custody during nonworking hours. "Periodic imprisonment" allows an inmate his freedom except for certain specified periods, e.g., weekends. "Community service" is a form of sentence whereby a convicted person is allowed to avoid incarceration in its traditional sense by performing a certain number of hours of work on a community project, such as picking up litter at a park on Saturday mornings.

Recently some states have adopted a plan that limits the sentencing discretion of judges and the release powers of parole boards, or even abolishes parole boards. Under this new system the judge is required to set a specific term according to more or less strict guidelines. The sentence may be reduced by "good time" allowance (for "good behavior") in prison, which is calculated by a set formula. When the inmate serves his sentence less "good time," he is automatically released.

In the federal system there are now fairly strict guidelines for sentences handed out by federal judges. The discretion of federal judges has been statutorily limited by ranges for sentences for particular offenses under set guidelines.

C. PROBATION

In certain types of cases, a judge is empowered, by statute, to grant "probation" to a convicted person. This means that instead of sending the defendant to the penitentiary the court permits him to remain at liberty but upon certain conditions prescribed by law and by the judge. His background must first be investigated by a probation officer for the purpose of determining whether he is the kind of person who may have "learned his lesson" by the mere fact of being caught and convicted, or whether he could be rehabilitated outside of prison better than behind prison walls. In other words, would any useful purpose be served for him or society by sending him to prison?

Among the conditions of a defendant's probation, the court may require him to make restitution of money stolen, or reparations to a person he injured. Some state statutes provide that for a period of up to six months in misdemeanor cases, and up to five years in felony cases, a defendant on probation will be subjected to the supervision of a probation officer and, in general, must remain on "good behavior" during the period fixed by the court. A failure to abide by the conditions prescribed by the court will subject the defendant to a sentence in the same manner and form as though he had been denied probation and sentenced immediately after his conviction for the offense.

D. PAROLE

A penitentiary sentence of a specified term or number of years does not necessarily mean that a convicted person will remain in the penitentiary for that particular period of time. Under certain conditions and circumstances he may be released earlier "on parole," which means a release under supervision until the expiration of his sentence or until the expiration of a period otherwise specified by law. For instance, a person sentenced "for life" is, in some states eligible for release "on parole" at the end of twenty years, with a subsequent five year period of parole supervision. One sentenced for a fixed number of years, for example 14 years for murder, may be eligible for parole in some states after he has served one-third that period of time. And a person who has been given an indeterminate minimum-maximum sentence, such as to 5 to 10 years for grand larceny, may be eligible for a parole after he has served the 5 year minimum, less time off for good behavior.

The manner of computing time off for good behavior, or "good time," varies among the states. Some states have a system based on yearly credits; under this arrangement, the amount of the credit granted increases as the amount of time served by the compliant prisoner increases. Accordingly, one month off is granted for good behavior in the first year, two months for the second year, and so on up to a maximum of six months off for good behavior in the sixth year and in each succeeding year. The inmate is allowed to accumulate these credits. Thus, under this system, a prisoner who received a minimum-maximum sentence of 3 to 5 years and who served "good time", would be eligible for parole after serving 2 years and 6 months of his sentence.

A violation of the conditions of the parole will subject the parolee to possible return to prison for the remainder of his unexpired sentence.

As previously noted, many states have practically abolished parole by providing mandatory release dates, less time off for good behavior, which means that there can be no parole release prior to that date.

In states maintaining the conventional parole system, revocation of probation or parole cannot be arbitrary. In either case there must be a hearing. The hearing need not be like a full scale trial, i.e., there is no jury, but it must be a fair determination of whether the conditions of probation and parole were violated.

E. POST-CONVICTION REMEDIES

The Appeal

After sentence has been pronounced, the defendant may appeal his conviction to a reviewing court. The reviewing court will examine all or part of the written record of what happened at the trial, and consider the written and oral arguments of both the defense attorney and the prosecutor. It will then render a written decision and opinion which will either reverse or affirm the trial court conviction and state the reasons for the decision. If the trial court's decision is "reversed and remanded," it means that the defendant's conviction is nullified, although he may be tried over again by another jury. A decision of "reversed" ordinarily means that in addition to an improper trial there appears to be insufficient competent evidence upon which to try the defendant again, and consequently the prosecuting attorney may not make a second attempt to win a conviction.

A decision of the state's highest court affirming a conviction is, in nearly all instances, a final disposition of the case, and there is nothing else the convicted person can do but submit to the judgment of the trial court. But if the appeal involved a *federal* constitutional question or issue the defendant is entitled to seek a review of the state appellate court decision by the Supreme Court of the United States. Such requests, known as petitions for a *writ of certiorari,* are rarely granted, however.

The courts may allow the defendant to remain free on bail pending appeal or they may increase the amount of bail or revoke bail entirely while the case is on appeal.

Whenever a defendant has succeeded in obtaining a reversal of his conviction, he may be retried unless the highest court to review the case has reversed for insufficiency of evidence. The reasons that a second trial after a reversal of a conviction for trial error does not constitute double jeopardy are three-fold, according to the courts which have been confronted with the issue. First of all, by appealing his conviction the accused is considered to "waive" (give up) his right not to be tried twice. Secondly, there is a strong societal interest in a final adjudication of the guilt or innocence of the accused. Thirdly, a retrial is in effect a continuation of the original proceeding.

Collateral Attacks

In addition to the appeal itself, nearly all states in recent years have provided additional post-conviction remedies by which a defendant may attack his conviction. Such "collateral" remedies are known, variously, as proceedings in habeas corpus, post-conviction petitions, or by other titles. A defendant may thereby seek a re-litigation, in a trial court, of an issue that had been considered and decided on the direct appeal; or he may attempt to raise an entirely new issue. Moreover, the decision with respect to a collateral attack may be the subject of an appeal to a reviewing court.

Even after a conviction is upheld against collateral attack in the state courts, if a federal constitutional question had been presented, the convicted person has yet another remedy available—the *federal* writ of habeas corpus. The Supreme Court of the United States has held that a state court judgment of conviction resulting from a trial which involved a substantial error of federal constitutional dimension is void, and a prisoner held pursuant to a void judgment is unlawfully confined and subject to release by a federal court upon a writ of habeas corpus. However, the Court has imposed some limitations upon this right. A state prisoner who claims that evidence used against him at trial was obtained in violation of constitutional rules governing arrest, search and seizure, cannot present those claims in a federal habeas corpus proceeding if he had the opportunity to make them in the state court.

In considering a petition for habeas corpus, a federal district court judge may order another "evidentiary hearing." And he has the power to remand the case to the state court for a new trial or for the outright release of the defendant, depending upon the kind of error committed and the evidence still available to the state. But his decision is appealable to higher federal courts, including the United States Supreme Court.

F. APPEALS BY PROSECUTION

Only the defendant has a right to appeal the result of a trial; to permit the prosecution to appeal from a verdict of acquittal or a trial judge's finding of not guilty has been held to violate the constitutional protection against double jeopardy.

In many jurisdictions, however, the prosecution is accorded the right to appeal certain decisions of a pre-trial nature. Some states now provide for prosecution appeals from a trial court order dismissing the charge against a defendant, or from an order suppressing a confession or other evidence alleged to have been illegally obtained.

The prosecution generally has the same right of appeal as the defense from an adverse decision of an intermediate appeals court. Many states and the federal government have two kinds of reviewing courts. The first, usually called a court of appeals, hears most appeals. The losing party may then ask the second court, usually called the supreme court, to rehear the appeal. This second court, the highest court, may rehear the appeal and render a final decision or it may simply refuse to rehear the case.

Chapter 2

CONSTITUTIONAL LIMITATIONS ON THE LEGISLATIVE POWER TO CREATE AND DEFINE CRIMINAL OFFENSES

A. FREEDOM OF SPEECH

1. POLITICAL SPEECH

MEYER v. GRANT

Supreme Court of the United States, 1988.
486 U.S. 414, 108 S.Ct. 1886.

JUSTICE STEVENS delivered the [unanimous] opinion of the Court.

In Colorado the proponents of a new law, or an amendment to the State Constitution, may have their proposal placed on the ballot at a general election if they can obtain enough signatures of qualified voters on an "initiative petition" within a six-month period. One section of the state law regulating the initiative process makes it a felony to pay petition circulators.[1] The question in this case is whether that provision is unconstitutional. The Court of Appeals for the Tenth Circuit, sitting en banc, held that the statute abridged the appellees' right to engage in political speech and therefore violated the First and Fourteenth Amendments to the Federal Constitution. We agree.

I

Colorado is one of several States that permits its citizens to place propositions on the ballot through an initiative process. Colo.Const., Art. V, § 1; Colo.Rev.Stat. §§ 1–40–101 to 1–40–119 (1980 and Supp. 1987). Under Colorado law, proponents of an initiative measure must submit the measure to the State Legislative Council and the Legislative

1. Colorado Rev.Stat. § 1–40–110 (1980) provides:

"Any person, corporation, or association of persons who directly or indirectly pays to or receives from or agrees to pay to or receive from any other person, corporation, or association of persons any money or other thing of value in consideration of or as an inducement to the circulation of an initiative or referendum petition or in consideration of or as an inducement to the signing of any such petition commits a class 5 felony and shall be punished as provided in section 13–1–105, C.R.S. (1973)."

Drafting Office for review and comment. The draft is then submitted to a three-member title board, which prepares a title, submission clause, and summary. After approval of the title, submission clause, and summary, the proponents of the measure then have six months to obtain the necessary signatures, which must be in an amount equal to at least five percent of the total number of voters who cast votes for all candidates for the Office of Secretary of State at the last preceding general election. If the signature requirements are met, the petitions may be filed with the Secretary of State, and the measure will appear on the ballot at the next general election. Colo.Rev.Stat. §§ 1–40–101 to 1–40–105 (1980 and Supp.1987).

State law requires that the persons who circulate the approved drafts of the petitions for signature be registered voters. Colo.Const., Art. V, § 1(6). Before the signed petitions are filed with the Secretary of State, the circulators must sign affidavits attesting that each signature is the signature of the person whose name it purports to be and that, to the best of their knowledge and belief, each person signing the petition is a registered voter. Colo.Rev.Stat. § 1–40–109 (Supp.1987). The payment of petition circulators is punished as a felony. Colo.Rev.Stat. § 1–40–110 (1980), n. 1, supra.

Appellees are proponents of an amendment to the Colorado Constitution that would remove motor carriers from the jurisdiction of the Colorado Public Utilities Commission. In early 1984 they obtained approval of a title, submission clause, and summary for a measure proposing the amendment and began the process of obtaining the 46,737 signatures necessary to have the proposal appear on the November 1984 ballot. Based on their own experience as petition circulators, as well as that of other unpaid circulators, appellees concluded that they would need the assistance of paid personnel to obtain the required number of signatures within the allotted time. They then brought this action under 42 U.S.C. § 1983 against the Secretary of State and the Attorney General of Colorado seeking a declaration that the statutory prohibition against the use of paid circulators violates their rights under the First Amendment.

After a brief trial, the District Judge entered judgment upholding the statute on alternative grounds. First, he concluded that the prohibition against the use of paid circulators did not burden appellees' First Amendment rights because it did not place any restraint on their own expression or measurably impair efforts to place initiatives on the ballot.[2]

2. In support of its conclusion that the prohibition against the use of paid circulators did not inhibit the placement of initiative measures on the general ballot, the District Court compared Colorado's experience with that of 20 States which have an initiative process but do not prohibit paid circulators. It noted that since 1910, Colorado has ranked fourth in the total number of initiatives placed on the ballot. This statistic, however, does not reject the possibility that even more petitions would have been successful if paid circulators had been available, or, more narrowly, that these respondents would have had greater success if they had been able to hire extra help. As the District Court itself noted, "the evidence indicates [appellees'] purposes would be enhanced if the corps of volunteers could be augmented by a cadre of paid workers."

The restriction on their ability to hire paid circulators to speak for them was not significant because they remained free to use their money to employ other spokesmen who could advertise their cause. Second, even assuming, *arguendo,* that the statute burdened appellees' right to engage in political speech, the District Judge concluded that the burden was justified by the State's interests in (a) making sure that an initiative measure has a sufficiently broad base to warrant its placement on the ballot, and (b) protecting the integrity of the initiative process by eliminating a temptation to pad petitions.

A divided panel of the Court of Appeals affirmed for the reasons stated by the District Court. After granting rehearing en banc, however, the court reversed. The en banc majority concluded that the record demonstrated that petition circulators engage in the communication of ideas while they are obtaining signatures and that the available pool of circulators is necessarily smaller if only volunteers can be used.

> "Thus, the effect of the statute's absolute ban on compensation of solicitors is clear. It impedes the sponsors' opportunity to disseminate their views to the public. It curtails the discussion of issues that normally accompanies the circulation of initiative petitions. And it shrinks the size of the audience that can be reached.... In short, like the campaign expenditure limitations struck down in *Buckley,* the Colorado statute imposes a direct restriction which 'necessarily reduces the quantity of expression....' *Buckley* [*v. Valeo*], 424 U.S. [1] at 19 [96 S.Ct. 612 at 634 (1976)]." 828 F.2d 1446, 1453–1454 (CA10 1987).

The Court of Appeals then rejected the State's asserted justifications for the ban. It first rejected the suggestion that the ban was necessary either to prevent fraud or to protect the public from circulators that might be too persuasive:

> "The First Amendment is a value-free provision whose protection is not dependent on 'the truth, popularity, or social utility of the ideas and beliefs which are offered.' NAACP v. Button, [371 U.S. 415, 445, 83 S.Ct. 328, 344, 9 L.Ed.2d 405 (1963)]. 'The very purpose of the First Amendment is to foreclose public authority from assuming a guardianship of the public mind.... In this field every person must be his own watchman for truth, because the forefathers did not trust any government to separate the true from the false for us.' Thomas v. Collins, [323 U.S. 516, 545 [65 S.Ct. 315, 329, 89 L.Ed. 430], (1945)] (Jackson, J., concurring)." 828 F.2d, at 1455.

The court then rejected the suggestion that the ban was needed to assure that the initiative had a broad base of public support because, in the court's view, that interest was adequately protected by the requirement that the petition be signed by five percent of the State's eligible voters. Finally, the Court of Appeals rejected an argument advanced by a dissenting judge that since Colorado had no obligation to afford its citizens an initiative procedure, it could impose this condition on its use. Having decided to confer the right, the State was obligated to do so in a manner consistent with the Constitution because, unlike Posadas de Puerto Rico Associates v. Tourism Co. of Puerto Rico, 478 U.S. 328, 106 S.Ct. 2968 (1986), which involved only commercial speech, this case involves "core political speech."

II

We fully agree with the Court of Appeals' conclusion that this case involves a limitation on political expression subject to exacting scrutiny. Buckley v. Valeo, 424 U.S. 1, 45, 96 S.Ct. 612, 647 (1976). The First Amendment provides that Congress "shall make no law ... abridging the freedom of speech, or of the press; or the right of people peaceably to assemble, and to petition the Government for a redress of grievances." U.S. Const., Amdt. 1. The Fourteenth Amendment makes that prohibition applicable to the State of Colorado. As we explained in Thornhill v. Alabama, 310 U.S. 88, 95, 60 S.Ct. 736, 740 (1940), "[t]he freedom of speech and of the press, which are secured by the First Amendment against abridgment by the United States, are among the fundamental personal rights and liberties which are secured to all persons by the Fourteenth Amendment against abridgment by a State."

Unquestionably, whether the trucking industry should be deregulated in Colorado is a matter of societal concern that appellees have a right to discuss publicly without risking criminal sanctions. "The freedom of speech and of the press guaranteed by the Constitution embraces at the least the liberty to discuss publicly and truthfully all matters of public concern without previous restraint or fear of subsequent punishment." Id., at 101–102, 60 S.Ct., at 744. The First Amendment "was fashioned to assure unfettered interchange of ideas for the bringing about of political and social changes desired by the people." Roth v. United States, 354 U.S. 476, 484, 77 S.Ct. 1304, 1308 (1957). Appellees seek by petition to achieve political change in Colorado; their right freely to engage in discussions concerning the need for that change is guarded by the First Amendment.

The circulation of an initiative petition of necessity involves both the expression of a desire for political change and a discussion of the merits of the proposed change. Although a petition circulator may not have to persuade potential signatories that a particular proposal should prevail to capture their signatures, he or she will at least have to persuade them that the matter is one deserving of the public scrutiny and debate that would attend its consideration by the whole electorate. This will in almost every case involve an explanation of the nature of the proposal and why its advocates support it.[3] Thus, the circulation of a petition

3. The record in this case demonstrates that the circulation of appellees' petition involved political speech. Paul Grant, one of the appellees, testified about the nature of his conversations with voters in an effort to get them to sign the petition:

involves the type of interactive communication concerning political change that is appropriately described as "core political speech." [4]

The refusal to permit appellees to pay petition circulators restricts political expression in two ways: First, it limits the number of voices who will convey appellees' message and the hours they can speak and, therefore, limits the size of the audience they can reach.[5] Second, it makes it less likely that appellees will garner the number of signatures necessary to place the matter on the ballot, thus limiting their ability to make the matter the focus of statewide discussion. The Colorado Supreme Court has itself recognized that the prohibition against the use of paid circulators has the inevitable effect of reducing the total quantum of speech on a public issue. When called upon to consider the constitutionality of the statute at issue here in another context in Urevich v.

"[T]he way we go about soliciting signatures is that you ask the person—first of all, you interrupt the person in their walk or whatever they are doing. You intrude upon them and ask them, Are you a registered voter?

* * *

"If you get a yes, then you tell the person your purpose, that you are circulating a petition to qualify the issue on the ballot in November, and tell them what about, and they say, 'Please let me know a little bit more.' Typically, that takes maybe a minute or two, the process of explaining to the persons that you are trying to put the initiative on the ballot to exempt Colorado transportation from [State Public Utilities Commission] regulations.

"Then you ask the person if they will sign your petition. If they hesitate, you try to come up with additional arguments to get them to sign.

* * *

"[We try] to explain the not just deregulation in this industry, that it would free up to industry from being cartelized, allowing freedom from moral choices, price competition for the first time, lowering price costs, which we estimate prices in Colorado to be $150 million a year in monopoly benefits. We have tried to convey the unfairness and injustice of the existing system, where some businesses are denied to go into business simply to protect the profits of existing companies.

"We tried to convey the unfairness of the existing system, which has denied individuals the right to start their own businesses. In many cases, individuals have asked for an authority and have been turned down because huge corporate organizations have opposed them." 2 Record 10–11.

This testimony provides an example of advocacy of political reform that falls squarely within the protections of the First Amendment.

4. Our recognition that the solicitation of signatures for a petition involves protected speech follows from our recognition in Schaumburg v. Citizens for a Better Environment, 444 U.S. 620, 100 S.Ct. 826 (1980), that the solicitation of charitable contributions often involves speech protected by the First Amendment and that any attempt to regulate solicitation would necessarily infringe that speech:

> "Prior authorities, therefore, clearly establish that charitable appeals for funds, on the street or door to door, involve a variety of speech interests—communication of information, the dissemination and propagation of views and ideas, and the advocacy of causes—that are within the protection of the First Amendment. Soliciting financial support is undoubtedly subject to reasonable regulation but the latter must be undertaken with due regard for the reality that solicitation is characteristically intertwined with informative and perhaps persuasive speech seeking support for particular causes or for particular views on economic, political, or social issues, and for the reality that without solicitation the flow of such information and advocacy would likely cease." Id., at 632, 100 S.Ct., at 833.

5. Paul Grant testified that compensation resulted in more people being "able and willing" to circulate petitions. 2 Record 19–20. As he succinctly concluded: "[M]oney either enables people to forego leaving a job, or enables them to have a job." Ibid.

Woodard, 667 P.2d 760, 763 (Colo.1983), that court described the burden the statute imposes on First Amendment expression:

> "As mentioned previously, statutes that limit the power of the people to initiate legislation are to be closely scrutinized and narrowly construed. That the statute in question acts as a limitation on ACORN's ability to circulate petitions cannot be doubted. We can take judicial notice of the fact that it is often more difficult to get people to work without compensation than it is to get them to work for pay. As the dissent in State v. Conifer Enterprises, Inc., 82 Wash.2d 94, 508 P.2d 149 (1973) (Rosellini, J., dissenting), observed:
>
> > 'The securing of sufficient signatures to place an initiative measure on the ballot is no small undertaking. Unless the proponents of a measure can find a large number of volunteers, they must hire persons to solicit signatures or abandon the project. I think we can take judicial notice of the fact that the solicitation of signatures on petitions is work. It is time-consuming and it is tiresome—so much so that it seems that few but the young have the strength, the ardor and the stamina to engage in it, unless, of course, there is some remuneration.' "

Appellants argue that even if the statute imposes some limitation on First Amendment expression, the burden is permissible because other avenues of expression remain open to appellees and because the State has the authority to impose limitations on the scope of the state-created right to legislate by initiative. Neither of these arguments persuades us that the burden imposed on appellees' First Amendment rights is acceptable.

That appellees remain free to employ other means to disseminate their ideas does not take their speech through petition circulators outside the bounds of First Amendment protection. Colorado's prohibition of paid petition circulators restricts access to the most effective, fundamental, and perhaps economical avenue of political discourse, direct one-on-one communication. That it leaves open "more burdensome" avenues of communication, does not relieve its burden on First Amendment expression. FEC v. Massachusetts Citizens For Life, Inc., 479 U.S. 238, 107 S.Ct. 616 (1986). Cf. Citizens Against Rent Control v. Berkeley, 454 U.S. 290, 296, 299, 102 S.Ct. 434, 437, 439 (1981). The First Amendment protects appellees' right not only to advocate their cause but also to select what they believe to be the most effective means for so doing.

Relying on Posadas de Puerto Rico Associates v. Tourism Co., 478 U.S. 328, 106 S.Ct. 2968 (1986), Colorado contends that because the power of the initiative is a state-created right, it is free to impose limitations on the exercise of that right. That reliance is misplaced. In *Posadas* the Court concluded that "the greater power to completely ban casino gambling necessarily includes the lesser power to ban advertising of casino gambling." Id., at 345–346, 106 S.Ct., at 2986. The Court of Appeals quite properly pointed out the logical flaw in Colorado's attempt to draw an analogy between the present case and *Posadas*. The decision in *Posadas* does not suggest that "the power to ban casino gambling entirely would include the power to ban public discussion of legislative proposals regarding the legalization and advertising of casino gambling." 828 F.2d, at 1456. Thus it does not support the position that the power to ban initiatives entirely includes the power to limit discussion of political issues raised in initiative petitions. And, as the Court of Appeals further observed:

> "*Posadas* is inapplicable to the present case for a more fundamental reason—the speech restricted in *Posadas* was merely 'commercial speech which does "no more than propose a commercial transaction...."' *Posadas,* [478 U.S., at 340, 106 S.Ct., at 2976], (quoting Virginia Pharmacy Board v. Virginia Citizens Consumer Council, Inc., [425 U.S. 748, 762, 96 S.Ct. 1817, 1825, 48 L.Ed.2d 346 (1976)])…. Here, by contrast, the speech at issue is 'at the core of our electoral process and of the First Amendment freedoms,' *Buckley,* [424 U.S., at 39, 96 S.Ct., at 644 (quoting Williams v. Rhodes, 393 U.S. 23, 32, 89 S.Ct. 5, 11, 21 L.Ed.2d 24 (1968)]—an area of public policy where protection of robust discussion is at its zenith." 828 F.2d, at 1456–1457.

We agree with the Court of Appeals' conclusion that the statute trenches upon an area in which the importance of First Amendment protections is "at its zenith." For that reason the burden that Colorado must overcome to justify this criminal law is well-nigh insurmountable.

III

We are not persuaded by the State's arguments that the prohibition is justified by its interest in making sure that an initiative has sufficient grass roots support to be placed on the ballot, or by its interest in protecting the integrity of the initiative process. As the Court of Appeals correctly held, the former interest is adequately protected by the requirement that no initiative proposal may be placed on the ballot unless the required number of signatures has been obtained. Id., at 1455.[6]

6. Colorado also seems to suggest that it is permissible to mute the voices of those who can afford to pay petition circulators. See Brief for Appellants 17. "But the concept that government may restrict the speech of some elements of our society in order to enhance the relative voice of others is wholly foreign to the First Amendment." Buckley, 424 U.S. 1, 48–49, 96 S.Ct. 612, 648–649 (1976). The concern that persons who can pay petition circulators may succeed in getting measures on the ballot when they might otherwise have failed cannot defeat First Amendment rights. As we said in First National Bank of Boston v. Bellotti, 435 U.S. 765, 790–791, 98 S.Ct. 1407, 1423–1424 (1978), paid advocacy "may influence the outcome of the vote; this would be its purpose. But the fact that advocacy may persuade the electorate is hardly a reason to suppress it…. '[T]he concept that government may restrict the speech of some elements of our society in order to enhance the relative voice of others is wholly foreign to the First Amendment….' Buckley, 424

The State's interest in protecting the integrity of the initiative process does not justify the prohibition because the State has failed to demonstrate that it is necessary to burden appellees' ability to communicate their message in order to meet its concerns. The Attorney General has argued that the petition circulator has the duty to verify the authenticity of signatures on the petition and that compensation might provide the circulator with a temptation to disregard that duty. No evidence has been offered to support that speculation, however, and we are not prepared to assume that a professional circulator—whose qualifications for similar future assignments may well depend on a reputation for competence and integrity—is any more likely to accept false signatures than a volunteer who is motivated entirely by an interest in having the proposition placed on the ballot.

Other provisions of the Colorado statute deal expressly with the potential danger that circulators might be tempted to pad their petitions with false signatures. It is a crime to forge a signature on a petition, Colo.Rev.Stat. § 1–13–106 (1980), to make false or misleading statements relating to a petition, Colo.Rev.Stat. § 1–40–119 (Supp.1987), or to pay someone to sign a petition, Colo.Rev.Stat. § 1–40–110 (1980). Further, the top of each page of the petition must bear a statement printed in red ink warning potential signatories that it is a felony to forge a signature on a petition or to sign the petition when not qualified to vote and admonishing signatories not to sign the petition unless they have read and understand the proposed initiative.[7] These provisions seem adequate to the task of minimizing the risk of improper conduct in the circulation of a petition, especially since the risk of fraud or corruption, or the appearance thereof, is more remote at the petition stage of an initiative than at the time of balloting. Cf. First National Bank of Boston v. Bellotti, 435 U.S., at 790, 98 S.Ct., at 1423 ("[t]he risk of corruption perceived in cases involving candidate elections ... simply is not present in a popular vote on a public issue").

> "[L]egislative restrictions on advocacy of the election or defeat of political candidates are wholly at odds with the guarantees of the First Amendment." Buckley v. Valeo, 424 U.S., at 50, 96 S.Ct., at 650. That principle applies equally to "the discussion of political policy generally or advocacy of the passage

U.S., at 48–49, 96 S.Ct., at 648–649.... [T]he people in our democracy are entrusted with the responsibility for judging and evaluating the relative merits of conflicting arguments." Cf. Brown v. Hartlage, 456 U.S. 45, 60, 102 S.Ct. 1523, 1532 (1982) ("[t]he State's fear that voters might make an ill-advised choice does not provide the State with a compelling justification for limiting speech").

7. Section 1–40–106 provides in part:

"(1) At the top of each page of every initiative or referendum petition shall be printed, in plain red letters no smaller than the impression of ten-point, boldface type, the following:

WARNING
IT IS A FELONY:

For anyone to sign any initiative or referendum petition with any name other than his or her own or to knowingly sign his or her name more than once for the same measure or to sign such petition when not a qualified elector.

DO NOT SIGN THIS PETITION UNLESS YOU ARE A QUALIFIED ELECTOR

or defeat of legislation." Id., at 48, 96 S.Ct., at 648. The Colorado statute prohibiting the payment of petition circulators imposes a burden on political expression that the State has failed to justify. The Court of Appeals correctly held that the statute violates the First and Fourteenth Amendments. Its judgment is therefore affirmed.

NOTE

In McIntyre v. Ohio Elections Commission, ___ U.S. ___, 115 U.S. 1511 (1995), the U.S. Supreme Court struck down, as unconstitutionally violative of the free speech guarantees of the First Amendment, an Ohio statute which prohibited the distribution of campaign literature that does not contain the name and address of the person or campaign official issuing the literature, i.e., anonymous political material. The Court ruled that the freedom to publish anonymously is protected by the First Amendment, and extends beyond the literary realm to the advocacy of political causes. It rejected the argument that the anonymous speech ban was justified by the state's asserted interests in preventing fraudulent and libelous statements and in providing the electorate with relevant information. It noted that the author's name and address would add little to the reader's ability to evaluate the document in the case of a flyer written by a private citizen unknown to the reader. Further, in relationship to the desire to prevent libel, the statute's prohibition of all anonymous leaflets, regardless of whether they are arguably false or misleading, went too far.

2. FREEDOM OF EXPRESSION BY INDIVIDUAL PROTESTERS

"It is by the goodness of God that in our country we have those three unspeakably precious things: freedom of speech, freedom of conscience, and the prudence never to practice either of them."

Mark Twain, Following the Equator (1903).

BRANDENBURG v. OHIO

Supreme Court of the United States, 1969.
395 U.S. 444, 89 S.Ct. 1827.

PER CURIAM.

The appellant, a leader of a Ku Klux Klan group, was convicted under the Ohio Criminal Syndicalism statute for "advocat[ing] . . . the duty, necessity, or propriety of crime, sabotage, violence, or unlawful methods of terrorism as a means of accomplishing industrial or political reform" and for "voluntarily assembl[ing] with any society, group, or assemblage of persons formed to teach or advocate the doctrines of criminal syndicalism." Ohio Rev.Code Ann. § 2923.13. He was fined $1,000 and sentenced to one to 10 years' imprisonment. The appellant challenged the constitutionality of the criminal syndicalism statute under the First and Fourteenth Amendments to the United States Constitution, but the intermediate appellate court of Ohio affirmed his conviction without opinion. The Supreme Court of Ohio dismissed his appeal,

. . . "for the reason that no substantial constitutional question exists herein." It did not file an opinion or explain its conclusions. Appeal was taken to this Court, and we noted probable jurisdiction. We reverse.

The record shows that a man, identified at trial as the appellant, telephoned an announcer-reporter on the staff of a Cincinnati television station and invited him to come to a Ku Klux Klan "rally" to be held at a farm in Hamilton County. With the cooperation of the organizers, the reporter and a cameraman attended the meeting and filmed the events. Portions of the films were later broadcast on the local station and on a national network.

The prosecution's case rested on the films and on testimony identifying the appellant as the person who communicated with the reporter and who spoke at the rally. The State also introduced into evidence several articles appearing in the film, including a pistol, a rifle, a shotgun, ammunition, a Bible, and a red hood worn by the speaker in the films.

One film showed 12 hooded figures, some of whom carried firearms. They were gathered around a large wooden cross, which they burned. No one was present other than the participants and the newsmen who made the film. Most of the words uttered during the scene were incomprehensible when the film was projected, but scattered phrases could be understood that were derogatory of Negroes and, in one instance, of Jews. Another scene on the same film showed the appellant, in Klan regalia, making a speech. The speech, in full, was as follows:

> "This is an organizers' meeting. We have had quite a few members here today which are—we have hundreds, hundreds of members throughout the State of Ohio. I can quote from a newspaper clipping from the Columbus, Ohio Dispatch, five weeks ago Sunday morning. The Klan has more members in the State of Ohio than does any other organization. We're not a revengent organization, but if our President, our Congress, our Supreme Court, continues to suppress the white, Caucasian race, it's possible that there might have to be some revengeance taken.
>
> "We are marching on Congress July the Fourth, four hundred thousand strong. From there we are dividing into two groups, one group to march on St. Augustine, Florida, the other group to march into Mississippi. Thank you."

The second film showed six hooded figures one of whom, later identified as the appellant, repeated a speech very similar to that recorded on the first film. The reference to the possibility of "revengeance" was omitted, and one sentence was added: "Personally, I believe the nigger should be returned to Africa, the Jew returned to

Israel." Though some of the figures in the films carried weapons, the speaker did not.

The Ohio Criminal Syndicalism Statute was enacted in 1919. From 1917 to 1920, identical or quite similar laws were adopted by 20 States and two territories. E. Dowell, A History of Criminal Syndicalism Legislation in the United States 21 (1939). In 1927, this Court sustained the constitutionality of California's Criminal Syndicalism Act, Cal.Penal Code §§ 11400–11402, the text of which is quite similar to that of the laws of Ohio. Whitney v. California, 274 U.S. 357, 47 S.Ct. 641 (1927). The Court upheld the statute on the ground that, without more, "advocating" violent means to effect political and economic change involves such danger to the security of the State that the State may outlaw it. But *Whitney* has been thoroughly discredited by later decisions. See Dennis v. United States, 341 U.S. 494, at 507, 71 S.Ct. 857, at 866 (1951). These later decisions have fashioned the principle that the constitutional guarantees of free speech and free press do not permit a State to forbid or proscribe advocacy of the use of force or of law violation except where such advocacy is directed to inciting or producing imminent lawless action and is likely to incite or produce such action. As we said in Noto v. United States, 367 U.S. 290, 297–298, 81 S.Ct. 1517, 1520–1521 (1961), "the mere abstract teaching ... of the moral propriety or even moral necessity for a resort to force and violence, is not the same as preparing a group for violent action and steeling it to such action." A statute which fails to draw this distinction impermissibly intrudes upon the freedoms guaranteed by the First and Fourteenth Amendments. It sweeps within its condemnation speech which our Constitution has immunized from governmental control.

Measured by this test, Ohio's Criminal Syndicalism Act cannot be sustained. The Act punishes persons who "advocate or teach the duty, necessity, or propriety" of violence "as a means of accomplishing industrial or political reform"; or who publish or circulate or display any book or paper containing such advocacy; or who "justify" the commission of violent acts "with intent to exemplify, spread or advocate the propriety of the doctrines of criminal syndicalism"; or who "voluntarily assemble" with a group formed "to teach or advocate the doctrines of criminal syndicalism." Neither the indictment nor the trial judge's instructions to the jury in any way refined the statute's bald definition of the crime in terms of mere advocacy not distinguished from incitement to imminent lawless action.[1]

1. The first count of the indictment charged that appellant "did unlawfully by word of mouth advocate the necessity, or propriety of crime, violence, or unlawful methods of terrorism as a means of accomplishing political reform...." The second count charged that appellant "did unlawfully voluntarily assemble with a group or assemblage of persons formed to advocate the doctrines of criminal syndicalism...." The trial judge's charge merely followed the language of the indictment. No construction of the statute by the Ohio courts has brought it within constitutionally permissible limits. The Ohio Supreme Court has considered the statute in only one previous case, State v. Kassay, 126 Ohio St. 177, 184 N.E. 521 (1932), where the constitutionality of the statute was sustained.

Accordingly, we are here confronted with a statute which, by its own words and as applied, purports to punish mere advocacy and to forbid, on pain of criminal punishment, assembly with others merely to advocate the described type of action.[2] Such a statute falls within the condemnation of the First and Fourteenth Amendments. The contrary teaching of Whitney v. California, supra, cannot be supported, and that decision is therefore overruled.

Reversed.

Mr. Justice Douglas, concurring.

While I join the opinion of the Court, I desire to enter a caveat.

The "clear and present danger" test was adumbrated by Mr. Justice Holmes in a case arising during World War I—a war "declared" by the Congress, not by the Chief Executive. The case was Schenck v. United States, 249 U.S. 47, 52, 39 S.Ct. 247, 249 where the defendant was charged with attempts to cause insubordination in the military and obstruction of enlistment. The pamphlets that were distributed urged resistance to the draft, denounced conscription, and impugned the motives of those backing the war effort. The First Amendment was tendered as a defense. Mr. Justice Holmes in rejecting that defense said:

> "The question in every case is whether the words used are used in such circumstances and are of such a nature as to create a clear and present danger that they will bring about the substantive evils that Congress has a right to prevent. It is a question of proximity and degree."

Frohwerk v. United States, 249 U.S. 204, 39 S.Ct. 249 also authored by Mr. Justice Holmes, involved prosecution and punishment for publication of articles very critical of the war effort in World War I. *Schenck* was referred to as a conviction for obstructing security "by words of persuasion." And the conviction in *Frohwerk* was sustained because "the circulation of the paper was in quarters where a little breath would be enough to kindle a flame." Id., at 209, 39 S.Ct., at 251.

Debs v. United States, 249 U.S. 211, 39 S.Ct. 252 was the third of the trilogy of the 1918 Term. Debs was convicted of speaking in opposition to the war where his "opposition was so expressed that its natural and intended effect would be to obstruct recruiting."

> "If that was intended and if, in all the circumstances, that would be its probable effect, it would not be protected by reason of its being part of a general program in expressions of a general and conscientious belief."

2. Statutes affecting the right of assembly, like those touching on freedom of speech, must observe the established distinctions between mere advocacy and incitement to imminent lawless action, for as Chief Justice Hughes wrote in De Jonge v. Oregon, supra, 299 U.S. at 364, 57 S.Ct. at 260:

> "The right of peaceable assembly is a right cognate to those of free speech and free press and is equally fundamental."

In the 1919 Term, the Court applied the *Schenck* doctrine to affirm the convictions of other dissidents in World War I. Abrams v. United States, 250 U.S. 616, 40 S.Ct. 17 was one instance. Mr. Justice Holmes, with whom Mr. Justice Brandeis concurred, dissented. While adhering to *Schenck,* he did not think that on the facts a case for overriding the First Amendment had been made out:

> "It is only the present danger of immediate evil or an intent to bring it about that warrants Congress in setting a limit to the expression of opinion where private rights are not concerned. Congress certainly cannot forbid all effort to change the mind of the country."

Another instance was Schaefer v. United States, 251 U.S. 466, 40 S.Ct. 259, in which Mr. Justice Brandeis, joined by Mr. Justice Holmes, dissented. A third was Pierce v. United States, 252 U.S. 239, 40 S.Ct. 205, in which again Mr. Justice Brandeis, joined by Mr. Justice Holmes, dissented.

Those, then, were the World War I cases that put the gloss of "clear and present danger" on the First Amendment. Whether the war power—the greatest leveler of them all—is adequate to sustain that doctrine is debatable. The dissents in *Abrams, Schaefer,* and *Pierce* show how easily "clear and present danger" is manipulated to crush what Brandeis called "[t]he fundamental right of free men to strive for better conditions through new legislation and new institutions" by argument and discourse even in time of war. Though I doubt if the "clear and present danger" test is congenial to the First Amendment in time of a declared war, I am certain it is not reconcilable with the First Amendment in days of peace.

The Court quite properly overrules Whitney v. California, 274 U.S. 357, 47 S.Ct. 641, which involved advocacy of ideas which the majority of the Court deemed unsound and dangerous.

Mr. Justice Holmes, though never formally abandoning the "clear and present danger" test, moved closer to the First Amendment ideal when he said in dissent in Gitlow [Gitlow v. People of State of New York, 268 U.S. 652, 45 S.Ct. 626]:

> "Every idea is an incitement. It offers itself for belief and if believed it is acted on unless some other belief outweighs it or some failure of energy stifles the movement at its birth. The only difference between the expression of an opinion and an incitement in the narrower sense is the speaker's enthusiasm for the result. Eloquence may set fire to reason. But whatever may be thought of the redundant discourse before us it had no chance of starting a present conflagration. If in the long run the beliefs expressed in proletarian dictatorship are destined to be accepted by the dominant forces of the community, the only meaning of free speech is that they should be given their chance and have their way."

We have never been faithful to the philosophy of that dissent.

The Court in Herndon v. Lowry, 301 U.S. 242, 57 S.Ct. 732, overturned a conviction for exercising First Amendment rights to incite insurrection because of lack of evidence of incitement. In Bridges v. California, 314 U.S. 252, 261–263, 62 S.Ct. 190, 192–194, we approved the "clear and present danger" test in an elaborate dictum that tightened it and confined it to a narrow category. But in Dennis v. United States, 341 U.S. 494, 71 S.Ct. 857, we opened wide the door, distorting the "clear and present danger" test beyond recognition.

In that case the prosecution dubbed an agreement to teach the Marxist creed a "conspiracy." The case was submitted to a jury on a charge that the jury could not convict unless it found that the defendants "intended to overthrow the Government 'as speedily as circumstances would permit.' " The Court sustained convictions under that charge, construing it to mean a determination of " 'whether the gravity of the "evil," discounted by its improbability, justifies such invasion of free speech as is necessary to avoid the danger.' " ...

I see no place in the regime of the First Amendment for any "clear and present danger" test, whether strict and tight as some would make it, or free-wheeling as the Court in *Dennis* rephrased it.

When one reads the opinions closely and sees when and how the "clear and present danger" test has been applied, great misgivings are aroused. First, the threats were often loud but always puny and made serious only by judges so wedded to the *status quo* that critical analysis made them nervous. Second, the test was so twisted and perverted in *Dennis* as to make the trial of those teachers of Marxism an all-out political trial which was part and parcel of the cold war that has eroded substantial parts of the First Amendment.

Action is often a method of expression and within the protection of the First Amendment.

Suppose one tears up his own copy of the Constitution in eloquent protest to a decision of this Court. May he be indicted?

Suppose one rips his own Bible to shreds to celebrate his departure from one "faith" and his embrace of atheism. May he be indicted?

Last Term the Court held in United States v. O'Brien, 391 U.S. 367, 382, 88 S.Ct. 1673, 1682, that a registrant under Selective Service who burned his draft card in protest of the war in Vietnam could be prosecuted. The First Amendment was tendered as a defense and rejected, the Court saying:

> "The issuance of certificates indicating the registration and eligibility classification of individuals is a legitimate and substantial administrative aid in the functioning of this system. And legislation to insure the continuing availability of issued certificates serves a legitimate and substantial purpose in the system's administration."

But O'Brien was not prosecuted for not having his draft card available when asked for by a federal agent. He was indicted, tried and convicted for burning the card. And this Court's affirmance of that conviction was not, with all respect consistent with the First Amendment.

The act of praying often involves body posture and movement as well as utterances. It is nonetheless protected by the Free Exercise Clause. Picketing, as we have said on numerous occasions, is "free speech plus." That means that it can be regulated when it comes to the "plus" or "action" side of the protest. It can be regulated as to the number of pickets and the place and hours ... because traffic and other community problems would otherwise suffer.

But none of these considerations are implicated in the symbolic protest of the Vietnam war in the burning of a draft card.

One's beliefs have long been thought to be sanctuaries which government could not invade. *Barenblatt* [360 U.S. 109, 79 S.Ct. 1081] is one example of the ease with which that sanctuary can be violated. The lines drawn by the Court between the criminal act of being an "active" Communist and the innocent act of being a nominal or inactive Communist mark the difference only between deep and abiding belief and casual or uncertain belief. But I think that all matters of belief are beyond the reach of subpoenas or the probings of investigators. That is why the invasions of privacy made by investigating committees were notoriously unconstitutional. That is the deep-seated fault in the infamous loyalty-security hearings which, since 1947 when President Truman launched them, have processed 20,000,000 men and women. Those hearings were primarily concerned with one's thoughts, ideas, beliefs, and convictions. They were the most blatant violations of the First Amendment we have ever known.

The line between what is permissible and not subject to control and what may be made impermissible and subject to regulation is the line between ideas and overt acts.

The example usually given by those who would punish speech is the case of one who falsely shouts fire in a crowded theatre.

This is, however, a classic case where speech is brigaded with action. See Speiser v. Randall, 357 U.S. 513, 536–537, 78 S.Ct. 1332, 1346, (Douglas J., concurring.) They are indeed inseparable and a prosecution can be launched for the overt acts actually caused. Apart from rare instances of that kind, speech is, I think, immune from prosecution. Certainly there is no constitutional line between advocacy of abstract ideas as in *Yates* and advocacy of political action as in *Scales*. The quality of advocacy turns on the depth of the conviction; and government has no power to invade that sanctuary of belief and conscience.

[The short concurring opinion of Mr. Justice Black is omitted.]

COHEN v. CALIFORNIA

Supreme Court of the United States, 1971.
403 U.S. 15, 91 S.Ct. 1780.

MR. JUSTICE HARLAN delivered the opinion of the Court.

This case may seem at first blush too inconsequential to find its way into our books, but the issue it presents is of no small constitutional significance.

Appellant Paul Robert Cohen was convicted in the Los Angeles Municipal Court of violating that part of California Penal Code § 415 which prohibits "maliciously and willfully disturb[ing] the peace or quiet of any neighborhood or person ... by ... offensive conduct...." He was given 30 days' imprisonment. The facts upon which his conviction rests are detailed in the opinion of the Court of Appeal of California, Second Appellate District, as follows:

> "On April 26, 1968, the defendant was observed in the Los Angeles County Courthouse in the corridor outside of division 20 of the municipal court wearing a jacket bearing the words 'Fuck the Draft' which were plainly visible. There were women and children present in the corridor. The defendant was arrested. The defendant testified that he wore the jacket knowing that the words were on the jacket as a means of informing the public of the depth of his feelings against the Vietnam War and the draft.
>
> "The defendant did not engage in, nor threaten to engage in, nor did anyone as the result of his conduct in fact commit or threaten to commit any act of violence. The defendant did not make any loud or unusual noise, nor was there any evidence that he uttered any sound prior to his arrest." ...

In affirming the conviction the Court of Appeal held that "offensive conduct" means "behavior which has a tendency to provoke *others* to acts of violence or to in turn disturb the peace," and that the State had proved this element because on the facts of this case, "[i]t was certainly reasonably foreseeable that such conduct might cause others to rise up to commit a violent act against the person of the defendant or attempt to forceably remove his jacket." ... The California Supreme Court declined review by a divided vote. ... We now reverse.

I

In order to lay hands on the precise issue which this case involves, it is useful first to canvass various matters which this record does *not* present.

The conviction quite clearly rests upon the asserted offensiveness of the *words* Cohen used to convey his message to the public. The only "conduct" which the State sought to punish is the fact of communication. Thus, we deal here with a conviction resting solely upon "speech," ... not upon any separately identifiable conduct which allegedly was intended by Cohen to be perceived by others as expressive of particular views but which, on its face does not necessarily convey any message and hence arguably could be regulated without effectively repressing Cohen's ability to express himself.

... Further, the State certainly lacks power to punish Cohen for the underlying content of the message the inscription conveyed. At least so long as there is no showing of an intent to incite disobedience to or disruption of the draft, Cohen could not, consistently with the First and Fourteenth Amendments, be punished for asserting the evident position on the inutility or immorality of the draft his jacket reflected....

Appellant's conviction, then, rests squarely upon his exercise of the "freedom of speech" protected from arbitrary governmental interference by the Constitution and can be justified, if at all, only as a valid regulation of the manner in which he exercised that freedom, not as a permissible prohibition on the substantive message it conveys. This does not end the inquiry, of course, for the First and Fourteenth Amendments have never been thought to give absolute protection to every individual to speak whenever or wherever he pleases or to use any form of address in any circumstances that he chooses. In this vein, too, however, we think it important to note that several issues typically associated with such problems are not presented here.

In the first place, Cohen was tried under a statute applicable throughout the entire State. Any attempt to support this conviction on the ground that the statute seeks to preserve an appropriately decorous atmosphere in the courthouse where Cohen was arrested must fail in the absence of any language in the statute that would have put appellant on notice that certain kinds of otherwise permissible speech or conduct would nevertheless, under California law, not be tolerated in certain places.... No fair reading of the phrase "offensive conduct" can be said sufficiently to inform the ordinary person that distinctions between certain locations are thereby created.

In the second place as it comes to us, this case cannot be said to fall within those relatively few categories of instances where prior decisions have established the power of government to deal more comprehensively with certain forms of individual expression simply upon a showing that such a form was employed. This is not, for example, an obscenity case. Whatever else may be necessary to give rise to the States' broader power to prohibit obscene expression, such expression must be, in some significant way, erotic. [Roth v. United States, infra this casebook]. It cannot plausibly be maintained that this vulgar allusion to the Selective Service System would conjure up such psychic stimulation in anyone likely to be confronted with Cohen's crudely defaced jacket.

This Court has also held that the States are free to ban the simple use, without a demonstration of additional justifying circumstances, of so-called "fighting words," those personally abusive epithets which, when addressed to the ordinary citizen, are, as a matter of common knowledge, inherently likely to provoke violent reaction. Chaplinsky v. New Hampshire, 315 U.S. 568, 62 S.Ct. 766 (1942). While the four-letter word displayed by Cohen in relation to the draft is not uncommonly employed in a personally provocative fashion, in this instance it was clearly not "directed to the person of the hearer." ... No individual actually or likely to be present could reasonably have regarded the words on appellant's jacket as a direct personal insult. Nor do we have here an instance of the exercise of the State's police power to prevent a speaker from intentionally provoking a given group to hostile reaction. Cf. Feiner v. New York, 340 U.S. 315, 71 S.Ct. 303 (1951); Terminiello v. Chicago, 337 U.S. 1, 69 S.Ct. 894 (1949). There is, as noted above, no showing that anyone who saw Cohen was in fact violently aroused or that appellant intended such a result.

Finally, in arguments before this Court much has been made of the claim that Cohen's distasteful mode of expression was thrust upon unwilling or unsuspecting viewers, and that the State might therefore legitimately act as it did in order to protect the sensitive from otherwise unavoidable exposure to appellant's crude form of protest. Of course, the mere presumed presence of unwitting listeners or viewers does not serve automatically to justify curtailing all speech capable of giving offense.... While this Court has recognized that government may properly act in many situations to prohibit intrusion into the privacy of the home of unwelcome views and ideas which cannot be totally banned from the public dialogue, ... we have at the same time consistently stressed that "we are often 'captives' outside the sanctuary of the home and subject to objectionable speech." ... The ability of government, consonant with the Constitution, to shut off discourse solely to protect others from hearing it is, in other words, dependent upon a showing that substantial privacy interests are being invaded in an essentially intolerable manner. Any broader view of this authority would effectively empower a majority to silence dissidents simply as a matter of personal predilections.

In this regard, persons confronted with Cohen's jacket were in a quite different posture than, say, those subjected to the raucous emissions of sound trucks blaring outside their residences. Those in the Los Angeles courthouse could effectively avoid further bombardment of their sensibilities simply by averting their eyes. And, while it may be that one has a more substantial claim to a recognizable privacy interest when walking through a courthouse corridor than, for example strolling through Central Park, surely it is nothing like the interest in being free from unwanted expression in the confines of one's own home. Given the subtlety and complexity of the factors involved, if Cohen's "speech" was otherwise entitled to constitutional protection, we do not think the fact that some unwilling "listeners" in a public building may have been briefly exposed to it can serve to justify this breach of the peace conviction where, as here, there was no evidence that persons powerless to avoid appellant's conduct did in fact object to it, and where that portion of the statute upon which Cohen's conviction rests evinces no concern, either on its face or as construed by the California courts, with the special plight of the captive auditor, but, instead, indiscriminately sweeps within its prohibitions all "offensive conduct" that disturbs "any neighborhood or person." ...

II

Against this background, the issue flushed by this case stands out in bold relief. It is whether California can excise, as "offensive conduct," one particular scurrilous epithet from the public discourse, either upon the theory of the court below that its use is inherently likely to cause violent reaction or upon a more general assertion that the States, acting as guardians of public morality, may properly remove this offensive word from the public vocabulary.

The rationale of the California court is plainly untenable. At most it reflects an "undifferentiated fear or apprehension of disturbance [which] is not enough to overcome the right to freedom of expression." Tinker v. Des Moines Indep. Community School Dist., 393 U.S. 503, 508, 89 S.Ct. 733, 737 (1969). We have been shown no evidence that substantial numbers of citizens are standing ready to strike out physically at whoever may assault their sensibilities with execrations like that uttered by Cohen. There may be some persons about with such lawless and violent proclivities, but that is an insufficient base upon which to erect, consistently with constitutional values, a governmental power to force persons who wish to ventilate their dissident views into avoiding particular forms of expression. The argument amounts to little more than the self-defeating proposition that to avoid physical censorship of one who has not sought to provoke such a response by a hypothetical coterie of the violent and lawless, the States may more appropriately effectuate that censorship themselves....

Admittedly, it is not so obvious that the First and Fourteenth Amendments must be taken to disable the States from punishing public utterance of this unseemly expletive in order to maintain what they regard as a suitable level of discourse within the body politic. We think, however, that examination and reflection will reveal the shortcomings of a contrary viewpoint.

At the outset, we cannot overemphasize that, in our judgment, most situations where the State has a justifiable interest in regulating speech will fall within one or more of the various established exceptions, discussed above but not applicable here, to the usual rule that governmental bodies may not prescribe the form or content of individual expression. Equally important to our conclusion is the constitutional backdrop against which our decision must be made. The constitutional right of free expression is powerful medicine in a society as diverse and populous as ours. It is designed and intended to remove governmental restraints from the arena of public discussion, putting the decision as to what views shall be voiced largely into the hands of each of us, in the hope that use of such freedom will ultimately produce a more capable citizenry and more perfect polity and in the belief that no other approach would comport with the premise of individual dignity and choice upon which our political system rests....

To many, the immediate consequence of this freedom may often appear to be only verbal tumult, discord, and even offensive utterance. These are however, within established limits, in truth necessary side effects of the broader enduring values which the process of open debate permits us to achieve. That the air may at times seem filled with verbal cacophony is, in this sense not a sign of weakness but of strength. We cannot lose sight of the fact that, in what otherwise might seem a trifling and annoying instance of individual distasteful abuse of a privilege, these fundamental societal values are truly implicated. That is why "[w]holly neutral futilities ... come under the protection of free speech as fully as do Keats' poems or Donne's sermons," ... and why "so long as the means are peaceful, the communication need not meet standards of acceptability," ...

Against this perception of the constitutional policies involved we discern certain more particularized considerations that peculiarly call for reversal of this conviction. First, the principle contended for by the State seems inherently boundless. How is one to distinguish this from any other offensive word? Surely the State has no right to cleanse public debate to the point where it is grammatically palatable to the most squeamish among us. Yet no readily ascertainable general principle exists for stopping short of that result were we to affirm the judgment below. For, while the particular four-letter word being litigated here is perhaps more distasteful than most others of its genre, it is nevertheless often true that one man's vulgarity is another's lyric. Indeed, we think it is largely because governmental officials cannot make principled distinctions in this area that the Constitution leaves matters of taste and style so largely to the individual.

Additionally, we cannot overlook the fact, because it is well illustrated by the episode involved here, that much linguistic expression serves a dual communicative function: it conveys not only ideas capable of relatively precise, detached explication, but otherwise inexpressible emotions as well. In fact, words are often chosen as much for their emotive as their cognitive force. We cannot sanction the view that the Constitution, while solicitous of the cognitive content of individual speech has little or no regard for that emotive function which practically speaking, may often be the more important element of the overall message sought to be communicated. Indeed, as Mr. Justice Frankfurter has said, "[o]ne of the prerogatives of American citizenship is the right to criticize public men and measures—and that means not only informed and responsible criticism but the freedom to speak, foolishly and without moderation." ...

Finally, and in the same vein, we cannot indulge the facile assumption that one can forbid particular words without also running a substantial risk of suppressing ideas in the process. Indeed, governments might soon seize upon the censorship of particular words as a convenient guise for banning the expression of unpopular views. We have been able, as noted above, to discern little social benefit that might result from running the risk of opening the door to such grave results.

It is, in sum, our judgment that, absent a more particularized and compelling reason for its actions, the State may not, consistently with the First and Fourteenth Amendments, make the simple public display here involved of this single four-letter expletive a criminal offense. Because that is the only arguably sustainable rationale for the conviction here at issue, the judgment below must be reversed.

Reversed.

MR. JUSTICE BLACKMUN, with whom THE CHIEF JUSTICE and MR. JUSTICE BLACK join.

I dissent, ...

Cohen's absurd and immature antic in my view, was mainly conduct and little speech. ... The California Court of Appeal appears so to have described it, ... and I cannot characterize it otherwise. Further, the case appears to me to be well within the sphere of Chaplinsky v. New Hampshire, ... where Mr. Justice Murphy, a known champion of First Amendment freedoms, wrote for a unanimous bench. As a consequence, this Court's agonizing over First Amendment values seem misplaced and unnecessary....

NOTES

1. The *Chaplinsky* case, to which the court referred in *Cohen,* involved a situation where the defendant on a public street, addressed another person as a "God damned racketeer" and a "damned Fascist", adding that the whole city government was composed of "Fascists or agents of Fascists". The defendant was charged with violating a statute providing that "No person shall address any offensive, derisive or annoying word to another person [in any public place] ..." His conviction was upheld by the Supreme Court, on the ground that the statute was intended to do no more than prohibit "face-to-face words plainly likely to cause a breach of the peace"; and that the limited scope of the statute was not an impingement of the constitutional right to free expression.

Compare Gooding, Warden v. Wilson, 405 U.S. 518, 92 S.Ct. 1103 (1972), which held unconstitutional, on grounds of violation of free speech as well as vagueness, a Georgia statute which provided that "[a]ny person who shall, without provocation, use to or of another, and in his presence ... opprobrious words or abusive language, tending to cause a breach of the peace ... shall be guilty of a misdemeanor."

The vagueness issue will be discussed in the Due Process section, infra.

2. See also, Lewis v. City of New Orleans, 415 U.S. 130, 94 S.Ct. 970 (1974), wherein the Court struck down, as unconstitutionally overbroad and therefore facially invalid, a New Orleans, Louisiana, ordinance providing:

> "It shall be unlawful and a breach of the peace for any person wantonly to curse or revile or to use obscene or opprobrious language toward or with reference to any member of the city police while in the actual performance of his duty."

The Court held that the ordinance had a broader sweep than the constitutional definition of "fighting words," saying, "At the least, the proscription of the use of 'opprobrious language,' embraces words that do not 'by their very utterance inflict injury or tend to incite an immediate breach of the peace.' ... In sum, [the ordinance] punishes only spoken words. It can therefore withstand appellant's attack upon its facial constitutionality only if, as authoritatively construed by the Louisiana Supreme Court, it is not susceptible of application to speech, although vulgar or offensive, that is protected by the First and Fourteenth Amendments." Since the Louisiana Supreme Court had not limited the ordinance by judicial decision, the United States Supreme Court reversed the conviction.

3. In Federal Communications Commission v. Pacifica Foundation, 438 U.S. 726, 98 S.Ct. 3026 (1978), the Supreme Court did approve an F.C.C. ban on seven "dirty words". The case was inspired by a father writing a letter to the F.C.C. after hearing an afternoon broadcast of a recorded monologue by comedian George Carlin. The comedian had identified seven words as "words you couldn't say on the public airwaves" and repeated them several times during his monologue. The commission later issued a declaratory order specifying that the words used could not be broadcast at the times of the day when children might be listening in.

The order was later approved by the U.S. Supreme Court in a 5–4 decision. All five Justices did not agree, however, as to the basis for upholding the ban. Justice Stevens' opinion, with which only two other Justices fully agreed, put forth the theory that speech with a certain content—such as indecent speech—is less valuable to society and therefore deserves less protection. Justice Powell's separate concurring opinion, which Justice Blackmun joined, disagreed with that theory, but upheld the F.C.C. action on the basis of the unique characteristics of the broadcast media, "combined with society's right to protect its children from speech generally agreed to be inappropriate for their years, and with the interest of unwilling adults in not being assaulted by such offensive speech in their homes."

4. "We'll take the fucking street later," spoken while facing a crowd at an antiwar demonstration while law enforcement officers were attempting to clear the street, could not be punished as obscene language or "fighting words" in Hess v. Indiana, 414 U.S. 105, 94 S.Ct. 326 (1973).

5. For a general discussion of the validity and construction of statutes and ordinances prohibiting profanity or profane swearing or cursing, see Annot., 5 A.L.R.4th 956 (1981). A similar discussion of statutes prohibiting the use of obscene language in public is contained in Annot., 2 A.L.R.4th 1331 (1980).

6. The CB radio message, "There is a Smokey taking pictures up the road," relayed by the defendant motorist to other motor vehicle operators, resulted in a conviction of obstructing governmental administration and a year's imprisonment. If attacked on appeal on First Amendment grounds, can the conviction stand? See People v. Case, 42 N.Y.2d 98, 396 N.Y.S.2d 841, 365 N.E.2d 872 (1977). Does the following ordinance unconstitutionally infringe upon free speech, "No person shall solicit a person to engage in sexual activity with the offender, when the offender knows such solicitation is offensive to the other person, or is reckless in that regard."? See City of Columbus v. Scott, 47 Ohio App.2d 287, 353 N.E.2d 858 (1975).

7. What about a clerical employee in a county constable's office who tells a fellow employee upon hearing that an attempt had been made on the life of the

President of the United States, "if they go for him again, I hope they get him"; can the employee be fired? No, according to the U.S. Supreme Court in Rankin v. McPherson, 483 U.S. 378, 107 S.Ct. 2891 (1987). The employee's speech was protected by the First Amendment because it dealt with a matter of "public concern." The Court ruled that the constable's interest in firing the employee as a matter of internal discipline was outweighed by the employee's right to free speech.

See also Waters v. Churchill, 511 U.S. ___, 114 S.Ct. 1878 (1994), which addresses the possible need for a public employer to conduct an investigation into what the employee actually said before taking disciplinary action against the employee for their speech.

8. In two interesting decisions, the U.S. Supreme Court addressed some of the outer perimeters of speech, focusing on state law "hate crimes" statutes. In R.A.V. v. St. Paul, 505 U.S. 377, 112 S.Ct. 2538 (1992), a defendant was charged with violation of a hate crimes ordinance after burning a cross on the lawn of an African-American family's home. The ordinance prohibited the display of a symbol which one knows or has reason to know "arouses anger, alarm or resentment in others on the basis of race, color, creed, religion or gender." The Court ruled that this ordinance unconstitutionally prohibited speech on the basis of the subjects the speech addresses. It was facially unconstitutional because it imposed "special prohibitions" on speakers expressing views on the disfavored subjects of "race, color, creed, religion or gender," while allowing "abusive invective" not addressed to those topics. The Court ruled that this was impermissible content based discrimination. In Wisconsin v. Mitchell, 508 U.S. 476, 113 S.Ct. 2194 (1993), on the other hand, the Court ruled that the enhancement of a defendant's sentence for aggravated battery because he intentionally selected his victim on account of the victim's race did not violate his First Amendment rights. The Court noted that a wide variety of factors may be taken into account in sentencing, and there is not absolute prohibition of the admission of evidence concerning one's beliefs and associations at sentencing simply because they are protected by the First Amendment. Further, the ordinance at issue in the case was explicitly directed at conduct unprotected by the First Amendment, rather than speech itself. The First Amendment allows previous declarations or statements to be used to establish the elements of a crime or to prove motive or intent.

9. As we go to press, there is a far-reaching controversy over "indecent" speech transmitted via interactive computer networks, such as the Internet and commercial on-line services (such as America On Line, Compuserve, Prodigy, etc.). On February 8, 1996, Congress passed and President Clinton signed into law the Communications Decency Act, 47 U.S.C.A. § 223. Section 223(d) makes it a federal crime, punishable by two year's imprisonment, to knowingly use any "interactive computer service" to send to a specific person under 18 years of age, or to "display" in a "manner available to" a person under the age of 18 certain "patently offensive" content. Section 223(a)(1)(B) of the same statute similarly imposes criminal penalties for using any "telecommunications device" to similarly transmit "indecent" material. Opponents of the Act argued that, given the difficulty inherent in restricting the access of minors to computer networks, this would effectively limit what was available to adults to what was deemed suitable for children. Proponents of the Act argued that restrictions imposed by the law were necessary to protect minors from exposure to harmful materials. Two lawsuits against the enforcement of the Act were filed almost immediately, and, based on provisions in the law itself providing for special streamlined judicial

review, the ultimate decision in the case may quickly be presented to the U.S. Supreme Court.

3. SYMBOLISM

UNITED STATES v. O'BRIEN

Supreme Court of the United States, 1968.
391 U.S. 367, 88 S.Ct. 1673.

[The defendant (in March, 1966) burned his Selective Service registration certificate (draft card) on the steps of a courthouse in the presence of a sizeable crowd. He said he did it to publicly influence others to adopt his anti war beliefs. He was arrested and charged with violating a federal statute making it a criminal offense for anyone to knowingly destroy or mutilate such certificates. In essence he claimed he was exercising his constitutional right to "symbolic free speech". Following are excerpts from the opinion of the Supreme Court upholding the defendant's conviction. The federal statute involved in the case is Section 462(b) of the Universal Military Training and Service Act of 1948—Title 50 (App.), United States Code, as amended in 1965.]

Mr. Chief Justice Warren delivered the opinion of the Court.

* * *

We note at the outset that the 1965 Amendment plainly does not abridge free speech on its face, and we do not understand O'Brien to argue otherwise. ... [It] deals with conduct having no connection with speech. It prohibits the knowing destruction of certificates issued by the Selective Service System, and there is nothing necessarily expressive about such conduct. The Amendment does not distinguish between public and private destruction, and it does not punish only destruction engaged in for the purpose of expressing views. ... A law prohibiting destruction of Selective Service certificates no more abridges free speech on its face than a motor vehicle law prohibiting the destruction of drivers' licenses, or a tax law prohibiting the destruction of books and records.

O'Brien nonetheless argues that the 1965 Amendment is unconstitutional in its application to him, and is unconstitutional as enacted because what he calls the "purpose" of Congress was "to suppress freedom of speech." We consider these arguments separately.

O'Brien first argues that the 1965 Amendment is unconstitutional as applied to him because his act of burning his registration certificate was protected "symbolic speech" within the First Amendment. His argument is that the freedom of expression which the First Amendment guarantees includes all modes of "communication of ideas by conduct," and that his conduct is within this definition because he did it in "demonstration against the war and against the draft."

We cannot accept the view that an apparently limitless variety of conduct can be labeled "speech" whenever the person engaging in the conduct intends thereby to express an idea. However, even on the assumption that the alleged communicative element in O'Brien's conduct is sufficient to bring into play the First Amendment, it does not necessarily follow that the destruction of a registration certificate is constitutionally protected activity. This Court has held that when "speech" and "nonspeech" elements are combined in the same course of conduct, a sufficiently important governmental interest in regulating the nonspeech element can justify incidental limitations on First Amendment freedoms. To characterize the quality of the governmental interest which must appear, the Court has employed a variety of descriptive terms: compelling; substantial; subordinating; paramount; cogent; strong. Whatever imprecision inheres in these terms, we think it clear that a government regulation is sufficiently justified if it is within the constitutional power of the Government; if it furthers an important or substantial governmental interest; if the governmental interest is unrelated to the suppression of free expression; and if the incidental restriction on alleged First Amendment freedoms is no greater than is essential to the furtherance of that interest. We find that the 1965 Amendment ... meets all of these requirements, and consequently that O'Brien can be constitutionally convicted for violating it.

The constitutional power of Congress to raise and support armies and to make all laws necessary and proper to that end is broad and sweeping.... The power of Congress to classify and conscript manpower for military service is "beyond question." ... Pursuant to this power, Congress may establish a system of registration for individuals liable for training and service, and may require such individuals within reason to cooperate in the registration system. The issuance of certificates indicating the registration and eligibility classification of individuals is a legitimate and substantial administrative aid in the functioning of this system. And legislation to insure the continuing availability of issued certificates serves a legitimate and substantial purpose in the system's administration.

O'Brien's argument to the contrary is necessarily premised upon his unrealistic characterization of Selective Service certificates. He essentially adopts the position that such certificates are so many pieces of paper designed to notify registrants of their registration or classification, to be retained or tossed in the wastebasket according to the convenience or taste of the registrant. Once the registrant has received notification, according to this view, there is no reason for him to retain the certificates. O'Brien notes that most of the information on a registration certificate serves no notification purpose at all; the registrant hardly needs to be told his address and physical characteristics. We agree that the registration certificate contains much information of which the registrant needs no notification. This circumstance, however, does not lead to the conclusion that the certificate serves no purpose, but that, like the classification certificate, it serves purposes in addition to initial notification. Many of these purposes would be defeated by the certificates' destruction or mutilation. Among these are:

1. The registration certificate serves as proof that the individual described thereon has registered for the draft. The classification certificate shows the eligibility classification of a named but undescribed individual. Voluntarily displaying the two certificates is an easy and painless way for a young man to dispel a question as to whether he might be delinquent in his Selective Service obligations. Correspondingly, the availability of the certificates for such display relieves the Selective Service System of the administrative burden it would otherwise have in verifying the registration and classification of all suspected delinquents. Further, since both certificates are in the nature of "receipts" attesting that the registrant has done what the law requires, it is in the interest of the just and efficient administration of the system that they be continually available, in the event, for example, of a mix-up in the registrant's file. Additionally, in a time of national crisis, reasonable availability to each registrant of the two small cards assures a rapid and uncomplicated means for determining his fitness for immediate induction, no matter now distant in our mobile society he may be from his local board.

2. The information supplied on the certificates facilitates communication between registrants and local boards, simplifying the system and benefiting all concerned. To begin with, each certificate bears the address of the registrant's local board, an item unlikely to be committed to memory. Further, each card bears the registrant's Selective Service number, and a registrant who has his number readily available so that he can communicate it to his local board when he supplies or requests information can make simpler the board's task in locating his file. Finally, a registrant's inquiry, particularly through a local board other than his own, concerning his eligibility status is frequently answerable simply on the basis of his classification certificate; whereas, if the certificate were not reasonably available and the registrant were uncertain of his classification, the task of answering his questions would be considerably complicated.

3. Both certificates carry continual reminders that the registrant must notify his local board of any change of address, and other specified changes in his status. The smooth functioning of the system requires that local boards be continually aware of the status and whereabouts of registrants, and the destruction of certificates deprives the system of a potentially useful notice device.

4. The regulatory scheme involving Selective Service certificates includes clearly valid prohibitions against the alteration, forgery, or similar deceptive misuse of certificates. The destruction or mutilation of certificates obviously increases the difficulty of detecting and tracing abuses such as these. Further, a mutilated certificate might itself be used for deceptive purposes.

The many functions performed by Selective Service certificates establish beyond doubt that Congress has a legitimate and substantial interest in preventing their wanton and unrestrained destruction and assuring their continuing availability by punishing people who knowingly and wilfully destroy or mutilate them. And we are unpersuaded that the pre-existence of the non-possession regulations in any way negates this interest....

... Finally, the 1965 Amendment ... is concerned with abuses involving *any* issued Selective Service certificates, not only with the registrant's own certificates. The knowing destruction or mutilation of someone else's certificates would therefore violate the statute....

* * *

... We perceive no alternative means that would more precisely and narrowly assure the continuing availability of issued Selective Service certificates than a law which prohibits their wilful mutilation or destruction.... The 1965 Amendment prohibits such conduct and does nothing more. In other words, both the governmental interest and the operation of the 1965 Amendment are limited to the noncommunicative aspect of O'Brien's conduct. The governmental interest and the scope of the 1965 Amendment are limited to preventing harm to the smooth and efficient functioning of the Selective Service System. When O'Brien deliberately rendered unavailable his registration certificate, he wilfully frustrated this governmental interest. For this noncommunicative impact of his conduct, and for nothing else, he was convicted....

MR. JUSTICE HARLAN, concurring.

The crux of the Court's opinion, which I join, is of course its general statement ... that:

> "a government regulation is sufficiently justified if it is within the constitutional power of the Government; if it furthers an important or substantial governmental interest; if the governmental interest is unrelated to the suppression of free expression; and if the incidental restriction on alleged First Amendment freedoms is no greater than is essential to the furtherance of that interest."

I wish to make explicit my understanding that this passage does not foreclose consideration of First Amendment claims in those rare instances when an "incidental" restriction upon expression, imposed by a regulation which furthers an "important or substantial" governmental interest and satisfies the Court's other criteria, in practice has the effect of entirely preventing a "speaker" from reaching a significant audience with whom he could not otherwise lawfully communicate. This is not such a case, since O'Brien manifestly could have conveyed his message in many ways other than by burning his draft card.

[Justice Douglas' dissent is omitted because it concerns itself only with the constitutionality of the draft and he wanted to have that issue decided by the Court.]

NOTES

1. With a rare coalition of Justices—some thought to be conservative, others liberal in their orientation—the Court in Texas v. Johnson, 491 U.S. 397, 109 S.Ct. 2533 (1989) held that laws prohibiting the burning of an American flag as part of a peaceful political expression are unconstitutional. Justices Brennan (who wrote the majority opinion), Blackmun, Kennedy, Marshall and Scalia forged a 5–4 decision. The majority said in part:

"After publicly burning an American flag as a means of political protest, Gregory Lee Johnson was convicted of desecrating a flag in violation of Texas law. This case presents the question whether his conviction is consistent with the First Amendment. We hold that it is not.

"While the Republican National Convention was taking place in Dallas in 1984, respondent Johnson participated in a political demonstration dubbed the 'Republican War Chest Tour.' ...

"The demonstration ended in front of Dallas City Hall, where Johnson unfurled the American flag, doused it with kerosene and set it on fire. While the flag burned, the protestors chanted, 'America, the red, white, and blue, we spit on you.' After the demonstrators dispersed, a witness to the flag-burning collected the flag's remains and buried them in his backyard. No one was physically injured or threatened with injury, though several witnesses testified that they had been seriously offended by the flag burning.

"Of the approximately 100 demonstrators, Johnson alone was charged with a crime. The only criminal offense with which he was charged was the desecration of a venerated object in violation of Texas Penal Code Ann. Sec. 42.09(a)(3) (1989). ['Desecration of a Venerated Object']. After a trial, he was convicted, sentenced to one year in prison and fined $2,000. The Court of Appeals for the Fifth District of Texas at Dallas affirmed Johnson's conviction, but the Texas Court of Criminal Appeals reversed, holding that the State could not, consistent with the First Amendment, punish Johnson for burning the flag in these circumstances....

"To justify Johnson's conviction for engaging in symbolic speech, the State asserted two interests: preserving the flag as a symbol of national unity and preventing breaches of the peace. The Court of Criminal Appeals held that neither interest supported his conviction.

"Acknowledging that this Court had not yet decided whether the Government may criminally sanction flag desecration in order to preserve the flag's symbolic value, the Texas court nevertheless concluded that our decision in *West Virginia Board of Education v. Barnette*, 319 U.S. 624 (1943), suggested that furthering this interest by curtailing speech was impermissible.

* * *

"The First Amendment literally forbids the abridgement only of 'speech,' but we have long recognized that its protection does not end at the spoken or written word....

* * *

"Especially pertinent to this case are our decisions recognizing the communicative nature of conduct relating to flags. Attaching a peace sign to the flag, *Spence v. Washington*, 1974; saluting the flag, *Barnette*, and displaying a red flag, *Stromberg v. California* (1931), we have held, all may find shelter under the

First Amendment.... That we have had little difficulty identifying an expressive element in conduct relating to flags should not be surprising. The very purpose of a national flag is to serve as a symbol of our country; it is, one might say, 'the one visible manifestation of two hundred years of nationhood.' ...

"Pregnant with expressive content, the flag as readily signifies this nation as does the combination of letters found in 'America.'

* * *

"The Government generally has a freer hand in restricting expressive conduct than it has in restricting the written or spoken word.... It may not, however, proscribe particular conduct *because* it has expressive elements.... It is, in short, not simply the verbal or nonverbal nature of the expression, but the governmental interest at stake, that helps to determine whether a restriction on that expression is valid.

* * *

"The State offers two separate interests to justify this conviction: preventing breaches of the peace, and preserving the flag as a symbol of nationhood and national unity. We hold that the first interest is not implicated on this record and that the second is related to the suppression of expression....

"We thus conclude that the State's interest in maintaining order is not implicated on these facts. The State need not worry that our holding will disable it from preserving the peace. We do not suggest that the First Amendment forbids a state to prevent 'imminent lawless action.' And, in fact, Texas already has a statute specifically prohibiting breaches of the peace, Texas Penal Code Ann. Sec. 42.01 (1989), which tends to confirm that Texas need not punish this flag desecration in order to keep the peace.

* * *

"We never before have held that the Government may insure that a symbol be used to express only one view of that symbol or its referents.... To conclude that the Government may permit designated symbols to be used to communicate only a limited set of messages would be to enter territory having no discernible or defensible boundaries.

* * *

"The First Amendment does not guarantee that other concepts virtually sacred to our nation as a whole—such as the principle that discrimination on the basis of race is odious and destructive—will go unquestioned in the marketplace of ideas. We decline, therefore, to create for the flag an exception to the joust of principles protected by the First Amendment."

* * *

Chief Justice Rehnquist wrote a dissenting opinion, joined by Justices O'Connor, Stevens and White. The minority opinion noted, "[s]urely one of the high purposes of a democratic society is to legislate against conduct that is regarded as evil and profoundly offensive to the majority of people—whether it be murder, embezzlement, pollution or flag burning." Justice Stevens also wrote a separate dissenting opinion.

Following *Texas v. Johnson,* Congress passed the Flag Protection Act of 1989, criminalizing the conduct of anyone who "knowingly mutilates, defaces, physically defiles, burns, maintains on the floor or ground, or tramples upon" a

U.S. flag, except conduct related to the disposal of a "worn or soiled" flag. A number of individuals were subsequently prosecuted for knowingly burning several flags while protesting various government policies, or for knowingly burning a flag while protesting the Act's passage. The U.S. Supreme Court, in a 5–4 decision, ruled that these prosecutions were "inconsistent" with the First Amendment, and that Congress, in passing the Act, had been concerned with the "communicative impact of flag destruction," particularly in light of the explicit exemption for disposal of "worn or soiled" flags, which protected certain acts traditionally associated with patriotic respect for the flag. United States v. Eichman, 496 U.S. 310 (1990).

2. In Street v. New York, 394 U.S. 576, 89 S.Ct. 1354 (1969), the defendant, a black person, heard a news report on the radio that civil rights leader James Meredith had been shot by a sniper in Mississippi. He thereupon took from a drawer an American flag, which he had formerly displayed on holidays, left his apartment, carried the flag to a nearby intersection, lit the flag with a match and dropped it to the pavement when it began to burn. A crowd gathered and when, soon thereafter, a police officer asked defendant whether he had burned the flag, he admitted doing so and said, "Yes, that's my flag, I burned it. If they let that happen to Meredith we don't need an American Flag." Defendant was thereafter convicted of violating a New York law which makes it a misdemeanor "publicly to mutilate, deface, defile or defy, trample upon or cast contempt upon either by words or act any flag of the United States." In reversing his conviction, Mr. Justice Harlan, writing for the majority found that it was unclear whether the jury verdict was based upon the words he had spoken—a constitutionally protected utterance—or his actions of burning the flag, which may not be constitutionally protected.

3. In Smith v. Goguen, 415 U.S. 566, 94 S.Ct. 1242 (1974), a plurality of the Court held that while nothing prevents a legislature from defining with substantial specificity what constitutes forbidden treatment of United States flags, a Massachusetts ban on "contemptuous" treatment is, at least absent narrowing judicial construction, unconstitutionally vague. The issue of vagueness is further discussed in Section H, infra.

4. DEMONSTRATIONS

CITY OF CHICAGO v. GREGORY

Supreme Court of Illinois, 1968.
39 Ill.2d 47, 233 N.E.2d 422.

MR. JUSTICE HOUSE delivered the opinion of the court.

These consolidated appeals involve the conviction of 40 civil rights marchers under two provisions of the disorderly conduct ordinance of the city of Chicago.[1] In cause number 39983 defendant Dick Gregory

[1. The disorderly conduct ordinance in effect at the time of the events described in this case (Section 193 of the Municipal Code of Chicago) read, in part, as follows:

"All persons who shall make, aid, countenance, or assist in making any improper noise, riot, disturbance, breach of the peace, or diversion tending to a breach of the peace, within the limits of the city; all persons who shall collect in bodies or crowds for unlawful purposes, or for any purpose, to the annoyance or disturbance

and four other defendants were found guilty in a jury trial before a magistrate in the circuit court of Cook County and each defendant was fined $200. In cause number 39984 the other 35 defendants were found guilty in a trial before a magistrate on a stipulation of facts adduced at the Gregory trial and each defendant was fined $25. The defendant Gregory was charged with disorderly conduct in that he "did make or aid in making an improper noise, disturbance, breach of peace, or diversion tending to a breach of the peace within the limits of the city." A constitutional question gives us jurisdiction.

The gist of the occurrence giving rise to the arrest and conviction of defendants was a march by 65 to 85 persons around the home of the mayor of Chicago. The marchers carried signs, sang songs and chanted slogans protesting the retention of Dr. Benjamin C. Willis as Superintendent of Schools of Chicago and his handling of school segregation problems in the city. In order to avert what the police believed would become a riot, the marchers were ordered to stop their demonstration and upon their refusal they were arrested.

The city in its brief has taken the position that residential picketing is *per se* a violation of the city ordinance. Extremely strong arguments have been advanced for the proposition that the constitutional rights of free speech, free assembly and freedom to petition for redress of grievances do not protect marches, demonstrations and picketing of a residence or residences—even of the privately owned homes of public officials. (See Kamin, Residential Picketing and the First Amendment, 61 N.W.L.Rev. 177 (1966); ... Furthermore, our legislature has now enacted a statute prohibiting residential picketing [infra note 3, p. 247] based on the following declaration of policy: "The Legislature finds and declares that men in a free society have the right to quiet enjoyment of their homes; that the stability of community and family life cannot be maintained unless the right to privacy and a sense of security and peace in the home are respected and encouraged; that residential picketing, however just the cause inspiring it disrupts home, family and communal life; that residential picketing is inappropriate in our society where the jealously guarded rights of free speech and assembly have always been associated with respect for the rights of others. For these reasons the Legislature finds this Article to be necessary." ... nine other States (Colorado, Connecticut, Florida, Hawaii, Kansas, Michigan, Nebraska, Utah and Wisconsin) have enacted statutory prohibitions of residential picketing.

A review of the record shows, however, that the arrests were not made on the basis of residential picketing nor did the trial proceed on that theory. Under these circumstances, we will assume, for the purposes of this opinion, as did the police and the magistrates below, that the residential picketing was not in and of itself a violation of the city ordinance.

of other persons; ... shall be deemed guilty of disorderly conduct, and upon conviction thereof, shall be severally fined not less than one dollar nor more than two hundred dollars for each offense."]

Lieutenant Hougeson testified that on August 2, 1965, he was in charge of the "task force" of the Chicago police department and that his assignment for that day was to protect a group of people who were going to march. He explained that the task force is a unit which provides extra police protection to a district to help handle crowds at a sporting or public event or to combat a high crime rate in a certain district. On this day he had 40 police officers and 4 sergeants. About 4:00 P.M. he went to Buckingham Fountain in Grant Park on Chicago's lake front just east of the Loop, where approximately 65 marchers had assembled. He observed Dick Gregory addressing the marchers and heard him say, "First we will go over to the snake pit [city hall]. When we leave there, we will go out to the snake's house [the mayor's home]. Then, we will continue to go out to Mayor Daley's home until he fires Ben Willis [Superintendent of Schools]."

About 4:30 P.M. the marchers, two abreast, walked out of the park and went to the city hall in the loop. The marchers then walked south on State Street to 35th Street and then proceeded west to Lowe Avenue, a distance of about 5 miles from the city hall. The mayor's home is at 3536 South Lowe Avenue. The demonstrators had increased in number to about 85 and they arrived at the mayor's home about 8:00 o'clock P.M. In addition to the police, the marchers were accompanied by their attorney and an assistant city counsel. At the suggestion of an assistant city counsel, Gregory had agreed that the group would quit singing at 8:30 P.M. Commander Pierson, district commander of the 9th police district which encompasses this area, met Lieutenant Hougeson at the corner of 35th and Lowe and assumed command of the police operations.

There were about 35 people on the corner and a group of about 6 or 8 youngsters carrying a sign "We love Mayor Daley" tried to join the marchers but the police stopped them. As the demonstrators started south into the 3500 block of Lowe Avenue, Gregory testified he went back through the line to tell everyone just to keep singing and to keep marching. "Don't stop and don't answer any one back. Don't worry about anything that is going to be said to you. Just keep marching. If anyone hits you or anything, try to remember what they look like, but above all means, do not hit them back. Keep the line straight and keep it tight." The demonstrators chanted "Ben Willis must go, Snake Daley, also;" "Ben Willis must go—When?—Now;" "We are going to the home of the snake, the snake pit is down the street;" "Hey, Hey, what do you know, Ben Willis must go" and "Hey, Hey, what do you know, Mayor Daley must go also." They carried signs which read: "Daley fire Willis;" "Defacto, Desmacto, it is still segregation;" "Ben Willis must go—now;" and "Mayor Daley, fire Ben Willis." They also sang the civil rights songs, "We Shall Overcome" and "We Shall Not Be Moved."

The police ordered the taverns closed during the march. Police from the task force, the 9th district and other districts surrounded the block in which the mayor's home is located. There were about 10 officers at each of the four intersections and about 10 officers spread along each of the four blocks. The rest of the 100 police officers assigned to the march accompanied the demonstrators as they marched around the block. The police tried to keep all spectators across the street from the marchers. They were equipped with walkie-talkie radios to relay reports of conditions to each other and they had a bullhorn with which they addressed the spectators and the demonstrators.

As the marchers started around the block the first time, the neighbors began coming out of their homes. On the second time around the block some of the residents had moved their lawn sprinklers onto the sidewalk and the demonstrators went into the street just long enough to get around the water. On the third trip around the block the water sprinklers had been removed, presumably by order of the police. Gregory himself testified to several instances when the police kept the crowd that was accumulating from interfering with the march. "One of the neighborhood people stood in front of the line, and we just stopped. This individual didn't move and we didn't move. After a few minutes, the officers standing on the corner asked him to move and he moved." He said that on their fourth trip around the block (about 8:30 P.M.) people were yelling out the windows and the police made spectators in door ways close the doors. About 8:30 P.M. the demonstrators quit their singing and chanting and marched quietly. Shortly before 9:00 P.M. 100 to 150 spectators formed a line of march ahead of the demonstrators. Gregory said "the lieutenant [Hougheson] asked me if I would hold up the line until they got those people out of the way. I said, I will hold up the line, but they have just as much right to march peacefully as we have." The spectators were ordered to move. In order to avoid the appearance that the marchers were following the 100 to 150 spectators who had been ordered to move, Gregory said his group marched straight south crossing 36th Street thus taking them one block south of the block which they had been marching. They had to stop when they crossed 36th Street while the police opened a pathway through about 300 spectators they had confined on the corner across the street.

Sergeant Golden testified that between 8:00 o'clock and 9:00 o'clock the crowd increased steadily to a few hundred, but that from 9:00 o'clock until about 9:20 o'clock the people just seemed to come from everywhere until it reached between 1,000 and 1,200. During this time the crowd became unruly. There was shouting and threats, "God damned nigger, get the hell out of here;" "Get out of here niggers—go back where you belong or we will get you out of here" and "Get the hell out of here or we will break your blankety-blank head open." Cars were stopped in the streets with their horns blowing. There were Ku Klux Klan signs and there was singing of the Alabama Trooper song. Children in the crowd were playing various musical instruments such as a cymbal, trumpet and drum.

Rocks and eggs were also being thrown at the marchers from the crowd. The police were dodging the rocks and eggs and attempted to catch the persons who threw them. Sergeant Golden explained the problem. "You could see these teen-agers behind the crowd. You could see a boil of activity and something would come over our heads and I or my partner would go down to try to apprehend who was doing it. You couldn't see who was doing it. They would vanish into the crowd." He further testified that about 9:25 P.M., "They were saying, 'Let's get them,' and with this they would step off the curb to try to cross 35th Street and we would push them back with force. Once in a while somebody would run out, and we would grab ahold of them and throw them back into the crowd."

About 9:30 P.M. Commander Pierson told Gregory the situation was dangerous and becoming riotous. He asked Gregory if he would co-operate and lead the marchers out of the area. The request to leave the area was made about five times. Pierson then told the marchers that any of them who wished to leave the area would be given a police escort. Three of the marchers accepted the proposal and were escorted out of the area. The remaining demonstrators were arrested and taken away in two police vans.

While we have gone into considerable detail in describing the events leading to the arrest of defendants, only a complete reading of the record can give one a true picture of the dilemma confronting the police. During the entire march from 4:30 P.M. until 9:30 P.M. the marchers were accompanied by their attorney who advised them, and the police were accompanied by an assistant city attorney who advised them. In short the record shows a determined effort by the police to allow the marchers to peacefully demonstrate and at the same time maintain order.

The defendants place heavy reliance on a footnote statement in Brown v. Louisiana, ... that "Participants in an orderly demonstration in a public place are not chargeable with the danger, unprovoked except by the fact of the constitutionally protected demonstration itself, that their critics might react with disorder or violence;" a statement in Watson v. City of Memphis, ... quoted in Cox v. Louisiana, ..., that "The compelling answer to this contention is that constitutional rights may not be denied simply because of hostility to their assertion or exercise;" and a statement in Wright v. Georgia, ... that "... the possibility of disorder by others cannot justify exclusion of persons from a place if they otherwise have a constitutional right ... to be present." They contend that their conduct was peaceful and that they were charged and convicted solely on the reaction of the crowd.

The Supreme Court in recent years has had occasion to reverse a number of breach-of-the-peace convictions based on civil rights activities. In none of these cases has there been a public disorder or imminent threat of public disorder. Garner v. Louisiana, ... involved sit-ins, by Negroes at lunch counters catering only to whites. The court pointed out, "Although the manager of Kress' Department Store testified the only conduct which he considered disruptive was the petitioners' mere presence at the counter, he did state that he called the police because he 'feared that some disturbance might occur.' However, his fear is completely unsubstantiated by the record." ... Taylor v. Louisiana, ...

concerned a sit-in by Negroes in a waiting room at a bus depot, reserved "for whites only." The court noted, "... immediately upon petitioners' entry into the waiting room many of the people therein became restless and that some onlookers climbed onto seats to get a better view. Nevertheless, respondent admits these persons moved on when ordered to do so by the police. There was no evidence of violence." ... Edwards v. South Carolina, ... involved a peaceful march by Negroes around the State House. The court commented, "There was no violence or threat of violence on their [marchers] part, or on the part of any member of the crowd watching them. Police protection was 'ample'." ... Wright v. Georgia, ... concerned 6 Negro boys playing basketball in a public park. The court noted, "The only evidence to support this contention is testimony of one of the police officers that 'The purpose of asking them to leave was to keep down trouble, which looked like to me might start—there were five or six cars driving around the park at the time, white people.' But that officer also stated that this 'was [not] unusual traffic for that time of day.' And the park was 50 acres in area." ... Cox v. Louisiana, ... involved the conviction of the leader of some 2,000 Negroes who demonstrated in the vicinity of a courthouse and jail to protest the arrest of fellow demonstrators. The court explained, "There is no indication, however, that any member of the white group threatened violence. ... As Inspector Trigg testified, they could have handled the crowd." ... Finally Brown v. Louisiana, ... concerned a sit-in by 5 Negroes in the reading room of a public library maintained on a racially segregated basis. The court mentioned, "There was ... no disorder, no intent to provoke a breach of the peace and no circumstances indicating that a breach might be occasioned by petitioners' actions." ... The court in two of these cases, *Cox* and *Edwards,* in commenting on the lack of violence or threat of violence remarked that the situations were "a far cry from the situation in Feiner v. New York,. . . ."

In Feiner v. New York, ... defendant was convicted of disorderly conduct when he refused a police order to stop haranguing about 80 "restless" listeners. The court pointed out: "The exercise of the police officers' proper discretionary power to prevent a breach of the peace was thus approved by the trial court and later by two courts on review. The courts below recognized petitioner's right to hold a street meeting at this locality, to make use of loudspeaking equipment in giving his speech, and to make derogatory remarks concerning public officials and the American Legion. They found that the officers in making the arrest were motivated solely by a proper concern for the preservation of order and protection of the general welfare, and that there was no evidence which could lend color to a claim that the acts of the police were a cover for suppression of petitioner's views and opinions." The court concluded, "The findings of the state courts as to the existing situation and the imminence of greater disorder coupled with petitioner's deliberate defiance of the police officers convince us that we should not reverse this conviction in the name of free speech." ...

In his dissenting opinion Justice Black stated "The Court's opinion apparently rests on this reasoning: The policeman, under the circumstances detailed, could reasonably conclude that serious fighting or even riot was imminent; therefore he could stop petitioner's speech to prevent a breach of peace; accordingly, it was 'disorderly conduct' for petitioner to continue speaking in disobedience of the officer's request." ... He then stated the record failed to show any imminent threat of riot or uncontrollable disorder. He next stated "The police of course have power to prevent breaches of the peace. But if, in the name of preserving order, they ever can interfere with a lawful public speaker, they first must make all reasonable efforts to protect him." ... Finally he disagreed with the majority's "statement that petitioner's disregard of the policeman's unexplained request amounted to such 'deliberate defiance' as would justify an arrest or conviction for disorderly conduct.... For at least where time allows, courtesy and explanation of commands are basic elements of good official conduct in a democratic society.... Petitioner was entitled to know why he should cease doing a lawful act." ...

Justice Frankfurter in a concurring opinion summarized the situation this way: "As was said in Hague v. C.I.O., ... uncontrolled official suppression of the speaker 'cannot be made a substitute for the duty to maintain order.' ... Where conduct is within the allowable limits of free speech, the police are peace officers for the speaker as well as for his hearers. But the power effectively to preserve order cannot be displaced by giving a speaker complete immunity.... *It is not a constitutional principle that, in acting to preserve order, the police must proceed against the crowd, whatever its size and temper, and not against the speaker.*" (Emphasis added.) ...

Applying the facts of this case to the rationale of the foregoing opinions we believe defendants were not denied their right to free speech, free assembly and freedom to petition for redress of grievances. First, the record is clear that there was some violence (throwing rocks and eggs) and an imminent threat of extreme public disorder. This immediately distinguishes this case from *Garner, Taylor, Edwards, Cox, Wright* and *Brown* discussed above. In fact the violence and imminent threat of a riot appears to have been greater here than in *Feiner.*

This brings us to the vital issue in the case of whether Justice Frankfurter's appraisal of *Feiner* that "It is not a constitutional principle that, in acting to preserve order, the police must proceed against the crowd, whatever its size and temper, and not against the speaker" can be reconciled with the Statement in *Brown* that "Participants in an orderly demonstration in a public place are not chargeable with the danger, unprovoked except by the fact of the constitutionally protected demonstration itself, that their critics might react with disorder or violence." We think the statements are harmonious when read in light of Justice Black's observation in his dissenting opinion in *Feiner* that "The police of course have power to prevent breaches of the peace. But, if, in the name of preserving order, they ever can interfere with a lawful public speaker, they first must make all reasonable efforts to protect him."

The record before us shows that the police made all reasonable efforts to protect the marchers before asking them to stop the demonstration. While no parade permit had been sought by the group and there had been no direct contact between representatives of the group and the police, the police did know of the planned march and a task force of 44 policemen were assigned to maintain order during the march. The 44 policemen went to Buckingham Fountain in Grant Park at 4:00 P.M. and accompanied the demonstrators while they marched to the city hall for a short demonstration and then marched about 5 miles south to 35th and Lowe. The police kept hostile spectators from interfering with the march around the block bounded by 35th Street, Union Avenue, 36th Street and Lowe Avenue. The taverns in the area were closed, barricades were placed at strategic points, there was radio communication among the police assigned to the area, and spectators were kept across the street. Water sprinklers which were turned on during the demonstration and interfered with the march were removed, persons in doorways were told to get back and close the doors, counterdemonstrators who tried to join the marchers were ordered across the street, a group of 150 countermarchers were ordered out of the demonstrators' line of march, and a pathway was cleared through several hundred spectators when the marchers deviated from their course around the block in which the mayor lived, and spectators who broke police lines and tried "to get" the demonstrators were forcefully thrown back into the crowd. Before the demonstration was ended there were about 100 policemen trying to maintain order in this one block area.

It is evident that there was adequate and determined police protection for the demonstrators from 4 o'clock in the afternoon until 9:30 in the evening while the demonstrators marched from Grant Park to the city hall and then to the mayor's home on the south side of Chicago. The demonstration around the mayor's home lasted 1½ hours during which the police were able to control the hostile crowd. It was between 9:00 and 9:25 that the crowd grew quickly in size and anger to the point where the police felt they could no longer control the situation.

Furthermore, we do not have here an "unexplained request" by the police as was apparently the case in *Feiner*. Commander Pierson told Gregory that the situation was becoming dangerous, that he was having difficulty containing the crowd and that there might be a riot. He asked Gregory five times to lead the marchers out. Gregory then went along the line of marchers and said "We will not leave; we have not broken any law; we will not resist if we are arrested." Commander Pierson then told the demonstrators that any of them who wished to leave would be given a police escort out of the area. After three of the demonstrators left, the rest were arrested.

We hold that under the circumstances of this case defendants were not denied any right of free speech, free assembly or freedom to petition for redress of grievances.

Defendants also argue that the disorderly conduct ordinance of the city is unconstitutionally vague as applied to free expression and free assembly. We interpret the ordinance as authorizing the action taken by police under the circumstances disclosed by this record. (See City of Chicago v. Williams, 45 Ill.App.2d 327, 195 N.E.2d 425.) It does not authorize the police to stop a peaceful demonstration merely because a hostile crowd may not agree with the views of the demonstrators. It is only where there is an imminent threat of violence, the police have made all reasonable efforts to protect the demonstrators, the police have requested that the demonstration be stopped and explained the request, if there be time, and there is a refusal of the police request, that an arrest for an otherwise lawful demonstration may be made. As so interpreted we believe the ordinance is not so overly broad in scope as to be unconstitutionally vague or that it delegates undue discretion to the police. This is the type of conduct with which we are here faced and which is prohibited by the ordinance....

The judgments of the circuit court of Cook County are affirmed.

NOTES

1. The foregoing Illinois Supreme Court decision was reversed by the Supreme Court of the United States in Gregory v. City of Chicago, 394 U.S. 111, 89 S.Ct. 946 (1969), in a short opinion by Mr. Chief Justice Warren, in which he stated, in part:

"Petitioners' march, if peaceful and orderly, falls well within the sphere of conduct protected by the First Amendment.... There is no evidence in this record that petitioners' conduct was disorderly. Therefore, ... convictions so totally devoid of evidentiary support violate due process.

"The opinion of the Supreme Court of Illinois suggests that petitioners were convicted not for the manner in which they conducted their march but rather for their refusal to disperse when requested to do so by Chicago police.... However reasonable the police request may have been and however laudable the police motives, petitioners were charged and convicted for holding a demonstration, not for a refusal to obey a police officer. ['The trial judge charged solely in terms of the Chicago ordinance. Neither the ordinance nor the charge defined disorderly conduct as the refusal to obey a police order.'] As we said in Garner v. Louisiana, ...: '[I]t is as much a denial of due process to send an accused to prison following conviction for a charge that was never made as it is to convict him upon a charge for which there is no evidence to support that conviction.'

"Finally, since the trial judge's charge permitted the jury to convict for acts clearly entitled to First Amendment protection, Stromberg v. California, ... independently requires reversal of these convictions."

Following are excerpts from the concurring opinion of Justice Black, in which he was joined by Justice Douglas:

"I agree with the Illinois Supreme Court that the 'record shows a determined effort by the police to allow the marchers to peacefully demonstrate and at the same time maintain order.' I also think the record shows that outside of the marching and propagandizing of their views and protests, Gregory and his group while marching did all in their power to maintain order. Indeed, in the face of jeers, insults, and assaults with rocks and eggs, Gregory and his group maintained a decorum that speaks well for their determination simply to tell their side of their grievances and complaints. Even the 'snake' and 'snake pit' invectives used by Gregory and his demonstrators, unlike some used by their hecklers, remained within the general give-and-take of heated political argument. Thus both police and demonstrators made their best efforts faithfully to discharge their responsibilities as officers and citizens, but they were nevertheless unable to restrain the hostile hecklers within decent and orderly bounds. These facts disclosed by the record point unerringly to one conclusion, namely, that when groups with diametrically opposed, deep-seated views are permitted to air their emotional grievances, side by side, on city streets, tranquility and order cannot be maintained even by the joint efforts of the finest and best officers and of those who desire to be the most law-abiding protestors of their grievances.

"It is because of this truth, and a desire both to promote order and to safeguard First Amendment freedoms, that this Court has repeatedly warned States and governmental units that they cannot regulate conduct connected with these freedoms through use of sweeping, dragnet statutes that may, because of vagueness, jeopardize these freedoms. In those cases, however, we have been careful to point out that the Constitution does not bar enactment of laws regulating conduct, even though connected with speech, press, assembly, and petition, if such laws specifically bar only the conduct deemed obnoxious and are carefully and narrowly aimed at that forbidden conduct. . . . The dilemma revealed by this record is a crying example of a need for some such narrowly drawn law. It is not our duty and indeed not within our power to set out and define with precision just what statutes can be lawfully enacted to deal with situations like the one confronted here by police and protestors, both of whom appear to us to have been conscientiously trying to do their duties as they understood them. Plainly, however, no mandate in our Constitution leaves States and governmental units powerless to pass laws to protect the public from the kind of boisterous and threatening conduct that disturbs the tranquility of spots selected by the people either for homes, wherein they can escape the hurly-burly of the outside business and political world, or for public and other buildings that require peace and quiet to carry out their functions, such as courts, libraries, schools, and hospitals.

"The disorderly conduct ordinance under which these petitioners were charged and convicted is not, however, a narrowly drawn law, particularly designed to regulate certain kinds of conduct such as marching or picketing or demonstrating along the streets or highways. Nor does it regulate the times or places or manner of carrying on such activities. To the contrary, it might better be described as a meat-ax ordinance, gathering in one comprehensive definition of an offense a number of words which have a multiplicity of meanings, some of which would cover activity specifically protected by the First Amendment. The average person charged with its violation is necessarily left uncertain as to what conduct and attitudes of mind would be enough to convict under it. Who, for example, could possibly foresee what kind of noise or protected speech would be held to be 'improper'? That, of course, would depend on sensibilities, nerves, tensions, and on countless other things. As pointed out in Cantwell v. Connecticut, . . . common-law breach of peace is at its best a confusing offense that may imperil First Amendment rights. But how infinitely more doubtful and uncertain are the boundaries of an offense including any 'diversion tending to a breach of the peace . . .'! Moreover, the ordinance goes on to state that it shall be a crime for persons to 'collect in bodies or crowds for unlawful purposes, or for any purpose, to the annoyance or disturbance of other persons. . . .' Such language could authorize conviction simply because the form of the protest displeased some of the onlookers, and of course a conviction on that ground would encroach on First Amendment rights.... And it must be remembered that only the tiniest bit of petitioners' conduct could possibly be thought illegal here—that is, what they did after the policeman's order to leave the area. The right 'peaceably to assemble, and to petition the Government for a redress of grievances' is specifically protected by the First Amendment. For the entire five-mile march, the walking by petitioners in a group, the language, and the chants and songs were all treated by the city's assistant attorney and its specially detailed policemen as lawful, not lawless, conduct.

"The so-called 'diversion tending to a breach of the peace' here was limited entirely and exclusively to the fact that when the policeman in charge of the special police detail concluded that the hecklers observing the march were dangerously close to rioting and that the demonstrators and others were likely to be engulfed in that riot, he ordered Gregory and his demonstrators to leave, and Gregory—standing on what he deemed to be his constitutional rights—refused to do so. The 'diversion' complained of on the part of Gregory and the other marchers was not any noise they made or annoyance or disturbance of 'other persons' they had inflicted. Their guilt of 'disorderly conduct' therefore turns out to be their refusal to obey instanter an individual policeman's command to leave the area of the Mayor's home. Since neither the city council nor the state legislature had enacted a narrowly drawn statute forbidding disruptive picketing or demonstrating in a residential neighborhood, the conduct involved here could become 'disorderly' only if the policeman's command was a law which the petitioners were bound to obey at their peril. But under our democratic system of government, lawmaking is not entrusted to the moment-to-moment judgment of the policeman on his beat. Laws, that is valid laws, are to be made by representatives chosen to make laws for the future, not by police officers whose duty is to enforce laws already enacted and to make arrests only for conduct already made criminal. One of our proudest boasts is that no man can be convicted of crime for conduct, innocent when engaged in, that is later made criminal.... To let a policeman's command become equivalent to a criminal statute comes dangerously near making our government one of men rather than of laws.... There are ample ways to protect the domestic tranquility without subjecting First Amendment freedoms to such a clumsy and unwieldy weapon.

"The City of Chicago, recognizing the serious First Amendment problems raised by the disorderly conduct ordinance as it is written, argues that these convictions should nevertheless be affirmed in light of the narrowing construction placed on the ordinance by the Illinois Supreme Court in this case. That court held that the ordinance

> 'does not authorize the police to stop a peaceful demonstration merely because a hostile crowd may not agree with the views of the demonstrators. It is only where there is an imminent threat of violence, the police have made all reasonable efforts to protect the demonstrators, the police have requested that the demonstration be stopped and explained the request, if there be time, and there is a refusal of the police request, that an arrest for an otherwise lawful demonstration may be made.'

This interpretation of the ordinance is, of course, binding on this Court, and the construction of the Illinois Supreme Court is as authoritative as if this limitation were written into the ordinance itself. But this cannot be the end of our problem. The infringement of First Amendment rights will not be cured if the narrowing construction is so unforeseeable that men of common intelligence could not have realized the law's limited scope at the only relevant time, when their acts were committed, ... or if the law remains excessively sweeping even as narrowed,.... Petitioners particularly press the Court to dispose of the case on this latter ground. They raise troublesome questions concerning the extent to which, even under the narrowed construction, guilt still depends on the mere refusal to obey a policeman's order. And they suggest that the scope of the police obligation to attempt first to deal with the hostile audience is still not made sufficiently clear.

"It is not necessary for the Court to resolve such issues in the present case, however, because the Chicago ordinance, as applied here, infringed on First Amendment rights for an even more fundamental reason. Whatever the validity of the Illinois Supreme Court's construction, this was simply not the theory on which these petitioners were convicted. In explaining the elements of the offense to the jury, the trial judge merely read the language of the ordinance. The jury was not asked to find whether, as the Illinois Supreme Court's construction apparently requires, there was 'an imminent threat of violence,' or whether the police had 'made all reasonable efforts to protect the demonstrators.' Rather, it was sufficient for the jury to decide that petitioners had made an 'improper noise' or a 'diversion tending to a breach of the peace,' or had 'collect[ed] in bodies or crowds for unlawful purposes, or for any purpose, to the annoyance or disturbance of other persons.'

"In fact, far from taking account of the limiting factors stressed by the Illinois Supreme Court, the judge's charge was based on precisely the opposite theory. The jury was instructed, over petitioners' objection, that 'the fact that persons other than these Defendants may or may not have violated any laws or may or may not have been arrested should not be considered by you in determining the guilt or innocence of these Defendants.' The significance of this instruction in the context of the evidence at trial is of course apparent—the jury was simply told to ignore questions concerning the acts of violence committed by the crowd of onlookers and attempts made by the police to arrest those directly responsible for them....

"At the time the petitioners were tried, the Illinois Supreme Court had not yet announced its narrowing construction of the Chicago disorderly conduct ordinance. The trial judge's instructions supplied the jury only with the unadorned language of the statute. Thus it is entirely possible that the jury convicted the petitioners on the ground that Gregory and the others who demonstrated with him had, in the language of the ordinance, 'collect[ed] in bodies or crowds ... to the annoyance or disturbance of other persons,' simply because the form of their protest had displeased some of the onlookers....

"In agreeing to the reversal of these convictions, however, I wish once more to say that I think our Federal Constitution does not render the States powerless to regulate the conduct of demonstrators and picketers, conduct which is more than 'speech,' more than 'press,' more than 'assembly,' and more than 'petition,' as those terms are used in the First Amendment. Narrowly drawn statutes regulating the conduct of demonstrators and picketers are not impossible to draft. And narrowly drawn statutes regulating these activities are not impossible to pass if the people who elect their legislators want them passed. Passage of such laws, however, like the passage of all other laws, constitutes in the final analysis a choice of policies by the elected representatives of the people.

"I, of course, do not mean to say or even to intimate that freedom of speech, press, assembly, or petition can be abridged so long as the First Amendment remains unchanged in our Constitution. But to say that the First Amendment grants those broad rights free from any exercise of governmental power to regulate conduct, as distinguished from speech, press, assembly, or petition, would subject all the people of the Nation to the uncontrollable whim and arrogance of speakers, and writers, and protesters, and grievance bearers.... Were the authority of government so trifling as to permit anyone with a complaint to have the vast power to do anything he pleased, wherever he pleased, and whenever he pleased, our customs and our habits of conduct, social, political, economic, ethical, and religious, would all be wiped out, and become no more than relics of a gone but not forgotten past. Churches would be compelled to welcome into their buildings invaders who came but to scoff and jeer; streets and highways and public buildings would cease to be available for the purposes for which they were constructed and dedicated whenever demonstrators and picketers wanted to use them for their own purposes. And perhaps worse than all other changes, homes, the sacred retreat to which families repair for their privacy and their daily way of living, would have to have their doors thrown open to all who desired to convert the occupants to new views, new morals, and a new way of life. Men and women who hold public office would be compelled, simply because they did hold public office, to lose the comforts and privacy of an unpicketed home. I believe that our Constitution, written for the ages, to endure except as changed in the manner it provides, did not create a government with such monumental weaknesses. Speech and press are, of course, to be free, so that public matters can be discussed with impunity. But picketing and demonstrating can be regulated like other conduct of men. I believe that the homes of men, sometimes the last citadel of the tired, the weary, and the sick, can be protected by government from noisy, marching, tramping, threatening picketers and demonstrators bent on filling the minds of men, women, and children with fears of the unknown."

2. Picketing by anti-obscenity groups of an "adult bookstore" was not enjoinable, even though the store suffered economic harm and an action at law for damages was inadequate. "Public issue" picketing is protected speech under the First Amendment, even though some aspects of the activity might be "intimidation" under a penal statute. Eagle Books, Inc. v. Jones, 130 Ill.App.3d 407, 85 Ill.Dec. 716, 474 N.E.2d 444 (1985). Consider the following case on residential picketing involving abortion issues.

FRISBY v. SCHULTZ

Supreme Court of the United States, 1988.
487 U.S. 474, 108 S.Ct. 2495.

JUSTICE O'CONNOR delivered the opinion of the Court.

Brookfield, Wisconsin, has adopted an ordinance that completely bans picketing "before or about" any residence. This case presents a facial First Amendment challenge to that ordinance.

I

Brookfield, Wisconsin, is a residential suburb of Milwaukee with a population of approximately 4,300. The appellees, Sandra C. Schultz and Robert C. Braun, are individuals strongly opposed to abortion and wish to express their views on the subject by picketing on a public street outside the Brookfield residence of a doctor who apparently performs abortions at two clinics in neighboring towns. Appellees and others engaged in precisely that activity, assembling outside the doctor's home on at least six occasions between April 20, 1985, and May 20, 1985, for periods ranging from one to one and a half hours. The size of the group varied from 11 to more than 40. The picketing was generally orderly and peaceful; the town never had occasion to invoke any of its various ordinances prohibiting obstruction of the streets, loud and unnecessary noises, or disorderly conduct. Nonetheless, the picketing generated substantial controversy and numerous complaints.

The Town Board therefore resolved to enact an ordinance to restrict the picketing. On May 7, 1985, the town passed an ordinance that prohibited all picketing in residential neighborhoods except for labor picketing. But after reviewing this Court's decision in Carey v. Brown, 447 U.S. 455, 100 S.Ct. 2286 (1980), which invalidated a similar ordinance as a violation of the Equal Protection Clause, the town attorney instructed the police not to enforce the new ordinance and advised the town Board that the ordinance's labor picketing exception likely rendered it unconstitutional. This ordinance was repealed on May 15, 1985, and replaced with the following flat ban on all residential picketing:

> "It is unlawful for any person to engage in picketing before or about the residence or dwelling of any individual in the Town of Brookfield." App. to Juris. Statement A–28.

The ordinance itself recites the primary purpose of this ban: "the protection and preservation of the home" through assurance "that members of the community enjoy in their homes and dwellings a feeling of well-being, tranquility, and privacy." Id., at A–26. The Town Board believed that a ban was necessary because it determined that "the practice of picketing before or about residences and dwellings causes emotional disturbance and distress to the occupants . . . [and] has as its object the harassing of such occupants." Id., at A–26—A–27. The ordinance also evinces a concern for public safety, noting that picketing obstructs and interferes with "the free use of public sidewalks and public ways of travel." Id., at A–27.

On May 18, 1985, appellees were informed by the town attorney that enforcement of the new, revised ordinance would begin on May 21, 1985. Faced with this threat of arrest and prosecution, appellees ceased picketing in Brookfield and filed this lawsuit in United States District Court for the Eastern District of Wisconsin. The complaint was brought under 42 U.S.C. § 1983 and sought declaratory as well as preliminary and permanent injunctive relief on the grounds that the ordinance violated the First Amendment. Appellees named appellants—the three members of the town Board, the Chief of Police, the town attorney, and the town itself—as defendants.

The District Court granted appellees' motion for a preliminary injunction. The court concluded that the ordinance was not narrowly tailored enough to restrict protected speech in a public forum. 619 F.Supp. 792, 797 (1985). The District Court's order specified that unless the appellants requested a trial on the merits within 60 days or appealed, the preliminary injunction would become permanent. Appellants requested a trial and also appealed the District Court's entry of a preliminary injunction.

A divided panel of the United States Court of Appeals for the Seventh Circuit affirmed. 807 F.2d 1339 (1986). The Court of Appeals subsequently vacated this decision, however, and reheard the case en banc. See 818 F.2d 1284 (1987). After rehearing, the Court of Appeals affirmed the judgment of the District Court by an equally divided vote. 822 F.2d 642 (1987). Contending that the Court of Appeals had rendered a final judgment holding the ordinance "to be invalid as repugnant to the Constitution," 28 U.S.C. § 1254(2), appellants attempted to invoke our mandatory appellate jurisdiction. App. to Juris. Statement A–25 (citing § 1254(2)). We postponed further consideration of our appellate jurisdiction until the hearing on the merits. 484 U.S. 1003, 108 S.Ct. 692 (1988).

* * *

II

The antipicketing ordinance operates at the core of the First Amendment by prohibiting appellees from engaging in picketing on an issue of public concern. Because of the importance of "uninhibited, robust, and wide-open" debate on public issues, New York Times Co. v. Sullivan, 376 U.S. 254, 270, 84 S.Ct. 710, 720–21 (1964), we have traditionally subjected restrictions on public issue picketing to careful scrutiny. See, e.g., Boos v. Barry, 485 U.S. 312, 318, 108 S.Ct. 1157, ___ (1988); United States v. Grace, 461 U.S. 171 (1983); Carey v. Brown, 447 U.S. 455, 100 S.Ct. 2286 (1980). Of course, "[e]ven protected speech is not equally permissible in all places and at all times." Cornelius v. NAACP Legal Defense and Educational Fund, Inc., 473 U.S. 788, 799, 105 S.Ct. 3439, 3447 (1985).

To ascertain what limits, if any, may be placed on protected speech, we have often focused on the "place" of that speech, considering the nature of the forum the speaker seeks to employ. Our cases have recognized that the standards by which limitations on speech must be evaluated "differ depending on the character of the property at issue." Perry Education Assn. v. Perry Local Educators' Assn., 460 U.S. 37, 44, 103 S.Ct. 948, 954 (1983). Specifically, we have identified three types of fora: "the traditional public forum, the public forum created by government designation, and the nonpublic forum." *Cornelius,* supra, 473 U.S. at 802, 105 S.Ct., at 3449.

The relevant forum here may be easily identified: appellees wish to picket on the public streets of Brookfield. Ordinarily, a determination of the nature of the forum would follow automatically from this identification; we have repeatedly referred to public streets as the archetype of a traditional public forum. See, e.g., Boos v. Barry, supra, 485 U.S., at 318, 108 S.Ct., at ___; *Cornelius,* supra, at 802, 105 S.Ct., at 3448–49;

Perry, supra, 460 U.S., at 45, 103 S.Ct., at 954–55. "[T]ime out of mind" public streets and sidewalks have been used for public assembly and debate, the hallmarks of a traditional public forum. See ibid.; Hague v. CIO, 307 U.S. 496, 515, 59 S.Ct. 954, 963–64 (1939) (Roberts, J.). Appellants, however, urge us to disregard these "cliches." Tr. of Oral Arg. 16. They argue that the streets of Brookfield should be considered a nonpublic forum. Pointing to the physical narrowness of Brookfield's streets as well as to their residential character, appellants contend that such streets have not by tradition or designation been held open for public communication. See Brief for Appellants 23 (citing *Perry,* supra, 460 U.S., at 46, 103 S.Ct., at 955–56).

We reject this suggestion. Our prior holdings make clear that a public street does not lose its status as a traditional public forum simply because it runs through a residential neighborhood. In *Carey v. Brown* —which considered a statute similar to the one at issue here, ultimately striking it down as a violation of the Equal Protection Clause because it included an exception for labor picketing—we expressly recognized that "public streets and sidewalks in residential neighborhoods," were "public for[a]." 447 U.S., at 460–461, 100 S.Ct., at 2289–2291. This rather ready identification virtually forecloses appellants' argument. See also Perry, supra, 460 U.S., at 54–55, 103 S.Ct., at 960 (noting that the "key" to Carey "was the presence of a public forum").

In short, our decisions identifying public streets and sidewalks as traditional public fora are not accidental invocations of a "cliche," but recognition that "[w]herever the title of streets and parks may rest, they have immemorially been held in trust for the use of the public." Hague v. CIO, supra, 307 U.S., at 515, 59 S.Ct., at 964 (Roberts, J.). No particularized inquiry into the precise nature of a specific street is necessary; all public streets are held in the public trust and are properly considered traditional public fora. Accordingly, the streets of Brookfield are traditional public fora. The residential character of those streets may well inform the application of the relevant test, but it does not lead to a different test; the antipicketing ordinance must be judged against the stringent standards we have established for restrictions on speech in traditional public fora:

> "In these quintessential public for[a], the government may not prohibit all communicative activity. For the State to enforce a content-based exclusion it must show that its regulation is necessary to serve a compelling state interest and that it is narrowly drawn to achieve that end.... The State may also enforce regulations of the time, place, and manner of expression which are content-neutral, are narrowly tailored to serve a significant government interest, and leave open ample alternative channels of communication." Perry, 460 U.S., at 45, 103 S.Ct., at 955 (citations omitted).

As *Perry* makes clear, the appropriate level of scrutiny is initially tied to whether the statute distinguishes between prohibited and permitted speech on the basis of content. Appellees argue that despite its facial content-neutrality, the Brookfield ordinance must be read as containing an implied exception for labor picketing. See Brief for Appellees 20–26. The basis for appellees' argument is their belief that an express protection of peaceful labor picketing in state law, see Wis.Stat. § 103.53(1) (1985–1986), must take precedence over Brookfield's contrary efforts. The District Court, however, rejected this suggested interpretation of state law, 619 F.Supp., at 796, and the Court of Appeals affirmed, albeit ultimately by an equally divided court. 822 F.2d 642 (1987). See also 807 F.2d 1339, 1347 (1986) (original panel opinion declining to reconsider District Court's construction of state law). Following our normal practice, "we defer to the construction of a state statute given it by the lower federal courts ... to reflect our belief that district courts and courts of appeal are better schooled in and more able to interpret the laws of their respective States." Brockett v. Spokane Arcades, Inc., 472 U.S. 491, 499–500, 105 S.Ct. 2794, 2800, 86 L.Ed.2d 394 (1985). See Virginia v. American Booksellers Assn., 484 U.S. 383, 395, 108 S.Ct. 636, 643 (1988) ("This Court rarely reviews a construction of state law agreed upon by the two lower federal courts"). Thus, we accept the lower courts' conclusion that the Brookfield ordinance is content-neutral. Accordingly, we turn to consider whether the ordinance is "narrowly tailored to serve a significant government interest" and whether it "leave[s] open ample alternative channels of communication." Perry, 460 U.S., at 45, 103 S.Ct., at 955.

Because the last question is so easily answered, we address it first. Of course, before we are able to assess the available alternatives, we must consider more carefully the reach of the ordinance. The precise scope of the ban is not further described within the text of the ordinance, but in our view the ordinance is readily subject to a narrowing construction that avoids constitutional difficulties. Specifically, the use of the singular form of the words "residence" and "dwelling" suggests that the ordinance is intended to prohibit only picketing focused on, and taking place in front of, a particular residence. As Justice White's concurring opinion recounts, the lower courts described the ordinance as banning "all picketing in residential areas." Post, at 2505. But these general descriptions do not address the exact scope of the ordinance and are in no way inconsistent with our reading of its text. "Picketing," after all, is defined as posting at a particular place, see Webster's Third New International Dictionary 1710 (1981), a characterization in line with viewing the ordinance as limited to activity focused on a single residence. Moreover, while we ordinarily defer to lower court constructions of state statutes, see supra, at 2500, we do not invariably do so, see Virginia v. American Booksellers Assn., supra, 484 U.S., at 395, 108 S.Ct., at ___. We are particularly reluctant to defer when the lower courts have fallen into plain error, see Brockett v. Spokane Arcades, Inc., supra, 472 U.S., at 500, n. 9, 105 S.Ct., at 2800, n. 9, which is precisely the situation presented here. To the extent they endorsed a broad reading of the ordinance, the lower courts ran afoul of the well-established principle that statutes will be interpreted to avoid constitutional difficulties. See, e.g., Erznoznik v. City of Jacksonville, 422 U.S. 205, 216, 95 S.Ct. 2268, 2276 (1975); Broadrick v. Oklahoma, 413 U.S. 601, 613, 93 S.Ct. 2908, 2916–2917 (1973). Cf. DeBartolo Corp. v. Florida Gulf Coast Building & Construction Trades Council, 485 U.S. 568, 575, 108 S.Ct. 1392, ___ (1988). Thus, unlike the lower courts' judgment that the ordinance does not contain an implied exception for labor picketing, we are unable to accept their potentially broader view of the ordinance's scope. We instead construe the ordinance more narrowly. This narrow reading is supported by the representations of counsel for the town at oral argument, which indicate that the town takes, and will enforce, a limited view of the "picketing" proscribed by the ordinance. Thus, generally speaking, "picketing would be having the picket proceed on a definite course or route in front of a home." Tr. of Oral Arg. 8. The picket need not be carrying a sign, id., at 14, but in order to fall within the scope of the ordinance the picketing must be directed at a single residence, id., at 9. General marching through residential neighborhoods, or even walking a route in front of an entire block of houses, is not prohibited by this ordinance. Id., at 15. Accordingly, we construe the ban to be a limited one; only focused picketing taking place solely in front of a particular residence is prohibited.

So narrowed, the ordinance permits the more general dissemination of a message. As appellants explain, the limited nature of the prohibition makes it virtually self-evident that ample alternatives remain:

> "Protestors have not been barred from the residential neighborhoods. They may enter such neighborhoods, alone or in groups, even marching.... They may go door-to-door to proselytize their views. They may distribute literature in this manner ... or through the mails. They may contact residents by telephone, short of harassment." Brief for Appellants 41–42 (citations omitted).

We readily agree that the ordinance preserves ample alternative channels of communication and thus move on to inquire whether the ordinance serves a significant government interest. We find that such an interest is identified within the text of the ordinance itself: the protection of residential privacy. See App. to Juris. Statement A–26.

"The State's interest in protecting the well-being, tranquility, and privacy of the home is certainly of the highest order in a free and civilized society." Carey v. Brown, 447 U.S., at 471, 100 S.Ct., at 2296. Our prior decisions have often remarked on the unique nature of the home, "the last citadel of the tired, the weary, and the sick," Gregory v. Chicago, 394 U.S. 111, 125 [89 S.Ct. 946, 954] (1969) (Black, J., concurring), and have recognized that "[p]reserving the sanctity of the home, the one retreat to which men and women can repair to escape from the tribulations of their daily pursuits, is surely an important value." Carey, supra, 447 U.S., at 471, 100 S.Ct., at 2295.

One important aspect of residential privacy is protection of the unwilling listener. Although in many locations, we expect individuals simply to avoid speech they do not want to hear, cf. Erznoznik v. Jacksonville, supra, 422 U.S., at 210–211, 95 S.Ct., at 2273–74; Cohen v. California, 403 U.S. 15, 21–22, 91 S.Ct. 1780, 1786–1787 (1971), the home is different. "That we are often 'captives' outside the sanctuary of the home and subject to objcctionable speech ... does not mean we must be captives everywhere." Rowan v. Post Office Dept., 397 U.S. 728, 738, 90 S.Ct. 1484, 1491 (1970). Instead, a special benefit of the privacy all citizens enjoy within their own walls, which the State may legislate to protect, is an ability to avoid intrusions. Thus, we have repeatedly held that individuals are not required to welcome unwanted speech into their own homes and that the government may protect this freedom. See, e.g., FCC v. Pacifica Foundation, 438 U.S. 726, 748–749, 98 S.Ct. 3026, 3039–3040 (1978) (offensive radio broadcasts); id., at 759–760, 98 S.Ct. at 3045–3047 (Powell, J., concurring in part and concurring in judgment) (same); *Rowan,* supra (offensive mailings); Kovacs v. Cooper, 336 U.S. 77, 86–87, 69 S.Ct. 448, 453–54 (1949) (sound trucks).

This principle is reflected even in prior decisions in which we have invalidated complete bans on expressive activity, including bans operating in residential areas. See, e.g., Schneider v. State, 308 U.S. 147, 162–163, 60 S.Ct. 146, 151–152 (1939) (handbilling); Martin v. Struthers, 319 U.S. 141, 63 S.Ct. 862 (1943) (door-to-door solicitation). In all such cases, we have been careful to acknowledge that unwilling listeners may be protected when within their own homes. In *Schneider,* for example, in striking down a complete ban on handbilling, we spoke of a right to distribute literature only "to one willing to receive it." Similarly, when we invalidated a ban on door-to-door solicitation in *Martin,* we did so on the basis that the "home owner could protect himself from such intrusion by an appropriate sign 'that he is unwilling to be disturbed.' " Kovacs, supra, 336 U.S., at 86, 69 S.Ct., at 453. We have "never intimated that the visitor could insert a foot in the door and insist on a hearing." Ibid. There simply is no right to force speech into the home of an unwilling listener.

It remains to be considered, however, whether the Brookfield ordinance is narrowly tailored to protect only unwilling recipients of the communications. A statute is narrowly tailored if it targets and eliminates no more than the exact source of the "evil" it seeks to remedy. City Council of Los Angeles v. Taxpayers for Vincent, 466 U.S. 789, 808–810, 104 S.Ct. 2118, 2130–2132 (1984). A complete ban can be narrowly tailored, but only if each activity within the proscription's scope is an appropriately targeted evil. For example, in *Taxpayers for Vincent* we upheld an ordinance that banned all signs on public property because the interest supporting the regulation, an esthetic interest in avoiding visual clutter and blight, rendered each sign an evil. Complete prohibition was necessary because "the substantive evil—visual blight—[was] not merely a possible byproduct of the activity, but [was] created by the medium of expression itself." Id., at 810, 104 S.Ct., at 2131.

The same is true here. The type of focused picketing prohibited by the Brookfield ordinance is fundamentally different from more generally directed means of communication that may not be completely banned in residential areas. See, e.g., Schneider, supra, 308 U.S., at 162–163, 60 S.Ct., at 151–152 (handbilling); Martin, supra (solicitation); Murdock v. Pennsylvania, 319 U.S. 105, 63 S.Ct. 870, 87 L.Ed. 1292 (1943) (solicitation. See also *Gregory v. Chicago,* supra (marching). Cf. Perry, 460 U.S., at 45, 103 S.Ct., at 954–55 (in traditional public forum, "the government may not prohibit all communicative activity"). In such cases "the flow of information [is not] into ... household[s], but to the public." Organization for a Better Austin v. Keefe, 402 U.S. 415, 420, 91 S.Ct. 1575, 1578 (1971). Here, in contrast, the picketing is narrowly directed at the household, not the public. The type of picketers banned by the Brookfield ordinance generally do not seek to disseminate a message to the general public, but to intrude upon the targeted resident, and to do so in an especially offensive way. Moreover, even if some such picketers have a broader communicative purpose, their activity nonetheless inherently and offensively intrudes on residential privacy. The devastating effect of targeted picketing on the quiet enjoyment of the home is beyond doubt:

> " 'To those inside ... the home becomes something less than a home when and while the picketing ... continue[s].... [The] tensions and pressures may be psychological, not physical, but they are not, for that reason, less inimical to family privacy and truly domestic tranquility.' " Carey, 447 U.S., at 478, 100 S.Ct., at 2299 (Rehnquist, J., dissenting) (quoting Wauwatosa v. King, 49 Wis.2d 398, 411–412, 182 N.W.2d 530, 537 (1971)).

In this case, for example, appellees subjected the doctor and his family to the presence of a relatively large group of protestors on their doorstep in an attempt to force the doctor to cease performing abortions. But the actual size of the group is irrelevant; even a solitary picket can invade residential privacy. See Carey, supra, 447 U.S., at 478, 100 S.Ct., at 2299 (Rehnquist, J., dissenting) ("Whether ... alone or accompanied by others ... there are few of us that would feel comfortable knowing that a stranger lurks outside our home"). The offensive and disturbing nature of the form of the communication banned by the Brookfield ordinance thus can scarcely be questioned. Cf. Bolger v. Youngs Drug Products Corp., 463 U.S. 60, 83–84, 103 S.Ct. 2875 (1983) (Stevens, J., concurring in judgment) (as opposed to regulation of communications due to the ideas expressed, which "strikes at the core of First Amendment values," "regulations of form and context may strike a constitutionally appropriate balance between the advocate's right to convey a message and the recipient's interest in the quality of his environment").

The First Amendment permits the government to prohibit offensive speech as intrusive when the "captive" audience cannot avoid the objectionable speech. See Consolidated Edison Co. v. Public Service Comm'n of New York, 447 U.S. 530, 542, 100 S.Ct. 2326 (1980). Cf. Bolger v. Youngs Drug Products Corp., supra, 463 U.S., at 72, 103 S.Ct., at 2883. The target of the focused picketing banned by the Brookfield ordinance is just such a "captive." The resident is figuratively, and perhaps literally, trapped within the home, and because of the unique and subtle impact of such picketing is left with no ready means of avoiding the unwanted speech. Cf. Cohen v. California, 403 U.S., at 21–22, 91 S.Ct., at 1786–1787 (noting ease of avoiding unwanted speech in other circumstances). Thus, the "evil" of targeted residential picketing, "the very presence of an unwelcome visitor at the home," Carey, supra, 447 U.S., at 478, 100 S.Ct., at 2299 (Rehnquist, J., dissenting), is "created by the medium of expression itself." See Taxpayers for Vincent, 466 U.S., at 810, 104 S.Ct., at 2131. Accordingly, the Brookfield ordinance's complete ban of that particular medium of expression is narrowly tailored.

Of course, this case presents only a facial challenge to the ordinance. Particular hypothetical applications of the ordinance—to, for example, a particular resident's use of his or her home as a place of business or public meeting, or to picketers present at a particular home by invitation of the resident—may present somewhat different questions. Initially, the ordinance by its own terms may not apply in such circumstances, since the ordinance's goal is the protection of residential privacy, App. to Juris. Statement A–26, and since it speaks only of a "residence or dwelling," not a place of business, id., at A–28. Cf. Carey, supra, 447 U.S., at 457, 100 S.Ct., at 2288 (quoting an antipicketing ordinance expressly rendered inapplicable by use of home as a place of business or to hold a public meeting). Moreover, since our First Amendment analysis is grounded in protection of the unwilling residential listener, the constitutionality of applying the ordinance to such hypotheticals remains open to question. These are, however, questions we need not address today in order to dispose of appellees' facial challenge.

Because the picketing prohibited by the Brookfield ordinance is speech directed primarily at those who are presumptively unwilling to receive it, the State has a substantial and justifiable interest in banning it. The nature and scope of this interest make the ban narrowly tailored. The ordinance also leaves open ample alternative channels of communication and is content-netrual. Thus, largely because of its narrow scope, the facial challenge to the ordinance must fail. The contrary judgment of the Court of Appeals is Reversed.

[The opinion of Justice White concurring in the judgment of the Court is omitted, as are the dissenting opinions of Justice Brennan (joined by Justice Marshall) and Justice Stevens.]

5. SURVEILLANCE OF PROTESTERS AND INFILTRATION OF SUSPECT GROUPS

ANDERSON v. SILLS

Supreme Court of New Jersey, 1970.
56 N.J. 210, 265 A.2d 678.

WEINTRAUB, C.J. This is a declaratory judgment suit brought as a class action against the Attorney General and local law enforcement officials, also as a class. The complaint alleges violation of plaintiffs' First Amendment rights of speech and association. The complaint revolves about a memorandum, entitled "Civil Disorders—The Role of Local, County and State Government" (herein Memorandum), prepared by the Attorney General of the State and sent to local law enforcement officials. . . .

I.

The Memorandum suggests guidelines based upon the intensity of the disorders and the ability of the municipality to cope with them. It describes the primary duty of each municipality, the basis for a call upon neighboring municipal and county resources, the basis for a call for limited State Police assistance, and finally the basis for State intervention. It recommends advance planning as to each of the stages just mentioned and in comprehensive fashion discusses the problems to be anticipated and the facilities and resources available.

Virtually at the end of the Memorandum appears the following statement which plaintiffs stress:

> Potential Problems
>
> Our State Police have been working closely with local police in various communities throughout the State in a continuing effort to keep abreast of potential civil disorder problems. In that respect, therefore, we are already familiar generally with basic problems in these communities. However, these problems change and we should never become over confident to the end that we lose sight of the cause, as well as the effect of civil disturbances. The State Police Central Security Unit has distributed Security Summary Reports Form 421 and Security Incident Reports Form 420 to each police department. It is necessary that these reports be used routinely to inform the State Police of the situation in your community. We urge you to see that this vital intelligence is communicated to this central bureau for evaluation and dissemination.

Plaintiffs say the Memorandum will result in police invasion of their First Amendment rights and build that complaint upon the content of forms 420 and 421 and the instructions for their preparation contained in the Memorandum.

Form 420 calls for a report of an "incident." As the instructions related to the form explain, the "incident" may be "anticipated" or "in progress" or "completed." The form calls for a statement of the "type" of incident and the instructions give as "*Examples:* Civil disturbance, riot, rally, protest, demonstration, march, confrontation, etc." The form calls for the names of the organizations of groups involved in the "incident," and the instructions suggest as "*Examples of types:* Left wing, Right wing, Civil Rights, Militant, Nationalistic, Pacifist, Religious, Black Power, Ku Klux Klan, Extremist, etc." and as "*Examples of How Involved:* Sponsor, co-sponsor, supporter, assembled group, etc."

Form 421 relates to an individual, as distinguished from an incident. Among the instructions appear: "*Spouses Full Name*—Type full name of spouse. If wife, include maiden name or names by any other marriages," and "*Associates*—Enter names and addresses of associates, include aliases and nicknames. List additional associates in Narrative." The "Narrative" portion of the forms reads: "citizenship/naturalization data—parental background/occupation—armed forces service/draft status—membership, affiliation and/or status with organizations or groups—education background—habits or traits—places frequented—parole/probation data on immediate family—financial/credit status—include other records of past activities, findings and/or observations."

On the basis of the several items we have just collated plaintiffs envision that a mere rally, protest, demonstration or march of a pacifist group will precipitate a police dossier of everyone who attends, including therein his butcher's and banker's opinion of his credit. Adverting then to the portion of the Memorandum quoted above which says it is "necessary that these reports be used routinely to inform the State Police of the situation in your community" and urges that the intelligence be communicated "to this central bureau for evaluation and dissemination," plaintiffs enlarge upon their hypothetical horribles and see each such citizen harried amid his family, friends, and business associates. There is not an iota of evidence that anything of the kind has occurred or will, or that any person has been deterred by that prospect.

The individual plaintiffs themselves do not claim to have been deterred. In their affidavits on the motion for judgment, one plaintiff says she is chairman of the Students for a Democratic Society at St. Peter's College, and as an example of her activity she tells of "a sit-in at the office of the President." She adds that during a student strike which followed, "pickets were photographed by two men in plain clothes in an unmarked car" but there is no evidence as to their identity. The husband of that affiant says he has participated in a number of marches, rallies, and protests in opposition to the Viet Nam war, in support of burners of draft cards, and in protest of some alleged "racist policies" of a large religious organization. He adds that he hopes to be a lawyer and fears the Memorandum "may hinder my chances at being accepted at the law school of my choice"; that although "I have thus far not been deterred from exercising my First Amendment rights by the existence of the aforesaid memorandum, its existence is a factor which I must weigh in deciding whether or not to speak or act on a particular occasion;" and that "as an organizer of rallies, marches, protests and demonstrations, I feel that I must warn potential participants that, pursuant to the Attorney General's Memorandum they are subject to being investigated and classified by the police despite the lawfulness of our activity." Another affiant says she is a member of an urban renewal association and has picketed in support of its aims and as well against some alleged "racist policies" of the religious organization already referred to but she says that she feels "the existence of the memorandum may deter me from exercising my First Amendment rights in the future." She says she is "particularly concerned lest a police investigation such as that directed by the memorandum lead my landlord to believe that I had done something illegal." Another affiant describes his activities, including picketing of police headquarters, a stand-in at a bank, a sit-in at a mayor's office, and the distribution of anti-war leaflets and peace marches. He says "I cannot say that I will be deterred in the future from exercising my First Amendment rights" but he believes that "police surveillance, investigation, and cataloguing, and ... disseminating the garnered information" may jeopardize his right to associate with others "should my activities become subject to the Attorney General's memorandum." The final affiant, the president of the Jersey City Branch of the NAACP, says that "once our organization and its members are investigated and categorized as per the memorandum, other persons in the community who are potential supporters ... will disassociate themselves from any NAACP activity and a valuable audience will be lost."

The foregoing is a resume of the record upon which the trial court held that the portion of the Memorandum we quoted above, entitled "Potential Problems," and forms 420 and 421 violate the First Amendment, and granted sweeping injunctive relief we will discuss later in this opinion. There was no evidence that the Memorandum was intended or has been read by local police officials to call for any action which invades a constitutionally protected area. There was no evidence that the Attorney General intended to intimidate anyone. Nor does it appear that he even sought to publicize the use of these forms. Indeed, according to the affidavit of Lieutenant Goch of the State Police submitted on the motion for reconsideration, there is no form 420 or 421 as to any of the plaintiffs, and there is no index file on any of them except one, and as to him only because of an arrest record going back to 1963.

II.

Defendants contend that since plaintiffs have not been harmed they lack "standing" to sue. We do not require that injury shall be experienced as a condition for suit, ... and there is good reason to permit the strong to speak for the weak or the timid in First Amendment matters. Nonetheless the prospect of wrongful conduct must be real and not fanciful, . . . for the chance of error is substantial if an issue is accepted in a setting that is merely hypothetical. . . . Especially is this so when the decision depends upon striking a balance between competing constitutional values.

In this connection it is important to note what is and is not before us. We are not dealing with a statute imposing criminal liability for its violation, ...

Here, the Memorandum imposes no liability or obligation or restriction whatever upon the citizen. Nor does it order the policeman to take action against a citizen upon the pain of discipline if the policeman does not comply. It is no more than a communication to law enforcement agencies about their respective powers and duties. It is wholly informative and advisory. It does not command; it merely encourages cooperation among all agencies concerned with the problem of civil disorders.

This is not to say that only statutes, regulations, or binding directives may spawn a First Amendment problem. But it would be unreasonable to require that intragovernmental communications be drafted with a precision the Constitution demands of a legislative enactment. The writer of the Memorandum could well assume the reader would be aware of the limitations of his office and would understand that the writer was not advocating anything arbitrary, oppressive, or foolish. The police are much too occupied for idle investigations. We think it preposterous to suppose that the Memorandum was intended or was understood to recommend round-the-clock surveillance of every person who attends an anti-war meeting.

When the Memorandum and forms 420 and 421 are read without strain, the common sense of the situation readily emerges. There have been serious disorders involving heavy losses of life and property. The police function is pervasive. It is not limited to the detection of past criminal events. Of at least equal importance is the responsibility to prevent crime. . . . In the current scene, the preventive role requires an awareness of group tensions and preparations to head off disasters as well as to deal with them if they appear. To that end the police must know what forces exist, what groups or organizations could be enmeshed in public disorders. This is not to ask the police to decide which are "good" and which are "bad." In terms of civil disorders, their respective virtues are irrelevant, for a group is of equal concern to the police whether it is potentially the victim or the aggressor. The police interest is in the explosive possibilities and not in the merits of the colliding philosophies. And it must be evident that a riot or the threat of one may best be ended with the aid of private citizens who because of their connections with the discordant groups can persuade them from a course of violence. Hence a police force would fail in its obligation if it did not know who could be called upon to help put out the burning fuse or the fire.

In the summer of 1967 there were serious riots. Both the President of the United States and the Governor of this State appointed commissions to study the problem and to make recommendations. The Report of the National Advisory Commission on Civil Disorders (March 1, 1968) in its "Supplement on Control of Disorders" encouraged the preparations which the Memorandum here involved seeks to achieve. It reads (p. 269):

> *Intelligence*—The absence of accurate information both before and during a disorder has created special control problems for police. Police departments must develop means to obtain adequate intelligence for planning purposes, as well as on-the-scene information for use in police operations during a disorder.
>
> An intelligence unit staffed with full-time personnel should be established to gather, evaluate, analyze, and disseminate information on potential as well as actual civil disorders. It should provide police administrators and commanders with reliable information essential for assessment and decisionmaking. It should use undercover police personnel and informants but it should also draw on community leaders, agencies, and organizations in the ghetto.

In his affidavit accepted by the trial court, Lieutenant Goch of the State Police described the activities of its Central Security Unit. He stated in part:

> At the present time information concerning crime and criminals is gathered by the intelligence unit in the Organized Crime Task Force in the New Jersey State Police and information concerning extremist organizations and incidents concerning disturbances arising out of racial, social and economic tensions is gathered by the central security unit, the human relations unit and the civil disturbance unit.
>
> Specifically, some of the past and present reasons for the accumulation of information by the State Police are: (a) to aid in the evaluation and determination of the probability of unlawful disorders, large-scale violence, and potential riots; (b) to aid in the determination of supplemental police manpower needs; (c) to facilitate decisions and planning for coping with disorders anticipated or in progress; (d) to aid in the assessment of tension within communities and possible causes of unrest; (e) to aid in familiarization with the past activities of professional agitators, their tactics and control over their followings; and (f) to furnish information for meetings of the Governor with officials of various State Departments including the Department of Community Affairs, Department of Education, Department of Institutions and Agencies, Division on Civil Rights, Office of Attorney General, and Division of State Police for their study of the causes of civil disorder, so that this information can be used

by the Governor and appropriate governmental agencies to alleviate present tensions and prevent future and potential disorders.

He pointed out that forms 420 and 421 were prepared prior to the Memorandum and were not devised for it. He emphasized that the forms deal with public incidents only, and are simply suggestive of the kinds of information the State Police believe should be on hand; that like information had always been received through liaison with police agencies; that in fact most of the information called for in these forms can be obtained from newspaper clippings; that such information as appears with respect to these plaintiffs was received from news clippings or other agencies, rather than by way of these forms; that information from all sources is integrated, and is available to public agencies only on a "need-to-know basis," and is never available to private interests.

Other affidavits accepted on the motion for reconsideration spell out the measures taken to keep up with a fast-moving scene and to anticipate explosive situations. They repel the notion that the program was intended or has been used to harass anyone....

The State Police have, for example, supplied information on occasion that a particular group would be holding a public meeting at a particular time and place and that a volatile situation could develop. Thereafter members of this agency and others contact these groups or mentioned leaders to avert the development of disorders....

It of course is not our purpose here to resolve a factual issue. We refer to the affidavits simply because on their face they assert a purpose to discharge a plain duty of government and thus confirm the purpose avowed in the Memorandum.

It is a serious matter for the judiciary to interfere with the preventive measures devised by the executive branch of government in response to its constitutional obligation to protect all the citizens. Surely, such interference may not rest upon a hypothetical exposition of what could happen under a set of forms in the hands of an officer indifferent to the restraints upon his office. Rather the premise must be accepted, absent proof the other way, that the Memorandum assumed a lawful exercise of the judgment and discretion vested in the local police. The Memorandum did not originate the duty of the local police unit to decide what situations harbor the potential of disaster and what data should be gathered for responsible performance in office. The forms do not enlarge upon that power and responsibility. Rather, being designed for many situations, the forms are necessarily comprehensive, leaving it to the local authorities to decide in their judgment what incidents are worthy of note and what information should be obtained as to the individuals concerned or involved.

Nor should an injunction issue on the assumption that there will be unwarranted police action because a judge cannot on the basis of his own experience understand the relevancy of the spouse's full name, or the employer's name, or of "armed forces service/draft status," or "data on immediate family" or "financial/credit status," to mention some items plaintiffs stress in their academic attack. Law enforcement is a speciality, and its needs may not be within the expertise of a court. That is why a hearing is essential for an informed decision in a case of this kind. It may well be that a hearing will establish that some of these items are wholly unrelated to the police obligation with respect to anyone involved in any type of incident, but we should not merely assume that this is so. We cannot know how little we know until we listen.

III.

For these reasons the issue as projected by plaintiffs on the motion for summary judgment was a mere abstraction. The trial court should have denied the motion on that account. For the same reasons we will not deal with the merits. Nonetheless some observations may be helpful upon the remand.

Here we are dealing with the critical power of government to gather intelligence to enable it to satisfy the very reason for its being—to protect the individual in his person and things. The question in the case is not merely whether there are some individuals who might be "chilled" in their speech or associations by reason of the police activity here involved. Rather the critical question is whether that activity is legal, and although the amount of "chill" might in a given case be relevant to the issue of legality, the fact of "chill" is not itself pivotal. Indeed, the very existence of this Court may "chill" some who would speak or act more freely if there were no accounting before us for trespasses against others. But government there must be, for without it no value could be worth very much. The First Amendment itself would be meaningless if there were no constituted authority to protect the individual from suppression by others who disapprove of him or the company he keeps. Hence the First Amendment rights must be weighed against the competing interests of the citizen. If there is no intent to control the content of speech, an overriding public need may be met even though the measure adopted to that end operates incidentally to limit the unfettered exercise of the First Amendment right.... If a properly drawn measure is within the power of government, it is no objection that the exercise of speech or association is thereby "chilled." ...

The power to investigate is basic. So the cases recognize a vast power to investigate in the legislative branch so long as the inquiry is relevant to the legislative function.... An administrative agency may on its own initiative investigate to see that there is compliance with law within the ambit of its responsibility.... So, too, a grand jury may inquire as to whether a crime occurred and who was the culprit, and its power to compel testimony does not depend upon the existence of "probable cause" either as to the fact of a crime or the culpability of the suspect.

The investigatory obligation of the police is surely no less extensive than the grand jury's. Indeed, the preventive role of the police necessarily implies a duty to gather data along a still wider range. The "stop-

and-frisk" rule rests upon that preventive duty,.... There is the power of surveillance. It includes even the deceptive use of undercover agents to infiltrate situations in which criminal events have occurred or may be anticipated....

No doubt there may be situations in which judicial intervention would be warranted. One court intervened when it found the police surveillance was conducted in a manner which was unnecessarily obtrusive and unnecessarily interfered with legitimate business activity, ... and another enjoined surveillance of a private meeting of a labor union when the presence of the police was manifest and operated to prevent free discussion,.... But the power of surveillance is so imperative that even though it was found in United States v. McLeod, 385 F.2d 734 (5 Cir.1967), that the police illegally intended by sham arrests and baseless prosecutions to frustrate the right to vote of a racial minority and should be enjoined in those respects, nonetheless the court would not restrain police surveillance of public meetings,....

The basic approach must be that the executive branch may gather whatever information it reasonably believes to be necessary to enable it to perform the police roles, detectional and preventive. A court should not interfere in the absence of proof of bad faith or arbitrariness....

We are not unmindful of the unfortunate polarization within our society, and we can understand how in that light some may fear that officials will unlawfully take sides. Yet, to deny to government, on that account, the authority it must have to fulfill its mission would heighten that fear or even make it a reality. Lawlessness has a tyranny of its own, and it would be folly to deprive government of its power to deal with that tyranny merely because of a figment of a fear that government itself may run amuck. It should be remembered, too, that our form of government has a built-in safeguard against tyranny in office. The total power of government is divided among the three branches to prevent despotic behavior within any of them. The delicate balance would be upset if the judiciary interfered with another branch upon nothing more than a fear that its officers will be unfaithful to their oaths or unequal to their responsibility. A public official who intentionally turns his office to an arbitrary end is already accountable under the criminal law for such misconduct. It will be time enough for a court to act injunctively when the threat of misbehavior is real....

NOTE

1. With regard to the constitutional right of "association" referred to in Anderson v. Sills, consider the following excerpts from the dissenting opinions of Justices White and Harlan in United States v. Robel, 389 U.S. 258, 88 S.Ct. 419 (1967): "The right of association is not mentioned in the Constitution. It is a judicial construct appended to the First Amendment rights to speak freely, to assemble, and to petition for redress of grievances.... If men may speak as individuals, they may speak in groups as well. If they may assemble and petition, they must have the right to associate to some extent. In this sense the right of association simply extends constitutional protection to First Amendment rights when exercised with others rather than by an individual alone...."

ALLIANCE TO END REPRESSION v. CITY OF CHICAGO

United States District Court, N.D. Illinois, E.D., 1985.
627 F.Supp. 1044.

MEMORANDUM OPINION AND ORDER

GETZENDANNER, DISTRICT JUDGE:

This civil rights action, brought under 42 U.S.C. § 1983, presents the question of whether the first amendment permits local police authorities to infiltrate, observe, record, and disseminate information gathered on the lawful speech activities of private individuals and private organizations when the police have no reasonable suspicion of criminal conduct. This question is now before the court on cross motions for summary judgment.

The moving plaintiffs are the only remaining named plaintiffs in this historic civil rights litigation. The class claims were resolved through a consent decree entered in 1981 and the claims of all other named plaintiffs have been resolved through settlements. The court's decision on the cross motions for summary judgment will end this litigation because the parties have agreed to settlement of any successful claim and all parties have agreed not to appeal this decision.

I. Background and Factual Summary

The parties have stipulated to the following material facts as to which there is no genuine dispute: Plaintiff Alliance to End Repression ("Alliance") is a civil liberties organization that seeks what it deems to be reforms in the criminal justice system of Chicago. Plaintiff Chicago Peace Council ("CPC") is a peace organization which advocates positions on peace issues and organizes demonstrations regarding United States foreign policy. Plaintiff William Hogan, a Roman Catholic priest, plaintiff Lucy Montgomery, a retired social worker, and plaintiff A.A. (Sammy) Rayner, Jr., a former Chicago alderman, are all United States citizens who in the past have actively exercised their first amendment rights. There is no evidence in the record that any of the plaintiffs conducted, or ever planned on conducting any violent or otherwise unlawful activity. Plaintiffs indicate that if the case were brought to trial, they would testify that their activities were always lawful. The only defendant in this case is the City of Chicago ("City"); claims against individual members of the Chicago Police Department have been settled and dismissed. The actions complained of in this case are deemed to have been done under color of state law and represent the official policy of the City of Chicago.

Plaintiffs, it is agreed, were the subjects of investigations carried out by a unit of the Chicago Police Department, the explicit purpose of which was to gather intelligence on non-criminal activity. The unit has been variously known as the Subversive Activities Section, the Subversive Activities Unit, and the Security Section. This unit investigated, without any reasonable suspicion of criminal conduct, the admittedly lawful activities of plaintiffs relating to their political speech and associations. The investigations were conducted by a variety of means. Among the more striking examples was the use of certain organization infiltrators. Specifically, some of the information accumulated on CPC was obtained by means of an informer who became CPC's treasurer and participated in the CPC decision-making process. Information was obtained on Alliance by means of an informer and an undercover agent, both of whom became Alliance board members and who participated in the Alliance decision-making process. More generally, a sizeable amount of information on the two organizations was obtained from newspaper clippings and clippings from other public sources of information. Intelligence was also gathered from various other informers whose level of infiltration or association with the plaintiffs is not specified. Finally, photographing, filming, videotaping and recording of plaintiffs' activities were also techniques employed in acquiring information. One such instance occurred when CPC, along with other groups, rented the grounds of a summer camp one weekend for a conference on nonviolent ways to "end war, racism, and repression." The police set up equipment opposite the camp and took photographs of all who were present at the conference.

Similarly, information gathered on the three individual plaintiffs was also obtained through the techniques of informer interviews, newspaper clippings and photographs. There does not, however, appear to be any evidence that the informers were (or were not) specifically recruited by the police to duplicitously befriend the individuals and obtain their confidence. Finally, there is no evidence that any of the five plaintiffs were electronically surveilled, wiretapped, or photographed in their homes or other private enclaves.

The various forms of information thus obtained were filed and recorded in police dossiers on each of the plaintiffs. These dossiers are extensive. There are 13 volumes of reports on Alliance, 1,760 reports on CPC, 499 reports on Hogan, 220 on Montgomery, and 513 on Rayner. The contents of these reports include the identities of many members of the CPC and Alliance, what was discussed at meetings, and who made particular comments during the discussions. The reports on the individual plaintiffs contain the identities of their political associates and numerous other details of their public and personal lives.

The parties agree that the police department maintained a policy, directed against Alliance, which sought to "neutralize" and "nullify" its political influence, financial organization and support, and operational activities. The parties also have stipulated that as a result of the surveillance of CPC at the summer camp, a reporter who "accompanied" the police to the camp published a newspaper story in the Chicago Tribune which stated that "radicals" and "Communists" had used the property for a "secret revolutionary planning session." There is evidence, the parties agree, that a Security Section police officer, an undercover officer, and an informer testified inaccurately before the

Senate Internal Security Subcommittee that Alliance was a "Communist Party front group." Alliance and CPC have indicated that, if the case were tried, they would testify that these statements were false and have injured their reputations. All five plaintiffs have indicated that they would testify that the entire surveillance operation has chilled their exercise of first amendment rights.

One year after this lawsuit was filed, the subversive unit of the Chicago Police Department was abolished. In 1981, the defendant City of Chicago agreed to a permanent injunction. Alliance to End Repression v. Chicago, 561 F.Supp. 537 (N.D.Ill.1982), rev'd on other grounds, 742 F.2d 1007 (7th Cir.1984). Consent decrees were also signed with the federal defendants. Alliance to End Repression v. Chicago, 91 F.R.D. 182 (N.D.Ill.1982). The only remaining issue in this case is the constitutional validity of the police department's tactics with respect to the five remaining plaintiffs.

II. Justiciability

Before the merits of the plaintiffs' claim can be decided the court must first address the defendant's argument that, under the authority of Laird v. Tatum, 408 U.S. 1, 92 S.Ct. 2318 (1972), the plaintiffs have no standing to bring this claim because it is nonjusticiable. Only if the plaintiffs can establish that their injury is justiciable can this court then undertake to determine whether the injury was inflicted in a manner inconsistent with the first amendment.

A. The Relevant Case Law

In *Laird v. Tatum,* the plaintiffs had alleged that the mere existence of an Army surveillance system which investigated lawful and peaceful civilian activity chilled the exercise of their first amendment rights. The Supreme Court held, in a 5–4 decision, that "in the absence of a showing of objective harm or a specific threatened future harm," any claimed chill is merely "subjective" and therefore not justiciable.

Although the surveillance system under attack in *Tatum* and the one in this case are similar in that much of the intelligence was garnered from news publications, none of the information in *Tatum* was obtained through the clandestine infiltration some of the plaintiffs experienced here. In *Tatum,* when news publications were insufficient to satisfy Army intelligence needs, the Army, which apparently was not claiming to have had any suspicion of criminal conduct, properly kept its surveillance limited to the public domain. The Court emphasized the public scope of the investigation as follows:

> The information itself was collected by a variety of means, but it is significant that the principal sources of information were the news media and publications in general circulation. Some of the information came from Army Intelligence agents who attended meetings that were open to the public and who wrote field reports describing the meetings, giving such data as the

> name of the sponsoring organization, the identity of speakers, the approximate number of persons in attendance, and an indication of whether any disorder occurred. And still other information was provided to the Army by civilian law enforcement agencies.

408 U.S. at 6, 92 S.Ct. at 2322.

It was in this context that the plaintiffs in *Tatum* claimed that the compilation and storage of the acquired information chilled their exercise of first amendment rights. The Court felt that the intrusions the plaintiffs were objecting to were unlike and much less significant than those the Court had previously condemned on first amendment grounds, so any "chill" the plaintiffs claimed to be suffering was purely "subjective." The types of intrusions which the Court felt would cause an objective chill occurred in cases like Baird v. State Bar of Arizona, 401 U.S. 1, 91 S.Ct. 702 (1971) (state may not compel a person to disclose that person's associations in order to be admitted to state bar); Keyishian v. Board of Regents, 385 U.S. 589, 87 S.Ct. 675 (1967) (state may not discharge employees because of their political associations); Lamont v. Postmaster General, 381 U.S. 301, 85 S.Ct. 1493 (1965), and Baggett v. Bullitt, 377 U.S. 360, 84 S.Ct. 1316 (1964). In those cases, "the challenged exercise of governmental power was regulatory, proscriptive, or compulsory in nature, and the complainant was either presently or prospectively subject to the regulations, proscriptions, or compulsions that he was challenging." 408 U.S. at 11, 92 S.Ct. at 2324. By contrast the chill involved in *Tatum,* based as it was on knowledge of the mere existence of a surveillance system, which collected data from information open to the public, and which caused no tangible harm to plaintiffs, could only have caused a subjective chill and was therefore nonjusticiable.

In the years since *Tatum,* courts have struggled to determine when a surveillance system became so intrusive as to create a reasonable or objective chill in a plaintiff and therefore present a justiciable controversy. As a substantial amount of time has elapsed since Tatum, it is possible to glean a pattern from these various court decisions. For example, as Tatum itself suggested, when the intelligence-gathering tactic involves only the use of police surveillance of meetings held open to the public, no objective chill is involved; conversely, when infiltration into private enclaves is present, a first amendment claim may be justiciable. See e.g., Berlin Democratic Club v. Rumsfeld, 410 F.Supp. 144 (D.D.C.1976) (surveillance by illegal wiretapping and infiltration into "meetings and private associations" held to be factors rendering Tatum distinguishable and the claim justiciable); Philadelphia Yearly Meeting of the Religious Society of Friends v. Tate, 519 F.2d 1335, 1337–38 (3d Cir.1975) (only public surveillance involved; Tatum governs); Socialist Workers Party v. Attorney General, 510 F.2d 253 (2d Cir.1974) (Socialist Workers Party convention open to any person under 29; surveillance by FBI informants did not present justiciable controversy under *Tatum*). When Justice Marshall was presented with the facts of

Socialist Workers Party as Circuit Justice on an application to stay the Court of Appeals decision, he decided the issue of justiciability differently. While not disagreeing with the Court of Appeals' holding that the openness of the convention was a factor against justiciability, he wrote that *Tatum* should nevertheless be distinguished and the claim considered justiciable because of the presence of other, apparently more important factors pertinent to an objective chill: "[T]he challenged investigative activity will have the concrete effects of dissuading some YSA delegates from participating actively in the convention and leading to possible loss of employment for those identified as being in attendance." Socialist Workers Party v. Attorney General, 419 U.S. 1314, 1319, 95 S.Ct. 425, 428 (1974). Subsequent lower court cases have picked up on the potential injury-to-employment factor as helping establish justiciability. See e.g., Paton v. La Prade, 524 F.2d 862 (3d Cir.1975) (justiciable claim presented when FBI maintained a "mail cover" file on plaintiff, pursuant to a regulation which directed an investigation and record-keeping on all persons who wrote letters to Socialist Workers Party; file was alleged to possibly cause injury to future employment prospects); Clark v. Library of Congress, 750 F.2d 89 (D.C.Cir.1984) (library worker who was investigated by FBI because of his political associations presented justiciable claim when he alleged the investigation cost him employment opportunities).

Thus it appears that in determining whether a claimed chill is objective, the Supreme Court in *Tatum* and the appellate courts in *Philadelphia Yearly* and *Socialist Workers Party* relied chiefly on the public nature of the surveillance tactics in concluding nonjusticiability. By contrast, Justice Marshall, *Paton,* and *Clark* focused on the specific adverse effects that the investigation was claimed to have on the plaintiffs. Some of the adverse effects which other courts have considered relevant to justiciability relate to issues other than employment, such as the damaged reputations caused by the dissemination of the accumulated information when such dissemination has occurred. See e.g., Jabara v. Kelley, 476 F.Supp. 561 (E.D.Mich.1979) (justiciability where false and misleading reports of plaintiff's activities were disseminated in course of FBI investigation causing injury to reputation); Berlin Democratic Club v. Rumsfeld, 410 F.Supp. 144 (D.D.C.1976) (public dissemination of accumulated information in a false or defamatory manner was a factor in rendering claim justiciable); Alliance to End Repression v. Rochford, 407 F.Supp. 115 (N.D.Ill.1975) (where police files were allegedly disseminated so as to damage academic and professional lives of plaintiffs, justiciable claim was presented).[1] Even police dissemination of truthful but

1. In their brief in answer to defendant's motion for summary judgment, plaintiffs argue that the *Alliance* opinion, written in response to defendant's motion to dismiss the complaint in this case ten years ago, governs whether *Tatum* applies to the facts of this case. It is true that *Alliance* held that *Tatum* and its progeny did not bar plaintiffs' claim, as set forth in the allegations of the complaint. However, that opinion is not dispositive of the current motions for summary judgment, since the court is no longer working with the same set of allegations. Instead, the court has been presented with a set of stipulated facts which are in many ways different from the

stigmatizing information, such as police statements that certain individuals are the subjects of police intelligence files, if done without any lawful purpose, may be justiciable. See Philadelphia Yearly, 519 F.2d at 1339.

Other adverse effects relevant to justiciability, and closely related to the issue of how the surveillance is conducted, pertain to the instability and disruption of political associations caused by intrusive infiltrators and investigators. See Founding Church of Scientology v. FBI, 459 F.Supp. 748 (D.D.C.1978) (surveillance and infiltration of church group presented justiciable claim where FBI activities had effect of disrupting plaintiff organization and its growth by deterring supporters from joining); Berlin Democratic Club, 410 F.Supp. at 149 (claim justiciable when infiltrators disrupted private organization by providing it with false information and soliciting illegal actions); Handschu v. Special Services Division, 349 F.Supp. 766 (S.D.N.Y.1972) (government may use infiltrators and informers generally, but not to solicit unlawful activity or create feelings of mutual distrust and suspicion among group members). See also Socialist Workers Party v. Attorney General, 419 U.S. 1314, 95 S.Ct. 425 (1974) (Marshall, Circuit Justice) (surveillance which has effect of deterring supporters from joining organization, even when surveillance conducted in public, may present justiciable claim); Jabara v. Kelley, 476 F.Supp. 561 (E.D.Mich.1979) (investigation of individual which has effect of deterring others from associating with him is factor in favor of justiciability), vacated in part on other grounds, 691 F.2d 272 (6th Cir.1982), *cert. denied*, 464 U.S. 863, 104 S.Ct. 193 (1983).

To summarize, these various considerations have been restated by the *Philadelphia Yearly* and *Berlin* opinions:

> We think it is clear that *Tatum* supports the action of the district court here [dismissing the complaint] to the extent the complaint alleges a constitutional violation on the basis of mere police photographing and data gathering at public meetings. We say this because such activity by law enforcement authorities, without more, is legally unobjectionable and creates at best a so-called subjective chill which the Supreme Court has said is not a substitute for a claim of specific present harm or a threat of specific future harm. [footnote omitted]

Philadelphia Yearly Meeting of the Religious Society of Friends, 519 F.2d at 1337. And in explaining when a claim presents a justiciable controversy, the *Berlin* court stated:

> Thus, while collection and retention of information, if collected in a legal manner, cannot be challenged, public dissemination of that information in a false or defamatory manner and with no lawful purpose, disruption of legitimate activities, termination of employment, illegal electronic surveillance, and other forms

allegations of the complaint. The court must therefore reassess the relevance of *Tatum* in light of this new set of facts.

of harassment are subject to challenge as beyond "legitimate surveillance activities."

Berlin Democratic Club, 410 F.Supp. at 151.

B. Application of Law to Parties

Having surveyed the case law, the court can now determine whether the parties here have presented a justiciable claim. Careful examination of the evidence leads this court to conclude that the actions of the police department with respect to Alliance, CPC, and Montgomery created justiciable claims, but there is insufficient evidence in the record to warrant a similar conclusion as to the individual plaintiffs Hogan and Rayner.

1. Alliance

The case for Alliance is the strongest of all the plaintiffs. The record establishes that the police surveillance of Alliance was far more intrusive than the "passive observational activities upheld in *Tatum*." Handschu, 349 F.Supp. 766, 771. First, an informer and an undercover agent both became board members of Alliance and participated in the Alliance decision-making process. This sort of infiltration, especially as to the undercover police officer, weighs heavily in the determination that Alliance's claimed chill is reasonable. The board of a political organization is certainly not open to the public. Almost by definition, the "board" is a select group of an organization's members who develop and decide the goals and directions that the organization is going to take. When the police are permitted to infiltrate and record comments made by the members of an organization's highest levels, and to participate in the organization's top decisional authority, there will inevitably be some distrust and suspicion bred among the organization's members. The use of police officers to infiltrate an organization and thereby cause disruption of the organization through the creation of distrust, has already been held to be a factor establishing justiciability. See e.g., Handschu, 349 F.Supp. 766.

These objections to the police undercover infiltrator can also be raised against the informer who also became an Alliance board member. In general, of course, there is nothing wrong with the police receiving and retaining information freely reported to it by informers. Plaintiffs themselves are willing to recognize this principle. See Plaintiff's Brief in Opposition to City's Motion for Summary Judgment at 6. Thus, if an Alliance board member decided to turn against her or his organization and inform the police of Alliance's activities, the police would be free to question the individual. But that is not what happened here. The record clearly states that an informer "became" a board member. The implication is that a person who had already been a police informer took on the additional duplicitous role of an Alliance board member. For the same reasons that the police may not use its own undercover agents to infiltrate the high, private levels of an organization—it risks fostering the disruptive feelings of organizational distrust—the police may not participate in a venture whereby existing informers are used to infiltrate the private levels of a political association. Admittedly, the record does not indicate as clearly as it might that the police here actually told its informer to become an Alliance board member. Possibly (though unlikely) the police played no role in encouraging the informer to become a board member. Nevertheless, the court cannot find any evidence in the record to lend support to this view. To the contrary, the evidence suggesting that the police did participate in the decision to have its informer become a board member is too weighty to ignore. In particular, the defendant has agreed that the police department targeted Alliance to "nullify" its sympathetic and political influence, its financial and organizational support, and its operational activities. This glaring admission not only supports the court's earlier conclusion that the effect of the infiltration into the private levels of the organization was to disrupt Alliance, but it also strongly suggests that the police participated in the decision to have the informer infiltrate the Alliance board.

Another factor relevant to justiciability present in this case is the evidence, uncontradicted in the record, that Alliance's reputation was injured as a result of the police surveillance activities. Specifically, there is uncontradicted evidence that a Security Section police officer, an undercover police officer, and an informer all testified inaccurately before the Senate Internal Security Subcommittee that Alliance was a "Communist Party Front Group." The police dissemination of false information pertaining to an organization or person under police surveillance has been previously discussed as rendering a chill more objective. While it is not clear that the defamatory statements about Alliance were intended to be false, the court is again able to infer such intent from the police department's admitted policy of targeting Alliance for "nullification" and "neutralization."

In sum, the police infiltration into the private high levels of the Alliance organization, the "nullification" policy, and the injury the police caused to Alliance's reputation through disseminating false information together make the "chill" Alliance has claimed reasonable and objective. Alliance's first amendment claim is therefore justiciable and not barred by Tatum. It remains to be decided, however, whether the claim is nevertheless defeated because the first amendment permits the sort of police activity involved here.

2. CPC

The CPC case, though perhaps not as strong as Alliance's, still demonstrates enough police intrusiveness so that the chill is objective. As with Alliance, the parties here agree that an informer became a treasurer of CPC and participated in CPC's decision-making process. However, unlike Alliance, there is no evidence that an undercover agent was involved, or that CPC was the target of a nullification plan. Therefore, it is not so easy to conclude that the police participated in the decision to have its informer become the treasurer. Nevertheless, because the position of treasurer is obviously one of the most select and sensitive of all possible levels, and because infiltration at such a level implicates the very essence of the first amendment right to freely associate, the court is willing to infer police complicity on less strong evidence. For CPC, sufficiently convincing evidence exists to infer police complicity. The record establishes that independent of its specific policy targeting Alliance for neutralization, the police department had a neutralization policy against other civic organizations that the defendant admits are peaceful, including the Spanish Action Committee of Chicago, the Citizens Action Program, and the National Lawyers Guild. The existence of such an extensive "neutralization" program against organizations which, like CPC, are peaceful, leads this court to conclude that the police department at least knew of and concurred in the CPC's informer's decision to move into the rank of treasurer, thus making the police accountable for the infiltration.

As with Alliance, there is also present here another factor in favor of justiciability—evidence of damaged reputation from disseminated information. The record shows that when the police took photographs of CPC members at the weekend camp conference from their position "opposite" the camp,[2] the police were accompanied by a reporter for the Chicago Tribune. Subsequently, the reporter wrote a story stating, falsely, that "radicals" and "Communists" had used the property for a "secret revolutionary planning session." In fact, the purpose of the conference was to study nonviolent ways "to end war, racism, and repression." The police, then, by inviting[3] the reporter to the camp scene and conveying some of their information about CPC to him, contributed to the dissemination of damaging information. The consequence, for which there is evidence in the record, was that CPC's reputation was injured.

In sum for the case of CPC, the court is convinced that the very high level of infiltration, and the damaged reputation from the police—caused disseminated information make CPC's chill objective. CPC's first amendment claim is therefore justiciable.

3. Rayner and Hogan

Unlike their organizational counterparts, these two individual plaintiffs have failed to produce evidence that establishes a justiciable contro-

2. It is not clear from the record whether the police position "opposite" the camp was open to the public, or whether CPC and the other groups had some reasonable expectation that no one would have access to that position without their permission. Plaintiffs do not argue that the police concealed their position or placed themselves somewhere that was not generally accessible to the public. In the absence of any arguments on the impropriety of the police setting up their equipment "opposite" the camp, the court will not rule on that question. It is worth noting, however, that police photography from places open to the public has been held not to produce a justiciable first amendment claim. See Philadelphia Yearly Meeting of the Religious Society of Friends v. Tate, 519 F.2d 1335, 1337 (3d Cir.1975).

3. Although the record indicates that the reporter merely "accompanied" the police to the camp, I think the conclusion is inescapable that the police invited the reporter to watch the conference events. To conclude otherwise would be to suggest the uncanny coincidence that the police and the reporter were investigating the same organization at the same time and place and just happened to independently arrive at the campsite together. Without at least some argument by defendant that this is what in fact happened, I must conclude that the reporter was actually invited to attend.

versy. These plaintiffs do claim that they have been chilled as a result of the police surveillance and record-keeping of their peaceful activities. But unlike the claims of the organizations, there is no evidence that the surveillance tactics resulted in any of the specific effects or was conducted in any of the ways which courts have previously identified as relevant to rendering the chill objective. For example, unlike the organizational plaintiffs, there is no evidence that police have damaged the plaintiffs' reputations or that the police created feelings of distrust among the plaintiffs' political associates. In particular, unlike *Jabara,* there is no evidence that other people are now deterred from associating with the individual plaintiffs. Unlike *Clark,* there is no evidence that plaintiffs' employment opportunities have been injured. Unlike *Founding Church of Scientology,* there is no showing that these two individual plaintiffs were harassed.

Finally, the police surveillance tactics, unlike the complaint allegations at issue in the *Alliance* opinion, were not shown to be illegal or otherwise an invasion of some reasonable expectation of privacy with respect to these individual plaintiffs. The Rayner file consists, almost entirely, of nothing more intrusive than clippings from Chicago newspapers. The Hogan file similarly contains many newspaper clippings. There is no showing of illegal wiretaps, or other forms of unlawful surveillance. Although informers gave the police some of the information in the files, there is no showing that the police directed or paid the informers to duplicitously befriend or remain friends with the plaintiffs while informing on them. Without any such evidence, and the burden of proof is on the plaintiffs, the court can only presume that these informers volunteered information to the police on their own initiative when the police interviewed them. There is certainly nothing illegal or unconstitutional about this, even in the absence of some reasonable suspicion of criminal conduct.[4] See e.g., Handschu, 349 F.Supp. 766, 769; Socialist Workers Party v. Attorney General, 510 F.2d 253, 257 (2d Cir.1974) ("no one has yet suggested that the FBI be restrained from receiving information freely reported to it"). Any chill resulting from this sort of activity must be considered subjective under *Tatum.*

4. A different question might be presented if plaintiffs had presented evidence showing that the police did more than simply interview informers who had come to the police with information on the plaintiffs. In particular, if after receiving information for the first time from an informer, the police directed the informer to keep up the appearance of a friendly relationship with the person informed on while continuing to inform on him, a constitutional claim might be stated since the police admit they never had any reasonable suspicion of criminal conduct. Although Hoffa v. United States, 385 U.S. 293, 87 S.Ct. 408 (1966) permits police participation in informer duplicity, the *Hoffa* investigation took place in the context of reasonable suspicion of criminal conduct. *Hoffa's* holding was based on the fourth amendment, but in Jabara v. Kelley, 476 F.Supp. 561, 570–75, after a lengthy discussion, the court held that a first amendment analysis leads to the same result. Thus, under *Jabara,* when police participate in getting an informer to maintain a duplicitous relationship with an individual, there must be a "good faith" investigation underway. There was no good faith investigation underway here. However, since the record for the individual plaintiffs does not establish any police complicity in getting the informers to maintain a duplicitous relationship with the individual plaintiffs, no constitutional claim is presented.

Thus, all that the court has in the record with respect to these two plaintiffs is a claim of a chill from a police surveillance system which acquired its information from various publications and from interviews with persons who knew the plaintiffs. This is the sort of situation which *Tatum* found nonjusticiable: a claim of chill based on the mere existence of a general system of public surveillance and no showing of any specific adverse effects. Under *Tatum,* such a chill is considered subjective and cannot support a justiciable claim.

4. Montgomery

The Montgomery file is troubling to the court. The file contains much more than newspaper clippings. Besides extensive biographical information, such as her date of birth, weight, eye color, schooling, marriages, and current address, the file contains a detailed chronology on Montgomery's political activities and her social and personal activities. Specifically, this chronology outlines when Montgomery participated in certain political and social groups, where the participation took place, and the nature and extent of the participation. There is even a report included in the file on the conversations that took place during a private cocktail party at Montgomery's home. The file contains other information that is generally not considered public. There is an extensive report on various checks Montgomery drafted and the accompanying bank statements. The file also contains details on her then current and former husbands. Specifically, the file describes where her then current husband went to college and law school, where he had positions of trustee and membership on boards of directors, and the clubs to which he belonged. Details on Montgomery's children, by both husbands, their names, ages, and schooling are all in the file. Medical information about the husband and one child are detailed in the file. Other details about Montgomery's past and then current political, social, and personal activities are enumerated at length.

If all this information was obtained from published sources or informants whom the police did not recruit, then *Tatum* would likely bar Montgomery's claim. Nevertheless, the information covers such a wide range of Montgomery's public and personal activities that one cannot help but get an entire character portrait from reading the file. It seems that there should come a point when, in tenaciously tracking and piecing together the details of a person's life from multifarious sources, the resulting probe becomes so intrusive as to amount to an invasion of privacy even if the individual pieces of the probe are from public sources. Such an intrusion has happened here. In these circumstances, the burden of proving that the information indeed did come from exclusively public sources, such as newspapers or volunteer informants whom the police did not direct themselves, should be on the defendant before *Tatum* bars the claim. Because the City has not presented any evidence suggesting that all the information was accumulated from public sources, and because it is reasonable to infer that much of the extensively personal information in the file could only be obtained from nonpublic sources, the court concludes that Montgomery's chill is reasonable, objective and justiciable.

III. The Merits of the First Amendment Claims

Having established that Alliance and CPC present justiciable claims, the court must now decide whether those claims are meritorious under first amendment doctrine. Put another way, given that the police tactics have reasonably chilled Alliance and CPC, is that chill nevertheless justified under first amendment standards?

The first amendment, of course, protects the rights of all citizens to hold differing political beliefs and belong to lawful political parties and associations. Elrod v. Burns, 427 U.S. 347, 356–60, 96 S.Ct. 2673, 2681–83 (1976); Buckley v. Valeo, 424 U.S. 1, 11, 96 S.Ct. 612, 630 (1976), NAACP v. Button, 371 U.S. 415, 430, 83 S.Ct. 328, 336 (1963). As stated before, the parties to this case do not dispute the lawfulness of the Alliance and CPC associations. Significant impairments of these first amendment rights, as in the case of an objective chill, must withstand exacting scrutiny and may not be justified on a showing of a mere legitimate state interest. Elrod v. Burns, 427 U.S. at 362, 96 S.Ct. at 2684, Buckley v. Valeo, 424 U.S. at 64, 96 S.Ct. at 656; Kusper v. Pontikes, 414 U.S. 51, 58, 94 S.Ct. 303, 308 (1973). The District of Columbia Circuit in *Clark v. Library of Congress* carefully articulated these first amendment standards as applied to the police surveillance context:

> Exacting scrutiny is especially appropriate where the government action is motivated solely by an individual's lawful beliefs or associations, for government action so predicated is imbued with the potential for subtle coercion of the individual to abandon his controversial beliefs or associations. Whether or not the government intended to punish or coerce the individual cannot be the sole test of legitimacy in such governmental action. Where the government action inflicts a palpable injury on the individual because of his lawful beliefs, it has the direct and consequent effect of chilling his rights to freedom of belief and association. For these reasons, the Supreme Court has held such governmental actions may be justified only upon a showing of a paramount or vital government interest. Elrod v. Burns, 427 U.S. at 362 [96 S.Ct. at 2684]. The burden is on the government to show the existence of such an interest. Id. Moreover, the government must demonstrate that the means chosen to further its compelling interest are those least restrictive of freedom of belief and association. Id. at 362–63 [96 S.Ct. at 2684–85].

Clark v. Library of Congress, 750 F.2d 89, 94 (D.C.Cir.1984).

1. Alliance

The City admits that the police surveillance of Alliance was conducted without any reasonable suspicion that Alliance was engaged in criminal conduct. Nevertheless, the police infiltrated the Alliance board pursuant to a "neutralization" policy and disseminated false and damaging information about Alliance while testifying to a congressional committee. In the discussion below I conclude that the City has not sustained its burden of demonstrating that these tactics were the least drastic means to achieving a compelling state interest.

There can be no doubt that, even in the absence of a reasonable suspicion of criminal activity, the government has an interest in investigating civilian conduct so that it may determine whether some further action is needed to protect the public from criminal behavior. This interest, including specifically the government's interest in using informers and infiltrators to investigate lawful conduct, has been described elsewhere as "legitimate." Handschu, 349 F.Supp. at 769. But, as *Elrod* teaches, a mere legitimate interest is insufficient to justify an investigatory tactic that creates an objective chill of first amendment rights. The City must show that infiltrating a high, private level of Alliance, without any reasonable suspicion of criminal activity, was the least drastic means in furtherance of a compelling state interest. Similarly, the City must show a compelling state interest in intentionally giving false testimony about Alliance at congressional hearings.

The court first examines the infiltration activities. The Alliance case is unlike the typical case of police surveillance. The City has not simply sent informers and infiltrators to open meetings to observe and record events. It has sent its agents to participate in private meetings which are reasonably expected to be open only to those who have a sincere interest in exercising responsibility for the organization. The court cannot find, and the City does not proffer, a compelling reason for permitting this sort of disruptive infiltration in the absence of any reasonable suspicion of criminal conduct. In similar cases, such police conduct, in the absence of any "good faith" basis for an investigation, has been held to be violative of the first amendment. See e.g., Jabara v. Kelley, 476 F.Supp. 561 (government cannot justify deterring political associations in the absence of a good faith criminal investigation); Clark, 750 F.2d 89 (objective chill can be justified only by a good faith investigation), Paton v. LaPrade, 469 F.Supp. 773 (D.N.J.1978) (good faith criminal investigation needed before a mail cover regulation can issue).[5] Even if there were a compelling interest in private, high level infiltration without a reasonable suspicion of criminal conduct, the City

5. None of the cases provides a precise definition of a "good faith" criminal investigation. However, it appears clear that a good faith investigation requires more than a mere "subjective perception of a threat." Jabara v. Kelley, 476 F.Supp. 561, 574 n. 7. Accordingly, the court is of the opinion that a good faith criminal investigation requires at least some reasonable suspicion of criminal conduct. While the standard of reasonable suspicion of criminal conduct is itself imprecise, it is not as stringent as probable cause. See Llaguno v. Mingey, 763 F.2d 1560, 1565 (7th Cir.1985). The Supreme Court has often recognized a difference between a reasonable suspicion of criminal conduct and—what is required for probable cause—a reasonable probability of criminal conduct. See United States v. Cortez, 449 U.S. 411, 421–22, 101 S.Ct. 690, 696–97 (1982); United States v. Brignoni–Ponce, 422 U.S. 873, 880, 95 S.Ct. 2574, 2579 (1975); Adams v. Williams, 407 U.S. 143, 145–46, 92 S.Ct. 1921, 1922–23 (1972); Terry v. Ohio, 392 U.S. 1, 21, 88 S.Ct. 1868, 1879 (1968).

has not shown why the information sought could not also be acquired by less drastic means, such as sending infiltrators to Alliance meetings open to the public. In short, the police infiltration into Alliance's board in the absence of any reasonable suspicion of criminal activity violated Alliance's first amendment rights.

The City has also failed to demonstrate, or even argue, any interest whatever in intentionally testifying falsely to a congressional committee. Although the City certainly has an interest, indeed the duty, to answer Congress' lawful requests for testimony as to the information the police have lawfully accumulated, this court can conceive of no reason, let alone a compelling one, which would justify the intentional giving of false testimony to that or any investigative body. Therefore, this particular action of the police also violated Alliance's first amendment rights.

2. CPC

The discussion as to the Alliance infiltration applies with equal force to CPC. The police, it is admitted, had no reasonable suspicion that CPC was engaged in any criminal conduct. Therefore, the police involvement in infiltrating one of its informers into the position of treasurer, and the inevitable disruption and distrust within the organization caused by such infiltration, cannot be justified on first amendment grounds, especially in the absence of any argument that the information thus obtained could have been acquired by less drastic means.

The police action in inviting the Tribune reporter to the CPC weekend conference at the camp location also unnecessarily infringed on CPC's first amendment rights. Even if this court were to assume that all of the statements the police made to the reporter about CPC were true, and it was only the reporter who then published the falsehoods, there is no reason why the police had to invite the reporter to the campsite at all. The court fails to see how the police investigation was advanced by the presence of a newspaper reporter at the scene of investigation. If anything, the published story may have made it more difficult for the police to conduct their investigation. In any event, the City offers, and I find, no compelling reason for permitting the police to render available to a reporter information about CPC's lawful conference activities to a newspaper, thereby enabling that reporter to write a story on those activities. See Philadelphia Yearly, 519 F.2d at 1338 ("It is not apparent how making information concerning the lawful activities of plaintiffs available to non-police groups [television broadcasters] or individuals could be considered within the proper ambit of law enforcement activity.") Therefore, the police action in inviting the newspaper reporter to the campsite violated CPC's first amendment rights.

3. Montgomery

As to Montgomery, the police again admit they had no reasonable suspicion of criminal conduct. Yet the police accumulated an extensive dossier detailing almost all facets of Montgomery's life, from her participation in political events to conversations at a cocktail party, to medical facts about her child. Without any reasonable suspicion of criminal conduct, the court cannot conceive of any remotely compelling interest the City has in recording which political activities an individual chooses to involve herself in, let alone to whom the individual writes her checks, and any family medical problems that may exist. The recordation of such information can only serve to stifle the very sort of lawful, robust dissent that the first amendment, from its inception, was intended to protect. Therefore, the police maintenance of a dossier on Montgomery which was so extensive as to create an entire portrait of her personal, family, financial, and political life, violated her first amendment rights in the absence of a reasonable suspicion of criminal conduct, and in the absence of any evidence that the information came from exclusively public sources.

IV. Conclusion

The defendant has violated the first amendment rights of Alliance, CPC, and Montgomery in the specific ways described above. Rayner and Hogan have not presented justiciable first amendment claims so the court does not consider the merits of those claims. In accordance with the agreement of the parties, the court enters judgment in favor of plaintiffs Alliance and CPC, and against defendant City of Chicago, for $20,625 apiece plus costs, and enters judgment in favor of plaintiff Montgomery for $10,000 plus costs. Judgment is entered in favor of defendant City of Chicago as against plaintiffs Hogan and Rayner for lack of justiciability.

It is so ordered.

WHITE v. DAVIS

Supreme Court of California, 1975.
13 Cal.3d 757, 120 Cal.Rptr. 94, 533 P.2d 222.

TOBRINER, JUSTICE.

Do the state and federal Constitutions permit police officers, posing as students, to enroll in a major university and engage in the covert practice of recording class discussions, compiling police dossiers and filing "intelligence" reports, so that the police have "records" on the professors and students? Is this "intelligence gathering" by the police covering discussions in university classes and in public and private meetings of university-sponsored organizations, constitutionally valid when such reports "pertain to no illegal activity or acts"? The complaint in the present action challenges this practice of police surveillance as violative of the federal and state constitutional guarantees of freedom of speech, assembly, privacy and due process of law. To this complaint the superior court sustained a demurrer without leave to amend, and thereafter entered judgment in favor of defendant.

We have determined that the superior court erred in sustaining the demurrer; we conclude that the allegations of the complaint state a prima facie violation of freedom of speech and of assembly as well as of the state constitutional right of privacy....

In light of this potentially grave threat to freedom of expression, constitutional authorities establish that the government bears the responsibility of demonstrating a compelling state interest which justifies such impingement and of showing that its purposes cannot be achieved by less restrictive means. At this stage of the proceedings, however, defendant has demonstrated no such justification; indeed, because the case arises upon the sustaining of a demurrer, defendant has yet even to file an answer in this litigation. Accordingly, we think that the demurrer should not have been sustained.

Moreover, the surveillance alleged in the complaint also constitutes a prima facie violation of the explicit "right of privacy" recently added to our state Constitution.... a principal aim of the constitutional provision is to limit the infringement upon personal privacy arising from the government's increasing collection and retention of data relating to all facets of an individual's life. The alleged accumulation in "police dossiers" of information gleaned from classroom discussions or organization meetings presents one clear example of activity which the constitutional amendment envisions as a threat to personal privacy and security. Though the amendment does not purport to invalidate all such information gathering, it does require that the government establish a compelling justification for such conduct. Once again, because the case arises after the sustaining of a demurrer, the government has not yet proffered any justification for the alleged covert information network and police dossiers. Consequently, the demurrer should have been overruled on this basis as well.

Accordingly, we reverse the judgment and remand for a trial on the merits.

* * *

At the outset we note that for purposes of the present appeal, defendant's demurrer admits the truthfulness of the properly pleaded factual allegations of the complaint. Accordingly, we must assume that the Los Angeles Police Department is conducting a regular, ongoing covert surveillance operation of university classes and university-recognized organizations, and is compiling police dossiers on "matters which pertain to no illegal activity or acts." The present pleadings do not indicate any limits on the scope or extent of these undercover activities.

In support of the trial court's ruling that these facts, even if true, do not demonstrate illegal governmental behavior, defendant argues that the undercover activities at issue here are no different than the "normal" undercover police operations which the courts have regularly sanctioned. In this connection, defendant relies heavily on the statement of the United States Supreme Court in Lewis v. United States (1966) 385 U.S. 206, 209, 87 S.Ct. 424, 426, declaring that "in the detection of many types of crime, the government is entitled to use decoys and to conceal the identity of its agents." The undercover police activity at issue in *Lewis*—involving the investigation of *specific criminal activity* by an undercover narcotics agent—is, however, a far cry from the police surveillance network at issue in this case. Moreover, even within the realm of the investigation of specific crimes, the *Lewis* court did not grant blanket approval to all covert operations, emphasizing that "in this area, each case must be judged on its own particular facts."

The gist of defendant's position, as we understand it, is that the gathering of intelligence information to enable the police to anticipate and perhaps prevent future criminal activity is a legitimate and important police function and consequently that under all circumstances the police may routinely utilize undercover agents to fulfill such a function. Although the police unquestionably pursue a legitimate interest in gathering information to forestall future criminal acts, the identification of that legitimate interest is just the beginning point of analysis in this case, not, as defendant suggests, the conclusion. The inherent legitimacy of the police "intelligence gathering" function does not grant the police the unbridled power to pursue that function by any and all means. In this realm, as in all others, the permissible limits of governmental action are circumscribed by the federal Bill of Rights and the comparable protections of our state Constitution.

* * *

... although police surveillance of university classrooms and organizations meetings may not constitute a direct prohibition of speech or association, such surveillance may still run afoul of the constitutional guarantee if the effect of such activity is to chill constitutionally protected activity. "In the domain of these indispensible liberties, whether of speech, press, or association, the decisions of this Court recognize that abridgement of such rights, even though unintended, may inevitably follow from varied forms of governmental action." As the United States Supreme Court stated recently in Healy v. James, 408 U.S. 169, 183, 92 S.Ct. 2338, 2347: "We are not free to disregard the practical realities. Mr. Justice Stewart has made the salient point: 'Freedoms such as these are protected not only against heavy-handed frontal attack, but also from being stifled by more subtle governmental interference.' "

As a practical matter, the presence in a university classroom of undercover officers taking notes to be preserved in police dossiers must inevitably inhibit the exercise of free speech both by professors and students. In a line of cases stretching over the past two decades, the United States Supreme Court has repeatedly recognized that to compel an individual to disclose his political ideas or affiliations to the government is to deter the exercise of First Amendment rights....

* * *

The crucible of new thought is the university classroom; the campus is the sacred ground of free discussion. Once we expose the teacher or the student to possible future prosecution for the ideas he may express, we forfeit the security that nourishes change and advancement. The censorship of totalitarian regimes that so often condemns developments in art, science and politics is but a step removed from the inchoate surveillance of free discussion in the university; such intrusion stifles creativity and to a large degree shackles democracy.

* * *

In the instant case, defendant's burden of justification is very heavy indeed. Not only does the alleged covert intrusion into university classes and meetings pose a grave threat to the freedom of expression necessary for the preservation of the university as we know it today, but the complaint also alleges that the information gathered by the undercover police officers "pertains to no illegal activity or acts." Because this case arises upon the sustaining of a demurrer, defendant has as yet given no explanation or justification for the alleged surveillance; indeed, defendant has yet to file any answer at all in this case. Thus, inasmuch as we have determined that the complaint does demonstrate a prima facie violation of First Amendment rights, the trial court erred in sustaining defendant's demurrer. The judgment must accordingly be reversed and the case remanded for a trial on the merits.

* * *

... Shortly after the court sustained the demurrer to the complaint, the people of California amended the state Constitution to provide explicit protection to every individual's interest in "privacy." Although the full contours of the new constitutional provision have as yet not even tentatively been sketched, we have concluded that the surveillance and data gathering activities challenged in this case do fall within the aegis of that provision.

* * *

... In the course of classroom debate some thoughts will be hazarded only as the trial balloons of new theories. Yet such propositions, that are tentative only, will nevertheless be recorded by police officers, filtered through the minds of the listening informers, often incorrectly misstated to their superiors and sometimes maliciously distended. Only a brave soul would dare to express anything other than orthodoxy under such circumstances. But the classroom of the university should be a forum of free expression; its very function would largely be destroyed by the practices described in the complaint before us.

The judgment is reversed.

* * *

NOTE

The present section has not dealt with the subject of surveillance of or intrusions upon private property; that falls within the purview of the subsequent chapter on Search and Seizure.

B. FREEDOM OF THE PRESS—THE OBSCENITY ISSUE

"The liberty of the press consists in printing without any previous license, subject to the consequences of law. The licentiousness of the press is Pandora's Box, the source of every evil. Miserable is the condition of individuals, dangerous is the condition of the State, if there is no certain law, or, which is the same thing, no certain administration of law, to protect individuals, or guard the State."

Lord Mansfield, C.J., R. v. Shipley, (1784) 4 Doug. 73, 170.

MILLER v. CALIFORNIA

Supreme Court of the United States, 1973.
413 U.S. 15, 93 S.Ct. 2607.

MR. CHIEF JUSTICE BURGER delivered the opinion of the Court....

Appellant conducted a mass mailing campaign to advertise the sale of illustrated books, euphemistically called "adult" material. After a jury trial, he was convicted of violating California Penal Code § 311.2(a), a misdemeanor, by knowingly distributing obscene matter,[1] and the Appellate Department, Superior Court of California, County of Orange, summarily affirmed the judgment without opinion. Appellant's conviction was specifically based on his conduct in causing five unsolicited advertising brochures to be sent through the mail in an envelope addressed to a restaurant in Newport Beach, California. The envelope was opened by the manager of the restaurant and his mother. They had not requested the brochures; they complained to the police.

1. At the time of the commission of the alleged offense, which was prior to June 25, 1969, §§ 311.2(a) and 311 of the California Penal Code read in relevant part:

"§ 311.2 Sending or bringing into state for sale or distribution; printing, exhibiting, distributing or possessing within state

"(a) Every person who knowingly: sends or causes to be sent, or brings or causes to be brought, into this state for sale or distribution, or in this state prepares, publishes, prints, exhibits, distributes, or offers to distribute, or has in his possession with intent to distribute or to exhibit or offer to distribute, any obscene matter is guilty of a misdemeanor...."

"§ 311. Definitions

"As used in this chapter:

"(a) 'Obscene' means that to the average person, applying contemporary standards, the predominant appeal of the matter, taken as a whole, is to prurient interest, i.e., a shameful or morbid interest in nudity, sex, or excretion, which goes substantially beyond customary limits of candor in description or representation of such matters and is matter which is utterly without redeeming social importance.

"(b) 'Matter' means any book, magazine, newspaper, or other printed or written material or any picture, drawing, photograph, motion picture, or other pictorial representation or any statue or other figure, or any recording, transcription or mechanical, chemical or electrical reproduction or any other articles, equipment, machines or materials.

"(c) 'Person' means any individual, partnership, firm, association, corporation, or other legal entity.

"(d) 'Distribute' means to transfer possession of, whether with or without consideration.

"(e) 'Knowingly' means having knowledge that the matter is obscene."

Section 311(e) of the California Penal Code, supra, was amended on June 25, 1969, to read as follows:

"(e) 'Knowingly' means being aware of the character of the matter."

The brochures advertise four books entitled, "Intercourse," "Man-Woman," "Sex Orgies Illustrated," and "An Illustrated History of Pornography," and a film entitled "Marital Intercourse." While the brochures contain some descriptive printed material, primarily they consist of pictures and drawings very explicitly depicting men and women in groups of two or more engaging in a variety of sexual activities, with genitals often prominently displayed.

This case involves the application of a State's criminal obscenity statute to a situation in which sexually explicit materials have been thrust by aggressive sales action upon unwilling recipients who had in no way indicated any desire to receive such materials. This Court has recognized that the States have a legitimate interest in prohibiting dissemination or exhibition of obscene material[2] when the mode of dissemination carries with it a significant danger of offending the sensibilities of unwilling recipients or of exposure to juveniles. It is in this context that we are called on to define the standards which must be used to identify obscene material that a State may regulate without infringing on the First Amendment as applicable to the States through the Fourteenth Amendment.

... In Roth v. United States, 354 U.S. 476, 77 S.Ct. 1304 (1957), the Court sustained a conviction under a federal statute punishing the mailing of "obscene, lewd, lascivious or filthy ... " materials. The key to that holding was the Court's rejection of the claim that obscene materials were protected by the First Amendment. Five Justices joined in the opinion stating:

> "All ideas having even the slightest redeeming social importance—unorthodox ideas, controversial ideas, even ideas hateful to the prevailing climate of opinion—have the full protection of the [First Amendment] guaranties, unless excludable because they encroach upon the limited area of more important inter-

2. This Court has defined "obscene material" as "material which deals with sex in a manner appealing to prurient interest," Roth v. United States, [354 U.S. 476], at 487, but the *Roth* definition does not reflect the precise meaning of "obscene" as traditionally used in the English language. Derived from the Latin *obscaenus, ob,* to, plus *caenum,* filth, "obscene" is defined in the Webster's Third New International Dictionary (Unabridged 1969) as "1a: disgusting to the senses ... b: grossly repugnant to the generally accepted notions of what is appropriate ... 2: offensive or revolting as countering or violating some ideal or principle." The Oxford English Dictionary (1933 ed.) gives a similar definition, "[o]ffensive to the senses, or to taste or refinement; disgusting, repulsive, filthy, foul, abominable, loathsome."

The material we are discussing in this case is more accurately defined as "pornography" or "pornographic material." "Pornography" derives from the Greek (*pornè,* harlot, and *graphos,* writing). The word now means "1: a description of prostitutes or prostitution 2: a depiction (as in writing or painting) of licentiousness or lewdness: a portrayal of erotic behavior designed to cause sexual excitement." Webster's Third New International Dictionary, supra. Pornographic material which is obscene forms a subgroup of all "obscene" expression, but not the whole, at least as the word "obscene" is now used in our language. We note, therefore, that the words "obscene material," as used in this case, have a specific judicial meaning which derives from the *Roth* case, i.e., obscene material "which deals with sex." *Roth* [infra 78]. See also ALI Model Penal Code § 251.4(1) "Obscene Defined." (Official Draft 1962.)

ests. But implicit in the history of the First Amendment is the rejection of obscenity as utterly without redeeming social importance.... This is the same judgment expressed by this Court in Chaplinsky v. New Hampshire, 315 U.S. 568, 571–572, 62 S.Ct. 766, 768–769:

"'... There are certain well-defined and narrowly limited classes of speech, the prevention and punishment of which have never been thought to raise any Constitutional problem. *These include the lewd and obscene.... It has been well observed that such utterances are no essential part of any exposition of ideas, and are of such slight social value as a step to truth that any benefit that may be derived from them is clearly outweighed by the social interest in order and morality....'* [Emphasis by Court in *Roth* opinion.]

"We hold that obscenity is not within the area of constitutionally protected speech or press."

Nine years later, in Memoirs v. Massachusetts, 383 U.S. 413, 86 S.Ct. 975 (1966), the Court veered sharply away from the *Roth* concept and, with only three Justices in the plurality opinion, articulated a new test of obscenity. The plurality held that under the *Roth* definition

"as elaborated in subsequent cases, three elements must coalesce: it must be established that (a) the dominant theme of the material taken as a whole appeals to a prurient interest in sex; (b) the material is patently offensive because it affronts contemporary community standards relating to the description or representation of sexual matters; and (c) the material is utterly without redeeming social value."

The sharpness of the break with *Roth,* represented by the third element of the *Memoirs* test and emphasized by Mr. Justice White's dissent, was further underscored when the *Memoirs* plurality went on to state:

"The Supreme Judicial Court erred in holding that a book need not be 'unqualifiedly worthless before it can be deemed obscene.' A book cannot be proscribed unless it is found to be *utterly* without redeeming social value." (emphasis in original).

While *Roth* presumed "obscenity" to be "utterly without redeeming social importance," *Memoirs* required that to prove obscenity it must be affirmatively established that the material is "*utterly* without redeeming social value." Thus, even as they repeated the words of *Roth,* the *Memoirs* plurality produced a drastically altered test that called on the prosecution to prove a negative, i.e., that the material was "*utterly* without redeeming social value"—a burden virtually impossible to discharge under our criminal standards of proof....

Apart from the initial formulation in the *Roth* case, no majority of the Court has at any given time been able to agree on a standard to determine what constitutes obscene, pornographic material subject to regulation under the States' police power. We have seen "a variety of views among the members of the Court unmatched in any other course of constitutional adjudication." Interstate Circuit, Inc. v. Dallas, 390 U.S. at 704–705, 88 S.Ct., at 1314 (Harlan, J., concurring and dissenting) (footnote omitted).[3] This is not remarkable, for in the area of freedom of speech and press the courts must always remain sensitive to any infringement on genuinely serious literary, artistic, political, or scientific expression. This is an area in which there are few eternal verities.

The case we now review was tried on the theory that the California Penal Code § 311 approximately incorporates the three-stage *Memoirs* test, supra. But now the *Memoirs* test has been abandoned as unworkable by its author, and no Member of the Court today supports the *Memoirs* formulation.

This much has been categorically settled by the Court, that obscene material is unprotected by the First Amendment. We acknowledge, however, the inherent dangers of undertaking to regulate any form of expression. State statutes designed to regulate obscene materials must be carefully limited. As a result, we now confine the permissible scope of such regulation to works which depict or describe sexual conduct. That conduct must be specifically defined by the applicable state law, as written or authoritatively construed. A state offense must also be limited to works which, taken as a whole, appeal to the prurient interest in sex, which portray sexual conduct in a patently offensive way, and which, taken as a whole, do not have serious literary, artistic, political, or scientific value.

The basic guidelines for the trier of fact must be: (a) whether "the average person, applying contemporary community standards" would find that the work, taken as a whole, appeals to the prurient interest; (b) whether the work depicts or describes, in a patently offensive way, sexual conduct specifically defined by the applicable state law; and (c) whether the work, taken as a whole, lacks serious literary, artistic, political, or scientific value. We do not adopt as a constitutional standard the "*utterly* without redeeming social value" test of Memoirs v. Massachusetts; that concept has never commanded the adherence of more than three Justices at one time. If a state law that regulates obscene material is thus limited, as written or construed, the First Amendment values applicable to the States through the Fourteenth Amendment are adequately protected by the ultimate power of appellate courts to conduct an independent review of constitutional claims when necessary.

3. In the absence of a majority view, this Court was compelled to embark on the practice of summarily reversing convictions for the dissemination of materials that at least five members of the Court, applying their separate tests, found to be protected by the First Amendment. Redrup v. New York, 386 U.S. 767, 87 S.Ct. 1414 (1967). Thirty-one cases have been decided in this manner. Beyond the necessity of circumstances, however, no justification has ever been offered in support of the *Redrup* "policy." See Walker v. Ohio, 398 U.S. 434–435, 90 S.Ct. 1884 (1970) (dissenting opinions of Burger, C.J., and Harlan, J.). The *Redrup* procedure has cast us in the role of an unreviewable board of censorship for the 50 States, subjectively judging each piece of material brought before us.

We emphasize that it is not our function to propose regulatory schemes for the States. That must await their concrete legislative efforts. It is possible, however, to give a few plain examples of what a state statute could define for regulation under part (b) of the standard announced in this opinion, supra:

(a) Patently offensive representations or descriptions of ultimate sexual acts, normal or perverted, actual or simulated.

(b) Patently offensive representations or descriptions of masturbation, excretory functions, and lewd exhibition of the genitals.

Sex and nudity may not be exploited without limit by films or pictures exhibited or sold in places of public accommodation any more than live sex and nudity can be exhibited or sold without limit in such public places. At a minimum, prurient, patently offensive depiction or description of sexual conduct must have serious literary, artistic, political, or scientific value to merit First Amendment protection. For example, medical books for the education of physicians and related personnel necessarily use graphic illustrations and descriptions of human anatomy. In resolving the inevitably sensitive questions of fact and law, we must continue to rely on the jury system, accompanied by the safeguards that judges, rules of evidence, presumption of innocence, and other protective features provide, as we do with rape, murder, and a host of other offenses against society and its individual members.

Mr. Justice Brennan, author of the opinions of the Court, or the plurality opinions, in Roth v. United States, supra; Jacobellis v. Ohio [378 U.S. 184 (1964)]; Ginzburg v. United States, 383 U.S. 463, 86 S.Ct. 952 (1966); Mishkin v. New York, 383 U.S. 502, 86 S.Ct. 958 (1966); and Memoirs v. Massachusetts, supra, has abandoned his former position and now maintains that no formulation of this Court, the Congress, or the States can adequately distinguish obscene material unprotected by the First Amendment from protected expression. Paradoxically, Mr. Justice Brennan indicates that suppression of unprotected obscene material is permissible to avoid exposure to unconsenting adults, as in this case, and to juveniles, although he gives no indication of how the division between protected and nonprotected materials may be drawn with greater precision for these purposes than for regulation of commercial exposure to consenting adults only. Nor does he indicate where in the Constitution he finds the authority to distinguish between a willing "adult" one month past the state law age of majority and a willing "juvenile" one month younger.

Under the holdings announced today, no one will be subject to prosecution for the sale or exposure of obscene materials unless these materials depict or describe patently offensive "hard core" sexual conduct specifically defined by the regulating state law, as written or construed. We are satisfied that these specific prerequisites will provide fair notice to a dealer in such materials that his public and commercial activities may bring prosecution. If the inability to define regulated materials with ultimate, god-like precision altogether removes the power of the States or the Congress to regulate, then "hard core" pornography may be exposed without limit to the juvenile, the passerby, and the consenting adult alike, as, indeed, Mr. Justice Douglas contends. In this belief, however, Mr. Justice Douglas now stands alone.

Mr. Justice Brennan also emphasizes "institutional stress" in justification of his change of view. Noting that "[t]he number of obscenity cases on our docket gives ample testimony to the burden that has been placed upon this Court," he quite rightly remarks that the examination of contested materials "is hardly a source of edification to the members of this Court." He also notes, and we agree, that "uncertainty of the standards creates a continuing source of tension between state and federal courts...." "The problem is ... that one cannot say with certainty that material is obscene until at least five members of this Court, applying inevitably obscure standards, have pronounced it so."

It is certainly true that the absence, since *Roth,* of a single majority view of this Court as to proper standards for testing obscenity has placed a strain on both state and federal courts. But today, for the first time since *Roth* was decided in 1957, a majority of this Court has agreed on concrete guidelines to isolate "hard core" pornography from expression protected by the First Amendment....

Under a National Constitution, fundamental First Amendment limitations on the powers of the States do not vary from community to community, but this does not mean that there are, or should or can be, fixed, uniform national standards of precisely what appeals to the "prurient interest" or is "patently offensive." These are essentially questions of fact, and our Nation is simply too big and too diverse for this Court to reasonably expect that such standards could be articulated for all 50 States in a single formulation, even assuming the prerequisite consensus exists. When triers of fact are asked to decide whether "the average person, applying contemporary community standards" would consider certain materials "prurient," it would be unrealistic to require that the answer be based on some abstract formulation. The adversary system, with lay jurors as the usual ultimate factfinders in criminal prosecutions, has historically permitted triers of fact to draw on the standards of their community, guided always by limiting instructions on the law. To require a State to structure obscenity proceedings around evidence of a *national* "community standard" would be an exercise in futility.

As noted before, this case was tried on the theory that the California obscenity statute sought to incorporate the tripartite test of *Memoirs*.... The jury, however, was explicitly instructed that, in determining whether the "dominant theme of the material as a whole ... appeals to the prurient interest" and in determining whether the material "goes substantially beyond customary limits of candor and affronts contemporary community standards of decency," it was to apply "contemporary community standards of the State of California."

During the trial, both the prosecution and the defense assumed that the relevant "community standards" in making the factual determination of obscenity were those of the State of California, not some hypothetical standard of the entire United States of America. Defense counsel at trial never objected to the testimony of the State's expert on community standards or to the instructions of the trial judge on "statewide" standards. On appeal to the Appellate Department, Superior Court of California, County of Orange, appellant for the first time contended that application of state, rather than national, standards violated the First and Fourteenth Amendments.

We conclude that neither the State's alleged failure to offer evidence of "national standards," nor the trial court's charge that the jury consider state community standards, were constitutional errors. Nothing in the First Amendment requires that a jury must consider hypothetical and unascertainable "national standards" when attempting to determine whether certain materials are obscene as a matter of fact....

It is neither realistic nor constitutionally sound to read the First Amendment as requiring that the people of Maine or Mississippi accept public depiction of conduct found tolerable in Las Vegas, or New York City. People in different States vary in their tastes and attitudes, and this diversity is not to be strangled by the absolutism of imposed uniformity. As the Court made clear in Mishkin v. New York, 383 U.S., at 508–509, 86 S.Ct., at 963, the primary concern with requiring a jury to apply the standard of "the average person, applying contemporary community standards" is to be certain that, so far as material is not aimed at a deviant group, it will be judged by its impact on an average person, rather than a particularly susceptible or sensitive person—or indeed a totally insensitive one. We hold that the requirement that the jury evaluate the materials with reference to "contemporary standards of the State of California" serves this protective purpose and is constitutionally adequate.

... The First Amendment protects works which, taken as a whole, have serious literary, artistic, political, or scientific value, regardless of whether the government or a majority of the people approve of the ideas these works represent. "The protection given speech and press was fashioned to assure unfettered interchange of *ideas* for the bringing about of political and social changes desired by the people." But the public portrayal of hard-core sexual conduct for its own sake, and for the ensuing commercial gain, is a different matter.

There is no evidence, empirical or historical, that the stern 19th century American censorship of public distribution and display of material relating to sex, in any way limited or affected expression of serious literary, artistic, political, or scientific ideas. On the contrary, it is beyond any question that the era following Thomas Jefferson to Theodore Roosevelt was an "extraordinarily vigorous period," not just in economics and politics, but in *belles lettres* and in "the outlying fields of social and political philosophies." We do not see the harsh hand of censorship of ideas—good or bad, sound or unsound—and "repression" of political liberty lurking in every state regulation of commercial exploitation of human interest in sex.

... One can concede that the "sexual revolution" of recent years may have had useful byproducts in striking layers of prudery from a subject long irrationally kept from needed ventilation. But it does not follow that no regulation of patently offensive "hard core" materials is needed or permissible; civilized people do not allow unregulated access to heroin because it is a derivative of medicinal morphine.

In sum, we (a) reaffirm the *Roth* holding that obscene material is not protected by the First Amendment; (b) hold that such material can be regulated by the States, subject to the specific safeguards enunciated above, without a showing that the material is "*utterly* without redeeming social value"; and (c) hold that obscenity is to be determined by applying "contemporary community standards," not "national standards." The judgment of the Appellate Department of the Superior Court, Orange County, California, is vacated and the case remanded to that court for further proceedings not inconsistent with the First Amendment standards established by this opinion.

[The dissenting opinion of Justice Douglas is omitted. He argued that the decision left courts with no guidelines for determining what is obscene. The dissenting opinion of Justice Brennan, joined by Justices Marshall and Stewart is also omitted. They argued that the statute was constitutionally overbroad.]

BROCKETT v. SPOKANE ARCADES, INC.

Supreme Court of the United States, 1985.
472 U.S. 491, 105 S.Ct. 2794.

JUSTICE WHITE delivered the opinion of the Court.

The question in this case is whether the Court of Appeals for the Ninth Circuit erred in invalidating in its entirety a Washington statute aimed at preventing and punishing the publication of obscene materials.

I

On April 1, 1982, the Washington state moral nuisance law became effective. Wash.Rev.Code § 7.48A.010—7.48A.900 (1983).[1] It sets forth a comprehensive scheme establishing criminal and civil penalties for those who deal in obscenity or prostitution. The statute declares to be a "moral nuisance" any place "where lewd films are publicly exhibited as a regular course of business" and any place of business "in which lewd publications constitute a principal part of the stock in trade." §§ 7.48A.020. (1), (3). Subsection (2) of the "Definitions" section of the

1. An earlier moral nuisance law, Wash. Rev.Code § 7.48.052 et seq. (1983), adopted as an initiative measure in 1977, was struck down as an impermissible prior restraint. See Spokane Arcades, Inc. v. Brockett, 631 F.2d 135 (CA9 1980), aff'd, 454 U.S. 1022 (1981).

statute provides that "lewd matter" is synonymous with "obscene matter," and defines these terms to mean any matter:

> "(a) Which the average person, applying contemporary community standards, would find, when considered as a whole, appeals to the prurient interest; and
>
> "(b) Which explicitly depicts or describes patently offensive representations or descriptions of:
>
> "(i) Ultimate sexual acts, normal or perverted, actual or simulated; or
>
> "(ii) Masturbation, fellatio, cunnilingus, bestiality, excretory functions, or lewd exhibition of the genitals or genital area; or
>
> "(iii) Violent or destructive sexual acts, including but not limited to human or animal mutilation, dismemberment, rape or torture; and
>
> "(c) Which, when considered as a whole, and in the context in which it is used, lacks serious literary, artistic, political, or scientific value." § 7.48A.010(2).

The word "prurient," as used in subsection (2)(a), is defined in subsection (8) to mean "that which incites lasciviousness or lust." § 7.48A.010(8).

On April 5, four days after the effective date of the statute, appellees—various individuals and corporations who purvey sexually oriented books and movies to the adult public—challenged the constitutionality of the statute in Federal District Court, seeking injunctive and declaratory relief. One of their assertions was that the statute's definition of "prurient" to include "that which incites ... lust" was unconstitutionally overbroad because it reached material that aroused only a normal, healthy interest in sex and that the statute was therefore to be declared invalid on its face. Appellees alleged that the sexually oriented films and books they sold were protected by the First Amendment, and that the state authorities would enforce the new legislation against them unless restrained by the Court. App. 33. On April 13, the District Court for the Eastern District of Washington issued a preliminary injunction against enforcement of the statute. Id., at 35.

After trial, the District Court rejected all of appellees' constitutional challenges to the validity of the statute. 544 F.Supp. 1034 (1982). A divided panel of the Court of Appeals for the Ninth Circuit reversed. 725 F.2d 482 (1984). It first held that a facial challenge to the allegedly overbroad statute was appropriate despite the fact that the law had not yet been authoritatively interpreted or enforced. This was necessary when First Amendment rights were at stake lest the very existence of the statute have a chilling effect on protected expression. The Court of Appeals acknowledged that facial invalidation required "substantial overbreadth," Broadrick v. Oklahoma, 413 U.S. 601 (1973), but concluded that the requirement applies only when the challenged statute regulates conduct, as opposed to "pure speech." 725 F.2d, at 487. Nor did the court find this to be an appropriate case for abstention. See Railroad Comm'n v. Pullman Co., 312 U.S. 496 (1941).

Reaching the merits, the Court of Appeals held that by including "lust" in its definition of "prurient," the Washington state legislature had intended the statute to reach material that merely stimulated normal sexual responses, material that it considered to be constitutionally protected. Because in its view the statute did not lend itself to a saving construction by a state court and any application of the statute would depend on a determination of obscenity by reference to the "unconstitutionally overbroad" definition, the Court of Appeals declared the statute as a whole to be null and void.[2]

The defendant state and county officials separately appealed to this Court. We noted probable jurisdiction in both cases, 469 U.S. ___.[3]

II

The Court of Appeals was of the view that neither Roth v. United States, 354 U.S. 476 (1957), nor later cases should be read to include within the definition of obscenity those materials that appeal to only normal sexual appetites. *Roth* held that the protection of the First Amendment did not extend to obscene speech, which was to be identified by inquiring "whether to the average person, applying contemporary community standards, the dominant theme of the material taken as a whole appeals to prurient interest." Id., at 489 (footnote omitted). Earlier in its opinion, id., at 487, n. 20, the Court had defined "material which deals with sex in a manner appealing to prurient interest" as:

> "I.e., material having a tendency to excite lustful thoughts. Webster's New International Dictionary (Unabridged, 2d ed., 1949) defines *prurient,* in pertinent part, as follows:
>
> " '... Itching; longing; uneasy with desire or longing; of persons, having itching, morbid, or lascivious longings; of desire, curiosity, or propensity, lewd...."
>
> "*Pruriency* is defined, in pertinent part, as follows:
>
> " '... Quality of being prurient; lascivious desire or thought....'
>
> "See also Mutual Film Corp. v. Industrial Comm'n, 236 U.S. 230, 242, where this Court said as to motion pictures: '... They take their attraction from the general interest, eager and

2. Having struck down the statute *in toto* on overbreadth grounds, the Court of Appeals nevertheless went on to conclude that the statute's civil fine provisions were constitutionally invalid, on the theory that "the legislature will undoubtedly try again." 725 F.2d, at 493. This part of the opinion was obviously unnecessary to the Court of Appeals' holding, and in view of our disposition of this case, will require reconsideration on remand.

3. Because there are no significant differences between the two cases, we do not distinguish between them in our discussion.

wholesome it may be, in their subjects, but a *prurient interest may be excited and appealed to....'"* (Emphasis added.)

"We perceive no significant difference between the meaning of obscenity developed in the case law and the definition of the A.L.I., Model Penal Code, § 207.10(2) (Tent. Draft No. 6, 1957), viz.:

"'... A thing is obscene if, considered as a whole, its predominant appeal is to prurient interest, i.e., a shameful or morbid interest in nudity, sex, or excretion, and if it goes substantially beyond customary limits of candor in description or representation of such matters...." See Comment, id., at 10, and the discussion at page 29 et seq."

Under *Roth,* obscenity was equated with prurience and was not entitled to First Amendment protection. Nine years later, however, the decision in Memoirs v. Massachusetts, 383 U.S. 413 (1966), established a much more demanding three-part definition of obscenity, a definition that was in turn modified in Miller v. California, 413 U.S. 15 (1973).[4] The *Miller* guidelines for identifying obscenity are:

"(a) whether 'the average person, applying contemporary community standards' would find that the work, taken as a whole, appeals to the prurient interest, Kois v. Wisconsin, [408 U.S.,] at 230, quoting *Roth v. United States,* supra, at 489; (b) whether the work depicts or describes, in a patently offensive way, sexual conduct specifically defined by the applicable state law; and (c) whether the work, taken as a whole, lacks serious literary, artistic, political, or scientific value." Id., at 24.

Miller thus retained, as had *Memoirs,* the *Roth* formulation as the first part of this test, without elaborating on or disagreeing with the definition of "prurient interest" contained in the *Roth* opinion.

The Court of Appeals was aware that *Roth* had indicated in footnote 20 that material appealing to the prurient interest was "material having a tendency to excite lustful thoughts" but did not believe that *Roth* had intended to characterize as obscene material that provoked only normal, healthy sexual desires. We do not differ with that view. As already noted, material appealing to the "prurient interest" was itself the definition of obscenity announced in *Roth;* and we are quite sure that by using the words "lustful thoughts" in footnote 20, the Court was referring to sexual responses over and beyond those that would be characterized as normal. At the end of that footnote, as the Court of Appeals observed, the *Roth* opinion referred to the Model Penal Code definition of obscenity—material whose predominate appeal is to "a shameful or morbid interest in nudity, sex, or excretion" and indicated

4. The basic difference between the *Memoirs* test and the *Miller* test was the *Memoirs* requirement that in order to be judged obscene, a work must be "utterly without redeeming social value." 383 U.S., at 418. *Miller* settled on the formulation, "whether the work, taken as a whole, lacks serious literary, artistic, political, or scientific value." 413 U.S., at 24.

that it perceived no significant difference between that definition and the meaning of obscenity developed in the case law. This effectively negated any inference that "lustful thoughts" as used earlier in the footnote was limited to or included normal sexual responses.[5] It would require more than the possible ambiguity in footnote 20 to lead us to believe that the Court intended to characterize as obscene and exclude from the protection of the First Amendment any and all speech that aroused any sexual responses, whether normal or morbid.

Appellants urge that because *Roth* defined prurience in terms of lust, the Washington obscenity statute cannot be faulted for defining "prurient" as that which "incites lasciviousness or lust." Whatever *Roth* meant by "lustful thoughts"—and the State agrees that the Court did not intend to include materials that provoked only normal sexual reactions—that meaning should be attributed to the term "lust" appearing in the state law. On this basis, the State submits that the statute cannot be unconstitutional for defining prurience in this manner.

The Court of Appeals rejected this view, holding that the term "lust" had acquired a far broader meaning since *Roth* was decided in 1957. The word had come to be understood as referring to a "healthy, wholesome, human reaction common to millions of well-adjusted persons in our society," rather than to any shameful or morbid desire. 725 F.2d, at 490. Construed in this way, the statutory definition of prurience would include within the first part of the *Miller* definition of obscenity material that is constitutionally protected by the First Amendment: material that, taken as a whole, does no more than arouse, "good, old fashioned, healthy" interest in sex. Id., at 492. The statute, the Court of Appeals held, was thus overbroad and invalid on its face.

Appellants fault the Court of Appeals for construing the statute in this manner. Normally, however we defer to the construction of a state statute given it by the lower federal courts. Chardon v. Fumero Soto, 462 U.S. 650, 654–655, n. 5 (1983); Haring v. Prosise, 462 U.S. 306, 314, n. 8 (1983); Pierson v. Ray, 386 U.S. 547, 558, n. 12 (1967); General Box Co. v. United States, 351 U.S. 159, 165 (1956). We do so not only to "render unnecessary review of their decisions in this respect," Cort v. Ash, 422 U.S. 66, 73, n. 6 (1975), but also to reflect our belief that

5. This conclusion is bolstered by a subsequent footnote, 354 U.S., at 489, n. 26, referring to a number of cases defining obscenity in terms of "lust" or "lustful." See Parmelee v. United States, 72 App.D.C. 203, 210, 113 F.2d 729, 736 (1940) (material is protected if "the erotic matter is not introduced to promote lust"); United States v. Dennett, 39 F.2d 564, 569 (CA2 1930) (sex education pamphlet not obscene because tendency is to "rationalize and dignify [sex] emotions rather than to arouse lust"); United States v. One Book Called "Ulysses," 5 F.Supp. 182, 184 (SDNY 1933), aff'd, 72 F.2d 705 (CA2 1934) (meaning of the word "obscene" is "[t]ending to stir the sex impulses or to lead to sexually impure and lustful thoughts"); Commonwealth v. Isenstadt, 318 Mass. 543, 549–550, 62 N.E.2d 840, 844 (1945) (material is obscene if it has "a substantial tendency to deprave or corrupt its readers by inciting lascivious thoughts or arousing lustful desire"); Missouri v. Becker, 364 Mo. 1079, 1085, 272 S.W.2d 283, 286 (1954) (materials are obscene if they "incite lascivious thoughts, arouse lustful desire"); Adams Theatre Co. v. Keenan, 12 N.J. 267, 272, 96 A.2d 519, 521 (1953) (Brennan, J.) (question is whether "dominant note of the presentation is erotic allurement 'tending to excite lustful and lecherous desire' ").

district courts and courts of appeals are better schooled in and more able to interpret the laws of their respective States. See Bishop v. Wood, 426 U.S. 341, 345–346 (1976); Gooding v. Wilson, 405 U.S. 518, 524, and n. 2 (1972). The rule is not ironclad, however, and we surely have the authority to differ with the lower federal courts as to the meaning of a state statute. It may also be that, other things being equal, this would not be a case for deferring to the Court of Appeals.[6] But we pretermit this issue, for the Court of Appeals fell into another error when it invalidated the statute on its face because of its "unconstitutionally overbroad" definition of obscenity.

III

Appellants insist that the error was in finding any invalidity in the statute, even accepting the court's construction of the word "lust." To be obscene under *Miller,* a publication must, taken as a whole, appeal to the prurient interest, must contain patently offensive depictions or descriptions of specified sexual conduct, and on the whole have no serious literary, artistic, political, or scientific value. Appellants submit that the latter two *Miller* guidelines, which the Washington statute faithfully follows, will completely cure any overbreadth that may inhere in the statute's definition of prurience as construed by the Court of Appeals. We are not at all confident that this would always be the case. It could be that a publication that on the whole arouses normal sexual responses would be declared obscene because it contains an isolated example of conduct required by the second guideline and because it also fails to have the redeeming value required by the third. Under the existing case law, material of that kind is not without constitutional protection.[7]

Facial invalidation of the statute was nevertheless improvident. We call to mind two of the cardinal rules governing the federal courts: " '[o]ne, never to anticipate a question of constitutional law in advance of the necessity of deciding it; the other never to formulate a rule of constitutional law broader than is required by the precise facts to which

6. Appellants make a strong argument that the Court of Appeals erred in construing the Washington statute. The Court of Appeals relied on dictionary definitions of "prurient" and "lust," saying that the most recent edition of Webster's Third New International Dictionary (Unabridged, 4th ed. 1976) did not include the word "lust" in its definition of "prurient." But neither did the edition of Webster cited by the *Roth* court. Webster's Second Edition defined "lust" as (excluding the obsolete meanings):

> "sensuous desire; bodily appetite; specif. and most commonly, sexual desire, as a violent or degrading passion." Webster's New International Dictionary (Unabridged, 2d ed., 1949).

Furthermore, and of some significance, the word "lust" is defined in Webster's Third New International (Unabridged, 5th ed., 1981) in pertinent part as follows:

> "1 *obs.* a: PLEASURE, GRATIFICATION, DELIGHT ... b: personal inclination: WISH, WHIM ... c: VIGOR, FERTILITY ... 2: sexual desire esp. of a violent self-indulgent character: LECHERY, LASCIVIOUSNESS ... 3 a: an intense longing: CRAVING ... b: EAGERNESS, ENTHUSIASM."

7. *Roth* specifically rejected a standard of obscenity that "allowed material to be judged merely by the effect of an isolated excerpt upon particularly susceptible persons." 354 U.S., at 488–489 (discussing *Queen v. Hicklin,* [1868] L.R. 3 Q.B. 360).

it is to be applied.'" United States v. Raines, 362 U.S. 17, 21 (1960), quoting Liverpool, New York & Philadelphia S.S. Co. v. Commissioners of Emigration, 113 U.S. 33, 39 (1885). Citing a long line of cases, *Raines* also held that "[k]indred to these rules is the rule that one to whom application of a statute is constitutional will not be heard to attack the statute on the ground that impliedly it might also be taken as applying to other persons or other situations in which its application might be unconstitutional." These guideposts are at the bottom of the "elementary principle that the same statute may be in part constitutional and in part unconstitutional, and that if the parts are wholly independent of each other, that which is constitutional may stand while that which is unconstitutional will be rejected." Allen v. Louisiana, 103 U.S. 80, 83–84 (1881), quoted with approval in Field v. Clark, 143 U.S. 649, 695–696 (1892). Absent "weighty countervailing" circumstances, *Raines,* 362 U.S. at 22, this is the course that the Court has adhered to. Reagan v. Farmers' Loan & Trust Co., 154 U.S. 362, 395–396 (1894); Champlin Refining Co. v. Corporation Comm'n, 286 U.S. 210, 234–235 (1932); Watson v. Buck, 313 U.S. 387, 395–396 (1941); Buckley v. Valeo, 424 U.S. 1, 108 (1976). Just this Term, in Tennessee v. Garner, 471 U.S. 1 (1985), we held unconstitutional a state statute authorizing the use of deadly force against fleeing suspects, not on its face, but only insofar as it authorized the use of lethal force against unarmed and nondangerous suspects.

Nor does the First Amendment involvement in this case render inapplicable the rule that a federal court should not extend its invalidation of a statute further than necessary to dispose of the case before it. *Buckley v. Valeo,* supra, illustrates as much. So does Cantwell v. Connecticut, 310 U.S. 296 (1940), where the Court did not invalidate the state offense of "breach of the peace" on its face but only to the extent that it was construed and applied to prevent the peaceful distribution of religious literature on the streets. In Marsh v. Alabama, 326 U.S. 501 (1946), the Court struck down a state trespass law only "[i]nsofar as the State has attempted to impose criminal punishment" on those distributing literature on the streets of a company town. Id., at 509. NAACP v. Button, 371 U.S. 415 (1963), did not facially invalidate the state's rules against solicitation by attorneys but only as they were sought to be applied to the activities of the NAACP involved in that case. Id., at 419, 439. More recently, in United States v. Grace, 461 U.S. 171 (1983), we declined to invalidate on its face a federal statute prohibiting demonstrations on the Supreme Court grounds and confined our holding to the invalidity of the statute as applied to picketing on the public sidewalks surrounding the building. Id., at 175.

For its holding that in First Amendment cases an overbroad statute must be stricken down on its face, the Court of Appeals relied on that line of cases exemplified by Thornhill v. Alabama, 310 U.S. 88 (1940), and more recently by Village of Schaumburg v. Citizens for a Better Environment, 444 U.S. 620 (1980). In those cases, an individual whose own speech or expressive conduct may validly be prohibited or sanctioned is permitted to challenge a statute on its face because it also threatens others not before the court—those who desire to engage in legally protected expression but who may refrain from doing so rather than risk prosecution or undertake to have the law declared partially invalid. If the overbreadth is "substantial," [8] the law may not be enforced against anyone, including the party before the court, until it is narrowed to reach only unprotected activity, whether by legislative action or by judicial construction or partial invalidation. Broadrick v. Oklahoma, 413 U.S. 601 (1973).

It is otherwise where the parties challenging the statute are those who desire to engage in protected speech that the overbroad statute purports to punish, or who seek to publish both protected and unprotected material. There is then no want of a proper party to challenge the statute, no concern that an attack on the statute will be unduly delayed or protected speech discouraged. The statute may forthwith be declared invalid to the extent that it reaches too far, but otherwise left intact.

The cases before us are ones governed by the normal rule that partial, rather than facial, invalidation is the required course. The Washington statute was faulted by the Court of Appeals only because it reached material that incited normal as well as unhealthy interest in sex, and appellees, or some of them, desiring to publish this sort of material, claimed that they faced punishment if they did so. Unless there are countervailing considerations, the Washington law should have been invalidated only insofar as the word "lust" is to be understood as reaching protected materials.

The Court of Appeals was of the view that the term "lust" did not lend itself to a limiting construction and that it would not be feasible to separate its valid and invalid applications. Even accepting the Court of Appeals' construction of "lust," however, we are unconvinced that the identified overbreadth is incurable and would taint all possible applications of the statute, as was the case in Secretary of State of Maryland v. Joseph H. Munson Co., 467 U.S. ___ (1984). See also City Council of Los Angeles v. Taxpayers for Vincent, 466 U.S. ___, ___, and nn. 12–16 (1984). If, as we have held, prurience may be constitutionally defined for the purposes of identifying obscenity as that which appeals to a shameful or morbid interest in sex, Roth v. United States, 354 U.S. 476 (1957), it is equally certain that if the statute at issue here is invalidated only insofar as the word "lust" is taken to include normal interest in sex, the statute would pass constitutional muster and would validly reach the whole range of obscene publications. Furthermore, had the Court of Appeals thought that "lust" refers *only* to normal sexual

8. The Court of Appeals erred in holding that the *Broadrick* substantial overbreadth requirement is inapplicable where pure speech rather than conduct is at issue. New York v. Ferber, 458 U.S. 747, 772 (1982), specifically held to the contrary. Because of our disposition of this case, we do not address the issue whether the overbreadth of the Washington statute, in relation to its legitimate reach, is substantial and warrants a declaration of facial invalidity. See Secretary of State of Maryland v. Joseph H. Munson Co., ___ U.S. 467, ___ (1984); CSC v. Letter Carriers, 413 U.S. 548, 580–581 (1973).

appetites, it could have excised the word from the statute entirely, since the statutory definition of prurience referred to "lasciviousness" as well as "lust." Even if the statute had not defined prurience at all, there would have been no satisfactory ground for striking the statute down in its entirety because of invalidity in all of its applications.[9]

Partial invalidation would be improper if it were contrary to legislative intent in the sense that the legislature had passed an inseverable Act or would not have passed it had it known the challenged provision was invalid. But here the statute itself contains a severability clause; and under Washington law, a statute is not to be declared unconstitutional in its entirety unless "the invalid provisions are unseverable and it cannot reasonably be believed that the legislature would have passed the one without the other, or unless the elimination of the invalid part would render the remainder of the act incapable of accomplishing the legislative purposes." State v. Anderson, 81 Wash.2d 234, 236, 501 P.2d 184, 185–186 (1972). It would be frivolous to suggest, and no one does, that the Washington Legislature, if it could not proscribe materials that

9. According to Appellees, the vast majority of state statutes either leave the word "prurient" undefined or adopt a definition using the words "shameful or morbid." Brief for Appellees 26–27. One State, New Hampshire, defines prurient interest as "an interest in lewdness or lascivious thoughts." N.H.Rev.Stat. Ann. 650:(1)(I)—(IV)(a) (Supp.1983). Mississippi is apparently the only state other than Washington to use the word "lust" in its definition of "prurient." Miss.Code Ann. § 97–29–103(1)(a) (Supp.1984) ("a lustful, erotic, shameful, or morbid interest in nudity, sex or excretion"). The District Court for the Northern District of Mississippi has issued a preliminary injunction against enforcement of the statute, partly on the ground that "[t]he inclusion of the terms lustful and erotic [in the definition of prurient] would permit the application of the statute to arguably protected materials." Goldstein v. Allain, 568 F.Supp. 1377, 1385 (1983), appeal stayed pending trial on the merits, Case No. 83–4452 (CA5, June 20, 1984).

Some lower courts considering the issue have used the words "shameful or morbid" in describing the "prurient interest" that distinguishes obscene materials. See, e.g., Red Bluff Drive-In, Inc. v. Vance, 648 F.2d 1020, 1026 (CA5 1981), cert. denied sub nom. Theatres West, Inc. v. Holmes, 455 U.S. 913 (1982); Leach v. American Booksellers Assn., Inc., 582 S.W.2d 738, 749–750 (Tenn.1979). Others, however, have used "lust" in connection with definitions of "prurient," reading the word as connoting a sense of shame or debasement, or relying on its use in *Roth*. See, e.g., United States v. 35 MM. Motion Picture Film Entitled "Language of Love," 432 F.2d 705, 711–712 (CA2 1970); Childs v. Oregon, 431 F.2d 272, 275 (CA9 1970); Flying Eagle Publications, Inc. v. United States, 273 F.2d 799, 803 (CA1 1960).

An obscenity statute that leaves the word "prurient" undefined, or rather, defined only by case law has been sustained. See Red Bluff Drive-In, Inc. v. Vance, supra, at 1026. See also Ward v. Illinois, 431 U.S. 767, 775 (1977) (state obscenity statute not overbroad for failure to expressly describe the kinds of sexual conduct intended to be referred to under part (b) of *Miller* guidelines, where state court had construed statute to incorporate the examples of sexual conduct mentioned in *Miller*. A predecessor of the Washington statute at issue here similarly used the word "prurient" without defining it. Wash.Rev.Code § 7.48.050 et seq. (1983). The Court of Appeals for the Ninth Circuit struck down the statute on other grounds, but apparently the use of the word "prurient" was not challenged. See Spokane Arcades v. Brockett, 631 F.2d, at 136, n. 1. An earlier predecessor statute used only the word "obscene," without any further definition whatsoever. The Washington Supreme Court construed the statute to incorporate the *Roth-Miller* test, saving it from unconstitutional vagueness. See State v. J–R Distributors, Inc., 82 Wash.2d 584, 602–603, 512 P.2d 1049, 1061 (1973). The evident likelihood that the Washington courts would construe the instant statute to conform with the *Miller* standards also counsels against facial invalidation in this case. Cf. Time, Inc. v. Hill, 385 U.S. 374 (1967).

appealed to normal as well as abnormal sexual appetites, would have refrained from passing the moral nuisance statute. And it is quite evident that the remainder of the statute retains its effectiveness as a regulation of obscenity. In these circumstances, the issue of severability is no obstacle to partial invalidation, which is the course the Court of Appeals should have pursued.

The judgment of the Court of Appeals is accordingly reversed, and the case is remanded for further proceedings consistent with this opinion.

So ordered.

JUSTICE POWELL took no part in the decision of these cases.

[The concurring opinion of JUSTICE O'CONNOR, and the dissenting opinion of JUSTICE BRENNAN, joined by JUSTICE MARSHALL, is omitted.]

NOTES

1. Paris Adult Theatre I v. Slaton, 413 U.S. 49, 93 S.Ct. 2628 (1973), decided the same day as Miller v. California, involved a proceeding brought against two movie theatre owners and managers to enjoin the exhibition of two allegedly obscene films. The trial court had dismissed the complaints, holding that the display of admittedly obscene movies in commercial theatres to consenting adults, after having taken reasonable precautions to exclude minors, was constitutionally permissible. The Georgia Supreme Court reversed, determining that the movies constituted "hard core pornography" which could be enjoined since they were not protected by the First Amendment. The Supreme Court of the United States vacated the Georgia Supreme Court order and remanded for a reconsideration in the light of Miller v. California. The Court, however, expressed sympathy as well as constitutional approval to state attempts to stamp out pornography:

> In particular we hold that there are legitimate state interests at stake in stemming the tide of commercialized obscenity, even assuming it is feasible to enforce effective safeguards against exposure to juveniles and to passersby. Rights and interests "other than those of the advocates are involved." These include the interest of the public in the quality of life and the total community environment, the tone of commerce in the great city centers, and, possibly, the public safety itself. . . .

2. If the *Miller* test is intended to reach only depiction of "patently offensive 'hard core' sexual conduct", does it make any difference whether the test is (1) that the material be "utterly without redeeming social value", or (2) that the material "lacks serious literary, artistic, political or scientific values"? Could a lay jury distinguish between the two tests? Could a lay jury distinguish between *state* contemporary community standards and *national* contemporary standards, and particularly when the Court held, in the companion case of Paris Adult Theatre v. Slaton, supra note 1, that expert testimony on this point is not constitutionally required?

In *Miller* the Court established a three-part test to determine the obscenity of printed material: (1) it must appeal to the "prurient interest," (2) it must be "patently offensive," and (3) it must, "taken as a whole, lack [ ] serious literary, artistic, political, or scientific value." In Pope v. Illinois, 481 U.S. 497, 107 S.Ct.

1918 (1987), the Court ruled that the "contemporary community standards" test applies only to prongs (1) and (2). For prong (3), the constitutional test is now the "reasonable person" standard, i.e., would a reasonable person (not an "ordinary member of any given community") find such value in the material in question. Five Justices found an instruction on prong (3) that used the "contemporary community standards" test to be harmless error. "[I]n the present cases the jurors were not precluded from considering the question of value.... While it was error to instruct the juries to use a state community standard in considering the value question, if a reviewing court concludes that no rational juror, if properly instructed, could find value in the magazines, the convictions should stand." Justice Scalia suggested that when a proper case is presented to the Court, the *Miller* test should be reexamined *in toto*.

3. A statute designed to prohibit the dissemination of "obscene" or "harmful" materials to minors, which materials may not be deemed to be so for adults, was held constitutionally valid by a 6 to 3 decision of the Supreme Court. The statutory expression "harmful to minors" was not considered so vague as to fail to put a legitimate disseminator on notice, and, consequently, a conviction under the statute was not in violation of due process. Ginsberg v. N.Y., 390 U.S. 629, 88 S.Ct. 1274 (1968). See New York v. Ferber, infra, for more on the issue of the regulation of obscene materials with respect to minors.

4. In Kaplan v. California, 413 U.S. 115, 93 S.Ct. 2680 (1973), the Court held that written material, without pictures, could be obscene.

5. Regulation and banning of topless-bottomless exhibitions, nude dancing, and massage parlor operations has been achieved by a number of jurisdictions by legislation or ordinances which sidestep First Amendment issues. In California v. LaRue, 409 U.S. 109, 93 S.Ct. 390 (1972), the Supreme Court upheld a state law which permitted withdrawal of liquor licenses of establishments which dispensed liquor at the same time that lewd or naked entertainment took place. The broad latitude given the California Department of Alcoholic Beverage Control under the Twenty-first Amendment permitted the prohibition of sensual performances such as nude dancing simultaneously in bars and cocktail lounges for which it had licensing responsibility. In New York State Liquor Authority v. Bellanca, 452 U.S. 714, 101 S.Ct. 2599 (1981), the Court upheld a New York statute prohibiting topless dancing at establishments licensed by the state to sell liquor, again relying on the broad power to regulate (or prohibit) liquor sales granted to the states by the Twenty-first Amendment. However, in a case decided the same term as *Bellanca*, the Court reversed the conviction of operators of an adult bookstore who presented nude dancing. Schad v. Borough of Mount Ephraim, 452 U.S. 61 (1981). *Schad* did not involve liquor sales, but rather a zoning ordinance that prohibited all live entertainment. Another earlier case, Doran v. Salem Inn, Inc., 422 U.S. 922, 95 S.Ct. 2561 (1975), had enjoined enforcement of an ordinance that prohibited topless dancing at "all" public places—both those that did and those that did not serve liquor.

Many jurisdictions have used zoning powers, health regulations, licensing laws, taxing powers, etc., to limit, disperse, regulate, or suppress such "adult" entertainment. The U.S. Supreme Court upheld Detroit's effort to disperse adult movie theaters through its zoning powers in Young v. American Mini Theatres, 427 U.S. 50, 96 S.Ct. 2440 (1976). For a general discussion, see, e.g., Finer & Grant, "Regulation and Prohibition of Sensual Performances Under Nonobscenity Statutes," 10 Crim.L.Bull. 717 (1975).

In City of Renton v. Playtime Theatres, Inc., 475 U.S. 41, 106 S.Ct. 925 (1986), the Court upheld as not violative of the First Amendment a municipal ordinance prohibiting the location of "adult motion picture theaters" within 1000 feet of any family dwelling, church, park or school. The ordinance was "content neutral," served a valid municipal interest—reduction of crime and maintenance of property values—and did not unreasonably limit alternative means of communication. In effect, the ordinance limited such movie houses to approximately 5 percent of the municipal area, a limitation that the Court did not believe was unreasonable. Significantly, the Court ruled that the municipality could rely upon the experience of other large cities in reaching its legislative conclusion culminating in the adoption of the ordinance, and did not have to conduct its own expensive study of the specific effects of such movie houses in its own community. Nor did the municipality need to be concerned whether such movie houses would be able to compete successfully in the real estate market after being relegated to such a small part of the city in order for the "alternative avenue of communication" to be "reasonable."

The U.S. Supreme Court explicitly reached the issue of the level of constitutional protection for nude dancing in Barnes v. Glen Theatre, Inc., 501 U.S. 560 (1991). Chief Justice Rehnquist, joined by Justices O'Connor and Kennedy, concluded that the enforcement of an Indiana public indecency law to prevent totally nude dancing in commercial establishments did not violate the First Amendment's guarantee of freedom of expression. While they acknowledged that such dancing was "expressive conduct" within the outer perimeters of the First Amendment, they commented that it was only marginally so. They found the governmental interest in promoting public health, safety and morals, the traditional police power of the state, was a governmental interest unrelated to the suppression of free expression, since public nudity was an evil the state sought to prevent, whether or not it was combined with expressive activity. The law in question did not prevent the dancers from conveying an "erotic" message. To the contrary, they were free to do so, as long as they wore a "scant" amount of clothing. Justice Scalia concurred in upholding the statute, analyzing the statute as a general law regulating conduct and not specifically aimed at expression, either in practice or on its face. He therefore concluded that the statute should not even be subject to normal First Amendment scrutiny, and could be upheld on the ground that moral opposition to nudity supplied a rational basis for its prohibition. Justice Souter also concurred in upholding the statute. He believed that the nude dancing in question had a "degree" of First Amendment protection, but that the state's interest in preventing the secondary effects of "adult entertainment" establishments, such as prostitution, sexual assaults, and other criminal activity was sufficient to justify the law's enforcement against nude dancing.

For a decision addressing some of the procedural safeguards required in enforcing restrictions on such "adult entertainment" establishments, see FW/PBS, Inc. v. Dallas, 493 U.S. 215 (1990).

6. An obscenity statute that defined "patently offensive," in terms of standards of "decency," was too broad. Obscenity can be constitutionally applied only to material that the community finds "intolerable," not the wider range of material it might deem "indecent." Another problem with the statute was its use of the term "accredited" in describing certain institutions in its exemption provisions. The term was vague. Also, a provision on "obscene devices" infringed on the right of privacy, while a presumption proceeding from the promotion of obscene materials to knowledge of their contents denied due

process. The court severed these portions from the statute and pronounced the rest fit to be enforced. Tooley v. Seven Thirty-Five East Colfax, Inc., 697 P.2d 348 (Colo.1985). The same court struck down a statute proscribing the display and sale of sexual material to minors because the "display" part of the statute was drawn so broadly as to infringe on the free speech right of adults. To comply with the provision, a retailer would have to adopt means the court deemed commercially unfeasible, such as banning children from his store or cordoning off "adults only" sections of his establishment. This statute also used the word "accredited," which is vague, but when the word was removed from the statute there was an impermissible distinction between private bookstores and those operated by educational institutions, which led to the entire statute's demise. Tattered Cover, Inc. v. Tooley, 696 P.2d 780 (Colo.1985).

7. Is a defendant in an obscenity trial entitled to introduce evidence of a public opinion poll conducted on his behalf showing that a film distributed at his adult book store was not obscene? This court agreed with the defendant stating that such surveys are "particularly relevant" at obscenity trials, although the court divided on the issue of what is necessary to establish the reliability of a poll as an indicator of community standards. Saliba v. State, 475 N.E.2d 1181 (Ind.App.1985).

8. In Arcara v. Cloud Books, Inc., 478 U.S. 697, 106 S.Ct. 3172 (1986), the Court ruled that a statute that authorized the closing of premises used for prostitution and lewdness could be applied to an establishment that also included an "adult bookstore" without offending the First Amendment. The main activity of the establishment—illegal sex acts—was a proper subject of enforcement action; the effect upon the bookselling activities of the establishment was "incidental." The Court stated that "... neither the press nor booksellers may claim special protection from governmental regulations of general applicability simply by virtue of their First Amendment protected activities.... Bookselling in an establishment used for prostitution does not confer First Amendment coverage to defeat a valid statute aimed at penalizing and terminating illegal uses of premises."

STANLEY v. GEORGIA

Supreme Court of the United States, 1969.
394 U.S. 557, 89 S.Ct. 1243.

MR. JUSTICE MARSHALL delivered the opinion of the Court.

An investigation of appellant's alleged bookmaking activities led to the issuance of a search warrant for appellant's home. Under authority of this warrant, federal and state agents secured entrance. They found very little evidence of bookmaking activity, but while looking through a desk drawer in an upstairs bedroom, one of the federal agents, accompanied by a state officer, found three reels of eight-millimeter film. Using a projector and screen found in an upstairs living room they viewed the films. The state officer concluded that they were obscene and seized them. Since a further examination of the bedroom indicated that appellant occupied it, he was charged with possession of obscene matter and placed under arrest. He was later indicted for "knowingly hav[ing] possession of obscene matter" in violation of Georgia law. Appellant was tried before a jury and convicted. The Supreme Court of Georgia affirmed....

Appellant raises several challenges to the validity of his conviction. We find it necessary to consider only one. Appellant argues here, and argued below, that the Georgia obscenity statute, insofar as it punishes mere private possession of obscene matter, violates the First Amendment, as made applicable to the States by the Fourteenth Amendment. For reasons set forth below, we agree that the mere private possession of obscene matter cannot constitutionally be made a crime.

The court below saw no valid constitutional objection to the Georgia statute, even though it extends further than the typical statute forbidding commercial sales of obscene material. It held that "[i]t is not essential to an indictment charging one with possession of obscene matter that it be alleged that such possession was 'with intent to sell, expose or circulate the same.' " ... The State and appellant both agree that the question here before us is whether "a statute imposing criminal sanctions upon the mere [knowing] possession of obscene matter" is constitutional. In this context, Georgia concedes that the present case appears to be one of "first impression ... on this exact point," but contends that since "obscenity is not within the area of constitutionally protected speech or press," ... the States are free, subject to the limits of other provisions of the Constitution, ... to deal with it any way deemed necessary, just as they may deal with possession of other things thought to be detrimental to the welfare of their citizens. If the State can protect the body of a citizen, may it not, argues Georgia, protect his mind?

It is true that *Roth* [354 U.S. 476, 77 S.Ct. 1304 (1957)] does declare, seemingly without qualification that obscenity is not protected by the First Amendment.... [However] none of the statements cited by the Court in *Roth* for the proposition that "this Court has always assumed that obscenity is not protected by the freedoms of speech and press" were made in the context of a statute punishing mere private possession of obscene material; the cases cited deal for the most part with use of the mails to distribute objectionable material or with some form of public distribution or dissemination. Moreover, none of this Court's decisions subsequent to *Roth* involved prosecution for private possession of obscene materials....

In this context, we do not believe that this case can be decided simply by citing *Roth*. *Roth* and its progeny certainly do mean that the First and Fourteenth Amendments recognize a valid governmental interest in dealing with the problem of obscenity. But the assertion of that interest cannot, in every context, be insulated from all constitutional protections.... That holding cannot foreclose an examination of the constitutional implications of a statute forbidding mere private possession of such material.

It is now well established that the Constitution protects the right to receive information and ideas. "This freedom [of speech and press] ... necessarily protects the right to receive...." ... This right to receive information and ideas, regardless of their social worth, ... is fundamental to our free society. Moreover, in the context of this case—a prosecution for mere possession of printed or filmed matter in the privacy of a person's own home—that right takes on an added dimension. For also fundamental is the right to be free, except in very limited circumstances, from unwanted governmental intrusions into one's privacy.

These are the rights that appellant is asserting in the case before us. He is asserting the right to read or observe what he pleases—the right to satisfy his intellectual and emotional needs in the privacy of his own home. He is asserting the right to be free from state inquiry into the contents of his library. Georgia contends that appellant does not have these rights, that there are certain types of materials that the individual may not read or even possess. Georgia justifies this assertion by arguing that the films in the present case are obscene. But we think that mere categorization of these films as "obscene" is insufficient justification for such a drastic invasion of personal liberties guaranteed by the First and Fourteenth Amendments. Whatever may be the justifications for other statutes regulating obscenity, we do not think they reach into the privacy of one's own home. If the First Amendment means anything, it means that a State has no business telling a man, sitting alone in his own house, what books he may read or what films he may watch. Our whole constitutional heritage rebels at the thought of giving government the power to control men's minds.

And yet, in the face of these traditional notions of individual liberty, Georgia asserts the right to protect the individual's mind from the effects of obscenity. We are not certain that this argument amounts to anything more than the assertion that the State has the right to control the moral content of a person's thoughts. To some, this may be a noble purpose, but it is wholly inconsistent with the philosophy of the First Amendment.... Nor is it relevant that obscenity in general or the particular films before the Court, are arguably devoid of any ideological content. The line between the transmission of ideas and mere entertainment is much too elusive for this Court to draw, if indeed such a line can be drawn at all.... Whatever the power of the state to control public dissemination of ideas inimical to the public morality, it cannot constitutionally premise legislation on the desirability of controlling a person's private thoughts.

Perhaps recognizing this, Georgia asserts that exposure to obscenity may lead to deviant sexual behavior or crimes of sexual violence. There appears to be little empirical basis for that assertion. But more importantly, if the State is only concerned about literature inducing antisocial conduct, we believe that in the context of private consumption of ideas and information we should adhere to the view that "[a]mong free men, the deterrents ordinarily to be applied to prevent crime are education and punishment for violations of the law...." ... Given the present state of knowledge, the State may no more prohibit mere possession of obscenity on the ground that it may lead to antisocial conduct than it may prohibit possession of chemistry books on the ground that they may lead to the manufacture of homemade spirits.

It is true that in *Roth* this Court rejected the necessity of proving that exposure to obscene material would create a clear and present danger of antisocial conduct or would probably induce its recipients to such conduct.... But that case dealt with public distribution of obscene materials and such distribution is subject to different objections. For example, there is always the danger that obscene material might fall into the hands of children, or that it might intrude upon the sensibilities or privacy of the general public.... No such dangers are present in this case.

Finally, we are faced with the argument that prohibition of possession of obscenity is a necessary incident to statutory schemes prohibiting distribution. That argument is based on alleged difficulties of proving an intent to distribute or in producing evidence of actual distribution. We are not convinced that such difficulties exist, but even if they did we do not think that they would justify infringement of the individual's right to read or observe what he pleases. Because that right is so fundamental to our scheme of individual liberty, its restriction may not be justified by the need to ease the administration of otherwise valid criminal laws.

We hold that the First and Fourteenth Amendments prohibit making mere private possession of obscene material a crime.... *Roth* and the cases following that decision are not impaired by today's holding. As we have said, the States retain broad power to regulate obscenity; that power simply does not extend to mere possession by the individual in the privacy of his own home. Accordingly, the judgment of the court below is reversed and the case is remanded for proceedings not inconsistent with this opinion.

It is so ordered.

Judgment reversed and case remanded.

[The concurring opinion of Justice Black is omitted. We have also omitted the concurring opinion by Justices Stewart, Brennan, and White, who considered the extent of the search to be a violation of the Fourth Amendment's prohibition against unreasonable searches and seizures—a subject we are leaving for criminal procedure casebook treatment.]

NOTES

1. In United States v. Orito, 413 U.S. 139, 93 S.Ct. 2674 (1973), the Court held that the federal government may lawfully ban the interstate shipment of obscenity for personal use, and in United States v. 12 200 Ft. Reels of Super 8mm. Film, 413 U.S. 123, 93 S.Ct. 2665 (1973), the same conclusion was reached as to the importation of such materials. Can these cases be squared with the rationale in *Stanley*?

2. A statute proscribing the distribution of "obscene devices" such as dildos and artificial vaginas did not violate the right to privacy protected by the Fourteenth Amendment. Such devices are more like obscene materials, the sale of which can be constitutionally banned, than contraceptive materials that would

be constitutionally protected. Yorko v. State, 690 S.W.2d 260 (Tex.Crim.App. 1985).

NEW YORK v. FERBER

United States Supreme Court, 1982.
458 U.S. 747, 102 S.Ct. 3348.

JUSTICE WHITE delivered the opinion of the Court.

At issue in this case is the constitutionality of a New York criminal statute which prohibits persons from knowingly promoting sexual performances by children under the age of 16 by distributing material which depicts such performances.

I

In recent years, the exploitive use of children in the production of pornography has become a serious national problem. The federal government and forty-seven States have sought to combat the problem with statutes specifically directed at the production of child pornography. At least half of such statutes do not require that the materials produced be legally obscene. Thirty-five States and the United States Congress have also passed legislation prohibiting the distribution of such materials; twenty States prohibit the distribution of material depicting children engaged in sexual conduct without requiring that the material be legally obscene.

New York is one of the twenty. In 1977, the New York legislature enacted Article 263 of its Penal Law. Section 263.05 criminalizes as a class C felony the use of a child in a sexual performance:

> "A person is guilty of the use of a child in a sexual performance if knowing the character and content thereof he employs, authorizes or induces a child less than sixteen years of age to engage in a sexual performance or being a parent, legal guardian or custodian of such child, he consents to the participation by such child in a sexual performance."

A "sexual performance is defined as 'any performance or part thereof which includes sexual conduct by a child less than sixteen years of age,' " § 263.1. "Sexual conduct" is in turn defined in § 263.3:

> " 'Sexual conduct' means actual or simulated sexual intercourse, deviate sexual intercourse, sexual bestiality, masturbation, sado-masochistic abuse, or lewd exhibition of the genitals."

A performance is defined as "any play, motion picture, photograph or dance" or "any other visual presentation exhibited before an audience." § 263.4

At issue in this case is § 263.15, defining a class D felony:

> "A person is guilty of promoting a sexual performance by a child when, knowing the character and content thereof, he

> produces, directs or promotes any performance which includes sexual conduct by a child less than sixteen years of age."

To "promote" is also defined:

> " 'Promote' means to procure, manufacture, issue, sell, give, provide, lend, mail, deliver, transfer, transmute, publish, distribute, circulate, disseminate, present, exhibit or advertise, or to offer or agree to do the same."

A companion provision bans only the knowing dissemination of obscene material. § 263.10.

This case arose when Paul Ferber, the proprietor of a Manhattan bookstore specializing in sexually oriented products, sold two films to an undercover police officer. The films are devoted almost exclusively to depicting young boys masturbating. Ferber was indicted on two counts of § 263.10 and two counts of § 263.15, the two New York laws controlling dissemination of child pornography. After a jury trial, Ferber was acquitted of the two counts of promoting an obscene sexual performance, but found guilty of the two counts under § 263.15, which did not require proof that the films were obscene. Ferber's convictions were affirmed without opinion by the Appellate Division of the New York State Supreme Court.

The New York Court of Appeals reversed, holding that § 263.15 violated the First Amendment. The court began by noting that in light of § 263.10's explicit inclusion of an obscenity standard, § 263.15 could not be construed to include such a standard. Therefore, "the statute would ... prohibit the promotion of materials which are traditionally entitled to constitutional protection from government interference under the First Amendment." Although the court recognized the State's "legitimate interest in protecting the welfare of minors" and noted that this "interest may transcend First Amendment concerns," it nevertheless found two fatal defects in the New York statute. Section 263.15 was underinclusive because it discriminated against visual portrayals of children engaged in sexual activity by not also prohibiting the distribution of films of other dangerous activity. It was also overbroad because it prohibited the distribution of materials produced outside the State, as well as materials, such as medical books and educational sources, which "deal with adolescent sex in a realistic but nonobscene manner." Two judges dissented. We granted the State's petition for certiorari, presenting the single question:

> "To prevent the abuse of children who are made to engage in sexual conduct for commercial purposes, could the New York State Legislature, consistent with the First Amendment, prohibit the dissemination of material which shows children engaged in sexual conduct, regardless of whether such material is obscene?"

II

The Court of Appeals proceeded on the assumption that the standard of obscenity incorporated in § 263.10, which follows the guidelines enunciated in Miller v. California, 413 U.S. 15, 93 S.Ct. 2607 (1973), constitutes the appropriate line dividing protected from unprotected expression by which to measure a regulation directed at child pornography. It was on the premise that "nonobscene adolescent sex" could not be singled out for special treatment that the court found § 263.15 "strikingly underinclusive." Moreover, the assumption that the constitutionally permissible regulation of pornography could not be more extensive with respect to the distribution of material depicting children may also have led the court to conclude that a narrowing construction of § 263.15 was unavailable.

The Court of Appeals' assumption was not unreasonable in light of our decisions. This case, however, constitutes our first examination of a statute directed at and limited to depictions of sexual activity involving children. We believe our inquiry should begin with the question of whether a State has somewhat more freedom in proscribing works which portray sexual acts or lewd exhibitions of genitalia by children....

B

The *Miller* standard, like its predecessors, was an accommodation between the state's interests in protecting the "sensibilities of unwilling recipients" from exposure to pornographic material and the dangers of censorship inherent in unabashedly content-based laws. Like obscenity statutes, laws directed at the dissemination of child pornography run the risk of suppressing protected expression by allowing the hand of the censor to become unduly heavy. For the following reasons, however, we are persuaded that the States are entitled to greater leeway in the regulation of pornographic depictions of children.

First. It is evident beyond the need for elaboration that a state's interest in "safeguarding the physical and psychological well being of a minor" is "compelling." Globe Newspapers v. Superior Court, 457 U.S. 596, ___, 102 S.Ct. 2613, 2621 (1982). "A democratic society rests, for its continuance, upon the healthy well-rounded growth of young people into full maturity as citizens." Prince v. Massachusetts, 321 U.S. 158, 168, 64 S.Ct. 438, 443, 88 L.Ed. 645 (1944). Accordingly, we have sustained legislation aimed at protecting the physical and emotional well-being of youth even when the laws have operated in the sensitive area of constitutionally protected rights. In Prince v. Massachusetts, supra, the Court held that a statute prohibiting use of a child to distribute literature on the street was valid notwithstanding the statute's effect on a First Amendment activity. In Ginsberg v. New York, 390 U.S. 629, 88 S.Ct. 1274 (1968), we sustained a New York law protecting children from exposure to nonobscene literature. Most recently, we held that the government's interest in the "well-being of its youth" justified special treatment of indecent broadcasting received by adults as well as children. FCC v. Pacifica Foundation, 438 U.S. 726, 98 S.Ct. 3026 (1978).

The prevention of sexual exploitation and abuse of children constitutes a government objective of surpassing importance. The legislative findings accompanying passage of the New York laws reflect this concern:

> "There has been a proliferation of children as subjects in sexual performances. The care of children is a sacred trust and should not be abused by those who seek to profit through a commercial network based on the exploitation of children. The public policy of the state demands the protection of children from exploitation through sexual performances." Laws of N.Y., 1977, ch. 910, § 1.

We shall not second-guess this legislative judgment. Respondent has not intimated that we do so. Suffice it to say that virtually all of the States and the United States have passed legislation proscribing the production of or otherwise combatting "child pornography." The legislative judgment, as well as the judgment found in the relevant literature, is that the use of children as subjects of pornographic materials is harmful to the physiological, emotional, and mental health of the child. That judgment, we think, easily passes muster under the First Amendment.

Second. The distribution of photographs and films depicting sexual activity by juveniles is intrinsically related to the sexual abuse of children in at least two ways. First, the materials produced are a permanent record of the children's participation and the harm to the child is exacerbated by their circulation. Second, the distribution network for child pornography must be closed if the production of material which requires the sexual exploitation of children is to be effectively controlled. Indeed, there is no serious contention that the legislature was unjustified in believing that it is difficult, if not impossible, to halt the exploitation of children by pursuing only those who produce the photographs and movies. While the production of pornographic materials is a low-profile, clandestine industry, the need to market the resulting products requires a visible apparatus of distribution. The most expeditious if not the only practical method of law enforcement may be to dry up the market for this material by imposing severe criminal penalties on persons selling, advertising, or otherwise promoting the product. Thirty-five States and Congress have concluded that restraints on the distribution of pornographic materials are required in order to effectively combat the problem, and there is a body of literature and testimony to support these legislative conclusions. Cf. United States v. Darby, 312 U.S. 100, 61 S.Ct. 451 (1941) (upholding federal restrictions on sale of goods manufactured in violation of Fair Labor Standards Act).

Respondent does not contend that the State is unjustified in pursuing those who distribute child pornography. Rather, he argues that it is enough for the State to prohibit the distribution of materials that are legally obscene under the *Miller* test. While some States may find that this approach properly accommodates its interests, it does not follow that the First Amendment prohibits a State from going further. The *Miller* standard, like all general definitions of what may be banned as obscene, does not reflect the State's particular and more compelling interest in prosecuting those who promote the sexual exploitation of children. Thus, the question under the *Miller* test of whether a work, taken as a whole, appeals to the prurient interest of the average person bears no connection to the issue of whether a child has been physically or psychologically harmed in the production of the work. Similarly, a sexually explicit depiction need not be "patently offensive" in order to have required the sexual exploitation of a child for its production. In addition, a work which, taken on the whole, contains serious literary, artistic, political, or scientific value may nevertheless embody the hardest core of child pornography. "It is irrelevant to the child [who has been abused] whether or not the material ... has a literary, artistic, political, or social value." Memorandum of Assemblyman Lasher in Support of § 263.15. We therefore cannot conclude that the *Miller* standard is a satisfactory solution to the child pornography problem.

Third. The advertising and selling of child pornography provides an economic motive for and is thus an integral part of the production of such materials, an activity illegal throughout the nation. "It rarely has been suggested that the constitutional freedom for speech and press extends its immunity to speech or writing used as an integral part of conduct in violation of a valid criminal statute." Giboney v. Empire Storage & Ice Co., 336 U.S. 490, 498, 69 S.Ct. 684, 688 (1949). We note that were the statutes outlawing the employment of children in these films and photographs fully effective, and the constitutionality of these laws have not been questioned, the First Amendment implications would be no greater than that presented by laws against distribution: enforceable production laws would leave no child pornography to be marketed.

Fourth. The value of permitting live performances and photographic reproductions of children engaged in lewd sexual conduct is exceedingly modest, if not *de minimis.* We consider it unlikely that visual depictions of children performing sexual acts or lewdly exhibiting their genitals would often constitute an important and necessary part of a literary performance or scientific or educational work. As the trial court in this case observed, if it were necessary for literary or artistic value, a person over the statutory age who perhaps looked younger could be utilized. Simulation outside of the prohibition of the statute could provide another alternative. Nor is there any question here of censoring a particular literary theme or portrayal of sexual activity. The First Amendment interest is limited to that of rendering the portrayal somewhat more "realistic" by utilizing or photographing children.

Fifth. Recognizing and classifying child pornography as a category of material outside the protection of the First Amendment is not incompatible with our earlier decisions. "The question whether speech is, or is not protected by the First Amendment often depends on the content of the speech." Young v. American Mini Theatres, 427 U.S. 50, 66, 96 S.Ct. 2440, 2450 (Opinion of Justice Stevens, joined by The Chief Justice, Justice White, and Justice Rehnquist). See also FCC v. Pacifica Foundation, 438 U.S. 726, 742–748, 98 S.Ct. 3026, 3036–3039 (1978)

(Opinion of Justice Stevens, joined by The Chief Justice, Justice White, and Justice Rehnquist). "It is the content of an utterance that determines whether it is a protected epithet or an unprotected 'fighting comment.'" Young v. American Mini Theatres, supra. See Chaplinsky v. New Hampshire, 315 U.S. 568, 62 S.Ct. 766 (1942). Leaving aside the special considerations when public officials are the target, a libelous publication is not protected by the Constitution. Thus, it is not rare that a content-based classification of speech has been accepted because it may be appropriately generalized that within the confines of the given classification, the evil to be restricted so overwhelmingly outweighs the expressive interests, if any, at stake, that no process of case-by-case adjudication is required. When a definable class of material, such as that covered by § 263.15, bears so heavily and pervasively on the welfare of children engaged in its production, we think the balance of competing interests is clearly struck and that it is permissible to consider these materials as without the protection of the First Amendment.

C

There are, of course, limits on the category of child pornography which, like obscenity, is unprotected by the First Amendment. As with all legislation in this sensitive area, the conduct to be prohibited must be adequately defined by the applicable state law, as written or authoritatively construed. Here the nature of the harm to be combatted requires that the state offense be limited to works that *visually* depict sexual conduct by children below a specified age. The category of "sexual conduct" proscribed must also be suitably limited and described.

The test for child pornography is separate from the obscenity standard enunciated in *Miller*, but may be compared to it for purpose of clarity. The *Miller* formulation is adjusted in the following respects: A trier of fact need not find that the material appeals to the prurient interest of the average person; it is not required that sexual conduct portrayed be done so in a patently offensive manner; and the material at issue need not be considered as a whole. We note that the distribution of descriptions or other depictions of sexual conduct, not otherwise obscene, which do not involve live performance or photographic or other visual reproduction of live performances, retains First Amendment protection. As with obscenity laws, criminal responsibility may not be imposed without some element of scienter on the part of the defendant....

NOTES

1. While all U.S. Supreme Court Justices agreed to uphold Ferber's conviction, there was substantial disagreement among the Justices as to how broadly the principles announced in the opinion should be applied.

2. In Sable Communications v. Federal Communications Commission, 492 U.S. 115, 109 S.Ct. 2829 (1989), the Court ruled 9–0 that a federal law banning all sexually explicit telephone messages ("dial-a-porn") violated the First Amendment. The law had banned "obscene or indecent communication for commercial purposes" over interstate telephone lines. The Court stated that "obscene"

phone calls could be prohibited but "indecent" phone calls could not be constitutionally prohibited for adults. Congress could seek to protect children from access to "indecent" calls, but the law swept too broadly. "The ban on indecent telephone messages violates the First Amendment since the law's denial of adult access to such messages far exceeds that which is necessary to serve the compelling interest of preventing minors from being exposed to the messages."

C. FREEDOM OF RELIGION

> O unbelievers, I will not worship that which ye worship; nor will ye worship that which I worship.... Ye have your religion, and I my religion.
>
> The Koran, Chap. 109.

WOOLEY v. MAYNARD

Supreme Court of the United States, 1977.
430 U.S. 705, 97 S.Ct. 1428.

MR. CHIEF JUSTICE BURGER delivered the opinion of the Court.

The issue on appeal is whether the State of New Hampshire may constitutionally enforce criminal sanctions against persons who cover the motto "Live Free or Die" on passenger vehicle license plates because that motto is repugnant to their moral and religious beliefs.

Since 1969 New Hampshire has required that noncommercial vehicles bear license plates embossed with the state motto, "Live Free or Die." Another New Hampshire statute makes it a misdemeanor "knowingly [to obscure] ... the figures or letters on any number plate." ...

Appellees George Maynard and his wife Maxine are followers of the Jehovah's Witnesses faith. The Maynards consider the New Hampshire State motto to be repugnant to their moral, religious, and political beliefs, and therefore assert it objectionable to disseminate this message by displaying it on their automobiles. Pursuant to these beliefs, the Maynards began early in 1974 to cover up the motto on their license plates.

On November 27, 1974, Mr. Maynard was issued a citation for violating N.H.Rev.Stat.Ann. § 262:27–c. On December 6, 1974, he appeared *pro se* in Lebanon, New Hampshire District Court to answer the charge. After waiving his right to counsel, he entered a plea of not guilty and proceeded to explain his religious objections to the motto. The state trial judge expressed sympathy for appellee's situation, but considered himself bound by the authority of State v. Hoskin, supra to hold Maynard guilty. A $25 fine was imposed, but execution was suspended during "good behavior."

On December 28, 1974, Mr. Maynard was again charged with violating § 262:27–c. He appeared in court on January 31, 1975, and again chose to represent himself; he was found guilty, fined $50 and sentenced for six months to the Grafton County House of Corrections.

The court suspended this jail sentence but ordered Mr. Maynard to also pay the $25 fine for the first offense. Maynard informed the court that, as a matter of conscience, he refused to pay the two fines. The court thereupon sentenced appellee to jail for a period of 15 days. Appellee has served the full sentence.

Prior to trial on the second offense Mr. Maynard was charged with yet a third violation of § 262:27–c on January 3, 1975. He appeared on this complaint on the same day as for the second offense, and was, again, found guilty. This conviction was "continued for sentence" so that Maynard received no punishment in addition to the 15 days.

On March 4, 1975, appellees brought the present action pursuant to 42 U.S.C.A. § 1983 in the United States District Court for the District of New Hampshire. They sought injunctive and declaratory relief against enforcement of N.H.Rev.Stat.Ann. §§ 262:27–c, 263:1, insofar as these required displaying the state motto on their vehicle license plates, and made it a criminal offense to obscure the motto. On March 11, 1975, the single District Judge issued a temporary restraining order against further arrests and prosecutions of the Maynards. Because the plaintiffs sought an injunction against a state statute on grounds of its unconstitutionality, a three-judge District Court was convened pursuant to 28 U.S.C.A. § 2281. Following a hearing on the merits the District Court entered an order enjoining the State "from arresting and prosecuting [the Maynards] at any time in the future for covering over that portion of their license plates that contains the motto 'Live Free or Die.' " ...

Appellants argue that the District Court was precluded from exercising jurisdiction in this case by the principles of equitable restraint enunciated in Younger v. Harris, 401 U.S. 37 (1971). In *Younger* the Court recognized that principles of judicial economy, as well as proper state-federal relations, preclude federal courts from exercising equitable jurisdiction to enjoin ongoing state prosecutions. Id., at 43. However, when a genuine threat of prosecution exists, a litigant is entitled to resort to a federal forum to seek redress for an alleged deprivation of federal rights. See Steffel v. Thompson, 415 U.S. 452 (1974); Doran v. Salem Inn, Inc., 422 U.S. 922, 930–931 (1975). *Younger* principles aside, a litigant is entitled to resort to a federal forum in seeking redress under 42 U.S.C. § 1983 for an alleged deprivation of federal rights. Huffman v. Pursue, Ltd., 420 U.S. 592, 609–610, n. 21 (1975). Mr. Maynard now finds himself placed "between the Scylla of intentionally flouting state law and the Charybdis of foregoing what he believes to be constitutionally protected activity in order to avoid becoming enmeshed in [another] criminal proceeding." Steffel v. Thompson, supra, 415 U.S., at 462. Mrs. Maynard, as joint owner of the family automobiles is no less likely than her husband to be subjected to state prosecution. Under these circumstances he cannot be denied consideration of a federal remedy.

* * *

The District Court held that by covering up the state motto "Live Free or Die" on his automobile license plate, Mr. Maynard was engaging in symbolic speech and that "New Hampshire's interest in the enforcement of its defacement statute is not sufficient to justify the restriction on [appellee's] constitutionally protected expression." 406 F.Supp., at 1389. We find it unnecessary to pass on the "symbolic speech" issue, since we find more appropriate First Amendment grounds to affirm the judgment of the District Court. We turn instead to what in our view is the essence of appellees' objection to the requirement that they display the motto "Live Free or Die" on their automobile license plates. This is succinctly summarized in the statement made by Mr. Maynard in his affidavit filed with the District Court:

> "I refuse to be coerced by the State into advertising a slogan which I find morally, ethically, religiously and politically abhorrent."

We are thus faced with the question of whether the State may constitutionally require an individual to participate in the dissemination of an ideological message by displaying it on his private property in a manner and for the express purpose that it be observed and read by the public. We hold that the State may not do so....

We begin with the proposition that the right of freedom of thought protected by the First Amendment against state action includes both the right to speak freely and the right to refrain from speaking at all. See Board of Education v. Barnette, 319 U.S. 624, 633–634, 645 (1943). A system which secures the right to proselytize religious, political, and ideological causes must also guarantee the concomitant right to decline to foster such concepts. The right to speak and the right to refrain from speaking are complementary components of the broader concept of "individual freedom of mind." ...

The Court in *Barnette,* supra, was faced with a state statute which required public school students to participate in daily public ceremonies by honoring the flag both with words and traditional salute gestures. In overruling its prior decision in Minersville District v. Gobitis, 310 U.S. 586, 60 S.Ct. 1010 (1940), the Court held that "a ceremony so touching matters of opinion and political attitude may [not] be imposed upon the individual by official authority under powers committed to any political organization under our Constitution." 319 U.S., at 636. Compelling the affirmative act of a flag salute involved a more serious infringement upon personal liberties than the passive act of carrying the state motto on a license plate, but the difference is essentially one of degree. Here, as in *Barnette,* we are faced with a state measure which forces an individual, as part of his daily life—indeed constantly while his automobile is in public view—to be an instrument for fostering public adherence to an ideological point of view he finds unacceptable. In doing so, the State "invades the sphere of intellect and spirit which it is the purpose of the First Amendment to our Constitution to reserve from all official control."

New Hampshire's statute in effect requires that appellees use their private property as a "mobile billboard" for the State's ideological message—or suffer a penalty, as Maynard already has. As a condition to driving an automobile—a virtual necessity for most Americans—the Maynards must display "Live Free or Die" to hundreds of people each day. The fact that most individuals agree with the thrust of New Hampshire's motto is not the test; most Americans also find the flag salute acceptable. The First Amendment protects the right of individuals to hold a point of view different from the majority and to refuse to foster, in the way New Hampshire commands, an idea they find morally objectionable.

Identifying the Maynards' interests as implicating First Amendment protections does not end our inquiry however. We must also determine whether the State's countervailing interest is sufficiently compelling to justify requiring appellees to display the state motto on their license plates. See, e.g., United States v. O'Brien, 391 U.S. 367, 376–377, 88 S.Ct. 1673, 1678–1679 (1968). The two interests advanced by the State are that display of the motto (1) facilitates the identification of passenger vehicles, and (2) promotes appreciation of history, individualism, and state pride.

The State first points out that passenger vehicles, but not commercial, trailer, or other vehicles are required to display the state motto. Thus, the argument proceeds, officers of the law are more easily able to determine whether passenger vehicles are carrying the proper plates. However, the record here reveals that New Hampshire passenger license plates normally consist of a specific configuration of letters and numbers, which makes them readily distinguishable from other types of plates, even without reference to the state motto. Even were we to credit the State's reasons and "even though the governmental purpose be legitimate and substantial, that purpose cannot be pursued by means that broadly stifle fundamental personal liberties when the end can be more narrowly achieved. The breadth of legislative abridgment must be viewed in the light of less drastic means for achieving the same basic purpose." Shelton v. Tucker, 364 U.S. 479, 488, 81 S.Ct. 247, 252 (1960) (footnotes omitted).

The State's second claimed interest is not ideologically neutral. The State is seeking to communicate to others an official view as to proper "appreciation of history, state pride, [and] individualism." Of course, the State may legitimately pursue such interests in any number of ways. However, where the State's interest is to disseminate an ideology, no matter how acceptable to some, such interest cannot outweigh an individual's First Amendment right to avoid becoming the courier for such message.

We conclude that the State of New Hampshire may not require appellees to display the state motto upon their vehicle license plates, and accordingly, we affirm the judgment of the District Court.

Affirmed.

[The dissenting opinion of Mr. Justice White with whom Mr. Justice Blackmun and Mr. Justice Rehnquist join in part, is omitted.]

MR. JUSTICE REHNQUIST, with whom MR. JUSTICE BLACKMUN joins, dissenting.

The Court holds that a State is barred by the Federal Constitution from requiring that the state motto be displayed on a state license plate. The path that the Court travels to reach this result demonstrates the difficulty in supporting it. The Court holds that the required display of the motto is an unconstitutional "required affirmation of belief." The District Court, however, expressly refused to consider this contention, and noted that, in an analogous case, a decision of the Supreme Court of New Hampshire had reached precisely the opposite result. See State v. Hoskin, 112 N.H. 332, 295 A.2d 454 (1972). The District Court found for appellees on the ground that the obscuring of the motto was protected "symbolic speech." This Court in relying upon a ground expressly avoided by the District Court, appears to disagree with the ground adopted by the District Court; indeed it points out that appellees' claim of symbolic expression has been "substantially undermined" by their very complaint in this action.

I not only agree with the Court's implicit recognition that there is no protected "symbolic speech" in this case, but I think that that conclusion goes far to undermine the Court's ultimate holding that there is an element of protected expression here. The State has not forced appellees to "say" anything; and it has not forced them to communicate ideas with nonverbal actions reasonably likened to "speech," such as wearing a lapel button promoting a political candidate or waving a flag as a symbolic gesture. The State has simply required that *all* noncommercial automobiles bear license tags with the state motto, "Live Free or Die." Appellees have not been forced to affirm or reject that motto; they are simply required by the State, under its police power, to carry a state auto license tag for identification and registration purposes.

The Court relies almost solely on Board of Education v. Barnette. The Court cites *Barnette* for the proposition that there is a constitutional right, in some cases, to "refrain from speaking." What the Court does not demonstrate is that there is any "speech" or "speaking" in the context of this case. The Court also relies upon the "right to decline to foster [religious, political, and ideological] concepts," ibid., and treats the state law in this case as if it were forcing appellees to proselytize, or to advocate an ideological point of view. But this begs the question. The issue, unconfronted by the Court, is whether appellees, in displaying, as they are required to do, state license tags, the format of which is known to all as having been prescribed by the State, would be considered to be advocating political or ideological views.

The Court recognizes, as it must, that this case substantially differs from *Barnette,* in which schoolchildren were forced to recite the pledge of allegiance while giving the flag salute. However, the Court states "the difference is essentially one of degree." But having recognized the rather obvious differences between these two cases, the Court does not explain why the same result should obtain. The Court suggests that the test is whether the individual is forced "to be an instrument for fostering public adherence to an ideological point of view he finds unacceptable." But, once again, these are merely conclusory words, barren of analysis. For example, were New Hampshire to erect a multitude of billboards, each proclaiming "Live Free or Die," and tax all citizens for the cost of erection and maintenance, clearly the message would be "fostered" by the individual citizen-taxpayers and just as clearly those individuals would be "instruments" in that communication. Certainly, however, that case would not fall within the ambit of *Barnette.* In that case, as in this case, there is no *affirmation* of belief. For First Amendment principles to be implicated, the State must place the citizen in the position of either apparently or actually "asserting as true" the message. This was the focus of *Barnette,* and clearly distinguishes this case from that one.

In holding that the New Hampshire statute does not run afoul of our holding in *Barnette,* the New Hampshire Supreme Court in *Hoskin* aptly articulated why there is no required affirmation of belief in this case:

> "The defendants' membership in a class of persons required to display plates bearing the State motto carries no implication and is subject to no requirement that they endorse that motto or profess to adopt it as matter of belief."

As found by the New Hampshire Supreme Court in *Hoskin,* there is nothing in state law which precludes appellees from displaying their disagreement with the state motto as long as the methods used do not obscure the license plates. Thus appellees could place on their bumper a conspicuous bumper sticker explaining in no uncertain terms that they do not profess the motto "Live Free or Die" and that they violently disagree with the connotations of that motto. Since any implication that they affirm the motto can be so easily displaced, I cannot agree that the state statutory system for motor vehicle identification and tourist promotion may be invalidated under the fiction that appellees are unconstitutionally forced to affirm, or profess belief in, the state motto.

The logic of the Court's opinion leads to startling, and I believe totally unacceptable, results. For example, the mottoes "In God We Trust" and "E Pluribus Unum" appear on the coin and currency of the United States. I cannot imagine that the statutes, see 18 U.S.C.A. §§ 331 and 333, proscribing defacement of United States currency impinge upon the First Amendment rights of an atheist. The fact that an atheist carries and uses United States currency does not, in any meaningful sense, convey any affirmation of belief on his part in the motto "In God We Trust." Similarly, there is no affirmation of belief involved in the display of state license tags upon the private automobiles involved here.

I would reverse the judgment of the District Court.

NOTES

1. In Wisconsin v. Yoder, 406 U.S. 205, 92 S.Ct. 1526 (1972), members of the Amish religion were convicted of violating Wisconsin's compulsory school-attendance law by declining to send their children to public or private school after they had graduated from the eighth grade. The U.S. Supreme Court, in overturning the convictions, balanced the state's interest in universal education against the religious beliefs of the Amish and the traditional interest of parents with respect to the religious upbringing of their children. Finding that enforcement of the law would gravely endanger if not destroy the free exercise of sincerely held religious beliefs in this instance, the Court held that the Amish had also "carried the ... difficult burden of demonstrating the adequacy of their alternative mode of continuing informal vocational education in terms of precisely those overall interests that the State advances in support of its program of compulsory high school education." 406 U.S. at 235, 92 S.Ct. at 1543.

2. In People v. Swartzentruber, 170 Mich.App. 682, 429 N.W.2d 225 (1988), the court ruled that the State of Michigan's interest in traffic safety was not so compelling as to override the Amish defendants' religious free exercise rights to drive "plain" horse-drawn buggies in violation of a statute requiring vehicles having a maximum speed of less than 25 miles per hour to display a slow-moving vehicle sign. "We can only echo the district court when it said '[t]here appears to be no "state interest of sufficient magnitude to override the interest claiming protection under the Free Exercise Clause." Wisconsin v. Yoder, supra, 406 U.S. at 214, 92 S.Ct. at 1532. In other words, the State has not argued to this Court a substantial traffic hazard or an increase in accidents involving horse drawn vehicles; the local Amish have consented to conformance to requirements set in the State of Ohio.' We therefore find that the state has failed to come forward with proof in court of a compelling state interest such as to override the imposition placed on defendants' free exercise rights." 429 N.W.2d at 229.

PEOPLE v. WOODY

Supreme Court of California, 1964.
61 Cal.2d 716, 40 Cal.Rptr. 69, 394 P.2d 813.

TOBRINER, JUSTICE. On April 28, 1962, a group of Navajos met in an Indian hogan in the desert near Needles, California, to perform a religious ceremony which included the use of peyote. Police officers, who had observed part of the ceremony, arrested defendants, who were among the Indians present. Defendants were later convicted of violating section 11500 of the Health and Safety Code, which prohibits the unauthorized possession of peyote. We have concluded that since the defendants used the peyote in a bona fide pursuit of a religious faith, and since the practice does not frustrate a compelling interest of the state the application of the statute improperly defeated the immunity of the First Amendment of the Constitution of the United States.

When the police entered the hogan and charged the participants with the use of peyote, one of the Indians handed the officers a gold-colored portrait frame containing a photostatic copy of the articles of incorporation of the Native American Church of the State of California. The articles declared: "That we as a people place explicit faith and hope and belief in the Almighty God and declare full, competent, and everlasting faith in our Church things which and by which we worship God. That we further pledge ourselves to work for unity with the sacramental use of peyote and its religious use."

The state stipulated at trial that at the time of the arrest defendants and the other Indians were performing a religious ceremony which involved the use of peyote. Defendants pleaded not guilty to the crime of illegal possession of narcotics, contending that their possession of peyote was incident to the observance of their faith and that the state could not constitutionally invoke the statute against them without abridging their right to the free exercise of their religion. The trial proceeded without a jury; the court held defendants guilty and imposed suspended sentences.

Defendants' defense, if any, must lie in their constitutional objection. We do not doubt that even though technically peyote is an "hallucinogen" rather than a narcotic, the state, pursuant to the police power, may proscribe its use.... Only if the application of the proscription improperly infringes upon the immunity of the First Amendment can defendants prevail; their case rests upon that Amendment, which is operative upon the states by means of the Fourteenth Amendment....

Although the prohibition against infringement of religious belief is absolute, the immunity afforded religious practices by the First Amendment is not so rigid.... But the state may abridge religious practices only upon a demonstration that some compelling state interest outweighs the defendants' interests in religious freedom....

The first step requires an exploration into the particulars of this case to determine whether section 11500 of the Health and Safety Code imposes any burden upon the free exercise of defendants' religion. An examination of the record as to the nature of peyote and its role in the religion practiced by defendants as members of the Native American Church of California compels the conclusion that the statutory prohibition most seriously infringes upon the observance of the religion.

The plant Lophophora williamsii, a small, spineless cactus, found in the Rio Grande Valley of Texas and northern Mexico, produces peyote, which grows in small buttons on the top of the cactus. Peyote's principal constituent is mescaline. When taken internally by chewing the buttons or drinking a derivative tea, peyote produces several types of hallucinations, depending primarily upon the user. In most subjects it causes extraordinary vision marked by bright and kaleidoscopic colors, geometric patterns, or scenes involving humans or animals. In others it engenders hallucinatory symptoms similar to those produced in cases of schizophrenia, dementia praecox, or paranoia. Beyond its hallucinatory effect, peyote renders for most users a heightened sense of comprehension; it fosters a feeling of friendliness toward other persons.

Peyote, as we shall see, plays a central role in the ceremony and practice of the Native American Church, a religious organization of Indians. Although the church claims no official prerequisites to membership, no written membership rolls, and no recorded theology, estimates of its membership range from 30,000 to 250,000, the wide variance deriving from differing definitions of a "member." As the anthropologists have ascertained through conversations with members, the theology of the church combines certain Christian teachings with the belief that peyote embodies the Holy Spirit and that those who partake of peyote enter into direct contact with God.

Peyotism discloses a long history. A reference to the religious use of peyote in Mexico appears in Spanish historical sources as early as 1560. Peyotism spread from Mexico to the United States and Canada; American anthropologists describe it as well established in this country during the latter part of the nineteenth century. Today, Indians of many tribes practice Peyotism. Despite the absence of recorded dogma, the several tribes follow surprisingly similar ritual and theology; the practices of Navajo members in Arizona practically parallel those of adherents in California, Montana, Oklahoma, Wisconsin, and Saskatchewan.

The "meeting," a ceremony marked by the sacramental use of peyote, composes the cornerstone of the peyote religion. The meeting convenes in an enclosure and continues from sundown Saturday to sunrise Sunday. To give thanks for the past good fortune or find guidance for future conduct, a member will "sponsor" a meeting and supply to those who attend both the peyote and the next morning's breakfast. The "sponsor," usually but not always the "leader," takes charge of the meeting; he decides the order of events and the amount of peyote to be consumed. Although the individual leader exercises an absolute control of the meeting, anthropologists report a striking uniformity of its ritual.

A meeting connotes a solemn and special occasion. Whole families attend together, although children and young women participate only by their presence. Adherents don their finest clothing, usually suits for men and fancy dresses for the women, but sometimes ceremonial Indian costumes. At the meeting the members pray, sing, and make ritual use of drum, fan, eagle bone, whistle, rattle and prayer cigarette, the symbolic emblems of their faith. The central event, of course, consists of the use of peyote in quantities sufficient to produce an hallucinatory state.

At an early but fixed stage in the ritual the members pass around a ceremonial bag of peyote buttons. Each adult may take four, the customary number, or take none. The participants chew the buttons, usually with some difficulty because of extreme bitterness; later, at a set time in the ceremony any member may ask for more peyote; occasionally a member may take as many as four more buttons. At sunrise on Sunday the ritual ends; after a brief outdoor prayer, the host and his family serve breakfast. Then the members depart. By morning the effects of the peyote disappear; the users suffer no aftereffects.

Although peyote serves as a sacramental symbol similar to bread and wine in certain Christian churches, it is more than a sacrament. Peyote constitutes in itself an object of worship; prayers are directed to it much as prayers are devoted to the Holy Ghost. On the other hand, to use peyote for nonreligious purposes is sacrilegious. Members of the church regard peyote also as a "teacher" because it induces a feeling of brotherhood with other members; indeed, it enables the participant to experience the Deity. Finally, devotees treat peyote as a "protector." Much as a Catholic carries his medallion, an Indian G.I. often wears around his neck a beautifully beaded pouch containing one large peyote button....

The record thus establishes that the application of the statutory prohibition of the use of peyote results in a virtual inhibition of the practice of defendants' religion. To forbid the use of peyote is to remove the theological heart of Peyotism. Having reached this conclusion, we must undertake the second step in the analysis of the constitutional issue: a determination of whether the state has demonstrated that "compelling state interest" which necessitates an abridgement of defendants' First Amendment right....

The state asserts that the compelling reason for the prohibition of Peyotism lies in its deleterious effects upon the Indian community, and even more basically, in the infringement such practice would place upon the enforcement of the narcotic laws because of the difficulty of detecting fraudulent claims of an asserted religious use of peyote. The prosecution further claims that the cases support these positions. We set forth the reasons why we believe the contentions to be unfounded.

The People urge that "the use of peyote by Indians in place of medical care, the threat of indoctrination of small children," and the "possible correlation between the use of this drug and the possible propensity to use some other more harmful drug" justify the statutory prohibition. The record, however, does not support the state's chronicle of harmful consequences of the use of peyote.

The evidence indicates that the Indians do not in fact employ peyote in place of proper medical care; and, as the Attorney General with fair objectivity admits, "there was no evidence to suggest that Indians who use peyote are more liable to become addicted to other narcotics than non-peyote-using Indians." Nor does the record substantiate the state's fear of the "indoctrination of small children"; it shows that Indian children never, and Indian teenagers rarely, use peyote. Finally, as the Attorney General likewise admits, the opinion of scientists and other experts is "that peyote ... works no permanent deleterious injury to the Indian...." Indeed, as we have noted, these experts regard the moral standards of members of the Native American Church as higher than those of Indians outside the church.

The Attorney General also argues that since "peyote could be regarded as a symbol, one that obstructs enlightenment and shackles the Indian to primitive conditions" the responsibility rests with the state to eliminate its use. We know of no doctrine that the state, in its asserted omniscience, should undertake to deny to defendants the observance of their religion in order to free them from the suppositious "shackles" of their "unenlightened" and "primitive condition."

Turning to the state's second contention, that the threat of fraudulent assertions of religious immunity will render impossible the effective enforcement of the narcotic laws, we note that [in earlier cases before this Court, and in this one] the state produced no evidence that spurious claims of religious immunity would in fact preclude effective administration of the law or that other "forms of regulation" would not accomplish the state's objectives.

That other states have excepted from the narcotic laws the use of peyote, and have not considered such exemption an impairment to enforcement, weakens the prosecution's forebodings. New Mexico in 1959, and Montana in 1957, amended their narcotics laws to provide that the prohibition against narcotics "shall not apply to the possession, sale or gift of peyote for religious sacramental purposes by any bona fide religious organization incorporated under the laws of the state." Arizona has reached a similar result by judicial decree.

That the state's showing of "compelling interest" cannot lie in untested assertions that recognition of the religious immunity will interfere with the enforcement of the state statute, finds illustration in the Minnesota litigation culminating in In re Jenison (1963) 267 Minn. 136, 125 N.W.2d 588 [which involved a criminal contempt conviction of a woman who refused to serve on a jury because of religious objections]. The United States Supreme Court reversed *per curiam* and remanded the case to the Minnesota Supreme Court.... Upon remand the state court reversed the conviction, stating that "there has been an inadequate showing that the state's interest in obtaining competent jurors requires us to override relator's right to the free exercise of her religion. Consequently we hold that until and unless further experience indicates that the indiscriminate invoking of the First Amendment poses a serious threat to the effective functioning of our jury system, any person whose religious convictions prohibit compulsory jury duty shall henceforth be exempt." ...

We turn to the several cases cited by the Attorney General which uphold statutes restricting religious practices. The People principally rely upon Reynolds v. United States which ruled that Congress could constitutionally apply to Mormons a prohibition against polygamy. The Mormon doctrine of polygamy rested in alleged divine origin and imposed upon male members, circumstances permitting, the observance of the practice upon pain of eternal damnation.

The Supreme Court held that the history of the laws against polygamy showed that the condemnation of the practice was a matter of the gravest social importance. It found in polygamy the seed of destruction of a democratic society. Viewing the practice as highly injurious to its female adherents, the Court classed polygamy with such religious rites as sacrifice of human beings and funereal immolation of widows.

Reynolds v. United States must be distinguished from the instant case for two fundamental reasons. The test of constitutionality calls for an examination of the degree of abridgement of religious freedom involved in each case. Polygamy, although a basic tenet in the theology of Mormonism, is not essential to the practice of the religion; peyote, on the other hand, is the *sine qua non* of defendants' faith. It is the sole means by which defendants are able to experience their religion; without peyote defendants cannot practice their faith. Second, the degree of danger to state interests in Reynolds far exceeded that in the instant case. The Court in Reynolds considered polygamy as a serious threat to democratic institutions and injurious to the morals and well-being of its practitioners. As we have heretofore indicated, no such compelling state interest supports the prohibition of the use of peyote....

Finally, we deal with the Attorney General's argument that our present conclusion requires an inquiry in each case into the bona fides of a particular defendant's beliefs, an inquiry which is both difficult and "repugnant to the spirit of our law...." Yet the trier of fact need inquire only into the question of whether the defendants' belief in Peyotism is honest and in good faith ... although judicial examination of the truth or validity of religious beliefs is foreclosed by the First Amendment, the courts of necessity must ask whether the claimant holds his belief honestly and in good faith or whether he seeks to wear the mantle of religious immunity merely as a cloak for illegal activities.

In so doing, we impose no undue burden upon the trier of fact. We do not doubt the capacity of judge and jury to distinguish between those who would feign faith in an esoteric religion and those who would honestly follow it.... Thus the court makes a factual examination of the bona fides of the belief and does not intrude into the religious issue at all; it does not determine the nature of the belief but the nature of defendants' adherence to it.

* * *

In the instant case, of course, we encounter no problem as to the bona fide nature of defendants' assertion of the free exercise clause. The state agrees, and the evidence amply demonstrates, that defendants' use of peyote was for a religious purpose.

We have weighed the competing values represented in this case on the symbolic scale of constitutionality. On the one side we have placed the weight of freedom of religion as protected by the First Amendment; on the other, the weight of the state's "compelling interest." Since the use of peyote incorporates the essence of the religious expression, the first weight is heavy. Yet the use of peyote presents only slight danger to the state and to the enforcement of its laws; the second weight is relatively light. The scale tips in favor of the constitutional protection....

NOTES

1. Also holding, in accord with *Woody,* that the use of peyote in the bona fide pursuit of religious faith is constitutionally protected by the First Amend-

ment is State v. Whittingham, 19 Ariz.App. 27, 504 P.2d 950 (1973), cert. denied 417 U.S. 946, 94 S.Ct. 3071 (1974), and Whitehorn v. State, 561 P.2d 539 (Okl.Cr.1977).

In reaching a result contrary to the Woody case, the Supreme Court of North Carolina said, in State v. Bullard, 267 N.C. 599, 148 S.E.2d 565 (1966), cert. denied 386 U.S. 917, 87 S.Ct. 876 (1967): "Even if he [the defendant] were sincere, the first amendment could not protect him. It is true that this amendment permits a citizen complete freedom of religion. He may belong to any church or to no church and may believe whatever he will, however fantastic, illogical or unreasonable, but nowhere does it authorize him in the exercise of his religion to commit acts, which constitute threats to the public safety, morals, peace and order.... The defendant may believe what he will as to peyote and marijuana and he may conceive that one is necessary and the other is advisable in connection with his religion. But it is not a violation of his constitutional rights to forbid him, in the guise of his religion, to possess a drug which will produce hallucinatory symptoms similar to those produced in cases of schizophrenia, dementia praecox, or paranoia, and his position cannot be sustained here—in law nor in morals."

The court's use of the phrases "guise of his religion" and "nor in morals" should probably be read in light of its earlier conclusion that "Some doubt may be cast upon the validity of the defendant's claim that he uses these drugs only in connection with his religion. The officers testified that in their discussion with him at the time the drugs were found in his apartment that the defendant made no mention of his religion nor the need for the drugs in connection therewith. A jury might well have found that this claim was a defense invented by the defendant long after his arrest", although, at the time of appeal, he claimed to be "a Peyotist with Buddhist leanings and that he has recently joined the Neo-American Church".

What about a personal belief that marijuana is a "gift from God"? Would this constitute a defense to a charge of possession? See State v. Brashear, 92 N.M. 622, 593 P.2d 63 (App.1979). For a general discussion of the free exercise of religion as a defense to prosecution for narcotic or psychedelic drug offenses, see Annot., 10 A.L.R.4th 246 (1981).

On the basis of an employment policy prohibiting the use of nonprescription drugs, two drug and alcohol abuse rehabilitation counselors in Oregon were discharged for ingesting a small quantity of peyote, a hallucinogenic drug, for sacramental purposes during a religious ceremony of the Native American Church. It was undisputed that they were members of the church and that their religious beliefs were sincere. They filed a claim for unemployment compensation benefits. In examining the claim, the U.S. Supreme Court in Employment Div., Dept. of Human Res. v. Smith, 485 U.S. 660, 108 S.Ct. 1444 (1988), remanded the case to the Oregon Supreme Court for a definitive ruling as to whether the religious use of peyote is legal in Oregon. If Oregon does prohibit the religious use of peyote, and if that prohibition is consistent with the U.S. Constitution (which the Court did not decide), there is no federal right to engage in that conduct in Oregon, and the State is then free to withhold unemployment benefits. If, however, the Court stated, Oregon is among those states that exempt the religious use of peyote from statutory controlled substances prohibitions, their conduct may be entitled to constitutional protection.

2. Compare the case of In re Jenison, cited by the court in the Woody case, supra, with In re Williams, 269 N.C. 68, 152 S.E.2d 317, 325, 327, cert. denied

388 U.S. 918, 87 S.Ct. 2137 (1967), where the court affirmed the contempt conviction of a Baptist minister who refused to testify in a case involving his parishioners. The court concluded that if a clergyman was protected by religious belief from testifying, absent a valid claim of privileged communication, "a layman having such belief would also be protected from compulsion to testify.... The consequence might well be to deprive the courts of testimony necessary in order to administer justice, or to require them to embark upon the hazardous undertaking of determining the sincerity of the belief asserted."

3. In refusing to follow Jenison, the North Carolina court held, "An entirely different situation is presented by the refusal of a witness to testify. In many instances the witness is the only person who can give the desired testimony. The 'compelling interest' of the state in the rendering of a just judgment in accordance with its law overrides the incidental infringement upon the religious belief of the witness that for him to testify is wrong."

4. What if the State desires to establish a uniform day of rest? Can people be prohibited by law from working on Sundays? What if they belong to religious groups that consider some day other than Sunday to be the sabbath? For the modern status of "Sunday closing" or "blue" laws, see Annot., 35 A.L.R.3d 939 (1971).

Thirty states have laws or regulations requiring employers to accommodate Sabbath observers in some way. Only a Connecticut statute, Conn.Gen.Stat. § 53–303e(b) made that obligation absolute and unqualified: "No person who states that a particular day of the week is observed as his Sabbath may be required to work on such day." In Estate of Thornton v. Caldor, 472 U.S. 703, 105 S.Ct. 2914 (1985), the Court ruled 8–1 that the statute violated the Establishment Clause of the First Amendment, because of its absolute prohibition. The decision does not affect Title VII of the Civil Rights Act of 1964 which requires employers to "reasonably accommodate" the religious practices of employees unless to do so would cause undue hardship to the employer's business.

In Hobbie v. Unemployment Appeals Comm'n, 480 U.S. 136, 107 S.Ct. 1046 (1987), the Court prohibited the denial of unemployment compensation to employees required to choose between fidelity to their religious beliefs and cessation of work. The Court said that the case involved conduct that was "perfectly legal"—refusal to work on Saturday.

In Frazee v. Illinois Department of Employment Sec., 489 U.S. 829, 109 S.Ct. 1514 (1989), the Court ruled that an unemployed worker could not be denied unemployment benefits because of religious objections to Sunday work based upon personally held beliefs. The Court stated that membership in an organized religion was not necessary to claim an exemption under the First Amendment to the state's requirement that the worker take a particular job referral from the unemployment compensation agency.

5. Although the cases in this section deal primarily with the exercise of religious beliefs, a recent ruling settled a major Establishment Clause issue. In Allegheny County v. Greater Pittsburgh, 492 U.S. 573, 109 S.Ct. 3086 (1989), the Court ruled that government sponsored religious holiday displays do not violate the First Amendment if they do not have the effect of "promoting or endorsing religious beliefs." The Court disapproved a Christmas Nativity scene on city property because it had a purely "religious message." If it had been part of a larger display including other religious symbols—like a Hanukkah menorah—it would have been constitutional. The context of such displays, therefore, is

critical to the constitutional issue. If a holiday display contains a variety of symbols of different religions—perhaps Christian and Jewish—the display will likely not violate the Establishment Clause.

6. In Employment Div., Ore. Dept. of Human Resources v. Smith, 494 U.S. 872 (1990), the U.S. Supreme Court ruled that the Free Exercise Clause of the First Amendment did not prevent the state of Oregon from prohibiting sacramental peyote use and therefore denying unemployment benefits to persons discharged for such use. The Court ruled that there was no right, based on religious freedom, to ignore laws of general applicability that were not supported by a "compelling governmental interest," particularly when those laws were not specifically aimed at restricting a religious practice.

In response to this case, Congress passed, and President Clinton signed into law, the Religious Freedom Restoration Act of 1993 (RFRA), 42 U.S.C.A. § 2000bb. This important new legislation explicitly overturned the U.S. Supreme Court decision in *Employment Division v. Smith,* which held that facially neutral laws of general applicability that burden the exercise of religion require no special justification to satisfy the Free Exercise of Religion Clause of the First Amendment—rejecting prior tests requiring a compelling state interest and use of the "least restrictive means."

The general standard set forth in the Religious Freedom Restoration Act of 1993, is that "government shall not substantially burden a person's exercise of religion even if the burden results from a rule of general applicability, except if it demonstrates that application of the burden to the person—(1) is in furtherance of a compelling governmental interest; and (2) is the least restrictive means of furthering that compelling governmental interest." The reasoning of the Act would appear to apply to state criminal laws, as well as civil statutes.

D. THE RIGHT OF PRIVACY

> "I give the fight up; let there be an end, a privacy, an obscure nook for me."
>
> Robert Browning, *Paracelsus,* Part V [1835].

1. ABORTION

PLANNED PARENTHOOD OF SOUTHEASTERN PA. v. CASEY

Supreme Court of the United States, 1992.
505 U.S. 833, 112 S.Ct. 2791.

JUSTICE O'CONNOR, JUSTICE KENNEDY, and JUSTICE SOUTER announced the judgment of the Court and delivered the opinion of the Court with respect to Parts I, II, III, V–A, V–C, and VI, an opinion with respect to Part V–E, in which JUSTICE STEVENS joins, and an opinion with respect to Parts IV, V–B, and V–D.

I

Liberty finds no refuge in a jurisprudence of doubt. Yet, 19 years after our holding that the Constitution protects a woman's right to terminate her pregnancy in its early stages, Roe v. Wade, 410 U.S. 113 (1973), that definition of liberty is still questioned. Joining the respondents as *amicus curiae*, the United States, as it has done in five other cases in the last decade, again asks us to overrule *Roe*. See Brief for Respondents 104–117; Brief for United States as *Amicus Curiae* 8.

At issue in these cases are five provisions of the Pennsylvania Abortion Control Act of 1982, as amended in 1988 and 1989. 18 Pa.Cons.Stat. §§ 3203–3220 (1990). Relevant portions of the Act are set forth in the Appendix. *Infra* at 60. The Act requires that a woman seeking an abortion give her informed consent prior to the abortion procedure, and specifies that she be provided with certain information at least 24 hours before the abortion is performed. § 3205. For a minor to obtain an abortion, the Act requires the informed consent of one of her parents, but provides for a judicial bypass option if the minor does not wish to or cannot obtain a parent's consent. § 3206. Another provision of the Act requires that, unless certain exceptions apply, a married woman seeking an abortion must sign a statement indicating that she has notified her husband of her intended abortion. § 3209. The Act exempts compliance with these three requirements in the event of a "medical emergency," which is defined in § 3203 of the Act. See §§ 3203, 3205(a), 3206(a), 3209(c). In addition to the above provisions regulating the performance of abortions, the Act imposes certain reporting requirements on facilities that provide abortion services. §§ 3207(b), 3214(a), 3214(f).

Before any of these provisions took effect, the petitioners, who are five abortion clinics and one physician representing himself as well as a class of physicians who provide abortion services, brought this suit seeking declaratory and injunctive relief. Each provision was challenged as unconstitutional on its face. The District Court entered a preliminary injunction against the enforcement of the regulations, and, after a 3–day bench trial, held all the provisions at issue here unconstitutional, entering a permanent injunction against Pennsylvania's enforcement of them. 744 F.Supp. 1323 (ED Pa.1990). The Court of Appeals for the Third Circuit affirmed in part and reversed in part, upholding all of the regulations except for the husband notification requirement. 947 F.2d 682 (1991). We granted certiorari. 502 U.S. 1056 (1992).

The Court of Appeals found it necessary to follow an elaborate course of reasoning even to identify the first premise to use to determine whether the statute enacted by Pennsylvania meets constitutional standards. See 947 F.2d, at 687–698. And at oral argument in this Court, the attorney for the parties challenging the statute took the position that none of the enactments can be upheld without overruling *Roe v. Wade*. Tr. of Oral Arg. 5–6. We disagree with that analysis; but we acknowledge that our decisions after *Roe* cast doubt upon the meaning and reach of its holding. Further, The CHIEF JUSTICE admits that he would overrule the central holding of *Roe* and adopt the rational relationship test as the sole criterion of constitutionality.... State and federal courts, as well as legislatures throughout the Union, must have guidance as they seek to address this subject in conformance with the Constitution. Given these premises, we find it imperative to review once more the principles that define the rights of the woman and the legitimate authority of the State respecting the termination of pregnancies by abortion procedures.

After considering the fundamental constitutional questions resolved by *Roe,* principles of institutional integrity, and the rule of *stare decisis,* we are led to conclude this: the essential holding of *Roe v. Wade* should be retained and once again reaffirmed.

It must be stated at the outset and with clarity that *Roe's* essential holding, the holding we reaffirm, has three parts. First is a recognition of the right of the woman to choose to have an abortion before viability and to obtain it without undue interference from the State. Before viability, the State's interests are not strong enough to support a prohibition of abortion or the imposition of a substantial obstacle to the woman's effective right to elect the procedure. Second is a confirmation of the State's power to restrict abortions after fetal viability if the law contains exceptions for pregnancies which endanger the woman's life or health. And third is the principle that the State has legitimate interests from the outset of the pregnancy in protecting the health of the woman and the life of the fetus that may become a child. These principles do not contradict one another; and we adhere to each.

II

Constitutional protection of the woman's decision to terminate her pregnancy derives from the Due Process Clause of the Fourteenth Amendment. It declares that no State shall "deprive any person of life, liberty, or property, without due process of law." The controlling word in the cases before us is "liberty." Although a literal reading of the Clause might suggest that it governs only the procedures by which a State may deprive persons of liberty, for at least 105 years, since Mugler v. Kansas, 123 U.S. 623, 660–661 (1887), the Clause has been understood to contain a substantive component as well, one "barring certain government actions regardless of the fairness of the procedures used to implement them." Daniels v. Williams, 474 U.S. 327, 331 (1986). As Justice Brandeis (joined by Justice Holmes) observed, [d]espite arguments to the contrary which had seemed to me persuasive, it is settled that the Due Process Clause of the Fourteenth Amendment applies to matters of substantive law, as well as to matters of procedure. Thus, all fundamental rights comprised within the term liberty are protected by the Federal Constitution from invasion by the States. Whitney v. California, 274 U.S. 357, 373 (1927) (concurring opinion). [T]he guaranties of due process, though having their roots in Magna Carta's "*per legem terrae*" and considered as procedural safeguards "against executive usurpation and tyranny," have in this country "become bulwarks also against arbitrary legislation." Poe v. Ullman, 367 U.S. 497, 541 (1961) (HARLAN, J., dissenting from dismissal on jurisdictional grounds) (quoting Hurtado v. California, 110 U.S. 516, 532 (1884)).

The most familiar of the substantive liberties protected by the Fourteenth Amendment are those recognized by the Bill of Rights. We have held that the Due Process Clause of the Fourteenth Amendment incorporates most of the Bill of Rights against the States. See, *e.g.*, Duncan v. Louisiana, 391 U.S. 145, 147–148 (1968). It is tempting, as a means of curbing the discretion of federal judges, to suppose that liberty encompasses no more than those rights already guaranteed to the individual against federal interference by the express provisions of the first eight amendments to the Constitution. See Adamson v. California, 332 U.S. 46, 68–92 (1947) (BLACK, J., dissenting). But of course this Court has never accepted that view.

It is also tempting, for the same reason, to suppose that the Due Process Clause protects only those practices, defined at the most specific level, that were protected against government interference by other rules of law when the Fourteenth Amendment was ratified. See Michael H. v. Gerald D., 491 U.S. 110, 127–128, n. 6 (1989) (opinion of SCALIA, J.). But such a view would be inconsistent with our law. It is a promise of the Constitution that there is a realm of personal liberty which the government may not enter. We have vindicated this principle before. Marriage is mentioned nowhere in the Bill of Rights, and interracial marriage was illegal in most States in the 19th century, but the Court was no doubt correct in finding it to be an aspect of liberty protected against state interference by the substantive component of the Due Process Clause in Loving v. Virginia, 388 U.S. 1, 12 (1967) (relying, in an opinion for eight Justices, on the Due Process Clause). Similar examples may be found in Turner v. Safley, 482 U.S. 78, 94–99 (1987); in Carey v. Population Services International, 431 U.S. 678, 684–686 (1977); in Griswold v. Connecticut, 381 U.S. 479, 481–482 (1965), as well as in the separate opinions of a majority of the Members of the Court in that case, *id.* at 486–488 (Goldberg, J., joined by Warren, C.J., and Brennan, J., concurring) (expressly relying on due process), *id.* at 500–502 (HARLAN, J., concurring in judgment) (same), *id.* at 502–507, (WHITE, J., concurring in judgment) (same); in Pierce v. Society of Sisters, 268 U.S. 510, 534–535 (1925); and in Meyer v. Nebraska, 262 U.S. 390, 399–403 (1923).

Neither the Bill of Rights nor the specific practices of States at the time of the adoption of the Fourteenth Amendment marks the outer limits of the substantive sphere of liberty which the Fourteenth Amendment protects. See U.S. Const., Amdt. 9. As the second Justice Harlan recognized:

> [T]he full scope of the liberty guaranteed by the Due Process Clause cannot be found in or limited by the precise terms of the specific guarantees elsewhere provided in the Constitution. This "liberty" is not a series of isolated points pricked out in terms of the taking of property; the freedom of speech, press, and religion; the right to keep and bear arms; the freedom from unreasonable searches and seizures; and so on. It is a rational continuum which, broadly speaking, includes a freedom

> from all substantial arbitrary impositions and purposeless restraints, ... and which also recognizes, what a reasonable and sensitive judgment must, that certain interests require particularly careful scrutiny of the state needs asserted to justify their abridgment. *Poe v. Ullman, supra,* 367 U.S., at 543 (dissenting from dismissal on jurisdictional grounds).

Justice Harlan wrote these words in addressing an issue the full Court did not reach in *Poe v. Ullman,* but the Court adopted his position four Terms later in *Griswold v. Connecticut, supra.* In *Griswold,* we held that the Constitution does not permit a State to forbid a married couple to use contraceptives. That same freedom was later guaranteed, under the Equal Protection Clause, for unmarried couples. See Eisenstadt v. Baird, 405 U.S. 438 (1972). Constitutional protection was extended to the sale and distribution of contraceptives in *Carey v. Population Services International, supra.* It is settled now, as it was when the Court heard arguments in *Roe v. Wade,* that the Constitution places limits on a State's right to interfere with a person's most basic decisions about family and parenthood, see *Carey v. Population Services International, supra;* Moore v. East Cleveland, 431 U.S. 494 (1977); *Eisenstadt v. Baird, supra; Loving v. Virginia, supra; Griswold v. Connecticut, supra;* Skinner v. Oklahoma ex rel. Williamson, 316 U.S. 535 (1942); *Pierce v. Society of Sisters, supra; Meyer v. Nebraska, supra,* as well as bodily integrity, see, *e.g.,* Washington v. Harper, 494 U.S. 210, 221–222 (1990); Winston v. Lee, 470 U.S. 753 (1985); Rochin v. California, 342 U.S. 165 (1952).

The inescapable fact is that adjudication of substantive due process claims may call upon the Court in interpreting the Constitution to exercise that same capacity which, by tradition, courts always have exercised: reasoned judgment. Its boundaries are not susceptible of expression as a simple rule. That does not mean we are free to invalidate state policy choices with which we disagree; yet neither does it permit us to shrink from the duties of our office. As Justice Harlan observed:

> "Due process has not been reduced to any formula; its content cannot be determined by reference to any code. The best that can be said is that, through the course of this Court's decisions, it has represented the balance which our Nation, built upon postulates of respect for the liberty of the individual, has struck between that liberty and the demands of organized society. If the supplying of content to this Constitutional concept has, of necessity, been a rational process, it certainly has not been one where judges have felt free to roam where unguided speculation might take them. The balance of which I speak is the balance struck by this country, having regard to what history teaches are the traditions from which it developed as well as the traditions from which it broke. That tradition is a living thing. A decision of this Court which radically departs from it could not long survive, while a decision which builds on what has

> survived is likely to be sound. No formula could serve as a substitute, in this area, for judgment and restraint." *Poe v. Ullman,* 367 U.S., at 542 (dissenting from dismissal on jurisdictional grounds).

See also *Rochin v. California, supra,* at 171–172 (FRANKFURTER, J., writing for the Court) ("To believe that this judicial exercise of judgment could be avoided by freezing 'due process of law' at some fixed stage of time or thought is to suggest that the most important aspect of constitutional adjudication is a function for inanimate machines, and not for judges").

Men and women of good conscience can disagree, and we suppose some always shall disagree, about the profound moral and spiritual implications of terminating a pregnancy, even in its earliest stage. Some of us as individuals find abortion offensive to our most basic principles of morality, but that cannot control our decision. Our obligation is to define the liberty of all, not to mandate our own moral code. The underlying constitutional issue is whether the State can resolve these philosophic questions in such a definitive way that a woman lacks all choice in the matter, except perhaps in those rare circumstances in which the pregnancy is itself a danger to her own life or health, or is the result of rape or incest.

It is conventional constitutional doctrine that, where reasonable people disagree, the government can adopt one position or the other. [. . .] That theorem, however, assumes a state of affairs in which the choice does not intrude upon a protected liberty. Thus, while some people might disagree about whether or not the flag should be saluted, or disagree about the proposition that it may not be defiled, we have ruled that a State may not compel or enforce one view or the other. See West Virginia Bd. of Ed. v. Barnette, 319 U.S. 624 (1943); Texas v. Johnson, 491 U.S. 397 (1989).

Our law affords constitutional protection to personal decisions relating to marriage, procreation, contraception, family relationships, child rearing, and education. Carey v. Population Services International, 431 U.S., at 685. Our cases recognize the right of the *individual,* married or single, to be free from unwarranted governmental intrusion into matters so fundamentally affecting a person as the decision whether to bear or beget a child. Eisenstadt v. Baird, *supra,* 405 U.S., at 453 (emphasis in original). Our precedents "have respected the private realm of family life which the state cannot enter." Prince v. Massachusetts, 321 U.S. 158, 166 (1944). These matters, involving the most intimate and personal choices a person may make in a lifetime, choices central to personal dignity and autonomy, are central to the liberty protected by the Fourteenth Amendment. At the heart of liberty is the right to define one's own concept of existence, of meaning, of the universe, and of the mystery of human life. Beliefs about these matters could not define the attributes of personhood were they formed under compulsion of the State.

These considerations begin our analysis of the woman's interest in terminating her pregnancy, but cannot end it, for this reason: though the abortion decision may originate within the zone of conscience and belief, it is more than a philosophic exercise. Abortion is a unique act. It is an act fraught with consequences for others: for the woman who must live with the implications of her decision; for the persons who perform and assist in the procedure; for the spouse, family, and society which must confront the knowledge that these procedures exist, procedures some deem nothing short of an act of violence against innocent human life; and, depending on one's beliefs, for the life or potential life that is aborted. Though abortion is conduct, it does not follow that the State is entitled to proscribe it in all instances. That is because the liberty of the woman is at stake in a sense unique to the human condition, and so, unique to the law. The mother who carries a child to full term is subject to anxieties, to physical constraints, to pain that only she must bear. That these sacrifices have from the beginning of the human race been endured by woman with a pride that ennobles her in the eyes of others and gives to the infant a bond of love cannot alone be grounds for the State to insist she make the sacrifice. Her suffering is too intimate and personal for the State to insist, without more, upon its own vision of the woman's role, however dominant that vision has been in the course of our history and our culture. The destiny of the woman must be shaped to a large extent on her own conception of her spiritual imperatives and her place in society.

It should be recognized, moreover, that in some critical respects, the abortion decision is of the same character as the decision to use contraception, to which *Griswold v. Connecticut, Eisenstadt v. Baird,* and *Carey v. Population Services International* afford constitutional protection. We have no doubt as to the correctness of those decisions. They support the reasoning in *Roe* relating to the woman's liberty, because they involve personal decisions concerning not only the meaning of procreation but also human responsibility and respect for it. As with abortion, reasonable people will have differences of opinion about these matters. One view is based on such reverence for the wonder of creation that any pregnancy ought to be welcomed and carried to full term, no matter how difficult it will be to provide for the child and ensure its wellbeing. Another is that the inability to provide for the nurture and care of the infant is a cruelty to the child and an anguish to the parent. These are intimate views with infinite variations, and their deep, personal character underlay our decisions in *Griswold, Eisenstadt,* and *Carey.* The same concerns are present when the woman confronts the reality that, perhaps despite her attempts to avoid it, she has become pregnant.

It was this dimension of personal liberty that *Roe* sought to protect, and its holding invoked the reasoning and the tradition of the precedents we have discussed, granting protection to substantive liberties of the person. *Roe* was, of course, an extension of those cases and, as the decision itself indicated, the separate States could act in some degree to further their own legitimate interests in protecting prenatal life. The extent to which the legislatures of the States might act to outweigh the interests of the woman in choosing to terminate her pregnancy was a subject of debate both in *Roe* itself and in decisions following it.

While we appreciate the weight of the arguments made on behalf of the State in the cases before us, arguments which in their ultimate formulation conclude that *Roe* should be overruled, the reservations any of us may have in reaffirming the central holding of *Roe* are outweighed by the explication of individual liberty we have given, combined with the force of *stare decisis*. We turn now to that doctrine.

III

A

The obligation to follow precedent begins with necessity, and a contrary necessity marks its outer limit. With Cardozo, we recognize that no judicial system could do society's work if it eyed each issue afresh in every case that raised it. See B. Cardozo, The Nature of the Judicial Process 149 (1921). Indeed, the very concept of the rule of law underlying our own Constitution requires such continuity over time that a respect for precedent is, by definition, indispensable. See Powell, Stare Decisis and Judicial Restraint, 1991 Journal of Supreme Court History 13, 16. At the other extreme, a different necessity would make itself felt if a prior judicial ruling should come to be seen so clearly as error that its enforcement was, for that very reason, doomed.

Even when the decision to overrule a prior case is not, as in the rare, latter instance, virtually foreordained, it is common wisdom that the rule of *stare decisis* is not an "inexorable command," and certainly it is not such in every constitutional case, see Burnet v. Coronado Oil & Gas Co., 285 U.S. 393, 405–411 (1932) (BRANDEIS, J., dissenting). See also Payne v. Tennessee, 501 U.S. 808, 842 (1991) (SOUTER, J., joined by KENNEDY, J., concurring); Arizona v. Rumsey, 467 U.S. 203, 212 (1984). Rather, when this Court reexamines a prior holding, its judgment is customarily informed by a series of prudential and pragmatic considerations designed to test the consistency of overruling a prior decision with the ideal of the rule of law, and to gauge the respective costs of reaffirming and overruling a prior case. Thus, for example, we may ask whether the rule has proven to be intolerable simply in defying practical workability, Swift & Co. v. Wickham, 382 U.S. 111, 116 (1965); whether the rule is subject to a kind of reliance that would lend a special hardship to the consequences of overruling and add inequity to the cost of repudiation, *e.g.*, United States v. Title Ins. & Trust Co., 265 U.S. 472, 486 (1924); whether related principles of law have so far developed as to have left the old rule no more than a remnant of abandoned doctrine, see Patterson v. McLean Credit Union, 491 U.S. 164, 173–174 (1989); or whether facts have so changed, or come to be seen so differently, as to have robbed the old rule of significant application or justification, *e.g.*, *Burnet, supra,* 285 U.S. at 412 (BRANDEIS, J., dissenting).

So in this case, we may enquire whether *Roe's* central rule has been found unworkable; whether the rule's limitation on state power could be removed without serious inequity to those who have relied upon it or significant damage to the stability of the society governed by it; whether the law's growth in the intervening years has left *Roe's* central rule a doctrinal anachronism discounted by society; and whether *Roe's* premises of fact have so far changed in the ensuing two decades as to render its central holding somehow irrelevant or unjustifiable in dealing with the issue it addressed.

1

Although *Roe* has engendered opposition, it has in no sense proven "unworkable," see Garcia v. San Antonio Metropolitan Transit Authority, 469 U.S. 528, 546 (1985), representing as it does a simple limitation beyond which a state law is unenforceable. While *Roe* has, of course, required judicial assessment of state laws affecting the exercise of the choice guaranteed against government infringement, and although the need for such review will remain as a consequence of today's decision, the required determinations fall within judicial competence.

2

The inquiry into reliance counts the cost of a rule's repudiation as it would fall on those who have relied reasonably on the rule's continued application. Since the classic case for weighing reliance heavily in favor of following the earlier rule occurs in the commercial context, see *Payne v. Tennessee, supra,* at 828, where advance planning of great precision is most obviously a necessity, it is no cause for surprise that some would find no reliance worthy of consideration in support of *Roe.*

While neither respondents nor their *amici* in so many words deny that the abortion right invites some reliance prior to its actual exercise, one can readily imagine an argument stressing the dissimilarity of this case to one involving property or contract. Abortion is customarily chosen as an unplanned response to the consequence of unplanned activity or to the failure of conventional birth control, and except on the assumption that no intercourse would have occurred but for *Roe's* holding, such behavior may appear to justify no reliance claim. Even if reliance could be claimed on that unrealistic assumption, the argument might run, any reliance interest would be *de minimis.* This argument would be premised on the hypothesis that reproductive planning could take virtually immediate account of any sudden restoration of state authority to ban abortions.

To eliminate the issue of reliance that easily, however, one would need to limit cognizable reliance to specific instances of sexual activity. But to do this would be simply to refuse to face the fact that, for two decades of economic and social developments, people have organized intimate relationships and made choices that define their views of themselves and their places in society, in reliance on the availability of abortion in the event that contraception should fail. The ability of women to participate equally in the economic and social life of the Nation has been facilitated by their ability to control their reproductive lives. See, *e.g.,* R. Petchesky, Abortion and Woman's Choice 109, 133, n. 7 (rev. ed. 1990). The Constitution serves human values, and while the effect of reliance on *Roe* cannot be exactly measured, neither can the certain cost of overruling *Roe* for people who have ordered their thinking and living around that case be dismissed.

3

No evolution of legal principle has left *Roe's* doctrinal footings weaker than they were in 1973. No development of constitutional law since the case was decided has implicitly or explicitly left *Roe* behind as a mere survivor of obsolete constitutional thinking.

It will be recognized, of course, that *Roe* stands at an intersection of two lines of decisions, but in whichever doctrinal category one reads the case, the result for present purposes will be the same. The *Roe* Court itself placed its holding in the succession of cases most prominently exemplified by Griswold v. Connecticut, 381 U.S. 479 (1965). See *Roe,* 410 U.S., at 152–153. When it is so seen, *Roe* is clearly in no jeopardy, since subsequent constitutional developments have neither disturbed, nor do they threaten to diminish, the scope of recognized protection accorded to the liberty relating to intimate relationships, the family, and decisions about whether or not to beget or bear a child. See, *e.g.,* Carey v. Population Services International, 431 U.S. 678 (1977); Moore v. East Cleveland, 431 U.S. 494 (1977).

Roe, however, may be seen not only as an exemplar of *Griswold* liberty but as a rule (whether or not mistaken) of personal autonomy and bodily integrity, with doctrinal affinity to cases recognizing limits on governmental power to mandate medical treatment or to bar its rejection. If so, our cases since *Roe* accord with *Roe's* view that a State's interest in the protection of life falls short of justifying any plenary override of individual liberty claims. Cruzan v. Director, Mo. Dept. of Health, 497 U.S. 261, 278 (1990); cf., *e.g.,* Riggins v. Nevada, 504 U.S. 127, 135 (1992); Washington v. Harper, 494 U.S. 210 (1990); see also, *e.g.,* Rochin v. California, 342 U.S. 165 (1952); Jacobson v. Massachusetts, 197 U.S. 11, 24–30 (1905).

Finally, one could classify *Roe* as *sui generis.* If the case is so viewed, then there clearly has been no erosion of its central determination. The original holding resting on the concurrence of seven Members of the Court in 1973 was expressly affirmed by a majority of six in 1983, see Akron v. Akron Center for Reproductive Health, Inc., 462 U.S. 416 (1983) (*Akron I*), and by a majority of five in 1986, see Thornburgh v. American College of Obstetricians and Gynecologists, 476 U.S. 747 (1986), expressing adherence to the constitutional ruling despite legislative efforts in some States to test its limits. More recently, in Webster v. Reproductive Health Services, 492 U.S. 490 (1989), although two of the present authors questioned the trimester framework in a way consistent with our judgment today, see *id.,* at 518 (REHNQUIST, C.J., joined by

WHITE and KENNEDY, JJ.); *id.*, at 529 (O'CONNOR, J., concurring in part and concurring in judgment), a majority of the Court either decided to reaffirm or declined to address the constitutional validity of the central holding of *Roe*. *See Webster,* 492 U.S., at 521 (REHNQUIST, C.J., joined by WHITE and KENNEDY, JJ.); *id.*, at 525–526 (O'CONNOR, J., concurring in part and concurring in judgment); *id.*, at 537, 553 (BLACKMUN, J., joined by BRENNAN and MARSHALL, JJ., concurring in part and dissenting in part); *id.*, at 561–563 (STEVENS, J., concurring in part and dissenting in part).

Nor will courts building upon *Roe* be likely to hand down erroneous decisions as a consequence. Even on the assumption that the central holding of *Roe* was in error, that error would go only to the strength of the state interest in fetal protection, not to the recognition afforded by the Constitution to the woman's liberty. The latter aspect of the decision fits comfortably within the framework of the Court's prior decisions, including Skinner v. Oklahoma ex rel. Williamson, 316 U.S. 535 (1942); *Griswold, supra;* Loving v. Virginia, 388 U.S. 1 (1967); and Eisenstadt v. Baird, 405 U.S. 438 (1972), the holdings of which are "not a series of isolated points," but mark a "rational continuum." Poe v. Ullman, 367 U.S., at 543 (HARLAN, J., dissenting). As we described in *Carey v. Population Services International, supra,* the liberty which encompasses those decisions

> includes "the interest in independence in making certain kinds of important decisions." While the outer limits of this aspect of [protected liberty] have not been marked by the Court, it is clear that among the decisions that an individual may make without unjustified government interference are personal decisions " 'relating to marriage, procreation, contraception, family relationships, and childrearing and education.' " 431 U.S., at 684–685 (citations omitted).

The soundness of this prong of the *Roe* analysis is apparent from a consideration of the alternative. If indeed the woman's interest in deciding whether to bear and beget a child had not been recognized as in *Roe,* the State might as readily restrict a woman's right to choose to carry a pregnancy to term as to terminate it, to further asserted state interests in population control, or eugenics, for example. Yet *Roe* has been sensibly relied upon to counter any such suggestions. *E.g.,* Arnold v. Board of Education of Escambia County, Ala., 880 F.2d 305, 311 (CA11 1989) (relying upon *Roe* and concluding that government officials violate the Constitution by coercing a minor to have an abortion); Avery v. County of Burke, 660 F.2d 111, 115 (CA4 1981) (county agency inducing teenage girl to undergo unwanted sterilization on the basis of misrepresentation that she had sickle cell trait); see also In re Quinlan, 70 N.J. 10, 355 A.2d 647, cert. denied sub nom. Garger v. New Jersey, 429 U.S. 922 (1976) (relying on *Roe* in finding a right to terminate medical treatment). In any event, because *Roe's* scope is confined by the fact of its concern with postconception potential life, a concern otherwise likely to be implicated only by some forms of contraception protected independently under *Griswold* and later cases, any error in *Roe* is unlikely to have serious ramifications in future cases.

4

We have seen how time has overtaken some of *Roe's* factual assumptions: advances in maternal health care allow for abortions safe to the mother later in pregnancy than was true in 1973, see *Akron I, supra,* 462 U.S. at 429, n. 11, and advances in neonatal care have advanced viability to a point somewhat earlier. *Compare Roe,* 410 U.S., at 160, with *Webster, supra,* 492 U.S., at 515–516 (opinion of REHNQUIST, C.J.); see *Akron I,* 462 U.S., at 457, and n. 5 (O'CONNOR, J., dissenting). But these facts go only to the scheme of time limits on the realization of competing interests, and the divergences from the factual premises of 1973 have no bearing on the validity of *Roe's* central holding, that viability marks the earliest point at which the State's interest in fetal life is constitutionally adequate to justify a legislative ban on nontherapeutic abortions. The soundness or unsoundness of that constitutional judgment in no sense turns on whether viability occurs at approximately 28 weeks, as was usual at the time of *Roe,* at 23 to 24 weeks, as it sometimes does today, or at some moment even slightly earlier in pregnancy, as it may if fetal respiratory capacity can somehow be enhanced in the future. Whenever it may occur, the attainment of viability may continue to serve as the critical fact, just as it has done since *Roe* was decided; which is to say that no change in *Roe's* factual underpinning has left its central holding obsolete, and none supports an argument for overruling it.

5

The sum of the precedential enquiry to this point shows *Roe's* underpinnings unweakened in any way affecting its central holding. While it has engendered disapproval, it has not been unworkable. An entire generation has come of age free to assume *Roe's* concept of liberty in defining the capacity of women to act in society, and to make reproductive decisions; no erosion of principle going to liberty or personal autonomy has left *Roe's* central holding a doctrinal remnant; *Roe* portends no developments at odds with other precedent for the analysis of personal liberty; and no changes of fact have rendered viability more or less appropriate as the point at which the balance of interests tips. Within the bounds of normal *stare decisis* analysis, then, and subject to the considerations on which it customarily turns, the stronger argument is for affirming *Roe's* central holding, with whatever degree of personal reluctance any of us may have, not for overruling it.

B

[. . .]

The Court's duty in the present case is clear. In 1973, it confronted the already-divisive issue of governmental power to limit personal choice to undergo abortion, for which it provided a new resolution based on the due process guaranteed by the Fourteenth Amendment. Whether or not a new social consensus is developing on that issue, its divisiveness is no less today than in 1973, and pressure to overrule the decision, like pressure to retain it, has grown only more intense. A decision to overrule *Roe's* essential holding under the existing circumstances would address error, if error there was, at the cost of both profound and unnecessary damage to the Court's legitimacy, and to the Nation's commitment to the rule of law. It is therefore imperative to adhere to the essence of *Roe's* original decision, and we do so today.

IV

From what we have said so far, it follows that it is a constitutional liberty of the woman to have some freedom to terminate her pregnancy. We conclude that the basic decision in *Roe* was based on a constitutional analysis which we cannot now repudiate. The woman's liberty is not so unlimited, however, that, from the outset, the State cannot show its concern for the life of the unborn and, at a later point in fetal development, the State's interest in life has sufficient force so that the right of the woman to terminate the pregnancy can be restricted.

That brings us, of course, to the point where much criticism has been directed at *Roe,* a criticism that always inheres when the Court draws a specific rule from what in the Constitution is but a general standard. We conclude, however, that the urgent claims of the woman to retain the ultimate control over her destiny and her body, claims implicit in the meaning of liberty, require us to perform that function. Liberty must not be extinguished for want of a line that is clear. And it falls to us to give some real substance to the woman's liberty to determine whether to carry her pregnancy to full term.

We conclude the line should be drawn at viability, so that, before that time, the woman has a right to choose to terminate her pregnancy. We adhere to this principle for two reasons. First, as we have said, is the doctrine of *stare decisis.* Any judicial act of line-drawing may seem somewhat arbitrary, but *Roe* was a reasoned statement, elaborated with great care. We have twice reaffirmed it in the face of great opposition. See Thornburgh v. American College of Obstetricians and Gynecologists, 476 U.S., at 759; Akron I, 462 U.S., at 419–420. Although we must overrule those parts of *Thornburgh* and *Akron I* which, in our view, are inconsistent with *Roe's* statement that the State has a legitimate interest in promoting the life or potential life of the unborn, see *infra,* at 40–41, the central premise of those cases represents an unbroken commitment by this Court to the essential holding of *Roe.* It is that premise which we reaffirm today.

The second reason is that the concept of viability, as we noted in *Roe,* is the time at which there is a realistic possibility of maintaining and nourishing a life outside the womb, so that the independent existence of the second life can, in reason and all fairness, be the object of state protection that now overrides the rights of the woman. See Roe v. Wade, 410 U.S., at 163. Consistent with other constitutional norms, legislatures may draw lines which appear arbitrary without the necessity of offering a justification. But courts may not. We must justify the lines we draw. And there is no line other than viability which is more workable. To be sure, as we have said, there may be some medical developments that affect the precise point of viability, see *supra,* at 17–18, but this is an imprecision within tolerable limits, given that the medical community and all those who must apply its discoveries will continue to explore the matter. The viability line also has, as a practical matter, an element of fairness. In some broad sense, it might be said that a woman who fails to act before viability has consented to the State's intervention on behalf of the developing child.

The woman's right to terminate her pregnancy before viability is the most central principle of *Roe v. Wade.* It is a rule of law and a component of liberty we cannot renounce.

On the other side of the equation is the interest of the State in the protection of potential life. The *Roe* Court recognized the State's "important and legitimate interest in protecting the potentiality of human life." *Roe, supra,* at 162. The weight to be given this state interest, not the strength of the woman's interest, was the difficult question faced in *Roe.* We do not need to say whether each of us, had we been Members of the Court when the valuation of the state interest came before it as an original matter, would have concluded, as the *Roe* Court did, that its weight is insufficient to justify a ban on abortions prior to viability even when it is subject to certain exceptions. The matter is not before us in the first instance, and, coming as it does after nearly 20 years of litigation in *Roe's* wake we are satisfied that the immediate question is not the soundness of *Roe's* resolution of the issue, but the precedential force that must be accorded to its holding. And we have concluded that the essential holding of *Roe* should be reaffirmed.

Yet it must be remembered that *Roe v. Wade* speaks with clarity in establishing not only the woman's liberty but also the State's "important and legitimate interest in potential life." *Roe, supra,* at 163. That portion of the decision in *Roe* has been given too little acknowledgment and implementation by the Court in its subsequent cases. Those cases decided that any regulation touching upon the abortion decision must survive strict scrutiny, to be sustained only if drawn in narrow terms to further a compelling state interest. See, *e.g., Akron I, supra,* at 427. Not all of the cases decided under that formulation can be reconciled with the holding in *Roe* itself that the State has legitimate interests in the health of the woman and in protecting the potential life within her. In resolving this tension, we choose to rely upon *Roe,* as against the later cases.

Roe established a trimester framework to govern abortion regulations. Under this elaborate but rigid construct, almost no regulation at all is permitted during the first trimester of pregnancy; regulations designed to protect the woman's health, but not to further the State's interest in potential life, are permitted during the second trimester; and, during the third trimester, when the fetus is viable, prohibitions are permitted provided the life or health of the mother is not at stake. *Roe, supra,* at 163–166. Most of our cases since *Roe* have involved the application of rules derived from the trimester framework. See, *e.g., Thornburgh v. American College of Obstetricians and Gynecologists, supra; Akron I, supra.*

The trimester framework no doubt was erected to ensure that the woman's right to choose not become so subordinate to the State's interest in promoting fetal life that her choice exists in theory, but not in fact. We do not agree, however, that the trimester approach is necessary to accomplish this objective. A framework of this rigidity was unnecessary, and, in its later interpretation, sometimes contradicted the State's permissible exercise of its powers.

Though the woman has a right to choose to terminate or continue her pregnancy before viability, it does not at all follow that the State is prohibited from taking steps to ensure that this choice is thoughtful and informed. Even in the earliest stages of pregnancy, the State may enact rules and regulations designed to encourage her to know that there are philosophic and social arguments of great weight that can be brought to bear in favor of continuing the pregnancy to full term, and that there are procedures and institutions to allow adoption of unwanted children as well as a certain degree of state assistance if the mother chooses to raise the child herself. "[T]he Constitution does not forbid a State or city, pursuant to democratic processes, from expressing a preference for normal childbirth." Webster v. Reproductive Health Services, 492 U.S., at 511 (opinion of the Court) (quoting Poelker v. Doe, 432 U.S. 519, 521 (1977)). It follows that States are free to enact laws to provide a reasonable framework for a woman to make a decision that has such profound and lasting meaning. This, too, we find consistent with *Roe's* central premises, and indeed the inevitable consequence of our holding that the State has an interest in protecting the life of the unborn.

We reject the trimester framework, which we do not consider to be part of the essential holding of *Roe.* See *Webster v. Reproductive Health Services, supra,* at 518 (opinion of REHNQUIST, C.J.); *id.,* at 529 (O'CONNOR, J., concurring in part and concurring in judgment) (describing the trimester framework as "problematic"). Measures aimed at ensuring that a woman's choice contemplates the consequences for the fetus do not necessarily interfere with the right recognized in *Roe,* although those measures have been found to be inconsistent with the rigid trimester framework announced in that case. A logical reading of the central holding in *Roe* itself, and a necessary reconciliation of the liberty of the woman and the interest of the State in promoting prenatal life, require, in our view, that we abandon the trimester framework as a rigid prohibition on all pre-viability regulation aimed at the protection of fetal life. The trimester framework suffers from these basic flaws: in its formulation, it misconceives the nature of the pregnant woman's interest; and in practice, it undervalues the State's interest in potential life, as recognized in *Roe.*

As our jurisprudence relating to all liberties save perhaps abortion has recognized, not every law which makes a right more difficult to exercise is, *ipso facto,* an infringement of that right. An example clarifies the point. We have held that not every ballot access limitation amounts to an infringement of the right to vote. Rather, the States are granted substantial flexibility in establishing the framework within which voters choose the candidates for whom they wish to vote. Anderson v. Celebrezze, 460 U.S. 780, 788 (1983); Norman v. Reed, 502 U.S. 279 (1992).

The abortion right is similar. Numerous forms of state regulation might have the incidental effect of increasing the cost or decreasing the availability of medical care, whether for abortion or any other medical procedure. The fact that a law which serves a valid purpose, one not designed to strike at the right itself, has the incidental effect of making it more difficult or more expensive to procure an abortion cannot be enough to invalidate it. Only where state regulation imposes an undue burden on a woman's ability to make this decision does the power of the State reach into the heart of the liberty protected by the Due Process Clause. [. . .]

For the most part, the Court's early abortion cases adhered to this view. In Maher v. Roe, 432 U.S. 464, 473–474 (1977), the Court explained: *Roe* did not declare an unqualified "constitutional right to an abortion," as the District Court seemed to think. Rather, the right protects the woman from unduly burdensome interference with her freedom to decide whether to terminate her pregnancy. See also Doe v. Bolton, 410 U.S. 179, 198 (1973) ("[T]he interposition of the hospital abortion committee is unduly restrictive of the patient's rights"); *Bellotti I, supra,* 428 U.S., at 147 (State may not "impose undue burdens upon a minor capable of giving an informed consent"); Harris v. McRae, 448 U.S. 297, 314 (1980) (citing *Maher, supra*). Cf. Carey v. Population Services International, 431 U.S., at 688 ("[T]he same test must be applied to state regulations that burden an individual's right to decide to prevent conception or terminate pregnancy by substantially limiting access to the means of effectuating that decision as is applied to state statutes that prohibit the decision entirely").

These considerations of the nature of the abortion right illustrate that it is an overstatement to describe it as a right to decide whether to have an abortion "without interference from the State." Planned Parenthood of Central Mo. v. Danforth, 428 U.S. 52, 61 (1976). All abortion regulations interfere to some degree with a woman's ability to decide whether to terminate her pregnancy. It is, as a consequence, not surprising that, despite the protestations contained in the original *Roe* opinion to the effect that the Court was not recognizing an absolute right, 410 U.S., at 154–155, the Court's experience applying the trimester framework has led to the striking down of some abortion regulations which in no real sense deprived women of the ultimate decision. Those decisions went too far, because the right recognized by *Roe* is a right to be free from unwarranted governmental intrusion into matters so fundamentally affecting a person as the decision whether to bear or beget a child. *Eisenstadt v. Baird,* 405 U.S., at 453. Not all governmental intrusion is, of necessity, unwarranted, and that brings us to the other basic flaw in the trimester framework: even in *Roe's* terms, in practice, it undervalues the State's interest in the potential life within the woman.

Roe v. Wade was express in its recognition of the State's important and legitimate interest[s] in preserving and protecting the health of the pregnant woman [and] in protecting the potentiality of human life. 410 U.S., at 162. The trimester framework, however, does not fulfill *Roe's* own promise that the State has an interest in protecting fetal life or potential life. *Roe* began the contradiction by using the trimester framework to forbid any regulation of abortion designed to advance that interest before viability. *Id.,* at 163. Before viability, *Roe* and subsequent cases treat all governmental attempts to influence a woman's decision on behalf of the potential life within her as unwarranted. This treatment is, in our judgment, incompatible with the recognition that there is a substantial state interest in potential life throughout pregnancy. Cf. Webster, 492 U.S., at 519 (opinion of REHNQUIST, C.J.); Akron I, supra, *462 U.S., at 461 (O'CONNOR, J., dissenting).*

The very notion that the State has a substantial interest in potential life leads to the conclusion that not all regulations must be deemed unwarranted. Not all burdens on the right to decide whether to terminate a pregnancy will be undue. In our view, the undue burden standard is the appropriate means of reconciling the State's interest with the woman's constitutionally protected liberty.

The concept of an undue burden has been utilized by the Court as well as individual Members of the Court, including two of us, in ways that could be considered inconsistent. [. . .] Because we set forth a standard of general application to which we intend to adhere, it is important to clarify what is meant by an undue burden.

A finding of an undue burden is a shorthand for the conclusion that a state regulation has the purpose or effect of placing a substantial obstacle in the path of a woman seeking an abortion of a nonviable fetus. A statute with this purpose is invalid because the means chosen by the State to further the interest in potential life must be calculated to inform the woman's free choice, not hinder it. And a statute which, while furthering the interest in potential life or some other valid state interest, has the effect of placing a substantial obstacle in the path of a woman's choice cannot be considered a permissible means of serving its legitimate ends. To the extent that the opinions of the Court or of individual Justices use the undue burden standard in a manner that is inconsistent with this analysis, we set out what, in our view, should be the controlling standard. Cf. McCleskey v. Zant, 499 U.S. 467, 489 (1991) (attempting "to define the doctrine of abuse of the writ with more precision" after acknowledging tension among earlier cases). In our considered judgment, an undue burden is an unconstitutional burden.

See Akron II, 497 U.S., at 519–520 (opinion of KENNEDY, J.). Understood another way, we answer the question, left open in previous opinions discussing the undue burden formulation, whether a law designed to further the State's interest in fetal life which imposes an undue burden on the woman's decision before fetal viability could be constitutional. See, *e.g.*, Akron I, 462 U.S. at 462–463 (O'CONNOR, J., dissenting). The answer is no.

Some guiding principles should emerge. What is at stake is the woman's right to make the ultimate decision, not a right to be insulated from all others in doing so. Regulations which do no more than create a structural mechanism by which the State, or the parent or guardian of a minor, may express profound respect for the life of the unborn are permitted, if they are not a substantial obstacle to the woman's exercise of the right to choose. See *infra,* at 899–900 (addressing Pennsylvania's parental consent requirement). Unless it has that effect on her right of choice, a state measure designed to persuade her to choose childbirth over abortion will be upheld if reasonably related to that goal. Regulations designed to foster the health of a woman seeking an abortion are valid if they do not constitute an undue burden.

Even when jurists reason from shared premises, some disagreement is inevitable. *Compare* Hodgson, 497 U.S., at 482–497 (KENNEDY, J., concurring in judgment in part and dissenting in part) *with id.,* at 458–460 (O'CONNOR, J., concurring in part and concurring in judgment in part). That is to be expected in the application of any legal standard which must accommodate life's complexity. We do not expect it to be otherwise with respect to the undue burden standard. We give this summary:

(a) To protect the central right recognized by *Roe v. Wade* while at the same time accommodating the State's profound interest in potential life, we will employ the undue burden analysis as explained in this opinion. An undue burden exists, and therefore a provision of law is invalid, if its purpose or effect is to place a substantial obstacle in the path of a woman seeking an abortion before the fetus attains viability.

(b) We reject the rigid trimester framework of *Roe v. Wade.* To promote the State's profound interest in potential life, throughout pregnancy, the State may take measures to ensure that the woman's choice is informed, and measures designed to advance this interest will not be invalidated as long as their purpose is to persuade the woman to choose childbirth over abortion. These measures must not be an undue burden on the right.

(c) As with any medical procedure, the State may enact regulations to further the health or safety of a woman seeking an abortion. Unnecessary health regulations that have the purpose or effect of presenting a substantial obstacle to a woman seeking an abortion impose an undue burden on the right.

(d) Our adoption of the undue burden analysis does not disturb the central holding of *Roe v. Wade,* and we reaffirm that holding. Regardless of whether exceptions are made for particular circumstances, a State may not prohibit any woman from making the ultimate decision to terminate her pregnancy before viability.

(e) We also reaffirm *Roe's* holding that, subsequent to viability, the State, in promoting its interest in the potentiality of human life, may, if it chooses, regulate, and even proscribe, abortion except where it is necessary, in appropriate medical judgment, for the preservation of the life or health of the mother. Roe v. Wade, 410 U.S., at 164–165.

These principles control our assessment of the Pennsylvania statute, and we now turn to the issue of the validity of its challenged provisions. [. . .]

[The remainder of Justices O'Connor, Kennedy, and Souter's decision is omitted, as are the separate opinions of Justice Stevens concurring in part and dissenting in part, the separate opinion of Justice Blackmun, concurring in part, concurring in the judgment in part, and dissenting in part, the opinion of Chief Justice Rehnquist concurring in the judgment in part and dissenting in part (joined by Justices White, Scalia, and Thomas), and the opinion of Justice Scalia, concurring in the judgment in part and dissenting in part (joined by Justices Rehnquist, White, and Thomas). At issue were separate provisions of the statute in question requiring a 24 hour waiting period for an abortion, parental consent for minors (with possible judicial bypass provisions; spousal notification; medical emergency exceptions to the other requirements; and certain information reporting requirements for abortion providers. A majority upheld the emergency exceptions, waiting period, information reporting requirements, and parental consent/judicial bypass requirements but overturned the spousal notification requirements as an "undue burden." Justice Scalia, joined by Chief Justice Rehnquist, Justice White, and Justice Thomas would have held that a woman's decision to abort her unborn child is not a constitutionally protected liberty at all, and that the state statute in question should be upheld in its entirety under the rational basis test.]

NOTE

The Supreme Court has dealt with issues relating to financial assistance and medicaid support of desired nontherapeutic abortions in Beal v. Doe, 432 U.S. 438, 97 S.Ct. 2366 (1977); Maher v. Roe, 432 U.S. 464, 97 S.Ct. 2376 (1977), and Poelker v. Doe, 432 U.S. 519, 97 S.Ct. 2391 (1977), all decided the same day.

It is obvious from these cases and simple reading of newspapers and other media that abortion continues to be one of the most volatile legal and social issues as the U.S. Supreme Court approaches the exit of the decade of the 1990's. Subsequent supplements of this book may well record drastic revisions to *Roe v. Wade* and related cases, if not outright reversal. Whatever ultimately happens to *Roe* and its progeny, the case will, however, stand as a landmark ruling on the constitutional development of the right to privacy.

2. SEXUALITY

BOWERS v. HARDWICK

Supreme Court of the United States, 1986.
478 U.S. 186, 106 S.Ct. 2841.

JUSTICE WHITE delivered the opinion of the Court.

In August 1982, respondent Hardwick (hereafter respondent) was charged with violating the Georgia statute criminalizing sodomy by committing that act with another adult male in the bedroom of respondent's home. After a preliminary hearing, the District Attorney decided not to present the matter to the grand jury unless further evidence developed.

Respondent then brought suit in the Federal District Court, challenging the constitutionality of the statute insofar as it criminalized consensual sodomy. He asserted that he was a practicing homosexual, that the Georgia sodomy statute, as administered by the defendants, placed him in imminent danger of arrest, and that the statute for several reasons violates the Federal Constitution. The District Court granted the defendants' motion to dismiss for failure to state a claim, relying on Doe v. Commonwealth's Attorney for the City of Richmond, 403 F.Supp. 1199 (E.D.Va.1975), which this Court summarily affirmed, 425 U.S. 901 (1976).

A divided panel of the Court of Appeals for the Eleventh Circuit reversed. 760 F.2d 1202 (1985). The court first held that, because *Doe* was distinguishable and in any event had been undermined by later decisions, our summary affirmance in that case did not require affirmance of the District Court. Relying on our decisions in Griswold v. Connecticut, 381 U.S. 479 (1965); Eisenstadt v. Baird, 405 U.S. 438 (1972); Stanley v. Georgia, 394 U.S. 557 (1969); and Roe v. Wade, 410 U.S. 113 (1973), the court went on to hold that the Georgia statute violated respondent's fundamental rights because his homosexual activity is a private and intimate association that is beyond the reach of state regulation by reason of the Ninth Amendment and the Due Process Clause of the Fourteenth Amendment. The case was remanded for trial, at which, to prevail, the State would have to prove that the statute is supported by a compelling interest and is the most narrowly drawn means of achieving that end.

Because other Courts of Appeals have arrived at judgments contrary to that of the Eleventh Circuit in this case, we granted the Attorney General's petition for certiorari questioning the holding that the sodomy statute violates the fundamental rights of homosexuals. We agree with petitioner that the Court of Appeals erred, and hence reverse its judgment.

This case does not require a judgment on whether laws against sodomy between consenting adults in general, or between homosexuals in particular, are wise or desirable. It raises no question about the right or propriety of state legislative decisions to repeal their laws that criminalize homosexual sodomy, or of state-court decisions invalidating those laws on state constitutional grounds. The issue presented is whether the Federal Constitution confers a fundamental right upon homosexuals to engage in sodomy and hence invalidates the laws of the many States that still make such conduct illegal and have done so for a very long time. The case also calls for some judgment about the limits of the Court's role in carrying out its constitutional mandate.

We first register our disagreement with the Court of Appeals and with respondent that the Court's prior cases have construed the Constitution to confer a right of privacy that extends to homosexual sodomy and for all intents and purposes have decided this case. The reach of this line of cases was sketched in Carey v. Population Services International, 431 U.S. 678, 685 (1977). Pierce v. Society of Sisters, 268 U.S. 510 (1925), and Meyer v. Nebraska, 262 U.S. 390 (1923), were described as dealing with child rearing and education; Prince v. Massachusetts, 321 U.S. 158 (1944), with family relationships; Skinner v. Oklahoma ex rel. Williamson, 316 U.S. 535 (1942), with procreation; Loving v. Virginia, 388 U.S. 1 (1967), with marriage; *Griswold v. Connecticut, supra,* and *Eisenstadt v. Baird, supra,* with contraception; and Roe v. Wade, 410 U.S. 113 (1973), with abortion. The latter three cases were interpreted as construing the Due Process Clause of the Fourteenth Amendment to confer a fundamental individual right to decide whether or not to beget or bear a child. *Carey v. Population Services International, supra,* at 688–689.

Accepting the decisions in these cases and the above description of them, we think it evident that none of the rights announced in those cases bears any resemblance to the claimed constitutional right of homosexuals to engage in acts of sodomy that is asserted in this case. No connection between family, marriage, or procreation on the one hand and homosexual activity on the other has been demonstrated, either by the Court of Appeals or by respondent. Moreover, any claim that these cases nevertheless stand for the proposition that any kind of private sexual conduct between consenting adults is constitutionally insulated from state proscription is unsupportable. Indeed, the Court's opinion in *Carey* twice asserted that the privacy right, which the *Griswold* line of cases found to be one of the protections provided by the Due Process Clause, did not reach so far. 431 U.S., at 688, n. 5, 694, n. 17.

Precedent aside, however, respondent would have us announce, as the Court of Appeals did, a fundamental right to engage in homosexual sodomy. This we are quite unwilling to do. It is true that despite the language of the Due Process Clauses of the Fifth and Fourteenth Amendments, which appears to focus only on the processes by which life, liberty, or property is taken, the cases are legion in which those Clauses have been interpreted to have substantive content, subsuming rights that to a great extent are immune from federal or state regulation or proscription. Among such cases are those recognizing rights that have little or no textual support in the constitutional language. *Meyer, Prince,* and *Pierce* fall in this category, as do the privacy cases from *Griswold* to *Carey.*

Striving to assure itself and the public that announcing rights not readily identifiable in the Constitution's text involves much more than the imposition of the Justices' own choice of values on the States and the Federal Government, the Court has sought to identify the nature of the rights qualifying for heightened judicial protection. In Palko v. Connecticut, 302 U.S. 319, 325, 326 (1937), it was said that this category includes those fundamental liberties that are "implicit in the concept of ordered liberty," such that "neither liberty nor justice would exist if [they] were sacrificed." A different description of fundamental liberties appeared in Moore v. East Cleveland, 431 U.S. 494, 503 (1977) (opinion of POWELL, J.), where they are characterized as those liberties that are "deeply rooted in this Nation's history and tradition." *Id.,* at 503 (POWELL, J.). See also Griswold v. Connecticut, 381 U.S., at 506.

It is obvious to us that neither of these formulations would extend a fundamental right to homosexuals to engage in acts of consensual sodomy. Proscriptions against that conduct have ancient roots. See generally, Survey on the Constitutional Right to Privacy in the Context of Homosexual Activity, 40 U.Miami L.Rev. 521, 525 (1986). Sodomy was a criminal offense at common law and was forbidden by the laws of the original 13 States when they ratified the Bill of Rights. In 1868, when the Fourteenth Amendment was ratified, all but 5 of the 37 States in the Union had criminal sodomy laws. In fact, until 1961, all 50 States outlawed sodomy, and today, 24 States and the District of Columbia continue to provide criminal penalties for sodomy performed in private and between consenting adults. See Survey, U.Miami L.Rev., *supra,* at 524, n. 9. Against this background, to claim that a right to engage in such conduct is "deeply rooted in this Nation's history and tradition" or "implicit in the concept of ordered liberty" is, at best, facetious.

Nor are we inclined to take a more expansive view of our authority to discover new fundamental rights imbedded in the Due Process Clause. The Court is most vulnerable and comes nearest to illegitimacy when it deals with judge-made constitutional law having little or no cognizable roots in the language or design of the Constitution. That this is so was painfully demonstrated by the face-off between the Executive and the Court in the 1930's, which resulted in the repudiation of much of the substantive gloss that the Court had placed on the Due Process Clauses of the Fifth and Fourteenth Amendments. There should be, therefore, great resistance to expand the substantive reach of those Clauses, particularly if it requires redefining the category of rights deemed to be fundamental. Otherwise, the Judiciary necessarily takes to itself further authority to govern the country without express constitutional authority. The claimed right pressed on us today falls short of overcoming this resistance.

Respondent, however, asserts that the result should be different where the homosexual conduct occurs in the privacy of the home. He relies on Stanley v. Georgia, 394 U.S. 557 (1969), where the Court held that the First Amendment prevents conviction for possessing and reading obscene material in the privacy of one's home: "If the First Amendment means anything, it means that a State has no business telling a man, sitting alone in his house, what books he may read or what films he may watch." *Id.*, at 565.

Stanley did protect conduct that would not have been protected outside the home, and it partially prevented the enforcement of state obscenity laws; but the decision was firmly grounded in the First Amendment. The right pressed upon us here has no similar support in the text of the Constitution, and it does not qualify for recognition under the prevailing principles for construing the Fourteenth Amendment. Its limits are also difficult to discern. Plainly enough, otherwise illegal conduct is not always immunized whenever it occurs in the home....

Accordingly, the judgment of the Court of Appeals is *Reversed.*

[The concurring opinions of Justices Burger and Powell are omitted, as are dissenting opinions by Justice Blackmun, joined by Justices Brennan, Marshall and Stevens, and by Justice Stevens joined by Justices Brennan & Marshall.

NOTE

A 6–3 majority of the U.S. Supreme Court ruled that it was a violation of the Equal Protection Clause of the 14th Amendment for an amendment to the Colorado State Constitution, "Amendment 2," to forbid any legislative, executive, or judicial action at any level of state or local government designed to protect homosexuals, lesbians or bisexuals as a class of persons. The amendment had been adopted by a statewide referendum after a number of municipalities adopted ordinances prohibiting discrimination based on sexual orientation in housing, employment, education, public accommodations, health and welfare services, and other transactions and activities.

The majority opinion, written by Justice Kennedy, acknowledged that "if a law neither burdens a fundamental right nor targets a suspect class, we will uphold the legislative classification so long as it bears a rational relation to some legitimate end." The Court ruled that "Amendment 2" failed this test, "imposing a broad and undifferentiated disability on a single named group," and lacked "a rational relationship to legitimate state interests." The Court found that the "sheer breadth" of the Amendment "is so discontinuous with the reasons offered for it that the amendment seems inexplicable by anything but animus toward the class that it affects." The effect of the Amendment would be to disqualify the named groups "from the right to seek specific protection from the law." The Court characterized this as "unprecedented in our jurisprudence." A "law declaring that in general it shall be more difficult for one group of citizens than for all others to seek aid from the government is itself a denial of equal protection of the laws in the most literal sense."

Rejecting the argument that the Amendment was designed to promote "respect for other citizens' freedom of association, and in particular the liberties of landlords or employers who have personal or religious objections to homosexuality," the Court found that "Amendment 2 classifies homosexuals not to further a proper legislative end but to make them unequal to everyone else. This Colorado cannot do. A State cannot deem a class of persons a stranger to its laws." Justice Kennedy's opinion was joined by Justices Stevens, O'Connor, Souter, Ginsburg, and Breyer.

A strong dissent by Justice Scalia, joined by Chief Justice Rehnquist and Justice Thomas, argued that Amendment 2 was "a modest attempt by seemingly tolerant Coloradans to preserve traditional sexual mores against the efforts of a politically powerful minority to revise those mores through use of the laws." The majority, Justice Scalia contended, by holding that "homosexuality cannot be singled out for disfavorable treatment," contradicted the ten-year-old decision in Bowers v. Hardwick, 478 U.S. 186, 106 S.Ct. 2841 (1986), which upheld the constitutionality of a state statute criminalizing homosexual conduct. The Bowers decision was not discussed or cited in the majority opinion. "If it is constitutionally permissible for a State to make homosexual conduct criminal," Justice Scalia stated, "surely it is constitutionally permissible for a State to enact other laws merely disfavoring homosexual conduct." Romer v. Evans, 116 S.Ct. 1620, 64 U.S.L.W. 4353 (May 20, 1996).

E. THE RIGHT TO BEAR ARMS

QUILICI v. VILLAGE OF MORTON GROVE

United States Court of Appeals, 7th Circuit, 1982.
695 F.2d 261, cert. denied 464 U.S. 863, 104 S.Ct. 194 (1983).

BAUER, CIRCUIT JUDGE.

This appeal concerns the constitutionality of the Village of Morton Grove's Ordinance No. 81–11, which prohibits the possession of handguns within the Village's borders. The district court held that the Ordinance was constitutional. We affirm.

I

Victor D. Quilici initially challenged Ordinance No. 81–11 in state court. Morton Grove removed the action to federal court where it was consolidated with two similar actions, one brought by George L. Reichert and Robert E. Metler (collectively Reichert) and one brought by Robert Stengl, Martin Gutenkauf, Alice Gutenkauf, Walter J. Dutchak and Geoffrey Lagonia (collectively Stengl). Plaintiffs alleged that Ordinance No. 81–11 violated article I, section 22 of the Illinois Constitution and the second, ninth and fourteenth amendments of the United States Constitution. They sought an order declaring the Ordinance unconstitutional and permanently enjoining its enforcement. The parties filed cross motions for summary judgment. The district court granted Morton Grove's motion for summary judgment and denied plaintiffs' motions for summary judgment.

In its opinion, Quilici v. Village of Morton Grove, 532 F.Supp. 1169 (N.D.Ill.1981), the district court set forth several reasons for upholding the handgun ban's validity under the state and federal constitutions.

First, it held that the Ordinance which banned only certain kinds of arms was a valid exercise of Morton Grove's police power and did not conflict with section 22's conditional right to keep and bear arms. Second, relying on Presser v. Illinois, 116 U.S. 252, 6 S.Ct. 580 (1886), the court concluded that the second amendment's guarantee of the right to bear arms has not been incorporated into the fourteenth amendment and, therefore, is inapplicable to Morton Grove. Finally, it stated that the ninth amendment does not include the right to possess handguns for self-defense. Appellants contend that the district court incorrectly construed the relevant constitutional provisions, assigning numerous errors based on case law, historical analysis, common law traditions and public policy concerns.

* * *

III

We next consider whether Ordinance No. 81–11 violates the second amendment to the United States Constitution. While appellants all contend that Ordinance No. 81–11 is invalid under the second amendment, they offer slightly different arguments to substantiate this contention. All argue, however, that the second amendment applies to state and local governments and that the second amendment guarantee of the right to keep and bear arms exists, not only to assist in the common defense, but also to protect the individual. While reluctantly conceding that Presser v. Illinois, 116 U.S. 252, 6 S.Ct. 580 (1886), held that the second amendment applied only to action by the federal government, they nevertheless assert that *Presser* also held that the right to keep and bear arms is an attribute of national citizenship which is not subject to state restriction. Reichert br. at 36. Finally, apparently responding to the district court's comments that "[p]laintiffs ... have not suggested that the Morton Grove Ordinance in any way interferes with the ability of the United States to maintain public security ..." Quilici v. Village of Morton Grove, supra, Quilici and Reichert argue in this court that the Morton Grove Ordinance interferes with the federal government's ability to maintain public security by preventing individuals from defending themselves and the community from "external or internal armed threats." These are the same arguments made in the district court. Accordingly, we comment only briefly on the points already fully analyzed in that court's decision.

As we have noted, the parties agree that *Presser* is controlling, but disagree as to what *Presser* held. It is difficult to understand how appellants can assert that *Presser* supports the theory that the second amendment right to keep and bear arms is a fundamental right which the state cannot regulate when the *Presser* decision plainly states that "[t]he Second Amendment declares that it shall not be infringed, but this ... means no more than that it shall not be infringed by Congress. This is one of the amendments that has no other effect than to restrict the powers of the National government...." Presser v. Illinois, 116 U.S. 252, 265, 6 S.Ct. 580, 584 (1886). As the district court explained in detail, appellants' claim that *Presser* supports the proposition that the second amendment guarantee of the right to keep and bear arms is not subject to state restriction is based on dicta quoted out of context. Quilici v. Village of Morton Grove, supra. This argument borders on the frivolous and does not warrant any further consideration.

Apparently recognizing the inherent weakness of their reliance on *Presser*, appellants urge three additional arguments to buttress their claim that the second amendment applies to the states. They contend that: (1) *Presser* is no longer good law because later Supreme Court cases incorporating other amendments into the fourteenth amendment have effectively overruled; (2) *Presser* is illogical; and (3) the entire Bill of Rights has been implicitly incorporated into the fourteenth amendment to apply to the states.

None of these arguments has merit. First, appellants offer no authority, other than their own opinions, to support their arguments that *Presser* is no longer good law or would have been decided differently today. Indeed, the fact that the Supreme Court continues to cite Presser, Malloy v. Hogan, 378 U.S. 1, 4 n. 2, 84 S.Ct. 1489, 1491 n. 2 (1964), leads to the opposite conclusion. Second, regardless of whether appellants agree with the *Presser* analysis, it is the law of the land and we are bound by it. Their assertion that *Presser* is illogical is a policy matter for the Supreme Court to address. Finally, their theory of implicit incorporation is wholly unsupported. The Supreme Court has specifically rejected the proposition that the entire Bill of Rights applies to the states through the fourteenth amendment.

Since we hold that the second amendment does not apply to the states, we need not consider the scope of its guarantee of the right to bear arms. For the sake of completeness, however, and because appellants devote a large portion of their briefs to this issue, we briefly comment on what we believe to be the scope of the second amendment.

The second amendment provides that "A well regulated Militia being necessary to the security of a free State, the right of the people to keep and bear Arms, shall not be infringed." U.S.Const. amend. II. Construing this language according to its plain meaning, it seems clear that the right to bear arms is inextricably connected to the preservation of a militia. This is precisely the manner in which the Supreme Court interpreted the second amendment in United States v. Miller, 307 U.S. 174, 59 S.Ct. 816 (1939), the only Supreme Court case specifically addressing that amendment's scope. There the Court held that the right to keep and bear arms extends only to those arms which are necessary to maintain a well regulated militia.

In an attempt to avoid the *Miller* holding that the right to keep and bear arms exists only as it relates to protecting the public security, appellants argue that "[t]he fact that the right to keep and bear arms is joined with language expressing one of its purposes in no way permits a construction which limits or confines the exercise of that right." Reichert br. at 35. They offer no explanation for how they have arrived at this conclusion. Alternatively, they argue that handguns are military weapons. Our reading of *Miller* convinces us that it does not support either of these theories. As the Village correctly notes, appellants are essentially arguing that *Miller* was wrongly decided and should be overruled. Such arguments have no place before this court. Under the controlling authority of *Miller* we conclude that the right to keep and bear handguns is not guaranteed by the second amendment.

Because the second amendment is not applicable to Morton Grove and because possession of handguns by individuals is not part of the right to keep and bear arms, Ordinance No. 81–11 does not violate the second amendment.

IV

Finally, we consider whether Ordinance No. 81–11 violates the ninth amendment. Appellants argue that, although the right to use commonly-owned arms for self-defense is not explicitly listed in the Bill of Rights, it is a fundamental right protected by the ninth amendment. Citing no authority which directly supports their contention, they rely on the debates in the First Congress and the writings of legal philosophers to establish that the right of an individual to own and possess firearms for self-defense is an absolute and inalienable right which cannot be impinged.

Since appellants do not cite, and our research has not revealed, any Supreme Court case holding that any specific right is protected by the ninth amendment, appellants' argument has no legal significance. Appellants may believe the ninth amendment should be read to recognize an unwritten, fundamental, individual right to own or possess firearms; the fact remains that the Supreme Court has never embraced this theory.

V

Reasonable people may differ about the wisdom of Ordinance No. 81–11. History may prove that the Ordinance cannot effectively promote peace and security for Morton Grove's citizens. Such issues, however, are not before the court. We simply hold the ordinance is a proper exercise of Morton Grove's police power and does not violate art. I, § 22 of the Illinois Constitution or the second, ninth, or fourteenth amendments of the United States Constitution. Accordingly, the decision of the district court is

Affirmed.

COFFEY, CIRCUIT JUDGE, dissenting.

The constitutions of the United States and the respective states define and delineate the powers of our various governmental units. As a fundamental principle, if a governing body (federal, state or local) should at any time overstep its limits the judiciary must act as a constitutional check. This was the intent of the framers of the Constitution as evidenced by their dividing the powers and responsibilities of the government into three separate and distinct branches. Specifically, if a legislative body enacts a law exceeding the constitutional limits of its authority, it is the responsibility and the duty of an independent judiciary to declare it void.

With this principle in mind and conscious of the magnitude of the political and social implications of this case, I am compelled to dissent from my brethren today. It is my opinion that the Village of Morton Grove has improperly legislated beyond the legitimate parameters of its authority.

* * *

Third, I believe that Morton Grove Ordinance No. 81–11, as a matter of constitutional law, impermissibly interferes with individual privacy rights. I join others who throughout history have recognized that an individual in this country has a protected right, within the confines of the criminal law, to guard his or her home or place of business from unlawful intrusions. In my view, today's majority decision marks a new nadir for the fundamental principle that "a man's home is his castle." It has been said that the greatest threat to our liberty is from well-meaning, and almost imperceptible governmental encroachments upon our personal freedom. Today's decision sanctions an intrusion on our basic rights as citizens which would no doubt be alarming and odious to our founding fathers. For the above-cited reasons, which I shall discuss in greater detail herein, I respectfully dissent from the opinion of this court.

* * *

III.

I find today's decision particularly disturbing as it sanctions governmental action which I feel impermissibly interferes with basic human freedoms. I cannot let this opportunity pass without expressing my concern with the erosion of these rights.

The majority cavalierly dismisses the argument that the right to possess commonly owned arms for self-defense and the protection of loved ones is a fundamental right protected by the Constitution. Justice Cardozo in Palko v. Connecticut, 302 U.S. 319, 325, 58 S.Ct. 149, 151 (1937), defined fundamental rights as those rights "implicit in the concept of ordered liberty." Surely nothing could be more fundamental to the "concept of *ordered* liberty" than the basic right of an individual, within the confines of the criminal law, to protect his home and family from unlawful and dangerous intrusions.

Article I, section 22 of the Illinois Constitution provides that subject to the "police power," the right of an individual to bear arms shall not be infringed. The United States Supreme Court has noted the difficulty in attempting to outline the parameters of a state's legitimate police power. In Berman v. Parker, 348 U.S. 26, 75 S.Ct. 98, (1954), addressing the concept of "police power," the Supreme Court stated that "an attempt to define its reach or trace its outer limits is fruitless, for each case must turn on its own facts." The term is neither "abstractly nor historically capable of complete definition." In enacting Ordinance No. 81–11, Morton Grove has gone beyond the "outer limits" of its legitimate police powers.

In Haller Sign Works v. Physical Culture Training School, 249 Ill. 436, 94 N.E. 920 (1911), the Illinois Supreme Court recognized that it is the responsibility of the courts to determine when constitutional limits have been exceeded in the enactment of police power legislation. It is the duty of the courts to determine whether there has been an "unreasonable invasion of private rights."

> "Necessarily there are limits beyond which legislation cannot constitutionally go in depriving individuals of their natural rights and liberties. To determine where the rights of the individual end and those of the public begin is a question which must be determined by the court."

In today's decision this court has refused to take cognizance of the natural right of an individual, within the confines of the criminal law, to protect his home and family from unlawful and dangerous intrusions. It is my opinion that Morton Grove Ordinance No. 81–11 impermissibly interferes with the rights of Illinois citizens to guard their personal security, subject to the limits of the criminal law, and that it is the duty of this court to so declare.

The court today has also refused to recognize the tremendous impact of Morton Grove Ordinance No. 81–11 on personal privacy rights. There is no doubt that the right to one's privacy is afforded constitutional protection. The United States Supreme Court has repeatedly recognized a right to privacy implicit in the federal constitution and Article I, section 6, of the Illinois Constitution expressly establishes a right to privacy. The Illinois provision has been interpreted by some members of the Illinois Supreme Court as creating a direct right to freedom from invasions of privacy by government or public officials.

The Morton Grove Ordinance, by prohibiting the possession of a handgun within the confines of the home, violates both the fundamental right to privacy and the fundamental right to defend the home against unlawful intrusion within the parameters of the criminal law. There is no area of human activity more protected by the right to privacy than the right to be free from unnecessary government intrusion in the confines of the home.

The unique importance of the home from time immemorial has been amply demonstrated in our constitutional jurisprudence. Among the enumerated rights in the Bill of Rights are the Third Amendment's prohibition of quartering of troops in a private house in peace-time and the right of citizens to be "secure in their ... houses ... against unreasonable searches and seizures ..." guaranteed by the Fourth Amendment. As early as 1886, the United States Supreme Court recognized that the Fifth Amendment protects against all governmental invasions "of the sanctity of a man's home and the privacies of life." Boyd v. United States, 116 U.S. 616, 630, 6 S.Ct. 524, 532 (1886). The First Amendment had been held to encompass the right to "privacy and freedom of association in the home."

In Stanley v. Georgia, 394 U.S. 557, 89 S.Ct. 1243 (1969), the Supreme Court overturned a state conviction for possession of obscene material, holding "that the First and Fourteenth Amendments prohibit making the private possession of obscene material a crime." The Supreme Court had previously held that obscenity is not protected by the First Amendment, but in *Stanley* the Court made a distinction between commercial distribution of obscene matter and the private possession of such materials in the home and held the Georgia statute unconstitutional because it prohibited the possession of such materials in the home. The Court recited:

> "For also fundamental is the right to be free, except in very limited circumstances, from unwanted governmental intrusions into one's privacy."

The Court has made it clear that its *Stanley* decision was not based on the idea that obscene matter is itself protected under the right of privacy. Rather, the focus in *Stanley* was on the fact that the activity prohibited by the Georgia statute occurred in the privacy of the home. In United States v. Reidel, 402 U.S. 351, 356, 91 S.Ct. 1410, 1412 (1971), the Court rejected the argument that commercial distribution of pornography is constitutionally protected and held that the "focus" of *Stanley* was "on freedom of mind and thought and on the privacy of one's home." Subsequently, the Court in United States v. Orito, 413 U.S. 139, 142, 93 S.Ct. 2674, 2677 (1973) stated "the Constitution extends special safeguards to the privacy of the home" and there exists a "myriad" of activities which may be prohibited in public but which may be lawfully conducted within the privacy and confines of the home.

Most importantly, the Supreme Court in Paris Adult Theatre I v. Slaton, 413 U.S. 49, 66, 93 S.Ct. 2628, 2639 (1973), held that *Stanley* was decided "on the narrow basis of the 'privacy of the home' which was hardly more than a reaffirmation that *'a man's home is his castle.'* " (emphasis added).

Privacy in the home is a fundamental right under both the federal and Illinois Constitutions. This does not mean, of course, that a person may do anything at anytime as long as the activity takes place within a person's home. Instead, the right to privacy is limited in two important respects. First, the Supreme Court strictly limited its *Stanley* holding to possession for purely private, noncommercial use in the home. Second, as noted in *Stanley*, the right to privacy must yield when it seriously interferes with the public welfare. The government bears a heavy burden when attempting to justify an expansion, as in gun control, of the "limited circumstances" in which intrusion into the privacy of a home is permitted.

Morton Grove has not met that heavy burden. Without question, the state may, should and has placed reasonable restrictions on the possession of handguns outside one's home to protect the public welfare. However, Morton Grove's prohibition of handgun possession within the confines of a person's own home has not been shown to be necessary to protect the public welfare and thus violates the fundamental right to privacy.

The right to privacy is one of the most cherished rights an American citizen has; the right to privacy sets America apart from totalitarian states in which the interests of the state prevail over individual rights. A fundamental part of our concept of ordered liberty is the right to protect one's home and family against dangerous intrusions subject to the criminal law. Morton Grove, acting like the omniscient and paternalistic "Big Brother" in George Orwell's novel, "1984", cannot, in the name of public welfare, dictate to its residents that they may not possess a handgun in the privacy of their home. To so prohibit the possession of handguns in the privacy of the home prevents a person from protecting his home and family, endangers law-abiding citizens and renders meaningless the Supreme Court's teaching that "a man's home is his castle."

IV.

In summary, I believe a truly independent judiciary must exercise its powers with discretion and reservation, giving due deference to the other branches of government. Our judicial responsibility, however, obligates us to declare an act by another governmental unit to be void if we believe the enacted law is contrary to the principles of the Constitution. Because I believe that the Morton Grove Ordinance as enacted is contrary to the principles of the Constitution, I must respectfully dissent from the opinion of this court.

NOTE

The Village of Morton Grove ordinance referred to in the principal case has additionally been found not to violate the Illinois Constitution's right to bear arms. Kalodimos v. Village of Morton Grove, 103 Ill.2d 483, 83 Ill.Dec. 308, 470 N.E.2d 266 (1984). In holding that the ordinance is a valid exercise of the police and home rule powers, the Illinois Supreme Court stated:

> "Article I, section 22, added to the Illinois Constitution in 1970, provides: "Subject only to the police power, the right of the individual citizen to keep and bear arms shall not be infringed." ... The section does not mirror the second amendment to the Federal Constitution ...; rather it adds the words '[s]ubject only to the police power,' omits prefatory language concerning the importance of a militia, and substitutes 'the individual citizen' for 'the people.' The majority report of the Bill of Rights Committee of the constitutional convention, which framed the provision, makes clear that the latter two changes were intended to broaden the scope of the right to arms from a collective one applicable only to weapons traditionally used by a regulated militia ... to an individual right covering a wider variety of arms....

"Equally distinctive, however, is the explicit recognition of 'the police power' as a limitation on the liberty the provision affords....

"The meaning of a constitutional provision depends, of course, on the common understanding of the citizens who, by ratifying the Constitution, gave it life... This understanding, however, is best determined by referring to the common meaning of the words used.... The plain language of the provision clearly leaves the right to bear any type of arms subject to the police power. This belies any assertion that a majority of the voters must have interpreted the plain words of the statute as ruling out any specific regulatory measure. The official explanation which all voters received also left considerable leeway for regulation of guns....

"Based on the floor debates and the official explanation, as well as on the language of the provision, it is apparent to us that section 22, as submitted to the voters, meant that a ban on all firearms that an individual citizen might use would not be permissible, but a ban on discrete categories of firearms, such as handguns, would be.... [W]e conclude, along with the Federal courts ... that a reasonable prohibition of handguns is constitutional in this State....

"We emphasize again that section 22 bestows upon individual citizens for the first time a right to possess some form of weapon suitable for self-defense or recreation, regardless of the adaptability of the weapon for use in an organized militia or of whether it is possessed for the purposes of forming a militia.

"The plaintiffs seek to apply a free-wheeling preemption rule to the exercise of home rule power. They argue in effect that a subject is preempted whenever it is of significant concern to the State or whenever a uniform statewide solution to the problems it entails might arguably be more manageable than individual control by local units of government. Home rule, however, is predicated on the assumption that problems in which local governments have a legitimate and substantial interest should be open to local solution and reasonable experimentation to meet local needs, free from veto by voters and elected representatives of other parts of the State who might disagree with the particular approach advanced by the representatives of the locality involved or fail to appreciate the local perception of the problem...."

F. THE SELF-INCRIMINATION PRIVILEGE

1. THE PHYSICAL EVIDENCE—COMMUNICATION DELINEATION

SCHMERBER v. CALIFORNIA

Supreme Court of the United States, 1966.
384 U.S. 757, 86 S.Ct. 1826.

MR. JUSTICE BRENNAN delivered the opinion of the Court.

Petitioner was convicted in Los Angeles Municipal Court of the criminal offense of driving an automobile while under the influence of intoxicating liquor. He had been arrested at a hospital while receiving treatment for injuries suffered in an accident involving the automobile that he had apparently been driving. At the direction of a police officer, a blood sample was then withdrawn from petitioner's body by a physician at the hospital. The chemical analysis of this sample revealed a percent by weight of alcohol in his blood at the time of the offense which indicated intoxication, and the report of this analysis was admitted in evidence at the trial. Petitioner objected to receipt of this evidence of the analysis on the ground that the blood had been withdrawn despite his refusal, on the advice of his counsel, to consent to the test. He contended that in that circumstance the withdrawal of the blood and the admission of the analysis in evidence denied him due process of law under the Fourteenth Amendment, as well as specific guarantees of the Bill of Rights secured against the States by that Amendment; his privilege against self-incrimination under the Fifth Amendment; his right to counsel under the Sixth Amendment; and his right not to be subjected to unreasonable searches and seizures in violation of the Fourth Amendment. The Appellate Department of the California Superior Court rejected these contentions and affirmed the conviction. In view of constitutional decisions since we last considered these issues we granted certiorari. We affirm.

[Only the self-incrimination portion of the case is included herein.]

[Breithaupt v. Abram, 352 U.S. 432, 77 S.Ct. 408 (1957)] summarily rejected an argument that the withdrawal of blood and the admission of the analysis report involved in that state case violated the Fifth Amendment privilege of any person not to "be compelled in any criminal case to be a witness against himself." Citing Twining v. State of New Jersey, 211 U.S. 78, 29 S.Ct. 14 (1964). But that case, holding that the protections of the Fourteenth Amendment do not embrace this Fifth Amendment privilege, has been succeeded by Malloy v. Hogan, 378 U.S. 1, 8, 84 S.Ct. 1489, 1493. We there held that "[t]he Fourteenth Amendment secures against state invasion the same privilege that the Fifth Amendment guarantees against federal infringement—the right of a person to remain silent unless he chooses to speak in the unfettered exercise of his own will, and to suffer no penalty ... for such silence." We therefore must now decide whether the withdrawal of the blood and admission in evidence of the analysis involved in this case violated petitioner's privilege. We hold that the privilege protects an accused only from being compelled to testify against himself, or otherwise provide the State with evidence of a testimonial or communicative nature,[1]

1. A dissent suggests that the report of the blood test was "testimonial" or "communicative," because the test was performed in order to obtain the testimony of others, communicating to the jury facts about petitioner's condition. Of course, all evidence received in court is "testimonial" or "communicative" if these words are thus used. But the Fifth Amendment relates only to acts on the part of the person to whom the privilege applies, and we use these words subject to the same limitations. A nod or headshake is as much a "testimonial" or "communicative" act in this sense as are spoken words. But the terms as we use them do not apply to evidence of acts noncommunicative in nature as to the person asserting the privilege, even though, as

and that the withdrawal of blood and use of the analysis in question in this case did not involve compulsion to these ends.

It could not be denied that in requiring petitioner to submit to the withdrawal and chemical analysis of his blood the State compelled him to submit to an attempt to discover evidence that might be used to prosecute him for a criminal offense. He submitted only after the police officer rejected his objection and directed the physician to proceed. The officer's direction to the physician to administer the test over petitioner's objection constituted compulsion for the purposes of the privilege. The critical question, then, is whether petitioner was thus compelled "to be a witness against himself." [2]

If the scope of the privilege coincided with the complex of values it helps to protect, we might be obliged to conclude that the privilege was violated. In Miranda v. Arizona ... [1966], the Court said of the interests protected by the privilege: "All these policies point to one overriding thought: the constitutional foundation underlying the privilege is the respect a government—state or federal—must accord to the dignity and integrity of its citizens. To maintain a 'fair state-individual balance,' to require the government 'to shoulder the entire load,' ... to respect the inviolability of the human personality, our accusatory system of criminal justice demands that the government seeking to punish an individual produce the evidence against him by its own independent labors, rather than by the cruel, simple expedient of compelling it from his own mouth." The withdrawal of blood necessarily involves puncturing the skin for extraction, and the percent by weight of alcohol in that blood, as established by chemical analysis, is evidence of criminal guilt. Compelled submission fails on one view to respect the "inviolability of the human personality." Moreover, since it enables the State to rely on evidence forced from the accused, the compulsion violates at least one meaning of the requirement that the State procure the evidence against an accused "by its own independent labors."

As the passage in *Miranda* implicitly recognizes, however, the privilege has never been given the full scope which the values it helps to protect suggest. History and a long line of authorities in lower courts have consistently limited its protection to situations in which the State seeks to submerge those values by obtaining the evidence against an accused through "the cruel, simple expedient of compelling it from his own mouth.... In sum, the privilege is fulfilled only when the person is

here, such acts are compelled to obtain the testimony of others.

2. Many state constitutions, including those of most of the original Colonies, phrase the privilege in terms of compelling a person to give "evidence" against himself. But our decision cannot turn on the Fifth Amendment's use of the word "witness." "[A]s the manifest purpose of the constitutional provisions, both of the states and of the United States, is to prohibit the compelling of testimony of a self-incriminating kind from a party or a witness, the liberal construction which must be placed upon constitutional provisions for the protection of personal rights would seem to require that the constitutional guaranties, however differently worded, should have as far as possible the same interpretation...." Counselman v. Hitchcock, 142 U.S. 547, 584–585, 12 S.Ct. 195, 206. 8 Wigmore, Evidence § 2252 (McNaughton rev. 1961).

guaranteed the right 'to remain silent unless he chooses to speak in the unfettered exercise of his own will.' " The leading case in this Court is Holt v. United States, 218 U.S. 245, 31 S.Ct. 2. There the question was whether evidence was admissible that the accused, prior to trial and over his protest, put on a blouse that fitted him. It was contended that compelling the accused to submit to the demand that he model the blouse violated the privilege. Mr. Justice Holmes, speaking for the Court, rejected the argument as "based upon an extravagant extension of the 5th Amendment," and went on to say: "[T]he prohibition of compelling a man in a criminal court to be witness against himself is a prohibition of the use of physical or moral compulsion to extort communications from him, not an exclusion of his body as evidence when it may be material. The objection in principle would forbid a jury to look at a prisoner and compare his features with a photograph in proof." [3]

It is clear that the protection of the privilege reaches an accused's communications, whatever form they might take, and the compulsion of responses which are also communications, for example, compliance with a subpoena to produce one's papers. Boyd v. United States, 116 U.S. 616, 6 S.Ct. 524. On the other hand, both federal and state courts have usually held that it offers no protection against compulsion to submit to fingerprinting, photographing, or measurements, to write or speak for identification, to appear in court, to stand, to assume a stance, to walk, or to make a particular gesture. The distinction which has emerged, often expressed in different ways, is that the privilege is a bar against compelling "communications" or "testimony," but that compulsion which makes a suspect or accused the source of "real or physical evidence" does not violate it.

Although we agree that this distinction is a helpful framework for analysis, we are not to be understood to agree with past applications in all instances. There will be many cases in which such a distinction is not readily drawn. Some tests seemingly directed to obtain "physical evidence," for example, lie detector tests measuring changes in body function during interrogation, may actually be directed to eliciting responses which are essentially testimonial. To compel a person to submit to testing in which an effort will be made to determine his guilt or innocence on the basis of physiological responses, whether willed or not, is to evoke the spirit and history of the Fifth Amendment. Such situations call to mind the principle that the protection of the privilege "is as broad as the mischief against which it seeks to guard." Counselman v. Hitchcock, 142 U.S. 547, 562, 12 S.Ct. 195, 198.

In the present case, however, no such problem of application is presented. Not even a shadow of testimonial compulsion upon or

3. Compare Wigmore's view, "that the privilege is limited to testimonial disclosures. It was directed at the employment of legal process to *extract from the person's own lips* an admission of guilt, which would thus take the place of other evidence." 8 Wigmore, Evidence § 2263 (McNaughton rev. 1961). California adopted the Wigmore formulation. Our holding today, however, is not to be understood as adopting the Wigmore formulation.

enforced communication by the accused was involved either in the extraction or in the chemical analysis. Petitioner's testimonial capacities were in no way implicated; indeed, his participation, except as a donor, was irrelevant to the results of the test, which depend on chemical analysis and on that alone.[4] Since the blood test evidence, although an incriminating product of compulsion, was neither petitioner's testimony nor evidence relating to some communicative act or writing by the petitioner, it was not inadmissible on privilege grounds.

* * *

[The concurring opinion of Justices Harlan and Stewart is omitted.]

MR. JUSTICE BLACK with whom MR. JUSTICE DOUGLAS joins, dissenting.

I would reverse petitioner's conviction. I agree with the Court that the Fourteenth Amendment made applicable to the States the Fifth Amendment's provision that "No person ... shall be compelled in any criminal case to be a witness against himself...." But I disagree with the Court's holding that California did not violate petitioner's constitutional right against self-incrimination when it compelled him, against his will, to allow a doctor to puncture his blood vessels in order to extract a sample of blood and analyze it for alcoholic content, and then used that analysis as evidence to convict petitioner of a crime.

The Court admits that "the State compelled [petitioner] to submit to an attempt to discover evidence [in his blood] that might be [and was] used to prosecute him for a criminal offense." To reach the conclusion that compelling a person to give his blood to help the State convict him is not equivalent to compelling him to be a witness against himself strikes me as quite an extraordinary feat. The Court, however, overcomes what had seemed to me to be an insuperable obstacle to its conclusion by holding that

> "... the privilege protects an accused only from being compelled to testify against himself, or otherwise provide the State with evidence of a testimonial or communicative nature, and that the withdrawal of blood and use of the analysis in question in this case did not involve compulsion to these ends."

I cannot agree that this distinction and reasoning of the Court justify denying petitioner his Bill of Rights' guarantee that he must not be compelled to be a witness against himself.

4. This conclusion would not necessarily govern had the State tried to show that the accused had incriminated himself when told that he would have to be tested. Such incriminating evidence may be an unavoidable by-product of the compulsion to take the test, especially for an individual who fears the extraction or opposes it on religious grounds. If it wishes to compel persons to submit to such attempts to discover evidence, the State may have to forego the advantage of any *testimonial* products of administering the test—products which would fall within the privilege. Indeed, there may be circumstances in which the pain, danger, or severity of an operation would almost inevitably cause a person to prefer confession to undergoing the "search," and nothing we say today should be taken as establishing the permissibility of compulsion in that case. But no such situation is presented in this case....

In the first place it seems to me that the compulsory extraction of petitioner's blood for analysis so that the person who analyzed it could give evidence to convict him had both a "testimonial" and a "communicative nature." The sole purpose of this project which proved to be successful was to obtain "testimony" from some person to prove that petitioner had alcohol in his blood at the time he was arrested. And the purpose of the project was certainly "communicative" in that the analysis of the blood was to supply information to enable a witness to communicate to the court and jury that petitioner was more or less drunk.

I think it unfortunate that the Court rests so heavily for its very restrictive reading of the Fifth Amendment's privilege against self-incrimination on the words "testimonial" and "communicative." These words are not models of clarity and precision as the Court's rather labored explication shows. Nor can the Court, so far as I know, find precedent in the former opinions of this Court for using these particular words to limit the scope of the Fifth Amendment's protection. There is a scholarly precedent, however, in the late Professor Wigmore's learned treatise on evidence. He used "testimonial" which, according to the latest edition of his treatise ... means "communicative" ... as a key word in his vigorous and extensive campaign designed to keep the privilege against self-incrimination "within limits the strictest possible." 8 Wigmore, Evidence § 2251 (3d ed. 1940), p. 318. Though my admiration for Professor Wigmore's scholarship is great, I regret to see the word he used to narrow the Fifth Amendment's protection play such a major part in any of this Court's opinions.

I am happy that the Court itself refuses to follow Professor Wigmore's implication that the Fifth Amendment goes no further than to bar the use of forced self-incriminating statements coming from a "person's own lips." It concedes, as it must so long as Boyd v. United States, stands, that the Fifth Amendment bars a State from compelling a person to produce papers he has that might tend to incriminate him. It is a strange hierarchy of values that allows the State to extract a human being's blood to convict him of a crime because of the blood's content but proscribes compelled production of his lifeless papers. Certainly there could be few papers that would have any more "testimonial" value to convict a man of drunken driving than would an analysis of the alcoholic content of a human being's blood introduced in evidence at a trial for driving while under the influence of alcohol. In such a situation blood, of course, is not oral testimony given by an accused but it can certainly "communicate" to a court and jury the fact of guilt.

The Court itself expresses its own doubts, if not fears, of its own shadowy distinction between compelling "physical evidence" like blood which it holds does not amount to compelled self-incrimination, and "eliciting responses which are essentially testimonial." And in explanation of its fears the Court goes on to warn that

> "To compel a person to submit to testing [by lie detectors for example] in which an effort will be made to determine his guilt or innocence on the basis of physiological responses, whether willed or not, is to evoke the spirit and history of the Fifth Amendment. Such situations call to mind the principle that the protection of the privilege 'is as broad as the mischief against which it seeks to guard.' Counselman v. Hitchcock."

A basic error in the Court's holding and opinion is its failure to give the Fifth Amendment's protection against compulsory self-incrimination the broad and liberal construction that *Counselman* and other opinions of this Court have declared it ought to have.

The liberal construction given the Bill of Rights' guarantee in Boyd v. United States, supra, which Professor Wigmore criticized severely, ... makes that one among the greatest constitutional decisions of this Court. In that case all the members of the Court decided that civil suits for penalties and forfeitures incurred for commission of offenses against the law,

> "... are within the reason of criminal proceedings for all the purposes of ... that portion of the fifth amendment which declares that no person shall be compelled in any criminal case to be a witness against himself; ... within the meaning of the fifth amendment to the constitution. ..."

Obviously the Court's interpretation was not completely supported by the literal language of the Fifth Amendment. Recognizing this, the Court announced a rule of constitutional interpretation that has been generally followed ever since, particularly in judicial construction of Bill of Rights guarantees:

> "A close and literal construction [of constitutional provisions for the security of persons and property] deprives them of half their efficacy, and leads to gradual depreciation of the right, as if it consisted more in sound than in substance. It is the duty of courts to be watchful for the constitutional rights of the citizen, and against any stealthy encroachments thereon."

The Court went on to say ... that to require "an owner to produce his private books and papers, in order to prove his breach of the laws, and thus to establish the forfeiture of his property, is surely compelling him to furnish evidence against himself." The Court today departs from the teachings of *Boyd*. Petitioner Schmerber has undoubtedly been compelled to give his blood "to furnish evidence against himself," yet the Court holds that this is not forbidden by the Fifth Amendment. With all deference I must say that the Court here gives the Bill of Rights' safeguard against compulsory self-incrimination a construction that would generally be considered too narrow and technical even in the interpretation of an ordinary commercial contract.

The Court apparently, for a reason I cannot understand, finds some comfort for its narrow construction of the Fifth Amendment in this

Court's decision in Miranda v. Arizona. I find nothing whatever in the majority opinion in that case which either directly or indirectly supports the holding in this case. In fact I think the interpretive constitutional philosophy used in *Miranda*, unlike that used in this case, gives the Fifth Amendment's prohibition against compelled self-incrimination a broad and liberal construction in line with the wholesome admonitions in the *Boyd* case. The closing sentence in the Fifth Amendment section of the Court's opinion in the present case is enough by itself, I think, to expose the unsoundness of what the Court here holds. That sentence reads:

> "Since the blood test evidence, although an incriminating product of compulsion, was neither petitioner's testimony nor evidence relating to some communicative act or writing by the petitioner, it was not inadmissible on privilege grounds."

How can it reasonably be doubted that the blood test evidence was not in all respects the actual equivalent of "testimony" taken from petitioner when the result of the test was offered as testimony, was considered by the jury as testimony, and the jury's verdict of guilt rests in part on that testimony? The refined, subtle reasoning and balancing process used here to narrow the scope of the Bill of Rights' safeguard against self-incrimination provides a handy instrument for further narrowing of that constitutional protection, as well as others, in the future. Believing with the Framers that these constitutional safeguards broadly construed by independent tribunals of justice provide our best hope for keeping our people free from governmental oppression, I deeply regret the Court's holding....

[The separate dissenting opinion of Justice Douglas and the one by Justice Fortas are omitted.]

NOTES

1. Consider the following alternative to the procedure utilized by the police in *Schmerber*—a provision of the Uniform Vehicle Code, prepared by the National Commission on Uniform Traffic Laws and Ordinances, as revised in 1987:

§ 6–207. Revocation of license for refusal to submit to chemical test or having BAC of 0.08 or more [generally known as the "implied consent law"]

(a) Any person who operates a motor vehicle upon the highways of this State shall be deemed to have given consent, subject to the provisions of § 11–903, to a test or tests of his blood, breath, or urine for the purpose of determining his alcohol concentration or the presence of other drugs. The test or tests shall be administered at the direction of a law enforcement officer who has probable cause to believe the person has been violating § 11–902(a), and one of the following conditions exists:

1. The person has been arrested for violating § 11–902(a) or any other offense alleged to have been committed while the person was violating § 11–902(a);

2. The person has been involved in an accident;

3. The person has refused to submit to the preliminary screening test authorized by § 6–208; or

4. The person has submitted to the preliminary screening test authorized by § 6–208; which disclosed an alcohol concentration of 0.08 or more.

The law enforcement agency by which such officer is employed shall designate which of the aforesaid tests shall be administered. (Revised, 1984.)

(b) Any person who is dead, unconscious or who is otherwise in a condition rendering him incapable of refusal, shall be deemed not to have withdrawn the consent provided by paragraph (a) of this section and the test or tests may be administered, subject to the provisions of § 11–903. (Revised, 1971.)

(c) A person requested to submit to a test as provided above shall be warned by the law enforcement officer requesting the test that a refusal to submit to the test will result in revocation of his license to operate a motor vehicle for (six months) (one year). Following this warning, if a person under arrest refuses upon the request of a law enforcement officer to submit to a test designated by the law enforcement agency as provided in paragraph (a) of this section, none shall be given. (Revised, 1984.)

(d) If the person refuses testing or submits to a test which discloses an alcohol concentration of 0.08 or more under this section, the law enforcement officer shall submit a sworn report to the department, certifying that the test was requested pursuant to subsection (a) and that the person refused to submit to testing or submitted to a test which disclosed an alcohol concentration of 0.08 or more. (New, 1984.)

(e) Upon receipt of the sworn report of a law enforcement officer submitted under subsection (d), the department shall revoke the driver's license of the person for the periods specified in § 6–213, (New, 1984.)

(f) On behalf of the department, the law enforcement officer submitting the sworn report under subsection (d) shall serve immediate notice of the revocation on the person, and the revocation shall be effective (7) (10) (15) days after the date of service. If the person has a valid license, the officer shall take the driver's license of the person, and issue a temporary license valid for the notice period. The officer shall send the license to the department along with the sworn report under subsection (d). (New, 1984.)

In cases where no notice has been served by the law enforcement officer, the department shall give notice as provided in § 2–314 and the revocation shall be effective (7) (10) (15) days after the date of service. If the address shown in the law enforcement officer's report differs from that shown on the department records, the notice shall be mailed to both addresses. (New, 1984; Section Renumbered, 1986.)

2. Where a driver has refused to submit to a chemical test for intoxication, a number of jurisdictions, either by statute or by decision law, permit comment to be made upon that fact at the trial. See Campbell v. Superior Court, 106 Ariz. 542, 479 P.2d 685 (1971), and the cases from other states cited therein. The physical characteristic of the test distinguishes such a holding from that of the United States Supreme Court in Griffin v. California, 380 U.S. 609, 85 S.Ct. 1229 (1965), prohibiting prosecutorial comment on the defendant's failure to *testify*. For the viewpoint contrary to the above Arizona case, and for the law that prevails in the various jurisdictions, consult 87 A.L.R.2d 370.

A number of recent U.S. Supreme Court cases have examined various state statutes on this subject. In South Dakota v. Neville, 459 U.S. 553, 103 S.Ct. 916 (1983), the Court upheld a statute that permits a person suspected of driving while intoxicated to refuse to submit to a blood-alcohol test, but also authorizes revocation of the driver's license of a person so refusing and permits such refusal to be used against him at trial. The contention that this violates the Fifth Amendment right against self-incrimination was rejected. Also see Mackey v. Montrym, 443 U.S. 1, 99 S.Ct. 2612 (1979) and Illinois v. Batchelder, 463 U.S. 1112, 103 S.Ct. 3513 (1983).

Under an implied consent statute that permits the use in evidence of a driver's refusal to submit to a chemical test, evidence of an initial refusal is not admissible if the driver changes his mind and submits to the test. To permit such evidence where the driver has taken the test would negate the legislature's intent "... to present a driver, as an incentive to submit, with the continuing option to prevent admission of evidence of his refusal to be tested by actually completing a test." People v. Naseef, 127 Ill.App.3d 70, 82 Ill.Dec. 204, 468 N.E.2d 466 (1984).

In California v. Trombetta, 467 U.S. 479, 104 S.Ct. 2528 (1984), the Court rejected a claim that the Fourteenth Amendment Due Process Clause requires police and prosecutors to preserve breath samples of suspected drunk drivers tested on chemical breath-alcohol measuring devices such as the Intoxilyzer or Breathalyzer. The Court adopted the rule that any duty the states may have to preserve evidence is limited to evidence that possesses an exculpatory value that is apparent before its destruction and that is unobtainable by the defendant by other reasonable means. In the case of breath samples saved for defense use, they would almost always confirm the results obtained by the state, and any inaccuracies in the state's results could be shown by other means such as cross-examination or independent tests obtained by the defendant after taking the state's chemical test. Thus, even if the police use a device such as the Breathalyzer that saves a breath sample (the Intoxilyzer does not save a sample), they have no constitutional duty to save it and make it available to the defendant.

3. For a discussion of the scientific and legal aspects of chemical tests for alcoholic intoxication, as well as many other types of scientific evidence, consult Moenssens, Inbau, and Starrs, Scientific Evidence in Criminal Cases (3d ed. 1986), Ch. 2.

4. Although of primary interest to lawyers rather than law enforcement personnel, we wish to point out that the continued vitality of the *Boyd* case referred to in the *Schmerber* case is highly questionable in view of the subsequent Supreme Court's decisions in Fisher v. United States, 425 U.S. 391, 96 S.Ct. 1569 (1976) and Andresen v. Maryland, 427 U.S. 463, 96 S.Ct. 2737 (1976).

5. A court order directing a defendant to furnish handwriting exemplars in response to dictation, in which the way he spelled certain words could be compared to writings that the police possessed, was a testimonial act protected by the Fifth Amendment, not a mere handwriting exemplar. In effect, the defendant was compelled to say, "This is how I spell this word." United States v. Campbell, 724 F.2d 812 (9th Cir.1984).

2. LIMITATIONS UPON COMPELLED COMMUNICATIONS

CALIFORNIA v. BYERS

Supreme Court of the United States, 1971.
402 U.S. 424, 91 S.Ct. 1535.

MR. CHIEF JUSTICE BURGER announced the judgment of the Court and an opinion in which MR. JUSTICE STEWART, MR. JUSTICE WHITE, and MR. JUSTICE BLACKMUN join.

This case presents the narrow but important question of whether the constitutional privilege against compulsory self-incrimination is infringed by California's so-called "hit and run" statute which requires the driver of a motor vehicle involved in an accident to stop at the scene and give his name and address. Similar "hit and run" or "stop and report" statutes are in effect in all 50 States and the District of Columbia.

* * *

Section 20002(a)(1) of the California Vehicle Code provides:

> "The driver of any vehicle involved in an accident resulting in damage to any property including vehicles shall immediately stop the vehicle at the scene of the accident and shall then and there ... [l]ocate and notify the owner or person in charge of such property of the name and address of the driver and owner of the vehicle involved...." [1]

Byers demurred on the ground that it violated his privilege against compulsory self-incrimination. His demurrer was ultimately sustained by the California Supreme Court. That court held that the privilege protected a driver who "reasonably believes that compliance with the statute will result in self-incrimination." Here the court found that Byers' apprehensions were reasonable because compliance with § 20002(a)(1) confronted him with "substantial hazards of self-incrimination." Nevertheless the court upheld the validity of the statute by inserting a judicially-created use restriction on the disclosures which it required. [Editors' note: What the California court held and said was that the compelled disclosures and the fruits of such disclosures may not be used in a criminal prosecution relating to the accident.] The court

1. As an alternative § 20002(a)(2) requires that the driver shall "[l]eave in a conspicuous place on the vehicle or other property damaged a written notice giving the name and address of the driver and of the owner of the vehicle involved and a statement of the circumstances thereof and shall without unnecessary delay notify the police department...."

The California Supreme Court did not pass upon this part of the statute, and we express no opinion as to its validity. The violation of either part of the statute leaves the driver liable to imprisonment for up to six months or to a fine of up to $500.

The California Vehicle Code also requires drivers involved in accidents resulting in personal injury or death to file accident reports, but there is a statutory use restriction for these compelled disclosures. §§ 20012–20013.

concluded, however, that it would be "unfair" to punish Byers for his failure to comply with the statute because he could not reasonably have anticipated the judicial promulgation of the use restriction.[2] We granted certiorari, to assess the validity of the California Supreme Court's premise that without a use restriction § 20002(a)(1) would violate the privilege against compulsory self-incrimination. We conclude that there is no conflict between the statute and the privilege.

(1)

Whenever the Court is confronted with the question of a compelled disclosure that has an incriminating potential, the judicial scrutiny is invariably a close one. Tension between the State's demand for disclosures and the protection of the right against self-incrimination are likely to give rise to serious questions. Inevitably these must be resolved in terms of balancing the public need on the one hand, and the individual claim to constitutional protections on the other; neither interest can be treated lightly.

An organized society imposes many burdens on its constituents. It commands the filing of tax returns for income; it requires producers and distributors of consumer goods to file informational reports on the manufacturing process and the content of products, on the wages, hours, and working conditions of employees. Those who borrow money on the public market or issue securities for sale to the public must file various information reports; industries must report periodically the volume and content of pollutants discharged into our waters and atmosphere. Comparable examples are legion.

In each of these situations there is some possibility of prosecution—often a very real one—for criminal offenses disclosed by or deriving from the information which the law compels a person to supply. Information revealed by these reports could well be "a link in a chain" of evidence leading to prosecution and conviction. But under our holdings the mere possibility of incrimination is insufficient to defeat the strong policies in favor of a disclosure called for by statutes like the one challenged here.

United States v. Sullivan, 274 U.S. 259, 47 S.Ct. 607 (1927), shows that an application of the privilege to the California statute is not warranted. There a bootlegger was prosecuted for failure to file an income tax return. He claimed that the privilege against compulsory self-incrimination afforded him a complete defense because filing a return would have tended to incriminate him by revealing the unlawful source of his income. Speaking for the Court, Mr. Justice Holmes rejected this claim on the ground that it amounted to "an extreme if not

2. Presumably the California holding contemplated that persons who fail to comply with the statute in the future will be subject to prosecution and conviction since the use restriction removed the justification for a reasonable apprehension of self-incrimination. Our disposition removes the

an extravagant application of the Fifth Amendment." at 607.[3] Sullivan's tax return, of course, increased his risk of prosecution and conviction for violation of the National Prohibition Act. But the Court had no difficulty in concluding that an extension of the privilege to cover that kind of mandatory report would have been unjustified. In order to invoke the privilege it is necessary to show that the compelled disclosures will themselves confront the claimant with "substantial hazards of self-incrimination."

The components of this requirement were articulated in Albertson v. SACB ... (1965), and later in Marchetti v. United States (1968), Grosso v. United States ... (1968), and Haynes v. United States ... (1968). In *Albertson* the Court held that an order requiring registration by individual members of a Communist organization violated the privilege. There *Sullivan* was distinguished:

> "In *Sullivan* the questions in the income tax return were neutral on their face and directed at the public at large, but here they are directed at a *highly selective group inherently suspect of criminal activities*. Petitioners' claims are not asserted in an *essentially noncriminal* and *regulatory area* of inquiry, but against an inquiry in an area permeated with criminal statutes, where response to any of the ... questions in context might involve the petitioners in the admission of a crucial element of a crime." (emphasis added).

Albertson was followed by *Marchetti* and *Grosso* where the Court held that the privilege afforded a complete defense to prosecutions for noncompliance with federal gambling tax and registration requirements. It was also followed in *Haynes* where petitioner had been prosecuted for failure to register a firearm as required by federal statute. In each of these cases the Court found that compliance with the statutory disclosure requirements would confront the petitioner with "substantial hazards of self-incrimination." ...

In all of these cases the disclosures condemned were only those extracted from a "highly selective group inherently suspect of criminal activities" and the privilege was applied only in "an area permeated with criminal statutes"—not in "an essentially noncriminal and regulatory area of inquiry." ...

Although the California Vehicle Code defines some criminal offenses, the statute is essentially regulatory, not criminal. The California Supreme Court noted that § 20002(a)(1) was not intended to facilitate criminal convictions but to promote the satisfaction of civil liabilities arising from automobile accidents. In *Marchetti* the Court rested on the

premise upon which the use restriction rested.

3. "As the defendant's income was taxed, the statute of course required a return.... In the decision that this was contrary to the Constitution we are of opinion that the protection of the Fifth Amendment was pressed too far. If the form of return provided called for answers that the defendant was privileged from making he could have raised the objection in the return, *but could not on that account refuse to make any return at all*." (emphasis added).

reality that almost everything connected with gambling is illegal under "comprehensive" state and federal statutory schemes. The Court noted that in almost every conceivable situation compliance with the statutory gambling requirements would have been incriminating. Largely because of these pervasive criminal prohibitions, gamblers were considered by the Court to be "a highly selective group inherently suspect of criminal activities."

In contrast, § 20002(a)(1), like income tax laws, is directed at all persons—here all persons who drive automobiles in California. This group, numbering as it does in the millions, is so large as to render § 20002(a)(1) a statute "directed at the public at large." ... It is difficult to consider this group as either "highly selective" or "inherently suspect of criminal activities." Driving an automobile, unlike gambling, is a lawful activity. Moreover, it is not a criminal offense under California law to be a driver "involved in an accident." An accident may be the fault of others; it may occur without any driver having been at fault. No empirical data is suggested in support of the conclusion that there is a relevant correlation between being a driver and criminal prosecution of drivers. So far as any available information instructs us, most accidents occur without creating criminal liability even if one or both of the drivers are guilty of negligence as a matter of tort law.

The disclosure of inherently illegal activity is inherently risky. Our decisions in *Albertson* and the cases following illustrate that truism. But disclosures with respect to automobile accidents simply do not entail the kind of substantial risk of self-incrimination involved in *Marchetti, Grosso,* and *Haynes.* Furthermore, the statutory purpose is noncriminal and self-reporting is indispensible to its fulfillment.

(2)

Even if we were to view the statutory reporting requirement as incriminating in the traditional sense, in our view it would be the "extravagant" extension of the privilege Justice Holmes warned against to hold that it is testimonial in the Fifth Amendment sense. Compliance with § 20002(a)(1) requires two things: first, a driver involved in an accident is required to stop at the scene; second, he is required to give his name and address. The act of stopping is no more testimonial—indeed less so in some respects—than requiring a person in custody to stand or walk in a police lineup, to speak prescribed words, to give samples of handwriting, fingerprints or blood.... Disclosure of name and address is an essentially neutral act. Whatever the collateral consequences of disclosing name and address, the statutory purpose is to implement the state police power to regulate use of motor vehicles.

* * *

Stopping in compliance with § 20002(a)(1) ... does not provide the State with "evidence of a testimonial or communicative nature" within the meaning of the Constitution. It merely provides the State and private parties with the driver's identity for, among other valid state needs, the study of causes of vehicle accidents and related purposes, always subject to the driver's right to assert a Fifth Amendment privilege concerning specific inquiries.

Petitioner argues that since the statutory duty to stop is imposed only on the "driver of any vehicle involved in an accident," a driver's compliance is testimonial because his action gives rise to an inference that he believes that he was the "driver of a vehicle involved in an accident." From this, the petitioner tells us, it can be further inferred that he was indeed the operator of an "accident involved" vehicle. In [United States v. Wade (1967)], however, the Court rejected the notion that such inferences are communicative or testimonial. There the petitioner was placed in a lineup to be viewed by persons who had witnessed a bank robbery. At one point he was compelled to speak the words alleged to have been used by the perpetrator. Despite the inference that the petitioner uttered the words in his normal undisguised voice, the Court held that the utterances were not of a "testimonial" nature in the sense of the Fifth Amendment privilege even though the speaking might well have led to identifying him as the bank robber. Furthermore, the Court noted in *Wade* that no question was presented as to the admissibility in evidence at trial of anything said or done at the lineup.... Similarly no such problem is presented here. Of course, a suspect's normal voice characteristics, like his handwriting, blood, fingerprints, or body may prove to be the crucial link in a chain of evidentiary factors resulting in prosecution and conviction. Yet such evidence may be used against a defendant.

After having stopped, a driver involved in an accident is required by § 20002(a)(1) to notify the driver of the other vehicle of his name and address. A name, linked with a motor vehicle, is no more incriminating than the tax return, linked with the disclosure of income,.... It identifies but does not by itself implicate anyone in criminal conduct.

Although identity, when made known, may lead to inquiry that in turn leads to arrest and charge, those developments depend on different factors and independent evidence. Here the compelled disclosure of identity could have led to a charge that might not have been made had the driver fled the scene; but this is true only in the same sense that a taxpayer can be charged on the basis of the contents of a tax return or failure to file an income tax form. There is no constitutional right to refuse to file an income tax return or to flee the scene of an accident in order to avoid the possibility of legal involvement.

The judgment of the California Supreme Court is vacated and the case is remanded for further proceedings not inconsistent with this opinion.

Vacated and remanded.

[Justice Harlan wrote a very lengthy concurring opinion. Due to its length, and to the fact that what he had to say is discussed in the dissenting opinion, we are herewith reporting what we consider to be the core of his viewpoint.]

[The concurring opinion of Justice Harlan, and dissenting opinions of Justice Black and Brennan are omitted.]

NOTES

1. Where a defendant introduces psychiatric testimony to rebut the intent element of a murder charge at trial, can he be compelled to submit to an examination by a state psychiatrist whose trial testimony will be used in rebuttal? This was held to violate the defendant's privilege against self-incrimination. It was distinguished from the situation in which a defendant presents an insanity defense. Such a defense impliedly admits the state's charges, while a challenge to the intent element does not admit the crime. The state also has other ways, besides compelling a psychiatric examination, in which to respond to a challenge to the intent element. State v. Vosler, 216 Neb. 461, 345 N.W.2d 806 (1984).

2. Where a prosecutor obtained a lawyer's bookkeeping records from a lawyer disciplinary board that had been obtained by the board during the course of an investigation, this did not violate the lawyer's Fifth Amendment privilege or the confidentiality provisions of ethics rules promulgated by the state. The state-imposed confidentiality was not intended to shield a lawyer's unethical or criminal activities against self-incrimination. State v. Stroger, 97 N.J. 391, 478 A.2d 1175 (1984).

3. Defendant, as the president of two closely held corporations, was presented with a subpoena for the records of the corporations in his custodial capacity; the subpoena did not require him to testify. Defendant and his family members were directors and officers of the corporations, but had no authority over the business affairs of the corporations. He resisted the subpoena on the basis of his Fifth Amendment privilege against self-incrimination.

The Court denied defendant's self-incrimination claim. Since the records were held by defendant in his representative capacity, rather than his personal capacity, the privilege did not apply. The privilege is personal in nature and not applicable to corporations. The result would not be changed even if production of the records would "tend" to incriminate the defendant. Because of his representative capacity, his claim of privilege was tantamount to a claim of privilege on behalf of the corporations. The act of production, however, is strictly an act of the corporation, and thus the prosecution could make no evidentiary use of the "individual act" of production against the defendant. Braswell v. United States, 487 U.S. 99, 108 S.Ct. 2284 (1988).

G. CRUEL AND UNUSUAL PUNISHMENT—THE DEATH PENALTY ISSUE

GREGG v. GEORGIA

Supreme Court of the United States, 1976.
428 U.S. 153, 96 S.Ct. 2909.

Judgment of the Court, and opinion of Mr. Justice Stewart, Mr. Justice Powell, and Mr. Justice Stevens, announced by Mr. Justice Stewart.

The issue in this case is whether the imposition of the sentence of death for the crime of murder under the law of Georgia violates the Eighth and Fourteenth Amendments.

I

The petitioner, Troy Gregg, was charged with committing armed robbery and murder. In accordance with Georgia procedure in capital cases, the trial was in two stages, a guilt stage and a sentencing stage. The evidence at the guilt trial established that on November 21, 1973, the petitioner and a traveling companion, Floyd Allen, while hitchhiking north in Florida were picked up by Fred Simmons and Bob Moore. Their car broke down, but they continued north after Simmons purchased another vehicle with some of the cash he was carrying. While still in Florida, they picked up another hitchhiker, Dennis Weaver, who rode with them to Atlanta, where he was let out about 11 p.m. A short time later the four men interrupted their journey for a rest stop along the highway. The next morning the bodies of Simmons and Moore were discovered in a ditch nearby.

On November 23, after reading about the shootings in an Atlanta newspaper, Weaver communicated with the Gwinnett County police and related information concerning the journey with the victims, including a description of the car. The next afternoon, the petitioner and Allen, while in Simmons' car, were arrested in Asheville, N.C. In the search incident to the arrest a .25-caliber pistol, later shown to be that used to kill Simmons and Moore, was found in the petitioner's pocket. After receiving the warnings required by Miranda v. Arizona, 384 U.S. 436, 86 S.Ct. 1602 (1966), and signing a written waiver of his rights, the petitioner signed a statement in which he admitted shooting, then robbing Simmons and Moore. He justified the slayings on grounds of self-defense. The next day, while being transferred to Lawrenceville, Ga., the petitioner and Allen were taken to the scene of the shootings. Upon arriving there, Allen recounted the events leading to the slayings. His version of these events was as follows: After Simmons and Moore left the car, the petitioner stated that he intended to rob them. The petitioner then took his pistol in hand and positioned himself on the car to improve his aim. As Simmons and Moore came up an embankment toward the car, the petitioner fired three shots and the two men fell near a ditch. The petitioner, at close range, then fired a shot into the head of each. He robbed them of valuables and drove away with Allen.

A medical examiner testified that Simmons died from a bullet wound in the eye and that Moore died from bullet wounds in the cheek and in the back of the head. He further testified that both men had several bruises and abrasions about the face and head which probably were sustained either from the fall into the ditch or from being dragged or pushed along the embankment. Although Allen did not testify, a police detective recounted the substance of Allen's statements about the slayings and indicated that directly after Allen had made these statements the petitioner had admitted that Allen's account was accurate.

The petitioner testified in his own defense. He confirmed that Allen had made the statements described by the detective, but denied their truth or ever having admitted to their accuracy. He indicated that he had shot Simmons and Moore because of fear and in self-defense, testifying they had attacked Allen and him, one wielding a pipe and the other a knife.

The trial judge submitted the murder charges to the jury on both felony-murder and nonfelony-murder theories. He also instructed on the issue of self-defense but declined to instruct on manslaughter. He submitted the robbery case to the jury on both an armed-robbery theory and on the lesser included offense of robbery by intimidation. The jury found the petitioner guilty of two counts of armed robbery and two counts of murder.

At the penalty stage, which took place before the same jury, neither the prosecutor nor the petitioner's lawyer offered any additional evidence. Both counsel, however, made lengthy arguments dealing generally with the propriety of capital punishment under the circumstances and with the weight of the evidence of guilt. The trial judge instructed the jury that it could recommend either a death sentence or a life prison sentence on each count. The judge further charged the jury that in determining what sentence was appropriate the jury was free to consider the facts and circumstances, if any, presented by the parties in mitigation or aggravation.

Finally, the judge instructed the jury that it "would not be authorized to consider [imposing] the penalty of death" unless it first found beyond a reasonable doubt one of these aggravating circumstances:

> "One—That the offense of murder was committed while the offender was engaged in the commission of two other capital felonies, to-wit the armed robbery of [Simmons and Moore].
>
> "Two—That the offender committed the offense of murder for the purpose of receiving money and the automobile described in the indictment.
>
> "Three—The offense of murder was outrageously and wantonly vile, horrible and inhuman, in that they [*sic*] involved the depravity of [the] mind of the defendant."

Finding the first and second of these circumstances, the jury returned verdicts of death on each count.

The Supreme Court of Georgia affirmed the convictions and the imposition of the death sentences for murder. After reviewing the trial transcript and the record, including the evidence, and comparing the evidence and sentence in similar cases in accordance with the requirements of Georgia law, the court concluded that, considering the nature of the crime and the defendant, the sentences of death had not resulted from prejudice or any other arbitrary factor and were not excessive or disproportionate to the penalty applied in similar cases. The death sentences imposed for armed robbery, however, were vacated on the grounds that the death penalty had rarely been imposed in Georgia for that offense and that the jury improperly considered the murders as aggravating circumstances for the robberies after having considered the armed robberies as aggravating circumstances for the murders. . . .

II

Before considering the issues presented it is necessary to understand the Georgia statutory scheme for the imposition of the death penalty. The Georgia statute, as amended after our decision in Furman v. Georgia, 408 U.S. 238, 92 S.Ct. 2726 (1972), retains the death penalty for six categories of crime: murder, kidnapping for ransom or where the victim is harmed, armed robbery, rape, treason, and aircraft hijacking. The capital defendant's guilt or innocence is determined in the traditional manner, either by a trial judge or a jury, in the first stage of a bifurcated trial.

If trial is by jury, the trial judge is required to charge lesser included offenses when they are supported by any view of the evidence. After a verdict, finding, or plea of guilty to a capital crime, a presentence hearing is conducted before whoever made the determination of guilt. The sentencing procedures are essentially the same in both bench and jury trials. At the hearing:

> "[T]he judge [or jury] shall hear additional evidence in extenuation, mitigation and aggravation of punishment, including the record of any prior criminal convictions and pleas of guilty or pleas of nolo contendere of the defendant, or the absence of any prior conviction and pleas: Provided, however, that only such evidence in aggravation as the State has made known to the defendant prior to his trial shall be admissible. The judge [or jury] shall also hear argument by the defendant or his counsel and the prosecuting attorney ... regarding the punishment to be imposed."

The defendant is accorded substantial latitude as to the types of evidence that he may introduce. Evidence considered during the guilt stage may be considered during the sentencing stage without being resubmitted.

In the assessment of the appropriate sentence to be imposed the judge is also required to consider or to include in his instructions to the jury "any mitigating circumstances or aggravating circumstances otherwise authorized by law and any of [10] statutory aggravating circumstances which may be supported by the evidence. . . ." The scope of the nonstatutory aggravating or mitigating circumstances is not delineated in the statute. Before a convicted defendant may be sentenced to death, however, except in cases of treason or aircraft hijacking, the jury, or the trial judge in cases tried without a jury, must find beyond a reasonable doubt one of the 10 aggravating circumstances specified in the statute.[1]

1. The statute provides in part:

"(a) The death penalty may be imposed for the offenses of aircraft hijacking or treason, in any case.

The sentence of death may be imposed only if the jury (or judge) finds one of the statutory aggravating circumstances and then elects to impose that sentence. If the verdict is death, the jury or judge must specify the aggravating circumstance(s) found. In jury cases, the trial judge is bound by the jury's recommended sentence.

In addition to the conventional appellate process available in all criminal cases, provision is made for special expedited direct review by the Supreme Court of Georgia of the appropriateness of imposing the sentence of death in the particular case. The court is directed to consider "the punishment as well as any errors enumerated by way of appeal," and to determine:

> "(1) Whether the sentence of death was imposed under the influence of passion, prejudice, or any other arbitrary factor, and

"(b) In all cases of other offenses for which the death penalty may be authorized, the judge shall consider, or he shall include in his instructions to the jury for it to consider, any mitigating circumstances or aggravating circumstances otherwise authorized by law and any of the following statutory aggravating circumstances which may be supported by the evidence:

"(1) The offense of murder, rape, armed robbery, or kidnapping was committed by a person with a prior record of conviction for a capital felony, or the offense of murder was committed by a person who has a substantial history of serious assaultive criminal convictions.

"(2) The offense of murder, rape, armed robbery, or kidnapping was committed while the offender was engaged in the commission of another capital felony, or aggravated battery, or the offense of murder was committed while the offender was engaged in the commission of burglary or arson in the first degree.

"(3) The offender by his act of murder, armed robbery, or kidnapping knowingly created a great risk of death to more than one person in a public place by means of a weapon or device which would normally be hazardous to the lives of more than one person.

"(4) The offender committed the offense of murder for himself or another, for the purpose of receiving money or any other thing of monetary value.

"(5) The murder of a judicial officer, former judicial officer, district attorney or solicitor or former district attorney or solicitor during or because of the exercise of his official duty.

"(6) The offender caused or directed another to commit murder or committed murder as an agent or employee of another person.

"(7) The offense of murder, rape, armed robbery, or kidnapping was outrageously or wantonly vile, horrible or inhuman in that it involved torture, depravity of mind, or an aggravated battery to the victim.

"(8) The offense of murder was committed against any peace officer, corrections employee or fireman while engaged in the performance of his official duties.

"(9) The offense of murder was committed by a person in, or who has escaped from, the lawful custody of a peace officer or place of lawful confinement.

"(10) The murder was committed for the purpose of avoiding, interfering with, or preventing a lawful arrest or custody in a place of lawful confinement, of himself or another.

"(c) The statutory instructions as determined by the trial judge to be warranted by the evidence shall be given in charge and in writing to the jury for its deliberation. The jury, if its verdict be a recommendation of death, shall designate in writing, signed by the foreman of the jury, the aggravating circumstance or circumstances which it found beyond a reasonable doubt. In non-jury cases the judge shall make such designation. Except in cases of treason or aircraft hijacking, unless at least one of the statutory aggravating circumstances enumerated in section 27–2534.1(b) is so found, the death penalty shall not be imposed." § 27–2534.1 (Supp.1975).

* * *

"(2) Whether, in cases other than treason or aircraft hijacking, the evidence supports the jury's or judge's finding of a statutory aggravating circumstance as enumerated in section 27.2534.1(b), and

"(3) Whether the sentence of death is excessive or disproportionate to the penalty imposed in similar cases, considering both the crime and the defendant."

If the court affirms a death sentence, it is required to include in its decision reference to similar cases that it has taken into consideration.

A transcript and complete record of the trial, as well as a separate report by the trial judge, are transmitted to the court for its use in reviewing the sentence. The report is in the form of a 6½-page questionnaire, designed to elicit information about the defendant, the crime, and the circumstances of the trial. It requires the trial judge to characterize the trial in several ways designed to test for arbitrariness and disproportionality of sentence. Included in the report are responses to detailed questions concerning the quality of the defendant's representation, whether race played a role in the trial, and, whether, in the trial court's judgment, there was any doubt about the defendant's guilt or the appropriateness of the sentence. A copy of the report is served upon defense counsel. Under its special review authority, the court may either affirm the death sentence or remand the case for resentencing. In cases in which the death sentence is affirmed there remains the possibility of executive clemency.

III

We address initially the basic contention that the punishment of death for the crime of murder is, under all circumstances, "cruel and unusual" in violation of the Eighth and Fourteenth Amendments of the Constitution....

The Court on a number of occasions has both assumed and asserted the constitutionality of capital punishment. In several cases that assumption provided a necessary foundation for the decision, as the Court was asked to decide whether a particular method of carrying out a capital sentence would be allowed to stand under the Eighth Amendment. But until Furman v. Georgia, 408 U.S. 238, 92 S.Ct. 2726 (1972) the Court never confronted squarely the fundamental claim that the punishment of death always, regardless of the enormity of the offense or the procedure followed in imposing the sentence, is cruel and unusual punishment in violation of the Constitution. Although this issue was presented and addressed in *Furman,* it was not resolved by the Court. Four Justices would have held that capital punishment is not unconstitutional *per se;* two Justices would have reached the opposite conclusion; and three Justices, while agreeing that the statutes then before the Court were invalid as applied, left open the question whether such punishment may ever be imposed. We now hold that the punishment of death does not invariably violate the Constitution....

The imposition of the death penalty for the crime of murder has a long history of acceptance both in the United States and in England.

Four years ago, the petitioners in *Furman* and its companion cases predicated their argument primarily upon the asserted proposition that standards of decency had evolved to the point where capital punishment no longer could be tolerated. The petitioners in those cases said, in effect, that the evolutionary process had come to an end, and that standards of decency required that the Eighth Amendment be construed finally as prohibiting capital punishment for any crime regardless of its depravity and impact on society. This view was accepted by two Justices. Three other Justices were unwilling to go so far; focusing on the procedures by which convicted defendants were selected for the death penalty rather than on the actual punishment inflicted, they joined in the conclusion that the statutes before the Court were constitutionally invalid.

The petitioners in the capital cases before the Court today renew the "standards of decency" argument, but developments during the four years since *Furman* have undercut substantially the assumptions upon which their argument rested. Despite the continuing debate, dating back to the 19th century, over the morality and utility of capital punishment, it is now evident that a large proportion of American society continues to regard it as an appropriate and necessary criminal sanction.

The most marked indication of society's endorsement of the death penalty for murder is the legislative response to *Furman*. The legislatures of at least 35 States have enacted new statutes that provide for the death penalty for at least some crimes that result in the death of another person. And the Congress of the United States, in 1974, enacted a statute providing the death penalty for aircraft piracy that results in death....

In the only statewide referendum occurring since *Furman* and brought to our attention, the people of California adopted a constitutional amendment that authorized capital punishment, in effect negating a prior ruling by the Supreme Court of California in People v. Anderson, 6 Cal.3d 628, 493 P.2d 880, cert. denied, 406 U.S. 958, 92 S.Ct. 2060 (1972), that the death penalty violated the California Constitution.

The jury also is a significant and reliable objective index of contemporary values because it is so directly involved. The Court has said that "one of the most important functions any jury can perform in making ... a selection [between life imprisonment and death for a defendant convicted in a capital case] is to maintain a link between contemporary community values and the penal system." Witherspoon v. Illinois, 391 U.S. 510, 519 n. 15, 88 S.Ct. 1770, 1775 (1968). It may be true that evolving standards have influenced juries in recent decades to be more discriminating in imposing the sentence of death. But the relative infrequency of jury verdicts imposing the death sentence does not indicate rejection of capital punishment *per se*.... Indeed, the actions of juries in many States since *Furman* are fully compatible with the legislative judgments, reflected in the new statutes, as to the continued utility and necessity of capital punishment in appropriate cases. At the close of 1974 at least 254 persons had been sentenced to death since *Furman,* and by the end of March 1976, more than 460 persons were subject to death sentences.

As we have seen, however, the Eighth Amendment demands more than that a challenged punishment be acceptable to contemporary society. The Court also must ask whether it comports with the basic concept of human dignity at the core of the Amendment. Trop v. Dulles, 356 U.S., at 100, 78 S.Ct., at 597 (plurality opinion). Although we cannot "invalidate a category of penalties because we deem less severe penalties adequate to serve the ends of penology," Furman v. Georgia, supra, 408 U.S., at 451, 92 S.Ct., at 2834 (Powell, J., dissenting), the sanction imposed cannot be so totally without penological justification that it results in the gratuitous infliction of suffering.

The death penalty is said to serve two principal social purposes: retribution and deterrence of capital crimes by prospective offenders.

In part, capital punishment is an expression of society's moral outrage at particularly offensive conduct. This function may be unappealing to many, but it is essential in an ordered society that asks its citizens to rely on legal processes rather than self-help to vindicate their wrongs.... "Retribution is no longer the dominant objective of the criminal law," Williams v. New York, 337 U.S. 241, 248, 69 S.Ct. 1079, 1084 (1949), but neither is it a forbidden objective nor one inconsistent with our respect for the dignity of men. Indeed, the decision that capital punishment may be the appropriate sanction in extreme cases is an expression of the community's belief that certain crimes are themselves so grievous an affront to humanity that the only adequate response may be the penalty of death.

Statistical attempts to evaluate the worth of the death penalty as a deterrent to crimes by potential offenders have occasioned a great deal of debate. The results simply have been inconclusive....

In sum, we cannot say that the judgment of the Georgia Legislature that capital punishment may be necessary in some cases is clearly wrong. Considerations of federalism, as well as respect for the ability of a legislature to evaluate, in terms of its particular State, the moral consensus concerning the death penalty and its social utility as a sanction, require us to conclude, in the absence of more convincing evidence that the infliction of death as a punishment for murder is not without justification and thus is not unconstitutionally severe.

Finally, we must consider whether the punishment of death is disproportionate in relation to the crime for which it is imposed. There is no question that death as a punishment is unique in its severity and irrevocability. When a defendant's life is at stake, the Court has been particularly sensitive to insure that every safeguard is observed. But we are concerned here only with the imposition of capital punishment for the crime of murder, and when a life has been taken deliberately by the offender,[2] we cannot say that the punishment is invariably disproportionate to the crime. It is an extreme sanction, suitable to the most extreme of crimes.

We hold that the death penalty is not a form of punishment that may never be imposed, regardless of the circumstances of the offense, regardless of the character of the offender, and regardless of the procedure followed in reaching the decision to impose it.

IV

We now consider whether Georgia may impose the death penalty on the petitioner in this case.

A

While *Furman* did not hold that the infliction of the death penalty *per se* violates the Constitution's ban on cruel and unusual punishments, it did recognize that the penalty of death is different in kind from any other punishment imposed under our system of criminal justice. Because of the uniqueness of the death penalty, *Furman* held that it could not be imposed under sentencing procedures that created a substantial risk that it would be inflicted in an arbitrary and capricious manner....

While some have suggested that standards to guide a capital jury's sentencing deliberations are impossible to formulate, the fact is that such standards have been developed. When the drafters of the Model Penal Code faced this problem, they concluded "that it is within the realm of possibility to point to the main circumstances of aggravation and of mitigation that should be weighed *and weighed against each other* when they are presented in a concrete case." ALI, Model Penal Code § 201.6, Comment 3, p. 71 (Tent.Draft No. 9, 1959, emphasis in original). While such standards are by necessity somewhat general, they do provide guidance to the sentencing authority and thereby reduce the likelihood that it will impose a sentence that fairly can be called capricious or arbitrary. Where the sentencing authority is required to specify the factors it relied upon in reaching its decision, the further safeguard of meaningful appellate review is available to ensure that death sentences are not imposed capriciously or in a freakish manner.

In summary, the concerns expressed in *Furman* that the penalty of death not be imposed in an arbitrary or capricious manner can be met by a carefully drafted statute that ensures that the sentencing authority is given adequate information and guidance. As a general proposition these concerns are best met by a system that provides for a bifurcated proceeding at which the sentencing authority is apprised of the information relevant to the imposition of sentence and provided with standards to guide its use of the information.

2. We do not address here the question whether the taking of the criminal's life is a proportionate sanction where no victim has been deprived of life—for example, when capital punishment is imposed for rape, kidnaping, or armed robbery that does not result in the death of any human being.

We do not intend to suggest that only the above-described procedures would be permissible under *Furman* or that any sentencing system constructed along these general lines would inevitably satisfy the concerns of *Furman,* for each distinct system must be examined on an individual basis. Rather, we have embarked upon this general exposition to make clear that it is possible to construct capital-sentencing systems capable of meeting *Furman's* constitutional concerns.

B

We now turn to consideration of the constitutionality of Georgia's capital-sentencing procedures. In the wake of *Furman,* Georgia amended its capital punishment statute, but chose not to narrow the scope of its murder provisions. See Part II, supra. Thus, now as before *Furman,* in Georgia "[a] person commits murder when he unlawfully and with malice aforethought, either express or implied, causes the death of another human being." All persons convicted of murder "shall be punished by death or by imprisonment for life."

Georgia did act, however, to narrow the class of murderers subject to capital punishment by specifying 10 statutory aggravating circumstances, one of which must be found by the jury to exist beyond a reasonable doubt before a death sentence can ever be imposed. In addition, the jury is authorized to consider any other appropriate aggravating or mitigating circumstances. The jury is not required to find any mitigating circumstance in order to make a recommendation of mercy that is binding on the trial court, but it must find a *statutory* aggravating circumstance before recommending a sentence of death. . . .

In short, Georgia's new sentencing procedures require as a prerequisite to the imposition of the death penalty, specific jury findings as to the circumstances of the crime or the character of the defendant. Moreover, to guard further against a situation comparable to that presented in *Furman,* the Supreme Court of Georgia compares each death sentence with the sentences imposed on similarly situated defendants to ensure that the sentence of death in a particular case is not disproportionate. On their face these procedures seem to satisfy the concerns of *Furman* . . . .

The petitioner contends, however, that the changes in the Georgia sentencing procedures are only cosmetic, that the arbitrariness and capriciousness condemned by *Furman* continue to exist in Georgia—both in traditional practices that still remain and in the new sentencing procedures adopted in response to *Furman.*

1

First, the petitioner focuses on the opportunities for discretionary action that are inherent in the processing of any murder case under Georgia law. He notes that the state prosecutor has unfettered authority to select those persons whom he wishes to prosecute for a capital offense and to plea bargain with them. Further, at the trial the jury may choose to convict a defendant of a lesser included offense rather than find him guilty of a crime punishable by death, even if the evidence would support a capital verdict. And finally, a defendant who is convicted and sentenced to die may have his sentence commuted by the Governor of the State and the Georgia Board of Pardons and Paroles.

The existence of these discretionary stages is not determinative of the issues before us. At each of these stages an actor in the criminal justice system makes a decision which may remove a defendant from consideration as a candidate for the death penalty. *Furman,* in contrast, dealt with the decision to impose the death sentence on a specific individual who had been convicted of a capital offense. Nothing in any of our cases suggests that the decision to afford an individual defendant mercy violates the Constitution. *Furman* held only that, in order to minimize the risk that the death penalty would be imposed on a capriciously selected group of offenders, the decision to impose it had to be guided by standards so that the sentencing authority would focus on the particularized circumstances of the crime and the defendant.

2

The petitioner further contends that the capital-sentencing procedures adopted by Georgia in response to *Furman* do not eliminate the dangers of arbitrariness and caprice in jury sentencing that were held in *Furman* to be violative of the Eighth and Fourteenth Amendments. He claims that the statute is so broad and vague as to leave juries free to act as arbitrarily and capriciously as they wish in deciding whether to impose the death penalty....

... We think that the Georgia court wisely has chosen not to impose unnecessary restrictions on the evidence that can be offered at such a hearing and to approve open and far-ranging argument. So long as the evidence introduced and the arguments made at the pre-sentence hearing do not prejudice a defendant, it is preferable not to impose restrictions. We think it desirable for the jury to have as much information before it as possible when it makes the sentencing decision.

3

Finally, the Georgia statute has an additional provision designed to assure that the death penalty will not be imposed on a capriciously selected group of convicted defendants. The new sentencing procedures require that the State Supreme Court review every death sentence to determine whether it was imposed under the influence of passion, prejudice, or any other arbitrary factor, whether the evidence supports the findings of a statutory aggravating circumstance, and "[w]hether the sentence of death is excessive or disproportionate to the penalty imposed in similar cases, considering both the crime and the defendant." In performing its sentence-review function, the Georgia court has held that "if the death penalty is only rarely imposed for an act or it is substantially out of line with sentences imposed for other acts it will be set aside as excessive." ...

It is apparent that the Supreme Court of Georgia has taken its review responsibilities seriously....

The provision for appellate review in the Georgia capital-sentencing system serves as a check against the random or arbitrary imposition of the death penalty. In particular, the proportionality review substantially eliminates the possibility that a person will be sentenced to die by the action of an aberrant jury. If a time comes when juries generally do not impose the death sentence in a certain kind of murder case, the appellate review procedures assure that no defendant convicted under such circumstances will suffer a sentence of death.

V

The basic concern of *Furman* centered on those defendants who were being condemned to death capriciously and arbitrarily. Under the procedures before the Court in that case, sentencing authorities were not directed to give attention to the nature or circumstances of the crime committed or to the character or record of the defendant. Left unguided, juries imposed the death sentence in a way that could only be called freakish. The new Georgia sentencing procedures, by contrast, focus the jury's attention on the particularized nature of the crime and the particularized characteristics of the individual defendant. While the jury is permitted to consider any aggravating or mitigating circumstances, it must find and identify at least one statutory aggravating factor before it may impose a penalty of death. In this way the jury's discretion is channeled. No longer can a jury wantonly and freakishly impose the death sentence; it is always circumscribed by the legislative guidelines. In addition, the review function of the Supreme Court of Georgia affords additional assurance that the concerns that prompted our decision in *Furman* are not present to any significant degree in the Georgia procedure applied here.

For the reasons expressed in this opinion, we hold that the statutory system under which Gregg was sentenced to death does not violate the Constitution. Accordingly, the judgment of the Georgia Supreme Court is affirmed.

[The concurring opinion of Mr. Justice White, with whom the Chief Justice and Mr. Justice Rehnquist join, is omitted. The statements of the Chief Justice and Mr. Justice Rehnquist, as well as the brief concurrence by Mr. Justice Blackmun, are also omitted.]

[The dissenting opinions of Justices Brennan and Marshall are omitted. They argued, as they have in almost every death penalty case since Gregg v. Georgia, that the penalty is unconstitutionally vague and does not serve as a deterrence.]

BALDWIN v. ALABAMA

Supreme Court of the United States, 1985.
472 U.S. 372, 105 S.Ct. 2727.

JUSTICE BLACKMUN delivered the opinion of the Court.

Between 1976 and 1981, an Alabama statute required a jury that convicted a defendant of any one of a number of specified crimes "with aggravation" to "fix the punishment at death." Ala.Code § 13–11–2(a) (1975).[1] The "sentence" imposed by the jury, however, was not dispositive. Instead, "[n]otwithstanding the fixing of the punishment at death by the jury," § 13–11–4, the trial judge then was to hear evidence of aggravating and mitigating circumstances and, after weighing those circumstances, to sentence the defendant to death or to life imprisonment without parole.

This case concerns the constitutionality of the peculiar and unusual requirement of the 1975 Alabama Act that the jury "shall fix the punishment at death," even though the trial judge is the actual sentencing authority.[2] The United States Court of Appeals for the Eleventh Circuit ruled that the scheme was facially unconstitutional. Ritter v. Smith, 726 F.2d 1505, 1515–1517, cert. denied, ___ U.S. ___ (1984). Shortly thereafter, however, the Supreme Court of Alabama, with two dissenting votes, ruled to the contrary in the present case. Ex Parte Baldwin, 456 So.2d 129, 138–139 (1984). We granted certiorari to resolve this significant conflict. ___ U.S. ___ (1984).

I

A

The facts are sordid, but a brief recital of them must be made. Petitioner Brian Keith Baldwin, then 18 years of age, escaped from a North Carolina prison camp on Saturday, March 12, 1977. That evening, he and a fellow escapee, Edward Horsley, came upon 16-year-old Naomi Rolon, who was having trouble with her automobile. The two forcibly took over her car and drove her to Charlotte, N.C. There, both men attempted to rape her, petitioner sodomized her, and the two attempted to choke her to death. They then ran over her with the car, locked her in its trunk, and left her there while they drove through

1. The originating statute was 1975 Ala. Acts, No. 213, effective March 7, 1976. Act No. 213 was enacted in response to this Court's decision in Furman v. Georgia, 408 U.S. 238 (1972), and revised the State's death-penalty statutes. Chapter 11 of Title 13 of the Alabama Code, as it thereafter stood, was repealed in its entirety and replaced by new death-penalty provisions set forth in 1981 Ala.Acts, No. 81–178, effective July 1, 1981. The repeal did not moot the present case because petitioner's offense was committed and his sentence was imposed in 1977 while the 1975 Act was in effect. See 1981 Ala.Acts, §§ 19 and 20, codified as Ala.Code, § 13A–5–57 (1982).

2. Our own research has disclosed no other death-penalty statute currently in effect that *requires* the jury to return a death "sentence," but then has the judge make the actual sentencing decision. Indeed, as is noted herein, Alabama has changed its death-penalty scheme and no longer has the requirement.

Georgia and Alabama. Twice, when they heard the young woman cry out, they stopped the car, opened the trunk, and stabbed her repeatedly. On Monday afternoon, they stole a pickup truck, drove both vehicles to a secluded spot, and, after again using the car to run over the victim, cut her throat with a hatchet. She died after this 40-hour ordeal.

Petitioner was apprehended the following day driving the stolen truck. He was charged with theft. While in custody, he confessed to the victim's murder and led the police to her body. He was then indicted for "robbery ... when the victim is intentionally killed," a capital offense, § 13–11–2(a)(2), and was tried before a jury in Monroe County. At the close of the evidence regarding guilt or innocence, the judge instructed the jury that if it found the petitioner guilty, "the Legislature of the State of Alabama has said this is a situation [in] which ... the punishment would be death by electrocution," Tr. 244–245, and the jury therefore would be required to sentence petitioner to death. Id., at 242. The jury found petitioner guilty, in the terms of the statute, of robbery with the aggravated circumstance of intentionally killing the victim, and returned a verdict form that stated: "We, the Jury, find the defendant guilty as charged in the indictment and fix his punishment at death by electrocution." App. 4.

B

Under Alabama's 1975 Death Penalty Act, once a defendant was convicted of any one of 14 specified aggravated offenses, see Ala.Code § 13–11–2(a) (1975), and the jury returned the required death sentence, the trial judge was obligated to hold a sentencing hearing:

> "[T]he court shall thereupon hold a hearing to aid the court to determine whether or not the court will sentence the defendant to death or to life imprisonment without parole. In the hearing, evidence may be presented as to any matter that the court deems relevant to sentence and shall include any matters relating to any of the aggravating or mitigating circumstances enumerated in sections 13–11–6 and 13–11–7." § 13–11–3.

The judge was then required to sentence the defendant to death or to life imprisonment without parole:

> "Notwithstanding the fixing of the punishment at death by the jury, the court, after weighing the aggravating and mitigating circumstances, may refuse to accept the death penalty as fixed by the jury and sentence the defendant to life imprisonment without parole, which shall be served without parole; or the court, after weighing the aggravating and mitigating circumstances, and the fixing of the punishment at death by the jury, may accordingly sentence the defendant to death." § 13–11–4.

If the court imposed a death sentence, it was required to set forth in writing the factual findings from the trial and the sentencing hearing, including the aggravating and mitigating circumstances that formed the basis for the sentence. Ibid. The judgment of conviction and sentence of death were subject to automatic review by the Court of Criminal Appeals, and, if that court affirmed, by the Supreme Court of Alabama. §§ 13–11–5, 12–22–150; Ala.Rules App.Proc. 39(c). See Beck v. State, 396 So.2d 645, 664 (Ala.1981); Evans v. Birtton, 472 F.Supp. 707, 713–714, 723–724 (SD Ala.1979), rev'd on other grounds, 628 F.2d 400 (CA5 1980), 639 F.2d 221 (CA5 1981), rev'd *sub nom.* Hopper v. Evans, 456 U.S. 605 (1982).

C

Following petitioner's conviction, the trial judge held the sentencing hearing required by § 13–11–3. The State reintroduced the evidence submitted at trial, and introduced petitioner's juvenile and adult criminal records, as well as Edward Horsley's statement regarding the crime. Petitioner then took the stand and testified that he had "a hard time growing up"; that he left home at the age of 13 because his father did not like him to come home late at night; that he dropped out of school after the ninth grade; that he made a living by "street hustling"; that he had been arrested approximately 30 times; and that he was a drug addict. App. 8–10. At the conclusion of petitioner's testimony, the trial judge stated:

> "Brian Keith Baldwin, today is the day you have in court to tell this judge whatever is on your mind . . ., now is your time to tell the judge anything that you feel like might be helpful to you in the position that you find yourself in. I want to give you every opportunity in the world that I know about. . . . Anything you feel like you can tell this Judge that will help you in your present position." Id., at 12.

Petitioner then complained about various aspects of his trial, and concluded: "I ain't saying I'm guilty but I might be guilty for murder but I ain't guilty for robbery down here. That's all I got to say." Id., at 13.

The judge stated that "having considered the evidence presented at the trial and at said sentence hearing," id., at 17–18, the court found the following aggravating circumstances: the capital offense was committed while petitioner was under a sentence of imprisonment in the State of North Carolina from which he had escaped; petitioner previously had pleaded guilty to a felony involving the use of violence to the person; the capital offense was committed while petitioner was committing a robbery or in flight after the robbery; and the offense was especially heinous, atrocious, or cruel.[3] The judge found that petitioner's age—18 at the

3. The sentencing judge found, as an additional aggravating factor, that petitioner had been adjudged delinquent in juvenile proceedings after being charged with kidnaping and rape. The Alabama Court of Criminal Appeals ruled that the delinquency adjudication was not valid as an aggravating circumstance, but held that the judge's consideration of it was harmless error. 456 So.2d 117, 125–128 (1983), aff'd, 456 So.2d 129 (Ala.1984). That issue was not raised in the petition for certiorari here, and we have no reason to consider it.

time of the crime—was the only mitigating circumstance. Id., at 18. He then stated:

> "The Court having considered the aggravating circumstances and the mitigating circumstances and after weighing the aggravating and mitigating circumstances, it is the judgment of the Court that the aggravating circumstances far outweigh the mitigating circumstances and that the death penalty as fixed by the jury should be and is hereby accepted." Ibid.

The Supreme Court of Alabama eventually affirmed the conviction and sentence. 456 So.2d 129 (1984).[4] In his argument to that court, petitioner contended that the 1975 Act was facially invalid. Tracking the reasoning of the Eleventh Circuit in Ritter v. Smith, 726 F.2d, at 1516–1517, he argued that the jury's mandatory sentence was unconstitutional because it was unguided, standardless, and reflected no consideration of the particular defendant or crime, and that the judge's sentence was unconstitutional because it was based in part upon consideration of the impermissible jury sentence and was infected by it. The court rejected petitioner's arguments, holding that even though the jury had no discretion regarding the "sentence" it would impose, the sentencing procedure was saved by the fact that it was the trial judge who was the true sentencing authority, and he considered aggravating and mitigating circumstances before imposing sentence. 456 So.2d, at 139.[5]

4. Petitioner's conviction and sentence were affirmed initially by the Alabama Court of Criminal Appeals, 372 So.2d 26 (1978), and by the Supreme Court of Alabama, 372 So.2d 32 (1979). This Court, however, 448 U.S. 903 (1980), vacated and remanded the case for reconsideration in the light of Beck v. Alabama, 447 U.S. 625 (1980), which held unconstitutional a clause in Alabama's 1975 Act that precluded the jury from considering lesser-included non-capital offenses. On remand, the Court of Criminal Appeals reversed the judgment of conviction on the basis of *Beck*. 405 So.2d 699 (1981). After this Court ruled that due process requires a lesser-included offense instruction only when warranted by the evidence, Hopper v. Evans, 456 U.S. 605 (1982), the Court of Criminal Appeals granted rehearing, rescinded its earlier reversal, and reaffirmed petitioner's conviction and sentence. 456 So.2d 117 (1983). The Supreme Court of Alabama affirmed that decision, 456 So.2d 129 (1984), and it is that judgment which we now review.

5. The Court of Criminal Appeals, as has been noted in the text, must review the decision of a trial court that imposes the death penalty, § 12–22–150, and if that court affirms the sentence, certiorari review by the Supreme Court of Alabama is automatic. Ala.Rule App.Proc. 39(c). Both appellate courts "review ... the aggravating and mitigating circumstances found in the case by the trial judge" and independently weigh those circumstances to determine whether the imposition of a death sentence is appropriate. Jacobs v. State, 361 So.2d 640, 647 (Ala.1978) (Torbert, C.J., concurring in part and dissenting in part), cert. denied, 439 U.S. 1122 (1979); see also Beck v. State, 396 So.2d 645, 664 (Ala.1981). In reviewing petitioner's sentence, neither appellate court gave any indication of including the jury's "sentence" in the weighing. In describing its review of petitioner's sentence, the Court of Criminal Appeals stated:

> "We have reviewed the aggravating and mitigating circumstances set out in the record and the trial court's findings relative to those circumstances.... After review of the hearing on aggravating and mitigating circumstances, we find no error on the part of the trial court in reaching the conclusion that the aggravating circumstances far outweigh the mitigating circumstances in this case. The sentence fits the crime." 372 So.2d, at 32.

Upon reaffirming petitioner's conviction in light of Hopper v. Evans, 456 U.S. 605 (1982), the Court of Criminal Appeals again noted its obligation to weigh independently the aggravating and mitigating circum-

II

If the jury's "sentence" were indeed the dispositive sentence, the Alabama scheme would be unconstitutional under the principles announced in Woodson v. North Carolina, 428 U.S. 280 (1976) (plurality opinion), and Roberts (Stanislaus) v. Louisiana, 428 U.S. 325 (1976) (plurality opinion). See also Roberts (Harry) v. Louisiana, 431 U.S. 633 (1977). In *Woodson,* the Court held that North Carolina's sentencing scheme, which imposed a mandatory death sentence for a broad category of homicidal offenses, violated the Eighth and Fourteenth Amendments in three respects. First, such mandatory schemes offend contemporary standards of decency, as evidenced by the frequency with which jurors avoid the imposition of mandatory death sentences by disregarding their oaths and refusing to convict, and by the consistent movement of the States and Congress away from such schemes. 428 U.S., at 288–301. Second, by refusing to convict defendants who the jurors think do not deserve the death penalty, juries exercise unguided and unchecked discretion regarding who will be sentenced to death. Id., at 302–303. Third, such mandatory schemes fail to allow particularized consideration of the character and record of the defendant and the circumstances of the offense. Id., at 303–305. Alabama's requirement that the jury impose a mandatory sentence for a wide range of homicides, standing alone, would suffer each of those defects.

The jury's mandatory "sentence," however, does not stand alone under the Alabama scheme. Instead, as has been described above, the trial judge thereafter conducts a separate hearing to receive evidence of aggravating and mitigating circumstances, and determines whether the aggravating circumstances outweigh the mitigating circumstances. The judge's discretion is guided by the requirement that the death penalty be imposed only if the judge finds the aggravating circumstance that serves to define the capital crime—in this case the fact that the homicide took place during the commission of a robbery—and only if the judge finds that the definitional aggravating circumstance, plus any other specified aggravating circumstance,[6] outweighs any statutory and nonstatutory mitigating circumstances. § 13–11–4. Petitioner accordingly does not argue that the judge's discretion under § 13–11–4 is not "suitably directed and limited so as to minimize the risk of wholly arbitrary and capricious action," Gregg v. Georgia, 428 U.S. 153, 189 (1976) (opinion of

stances, and found that petitioner's death sentence was appropriate. 456 So.2d, at 128. The State Supreme Court also found that the "aggravating circumstances greatly outweighed the mitigating circumstances." 456 So.2d, at 140.

6. See § 13–11–6. The 1975 Act required the judge to weigh aggravating circumstances specified in § 13–11–6 against mitigating circumstances. The Alabama courts interpreted the Act, however, to require the judge to find the presence of the § 13–11–2(a) definitional aggravating circumstance (in other words, to agree with the jury's finding that the defendant is guilty of the offense charged in the indictment) before weighing any § 13–11–6 aggravating circumstances against mitigating circumstances. Ex Parte Kyzer, 399 So.2d 330 (Ala.1981). Generally, the definitional aggravating circumstances of § 13–11–2(a) have counterparts in § 13–11–6. Where there is no counterpart, the judge must find the definitional aggravating circumstance or no death sentence can be imposed, even though § 13–11–6 aggravating circumstances outweigh mitigating circumstances. 399 So.2d, at 337.

STEWART, POWELL, and STEVENS, JJ.). Nor is there any issue before this Court that the 1975 Act did not allow "the type of individualized consideration of mitigating factors" by the sentencing judge that has been held constitutionally indispensable in capital cases.[7] Lockett v. Ohio, 438 U.S. 586, 606 (1978) (plurality opinion); see also Eddings v. Oklahoma, 455 U.S. 104 (1982); Woodson v. North Carolina, 428 U.S., at 304 (plurality opinion).

Petitioner's challenge to the Alabama scheme rests instead on the provision of the 1975 Act that allows the judge to weigh "the aggravating and mitigating circumstances, and the fixing of the punishment at death by the jury" in determining whether death is the appropriate sentence. § 13–11–4. This Court has stated that a death sentence based upon consideration of "factors that are constitutionally impermissible or totally irrelevant to the sentencing process, such as for example the race, religion, or political affiliation of the defendant," would violate the Constitution. Zant v. Stephens, 462 U.S. 862, 885 (1983). Relying upon *Zant,* petitioner contends that, because the jury's mandatory "sentence" would be unconstitutional standing alone, it is an impermissible factor for the trial judge to consider, as the statute appears to require, in the sentencing process. That argument conceivably might have merit if the judge actually were required to consider the jury's "sentence" as a recommendation as to the sentence the jury believed would be appropriate, cf. Proffitt v. Florida, 428 U.S. 242 (1976), and if the judge were obligated to accord some deference to it. The jury's verdict is not considered in that fashion, however, as the Alabama appellate courts' construction of the Act, as well as the judge's statements regarding the process by which he arrived at the sentence, so definitely indicate.

A

The language of § 13–11–4, to be sure, in so many words does not preclude the sentencing judge from considering the jury's "sentence" in determining whether the death penalty is appropriate. The first clause of the section—"the court, after weighing the aggravating and mitigating circumstances, may refuse to accept the death penalty as fixed by the

7. In his statement of facts, petitioner asserts that the sentencing judge limited his consideration of mitigating circumstances to those specified by § 13–11–7, in violation of Lockett v. Ohio, 438 U.S. 586 (1978) (plurality opinion). That issue was not addressed by the Supreme Court of Alabama in the decision under review, and was not raised in the petition for certiorari. We have no reason to consider the issue here. We note, however, that in its first review of petitioner's sentence, the Court of Criminal Appeals held that petitioner "was given the opportunity to present *any* mitigating circumstance" (emphasis supplied), and that the 1975 Act did not preclude consideration of any aspect of petitioner's character or of the circumstances of the offense. 372 So.2d, at 32. We already have noted that the sentencing judge asked petitioner to "tell the judge anything that you feel like might be helpful to you in the position you find yourself in." App. 12. Petitioner's counsel three times asked petitioner while he was on the stand if there was "anything else you would like for the judge to know or to be able to tell him at this point?" Id., at 10–11. Finally, at the conclusion of petitioner's testimony, the judge asked petitioner's counsel if he had "anything else that you might be able to offer in the way of mitigating circumstances." Id., at 14.

jury and sentence the defendant to life imprisonment without parole"—does not authorize or require the court to weigh the jury's "sentence" in determining whether to refuse to impose the death penalty. The second clause—"or the court, after weighing the aggravating and mitigating circumstances, and the fixing of death by the jury, may accordingly sentence the defendant to death"—does seem to authorize consideration of the jury's "sentence." It is not clear whether the second clause allows consideration of the jury's "sentence" only if the weighing of the aggravating and mitigating circumstances authorized in the first clause has indicated that the "sentence" should not be rejected, or whether the second clause allows the judge to ignore the first clause and count the jury's "sentence" as a factor, similar to an aggravating circumstance, weighing in favor of the death penalty. We therefore look to the Alabama courts' construction of § 13–11–4. See Proffitt v. Florida, supra; Jurek v. Texas, 428 U.S. 262, 272–273 (1976) (opinion of STEWART, POWELL, and STEVENS, JJ.).

The Alabama appellate courts have interpreted the 1975 Act expressly to mean that the sentencing judge is to impose a sentence without regard to the jury's mandatory "sentence." The Alabama Court of Criminal Appeals has stated: "The jury's function is only to find guilt or innocence. The jury is not the sentencing authority." Jacobs v. State, 361 So.2d 607, 631 (1977), aff'd, 361 So.2d 640 (Ala.1978), cert. denied, 439 U.S. 1122 (1979). Indeed, the court has gone so far as to state:

> "No sentence exists until the pronouncement by the trial judge at the conclusion of the sentence hearing. It is for this reason that the court cannot be said to be commuting a sentence of death imposed by the jury, but, in truth and in fact, it is sentencing the accused after a jury's finding of guilt." Beck v. State, 365 So.2d 985, 1005, aff'd, 365 So.2d 1006 (Ala.1978), rev'd on other grounds, 447 U.S. 625 (1980).

The court further has described the judge's role as follows:

> "The sentencing hearing is one of the most important and critical stages under Alabama's death penalty law. The guilt stage has passed. Now an experienced trial judge must consider the particularized circumstances surrounding the offense and the offender and determine if the accused is to die or be sentenced to life imprisonment without parole.... The trial evidence must be reviewed to determine all of the aggravating circumstances leading up to and culminating in the death of the victim and then all the mitigating circumstances must be considered in determining if any outweigh the aggravating circumstances so found in the trial court's findings of fact." Richardson v. State, 376 So.2d 205, 224 (1978), aff'd, 376 So.2d 228 (Ala.1979).

Conspicuously absent from the court's description of the judge's duty is any mention of according weight or deference to the jury's "sentence."

The Supreme Court of Alabama agrees that "the jury is not the sentencing authority in ... Alabama," and has described the sentencing judge not as a reviewer of the jury's "sentence," but as *the* sentencer:

> "In Alabama, the jury is not the body which finally determines which murderers must die and which must not. In fact, Alabama's statute *mandatorily* requires the court to 'hold a hearing to aid the court to determine whether or not the court will *sentence* the defendant to death or to life imprisonment without parole,' and specifically provides that the court may refuse to accept the death penalty as fixed by the jury and may 'sentence' the defendant to death or life without parole. Code of Ala.1975, § 13–11–4. That section provides that if the *court* imposes a 'sentence of death' it must set forth, in writing, the basis for the sentence." Jacobs v. State, 361 So.2d 640, 644 (1978), cert. denied, 439 U.S. 1122 (1979) (emphasis in original; footnote omitted).

See also Ritter v. State, 429 So.2d 928, 935–936 (Ala.1983); Beck v. State, 396 So.2d 645, 659 (Ala.1981).

B

In this case, moreover, it is clear that the sentencing judge did not interpret the statute as requiring him to consider the jury's "sentence," because he never described the "sentence" as a factor in his deliberations. After the jury returned its verdict, the trial judge informed petitioner:

> "Let me say this: The jury has found you guilty of the crime of robbery with the aggravated circumstances of intentionally killing the victim ... and set your punishment at death by electrocution but the law of this state provides first that there will be an additional hearing in this case at which time *the Court will consider aggravating circumstances, extenuating and all other circumstances, concerning the commission of this particular offense* " (emphasis added). Tr. 249.

In addition, in imposing the sentence, the judge stated:

> "The Court *having considered the aggravating circumstances and the mitigating circumstances and after weighing the aggravating and mitigating circumstances,* it is the judgment of the Court that the aggravating circumstances far outweigh the mitigating circumstances and the death penalty as fixed by the jury should be and is hereby accepted" (emphasis added). App. 18.

None of these statements indicates that the judge considered the jury's verdict to be a factor that he added, or that he was required to add, to the scale in determining the appropriateness of the death penalty, or that he believed the jury's verdict was entitled to a presumption of correctness. The judge, of course, knew the Alabama system and all that it signified, knew that the jury's "sentence" was mandatory, and knew that it did not reflect consideration of any mitigating circumstance. The judge logically, therefore, would not have thought that he owed any deference to the jury's "sentence" on the issue whether the death penalty was appropriate for petitioner.[8]

III

Petitioner contends, nevertheless, that a judge's decision to impose the death penalty *must* be swayed by the fact that the jury returned a "sentence" of death. He points to this Court's opinion in Beck v. Alabama, 447 U.S. 625, 645 (1980), which expressed some skepticism about the influence the jury's "sentence" would have on a judge. *Beck* held unconstitutional the provision of the 1975 Act that precluded the jury from considering lesser-included noncapital offenses. The Court reasoned that the provision violated due process, because where the jury's only choices were to convict a defendant of the capital offense and "sentence" him to death, or to acquit him, but the evidence would have supported a lesser-included offense verdict, the factfinding process was tainted with irrelevant considerations. On the one hand, the Court reasoned, the unavailability of the option of convicting on a lesser-included offense may encourage the jury to convict the defendant of a capital crime because it believes that the defendant is guilty of some serious crime and should be punished. On the other hand, the apparently mandatory nature of the death penalty may encourage the jury to acquit because it believes the defendant does not deserve the death penalty. The unavailability of the lesser-included offense option, when it is warranted by the evidence, thus "introduce[s] a level of uncertainty and unreliability into the factfinding process that cannot be tolerated in a capital case." Id., at 642–643.

In so holding, this Court rejected Alabama's argument that, even if the unavailability of a lesser-included offense led a jury erroneously to convict a defendant, the fact that the judge was the true sentencer would ensure that the defendant was not improperly sentenced to death. It reasoned:

> "[I]t is manifest that the jury's verdict must have a tendency to motivate the judge to impose the same sentence that the jury did. Indeed, according to statistics submitted by the State's Attorney General, it is fair to infer that the jury verdict will ordinarily be followed by the judge even though he must hold a separate hearing in aggravation and mitigation before he imposes sentence. Under these circumstances, we are unwilling to presume that a post-trial hearing will always correct whatever mistakes have occurred in the performance of the jury's factfinding function." Id., at 645–646 (footnote omitted).

8. We express no view regarding the constitutionality of a death sentence imposed by a judge who did consider the jury's verdict in this Alabama statutory structure as a factor that weighed in favor of the imposition of the death penalty.

This Court's concern in *Beck* was that the judge would be inclined to accept the jury's factual finding that the defendant was guilty of a capital offense, not that the judge would be influenced by the jury's "sentence" of death. To "correct" an erroneous guilty verdict, the sentencing judge would have to determine that death was an inappropriate punishment, not because mitigating circumstances outweighed aggravating circumstances, but because the defendant had not been proved guilty beyond a reasonable doubt. Obviously, a judge will think hard about the jury's guilty verdict before basing a sentence on the belief that the defendant was not proved guilty of the capital offense. Indeed, the judge should think hard before rejecting the guilty verdict, because the determination of guilt is properly within the province of the jury, and the jury heard the same evidence regarding guilt as the judge.

It does not follow, however, that the judge will be swayed to impose a sentence of death merely because the jury returned a mandatory death "sentence," when it had no opportunity to consider mitigating circumstances. The judge knows that determination of the appropriate sentence is not within the jury's province, and that the jury does not consider evidence in mitigation in arriving at its "sentence." The jury's "sentence" means only that the jury found the defendant guilty of a capital crime—that is, that it found the fact of intentional killing in the course of a robbery—and that if the judge finds that the aggravating circumstances outweigh the mitigating circumstances, the judge is authorized to impose a sentence of death. The "sentence" thus conveys nothing more than the verdict of guilty, when it is read in conjunction with the provisions of the 1975 Act making the offense a capital crime, would convey. It defies logic to assume that a judge will be swayed to impose the death penalty by a "sentence" that has so little meaning. Despite its misdescribed label, it is not a sentence of death.

Petitioner also argues that the requirement that the jury return a "sentence" of death "blurs" the issue of guilt with the issue whether death is the appropriate punishment, and may cause the jury arbitrarily to nullify the mandatory death penalty by acquitting a defendant who is proved guilty, but who the jury, without any guidance, finds undeserving of the death penalty. Petitioner's argument stems from *Woodson,* where the plurality opinion noted that American juries "persistently" have refused to convict "a significant portion" of those charged with first degree murder in order to avoid mandatory death-penalty statutes, and expressed concern that the unguided exercise of the power to nullify a mandatory sentence would lead to the same "wanton" and "arbitrary" imposition of the death penalty that troubled the Court in *Furman.* 428 U.S., at 302–303. The Alabama scheme, however, has not resulted in such arbitrariness. Juries deliberating under the 1975 statute did not act to nullify the mandatory "sentence" by refusing to convict in a significant number of cases; indeed, only 2 of the first 50 defendants tried for capital crimes during the time the 1975 Act was in effect were acquitted. See Beck v. Alabama, 447 U.S., at 641, n. 18. Thus, while the specter of a mandatory death sentence may have made juries more prone to acquit, thereby benefiting the two defendants acquitted, it did not render Alabama's scheme unconstitutionally arbitrary.

IV

The wisdom and phraseology of Alabama's curious 1975 statute surely are open to question, as Alabama's abandonment of the statutory scheme in 1981 perhaps indicates.[9] This Court has made clear, however, that "we are unwilling to say that there is any one right way for a State to set up its capital-sentencing scheme." Spaziano v. Florida, ___ U.S. ___, ___ (1984) (slip op. 16). See also Zant v. Stephens, 462 U.S., at 884 (slip op. 22); Gregg v. Georgia, 428 U.S., at 195 (opinion of STEWART, POWELL, and STEVENS, JJ.). Alabama's requirement that the jury return a "sentence" of death along with its guilty verdict, while unusual, did not render unconstitutional the death sentence the trial judge imposed after independently considering petitioner's background and character and the circumstances of his crime.

The judgment of the Supreme Court of Alabama is affirmed.

It is so ordered.

CHIEF JUSTICE BURGER, concurring in the judgment.

It seems to me that the Court evades the constitutional issue presented, see ante, at 13, n. 8, and resolves this case on the basis of a construction of state law (a) that is inconsistent with the relevant state statute, (b) that does not appear in the opinion of the Alabama Supreme Court in this or any other case, and (c) that was not asserted by the State in its arguments before this Court.

The statute at issue states:

> "*Notwithstanding the fixing of punishment at death by the jury,* the court, after weighing the aggravating and mitigating circumstances, may *refuse to accept the death penalty as fixed by the jury* and sentence the defendant to life imprisonment without parole, which shall be served without parole; or the court, after weighing the aggravating and mitigating circumstances,

9. Following this Court's decisions in Beck v. Alabama, 447 U.S. 625 (1980), and Hopper v. Evans, 456 U.S. 605 (1982), the Supreme Court of Alabama held that in a capital case in which the jury is instructed regarding a lesser-included noncapital offense

> "the requirement in § 13–11–2(a), that the jury 'shall fix the punishment at death' [is construed] to be *permissive and to mean that the jury cannot fix punishment at death until it takes into account the circumstances of the offense together with the character and propensity of the offender, under sentencing procedures which will minimize the risk of an arbitrary and capricious imposition of the death penalty*" (emphasis in original).

Beck v. State, 396 So.2d 645, 660 (1981).

The Alabama Legislature then repealed the 1975 Act, and replaced it with a trifurcated proceeding in which the jury first determines guilt or innocence, and, if it returns a guilty verdict, hears evidence concerning aggravation and mitigation. On the basis of that evidence, the jury issues an advisory sentence. If the verdict is for death, that sentence is not binding on the trial judge, who then is required to hold another hearing regarding aggravating and mitigating circumstances before determining the actual sentence. Ala.Code § 13A–5–39 to 13A–5–59 (1982).

and the fixing of the punishment at death by the jury, may accordingly sentence the defendant to death."

Ala.Code § 13–11–4 (1975) (emphasis added).

The statutory language, particularly the underscored portions, clearly contemplates that a trial judge sentencing a capital defendant is to consider the jury's "fixing of the punishment at death" along with the aggravating and mitigating circumstances. But according to the Court's opinion, the statute is ambiguous as to whether the judge must consider the jury's "sentence" in all cases or only in cases where he has decided that the death penalty may be appropriate. See ante, at 10–11. Even if the Court is correct on this point, the ambiguity is irrelevant in every case, including this one, in which the trial judge *does in fact* impose the death sentence.

Given the clear import of the statutory language, it is difficult to see any reason to depart from the statute absent an equally clear contrary statement by a state court. Throughout its discussion of Alabama case law, however, the Court simply draws inferences from omissions. No Alabama decision holds affirmatively that the trial judge is *not* to consider the jury's "sentence." The passages quoted by the Court, see id., at 11–12, establish only that the judge, not the jury, is the sentencing authority. This proposition is not inconsistent with the judge's having to consider the jury's "sentence" in the sentencing process.

The opinion of the Alabama Supreme Court does not support the Court's construction of Alabama law. Indeed, the Supreme Court's opinion quotes the statement of the Eleventh Circuit Court of Appeals that " 'the statute [§ 13–11–4] requires the judge to weigh the mandatory death sentence factor in the balance with his consideration of aggravating and mitigating circumstances in deciding to impose the death penalty.' " Ex parte Baldwin, 456 So.2d 129, 138 (Ala.1984) (quoting Ritter v. Smith, 726 F.2d 1505, 1516 (CA11 1984)); accord id., at 141 (JONES, J., concurring in part and dissenting in part). The Alabama court did not refute this construction of the statute; instead, it upheld the statute on the grounds that the jury's "sentence" was not binding on the trial judge and that the statute required the trial judge to consider the circumstances of the particular offense and the character and propensities of the offender. There is no inconsistency between this reasoning and the sentencing judge having to consider the jury's conclusion along with the other relevant factors.

If state law were as clear as the Court suggests, one would expect the State's otherwise thorough brief to include some support for the Court's view of Alabama law. According to the petitioner, the "very flaw which kills the statute" is that it requires the trial judge to consider the jury's "sentence" "as a factor in the sentencing process." Brief for Petitioner 13. In the face of this contention, it seems that if "[t]he Alabama appellate courts have interpreted the 1975 Act *expressly* to mean that the sentencing judge is to impose a sentence *without regard* to the jury's mandatory 'sentence,' " ante, at 11 (emphasis added), the State would have mentioned that fact in its arguments here. It did not.

The Court should decide whether the 1975 Alabama statute is unconstitutional *because* it requires the trial judge to consider the jury's "sentence" in determining the sentence actually to be imposed. In my view the statute passes constitutional muster.

The 1975 statutory scheme limits capital offenses to murders involving statutorily specified aggravating circumstances. Because each capital offense already includes an aggravating circumstance in the definition of the offense, the jury's mandatory death "sentence" reflects the jury's determination that the State has proved the defined aggravating circumstance beyond a reasonable doubt. Because the trial judge must weigh that circumstance along with the other aggravating circumstances and the mitigating circumstances, Ex parte Kyzer, 399 So.2d 330, 338 (Ala.1981), it makes complete sense for the judge to take into account the jury's finding on that issue. The statute requires no more in having the trial judge take into account the jury's "sentence" in the process of weighing the aggravating and mitigating circumstances.

[The dissenting opinions of Justices Brennan and Stevens (joined by Justices Brennan and Marshall) are omitted.]

NOTES

1. *Gregg* was one of a series of cases handed down the same day. In Proffitt v. Florida, 428 U.S. 242, 96 S.Ct. 2960 (1976), the Court sustained imposition of the death penalty under a Florida capital crimes scheme similar to Georgia's except that the jury role on sentencing is advisory. Mr. Justice Powell, writing the Court's plurality opinion, distinguished the two schemes thusly:

"On their face these procedures, like those used in Georgia appear to meet the constitutional deficiencies identified in *Furman*. The sentencing authority in Florida, the trial judge, is directed to weigh eight aggravating factors against seven mitigating factors to determine whether the death penalty shall be imposed. This determination requires the trial judge to focus on the circumstances of the crime and the character of the individual defendant. He must, *inter alia*, consider whether the defendant has a prior criminal record, whether the defendant acted under duress or under the influence of extreme mental or emotional disturbance, whether the defendant's role in the crime was that of a minor accomplice, and whether the defendant's youth argues in favor of a more lenient sentence than might otherwise be imposed. The trial judge must also determine whether the crime was committed in the course of one of several enumerated felonies, whether it was committed for pecuniary gain, whether it was committed to assist in an escape from custody or to prevent a lawful arrest, and whether the crime was especially heinous, atrocious, or cruel. To answer these questions, which are not unlike those considered by a Georgia sentencing jury, . . . the sentencing judge must focus on the individual circumstances of each homicide and each defendant.

"The basic difference between the Florida system and the Georgia system is that in Florida the sentence is determined by the trial judge rather than by the jury. This Court has pointed out that jury sentencing in a capital case can perform an important societal function, Witherspoon v. Illinois, 391 U.S. 510,

519 n. 15, 88 S.Ct. 1770, 1775, but it has never suggested that jury sentencing is constitutionally required. And it would appear that judicial sentencing should lead, if anything, to even greater consistency in the imposition at the trial court level of capital punishment, since a trial judge is more experienced in sentencing than a jury, and therefore is better able to impose sentences similar to those imposed in analogous cases.

"The Florida capital-sentencing procedures thus seek to assure that the death penalty will not be imposed in an arbitrary or capricious manner. Moreover, to the extent that any risk to the contrary exists, it is minimized by Florida's appellate review system, under which the evidence of the aggravating and mitigating circumstances is reviewed and reweighed by the Supreme Court of Florida 'to determine independently whether the imposition of the ultimate penalty is warranted.' Songer v. State, 322 So.2d 481, 484 (1975).... The Supreme Court of Florida, like that of Georgia, has not hesitated to vacate a death sentence when it has determined that the sentence should not have been imposed. Indeed, it has vacated eight of the 21 death sentences that it has reviewed to date.

"Under Florida's capital-sentencing procedures, in sum, trial judges are given specific and detailed guidance to assist them in deciding whether to impose a death penalty or imprisonment for life. Moreover, their decisions are reviewed to ensure that they are consistent with other sentences imposed in similar circumstances. Thus, in Florida, as in Georgia, it is no longer true that there is ' "no meaningful basis for distinguishing the few cases in which [the death penalty] is imposed from the many cases where it is not." ' On its face the Florida system thus satisfies the constitutional deficiencies identified in *Furman*."

The Court also sustained the Texas death penalty statute procedures in Jurek v. Texas, 428 U.S. 262, 96 S.Ct. 2950 (1976). The Texas procedure was outlined as follows in *Jurek:*

"... The new Texas Penal Code limits capital homicides to intentional and knowing murders committed in five situations: murder of a peace officer or fireman; murder committed in the course of kidnapping, burglary, robbery, forcible rape, or arson; murder committed for remuneration; murder committed while escaping or attempting to escape from a penal institution; and murder committed by a prison inmate when the victim is a prison employee. See Texas Penal Code § 19.03 (1974).

"In addition, Texas adopted a new capital-sentencing procedure. See Texas Code of Crim.Proc., Art. 37.071 (Supp.1975–1976). That procedure requires the jury to answer three questions in a proceeding that takes place subsequent to the return of a verdict finding a person guilty of one of the above categories of murder. The questions the jury must answer are these:

"(1) whether the conduct of the defendant that caused the death of the deceased was committed deliberately and with the reasonable expectation that the death of the deceased or another would result;

"(2) whether there is a probability that the defendant would commit criminal acts of violence that would constitute a continuing threat to society; and

"(3) if raised by the evidence, whether the conduct of the defendant in killing the deceased was unreasonable in response to the provocation, if any, by the deceased." Texas Code Crim.Proc., Art. 37.071(b) (Supp. 1975–1976).

"If the jury finds that the State has proved beyond a reasonable doubt that the answer to each of the three questions is yes, then the death sentence is imposed. If the jury finds that the answer to any question is no, then a sentence of imprisonment results. The law also provides for an expedited review by the Texas Court of Criminal Appeals.

* * *

"While Texas has not adopted a list of statutory aggravating circumstances the existence of which can justify the imposition of the death penalty as have Georgia and Florida, its action in narrowing the categories of murders for which a death sentence may never be imposed serves much the same purpose. In fact, each of the five classes of murders made capital by the Texas statute is encompassed in Georgia and Florida by one or more of their statutory aggravating circumstances. For example, the Texas statute requires the jury at the guilt determining stage to consider whether the crime was committed in the course of a particular felony, whether it was committed for hire, or whether the defendant was an inmate of a penal institution at the time of its commission. Thus, in essence, the Texas statute requires that the jury find the existence of a statutory aggravating circumstance before the death penalty may be imposed. So far as consideration of aggravating circumstances is concerned, therefore, the principal difference between Texas and the other two States is that the death penalty is an available sentencing option—even potentially—for a smaller class of murders in Texas. Otherwise the statutes are similar. Each requires the sentencing authority to focus on the particularized nature of the crime.

* * *

"Thus, Texas law essentially requires that one of five aggravating circumstances be found before a defendant can be found guilty of capital-murder, and that in considering whether to impose a death sentence the jury may be asked to consider whatever evidence of mitigating circumstances the defense can bring before it. It thus appears that, as in Georgia and Florida, the Texas capital-sentencing procedure guides and focuses the jury's objective consideration of the particularized circumstances of the individual offense and the individual offender before it can impose a sentence of death.

* * *

"We conclude that Texas' capital-sentencing procedures, like those of Georgia and Florida, do not violate the Eighth and Fourteenth Amendments. By narrowing its definition of capital murder, Texas has essentially said that there must be at least one statutory aggravating circumstance in a first-degree murder case before a death sentence may even be considered. By authorizing the defense to bring before the jury at the separate sentencing hearing whatever mitigating circumstances relating to the individual defendant can be adduced, Texas has ensured that the sentencing jury will have adequate guidance to enable it to perform its sentencing function. By providing prompt judicial review of the jury's decision in a court with state-wide jurisdiction, Texas has provided a means to promote the evenhanded, rational, and consistent imposition of death sentences under law. Because this system serves to assure that sentences of death will not be 'wantonly' or 'freakishly' imposed, it does not violate the Constitution."

2. In Woodson v. North Carolina, 428 U.S. 280, 96 S.Ct. 2978 (1976), however, the Court struck down the North Carolina capital punishment scheme. That state had previously provided that the jury could, in its unbridled discretion, impose the death penalty for certain crimes, but subsequent to *Furman* had changed its statute to make the death penalty mandatory in first-degree murder cases. Petitioners' convictions under this new statutory scheme were reversed. The Court said, in part:

* * *

"Although it seems beyond dispute that, at the time of the *Furman* decision in 1972, mandatory death penalty statutes had been renounced by American juries and legislatures, there remains the question whether the mandatory statutes adopted by North Carolina and a number of other States following *Furman* evince a sudden reversal of societal values regarding the imposition of capital punishment. In view of the persistent and unswerving legislative rejection of mandatory death penalty statutes beginning in 1838 and continuing for more than 130 years until *Furman,* it seems evident that the post-*Furman* enactments reflect attempts by the States to retain the death penalty in a form consistent with the Constitution, rather than a renewed societal acceptance of mandatory death sentencing.

* * *

"It is now well established that the Eighth Amendment draws much of its meaning from 'the evolving standards of decency that mark the progress of a maturing society.' Trop v. Dulles, 356 U.S., at 101, 78 S.Ct., at 598 (plurality opinion). As the above discussion makes clear, one of the most significant developments in our society's treatment of capital punishment has been the rejection of the common-law practice of inexorably imposing a death sentence upon every person convicted of a specified offense. North Carolina's mandatory death penalty statute for first-degree murder departs markedly from contemporary standards respecting the imposition of the punishment of death and thus cannot be applied consistently with the Eighth and Fourteenth Amendments' requirement that the State's power to punish 'be exercised within the limits of civilized standards.'

"A separate deficiency of North Carolina's mandatory death sentence statute is its failure to provide a constitutionally tolerable response to *Furman's* rejection of unbridled jury discretion in the imposition of capital sentences. Central to the limited holding in *Furman* was the conviction that the vesting of standardless sentencing power in the jury violated the Eighth and Fourteenth Amendments. It is argued that North Carolina has remedied the inadequacies of the death penalty statutes held unconstitutional in *Furman* by withdrawing all sentencing discretion from juries in capital cases. But when one considers the long and consistent American experience with the death penalty in first-degree murder cases, it becomes evident that mandatory statutes enacted in response to *Furman* have simply papered over the problem of unguided and unchecked jury discretion.

* * *

"A third constitutional shortcoming of the North Carolina statute is its failure to allow the particularized consideration of relevant aspects of the character and record of each convicted defendant before the imposition upon him of a sentence of death. In *Furman,* members of the Court acknowledged what cannot fairly be denied—that death is a punishment different from all other sanctions in kind rather than degree.... A process that accords no significance to relevant facets of the character and record of the individual offender or the circumstances of the particular offense excludes from consideration in fixing the ultimate punishment of death the possibility of compassionate or mitigating factors stemming from the diverse frailties of humankind. It treats all persons convicted of a designated offense not as uniquely individual human beings, but as members of a faceless, undifferentiated mass to be subjected to the blind infliction of the penalty of death.

"This Court has previously recognized that '[f]or the determination of sentences, justice generally requires consideration of more than the particular acts by which the crime was committed and that there be taken into account the circumstances of the offense together with the character and propensities of the offender.' Pennsylvania v. Ashe, 302 U.S. 51, 55, 58 S.Ct. 59, 61 (1937). Consideration of both the offender and the offense in order to arrive at a just and appropriate sentence has been viewed as a progressive and humanizing development. While the prevailing practice of individualizing sentencing determinations generally reflects simply enlightened policy rather than a constitutional imperative, we believe that in capital cases the fundamental respect for humanity underlying the Eighth Amendment, see Trop v. Dulles, 356 U.S., at 100, 78 S.Ct., at 597 (plurality opinion), requires consideration of the character and record of the individual offender and the circumstances of the particular offense as a constitutionally indispensable part of the process of inflicting the penalty of death.

"This conclusion rests squarely on the predicate that the penalty of death is qualitatively different from a sentence of imprisonment, however long. Death, in its finality, differs more from life imprisonment than a 100-year prison term differs from one of only a year or two. Because of that qualitative difference, there is a corresponding difference in the need for reliability in the determination that death is the appropriate punishment in a specific case."

Louisiana's death penalty statute, enacted in the wake of *Furman,* was also invalidated by the Court in Roberts v. Louisiana, 428 U.S. 325, 96 S.Ct. 3001 (1976). The Louisiana statute required imposition of the death penalty for five different types of homicides, if the jury should find that the defendant specifically intended to kill or do great bodily harm. The *Roberts* homicide was a felony-murder (killing during the commission of an armed robbery). Despite the narrower definition of murder than under the North Carolina scheme reviewed in *Woodson,* the plurality opinion identified these reasons for the statute's invalidity:

"That Louisiana has adopted a different and somewhat narrower definition of first-degree murder than North Carolina is not of controlling constitutional significance. The history of mandatory death penalty statutes indicates a firm societal view that limiting the scope of capital murder is an inadequate response to the harshness and inflexibility of a mandatory death sentence statute. A large group of jurisdictions first responded to the unacceptable severity of the common-law rule of automatic death sentences for all murder convictions by narrowing the definition of capital homicide. Each of these jurisdictions found that approach insufficient and subsequently substituted discretionary sentencing for mandatory death sentences.

"The futility of attempting to solve the problems of mandatory death penalty statutes by narrowing the scope of the capital offense stems from our society's rejection of the belief that 'every offense in a like legal category calls for an identical punishment without regard to the past life and habits of a particular offender.' As the dissenting justices in *Furman* noted, the 19th century movement away from mandatory death sentences was rooted in the recognition that 'individual culpability is not always measured by the category of crime committed.' 408 U.S. 238, 402, 92 S.Ct. at 2810 (1972) (Burger, C.J., dissenting).

"The constitutional vice of mandatory death sentence statutes—lack of focus on the circumstances of the particular offense and the character and propensities of the offender—is not resolved by Louisiana's limitation of first-degree murder to various categories of killings. The diversity of circumstances presented in cases falling within the single category of killings during the commission of a specified felony, as well as the variety of possible offenders involved in such crimes, underscores the rigidity of Louisiana's enactment and its similarity to the North Carolina statute. Even the other more narrowly drawn categories of first-degree murder in the Louisiana law afford no meaningful opportunity for consideration of mitigating factors presented by the circumstances of the particular crime or by the attributes of the individual offender."

3. In Coker v. Georgia, 433 U.S. 584, 97 S.Ct. 2861 (1977) the Supreme Court struck down a death sentence for the crime of rape as grossly disproportionate and excessive punishment forbidden by the Eighth Amendment. The rape and armed robbery had been committed by an escaped felon and the death sentence had been imposed because of that aggravated factor. Mr. Justice White, in authoring the plurality opinion, stressed that the Eighth Amendment bars not only those punishments that are barbaric, but also those that are excessive in relation to the crime committed. A punishment is excessive and therefore unconstitutional if it "(1) makes no measurable contribution to acceptable goals of punishment and hence is nothing more than a purposeless and needless imposition of pain and suffering; or (2) is grossly out of proportion to the severity of the crime."

While rape is deserving of serious punishment, the Court's opinion suggested that the imposition of the death sentence for the rape, even though committed by a person with prior felony convictions, was excessive where under Georgia law a deliberate killer cannot be sentenced to death absent aggravating circumstances. It seemed incongruous to the Court that a rapist who does not take life should be punished more severely than a deliberate killer.

4. See also, Gardner v. Florida, 430 U.S. 349, 97 S.Ct. 1197 (1977), where the United States Supreme Court vacated a death sentence and remanded to the state supreme court because of the manner in which the sentence was imposed.

The problem in *Gardner* is that the judge had imposed the death sentence, at least in part, on the basis of information that the defendant had no opportunity to deny or explain—a confidential presentence investigation report that contained portions not disclosed to defense counsel.

5. What about the imposition of a death penalty on a defendant who aids and abets in a felony during the course of which a murder is committed by others but who does not himself kill, attempt to kill or intend that killing take place or that lethal force will be employed? Such a death penalty was struck down as violative of the Eighth Amendment in Enmund v. Florida, 458 U.S. 782, 102 S.Ct. 3368 (1982).

In Tison v. Arizona, 481 U.S. 137, 107 S.Ct. 1676 (1987), the Court approved the use of the death penalty in felony murder cases. In *Tison* two brothers planned and carried out their father's armed prison break. After the break their car stalled and they commandeered a car carrying a family. The brothers looked on while their father executed the family in cold blood to facilitate their common criminal adventure. The brothers were convicted and sentenced to death for felony murder. In approving the death penalty the Court established guidelines for determining the constitutionality of the death penalty in felony murder cases. If a defendant participates in a felony where the victim is killed but not by the defendant, the defendant may be sentenced to death without violating the Eighth Amendment's "proportionality" requirement, if the defendant's participation in the felony was "major" and he is found to have a mental state of "reckless indifference" to human life. The test does *not* turn on whether the defendant actually "intended to kill." It turns on the crucial finding of "reckless indifference to the value of human life," which the Court said is "every bit as shocking to the moral sense as 'intent to kill.' "

6. Is it cruel and unusual punishment to impose the death penalty on a minor or a mentally retarded person? In 1988 the U.S. Supreme Court squarely considered the issue of whether the Eighth Amendment permits the imposition of the death penalty on juveniles who were less than 16 years old at the time of an offense. The case arose in a state that had no minimum age for imposition of the death penalty and permitted juveniles to be tried as adults in some cases. The Court was unable to put together a majority opinion on the constitutional issue. Four Justices joined in an opinion by Justice Stevens to the effect that the Eighth Amendment proscribed the death penalty for juveniles. A concurring opinion by Justice O'Connor argued that the death penalty for juveniles was not unconstitutional in theory, but that it could only be imposed pursuant to a statute specifically setting forth the penalty for juveniles (instead of the situation in the instant case where a combination of two statutes indirectly permitted the penalty to be imposed on a juvenile). Thompson v. Oklahoma, 487 U.S. 815, 108 S.Ct. 2687 (1988).

Finally in 1989 the Court ruled 5–4 in two cases that the Eighth Amendment does not proscribe the imposition of the death penalty for murderers who committed their crimes when they were 16 or 17 years old. However, sentencing juries in such cases must be allowed to take into consideration the youthfulness of the defendant. Stanford v. Kentucky, 492 U.S. 361, 109 S.Ct. 2969 (1989).

In a companion case, Penry v. Lynaugh, 492 U.S. 302, 109 S.Ct. 2934 (1989), a 5–4 Court ruled that the execution of a mentally retarded murderer is not "categorically prohibited" by the Eighth Amendment, although the fact of mental retardation must be taken into consideration by the sentencing jury. The Court declared "[t]here is insufficient evidence of a national consensus against executing mentally retarded people convicted of capital offenses for us to conclude that it is categorically prohibited by the Eighth Amendment." The Court noted that only two states—Georgia and Maryland—prohibit the execution of the mentally retarded.

In Ford v. Wainwright, 477 U.S. 399, 106 S.Ct. 2595 (1986), the U.S. Supreme Court held that it is a violation of the Eighth Amendment cruel and unusual punishment proscription to execute a condemned prisoner who is insane. The Court found violative of due process a state statutory scheme for determining whether an inmate is competent to be executed under which the governor appointed a commission of three psychiatrists to examine the prisoner ex parte and report on his sanity, and then made an ex parte and unreviewable determination of whether the sentence will be carried out. The procedure was defective: (1) because it failed to include the prisoner in the "truth-seeking process," (2) denied the prisoner an opportunity to challenge or impeach the state-appointed psychiatrists, and (3) for placing the ultimate decision wholly in the executive branch of government (the governor). The Court indicated that the states could satisfy due process by providing an impartial officer or board that could receive evidence and argument from the prisoner's counsel, including expert psychiatric evidence, and that beyond these requirements, the states retain substantial discretion to create appropriate procedures. The tests for determining whether a prisoner is insane for Eighth Amendment purposes is simply whether the prisoner is aware of his impending execution and of the reason for it.

In McCleskey v. Kemp, 481 U.S. 279, 107 S.Ct. 1756 (1987), a statistical study of death penalty judgments in the State of Georgia indicating that defendants charged with the murder of whites were 4.3 times more likely to receive the death penalty than defendants charged with the murder of blacks, and that black defendants were 1.1 times more likely to receive the death penalty than whites, failed to convince the Court that the death penalty was imposed in a discriminatory manner in that State or that the jury in this case abused its discretion and acted with a discriminatory purpose. "Because discretion is essential to the criminal justice process, we would demand exceptionally clear proof before we would infer that the discretion has been abused." The Court rejected arguments raised by the defendant that (1) the State maintains the death penalty for a "discriminatory purpose," (2) application of the death penalty under these circumstances violates the cruel and unusual punishment provisions of the Eighth Amendment, and (3) racial disparities in the death penalty constitute "invidious" discrimination (such disparities, the court noted, are "ineviable").

The imposition of the death penalty does not require a specific jury finding on whether a defendant killed or intended to kill. *Enmund,* supra, is satisfied if the appellate court is able to determine from the record that the required level of culpability exists. It might be desirable to have a specific jury finding on intent, but it is not constitutionally required. Ross v. Kemp, 756 F.2d 1483 (11th Cir.1985). In Cabana v. Bullock, 474 U.S. 376, 106 S.Ct. 689 (1986), the U.S. Supreme Court ruled that the factual finding necessary to impose the death sentence articulated in *Enmund* need not be made by the trier of facts at the guilt determining phase of the proceedings or even at the sentencing phase of the proceedings by the trial judge, but can be made subsequent to trial by an appellate court. A defendant, the Court ruled, has a constitutional right to a jury determination of his guilt or innocence, but has no similar right to have a jury determine the penalty, and *Enmund* did not impose any particular form of procedure for making the necessary finding of appropriateness for the death penalty (murderous intent). So long as the record of state court proceedings contains the necessary *Enmund* determination, such determination is entitled to a presumption of correctness in federal habeas corpus; otherwise a case should be remanded to give the state courts a reasonable time to make an *Enmund*-required determination.

7. In Zant v. Stephens, 462 U.S. 862, 103 S.Ct. 2733 (1983), a jury found the defendant guilty of murder and imposed the death penalty, stating in writing that it found three statutory aggravating circumstances: 1) prior conviction of a capital felony, 2) a substantial history of serious assaultive criminal convictions and 3) that the murder was committed by an escapee. While the defendant's appeal was pending, the Georgia Supreme Court held in another case that one of these—the "substantial history of serious assaultive criminal convictions"—was unconstitutionally vague. The U.S. Supreme Court ultimately upheld the imposition of the death penalty because the other two grounds were sufficient and the

jury specifically indicated that it found the other two aggravating circumstances rather than simply returning a general verdict.

8. Some additional recent U.S. Supreme Court rulings on various death penalty issues include these:

In California v. Ramos, 463 U.S. 992, 103 S.Ct. 3446 (1983), the Court upheld a requirement that the judge inform the jury that a sentence of life imprisonment without the possibility of parole may be commuted by the Governor to a sentence that includes the possibility of parole (the so-called Briggs instruction). After receiving this instruction, the jury returned a verdict of death. The Court said that this merely accurately informed the jury of the meaning of the meaning of the phrase "life imprisonment without possibility of parole."

In Barclay v. Florida, 463 U.S. 939, 103 S.Ct. 3418 (1983), the trial judge who imposed the death penalty improperly found that the defendant's prior criminal record was an aggravating circumstance, since the state statute did not list it as one. However, other valid statutory aggravating circumstances were also contained in the judge's findings. In a plurality opinion, with Justices Stevens and Powell separately concurring in the judgment, Justice Rehnquist stated that the Court's review of the sentence was limited to the question of whether the findings of the Florida trial court, approved by the Florida Supreme Court under the laws of that state, were so unprincipled or arbitrary as to violate the Federal Constitution. He concluded that they were not, and also rejected the argument that the sentence should be vacated because the trial judge, in the course of explaining his sentence, discussed racial motives involved in the murder and compared it with his own Army experiences in the Second World War, when he saw Nazi concentration camps and their victims.

In Barefoot v. Estelle, 463 U.S. 880, 103 S.Ct. 3383 (1983), the Court approved the expedited handling of death penalty appeals by the federal courts and suggested procedural guidelines for handling stays of execution on habeas corpus appeals pursuant to a certificate of probable cause. In an attempt to avoid a multiplicity of appeals, the Court suggested that a certificate of probable cause in such a case requires more than merely the showing of the absence of frivolity of the appeal—a substantial showing of the denial of a federal right must be made. The Court approved of the procedure of expediting the appeal by deciding the merits of the appeal on the motion for a stay. And the Court stated that stays of execution are not automatic pending the filing and consideration of a petition for certiorari from the U.S. Supreme Court to a court of appeals which has denied a writ of habeas corpus. The Court also suggested that federal district courts expedite consideration of a second or successive federal habeas petition in the same case.

In Skipper v. South Carolina, 476 U.S. 1, 106 S.Ct. 1669 (1986), the Court held that a capital defendant's good behavior in jail awaiting trial must be allowed as mitigating evidence in sentencing proceedings. Although the defendant and his wife were allowed to testify that defendant behaved well in jail during the seven and one-half months before his capital trial for rape, the trial court barred other evidence by his jailers and a regular visitor of his good conduct in jail, while the prosecutor suggested in closing argument that the defendant would be a disciplinary problem in prison and might rape other prisoners. Reversing the defendant's death sentence, the Court held that "(c)onsideration of a defendant's past conduct as indicative of his probable future behavior is an inevitable and not undesirable element of criminal sentencing," and it was reversible error not to allow such evidence in mitigation at defendant's sentencing hearing. The Court rejected an argument that such evidence was improper lay opinion testimony and that it was "cumulative." It was not the latter, since the defendant's and wife's testimony "was the sort of evidence that a jury naturally would tend to discount as self-serving."

In light of *Skipper,* it was reversible error for a trial court in a death penalty case to now allow an advisory jury to consider mitigating factors in addition to those established in the State's death penalty statute. The trial judge made the same mistake in setting the sentence; preclusion of *any* mitigating factors is unconstitutional in death penalty cases. Hitchcock v. Dugger, 481 U.S. 393, 107 S.Ct. 1821 (1987).

In Mills v. Maryland, 486 U.S. 367, 108 S.Ct. 1860 (1988), the Court ruled that a verdict form and jury instructions used in a capital case, which were confusing and vague, and which created a substantial probability that the jurors did not realize that all mitigating evidence could be taken into consideration in setting the death penalty, spoiled the death sentence. The Court had previously ruled in Lockett v. Ohio, 438 U.S. 586, 98 S.Ct. 2954 (1978), and Eddings v. Oklahoma, 455 U.S. 104, 102 S.Ct. 869 (1982), that a capital defendant is constitutionally entitled to have the jury consider all possible mitigating evidence in setting the death penalty. The instructions in the instant case could have led the jury to believe that they could not consider certain mitigating evidence unless all 12 members of the jury agreed that a particular mitigating circumstance existed. The case was remanded for resentencing.

In Franklin v. Lynaugh, 487 U.S. 164, 108 S.Ct. 2320 (1988), under state law a jury in a capital case was instructed by the trial court that if it answered "yes" to two "Special Issues", finding beyond a reasonable doubt that (1) the murder was committed deliberately and with a reasonable expectation that death would result, and (2) that there was a probability that the defendant was a continuing threat to society, it could impose the death penalty. The trial court refused to instruct the jury that it could consider any evidence it thought to be mitigating in responding to the "Special Issues", and could acquit the defendant of the death penalty even if in consideration of such mitigating evidence, it believed that the "Special Issues" were established against the defendant. In affirming the jury's death verdict, the Court, found no constitutional error. The instruction did not unconstitutionally limit the jury's consideration of relevant mitigating evidence where the only mitigating factors brought forward by the defendant were his good prison record and some asserted "residual doubts" that the jury may have had about his guilt. The state procedure adequately allowed for consideration of mitigating evidence and sufficiently allowed jury discretion.

In Johnson v. Mississippi, 486 U.S. 578, 108 S.Ct. 1981 (1988), the defendant was sentenced to death for murder of a police officer in Mississippi. The sentencing jury relied on three aggravating circumstances, one of which was an 18-year-old conviction in New York for assault with intent to commit rape. After the death sentence was handed down, defendant's N.Y. conviction was reversed in a collateral proceeding because of a coerced confession. The Court set aside the Mississippi death sentence. Inasmuch as there was a "possibility" that the New York conviction was "decisive" in the Mississippi jury's determination of the death sentence, the Eighth Amendment's requirement that death be dealt out only in a "reliable" proceeding, required reversal of the death sentence. A later reversed conviction is an invalid aggravating circumstance in a death penalty proceeding. The use of it by the death sentencing jury created a risk that the sentence imposed was "arbitrary."

Finally, in Lowenfield v. Phelps, 484 U.S. 231, 108 S.Ct. 546 (1988), the Court ruled that an "Allen" ("dynamite") charge to a jury deadlocked on whether to give the defendant the death penalty did not violate the Constitution. The Court spoke approvingly of the "Allen" charge, noting that it has long been approved. In this case the trial judge did not urge the minority jurors to consider the views of the majority, which is said to be the chief objection (coercion) to the Allen charge. And although the trial judge polled the jury, it confined the poll to whether further deliberations would be helpful, not the numerical split of the jury (which would be coercive). The result in this case was not changed by the fact that a jury split on the death penalty would not mean a retrial, but only an automatic life sentence. The State is entitled to a decisive determination on the death penalty. The Court also approved a statutory death sentence scheme that made an aggravating factor for the death sentence the same as one of the elements of the underlying crime.

9. Although the question of "cruel and unusual punishment" frequently arises in the context of the death penalty, two recent cases examined it in the context of a life sentence.

A mandatory life sentence imposed under the Texas recidivist statute following the defendant's third felony conviction for obtaining $120.75 by false pretenses was upheld by the Court. The two previous convictions involved use of a credit card to obtain $80 worth of goods or services and passing a forged check in the amount of $28.36. Rummel v. Estelle, 445 U.S. 263, 100 S.Ct. 1133 (1980).

More recently, the Court held that a life sentence without possibility of parole under the South Dakota recidivist statute was cruel and unusual punishment because it was disproportionate to the crime committed. In this case, the defendant was convicted of passing a bad $100 check, but had six prior felony convictions—three for third-degree burglary and convictions for obtaining money under false pretenses, grand larceny, and third-offense driving while intoxicated. The Court relied on the fact that the most recent offense involved neither violence or threat of violence and the previous felonies were all nonviolent and none was a crime against a person. The Court distinguished this case from *Rummel* on the basis that the defendant in that case was eligible for parole, while the South Dakota statute only provided the possibility of commutation, which is more difficult to obtain. Solem v. Helm, 463 U.S. 277, 103 S.Ct. 3001 (1983).

10. In Robinson v. California, 370 U.S. 660, 82 S.Ct. 1417 (1962), the Court held that it was cruel and unusual punishment to provide criminal penalties for being "addicted to the use of narcotics" as a status even though the defendant may not have possessed any narcotics within the state. See Manak, Recent Decisions, The Narcotics Problem: Outlook for Reform, 12 Buffalo Law Review 605 (1963). For a discussion of the application of this principle to chronic alcoholics, see Annot., 40 A.L.R.3d 321 (1971).

H. DUE PROCESS OF LAW—POLICE POWER AND STATUTORY VAGUENESS

PAPACHRISTOU ET AL. v. CITY OF JACKSONVILLE

Supreme Court of the United States, 1972.
405 U.S. 156, 92 S.Ct. 839.

MR. JUSTICE DOUGLAS delivered the opinion of the Court.

This case involves eight defendants who were convicted in a Florida municipal court of violating a Jacksonville, Florida, vagrancy ordinance.[1] Their convictions, entailing fines and jail sentences (some of which were suspended), were affirmed by the Florida Circuit Court in a consolidated appeal, and their petition for certiorari was denied by the District Court of Appeals,.... The case is here on a petition for certiorari, which we granted.... For reasons which will appear, we reverse.[2]

At issue are five consolidated cases. Margaret Papachristou, Betty Calloway, Eugene Eddie Melton, and Leonard Johnson were all arrested early on a Sunday morning, and charged with vagrancy—"prowling by auto."

Jimmy Lee Smith and Milton Henry were charged with vagrancy—"vagabonds."

1. Jacksonville Ordinance Code § 26–57 provided at the time of these arrests and convictions as follows:

> "Rogues and vagabonds, or dissolute persons who go about begging, common gamblers, persons who use juggling or unlawful games or plays, common drunkards, common night walkers, thieves, pilferers or pickpockets, traders in stolen property, lewd, wanton and lascivious persons, keepers of gambling places, common railers and brawlers, persons wandering or strolling around from place to place without any lawful purpose or object, habitual loafers, disorderly persons, persons neglecting all lawful business and habitually spending their time by frequenting houses of ill fame, gaming houses, or places where alcoholic beverages are sold or served, persons able to work but habitually living upon the earnings of their wives or minor children shall be deemed vagrants and, upon conviction in the Municipal Court shall be punished [90 days imprisonment, $500 fine, or both.]

We are advised that at present the Jacksonville vagrancy ordinance is § 330.107 and identical with the earlier one except that "juggling" has been eliminated.

2. Florida also has a vagrancy statute ... which reads quite closely on the Jacksonville ordinance.... [It] makes the commission of any Florida misdemeanor a Class D offense against the City of Jacksonville. In 1971 Florida made minor amendments to its statute.

[The statute] was declared unconstitutionally overbroad in Lazarus v. Faircloth, D.C., 301 F.Supp. 266. The Court said: "All loitering, loafing, or idling on the streets and highways of a city, even though habitual, is not necessarily detrimental to the public welfare nor is it under all circumstances an interference with travel upon them. It may be and often is entirely innocuous. The statute draws no distinction between conduct that is calculated to harm and that which is essentially innocent." See also Smith v. Florida, 405 U.S. 172, 92 S.Ct. 848 (1972).

The Florida disorderly conduct ordinance, covering "loitering about any hotel, block, barroom, dramshop, gambling house or disorderly house, or wandering about the streets either by night or by day without any known lawful means of support or without being able to give a satisfactory account of themselves" has also been held void for "excessive broadness and vagueness" by the Florida Supreme Court, Headley v. Selkowitz, 171 So.2d 368, 370.

Henry Edward Heath and a co-defendant were arrested for vagrancy—"loitering" and "common thief."

Thomas Owen Campbell was charged with vagrancy—"common thief."

Hugh Brown was charged with vagrancy—"disorderly loitering on street" and "disorderly conduct—resisting arrest with violence."

The facts are stipulated. Papachristou and Calloway are white females. Melton and Johnson are black males. Papachristou was enrolled in a job-training program sponsored by the State Employment Service at Florida Junior College in Jacksonville. Calloway was a typing and shorthand teacher at a state mental institution located near Jacksonville. She was the owner of the automobile in which the four defendants were arrested. Melton was a Vietnam war veteran who had been released from the Navy after nine months in a veterans' hospital. On the date of his arrest he was a part-time computer helper while attending college as a full-time student in Jacksonville. Johnson was a tow-motor operator in a grocery chain warehouse and was a lifelong resident of Jacksonville.

At the time of their arrest the four of them were riding in Calloway's car on the main thoroughfare in Jacksonville. They had left a restaurant owned by Johnson's uncle where they had eaten and were on their way to a night club. The arresting officers denied that the racial mixture in the car played any part in the decision to make the arrest. The arrest they said, was made because the defendants had stopped near a used-car lot which had been broken into several times. There was, however, no evidence of any breaking and entering on the night in question.

Of these four charged with "prowling by auto" none had been previously arrested except Papachristou who had once been convicted of a municipal offense.

Jimmy Lee Smith and Milton Henry (who is not a petitioner) were arrested between 9 and 10 a.m. on a weekday in downtown Jacksonville, while waiting for a friend who was to lend them a car so they could apply for a job at a produce company. Smith was a part-time produce worker and part-time organizer for a Negro political group. He had a common-law wife and three children supported by him and his wife. He had been arrested several times but convicted only once. Smith's companion, Henry, was an 18-year-old high school student with no previous record of arrest.

This morning it was cold, and Smith had no jacket, so they went briefly into a dry cleaning shop to wait, but left when requested to do so. They thereafter walked back and forth two or three times over a two-block stretch looking for their friend. The store owners, who apparently were wary of Smith and his companion, summoned two police officers who searched the men and found neither had a weapon. But they were arrested because the officers said they had no identification and because the officers did not believe their story.

Heath and a codefendant were arrested for "loitering" and for "common thief." Both were residents of Jacksonville, Heath having lived there all his life and being employed at an automobile and body shop. Heath had previously been arrested but his codefendant had no arrest record. Heath and his companion were arrested when they drove up to a residence shared by Heath's girlfriend and some other girls. Some police officers were already there in the process of arresting another man. When Heath and his companion started backing out of the driveway, the officers signaled to them to stop and asked them to get out of the car, which they did. Thereupon they and the automobile were searched. Although no contraband or incriminating evidence was found, they were both arrested, Heath being charged with being a "common thief" because he was reputed to be a thief. The codefendant was charged with "loitering" because he was standing in the driveway, an act which the officers admitted was done only at their command.

Campbell was arrested as he reached his home very early one morning and was charged with "common thief." He was stopped by officers because he was traveling at a high rate of speed, yet no speeding charge was placed against him.

Brown was arrested when he was observed leaving a downtown, Jacksonville, hotel by a police officer seated in a cruiser. The police testified he was reputed to be a thief, narcotics pusher, and generally opprobrious character. The officer called Brown over to the car, intending at that time to arrest him unless he had a good explanation for being on the street. Brown walked over to the police cruiser, as commanded, and the officer began to search him, apparently preparatory to placing him in the car. In the process of the search he came on two small packets which were later found to contain heroin. When the officer touched the pocket where the packets were, Brown began to resist. He was charged with "disorderly loitering on the street" and "disorderly conduct—resisting arrest with violence." While he was also charged with a narcotics violation, that charge was *nolled.*

Jacksonville's ordinance and Florida's statute were "derived from early English law," ... and employ "archaic language" in their definitions of vagrants. The history is an often-told tale. The breakup of feudal estates in England led to labor shortages which in turn resulted in the Statutes of Laborers, designed to stabilize the labor force by prohibiting increases in wages and prohibiting the movement of workers from their home areas in search of improved conditions. Later vagrancy laws became criminal aspects of the poor laws. The series of laws passed in England on the subject became increasingly severe. But "the theory of the Elizabethan poor laws no longer fits the facts," ... The conditions which spawned these laws may be gone, but the archaic classifications remain.

This ordinance is void-for-vagueness, both in the sense that it "fails to give a person of ordinary intelligence fair notice that his contemplated conduct is forbidden by the statute," ... and because it encourages arbitrary and erratic arrests and convictions....

Living under a rule of law entails various suppositions, one of which is that "All [persons] are entitled to be informed as to what the State commands or forbids." Lanzetta v. New Jersey,....

Lanzetta is one of a well-recognized group of cases insisting that the law give fair notice of the offending conduct.... In the field of regulatory statutes governing business activities, where the acts limited are in a narrow category, greater leeway is allowed....

The poor among us, the minorities, the average householder are not in business and not alerted to the regulatory schemes of vagrancy laws; and we assume they would have no understanding of their meaning and impact if they read them. Nor are they protected from being caught in the vagrancy net by the necessity of having a specific intent to commit an unlawful act....

The Jacksonville ordinance makes criminal activities which by modern standards are normally innocent. "Nightwalking" is one. Florida construes the ordinance not to make criminal one night's wandering, ... only the "habitual" wanderer or as the ordinance describes it "common night walkers." We know, however, from experience that sleepless people often walk at night, perhaps hopeful that sleep-inducing relaxation will result.

Luis Munoz-Marin, former Governor of Puerto Rico, commented once that "loafing" was a national virtue in his Commonwealth and that it should be encouraged. It is, however, a crime in Jacksonville.

"Persons able to work but habitually living on the earnings of their wives or minor children"—like habitually living "without visible means of support"—might implicate unemployed pillars of the community who have married rich wives.

"Persons able to work but habitually living on the earnings of their wives or minor children" may also embrace unemployed people out of the labor market, by reason of a recession or disemployed by reason of technological or so-called structural displacements.

Persons "wandering or strolling" from place to place have been extolled by Walt Whitman and Vachel Lindsay. The qualification "without any lawful purpose or object" may be a trap for innocent acts. Persons "neglecting all lawful business and habitually spending their time by frequenting ... places where alcoholic beverages are sold or served" would literally embrace many members of golf clubs and city clubs.

Walkers and strollers and wanderers may be going to or coming from a burglary. Loafers or loiterers may be "casing" a place for a holdup. Letting one's wife support him is an intra-family matter, and normally of no concern to the police. Yet it may, of course, be the setting for numerous crimes.

The difficulty is that these activities are historically part of the amenities of life as we have known it. They are not mentioned in the Constitution or in the Bill of Rights. These unwritten amenities have been in part responsible for giving our people the feeling of independence and self-confidence, the feeling of creativity. These amenities have dignified the right of dissent and have honored the right to be nonconformists and the right to defy submissiveness. They have encouraged lives of high spirits rather than hushed, suffocating silence.

They are embedded in Walt Whitman's writings especially in his Song of the Open Road. They are reflected too, in the spirit of Vachel Lindsay's I Want to go Wandering and by Henry D. Thoreau.

This aspect of the vagrancy ordinance before us is suggested by what this Court said in 1875 about a broad criminal statute enacted by Congress: "It would certainly be dangerous if the legislature could set a net large enough to catch all possible offenders, and leave it to the courts to step inside and say who could be rightfully detained, and who should be set at large." ...

While that was a federal case, the due process implications are equally applicable to the States and to this vagrancy ordinance. Here the net cast is large, not to give the courts the power to pick and choose but to increase the arsenal of the police....

* * *

Where the list of crimes is so all-inclusive and generalized as that one in this ordinance, those convicted may be punished for no more than vindicating affronts to police authority: ....

Another aspect of the ordinance's vagueness appears when we focus, not on the lack of notice given a potential offender, but on the effect of the unfettered discretion it places in the hands of the Jacksonville police. Caleb Foote, an early student of this subject, has called the vagrancy-type law as offering "punishment by analogy." Such crimes, though long common in Russia, are not compatible with our constitutional system. We allow our police to make arrests only on "probable cause," a Fourth and Fourteenth Amendment standard applicable to the States as well as to the Federal Government. Arresting a person on suspicion, like arresting a person for investigation, is foreign to our system, even when the arrest is for past criminality. Future criminality, however, is the common justification for the presence of vagrancy statutes.... Florida has indeed construed her vagrancy statute "as necessary regulations," *inter alia,* "to deter vagabondage and prevent crimes." ...

A direction by a legislature to the police to arrest all "suspicious" persons would not pass constitutional muster. A vagrancy prosecution may be merely the cloak for a conviction which could not be obtained on the real but undisclosed grounds for the arrest....

Those generally implicated by the imprecise terms of the ordinance—poor people, nonconformists, dissenters, idlers—may be required to comport themselves according to the life-style deemed appropriate by the Jacksonville police and the courts. Where, as here, there are no standards governing the exercise of the discretion granted by the ordinance, the scheme permits and encourages an arbitrary and discriminatory enforcement of the law. It furnishes a convenient tool for "harsh and discriminatory enforcement by prosecuting officials, against particular groups deemed to merit their displeasure." ... It results in a regime in which the poor and the unpopular are permitted to "stand on a public sidewalk ... only at the whim of any police officer." ...

A presumption that people who might walk or loaf or loiter or stroll or frequent houses where liquor is sold, or who are supported by their wives or who look suspicious to the police are to become future criminals is too precarious for a rule of law. The implicit presumption in these generalized vagrancy standards—that crime is being nipped in the bud—is too extravagant to deserve extended treatment. Of course, vagrancy statutes are useful to the police. Of course they are nets making easy the round-up of so-called undesirables. But the rule of law implies equality and justice in its application. Vagrancy laws of the Jacksonville type teach that the scales of justice are so tipped that even-handed administration of the law is not possible. The rule of law, evenly applied to minorities as well as majorities, to the poor as well as the rich, is the great mucilage that holds society together.

The Jacksonville ordinance cannot be squared with our constitutional standards and is plainly unconstitutional.

Reversed.

Mr. Justice Powell and Mr. Justice Rehnquist took no part in the consideration or decision of this case.

COATES v. CITY OF CINCINNATI

Supreme Court of the United States, 1971.
402 U.S. 611, 91 S.Ct. 1686.

MR. JUSTICE STEWART delivered the opinion of the Court.

A Cincinnati, Ohio, ordinance makes it a criminal offense for "three or more persons to assemble ... on any of the sidewalks ... and there conduct themselves in a manner annoying to persons passing by...." The issue before us is whether this ordinance is unconstitutional on its face.

The appellants were convicted of violating the ordinance, and the convictions were ultimately affirmed by a closely divided vote in the Supreme Court of Ohio, upholding the constitutional validity of the ordinance.... The record brought before the reviewing courts tells us no more than that the appellant Coates was a student involved in a demonstration and the other appellants were pickets involved in a labor dispute. For throughout this litigation it has been the appellants' position that the ordinance on its face violates the First and Fourteenth Amendments of the Constitution....

In rejecting this claim and affirming the convictions the Ohio Supreme Court did not give the ordinance any construction at variance with the apparent plain import of its language. The court simply stated:

> "The ordinance prohibits, *inter alia,* 'conduct ... annoying to persons passing by.' The word 'annoying' is a widely used and well understood word; it is not necessary to guess its meaning. 'Annoying' is the present participle of the transitive verb 'annoy' which means to trouble, to vex, to impede, to incommode, to provoke, to harass or to irritate.
>
> "We conclude, as did the Supreme Court of the United States in Cameron v. Johnson, ... in which the issue of the vagueness of a statute was presented, that the ordinance 'clearly and precisely delineates its reach in words of common understanding. It is a "precise and narrowly drawn regulatory statute [ordinance] evincing a legislative judgment that certain specific conduct be ... proscribed." ' " ...

Beyond this, the only construction put upon the ordinance by the state court was its unexplained conclusion that "the standard of conduct which it specifies is not dependent upon each complainant's sensitivity." But the court did not indicate upon whose sensitivity a violation does depend—the sensitivity of the judge or jury, the sensitivity of the arresting officer, or the sensitivity of a hypothetical reasonable man.

We are thus relegated, at best, to the words of the ordinance itself. If three or more people meet together on a sidewalk or street corner, they must conduct themselves so as not to annoy any police officer or other person who should happen to pass by. In our opinion this ordinance is unconstitutionally vague because it subjects the exercise of the right of assembly to an unascertainable standard, and unconstitutionally broad because it authorizes the punishment of constitutionally protected conduct.

Conduct that annoys some people does not annoy others. Thus, the ordinance is vague, not in the sense that it requires a person to conform his conduct to an imprecise but comprehensible normative standard, but rather in the sense that no standard of conduct is specified at all. As a result, "men of common intelligence must necessarily guess at its meaning." ...

It is said that the ordinance is broad enough to encompass many types of conduct clearly within the city's constitutional power to prohibit. And so, indeed, it is. The city is free to prevent people from blocking sidewalks, obstructing traffic, littering streets, committing assaults, or engaging in countless other forms of antisocial conduct. It can do so through the enactment and enforcement of ordinances directed with reasonable specificity toward the conduct to be prohibited.... It cannot constitutionally do so through the enactment and enforcement of an ordinance whose violation may entirely depend upon whether or not a policeman is annoyed.

But the vice of the ordinance lies not alone in its violation of the due process standard of vagueness. The ordinance also violates the constitutional right of free assembly and association. Our decisions establish that mere public intolerance or animosity cannot be the basis for abridgment of these constitutional freedoms.... The First and Fourteenth Amendments do not permit a State to make criminal the exercise of the right of assembly simply because its exercise may be "annoying" to some people. If this were not the rule, the right of the people to gather in public places for social or political purposes would be continually subject to summary suspension through the good-faith enforcement of a prohibition against annoying conduct. And such a prohibition, in addition, contains an obvious invitation to discriminatory enforcement against those whose association together is "annoying" because their ideas, their lifestyle, or their physical appearance is resented by the majority of their fellow citizens.

The ordinance before us makes a crime out of what under the Constitution cannot be a crime. It is aimed directly at activity protected by the Constitution. We need not lament that we do not have before us the details of the conduct found to be annoying. It is the ordinance on its face that sets the standard of conduct and warns against transgression. The details of the offense could no more serve to validate this ordinance than could the details of an offense charged under an ordinance suspending unconditionally the right of assembly and free speech.

The judgment is reversed.

MR. JUSTICE BLACK.

* * *

This Court has long held that laws so vague that a person of common understanding cannot know what is forbidden are unconstitutional on their face.... Likewise, laws which broadly forbid conduct or activities which are protected by the Federal Constitution, such as, for instance, the discussion of political matters, are void on their face.... On the other hand, laws which plainly forbid conduct which is constitutionally within the power of the State to forbid but also restrict constitutionally protected conduct may be void either on their face or merely as applied in certain instances. As my Brother White states in his opinion (with which I substantially agree), this is one of those numerous cases where the law could be held unconstitutional because it prohibits both conduct which the Constitution safeguards and conduct which the State may constitutionally punish. Thus, the First Amendment which forbids the State to abridge freedom of speech, would invalidate this city ordinance if it were used to punish the making of a political speech, even if that speech were to annoy other persons. In contrast, however, the ordinance could properly be applied to prohibit the gathering of persons in the mouths of alleys to annoy passersby by throwing rocks or by some other conduct not at all connected with speech. It is a matter of no little difficulty to determine when a law can be held void on its face and when such summary action is inappropriate. This difficulty has been aggravated in this case, because the record fails to show in what conduct these defendants had engaged to annoy other people. In my view, a record showing the facts surrounding the conviction is essential to adjudicate the important constitutional issues in this case. I would therefore vacate the judgment and remand the case with instructions that the trial court give both parties an opportunity to supplement the record so that we may determine whether the conduct actually punished is the kind of conduct which it is within the power of the State to punish.

[The dissenting opinion of Justice White, joined by the Chief Justice and Justice Blackmun, is omitted.]

NOTES

1. A Kentucky statute provided that "a person is guilty of disorderly conduct if, with intent to cause public inconvenience, annoyance or alarm, or recklessly creating a risk thereof, he ... congregates with other persons in a public place and refuses to comply with a lawful order of the police to disperse ..." Ky.Rev.Stat. § 437.016(1)(f). In Colten v. Kentucky, 407 U.S. 104, 92 S.Ct. 1953 (1972), a police officer requested the defendant several times to leave a congested roadside where a friend of his in another car was being ticketed for a traffic offense. Defendant refused, was arrested for disorderly conduct, and convicted. The majority of the Court held that the statute was not impermissibly vague or broad. It laid down these basic principles:

> "The root of the vagueness doctrine is a rough idea of fairness. It is not a principle designed to convert into a constitutional dilemma the practical difficulties in drawing criminal statutes both general enough to take into account a variety of human conduct and sufficiently specific to provide fair warning that certain kinds of conduct are prohibited. We agree with the Kentucky court when it said: 'We believe that citizens who desire to obey the statute will have no difficulty in understanding it....'
>
> * * *
>
> "As the Kentucky statute was construed by the state court, a crime is committed only where there is no bona fide intention to exercise a constitutional right—in which event, by definition, the statute infringes no protected speech or conduct—or where the interest so clearly outweighs the collective interest sought to be asserted that the latter must be deemed insubstantial."

2. In Plummer v. Columbus, 414 U.S. 2, 94 S.Ct. 17 (1973), the defendant was convicted of violating a city code provision which prohibits any person from abusing another by using menacing, insulting, slanderous or profane language. The Supreme Court held that even though as applied to the defendant, the ordinance might be neither vague, nor overbroad, nor otherwise constitutionally infirm, he nevertheless could raise its vagueness or constitutional overbreadth as applied to others. In holding the ordinance facially unconstitutional in the absence of a satisfactory limiting construction by the state courts, the defendant's conviction was reversed.

In Hynes v. Mayor of Oradell, 425 U.S. 610, 96 S.Ct. 1755 (1976), a municipal ordinance required door-to-door canvassers to give advance notice of their intent to do so to the police department. The ordinance was held invalid for vagueness in that it covers "recognized charitable causes" without explaining which causes are so recognized. Other constitutional defects were noted as well.

3. A Sunday closing law exempts stores that have no more than four employees on duty at any one time on Sunday. Is such statute sufficiently precise? Does "employees" include the owner of a business, members of his family, whether paid or unpaid, a clean-up man, bag boy, or security guard? See Simonetti v. City of Birmingham, 55 Ala.App. 163, 314 So.2d 83 (1975), cert. denied 294 Ala. 192, 314 So.2d 99. A City of Columbus ordinance makes it unlawful to appear in public in a dress not belonging to the wearer's sex. Is such an ordinance constitutional if attached on vagueness grounds? See City of Columbus v. Rogers, 41 Ohio St.2d 161, 324 N.E.2d 563 (1975), and Annot., 12 A.L.R. 4th 1249 (1982). Is a statute unconstitutionally vague which makes it a misdemeanor when a person "intentionally interferes with a person recognized to be a law enforcement official seeking to effect an arrest or detention of himself or another regardless of whether there is a legal basis for the arrest?" See, State v. Bradshaw, 541 P.2d 800 (Utah 1975). How about a statute that prohibits a person from peeping through doors, windows, or similar places of another while on another's premises with intent or purpose to spy on such person or to invade his privacy, or going into another's premises for that purpose? See Lemon v. State, 235 Ga. 74, 218 S.E.2d 818 (1975), cert. denied, 425 U.S. 906, 96 S.Ct. 1499 (1976).

4. Is Virginia Code § 18.2–388 (1982), defining the crime of profane swearing and drunkenness, constitutionally valid? The statute provides: "If any person profanely curse or swear or be drunk in public he shall be deemed guilty of a Class 4 misdemeanor." What about Virginia Code § 18.2–416 which states: "If any person shall, in the presence or hearing of another, curse or abuse such other person, or use any violent abusive language to such person concerning himself or any of his relations, or otherwise use such language, under circumstances reasonably calculated to provoke a breach of the peace, he shall be guilty of a Class 3 misdemeanor."

5. A California statute requiring persons who loiter or wander on the streets to provide "credible and reliable" identification and account for their presence when requested by a police officer was held to be unconstitutionally vague on its face in Kolender v. Lawson, 461 U.S. 352, 103 S.Ct. 1855 (1983). The Court found vagueness because the statute failed to clarify what "credible and reliable" identification is. Therefore, the statute gave virtually complete discretion to the officer to determine whether the suspect has satisfied the statute and must be permitted to go on his way in the absence of probable cause to arrest.

The Wisconsin Supreme Court upheld a demand for identification by a police officer in a case where a burglary of a sporting goods shop had just occurred and one of the persons stopped fit the description of those seen breaking into the store a half hour earlier. State v. Flynn, 92 Wis.2d 427, 285 N.W.2d 710 (1979), cert. denied sub nom. Flynn v. Wisconsin, 449 U.S. 846, 101 S.Ct. 130 (1980).

A loitering ordinance based on the American Law Institute's 1962 Model Penal Code which permits an officer to approach and detain a person only under circumstances that would justify a stop pursuant to *Terry v. Ohio,* see Chapter 14, p. 1071, and under which the officer must be able to conclude that peace and order are threatened or that the safety of persons or property is jeopardized, and the officer has to give the suspect an opportunity to identify himself and explain his conduct, and a suspect may not be convicted if the officer *should* have believed his explanation, is not unconstitutional on its face under the ruling in Kolender v. Lawson. Porta v. Mayor, City of Omaha, 593 F.Supp. 863 (D.Neb. 1984).

6. A statute that proscribed "neglect of a dependent" has been held to be constitutionally vague and overbroad. The custodian of a dependent had a statutory duty not to "[p]lace the dependent in a situation that may endanger his life or health" (West's Ann.Ind.Code 35–46–1–4). This language did not sufficiently inform persons of ordinary intelligence of the prohibited conduct.

> "The word 'may' expresses ability, possibility, or contingency.... Therefore, the statute must be read to proscribe placements which to some degree are likely to bring a dependent into a situation in which he is exposed to harm. Thus the statute does not require that the placement expose a dependent to harm. It need only expose one to the risk of a risk of harm. Under this language, it would be a crime to raise a child in a highrise apartment or to mop the kitchen floor with a bucket of water in the presence of a small child." State v. Downey, 476 N.E.2d 121 (Ind.1985).

GOODING, WARDEN v. WILSON

Supreme Court of the United States, 1972.
405 U.S. 518, 92 S.Ct. 1103.

MR. JUSTICE BRENNAN delivered the opinion of the Court.

Appellee was convicted in Superior Court, Fulton County, Georgia, on two counts of using opprobrious words and abusive language in violation of Georgia Code § 26–6303, which provides: "Any person who shall, without provocation, use to or of another, and in his presence ... opprobrious words or abusive language, tending to cause a breach of the peace ... shall be guilty of a misdemeanor."

* * *

Section 26–6303 punishes only spoken words. It can therefore withstand appellee's attack upon its facial constitutionality only if, as authoritatively construed by the Georgia courts, it is not susceptible of application to speech, although vulgar or offensive, that is protected by the First and Fourteenth Amendments,.... Only the Georgia courts can supply the requisite construction, since of course "we lack jurisdiction authoritatively to construe state legislation." ... It matters not that the words appellee used might have been constitutionally prohibited under a narrowly and precisely drawn statute. At least when statutes regulate or proscribe speech and when "no readily apparent construction suggests itself as a vehicle for rehabilitating the statutes in a single prosecution," ... the transcendent value to all society of constitutionally protected expression is deemed to justify allowing "attacks on overly broad statutes with no requirement that the person making the attack demonstrate that his own conduct could not be regulated by a statute drawn with the requisite narrow specificity," ... This is deemed necessary because persons whose expression is constitutionally protected may well refrain from exercising their rights for fear of criminal sanctions provided by a statute susceptible of application to protected expression.

* * *

The constitutional guarantees of freedom of speech forbid the States from punishing the use of words or language not within "narrowly limited classes of speech." Chaplinsky v. New Hampshire,.... Even as to such a class, however, because "the line between speech unconditionally guaranteed and speech which may legitimately be regulated, suppressed, or punished is finely drawn,".... "[i]n every case the power to regulate must be so exercised as not, in attaining a permissible end, unduly to infringe the protected freedom,".... In other words, the statute must be carefully drawn or be authoritatively construed to punish only unprotected speech and not be susceptible of application to protected expression. "Because First Amendment freedoms need breathing space to survive, government may regulate in the area only with narrow specificity." ...

Appellant does not challenge these principles but contends that the Georgia statute is narrowly drawn to apply only to a constitutionally unprotected class of words—"fighting" words—"those which by their very utterance inflict injury or tend to incite an immediate breach of the peace." ... In *Chaplinsky,* we sustained a conviction under Chapter 378, § 2, of the Public Laws of New Hampshire, which provided: "No person shall address any offensive, derisive or annoying word to any other person who is lawfully in any street or other public place, nor call him by any offensive or derisive name...." Chaplinsky was convicted for addressing to another on a public sidewalk the words, "You are a God damned racketeer," and "a damned Fascist and the whole government of Rochester are Fascists or agents of Fascists." Chaplinsky challenged the constitutionality of the statute as inhibiting freedom of expression because it was vague and indefinite. The Supreme Court of New Hampshire, however, "long before the words for which Chaplinsky was convicted," sharply limited the statutory language "offensive, derisive or annoying word" to "fighting" words....

* * *

Appellant argues that the Georgia appellate courts have by construction limited the proscription of § 26–6303 to "fighting" words, as the New Hampshire Supreme Court limited the New Hampshire statute.... We have however, made our own examination of the Georgia cases, both those cited and others discovered in research. That examination brings us to the conclusion, in agreement with the courts below, that the Georgia appellate decisions have not construed § 26–6303 to be limited in application, as in *Chaplinsky,* to words that "have a direct tendency to cause acts of violence by the person to whom, individually, the remark is addressed."

The dictionary definitions of "opprobrious" and "abusive" give them greater reach than "fighting" words. . . .

* * *

Mr. Justice Powell and Mr. Justice Rehnquist, took no part in the consideration or decision of this case.

MR. CHIEF JUSTICE BURGER, dissenting.

I fully join in Mr. Justice Blackmun's dissent against the bizarre result reached by the Court. It is not merely odd, it is nothing less than remarkable that a court can find a state statute void on its face, not because of its language—which is the traditional test—but because of the way courts of that State have applied the statute in a few isolated cases, decided as long ago as 1905 and generally long before this Court's decision in Chaplinsky v. New Hampshire,. . . . Even if all of those cases had been decided yesterday, they do nothing to demonstrate that the narrow language of the Georgia statute has any significant potential for sweeping application to suppress or deter important protected speech.

In part the Court's decision appears to stem from its assumption that a statute should be regarded in the same light as its most vague clause, without regard to any of its other language. . . . The statute at bar, however, does not prohibit language "tending to cause a breach of the peace." Nor does it prohibit the use of "opprobrious words or abusive language" without more. Rather, it prohibits use "to or of another, and in his presence opprobrious words or abusive language, tending to cause a breach of the peace." If words are to bear their common meaning, and are to be considered in context, rather than dissected with surgical precision using a semantical scalpel, this statute has little potential for application outside the realm of "fighting words" which this Court held beyond the protection of the First Amendment in *Chaplinsky*. Indeed, the language used by the *Chaplinsky* Court to describe words properly subject to regulation bears a striking resemblance to that of the Georgia statute, which was enacted many, many years before *Chaplinsky* was decided. And, if the early Georgia cases cited by the majority establish any proposition, it is that the statute, as its language so clearly indicates, is aimed at preventing precisely that type of personal, face-to-face abusive and insulting language likely to provoke a violent retaliation—self help, as we euphemistically call it—which the *Chaplinsky* case recognized could be validly prohibited. The facts of the case now before the Court demonstrate that the Georgia statute is serving that valid and entirely proper purpose. There is no persuasive reason to wipe the statute from the books, unless we want to encourage victims of such verbal assaults to seek their own private redress.

* * *

MR. JUSTICE BLACKMUN, with whom THE CHIEF JUSTICE joins, dissenting.

It seems strange indeed that in this day a man may say to a police officer, who is attempting to restore access to a public building, "White son of a bitch, I'll kill you" and "You son of a bitch, I'll choke you to death," and say to an accompanying officer, "You son of a bitch, if you ever put your hands on me again, I'll cut you all to pieces," and yet constitutionally cannot be prosecuted and convicted under a state statute which makes it a misdemeanor to "use to or of another, and in his presence, opprobrious words or abusive language, tending to cause a breach of the peace...." This, however, is precisely what the Court pronounces as the law today.

The Supreme Court of Georgia, when the conviction was appealed, unanimously held the other way.... Surely any adult who can read—and I do not exclude this appellee-defendant from that category—should reasonably expect no other conclusion. The words of Georgia Code § 26–6303 are clear. They are also concise. They are not, in my view, overbroad or incapable of being understood. Except perhaps for the "big" word "opprobrious"—and no point is made of its bigness—any Georgia schoolboy would expect that this defendant's fighting and provocative words to the officers were covered by § 26–6303. Common sense permits no other conclusion. This is demonstrated by the fact that the appellee, and this Court, attacks the statute not as it applies to the appellee, but as it conceivably might apply to others who might utter other words.

The Court reaches its result by saying that the Georgia statute has been interpreted by the State's courts so as to be applicable in practice to otherwise constitutionally protected speech. It follows, says the Court, that the statute is overbroad and therefore is facially unconstitutional and to be struck down in its entirety. Thus Georgia apparently is to be left with no valid statute on its books to meet Wilson's bullying tactic. This result, achieved by what is indeed a very strict construction, will be totally incomprehensible to the State of Georgia, to its courts, and to its citizens.

The Court would justify its conclusion by unearthing a 66-year-old decision, ..., of the Supreme Court of Georgia, and two intermediate appellate court cases over 55 years old, ... broadly applying the statute in those less permissive days, and by additional reference to (a) a 1956 Georgia intermediate appellate court decision, ... which, were it the first and only Georgia case, would surely not support today's decision, and (b) another intermediate appellate court decision ... (1961), relating not to § 26–6303, but to another statute.

This Court appears to have developed its overbreadth rationale in the years since these early Georgia cases. The State's statute, therefore, is condemned because the State's courts have not had an opportunity to adjust to this Court's modern theories of overbreadth.

I wonder, now that § 26–6303 is voided, just what Georgia can do if it seeks to proscribe what the Court says it still may constitutionally proscribe. The natural thing would be to enact a new statute reading just as § 26–6303 reads. But it, too, presumably would be overbroad unless the legislature would add words to the effect that it means only what this Court says it may mean and no more.

* * *

For me, Chaplinsky v. New Hampshire ... was good law when it was decided and deserves to remain as good law now. A unanimous Court, including among its members Chief Justice Stone and Justices Black, Reed, Douglas and Murphy, obviously thought it was good law. But I feel that by decisions such as this one ..., despite its protestations to the contrary, is merely paying lip service to *Chaplinsky.* As the appellee states in a footnote to his brief, p. 14, "Although there is no doubt that the state can punish 'fighting words' this appears to be about all that is left of the decision in *Chaplinsky.*" If this is what the overbreadth doctrine means, and if this is what it produces, it urgently needs reexamination. The Court has painted itself into a corner from which it, and the States, can extricate themselves only with difficulty.

NOTE

A disorderly conduct statute that proscribed "[t]he causing or making of an unnecessarily loud noise or shouting or yelling or uncooperative or unseemly behavior toward or in the presence of a police officer" was facially unconstitutional for prohibiting both protected as well as unprotected speech and no amount of judicial interpretation could save it. "There is no way that the phrase 'unseemly behavior toward or in the presence of a police officer' ... can be so limited by judicial construction. The term 'unseemly' is defined as 'not according with established standards of good form or taste.' ... An unending list of examples of utterances could be conjured up which do not comport with 'good form or taste' but which are clearly protected by the First Amendment." City of Jackson v. Oliver, 680 S.W.2d 406 (Mo.App.1984).

In City of Houston, Texas v. Hill, 482 U.S. 451, 107 S.Ct. 2502 (1987), a city ordinance penalized interruption of police officers while they were performing official duties. Part of the ordinance covered physical assaults on the police, but that part was inoperative because of pre-emption by a separate state statute covering assaultive conduct. The operative part of the ordinance was used to convict a defendant who verbally intervened in a police encounter with a friend, telling the police to "pick on somebody my size." The U.S. Supreme Court found the ordinance overbroad in violation of the First Amendment because of its applicability to pure speech and for giving too much discretion to the police. This was *not* an ordinance penalizing "fighting words," which would be constitutional, see *Gooding, Warden v. Wilson,* p. 227 in the book. It covered mere verbal "criticism and challenge." "The freedom of individuals verbally to oppose or challenge police action without thereby risking arrest is one of the principal characteristics by which we distinguish a free nation from a police state." The Court's rule is narrow and specific: "pure speech" cannot be punished by such an ordinance, even if it is "criticism" or "challenging," but "fighting words" or physical assaultive conduct *can* be penalized, usually under an appropriately worded disorderly conduct statute.

A statute proscribing "making an offensively coarse utterance, gesture or display, or addressing abusive language to any person present [with the] intent to harass, annoy, or alarm another person, "was struck down as constitutionally overbroad, and the Court refused to "authoritatively construe" it to make it constitutional by applying only to "fighting words," since to do so might well change the statute from what was actually intended by the legislature. Musselman v. Commonwealth, 705 S.W.2d 476 (Ky.1986).

A disturbing of the peace ordinance defining the offense as "wilfully disturbing the peace and quiet of any person, family, or neighborhood" was struck down in Wichita v. Hughes, 12 Kan.App.2d 621, 752 P.2d 1086 (1988), as unconstitutionally vague. The language in the ordinance failed to give specific guidance as to how the law was or was not violated (what is "peace and quiet"?). In some cases courts have put a limiting construction on similar ordinances in order to save them from constitutional infirmity, but the court in this case refused to do so.

I. EQUAL PROTECTION OF THE LAW

"The least considerable man among us has an interest equal to the proudest nobleman, in the laws and constitution of his country...."

Junius, To the Printer of the Public Advertiser (March 19, 1770).

McLAUGHLIN v. FLORIDA

Supreme Court of the United States, 1964.
379 U.S. 184, 85 S.Ct. 283.

MR. JUSTICE WHITE delivered the opinion of the Court.

At issue in this case is the validity of a conviction under § 798.05 of the Florida statutes, providing that:

"Any negro man and white woman, or any white man and negro woman, who are not married to each other, who shall habitually live in and occupy in the nighttime the same room shall each be punished by imprisonment not exceeding twelve months, or by fine not exceeding five hundred dollars."

Because the section applies only to a white person and a Negro who commit the specified acts and because no couple other than one made up of a white and a Negro is subject to conviction upon proof of the elements comprising the offense it proscribes, we hold § 798.05 invalid as a denial of the equal protection of the laws guaranteed by the Fourteenth Amendment....

The elements of the offense as described by the trial judge are the (1) habitual occupation of a room at night, (2) by a Negro and a white person (3) who are not married. The State presented evidence going to each factor, appellants' constitutional contentions were overruled and the jury returned a verdict of guilty. Solely on the authority of Pace v. Alabama, ... the Florida Supreme Court affirmed and sustained the validity of § 798.05 as against appellants' claims that the section denied them equal protection of the laws guaranteed by the Fourteenth Amendment....

It is readily apparent that § 798.05 treats the interracial couple made up of a white person and a Negro differently than it does any other couple. No couple other than a Negro and a white person can be convicted under § 798.05 and no other section proscribes the precise conduct banned by § 798.05. Florida makes no claim to the contrary in this Court. However, all whites and Negroes who engage in the forbidden conduct are covered by the section and each member of the interracial couple is subject to the same penalty.

In this situation, Pace v. Alabama is relied upon as controlling authority. In our view, however, *Pace* represents a limited view of the Equal Protection Clause which has not withstood analysis in the subsequent decisions of this Court. In that case, the Court let stand a conviction under an Alabama statute forbidding adultery or fornication between a white person and a Negro and imposing a greater penalty than allowed under another Alabama statute of general application and proscribing the same conduct whatever the race of the participants. The opinion acknowledged that the purpose of the Equal Protection Clause "was to prevent hostile and discriminating State legislation against any person or class of persons" and that equality of protection under the laws implies that any person, "whatever his race ... shall not be subjected, for the same offence, to any greater or different punishment." But taking quite literally its own words, "for the same *offence*" (emphasis supplied), the Court pointed out that Alabama had designated as a separate offense the commission by a white person and a Negro of the identical acts forbidden by the general provisions. There was, therefore, no impermissible discrimination because the difference in punishment was "directed against the offence designated" and because in the case of each offense all who committed it, white and Negro were treated alike. Under *Pace* the Alabama law regulating the conduct of both Negroes and whites satisfied the Equal Protection Clause since it applied equally to and among the members of the class which it reached without regard to the fact that the statute did not reach other types of couples performing the identical conduct and without any necessity to justify the difference in penalty established for the two offenses. Because each of the Alabama laws applied equally to those to whom it was applicable, the different treatment accorded interracial and intraracial couples was irrelevant.[1]

1. Had the Court been presented with a statute that, for example, prohibited any Negro male from having carnal knowledge of a white female and penalized only the Negro, such a statute would unquestionably have been held to deny equal protection even though it applied equally to all to whom it applied. See Strauder v. West Virginia, 100 U.S. 303, 306–308; Ho Ah Kow v. Nunan, 12 Fed.Cas. 252 (No. 6546) (C.C.D.Cal.1879) (Field, J.) ("Chinese Pigtail" case). Because of the manifest inadequacy of any approach requiring only equal application to the class defined in the statute, one may conclude that in *Pace* the Court actually ruled *sub silentio* that the different treatment meted out to interracial and intraracial couples was based on a reasonable legislative purpose. If the Court did reach that conclusion it failed to articulate it or to give its reasons and for the

This narrow view of the Equal Protection Clause was soon swept away. While acknowledging the currency of the view that "if the law deals alike with all of a certain class" it is not obnoxious to the Equal Protection Clause and that "as a general proposition, this is undeniably true," the Court in Gulf, C. & S.F.R. Co. v. Ellis, ... said that it was "equally true that such classification cannot be made arbitrarily...." Classification "must always rest upon some difference which bears a reasonable and just relation to the act in respect to which the classification is proposed, and can never be made arbitrarily and without any such basis." "[A]rbitrary selection can never be justified by calling it classification." ...

Judicial inquiry under the Equal Protection Clause, therefore, does not end with a showing of equal application among the members of the class defined by the legislation. The courts must reach and determine the question whether the classifications drawn in a statute are reasonable in light of its purpose—in this case, whether there is an arbitrary or invidious discrimination between those classes covered by Florida's cohabitation law and those excluded. That question is what *Pace* ignored and what must be faced here.

Normally, the widest discretion is allowed the legislative judgment in determining whether to attack some, rather than all, of the manifestations of the evil aimed at; and normally that judgment is given the benefit of every conceivable circumstance which might suffice to characterize the classification as reasonable rather than arbitrary and invidious.... But we deal here with a classification based upon the race of the participants, which must be viewed in light of the historical fact that the central purpose of the Fourteenth Amendment was to eliminate racial discrimination emanating from official sources in the States. This strong policy renders racial classifications "constitutionally suspect" ...; and subject to the "most rigid scrutiny" ...; and "in most circumstances irrelevant" to any constitutionally acceptable legislative purpose.... Thus it is that racial classifications have been held invalid in a variety of contexts. See, e.g., Virginia Board of Elections v. Hamm ... (designation of race in voting and property records); Anderson v. Martin ... (designation of race on nomination papers and ballots); Watson v. City of Memphis ... (segregation in public parks and playgrounds); Brown v. Board of Education ... (segregation in public schools).

We deal here with a racial classification embodied in a criminal statute. In this context, where the power of the State weighs most heavily upon the individual or the group, we must be especially sensitive to the policies of the Equal Protection Clause which, as reflected in congressional enactments dating from 1870, were intended to secure "the full and equal benefit of all laws and proceedings for the security of persons and property" and to subject all persons "to like punishment,

reasons stated infra we reject the contention presented here that the criminal statute presently under review is grounded in a reasonable legislative policy.

pains, penalties, taxes, licenses, and exactions of every kind, and to no other."

Our inquiry, therefore, is whether there clearly appears in the relevant materials some overriding statutory purpose requiring the proscription of the specified conduct when engaged in by a white person and a Negro, but not otherwise. Without such justification the racial classification contained in § 798.05 is reduced to an invidious discrimination forbidden by the Equal Protection Clause.

The Florida Supreme Court, relying upon Pace v. Alabama, found no legal discrimination at all and gave no consideration to statutory purpose. The State in its brief in this Court, however, says that the legislative purpose of § 798.05, like the other sections of chapter 798, was to prevent breaches of the basic concepts of sexual decency; and we see no reason to quarrel with the State's characterization of this statute, dealing as it does with illicit extramarital and premarital promiscuity.

We find nothing in this suggested legislative purpose, however, which makes it essential to punish promiscuity of one racial group and not that of another. There is no suggestion that a white person and a Negro are any more likely habitually to occupy the same room together than the white or the Negro couple or to engage in illicit intercourse if they do. Sections 798.01–798.05 indicate no legislative conviction that promiscuity by the interracial couple presents any particular problems requiring separate or different treatment if the suggested over-all policy of the chapter is to be adequately served. Sections 798.01–798.03 deal with adultery, lewd cohabitation and fornication, in that order. All are of general application. Section 798.04 prohibits a white and a Negro from living in a state of adultery or fornication and imposes a lesser period of imprisonment than does either § 798.01 or § 798.02, each of which is applicable to all persons. Simple fornication by the interracial couple is covered only by the general provision of § 798.03. This is not, therefore, a case where the class defined in the law is that from which "the evil mainly is to be feared," Patsone v. Pennsylvania . . .; or where the "[e]vils in the same field may be of different dimensions and proportions, requiring different remedies" . . .; or even one where the State has done as much as it can as fast as it can. . . . That a general evil will be partially corrected may at times, and without more, serve to justify the limited application of a criminal law; but legislative discretion to employ the piecemeal approach stops short of permitting State to narrow statutory coverage to focus on a racial group. Such classifications bear a far heavier burden of justification. . . .

Florida's remaining argument is related to its law against interracial marriage . . . which, in the light of certain legislative history of the Fourteenth Amendment, is said to be immune from attack under the Equal Protection Clause. Its interracial cohabitation law, § 798.05, is likewise valid, it is argued, because it is ancillary to and serves the same purpose as the miscegenation law itself.

We reject this argument, without reaching the question of the validity of the State's prohibition against interracial marriage or the soundness of the arguments rooted in the history of the Amendment. For even if we posit the constitutionality of the ban against the marriage of a Negro and a white, it does not follow that the cohabitation law is not to be subjected to independent examination under the Fourteenth Amendment. "[A]ssuming, for purposes of argument only, that the basic prohibition is constitutional," in this case the law against interracial marriage, "it does not follow that there is no constitutional limit to the means which may be used to enforce it." ... Section 798.05 must therefore itself pass muster under the Fourteenth Amendment; and for reasons quite similar to those already given, we think it fails the test.

There is involved here an exercise of the state police power which trenches upon the constitutionally protected freedom from invidious official discrimination based on race. Such a law, even though enacted pursuant to a valid state interest, bears a heavy burden of justification, as we have said, and will be upheld only if it is necessary, and not merely rationally related, to the accomplishment of a permissible state policy.... Those provisions of chapter 798 which are neutral as to race express a general and strong state policy against promiscuous conduct, whether engaged in by those who are married, those who may marry or those who may not. These provisions, if enforced, would reach illicit relations of any kind and in this way protect the integrity of the marriage laws of the State, including what is claimed to be a valid ban on interracial marriage. These same provisions, moreover, punish premarital sexual relations as severely or more severely in some instances than do those provisions which focus on the interracial couple. Florida has offered no argument that the State's policy against interracial marriage cannot be as adequately served by the general, neutral, and existing ban on illicit behavior as by a provision such as § 798.05 which singles out the promiscuous interracial couple for special statutory treatment. In short, it has not been shown that § 798.05 is a necessary adjunct to the State's ban on interracial marriage. We accordingly invalidate § 798.05 without expressing any views about the State's prohibition of interracial marriage, and reverse these convictions.

Reversed.

MR. JUSTICE STEWART, with whom MR. JUSTICE DOUGLAS joins, concurring.

I concur in the judgment and agree with most of what is said in the Court's opinion. But the Court implies that a criminal law of the kind here involved might be constitutionally valid if a State could show "some overriding statutory purpose." This is an implication in which I cannot join, because I cannot conceive of a valid legislative purpose under our Constitution for a state law which makes the color of a person's skin the test of whether his conduct is a criminal offense. These appellants were convicted, fined, and imprisoned under a statute which made their conduct criminal only because they were of different races. So far as this statute goes, their conduct would not have been illegal had they both been white, or both Negroes. There might be limited room under the Equal Protection Clause for a civil law requiring the keeping of racially segregated public records for statistical or other valid public purposes.... But we deal here with a criminal law which imposes criminal punishment. And I think it is simply not possible for a state law to be valid under our Constitution which makes the criminality of an act depend upon the race of the actor. Discrimination of that kind is invidious *per se.*

NOTES

1. In Loving v. Virginia, 388 U.S. 1, 87 S.Ct. 1817 (1967), the Court, on the authority of the McLaughlin case, voided prohibitions against interracial marriage.

2. The limitations imposed upon state action in the creation and definition of crime are not always concerned with unequal application based on race. For example, in State ex rel. Flores v. Tahash, 272 Minn. 451, 138 N.W.2d 626 (1965), the petitioner, convicted of the unlawful possession of 85 bottles of empirin compound with codeine phosphate, and sentenced to 10 to 40 years in the penitentiary, attacked the statute defining the offense on the ground that the legislature had not outlawed the possession of other exempt narcotics containing a higher percentage of codeine. Consider the following excerpt from the court's opinion affirming the conviction:

"... A pharmaceutical expert called by counsel for defendant testified in the following manner:

> 'Q. Now Doctor, can you make some comparison for us as to the amount of codeine which would be consumed, say, in a teaspoonful of syrup, cough syrup, as compared with one tablet of empirin compound with codeine phosphate, assuming that this was a ⅛ grain tablet of codeine?
>
> 'A. The maximum amount of codeine that an exempt codeine-containing cough syrup may contain, as you stated, is one grain of codeine phosphate per fluid ounce. The usual dose of such a preparation would be one teaspoonful. This would be approximately ⅙ of an ounce. So that the amount of codeine contained in a teaspoonful of such a cough syrup would be about ⅙ grain.
>
> 'Q. ⅙ grain?
>
> 'A. A teaspoonful of such an exempt codeine containing cough syrup would therefore contain more codeine phosphate than would be contained in one—⅛ grain codeine phosphate empirin compound with codeine phosphate.'

"While the defendant concedes that possession of tablets containing codeine in the amounts found on his person is a violation of the statute, he asserts that under the evidence the statute denies him the equal protection of the laws guaranteed by the State and Federal Constitutions. It is essentially defendant's position that to prohibit the sale of a tablet with ⅛ of a grain of codeine and at the same time exempt the sale of cough syrup containing as much as ⅙ of a grain of codeine per teaspoon results in an arbitrary and unreasonable classification. The state, on the other hand, argues that the classification is proper because (1) liquid cough syrup is more difficult to conceal than tablets; (2) its costs would be prohibitive if available only by prescription; and (3) the benefit and convenience to the public in securing cough syrup over the counter outweigh the potential dangers inherent in permitting its purchase without a prescription.

"With respect to the test to be applied in considering the propriety of a legislative classification, we have recently held ... 'In deciding whether classification in a given situation offends constitutional principles, the rules of construction generally governing legislation are relevant. In this area there is a growing judicial tendency to permit the exercise of broad discretion. The fact that measures taken are not directed at all of the evils to be corrected does not invalidate the application of the statute if the problem is dealt with according to practical exigencies and experience in a manner which is germane to its solution.' For the reasons advanced by the state, we are of the opinion the classification is reasonable and the statute therefore valid...."

3. Sometimes the contention of a denial of equal protection of the laws is raised against a statutory scheme which, because it strives for flexibility in sentencing, may make different defendants liable for varying penalties for committing the same act. In Black v. Gladden, 237 Or. 631, 393 P.2d 190 (1964), the defendant was convicted of shoplifting goods valued at $2.30 and sentenced to a term not to exceed six years. In seeking post-conviction release he contended that he was denied equal protection of the laws since there was "no rational distinction between the acts proscribed in ... the larceny statute [a misdemeanor], and the acts proscribed in ... the shoplifting statute [a felony], and that, therefore, if two persons do identical acts of taking, one may be charged by the grand jury or magistrate with a felony and the other with a misdemeanor without any guiding standard to guide them in making the distinction". This, said the petitioner, violates the rule which says "that if there is no rational basis for distinguishing the acts committed by one person from the acts committed by another, the acts of one cannot be treated solely as a felony and the acts of the other solely as a misdemeanor."

In rejecting the argument, the court held that since there "is a reasonable basis for regarding theft committed in a store or other mercantile establishment as a *separate social evil,* distinct from theft committed under other circumstances", it was "clearly a matter for legislative discretion" which did not "give rise to a constitutional objection". (Emphasis added.)

In People v. Harper, 1 Mich.App. 480, 136 N.W.2d 768 (1965), appeal dismissed sub. nom. Harper v. Michigan, 392 U.S. 644, 88 S.Ct. 2296 (1967), the court held constitutional a statutory scheme of regulation which punished the unlawful sale of narcotics by unlicensed persons with greater severity than it punished unlawful sale by licensed persons. Portions of the court's opinion are set forth below:

"Quinn, Judge.

"... The gist of appellant's argument to establish unconstitutionality is that because a licensed person who sells narcotics unlawfully is subject to a maximum penalty of 10 years ... and an unlicensed person who does the same thing is subject to a minimum sentence of 20 years and a maximum of life ... the latter is denied equal protection of the law as guaranteed by U.S.Const. art. 14 and Const.1908, art. 2, § 1. Appellant is not licensed. The precise question for decision is whether the classification 'licensed' and 'unlicensed' is reasonable....

"The standards of classification are:

" '1. The equal-protection clause of the 14th Amendment does not take from the state the power to classify in the adoption of police laws, but admits of the exercise of a wide scope of discretion in that regard, and avoids what is done only when it is without any reasonable basis, and therefore is purely arbitrary. 2. A classification having some reasonable basis does not offend against that clause merely because it is not made with mathematical nicety, or because in practice it results in some inequality. 3. When the classification in such a law is called in question, if any state of facts reasonably can be conceived that would sustain it, the existence of that state of facts at the time the law was enacted must be assumed. 4. One who assails the classification in such a law must carry the burden of showing that it does not rest upon any reasonable basis, but is essentially arbitrary.' "

"The statutes here involved were enacted to control manufacture, possession, and distribution of narcotic drugs. In order to facilitate and regulate the legitimate trade in these products, certain people are licensed.... By licensing this group, the legislature places severe controls over their contact with narcotics.... Every transaction that they make is governed by law and the records that they keep are subject to close scrutiny by the appropriate authorities.... The licensing act is aimed primarily at safeguarding and regulating legitimate trade of narcotics. The act under which respondent was convicted and sentenced is directed solely at suppressing illegal traffic in narcotics. The purpose of the two acts is entirely different, and it is a reasonable basis for the classifications 'licensed' and 'unlicensed'.

"The statutes involved are not unconstitutional. Writ denied."

4. A Massachusetts statute made it a criminal offense for "whoever ... gives away ... any drug, medicine, instrument or article whatever for the prevention of conception", except that a registered physician could administer to or prescribe the same for any *married* person. It also authorized the sale by a pharmacist to any *married* person presenting a physician's prescription. The defendant, who was neither a physician nor a pharmacist, exhibited contraceptive articles in the course of delivering a lecture to a group of college students, and at the end of his lecture he gave a young *unmarried woman* a contraceptive vaginal foam. His Massachusetts conviction was reversed by the Supreme Court of the United States—Eisenstadt v. Baird, 405 U.S. 438, 92 S.Ct. 1029 (1972)—upon the privacy principle and also because of its violation of the rights of single persons under the Equal Protection Clause of the Fourteenth Amendment.

5. An all-male draft registration requirement was upheld by the U.S. Supreme Court in Rostker v. Goldberg, 453 U.S. 57, 101 S.Ct. 2646 (1981), finding that women, because of the congressional determination to exclude them from combat, were not similarly situated for purposes of a draft or registration for a draft.

6. A Georgia statute provided that a parent who willfully and voluntarily abandons their dependent child is guilty of a misdemeanor and that those parents who commit the offense within Georgia and thereafter leave the state are guilty of a felony. The U.S. Supreme Court rejected arguments that this infringed on the constitutional right to travel, since the departure aggravates the consequences of conduct that is otherwise punishable. Further, the Court held that there was no violation of equal protection, since the clause involved applied equally to all parents residing in Georgia. Jones v. Helms, 452 U.S. 412, 101 S.Ct. 2434 (1981).

A 1901 Alabama constitutional provision that required the disenfranchisement of persons convicted of certain felonies and misdemeanors, including, "any crime ... involving moral turpitude," was held unanimously by the U.S. Supreme Court to violate equal protection principles because it was applied in a racially discriminatory manner. By examination of legislative history there was little doubt that the provision was originally designed to keep blacks from voting, even though on its face it applied to no particular racial or ethnic group. A facially neutral law that has a racially disproportionate impact must pass a test requiring its proponent to demonstrate that the law would have been passed even without a discriminatory motivation, a burden that was not met in this case. Hunter v. Underwood, 471 U.S. 222, 105 S.Ct. 1916 (1985).

Chapter 3

FEDERAL CRIMINAL JURISDICTION

A. THE UNITED STATES CONSTITUTION AND FEDERAL "COMMON LAW"

* * *

ARTICLE I

Section 1. All legislative Powers herein granted shall be vested in a Congress of the United States, which shall consist of a Senate and House of Representatives.

* * *

Section 8. The Congress shall have Power To lay and collect Taxes, Duties, Imposts and Excises, to pay the Debts and provide for the common Defence and general Welfare of the United States; but all Duties, Imposts and Excises shall be uniform throughout the United States;

To borrow Money on the credit of the United States;

To regulate Commerce with foreign Nations, and among the several States, and with the Indian Tribes;

To establish an uniform Rule of Naturalization, and uniform Laws on the subject of Bankruptcies throughout the United States;

To coin Money, regulate the Value thereof, and of foreign Coin, and fix the Standard of Weights and Measures;

To provide for the Punishment of counterfeiting the Securities and current Coin of the United States;

To establish Post Offices and post Roads;. . . .

To define and punish Piracies and Felonies committed on the high Seas, and Offences against the Law of Nations;

To declare War, grant Letters of Marque and Reprisal, and make Rules concerning Captures on Land and Water;

To raise and support Armies, but no Appropriation of Money to that Use shall be for a longer Term than two Years;

To provide and maintain a Navy;

To make Rules for the Government and Regulation of the land and naval Forces;. . . .

To exercise exclusive Legislation in all Cases whatsoever, over such District (not exceeding ten Miles square) as may, by Cession of particular States, and the Acceptance of Congress, become the Seat of the Government of the United States, and to exercise like Authority over all Places purchased by the Consent of the Legislature of the State in which the Same shall be, for the Erection of Forts, Magazines, Arsenals, dock-Yards, and other needful Buildings;—And

To make all Laws which shall be necessary and proper for carrying into Execution the foregoing Powers, and all other Powers vested by this Constitution in the Government of the United States, or in any Department or Officer thereof. * * *

ARTICLE [XIV]

Section 1. All persons born or naturalized in the United States, and subject to the jurisdiction thereof, are citizens of the United States and of the State wherein they reside. No State shall make or enforce any law which shall abridge the privileges or immunities of citizens of the United States; nor shall any State deprive any person of life, liberty, or property, without due process of law; nor deny to any person within its jurisdiction the equal protection of the laws.

* * *

Section 5. The Congress shall have power to enforce, by appropriate legislation, the provisions of this article.

THE UNITED STATES v. HUDSON AND GOODWIN

Supreme Court of the United States, 1812.
11 U.S. (7 Cranch) 32.

This was a case certified from the Circuit Court for the District of *Connecticut,* in which, upon argument of a general demurrer to an *indictment* for a libel on the President and Congress of the United States, contained in the *Connecticut Courant,* of the 7th of May, 1806, charging them with having in secret voted two millions of dollars as a present to Bonaparte for leave to make a treaty with Spain, the judges of that Court were divided in opinion upon the question, *whether the Circuit Court of the United States had a common law jurisdiction in cases of libel.*

The Court having taken time to consider, the following opinion was delivered (on the last day of the term, all the judges being present) by JOHNSON, J.

The only question which this case presents is, whether the Circuit Courts of the United States can exercise a common law jurisdiction in criminal cases. We state it thus broadly because a decision on a case of libel will apply to every case in which jurisdiction is not vested in those courts by statute.

Although this question is brought up now for the first time to be decided by this Court, we consider it as having been long since settled in public opinion. In no other case for many years has this jurisdiction been asserted; and the general acquiescence of legal men shews the prevalence of opinion in favor of the negative of the proposition.

The course of reasoning which leads to this conclusion is simple, obvious, and admits of but little illustration. The powers of the general Government are made up of concessions from the several states—whatever is not expressly given to the former, the latter expressly reserve. The judicial power of the United States is a constituent part of those concessions—that power is to be exercised by Courts organized for the purpose, and brought into existence by an effort of the legislative power of the Union. Of all the Courts which the United States may, under their general powers, constitute, one only, the Supreme Court, possesses jurisdiction derived immediately from the Constitution, and of which the legislative power cannot deprive it. All other Courts created by the general Government possess no jurisdiction but what is given them by the power that creates them, and can be vested with none but what the power ceded to the general Government will authorize them to confer.

It is not necessary to inquire whether the general Government, in any and what extent, possesses the power of conferring on its Courts a jurisdiction in cases similar to the present; it is enough that such jurisdiction has not been conferred by any legislative act, if it does not result to those Courts as a consequence of their creation.

And such is the opinion of a majority of this court: For, the power which Congress possess to create Courts of inferior jurisdiction, necessarily implies the power to limit the jurisdiction of those Courts to particular objects; and when a Court is created, and its operations confined to certain specific objects, with what propriety can it assume to itself a jurisdiction—much more extended—in its nature very indefinite—applicable to a great variety of subjects—varying in every State in the Union—and with regard to which there exists no definite criterion of distribution between the district and Circuit Courts of the same district?

The only ground on which it has ever been contended that this jurisdiction could be maintained is, that, upon the formation of any political body, an implied power to preserve its own existence and promote the end and object of its creation, necessarily results to it. But, without examining how far this consideration is applicable to the peculiar character of our constitution, it may be remarked that it is a principle by no means peculiar to the common law. It is coeval, probably, with the first formation of a limited Government; belongs to a system of universal law, and may as well support the assumption of many other powers as those more peculiarly acknowledged by the common law of England.

But if admitted as applicable to the state of things in this country, the consequence would not result from it which is here contended for. If it may communicate certain implied powers to the general Government, it would not follow that the Courts of that Government are vested with jurisdiction over any particular act done by an individual in supposed violation of the peace and dignity of the sovereign power. The legislative authority of the Union must first make an act a crime, affix a punishment to it, and declare the Court that shall have jurisdiction of the offence.

Certain implied powers must necessarily result to our Courts of justice from the nature of their institution. But jurisdiction of crimes against the state is not among those powers. To fine for contempt—imprison for contumacy—inforce the observance of order, &c. are powers which cannot be dispensed with in a Court, because they are necessary to the exercise of all others: and so far our Courts no doubt possess powers not immediately derived from statute; but all exercise of criminal law cases we are of opinion is not within their implied powers.

B. DIRECT FEDERAL INTEREST OFFENSES

HISTORY OF INTERNAL REVENUE LAWS

LAWS PRIOR TO 1939*

The first internal-revenue tax law was enacted on March 3, 1791, and imposed a tax on distilled spirits and stills. This was followed by legislation imposing taxes upon carriages, retail dealers in wines and foreign spirituous liquors, snuff, refined sugar, property sold at auction, legal instruments, real estate, and slaves. All of these taxes and the offices created for their enforcement were abolished in 1802. During this first era of taxation the internal-revenue receipts amounted to only $6,758,764.26. Comparing this with the receipts for the fiscal year 1938, amounting to $5,658,765,314, it will be noted that the Internal Revenue Service collects at the present time more than twice as much from internal-revenue taxes in one day as the original organization collected in 10 years.

Due to the necessities occasioned by the War of 1812, internal-revenue taxes were again imposed in 1813. These taxes were levied on refined sugar, carriages, distillers, sales at auction, distilled spirits, manufactured articles, household furniture, watches, gold, silver, plated ware, jewelry, real estate, and slaves. An officer known as the Commissioner of Revenues was in charge of the administration of such taxes. All these taxes were repealed by the act of December 23, 1817, and the office of Commissioner of Revenues was discontinued, effective, upon the completion of the collection of the outstanding taxes. The collections during the 5-year period from 1813 to 1818 amounted to $25,833,449.43.

For a period of 43 years, namely, 1818 to 1861, no internal-revenue taxes were imposed. On July 6, 1861, an act was passed imposing a tax on incomes and real property. No income tax was ever collected under

* From Report of Joint Committee on Internal Revenue Taxation, appearing in Pamphlet entitled "Codification of Internal Revenue Laws", 1939, p. IX.

this act, and all of the tax collected on real property was returned to the States under authority of the act of March 2, 1891.

The act of July 1, 1862, is largely the basis of our present system of taxation. It contained the first law under which any income tax was collected, and it created the office of Commissioner of Internal Revenue. It taxed practically everything which Congress thought was susceptible of yielding revenue. The three sources of revenue which remained for a long time the backbone of the internal revenue system, namely, spirits, tobacco, and beer, received particular attention from the lawmakers.

SONZINSKY v. UNITED STATES

Supreme Court of the United States, 1937.
300 U.S. 506, 57 S.Ct. 554.

MR. JUSTICE STONE delivered the opinion of the Court.

The question for decision is whether § 2 of the National Firearms Act of June 26, 1934, ... 26 U.S.C.A., §§ 1132–1132q, which imposes a $200 annual license tax on dealers in firearms, is a constitutional exercise of the legislative power of Congress.

Petitioner was convicted by the District Court for Eastern Illinois on two counts of an indictment, the first charging him with violation of § 2, by dealing in firearms without payment of the tax. On appeal the Court of Appeals set aside the conviction on the second count and affirmed on the first. 86 F.2d 486. On petition of the accused we granted certiorari, limited to the question of the constitutional validity of the statute in its application under the first count in the indictment.

Section 2 of the National Firearms Act requires every dealer in firearms to register with the Collector of Internal Revenue in the district where he carries on business, and to pay a special excise tax of $200 a year. Importers or manufacturers are taxed $500 a year. Section 3 imposes a tax of $200 on each transfer of a firearm, payable by the transferor, and § 4 prescribes regulations for the identification of purchases. The term "firearm" is defined by § 1 as meaning a shotgun or a rifle having a barrel less than eighteen inches in length, or any other weapon, except a pistol or revolver, from which a shot is discharged by an explosive, if capable of being concealed on the person, or a machine gun, and includes a muffler or silencer for any firearm....

In the exercise of its constitutional power to lay taxes, Congress may select the subjects of taxation, choosing some and omitting others.... Its power extends to the imposition of excise taxes upon the doing of business.... Petitioner does not deny that Congress may tax his business as a dealer in firearms. He insists that the present levy is not a true tax, but a penalty imposed for the purpose of suppressing traffic in a certain noxious type of firearms, the local regulation of which is reserved to the states because not granted to the national government. To establish its penal and prohibitive character, he relies on the amounts of the tax imposed by § 2 on dealers, manufacturers and importers, and of the tax imposed by § 3 on each transfer of a "firearm," payable by the transferor. The cumulative effect on the distribution of a limited class of firearms, of relatively small value, by the successive imposition of different taxes, one on the business of the importer or manufacturer, another on that of the dealer, and a third on the transfer to a buyer, is said to be prohibitive in effect and to disclose unmistakably the legislative purpose to regulate rather than to tax.

The case is not one where the statute contains regulatory provisions related to a purported tax in such a way as has enabled this Court to say in other cases that the latter is a penalty resorted to as a means of enforcing the regulations.... Nor is the subject of the tax described or treated as criminal by the taxing statute.... Here § 2 contains no regulation other than the mere registration provisions, which are obviously supportable as in aid of a revenue purpose. On its face it is only a taxing measure, and we are asked to say that the tax, by virtue of its deterrent effect on the activities taxed, operates as a regulation which is beyond the congressional power.

Every tax is in some measure regulatory. To some extent it interposes an economic impediment to the activity taxed as compared with others not taxed. But a tax is not any the less a tax because it has a regulatory effect, ... and it has long been established that an Act of Congress which on its face purports to be an exercise of the taxing power is not any the less so because the tax is burdensome or tends to restrict or suppress the thing taxed....

Inquiry into the hidden motives which may move Congress to exercise a power constitutionally conferred upon it is beyond the competency of courts.... They will not undertake, by collateral inquiry as to the measure of the regulatory effect of a tax, to ascribe to Congress an attempt, under the guise of taxation, to exercise another power denied by the Federal Constitution....

Here the annual tax of $200 is productive of some revenue.[1] We are not free to speculate as to the motives which moved Congress to impose it, or as to the extent to which it may operate to restrict the activities taxed. As it is not attended by an offensive regulation, and since it operates as a tax, it is within the national taxing power....

Affirmed.

NOTE

The judiciary has taken the position that, given the broad grant of constitutional power vested in Congress to collect taxes, it will not restrain an exercise of the taxing power because of the onerous and burdensome results to taxpayers. McCray v. United States, 195 U.S. 27, 24 S.Ct. 769 (1904). Congress, not the courts, has the right to select the objects of taxation and the measures for implementing the collection process. Thus, without inquiring into the reasons underlying Congress' decision to select a particular subject for taxation the

1. The $200 tax was paid by 27 dealers in 1934, and by 22 dealers in 1935. Annual Report of the Commissioner of Internal Revenue, Fiscal Year Ended June 30, 1935, pp. 129–131; id., Fiscal Year ended June 30, 1936, pp. 139–141.

courts will not limit any tax unless there are provisions in the tax statute extraneous to a constitutionally authorized taxing need. United States v. Kahriger, 345 U.S. 22, 73 S.Ct. 510 (1953).

In this manner, the courts have recognized Congress' power to collect taxes whether the business involved is lawful or unlawful, Wainer v. United States, 299 U.S. 92, 57 S.Ct. 79 (1936), although the method of reporting the income subject to taxation may generate Fifth Amendment self incrimination problems. See Marchetti v. United States, 390 U.S. 39, 88 S.Ct. 697 (1968).

C. THE "NECESSARY AND PROPER" CLAUSE OFFENSES

In conjunction with the specific authority to create laws in a number of enumerated areas, the Necessary and Proper clause of the Constitution, U.S.Const. Art. 1, § 8, cl. 18, provides Congress with the power to legislate in areas that will facilitate the execution of the powers vested in the federal government. In Logan v. United States, 144 U.S. 263, 12 S.Ct. 617 (1892), the Supreme Court recognized the applicability of this clause. There, taking cognizance of the propriety of the civil rights conspiracy statute, the Court upheld the right of federal authorities to protect prisoners in their custody:

> Among the powers which the Constitution expressly confers upon Congress is the power to make all laws necessary and proper for carrying into execution the powers specifically granted to it, and all other powers vested by the Constitution in the government of the United States, or in any department or officer thereof. In the exercise of this general power of legislation, Congress may use any means, appearing to it most eligible and appropriate, which are adapted to the end to be accomplished, and are consistent with the letter and the spirit of the Constitution.
>
> Although the Constitution contains no grant, general or specific, to Congress of the power to provide for the punishment of crimes, except piracies and felonies on the high seas, offences against the law of nations, treason, and counterfeiting the securities and current coin of the United States, no one doubts the power of Congress to provide for the punishment of all crimes and offences against the United States, whether committed within one of the States of the Union, or within territory over which Congress has plenary and exclusive jurisdiction.
>
> To accomplish this end, Congress has the right to enact laws for the arrest and commitment of those accused of any such crime or offence, and for holding them in safe custody until indictment and trial; and persons arrested and held pursuant to such laws are in the exclusive custody of the United States, and are not subject to the judicial process or executive warrant of any State. The United States, having the absolute right to hold

such prisoners, have an equal duty to protect them, while so held, against assault or injury from any quarter. The existence of that duty on the part of the government necessarily implies a corresponding right of the prisoners to be so protected; and this right of the prisoners is a right secured to them by the Constitution and laws of the United States.

Therefore, notwithstanding the fact that the Constitution may not specifically grant Congress the power to regulate conduct in certain areas, where a given piece of legislation may be characterized as an incident of sovereignty which inheres in the government, it will be upheld under the Necessary and Proper Clause. Congress, thus, has the power to create, define and punish offenses whenever it is necessary and proper, by law, to do so to effectuate the objects of government.

McNALLY v. UNITED STATES

Supreme Court of the United States, 1987.
483 U.S. 350, 107 S.Ct. 2875.

JUSTICE WHITE delivered the opinion of the Court.

This action involves the prosecution of petitioner Gray, a former public official of the Commonwealth of Kentucky, and petitioner McNally, a private individual, for alleged violation of the federal mail fraud statute, 18 U.S.C. § 1341.[1] The prosecution's principal theory of the case, which was accepted by the courts below, was that petitioners' participation in a self-dealing patronage scheme defrauded the citizens and government of Kentucky of certain "intangible rights," such as the right to have the Commonwealth's affairs conducted honestly.

We accept for the sake of argument the Government's view of the evidence, as follows. The petitioners and a third individual, Howard P. "Sonny" Hunt, were politically active in the Democratic Party in the Commonwealth of Kentucky during the 1970's. After Democrat Julian Carroll was elected Governor of Kentucky in 1974, Hunt was made chairman of the state Democratic Party and given *de facto* control over selecting the insurance agencies from which the State would purchase its policies. In 1975, the Wombwell Insurance Company of Lexington, Kentucky (Wombwell), which since 1971 had acted as the Commonwealth's agent for securing a workmen's compensation policy, agreed with Hunt that in exchange for a continued agency relationship it would share any resulting commissions in excess of $50,000 a year with other insurance agencies specified by him. The commissions in question were paid to Wombwell by the large insurance companies from which it secured coverage for the State.

1. Section 1341 provides in pertinent part:

"Whoever, having devised or intending to devise any scheme or artifice to defraud, or for obtaining money or property by means of false or fraudulent pretenses, representations, or promises, ... for the purpose of executing such scheme or artifice or attempting so to do [uses the mails or causes them to be used,] shall be fined not more than $1,000 or imprisoned not more than five years, or both."

From 1975 to 1979, Wombwell funneled $851,000 in commissions to 21 separate insurance agencies designated by Hunt. Among the recipients of these payments was Seton Investments, Inc. (Seton), a company controlled by Hunt and petitioner Gray and nominally owned and operated by petitioner McNally.

Gray served as Secretary of Public Protection and Regulation from 1976 to 1978 and also as Secretary of the Governor's Cabinet from 1977 to 1979. Prior to his 1976 appointment, he and Hunt established Seton for the sole purpose of sharing in the commissions distributed by Wombwell. Wombwell paid some $200,000 to Seton between 1975 and 1979, and the money was used to benefit Gray and Hunt. Pursuant to Hunt's direction, Wombwell also made excess commission payments to the Snodgrass Insurance Agency, which in turn gave the money to McNally.

On account of the foregoing activities, Hunt was charged with and pleaded guilty to mail and tax fraud and was sentenced to three years' imprisonment. The petitioners were charged with one count of conspiracy and mail fraud. The mail fraud count was based on the mailing of a commission check to Wombwell by the insurance company from which it had secured coverage for the State. This count alleged that petitioners had devised a scheme (1) to defraud the citizens and government of Kentucky of their right to have the Commonwealth's affairs conducted honestly, and (2) to obtain, directly and indirectly, money and other things of value by means of false pretenses and the concealment of material facts. The conspiracy count alleged that petitioners had (1) conspired to violate the mail fraud statute through the scheme just described and (2) conspired to defraud the United States by obstructing the collection of federal taxes.

After informing the jury of the charges in the indictment, the District Court instructed that the scheme to defraud the citizens of Kentucky and to obtain money by false pretenses and concealment could be made out by either of two sets of findings: (1) that Hunt had *de facto* control over the award of the workmen's compensation insurance contract to Wombwell from 1975 to 1979; that he directed payments of commissions from this contract to Seton, an entity in which he had an ownership interest, without disclosing that interest to persons in state government whose actions or deliberations could have been affected by the disclosure; and that petitioners, or either of them, aided and abetted Hunt in that scheme; or (2) that Gray, in either of his appointed positions, had supervisory authority regarding the Commonwealth's workmen's compensation insurance at a time when Seton received commissions; that Gray had an ownership interest in Seton and did not disclose that interest to persons in state government whose actions or deliberations could have been affected by that disclosure; and that McNally aided and abetted Gray (the latter finding going only to McNally's guilt).

The jury convicted petitioners on both the mail fraud and conspiracy counts, and the Court of Appeals affirmed the convictions. In affirming the substantive mail fraud conviction, the court relied on a line of decisions from the Courts of Appeals holding that the mail fraud statute proscribes schemes to defraud citizens of their intangible rights to honest and impartial government. Under these cases, a public official owes a fiduciary duty to the public, and misuse of his office for private gain is a fraud. Also, an individual without formal office may be held to be a public fiduciary if others rely on him " 'because of a special relationship in the government' " and he in fact makes governmental decisions. 790 F.2d, at 1296 (quoting United States v. Margiotta, 688 F.2d 108, 122 (CA2 1982), cert. denied, 461 U.S. 913, 103 S.Ct. 1891 (1983)). The Court of Appeals held that Hunt was such a fiduciary because he "substantially participated in governmental affairs and exercised significant, if not exclusive, control over awarding the workmen's compensation insurance contract to Wombwell and the payment of monetary kick-backs to Seton."

We granted certiorari, and now reverse.

The mail fraud statute clearly protects property rights, but does not refer to the intangible right of the citizenry to good government. As first enacted in 1872, as part of a recodification of the postal laws, the statute contained a general proscription against using the mails to initiate correspondence in furtherance of "any scheme or artifice to defraud." The sponsor of the recodification stated, in apparent reference to the anti-fraud provision, that measures were needed "to prevent the frauds which are mostly gotten up in the large cities ... by thieves, forgers, and rapscallions generally, for the purpose of deceiving and fleecing the innocent people in the country." Insofar as the sparse legislative history reveals anything, it indicates that the original impetus behind the mail fraud statute was to protect the people from schemes to deprive them of their money or property.

Durland v. United States (1896), the first case in which this Court construed the meaning of the phrase "any scheme or artifice to defraud," held that the phrase is to be interpreted broadly insofar as property rights are concerned, but did not indicate that the statute had a more extensive reach. It construed the statute to "includ[e] everything designed to defraud by representations as to the past or present, or suggestions and promises as to the future." Accordingly, the defendant's use of the mails to sell bonds which he did not intend to honor was within the statute. The Court explained that "[i]t was with the purpose of protecting the public against all such intentional efforts to despoil, and to prevent the post office from being used to carry them into effect, that this statute was passed...." Id., at 314, 16 S.Ct., at 511.

Congress codified the holding of *Durland* in 1909, and in doing so gave further indication that the statute's purpose is protecting property rights. The amendment added the words "or for obtaining money or property by means of false or fraudulent pretenses, representations, or promises" after the original phrase "any scheme or artifice to defraud." The new language is based on the statement in *Durland* that the statute reaches "everything designed to defraud by representations as to the past or present, or suggestions and promises as to the future." However, instead of the phrase "everything designed to defraud" Congress used the words "[any scheme or artifice] for obtaining money or property."

After 1909, therefore, the mail fraud statute criminalized schemes or artifices "to defraud" or "for obtaining money or property by means of false or fraudulent pretenses, representation, or promises...." Because the two phrases identifying the proscribed schemes appear in the disjunctive, it is arguable that they are to be construed independently and that the money-or-property requirement of the latter phrase does not limit schemes to defraud to those aimed at causing deprivation of money or property. This is the approach that has been taken by each of the Courts of Appeals that has addressed the issue: schemes to defraud include those designed to deprive individuals, the people or the government of intangible rights, such as the right to have public officials perform their duties honestly. See, e.g., United States v. States, 488 F.2d 761, 764 (CA8 1973).

As the Court long ago stated, however, the words "to defraud" commonly refer "to wronging one in his property rights by dishonest methods or schemes," and "usually signify the deprivation of something of value by trick, deceit, chicane or overreaching." *Hammerschmidt v. United States*. The codification of the holding in *Durland* in 1909 does not indicate that Congress was departing from this common understanding. As we see it, adding the second phrase simply made it unmistakable that the statute reached false promises and misrepresentations as to the future as well as other frauds involving money or property.

We believe that Congress' intent in passing the mail fraud statute was to prevent the use of the mails in furtherance of such schemes. The Court has often stated that when there are two rational readings of a criminal statute, one harsher than the other, we are to choose the harsher only when Congress has spoken in clear and definite language. *United States v. Bass* (1971); *United States v. Universal C.I.T. Credit Corp.* (1952). As the Court said in a mail fraud case years ago, "There are no constructive offenses; and before one can be punished, it must be shown that his case is plainly within the statute." *Fasulo v. United States* (1926). Rather than construe the statute in a manner that leaves its outer boundaries ambiguous and involves the Federal Government in setting standards of disclosure and good government for local and state officials, we read § 1341 as limited in scope to the protection of property rights. If Congress desires to go further, it must speak more clearly than it has.

For purposes of this action, we assume that Hunt, as well as Gray, was a state officer. The issue is thus whether a state officer violates the mail fraud statute if he chooses an insurance agent to provide insurance for the State but specifies that the agent must share its commissions with other named insurance agencies, in one of which the officer has an ownership interest and hence profits when his agency receives part of the commissions. We note that as the action comes to us, there was no charge and the jury was not required to find that the Commonwealth itself was defrauded of any money or property. It was not charged that in the absence of the alleged scheme the Commonwealth would have paid a lower premium or secured better insurance. Hunt and Gray received part of the commissions but those commissions were not the Commonwealth's money. Nor was the jury charged that to convict it must find that the Commonwealth was deprived of control over how its money was spent. Indeed, the premium for insurance would have been paid to some agency, and what Hunt and Gray did was to assert control that the Commonwealth might not otherwise have made over the commissions paid by the insurance company to its agent.[2] Although the Government now relies in part on the assertion that the petitioners obtained property by means of false representations to Wombwell, there was nothing in the jury charge that required such a finding. We hold, therefore, that the jury instruction on the substantive mail fraud count permitted a conviction for conduct not within the reach of § 1341.

The Government concedes that if petitioners' substantive mail fraud convictions are reversed their conspiracy convictions should also be reversed.

It is so ordered.

JUSTICE STEVENS, with whom JUSTICE O'CONNOR joins as to Parts I, II and III, dissenting.

[w]e must decide whether the statute's prohibition embraces a secret agreement by state officials to place the State's workmen's compensation insurance with a particular agency in exchange for that company's agreement to share a major portion of its commissions with a

2. Justice Stevens would affirm the convictions even though it was not charged that requiring the Wombwell agency to share commissions violated state law. We should assume that it did not. For the same reason we should assume that it was not illegal under state law for Hunt and Gray to own one of the agencies sharing in the commissions and hence to profit from the arrangement, whether or not they disclosed it to others in the state government. It is worth observing as well that it was not alleged that the mail fraud statute would have been violated had Hunt and Gray reported to state officials the fact of their financial gain. The violation asserted is the failure to disclose their financial interest, even if state law did not require it, to other persons in the state government whose actions could have been affected by the disclosure. It was in this way that the indictment charged that the people of Kentucky had been deprived of their right to have the Commonwealth's affairs conducted honestly.

It may well be that Congress could criminalize using the mails to further a state officer's efforts to profit from governmental decisions he is empowered to make or over which he has some supervisory authority, even if there is no state law proscribing his profiteering or even if state law expressly authorized it. But if state law expressly permitted or did not forbid a state officer such as Gray to have an ownership interest in an insurance agency handling the State's insurance, it would take a much clearer indication than the mail fraud statute evidences to convince us that having and concealing such an interest defrauds the State and is forbidden under federal law.

list of agents provided by the officials, including sham agencies under the control of the officials themselves.

The same question of statutory construction has arisen in a variety of contexts over the past few decades. In the public sector, judges, state Governors, chairmen of state political parties, state cabinet officers, city aldermen, congressmen and many other state and federal officials have been convicted of defrauding citizens of their right to the honest services of their governmental officials.[1] In most of these cases, the officials have secretly made governmental decisions with the objective of benefiting themselves or promoting their own interests, instead of fulfilling their legal commitment to provide the citizens of the State or local government with their loyal service and honest government. Similarly, many elected officials and their campaign workers have been convicted of mail fraud when they have used the mails to falsify votes, thus defrauding the citizenry of its right to an honest election.[2] In the private sector, purchasing agents, brokers, union leaders, and others with clear fiduciary duties to their employers or unions have been found guilty of defrauding their employers or unions by accepting kickbacks or selling confidential information.[3] In other cases, defendants have been found guilty of using the mails to defraud individuals of their rights to privacy, and other nonmonetary rights.[4] All of these cases have something in

1. See e.g., *United States v. Holzer* (CA7 1987) (county judge); *United States v. Silvano* (CA1 1987) (city budget director); *United States v. Barber* (CA4) (state Alcoholic Beverage Control Commissioner), (1982); *United States v. Margiotta,* (CA2 1982) (party leader); *United States v. Diggs* (1979) (Congressman), *United States v. Mandel,* (CA4 1979) (Governor of Maryland); *United States v. Brown* (CA8 1976) (city building commissioner); *United States v. Bush,* (CA7 1975) (city Director of Public Relations); *United States v. Keane,* (CA7 1975) (city alderman); *United States v. Staszcuk,* (CA7 1974) (city alderman); *United States v. Isaacs* (CA7) (ex-Governor of Illinois & ex-Director of Illinois Department of Revenue).

Some private defendants have also been convicted of devising schemes through which public servants defraud the public. See, *e.g., United States v. Lovett* (CA7 1987) (bribing mayor); *United States v. Alexander,* (CA7 1984) (bribing judge); *United States v. Rauhoff* (CA7 1975) (bribing state Secretary of State).

In Shushan v. United States, 117 F.2d 110 (CA5 1941), cert. denied, 313 U.S. 574, 61 S.Ct. 1085, 85 L.Ed. 1531 (1941), the Fifth Circuit upheld the mail fraud prosecution of a member of a Louisiana parish levy board for receiving kickbacks from the underwriters of a plan to refund outstanding bonds of the levy district. Explaining why it rejected the argument that no actual fraud had occurred because the refunding operation had actually been profitable to the levy board, the court stated:

> "No trustee has more sacred duties than a public official and any scheme to obtain an advantage by corrupting such a one must in the federal law be considered a scheme to defraud." 117 F.2d, at 115.

2. See e.g., *United States v. Girdner* (CA10 1985) (candidate for state legislature); *United States v. Odom* (CA4 1984) (sheriff); *United States v. Clapps,* (CA3 1984) (party chairman); *United States v. States,* (CA8 1973) (candidates for city office).

3. *United States v. Curry* (CA5 1982) (chairman of political action committee); *United States v. Bronston* (CA2 1981) (attorney); *United States v. Von Barta* (CA2 1980) (securities trader), (1981); *United States v. Bohonus* (CA9) (insurance manager); *United States v. Bryza* (CA7 1975) (purchasing agent); *United States v. George* (CA7) (purchasing agent); *United States v. Procter & Gamble Co.* (Mass.1942) (attempt to bribe competitor's employee).

4. See e.g., *United States v. Condolon* (CA4 1979) (wire fraud conviction related to bogus talent agency designed to seduce women); *United States v. Louderman* (CA9) (scheme to fraudulently obtain confidential personal information); see also *United States v. Castor* (CA7 1977) (fraudulent information on application for liquor license).

common—they involved what the Court now refers to as "intangible rights." They also share something else in common. The many federal courts that have confronted the question whether these sorts of schemes constitute a "scheme or artifice to defraud" have uniformly and consistently read the statute in the same, sensible way. They have realized that nothing in the words "any scheme or artifice to defraud," or in the purpose of the statute, justifies limiting its application to schemes intended to deprive victims of money or property.

I

The mail fraud statute sets forth three separate prohibitions. It prohibits the use of the United States mails for the purpose of executing

> "[1] *any* scheme or artifice to defraud, [2] *or* for obtaining money or property by means of false or fraudulent pretenses, representations, or promises, [3] *or* to sell, dispose of, loan, exchange, alter, give away, distribute, supply, or furnish or procure for unlawful use any counterfeit or spurious coin, obligation, security, or other article, or anything represented to be or intimated or held out to be such counterfeit or spurious article ..." 18 U.S.C. § 1341 (emphasis and brackets added).

As the language makes clear, each of these restrictions is independent. One can violate the second clause—obtaining money or property by false pretenses—even though one does not violate the third clause—counterfeiting. Similarly, one can violate the first clause—devising a scheme or artifice to defraud—without violating the counterfeiting provision. Until today it was also obvious that one could violate the first clause by devising a scheme or artifice to defraud, even though one did not violate the second clause by seeking to obtain money or property from his victim through false pretenses. Every court to consider the matter had so held. Yet, today, the Court, for all practical purposes, rejects this longstanding construction of the statute by imposing a requirement that a scheme or artifice to defraud does not violate the statute unless its purpose is to defraud someone of money or property. I am at a loss to understand the source or justification for this holding. Certainly no canon of statutory construction requires us to ignore the plain language of the provision.

In considering the scope of the mail fraud statute it is essential to remember Congress' purpose in enacting it. Congress sought to protect the integrity of the United States mails by not allowing them to be used as "instruments of crime." "The focus of the statute is upon the misuse of the Postal Service, not the regulation of state affairs, and Congress clearly has the authority to regulate such misuse of the mails. Once this purpose is considered, it becomes clear that the construction the Court adopts today is senseless. Can it be that Congress sought to purge the mails of schemes to defraud citizens of money but was willing to tolerate schemes to defraud citizens of their right to an honest government, or to unbiased public officials? Is it at all rational to assume that Congress wanted to ensure that the mails not be used for petty crimes, but did not prohibit election fraud accomplished through mailing fictitious ballots? Given Congress' "broad purpose," I "find it difficult to believe, absent some indication in the statute itself or the legislative history, that Congress would have undercut sharply that purpose by hobbling federal prosecutors in their effort to combat" use of the mails for fraudulent schemes. *McElroy v. United States* (1982).

The limitation the Court adopts today shows no fidelity to Congress' words or purpose. The Court recognizes that the "money or property" limitation of the second clause does not actually apply to prosecutions under the first clause. But where else can such a limitation be derived from? A few examples of the types of frauds that have been prosecuted under the "intangible right" theory reveals that these schemes constitute "fraud" in every sense of the word, and that the "intangible right" theory plays an indispensable role in effectuating Congress' goal of preserving the integrity of the Postal Service.

In *States,* supra, two candidates running for the office of Committeemen in St. Louis, Missouri, used the United States mails in their scheme to falsify voter registration affidavits in order to carry out an extensive fraudulent write-in scheme. The candidates had their campaign workers fill in the affidavits with fictitious names and addresses, making sure that the mailing addresses were accessible to the campaign. Applications for absentee ballots were filed, and when they arrived through the mail, they were filled in with the candidates' names and mailed back. The candidates and one of their aides were convicted of mail fraud for having devised a scheme to defraud the voters, the residents, and the Board of Election Commissioners. The Court of Appeals affirmed the convictions, rejecting the defendants' arguments that they had not defrauded anyone since they never sought money or property. The court explained that the term "defraud" must be "construed to further the purpose of the statute; namely, to prohibit the misuse of the mails to further fraudulent enterprises." 488 F.2d, at 764.

In *United States v. Rauhoff,* 525 F.2d 1170 (CA7 1975), the defendant was part of a scheme that used the United States mail to facilitate its paying the Illinois Secretary of State approximately $50,000 a year in return for the Secretary's awarding the State's license plate contract to a certain company. In response to the argument that all parties to the scheme were reaping profits, and that nobody was defrauded, the Court of Appeals explained that the victims of the scheme were the "people of Illinois, who were defrauded of their right to have the business of the office of the Secretary of State conducted free from bribery." Id., at 1175. Although it was not proven that the State or its citizens lost any money, it was and is clear that this was a scheme to defraud under § 1341.

There are scores of other examples of such schemes which, although not depriving anyone of money or property, are clearly schemes to defraud, and are clearly within the scope of Congress' purpose in enacting the mail fraud statute. Discussing the peculiar facts of each of them would only confirm the observation that fraud is "as old as falsehood and as versable as human ingenuity." Weiss v. United States, 122 F.2d 675, 681 (CA5 1941). But, taken as a whole, these cases prove just how unwise today's judicial amendment of the mail fraud statute is.

II

The cases discussed above demonstrate that the construction the courts have consistently given the statute is consistent with the common understanding of the term "fraud," and Congress' intent in enacting the statute. It is also consistent with the manner in which the term has been interpreted in an analogous federal statute; the way the term was interpreted at the time of this statute's enactment; and the statute's scant legislative history. There is no reason, therefore, to upset the settled, sensible construction that the federal courts have consistently endorsed.

The term "defraud" is not unique to § 1341. Another federal statute, 18 U.S.C. § 371, uses the identical term in prohibiting conspiracies to "defraud the United States," and the construction we have given to that statute should be virtually dispositive here. In *Haas v. Henkel* (1910), the Court, dealing with the predecessor to § 371, rejected the argument that there could be no conspiracy to defraud in the absence of contemplated monetary or property loss. "The statute is broad enough in its terms to include any conspiracy for the purpose of impairing, obstructing or defeating the lawful function of any department of Government." Again, in *Hammerschmidt v. United States* (1924), the Court described the scope of the statute as prohibiting not only conspiracies to "cheat the Government out of property or money, but it also means to interfere with or obstruct one of its lawful governmental functions by deceit, craft or trickery, or at least by means that are dishonest." It is thus clear that a conspiracy to defraud the United States does not require any evidence that the Government has suffered any property or pecuniary loss. See also United States v. Barnow, 239 U.S. 74, 79, 36 S.Ct. 19, 21 (1915).

There is no basis for concluding that the term "defraud" means something different in § 1341 (first enacted in 1872) than what it means in § 371 (first enacted in 1867). Although § 371 includes the words "in any manner or for any purpose," those words only modify the underlying act—fraud, and if that term does not include nonproperty interests then our longstanding interpretation of § 371 is unjustified. In any event, § 1341 itself includes the expansive phrase "any scheme or artifice to defraud."

The Court nonetheless suggests that interpreting the two statutes differently can be justified because § 371 applies exclusively to frauds against the United States, while § 1341 benefits private individuals. This argument is wide of the mark. The purpose of § 1341 is to protect the integrity of the United States Postal Service, and, as I have explained, it is ludicrous to think that a Congress intent on preserving the integrity of the Postal Service would have used the term "defraud" in a narrow sense so as to allow mailings whose purpose was merely to defraud citizens of rights other than money or property. There is, therefore, no reason to believe that Congress used the term "defraud" in a more limited way in § 1341 than it did in § 371. The Court is correct in pointing out that Congress intended to go beyond any common-law meaning of the word "defraud" in enacting § 371. But we have also rejected the argument that the common-law meaning of the term "defraud" confines the scope of § 1341. See *Durland v. United States* (1896). The general definition of the term "defraud" does not support, much less compel, today's decision.

Even if there were historical evidence of a limited definition of "fraud," the Court's holding would reflect a strange interpretation of legislation enacted by the Congress in the 19th Century. Statutes like the Sherman Act, the civil rights legislation, and the mail fraud statute were written in broad general language on the understanding that the courts would have wide latitude in construing them to achieve the remedial purposes that Congress had identified. The wide open spaces in statutes such as these are most appropriately interpreted as implicit delegations of authority to the courts to fill in the gaps in the common-law tradition of case by case adjudication. The notion that the meaning of the words "any scheme or artifice to defraud" was frozen by a special conception of the term recognized by Congress in 1872 is manifestly untenable.

* * *

Finally, there is nothing in the legislative history of the mail fraud statute that suggests that Congress intended the word "fraud" to have a narrower meaning in that statute than its common meaning and the meaning that it has in § 371. As originally enacted in 1872, the statute had but one class of prohibition: use of the mails as part of "any scheme or artifice to defraud." The second clause, which prohibits "any scheme . . . for obtaining money or property by means of false or fraudulent pretenses, representations, or promises," was added in 1909. The purpose of the second clause was to codify this Court's holding in *Durland* that the Act prohibits false promises even if they did not qualify as "fraud" at common law. See *Durland,* 161 U.S., at 312–314. There is no evidence to suggest that Congress sought to limit the scope of the original prohibition, and its use of the disjunctive "or" demonstrates that it was adding to, not modifying, the original prohibition.

. . . The general language in the mail fraud statute has repeatedly been construed to cover novel species of fraud, and Congress has repeatedly amended the statute in ways that support a broad interpretation of its basic thrust. That long history is accurately summarized in the following observations:

> "First enacted in 1872, the mail fraud statute, together with its lineal descendant, the wire fraud statute, has been characterized as the 'first line of defense' against virtually every new area of fraud to develop in the United States in the past century. Its

applications, too numerous to catalog, cover not only the full range of consumer frauds, stock frauds, land frauds, bank frauds, insurance frauds, and commodity stock frauds, but have extended even to such areas as blackmail, counterfeiting, election fraud, and bribery. In many of these and other areas, where legislatures have sometimes been slow to enact specific prohibitory legislation, the mail fraud statute has frequently represented the sole instrument of justice that could be wielded against the ever-innovative practitioners of deceit.

"During the past century, both Congress and the Supreme Court have repeatedly placed their stamps of approval on expansive use of the mail fraud statute. Indeed, each of the five legislative revisions of the statute has served to enlarge its coverage." Rakoff, The Federal Mail Fraud Statute, 18 Duquesne L.Rev. 772–773 (1980).

III

To support its crabbed construction of the Act, the Court makes a straight-forward but unpersuasive argument. Since there is no explicit, unambiguous evidence that Congress actually contemplated "intangible rights" when it enacted the mail fraud statute in 1872, the Court explains, any ambiguity in the meaning of the criminal statute should be resolved in favor of lenity. The doctrine of lenity is, of course, sound, for the citizen is entitled to fair notice of what sort of conduct may give rise to punishment. But the Court's reliance on that doctrine in this case is misplaced for several reasons.

To begin with, "although 'criminal statutes are to be construed strictly ... this does not mean that every criminal statute must be given the narrowest possible meaning in complete disregard of the purpose of the legislature.' " *United States v. Bramblett.* Especially in light of the statutory purpose, I believe that § 1341 unambiguously prohibits all schemes to defraud that use the United States mails—whether or not they involve money or property.

In any event, this asserted ambiguity in the meaning of the word "defraud," if it ever existed, was removed by judicial construction long ago. Even if Chief Justice Taft's opinion for the Court in the *Hammerschmidt* case was not sufficient to make it perfectly clear that a fraud on the public need not deprive it of tangible property, the series of Court of Appeals' opinions applying this very statute to schemes to defraud a State and its citizens of their intangible right to honest and faithful government, notwithstanding the absence of evidence of tangible loss, removed any relevant ambiguity in this statute. Surely these petitioners knew that it would be unlawful to place Kentucky's insurance coverage with an agent who would secretly make hundreds of thousands of dollars available for the private use of petitioners, their relatives, and their paramours. This is, indeed, a strange application of the doctrine of lenity.[5]

I recognize that there may have been some overly expansive applications of § 1341 in the past. With no guidance from this Court, the Courts of Appeals have struggled to define just when conduct which is clearly unethical is also criminal. In some instances, however, such as voting fraud cases, the criminality of the scheme and the fraudulent use of the mails could not be clearer. It is sometimes difficult to define when there has been a scheme to defraud someone of intangible rights. But it is also sometimes difficult to decide when a tangible loss was caused by fraud. The fact that the exercise of judgment is sometimes difficult is no excuse for rejecting an entire doctrine that is both sound and faithful to the intent of Congress.

IV

In the long run, it is not clear how grave the ramifications of today's decision will be. Congress can, of course, negate it by amending the statute. Even without Congressional action, prosecutions of corrupt officials who use the mails to further their schemes may continue since it will frequently be possible to prove some loss of money or property.[6] But many other types of fraudulent use of the mail will now be immune from prosecution. The possibilities that the decision's impact will be mitigated do not moderate my conviction that the Court has made a serious mistake. Nor do they erase my lingering questions about why a Court that has not been particularly receptive to the rights of criminal defendants in recent years has acted so dramatically to protect the elite class of powerful individuals who will benefit from this decision.

I respectfully dissent.

NOTES

1. The opinions in *McNally* did make it clear that Congress did have the power to enact laws punishing the conduct of McNally and other public officials like him. The reasons not to do so are expressed in another case by Justice Stevens (who dissented in *McNally*). In Garcia v. United States, 469 U.S. 70, 105 S.Ct. 479 (1984) the petitioners assaulted an undercover Secret Service agent with a pistol in an attempt to rob him of $1,800 of government "flash money"

5. When considering how much weight to accord to the doctrine of lenity, it is appropriate to identify the class of litigants that will benefit from the Court's ruling today. They are not uneducated, or even average, citizens. They are the most sophisticated practitioners of the art of government among us. There is an element of fiction in the presumption that every citizen is charged with a responsibility to know what the law is. But the array of government executives, judges, and legislators who have been accused, and convicted, of mail fraud under the well-settled construction of the statute that the Court renounces today are people who unquestionably knew that their conduct was unlawful.

6. When a person is being paid a salary for his loyal services, any breach of that loyalty would appear to carry with it some loss of money to the employer—who is not getting what he paid for. Additionally, "[i]f an agent receives anything as a result of his violation of a duty of loyalty to the principal, he is subject to a liability to deliver it, its value, or its proceeds, to the principal." Restatement (Second) of Agency § 403 (1958). This duty may fulfill the Court's "money or property" requirement in most kickback schemes.

that the agent was using to buy counterfeit currency from them. The Court upheld a prosecution under a statute (18 U.S.C.A. § 2114) originally enacted to punish assault and robbery of postal employees and rejected a claim that petitioners could be convicted only under a statute (18 U.S.C.A. § 111) prohibiting assaults on federal officers and carrying a much lesser penalty. The issue before the Court was quite technical, involving disputes over legislative history and prior conflicting positions taken by the government. In dissent, Justice Stevens said, "It is Congress, rather than the Executive, that must define the dimensions of the federal law enforcement program. Law enforcement remains, and should remain, the primary responsibility of the several States. Every increase in the power of the federal prosecutor moves us a step closer to a national police force with its attendant threats to individual liberty. For that reason, I believe we have a special obligation to make sure that Congress intended to authorize a novel assertion of federal criminal jurisdiction.... There is, of course, no doubt that Congress has the authority to enact a law with the meaning the Court finds in § 2114 today. I am not, however, convinced that Congress actually intended to do so."

2. In 1988 Congress exercised its authority to punish defendants like McNally. It enacted 18 U.S.C.A. § 1346 which provides that the term "scheme or artifice to defraud" includes a scheme or artifice to deprive another of the intangible right of honest services.

D. THE COMMERCE CLAUSE OFFENSES

PEREZ v. UNITED STATES

Supreme Court of the United States, 1971.
402 U.S. 146, 91 S.Ct. 1357.

MR. JUSTICE DOUGLAS delivered the opinion of the Court.

The question in this case is whether Title II of the Consumer Credit Protection Act, 18 U.S.C.A. § 891 et seq., as construed and applied to petitioner, is a permissible exercise by Congress of its powers under the Commerce Clause of the Constitution.

Petitioner is one of the species commonly known as "loan sharks" which Congress found are in large part under the control of "organized crime." [1] "Extortionate credit transactions" are defined as those char-

1. Section 201(a) of Title II contains the following findings by Congress:

"(1) Organized crime is interstate and international in character. Its activities involve many billions of dollars each year. It is directly responsible for murders, willful injuries to person and property, corruption of officials, and terrorization of countless citizens. A substantial part of the income of organized crime is generated by extortionate credit transactions.

"(2) Extortionate credit transactions are characterized by the use, or the express or implicit threat of the use, of violence or other criminal means to cause harm to person, reputation, or property as a means of enforcing repayment. Among the factors which have rendered past efforts at prosecution almost wholly ineffective has been the existence of exclusionary rules of evidence stricter than necessary for the protection of constitutional rights.

"(3) Extortionate credit transactions are carried on to a substantial extent in interstate and foreign commerce and through the means and instrumentalities of such commerce. Even where extor-

acterized by the use or threat of the use of "violence or other criminal means" in enforcement.[2] There was ample evidence showing petitioner was a "loan shark" who used the threat of violence as a method of collection. He loaned money to one Miranda, owner of a new butcher shop, making a $1,000 advance to be repaid in installments of $105 per week for 14 weeks. After paying at this rate for six or eight weeks, petitioner increased the weekly payment to $130. In two months Miranda asked for an additional loan of $2,000 which was made, the agreement being that Miranda was to pay $205 a week. In a few weeks petitioner increased the weekly payment to $330. When Miranda objected, petitioner told him about a customer who refused to pay and ended up in a hospital. So Miranda paid. In a few months petitioner increased his demands to $500 weekly which Miranda paid, only to be advised that at the end of the week petitioner would need $1,000. Miranda made that payment by not paying his suppliers; but faced with a $1,000 payment the next week, he sold his butcher shop. Petitioner pursued Miranda, first making threats to Miranda's wife and then telling Miranda he could have him castrated. When Miranda did not make more payments, petitioner said he was turning over his collections to people who would not be nice but who would put him in the hospital if he did not pay. Negotiations went on, Miranda finally saying he could only pay $25 a week. Petitioner said that was not enough, that Miranda should steal or sell drugs if necessary to get the money to pay the loan, and that if he went to jail it would be better than going to a hospital with a broken back or legs. He added, "I could have sent you to the hospital, you and your family, any moment I want with my people."

Petitioner's arrest followed. Miranda, his wife and an employee gave the evidence against petitioner who did not testify or call any witnesses. Petitioner's attack was on the constitutionality of the Act, starting with a motion to dismiss the indictment.

The constitutional question is a substantial one.

Two "loan shark" amendments to the bill that became this Act were proposed in the House—one by Congressman Poff of Virginia, 114 Cong.Rec. 1605–1606 and another one by Congressman McDade of Pennsylvania. Id., at 1609–1610.

The House debates include a long article from the New York Times Magazine for January 28, 1968, on the connection between the "loan

tionate credit transactions are purely intrastate in character, they nevertheless directly affect interstate and foreign commerce."

2. Section 891 of 18 U.S.C.A. (1964 ed., Supp. V) provides in part:

"(6) An extortionate extension of credit is any extension of credit with respect to which it is the understanding of the creditor and the debtor at the time it is made that delay in making repayment or failure to make repayment could result in the use of violence or other criminal means to cause harm to the person, reputation, or property of any person.

"(7) An extortionate means is any means which involves the use, or an express or implicit threat of use, of violence or other criminal means to cause harm to the person, reputation, or property of any person."

shark" and organized crime. The gruesome and stirring episodes related have the following as a prelude:

> "The loan shark, then, is the indispensable 'money-mover' of the underworld. He takes 'black' money tainted by its derivation from the gambling or narcotics rackets and turns it 'white' by funneling it into channels of legitimate trade. In so doing, he exacts usurious interest that doubles the black-white money in no time; and, by his special decrees, by his imposition of impossible penalties, he greases the way for the underworld takeover of entire businesses."

There were objections on constitutional grounds. Congressman Eckhardt of Texas said:

> "Should it become law, the amendment would take a long stride by the Federal Government toward occupying the field of general criminal law and toward exercising a general Federal police power; and it would permit prosecution in Federal as well as State courts of a typically State offense.
>
> * * *
>
> "I believe that Alexander Hamilton, though a federalist, would be astonished that such a deep entrenchment on the rights of the States in performing their most fundamental function should come from the more conservative quarter of the House." Id., at 1610.

Senator Proxmire presented to the Senate the Conference Report approving essentially the "loan shark" provision suggested by Congressman McDade, saying:

> "Once again these provisions raised serious questions of Federal-State responsibilities. Nonetheless, because of the importance of the problem, the Senate conferees agreed to the House provision. Organized crime operates on a national scale. One of the principal sources of revenue of organized crime comes from loan sharking. If we are to win the battle against organized crime we must strike at their source of revenue and give the Justice Department additional tools to deal with the problem. The problems simply cannot be solved by the States alone. We must bring into play the full resources of the Federal Government." Id., at 14490.

The Commerce Clause reaches, in the main, three categories of problems. First, the use of channels of interstate or foreign commerce which Congress deems are being misused, as, for example, the shipment of stolen goods (18 U.S.C.A. §§ 2312–2315) or of persons who have been kidnaped (18 U.S.C.A. § 1201). Second, protection of the instrumentalities of interstate commerce, as, for example, the destruction of an aircraft (18 U.S.C.A. § 32), or persons or things in commerce, as, for example, thefts from interstate shipments (18 U.S.C.A. § 659). Third, those activities affecting commerce. It is with this last category that we are here concerned.

Chief Justice Marshall in Gibbons v. Ogden, 9 Wheat. 1, 195, said:

> "The genius and character of the whole government seem to be, that its action is to be applied to all the external concerns of the nation, and to those internal concerns which affect the States generally; but not to those which are completely within a particular State, which do not affect other States, and with which it is not necessary to interfere, for the purpose of executing some of the general powers of the government. The completely internal commerce of a State, then, may be considered as reserve for the State itself."

Decisions which followed departed from that view; but by the time of United States v. Darby, 312 U.S. 100, 61 S.Ct. 451 and Wickard v. Filburn, 317 U.S. 111, 63 S.Ct. 82 the broader view of the Commerce Clause announced by Chief Justice Marshall had been restored.

[In] Wickard v. Filburn, 317 U.S. 111, 63 S.Ct. 82, a unanimous Court held that wheat grown wholly for home consumption was constitutionally within the scope of federal regulation of wheat production because, though never marketed interstate, it supplied the need of the grower which otherwise would be satisfied by his purchases in the open market. We said:

> "[E]ven if appellee's activity be local and though it may not be regarded as commerce, it may still, whatever its nature, be reached by Congress if it exerts a substantial economic effect on interstate commerce, and this irrespective of whether such effect is what might at some earlier time have been defined as 'direct' or 'indirect.' " 317 U.S., at 125, 63 S.Ct., at 89.

In United States v. Darby, 312 U.S. 100, 61 S.Ct. 451, the decision sustaining an Act of Congress which prohibited the employment of workers in the production of goods "for interstate commerce" at other than prescribed wages and hours, *a class of activities* was held properly regulated by Congress without proof that the particular intrastate activity against which a sanction was laid had an effect on commerce. A unanimous Court said:

> "Congress has sometimes left it to the courts to determine whether the intrastate activities have the prohibited effect on the commerce, as in the Sherman Act. It has sometimes left it to an administrative board or agency to determine whether the activities sought to be regulated or prohibited have such effect, as in the case of the Interstate Commerce Act, and the National Labor Relations Act, or whether they come within the statutory definition of the prohibited Act, as in the Federal Trade Commission Act. And sometimes Congress itself has said that a particular activity affects the commerce, as it did in the present Act, the Safety Appliance Act and the Railway Labor Act. In

passing on the validity of legislation of the *class* last mentioned the only function of courts is to determine whether the particular activity regulated or prohibited is within the reach of the federal power."

That case is particularly relevant here because it involved a criminal prosecution, a unanimous Court holding that the Act was "sufficiently definite to meet constitutional demands." Petitioner is clearly *a member of the class* which engages in "extortionate credit transactions" as defined by Congress and the description of that class has the required definiteness.

It was the "class of activities" test which we employed in Atlanta Motel v. United States, 379 U.S. 241, 85 S.Ct. 348, to sustain an Act of Congress requiring hotel or motel accommodations for Negro guests. The Act declared that " 'any inn, hotel, motel, or other establishment which provides lodging to transient guests' affects commerce *per se*." That exercise of power under the Commerce Clause was sustained.

> "[O]ur people have become increasingly mobile with millions of people of all races traveling from State to State; ... Negroes in particular have been the subject of discrimination in transient accommodations, having to travel great distances to secure the same; ... often they have been unable to obtain accommodations and have had to call upon friends to put them up overnight ... and ... these conditions had become so acute as to require the listing of available lodging for Negroes in a special guidebook...."

In a companion case, Katzenbach v. McClung, 379 U.S. 294, 85 S.Ct. 377, we ruled on the constitutionality of the restaurant provision of the same Civil Rights Act which regulated the restaurant "if ... it serves or offers to serve interstate travelers or a substantial portion of the food which it serves ... has moved in commerce." Apart from the effect on the flow of food in commerce to restaurants, we spoke of the restrictive effect of the exclusion of Negroes from restaurants on interstate travel by Negroes.

> "[T]here was an impressive array of testimony that discrimination in restaurants had a direct and highly restrictive effect upon interstate travel by Negroes. This resulted, it was said, because discriminatory practices prevent Negroes from buying prepared food served on the premises while on a trip, except in isolated and unkempt restaurants and under most unsatisfactory and often unpleasant conditions. This obviously discourages travel and obstructs interstate commerce for one can hardly travel without eating. Likewise it was said, that discrimination deterred professional, as well as skilled, people from moving into areas where such practices occurred and thereby caused industry to be reluctant to establish there."

In emphasis of our position that it was the *class of activities* regulated that was the measure, we acknowledged that Congress appropriately considered the "total incidence" of the practice on commerce.

Where the *class of activities* is regulated and that *class* is within the reach of federal power, the courts have no power "to excise, as trivial, individual instances" of the class. Maryland v. Wirtz, 392 U.S. 183, 193, 88 S.Ct. 2017.

Extortionate credit transactions, though purely intrastate, may in the judgment of Congress affect interstate commerce. In an analogous situation, Mr. Justice Holmes, speaking for a unanimous Court, said: "[W]hen it is necessary in order to prevent an evil to make the law embrace more than the precise thing to be prevented it may do so." Westfall v. United States, 274 U.S. 256, 259, 47 S.Ct. 629. In that case an officer of a state bank which was a member of the Federal Reserve System issued a fraudulent certificate of deposit and paid it from the funds of the state bank. It was argued that there was no loss to the Reserve Bank. Mr. Justice Holmes replied, "But every fraud like the one before us weakens the member bank and therefore weakens the System." In the setting of the present case there is a tie-in between local loan sharks and intrastate crime.

The findings by Congress are quite adequate on that ground. The McDade Amendment in the House, as already noted, was the one ultimately adopted. As stated by Congressman McDade it grew out of a "profound study of organized crime, its ramifications and its implications" undertaken by some 22 Congressmen in 1966–1967. 114 Cong. Rec. 14391. The results of that study were included in a report, The Urban Poor and Organized Crime, submitted to the House on August 29, 1967, which revealed that "organized crime takes over $350 million a year from America's poor through loansharking alone." See 113 Cong. Rec. 24460–24464. Congressman McDade also relied on The Challenge of Crime in a Free Society, A Report by the President's Commission on Law Enforcement and Administration of Justice (February 1967) which stated that loan sharking was "the second largest source of revenue for organized crime," and is one way by which the underworld obtains control of legitimate businesses.

The Congress also knew about New York's Report, An Investigation of the Loan Shark Racket (1965). See 114 Cong.Rec. 1428–1431. That report shows the loan shark racket is controlled by organized criminal syndicates, either directly or in partnership with independent operators; that in most instances the racket is organized into three echelons, with the top underworld "bosses" providing the money to their principal "lieutenants," who in turn distribute the money to the "operators" who make the actual individual loans; that loan sharks serve as a source of funds to bookmakers, narcotics dealers, and other racketeers; that victims of the racket include all classes, rich and poor, businessmen and laborers; that the victims are often coerced into the commission of criminal acts in order to repay their loans; that through loan sharking the organized underworld has obtained control of legitimate businesses, including securities brokerages and banks which are then exploited; and that "[e]ven where extortionate credit transactions are purely intrastate in character, they nevertheless directly affect interstate and foreign commerce."

Shortly before the Conference bill was adopted by Congress a Senate Committee had held hearings on loan sharking and that testimony was made available to members of the House. See 114 Cong.Rec. 14390.

The essence of all these reports and hearings was summarized and embodied in formal congressional findings. They supplied Congress with the knowledge that the loan shark racket provides organized crime with its second most lucrative source of revenue, exacts millions from the pockets of people, coerces its victims into the commission of crimes against property, and causes the takeover by racketeers of legitimate businesses. See generally 114 Cong.Rec. 14391, 14392, 14395, 14396.

We have mentioned in detail the economic, financial, and social setting of the problem as revealed to Congress. We do so not to infer that Congress need make particularized findings in order to legislate. We relate the history of the Act in detail to answer the impassioned plea of petitioner that all that is involved in loan sharking is a traditionally local activity. It appears, instead, that loan sharking in its national setting is one way organized interstate crime holds its guns to the heads of the poor and the rich alike and syphons funds from numerous localities to finance its national operations.

Affirmed.

MR. JUSTICE STEWART, dissenting.

Congress surely has power under the Commerce Clause to enact criminal laws to protect the instrumentalities of interstate commerce, to prohibit the misuse of the channels or facilities of interstate commerce, and to prohibit or regulate those intrastate activities that have a demonstrably substantial effect on interstate commerce. But under the statute before us a man can be convicted without any proof of interstate movement, of the use of the facilities of interstate commerce, or of facts showing that his conduct affected interstate commerce. I think the Framers of the Constitution never intended that the National Government might define as a crime and prosecute such wholly local activity through the enactment of federal criminal laws.

In order to sustain this law we would, in my view, have to be able at the least to say that Congress could rationally have concluded that loan sharking is an activity with interstate attributes that distinguish it in some substantial respect from other local crime. But it is not enough to say that loan sharking is a national problem, for all crime is a national problem. It is not enough to say that some loan sharking has interstate characteristics, for any crime may have an interstate setting. And the circumstance that loan sharking has an adverse impact on interstate business is not a distinguishing attribute, for interstate business suffers from almost all criminal activity, be it shoplifting or violence in the streets.

Because I am unable to discern any rational distinction between loan sharking and other local crime, I cannot escape the conclusion that this statute was beyond the power of Congress to enact. The definition and prosecution of local, intrastate crime are reserved to the States under the Ninth and Tenth Amendments.

UNITED STATES v. LOPEZ

Supreme Court of the United States, 1995.
___ U.S. ___, 115 S.Ct. 1624.

CHIEF JUSTICE REHNQUIST delivered the opinion of the Court.

In the Gun–Free School Zones Act of 1990, Congress made it a federal offense "for any individual knowingly to possess a firearm at a place that the individual knows, or has reasonable cause to believe, is a school zone."[1] 18 U.S.C. § 922(q)(1)(A) (1988 ed., Supp. V). The Act neither regulates a commercial activity nor contains a requirement that the possession be connected in any way to interstate commerce. We hold that the Act exceeds the authority of Congress "[t]o regulate Commerce ... among the several States...." U.S. Const., Art. I, § 8, cl. 3.

On March 10, 1992, respondent, who was then a 12th–grade student, arrived at Edison High School in San Antonio, Texas, carrying a concealed .38 caliber handgun and five bullets. Acting upon an anonymous tip, school authorities confronted respondent, who admitted that he was carrying the weapon.

A federal grand jury indicted respondent on one count of knowing possession of a firearm at a school zone, in violation of § 922(q). The District Court conducted a bench trial, found him guilty of violating § 922(q), and sentenced him to six months' imprisonment and two years' supervised release.

We start with first principles. The Constitution creates a Federal Government of enumerated powers. See U.S. Const., Art. I, § 8. As James Madison wrote, "[t]he powers delegated by the proposed Constitution to the federal government are few and defined. Those which are to remain in the State governments are numerous and indefinite." The Federalist No. 45, pp. 292–293 (C. Rossiter ed. 1961). This constitutionally mandated division of authority "was adopted by the Framers to ensure protection of our fundamental liberties." *Gregory v. Ashcroft* (1991). "Just as the separation and independence of the coordinate branches of the Federal Government serves to prevent the accumulation of excessive power in any one branch, a healthy balance of power

1. The term "school zone" is defined as "in, or on the grounds of, a public, parochial or private school" or "within a distance of 1,000 feet from the grounds of a public, parochial or private school." § 921(a)(25).

between the States and the Federal Government will reduce the risk of tyranny and abuse from either front." *Ibid.*

The Constitution delegates to Congress the power "[t]o regulate Commerce with foreign Nations, and among the several States, and with the Indian Tribes." U.S. Const., Art. I, § 8, cl. 3. The Court, through Chief Justice Marshall, first defined the nature of Congress' commerce power in *Gibbons v. Ogden* (1824):

> "Commerce, undoubtedly, is traffic, but it is something more: it is intercourse. It describes the commercial intercourse between nations, and parts of nations, in all its branches, and is regulated by prescribing rules for carrying on that intercourse."

The commerce power "is the power to regulate; that is, to prescribe the rule by which commerce is to be governed. This power, like all others vested in Congress, is complete in itself, may be exercised to its utmost extent, and acknowledges no limitations, other than are prescribed in the constitution." The *Gibbons* Court, however, acknowledged that limitations on the commerce power are inherent in the very language of the Commerce Clause.

> "It is not intended to say that these words comprehend that commerce, which is completely internal, which is carried on between man and man in a State, or between different parts of the same State, and which does not extend to or affect other States. Such a power would be inconvenient, and is certainly unnecessary.
>
> "Comprehensive as the word 'among' is, it may very properly be restricted to that commerce which concerns more States than one.... The enumeration presupposes something not enumerated; and that something, if we regard the language or the subject of the sentence, must be the exclusively internal commerce of a State."

[W]e have identified three broad categories of activity that Congress may regulate under its commerce power. First, Congress may regulate the use of the channels of interstate commerce. (" '[T]he authority of Congress to keep the channels of interstate commerce free from immoral and injurious uses has been frequently sustained, and is no longer open to question.' " (*Caminetti v. United States* (1917)). Second, Congress is empowered to regulate and protect the instrumentalities of interstate commerce, or persons or things in interstate commerce, even though the threat may come only from intrastate activities. See, *Southern R. Co. v. United States* (1911) (upholding amendments to Safety Appliance Act as applied to vehicles used in intrastate commerce). Finally, Congress' commerce authority includes the power to regulate those activities having a substantial relation to interstate commerce, *i.e.,* those activities that substantially affect interstate commerce.

We now turn to consider the power of Congress, in the light of this framework, to enact § 922(q). The first two categories of authority may be quickly disposed of: § 922(q) is not a regulation of the use of the channels of interstate commerce, nor is it an attempt to prohibit the interstate transportation of a commodity through the channels of commerce; nor can § 922(q) be justified as a regulation by which Congress has sought to protect an instrumentality of interstate commerce or a thing in interstate commerce. Thus, if § 922(q) is to be sustained, it must be under the third category as a regulation of an activity that substantially affects interstate commerce.

We have upheld a wide variety of congressional Acts regulating intrastate economic activity where we have concluded that the activity substantially affected interstate commerce. Examples include the regulation of intrastate coal mining; intrastate extortionate credit transactions, restaurants utilizing substantial interstate supplies, inns and hotels catering to interstate guests, and production and consumption of home-grown wheat, *Wickard v. Filburn* (1942). These examples are by no means exhaustive, but the pattern is clear. Where economic activity substantially affects interstate commerce, legislation regulating that activity will be sustained.

Even *Wickard,* which is perhaps the most far reaching example of Commerce Clause authority over intrastate activity, involved economic activity in a way that the possession of a gun in a school zone does not. Roscoe Filburn operated a small farm in Ohio, on which, in the year involved, he raised 23 acres of wheat. It was his practice to sow winter wheat in the fall, and after harvesting it in July to sell a portion of the crop, to feed part of it to poultry and livestock on the farm, to use some in making flour for home consumption, and to keep the remainder for seeding future crops. The Secretary of Agriculture assessed a penalty against him under the Agricultural Adjustment Act of 1938 because he harvested about 12 acres more wheat than his allotment under the Act permitted. The Act was designed to regulate the volume of wheat moving in interstate and foreign commerce in order to avoid surpluses and shortages, and concomitant fluctuation in wheat prices, which had previously obtained. The Court said, in an opinion sustaining the application of the Act to Filburn's activity:

> "One of the primary purposes of the Act in question was to increase the market price of wheat and to that end to limit the volume thereof that could affect the market. It can hardly be denied that a factor of such volume and variability as home-consumed wheat would have a substantial influence on price and market conditions. This may arise because being in marketable condition such wheat overhangs the market and, if induced by rising prices, tends to flow into the market and check price increases. But if we assume that it is never marketed, it supplies a need of the man who grew it which would otherwise be reflected by purchases in the open market. Home-grown wheat in this sense competes with wheat in commerce." 317 U.S., at 128, 63 S.Ct., at 90–91.

Section 922(q) is a criminal statute that by its terms has nothing to do with "commerce" or any sort of economic enterprise, however broadly one might define those terms.[2] Section 922(q) is not an essential part of a larger regulation of economic activity, in which the regulatory scheme could be undercut unless the intrastate activity were regulated. It cannot, therefore, be sustained under our cases upholding regulations of activities that arise out of or are connected with a commercial transaction, which viewed in the aggregate, substantially affects interstate commerce.

* * *

Although as part of our independent evaluation of constitutionality under the Commerce Clause we of course consider legislative findings, and indeed even congressional committee findings, regarding effect on interstate commerce, see, *e.g., Preseault v. ICC* (1990), the Government concedes that "[n]either the statute nor its legislative history contain[s] express congressional findings regarding the effects upon interstate commerce of gun possession in a school zone." We agree with the Government that Congress normally is not required to make formal findings as to the substantial burdens that an activity has on interstate commerce.

But to the extent that congressional findings would enable us to evaluate the legislative judgment that the activity in question substantially affected interstate commerce, even though no such substantial effect was visible to the naked eye, they are lacking here.[3]

The Government's essential contention, *in fine,* is that we may determine here that § 922(q) is valid because possession of a firearm in a local school zone does indeed substantially affect interstate commerce. The Government argues that possession of a firearm in a school zone may result in violent crime and that violent crime can be expected to affect the functioning of the national economy in two ways. First, the costs of violent crime are substantial, and, through the mechanism of insurance, those costs are spread throughout the population. Second, violent crime reduces the willingness of individuals to travel to areas within the country that are perceived to be unsafe. The Government

2. Under our federal system, the " 'States possess primary authority for defining and enforcing the criminal law.' " *Brecht v. Abrahamson* (1993). When Congress criminalizes conduct already denounced as criminal by the States, it effects a " 'change in the sensitive relation between federal and state criminal jurisdiction.' " The Government acknowledges that § 922(q) "displace[s] state policy choices in ... that its prohibitions apply even in States that have chosen not to outlaw the conduct in question."

3. We note that on September 13, 1994, President Clinton signed into law the Violent Crime Control and Law Enforcement Act of 1994, Pub.L. 103–322, 108 Stat. 1796. Section 320904 of that Act, *id.,* at 2125, amends § 922(q) to include congressional findings regarding the effects of firearm possession in and around schools upon interstate and foreign commerce. The Government does not rely upon these subsequent findings as a substitute for the absence of findings in the first instance. ("[W]e're not relying on them in the strict sense of the word, but we think that at a very minimum they indicate that reasons can be identified for why Congress wanted to regulate this particular activity").

also argues that the presence of guns in schools poses a substantial threat to the educational process by threatening the learning environment. A handicapped educational process, in turn, will result in a less productive citizenry. That, in turn, would have an adverse effect on the Nation's economic well-being. As a result, the Government argues that Congress could rationally have concluded that § 922(q) substantially affects interstate commerce.

We pause to consider the implications of the Government's arguments. The Government admits, under its "costs of crime" reasoning, that Congress could regulate not only all violent crime, but all activities that might lead to violent crime, regardless of how tenuously they relate to interstate commerce. Similarly, under the Government's "national productivity" reasoning, Congress could regulate any activity that it found was related to the economic productivity of individual citizens: family law (including marriage, divorce, and child custody), for example. Under the theories that the Government presents in support of § 922(q), it is difficult to perceive any limitation on federal power, even in areas such as criminal law enforcement or education where States historically have been sovereign. Thus, if we were to accept the Government's arguments, we are hard-pressed to posit any activity by an individual that Congress is without power to regulate.

Justice BREYER [in] dissent reasons that (1) gun-related violence is a serious problem; (2) that problem, in turn, has an adverse effect on classroom learning; and (3) that adverse effect on classroom learning, in turn, represents a substantial threat to trade and commerce. This analysis would be equally applicable, if not more so, to subjects such as family law and direct regulation of education.

For instance, if Congress can, pursuant to its Commerce Clause power, regulate activities that adversely affect the learning environment, then, *a fortiori,* it also can regulate the educational process directly. Congress could determine that a school's curriculum has a "significant" effect on the extent of classroom learning. As a result, Congress could mandate a federal curriculum for local elementary and secondary schools because what is taught in local schools has a significant "effect on classroom learning," and that, in turn, has a substantial effect on interstate commerce.

JUSTICE BREYER rejects our reading of precedent and argues that "Congress ... could rationally conclude that schools fall on the commercial side of the line." Again, JUSTICE BREYER's rationale lacks any real limits because, depending on the level of generality, any activity can be looked upon as commercial. Under the dissent's rationale, Congress could just as easily look at child rearing as "fall[ing] on the commercial side of the line" because it provides a "valuable service—namely, to equip [children] with the skills they need to survive in life and, more specifically, in the workplace." We do not doubt that Congress has authority under the Commerce Clause to regulate numerous commercial activities that substantially affect interstate commerce and also affect the educational process. That authority, though broad, does not include the authority to regulate each and every aspect of local schools.

Admittedly, a determination whether an intrastate activity is commercial or noncommercial may in some cases result in legal uncertainty. But, so long as Congress' authority is limited to those powers enumerated in the Constitution, and so long as those enumerated powers are interpreted as having judicially enforceable outer limits, congressional legislation under the Commerce Clause always will engender "legal uncertainty."

These are not precise formulations, and in the nature of things they cannot be. But we think they point the way to a correct decision of this case. The possession of a gun in a local school zone is in no sense an economic activity that might, through repetition elsewhere, substantially affect any sort of interstate commerce. [Lopez] was a local student at a local school; there is no indication that he had recently moved in interstate commerce, and there is no requirement that his possession of the firearm have any concrete tie to interstate commerce.

To uphold the Government's contentions here, we would have to pile inference upon inference in a manner that would bid fair to convert congressional authority under the Commerce Clause to a general police power of the sort retained by the States. Admittedly, some of our prior cases have taken long steps down that road, giving great deference to congressional action. The broad language in these opinions has suggested the possibility of additional expansion, but we decline here to proceed any further. To do so would require us to conclude that the Constitution's enumeration of powers does not presuppose something not enumerated, and that there never will be a distinction between what is truly national and what is truly local. This we are unwilling to do.

JUSTICE KENNEDY, with whom JUSTICE O'CONNOR joins, concurring.

While it is doubtful that any State, or indeed any reasonable person, would argue that it is wise policy to allow students to carry guns on school premises, considerable disagreement exists about how best to accomplish that goal. In this circumstance, the theory and utility of our federalism are revealed, for the States may perform their role as laboratories for experimentation to devise various solutions where the best solution is far from clear.

If a State or municipality determines that harsh criminal sanctions are necessary and wise to deter students from carrying guns on school premises, the reserved powers of the States are sufficient to enact those measures. Indeed, over 40 States already have criminal laws outlawing the possession of firearms on or near school grounds.

Other, more practicable means to rid the schools of guns may be thought by the citizens of some States to be preferable for the safety and welfare of the schools those States are charged with maintaining. See Brief for National Conference of State Legislatures et al., as *Amici Curiae* 26–30 (injection of federal officials into local problems causes friction and diminishes political accountability of state and local governments). These might include inducements to inform on violators where the information leads to arrests or confiscation of the guns, see C. Lima, Schools May Launch Weapons Hot Line, L.A. Times, Jan. 13, 1995, part B, p. 1, col. 5; Reward for Tips on Guns in Tucson Schools, The Arizona Republic, Jan. 7, 1995, p. B2; programs to encourage the voluntary surrender of guns with some provision for amnesty, see A. Zaidan, Akron Rallies to Save Youths, The Plain Dealer, Mar. 2, 1995, p. 1B; penalties imposed on parents or guardians for failure to supervise the child, see, *e.g.*, Okla.Stat., Tit. 21, § 858 (Supp.1995) (fining parents who allow students to possess firearm at school); Tenn.Code Ann. § 39–17–1312 (Supp.1992) (misdemeanor for parents to allow student to possess firearm at school); Straight Shooter: Gov. Casey's Reasonable Plan to Control Assault Weapons, Pittsburgh Post–Gazette, Mar. 14, 1994, p. B2 (proposed bill); laws providing for suspension or expulsion of gun-toting students, see, *e.g.*, Ala.Code § 16–1–24.1 (Supp.1994); Ind.Code § 20–8.1–5–4(b)(1)(D) (1993); Ky.Rev.Stat.Ann. § 158.150(1)(a) (Michie 1992); Wash.Rev.Code § 9.41.280 (1994), or programs for expulsion with assignment to special facilities, see J. Martin, Legislators Poised to Take Harsher Stand on Guns in Schools, The Seattle Times, Feb. 1, 1995, p. B1 (automatic-year-long expulsion for students with guns and intense semester-long reentry program).

The statute now before us forecloses the States from experimenting and exercising their own judgment in an area to which States lay claim by right of history and expertise, and it does so by regulating an activity beyond the realm of commerce in the ordinary and usual sense of that term. The tendency of this statute to displace state regulation in areas of traditional state concern is evident from its territorial operation. There are over 100,000 elementary and secondary schools in the United States. Each of these now has an invisible federal zone extending 1,000 feet beyond the (often irregular) boundaries of the school property. In some communities no doubt it would be difficult to navigate without infringing on those zones. Yet throughout these areas, school officials would find their own programs for the prohibition of guns in danger of displacement by the federal authority unless the State chooses to enact a parallel rule.

While the intrusion on state sovereignty may not be as severe in this instance as in some of our recent cases, the intrusion is nonetheless significant. Absent a stronger connection or identification with commercial concerns that are central to the Commerce Clause, that interference contradicts the federal balance the Framers designed and that this Court is obliged to enforce.

For these reasons, I join in the opinion and judgment of the Court.

JUSTICE THOMAS, concurring.

The Court today properly concludes that the Commerce Clause does not grant Congress the authority to prohibit gun possession within 1,000 feet of a school, as it attempted to do in the Gun–Free School Zones Act of 1990, Pub.L. 101–647, 104 Stat. 4844. Although I join the majority, I write separately to observe that our case law has drifted far from the original understanding of the Commerce Clause. In a future case, we ought to temper our Commerce Clause jurisprudence in a manner that both makes sense of our more recent case law and is more faithful to the original understanding of that Clause.

Apart from its recent vintage and its corresponding lack of any grounding in the original understanding of the Constitution, the substantial effects test suffers from the further flaw that it appears to grant Congress a police power over the Nation. When asked at oral argument if there were *any* limits to the Commerce Clause, the Government was at a loss for words. Likewise, the principal dissent insists that there are limits, but it cannot muster even one example. Indeed, the dissent implicitly concedes that its reading has no limits when it criticizes the Court for "threaten[ing] legal uncertainty in an area of law that ... seemed reasonably well settled." The one advantage of the dissent's standard is certainty: it is certain that under its analysis everything may be regulated under the guise of the Commerce Clause.

The substantial effects test suffers from this flaw, in part, because of its "aggregation principle." Under so-called "class of activities" statutes, Congress can regulate whole categories of activities that are not themselves either "interstate" or "commerce." In applying the effects test, we ask whether the class of activities *as a whole* substantially affects interstate commerce, not whether any specific activity within the class has such effects when considered in isolation.

The aggregation principle is clever, but has no stopping point. Suppose all would agree that gun possession within 1,000 feet of a school does not substantially affect commerce, but that possession of weapons generally (knives, brass knuckles, nunchuks, etc.) does. Under our substantial effects doctrine, even though Congress cannot single out gun possession, it can prohibit weapon possession generally. But one *always* can draw the circle broadly enough to cover an activity that, when taken in isolation, would not have substantial effects on commerce. Under our jurisprudence, if Congress passed an omnibus "substantially affects interstate commerce" statute, purporting to regulate every aspect of human existence, the Act apparently would be constitutional. Even though particular sections may govern only trivial activities, the statute in the aggregate regulates matters that substantially affect commerce.

* * *

At an appropriate juncture, I think we must modify our Commerce Clause jurisprudence. Today, it is easy enough to say that the Clause certainly does not empower Congress to ban gun possession within 1,000 feet of a school.

JUSTICE STEVENS, dissenting.

[OMITTED]

JUSTICE SOUTER, dissenting.

[OMITTED]

JUSTICE BREYER, with whom JUSTICE STEVENS, JUSTICE SOUTER, and JUSTICE GINSBURG join, dissenting.

I

I apply three basic principles of Commerce Clause interpretation. First, the power to "regulate Commerce ... among the several States," U.S. Const., Art. I, § 8, cl. 3, encompasses the power to regulate local activities insofar as they significantly affect interstate commerce. As the majority points out, the Court, in describing how much of an effect the Clause requires, sometimes has used the word "substantial" and sometimes has not. And, as the majority also recognizes in quoting Justice Cardozo, the question of degree (how *much* effect) requires an estimate of the "size" of the effect that no verbal formulation can capture with precision. I use the word "significant" because the word "substantial" implies a somewhat narrower power than recent precedent suggests. But, to speak of "substantial effect" rather than "significant effect" would make no difference in this case.

Second, in determining whether a local activity will likely have a significant effect upon interstate commerce, a court must consider, not the effect of an individual act (a single instance of gun possession), but rather the cumulative effect of all similar instances (*i.e.*, the effect of all guns possessed in or near schools).

Third, the Constitution requires us to judge the connection between a regulated activity and interstate commerce, not directly, but at one remove. Courts must give Congress a degree of leeway in determining the existence of a significant factual connection between the regulated activity and interstate commerce—both because the Constitution delegates the commerce power directly to Congress and because the determination requires an empirical judgment of a kind that a legislature is more likely than a court to make with accuracy. The traditional words "rational basis" capture this leeway. Thus, the specific question before us, as the Court recognizes, is not whether the "regulated activity sufficiently affected interstate commerce," but, rather, whether Congress could have had "*a rational basis*" for so concluding.

I recognize that we must judge this matter independently. "[S]imply because Congress may conclude that a particular activity substantially affects interstate commerce does not necessarily make it so." And, I also recognize that Congress did not write specific "interstate commerce" findings into the law under which Lopez was convicted. Nonetheless, as I have already noted, the matter that we review independently (*i.e.*, whether there is a "rational basis") already has considerable leeway built into it. And, the absence of findings, at most, deprives a statute of the benefit of some *extra* leeway. This extra deference, in principle, might change the result in a close case, though, in practice, it has not made a critical legal difference. It would seem particularly unfortunate to make the validity of the statute at hand turn on the presence or absence of findings. Because Congress did make findings (though not until after Lopez was prosecuted), doing so would appear to elevate form over substance. See Pub.L. 103–322, §§ 320904(2)(F), (G), 108 Stat. 2125, 18 U.S.C.A. § 922(q)(1)(F), (G) (Nov. 1994 Supp.).

In addition, there is no special need here for a clear indication of Congress' rationale. The statute does not interfere with the exercise of state or local authority.

Moreover, any clear statement rule would apply only to determine Congress' intended result, *not* to clarify the source of its authority or measure the level of consideration that went into its decision, and here there is no doubt as to which activities Congress intended to regulate.

Applying these principles to the case at hand, we must ask whether Congress could have had a *rational basis* for finding a significant (or substantial) connection between gun-related school violence and interstate commerce. Or, to put the question in the language of the *explicit* finding that Congress made when it amended this law in 1994: Could Congress rationally have found that "violent crime in school zones," through its effect on the "quality of education," significantly (or substantially) affects "interstate" or "foreign commerce"? 18 U.S.C.A. §§ 922(q)(1)(F), (G) (Nov. 1994 Supp.). As long as one views the commerce connection, not as a "technical legal conception," but as "a practical one," *Swift & Co. v. United States,* 196 U.S. 375, 398, 25 S.Ct. 276, 280, 49 L.Ed. 518 (1905) (Holmes, J.), the answer to this question must be yes. Numerous reports and studies—generated both inside and outside government—make clear that Congress could reasonably have found the empirical connection that its law, implicitly or explicitly, asserts.

For one thing, reports, hearings, and other readily available literature make clear that the problem of guns in and around schools is widespread and extremely serious. These materials report, for example, that four percent of American high school students (and six percent of inner-city high school students) carry a gun to school at least occasionally, that 12 percent of urban high school students have had guns fired at them, that 20 percent of those students have been threatened with guns, and that, in any 6–month period, several hundred thousand schoolchildren are victims of violent crimes in or near their schools. And, they report that this widespread violence in schools throughout the Nation significantly interferes with the quality of education in those schools. Based on reports such as these, Congress obviously could have thought that guns and learning are mutually exclusive. And, Congress could therefore have found a substantial educational problem—teachers unable to teach, students unable to learn—and concluded that guns near schools contribute substantially to the size and scope of that problem.

Having found that guns in schools significantly undermine the quality of education in our Nation's classrooms, Congress could also have found, given the effect of education upon interstate and foreign commerce, that gun-related violence in and around schools is a commercial, as well as a human, problem. Education, although far more than a matter of economics, has long been inextricably intertwined with the Nation's economy. When this Nation began, most workers received their education in the workplace, typically (like Benjamin Franklin) as apprentices. As late as the 1920's, many workers still received general education directly from their employers—from large corporations, such as General Electric, Ford, and Goodyear, which created schools within their firms to help both the worker and the firm. (Throughout most of the 19th century fewer than one percent of all Americans received secondary education through attending a high school.) As public school enrollment grew in the early 20th century, the need for industry to teach basic educational skills diminished. But, the direct economic link between basic education and industrial productivity remained. Scholars estimate that nearly a quarter of America's economic growth in the early years of this century is traceable directly to increased schooling, that investment in "human capital" (through spending on education) exceeded investment in "physical capital" by a ratio of almost two to one); and that the economic returns to this investment in education exceeded the returns to conventional capital investment.

In recent years the link between secondary education and business has strengthened, becoming both more direct and more important. Scholars on the subject report that technological changes and innovations in management techniques have altered the nature of the workplace so that more jobs now demand greater educational skills. There is evidence that "service, manufacturing or construction jobs are being displaced by technology that requires a better-educated worker or, more likely, are being exported overseas," that "workers with truly few skills by the year 2000 will find that only one job out of ten will remain," ...

Increasing global competition also has made primary and secondary education economically more important. The portion of the American economy attributable to international trade nearly tripled between 1950 and 1980, and more than 70 percent of American-made goods now compete with imports. Yet, lagging worker productivity has contributed to negative trade balances and to real hourly compensation that has fallen below wages in 10 other industrialized nations. At least some significant part of this serious productivity problem is attributable to students who emerge from classrooms without the reading or mathematical skills necessary to compete with their European or Asian counterparts, and, presumably, to high school dropout rates of 20 to 25 percent (up to 50 percent in inner cities). Indeed, Congress has said, when writing other statutes, that "functionally or technologically illiterate" Americans in the work force "erod[e]" our economic "standing in the international marketplace," Pub.L. 100–418, § 6002(a)(3), 102 Stat. 1469, and that "our Nation is ... paying the price of scientific and technological illiteracy, with our productivity declining, our industrial base ailing, and our global competitiveness dwindling." H.R.Rep. No. 98–6, pt. 1, p. 19 (1983).

Finally, there is evidence that, today more than ever, many firms base their location decisions upon the presence, or absence, of a work force with a basic education. Scholars on the subject report, for example, that today, "[h]igh speed communication and transportation make it possible to produce most products and services anywhere in the world," that "[m]odern machinery and production methods can therefore be combined with low wage workers to drive costs down," that managers can perform " 'back office functions anywhere in the world now,' " and say that if they " 'can't get enough skilled workers here' " they will " 'move the skilled jobs out of the country,' " with the consequence that "rich countries need better education and retraining, to reduce the supply of unskilled workers and to equip them with the skills they require for tomorrow's jobs." In light of this increased importance of education to individual firms, it is no surprise that half of the Nation's manufacturers have become involved with setting standards and shaping curricula for local schools, that 88 percent think this kind of involvement is important, that more than 20 States have recently passed educational reforms to attract new business, and that business magazines have begun to rank cities according to the quality of their schools.

The economic links I have just sketched seem fairly obvious. Why then is it not equally obvious, in light of those links, that a widespread, serious, and substantial physical threat to teaching and learning *also* substantially threatens the commerce to which that teaching and learning is inextricably tied? That is to say, guns in the hands of six percent of inner-city high school students and gun-related violence throughout a city's schools must threaten the trade and commerce that those schools support. The only question, then, is whether the latter threat is (to use the majority's terminology) "substantial." And, the evidence of (1) the *extent* of the gun-related violence problem, (2) the *extent* of the resulting negative effect on classroom learning, and (3) the *extent* of the consequent negative commercial effects, when taken together, indicate a threat to trade and commerce that is "substantial." At the very least, Congress could rationally have concluded that the links are "substantial."

Specifically, Congress could have found that gun-related violence near the classroom poses a serious economic threat (1) to consequently inadequately educated workers who must endure low paying jobs, and (2) to communities and businesses that might (in today's "information society") otherwise gain, from a well-singularly disruptive potential on interstate commerce that acts of violence may have. See *Perez.* For another thing, the immediacy of the connection between education and the national economic well-being is documented by scholars and accepted by society at large in a way and to a degree that may not hold true for other social institutions. It must surely be the rare case, then, that a statute strikes at conduct that (when considered in the abstract) seems so removed from commerce, but which (practically speaking) has so significant an impact upon commerce.

In sum, a holding that the particular statute before us falls within the commerce power would not expand the scope of that Clause. Rather, it simply would apply preexisting law to changing economic circumstances. It would recognize that, in today's economic world, gun-related violence near the classroom makes a significant difference to our economic, as well as our social, well-being. In accordance with well-accepted precedent, such a holding would permit Congress "to act in terms of economic ... realities," would interpret the commerce power as "an affirmative power commensurate with the national needs," and would acknowledge that the "commerce clause does not operate so as to render the nation powerless to defend itself against economic forces that Congress decrees inimical or destructive of the national economy." *North American Co. v. SEC.*

The legal problem created by the Court's holding is that it threatens legal uncertainty in an area of law that, until this case, seemed reasonably well settled. Congress has enacted many statutes (more than 100 sections of the United States Code), including criminal statutes (at least 25 sections), that use the words "affecting commerce" to define their scope, see, *e.g.,* 18 U.S.C. § 844(i) (destruction of buildings used in activity affecting interstate commerce), and other statutes that contain no jurisdictional language at all, see, *e.g.,* 18 U.S.C. § 922(*o*)(1) (possession of machine guns). Do these, or similar, statutes regulate noncommercial activities? If so, would that alter the meaning of "affecting commerce" in a jurisdictional element? Cf. *United States v. Staszcuk,* 517 F.2d 53, 57–58 (CA7 1975) (en banc) (Stevens, J.) (evaluation of Congress' intent "requires more than a consideration of the consequences of the particular transaction"). More importantly, in the absence of a jurisdictional element, are the courts nevertheless to take *Wickard,* 317 U.S., at 127–128, 63 S.Ct., at 90–91 (and later similar cases) as inapplicable, and to judge the effect of a single noncommercial activity on interstate commerce without considering similar instances of the forbidden conduct? However these questions are eventually resolved, the legal uncertainty now created will restrict Congress' ability to enact criminal laws aimed at criminal behavior that, considered problem by problem rather than instance by instance, seriously threatens the economic, as well as social, well-being of Americans.

NOTE

The decision in *Lopez* surprised many lawyers. There had been no successful challenges to federal jurisdiction for a very long time. In the aftermath of *Lopez,* a variety of statutes were challenged.

In United States v. Wilks, 58 F.3d 1518 (10th Cir.1995), the federal statute banning transfer or possession of a machine gun was challenged as an act having no basis in the Commerce Clause. The Court found that machine guns were a commodity in interstate commerce, a product transferred across state lines for profit by business entities and part of a national market for machine guns, all of which was implicitly found to be true by Congress when it passed the law. The same result was reached in United States v. Kirk, 70 F.3d 791 (5th Cir.1995), over a vigorous dissent that found too little evidence that Congress ever found a relation to commerce.

The federal statute which prohibits carjacking was similarly approved in United States v. Oliver, 60 F.3d 547 (9th Cir.1995), for the simple reason that the statute applies only to automobiles that have actually been "transported, shipped, or received in interstate or foreign commerce." Moreover, Congress had evidence that carjacking itself was in interstate commerce as part of a stolen car industry that removes cars to other states for retitling and distributes chopped parts on an interstate basis. The result was approved in United States v. Bishop, 66 F.3d 569 (3d Cir.1995), but this time over a rigorous dissent by Judge Becker who believed that *Lopez* had changed the rules. He noted that a carjacking itself is not a commercial transaction and can only be within federal jurisdiction if there is actual proof of the carjacking's relationship to interstate commercial activity. The fact that the car itself had once been shipped across state lines is not enough to establish federal jurisdiction. If it were, the dissent argued, Congress could outlaw the act of a child who steals a Hershey Kiss from a store in Ohio because the Kiss was made in and shipped from Pennsylvania. So, too, the fact that cars are sometimes instrumentalities of interstate commerce does not mean Congress can legislate all aspects of automobiles and their use. Finally, he argues that Congress really made no findings of effect on interstate commerce. The legislative record showed the purpose of Congress was to act against a violent crime and not to regulate commerce, and that is the task of the states, all of whom can (and have) legislated against carjacking.

There will be other challenges to an expanding range of federal laws which address acts traditionally governed by state law, such as the Child Support Recovery Act.

Lopez will also affect cases in which a statute itself is not challenged, rather the application is disputed. There is no question that Congress may pass a federal law punishing arson of property used in interstate commerce or in any activity affecting interstate commerce. In United States v. Pappadopoulous, 64 F.3d 522 (9th Cir.1995), defendant burned his own home to get insurance proceeds. The prosecution argued that the home used natural gas for power and this gas came across state lines. The home itself was not used in interstate commerce, so the only question was whether its use of out-of-state natural gas "substantially affected" interstate commerce. The Court said that even this trivial use would have been enough for jurisdiction prior to *Lopez;* It was not enough after *Lopez* which requires a substantial effect on interstate commerce. Either the government must identify a substantial, non-trivial, effect on or connection to commerce, or the connection must be obvious, or the connection must be "illuminated by express Congressional findings." If none of these is present then Congress cannot regulate an interstate activity that, like arson, has traditionally been subject to state and local jurisdiction.

UNITED STATES v. DeMET

United States Court of Appeals, Seventh Circuit, 1973.
486 F.2d 816.

FAIRCHILD, CIRCUIT JUDGE. Defendant was convicted by a jury of obstructing, delaying and affecting commerce and the movement of articles in commerce by extortion in violation of 18 U.S.C. § 1951, commonly called the Hobbs Act.[1] On this appeal defendant asserts error in ... insufficiency of the evidence as to extortion and effect on interstate commerce.... We have considered these contentions, find none meritorious and affirm the conviction.

Viewing the evidence in a light most favorable to support the verdict, the following facts appear:

Louis King owned a Chicago cocktail lounge called "The Scene" during the period covered by the indictment, November, 1969 to February, 1970. King purchased some of the beer for his business from the Chicago branch of Anheuser-Busch. It was brewed outside Illinois. Some of the liquor he purchased came from distilleries in other states or countries.

During the period of the indictment, defendant was a Chicago police officer and vice coordinator assigned to the district where the Scene was located.

In late November or early December, 1969, defendant and several other police officers visited the Scene. They sat at the bar and defendant asked King how it was going and whether King had any problems. King described how a police sergeant would come into the lounge on weekend nights and require payment of $10 or $20 in exchange for not enforcing a late night parking ordinance which went into effect one hour before closing. King also told defendant that police officers would come on week nights and unjustifiably accuse him of staying open after hours.

This conversation occurred at about 2:00 A.M. when the lounge was busy. Defendant asked if there was a more quiet place where they could talk. King led defendant to a back room. Once in the room, defendant said, "In order to avoid all this bullshit why don't you pay so much a month." King asked, "Now, what's the mutuels?" To which defendant replied, "Well you tell us." King offered $50.00 a month, a sum which defendant found acceptable. King and his wife made the payment to defendant.

King testified that he paid the money to defendant because he feared that if he did not pay it might jeopardize his liquor license and lead to more "harassment."

1. In pertinent part, § 1951 provides:

"(a) Whoever in any way or degree obstructs, delays, or affects commerce or the movement of any article or commodity in commerce, by robbery or extortion or attempts or conspires so to do, or commits or threatens physical violence to any person or property in furtherance of a plan or purpose to do anything in violation of this section shall be fined not more than $10,000 or imprisoned not more than twenty years, or both.

"(b) As used in this section—

"(1) ....

"(2) The term 'extortion' means the obtaining of property from another, with his consent, induced by wrongful use of actual or threatened force, violence, or fear, or under color of official right.

"(3) The term 'commerce' means commerce within the District of Columbia, or any Territory or Possession of the United States; all commerce between any point in a State, Territory, Possession, or the District of Columbia and any point outside thereof; all commerce between points within the same State through any place outside such State; and all other commerce over which the United States has jurisdiction."

Just before Christmas, 1969, defendant and three other officers all in plain clothes entered the Scene Lounge. During conversation with King one of the officers mentioned that a gift had been given or would be given to the "Commander." One of the officers asked what King was going to give. King displayed a bottle of Grand Metaxa. Then one of the officers asked, "Well what about us?" King replied, "O.K. Stop around Christmas and I will have something for you."

King testified that he inferred from this conversation that if he didn't cooperate he might be charged with liquor violations or risk loss of his license.

Later during the Christmas week, defendant stopped at the Scene between 7:00 and 8:00 P.M. before it had opened for business. He had previously called to make sure someone would be there. King had two cases of liquor and two extra bottles waiting for him when he arrived, and assisted in loading the cases into defendant's car. King estimated the value to be over $300.00.

Sometime between Christmas, 1969 and New Year's Day, King had another conversation with defendant at the police station. King complained to defendant that even though he was paying $50.00 a month, he had been forced to pay $300.00 to a sergeant and a patrolman the previous evening. Defendant professed ignorance of the incident and suggested that they go see the "boss." Defendant and King then went to the district commander's office. Defendant went in to see the commander and, after a few minutes, King was invited into his office.

In the presence of defendant, King related to the commander the incident of the previous night. King then asked, "Why am I paying $50.00 a month when I am brought into the station for after hours and forced to pay $300.00 a month?" The commander replied, "I will take care of this. Don't worry about it."

In January, 1970, defendant again visited King at the Scene in the company of other police officers. Defendant asked to see King for a few minutes. The two then went to a back room. King called his wife; Mrs. King came in and gave defendant $50.00.

Following the payments, the Scene had no further parking problems.

* * *

Alleged Failure to Prove Extortion.

Under § 1951 extortion is defined as "the obtaining of property from another, with his consent, induced by wrongful use of actual or threatened fear, or under color of official right." The government's proof was directed to showing that King feared economic loss should he not comply with defendant's demands.

Defendant contends that the government's proof was an insufficient basis upon which to convict for extortion. Because King admitted his encounters with the defendant were friendly and defendant never said nor intimated he would cause "trouble," defendant contends that King's conduct was not motivated by fear as required by § 1951. Rather, defendant argues, King willingly gave money to defendant because it brought certain advantages (such as non-enforcement of parking restrictions) to which he was not lawfully entitled. Thus, in essence, defendant argues that he was merely receiver of bribes and could therefore not be guilty of extortion.

Fear, as used in § 1951, includes not only fear of physical violence but fear of economic harm, as well.... It is not necessary that this fear be a consequence of a direct threat, it is enough that the circumstances surrounding the alleged extortion render the victim's fear reasonable....

Indeed, fear may be present even if confrontations between the victim and the alleged extorter appear friendly:

> "The fact that relations between the victims and the extorters were often cordial is not inconsistent with extortion. Knowing that they were at the mercy of the Attorney General's office, it is a fair inference that the victims felt that to save their businesses they had to keep the extorters satisfied." United States v. Hyde (1971).

Finally, it is important to note that the economic loss which the victim fears may be a consequence of action which the alleged extorter has a duty to take:

> "It is the wrongful use of an otherwise valid power that converts dutiful action into extortion. If the purpose and effect are to intimidate others, forcing them to pay, the action constitutes extortion. Put another way, it is the right to impartial determination of the issue on the merits (i.e. whether to enforce the law or whether to picket or strike) that the victim is deprived of when these actions are taken for the purpose of coercing him into paying. The distinction from bribery is therefore the initiative and purpose on the part of the official and the fear and lack of voluntariness on the part of the victim." United States v. Hyde, supra.

While portions of King's testimony taken with other evidence may be consistent with defendant's view that King freely gave money and liquor to obtain advantages, the jury could reasonably infer from all the circumstances, including defendant's official position, that King was in fear of harm to his business, his fear was reasonable, and defendant exploited it to extort money and liquor.

If early morning customers of the Scene had their cars ticketed, they might take their business elsewhere or at least leave earlier. An arrest for staying open after hours could lead to loss of the liquor license. Defendant, the vice coordinator of the district, promised to eliminate these concerns in exchange for a monthly payment. There was support for a finding that King believed that implicit in defendant's offer was the threat of continued "parking problems" and other harassment if the money (and later liquor) was not forthcoming.

In arguing for acquittal, defendant's counsel presented his view of the facts, i.e. that King was a willing participant and that any fear which King felt was unreasonable. The jury was instructed that in order for defendant's conduct to be considered extortion defendant must obtain the money through a wrongful use of fear, including fear of economic harm, and that the fear must be reasonable. Thus the issue of whether King gave money to defendant voluntarily in order to obtain certain advantages or out of fear that if the money was not forthcoming he would be subject to police harassment was squarely presented to the jury.

The jury apparently thought King's conduct was induced by fear and that defendant's conduct constituted extortion. We cannot say the verdict was not supported by substantial evidence.

Alleged Failure to Affect Interstate Commerce.

Extortion is an offense against the United States when the extorter "in any way or degree obstructs, delays or affects commerce or the movement of any article or commodity in commerce, . . ." 18 U.S.C. § 1951(a). In order to satisfy the interstate commerce element, the government offered proof that some of the beer and liquor purchased for the Scene had out of state origins, that in one instance a national corporation shipped its product across state lines to a Chicago warehouse from which it was delivered to the Scene and that in another instance a local company purchased liquor from out of state producers and then resold it to the Scene and others.

Relying primarily on cases applying the Fair Labor Standards Act, defendant argues that by the time the Scene acquired these beverages they were no longer in interstate commerce and that any extortion therefore could have no effect on interstate commerce. Because of differences in the statutes, such decisions are not controlling as to the requisite manner or degree of interference with commerce that may justify conviction under the Hobbs Act. . . .

Although King's business was primarily local, depletion of King's assets by the goods and money extorted, or the cessation of his business if he did not yield and his fears were realized, would tend to reduce the demand for and amount of beer and liquor moving into Illinois. The effect on interstate commerce would exist, though small by most standards, and only indirectly caused by defendant's acts. There are obvious questions as to the most desirable division between the states and the federal government of the function of enforcing good order, but given the existence of an impact of defendant's conduct on interstate commerce, the question is whether the Hobbs Act must be construed as stopping some margin short of full application of the commerce power.

"The commerce clause endows Congress with full and plenary power to do anything and everything necessary to protect interstate commerce—The specific question is whether in the statute involved the Congress has seen fit to exercise all of its power." Walling v. Goldblatt Bros. (1942).

When a law purports to regulate activities "in commerce" something less than the full commerce power is exercised. On the other hand, a law which regulates matters "affecting" interstate commerce is within, though a more nearly full application of, the commerce power.

Section 1951 clearly contemplates a full application of the commerce power. It proscribes extortion which "in any way or degree obstructs, delays, or affects commerce or the movement of any article or commodity in commerce...." In United States v. Stirone, 361 U.S. 212, 215, 4 L.Ed.2d 252, 255 (1960), the Supreme Court said of the Hobbs Act:

> " 'That Act speaks in broad language, manifesting a purpose to use all the constitutional power Congress has to punish interference with interstate commerce by extortion, robbery or physical violence.' The Act outlaws such interference 'in any way or degree.' "[2]

Because Congress has seen fit to exercise its full power under the commerce clause, extortionate conduct having an arguably *de minimis* effect on commerce may nevertheless be punished. Battaglia v. United States (1967) (extortion resulted in a pool table from an out-of-state source being kept from use); United States v. Augello (1971) (assets of drive-in restaurant which purchased mostly from an out-of-state concern depleted by $100; proprietor, in addition, gave $200 from his personal funds.)....

Where the victim of extortion, as here, customarily obtains inventory which has come from outside the state, obstruction and delay of, and effect upon commerce may, for the purpose of the Hobbs Act, be found in curtailment of the victim's potential as a buyer of such goods. This may be traced either through the depletion of his assets by his fulfillment of the extortionate demands or the harm which would follow if the threats were carried out.

* * *

The judgment is affirmed.

SWYGERT, CHIEF JUDGE, concurring.

Several years ago I took issue by dissent with a holding of this court that a depletion of corporate reserves comprised an "interference with

2. We have considered the Supreme Court's 1971 interpretation of the Travel Act as a less than full application of the commerce power, and the policy factors the Court suggests Congress may have considered, Rewis v. United States, 401 U.S. 808, 812 (1971). The two statutes are differently structured. We do not conclude that we are authorized, in a Hobbs Act case, to create a formula under which an impact on interstate commerce is to be dismissed as *de minimis*.

interstate commerce" within the meaning of the Hobbs Act where a corporation was engaged in interstate commerce. My concern was centered on the unlimited reach of the doctrine espoused by the majority:

> "If a depletion of reserves is all that is necessary to show the requisite effect on commerce, then a threat of any kind to extract money made to a person who happens to operate a business engaged to any extent in interstate commerce comes within the statute's proscription. Under this rationale, a retail store owner, for example, would be afforded federal protection from extortion, regardless of the nature or the likely effect of the threat, simply because his stock of merchandise had in some measure moved in interstate commerce."

Exactly what I apprehended in 1968 has today come to pass. My misgivings, however, did not persuade my brethren in *Amabile* [395 F.2d 47, 54], and I stand by the decision reached in this case as the law of the circuit.

I would also narrow what some might read to be the holding of the majority on the question of extortion under the Hobbs Act. DeMet was prosecuted below for a violation of that portion of the Hobbs Act which makes illegal "the obtaining of property from another, with his consent, induced by wrongful use of actual or threatened fear." As my colleagues recognize, the proof of the Government was directed to demonstrating a fear of economic loss on the part of King. Proof of fear may not have been necessary had the Government chosen to rely on another provision to the Hobbs Act, namely, that prohibiting "the obtaining of property from another, with his consent, ... *under color of official right.*" (emphasis supplied.) It is, of course, hardly appropriate to render a decision on that issue in this case, and I express no views on it.*

NOTES

1. The Hobbs Act "speaks in broad language, manifesting a purpose to use all the constitutional power Congress has to punish interference with interstate commerce by extortion...." Stirone v. United States, 361 U.S. 212, 215, 80 S.Ct. 270, 271 (1960). Thus, *DeMet* correctly held that "extortionate conduct having an arguably *de minimus* effect on commerce may nevertheless be punished". In this manner, the courts recognized that "the Hobbs Act not only forbids extortion which interferes with interstate commerce but also extortion which affects interstate commerce". United States v. Gill, 490 F.2d 233 (7th Cir., 1973). See also United States v. Malinsky, 19 F.R.D. 426, 428 (S.D.N.Y. 1956) ("The substantiality of the effect is not left to judicial determination. The

* It is worthy of note, however, that an argument has been made in the literature that this provision renders criminal any reception of money (not rightfully due) "under color of official right" by a police officer or other public official, without reference to whether the facts which surround the receipt characterize the action as bribery or extortion. See Stern, Prosecutions of Local Political Corruption Under the Hobbs Act: The Unnecessary Distinction Between Bribery and Extortion. 3 Seton Hall L.Rev. 1 (1971).

only question is whether the prohibited activity is within the reach of Congress").

Commerce may be affected either as a direct result of the extortionate transaction or by a depletion of the resources of a business operating in interstate commerce. The latter theory is predicated on the notion that the business would have been in a position to purchase more or better quality merchandise from out of state if the extortionate payment had not been made. For example, in United States v. Tropiano, 418 F.2d 1069 (2d Cir.1969), cert. denied 397 U.S. 1021, 90 S.Ct. 1262 (1970), defendants, engaged in the rubbish removal business, were charged with threatening to harm certain individuals engaged in the same business for soliciting accounts in the city in which defendants operated. At trial, the government's sole evidence in support of the interstate commerce aspect of the offense was the fact that the victim purchased refuse removal trucks from an out of state corporation. In response to defendants' claim that this proof was insufficient, the court said:

> "[The victim's] surrender of his right to solicit additional customers in [the city] automatically limited his future orders for receptacles for new customers and the trucks required to serve such customers."

Tropiano not only recognized the depletion of resources theory, but it also indicated that a potential effect on commerce is sufficient to confer federal jurisdiction. Because "Congress has the power to deal with extortion or attempted extortion actually or *potentially* affecting interstate commerce," Hulahan v. United States, 214 F.2d 441, 445 (8th Cir.), cert. denied 348 U.S. 856, 75 S.Ct. 81 (1954), "it is enough that the extortion 'in any way or degree' ... affects commerce, though its effect be merely potential or subtle". United States v. Augello, 451 F.2d 1167, 1169–70 (2d Cir.1971), cert. denied 405 U.S. 1070, 92 S.Ct. 1518 (1972). Thus, in United States v. Pranno, 385 F.2d 387 (7th Cir.1967), cert. denied 390 U.S. 944, 88 S.Ct. 1028 (1968), the court affirmed the Hobbs Act conviction of two defendants who extorted a large sum from the owner and contractor of a proposed manufacturing plant by threatening to withhold a building permit. Because the extortionate demands were met, the permit was granted and the construction of the plant was not delayed. The movement of construction materials in interstate commerce was not, therefore, actually affected. The court, nevertheless, held that "it was only necessary to prove that delay *would have been caused* had the owner and contractor refused payment...." (emphasis added).

Pranno is consistent with the cases which have considered similar situations. For example, in United States v. Hyde, 448 F.2d 815 (5th Cir.1971), cert. denied 404 U.S. 1058, 92 S.Ct. 736 (1972), defendant claimed that the extorted companies had not commenced interstate operations until several months after payment was made. This claim was rejected on the ground that the interstate commerce element can be established by expectation at the time of the extortionate transaction:

> "The companies were formed, and registration for a stock sale was sought, with a stated purpose of going into the activities that support a finding of interstate commerce. Neither the statute nor the Constitution requires that the company be engaged in an interstate transaction at the moment of the extortion to support federal jurisdiction."

3. For a case which appears to extend the Hobbs Act coverage to its outer limits, consider United States v. Staszcuk, 517 F.2d 53 (7th Cir.), cert. denied 423 U.S. 837, 96 S.Ct. 65 (1975). The defendant, a Chicago alderman, was

convicted of extorting $9000 for a favorable zoning ruling with respect to the planned construction of an animal hospital. The commerce clause connection was based upon the fact that the building contractor needed various materials such as a furnace, plate glass, plumbing, and electrical fixtures which would be purchased from out-of-state suppliers.

4. Does the extraordinarily broad reading of the Hobbs Act trench upon state's rights? See Note, The Scope of Federal Criminal Jurisdiction Under the Commerce Clause, 1972 U.Ill.L.F. 805, 822:

"[I]t should be noted that the use of the commerce clause as an expansive basis for federal intervention in the area of crime control has not been opposed by the states, though similar federal intervention in economic affairs faced heavy resistance. State acquiescence, if not encouragement, can be attributed to several factors: the federal government has not preempted state powers; federal intervention has helped states deal with problems serious enough to override the usual states' rights fears; and the federal government has entered this area gradually, reluctantly, and primarily with programs aimed at organized crime, a problem generally felt to be incapable of solution by the states acting alone."

CAMINETTI v. UNITED STATES
DIGGS v. UNITED STATES
HAYS v. UNITED STATES

Supreme Court of the United States, 1916.
242 U.S. 470, 37 S.Ct. 192.

MR. JUSTICE DAY delivered the opinion of the court:

These three cases were argued together, and may be disposed of in a single opinion. In each of the cases there was a conviction and sentence for violation of the so-called White Slave Traffic Act of June 25, 1910 (36 Stat. at L. 825, chap. 395, Comp.Stat.1913, § 8813),[1] the judgments were affirmed by the circuit courts of appeals, and writs of certiorari bring the cases here.

In the *Caminetti* Case, the petitioner was indicted in the United States district court for the northern district of California, upon the 6th day of May 1913, for alleged violations of the act. The indictment was in

1. The White Slave Traffic Act, U.S.C.A., Title 18, § 2421, currently provides as follows:

"Whoever knowingly transports in interstate or foreign commerce, or in the District of Columbia or in any Territory or Possession of the United States, any woman or girl for the purpose of prostitution or debauchery, or for any other immoral purpose, or with the intent and purpose to induce, entice, or compel such woman or girl to become a prostitute or to give herself up to debauchery, or to engage in any other immoral practice; or

"Whoever knowingly procures or obtains any ticket or tickets, or any form of transportation or evidence of the right thereto, to be used by any woman or girl in interstate or foreign commerce, or in the District of Columbia or any Territory or Possession of the United States, in going to any place for the purpose of prostitution or debauchery, or for any other immoral purpose, or with the intent or purpose on the part of such person to induce, entice, or compel her to give herself up to the practice of prostitution, or to give herself up to debauchery, or any other immoral practice, whereby any such woman or girl shall be transported in interstate or foreign commerce, or in the District of Columbia or any Territory or Possession of the United States—

"Shall be fined not more than $5,000 or imprisoned not more than five years, or both." [Eds.]

four counts, the first of which charged him with transporting and causing to be transported, and aiding and assisting in obtaining transportation for a certain woman from Sacramento, California, to Reno, Nevada, in interstate commerce, for the purpose of debauchery, and for an immoral purpose, to wit, that the aforesaid woman should be and become his mistress and concubine. A verdict of not guilty was returned as to the other three counts of this indictment. As to the first count, defendant was found guilty and sentenced to imprisonment for eighteen months and to pay a fine of $1,500. Upon writ of error to the United States circuit court of appeals for the ninth circuit, that judgment was affirmed....

Diggs was indicted at the same time as was Caminetti.... The first count charged the defendant with transporting and causing to be transported, and aiding and assisting in obtaining transportation for, a certain woman from Sacramento, California, to Reno, Nevada, for the purpose of debauchery, and for an immoral purpose, to wit, that the aforesaid woman should be and become his concubine and mistress. The second count charged him with a like offense as to another woman (the companion of Caminetti) in transportation, etc., from Sacramento to Reno, that she might become the mistress and concubine of Caminetti. The third count charged him (Diggs) with procuring a ticket for the first-mentioned woman from Sacramento to Reno in interstate commerce, with the intent that she should become his concubine and mistress. The fourth count made a like charge as to the girl companion of Caminetti. Upon trial and verdict of guilty on these four counts, he was sentenced to imprisonment for two years and to pay a fine of $2,000. As in the *Caminetti* Case, that judgment was affirmed by the circuit court of appeals....

In the *Hays* Case, upon June 26th, 1914, an indictment was returned in the United States district court for the western district of Oklahoma against Hays and another, charging violations of the act. The first count charged the said defendants with having, on March 17th, 1914, persuaded, induced, enticed, and coerced a certain woman, unmarried and under the age of eighteen years, from Oklahoma City, Oklahoma, to the city of Wichita, Kansas, in interstate commerce and travel, for the purpose and with intent then and there to induce and coerce the said woman, and intending that she should be induced and coerced to engage in prostitution, debauchery, and other immoral practices, and did then and there, in furtherance of such purposes, procure and furnish a railway ticket entitling her to passage over the line of railway, to wit, the Atchison, Topeka, & Santa Fe Railway, and did then and there and thereby, knowingly entice and cause the said woman to go and to be carried and transported as a passenger in interstate commerce upon said line of railway. The second count charged that on the same date the defendants persuaded, induced, enticed, and coerced the same woman to be transported from Oklahoma City to Wichita, Kansas, with the purpose and intent to induce and coerce her to engage in prostitution, debauchery, and other immoral practices at and within the state of

Kansas, and that they enticed her and caused her to go and be carried and transported as a passenger in interstate commerce from Oklahoma City, Oklahoma, to Wichita, Kansas, upon a line and route of a common carrier, to wit: The Atchison, Topeka, & Santa Fe Railway. Defendants were found guilty by a jury upon both counts, and Hays was sentenced to imprisonment for eighteen months. Upon writ of error to the circuit court of appeals for the eighth circuit, judgment was affirmed....

It is contended that the act of Congress is intended to reach only "commercialized vice," or the traffic in women for gain, and that the conduct for which the several petitioners were indicted and convicted, however, reprehensible in morals, is not within the purview of the statute when properly construed in the light of its history and the purposes intended to be accomplished by its enactment. In none of the cases was it charged or proved that the transportation was for gain or for the purpose of furnishing women for prostitution for hire, and it is insisted that, such being the case, the acts charged and proved, upon which conviction was had, do not come within the statute.

It is elementary that the meaning of a statute must, in the first instance, be sought in the language in which the act is framed, and if that is plain, and if the law is within the constitutional authority of the law-making body which passed it, the sole function of the courts is to enforce it according to its terms....

Where the language is plain and admits of no more than one meaning, the duty of interpretation does not arise, and the rules which are to aid doubtful meanings need no discussion.... There is no ambiguity in the terms of this act. It is specifically made an offense to knowingly transport or cause to be transported, etc., in interstate commerce, any woman or girl for the purpose of prostitution or debauchery, or for "any other immoral purpose," or with the intent and purpose to induce any such woman or girl to become a prostitute or to give herself up to debauchery, or to engage in any other immoral practice.

Statutory words are uniformly presumed, unless the contrary appears, to be used in their ordinary and usual sense, and with the meaning commonly attributed to them. To cause a woman or girl to be transported for the purposes of debauchery, and for an immoral purpose, to wit, becoming a concubine or mistress, for which Caminetti and Diggs were convicted; or to transport an unmarried woman, under eighteen years of age, with the intent to induce her to engage in prostitution, debauchery, and other immoral practices, for which Hays was convicted, would seem by the very statement of the facts to embrace transportation for purposes denounced by the act, and therefore fairly within its meaning.

While such immoral purpose would be more culpable in morals and attributed to baser motives if accompanied with the expectation of pecuniary gain, such considerations do not prevent the lesser offense against morals of furnishing transportation in order that a woman may be debauched, or become a mistress or a concubine, from being the execution of purposes within the meaning of this law. To say the contrary would shock the common understanding of what constitutes an immoral purpose when those terms are applied, as here, to sexual relations.

In United States v. Bitty . . ., it was held that the act of Congress against the importation of alien women and girls for the purpose of prostitution "and any other immoral purpose" included the importation of an alien woman to live in concubinage with the person importing her. In that case this court said:

"All will admit that full effect must be given to the intention of Congress as gathered from the words of the statute. There can be no doubt as to what class was aimed at by the clause forbidding the importation of alien women for purposes of 'prostitution.' It refers to women who, for hire or without hire, offer their bodies to indiscriminate intercourse with men. The lives and example of such persons are in hostility to "the idea of the family, as consisting in and springing from the union for life of one man and one woman in the holy estate of matrimony; the sure foundation of all that is stable and noble in our civilization; the best guaranty of that reverent morality which is the source of all beneficent progress in social and political improvement.' . . . Now the addition in the last statute of the words, 'or for any other immoral purpose,' after the word 'prostitution,' must have been made for some practical object. Those added words show beyond question that Congress had in view the protection of society against another class of alien women other than those who might be brought here merely for purposes of 'prostitution.' In forbidding the importation of alien women 'for any other immoral purpose,' Congress evidently thought that there were purposes in connection with the importations of alien women which, as in the case of importations for prostitution, were to be deemed immoral. It may be admitted that, in accordance with the familiar rule of *ejusdem generis,* the immoral purpose referred to by the words 'any other immoral purpose' must be one of the same general class or kind as the particular purpose of 'prostitution' specified in the same clause of the statute. 2 Lewis' Sutherland Stat.Constr. § 423, and authorities cited. But that rule cannot avail the accused in this case; for the immoral purpose charged in the indictment is of the same general class or kind as the one that controls in the importation of an alien woman for the purpose strictly of prostitution. The prostitute may, in the popular sense, be more degraded in character than the concubine, but the latter none the less must be held to lead an immoral life, if any regard whatever be had to the views that are almost universally held in this country as to the relations which may rightfully, from the standpoint of morality, exist between man and woman in the matter of sexual intercourse."

This definition of an immoral purpose was given prior to the enactment of the act now under consideration, and must be presumed to have been known to Congress when it enacted the law here involved. . . .

But it is contended that though the words are so plain that they cannot be misapprehended when given their usual and ordinary interpretation, and although the sections in which they appear do not in terms limit the offense defined and punished to acts of "commercialized vice," or the furnishing or procuring of transportation of women for debauchery, prostitution, or immoral practices for hire, such limited purpose is to be attributed to Congress and engrafted upon the act in view of the language of § 8 and the report which accompanied the law upon its introduction into and subsequent passage by the House of Representatives.

In this connection, it may be observed that while the title of an act cannot overcome the meaning of plain and unambiguous words used in its body ..., the title of this act embraces the regulation of interstate commerce "by prohibiting the transportation therein for immoral purposes of women and girls, and for other purposes." It is true that § 8 of the act provides that it shall be known and referred to as the "White Slave Traffic Act," and the report accompanying the introduction of the same into the House of Representatives set forth the fact that a material portion of the legislation suggested was to meet conditions which had arisen in the past few years, and that the legislation was needed to put a stop to a villainous interstate and international traffic in women and girls. Still, the name given to an act by way of designation or description, or the report which accompanies it, cannot change the plain import of its words. If the words are plain, they give meaning to the act, and it is neither the duty nor the privilege of the courts to enter speculative fields in search of a different meaning.

Reports to Congress accompanying the introduction of proposed laws may aid the courts in reaching the true meaning of the legislature in cases of doubtful interpretation.... But, as we have already said, and it has been so often affirmed as to become a recognized rule, when words are free from doubt they must be taken as the final expression of the legislative intent, and are not to be added to or subtracted from by considerations drawn from titles or designating names or reports accompanying their introduction, or from any extraneous source. In other words, the language being plain, and not leading to absurd or wholly impracticable consequences, it is the sole evidence of the ultimate legislative intent....

The fact, if it be so, that the act as it is written opens the door to blackmailing operations upon a large scale, is no reason why the courts should refuse to enforce it according to its terms, if within the constitutional authority of Congress. Such considerations are more appropriately addressed to the legislative branch of the government, which alone had authority to enact and may, if it sees fit, amend the law.

It is further insisted that a different construction of the act than is to be gathered from reading it is necessary in order to save it from constitutional objections, fatal to its validity. The act has its constitutional sanction in the power of Congress over interstate commerce. The broad character of that authority was declared once for all in the judgment pronounced by this court, speaking by Chief Justice Marshall, ... and has since been steadily adhered to and applied to a variety of new conditions as they have arisen.

It may be conceded, for the purpose of the argument, that Congress has no power to punish one who travels in interstate commerce merely because he has the intention of committing an illegal or immoral act at the conclusion of the journey. But this act is not concerned with such instances. It seeks to reach and punish the movement in interstate commerce of women and girls with a view to the accomplishment of the unlawful purposes prohibited.

The transportation of passengers in interstate commerce, it has long been settled, is within the regulatory power of Congress, under the commerce clause of the Constitution, and the authority of Congress to keep the channels of interstate commerce free from immoral and injurious uses has been frequently sustained, and is no longer open to question....

The judgment in each of the cases is affirmed.

MR. JUSTICE MCKENNA, with whom concurred the CHIEF JUSTICE and MR. JUSTICE CLARKE, dissenting:

Undoubtedly, in the investigation of the meaning of a statute we resort first to its words, and, when clear, they are decisive. The principle has attractive and seemingly disposing simplicity, but that it is not easy of application, or, at least, encounters other principles, many cases demonstrate. The words of a statute may be uncertain in their signification or in their application. If the words be ambiguous, the problem they present is to be resolved by their definition; the subject matter and the lexicons become our guides. But here, even, we are not exempt from putting ourselves in the place of the legislators. If the words be clear in meaning, but the objects to which they are addressed be uncertain, the problem then is to determine the uncertainty. And for this a realization of conditions that provoked the statute must inform our judgment. Let us apply these observations to the present case.

The transportation which is made unlawful is of a woman or girl "to become a prostitute or to give herself up to debauchery, or to engage in any other immoral practice." Our present concern is with the words "any other immoral practice," which, it is asserted, have a special office. The words are clear enough as general descriptions; they fail in particular designation; they are class words, not specifications. Are they controlled by those which precede them? If not, they are broader in generalization and include those that precede them, making them unnecessary and confusing. To what conclusion would this lead us? "Immoral" is a very comprehensive word. It means a dereliction of morals. In such sense it covers every form of vice, every form of conduct that is contrary to good order. It will hardly be contended that in this sweeping sense it is used in the statute. But, if not used in such sense, to what is it limited and by what limited? If it be admitted that it is limited at all, that ends the imperative effect assigned to it in the opinion of the court. But not insisting quite on that, we ask again, By what is it limited? By its context, necessarily, and the purpose of the statute.

For the context I must refer to the statute; of the purpose of the statute Congress itself has given us illumination. It devotes a section to the declaration that the "act shall be known and referred to as the 'White Slave Traffic Act.'" And its prominence gives it prevalence in the construction of the statute. It cannot be pushed aside or subordinated by indefinite words in other sentences, limited even there by the context. It is a peremptory rule of construction that all parts of a statute must be taken into account in ascertaining its meaning, and it cannot be said that § 8 has no object. Even if it gives only a title to the act, it has especial weight.... But it gives more than a title; it makes distinctive the purpose of the statute. The designation "white slave traffic" has the sufficiency of an axiom. If apprehended, there is no uncertainty as to the conduct it describes. It is commercialized vice, immoralities having a mercenary purpose, and this is confirmed by other circumstances.

The author of the bill was Mr. Mann, and in reporting it from the House committee on interstate and foreign commerce he declared for the committee that it was not the purpose of the bill to interfere with or usurp in any way the police power of the states, and further, that it was not the intention of the bill to regulate prostitution or the places where prostitution or immorality was practiced, which were said to be matters wholly within the power of the states,[2] and over which the Federal

2. State statutory coverage of prostitution and related activities is extensive. Although these statutes vary greatly in their wording, they are fairly uniform with respect to the specific matters dealt with. For purposes of illustration, the Wisconsin provisions, which are uncommonly succinct, are set forth below:

§ 944.30. *Prostitution.* Any female who intentionally does any of the following may be fined not more than $500 or imprisoned not more than one year or both:

(1) Has or offers to have non-marital sexual intercourse for money; or

(2) Commits or offers to commit an act of sexual perversion for money; or

(3) Is an inmate of a place of prostitution.

§ 944.31. *Patronizing Prostitutes.* Any male who enters or remains in any place of prostitution with intent to have non-marital sexual intercourse or to commit an act of sexual perversion may be fined not more than $100 or imprisoned not more than 3 months or both.

§ 944.32. *Soliciting Prostitutes.* Whoever intentionally solicits or causes any female to practice prostitution or establishes any female in a place of prostitution may be fined not more than $1,000 or imprisoned not more than 5 years or both. If the female is under the age of 18, the defendant may be fined not more than $2,000 or imprisoned not more than 10 years or both.

§ 944.33. *Pandering.* (1) Whoever does any of the following may be fined not more than $200 or imprisoned not more than 6 months or both:

(a) Solicits another to have non-marital sexual intercourse or to commit an act of sexual perversion with a female he knows is a prostitute; or

(b) With intent to facilitate another in having non-marital intercourse or committing an act of sexual perversion with a prostitute, directs or transports him to a prostitute or directs or transports a prostitute to him.

(2) If the accused received compensation from the earnings of the prostitute, he may be fined not more than $5,000 or imprisoned not more than 10 years or both....

§ 944.34. *Keeping Place of Prostitution.* Whoever intentionally does any of the fol-

government had no jurisdiction. And further explaining the bill, it was said that the sections of the act had been "so drawn that they are limited to the cases in which there is an act of transportation in interstate commerce of women for the purposes of prostitution." and again:

"The White Slave Trade.—A material portion of the legislation suggested and proposed is necessary to meet conditions which have arisen within the past few years. The legislation is needed to put a stop to a villainous interstate and international traffic in women and girls. The legislation is not needed or intended as an aid to the states in the exercise of the police powers in the suppression or regulation of immorality in general. It does not attempt to regulate the practice of voluntary prostitution, but aims solely to prevent panderers and procurers from compelling thousands of women and girls against their will and desire to enter and continue in a life of prostitution." . . .

In other words, it is vice as a business at which the law is directed, using interstate commerce as a facility to procure or distribute its victims.

In 1912 the sense of the Department of Justice was taken of the act in a case where a woman of twenty-four years went from Illinois, where she lived, to Minnesota, at the solicitation and expense of a man. She was there met by him and engaged with him in immoral practices like those for which petitioners were convicted. The assistant district attorney forwarded her statement to the Attorney General, with the comment that the element of traffic was absent from the transaction and that therefore, in his opinion, it was not "within the spirit and intent of the Mann Act." Replying, the Attorney General expressed his concurrence in the view of his subordinate.

Of course, neither the declarations of the report of the committee on interstate commerce of the House nor the opinion of the Attorney General are conclusive of the meaning of the law, but they are highly persuasive. The opinion was by one skilled in the rules and methods employed in the interpretation or construction of laws, and informed, besides, of the conditions to which the act was addressed. The report was by the committee charged with the duty of investigating the necessity for the act, and to inform the House of the results of that investigation, both of evil and remedy. The report of the committee has, therefore, a higher quality than debates on the floor of the House. The representations of the latter may indeed be ascribed to the exaggerations of advocacy or opposition. The report of a committee is the execution of a duty and has the sanction of duty. There is a presumption, therefore, that the measure it recommends has the purpose it declares and will accomplish it as declared.

lowing may be fined not more than $5,000 or imprisoned not more than 5 years or both:

(1) Keeps a place of prostitution; or

(2) Grants the use or allows the continued use of a place as a place of prostitution. [Eds.]

This being the purpose, the words of the statute should be construed to execute it, and they may be so construed even if their literal meaning be otherwise....

There is much in the present case to tempt to a violation of the rule. Any measure that protects the purity of women from assault or enticement to degradation finds an instant advocate in our best emotions; but the judicial function cannot yield to emotion—it must, with poise of mind, consider and decide. It should not shut its eyes to the facts of the world and assume not to know what everybody else knows. And everybody knows that there is a difference between the occasional immoralities of men and women and that systematized and mercenary immorality epitomized in the statute's graphic phrase "white slave traffic." And it was such immorality that was in the legislative mind, and not the other. The other is occasional, not habitual,—inconspicuous,—does not offensively obtrude upon public notice. Interstate commerce is not its instrument as it is of the other, nor is prostitution its object or its end. It may, indeed, in instances, find a convenience in crossing state lines, but this is its accident, not its aid.

There is danger in extending a statute beyond its purpose, even if justified by a strict adherence to its words. The purpose is studied, all effects measured, not left at random,—one evil practice prevented, opportunity given to another. The present case warns against ascribing such improvidence to the statute under review. Blackmailers of both sexes have arisen, using the terrors of the construction now sanctioned by this court as a help—indeed, the means—for their brigandage. The result is grave and should give us pause. It certainly will not be denied that legal authority justifies the rejection of a construction which leads to mischievous consequences, if the statute be susceptible of another construction....

NOTES

1. William Seagle, in his article, The Twilight of the Mann Act, 55 A.B.A.J. 641, 642 (1969), dispels the notion that the *Caminetti* case involved as innocent an episode of private interstate sex as the opinion seems to suggest:

> It has been the habit of commentators to pretend that the *Caminetti* case involved a mere interstate weekend on which two men took their mistresses. Actually the affair was more serious. The interstate weekend was the culmination of the seduction of two girls of Sacramento, California, ages respectively 19 and 20, by two married men who apparently had concealed their matrimonial state, as well as their fatherhood, from the objects of their passion. The seducers were Drew Caminetti, who was the son of Anthony Caminetti, then Commissioner of Immigration (a circumstance that was undoubtedly part of the explanation for the excited national interest in the case), and Maury Diggs, a boon companion. When the girls discovered the truth of the situation and indignation in Sacramento began to mount, Drew Caminetti and Maury Diggs decided it was time to get out of town. To induce the girls to run away with them to Reno, Nevada, they told them

that their wives would hale them before the juvenile court and have them put away in a reformatory.

2. Consider Cleveland v. United States, 329 U.S. 14, 67 S.Ct. 13 (1946), a 6 to 3 decision sustaining Mann Act convictions of fundamentalist Utah Mormon adherents of polygamy who transported one or more of their "celestial" wives across state lines. Also see critical comment on the Caminetti and Cleveland decisions in 56 Yale L.J. 718, 727 (1947).

For another holding relying upon the principal case, see United States v. Reginelli, 133 F.2d 595 (3d Cir.1943), cert. denied 318 U.S. 783, 63 S.Ct. 856 (1943). (Defendant went from his home in New Jersey to Miami, Florida for a visit. Enroute, as well as after arrival, he repeatedly telegraphed and telephoned a woman friend in New Jersey urging her to come to Miami. Pursuant to his requests, the woman, at defendant's expense, flew to Miami and there shared a hotel room with defendant for a period of ten days. During that time, they occupied the same bed and had sexual relations. Defendant was convicted of violating the Mann Act, and his conviction was affirmed.) See also Batsell v. United States, 217 F.2d 257 (8th Cir.1954) (Defendant, in an attempt to procure work for a woman in a house of prostitution, drove her from Minneapolis, Minnesota, to Duluth, Minnesota, passing briefly through a portion of Wisconsin in order to avoid road difficulties. In upholding his conviction, the Court of Appeals stated: "While it had been first intended that they would cross no state lines ..., exigencies of the situation made it necessary for them to cross into Wisconsin ... and return again into Minnesota. This, in the opinion of the Court, constituted interstate commerce and established a violation of the act").

3. The following excerpts from a 1971 federal appeals court opinion in a Mann Act case, United States v. Jenkins, 442 F.2d 429 (5th Cir.1971), present an interesting point of law entwined in an almost incredible series of events:

"Bell, Circuit Judge:

"This is a Mann Act case. Appellant, a practicing lawyer in St. Petersburg, Florida, was tried before a jury and convicted on a one count indictment charging a violation of [the Mann Act]. He was sentenced to four years imprisonment and fined $5,000. The trial consumed approximately six weeks and was a vigorous contest throughout. One indicia of this vigor is seen in the fact that appellant now urges fifty assignments of error. Upon consideration of the record and all assignments of error, and after extended oral argument, we find no error and accordingly affirm the judgment of the district court.

"The indictment charged that Jenkins induced Diane Feldman to go from Atlanta, Georgia to St. Petersburg, Florida, via a common carrier in interstate commerce, for the purpose of prostitution and debauchery in violation of the statute. The essence of Jenkins' defense was that his conduct, whatever it may have been, was not the moving force in the inducement of Feldman to travel as charged....

"On November 11, 1966 Jenkins accompanied members of the St. Petersburg Quarterback Club to Atlanta, Georgia for a weekend of football games. The members of the club stayed at the Atlanta Baltimore Hotel. Upon arrival Jenkins was assigned to a suite with another member on the fifth floor.

"That evening, through the efforts of some of the members and various other persons, several prostitutes came to the hotel and began successfully plying their trade. Diane Feldman, a professional prostitute accompanied three of the members to a room in the hotel. After completing her business in their room she left and went to the elevator. There she met another member of the St. Petersburg group who invited her to a party then in progress in Jenkins' suite.

"She was introduced to Jenkins and had sexual intercourse with him and others in the group who were attending the party. During the course of the evening Jenkins told her that he recognized her and recalled that he had seen a warrant for her arrest in St. Petersburg. She was charged in the warrant with grand larceny. He told her that she could get in serious trouble if she did not return and that he could handle her case and get her off. He urged her to return to the Biltmore the following night when he would introduce her to the judge (a committing magistrate), who had signed the warrant, and they could discuss it.

"On the following night, Saturday, Feldman returned to Jenkins' hotel suite. She again participated in acts of sexual intercourse with various persons in the room as did several other prostitutes who were there. While there she met Justice of the Peace Dadswell. They discussed her case and he urged her to return to Florida, stating that Jenkins was a fine lawyer and that he could handle things so that she would not have to go to jail.

"She talked further with Jenkins about the charges at which time he told her that the offense of grand larceny was a serious one and that she could be extradited and held without bond. He again offered to represent her in the case. The fee was to be that she would have to furnish her services as a prostitute to Jenkins and his law partner one time. He also assured her that she could find plenty of work as a prostitute in St. Petersburg and that he would help her find a job as a go-go dancer. He then stated that he wanted her to ride back to St. Petersburg on the train with him and that he would pay her way. She declined this offer to return on the train.

"On Sunday Feldman talked with her husband who was then in Florida. After relating the incident with Jenkins, he told her that she should return if she thought Jenkins could clear up the charges against her. Feldman also called the St. Petersburg Police Department and verified that there was an outstanding grand larceny warrant against her. She then called Jenkins at his hotel to accept his offer, but he had already checked out. Later that night she took a plane to St. Petersburg.

"On Monday she contacted Jenkins and went to his office. He arranged for a bondsman, and agreed to represent her for the previously discussed fee.

"On November 16, 1966 she appeared in Justice of the Peace Court for a preliminary hearing on the grand larceny charge. She was transported to court in a black cadillac owned by Jenkins from the hotel where she was staying at the direction of Jenkins. Jenkins, his partner Abernathy, Estes the bondsman, and a law clerk were all in the vehicle.

"She was represented at the hearing by Jenkins and Abernathy. During the hearing, argument became quite heated. The judge and counsel retired to chambers. Jenkins came out and told Feldman that something was wrong because a different judge from the one he expected was presiding and that she would have to go to bed with the judge and the prosecutor in order to get the charges dismissed. She agreed. The case was dismissed.

"That evening or the next, she was taken to the Gulf Winds Motel where she engaged in sexual relations with seven men, according to her testimony, which was corroborated by some of the participants. Included in the group were Jenkins, Abernathy, the state's attorney who had prosecuted her that afternoon,

Estes the bondsman, and Manderscheid, the owner of the motel. The trial judge was not involved.

"Jenkins continued his association with Feldman during the next several days....

"On November 22, 1966, Feldman appeared before Judge Richard Carr, a Justice of the Peace, on a traffic ticket charge and was again represented by Jenkins and Abernathy. Jenkins again reminded her that she could get into serious trouble. She agreed with Jenkins to have sexual relations with Jenkins, Abernathy, and the judge in return for their services. There is no evidence that Feldman responded immediately following this court appearance.

"Several days later Jenkins arranged for Feldman to contact Jemison, one of his clients or friends. Jemison had customers who were arriving in Florida. For a negotiated price of $100.00, Feldman spent a night with one of these customers at the Happy Dolphin Inn....

"On December 9, 1966, Feldman made a third court appearance, this time appearing only with Abernathy. That evening, at the instruction of Jenkins, she met Judge Carr at the Office Lounge. They went from there to the Venice Motel where she engaged in sexual relations with Carr. She testified that Jenkins told her to do this....

"She later phoned Carr and Estes and asked them for money. Estes directed her to come to his office where she was met by Abernathy and Jenkins. After refusing her demands for money, she testified that they threatened to harm her for having 'talked'. She also testified that Abernathy threatened her by waving a letter opener or a knife in her face and advised her to keep quiet and leave town.

"It developed that Feldman had previously related her story to the vice squad of the St. Petersburg police force. The police advised her to leave town. She also tried to sell her story without success to a local newspaper. The newspaper referred her to the county sheriff who listened to her story and then referred her to the FBI. This prosecution followed.

"One group of appellant's contentions turns on the notion that judgment for acquittal should have been granted because the evidence allegedly shows that Jenkins was not the moving inducement for Feldman's travel in interstate commerce. This argument is based on what appellant characterizes as a rejection of his illicit offer to return to St. Petersburg on the train with the Quarterback Club.... [But] she only temporarily rejected his offer. [She] was unable to contact appellant at his hotel prior to his departure.

"The interstate transportation here by United Airlines, a common carrier, was not disputed. The fact of prostitution and debauchery in St. Petersburg was clearly established by direct evidence. There was also direct evidence of inducement on the part of Jenkins. This meets the test of Nunnally v. United States, (5 Cir., 1961) 291 F.2d 205, and makes a question for the jury....

"Nunnally v. United States, supra, also forecloses the claim that the evidence was insufficient as to prostitution because Feldman and Jenkins had another purpose in mind, i.e., having the warrant dismissed. *Nunnally* teaches that there can be dual purposes under this statute—prostitution need only be one of the principal purposes. *Nunnally* also destroys the argument that Jenkins did not know an interstate carrier would be employed in the trip to St. Petersburg. It is sufficient as here that a common carrier in interstate commerce would likely be and was utilized...."

E. CIVIL RIGHTS OFFENSES

A number of statutes, both federal and state, make it a criminal offense to deprive a person of his constitutional rights. Foremost are the following two federal enactments.

Section 241 of Title 18 of the United States Code provides:

> "If two or more persons conspire to injure, oppress, threaten, or intimidate any citizen in the free exercise or enjoyment of any right or privilege secured to him by the Constitution or laws of the United States, or because of his having so exercised the same: or
>
> "If two or more persons go in disguise on the highway, or on the premises of another, with intent to prevent or hinder his free exercise or enjoyment of any right or privilege so secured—
>
> "They shall be fined not more than $10,000 or imprisoned not more than ten years, or both; and if death results, they shall be subject to imprisonment for any term of years or for life."

A companion provision, Section 242, reads:

> "Whoever, under color of any law, statute, ordinance, regulation, or custom, willfully subjects any inhabitant of any State, Territory, or District to the deprivation of any rights, privileges, or immunities secured or protected by the Constitution or laws of the United States, or to different punishments, pains, or penalties, on account of such inhabitant being an alien, or by reason of his color, or race, than are prescribed for the punishment of citizens, shall be fined not more than $1,000 or imprisoned not more than one year, or both; and if death results shall be subject to imprisonment for any term of years or for life."

There is also the Federal Civil Rights Act of 1871 (42 U.S.C.A. § 1983), under which a civil action may be brought by any person who has been deprived of his constitutional rights by a person who acts "under color of any statute, ordinance, regulation, custom, or usage of any State or territory." The language of the statute obviously confines its application to agents of state governments. However, the United States Supreme Court has held (in a 6 to 3 decision) that federal law enforcement officials may be subject to a civil action in the federal courts where such officials violate a person's Fourth Amendment protection against unreasonable searches and seizures. The dissenting justices were of the view that congressional authorization was needed for according such civil actions against federal officers. Bivens v. Six Unknown Named Agents of Federal Bureau of Narcotics, 403 U.S. 388, 91 S.Ct. 1999 (1971).

F. FEDERAL PROSECUTORIAL DISCRETION AND STATE LAW ENFORCEMENT

The relationship of federal and state law enforcement authorities in acting upon offenses and offenders within a common sphere is a delicate and critical one. Apart from an early article, Schwartz, Federal Criminal Jurisdiction and Prosecutorial Discretion, 13 Law & Contemp.Prob. 64, 69 (1948), little has been written on the subject.

Two areas deserve focus. The first is the notion that primary and plenary law enforcement is the task of the states. The second is the growing reach of federal jurisdiction—by Congressional enactment and judicial construction—in areas where state jurisdiction has not been satisfactorily used, e.g., extortion, theft, bribery, especially in organized crime and official corruption cases.

In these circumstances, how does the federal prosecutor—newly armed with broadened jurisdictional powers, all-encompassing immunity statutes, and federal resources—define his area of activity and avoid federal-state tensions by supplanting, in whole or in part, the state prosecutor and police? Does vigorous federal prosecution of essentially local offenses weaken local law enforcement in the long run by encouraging lethargy or inactivity on the part of the local prosecutor who has other resource allocation problems, e.g., violent street crime, narcotics and the so-called "victimless" offenses in the areas of gambling, prostitution and drunkenness?

What standards should a federal prosecutor employ to guide his prosecutorial discretion in the overlap area? Perhaps the threshold consideration for the federal prosecutor is to determine whether he has—or can obtain—the resources and manpower to broaden his prosecutorial base and, at the same time, continue to deter the commission of uniquely federal offenses. Assuming that he can, the question is reduced to whether he should branch out into the area of overlap between state and federal jurisdiction.

A key yardstick for measuring the degree to which the federal government should enter into this area is the quality of the local prosecutor's office. While some part of this evaluation may be subjective, factors such as community confidence in local authorities, as reflected by the media, the extent of local resources devoted to the prosecutor's office and the relationship between that office and local judges are relatively objective considerations in the overall determination. Moreover, where the same political party that controls a large part of the local government also controls the prosecutor's office, it is inconceivable, either because of pursestring control or political association, that local officials can always deal satisfactorily with the problems of official corruption. And where corruption appears in the local prosecutor's own investigative force—the community police—it is virtually impossible for him to take any extensive action because of the cohesion within the police fraternity. In instances such as this, an independent investigative agency, such as the FBI, is essential.

Thus, there may be some legitimate areas of prosecutorial concern in which the local officials are unwilling or unable to act. It is in these areas that the federal prosecutor must employ the existing federal statutes—and some degree of imagination—to combat and deter crime. But the decision to enter into this area depends upon a balancing of the factors outlined above in the particular circumstances of the jurisdiction over which the federal prosecutor presides. Are there any other factors that should be considered in reaching this ultimate decision?

Chapter 4
HOMICIDE

A. MURDER

1. EARLY, TRADITIONAL LAW—THE MALICE FACTOR

COMMONWEALTH v. WEBSTER

Supreme Judicial Court of Massachusetts, 1850.
59 Mass. 295, 386.

The defendant, professor of chemistry, in the medical college, in Boston, attached to the university at Cambridge, was indicted in the municipal court at the January term, 1850, for the murder of Dr. George Parkman, at Boston, on the 23d of November, 1849. . . .

The government introduced evidence, that George Parkman, quite peculiar in person and manners, and very well known to most persons in the city of Boston, left his home in Walnut Street in Boston in the forenoon of the 23d of November, 1849, in good health and spirits; and that he was traced through various streets of the city until about a quarter before two o'clock of that day, when he was seen going towards and about to enter the medical college: That he did not return to his home: That on the next day a very active, particular, and extended search was commenced in Boston and the neighboring towns and cities, and continued until the 30th of November; and that large rewards were offered for information about Dr. Parkman: That on the 30th of November certain parts of a human body were discovered, in and about the defendant's laboratory in the medical college; and a great number of fragments of human bones and certain blocks of mineral teeth, imbedded in slag and cinders, together with small quantities of gold, which had been melted, were found in an assay furnace of the laboratory: That in consequence of some of these discoveries the defendant was arrested on the evening of the 30th of November: That the parts of a human body so found resembled in every respect the corresponding portions of the body of Dr. Parkman, and that among them all there were no duplicate parts; and that they were not the remains of a body which had been dissected: That the artificial teeth found in the furnace were made for Dr. Parkman by a dentist in Boston in 1846, and refitted in his mouth by the same dentist a fortnight before his disappearance: That the defendant was indebted to Dr. Parkman on certain notes, and was pressed by him for payment; that the defendant has said that on the 23d of November, about nine o'clock in the morning, he left word at Dr. Parkman's house, that if he would come to the medical college at half past one o'clock on that day, he would pay him; and that, as he said, he accordingly had an interview with Dr. Parkman at half past one o'clock on that day, at his laboratory in the medical college: That the defendant then had no means of paying, and that the notes were afterwards found in his possession....

[The defendant was tried before the Chief Justice, and Justices Wilde, Dewey and Metcalf. The opinion of the court on the law of the case was given in the charge to the jury as follows:]

SHAW, C.J. Homicide, of which murder is the highest and most criminal species, is of various degrees, according to circumstances. The term, in its largest sense, is generic, embracing every mode by which the life of one man is taken by the act of another. Homicide may be lawful or unlawful; it is lawful when done in lawful war upon an enemy in battle, it is lawful when done by an officer in the execution of justice upon a criminal, pursuant to a proper warrant. It may also be justifiable, and of course lawful, in necessary self-defence. But it is not necessary to dwell on these distinctions; it will be sufficient to ask attention to the two species of criminal homicide, familiarly known as murder and manslaughter.

In seeking for the sources of our law upon this subject, it is proper to say, that whilst the statute law of the commonwealth declares that "Every person who shall commit the crime of murder shall suffer the punishment of death for the same;" yet it nowhere defines the crimes of murder or manslaughter, with all their minute and carefully-considered distinctions and qualifications. For these, we resort to that great repository of rules, principles, and forms, the common law. This we commonly designate as the common law of England; but it might now be properly called the common law of Massachusetts. It was adopted when our ancestors first settled here, by general consent. It was adopted and confirmed by an early act of the provincial government, and was formally confirmed by the provision of the constitution declaring that all the laws which had theretofore been adopted, used, and approved, in the province or state of Massachusetts bay, and usually practiced on in the courts of law, should still remain and be in full force until altered or repealed by the legislature. So far, therefore, as the rules and principles of the common law are applicable to the administration of criminal law, and have not been altered and modified by acts of the colonial or provincial government or by the state legislature, they have the same force and effect as laws formally enacted.

By the existing law, as adopted and practiced on, unlawful homicide is distinguished into murder and manslaughter.

Murder, in the sense in which it is now understood, is the killing of any person in the peace of the commonwealth, with *malice aforethought,* either express or implied by law. Malice, in this definition, is used in a technical sense, including not only anger, hatred, and revenge, but every other unlawful and unjustifiable motive. It is not confined to ill-will towards one or more individual persons, but is intended to denote an action flowing from any wicked and corrupt motive, a thing done *malo animo,* where the fact has been attended with such circumstances as carry in them the plain indications of a heart regardless of social duty, and fatally bent on mischief. And therefore malice is implied from any deliberate or cruel act against another, however sudden.

Manslaughter is the unlawful killing of another without malice; and may be either voluntary, as when the act is committed with a real design and purpose to kill, but through the violence of sudden passion, occasioned by some great provocation, which in tenderness for the frailty of human nature the law considers sufficient to palliate the criminality of the offence; or involuntary, as when the death of another is caused by some unlawful act not accompanied by any intention to take life.

From these two definitions, it will be at once perceived, that the characteristic distinction between murder and manslaughter is malice, express or implied. It therefore becomes necessary, in every case of homicide proved, and in order to [make] an intelligent inquiry into the legal character of the act, to ascertain with some precision the nature of legal malice, and what evidence is requisite to establish its existence.

Upon this subject, the rule as deduced from the authorities is, that the implication of malice arises in every case of intentional homicide; and, the fact of killing being first proved, all the circumstances of accident, necessity, or infirmity, are to be satisfactorily established by the party charged, unless they arise out of the evidence produced against him to prove the homicide, and the circumstances attending it. If there are, in fact, circumstances of justification, excuse, or palliation, such proof will naturally indicate them. But where the fact of killing is proved by satisfactory evidence, and there are no circumstances disclosed, tending to show justification or excuse, there is nothing to rebut the natural presumption of malice. This rule is founded on the plain and obvious principle, that a person must be presumed to intend to do that which he voluntarily and wilfully does in fact do, and that he must intend all the natural, probable, and usual consequences of his own acts. Therefore, when one person assails another violently with a dangerous weapon likely to kill and which does in fact destroy the life of the party assailed, the natural presumption is, that he intended death or other great bodily harm; and, as there can be no presumption of any proper motive or legal excuse for such a cruel act, the consequence follows, that, in the absence of all proof to the contrary, there is nothing to rebut the presumption of malice. On the other hand, if death, though wilfully intended, was inflicted immediately after provocation given by the deceased, supposing that such provocation consisted of a blow or an assault, or other provocation on his part, which the law deems adequate to excite sudden and angry passion and create heat of blood, this fact rebuts the presumption of malice; but still, the homicide being unlawful, because a man is bound to curb his passions, is criminal, and is manslaughter.

In considering what is regarded as such adequate provocation, it is a settled rule of law, that no provocation by words only, however opprobrious, will mitigate an intentional homicide, so as to reduce it to manslaughter. Therefore, if, upon provoking language given, the party immediately revenges himself by the use of a dangerous and deadly weapon likely to cause death, such as a pistol discharged at the person, a heavy bludgeon, an axe, or a knife; if death ensues, it is a homicide not mitigated to manslaughter by the circumstances, and so is homicide by malice aforethought, within the true definition of murder. It is not the less malice aforethought, within the meaning of the law, because the act is done suddenly after the intention to commit the homicide is formed; it is sufficient that the malicious intention precedes and accompanies the act of homicide. It is manifest, therefore, that the words "malice aforethought," in the description of murder, do not imply deliberation, or the lapse of considerable time between the malicious intent to take life and the actual execution of that intent, but rather denote purpose and design, in contradistinction to accident and mischance.

In speaking of the use of a dangerous weapon, and the mode of using it upon the person of another, I have spoken of it as indicating an intention to kill him, or do him great bodily harm. The reason is this. Where a man, without justification or excuse, causes the death of another by the intentional use of a dangerous weapon likely to destroy life, he is responsible for the consequences, upon the principle already stated, that he is liable for the natural and probable consequences of his act. Suppose, therefore, for the purpose of revenge, one fires a pistol at another, regardless of consequences, intending to kill, maim, or grievously wound him, as the case may be, without any definite intention to take his life; yet, if that is the result, the law attributes the same consequences to homicide so committed, as if done under an actual and declared purpose to take the life of the party assailed....

The true nature of manslaughter is, that it is homicide mitigated out of tenderness to the frailty of human nature. Every man, when assailed with violence or great rudeness, is inspired with a sudden impulse of anger, which puts him upon resistance before time for cool reflection; and if, during that period, he attacks his assailant with a weapon likely to endanger life, and death ensues, it is regarded as done through heat of blood or violence of anger, and not through malice, or that cold-blooded desire of revenge which more properly constitutes the feeling, emotion, or passion of malice.

The same rule applies to homicide in mutual combat, which is attributed to sudden and violent anger occasioned by the combat, and not to malice. When two meet, not intending to quarrel, and angry words suddenly arise, and a conflict springs up in which blows are given on both sides, without much regard to who is the assailant, it is mutual combat. And if no unfair advantage is taken in the outset, and the occasion is not sought for the purpose of gratifying malice, and one seizes a weapon and strikes a deadly blow, it is regarded as homicide in heat of blood; and though not excusable, because a man is bound to control his angry passions, yet it is not the higher offence of murder.

We have stated these distinctions, not because there is much evidence in the present case which calls for their application, but that the jury may have a clear and distinct view of the leading principles in the law of homicide. There seems to have been little evidence in the present case that the parties had a contest. There is some evidence tending to show the previous existence of angry feelings; but unless these feelings resulted in angry words, and words were followed by blows, there would be no proof of heat of blood in mutual combat, or under provocation of an assault, on the one side or the other; and the proof of the defendant's declarations, as to the circumstances under which the parties met and parted, as far as they go, repel the supposition of such a contest.

With these views of the law of homicide, we will proceed to the further consideration of the present case. The prisoner at the bar is charged with the wilful murder of Dr. George Parkman. This charge divides itself into two principal questions, to be resolved by the proof: first, whether the party alleged to have been murdered came to his death by an act of violence inflicted by any person; and if so, secondly, whether the act was committed by the accused....

This case is to be proved, if proved at all, by circumstantial evidence; because it is not suggested that any direct evidence can be given, or that any witness can be called to give direct testimony, upon the main fact of the killing. It becomes important, therefore, to state what circumstantial evidence is; to point out the distinction between that and positive or direct evidence.

The distinction, then, between direct and circumstantial evidence, is this. Direct or positive evidence is when a witness can be called to testify to the precise fact which is the subject of the issue on trial; that is, in a case of homicide, that the party accused did cause the death of the deceased. Whatever may be the kind of force of the evidence, that is the fact to be proved. But suppose no person was present on the occasion of the death, and of course that no one can be called to testify to it; is it wholly unsusceptible of legal proof? Experience has shown that circumstantial evidence may be offered in such a case; that is, that a body of facts may be proved of so conclusive a character, as to warrant a firm belief of the fact, quite as strong and certain as that on which discreet men are accustomed to act, in relation to their most important concerns. It would be injurious to the best interests of society, if such proof could not avail in judicial proceedings. If it was necessary always to have positive evidence how many criminal acts committed in the community, destructive of its peace and subversive of its order and security, would go wholly undetected and unpunished?

The necessity, therefore, of resorting to circumstantial evidence, if it is a safe and reliable proceeding, is obvious and absolute. Crimes are secret. Most men, conscious of criminal purposes, and about the execution of criminal acts, seek the security of secrecy and darkness. It is therefore necessary to use all modes of evidence besides that of direct testimony, provided such proofs may be relied on as leading to safe and satisfactory conclusions; and, thanks to a beneficent providence, the laws of nature and the relations of things to each other are so linked and combined together, that a medium of proof is often thereby furnished, leading to inferences and conclusions as strong as those arising from direct testimony.... The evidence must establish the *corpus delicti,* as it is termed, or the offence committed as charged; and, in case of homicide, must not only prove a death by violence, but must, to a reasonable extent, exclude the hypothesis of suicide, and a death by the act of any other person. This is to be proved beyond reasonable doubt.

Then, what is reasonable doubt? It is a term often used, probably pretty well understood, but not easily defined. It is not mere possible doubt; because every thing relating to human affairs, and depending on moral evidence, is open to some possible or imaginary doubt. It is that state of the case, which, after the entire comparison and consideration of all the evidence, leaves the minds of the jurors in that condition and they cannot say they feel an abiding conviction, to a moral certainty, of the truth of the charge. The burden of proof is upon the prosecutor. All the presumptions of law independent of evidence are in favor of innocence; and every person is presumed to be innocent until he is proved guilty. If upon such proof there is reasonable doubt remaining, the accused is entitled to the benefit of it by an acquittal. For it is not sufficient to establish a probability, though a strong one arising from the doctrine of chances, that the fact charged is more likely to be true than the contrary; but the evidence must establish the truth of the fact to a reasonable and moral certainty; a certainty that convinces and directs the understanding, and satisfies the reason and judgment of those who are bound to act conscientiously upon it. This we take to be proof beyond reasonable doubt; because if the law, which mostly depends upon considerations of a moral nature, should go further than this, and require absolute certainty, it would exclude circumstantial evidence altogether....

The jury returned a verdict of guilty, and the defendant's sentence of death by hanging was sustained by the Supreme Judicial Court of Massachusetts. Subsequently, Dr. Webster confessed:

"On Tuesday the 20th of November, I sent the note to Dr. Parkman.... It was to ask Dr. Parkman to call at my rooms on Friday the 23d, after my lecture.... My purpose was, if he should accede to the proposed interview, to state to him my embarrassments and utter inability to pay him at present, to apologize for those things in my conduct which had offended him, to throw myself upon his mercy, to beg for further time and indulgence for the sake of my family, if not for my own, and to make as good promises to him as I could have any hope of keeping....

"Dr. Parkman agreed to call on me as I proposed.

"He came, accordingly, between half-past one and two.... He immediately addressed me with great energy: 'Are you ready for me, sir? Have you got the money?' I replied, 'No, Dr. Parkman'; and was then beginning to state my condition and make my appeal to him. He would not listen to me, but interrupted me with much vehemence. He called me 'scoundrel' and 'liar', and went on heaping upon me the most bitter taunts and opprobrious epithets.... I cannot tell how long the torrent of threats and invectives continued, and I can now recall to memory but a small portion of what he said. At first I kept interposing, trying to pacify him, so that I might obtain the object for which I had sought the interview. But I could not stop him, and soon my own temper was up. I forgot everything. I felt nothing but the sting of his words. I was excited to the highest degree of passion; and while he was speaking and gesticulating in the most violent and menacing manner, thrusting the letter and his fist into my face, in my fury I seized whatever was the handiest,—it was a stick of wood,—and dealt him an instantaneous blow with all the force that passion could give it. I did not know, nor think, nor care where I should hit him, nor how hard nor what the effect would be. It was on the side of his head, and there was nothing to break the force of the blow. He fell instantly upon the pavement.... Perhaps I spent ten minutes in attempts to resuscitate him; but I found that he was absolutely dead....

"My next move was to get the body into the sink which stands in the small private room. By setting the body partially erect against the corner, and getting up into the sink myself, I succeeded in drawing it up. There it was entirely dismembered....

"There was a fire burning in the furnace of the lower laboratory.... The head and viscera were put into that furnace that day....

"When the body had been thus all disposed of, I cleared away all traces of what had been done. I took up the stick with which the fatal blow had been struck. It proved to be the stump of a large grape vine, say two inches in diameter, and two feet long.... I had carried it in from Cambridge ... for the purpose of showing the effect of certain chemical fluids in coloring wood.... I put it into the fire...."

The full confession appears in Bemis, Report of the Case of John W. Webster, pp. 564–71 (1850).

Had the above story been told at the trial, and believed, should the jury, in light of the judge's charge, have convicted Dr. Webster of murder or manslaughter? *

* For an interesting account of the trial of Dr. Webster, see the article by Justice Robert Sullivan, "The Murder Trial of Dr. Webster, Boston, 1850", in 51 Mass.L.Q. 367 (1966) and 52 ibid., 67 (1967). Also see the same author's book "The Disappearance of Dr. Parkman" (1971), in which he states that the "charge to the jury" by Justice Shaw was not the one actually delivered, but rather an extensively rewritten and moderated third draft, partly composed after Webster's execution. See also, Borowitz, The Janitor's Story: An Ethical Dilemma in the Harvard Murder Case, 66

NOTES

Malice Aforethought

1. As Chief Justice Shaw noted in his charge to the jury in the Webster case, supra, "[T]he characteristic distinction between murder and manslaughter is malice, express or implied."

With respect to the meaning and significance of the term "malice," consider the following:

"The meaning of 'malice aforethought', which is the distinguishing criterion of murder, is certainly not beyond the range of controversy. The first thing that must be said about it is that neither of the two words is used in its ordinary sense.... 'It is now only an arbitrary symbol. For the "malice" may have in it nothing really malicious; and need never be really "aforethought", except in the sense that every desire must necessarily come before—though perhaps only an instant before—the act which is desired. The word "aforethought", in the definition, has thus become either false or else superfluous. The word "malice" is neither; but it is apt to be misleading, for it is not employed in its original (and its popular) meaning.' 'Malice aforethought' is simply a comprehensive name for a number of different mental attitudes which have been variously defined at different stages in the development of the law, the presence of any one of which in the accused has been held by the courts to render a homicide particularly heinous and therefore to make it murder.... As Stephen put it '... when a particular state of mind came under their notice the Judges called it malice or not according to their view of the propriety of hanging particular people....'" Report of the Royal Commission on Capital Punishment, 26–28 (1953).

With respect to the meaning of "afore thought" see State v. Moore, 481 N.W.2d 355 (Minn.1992) (some time is required for the existence of malice prior to killing) and Willey v. State, 328 Md. 126, 613 A.2d 956 (1992) (the time period required may be very short).

2. The following definition of "malice aforethought" is deserving of consideration: "an unjustifiable, inexcusable and unmitigated man-endangering-state-of-mind." Perkins, Criminal Law (1957) 40.

A good example within Professor Perkins' definition is the early case of Banks v. State, 85 Tex.Cr.R. 165, 211 S.W. 217 (1919), which involved the firing of shots into a moving train and resulted in the death of one of the crew, and where the court said:

"One who deliberately used a deadly weapon in such reckless manner as to evince a heart regardless of social duty and fatally bent on mischief, as is shown by firing into a moving train upon which human beings necessarily are, cannot shield himself from the consequences of his acts by disclaiming malice. Malice may be toward a group of persons as well as toward an individual. It may exist without former grudges or antecedent menaces. The intentional doing of any wrongful act in such manner and under such circumstances as that the death of a human being may result therefrom is malice."

Another example is Commonwealth v. Ashburn, 459 Pa. 625, 331 A.2d 167 (1975), where the defendant was convicted of murder for killing a friend in a game of Russian Roulette. Only one chamber of the revolver had been loaded

A.B.A.J. 1540 (1980), suggesting that the confession was a "hoax" and was viewed by the press as a last-ditch effort by Webster to save his life.

with live ammunition. When defendant argued there was only one chance in six that the victim would be killed and that such odds do not make it highly foreseeable that death would result, the Pennsylvania Supreme Court stated that the finding of malice does not depend on any precise mathematical calculation of the probable consequences of defendant's acts. A somewhat similar case is Commonwealth v. Malone, 354 Pa. 180, 47 A.2d 445 (1946), in which the defendant's conviction for murder was affirmed when it was shown he had placed a gun against the decedent and pulled the trigger three times. He erroneously believed that he had placed the bullet in such a manner that the gun would not fire.

A 15½-year-old high school student deliberately loaded a mix of live and dummy rounds into the magazine of a 12–gauge shotgun, pumped a round into the firing chamber and then, not knowing what sort of shell was in front of the firing pin, pointed the weapon at a 13-year-old boy. "Let's play Polish roulette," he said. "Who's first?" He pulled the trigger discharging the live round into the other boy's chest, killing him. The Court of Appeals found that this was murder where the statute required only that the defendant acted recklessly. The difference between recklessness leading to a conviction of manslaughter and that leading to a conviction of murder lies in the facts of the case. Is the conduct such that it creates a very substantial risk of death? The Court held that pointing and pulling the trigger of a shotgun at someone else is such conduct where the defendant knew the round might be live. People v. Roe, 74 N.Y.2d 20, 544 N.Y.S.2d 297, 542 N.E.2d 610 (1989).

3. Consider the following interesting definition of malice in the present California Penal Code, Title 8, § 188 (which provision was enacted in 1872): "[M]alice may be express or implied. It is express when there is manifested a deliberate intention unlawfully to take away the life of a fellow creature. It is implied, when no considerable provocation appears, or when the circumstances attending the killing show an abandoned and malignant heart."

The Illinois Criminal Code provides, in 720 ILCS 5/9–1, that

(a) A person who kills an individual without lawful justification commits first degree murder if, in performing the acts which cause the death:

> (1) He either intends to kill or do great bodily harm to that individual or another, or knows that such acts will cause death to that individual or another; or
>
> (2) He knows that such acts create a strong probability of death or great bodily harm to that individual or another; or
>
> (3) He is attempting or committing a forcible felony other than second degree murder.

4. Malice aforethought is a difficult concept to use since its plain meaning would be taken by many to require an intent to kill, out of hatred and spite, conceived before the homicide itself. This meaning has been, for centuries, clearly too restrictive for the definition of murder accepted by most people. One way to loosen its meaning was to redefine it as Prof. Perkins did (note 2, supra). Another method is to abandon it entirely as nearly all statutes do today. In 2 La Fave and Scott, 2 Substantive Criminal Law, 191–206 (1986) the common-law malice requirement for murder is broken down into three categories: (1) Intent to kill, (2) Intent to do serious bodily injury, (3) Depraved-heart murder—this state of mind exists when one engages in conduct which has a high degree of risk that it will result in death or serious bodily injury to someone—such as in the

cases of Russian Roulette, firing a bullet at a moving car, selling uncut heroin, etc.

The depraved-heart doctrine may be applied where management engages in workplace practices that injure employees. See 1 K. Brickey, Corporate Criminal Liability (1984 & 1988 Supp.); Brickey, Death in the Workplace: Corporate Liability for Criminal Homicide, 2 Notre Dame J.L. Ethics & Pub. Pol'y 753 (1987); Comment, The Application of Criminal Homicide Statutes to Work–Related Deaths: Mens Rea and Deterrence, 1986 U.Ill.L.Rev. 969 (1986). See People v. O'Neil, 194 Ill.App.3d 79, 141 Ill.Dec. 44, 550 N.E.2d 1090 (1990).

2. EUTHANASIA—"MERCY KILLINGS"

Malice may be present even though the motive for a killing is of the highest order. Thus, a "mercy killing" is usually murder, inasmuch as it constitutes an intentional taking of life without provocation or other mitigation, and without legal justification or excuse. The law concerning euthanasia is well summarized in the following excerpt from Williams, The Sanctity of Life and the Criminal Law, 318–26 (1957):

"Under the present law, voluntary euthanasia would, except in certain narrow circumstances, be regarded as suicide, in the patient who consents and murder in the doctor who administers; even on a lenient view, most lawyers would say that it could not be less than manslaughter in the doctor, the punishment for which, according to the jurisdiction and the degree of manslaughter, can be anything up to imprisonment for life.

"More specifically, the following principles may be stated:

"(a) If the doctor gives the patient a fatal injection with the intention of killing him, and the patient dies in consequence, the doctor is a common murderer because it is his hand that caused the death. Neither the consent of the patient, nor the extremity of his suffering, nor the imminence of death by natural causes, nor all of these factors taken together, is a defence....

"(b) If the doctor furnishes poison (for example, an overdose of sleeping tablets) for the purpose of enabling the patient to commit suicide, and the patient takes it accordingly and dies, this is suicide and a kind of self-murder in the patient, and the doctor, as an abettor, again becomes guilty of murder. So, at any rate, is it in strict legal theory....

"(c) A case that may be thought to be distinguishable from both of those already considered is that of the administration of a fatal dose of a drug where this dose is in fact the minimum necessary to deaden pain. Where a patient is suffering from an incurable and agonizing disease, and ordinary quantities of a drug fail to render the pain tolerable, many doctors will give the minimum dose necessary to kill the pain, knowing that this minimum is at the same time an amount that is likely to kill the patient. In other words, with the choice of either doing nothing, or killing both the pain and the patient, the doctor chooses the latter course.... Thus a point is reached at which, proceeding upon the same principles as he has followed heretofore, and which have so far been lawful, the doctor is led to give what he knows is likely to be an immediately fatal dose. It would be extremely artificial to say that this last dose, which is administered upon the same principle as all the previous ones, is alone unlawful.... [The physician's] legal excuse ... rests upon the doctrine of necessity, there being at this junction no way of relieving pain without ending life. In this limited form the excuse of necessity would be likely to be accepted by a judge, and to this extent it may be held that euthanasia is permitted under the existing law....

"(d) We come, finally, to the problem of killing by inaction. 'Mercy-killing' by omission to use medical means to prolong life is probably lawful. Although a physician is normally under a duty to use reasonable care to conserve his patient's life, he is probably exempted from that duty if life has become a burden to the patient."

NOTES

1. Administration of the law in this area reflects a contemporary conflict between the thought that euthanasia is less reprehensible than other forms of murder, and the idea that, morally, such homicide cannot be condoned. Consider the following histories of several cases of euthanasia:

(a) Louis Rapouille filed a petition for naturalization on September 22, 1944, and the federal district court entered an order granting the petition. The federal district attorney appealed on the ground that the petitioner had not established the fact of "good moral character" for the five-year period preceding his petition in that it was alleged and proved at the district court hearing that the petitioner had, during that period, deliberately put to death his thirteen-year-old son. The Court of Appeals for the Second Circuit reversed the order of the district court and dismissed Repouille's petition, but without prejudice to the filing of a second petition. 165 F.2d 152 (1947). In rendering the court's decision, Judge Learned Hand stated:

"His reason for this tragic deed was that the child had 'suffered from birth from a brain injury which destined him to be an idiot and a physical monstrosity malformed in all four limbs. The child was blind, mute, and deformed. He had to be fed; the movements of his bladder and bowels were involuntary, and his entire life was spent in a small crib'. Repouille had four other children at the time, towards whom he has always been a dutiful and responsible parent; it may be assumed that his act was to help him in their nurture, which was being compromised by the burden imposed upon him in the care of the fifth. The family was altogether dependent upon his industry for its support. He was indicted for manslaughter in the first degree; but the jury brought in a verdict of manslaughter in the second degree with a recommendation of the 'utmost clemency'; and the judge sentenced him to not less than five years or more than ten, execution to be stayed, and the defendant to be placed on probation, from which he was discharged in December, 1945. Concededly, except for this act he conducted himself as a person of 'good moral character' during the five years before he filed his petition. Indeed, if he had waited before filing his petition from September 22, to October 14, 1944, he would have had a clear record for the necessary period, and would have been admitted without question....

"It is reasonably clear that the jury which tried Repouille did not feel any moral repulsion at his crime. Although it was inescapably murder in the first degree, not only did they bring in a verdict that was flatly in the face of the facts and utterly absurd—for manslaughter in the second degree presupposes that the killing has not been deliberate—but they coupled even that with a recommendation which showed that in substance they wished to exculpate the offender. Moreover, it is also plain, from the sentence which he imposed, that the judge could not have seriously disagreed with their recommendation.

"One might be tempted to seize upon all this as a reliable measure of current morals; and no doubt it should have its place in the scale; but we should hesitate to accept it as decisive, when, for example, we compare it with the fate of a similar offender in Massachusetts, who, although he was not executed, was imprisoned for life. Left at large as we are, without means of verifying our conclusion, and without authority to substitute our individual beliefs, the outcome must needs be tentative; and not much is gained by discussion. We can say no more than that, quite independently of what may be the current moral feeling as to legally administered euthanasia, we feel reasonably secure in holding that only a minority of virtuous persons would deem the practice morally justifiable, while it remains in private hands, even when the provocation is as overwhelming as it was in this instance."

(b) The Massachusetts case referred to by the Court in the preceding paragraph was Commonwealth v. Noxon, 319 Mass. 495, 66 N.E.2d 814 (1946). The history of the Noxon case, particularly that portion of it occurring after the above decision on the Repouille petition, sheds light on the many factors which affect the ultimate outcome of such cases. The following brief history is taken from the January 17, 1949, issue of Newsweek Magazine:

"When John F. Noxon was charged in 1943 with electrocuting his incurably Mongoloid 6-month-old son Larry, the newspapers labeled the case a 'mercy killing.' Noxon pleaded innocent. He insisted that the death had been accidental—that it was only by chance the boy had come in contact with a metal tray that touched a short-circuited radio wire.

"The wealthy Pittsfield, Mass., lawyer's trial became much more than a simple attempt to arrive at facts. In a heavily Catholic state, the idea of mercy killing was anathema. Noxon's social position and his personality—dour and uncommunicative—lost him much sympathy among those who might have supported him. After a sensational trial, he was found guilty and sentenced to the electric chair.

"But Noxon's lawyer, ex-Gov. Joseph B. Ely, did not give up. When the State Supreme Court rejected his appeal, Ely turned to Gov. Maurice J. Tobin. His argument: Noxon, half-crippled by infantile paralysis, would be punished enough if his sentence was commuted to life imprisonment. Although a Catholic, Tobin agreed and won the approval of his nine-man Executive Council. Noxon was moved from the condemned row in the state prison at Charleston to the Norfolk prison colony where thenceforth he served as prison librarian.

"Last month Gov. Robert F. Bradford, Ely's onetime law partner, who was defeated for reelection in November, asked the Pardon and Parole Committee of his council to consider a further reduction of Noxon's sentence—from life to six-years-to-life, making parole possible at once. This time, Tobin, now Secretary of Labor, advised against further leniency. More sensationally, District Attorney William J. Foley openly charged that Bradford was deliberately turning loose murderers in the last days of his administration and hinted at corruption.

"In the midst of the hullabaloo, Bradford's committee, headed by Lt. Gov. Arthur Coolidge, approved the governor's recommendation. Then the full council, by a 6-to-3 vote, granted the reduction in sentence. Last week the State

Parole Board closed the books on the controversial case by releasing Noxon. On Friday, Jan. 7, 1949, he walked out of the Norfolk prison colony."

Another unusual case history is discussed in Note, 34 Notre Dame Law. 460 (1959).

(c) An interesting "mercy killing" case occurred in Belgium in 1962. A child was born very badly malformed as a result of the mother having taken thalidomide while pregnant. The parents and a doctor arranged for killing the child 8 days old, by placing barbiturates with honey in a bottle of milk.

Following are portions of a news report (Chicago Daily News, Nov. 12, 1962) of the public reaction to the acquittal:

> "When the verdict was announced yesterday, spectators in the courtroom, who earlier in the day had applauded the defense and hissed the prosecutor, cheered, stamped, jumped in the air, and shouted, 'Bravo!'
>
> "A woman in the crowds suffered a broken leg."

2. Present attitudes regarding legislative change in the law concerning euthanasia include (1) the view that the status quo has sufficient flexibility, through such factors as the jury system and the pardoning power, to afford just treatment in each case according to its merits; (2) the position that the penalty for a killing motivated by mercy should be reduced; and (3) the view that euthanasia should be legalized within certain narrow bounds and placed under state supervision and control.

3. With respect to "the right to die", there is the case of Matter of Quinlan, 70 N.J. 10, 355 A.2d 647 (1976). It involved the issue of the legality of removing life sustaining equipment from a person whom physicians consider hopelessly ill. The patient, a young female named Karen Quinlan, was pronounced medically to be in a "chronic persistent vegetative state"—one who "remains with the capacity to maintain the vegetative parts of neurological function but who no longer has any cognitive function." Her condition having been considered hopeless, and her parents reconciled to the certainty of impending death, a request was made by them for the withdrawal of the life supporting mechanisms. The attending physician, however, refused to comply, because of his conception of medical standards, practice and ethics, compounded perhaps by a concern as to the legality of such action. The latter issue was decided by the court in favor of the parents' wishes. The court reasoned that as a matter of a constitutional "right to privacy" the patient, if competent to make a decision, would have been entitled to the removal of the life supporting mechanisms, and that since she was incompetent to do so, her parents, as her legal guardians, were entitled to make the decision on her behalf. The court added that the removal of the support system would not subject a physician or anyone else to criminal or civil liability. To the same effect: Barber v. Superior Court, 147 Cal.App.3d 1006, 195 Cal. Rptr. 484 (1983). See generally G. Grisez and J. Boyle, Life and Death with Liberty and Justice (1979).

4. Relevant to the euthanasia issue is the question as to the legality of suicide. At common law it was a felony, punishable by forfeiture of goods and ignominious burial; attempted suicide was a misdemeanor. Since forfeiture of goods as a punishment for crime has largely been abandoned, and ignominious burial is no longer practiced, it might be said that the successful suicide has not committed any offense, since he cannot be punished. Some states still punish

the unsuccessful (attempted) suicide by statute, although the attempting person is usually referred to a mental diagnosis and treatment facility.

The issue in recent times has been the legality of physician assistance to one who wishes to end life. Michigan barred physicians from assisting suicides, and its legislation was upheld in People v. Kevorkian, 447 Mich. 436, 527 N.W.2d 714 (1994), which held that there was no constitutional right to commit suicide. The issue divided judges in Michigan which has no law criminalizing either suicide or its attempt.

The difficulty of the issue is best shown by the fact that Washington banned physician-assisted suicide, and its law was found to be unconstitutional while Oregon legalized physician-assisted suicide, and its law was also found to be unconstitutional. Compare Compassion in Dying v. State of Washington, 850 F.Supp. 1454 (W.D.Wash.1994), rev'd 49 F.3d 586 (9th Cir.1995), r'hg en banc granted 62 F.3d 299 (9th Cir.1995) with Lee v. Oregon, 891 F.Supp. 1429 (D.Or.1995).

3. DESTRUCTION OF THE UNBORN CHILD

Since the common law of homicide refers to the killing of a "human being," the courts in this country have generally not considered the aborting of an unborn child to be a homicide. The child must be shown to have achieved an independent circulation.

NOTES

1. In State v. Gyles, 313 So.2d 799 (La.1975), the Supreme Court of Louisiana observed that "The common law crime of murder ... contemplates only the killing of those human beings who have been born alive and who thus have an existence independent of their mothers at the time of their death. The crime does not punish conduct which causes the death of a fetus not born alive due to an assault on the mother, in the absence of a statute expressly changing the common law definition of the crime. The uniform authority in all American jurisdictions is to this effect." A dissenting judge would have defined a child in the mother's womb at eight months of pregnancy a human being.

Taking its cue from *Gyles,* in 1976 the Louisiana legislature amended the definition of "person" to include "a human being from the moment of fertilization and implantation * * *." LSA–R.S. 14:2(7) (1977). But in State v. Brown, 378 So.2d 916 (La.1979), the Supreme Court of Louisiana held that this language did not criminalize feticide because the Louisiana Criminal Code defined homicide as the unlawful killing of a "human being", not a "person." Is the *Brown* court's distinction between a "person" and a "human being" persuasive? See Meadows v. State, 291 Ark. 105, 722 S.W.2d 584 (1987) and Commonwealth v. Cass, 392 Mass. 799, 467 N.E.2d 1324 (1984), noting that the common law definitions of "person" and "human being" are synonymous. For one commentator's assessment of *Brown* (negative) see Note, Feticide is Still Legal in Louisiana, 26 Loy.L.Rev. 422 (1980).

An excellent discussion of the issue of whether a fetus is (or should be) a "human being" for purposes of the law is contained in H. Arkes, *First Things* ch. 16 (1986). And a thorough discussion of the born alive rule can be found in Forsythe, Homicide of the Unborn Child: The Born Alive Rule and Other Legal Anachronisms, 21 Val.U.L.Rev. 563 (1987).

2. Once the fetus has emerged totally and the breathing process started, it is not needed that the umbilical cord be severed; it achieves the status of a "human being". Jackson v. Commonwealth, 265 Ky. 295, 96 S.W.2d 1014 (1936). But see, Morgan v. State, 148 Tenn. 417, 256 S.W. 433 (1923), suggesting that an independent circulation cannot be established until after the umbilical cord is severed.

3. The infliction of injuries upon an unborn child who dies after having been born alive may be considered homicide. In Abrams v. Foshee, 3 Iowa 274 (1856), the court held that if a child is born alive and subsequently dies as a result of potions or bruises while still in the womb, the person administering the potions or bruises with intent to produce a miscarriage could be convicted of murder. And in State v. Anderson, 135 N.J.Super. 423, 343 A.2d 505 (1975), where a mother seven months pregnant with twin fetuses, received a gunshot wound and was delivered of the fetuses after the injury by Caesarian section. After the operation both fetuses were alive, but they died shortly thereafter. One of the fetuses was said to have died from a bullet wound across the back as the missile passed through the mother, the other was not struck by the bullet and death was said to be immaturity. The court held that "fetuses which are the victim of a criminal blow or wound upon their mother and are subsequently born alive, and thereafter die by reason of a chain of circumstances precipitated by such blow or wound, may be the victims of murder" and would be considered "persons" within the meaning of the state's homicide statutes.

4. Following the California decision in Keeler v. Superior Court, 2 Cal.3d 619, 87 Cal.Rptr. 481, 470 P.2d 617 (1970), holding that the destruction of a fetus caused by a criminally inflicted blow to its mother was not a homicide because it was not a "human being," the legislature declared that murder included the "killing of a fetus" with "malice aforethought." Exceptions were made, of course, as regards authorized abortions. Calif. Penal Code, Title 8, Ch. 1, § 187. The California Supreme Court upheld this statute against constitutional challenge in People v. Bunyard, 45 Cal.3d 1189, 249 Cal.Rptr. 71, 756 P.2d 795 (1988). Another case holding that an unborn fetus is not a "person" or "human being" is State v. Larsen, 578 P.2d 1280 (Utah 1978).

Compare the provisions of 720 ILCS 5/9–1.2:

§ 9–1.2. Intentional Homicide of an Unborn Child. (a) A person commits the offense of intentional homicide of an unborn child if, in performing acts which cause the death of an unborn child, he without lawful justification:

(1) either intended to cause the death of or do great bodily harm to the pregnant woman or her unborn child or knew that such acts would cause death or great bodily harm to the pregnant woman or her unborn child; or

(2) he knew that his acts created a strong probability of death or great bodily harm to the pregnant woman or her unborn child; and

(3) he knew that the woman was pregnant.

(b) For purposes of this Section, (1) "unborn child" shall mean any individual of the human species from fertilization until birth, and (2) "person" shall not include the pregnant woman whose unborn child is killed.

(c) This Section shall not apply to acts which cause the death of an unborn child if those acts were committed during any abortion, as defined in Section 2 of the Illinois Abortion Law of 1975, as amended, to which the pregnant woman has consented. This Section shall not apply to acts which were committed pursuant to usual and customary standards of medical practice during diagnostic testing or therapeutic treatment.

5. Because it is sometimes very difficult to establish that the issue was born alive, which proof is needed to support a prosecution for murder or manslaughter, some states have specially provided that concealment of an infant death is a misdemeanor.

In Williams v. People, 114 Colo. 207, 158 P.2d 447 (1945), the court affirmed a conviction of murder and of concealing the death of a bastard, but a strong dissent suggested there was no proof the child was ever born alive. The dissenting opinion analyzed in great detail the requirement of the corpus delicti in infanticides and reviewed the case law in other states on the issue.

This problem is discussed in Bales, Legal Criteria for Distinguishing Between Live and Dead Foetuses and Newborn Children, 6 U. New S. Wales L.J. 143 (1983).

4. THE "CORPUS DELICTI"

R. v. ONUFREJCZYK

Court of Criminal Appeals.
[1955] 1 All Eng.R. 247.

[The evidence was that the defendant and one Sykut had a farm which was a financial failure. The defendant was trying, unsuccessfully, to borrow money to buy out Sykut's interest, in order to avoid a sale of the farm by auction. On or about December 14th, Sykut disappeared. On December 18th, defendant told a sheriff's officer that Sykut had gone to another city to see a doctor. Later, however, he said that three men had forced Sykut into a car at gun point and driven him away from the farm. He also wrote letters suggesting that Sykut had returned to Poland. Sykut's wife, who lived in Poland, had not heard from him, however, well after the time it would have taken him to reach Poland. The defendant was still trying to borrow money, and he tried to persuade a friend to go to a solicitor with him and impersonate Sykut. He was also arranging for a woman to draft some supposed agreements and forge Sykut's signature to them. In addition, he tried to get a blacksmith to say that Sykut had fetched a horse at the blacksmith's on December 17th, when Sykut had actually called for the horse on the 14th.]

LORD GODDARD, C.J., delivered the judgment of the court: The appellant, who is a Pole and who has been in this country since 1947, was convicted of the murder of another Pole, Sykut, his partner.

The principal question that has been argued, is whether there was proof of what the law calls a corpus delicti. In this case the remarkable fact, which has remained remarkable and unexplained, is that the body of this man, who was last seen so far as anybody knows on Dec. 14, 1953, has completely disappeared and there is no trace whatever either of him, or of his clothes, or of his ashes. It has been submitted to us that the law is that, unless the body can be found or an account can be given of the death, there is no proof of a corpus delicti. Corpus delicti means, first, that a crime has been committed, that is to say that the man is dead, and that his death has been caused by a crime.

There is, apparently, no reported case in English law where a man has been convicted of murder and there has been no trace of the body at all. But it is, we think, clear that the fact of death can be proved, like any other fact can be proved, by circumstantial evidence, that is to say, by evidence of facts which lead to one conclusion, provided the jury are satisfied and are warned that the evidence must lead to one conclusion only....

... The case for the prosecution was:—This man has disappeared. He has completely gone from the ken of mankind. It is impossible to believe that he is alive now. I suppose it would have been possible for him to have got out of the country and become immured behind what is sometimes called the Iron Curtain; but here you have facts which point irresistably towards the appellant being the person who knows and who disposed of that man in one form or another. It may be that it would be desirable to emphasize to the jury that the first thing to which they must apply their mind is: Was a murder committed? Speaking for myself, I think that the way the learned judge put it in the two passages which I have read did sufficiently direct the attention of the jury to the fact that they had to be satisfied of that, and, if they were satisfied of the death, and the violent death, of this man, they need not go any further. It is, no doubt, true that the prosecution relied considerably on certain minute spots of blood which were found in the kitchen when it was scientifically examined, spots so small that they might easily have escaped the attention of somebody who was trying to wash or wipe up blood. The appellant did not deny that the blood that was found, although it was a minute quantity, on the wall of the kitchen, and, I think, on the ceiling of the kitchen, was the blood of his partner. He said that its presence there was due to the fact that his partner had cut his hand in the field with, I think, one of the tractors, and on coming in must have shaken his hand and shaken off some blood. That, of course, was a possibility and it was put to the jury. It was also a possibility that Sykut was disposed of in the kitchen, but there is no evidence that he was and, a matter which has been very properly stressed by counsel for the appellant, there is no evidence here how Sykut met his death. This court is of the opinion, however, that there was evidence on which the jury could infer that he met his death, that he was dead; and, if he was dead, the circumstances of the case point to the fact that his death was not a natural death. Then, if that establishes, as it would, a corpus delicti, the evidence was such that the jury were entitled to find that the appellant murdered his partner....

We have come to the conclusion that there was evidence on which the jury were entitled to find that the appellant's partner was murdered and that the appellant was the murderer. Accordingly, this appeal is dismissed.

NOTES

1. For other murder cases in which the corpus delicti was established by circumstantial evidence alone, consider the following:

(a) In People v. Scott, 176 Cal.App.2d 458, 1 Cal.Rptr. 600 (1959), the defendant's wife, a woman in excellent health, disappeared. Although her glasses and dentures were found in a trash pile, no traces of her body were ever found. Before his arrest the defendant had told his friends a number of conflicting stories and lies by way of trying to explain his wife's disappearance. He also forged her name on checks and had obtained large sums of her money. The affirmance of his murder conviction was disapproved in 34 Tul.L.Rev. 820 (1960).

In another California case, the multiple killer Charles Manson was convicted of one murder where the victim's body was never found. His conviction was affirmed, and the United States Supreme Court declined review. People v. Manson, 71 Cal.App.3d 1, 139 Cal.Rptr. 275 (1977), cert. denied 435 U.S. 953, 98 S.Ct. 1582 (1978). See also State v. Lerch, 296 Or. 377, 677 P.2d 678 (1984) (defendant convicted of murder although victim's body was never found).

(b) In Commonwealth v. Burns, 409 Pa. 619, 187 A.2d 552 (1963), the Supreme Court of Pennsylvania held that circumstantial evidence, which included proof of complete, sudden termination of a long-established, consistent pattern of living of the alleged victim, a healthy, 49-year old woman, who was last seen lying on the floor in defendant's presence in an apparently helpless condition with blood on her head, was sufficient to prove the corpus delicti.

(c) In King v. Horry, [1952] N.Z.L.R. 111, the defendant, George Horry, in 1942, while using an alias, married one Eileen Turner, in New Zealand. He had told her and her parents a number of fine things about himself; however, he concealed the fact that he was an ex-convict. After marriage Eileen converted all of her assets, about 1,000 pounds, into cash to take on their honeymoon. The day after the marriage, and while at a sea resort, she and George talked to her attorney about her finances. They also visited some friends to whom they told of plans to leave New Zealand the next day. George told them that a secret military mission precluded his giving them any further details about their trip. This was the last time Eileen was seen. The next day George, alone, was back in the town where he and Eileen had been married. (It was later established that he had never left New Zealand.) He opened a bank account in an amount of 767 pounds. Five months later he married another woman.

Shortly after Eileen's disappearance her parents received a letter, postmarked "Australia" and signed "George and Eileen," in which it was stated that they were leaving Australia for England. George said Eileen was busy visiting someone else. (It was later established that George, while still in New Zealand, had arranged for another person in Australia to mail the letter from there.) Thereafter George called on Eileen's parents and told them that he and Eileen had left Australia for England on the "Empress of India", and that the ship had been torpedoed and that he last saw Eileen in a life boat. He said he had been picked up by a British warship. In fact, no "Empress of India" ever existed.

Nine years after Eileen's disappearance George was prosecuted for murder and his conviction was sustained on appeal. See comment on the case in Morris, Corpus Delicti and Circumstantial Evidence, 68 L.Q.R. 391 (1952).

(d) In Phillips v. State, 133 Ga.App. 461, 211 S.E.2d 411 (1974), the court, after reading through 454 pages of trial transcript and studying hospital charts, held that there was insufficient evidence of guilt (corpus delicti?) where the attending physician was puzzled as to the cause of the victim's death.

(e) For other interesting cases and readings upon the subject, consult R. v. Workman and Huculak (Alberta App.Div., Dec. 19, 1962), 5 Cr.L.Q. 403; Commonwealth v. Lettrich, 346 Pa. 497, 31 A.2d 155 (1943); and People v. Kirby, 223 Mich. 440, 194 N.W. 142 (1923). And for a very interesting discussion of a case somewhat similar to the *Onufrejczyk* case, see Hilling, The Case of Decasto Earl Mayer and Marry Ellen Smith, 22 Wash.L.Rev. 79 (1947).

Also, for an account of case convictions for murders where no killings had ever occurred, see Borchand, Convicting the Innocent (1932). For another case involving the corpus delicti issue, see Commonwealth v. Burns, 409 Pa. 619, 187 A.2d 552 (1963).

2. Important legal issues arise when a vital organ is removed, for transplant purposes, from a crime victim who is considered medically "dead." Consider the following case situations:

Police arrive at a crime scene where they find a young man lying in a pool of blood with a bullet in his brain. Upon arrival at the hospital, the victim is comatose and given "one chance in a million" to survive after having been hooked up to life support systems which kept his heart beating. Two days later doctors decide the victim is dead because his brain stopped functioning and they proceed to remove his still beating heart to rush it to a university medical school where it is transplanted into the chest of a person with a defective heart. The person who fired the shot into the young man's brain is indicted for murder. Was there proof of the corpus delicti?

A like instance was reported in 1974 in Trial Magazine (Jan.-Feb.) under the headline "Unusual Death". The story reads:

"A Santa Rosa, California judge has ruled that a 12-year-old girl died because her heart was removed for transplant purposes and not because of brain injuries suffered in an auto accident.

"The judge's decision resulted in an acquittal for a man charged with manslaughter in connection with the girl's death.

"A doctor from the Stanford Medical Center had testified that the girl was the victim of 'cerebral death' or 'brain death syndrome,' i.e., her brain was not performing its normal function.

"Three other physicians concluded that without the life-support systems, the girl would have died within three hours of the accident, and with the support systems, she might have lived a week.

"The defendant's lawyer argued that death is defined as 'a total stoppage of the circulation of blood and a cessation of the animal and vital functions of the body such as respiration and pulsation.'

"In his ruling, the judge said that the evidence showed that the girl had 'a healthy body' and 'was in good shape except for her brain.' He said, furthermore, that a person is not legally dead until he ceases to exist."

A similar case is State v. Fierro, 124 Ariz. 182, 603 P.2d 74 (1979).

Some states hold that death occurs when the end of life is confirmed by the cessation of all electrical impulses in the brain—the so-called "flat EEG." Other states still adhere to the common law view that death occurs only when there is a cessation of breathing and a stopping of the heart.

3. A majority of courts hold that the corpus delicti cannot be established solely by the out of court confession of an accused. Some independent corroboration is required. Opper v. United States, 348 U.S. 84, 75 S.Ct. 158 (1954); People v. Holmes, 38 Ill.App.3d 122, 347 N.E.2d 407 (1976), containing a thorough analysis of the corpus delicti problem; Hogan v. State, 235 Ind. 271, 132 N.E.2d 908 (1956). Anno. 45 ALR2d 1316.

4. Contrary to a prevailing misconception, proof of corpus delicti is a requirement of all criminal cases and not merely in homicide cases. See, e.g., State v. Manzella, 306 Or. 303, 759 P.2d 1078 (1988) (driving on suspended license); Bussey v. State, 474 S.W.2d 708 (Tex.Crim.App.1972) (arson); People v. Brooks, 334 Ill. 549, 166 N.E. 35 (1929) (robbery).

5. STATUTORY DEGREES OF MURDER

At the common law, there were no degrees of murder. Any homicide, committed with malice aforethought, express or implied, constituted murder. The penalty for murder under the common law was death.

In order to lessen the penalty attaching to certain forms of murder not thought to warrant the punishment of death, many states have statutorily divided the crime of murder into degrees, with a sliding scale of penalties appropriate to the various degrees. This issue is well discussed in LaFave & Scott, 2 Substantive Criminal Law 236–46 (1986).

6. FELONY-MURDER

COMMONWEALTH v. ALMEIDA

Supreme Court of Pennsylvania, 1949.
362 Pa. 596, 68 A.2d 595.

[During an exchange of shots between robbers and police, Ingling, a police officer, was killed. The prosecution claimed that one of the felons killed Ingling; the defense, on the other hand, contended that Ingling was shot by a fellow officer. The defendant was convicted of first degree murder committed in the course of the robbery and sentenced to death.]

MAXEY, CHIEF JUSTICE. ... The defendant's thirteenth point for charge which the trial judge correctly rejected was in effect a request that the court instruct the jury that in order to convict the defendant of the death of Officer Ingling, the jury would have to find that the fatal shot was fired by one of the three robbers....

... The *legal* question presented [is] ... when men who are feloniously shot at by robbers return their fire in self-defense and a third person is killed by a shot fired by the defenders, are the robbers whose felonious action caused the shooting guilty of murder? ...

[In] the instant case, we have a band of robbers engaged in an exchange of shots with city policemen *whose duty it is to subdue the bandits if possible.* In the course of the exchange of deadly bullets Officer Ingling is slain. The policemen cannot be charged with any wrongdoing because their participation in the exchange of bullets with the bandits was both in justifiable self-defense and *in the performance of their duty.* The felonious acts of the robbers in firing shots at the policemen, well knowing that their fire would be returned, as it should have been, was the proximate cause of Officer Ingling's death....

... Their acts were "the cause of the cause" of the murder. They "set in motion the physical power" which resulted in Ingling's death and they are criminally responsible for that result. Whether the fatal bullet was fired by one of the bandits or by one of the policemen who were performing their duty in repelling the bandit's assault and defending themselves and endeavoring to prevent the escape of the felons is immaterial. Whoever fired the fatal shot, the killing of Officer Ingling had its genesis in the robbing by the defendant and his confederates ... and in their firing upon the police officers who in the performance of their duty were attempting to take them into custody....

There can be no doubt about the "justice" of holding that felon guilty of murder in the first degree who engages in a robbery or burglary and thereby inevitably calls into action defensive forces against him, the activity of which forces result in the death of a human being. Neither can there be any doubt about the "general utility" of a ruling which holds this defendant Almeida guilty of the murder of Officer Ingling, even if it had been established that the bullet which killed that officer was fired by one of the police officers who were returning the fire of Almeida and his confederates and were attempting to prevent their escape....

A knave who feloniously and maliciously starts "a chain reaction" of acts dangerous to human life must be held responsible for the natural fatal results of such acts. This is the doctrine enunciated by the textbook writers on criminal law, and which has been applied by the courts.

When men engaged in a scheme of robbery arm themselves with loaded revolvers they show that they expect to encounter forcible opposition and that to overcome it they are prepared to kill anyone who stands in their way. If in the course of their felonious enterprise they open deadly fire upon policemen or others and if in self-defense and to vindicate the law the fire is returned and someone is killed by a bullet fired in the exchange of shots, who can challenge the conclusion that the *proximate cause* of the killing was the malicious criminal action of the felons? No *other* genesis can justly be assigned to the homicide. The felons should be adjudged guilty of murder in the perpetration of a robbery, that is, murder in the first degree....

The judgment is affirmed and the record is remitted to the court below so that the sentence imposed may be carried out....

JONES, JUSTICE (dissenting). I would reverse the judgment and remand the case for a retrial because of fundamental error in the trial court's charge to the jury. The case was submitted on the felony murder theory) yet, the trial judge charged in effect that, even though the fatal shot was not fired by one of the felons but by someone attempting to frustrate the robbery, all the jury would need find in order to hold the defendant guilty of murder was that he was engaged in a robbery at the time of the killing. That instruction inadequately stated the law applicable to the circumstances.

On proof of no more than the perpetration of a felony and an incidental killing, liability for murder can be visited upon the participating felons *only* where the causation of the homicide is direct, i.e., where one of the felons or one acting in furtherance of the felonious design inflicted the fatal wound ... [E]ven though a felon or one acting in his aid does not fire the fatal bullet, his conduct may have initiated such a causative chain of events as to render him legally chargeable with having been the causa causans of the homicide.... In such circumstances, the felony murder theory supplies the malice necessary to make the killing murder while the proximate (although indirect) causation of the death is capable of fastening on the felon responsibility for the homicide. Sufficiency of the evidence to support a finding of the "chain of events" is, of course, a question of law for a court, but whether the "chain of events" existed unbroken and was the proximate cause of the homicide are questions of fact that only *a jury* can properly resolve.... Those important factual inquiries were not submitted in the instant case. Causation was assumed by the learned trial judge and all that was left to the jury to determine, in order to hold the defendant guilty of murder, was that he was engaged in a "holdup" at the time of the killing notwithstanding there was evidence that someone other than the felons had fired the fatal bullet....

... Whether the acts of Almeida and his confederates *were sufficient* to constitute the proximate cause of the killing was a question of law but whether they *did constitute* the proximate cause was a question of fact for the jury....

The jury should have been instructed that, in order to find the defendant guilty of murder, it was not only necessary for them to find the killing to have been coincidental with the perpetration of a felony in which the defendant was at the time participating but that they would also have to find that the fatal shot was fired by one of the felons or, if not fired by one of them, that the conduct of the defendant or his accomplices set in motion a chain of events among whose reasonably foreseeable consequences was a killing such as actually occurred. The only way that the question of the defendant's guilt can any longer be properly adjudicated upon adequate instructions to the jury is by the medium of a new trial....

NOTES

1. Subsequent to the *Almeida* case the Pennsylvania Supreme Court was required to rule on the following fact situation, in Commonwealth v. Thomas, 382 Pa. 639, 117 A.2d 204 (1955): Thomas and a confederate committed a robbery. While fleeing from the scene, the confederate was shot and killed by the store owner. Thomas was indicted for murder of his co-felon. However, the

trial court sustained Thomas' demurrer to the commonwealth's evidence and the decision was appealed. The Supreme Court, with three justices dissenting, reversed the judgment of the lower court. In so doing, the court stated:

"The sole question is whether defendant can be convicted of murder under this state of facts. That is, can a co-felon be found guilty of murder where the victim of an armed robbery justifiably kills the other felon as they flee from the scene of the crime? ... If the defendant sets in motion the physical power of another, he is liable for its result.... Commonwealth v. Almeida.... As has been said many times, such a rule is equally consistent with reason and sound public policy, and is essential to the protection of human life. The felon's robbery set in motion a chain of events which were or should have been within his contemplation when the motion was initiated. He therefore should be held responsible for *any death* which by direct and almost inevitable sequence results from the initial criminal act.... We can see no sound reason for distinction merely because the one killed was a co-felon."

Following the above action of the Supreme Court in the *Thomas* case, the District Attorney of Philadelphia moved the trial court for entry of a *nolle prosequi* on the murder indictment, and the court approved the motion. At the same time, Thomas pleaded guilty to an indictment charging him with armed robbery and was sentenced to the penitentiary. The Pennsylvania penalty for armed robbery is a fine not exceeding ten thousand dollars, or imprisonment in solitary confinement at labor for not exceeding twenty years, or both.

2. A few years later, the Pennsylvania Supreme Court again found it necessary to struggle with the felony-murder concept. The occasion was the case of Commonwealth v. Redline, 391 Pa. 486, 137 A.2d 472 (1958), where the defendant and his accomplice perpetrated a robbery and, while fleeing from the scene, engaged in a gun battle with the police. The accomplice was killed by a policeman, and defendant was indicted for and convicted of the murder of the accomplice. Here, the Supreme Court changed its mind and overruled *Thomas,* holding that felony-murder applies only if the killing is done by one of the felons, and not if the killing is done by a police officer or a bystander. The court did not overrule *Almeida,* although it expressed its dissatisfaction with that case, because the two cases could be distinguished on the basis that in *Almeida* the victim of the killing was a police officer, while in *Redline,* the victim was one of the felons.

3. On the same day that the Supreme Court of Pennsylvania decided the *Redline* case, it handed down a decision in Commonwealth v. Bolish, 391 Pa. 550, 138 A.2d 447 (1958). Bolish and one Flynn planned an arson, and in carrying out the plan Flynn was fatally injured by an explosion which occurred when he placed a jar of gasoline on an electric hot plate. Bolish was convicted of first degree murder and sentenced to life imprisonment. The judgment was affirmed on appeal, the court rejecting the defendant's contention that the felony-murder doctrine does not apply to the death of an accomplice resulting from the accomplice's own act. The court stated that the defendant "was actively participating in the felony which resulted in death. The element of malice, present in the design of defendant, necessarily must be imputed to the resulting killing, and made him responsible for the death.... The fact that the victim was an accomplice does not alter the situation, since his own act which caused his death was in furtherance of the felony." Two justices dissented.

Is the *Bolish* case distinguishable from *Redline*?

Was the majority holding in *Bolish* correct in view of the wording of the Pennsylvania statute which provides, in part, as follows: "All murder which shall be ... committed in the perpetration of ... arson ... shall be murder in the first degree"?

4. The conviction in the *Almeida* case was set aside by a federal district court, upon a habeas corpus hearing because of the fact that the prosecution had suppressed evidence establishing that the fatal bullet was actually fired by a police officer and not by one of the felons. 104 F.Supp. 321 (E.D.Pa.1951), affirmed 195 F.2d 815 (3d Cir.1952). Almeida was retried. He pled guilty and received a life sentence.

After the court's decision in *Redline,* Almeida appealed on the basis that under the new (Redline) rule he was not guilty of murder. The Pennsylvania Supreme Court held that the *Redline* decision was not relevant because the legality of Almeida's conviction must be governed by the law as it existed at that time. Commonwealth ex rel. Almeida v. Rundle, 409 Pa. 460, 187 A.2d 266 (1963). To the same effect see United States ex rel. Almeida v. Rundle, 383 F.2d 421 (3d Cir.1967).

COMMONWEALTH EX REL. SMITH v. MYERS

Supreme Court of Pennsylvania, 1970.
438 Pa. 218, 261 A.2d 550.

O'BRIEN, JUSTICE. This is an appeal from the order of the Court of Common Pleas of Philadelphia County, denying James Smith's petition for a writ of habeas corpus. The facts upon which the convictions of appellant and his co-felons, Almeida and Hough, rest are well known to this Court and to the federal courts. In addition to vexing the courts, these cases have perplexed a generation of law students, both within and without the Commonwealth, and along with their progeny, have spawned reams of critical commentary.[1]

Briefly, the facts of the crime are these. On January 30, 1947, Smith, along with Edward Hough and David Almeida, engaged in an armed robbery of a supermarket in the City of Philadelphia. An off-duty policeman, who happened to be in the area, was shot and killed while attempting to thwart the escape of the felons. Although the evidence as to who fired the fatal shot was conflicting in appellant's 1948 trial, the court charged the jury that it was irrelevant who fired the fatal bullet:

> "Even if you should find from the evidence that Ingling was killed by a bullet from the gun of one of the policemen, that policeman having shot at the felons in an attempt to prevent the robbery or the escape of the robbers, or to protect Ingling, the felons would be guilty of murder, or if they did that in returning the fire of the felons that was directed toward them."

1. It would be virtually impossible to catalogue all of the articles on these cases which have been published in the learned journals. Some of the more enlightening include Morris, The Felon's Responsibility for the Lethal Acts of Others, 105 U.Pa. L.Rev. 50 (1956); Ludwig, Foreseeable Death in Felony Murder, 18 U.Pitt.L.Rev. 51 (1956); and Case Notes, 71 Harv.L.Rev. 1565 (1958), and 106 U.Pa.L.Rev. 1176 (1958).

To this part of the charge appellant took a specific exception.

The jury convicted Smith of first degree murder, with punishment fixed at life imprisonment. He filed no post-trial motions, and took no appeal. Nor did Smith initiate any post conviction proceedings until the instant case, despite the litigious propensities of his co-felons.

On February 4, 1966, appellant filed the present petition for a writ of habeas corpus. . . .

. . . The court below held that appellant had knowingly waived his right to appeal, and although the opinion does not discuss the question, the denial of relief necessarily manifested a belief by the court below that appellant was aware of his right to counsel on appeal. The other issues raised by appellant were not mentioned by the court, apparently of the view that they were cognizable only if it appeared that appellant had been denied his right to appeal, and was entitled to an appeal nunc pro tunc.

We reverse, grant the writ, allow an appeal nunc pro tunc, and grant a new trial. . . .

Appellant urges that he was denied due process by virtue of the trial court's charge that it was irrelevant who fired the fatal bullet. Such a charge was consistent with the dictum of this Court in Commonwealth v. Moyer and Byron, 357 Pa. 181, 53 A.2d 736 (1947), and with the holding shortly thereafter in the appeal of appellant's co-felon, David Almeida, in Commonwealth v. Almeida, . . . (1949). In the latter case, by a stretch of the felony-murder rule, we held that Almeida could indeed be found guilty of murder even though the fatal bullet was fired by another officer acting in opposition to the felony. We adopted a proximate cause theory of murder: "[H]e whose felonious act is the *proximate* cause of another's death is *criminally* responsible for that death and must answer to society for it exactly as he who is *negligently* the *proximate cause* of another's death is civilly responsible for that death and must answer in damages for it." . . .

The proximate cause theory was taken a millimeter further by this Court in Commonwealth v. Thomas, . . . (1955). In that case the victim of an armed robbery shot and killed one of the felons, Jackson; the other felon, Thomas, was convicted of the murder.

Thomas was repudiated by this Court in Commonwealth v. Redline, . . . (1958). The facts there were virtually identical to those of *Thomas;* a policeman shot one fleeing felon and the other was convicted of murder. In a famous opinion by the late Chief Justice Charles Alvin Jones, this Court interred *Thomas* and dealt a fatal blow to *Almeida.* At the outset of this Court's opinion in *Redline,* we stated: "The decision in the Almeida case was a radical departure from common law criminal jurisprudence." The thorough documentation which followed in this lengthy opinion proved beyond a shadow of a doubt that *Almeida* and *Thomas* constituted aberrations in the annals of Anglo-American adjudicature.

Redline began with a rather general review of the entire felony-murder theory. If we may presume to elaborate a bit on that review, we should point out that the felony-murder rule really has two separate branches in Pennsylvania. The first, and the easier concept, is statutory. The Act of June 24, 1939 provides, *inter alia:* "All murder which shall ... be committed in the perpetration of, or attempting to perpetrate any arson, rape, robbery, burglary, or kidnapping, shall be murder in the first degree. All other kinds of murder shall be murder in the second degree." Clearly this statutory felony-murder rule merely serves to raise the degree of certain murders to first degree; it gives no aid to the determination of what constitutes murder in the first place. *Redline,* pointing out that except for one isolated situation there is no statutory crime of murder, directed us to the common law for a determination of what constitutes murder. It is here that the other branch of the felony-murder rule, the common law branch, comes into play. Citing Commonwealth v. Drum, 58 Pa. 9 (1868), the early leading case on murder in the Commonwealth, and Blackstone, Commentaries, *Redline* reaffirmed that the distinguishing criterion of murder is malice. The common law felony-murder rule is a means of imputing malice where it may not exist expressly. Under this rule, the malice necessary to make a killing, even an accidental one, murder, is constructively inferred from the malice incident to the perpetration of the initial felony.

The common law felony-murder rule as thus explicated has been subjected to some harsh criticism, most of it thoroughly warranted....

In fact, not only is the felony-murder rule non-essential, but it is very doubtful that it has the deterrent effect its proponents assert.[2] On the contrary, it appears that juries rebel against convictions, adopting a homemade rule against fortuities, where a conviction must result in life imprisonment.... To similar effect, Justice Oliver Wendell Holmes, in The Common Law, argued that the wise policy is not to punish the fortuity, but rather to impose severe penalties on those types of criminal activity which experience has demonstrated carry a high degree of risk to human life....

We have gone into this lengthy discussion of the felony-murder rule not for the purpose of hereby abolishing it. That is hardly necessary in the instant case. But we do want to make clear how shaky are the basic premises on which it rests. With so weak a foundation, it behooves us not to extend it further and indeed, to restrain it within the bounds it has always known. As stated above, *Redline,* ... demolished the exten-

2. See, e.g. the dissenting opinion of Justice (now Chief Justice) Bell in Commonwealth v. Redline, supra, where he stated: "The brutal crime wave which is sweeping and appalling our Country can be halted only if the Courts stop coddling, and stop freeing murderers, communists and criminals on technicalities made of straw." To similar effect is the statement in Commonwealth v. Kelly, 333 Pa. 280, 287, 4 A.2d 805 (1939): "To this Commonwealth one must answer as a malicious criminal for any fatal injury he here causes a human being by anything done by him intentionally or unintentionally during the commission or attempted commission of any of the specified felonies, for malice is the mainspring of his outlawed enterprise and his every act within the latter's ambit is imputable to that base quality. *Such a rule is essential to the protection of human life.*" (Emphasis added).

sion to the felony-murder rule made in *Almeida:* "In adjudging a felony-murder, it is to be remembered at all times that the thing which is imputed to a felon for a killing incidental to his felony is *malice* and *not the act of killing*.... 'The malice of the *initial* offense attaches to whatever else the *criminal* may do in connection therewith.' ... And so, until the decision of this court in Commonwealth v. Almeida, supra, in 1949, the rule which was uniformly followed, whether by express statement or by implication, was that in order to convict for felony-murder, *the killing must have been done by the defendant or by an accomplice or confederate or by one acting in furtherance of the felonious undertaking.* [citing a long line of cases.]

"Until the Almeida case there was no reported instance in this State of a jury ever having been instructed on the trial of an indictment for murder for a killing occurring contemporaneously with the perpetration of a felony that the defendant was guilty of murder regardless of the fact that the fatal shot was fired by a third person acting in hostility and resistance to the felon and in deliberate opposition to the success of the felon's criminal undertaking." (Emphasis in original).

Redline proceeded to discuss the cases, both within and without Pennsylvania, which establish the rule that murder is not present where the fatal shot is fired by a third person acting in opposition to the felon....

We then proceeded to distinguish the cases relied upon in *Almeida.* Chief among those cases was Commonwealth v. Moyer and Byron,.... We referred to the statement in that case to the effect that a felon can be convicted of murder if the shot is fired by the intended victim as "a palpable gratuity," since the court below had charged that the defendant was entitled to an acquittal unless the Commonwealth proved beyond a reasonable doubt that one of the felons had fired the fatal bullet. We further distinguished the cases, cited in *Almeida,* in which the death-dealing act was committed by one participating in the initial felony....

Finally, we distinguished the *express* malice cases. These included the so-called "shield" cases, where a felon used the interposition of the body of an innocent person to escape harm in flight from the scene of the crime.... These cases were not based on the felony-murder rule and imputed malice, but on the express malice found in the use of an innocent person as a shield or breastwork against hostile bullets....

This lengthy review of *Redline* should have made it clear that the cases on which *Almeida* was based did not support the result reached therein, nor do the later cases. However, *Redline,* was not limited merely to a factual explication of the cases on which *Almeida* relied. *Redline,* ... rejected the proximate cause tort analogy which Almeida found so appealing: "As we have already seen, the 'causation' requirement for responsibility in a felony-murder is that the homicide stem from the commission of the felony. Obviously, the assumed analogy between that concept and the tort-liability requirement of proximate cause is not conclusive. If it were, then the doctrine of supervening cause, which, for centuries courts have recognized and rendered operative on questions of proximate cause, would have to be considered and passed upon by the jury. But, that qualification, the Almeida case entirely disregarded."

The issue of the application of tort proximate cause principles to homicide prosecutions again arose a few years after *Redline* in Commonwealth v. Root [infra p. 501] (1961). In that case the defendant was engaged in a drag race on a public highway with another person who swerved to the left side of the road, crashed head-on into an oncoming truck, and was killed. This Court reversed Root's conviction for involuntary manslaughter, and rejected utterly the tort concept of proximate cause in criminal homicide prosecutions:

"While precedent is to be found for application of the tort law concept of 'proximate cause' in fixing responsibility for criminal homicide, the want of any rational basis for its use in determining criminal liability can no longer be properly disregarded. When proximate cause was first borrowed from the field of tort law and applied to homicide prosecutions in Pennsylvania, the concept connoted a much more direct causal relation in producing the alleged culpable result than it does today. Proximate cause, as an essential element of a tort founded in negligence, has undergone in recent times, and is still undergoing, a marked extension. More specifically, this area of civil law has been progressively liberalized in favor of claims for damages for personal injuries to which careless conduct of others can in some way be associated. To persist in applying the tort liability concept of proximate cause to prosecutions for criminal homicide after the marked expansion of *civil* liability of defendants in tort actions for negligence would be to extend possible *criminal* liability to persons chargeable with unlawful or reckless conduct in circumstances not generally considered to present the likelihood of a resultant death. . . .

After this review of *Redline,* the uninitiated might be surprised to learn that *Redline* did not specifically overrule *Almeida.* This Court did overrule *Thomas,* holding that no conviction was possible for a *justifiable* homicide where a policeman shot a felon, but "distinguished" *Almeida* on the ground that the homicide there, where an innocent third party was killed by a policeman, was only *excusable.*

The "distinction" *Redline* half-heartedly tries to draw has not escaped criticism from the commentators. While the result reached in *Redline* and most of its reasoning have met with almost unanimous approval, the *deus ex machina* ending has been condemned. One learned journal has commented:

"It seems, however, that Almeida cannot validly be distinguished from [Redline]. The probability that a felon will be killed seems at least as great as the probability that the victim will be an innocent bystander. Any distinction based on the fact that the killing of a felon by a policeman is sanctioned by the law and therefore justifiable, while the killing of an innocent bystander is merely excusable, seems unwarranted.

No criminal sanctions now attach to either in other areas of criminal law, and any distinction here would seem anomalous. Indeed, to make the result hinge on the character of the victim is, in many instances, to make it hinge on the marksmanship of resisters. Any attempt to distinguish between the cases on the theory that the cofelon assumes the risk of being killed would also be improper since this tort doctrine has no place in the criminal law in which the wrong to be redressed is a public one—a killing with the victim's consent is nevertheless murder. It is very doubtful that public desire for vengeance should alone justify a conviction of felony murder for the death of an innocent bystander when no criminal responsibility will attach for the death of a cofelon." ...

Appellant is therefore in no way precluded from asserting his claim that *Almeida* should be overruled. We thus give *Almeida* burial, taking it out of its limbo, and plunging it downward into the bowels of the earth.[3]

The order of the court below is reversed, an appeal is allowed *nunc pro tunc,* and a new trial is granted.

EAGEN, J., concurs in the result.

BELL, C.J., files a dissenting opinion.

This is the age of Crime and Criminals, and the peace-loving citizen is the forgotten man. Murder, robbery and rape are rampant, and this tidal wave of ruthless crime, violence and widespread lawlessness which too often goes unpunished is due in considerable part to recent pro-criminal decisions of the highest Courts in our State and Country. No matter how guilty a convicted criminal undoubtedly is, no matter how terrible his crime was, or how many crimes he has previously committed, the highest Courts of our Country (1) have in recent years extended and continue to *expand* the so-called rights of criminals, and (2) are completely oblivious of the rights, the security, the safety and the welfare of the law-abiding public....

The Majority specifically hold that if a killing occurs during the commission or attempted perpetration of robbery or other major felony, or during the attempted escape of one of the robbers or any of the dangerous co-felons, none of the robbers and *none of the co-felons is guilty of murder—if the fatal shot was fired by the holdup victim or by a policeman* or other law enforcement officer, or by a person attempting to prevent the robbery or the robber's (or felon's) escape, *or by anyone except one of the robbers or a co-felon.* This decision, which is so disastrous to Society, is reached by unrealistic, and at times far-fetched reasoning which together with its predecessor, Commonwealth v. Redline, ... which it expands, will produce the most harmful damage to law-

3. See fn # 14, ... of the Dissenting Opinion in *Redline,* where Justice (now Chief Justice) Bell laments: "In the majority opinion, Commonwealth v. Almeida, like Mohammed's coffin, is suspended between Heaven and earth. However, unlike Mohammed's coffin, which is headed upward toward Heaven, the coffin containing Commonwealth v. Almeida is pointed downward in preparation for a speedy flight into the bowels of the earth."

abiding citizens ever inflicted sua sponte by the Supreme Court of Pennsylvania....

For ages, it has been the well-settled and wisely-established law that when a person intentionally commits or joins or conspires with another to commit a felonious act, or sets or joins another in setting in motion a chain of circumstances the natural and probable or reasonably foreseeable result of which will be death or serious bodily harm to some person, he and his co-felons are guilty of the crime which was a product or result of the aforesaid criminal act or chain of circumstances. If the felon or co-felons possessed legal malice, and death resulted, all the felons who participated in the felonious act or in the aforesaid chain of circumstances would be guilty of murder.

In the leading case of Commonwealth v. Moyer and Commonwealth v. Byron, 357 Pa. 181, 53 A.2d 736, the Court unanimously held that every person who committed or attempted to commit a felony such as robbery, or feloniously participated therein, was guilty of murder in the first degree, even though the fatal bullet is fired by the intended victim in repelling the robbery. Chief Justice Maxey, speaking for a unanimous Court, relevantly and wisely said (pages 190–191, 53 A.2d pages 741–742):

"The doctrine that when malice is the mainspring of a criminal act the actor will be held responsible for any consequence of his act though it was not the one intended was recognized centuries ago when it was held that, quoting from Blackstone, Book IV, page 1599, Sec. 201, 'if one shoots at A and misses him, but kills B, this is murder, because of the previous felonious intent, *which the law transfers from one to the other.*' (Italics supplied.) It is equally consistent with reason and sound public policy to hold that when a felon's attempt to commit robbery or burglary sets in motion a chain of events which were or should have been within his contemplation when the motion was initiated, he should be held responsible for any death which by direct and almost inevitable sequence results from the initial criminal act. For any individual forcibly to defend himself or his family or his property from criminal aggression is a primal human instinct. It is the right and duty of both individuals and nations to meet criminal aggression with effective countermeasures. Every robber or burglar knows when he attempts to commit his crime that he is inviting dangerous resistance. Any robber or burglar who carries deadly weapons (as most of them do and as these robbers did) thereby reveals that he expects to meet and overcome forcible opposition.... Every robber or burglar knows that a likely later act in the chain of events he inaugurates will be the use of deadly force against him on the part of the selected victim. For whatever results follow from that natural and legal use of retaliating force, the felon must be held responsible. For Earl Shank, the proprietor of a gas station in Ridley Township, Delaware County, which at 11 P.M. on July 13, 1946, was being attacked by armed robbers, to return the fire of these robbers with a pistol which he had at hand was as proper and as inevitable as it was for the American forces at Pearl Harbor on the morning of December 7,

1941, to return the fire of the Japanese invaders. The Japanese felonious invasion of the Hawaiian Islands on that date was in law and morals the proximate cause of all the resultant fatalities. The Moyer-Byron felonious invasion of the Shank gas station on July 13, 1946, was likewise the proximate cause of the resultant fatality." ...

In Commonwealth v. Lowry, ... we held that the driver of the alleged get-away car was guilty of first-degree murder, and in an unanimous Opinion said: "Where a killing occurs in the course of a robbery, all who participate in the robbery including the driver of the get-away car are equally guilty of murder in the first degree even though some one other than the defendant fired the fatal shot...."

In Commonwealth v. Robb, the defendant was indicted and convicted of murder. He was a lookout and had nothing to do with the burglary or the murder. The Court said: "If defendants 'combine to commit a felony or make an assault, and, in carrying out the common purpose, another is killed, the one who enters into the combination but does not personally commit the wrongful act is equally responsible for the homicide with the one who directly causes it.'" ...

In Commonwealth v. Bolish ... this Court said: "We may thus summarize what has become the settled law of Pennsylvania: If a person with legal malice commits an act or sets off a chain of events from which, in the common experience of mankind, the death of another is a natural or reasonably foreseeable result, that person is guilty of murder, if death results from that act or from the events which it naturally produced. If the original malicious act was arson, rape, robbery, burglary or kidnapping, the original actor is guilty of murder in the first degree."....

Mr. Justice Cardozo in "The Nature of the Judicial Process," wisely said: "When they [judges] are called upon to say how far existing rules are to be extended or restricted, they must let the welfare of society fix the path, its direction and its distance.... The final cause of law is the welfare of society...."

Blackstone, ...: "If a man, however, does such an act of which the probable consequences may be, and eventually is, death; such killing may be murder, although no stroke be struck by himself and no killing primarily intended."

All of the aforesaid cases were actually or in practical effect overruled when there was a change of personnel in the Supreme Court of Pennsylvania, at which time they ignored all the reasoning and the principles and the prior decisions of this Court and changed the law and decided Commonwealth v. Redline, 391 Pa. 486, 137 A.2d 472. This was until today, I repeat, the most damaging blow to the protection and safety of Society ever delivered by the Supreme Court of Pennsylvania.

For all of the reasons hereinabove mentioned, I very vigorously dissent.

The decision of the Majority giving Smith a new trial—Smith never took any kind of appeal or any post-conviction petition until the present appeal—is inexcusably unfair and unjust to Almeida and Hough, whose repeated petitions for a new trial and their appeals from the judgment of sentence of murder were rejected and dismissed by this Court.

It has often been said that "Justice is blind," meaning thereby that Justice is absolutely fair to each and every one and is not subject to any outside influence whatsoever. In this case, Justice is certainly blind, but its blindness is real and realistic and not figurative blindness, and what it erroneously terms "Justice" is "gross injustice."

NOTES

1. The *Redline* rationale was adopted in People v. Morris, 1 Ill.App.3d 566, 274 N.E.2d 898 (1971), holding that the felony-murder doctrine is not applicable to convict the surviving felon when his accomplice was justifiably killed during the commission of a forcible felony. However, in People v. Hickman, 59 Ill.2d 89, 319 N.E.2d 511 (1974), the Illinois Supreme Court specifically rejected the approach of *Redline* and Commonwealth ex rel. Smith v. Myers as well as that reached in Taylor v. Superior Court of Alameda County (infra Note 3), and held that a felony murder conviction is possible for fleeing perpetrators of a forcible felony when a pursuing police officer is shot by a fellow officer. In discussing the cases cited above, the court stated, "Our statutory and case law, however, dictate a different, and we believe preferable, result."

Other state courts hold that their felony-murder statutes should apply only when an innocent person is killed, and not when the deceased is one of the felons. See Campbell v. State, 293 Md. 438, 444 A.2d 1034 (1982) (collecting cases). State v. Bonner, 330 N.C. 536, 411 S.E.2d 598 (1992) (same). Compare State v. Branson, 487 N.W.2d 880 (Minn.1992) (no felony murder when bystander is killed by police).

New York had decided in the early 1960s that no felony murder could be found where neither the defendant nor a co-defendant fired the fatal shot. In 1965 the Legislature sought to change the rule and, after years of controversy the highest court of New York held that the Legislature had succeeded, and that it was consistent with fundamental principles of criminal law to convict a felon for murder even though the bullet that caused a police officer's death was fired by another officer. People v. Santana, 82 N.Y.2d 309, 604 N.Y.S.2d 524, 624 N.E.2d 661 (1993).

2. In People v. Washington, 62 Cal.2d 777, 44 Cal.Rptr. 442, 402 P.2d 130 (1965), the defendant was convicted of murder for participating in a robbery in which his accomplice was killed by the victim of the robbery. Upon his appeal he urged the court to confine a felon's homicide responsibility to situations where the victim was an *innocent* person. Here, of course, the person killed was one of the felons. Although ultimately reversing the defendant's conviction the majority of the California Supreme Court (per Chief Justice Traynor) expressed the view that a distinction based upon a consideration of the person killed would make the defendant's criminal liability turn upon the marksmanship of the police and the victims of the felony during which the killing occurred. The court preferred to face up to the basic issue as to whether a felon can be convicted of murder for the killing of *any* person by another who is resisting the robbery; and it held that there could be no conviction in such instances. It interpreted the language of the California felony-murder statute to mean that for a killing to occur in the "perpetration", or in an "attempt to perpetrate" a felony, it had to be done by one of the felons; in other words, in furtherance of the felony. The

court rejected the causation theory upon which the opposite result would have been reached. Also, as regards the prosecution's contention that responsibility for any death would serve to prevent dangerous felonies, the court said:

"Neither the common-law rationale of the rule nor the Penal Code supports this contention. In every robbery there is a possibility that the victim will resist and kill. The robber has little control over such a killing once the robbery is undertaken as this case demonstrates. To impose an additional penalty for the killing would discriminate between robbers, not on the basis of any difference in their own conduct, but solely on the basis of the response by others that the robber's conduct happened to induce. An additional penalty for a homicide committed by the victim would deter robbery haphazardly at best."

Two justices dissented; they expressed the view that the rule adopted by the court contained the following implicit advice to would-be felons:

"Henceforth in committing certain crimes, including robbery, rape and burglary, you are free to arm yourselves with a gun and brandish it in the faces of your victims without fear of a murder conviction unless you or your accomplice pulls the trigger. If the menacing effect of your gun causes a victim or policeman to fire and kill an innocent person or a cofelon, you are absolved of responsibility for such killing unless you shoot first."

They added:

"Obviously this advance judicial absolution removes one of the most meaningful deterrents to the commission of armed felonies."

3. On the other hand, in Taylor v. Superior Court, 3 Cal.3d 578, 477 P.2d 131 (1970), a sharply divided California Supreme Court upheld the conviction of murder of the driver of a getaway car where one of his accomplices, who were engaged in a robbery and assault with a deadly weapon, was shot and killed by the robbery victim. The court cited with approval the following language from its earlier case of People v. Gilbert:

> When the defendant or his accomplice, with a conscious disregard for life, intentionally commits an act that is likely to cause death, and his victim or a police officer kills in reasonable response to such act, the defendant is guilty of murder. In such a case, the killing is attributable, not merely to the commission of a felony, but to the intentional act of the defendant or his accomplice committed with conscious disregard for life.

4. In People v. Phillips, 42 Cal.Rptr. 868 (Cal.App.1965), the California District Court of Appeal refused to extend what it called the "archaic and much criticized" felony-murder doctrine to non-dangerous felonies. Here a chiropractor falsely induced the parents of a child who had cancer of the eye to forego surgery and accept his "treatments" for a considerable fee. The child died and defendant was found guilty of murder in the second degree. Defendant's conviction was reversed because of the error of giving a felony-murder instruction.

Similarly, the felony of possession of a concealed firearm by a felon was deemed not in itself to be a felony inherently dangerous to human life. It was therefore deemed improper to dispense with the requirement of proof of malice for murder. People v. Satchell, 6 Cal.3d 28, 98 Cal.Rptr. 33, 489 P.2d 1361 (1971). The felony of escape from a county jail was another offense which was deemed incapable as serving as a basis for the imputation of malice aforethought in a murder prosecution. People v. Lopez, 6 Cal.3d 45, 98 Cal.Rptr. 44, 489 P.2d

1372 (1971). Selling liquor, under circumstances amounting to a felony, to a purchaser who became drunk and died from exposure, was found not to be an act in itself directly and naturally dangerous to life sufficient to support a murder conviction. People v. Pavlic, 227 Mich. 562, 199 N.W. 373 (1924).

5. Where an offender seizes hostages to be used as shields, and one of the hostages is killed by a policeman or other victim of the crime, the felony-murder rule applies. Thus, in Johnson v. State, 482 S.W.2d 600 (Ark.1972), a burglar who had been discovered seized the daughter of the householder as a shield. A struggle ensued in the course of which the householder shot his daughter. The murder conviction was upheld because the defendant had placed the deceased in the perilous position. Also, to the same effect: Pizano v. Superior Ct., 145 Cal.Rptr. 524, 21 Cal.3d 128, 577 P.2d 659 (1978).

6. Some states list or define, in their statutes, the felonies which trigger the applicability of the felony-murder rule. The California Penal Code, in § 189, includes among its first degree murders killings occurring during the commission or attempted commission of "arson, rape, robbery, burglary, mayhem, or any act punishable under Section 288 [lewd or lascivious acts, willfully and lewdly committed upon children under 14]." Pennsylvania, on the other hand, views felony-murder in a broader context and considers such acts essentially murders in the second degree. Purdon's Penna.Consol.Stats.Ann. 18 § 2502, in subsection (b), provides: "(b) Murder of the second degree.—A criminal homicide constitutes murder of the second degree when it is committed while defendant was engaged as a principal or an accomplice in the perpetration of a felony."

Illinois defines the crimes which give rise to felony-murder charges in a way which is much broader than do Virginia and California, supra, but not so broad as the Pennsylvania statute. 720 ILCS 5/9–1(a)(3) (Illinois) defines as felony-murders those killings which occur during the commission or attempted commission of "a forcible felony other than second degree murder." § 2–8 defines "forcible felonies" as "treason, first degree murder, second degree murder, aggravated criminal sexual assault, criminal sexual assault, robbery, burglary, arson, kidnaping, aggravated battery *and any other felony which involves the use or threat of physical force or violence against any individual.*" (Emphasis supplied.)

Virginia, apart from its first degree murder statute (a Class 2 felony), also has a separate Class 3 felony offense called Felony Homicide, which is defined as, "The killing of one accidentally, contrary to the intention of the parties, while in the prosecution of some felonious act other than those specified in §§ 18.2–31 [capital murders] and 18.2–32 [first degree murders]." Va.Code § 18.2–33.

7. Is it felony murder if the perpetrator commits arson and a firefighter dies while battling the blaze if the reason for the death was the firefighter's failure to get a new air bottle after the air bottle exhaustion alarm sounded in his air mask? See State v. Leech, 114 Wash.2d 700, 790 P.2d 160 (1990).

PEOPLE v. SALAS

Supreme Court of California, 1972.
7 Cal.3d 812, 103 Cal.Rptr. 431, 500 P.2d 7.

WRIGHT, CHIEF JUSTICE.

* * *

On the morning of June 7, 1968, five or ten minutes after midnight, defendant entered the Hub Bar in Sacramento and asked the bartender,

George Finnegan, for a six-pack of beer. After Finnegan reached into the cooler for the beer he saw that defendant was pointing a pistol directly at him. David Wright, a customer, and Richard Schwab, an insurance salesman who entered the bar at this moment, were ordered to lie down on the floor at the back of the barroom. Defendant then ordered Finnegan to deliver all the money in the bar's cash register.

The cash register had two drawers and after Finnegan had emptied the contents of one of them (amounting to about $150) into a cloth bank bag, defendant asked, "How about the the other drawer on the register?" Upon being satisfied that the second drawer was empty defendant took the bank bag, ordered Finnegan to lie down near the other men, told them not to move or he would shoot them and backed out of the front door.

Defendant had been driven to the bar by Arlin Damion, a friend who remained in the car during the robbery. When defendant emerged from the bar and entered the vehicle on the passenger's side of the front seat, Damion drove away.

Shortly after midnight Deputy Sheriff George O'Neal received a radio broadcast advising that the Hub Bar had just been robbed. He immediately drove his patrol car three-tenths of a mile to an intersection 1.2 miles from the bar. He knew that this intersection was on a route frequently used by robbers in making escapes from the general area. Just as he reached the intersection he saw an approaching car with two men who appeared to be of Mexican descent. The car approached from the direction of the bar and was the only vehicle in sight. The deputy followed the car and was then advised by radio that the suspect was a "male Mexican." After further radio communication the deputy activated the red light and siren of the police vehicle and the suspects eventually stopped their vehicle.

The deputy halted his patrol car about 15 to 18 feet behind the suspects' car, stepped out and shouted to the two men to put their hands out of the car windows. Neither suspect responded to the demand; the deputy thereupon reached for his shotgun. Damion opened the door on the driver's side of his car and fled on foot into an open field. Defendant, however, did not respond to the officer's further demands.

A second deputy sheriff, Kenneth B. Royal, arrived in his patrol car. Royal drew his service revolver and walked toward the suspects' car on the driver's side. O'Neal heard shots fired and saw Royal fall to the ground. Defendant emerged from the car on the passenger's side with a gun in his hand. O'Neal fired his shotgun at defendant. Defendant fell to the ground and then arose. Royal fired his revolver, and O'Neal fired his shotgun a second time. Defendant again fell to the ground, but once more got up and continued down the road away from the deputies. Defendant fell to the ground again and was then apprehended by another officer who had arrived at the scene. Royal died of a single gunshot wound in the neck.

* * *

We deal next with defendant's contention that, as a matter of law, the robbery had been completed prior to the time of and at a different place than the killing; that the homicide therefore could not have been committed in the course of the robbery within the felony-murder rule and that the trial court erred in instructing the jury on such rule. Defendant further contends that, even assuming that instructions on the felony-murder rule were appropriate, it was error for the court to refuse to define the term "scrambling possession" as applied to the proceeds of the robbery when requested to do so by the jury.

Section 189, which establishes the limits of the felony-first-degree-murder rule, provides that all "murder ... which is committed in the perpetration of, or attempt to perpetrate ... robbery ... is murder of the first degree...." Our particular concern is whether the killing of the deputy after defendant had been stopped while fleeing from the scene of the robbery, was a killing in the "perpetration" of the robbery. The trial court gave four instructions which we have numbered and set forth in the margin concerning the time within which a robbery is still in progress for purposes of application of the felony-murder rule.[1]

After retiring to deliberate, the jury returned to the court requesting further instructions on ... the law applying to "zone of danger," that is, how long a felony continues in progress. Included in the instructions read by the court pursuant to the request were the four instructions heretofore quoted. Some of them, after questions by the jurors, were read more than once. Two jurors requested that the court define "scrambling." The court, after saying that the dictionary definition

1. (1) "A robbery is still in commission while the perpetrator is being pursued immediately after the commission of the act of taking the property of another by force or fear with the fruits of the crime in his possession so long as the culprit has not won his way even momentarily to a place of temporary safety and the possession of the plunder is nothing more than a scrambling possession."

(2) "A robbery is still in commission during the continuous, integrated attempt to successfully leave with the loot."

(3) "If the robbery has been completed and terminated prior to the killing, then the robbery may not be used to find the defendant guilty of murder of the first degree. Whether the killing was committed during the perpetration of the robbery must be decided by the jury.

"A robbery is still being committed, no matter how far from the scene of the robbery, nor how long afterward, if the robber has not won his way even momentarily to a place of temporary safety and the possession of the plunder is nothing more than a scrambling possession." (This instruction was given at defendant's request.)

(4) "If the robbery has been completed and terminated prior to the killing then the robbery may not be used to find the defendant guilty of the murder of the first degree. On the other hand, the unlawful killing of a human being which is committed in the perpetration or attempt to perpetrate robbery, the commission of which crime itself must be proved beyond a reasonable doubt, is murder of the first degree whether the killing was intentional, unintentional or even accidental.

"Whether the killing was committed during the perpetration of robbery must be decided by the jury.

"A robbery is still being committed no matter how far from the scene of the robbery nor how long afterward if the robber has not won his way, even momentarily, to a place of temporary safety. That is to say, that a robbery is not completed at the moment the robber obtains possession of the stolen property, but is still in progress during the robber's attempt to escape with the loot. In other words, the escape of the robbers with the loot is a part of the robbery itself." (This instruction was given at the request of the prosecution.)

would not help and that the jurors should consider the word in the context of a person fleeing from the scene of a robbery with the plunder. Approximately two hours later, the jury again returned and a juror asked the court to reread the instructions in connection with whether the robbery was in progress. The court read the instructions designated as (1) through (4) in footnote [1] several times enabling the jurors to write them down. The jury deliberated for a little more than an hour before retiring for the night and returned its verdict shortly after reconvening the following morning.

Instructions (1) and (3) appear to require that the jury find *both* that the robber did not win his way to a "place of temporary safety" *and* that his possession of the plunder was no more than a "scrambling possession" before it could find that the robbery was still in progress. Instruction (1) further requires pursuit "immediately" after the physical taking of the property. Instructions (2) and (4), on the other hand, appear to require that the jury find only that the robber did not win his way to a "place of temporary safety"—that is, that the robber was still attempting to escape—to find that the robbery was still in progress.

The phrases "place of temporary safety" and "scrambling possession" are derived from the landmark case of People v. Boss (1930) 210 Cal. 245, 290 P. 881. In that case two defendants robbed a store and ran into the street; an employee immediately pursued them and was shot by Boss a moment later when the furthermost defendant was no more than 125 feet from the store. We held that the trial court properly instructed the jury as to first degree felony murder as the homicide was committed in the perpetration of a robbery and we stated: "It is a sound principle of law which inheres in common reason that where two or more persons engaged in a conspiracy to commit robbery and an officer or citizen is murdered while in immediate pursuit of one of their number who is fleeing from the scene of the crime with the fruits thereof in his possession, or in the possession of a coconspirator, the crime is not complete in the purview of the law, inasmuch as said conspirators have not won their way even momentarily to a place of temporary safety and the possession of the plunder is nothing more than a scrambling possession. In such a case the continuation of the use of arms which was necessary to aid the felon in reducing the property to possession is necessary to protect him in its possession and in making good his escape. Robbery, unlike burglary, is not confined to a fixed *locus,* but is frequently spread over considerable distance and varying periods of time. The escape of the robbers with the loot, by means of arms, necessarily is as important to the execution of the plan as gaining possession of the property. Without revolvers to terrify, or, if occasion requires, to kill any person, who attempts to apprehend them at the time of or immediately upon gaining possession of said property, their plan would be childlike. The defense of felonious possession which is challenged immediately upon the forcible taking is a part of the plan of robbery, or, as the books express it, it is *res gestae* of the crime."

* * *

The great majority of felony-murder rule cases involving robbery as the underlying felony decided by this court since *Boss* involve fact situations with both elements, continuous flight (lack of a "place of temporary safety") and continuous challenging pursuit ("scrambling possession") and generally set forth the language of *Boss* without further analysis. Thus these cases do little to clarify the question whether *both* elements are required for a robbery to be considered continuing for purposes of the felony-murder rule.

In People v. Kendrick (1961) 56 Cal.2d 71, 14 Cal.Rptr. 13, 363 P.2d 13, however, the element of "scrambling possession" was clearly missing. It was nevertheless held in that case that instructions on the felony-murder rule were properly given when the killing occurred about 48 minutes after the robbery victim had first been accosted by the defendant and when the police officer who was fatally shot by the defendant had apparently stopped him for a traffic violation and had no information about the robbery. We ignored the language in *Boss* concerning "place of temporary safety" and "scrambling possession" and quoted that part of *Boss* which stresses the importance of "[t]he escape ... with the loot ... to the execution of the plan,".... Although not expressly so described, the "rule" as applied in *Kendrick* required only the element of the defendant's failure to have reached a "place of temporary safety."

People v. Ketchel (1963) 59 Cal.2d 503, 30 Cal.Rptr. 538, 381 P.2d 394 involved a fact situation with both elements present: "place of temporary safety" and "scrambling possession." Defendants attempted to bring themselves within *Boss* and relied upon the language in that case which spoke of both "a place of temporary safety" and "scrambling possession." In rejecting their contention we relied only upon facts which established that the defendants had not reached a place of temporary safety and ignored the element of scrambling possession. That case like *Kendrick* must stand for the proposition that a fleeing robber's failure to reach a place of temporary safety is alone sufficient to establish the continuity of the robbery within the felony-murder rule.

In the present case as in *Ketchel,* the homicide was committed before defendant had reached a place of safety while he "was in hot flight with the stolen property and in the belief that the officer was about to arrest him for the robbery." Deputy O'Neal commenced to follow defendant's vehicle within three minutes of the time defendant left the bar and the killing occurred within six or seven minutes of that time. Thus the robbery was still in the escape stage, as conceded by defendant at trial. Defendant testified not only that he was caught while attempting to escape with the loot, but also that he did not know whether he would split the loot with Damion as they had had no opportunity to make that determination.

Under the circumstances here present and even if the killing were accidental or unintentional as contended by defendant, it occurred while the robbery continued in progress and constituted first degree murder under the felony-murder rule. Although the introduction in the instructions to the jury of concepts of immediate pursuit together with scrambling possession and the court's refusal to define "scrambling possession" may have been erroneous, no prejudice resulted to defendant as in any event the jurors were compelled to find that the homicide was committed before defendant had reached a place of safety. The introduction of the pursuit and scrambling concepts did in fact confer benefits to which defendant was not entitled.

Defendant's various attacks upon the propriety of the penalty trial proceedings are rendered moot by our decision in People v. Anderson, supra, 6 Cal.3d 628, 100 Cal.Rptr. 152, 493 P.2d 880, holding that the death penalty may not be constitutionally imposed.

The judgment, insofar as it provides for the penalty of death, is modified to provide in place of the death penalty a punishment of life imprisonment and as so modified is affirmed in all other respects.

TOBRINER, MOSK, BURKE, and SULLIVAN, JJ., concur.

PETERS, J., dissenting.

I dissent.

The majority have extended the felony-murder rule and repudiated in part the landmark decision in People v. Boss (1930) 210 Cal. 245, 290 P. 881. I would adhere to the decision in *Boss,* and when this is done, it is clear that prejudicial error occurred in instructing the jury on the felony-murder doctrine thus requiring reversal of the judgment.

Section 189 of the Penal Code, which establishes the felony-first-degree-murder rule, provides that all "murder . . . which is committed in the perpetration of, or attempt to perpetrate . . . robbery . . . is murder of the first degree; . . . ."

Section 211 of the Penal Code defines robbery as "the felonious taking of personal property in the possession of another, from his person or immediate presence, and against his will, accomplished by means of force or fear."

A literal reading of the sections, in light of the requirement of commission in the perpetration of the robbery and in light of the definition of robbery, would mean that the homicide must occur during the taking of the property and prior to the termination of the force and fear by which the taking was accomplished.

However, this court rejected a literal construction of the two statutes in People v. Boss, supra, and established a broader rule for determining whether a homicide occurred in the perpetration of the robbery or after its termination. In expanding the operation of the felony-murder rule in the robbery situation, the court in *Boss* established two limitations on the continuation of the robbery. Today, the majority repudiate one of the limitations and to that extent overrule *Boss*. I cannot agree with the further expansion of the felony-murder doctrine. . . .

The court [in *Boss*] thus established two requirements to establish that the robbery was not complete. First, there must be "immediate pursuit" which means that the possession is merely a "scrambling possession." This limitation finds some support in the language of the robbery statute because, so long as there is "immediate pursuit" and a mere "scrambling possession," it can be argued that the "taking" of the property is not complete because it is being physically disputed. Second, the robbers must not have reached "a place of temporary safety."

The majority today recognize but repudiate the first limitation, holding that the sole test is a place of temporary safety. In doing so, the majority rely upon People v. Ketchel, 59 Cal.2d 503, 30 Cal.Rptr. 538, 381 P.2d 394, and People v. Kendrick, 56 Cal.2d 71, 14 Cal.Rptr. 13, 363 P.2d 13. *Ketchel,* however, on its facts involved a homicide which occurred within both limitations. There was immediate pursuit with the resulting mere scrambling possession, and the robbers had not reached a place of temporary safety. Although the court spoke only of the failure to reach a place of temporary safety in connection with the defendants' contention, this was because the defendants' contention was based on the temporary-safety language in *Boss*. There was no intent to depart from the immediate pursuit and scrambling possession limitation, the court in fact quoted that limitation from *Boss.*

It is true that in *Kendrick* there was no immediate pursuit or scrambling possession and that the court, although citing and relying upon *Boss,* merely relied upon the failure of the robber to reach a point of temporary safety in upholding instructions on the felony-murder rule. However, I do not believe that *Kendrick* may be viewed as substantial authority warranting repudiation of the limitation of immediate pursuit and scrambling possession and of *Boss* and the numerous cases which have followed it. The defendant in that case urged that the homicide was too distant in time and place to classify it as having occurred during perpetration of the robbery. So far as appears, the defendant did not rely on the limitation of immediate pursuit and scrambling possession, and in answering the specific contention of defendant, it was proper to point out that *Boss* had established a rule which meant that it was not determinative that the homicide occurred some distance from the robbery and sometime later. Under the circumstances, it seems improper to hold that the court intended to repudiate one of the requirements of *Boss,* the case which was quoted from and principally relied upon.

Apart from their reliance on *Ketchel* and *Kendrick,* the majority give no reason to repudiate the first limitation of *Boss,* and in my view, those cases provide a weak foundation for the majority's action. . . .

The felony-murder doctrine ascribes malice aforethought to the felon who kills in the perpetration of an inherently dangerous felony and classifies the offense as murder of the first degree in homicides which are the direct result of those six felonies enumerated in section 189 of the Penal Code. . . .

"The felony-murder rule has been criticized on the grounds that in almost all cases in which it is applied it is unnecessary and that it erodes the relation between criminal liability and moral culpability." (People v. Washington, 62 Cal.2d 777, 783, 44 Cal.Rptr. 442, 446, 402 P.2d 130, 134.) The rule has been abolished in England where it had its origin (English Homicide Act, § 1, 1957, 5 & 6 Eliz. II, ch. 11.) We have recently pointed out that the rule "expresses a highly artificial concept that deserves no extension beyond its required application." (People v. Phillips, 64 Cal.2d 574, 582, 51 Cal.Rptr. 225, 232, 414 P.2d 353, 360.) Although the rule remains the law in this state, I do not believe we should extend its applicability by broadly defining the term robbery; instead in furtherance of the policy to equate criminal liability with culpability we should strictly limit the meaning of the term robbery as used in section 189.

To extend the felony-murder rule until the robber has reached a place of temporary safety, without regard to whether the decedent is a victim or witness of the crime and without regard to whether there has been a break in the pursuit, would mean that the death of victims of automobile collisions or of pedestrians occurring accidentally during an escape may constitute first degree murder. In the absence of a direct pursuit by victims or witnesses, such a broad application of the first degree felony-murder rule to accidental killings is not in accord with the purpose of the rule or the language of the statutes.

Once we depart from the literal definition of robbery in section 211 of the Penal Code, any test that might be used to determine whether a robbery is complete for purposes of the felony-murder rule is necessarily arbitrary. The place of temporary safety, or continuous flight, test is not directly related either to the increased foreseeable danger caused by the robbery or to the robber's motive in seeking to escape detection. The increased risk of a killing occurring due to the commission of the robbery continues long after the robber reaches a place of temporary safety for he will continue to have the motive to kill to escape apprehension. In other words, the risk of injury or death to investigating officers seeking to apprehend the criminal may relate to whether the robber has the loot, is armed, or anticipates conviction, but it bears little relationship to whether the robber has reached a place of temporary safety.

A test based solely on place of temporary safety makes the *length* of the escape route the decisive consideration. If the robber leaves the scene of the robbery and reaches his hideout or home near the scene, the felony-murder rule is inapplicable under the place-of-temporary-safety test whether he is armed or still in possession of the loot, but if he must cross the city to his hideout and the homicide occurs prior to his doing so, the test would make the felony-murder rule applicable although the robber was not armed, he had lost or disposed of the loot, a pedestrian was killed, and the homicide occurred a substantial time after the taking of the property and the termination of the force and fear incident to it....

On the other hand, the limitation to immediate pursuit and scrambling possession, as we have seen, finds some support in the definition of robbery in section 211 of the Penal Code. Although this court may refuse to adhere to the literal wording of the statute as was done in *Boss* and the case following it, we should not ignore the terms of the statute entirely. Where there is immediate pursuit by victims or witnesses of the taking or of the force and fear used in the robbery, the risk of injury or death is greatly increased, and it is not the same risk as exists with regard to apprehension occurring subsequent to the taking....

Accordingly, I would not repudiate either of the limitations established in *Boss* and the cases which have followed it.

As the majority point out, the evidence in the instant case is sufficient to warrant a finding of first degree murder on a theory of premeditation.... The felony-murder instructions, however, permitted a finding of first degree murder even if the shooting was inadvertent or unintentional, and in view of the jury's express concern with the felony-murder instructions, the error must be held prejudicial.

I would reverse the judgment.

NOTES

1. A determination of this issue has varied among the state courts. Consider the early case of Commonwealth v. Doris, 287 Pa. 547, 135 A. 313 (1926). Doris and three companions robbed the occupants of a bank car transporting funds. In the course of the robbery, Doris was captured; however, his companions fled from the scene. In the chase that followed, one of the pursuing policemen was shot and killed by the felons, who were captured a short time thereafter. Doris was separately tried, convicted of first degree murder committed "in the perpetration of ... robbery", and sentenced to death. The Pennsylvania Supreme Court affirmed. "The proof of the common purpose to take, by force, the money of the bank, carry it away, and make a safe escape, may be inferred from the attending circumstances. Whether such a criminal intent existed was a question for the jury, and the evidence warranted their conclusion.... It is urged that the escape and flight are not to be considered as part of the perpetration of the robbery, which, it is claimed, had been completed ... and thereafter no responsibility attached to any individual for the act of the other.... Whether the act of departing is a continuous part of the attempted or accomplished crime is for the jury."

Also consider the subsequent Pennsylvania case of Commonwealth v. DeMoss, 401 Pa. 395, 165 A.2d 14 (1960), in which the felony-murder was applied to convict for murder a robbery conspirator who was in another state at the time of the robbery-murder.

2. In People v. Walsh, 262 N.Y. 140, 186 N.E. 422 (1933), two robbers were convicted of felony-murder in a case situation where one of the other robbers shot and killed a police officer while making his escape, even though his co-felony defendants were under arrest and lying down on the floor of the premises when the fatal shot was fired.

THE LINDBERGH–HAUPTMANN CASE

"During the evening of March 1, 1932, between the hours of eight and ten o'clock, little Charles A. Lindbergh, Jr., disappeared from the home of his parents at East Amwell, New Jersey. In the baby's room was left a letter, demanding $50,000 in ransom, and stating that later instructions as to the method of payment and the return of the child would be forthcoming. Immediately negotiations were begun by the child's father, through one Dr. J.F. Condon, with supposed agents of the child's abductors, during the course of which the baby's sleeping suit was sent by mail to Condon as evidence that the family was 'dealing with the right parties.' Subsequently, on April 2, the ransom was paid, in marked money, to a man who met Condon in a cemetery in the Bronx, New York. The baby was never returned. On May 12 his body was found in the adjoining county of Mercer, several miles from the home of his parents. An autopsy disclosed that the child had suffered three violent fractures of the skull, and that death had been instantaneous.

"As a result of investigations covering many months, the defendant was arrested on October 8, 1934, and indicted for first-degree murder. The indictment charged the killing of a human being during the commission of a burglary. On this charge he was convicted and sentenced to death. Held: on appeal, affirmed. There was adequate evidence to establish common-law burglary and a killing resulting therefrom: State v. Hauptmann, 115 N.J.L. 412, 180 A. 809 (1935)." [1]

The burglary with which the defendant was charged in the indictment was breaking and entering the Lindbergh home, in the nighttime, with intent to steal *the sleeping suit of the child.* Legally, Hauptmann was electrocuted because he caused the death of a child in the course of stealing its sleeping suit.

Why did the result in the Hauptmann case rest upon such a technicality? Although any child kidnapping case attracts a great deal of public attention, there was an added factor here: the victim was the son of the famous Charles A. Lindbergh, the first person to fly the Atlantic Ocean alone, and his flight was only six years old in the public memory. Accordingly, the public demanded a death penalty. In this regard, however, the prosecution was faced with several difficulties. Kidnapping itself was only a "high misdemeanor" in New Jersey and not punishable with death. The death penalty could be awarded only for premeditated murder, common law felony murder, and statutory felony murder—the killing of another during the commission of (or attempt to commit) arson, burglary, rape, robbery or sodomy. Since the state had no evidence that Hauptmann had a preconceived intent to kill the child, and accordingly could not proceed on the theory of premeditated murder, the prosecution was forced to seek a conviction of felony murder, either at common law or under the statute. Since kidnapping was not among the crimes enumerated in the felony murder statute, and inasmuch as it was not a felony under the common law, a killing arising out of a kidnapping would not sustain a death penalty sentence. Accordingly, the prosecution's only possible course lay in charging that the killing occurred

1. The foregoing statement of facts is taken from a student comment on this case which appeared in 26 J.Crim.L. & C. 759 (1935).

during the commission of a burglary, although the only thing which Hauptmann took in addition to the child (who, under the common law, could not be a subject of larceny) was the sleeping suit it wore.

The defense contended that the evidence did not show the commission of a burglary. It was argued that there was no evidence of the required intent to steal the sleeping garment, since it was surrendered by the defendant of his own volition. It was held, however, that the evidence showed the commission of a burglary, in that the jury could find that the defendant took the sleeping suit for his own advantage in furthering the plan of extortion, and that he would not have returned the sleeping suit had the preliminaries of the extortion been unsuccessful.

Thus the felony murder doctrine, possibly stretched to the utmost limits of application, was employed to obtain the result desired by the prosecution and demanded by public sentiment. The case affords an interesting study of the effect a heinous offense may have upon judicial reasoning and the criminal law generally.

NOTES

1. Modern kidnaping statutes typically are felonies, thereby avoiding the dilemma created for the prosecution in the *Hauptmann* case.

2. An interesting sequel to the *Hauptmann* case developed almost fifty years after his trial and execution. In 1982, his widow filed a $100,000,000 suit against the State of New Jersey based upon her claim that he was innocent of any involvement in the crime.

Prior to the filing of the suit, but after legal action had been taken to obtain access to the New Jersey State Police files, a lengthy article appeared in the press of October 10, 1981, under the title: "Lindbergh Case Still on Trial in Many Minds," written by Stephen Salisbury. Among the papers that carried it was the Chicago Tribune, in which the distinct impression was created that Hauptmann was innocent. A similar impression appeared in another lengthy feature article published after the $100,000,000 suit had been filed. It was carried in the Chicago Tribune of August 29, 1982. Authored by Cheryl Lavin, it bore the title, "Widow's Mission: Clearing Husband in Lindbergh Case." The article concluded with the following italicized note: "Contributions to the Richard Hauptmann Memorial Fund to help defray legal costs may be sent to Robert Bryan, 506 Pixie Trail, Mill Valley, Calif." This is the name and address of the attorney who filed the suit, although in the second paragraph of the article that carried the fund solicitation note reference was made to the attorney as being Robert Bryan of San Francisco. The 1981 article also identified him as such. Despite the middle initial difference, the person who filed the suit is both the attorney and the solicitor of contributions to defray the legal costs.

Mrs. Hauptmann's suit was dismissed by the federal district court on August 11, 1983.

The foregoing articles correctly stated that the newspaper reporters and photographers covering the trial made the New Jersey courtroom like a circus, and the ransom intermediary's behind-the-wall identification of Hauptmann's voice lacks credibility, but there were the following facts establishing Hauptmann's guilt: on a board in a dark closet of Hauptmann's home there was the name and telephone number of the ransom intermediary, for which Hauptmann offered no explanation; as regards the substantial amount of the marked ransom money that was found buried in Hauptmann's garage, he said he was holding it for a friend, Isadore Fisch, whose whereabouts Hauptmann did not know; parts of the kidnap ladder matched exactly with sawed off boards in Hauptmann's attic; hand-plane markings on the crudely constructed kidnap ladder matched perfectly with marks left on wood samples planed with Hauptmann's plane; and the photographically illustrated testimony of eight of the country's top professional document examiners established positively that the ransom notes were written by Hauptmann. The scientific evidence that was used against Hauptmann is described in: Sellers, The Handwriting Evidence Against Hauptmann, 27 J.Crim.L. & C. 874 (1937); and, Koehler, Technique Used in Tracing the Lindbergh Kidnapping Ladder, 27 J.Crim.L. & C. 712 (1937).

SHOULD THE FELONY–MURDER RULE BE ABOLISHED?

Some jurisdictions, either by court decisions or statutes have abolished the felony-murder rule. Following are the reasons stated by the Supreme Court of Michigan for its abolition, as they appear in the concluding portions of its opinion in the 1980 case of People v. Aaron, 409 Mich. 672, 299 N.W.2d 304:

"The Pennsylvania Supreme Court has called the felony-murder rule 'nonessential', and the commentators to the Hawaii statute abolishing felony murder concluded that '[t]he rule certainly is not an indispensable ingredient in a system of criminal justice.' The penal code of India has done away with felony murder and the doctrine is also unknown as such in continental Europe. England, the birthplace of the felony-murder doctrine, has been without the rule for over 20 years and 'its passing apparently has not been mourned'. One writer suggests that the experience in England demonstrates that its demise would have little effect on the rate of convictions for murders occurring in the perpetration of felonies.

* * *

"Whatever reasons can be gleaned from the dubious origin of the felony-murder rule to explain its existence, those reasons no longer exist today. Indeed, most states, including our own, have recognized the harshness and inequity of the rule as is evidenced by the numerous restrictions placed on it. The felony-murder doctrine is unnecessary and in many cases unjust in that it violates the basic premise of individual moral culpability upon which our criminal law is based.

"We conclude that Michigan has no statutory felony-murder rule which allows the mental element of murder to be satisfied by proof of the intention to commit the underlying felony. Today we exercise our role in the development of the common law by abrogating the common-law felony-murder rule. We hold that in order to convict a defendant of murder, as that term is defined by Michigan case law, it must be shown that he acted with intent to kill or to inflict great bodily harm or with a wanton and willful disregard of the likelihood that the natural tendency of his behavior is to cause death or great bodily harm. We further hold that the issue of malice must always be submitted to the jury.

"The first-degree murder statute will continue to operate in that all *murder* committed in the perpetration or attempted perpetration of the enumerated felonies will be elevated to first-degree murder."

See Annot., 13 A.L.R.4th 1180 and Annot., 13 A.L.R.4th 1226 (1982 & 1988 Supp.).

A reason to believe that felony murder rules will not soon be abolished is their use in domestic violence cases. State v. Robinson, 539 N.W.2d 231 (Minn.1995) (statute establishes first degree murder if the homicide is an act of domestic abuse *and* the perpetrator has engaged in a past pattern of domestic abuse *and* the circumstances manifest indifference to human life.)

B. VOLUNTARY MANSLAUGHTER

STATE v. FLORY

Supreme Court of Wyoming, 1929.
40 Wyo. 184, 276 P. 458.

BLUME, C.J. The defendant was convicted of murder in the second degree for killing E.T. Ostrum on January 16, 1928, and he appeals.

The deceased, aged between 65 to 70 years, was the father of Daisy Flory, the wife of defendant, who is about 21 years of age, and who married defendant in 1923. The mother and father of Daisy were, it seems, divorced, for a number of years prior to the homicide in question in this case. The father apparently was not well acquainted with his daughter and paid little attention to her, although he sent her some small presents when her two children, age 3 years and 1 year, respectively, were born. At the time of the homicide and for some time prior thereto, the deceased lived on a farm in Campbell county, Wyo., the defendant on a farm in Montana; the distance, by road, between the two places being about 50 miles. The deceased was engaged in farming and in performing common labor. The defendant was a "dry farmer" in the summer and a trapper in the winter. Deceased wrote to his daughter in the summer of 1927, wanting to visit her, and she and her husband invited him to come. He arrived on the day after Thanksgiving, during the absence of the defendant, who came home on November 30th. The visit between the deceased and defendant was pleasant, and it was agreed, in fact, upon suggestion of the deceased, that the latter might somewhat later, move over to defendant's place, build himself a house, and in the meantime occupy the "bunkhouse" on defendant's place. He was invited to continue his visit at that time until after Christmas, which he agreed to do. Defendant left home, to go trapping, about the middle of December, and returned, as was expected, on the afternoon of December 23d. He claims that during this time the deceased made indecent proposals to Daisy Flory, defendant's wife, and raped her and committed incest upon her on the morning of December 23d. According to the testimony, defendant was not told thereof until later, although she immediately indicated to him that she did not want her father to stay longer and did not want him to move as had been planned. Deceased left on December 26th, first to visit at another place and then to go home. On January 3, 1928, defendant had occasion to go to Ostrum's place to get some poison for coyotes and to tell him not to move. During this time the deceased mentioned to defendant that he had discussed with Daisy the subject of not having any more children, and he gave defendant a package containing a silk sponge and three rubbers, used for prevention of conception, stating that while at Sheridan, a few days previously he had bought nine of them. Defendant had never discussed the subject with his wife, and when he arrived home and showed her the package, she was perturbed, exclaimed, "O, God!" and from that time to the morning of January 15th she gradually told him of the details of the indecent advances and rape above mentioned, telling the final scenes on the morning of the date last mentioned, and that deceased had said: "Don't be foolish and say anything about this." The defendant thereupon took his gun, as he was accustomed to do when going on trips, with the intention, as he testified, of going to deceased's home and getting an explanation of the latter's conduct. He stopped overnight at the house of Mr. Hudsonpillar, and the next morning went to the house of deceased, arriving there about 11 o'clock in the forenoon, finding the deceased at home. The house is nearly 24 feet square, entered by a door in the south into a large room occupying the whole of the south 13 feet. The north side of the house is divided between a kitchen, about 9 × 10 feet in area, in the northwest corner, and a storeroom in the northeast corner, each being connected with the large room by a door. No one else was there, and the only living witness to the tragedy is the defendant himself. He testified at length, and his testimony, condensed, is about as follows:

"I took the gun along in because I knew he was stouter than I and I knew he could handle me. I had no intentions when I went in of killing the man at all. He says 'Hello' to me, and I walked towards him, and I said 'What made you rape Daisy.' And he came right straight towards me. I looked at both hands, but he didn't have anything in them, and he says to me 'Let's talk it over,' and I says to him, 'Don't come any closer,' and he turned around and walked back, and I walked after him—to see what he was going to do, and when he got to the stove (in the northwest corner of the kitchen) he says 'Let's talk it over.' He was facing me in a stooped-over position and I says to him 'Charley, do you know you just about ruined my home?' And he says, 'I will keep the girl,' and when he said that, I says 'You are a pretty son of a bitch to keep your daughter.' I was thinking of some of the things he had done, was pretty nervous, and that man he just sprang after me, and when he did I jerked the rifle back, and just then I heard the report of the gun, and I saw him fall, and I turned around and went out. At no time did he deny he didn't rape his daughter. When I jerked the rifle back, I have no recollection of pulling the trigger with my finger. I didn't intend to shoot him when I jerked the rifle back, and it surprised me, and I turned around and went out. I had fear when he came at me. He had the meanest look in his face of any man I ever saw, and I knew he could handle me, if he got hold of me. I was giddy when I went out."

On cross-examination he testified, among other things:

"I was mad on my way over there and when I got there, but not any madder than any one else under the circumstances. I didn't tell Hudsonpillar I was going to Ostrum's. I didn't want to talk to him about it. I can't say that I was mad when I got to Hudsonpillar's. The gun was cocked when I took it out of the scabbard; I didn't examine it, but usually carry it with the safety on. I didn't rap when I went in. As I was opening the door, on the south, he showed up in the kitchen. I went right in; had the gun in the right hand. I walked towards the deceased; deceased was in the kitchen; I walked close to the kitchen door, keeping my eyes on deceased; I pointed the gun at him, when he came toward me the first time, and shouted at him 'Don't come any closer,' and he went back into the kitchen. I went next to the door. He had nothing in his hands, but when he sprang for me, I don't think so. I saw nothing in them. When he said 'I can keep the girl' it made me mad. I didn't take my eyes off Ostrum. I must have taken the safety off the gun when he rushed at me the first time. It looked like to me he was rushing for the rifle, and when he rushed towards me, I jerked the rifle, and that was when the shot was fired. I didn't intend to shoot him. The gun went off accidentally. I didn't intend to shoot him, and it got me so I couldn't stay there and look at him, I was intending to get away from him as he came toward me. I jerked the gun back and went backwards, and the gun went off. I was standing right in the door (leading to the kitchen). I knew he was dead the way he fell. I later gave myself up at Sheridan."

On re-examination he testified that he wept twice while going to Ostrum's....

The defendant contends that the information given him by his wife as to the rape and incest committed upon her by the decedent so aroused his passions and deprived him of such self-control that his act cannot be held to be murder. The incest and rape, if true, could not justify the killing of the deceased.... But the evidence may be admissible for the purpose of mitigation and to reduce the crime to manslaughter.... The state contends that the testimony was not admissible in this case, because ample time—at least a day and probably longer—had elapsed after the defendant had been informed of the acts of decedent; further, that defendant's own testimony shows that when he was at Hudsonpillar's during the evening and night of January 15, 1928, his blood had cooled and he was no longer perturbed. Counsel for the defendant say that when he, on the morning of January 16th, met the deceased, and the latter did not deny the rape and said that he would keep his daughter, this was heaping insult upon injury and vividly recalled to defendant's mind what had been told him on the previous days. There is other testimony which shows to some extent at least that defendant's mind was perturbed on his way to Ostrum's. We are inclined to agree with defendant's contention. The crime of deceased, if true, was most heinous and was calculated to create a most violent passion in the mind of the defendant, and it is hardly to be expected that it would, as a matter of law, subside within so short a time, especially when, as testified, a situation arose by which past facts were clearly recalled. Courts are not altogether agreed as to whether the question of cooling time is one of law or one for the jury. Some hold it to be a question of law and that 24 hours is sufficient for the mind to cool.... We think, however, that the weight of authority is that, in cases like that at bar, the question of cooling time depends on the circumstances and is ordinarily one for the jury....

In [State v. Thomas, 169 Iowa 591, 151 N.W. 842] it is said: "Where the want of provocation is so clear as to admit of no reasonable doubt that the alleged provocation could not have had any tendency to produce such state of mind in ordinary men, the evidence thereof should be excluded; but if there be a reasonable doubt as to whether the alleged provocation had such tendency, it is the safer rule to let the issue go to the jury under proper instructions. Of course, the reasonableness or adequacy of the provocation must depend on the facts of each particular case. In some cases, the courts declare that only actual personal knowledge of the wife's infidelity will extenuate the crime of killing by the husband to manslaughter.... But others with better reason hold that information of the recent liaison of the wife with a paramour, reaching the husband for the first time, may be shown as likely to have thrown him into ungovernable passion.... The circumstances of each case necessarily must determine the admissibility of the evidence as well as its bearing on the different issues presented. Again, it is to be remarked that there is no definite time within which the passions when aroused by such a wrong may be said to have so far subsided and reason to have resumed its sway to such an extent as that thereafter the killing may be denounced as in vengeance alone. The question is one of reasonable time and dependent on all the facts of the case. While the time may be so long as to exclude all doubt on the subject and exact the exclusion of the evidence in so far as offered in extenuation, more frequently it should be submitted to the jury under proper instructions...."

The court, in fact, permitted the defendant to show that the wife of the defendant told him of the commission of the rape and incest, but excluded all details, and collateral facts tending to show the state of the defendant's mind. In this we think there was error. While no cases discuss the point directly ..., courts seems to have admitted the details told a defendant as a matter of course, and the reasons for that are plain. In the first place, a bare statement of the ultimate fact might give the jury the impression that it is fabricated, while a detailed statement might add credibility to the witness. Again, the pertinent inquiry is as to what was the condition of the defendant's mind as the result of what has been told him. In order to determine that, the jury must, mentally, be placed as near as possible in the position of the defendant, in order to be able to judge properly. Details of an atrocious character would be more apt to affect the mind of the defendant, just as details are more apt to affect the mind of any one else.... It is true of course, as argued, that the details might prejudice and inflame the minds of the jury; if so, the same details would be apt to inflame the mind of the defendant, and that is the very point that was to be determined by the jury....

We have a case here, accordingly, in which we find that there is no error in the case, except as to the refusal to admit evidence which, if admitted, might have induced the jury to find the degree of the crime to be no greater than that of manslaughter.... [T]he state may elect by writing, filed in this case within 30 days, to take a new trial, in which event the judgment will be reversed and the cause remanded for a new trial. Unless that is done, the judgment will stand reversed as to murder in the second degree and affirmed for manslaughter, and the case will be remanded to the district court with direction to cause the prisoner to be brought before it to be resentenced for that crime, taking into consideration the time already served by the defendant, and to make all other necessary orders not inconsistent herewith.

Remanded, with directions.

BEDDER v. DIRECTOR OF PUBLIC PROSECUTIONS

House of Lords, 1954.
2 All Eng.R. 801.

LORD SIMONDS, L.C.: My Lords, this appeal raises once more a question of importance in the criminal law. Your Lordships, I think, agree with me that, on examination, the question appears to be amply covered by the highest authority, but the answer can usefully be restated.

The appellant, a youth of eighteen years, was convicted on May 27, 1954, at Leicester Assizes of the murder of Doreen Mary Redding, a prostitute. He appealed to the Court of Criminal Appeal on the substantial ground of misdirection, claiming that the learned judge who tried the case had wrongly directed the jury on the test of provocation and that, had they been rightly directed, they might have found him guilty not of murder but of manslaughter only. The Court of Criminal Appeal dismissed his appeal, holding that the jury had been rightly directed.

The relevant facts, so far as they bear on the question of provocation, can be shortly stated. The appellant has the misfortune to be sexually impotent, a fact which he naturally well knew and, according to his own evidence had allowed to prey on his mind. On the night of the crime he saw the prostitute with another man, and when they had parted, went and spoke to her and was led by her to a quiet court off a street in Leicester. There he attempted in vain to have intercourse with her whereupon—and I summarise the evidence in the way most favourable to him—she jeered at him and attempted to get away. He tried still to hold her and then she slapped him in the face and punched him in the stomach: he grabbed her shoulders and pushed her back from him whereat (I use his words),

"She kicked me in the privates. Whether it was her knee or foot, I do not know. After that I do not know what happened till she fell".

She fell, because he had taken a knife from his pocket and stabbed her with it twice, the second blow inflicting a mortal injury. It was in these circumstances that the appellant pleaded that there had been such provocation by the deceased as to reduce the crime from murder to manslaughter, and the question is whether the learned judge rightly directed the jury on this issue. In my opinion, the summing-up of the learned judge was impeccable. Adapting the language used in this House in the cases of Mancini v. Public Prosecutions Director, [1941] 3 All E.R. 272; and Holmes v. Public Prosecutions Director, [1946] 2 All E.R. 124 . . . , he thus directed the jury:

"Provocation would arise if the conduct of the deceased woman, Mrs. Redding, to the prisoner was such as would cause a reasonable person, and actually caused the person to lose his self-control suddenly and to drive him into such a passion and lack of self-control that he might use violence of the degree and nature which the prisoner used here. The provocation must be such as would reasonably justify the violence used, the use of a knife", . . . and a little later he addressed them thus:

"The reasonable person, the ordinary person, is the person you must consider when you are considering the effect which any acts, any conduct, any words, might have to justify the steps which were taken in response thereto, so that an unusually excitable or pugnacious individual, or a drunken one or a man who is sexually impotent is not entitled to rely on provocation which would not have led an ordinary person to have acted in the way which was in fact carried out. There may be, members of the jury, infirmity of mind and instability of character, but if it does not amount to insanity, it is no defence. Likewise infirmity of body or affliction of the mind of the assailant is not material in testing whether there has been provocation by the deceased to justify the violence used so as to reduce the act of killing to manslaughter. They must be tested throughout this by the reactions of a reasonable man to the acts, or series of acts, done by the deceased woman". . . .

My Lords, . . . I am at a loss to know what other direction than that which he gave could properly have been given by the learned judge to the jury in this case. The argument, as I understood it, for the appellant was that the jury, in considering the reaction of the hypothetical reasonable man to the acts of provocation, must not only place him in the circumstances in which the accused was placed, but must also invest him with the personal physical peculiarities of the accused. Learned counsel, who argued the case for the appellant with great ability, did not, I think, venture to say that he should be invested with mental or temperamental qualities which distinguished him from the reasonable man: for this would have been directly in conflict with ... the recent decision of the House in Mancini's case which I have cited. But he urged that the reasonable man should be invested with the peculiar physical qualities of the accused, as in the present case with the characteristic of impotence, and the question should be asked: what would be the reaction of the impotent reasonable man in the circumstances? For that proposition I know of no authority: nor can I see any reason in it. It would be plainly illogical not to recognise an unusually excitable or pugnacious temperament in the accused as a matter to be taken into account but yet to recognise for that purpose some unusual physical characteristic, be it impotence or another. Moreover, the proposed distinction appears to me to ignore the fundamental fact that the temper of a man which leads him to react in such and such a way to provocation is, or may be, itself conditioned by some physical defect. It is too subtle a refinement for my mind or, I think, for that of a jury to grasp that the temper may be ignored but the physical defect taken into account.

It was urged on your Lordships that the hypothetical reasonable man must be confronted with all the same circumstances as the accused, and that this could not be fairly done unless he was also invested with the peculiar characteristics of the accused. But this makes nonsense of the test. Its purpose is to invite the jury to consider the act of the accused by reference to a certain standard or norm of conduct and with this object the "reasonable" or the "average" or the "normal" man is invoked. If the reasonable man is then deprived in whole or in part of his reason, or the normal man endowed with abnormal characteristics, the test ceases to have any value. This is precisely the consideration which led this House in Mancini's case to say that an unusually excitable or pugnacious person is not entitled to rely on provocation which would not have led an ordinary person to act as he did. In my opinion, then, the Court of Criminal Appeal was right in approving the direction given to the jury by the learned judge and this appeal must fail.

NOTES

1. The Test of the "Reasonable Man"

(a) Compare the approach of the Lords in the above case with the comments regarding provocation contained in the 1953 Report of the Royal Commission on Capital Punishment, pp. 51–53.

"[The proposal has been put before us that], in considering whether there is provocation sufficient to reduce the crime to manslaughter, the sole test should be whether the accused was in fact deprived of self-control and that the jury should not be required to consider also whether a 'reasonable man' would have been so deprived....

"[The suggestion is] prompted by the feeling that objective tests of provocation are unsatisfactory and inequitable, and that the question whether a crime is murder or manslaughter ought to depend only on whether the accused did in fact commit it in ungovernable passion caused by sudden provocation, of whatever kind....

"[The argument suggesting] that this test of the 'reasonable man' should be abolished ... was simple and direct. This test, it is said, is inequitable.... As Mr. Nield put it, 'the jury should be permitted to determine the effect of the provocation on this particular man whom they have seen and may have heard and whose circumstances have probably been described to them.'

"This proposal was strongly opposed by the Judges who gave evidence before us.... Lord Cooper observed that if the existing rule was changed, 'there might be circumstances in which a bad-tempered man would be acquitted and a good-tempered man would be hanged, which, of course, is neither law nor sense.'

"We recognize the force of the Judge's objections.... We think that this argument is in principle sound, at least so far as minor abnormalities of character are concerned....

"Nevertheless we feel sympathy with the view which prompted the proposal that provocation should be judged by the standard of the accused. The objections of the Judges take no account of that fundamental difference between the law of murder and the law applicable to all other crimes.... In the case of the other crimes the court can and does take account of extenuating circumstances in assessing the sentence; in the case of murder alone the sentence is fixed and automatic. Provocation is in essence only an extenuating circumstance.... The rule of law that provocation may, within narrow bounds, reduce murder to manslaughter, represents an attempt by the courts to reconcile the preservation of the fixed penalty for murder with a limited concession to natural human weakness, but it suffers from the common defects of a compromise....

"We have indeed no doubt that if the criterion of the 'reasonable man' was strictly applied by the courts and the sentence of death was carried out in cases where it was so applied, it would be too harsh in its operation. In practice, however, the courts not infrequently give weight to factors personal to the prisoner in considering a plea of provocation, and where there is a conviction of murder such factors are taken into account by the Home Secretary and may often lead to commutation of the sentence. The application of the test does not therefore lead to any eventual miscarriage of justice. At the same time, as we have seen, there are serious objections of principle to its abrogation. In these circumstances we do not feel justified in recommending any change in the existing law."

(b) The objective, rather than subjective, test was held to have been properly used as the standard in determining "serious provocation" to reduce murder to manslaughter in Commonwealth v. Miller, 473 Pa. 398, 374 A.2d 1273 (1977).

2. Provocation

In situations where a homicide is committed in the heat of passion brought on by provoking circumstances, several types of provocation have traditionally been recognized as legally sufficient to reduce the grade of the homicide from murder to voluntary manslaughter.

(a) *Assault and battery.* The law takes account of the possibility that an assault and battery may so provoke a "reasonable man" that he may lose his powers of reason and judgment and kill as a consequence. The states are not uniform, however, in their treatment of this type of provocation.

Some jurisdictions follow a flexible rule and regard assault alone as legally adequate provocation where the particular circumstances appear sufficient to excite the passions of a reasonable man. Thus, in Beasley v. State, 64 Miss. 518, 1 So. 736 (1886), adequate provocation was held to exist where the defendant shot the deceased after the latter had first fired at the defendant and then turned to run.

Other jurisdictions, notably Missouri, require an actual battery, as a matter of law, before sufficient provocation is deemed to exist. Under this rule, it was held, for example, that where the deceased had chased the defendant with an axe and then broke into the latter's house, threatening to kill him, the defendant, who shot the deceased, had no right to an instruction on voluntary manslaughter, since there had been no actual battery. State v. Kizer, 360 Mo. 744, 230 S.W.2d 690 (1950).

Ordinarily, a battery that is no more than "technical" is regarded as too slight to qualify as legal incitement to homicide. Commonwealth v. Cisneros, 381 Pa. 447, 113 A.2d 293 (1955). Moreover, a battery that is somewhat more than "technical" may occasionally be held insufficient as a matter of law where the court concludes that the provocation was insufficient under the circumstances to cause a reasonable person to kill. In Com. v. Webb, 252 Pa. 187, 97 A. 189 (1916), the defendant's wife (5′7″; 200+ lbs.) hit the defendant (6′; 165 lbs.) with a fifteen inch poker. He retaliated with five mortal razor slashes. The Supreme Court of Pennsylvania, after discussing the comparative sizes of defendant and his wife, and noting that the defendant was not left with a mark on his head from the blow he received, concluded that there was not adequate provocation for the homicide. Normally such considerations would probably be left to the jury; the court apparently felt, however, that the defendant's brutality was out of all proportion to the nature of the provocation.

(b) *Adultery.* Adultery, under common law principles, constituted sufficient provocation where a husband discovered his wife in the act of intercourse and kills either her or her paramour. Sheppard v. State, 243 Ala. 498, 10 So.2d 822 (1942). It had also been held that adequate provocation exists where a mistake of fact could lead to the homicide, as in the case of the husband finding his wife in suspicious circumstances and having a reasonable belief that she has committed adultery. State v. Yanz, 74 Conn. 177, 50 A. 37 (1901).

In marked contrast to the common law, under which paramour killings are manslaughter at least, several states had statutes, now repealed, which provided that such killings were *justifiable.* The following provision was contained in the Texas Penal Code (Vernon's Ann.P.C. art. 1220):

> Homicide is justifiable when committed by the husband upon one taken in the act of adultery with the wife, provided the killing takes place before the parties to the act have separated. Such circumstances cannot justify a homicide when it appears that there has been on the part of the husband, any connivance in or assent to the adulterous connection.

As interpreted in Price v. State, 18 Tex.App. 474 (1885), the above statement "taken in the act of adultery" did not mean that the husband must be an actual eyewitness to the physical act. "It is sufficient if he sees them in bed together, or leaving that position, or in such a position as indicates with reasonable certainty to a rational mind that they have just then committed the adulterous act, or were then about to commit it."

Although a husband in Texas, under this earlier law, was justified in killing his wife's paramour, there was no privilege to use a razor merely to maim and torture. Sensobaugh v. State, 92 Tex.Cr.R. 417, 244 S.W. 379 (1922). Also see Shaw v. State, 510 S.W.2d 926 (Tex.Cr.App.1974).

Similar statutes were in effect in New Mexico and Utah, but they, along with the Texas statute, have been repealed.

Apart from other considerations behind the repeal of such adultery killing statutes, it will be observed that they accorded such "open season" privileges only to the husband; the wife was not accorded the same privilege as regards her adulterous husband.

For a discussion of the so-called "unwritten law" by which jury acquittals are often achieved in paramour killing cases under color of self-defense, see Inbau, Scientific Reasoning and Jury Verdicts, 16 Postgraduate Medicine, No. 4 (1954). The frequently successful use of the defense of insanity in such cases is described in 19 Neb.Law Bull. 146 (1940).

(c) *Trespass.* By one view, trespass constitutes legally sufficient provocation for a homicide committed in the heat of passion. Pearce v. State, 154 Fla. 656, 18 So.2d 754 (1944). Under another view, however, trespass is regarded as too minor an incident to qualify as legal incitement. People v. Free, 37 Ill.App.3d 1050, 347 N.E.2d 505 (1976).

(d) *Acts against third persons.* It is generally held that certain acts committed by one against a close relative of the slayer constitute sufficient provocation. See, e.g., People v. Rice, 351 Ill. 604, 184 N.E. 894 (1933) (murder or felonious injury); State v. Flory, 40 Wyo. 184, 276 P. 458 (1929) (rape); Toler v. State, 152 Tenn. 1, 260 S.W. 134 (1924) (seduction); State v. Burnett, 354 Mo. 45, 188 S.W.2d 51 (1945) (illegal arrest). In Commonwealth v. Paese, 220 Pa. 371, 69 A. 891 (1908), a severe beating of a friend was held to be insufficient as a matter of law, inasmuch as there was no family relationship between the slayer and the victim of the beating.

(e) *Words and gestures.* Strongly entrenched in the United States is the almost uniform rule that words or gestures, alone, are never sufficient provocation for an intentional homicide. People v. Pouncey, 437 Mich. 382, 471 N.W.2d 346 (1991). A few legislatures have altered this doctrine. See, e.g., People v. Valentine, 28 Cal.2d 121, 169 P.2d 1 (1946), and Elsmore v. State, 132 Tex.Cr.R. 261, 104 S.W.2d 493 (1937), interpreting legislative omission of former codification of the rule as abolishing it. For the most part, however, the states have firmly adhered to the rule, and the courts have rigidly applied it, often with harsh results. See, e.g., Freddo v. State, 127 Tenn. 376, 155 S.W. 170 (1913) (deceased intentionally and continuously used epithets which he knew were highly upsetting to the defendant); Commonwealth v. Cisneros, 381 Pa. 447, 113 A.2d 293 (1955) (deceased, defendant's estranged wife, refused reconciliation, explaining in strongly insulting terms that she would not live with or have children by one who was half-Mexican and half-Puerto Rican). Occasionally sufficient provocation is held to exist where the words or gestures are accompanied by a technical battery or other minor incident. See Lamp v. State, 38 Ga.App. 36, 142 S.E. 202 (1928); State v. Davis, 34 S.W.2d 133 (Mo.1930). Such additional aggravations, however, are not always permitted to alter the rule. See Commonwealth v. Cisneros, 381 Pa. 447, 113 A.2d 293 (1955).

Under one view, informational language, as opposed to words which in themselves constitute the incitement, may qualify as adequate provocation where the fact communicated would be sufficient, and where the slayer has not previously known of the matter revealed. See Commonwealth v. Berry, 461 Pa.

233, 336 A.2d 262 (1975); People v. Rice, 351 Ill. 604, 184 N.E. 894 (1933). Another view, however, does not admit of this exception. See Humphreys v. State, 175 Ga. 705, 165 S.E. 733 (1932).

Contemporary appraisal of the law concerning words as provocation indicates dissatisfaction with the inflexibility of a rule which fails to grant legal recognition to the inciting character of language which may be regarded as highly provoking by the general community. The 1953 Report of the Royal Commission on Capital Punishment, pp. 53–56, contains the following remarks on this subject:

"The suggestion is not new that the ancient rule excluding words and gestures from the scope of 'reasonable provocation' is itself unreasonable.... [I]t would appear that provocation by words is ... admissible in most of the [countries of the Commonwealth]. We understand too that provocation, whether by assault or by words, would be regarded in most countries of Western Europe as a mitigating circumstance which might justify reduction of the maximum penalty for homicide. On the other hand we were informed that in the United States ... it is the almost universal rule that words, no matter how opprobrious, will not constitute sufficient provocation.

"The witnesses in favour of admitting provocation based on words alone ... thought it beyond doubt that words might constitute provocation as gross as blows, even to a reasonable man, and considered that the right course was to leave it to the jury to decide whether in any particular case the provocation was sufficient to reduce the crime to manslaughter....

"We have no doubt that cases from time to time occur where words are grossly provocative and ought to be accepted as provocation sufficient to reduce murder to manslaughter....

"Our conclusion is as follows: Where the jury are satisfied that the accused killed the deceased upon provocation, that he was deprived of his self-control as a result of that provocation and that a reasonable man might have been so deprived, the nature (as distinct from the degree) of the provocation should be immaterial and it should be open to them to return a verdict of manslaughter.... We fully recognise that words alone will seldom constitute adequate provocation to a reasonable man, but we agree with those witnesses who considered that the question whether such provocation was given is essentially one for the determination of the jury. We think that if the issue is left to the jury and they are allowed to consider each case on its merits, irrespective of whether the alleged provocation was by word or deed, they can be trusted to arrive at a just and reasonable decision and will not hesitate to convict the accused of murder where he has acted on only slight provocation, whether by words or otherwise."

Compare the Commission's conclusion with the provisions of Section 3 of the English Homicide Act of 1957, which provided as follows:

> *Provocation.* Where on a charge of murder there is evidence on which the jury can find that the person charged was provoked (whether by things done or by things said or both together) to lose his self-control, the question whether the provocation was enough to make a reasonable man do as he did shall be left to be determined by the jury; and in determining that question the jury shall take into account everything

both done and said according to the effect which, in their opinion, it would have on a reasonable man.

3. Cooling of Blood

(a) Consider the following comments of the court in In re Fraley, 3 Okl.Cr. 719, 109 P. 295 (1910), and compare them with the statements of the court on this subject in State v. Flory.

"[I]t was stated by counsel for the petitioner ... that the deceased, some nine or ten months previously, had shot and killed the son of the petitioner ... and it is urged here that when the petitioner saw the deceased ... the recollection of that event must have engendered in him a passion which overcame him; that the killing was committed in the heat of such passion, was without premeditation, and therefore was not murder. To this we cannot assent.... In Ragland v. State ..., four hours intervening between the provocation and the killing was held as a matter of law to be sufficient cooling time to preclude the reduction of a homicide to manslaughter. Perry v. State ... and Rockmore v. State ... each hold three days as a matter of law sufficient cooling time. Commonwealth v. Aiello ... holds from one to two hours sufficient, and State v. Williams ... holds fifteen minutes sufficient. And the authorities are all agreed that the question is not alone whether the defendant's passion in fact cooled, but also was there sufficient time in which the passion of a reasonable man would cool. If in fact the defendant's passion did cool, which may be shown by circumstances, such as the transaction of other business in the meantime, rational conversations upon other subjects, evidence of preparation for the killing, etc., then the length of time intervening is immaterial. But if in fact it did not cool, yet if such time intervened between the provocation and the killing that the passion of the average man would have cooled and his reason have resumed its sway, then still there is not reduction of the homicide to manslaughter.... If the fatal wound be inflicted immediately following a sufficient provocation given, then the question as to whether the defendant's passion thereby aroused had in fact cooled, or as to whether or not such time had elapsed that the passion of a reasonable man would have cooled, is a question of fact to be determined upon a consideration of all the facts and circumstances in evidence; but when an unreasonable period of time has elapsed between the provocation and the killing, then the court is authorized to say as a matter of law that the cooling time was sufficient."

Also see Farr v. State, 54 Ala.App. 80, 304 So.2d 898 (1974).

(b) With regard to the application of the "reasonable man" test in this area, compare the following statement of the court in State v. Hazlett, 16 N.D. 426, 113 N.W. 374 (1907):

"Where the evidence shows that a homicide was committed, in the heat of passion and with provocation, we think the jury, in determining whether there was sufficient cooling time for the passion to subside and reason to resume its sway, should be governed, not by the standard of an ideal, reasonable man, but they should determine such question from the standpoint of the defendant in the light of all the facts and circumstances disclosed by the evidence.... We are aware that some courts have held to the contrary, but we are convinced that the rule as above announced is the more reasonable and just one."

C. JUSTIFIABLE USE OF DEADLY FORCE

1. SELF DEFENSE

The use of force to defend one's self is an undisputed right. It is only with respect to the manner in which he does it, or the circumstances under which it occurs, that there are differences and uncertainties in the law. For instance, when a person who is free from fault is faced with a threat of great bodily danger, may he stand his ground and kill his assailant, or is he under an obligation to retreat?

The American Law Institute, in its Model Penal Code provides (in § 3.04(b)(ii) (1985)) that:

> The use of deadly force is not justifiable ... if the actor knows that he can avoid the necessity of using such force with complete safety by retreating or by surrendering possession of a thing to a person asserting a claim of right thereto or by complying with a demand that he abstain from any action which he has no duty to take, except that:
>
> (A) the actor is not obliged to retreat from his dwelling or place of work, unless he was the initial aggressor....

In adopting the "retreat to the wall" doctrine the drafters of the code, in their commentary, offer the following justification (id. at comment 4(c) (footnotes omitted)):

"There is a sense in which a duty to retreat may be regarded as a logical derivative of the underlying justifying principle of self-defense: belief in the necessity of the protective action. The actor who knows he can retreat with safety also knows that the necessity can be avoided in that way. The logic of this position never has been accepted when moderate force is used in self-defense; here all agree that the actor may stand his ground and estimate necessity upon that basis. When the resort is to deadly force, however, Beale argued that the common law was otherwise—that the law of homicide demanded that the estimation of necessity take account of the possibility of safe retreat. Perkins challenged this conclusion in the case of actors free from fault in bringing on the struggle, urging that it was only true with respect to aggressors or cases of mutual combat. American jurisdictions, prior to approval of the Model Code, divided on the question, no less in crime than tort, with the preponderant position favoring the right to stand one's ground. In a famous opinion, Justice Holmes advanced what seems to be a median position: 'Rationally the failure to retreat is a circumstance to be considered with all the others in order to determine whether the defendant went farther than he was justified in doing; not a categorical proof of guilt.' This would apparently remit the issue to the jury, without a legal mandate on the point.

* * *

"Considerations of this sort, decisive with respect to torts, apply with equal force to penal law."

Some states have codified this rule into statute. See, for example N.Y. Penal Law § 35.15 (McKinney 1987):

"...

"2. A person may not use deadly physical force upon another person under circumstances specified in subdivision one unless:

> "(a) He reasonably believes that such other person is using or about to use deadly physical force. Even in such case, however, the actor may not use deadly physical force if he knows that he can with complete safety as to himself and others avoid the necessity of so doing by retreating; except that he is under no duty to retreat if he is:
>
> > "(i) in his dwelling and not the initial aggressor; or
> >
> > "(ii) a police officer or peace officer or a person assisting a police officer or a peace officer...."

In rejecting the rationale of the retreat rule, Mr. Justice Holmes said this in an early case:

"Rationally, the failure to retreat is a circumstance to be considered with all the others in order to determine whether the defendant went farther than he was justified in doing; not a categorical proof of guilt. The law has grown, and even if historical mistakes have contributed to its growth, it has tended in the direction of rules consistent with human nature. Many respectable writers agree that if a man reasonably believes that he is in immediate danger of death or grievous bodily harm from his assailant, he may stand his ground, and that if he kills him, he has not exceeded the bounds of lawful self-defense. That has been the decision of this court.... Detached reflection cannot be demanded in the presence of an uplifted knife. Therefore, in this court, at least, it is not a condition of immunity that one in that situation should pause to consider whether a reasonable man might not think it possible to fly with safety, or to disable his assailant rather than to kill him." *

The majority of states permit one to stand his own ground and meet force with force, as long as the defender is not the original aggressor.[1]

Even in those jurisdictions following the so-called "true man" rule that permits a self-defender to stand his ground, a person who "brings on the difficulty" will find that his self-defense right becomes an "imperfect" one. He may then be required to retreat before he can excusably kill, even though he used non-deadly force at the outset; and under some circumstances he is completely foreclosed and must settle, as a minimum, for a manslaughter conviction.[2]

* Brown v. United States, 256 U.S. 335, 343, 41 S.Ct. 501, 502 (1921).

1. LaFave & Scott, 2 Substantive Criminal Law § 7.11(a) (1986).

2. For a general discussion of the "per-

2. DEFENSE OF OTHERS

The law recognizes the right of a person to kill in defense of not only his own life but also that of another. Two doctrines bear upon this privilege to defend others: (1) the rule that one may defend a close relative, and (2) the rule that one may take life if necessary to prevent a dangerous or forcible felony. In application to specific situations, these principles are frequently cumulative. Thus, if one kills the assailant of a near relative, he may invoke his specific right to defend a member of his family, as well as his general privilege to interfere to prevent a felonious assault.

Cases involving defense of a party who, at the time of the killing, was engaged in an affray brought on by his own misconduct have resulted in disagreement among the courts as to whether the "assistant" must "stand in the shoes" of the wrongdoer, or instead be judged according to the reasonableness of his own conduct in interfering to protect one whose life seemed to be unlawfully endangered.[3]

It is a matter of speculation as to which view is the more socially tolerable. In other words, will a person who sees a close relative in great and immediate danger pause to determine whether the relative was himself free from fault?

Nebraska enacted a statute which read in part as follows: "No person in this state shall be placed in legal jeopardy of any kind whatsoever for protecting, by any means necessary, himself, his family, or his real or personal property, or when coming to the aid of another who is in imminent danger of or the victim of aggravated assault, armed robbery, holdup, rape, murder, or other heinous crime." It was held unconstitutional on the ground that the legislature could not delegate to private citizens the power to fix and execute punishment.[4]

3. PREVENTION OF A FELONY AND APPREHENSION OF DANGEROUS FELONS

The right to take life to prevent the commission of a felony is confined to the prevention of a *dangerous* felony. A corollary of this principle is the rule that homicide is not justifiable when committed for the protection of mere property rights or interests, although the punishment for such killings is usually of the manslaughter grade rather than murder.[5]

fect" as well as the "imperfect" right to self-defense, consult Perkins, Self-Defense Re-Examined, 1 U.C.L.A.L.Rev. 133, 154–159 (1954).

3. This concept is further explored in the materials on "Mistake of Fact".

4. State v. Goodseal, 186 Neb. 359, 183 N.W.2d 258 (1971).

5. See State v. Green, 118 S.C. 279, 110 S.E. 145, 19 A.L.R. 1431 (1921) ("spring gun" killing). Thus a burglar or robber—but not a larcenist or trespasser—may be killed, if such a measure reasonably seems necessary to frustrate the criminal. In Commonwealth v. Beverly, 237 Ky. 35, 34 S.W.2d 941 (1931), which involved the shooting of chicken thieves, the court said:

4. DEFENSE OF HABITATION

Defense of the habitation against a dangerous intruder is a right which stems from the law's early view that a man's home is his "fortress" or "castle." This privilege permits one to take the life of an intending trespasser, if the dweller reasonably believes that the threatened entry is for the purpose of committing a felony or inflicting great bodily harm upon an occupant of the house.[6] The rule is even broader in some jurisdictions, allowing the occupant to prevent an intrusion the apparent purpose of which is an assault or other violence non-felonious in nature.[7] The right to defend the habitation permits one to use non-deadly force to prevent a mere civil trespass, although it does not countenance the use of deadly force for that purpose.[8] Where deadly force is inflicted upon a trespasser, however, aggravating circumstances of the trespass may constitute such provocation as to make the killing manslaughter, rather than murder.[9]

The rule allows defense of the habitation by guests or servants of the household, where the occupant himself would be justified in making a defense.[10] It has also been held to encompass the protection of one's

"The law does not justify the taking of human life to prevent a mere trespass without felonious intention, nor to prevent a felony not involving the security of the person or the home or in which violence is not a constituent part."

The right to kill to prevent a felony applies at any stage prior to completion of the crime. In Viliborghi v. State, 45 Ariz. 275, 291, 43 P.2d 210, 217 (1935), the court stated: "... the owner of the premises burglarized may, at any stage of a burglary, kill the burglar if it be reasonably necessary to prevent the final completion of his felonious purpose, regardless at what stage of the crime the shooting occurs. He may, even after the burglary has been completed, and the burglar is withdrawing from the scene of his crime, if the latter attempts to resist or flee from arrest, use such force as is reasonably necessary for the apprehension of the offender, even to the taking of life."

An individual not only has a right but also an obligation to prevent the commission of a felony in his presence. "According to the common law, it is the duty of everyone, seeing any felony attempted, by force to prevent it, if need be, by the extinguishment of the felon's existence. This is a public duty, and the discharge of it is regarded as promotive of justice. Any one who fails to discharge it is guilty of an indictable misdemeanor, called misprision of felony." Carpenter v. State, 62 Ark. 286, 308, 36 S.W. 900, 906 (1896).

Also see Sykes v. Dir. of Public Prosecutions [1961] 3 W.L.R. 371 [1961] 3 All Eng.R. 33, holding as misprision (and punishable as a misdemeanor) the failure to report a felony, even though the defendant committed no positive act of concealment. The case is reproduced in the subsequent section on "Parties to the Crime" in Chapter 8.

6. 52 A.L.R.2d 1458.

7. See, e.g., Hayner v. People, 213 Ill. 142, 72 N.E. 792 (1904), and also § 7–2 of the 1961 Illinois Criminal Code which permits the use of deadly force if the entry into a dwelling is made in a "violent, riotous, or tumultuous manner, and he reasonably believes that such force is necessary to prevent an assault upon, or offer personal violence to him or another then in the dwelling. . . ." See also Rex v. Hussey, 18 Cr.App.R. 160 (1924), criticized in 2 Cambridge L.Q. 231 (1925), as carrying the defense of one in his home to an "extreme limit."

8. State v. Hibler, 79 S.C. 170, 60 S.E. 438 (1907).

9. State v. Welch, 37 N.M. 549, 25 P.2d 211 (1933); State v. Adams, 78 Iowa 292, 43 N.W. 194 (1889).

10. Davis v. Commonwealth, 252 S.W.2d 9 (Ky.1952).

place of business, in addition to his dwelling.[11]

One is not bound to retreat from his own house, even if he may do so with safety, in order to avoid taking the life of an assailant. He may stand his ground and kill the aggressor if it becomes necessary.[12]

The use of spring guns or traps for the protection of property or dwellings, resulting in the death of an intruder, may expose the owner of the property to liability for homicide,[13] although some cases have suggested that where the landowner would have been entitled to use similar force if he had been present, the use of the device was lawful.[14]

Colorado excuses the use of deadly force when the victim has made an unlawful entry and the defendant reasonably believes the intruder committed or intended to commit a crime. The law has been dubbed the "Make May Day Statute" see People v. McNeese, 892 P.2d 304 (Colo. 1995).

5. DEFENSE OF PROPERTY OTHER THAN DWELLING

Ordinarily, deadly force cannot be used to protect property or to preserve a lawful right of possession. Use of such force, to be justified, must be sanctioned under a different principle, such as that of self defense, defense of dwelling, or preventing a felony.[15]

Consider the following provision of the Illinois Criminal Code 720 ILCS 5/7–3):

> § 7–3. **Use of Force in Defense of Other Property.** A person is justified in the use of force against another when and to the extent that he reasonably believes that such conduct is necessary to prevent or terminate such other's trespass on or other tortious or criminal interference with either real property (other than a dwelling) or personal property, lawfully in his possession or in the possession of another who is a member of his immediate family or household or of a person whose property he has a legal duty to protect. However, he is justified in the use of force which is intended or likely to cause death or great bodily harm only if he reasonably believes that such force is necessary to prevent the commission of a forcible felony.

11. Suell v. Derricott, 161 Ala. 259, 49 So. 895 (1909). Commonwealth v. Johnston, 438 Pa. 485, 263 A.2d 376 (1970). See, also, 41 A.L.R.3d 584.

12. Jones v. State, 76 Ala. 8 (1884).

13. State v. Childers, 133 Ohio St. 508, 14 N.E.2d 767 (1938); Pierce v. Commonwealth, 135 Va. 635, 115 S.E. 686 (1923); Katko v. Briney, 183 N.W.2d 657 (Iowa 1971); People v. Ceballos, 12 Cal.3d 470, 116 Cal.Rptr. 233, 526 P.2d 241 (1974).

14. State v. Beckham, 306 Mo. 566, 267 S.W. 817 (1924); State v. Barr, 11 Wash. 481, 39 P. 1080 (1895). However, in State v. Marfaudille, 48 Wash. 117, 92 P. 939 (1907), the court indicated that use of a device could be sanctioned only to prevent atrocious and violent felonies creating danger to human life.

15. Commonwealth v. Beverly, 237 Ky. 35, 34 S.W.2d 941 (1931); Montgomery v. Commonwealth, 98 Va. 840, 36 S.E. 371 (1900).

6. DEADLY FORCE BY POLICE OFFICERS

TENNESSEE v. GARNER

Supreme Court of the United States, 1985.
471 U.S. 1, 105 S.C. 1694.

JUSTICE WHITE delivered the opinion of the Court.

This case requires us to determine the constitutionality of the use of deadly force to prevent the escape of an apparently unarmed suspected felon. We conclude that such force may not be used unless it is necessary to prevent the escape and the officer has probable cause to believe that the suspect poses a significant threat of death or serious physical injury to the officer or others.

I

At about 10:45 p.m. on October 3, 1974, Memphis Police Officers Elton Hymon and Leslie Wright were dispatched to answer a "prowler inside call." Upon arriving at the scene they saw a woman standing on her porch and gesturing toward the adjacent house. She told them she had heard glass breaking and that "they" or "someone" was breaking in next door. While Wright radioed the dispatcher to say that they were on the scene, Hymon went behind the house. He heard a door slam and saw someone run across the back yard. The fleeing suspect, who was appellee-respondent's decedent, Edward Garner, stopped at a 6–feet–high chain link fence at the edge of the yard. With the aid of a flashlight, Hymon was able to see Garner's face and hands. He saw no sign of a weapon, and, though not certain, was "reasonably sure" and "figured" that Garner was unarmed. He thought Garner was 17 or 18 years old and about 5′5″ or 5′7″ tall.[1] While Garner was crouched at the base of the fence, Hymon called out "police, halt" and took a few steps toward him. Garner then began to climb over the fence. Convinced that if Garner made it over the fence he would elude capture,[2] Hymon shot him. The bullet hit Garner in the back of the head. Garner was

1. In fact, Garner, an eighth-grader, was 15. He was 5′ 4″ tall and weighed somewhere around 100 or 110 pounds. App. to Pet. for Cert. A5.

2. When asked at trial why he fired, Hymon stated:

> "Well, first of all it was apparent to me from the little bit that I knew about the area at the time that he was going to get away because, number 1, I couldn't get to him. My partner then couldn't find where he was because, you know, he was late coming around. He didn't know where I was talking about. I couldn't get to him because of the fence here, I couldn't have jumped this fence and come up, consequently jumped this fence and caught him before he got away because he was already up on the fence, just one leap and he was already over the fence, and so there is no way that I could have caught him."

He also stated that the area beyond the fence was dark, that he could not have gotten over the fence easily because he was carrying a lot of equipment and wearing heavy boots, and that Garner, being younger and more energetic, could have outrun him.

taken by ambulance to a hospital, where he died on the operating table. Ten dollars and a purse taken from the house were found on his body.[3]

In using deadly force to prevent the escape, Hymon was acting under the authority of a Tennessee statute and pursuant to Police Department policy. The statute provides that "[i]f, after notice of the intention to arrest the defendant, he either flee or forcibly resist, the officer may use all the necessary means to effect the arrest." Tenn.Code Ann. § 40–7–108 (1982). The Department policy was slightly more restrictive than the statute, but still allowed the use of deadly force in cases of burglary. The incident was reviewed by the Memphis Police Firearm's Review Board and presented to a grand jury. Neither took any action.

Garner's father then brought this action in the Federal District Court ... seeking damages under 42 U.S.C. § 1983 for asserted violations of Garner's constitutional rights. The complaint alleged that the shooting violated the Fourth, Fifth, Sixth, Eighth, and Fourteenth Amendments of the United States Constitution. It named as defendants Officer Hymon, the Police Department, its Director, and the Mayor and city of Memphis. After a 3–day bench trial, the District Court entered judgment for all defendants. It dismissed the claims against the Mayor and the Director for lack of evidence. It then concluded that Hymon's actions were authorized by the Tennessee statute, which in turn was constitutional. Hymon had employed the only reasonable and practicable means of preventing Garner's escape. Garner had "recklessly and heedlessly attempted to vault over the fence to escape, thereby assuming the risk of being fired upon."

The Court of Appeals for the Sixth Circuit affirmed with regard to Hymon, finding that he had acted in good-faith reliance on the Tennessee statute and was therefore within the scope of his qualified immunity. 600 F.2d 52 (1979). It remanded for reconsideration of the possible liability of the city.... The District Court was directed to consider whether a city enjoyed a qualified immunity, whether the use of deadly force and hollow point bullets in these circumstances was constitutional....

The District Court concluded that ... the statute and Hymon's actions, were constitutional....

The Court of Appeals reversed and remanded. It reasoned that the killing of a fleeing suspect is a "seizure" under the Fourth Amendment, and is therefore constitutional only if "reasonable." The Tennessee statute failed as applied to this case because it did not adequately limit the use of deadly force by distinguishing between felonies of different magnitudes—"the facts, as found, did not justify the use of deadly force

3. Garner had rummaged through one room in the house, in which, in the words of the owner, "[a]ll the stuff was out on the floors, all the drawers was pulled out, and stuff was scattered all over." The owner testified that his valuables were untouched but that, in addition to the purse and the 10 dollars, one of his wife's rings was missing. The ring was not recovered.

under the Fourth Amendment." Officers cannot resort to deadly force unless they "have probable cause ... to believe that the suspect [has committed a felony and] poses a threat to the safety of the officers or a danger to the community if left at large."

The State of Tennessee, which had intervened to defend the statute, appealed to this Court....

II

Whenever an officer restrains the freedom of a person to walk away, he has seized that person. United States v. Brignoni–Ponce. While it is not always clear just when minimal police interference becomes a seizure, see United States v. Mendenhall, there can be no question that apprehension by the use of deadly force is a seizure subject to the reasonableness requirement of the Fourth Amendment.

A

A police officer may arrest a person if he has probable cause to believe that person committed a crime. Petitioners and appellant argue that if this requirement is satisfied the Fourth Amendment has nothing to say about *how* that seizure is made. This submission ignores the many cases in which this Court, by balancing the extent of the intrusion against the need for it, has examined the reasonableness of the manner in which a search or seizure is conducted. To determine the constitutionality of a seizure "[w]e must balance the nature and quality of the intrusion on the individual's Fourth Amendment interests against the importance of the governmental interests alleged to justify the intrusion." United States v. Place. We have described "the balancing of competing interests" as "the key principle of the Fourth Amendment." Michigan v. Summers. Because one of the factors is the extent of the intrusion, it is plain that reasonableness depends on not only when a seizure is made, but also how it is carried out.

Applying these principles to particular facts, the Court has held that governmental interests did not support a lengthy detention of luggage, an airport seizure not "carefully tailored to its underlying justification," surgery under general anesthesia to obtain evidence, or detention for fingerprinting without probable cause. On the other hand, under the same approach it has upheld the taking of fingernail scrapings from a suspect, an unannounced entry into a home to prevent the destruction of evidence, administrative housing inspections without probable cause to believe that a code violation will be found, and a blood test of a drunk-driving suspect. In each of these cases, the question was whether the totality of the circumstances justified a particular sort of search or seizure.

B

The same balancing process applied in the cases cited above demonstrates that, notwithstanding probable cause to seize a suspect, an officer may not always do so by killing him. The intrusiveness of a seizure by means of deadly force is unmatched. The suspect's fundamental interest in his own life need not be elaborated upon. The use of deadly force also frustrates the interest of the individual, and of society, in judicial determination of guilt and punishment. Against these interests are ranged governmental interests in effective law enforcement.[4] It is argued that overall violence will be reduced by encouraging the peaceful submission of suspects who know that they may be shot if they flee. Effectiveness in making arrests requires the resort to deadly force, or at least the meaningful threat thereof. "Being able to arrest such individuals is a condition precedent to the state's entire system of law enforcement."

Without in any way disparaging the importance of these goals, we are not convinced that the use of deadly force is a sufficiently productive means of accomplishing them to justify the killing of nonviolent suspects. The use of deadly force is a self-defeating way of apprehending a suspect and so setting the criminal justice mechanism in motion. If successful, it guarantees that that mechanism will not be set in motion. And while the meaningful threat of deadly force might be thought to lead to the arrest of more live suspects by discouraging escape attempts,[5] the pres-

4. The dissent emphasizes that subsequent investigation cannot replace immediate apprehension. We recognize that this is so, see infra, n. 13; indeed, that is the reason why there is any dispute. If subsequent arrest were assured, no one would argue that use of deadly force was justified. Thus, we proceed on the assumption that subsequent arrest is not likely. Nonetheless, it should be remembered that failure to apprehend at the scene does not necessarily mean that the suspect will never be caught.

In lamenting the inadequacy of later investigation, the dissent relies on the report of the President's Commission on Law Enforcement and Administration of Justice. It is worth noting that, notwithstanding its awareness of this problem, the Commission itself proposed a policy for use of deadly force arguably even more stringent than the formulation we adopt today. See President's Commission on Law Enforcement and Administration of Justice, Task Force Report: The Police 189 (1967). The Commission proposed that deadly force be used only to apprehend "perpetrators who, in the course of their crime threatened the use of deadly force, or if the officer believes there is a substantial risk that the person whose arrest is sought will cause death or serious bodily harm if his apprehension is delayed." In addition, the officer would have "to know, as a virtual certainty, that the suspect committed an offense for which the use of deadly force is permissible." Ibid.

5. We note that the usual manner of deterring illegal conduct—through punishment—has been largely ignored in connection with flight from arrest. Arkansas, for example, specifically excepts flight from arrest from the offense of "obstruction of governmental operations." The commentary notes that this "reflects the basic policy judgment that, absent the use of force or violence, a mere attempt to avoid apprehension by a law enforcement officer does not give rise to an independent offense." Ark. Stat.Ann. § 41–2802(3)(a) (1977) and commentary. In the few States that do outlaw flight from an arresting officer, the crime is only a misdemeanor. See, e.g., Ind.Code § 35–44–3–3 (1982). Even forceful resistance, though generally a separate offense, is classified as a misdemeanor. E.g., Ill. Rev.Stat., ch. 38, § 31–1 (1984); Mont.Code Ann. § 45–7–301 (1984); N.H.Rev.Stat. Ann. § 642:2 (Supp.1983); Ore.Rev.Stat. § 162.315 (1983).

This lenient approach does avoid the anomaly of automatically transforming every fleeing misdemeanant into a fleeing felon—subject, under the common-law rule, to apprehension by deadly force—solely by virtue of his flight. However, it is in real tension with the harsh consequences of flight in cases where deadly force is employed. For example, Tennessee does not outlaw fleeing from arrest. The Memphis City Code does, § 30–15, subjecting the offender to a maximum fine of $50, § 1–8. Thus, Garner's attempted escape subjected him to (a) a $50 fine, and (b) being shot.

ently available evidence does not support this thesis.[6] The fact is that a majority of police departments in this country have forbidden the use of deadly force against nonviolent suspects. If those charged with the enforcement of the criminal law have abjured the use of deadly force in arresting nondangerous felons, there is a substantial basis for doubting that the use of such force is an essential attribute of the arrest power in all felony cases. Petitioners and appellant have not persuaded us that shooting nondangerous fleeing suspects is so vital as to outweigh the suspect's interest in his own life.

The use of deadly force to prevent the escape of all felony suspects, whatever the circumstances, is constitutionally unreasonable. It is not better that all felony suspects die than that they escape. Where the suspect poses no immediate threat to the officer and no threat to others, the harm resulting from failing to apprehend him does not justify the use of deadly force to do so. It is no doubt unfortunate when a suspect who is in sight escapes, but the fact that the police arrive a little late or are a little slower afoot does not always justify killing the suspect. A police officer may not seize an unarmed, nondangerous suspect by shooting him dead. The Tennessee statute is unconstitutional insofar as it authorizes the use of deadly force against such fleeing suspects.

It is not, however, unconstitutional on its face. Where the officer has probable cause to believe that the suspect poses a threat of serious physical harm, either to the officer or to others, it is not constitutionally unreasonable to prevent escape by using deadly force. Thus, if the suspect threatens the officer with a weapon or there is probable cause to believe that he has committed a crime involving the infliction or threatened infliction of serious physical harm, deadly force may be used if necessary to prevent escape, and if, where feasible, some warning has been given. As applied in such circumstances, the Tennessee statute would pass constitutional muster.

III

A

It is insisted that the Fourth Amendment must be construed in light of the common-law rule, which allowed the use of whatever force was necessary to effect the arrest of a fleeing felon, though not a misdemeanant. As stated in Hale's posthumously published Pleas of the Crown:

> "[I]f persons that are pursued by these officers for felony or the just suspicion thereof ... shall not yield themselves to these officers, but shall either resist or fly before they are apprehended or being apprehended shall rescue themselves and resist or fly, so that they cannot be otherwise apprehended, and are upon necessity slain therein, because they cannot be otherwise

6. See Sherman, Reducing Police Gun Use, in Control in the Police Organization 98, 120–123 (M.Punch, ed. 1983); Fyfe, Observations on Police Deadly Force, 27 Crime & Delinquency 376, 378–381 (1981); W. Geller & K. Karales, Split-Second Decisions 67 (1981); App. 84 (Affidavit of William Bracey, Chief of Patrol, New York City Police Department). See generally Brief for Police Foundation et al. as *Amici Curiae.*

taken, it is no felony." 2 M. Hale, Historia Placitorum Coronae 85 (1736). See also 4 W. Blackstone, Commentaries * 289.

Most American jurisdictions also imposed a flat prohibition against the use of deadly force to stop a fleeing misdemeanant, coupled with a general privilege to use such force to stop a fleeing felon; see generally R. Perkins & R. Boyce, Criminal Law 1098–1102 (3d ed. 1982); Day, Shooting the Fleeing Felon: State of the Law, 14 Crim.L.Bull. 285, 286–287 (1978); Wilgus, Arrest Without a Warrant, 22 Mich.L.Rev. 798, 807–816 (1924).

The State and city argue that because this was the prevailing rule at the time of the adoption of the Fourth Amendment and for some time thereafter, and is still in force in some States, use of deadly force against a fleeing felon must be "reasonable." It is true that this Court has often looked to the common law in evaluating the reasonableness, for Fourth Amendment purposes, of police activity. See, e.g., United States v. Watson. On the other hand, it "has not simply frozen into constitutional law those law enforcement practices that existed at the time of the Fourth Amendment's passage." Payton v. New York. Because of sweeping change in the legal and technological context, reliance on the common-law rule in this case would be a mistaken literalism that ignores the purposes of a historical inquiry.

B

It has been pointed out many times that the common-law rule is best understood in light of the fact that it arose at a time when virtually all felonies were punishable by death. "Though effected without the protections and formalities of an orderly trial and conviction, the killing of a resisting or fleeing felon resulted in no greater consequences than those authorized for punishment of the felony of which the individual was charged or suspected." American Law Institute, Model Penal Code § 3.07, Comment 3, p. 56 (Tentative Draft No. 8, 1958) (hereinafter Model Penal Code Comment). Courts have also justified the common-law rule by emphasizing the relative dangerousness of felons.

Neither of these justifications makes sense today. Almost all crimes formerly punishable by death no longer are or can be. And while in earlier times "the gulf between the felonies and the minor offences was broad and deep," today the distinction is minor and often arbitrary. Many crimes classified as misdemeanors, or nonexistent, at common law are now felonies. These changes have undermined the concept, which was questionable to begin with, that use of deadly force against a fleeing felon is merely a speedier execution of someone who has already forfeited his life. They have also made the assumption that a "felon" is more dangerous than a misdemeanant untenable. Indeed, numerous misdemeanors involve conduct more dangerous than many felonies.[7]

7. White collar crime, for example, poses a less significant physical threat than, say, drunken driving.

There is an additional reason why the common-law rule cannot be directly translated to the present day. The common-law rule developed at a time when weapons were rudimentary. Deadly force could be inflicted almost solely in a hand-to-hand struggle during which, necessarily, the safety of the arresting officer was at risk. Handguns were not carried by police officers until the latter half of the last century. L. Kennett & J. Anderson, The Gun in America 150–151 (1975). Only then did it become possible to use deadly force from a distance as a means of apprehension. As a practical matter, the use of deadly force under the standard articulation of the common-law rule has an altogether different meaning—and harsher consequences—now than in past centuries. See Wechsler & Michael, A Rationale for the Law of Homicide: I, 37 Colum.L.Rev. 701, 741 (1937).[8]

One other aspect of the common-law rule bears emphasis. It forbids the use of deadly force to apprehend a misdemeanant, condemning such action as disproportionately severe.

In short, though the common law pedigree of Tennessee's rule is pure on its face, changes in the legal and technological context mean the rule is distorted almost beyond recognition when literally applied.

C

In evaluating the reasonableness of police procedures under the Fourth Amendment, we have also looked to prevailing rules in individual jurisdictions. The rules in the States are varied. See generally Comment, 18 Ga.L.Rev. 137, 140–144 (1983). Some 19 States have codified the common-law rule, though in two of these the courts have significantly limited the statute. Four States, though without a relevant statute, apparently retain the common-law rule. Two States have adopted the Model Penal Code's provision verbatim. Eighteen others allow, in slightly varying language, the use of deadly force only if the suspect has committed a felony involving the use or threat of physical or deadly force, or is escaping with a deadly weapon, or is likely to endanger life or inflict serious physical injury if not arrested. Louisiana and Vermont, though without statutes or case law on point, do forbid the use of deadly force to prevent any but violent felonies. The remaining States either have no relevant statute or case-law, or have positions that are unclear.

It cannot be said that there is a constant or overwhelming trend away from the common-law rule. In recent years, some States have

8. It has been argued that sophisticated techniques of apprehension and increased communication between the police in different jurisdictions have made it more likely that an escapee will be caught than was once the case, and that this change has also reduced the "reasonableness" of the use of deadly force to prevent escape. E.g., Sherman, Execution Without Trial: Police Homicide and the Constitution, 33 Vand. L.Rev. 71, 76 (1980). We are unaware of any data that would permit sensible evaluation of this claim. Current arrest rates are sufficiently low, however, that we have some doubt whether in past centuries the failure to arrest at the scene meant that the police had missed their only chance in a way that is not presently the case. In 1983, 21% of the offenses in the FBI crime index were cleared by arrest. Federal Bureau of Investigation, Uniform Crime Reports, Crime in the United States 159 (1984). The clearance rate for burglary was 15%. Ibid.

reviewed their laws and expressly rejected abandonment of the common-law rule. Nonetheless, the longterm movement has been away from the rule that deadly force may be used against any fleeing felon, and that remains the rule in less than half the States.

This trend is more evident and impressive when viewed in light of the policies adopted by the police departments themselves. Overwhelmingly, these are more restrictive than the common-law rule. C. Milton, J. Halleck, J. Lardner, & G. Abrecht, Police Use of Deadly Force 45–46 (1977). The Federal Bureau of Investigation and the New York City Police Department, for example, both forbid the use of firearms except when necessary to prevent death or grievous bodily harm. For accreditation by the Commission on Accreditation for Law Enforcement Agencies, a department must restrict the use of deadly force to situations where "the officer reasonably believes that the action is in defense of human life ... or in defense of any person in immediate danger of serious physical injury." Commission on Accreditation for Law Enforcement Agencies, Inc., Standards for Law Enforcement Agencies 1–2 (1983) (italics deleted). A 1974 study reported that the police department regulations in a majority of the large cities of the United States allowed the firing of a weapon only when a felon presented a threat of death or serious bodily harm. Boston Police Department, Planning & Research Division, The Use of Deadly Force by Boston Police Personnel (1974). Overall, only 7.5% of departmental and municipal policies explicitly permit the use of deadly force against any felon; 86.8% explicitly do not. K. Matulia, A Balance of Forces: A Report of the International Association of Chiefs of Police 161 (1982) (table). See generally W. Geller & K. Karales, Split-Second Decisions 33–42 (1981); Brief for Police Foundation et al. as *Amici Curiae*. In light of the rules adopted by those who must actually administer them, the older and fading common-law view is a dubious indicium of the constitutionality of the Tennessee statute now before us.

Actual departmental policies are important for an additional reason. We would hesitate to declare a police practice of long standing "unreasonable" if doing so would severely hamper effective law enforcement. But the indications are to the contrary. There has been no suggestion that crime has worsened in any way in jurisdictions that have adopted, by legislation or departmental policy, rules similar to that announced today. *Amici* noted that "[a]fter extensive research and consideration, [they] have concluded that laws permitting police officers to use deadly force to apprehend unarmed, non-violent fleeing felony suspects actually do not protect citizens or law enforcement officers, do not deter crime or alleviate problems caused by crime, and do not improve the crime-fighting ability of law enforcement agencies." Brief for Police Foundation et al. as *Amici Curiae* 11. The submission is that the obvious state interests in apprehension are not sufficiently served to warrant the use of lethal weapons against all fleeing felons. See supra, at 1700–1701, and n. 10.

Nor do we agree with petitioners and appellant that the rule we have adopted requires the police to make impossible, split-second evaluations of unknowable facts. We do not deny the practical difficulties of attempting to assess the suspect's dangerousness. However, similarly difficult judgments must be made by the police in equally uncertain circumstances. See, e.g., *Terry v. Ohio.* Nor is there any indication that in States that allow the use of deadly force only against dangerous suspects, the standard has been difficult to apply or has led to a rash of litigation involving inappropriate second-guessing of police officers' split-second decisions. Moreover, the highly technical felony/misdemeanor distinction is equally, if not more, difficult to apply in the field. An officer is in no position to know, for example, the precise value of property stolen, or whether the crime was a first or second offense. Finally, as noted above, this claim must be viewed with suspicion in light of the similar self-imposed limitations of so many police departments.

IV

* * *

In reversing, the Court of Appeals accepted the District Court's factual conclusions and held that "the facts, as found, did not justify the use of deadly force." We agree. Officer Hymon could not reasonably have believed that Garner—young, slight, and unarmed—posed any threat. Indeed, Hymon never attempted to justify his actions on any basis other than the need to prevent an escape. The District Court stated in passing that "[t]he facts of this case did not indicate to Officer Hymon that Garner was 'non-dangerous.'" This conclusion is not explained, and seems to be based solely on the fact that Garner had broken into a house at night. However, the fact that Garner was a suspected burglar could not, without regard to the other circumstances, automatically justify the use of deadly force. Hymon did not have probable cause to believe that Garner, whom he correctly believed to be unarmed, posed any physical danger to himself or others.

The dissent argues that the shooting was justified by the fact that Officer Hymon had probable cause to believe that Garner had committed a nighttime burglary. While we agree that burglary is a serious crime, we cannot agree that it is so dangerous as automatically to justify the use of deadly force. The FBI classifies burglary as a "property" rather than a "violent" crime. See Federal Bureau of Investigation, Uniform Crime Reports, Crime in the United States 1 (1984). Although the armed burglar would present a different situation, the fact that an unarmed suspect has broken into a dwelling at night does not automatically mean he is physically dangerous. This case demonstrates as much. In fact, the available statistics demonstrate that burglaries only rarely involve physical violence. During the 10–year period from 1973–1982, only 3.8% of all burglaries involved violent crime. Bureau of Justice Statistics, Household Burglary, p. 4 (1985).[9] See also T. Reppetto,

9. The dissent points out that three-fifths of all rapes in the home, three-fifths of all home robberies, and about a third of home assaults are committed by burglars.

Residential Crime 17, 105 (1974); Conklin & Bittner, Burglary in a Suburb, 11 Criminology 208, 214 (1973).

* * *

The judgment of the Court of Appeals is affirmed, and the case is remanded for further proceedings consistent with this opinion.

So ordered.

JUSTICE O'CONNOR, with whom THE CHIEF JUSTICE and JUSTICE REHNQUIST join, dissenting.

The Court today holds that the Fourth Amendment prohibits a police officer from using deadly force as a last resort to apprehend a criminal suspect who refuses to halt when fleeing the scene of a nighttime burglary. This conclusion rests on the majority's balancing of the interests of the suspect and the public interest in effective law enforcement. Notwithstanding the venerable common-law rule authorizing the use of deadly force if necessary to apprehend a fleeing felon, and continued acceptance of this rule by nearly half the States, the majority concludes that Tennessee's statute is unconstitutional inasmuch as it allows the use of such force to apprehend a burglary suspect who is not obviously armed or otherwise dangerous. Although the circumstances of this case are unquestionably tragic and unfortunate, our constitutional holdings must be sensitive both to the history of the Fourth Amendment and to the general implications of the Court's reasoning. By disregarding the serious and dangerous nature of residential burglaries and the longstanding practice of many States, the Court effectively creates a Fourth Amendment right allowing a burglary suspect to flee unimpeded from a police officer who has probable cause to arrest, who has ordered the suspect to halt, and who has no means short of firing his weapon to prevent escape. I do not believe that the Fourth Amendment supports such a right, and I accordingly dissent.

I

The facts below warrant brief review because they highlight the difficult, split-second decisions police officers must make in these circumstances. Memphis Police Officers Elton Hymon and Leslie Wright responded to a late-night call that a burglary was in progress at a private residence. When the officers arrived at the scene, the caller said that "they" were breaking into the house next door. The officers found the

Post, at 1709. These figures mean only that if one knows that a suspect committed a rape in the home, there is a good chance that the suspect is also a burglar. That has nothing to do with the question here, which is whether the fact that someone has committed a burglary indicates that he has committed, or might commit, a violent crime.

The dissent also points out that this 3.8% adds up to 2.8 million violent crimes over a 10–year period, as if to imply that today's holding will let loose 2.8 million violent burglars. The relevant universe is, of course, far smaller. At issue is only that tiny fraction of cases where violence has taken place and an officer who has no other means of apprehending the suspect is unaware of its occurrence.

residence had been forcibly entered through a window and saw lights on inside the house. Officer Hymon testified that when he saw the broken window he realized "that something was wrong inside," but that he could not determine whether anyone—either a burglar or a member of the household—was within the residence. As Officer Hymon walked behind the house, he heard a door slam. He saw Edward Eugene Garner run away from the house through the dark and cluttered backyard. Garner crouched next to a 6–foot–high fence. Officer Hymon thought Garner was an adult and was unsure whether Garner was armed because Hymon "had no idea what was in the hand [that he could not see] or what he might have had on his person." In fact, Garner was 15–years old and unarmed. Hymon also did not know whether accomplices remained inside the house. The officer identified himself as a police officer and ordered Garner to halt. Garner paused briefly and then sprang to the top of the fence. Believing that Garner would escape if he climbed over the fence, Hymon fired his revolver and mortally wounded the suspected burglar.

* * *

... The precise issue before the Court deserves emphasis, because both the decision below and the majority obscure what must be decided in this case. The issue is not the constitutional validity of the Tennessee statute on its face or as applied to some hypothetical set of facts. Instead, the issue is whether the use of deadly force by Officer Hymon under the circumstances of this case violated Garner's constitutional rights. Thus, the majority's assertion that a police officer who has probable cause to seize a suspect "may not always do so by killing him," is unexceptionable but also of little relevance to the question presented here. The same is true of the rhetorically stirring statement that "[t]he use of deadly force to prevent the escape of all felony suspects, whatever the circumstances, is constitutionally unreasonable." The question we must address is whether the Constitution allows the use of such force to apprehend a suspect who resists arrest by attempting to flee the scene of a nighttime burglary of a residence.

II

For purposes of Fourth Amendment analysis, I agree with the Court that Officer Hymon "seized" Garner by shooting him. Whether that seizure was reasonable and therefore permitted by the Fourth Amendment requires a careful balancing of the important public interest in crime prevention and detection and the nature and quality of the intrusion upon legitimate interests of the individual. In striking this balance here, it is crucial to acknowledge that police use of deadly force to apprehend a fleeing criminal suspect falls within the "rubric of police conduct ... necessarily [involving] swift action predicated upon the on-the-spot observations of the officer on the beat." Terry v. Ohio. The clarity of hindsight cannot provide the standard for judging the reasonableness of police decisions made in uncertain and often dangerous circumstances. Moreover, I am far more reluctant than is the Court to conclude that the Fourth Amendment proscribes a police practice that was accepted at the time of the adoption of the Bill of Rights and has continued to receive the support of many state legislatures. Although the Court has recognized that the requirements of the Fourth Amendment must respond to the reality of social and technological change, fidelity to the notion of *constitutional*—as opposed to purely judicial—limits on governmental action requires us to impose a heavy burden on those who claim that practices accepted when the Fourth Amendment was adopted are now constitutionally impermissible.

The public interest involved in the use of deadly force as a last resort to apprehend a fleeing burglary suspect relates primarily to the serious nature of the crime. Household burglaries represent not only the illegal entry into a person's home, but also "pos[e] real risk of serious harm to others." Solem v. Helm (1983) (Burger, C.J., dissenting). According to recent Department of Justice statistics, "[t]hree-fifths of all rapes in the home, three-fifths of all home robberies, and about a third of home aggravated and simple assaults are committed by burglars." Bureau of Justice Statistics Bulletin. Household Burglary 1 (January 1985). During the period 1973–1982, 2.8 million such violent crimes were committed in the course of burglaries. Ibid. Victims of a forcible intrusion into their home by a nighttime prowler will find little consolation in the majority's confident assertion that "burglaries only rarely involve physical violence." Ante, at 1706. Moreover, even if a particular burglary, when viewed in retrospect, does not involve physical harm to others, the "harsh potentialities for violence" inherent in the forced entry into a home preclude characterization of the crime as "innocuous, inconsequential, minor, or 'nonviolent.'" Solem v. Helm. (Burger, C.J., dissenting). See also Restatement of Torts § 131, Comment *g* (1934) (burglary is among felonies that normally cause or threaten death or serious bodily harm); R. Perkins & R. Boyce, Criminal Law 1110 (3d ed. 1982) (burglary is dangerous felony that creates unreasonable risk of great personal harm).

Because burglary is a serious and dangerous felony, the public interest in the prevention and detection of the crime is of compelling importance. Where a police officer has probable cause to arrest a suspected burglar, the use of deadly force as a last resort might well be the only means of apprehending the suspect. With respect to ... burglary, subsequent investigation simply cannot represent a substitute for immediate apprehension of the criminal suspect at the scene. See Report of President's Commission on Law Enforcement and Administration of Justice, The Challenge of Crime in a Free Society 97 (1967). Indeed, the Captain of the Memphis Police Department testified that in his city, if apprehension is not immediate, it is likely that the suspect will not be caught. Although some law enforcement agencies may choose to assume the risk that a criminal will remain at large, the Tennessee statute reflects a legislative determination that the use of deadly force in prescribed circumstances will serve generally to protect the public. Such statutes assist the police in apprehending suspected perpetrators of serious crimes and provide notice that a lawful police order to stop and submit to arrest may not be ignored with impunity.

The Court unconvincingly dismisses the general deterrence effects by stating that "the presently available evidence does not support [the] thesis" that the threat of force discourages escape and that "there is a substantial basis for doubting that the use of such force is an essential attribute to the arrest power in all felony cases." There is no question that the effectiveness of police use of deadly force is arguable and that many States or individual police departments have decided not to authorize it in circumstances similar to those presented here. But it should go without saying that the effectiveness or popularity of a particular police practice does not determine its constitutionality. Cf. Spaziano v. Florida. ("The Eighth Amendment is not violated every time a State reaches a conclusion different from a majority of its sisters over how best to administer its criminal laws"). Moreover, the fact that police conduct pursuant to a state statute is challenged on constitutional grounds does not impose a burden on the State to produce social science statistics or to dispel any possible doubts about the necessity of the conduct. This observation, I believe, has particular force where the challenged practice both predates enactment of the Bill of Rights and continues to be accepted by a substantial number of the States.

Against the strong public interests justifying the conduct at issue here must be weighed the individual interests implicated in the use of deadly force by police officers. The majority declares that "[t]he suspect's fundamental interest in his own life need not be elaborated upon." This blithe assertion hardly provides an adequate substitute for the majority's failure to acknowledge the distinctive manner in which the suspect's interest in his life is even exposed to risk. For purposes of this case, we must recall that the police officer, in the course of investigating a nighttime burglary, had reasonable cause to arrest the suspect and ordered him to halt. The officer's use of force resulted because the suspected burglar refused to heed this command and the officer reasonably believed that there was no means short of firing his weapon to apprehend the suspect. Without questioning the importance of a person's interest in his life, I do not think this interest encompasses a right to flee unimpeded from the scene of a burglary. The legitimate interests of the suspect in these circumstances are adequately accommodated by the Tennessee statute: to avoid the use of deadly force and the consequent risk to his life, the suspect need merely obey the valid order to halt.

A proper balancing of the interests involved suggests that use of deadly force as a last resort to apprehend a criminal suspect fleeing from the scene of a nighttime burglary is not unreasonable within the meaning of the Fourth Amendment. Admittedly, the events giving rise to this case are in retrospect deeply regrettable. No one can view the death of an unarmed and apparently nonviolent 15–year old without sorrow, much less disapproval. Nonetheless, the reasonableness of Officer Hymon's conduct for purposes of the Fourth Amendment cannot be evaluated by what later appears to have been a preferable course of police action. The officer pursued a suspect in the darkened backyard of a house that from all indications had just been burglarized. The police officer was not certain whether the suspect was alone or unarmed; nor did he know what had transpired inside the house. He ordered the suspect to halt, and when the suspect refused to obey and attempted to flee into the night, the officer fired his weapon to prevent escape. The reasonableness of this action for purposes of the Fourth Amendment is not determined by the unfortunate nature of this particular case; instead, the question is whether it is constitutionally impermissible for police officers, as a last resort, to shoot a burglary suspect fleeing the scene of the crime.

* * *

III

Even if I agreed that the Fourth Amendment was violated under the circumstances of this case, I would be unable to join the Court's opinion. The Court holds that deadly force may be used only if the suspect "threatens the officer with a weapon or there is probable cause to believe that he has committed a crime involving the infliction or threatened infliction of serious physical harm." The Court ignores the more general implications of its reasoning. Relying on the Fourth Amendment, the majority asserts that it is constitutionally unreasonable to *use* deadly force against fleeing criminal suspects who do not appear to pose a threat of serious physical harm to others. By declining to limit its holding to the use of firearms, the Court unnecessarily implies that the Fourth Amendment constrains the use of any police practice that is potentially lethal, no matter how remote the risk.

Although it is unclear from the language of the opinion, I assume that the majority intends the word "use" to include only those circumstances in which the suspect is actually apprehended. Absent apprehension of the suspect, there is no "seizure" for Fourth Amendment purposes. I doubt that the Court intends to allow criminal suspects who successfully escape to return later with § 1983 claims against officers who used, albeit unsuccessfully, deadly force in their futile attempt to capture the fleeing suspect. The Court's opinion, despite its broad language, actually decides only that the shooting of a fleeing burglary suspect who was in fact neither armed nor dangerous can support a § 1983 action.

The Court's silence on critical factors in the decision to use deadly force simply invites second-guessing of difficult police decisions that must be made quickly in the most trying of circumstances. Police are given no guidance for determining which objects, among an array of potentially lethal weapons ranging from guns to knives to baseball bats to rope, will justify the use of deadly force. The Court also declines to outline the additional factors necessary to provide "probable cause" for believing that a suspect "poses a significant threat of death or serious physical injury," when the officer has probable cause to arrest and the suspect refuses to obey an order to halt. But even if it were appropriate in this case to limit the use of deadly force to that ambiguous class of suspects, I believe the class should include nighttime residential burglars who resist arrest by attempting to flee the scene of the crime. We can expect an escalating volume of litigation as the lower courts struggle to determine if a police officer's split-second decision to shoot was justified by the danger posed by a particular object and other facts related to the crime. Thus, the majority opinion portends a burgeoning area of Fourth Amendment doctrine concerning the circumstances in which police officers can reasonably employ deadly force.

IV

The Court's opinion sweeps broadly to adopt an entirely new standard for the constitutionality of the use of deadly force to apprehend fleeing felons. Thus, the Court "lightly brushe[s] aside," Payton v. New York, supra, at 600, 100 S.Ct., at 1387, a long-standing police practice that predates the Fourth Amendment and continues to receive the approval of nearly half of the state legislatures. I cannot accept the majority's creation of a constitutional right to flight for burglary suspects seeking to avoid capture at the scene of the crime. Whatever the constitutional limits on police use of deadly force in order to apprehend a fleeing felon, I do not believe they are exceeded in a case in which a police officer has probable cause to arrest a suspect at the scene of a residential burglary, orders the suspect to halt, and then fires his weapon as a last resort to prevent the suspect's escape into the night. I respectfully dissent.

NOTES

1. In Graham v. Connor, 490 U.S. 386, 109 S.Ct. 1865 (1989) the Court adopted an "objective reasonableness" standard for deciding civil liability cases based upon claimed excessive use of force, rather than a substantive due process standard. In determining whether a particular use of force was objectively reasonable, the Court ruled a trial court should focus upon three factors: (1) the severity of the crime, (2) the apparent threat posed by the suspect, and (3) whether the suspect was attempting to resist or flee. The officer's subjective intentions are not relevant under this test. His "evil intentions will not make a Fourth Amendment violation out of an objectively reasonable use of force; nor will an officer's good intentions make an objectively unreasonable use of force constitutional."

2. Pursuant to a grant from the National Institute of Justice (United States Department of Justice), the International Association of Chiefs of Police conducted an eighteen month study of police homicides from 1970 through 1979 in the nation's fifty-seven largest municipal police agencies. The report was published in 1981 under the title of A Balance of Forces: A Study of Justifiable Homicide by the Police. A brief summary of the report appears in the IACP Newsletter of December, 1981. The summary reads as follows:

"The authority to use deadly force is the most critical responsibility that will ever be placed on a police officer. No other single person has the right and the immediate means to lawfully take another's life.

"The consequences of a decision to use deadly force are irreversible after the fact—it is a final action. No court of competent jurisdiction, administrative tribunal, or Presidential grant of clemency can ever reverse the decision. Similarly, a decision not to use deadly force can also mean finality. A hesitation, or conscious decision on the part of the police officer could very well result in the death of the officer or another person the officer is sworn to safeguard. These are decisions unlike any other which are required by our society.

"The control of deadly force through the development of policy is also an awesome responsibility for the police administrator. The police administrator must promulgate use of deadly force policy that will provide sufficient protection to his officers; provide officers with guidance yet allow for a realistic exercise of discretion; provide all citizens with an assurance of safety; and provide all persons with the guarantees granted to them by the Constitution of the United States. Policy statements which meet these criteria can only be set forth after extensive research.

"The object of this study was to provide the police administrator with sufficient research data from which to:

- Identify factors of law enforcement that underlie and determine the frequency of use of deadly force by police officers.
- Gain an understanding of the interrelationships of these factors and their causal role in homicides by police officers.
- Develop 'model' policy and procedure designed to reduce police homicides while preserving the officer's ability to fulfill his law enforcement duties and protect himself from death or personal harm.

"This study primarily addresses those justifiable homicides which *may* be preventable through the adoption of new policy, training, equipment, and operational techniques.

"On the premise that a significant number of law enforcement-related homicides occur within urban areas, this study is focused on the 57 police agencies operating in urban areas having a population of 250,000 or more.

"The study included both empirical research and analytical review of factors considered to be associated with the use of deadly force by the police. The format of the final report includes:

- An introduction of the issues
- A legal review of the deadly force issues
- A statistical review which compares crime to justifiable homicide
- A survey and analysis of deadly force factors in 54 law enforcement agencies (three did not respond)
- A content analysis of deadly force policy in 53 law enforcement agencies (four did not respond)
- Recommended 'deadly force' policy guidelines

"Legal Review

"A review of the judicial holdings indicates that courts nationwide have been unable to establish a standard of law regarding the use of deadly force by the police. Secondly, it was found that at least four somewhat distinct standards of law exist in the 50 states. The Common Law which has its origination in the early days of our country permits an officer to stop a fleeing felon by whatever means he determines to be necessary. In the 23 states that have adopted the Common Law rule, the felon is not defined and courts have reverted to the original historical definition when all felonies were punishable by death.

"Many crimes which are today not punishable by death (larceny, burglary, embezzlement, check fraud, auto theft, and many others) nevertheless remain classified as felonies. Findings in this study show that police agencies in the Common Law states experience the highest (.33) mean justifiable homicide rate.

"Twelve states have adopted a 'Modified' Common Law rule. These states permit officers to employ deadly force to stop *specified* fleeing felons. The specified felonies, usually denoted as 'atrocious' or 'dangerous,' are commonly identified to include such crimes as murder, arson, mayhem, burglary, aggravated assault, rape, kidnap, extortion, and robbery. The findings of this study indicate that police agencies in the 'Modified' Common Law states experienced the lowest (.22) mean justifiable homicide rate.

"Seven states have been identified as adopting the 'Model Penal Code.' This code recommends that officers should be permitted to use deadly force to effect an arrest when: (1) the arrest is for a felony; (2) the person effecting the arrest is authorized to act as a police officer or is assisting a person whom he believes to be authorized to act as a peace officer; and (3) the officer believes the crime for which the arrest is being made involved conduct including the use or threatened use of deadly force; or (4) the officer believes there is a substantial risk that the person to be arrested will cause death or serious bodily harm if his apprehension is delayed.

"The remaining states (8) and the District of Columbia are governed by court holding rather than state law regarding deadly force. These holdings have ranged from a Common Law philosophy to a Model Penal Code with the majority leaning to the Common Law.

"In spite of these four categories of state law, it was found that most police agencies have a more restrictive firearms policy than is required by law. This is somewhat interesting in light of the fact that court opinion as to the legality of such restrictions has been mixed. For example, a number of courts have indicated that a more restrictive policy could be used as the standard of conduct in a civil case against a police officer while several other courts have held that a more restrictive policy cannot be used against an officer.

"Statistical Comparison of Crime to Justifiable Homicide

"Various authors have indicated that there may be a serious flaw in the statistical reporting of justifiable homicides by the police. Other criminal justice authorities who recognized the limitations have called for mandatory reporting of justifiable homicides. Despite the known limitations, it is felt that a careful analysis of justifiable homicide data would yield significant information. Accordingly, it was possible to secure from the FBI Uniform Crime Reports unpublished data regarding justifiable homicide for the years 1970 through 1979. For the 57 cities, the justifiable homicide totals were 291 in 1970, 388 in 1971, 314 in 1972, 317 in 1973, 356 in 1974, 360 in 1975, 268 in 1976, 262 in 1977, 249 in 1978 and 289 in 1979.

"For the years 1975–79, this data was verified with the reporting police agencies. Although the data was not always immediately parallel, it was ultimately possible to resolve any discrepancies that existed between the FBI data and the data submitted directly to IACP.

"Using the justifiable homicide totals as the common denominator, a comparison was made of the totals of selected crimes and justifiable homicide from the same cities. The following were found to be significantly related to justifiable homicide by the police:

· robbery offenses

· police officer murdered

· justifiable homicide by civilian

· total community homicide

Next, a comparison was made of *each* individual city's justifiable homicides by the police to selected crimes and justifiable homicide. This comparison was made by using a five-year average of justifiable homicide with the five-year average of crime. The significant correlations were:

· homicide

· violent crime

· robbery

· justifiable homicide by civilian

· police officers murdered

These correlations constitute the central research findings of this report. The findings imply that the use of deadly force by the police is concentrated within an environment of community violence in general.

"The Issue of Race

"It has been known that blacks are overrepresented among victims of justifiable homicide by the police. But never has the issue been presented in such a manner as in recent years. For example:

> 'Police have one trigger finger for whites and another for blacks.' (Dr. Paul Takagi, University of California researcher, in a speech before United Methodist Clergy and Laity, April 1979.)
>
> 'In the absence of more conclusive evidence, the demonstrably higher rates of police homicide of blacks strongly suggest racial discrimination on a national basis.' (Lawrence W. Sherman, Execution Without Trial: Police Homicide and the Constitution, Vanderbilt Law Review, January 1981, p. 97.)
>
> 'While we meet here, some police officer somewhere in America is shooting a civilian. And if today's case is typical, that civilian will be a black or a Hispanic person. If that incident follows the averages, it is likely the victim is a young person. It is likely that the incident involved a non-felony offense. It is possible the victim was unarmed. It is possible that the shooting could have been avoided. And it is certain that no punitive action will be taken against the policeman doing the shooting.' (Vernon E. Jordan, Jr., President, National Urban League, National Consultation on Safety and Force Summary Report, U.S. Department of Justice, Dec. '79, p. 7.)

"Like other researchers before us, this study found that blacks are overrepresented (59.6) as victims of police use of deadly force. However, our findings show that blacks are also overrepresented in other areas of violence:

· Justifiable homicide by police (59.6)

· Victims of justifiable homicide by civilians (73.1)

· Persons arrested for robbery (71.0)

· Persons arrested for violent crimes (63.7)

· Persons arrested for weapon violations (57.9)

"Concerning the shooters, 15.7 percent of all police officers who shoot civilians are black, 58.3 percent are white, 25.1 percent are of unreported race, and 0.9 percent are of 'other' races.

"These research findings do not statistically prove or disprove the existence of police discrimination. What the data are consistent with is that the disproportionate rate of black victims of police justifiable homicide is in proportion to the level of police exposure to blacks as represented by blacks arrested for crime.

"Survey and Analyses of Potential Deadly Force Factors

"Using the number of justifiable homicides identified (1975–79) and the number of police officers, a Justifiable Homicide Rate (JHR) was established for each city. The rate ranged from a low of .04 justifiable homicides per 100 officers per year to a high of .77 with the mean being .28.

"A survey instrument consisting of more than 300 data points was developed and mailed to 57 major police agencies (fifty-four agencies completed the survey). The instrument was designed to identify pertinent data relative to each agency's personnel practices, training, firearms equipment, organizational units, policy, and procedure which could lead to answers as to why police agencies use deadly force in differing frequencies. Responses to the survey were statistically compared to the JHR in each city. One or more statistical tests were used to test hypotheses concerning the independent variables represented by the survey responses and the dependent variable represented by the JHR.

"The results of this analysis showed the following variables to be associated with high justifiable homicide rates:

1. A high supervisory/officer ratio
2. The use of semi-automatic handguns by SWAT [Special Weapons and Tactics] units
3. In-service SWAT unit training
4. The absence of policy for the management of stake-out units
5. The absence of policy for the management of decoy units
6. Patrol command response to the scene of deadly force incidents
7. Police chief and district attorney review of deadly force incidents
8. In-service crisis intervention training
9. Exertion type of pre-service firearms training
10. Exertion and stress in-service firearms training
11. The awarding of incentives for firearms marksmanship
12. In-service officer survival training
13. The issuance of on-duty firearms larger than .38 caliber
14. The issuance of shotguns

"These findings should be interpreted with caution since it was not always possible to clearly establish a cause/effect relationship using this research approach. For example, patrol command, police chief and district attorney response to deadly force may be the effect of a high JHR rather than the cause; likewise, the emphasis on training may have come about as a result of a high justifiable homicide rate.

"Policy Content Analysis

"Selected national deadly force policy recommendations were reviewed in an effort to obtain a "feel" for the community desires. Such reviews included policy, resolutions, or recommendations offered by: (1) the American Law Institute, (2) Federal Bureau of Investigation, (3) International Association of Chiefs of Police, (4) the President's Commission on Law Enforcement and Administration of Justice, (5) the Wisconsin Institute of Government Affairs, (6) the American Bar Association, (7) the National Organization of Black Law Enforcement Executives, (8) the United Nations, and (9) the American Civil Liberties Union. These recommendations were found to be inconsistent, vague, and generally less than comprehensive.

"Next a cursory analysis of a limited number of deadly force directives submitted by federal law enforcement agencies was conducted. This analysis shed only a little light on the issue of municipal police use of deadly force. Their statements are more general in nature than are the guidelines issued by municipal agencies. The differences in federal law enforcement missions was evident in the directives.

"A similar analysis was undertaken of state police and state patrol agencies. Their deadly force directives were found to be generally consistent with state law but not more restrictive than law.

"Fifty-three municipal police agencies responded to our request for a copy of their deadly force directives. These directives (policy, general order, operating procedure, training bulletin) were evaluated in relationship to each agency's justifiable homicide rate in an effort to determine if any relationships existed.

"Recommended Policy Guidelines

"The research report is concluded with a chapter which details 'model' use of deadly force policy and procedural guidelines which are designed to aid the police chief executive in determining specific agency directives. These 'model' guidelines are based on the report's (1) legal findings, (2) statistical testing of 40 hypotheses which took into account more than 300 management and operational factors which were considered as possible influences on the rate of justifiable homicide, (3) analysis and statistical testing of 53 agencies' written directives which deal with the use of deadly force issue, and (4) the thorough review of findings from other deadly force research efforts.

"The 'model' guidelines specifically address the policy, procedural, and equipment issues related to defense of life, reasonable danger, imminent threat, prevention of felonies, fleeing felons, juveniles, moving vehicles, warning shots, shooting of animals, on-duty firearms, off-duty firearms, secondary firearms, control of all firearms, type and frequency of certification training, post-shooting legal services, post-shooting psychological services, the shooting investigation, and the shooting review process.

"Deadly force policy decisions are not easily made by the chief executive, nor is the ultimate decision to shoot an easy one for the law enforcement officer.

The consequences of deadly force policy and action decisions are far-reaching. It is, however, far better that most of the decision considerations be critically researched and developed from within a calm, rational atmosphere of the administrator's office than from the explosive, irrational, and unpredictable 'office' (the street) of the police officer.

"Consequently, each police chief executive must promulgate and continuously update use of deadly force directives. The executive is encouraged to use the 'model' guidelines and supporting research as a framework to develop local deadly force training standards, equipment standards, and policy and procedural directives."

See the 1982 article by Professor James J. Fyfe, Blind Justice: Police Shootings in Memphis, 73 J.Crim.L. & C. 707 (1982), and also, Geller, Deadly Force, What We Know, 10 J.Police Sci. & Adm. 151 (1982).

D. INVOLUNTARY MANSLAUGHTER

STATE v. HORTON

Supreme Court of North Carolina, 1905.
139 N.C. 588, 51 S.E. 945.

[The defendant, Horton, in violation of a statute, was hunting turkeys on the land of another without the written consent of the owner of the land or his lawful agent. While hunting, Horton unintentionally killed one Hunt, mistaking him for a wild turkey. Horton was indicted for manslaughter, convicted and sentenced to four months in the county jail. Thereupon, the defendant appealed.]

HOKE, JUSTICE. It will be noted that the finding of the jury declares that the act of the defendant was not in itself dangerous to human life, and excludes every element of criminal negligence, and rests the guilt or innocence of the defendant on the fact alone that at the time of the homicide the defendant was hunting on another's land without written permission from the owner. The act ... makes the conduct a misdemeanor, and imposes a punishment on conviction of not less than $5 nor more than $10. The statement sometimes appears in works of approved excellence to the effect that an unintentional homicide is a criminal offense when occasioned by a person engaged at the time in an unlawful act. In nearly every instance, however, will be found the qualification that if the act in question is free from negligence, and not in itself of dangerous tendency, and the criminality must arise, if at all, entirely from the fact that it is unlawful, in such case, the unlawful act must be one that is "malum in se," and not merely "malum prohibitum," and this we hold to be the correct doctrine....

... Bishop, in his work entitled New Criminal Law (volume 1, § 332), treats of the matter as follows: "In these cases of an unintended evil result, the intent whence the act accidentally sprang must probably be, if specific, to do a thing which is malum in se, and not merely malum prohibitum." Thus Archbold says: "When a man in the execution of one act, by misfortune or chance, and not designedly, does another act, for which, if he had willfully committed it, he would be liable to be punished, in that case, if the act he were doing were lawful, or merely malum prohibitum, he shall not be punishable for the act arising from misfortune or chance; but, if it be malum in se, it is otherwise. To illustrate: Since it is malum prohibitum, not malum in se, for an unauthorized person to kill game in England contrary to the statutes, if, in unlawfully shooting at game, he accidentally kills a man, it is no more criminal in him than if he were authorized. But to shoot at another's fowls, wantonly or in sport, an act which is malum in se, though a civil trespass, and thereby accidentally to kill a human being, is manslaughter. If the intent in the shooting were to commit larceny of the fowls, we have seen that it would be murder." To same effect is Estell v. State, 51 N.J.L. 182, 17 A. 118; Com. v. Adams, 114 Mass. 323, 19 Am.Rep. 362. An offense malum in se is properly defined as one which is naturally evil as adjudged by the sense of a civilized community, whereas an act malum prohibitum is wrong only because made so by statute. For the reason that acts malum in se have, as a rule, become criminal offenses by the course and development of the common law, an impression has sometimes obtained that only acts can be so classified which the common law makes criminal; but this is not at all the test. An act can be, and frequently is, malum in se, when it amounts only to a civil trespass, provided it has a malicious element or manifests an evil nature or wrongful disposition to harm or injure another in his person or property. Bishop, Cr.Law, supra; Com. v. Adams, supra. The distinction between the two classes of acts is well stated in 19 Am. & Eng.Enc. (2d Ed.), at page 705: "An offense malum in se is one which is naturally evil, as murder, theft, and the like. Offenses at common law are generally malum in se. An offense malum prohibitum, on the contrary, is not naturally an evil, but becomes so in consequence of being forbidden."

We do not hesitate to declare that the offense of the defendant in hunting on the land without written permission of the owner was malum prohibitum, and, the special verdict having found that the act in which the defendant was engaged was not in itself dangerous to human life and negatived all idea of negligence, we hold that the case is one of excusable homicide, and the defendant should be declared not guilty....

... [It] has been called to our attention that courts of the highest authority have declared that the distinction between malum prohibitum and malum in se is unsound, and has now entirely disappeared. Our own court so held in Sharp v. Farmer, 20 N.C. 255, and decisions to the same effect have been made several times since. Said Ruffin, C.J., in Sharp v. Farmer: "The distinction between an act malum in se and one malum prohibitum was never sound, and is entirely disregarded; for the law would be false to itself if it allowed a party through its tribunals to derive advantage from a contract made against the intent and express provisions of the law." It will be noted that this decision was on a case involving the validity of a contract, and the principle there established is undoubtedly correct. The fact, however, that the judge who delivered the opinion uses the words "was never sound," and that other opinions to the same effect use the words "has disappeared," shows that the distinction has existed; and it existed, too, at a time when this feature in the law of homicide was established. And we are well assured that because the courts, in administering the law on the civil side of the docket, have come to the conclusion that a principle once established is unsound and should be rejected, this should not have the effect of changing the character of an act from innocence to guilt, which had its status fixed when the distinction was recognized and enforced....

There was error in holding the defendant guilty, and, on the facts declared, a verdict of not guilty should be directed, and the defendant discharged.

Reversed.

NOTE

Compare the following statement of the court in State v. Brown, 205 S.C. 514, 519, 32 S.E.2d 825, 827 (1945):

"The responsibility for a death is sometimes made to depend on whether the unlawful act is malum in se or malum prohibitum. The authorities agree, however, without regard to this distinction, that if the act is a violation of a statute intended and designated to prevent injury to the person, and is itself dangerous, and death ensues, the person violating the statute is guilty of manslaughter at least."

COMMONWEALTH v. FEINBERG

Superior Court of Pennsylvania, 1967.
211 Pa.Super. 100, 234 A.2d 913, aff'd 433 Pa. 558, 253 A.2d 636.

MONTGOMERY, JUDGE. These appeals are from judgments of sentence imposed following appellant's conviction on five charges of involuntary manslaughter. They arose by reason of the deaths of five individuals from methyl alcohol (methanol) poisoning due to their consumption of Sterno, a jelly-like substance prepared and intended for heating purposes. It is solidified alcohol popularly called "canned heat" but has additives specified by the United States government to render it unfit for drinking purposes.

Appellant Max Feinberg was the owner of a cigar store handling tobacco, candy, etc., in the skid-row section of Philadelphia and sold to residents of that area Sterno in two types of containers, one for home use and one for institutional use. Such sales were made under circumstances from which it could be reasonably concluded that appellant knew the purchasers were intending to use it for drinking purposes by diluting it with water or other beverages, and not for its intended use. Prior to December, 1963, there had been no known fatal consequences resulting from this practice, presumably for the reason that the product then sold by appellant contained only four per cent methyl alcohol (methanol). However, on December 21, 1963 appellant bought from the Richter

Paper Company ten additional cases of institutional Sterno containing seventy-two cans each, unaware that it contained fifty-four per cent methanol, although the lid of each container was marked "Institutional Sterno. Danger. Poison; Not for home use. For commercial and industrial use only", and had a skull and crossbones imprinted thereon. Nevertheless appellant ignored this warning and sold part of this supply in the same manner he had previously dispensed his other supply of the product. The containers of the regular Sterno and the institutional type previously sold contained no such warning and were merely marked "Caution. Flammable. For use only as a fuel." The only difference in the containers previously sold was that the institutional type was so marked but had no wrap-around label as was affixed to the container intended for regular use. Both containers were the same size, as were the containers sold after December 21st which did not contain wrap-around labels. Between December 23 and December 30, 1963, thirty-one persons died in this area as a result of methyl alcohol poisoning. After hearing of their deaths, appellant, on December 28, 1963 returned to the Richter Paper Company four cases and forty-two cans which remained unsold from the ten cases he had purchased on December 21, 1963, at which time he remarked about the change in markings on the cans. Appellant was the only purchaser in the Philadelphia area of this new institutional product from the Richter Company. The methanol content of institutional Sterno had been increased by the manufacturer from four per cent to fifty-four per cent in September, 1963 but the new product was not marketed until December, 1963. Richter received the first shipment of it on December 11, and another on December 17, 1963. The chemical contents of the new institutional product were not stated on the container; nor was the appellant informed otherwise of any change in the contents of that product except by the notice of its dangerous contents for home use, as previously recited.

It is the contention of the appellant that his convictions on the charges of involuntary manslaughter cannot be sustained . . . as a result of any criminal negligence on his part. . . .

There remains the question of whether the Commonwealth has established that the deaths under consideration were due to the criminal negligence of the appellant. Involuntary manslaughter consists of the killing of another person without malice and unintentionally, but in doing some unlawful act not amounting to a felony, or in doing some lawful act in an unlawful way. Where the act in itself is not unlawful, to make it criminal the negligence must be of such a departure from prudent conduct as to evidence a disregard of human life or an indifference to consequences. . . .

We are satisfied that the record clearly establishes that appellant, in the operation of his small store with part-time help, knew that he was selling Sterno in substantial quantities to a clientele that was misusing it; that in order to profit more from such sales he induced Richter Paper Company to procure for him a supply of the institutional product because the cost of same was less than the regular type with labels; that he was aware of the "poison" notice and warning of harmful effects of the new shipment received on December 21, 1963 but nevertheless placed it in stock for general sale by himself and his employees; and thereafter sold several hundred cans of it; and that he dispensed it without warning his purchasers of the harmful effect it would have if misused for drinking purposes, and without directing their attention to the warning on the containers.

If the deaths of these five persons were the result of appellant's actions, it justifies his conviction for involuntary manslaughter. Although a more culpable degree of negligence is required to establish a criminal homicide than is required in a civil action for damages, we find the appellant's actions as fully meeting the definition and requirement of proof set forth in Commonwealth v. Aurick, 342 Pa. 282, 19 A.2d 920 (1941). In the light of the recognized weaknesses of the purchasers of the product, and appellant's greater concern for profit than with the results of his actions, he was grossly negligent and demonstrated a wanton and reckless disregard for the welfare of those whom he might reasonably have expected to use the product for drinking purposes. . . .

We find no merit in appellant's argument that there is no evidence to prove he ever sold a can of the new institutional Sterno. The evidence clearly shows that he was in full charge of the operation of the store when the bulk of the new product was sold. Harold was only a part-time employe coming in after school and on Saturdays, and during this period appellant's wife and family were in Florida, which left appellant as the one who made the bulk of the sales.

Nor do we find any merit in his argument that he was unaware of the warning on the cans. He must have handled many of them during the course of events when almost four hundred cans were sold. The circumstances established by the evidence sufficiently supports a finding that he did know of the change in markings but disregarded it. As far as instructing anyone else to sell the product, the fact that it was available for sale in an opened carton under the counter is sufficient to indicate an implied authorization.

The facts in this case do not indicate the prosecution of a person for acts done by another without his knowledge or consent. Appellant was the active participant with full knowledge. He, personally, and through his part-time employe, acting under his orders, committed the crimes. . . .

The judgments of sentence, therefore, are affirmed in the cases of Lynwood Scott; John Streich; James Newsome; and Juanita Williams; and the judgment is reversed and appellant discharged in the case of Edward Harrell.

HOFFMAN, J., files a dissenting opinion.

* * *

NOTES

1. When death is caused through an overdose of drugs or excessive use of liquor, the courts generally require that the person furnishing the drugs or liquor be shown to have unlawfully furnished the substances. Also, it must be established that the unlawful furnishing is the proximate cause of the death. In People v. Cruciani, 70 Misc.2d 528, 334 N.Y.S.2d 515 (Suffolk County Ct.1972), an indictment of criminally negligent homicide was sustained when it was shown to be predicated upon the defendant having injected a 19-year old girl with a hypodermic syringe containing heroin. The court held it was proper for the jury to determine whether the defendant's administering of the heroin created a substantial and unjustifiable risk of death.

Depending upon the degree of foreseeability of death under the circumstances of a case, the charge could properly be murder. In Ureta v. Superior Court, 199 Cal.App.2d 672, 18 Cal.Rptr. 873 (1962), a murder prosecution for a death produced by morphine poisoning, the court stated it made no difference whether the decedent or the defendant who furnished the drug actually injected it. Where the victim injected himself with narcotics delivered by defendant, a manslaughter conviction may be valid. State v. Wassil, 233 Conn. 174, 658 A.2d 548 (1995).

2. If, during a legal abortion, a doctor fails to take steps to keep an aborted fetus alive, can the doctor be convicted of involuntary manslaughter? A Massachusetts jury answered affirmatively in the 1975 trial of Dr. Kenneth C. Edelin, chief resident in surgery in a Boston hospital, who aborted a fetus during a legal hysterotomy performed on a woman between 22 and 24 weeks pregnant. Superior Court Judge James P. McGuire sentenced Dr. Edelin to one year's probation, but stayed the sentence pending an appeal. The Massachusetts Supreme Judicial Court reversed the conviction and ordered that a judgment of acquittal be entered. Commonwealth v. Edelin, 371 Mass. 497, 359 N.E.2d 4 (1976).

3. In People v. Nelson, 309 N.Y. 231, 128 N.E.2d 391 (1955), the owner of an apartment building which was in violation of the New York Multiple Dwelling Law and constituted a fire hazard was convicted of manslaughter when two tenants died in a fire. The court held that failure to comply with various building codes regarding fire safety constituted conduct of such a nature that human life was endangered.

PEOPLE v. MARSHALL

Supreme Court of Michigan, 1961.
362 Mich. 170, 106 N.W.2d 842.

SMITH, JUSTICE. At approximately 3:00 a.m. on the morning of February 4, 1958, a car driven by Neal McClary, traveling in the wrong direction on the Edsel Ford Expressway, crashed head-on into another vehicle driven by James Coldiron. The drivers of both cars were killed. Defendant William Marshall has been found guilty of involuntary manslaughter of Coldiron. At the time that the fatal accident took place, he, the defendant William Marshall, was in bed at his place of residence. His connection with it was that he owned the car driven by McClary, and as the evidence tended to prove, he voluntarily gave his keys to the car to McClary, with knowledge that McClary was drunk.

The principal issue in the case is whether, upon these facts, the defendant may be found guilty of involuntary manslaughter. It is axiomatic that "criminal guilt under our law is personal fault." ... As Sayre ... puts the doctrine "it is of the very essence of our deep-rooted notions of criminal liability that guilt be personal and individual." This was not always true in our law, nor is it universally true in all countries even today, but for us it is settled doctrine.

The State relies on a case, Story v. United States, ... in which the owner, driving with a drunk, permitted him to take the wheel, and was held liable for aiding and abetting him "in his criminal negligence." The owner, said the court, sat by his side and permitted him "without protest so recklessly and negligently to operate the car as to cause the death of another." ... If defendant Marshall had been by McClary's side an entirely different case would be presented, but on the facts before us Marshall, as we noted, was at home in bed. The State also points out that although it is only a misdemeanor to drive while drunk, yet convictions for manslaughter arising out of drunk driving have often been sustained. It argues from these cases that although it was only a misdemeanor for an owner to turn his keys over to a drunk driver, nevertheless a conviction for manslaughter may be sustained if such driver kills another. This does not follow from such cases as Story, supra. In the case before us death resulted from the misconduct of driver. The accountability of the owner must rest as a matter of general principle, upon his complicity in such misconduct. In turning his keys over, he was guilty of a specific offense, for which he incurred a specific penalty. Upon these facts he cannot be held a principal with respect to the fatal accident: the killing of Coldiron was not counselled by him, accomplished by another acting jointly with him, nor did it occur in the attempted achievement of some common enterprise.

This is not to say that defendant is guilty of nothing. He was properly found guilty of violation of paragraph (b) of section 625 of the Michigan vehicle code which makes it punishable for the owner of an automobile knowingly to permit it to be driven by a person "who is under the influence of intoxicating liquor." The State urges that this is not enough, that its manslaughter theory, above outlined, "was born of necessity," and that the urgency of the drunk-driver problem "has made it incumbent upon responsible and concerned law enforcement officials to seek new approaches to a new problem within the limits of our law." What the State actually seeks from us is an interpretation that the manslaughter statute imposes an open-end criminal liability. That is to say, whether the owner may ultimately go to prison for manslaughter or some lesser offense will depend upon whatever unlawful act the driver commits while in the car. Such a theory may be defensible as a matter of civil liability but [in his American Rights, 85, 86] Gellhorn's language in another criminal context is equally applicable here: "It is a basic proposition in a constitutional society that crimes should be defined in advance, and not after action has been taken." We are not unaware of the magnitude of the problem presented, but the new approaches demanded for its solution rest with the legislature, not the courts.

The view we have taken of the case renders it unnecessary to pass upon other allegations of error. The verdict and sentence on that count of the information dealing with involuntary manslaughter are set aside and the case remanded to the circuit court for sentencing on the verdict of the jury respecting the violation, as charged, of section 625(b) of the Michigan Vehicle Code, discussed hereinabove.

PEOPLE v. DECINA

Court of Appeals of New York, 1956.
2 N.Y.2d 133, 157 N.Y.S.2d 558, 138 N.E.2d 799.

FROESSEL, JUDGE. At about 3:30 p.m. on March 14, 1955, a bright, sunny day, defendant was driving, alone in his car, in a northerly direction on Delaware Avenue in the city of Buffalo. The portion of Delaware Avenue here involved is 60 feet wide. At a point south of an overhead viaduct of the Erie Railroad, defendant's car swerved to the left, across the center line in the street, so that it was completely in the south lane, traveling 35 to 40 miles per hour.

It then veered sharply to the right, crossing Delaware Avenue and mounting the easterly curb at a point beneath the viaduct and continued thereafter at a speed estimated to have been about 50 or 60 miles per hour or more. During this latter swerve, a pedestrian testified that he saw defendant's hand above his head; another witness said he saw defendant's left arm bent over the wheel, and his right hand extended towards the right door.

A group of six schoolgirls were walking north on the easterly sidewalk of Delaware Avenue, two in front and four slightly in the rear, when defendant's car struck them from behind. One of the girls escaped injury by jumping against the wall of the viaduct. The bodies of the children struck were propelled northward onto the street and the lawn in front of a coal company, located to the north of the Erie viaduct on Delaware Avenue. Three of the children, 6 to 12 years old, were found dead on arrival by the medical examiner, and a fourth child, 7 years old, died in a hospital two days later as a result of injuries sustained in the accident.

After striking the children, defendant's car continued on the easterly sidewalk, and then swerved back onto Delaware Avenue once more. It continued in a northerly direction passing under a second viaduct before it again veered to the right and remounted the easterly curb, striking and breaking a metal lamppost. With its horn blowing steadily—apparently because defendant was "stooped over" the steering wheel—the car proceeded on the sidewalk until it finally crashed through a 7¼-inch brick wall of a grocery store, injuring at least one customer and causing considerable property damage.

When the car came to a halt in the store, with its horn still blowing, several fires had been ignited. Defendant was stooped over in the car and was "bobbing a little". To one witness he appeared dazed, to another unconscious, lying back with his hands off the wheel. Various people present shouted to defendant to turn off the ignition of his car, and "within a matter of seconds the horn stopped blowing and the car did shut off."

Defendant was pulled out of the car by a number of bystanders and laid down on the sidewalk. To a policeman who came on the scene shortly he appeared "injured, dazed"; another witness said that "he looked as though he was knocked out, and his arm seemed to be bleeding". An injured customer in the store, after receiving first aid, pressed defendant for an explanation of the accident and he told her: "I blacked out from the bridge".

When the police arrived, defendant attempted to rise, staggered and appeared dazed and unsteady. When informed that he was under arrest, and would have to accompany the police to the station house, he resisted and, when he tried to get away, was handcuffed. The foregoing evidence was adduced by the People, and is virtually undisputed—defendant did not take the stand nor did he produce any witnesses.

From the police station defendant was taken to the E.J. Meyer Memorial Hospital. . . .

[There,] defendant proceeded to relate to Dr. Wechter his past medical history, namely, that at the age of 7 he was struck by an auto and suffered a marked loss of hearing. In 1946 he was treated in this same hospital for an illness during which he had some convulsions. Several burr holes were made in his skull and a brain abscess was drained. Following this operation defendant had no convulsions from 1946 through 1950. In 1950 he had four convulsions, caused by scar tissue on the brain. From 1950 to 1954 he experienced about 10 or 20 seizures a year, in which his right hand would jump although he remained fully conscious. In 1954, he had 4 or 5 generalized seizures with loss of consciousness, the last being in September, 1954, a few months before the accident. Thereafter he had more hospitalization, a spinal tap, consultation with a neurologist, and took medication daily to help prevent seizures.

On the basis of this medical history, Dr. Wechter made a diagnosis of Jacksonian epilepsy, and was of the opinion that defendant had a seizure at the time of the accident. Other members of the hospital staff performed blood tests and took an electroencephalogram during defendant's three-day stay there. The testimony of Dr. Wechter is the only testimony before the trial court showing that defendant had epilepsy, suffered an attack at the time of the accident, and had knowledge of his susceptibility to such attacks.

Defendant was indicted and charged with violating section 1053–a of the Penal Law, Consol.Laws, c. 40.[1] Following his conviction, after a

1. "Any person who operates or drives any vehicle of any kind in a reckless or culpably negligent manner, whereby a human being is killed, is guilty of criminal negligence in the operation of a vehicle resulting in death". (A person convicted of

demurrer to the indictment was overruled, the Appellate Division, while holding that the demurrer was properly overruled, reversed on the law, the facts having been "examined" and found "sufficient". It granted a new trial upon the ground that the "transactions between the defendant and Dr. Wechter were between physician and patient for the purpose of treatment and that treatment was accomplished", and that evidence thereof should not have been admitted. From its determination both parties have appealed.

We turn first to the subject of defendant's cross appeal, namely, that his demurrer should have been sustained, since the *indictment* here does not charge a crime. The indictment states essentially that defendant, *knowing* "that he was subject to epileptic attacks or other disorder rendering him likely to lose consciousness for a considerable period of time", was culpably negligent "in that he *consciously* undertook to and *did operate* his Buick sedan on a public highway" (emphasis supplied) and "while so doing" suffered such an attack which caused said automobile "to travel at a fast and reckless rate of speed, jumping the curb and driving over the sidewalk" causing the death of 4 persons. In our opinion, this clearly states a violation of section 1053–a of the Penal Law. The statute does not require that a defendant must deliberately intend to kill a human being, for that would be murder. Nor does the statute require that he knowingly and consciously follow the precise path that leads to death and destruction. It is sufficient, we have said, when his conduct manifests a "disregard of the consequences which may ensue from the act, and indifference to the rights of others. No clearer definition, applicable to the hundreds of varying circumstances that may arise, can be given. Under a given state of facts, whether negligence is culpable is a question of judgment." . . .

Assuming the truth of the indictment, as we must on a demurrer, this defendant knew he was subject to epileptic attacks and seizures that might strike *at any time*. He also knew that a moving motor vehicle uncontrolled on a public highway is a highly dangerous instrumentality capable of unrestrained destruction. With this *knowledge*, and without anyone accompanying him, he deliberately took a chance by making a conscious choice of a course of action, in disregard of the consequences which he knew might follow from his conscious act, and which in this case did ensue. How can we say as a matter of law that this did not amount to culpable negligence within the meaning of section 1053–a?

To hold otherwise would be to say that a man may freely indulge himself in liquor in the same hope that it will not affect his driving, and if it later develops that ensuing intoxication causes dangerous and reckless driving resulting in death, his unconsciousness or involuntariness at that time would relieve him from prosecution under the statute. His awareness of a condition which he knows may produce such consequences as here, and his disregard of the consequences, renders him

violating § 1053–a is punishable by imprisonment up to 5 years, or a fine up to $1,000, or both. § 1053–b.)

liable for culpable negligence, as the courts below have properly held.... To have a sudden sleeping spell, an unexpected heart or other disabling attack, without any prior knowledge or warning thereof, is an altogether different situation, see Jenson v. Fletcher, ... and there is simply no basis for comparing such cases with the flagrant disregard manifested here....

Accordingly, the Appellate Division properly sustained the lower court's order overruling the demurrer, as well as its denial of the motion in arrest of judgment on the same ground....

DESMOND, JUDGE (dissenting in part).... The indictment charges that defendant knowing that "he was subject to epileptic attacks or other disorder rendering him likely to lose consciousness" suffered "an attack and loss of consciousness which caused the said automobile operated by the said defendant to travel at a fast and reckless rate of speed" and to jump a curb and run onto the sidewalk "thereby striking and causing the death" of 4 children. Horrible as this occurrence was and whatever necessity it may show for new licensing and driving laws, nevertheless this indictment charges no crime known to the New York statutes. Our duty is to dismiss it.

Section 1053–a of the Penal Law describes the crime of "criminal negligence in the operation of a vehicle resulting in death". Declared to be guilty of that crime is "A person who operates or drives any vehicle of any kind in a reckless or culpably negligent manner, whereby a human being is killed". The essentials of the crime are, therefore, first, vehicle *operation* in a culpably negligent *manner*, and second, the resulting death of a person. This indictment asserts that defendant violated section 1053–a, but it then proceeds in the language quoted in the next-above paragraph of this opinion to describe the way in which defendant is supposed to have offended against that statute. That descriptive matter (an inseparable and controlling ingredient of the indictment, ...) shows that defendant did *not* violate section 1053–a. No *operation* of an automobile in a reckless manner is charged against defendant. The excessive speed of the car and its jumping the curb were "caused", says the indictment itself, by defendant's prior "attack and loss of consciousness". Therefore, what defendant is accused of is *not* reckless or culpably negligent driving, which necessarily connotes and involves consciousness and volition. The fatal assault by this car was after and because of defendant's failure of consciousness. To say that one drove a car in a reckless manner in that his unconscious condition caused the car to travel recklessly is to make two mutually contradictory assertions. One cannot be "reckless" while unconscious. One cannot while unconscious "operate" a car in a culpably negligent manner or in any other "manner". The statute makes criminal a particular kind of knowing, voluntary, immediate operation. It does not touch at all the involuntary presence of an unconscious person at the wheel of an uncontrolled vehicle. To negative the possibility of applying section 1053–a to these alleged facts we do not even have to resort to the rule that all criminal statutes are closely and strictly construed in favor of the citizen and that no act or omission is criminal unless specifically and in terms so labeled by a clearly worded statute,. . . .

Tested by its history section 1053–a has the same meaning: penalization of conscious operation of a vehicle in a culpably negligent manner. It is significant that until this case ... no attempt was ever made to penalize, either under section 1053–a or as manslaughter, the wrong done by one whose foreseeable blackout while driving had consequences fatal to another person.

The purpose of and occasion for the enactment of section 1053–a is well known (see Governor's Bill Jacket on L.1936 ch. 733). It was passed to give a new label to, and to fix a lesser punishment for, the culpably negligent automobile driving which had formerly been prosecuted under section 1052 of the Penal Law defining manslaughter in the second degree. It had been found difficult to get manslaughter convictions against death-dealing motorists. But neither of the two statutes has ever been thought until now to make it a crime to drive a car when one is subject to attacks or seizures such as are incident to certain forms and levels of epilepsy and other diseases and conditions.

Now let us test by its consequences this new construction of section 1053–a. Numerous are the diseases and other conditions of a human being which make it possible or even likely that the afflicted person will lose control of his automobile. Epilepsy, coronary involvements, circulatory diseases, nephritis, uremic poisoning, diabetes, Meniere's syndrome, a tendency to fits of sneezing, locking of the knee, muscular contractions—any of these common conditions may cause loss of control of a vehicle for a period long enough to cause a fatal accident. An automobile traveling at only 30 miles an hour goes 44 feet in a second. Just what is the court holding here? No less than this: that a driver whose brief blackout lets his car run amuck and kill another has killed that other by reckless driving. But any such "recklessness" consists necessarily not of the erratic behavior of the automobile while its driver is unconscious, but of his driving at all when he knew he was subject to such attacks. Thus, it must be that such a blackout-prone driver is guilty of reckless driving, Vehicle and Traffic Law, Consol.Laws, c. 71, § 58, whenever and as soon as he steps into the driver's seat of a vehicle. Every time he drives, accident or no accident, he is subject to criminal prosecution for reckless driving or to revocation of his operator's license, Vehicle and Traffic Law, § 71, subd. 3. And how many of this State's 5,000,000 licensed operators are subject to such penalties for merely driving the cars they are licensed to drive? No one knows how many citizens or how many or what kind of physical conditions will be gathered in under this practically limitless coverage of section 1053–a of the Penal Law and section 58 and subdivision 3 of section 71 of the Vehicle and Traffic Law. It is no answer that prosecutors and juries will be reasonable or compassionate. A criminal statute whose reach is so unpredictable violates constitutional rights, as we shall now show.

When section 1053–a was new it was assailed as unconstitutional on the ground that the language "operate or drives any vehicle of any kind in a reckless or culpably negligent manner" was too indefinite since a driver could only guess as to what acts or omissions were meant. Constitutionality was upheld in People v. Gardner,.... The then Justice Lewis, later of this court, wrote in People v. Gardner that the statutory language was sufficiently explicit since "reckless driving" and "culpable negligence" had been judicially defined in manslaughter cases as meaning the operation of an automobile in such a way as to show a disregard of the consequences,.... The *manner* in which a car is driven may be investigated by a jury, grand or trial, to see whether the manner was such as to show a reckless disregard of consequences. But giving section 1053–a the new meaning assigned to it permits punishment of one who did not drive in any forbidden manner but should not have driven at all, according to the present theory. No motorist suffering from any serious malady or infirmity can with impunity drive any automobile at any time or place, since no one can know what physical conditions make it "reckless" or "culpably negligent" to drive an automobile. Such a construction of a criminal statute offends against due process and against justice and fairness. The courts are bound to reject such conclusions when, as here, it is clearly possible to ascribe a different but reasonable meaning,....

A whole new approach may be necessary to the problem of issuing or refusing drivers' licenses to epileptics and persons similarly afflicted.... But the absence of adequate licensing controls cannot in law or in justice be supplied by criminal prosecutions of drivers who have violated neither the language nor the intendment of any criminal law.

Entirely without pertinence here is any consideration of driving while intoxicated or while sleepy, since those are conditions presently known to the driver, not mere future possibilities or probabilities.

The demurrer should be sustained and the indictment dismissed.

CONWAY, CH. J., DYE and BURKE, JJ., concur with FROESSEL, J.; DESMOND, J., concurs in part and dissents in part in an opinion in which FULD and VAN VOORHIS, JJ., concur.

Order affirmed.

NOTES

1. For an interesting note on the Decina case, supra, and its companion case, People v. Eckert, 2 N.Y.2d 126, 138 N.E.2d 794 (1956), see 43 Cornell L.Q. 117 (1957).

2. Many states have enacted "Negligent Homicide" or "Reckless Homicide" statutes similar to the one in the Decina case. An Oregon statute, repealed in 1971, provided that death caused by the driving of a motor vehicle in a "negligent manner" constitutes "negligent homicide", and "negligent" is defined as "a want of such attention to the natural or probable consequences of the act or omission referred to as a prudent man ordinarily bestows in acting in his own concerns." In State v. Wojahn, 204 Or. 84, 282 P.2d 675 (1955), the Supreme Court of Oregon upheld the constitutionality of this statute against the

contention that it was vague, indefinite and a violation of due process. In discussing the purpose of this type of legislation, the court said: "Negligent homicide statutes were adopted after the manslaughter acts had proved ineffective as a means of repressing the negligence in motor vehicle operation which was causing deaths upon the public thoroughfares. Possibly the success of the new legislation, if it in truth achieved any, resulted from the fact that in common understanding manslaughter acts deal with brutal killings by a debased type of individual, whereas the motorist is generally a reputable citizen, and the wrong committed by him which brought someone to his death finds its counterpart in the driving of many others."

E. THE "PROXIMATE CAUSE" ISSUE IN HOMICIDE CASES

COMMONWEALTH v. ROOT

Supreme Court of Pennsylvania, 1961.
403 Pa. 571, 170 A.2d 310.

CHARLES ALVIN JONES, CHIEF JUSTICE. The appellant was found guilty of involuntary manslaughter for the death of his competitor in the course of an automobile race between them on a highway. The trial court overruled the defendant's demurrer to the Commonwealth's evidence and, after verdict, denied his motion in arrest of judgment. On appeal from the judgment of sentence entered on the jury's verdict, the Superior Court affirmed. We granted allocatur because of the important question present as to whether the defendant's unlawful and reckless conduct was a sufficiently direct cause of the death to warrant his being charged with criminal homicide.

The testimony, which is uncontradicted in material part, discloses that, on the night of the fatal accident, the defendant accepted the deceased's challenge to engage in an automobile race; that the racing took place on a rural 3-lane highway; that the night was clear and dry, and traffic light; that the speed limit on the highway was 50 miles per hour; that, immediately prior to the accident, the two automobiles were being operated at varying speeds of from 70 to 90 miles per hour; that the accident occurred in a no-passing zone on the approach to a bridge where the highway narrowed to two directionally-opposite lanes; that, at the time of the accident, the defendant was in the lead and was proceeding in his right hand lane of travel; that the deceased, in an attempt to pass the defendant's automobile, when a truck was closely approaching from the opposite direction, swerved his car to the left, crossed the highway's white dividing line and drove his automobile on the wrong side of the highway head-on into the oncoming truck with resultant fatal effect to himself.

This evidence would of course amply support a conviction of the defendant for speeding, reckless driving and, perhaps, other violations of The Vehicle Code of May 1, 1929, P.L. 905, as amended. In fact, it may be noted, in passing, that the Act of January 8, 1960, ... makes automobile racing on a highway an independent crime punishable by fine or imprisonment or both up to $500 and three years in jail. As the highway racing in the instant case occurred prior to the enactment of the Act of 1960, ... that statute is, of course, not presently applicable. In any event, unlawful or reckless conduct is only one ingredient of the crime of involuntary manslaughter. Another essential and distinctly separate element of the crime is that the unlawful or reckless conduct charged to the defendant was the *direct* cause of the death in issue. The first ingredient is obviously present in this case but, just as plainly, the second is not.

While precedent is to be found for application of the tort law concept of "proximate cause" in fixing responsibility for criminal homicide, the want of any rational basis for its use in determining criminal liability can no longer be properly disregarded. When proximate cause was first borrowed from the field of tort law and applied to homicide prosecutions in Pennsylvania, the concept connoted a much more direct causal relation in producing the alleged culpable result than it does today. Proximate cause, as an essential element of a tort founded in negligence, has undergone in recent times, and is still undergoing, a marked extension. More specifically, this area of civil law has been progressively liberalized in favor of claims for damages for personal injuries to which careless conduct of others can in some way be associated. To persist in applying the tort liability concept of proximate cause to prosecutions for criminal homicide after the marked expansion of *civil* liability of defendants in tort actions for negligence would be to extend possible *criminal* liability to persons chargeable with unlawful or reckless conduct in circumstances not generally considered to present the likelihood of a resultant death....

The instant case is one of first impression in this State; and our research has not disclosed a single instance where a district attorney has ever before attempted to prosecute for involuntary manslaughter on facts similar to those established by the record now before us. The closest case, factually, would seem to be Commonwealth v. Levin, ... which affirmed the defendant's conviction of involuntary manslaughter. In the Levin case two cars were racing on the streets of Philadelphia at speeds estimated at from 85 to 95 miles per hour. The defendant's car, in the left hand lane, was racing alongside of the car in which the deceased was a passenger when the defendant turned his automobile sharply to the right in front of the other car thereby causing the driver of the latter car to lose control and smash into a tree, the passenger being thrown to the road and killed as a result of the impact. It is readily apparent that the elements of causation in the Levin case were fundamentally different from those in the present case. Levin's act of cutting his automobile sharply in front of the car in which the deceased was riding directly forced that car off of the road and into the tree. The defendant's reckless and unlawful maneuver was the direct cause of the crucial fatality. In the instant case, the defendant's conduct was not even remotely comparable. Here, the action of the deceased driver in recklessly and suicidally swerving his car to the left lane of a 2-lane highway into the path of an oncoming truck was not forced upon him by any act of the defendant; it was done by the deceased and by him alone, who thus directly brought about his own demise. The Levin case was properly decided but it cannot, by any ratiocination, be utilized to justify a conviction in the present case.

Legal theory which makes guilt or innocence of criminal homicide depend upon such accidental and fortuitous circumstances as are now embraced by modern tort law's encompassing concept of proximate cause is too harsh to be just....

Even if the tort liability concept of proximate cause were to be deemed applicable, the defendant's conviction of involuntary manslaughter in the instant case could not be sustained under the evidence. The operative effect of a supervening cause would have to be taken into consideration. Commonwealth v. Redline,.... But, the trial judge refused the defendant's point for charge to such effect and erroneously instructed the jury that "negligence or want of care on the part of [the deceased] is no defense to the criminal responsibility of the defendant...."

The Superior Court, in affirming the defendant's conviction in this case, approved the charge above mentioned, despite a number of decisions in involuntary manslaughter cases holding that the conduct of the deceased victim must be considered in order to determine whether the defendant's reckless acts were the proximate (i.e., sufficiently direct) cause of his death.... The Superior Court dispensed with this decisional authority.... It did so on the ground that there can be more than one proximate cause of death. The point is wholly irrelevant. Of course there can be more than one proximate cause of death just as there can also be more than one *direct* cause of death. For example, in the so-called "shield" cases where a felon interposes the person of an innocent victim between himself and a pursuing officer, if the officer should fire his gun at the felon to prevent his escape and fatally wound the person used as a shield, the different acts of the policeman and the felon would each be a direct cause of the victim's death.

If the tort liability concept of proximate cause were to be applied in a criminal homicide prosecution, then the conduct of the person whose death is the basis of the indictment would have to be considered, not to prove that it was merely an *additional* proximate cause of the death, but to determine under fundamental and long recognized law applicable to proximate cause, whether the subsequent wrongful act *superseded* the original conduct chargeable to the defendant. If it did in fact supervene, then the original act is so insulated from the ensuing death as not to be its proximate cause.

Under the uncontradicted evidence in this case, the conduct of the defendant was not the proximate cause of the decedent's death as a matter of law. In Kline v. Moyer and Albert, 1937 ..., the rule is stated as follows: "Where a second actor has become aware of the existence of a potential danger created by the negligence of an original tort-feasor, and thereafter, by an independent act of negligence, brings about an accident, the first tort-feasor is relieved of liability, because the condition created by him was merely a circumstance of the accident and not its proximate cause." ...

In [Johnson v. Angretti, 1950, the defendant] was driving his truck eastward along a highway, a bus traveling in the same direction in front of him, stopped to take on a passenger. Angretti swerved his truck to the left into the lane of oncoming traffic in an attempt to pass the bus but collided with a tractor-trailer driven by the plaintiff's decedent, who was killed as a result of the collision. In affirming the entry of judgment n.o.v. in favor of the defendant bus company, we held that any negligence on the part of the bus driver, in suddenly bringing his bus to a halt in order to pick up a passenger was not a proximate cause of the death of the plaintiff's decedent since the accident "was due entirely to the intervening and superseding negligence of Angretti in allowing his truck to pass over into the pathway of the westbound tractor-trailer...."

In the case now before us, the deceased was aware of the dangerous condition created by the defendant's reckless conduct in driving his automobile at an excessive rate of speed along the highway but, despite such knowledge, he recklessly chose to swerve his car to the left and into the path of an oncoming truck, thereby bringing about the head-on collision which caused his own death....

The judgment of sentence is reversed and the defendant's motion in arrest of judgment granted.

BELL, JUSTICE (concurring). I concur in the result reached by the majority opinion. I also agree that in recent years the doctrine of tort liability in civil cases has been extended and stretched to such an extent that it should no longer be applied in criminal cases. This is especially necessary because the tests for involuntary manslaughter, particularly in cases arising out of automobile accidents, have been different and varying in the Superior Court and in the lower Courts, with no clear standard. This was due to an attempt by these Courts to apply a proper test to the different circumstances of each particular case. For example the following tests have been applied by the Superior Court: Rash or reckless conduct; proximate cause; legal cause; substantial factor; natural and probable consequence such as should have been foreseen; efficient cause; concurring cause; must be more than remote cause—substantial factor; natural result or probable consequence....

What is involuntary manslaughter? Involuntary manslaughter is a misdemeanor and is very different from murder and from voluntary manslaughter. The prime difference between murder, voluntary manslaughter, and involuntary manslaughter may be thus summarized: Murder is an unlawful killing of another person with malice aforethought, expressed or implied....

Voluntary manslaughter is the intentional killing of another person which is committed under the influence of passion. . . .

Involuntary manslaughter is an unintentional and nonfelonious killing of another person without malice or passion, which results from conduct by defendant which is so unlawful as to be outrageous, provided such conduct is a direct cause of the killing.

The unlawful racing by this defendant was not only unlawful, it was outrageous, but it was not a direct cause, i.e., one of the direct causes, of the killing.

EAGEN, JUSTICE (dissenting). The opinion of the learned Chief Justice admits, under the uncontradicted facts, that the defendant, at the time of the fatal accident involved, was engaged in an unlawful and reckless course of conduct. Racing an automobile at 90 miles per hour, trying to prevent another automobile going in the same direction from passing him, in a no-passing zone on a two-lane public highway, is certainly all of that. Admittedly also, there can be more than one direct cause of an unlawful death. To me, this is self-evident. But, says the majority opinion, the defendant's recklessness was not a direct cause of the death. With this, I cannot agree.

If the defendant did not engage in the unlawful race and so operate his automobile in such a reckless manner, this accident would never have occurred. He helped create the dangerous event. He was a vital part of it. The victim's acts were a natural reaction to the stimulus of the situation. The race, the attempt to pass the other car and forge ahead, the reckless speed, all of these factors the defendant himself helped create. He was part and parcel of them. That the victim's response was normal under the circumstances, that his reaction should have been expected and was clearly foreseeable, is to me beyond argument. That the defendant's recklessness was a substantial factor is obvious. All of this, in my opinion, makes his unlawful conduct a direct cause of the resulting collision.

The cases cited in support of the majority opinion are not in point. For instance, in Johnson v. Angretti, 1950, . . . this Court, in affirming the trial court, found that the bus driver *was not guilty of any negligence or violation of the Motor Vehicle Code* in bringing the bus to a stop. The Court, as dicta, then went on to say,. . . . "Moreover it is clear that such alleged violation bore no causal relation whatever to the happening of the accident which was due entirely to the intervening and superseding negligence of Angretti in allowing his truck to pass over into the pathway of the westbound tractor-trailer instead of bringing his vehicle to a stop as Osterling [the driver of the truck directly behind the bus and in front of Angretti] had done and *as he admitted he could readily have done without colliding with the truck ahead of him.* The situation created by the stopping of the bus was merely a circumstance of the accident and not its proximate cause: (citing cases)." It is readily apparent that the instant case and the Angretti case are distinguishable in all the important factors. In the present case there was, (1) recklessness and a violation of the Motor Vehicle Code; (2) a joint venture or common enterprise of racing; (3) no proof that Hall could have guided his car back into the right-hand lane behind Root after he became aware of the danger of the oncoming truck.

Nor does the case of Kline v. Moyer and Albert, 1937, ... lend support. Quite to the contrary, both the facts and the law oppose it. The majority omits the pertinent part of the rule cited, ... the whole of which is as follows: "Where a second actor has become aware of the existence of a potential danger created by the negligence of an original tort-feasor, and thereafter, by an independent act of negligence, brings about an accident, the first tort-feasor is relieved of liability, because the condition created by him was merely a circumstance of the accident and not its proximate cause. *Where, however, the second actor does not become apprised of such danger until his own negligence, added to that of the existing perilous condition, has made the accident inevitable, the negligent acts of the two tort-feasors are contributing causes and proximate factors in the happening of the accident and impose liability upon both of the guilty parties.*" The Kline case involved a truck, operated by Albert, which he abandoned on a highway without any lights to warn approaching motorists of the danger. Moyer drove down the highway and upon seeing the truck, failed to reduce his speed and went into the lane of oncoming traffic and crashed into Kline. This Court said.... "It is clear that when an unlighted, parked truck is seen by the operator of an approaching vehicle, the fact of its being unlighted becomes *thereafter* of legal inconsequence, because the purpose of a light as warning has been otherwise accomplished. *If already at that time, by the negligence of its driver, the moving vehicle is in such a position and under such impetus that an accident cannot be avoided, the negligence of the truck owner is as much a proximate cause of the accident as is the negligence of the driver of the car; the negligence of each has contributed to the result.* But if, after seeing the unlighted truck, although he would still have been able to guide his car without accident, the driver proceeds in such negligent manner that an accident results, the original negligence of the truck owner has become a non-causal factor divested of legal significance; as to it the chain of causation is broken, and responsibility remains solely with the operator of the moving car." Because the evidence was not undisputed that Moyer became aware of the presence of the abandoned truck on the highway in time to stop, we stated that the question of causal connection was for the jury and not for the court as a matter of law. In the present case, there wasn't any evidence that Hall saw the oncoming truck when he pulled out to pass Root. This would have been suicide, against which there is a presumption.... The act of passing was not an "extraordinarily negligent" act, but rather a "normal response" to the act of "racing." Furthermore, as Hall pulled out to pass, Root "dropped off" his speed to 90 miles an hour. Such a move probably prevented Hall from getting back into the right-hand lane since he was alongside of Root at the time and to brake the car at that speed would have been fatal to both himself and Root. Moreover, the dangerous condition of which the deceased had to become aware of before the defendant was relieved of his direct causal connection with the ensuing accident, was not the fact that the defendant was driving at an excessive rate of speed along the highway. He knew that when the race began many miles and minutes earlier. *The dangerous condition necessary was an awareness of the oncoming truck and the fact that at the rate of speed Root was traveling he couldn't safely pass him.* This important fact was not shown and, therefore, was a question for the fact-finders and not a question that could be decided as a matter of law....

Professor Joseph Beale, late renowned member of the Harvard Law School faculty, in an article entitled, The Proximate Consequence of an Act, 33 Harv.L.Rev. 633, 646, said, "Though there is an active force intervening after defendant's act, the result will nevertheless be proximate if the defendant's act actually caused the intervening force. In such a case the defendant's force is really continuing in active operation *by means of the force it stimulated into activity.*" Professor Beale, at 658, sums up the requirements of proximity of result in this manner: "1. The defendant must have acted (or failed to act in violation of a duty). 2. The force thus created must (a) have remained active itself or created another *force* which remained active until it directly caused the result; or (b) have created a new active *risk* of being acted upon by the active force that caused the result." 2 Bishop, New Criminal Law § 424 (1913), says: "He whose act causes in any way, directly or indirectly, the death of another, kills him, within the meaning of felonious homicide. It is a rule of both reason and the law that whenever one's will contributes to impel a physical force, whether another's, his own, or a combined force, proceeding from whatever different sources, he is responsible for the result, the same as though his hand, unaided, had produced it."

But, says the majority opinion, these are principles of tort law and should not in these days be applied to the criminal law. But such has been the case since the time of Blackstone. These same principles have always been germane to both crimes and tort. See, Beale, Recovery for Consequence of an Act, 9 Harv.L.Rev. 80; Greene, Rationale of Proximate Cause, 132–133 (1927); Frederick C. Moesel, Jr., A Survey of Felony Murder, 28 Temp.L.Q. 453, 459–466. They have been repeatedly so applied throughout the years and were employed in a criminal case in Pennsylvania as long as one hundred and seventeen years ago. See, Commonwealth v. Hare, 1844, 2 Clark 467. In that case, two separate bands of men were fighting each other with firearms in a public street and, as a result, an innocent citizen was shot and killed. The person firing the fatal shot could not be ascertained. Hare, one of the rioters, was convicted of homicide and the judgment was affirmed. Can anyone question the logic or correctness of this decision? Under the rationale of the majority opinion, what would be the result in the Hare case? Certainly, under its reasoning, if the truck driver met death under the circumstances the case at hand presents, the defendant would not be legally responsible. Again with this conclusion, I cannot agree.

While the victim's foolhardiness in this case contributed to his own death, he was not the only one responsible and it is not he alone with whom we are concerned. It is the people of the Commonwealth who are harmed by the kind of conduct the defendant pursued. Their interests must be kept in mind.

I, therefore, dissent and would accordingly affirm the judgment of conviction.

NOTES

1. Compare the decision of the Supreme Court of Montana in State v. Strobel, 130 Mont. 442, 304 P.2d 606 (1956). In that case, the defendant, while driving to the left of the centerline of the highway, collided with a gasoline truck driven by one Little. The truck overturned and exploded causing Little's death. The defendant was convicted of manslaughter and appealed. In reversing the judgment and ordering a new trial, the court stated:

"Instruction No. 7, submitting the question of driving on the wrong side of the road in violation of the statutes, was apparently intended to present to the jury the issue of defendant's guilt in the unlawful killing of a human being 'in the commission of an unlawful act, not amounting to felony.' ...

"The driving of an automobile to the left of the centerline of the highway appears to be an act merely *malum prohibitum*.... In some jurisdictions it is held that when one commits an act expressly prohibited by law which results in the death of a human being he is thereby guilty of manslaughter and that in such a case an instruction on criminal negligence is neither necessary nor proper.... [That] rule ... has not been followed in Montana.... This court has committed itself to the rule that the unlawful killing of a human being, 'in the commission of an unlawful act, not amounting to felony,' does not constitute involuntary manslaughter unless the element of criminal negligence is also present....

"It is not incumbent upon us to go further and determine the character of the unlawful act, *aside from such criminal negligence,* which makes a person guilty of manslaughter should death ensue. Irrespective of the character of the unlawful act, whether *malum in se* or merely *malum prohibitum,* the criminality of the act resulting in death is established if that act was done negligently in such a manner as to evince a disregard for human life or an indifference to consequences. Negligence of this character is culpable in itself. Hence it is wholly unnecessary in involuntary manslaughter cases to superimpose upon the requirement of the element of criminal negligence the further requirement that a determination must be made as to whether the act resulting in death might ordinarily be classified as *malum in se* or *malum prohibitum,* for, if that act is done in a manner which is criminally negligent, it thereby becomes *malum in se* and thereby includes the element of *mens rea*....

"Applying the foregoing discussion to the case at bar, we hold that Instruction No. 7 ... was erroneous in advising that jury that they might find the defendant guilty if she was driving on the wrong side of the road in violation of the statutes and if she thereby caused the death of Gerald Little...."

2. Deaths resulting from traffic offenses are viewed as possible involuntary manslaughter offenses if the degree of foreseeability of death was fairly high, but not if the causal connection is less obvious. Thus, in Beck v. Commonwealth, 216 Va. 1, 216 S.E.2d 8 (1975), the court affirmed a conviction of involuntary

manslaughter where the defendant had consumed "around seven beers" in a very short period of time, was unsteady on his feet and had difficulty closing his car door, failed to see seven young men with his lights on and after striking something in "a blur" was reported by other witnesses to have departed at high speed. The finding of driving while intoxicated was deemed to be the proximate cause of the resulting homicide which occurred during the performance of an unlawful act. On the other hand, in King v. Commonwealth, 217 Va. 601, 231 S.E.2d 312 (1977), the defendant was operating a motor vehicle without headlights at night, in violation of a state statute, as a result of which a death occurred and she was convicted of involuntary manslaughter. The Virginia Supreme Court reversed, stating that the operation of an automobile without headlights in violation of law amounted only to ordinary negligence and was therefore an insufficient predicate for a conviction of involuntary manslaughter. The court said: "In the operation of motor vehicles violation of a safety statute amounting to mere negligence proximately causing an accidental death is not sufficient to support a conviction of involuntary manslaughter. Likewise, the improper performance of a lawful act proximately causing an accidental killing is also insufficient unless that improper performance constitutes criminal negligence."

3. If there has been a violation of the "Inland Rules of the Road," as stated in the U.S. Coast Guard pamphlet, resulting in a collision of two pleasure motorboats causing the death of a passenger of one of the boats, can the pilot be convicted of involuntary manslaughter? For a case dealing with the statutory law, see Allen v. State, 39 Md.App. 686, 389 A.2d 909 (1978).

4. Consider a case situation involving the death of a participant in the "game" of "Russian Roulette." May the surviving participants be held guilty of manslaughter? Such a conviction was upheld in Commonwealth v. Atencio, 345 Mass. 627, 189 N.E.2d 223 (1963), in which the court distinguished the Root case on the ground that "skill" is involved in a "drag race," whereas "Russian Roulette" involves only a matter of chance and someone is very likely to be killed.

COMMONWEALTH v. CHEEKS

Supreme Court of Pennsylvania, 1966.
423 Pa. 67, 223 A.2d 291.

EAGEN, JUSTICE. On May 22, 1964, after a nine-day trial, the appellant, Bernard Cheeks, was convicted by a jury of murder in the first degree and punishment was fixed at life imprisonment....

The crime involved the robbery and stabbing on October 11, 1963, of Joe Henry Howell by four young males on a public street in Philadelphia....

The Commonwealth's medical trial testimony may be summarized as follows: Upon Howell's admission to the hospital at 2:10 a.m. o'clock in the early morning following the occurrence, an examination disclosed an obvious penetrating wound of the abdomen in the area of the umbilicus. Since the extent of the wound was not ascertainable from an exterior examination, an operation was deemed necessary and was performed. It disclosed a puncture of the abdominal cavity, measuring about one inch in length, and it also disclosed that the only interior damage therefrom was to the mesentery, a leaf of tissue attached to the intestines through which the blood vessels course and supply nourishment to these organs. However, during the operation the whole gastro-intestinal tract was manually handled and checked for wounds.

In order to prevent a common post-operative complication,[1] a "Levin" tube was inserted in the patient through the nostril to the stomach to suction off damaging secretions and air that might accumulate in that organ. Following the operation and after coming out of the anesthesia, the patient, Howell, was uncooperative, disorientated, resisted treatment, demonstrated delirium tremens, hallucinations, wouldn't stay in bed and wandered into the hospital halls and the rooms of other patients. Out of precaution, he was then tied to the bed. However, he managed to pull out the tube three times and developed hiccups.[2]

On October 15th, the abdomen became markedly distended. This followed a period during which the patient had continued to be uncooperative and had again extracted the tube. However, the abdominal distention was described as "secondary to the operation, and not secondary to pulling out the tube." It was also stated that the operation itself "produced a temporary paralysis in the intestine which caused accumulation of the gas and fluids and it was necessary to remove the fluids to keep the man alive."

As a result of the above described complication, another longer "Cantor" tube was inserted. This had a bag of mercury at the end for weight purposes and had to be positioned under a fluoroscope or x-ray machine. Howell pulled out this tube on at least two occasions, the second of these instances occurred on October 18th, in the x-ray room, just as the process of inserting the tube was about completed. As a result a gag reaction immediately followed, causing a large amount of gastric material in the stomach to be sucked into the lungs. A tracheotomy was hurriedly performed without material result. Howell expired about 1:30 p.m. o'clock on the same day from suffocation, resulting in heart stoppage due to lack of oxygen in the lungs.

Under this proof, it is our studied conclusion that the question of causal connection was for the jury to resolve. The fact that the stabbing was not the immediate cause of death is not controlling. [As pointed out in the *Peters* case, Pa.1964], one charged with homicide cannot escape liability merely because the blow he inflicted is not mortal, or the immediate cause of death. If his blow is the legal cause, i.e., if it started a chain of causation which led to the death, he is guilty of homicide. . . .

In this case, the stabbing necessitated the operation; the operation was the direct cause of the stomach complication and abdominal disten-

1. Following such an operation, the intestines and bowels frequently do not function normally causing secretions and air to remain unduly in the stomach, resulting in abnormal distention and possible serious consequences.

2. One medical expert stated that this condition and behavior was in no way attributable to the operation or medication. However, another such expert testified, that the abnormal retention of fluids and gases in the stomach produced a chemical reaction and the mental confusion, which in turn caused the confused behavior of the patient and resulted in his pulling out the tubes.

tion; the insertion of the tubes was required to alleviate this condition and to save the victim's life. The fact that the victim, while in a weakened physical condition and disorientated mental state, pulled out the tubes and created the immediate situation, which resulted in his death, is not such an intervening and independent act sufficient to break the chain of causation or events between the stabbing and the death. See, Beale, The Proximate Consequences of an Act, 33 Harv.L.Rev. 633 (1920); Levitt, Cause, Legal Cause & Proximate Cause, 21 Mich.L.Rev. 34 (1922); Edgerton, Legal Cause, 72 U.Pa.L.Rev. 211 (1924); and McLaughlin, Proximate Cause, 39 Harv.L.Rev. 149 (1925).

COHEN, JUSTICE (dissenting). In Commonwealth v. Root [reproduced supra] we held that "the tort liability concept of proximate cause has no proper place in prosecutions for criminal homicide and more direct causal connection is required for conviction". A reading of the majority opinion discloses that in concluding that defendant's act was the proximate cause of death and that defendant is criminally responsible therefor, a weighty reliance has been placed upon precedent grounded upon the application of the tort liability concept of proximate cause. This reliance blatantly violates the principles of Root. I, accordingly, dissent.

NOTES

1. In State v. Preslar, 48 N.C. 421 (1856), the defendant and his wife had quarrelled, and the defendant inflicted a severe beating upon her. She left the house and sat down in the yard. A short time later, she walked to the home of her father. Instead of entering the house, however, she laid down on a bed-quilt in the woods, telling her son, who had accompanied her, that she would wait until morning to go inside. The next morning she was unable to walk, from the effects of exposure. She died the next day. The defendant was convicted of murder, but the conviction was set aside on appeal. The court stated that "if, to avoid the rage of a brutal husband, a wife is compelled to expose herself, by wading through a swamp, or jumping into a river, the husband is responsible for the consequences." The court further stated, however, that "if she exposes herself thus, without necessity, and of her own accord, we know of no principle of law, by which he is held responsible. . . ."

Consider the language of the Supreme Court of Missouri in State v. Glover, 330 Mo. 709, 50 S.W.2d 1049 (1932), where the defendant was convicted of first degree murder as a result of the death of a fireman who died fighting a fire allegedly set by the defendant for the purpose of collecting insurance proceeds on the premises and contents:

"If the appellant had reason to think members of the fire department of Kansas City and citizens generally would congregate at the drug store to fight the fire, and thus would place themselves within perilous range of the flames and potentially destructive forces that had been set at work, the ensuing homicide was a natural and probable consequence of the arson; and the fact that the deceased fireman came after the fire began to burn did not break the causal relation between the arson and the homicide or constitute an independent intervening cause."

See also State v. Leopold, 110 Conn. 55, 147 A. 118 (1929), where defendant was convicted of the murder of two boys who died in a fire maliciously set by the defendant. The boys, in the building when the fire was set, had ample opportunity to escape; however, after starting to leave (or in fact leaving the building), they returned to save some property and as a result died in the fire. The Supreme Court of Connecticut noted that the boys' efforts to save property from destruction was "such a natural and ordinary course of conduct that it cannot be said to break the sequence of cause and effect."

In light of the statement in State v. Leopold, supra, that the failure of a deceased to use due care is not a defense available to the accused, how can the result in the Preslar case be explained? Consider the following excerpt from Beale, The Proximate Consequences of an Act, 33 Harv.L.Rev. 633, 651, 652 (1920): "Where defendant's active force has come to rest in a position of apparent safety, the court will follow it no longer; if some new force later combines with this condition to create harm, the result is remote from defendant's act.... The form of rule above stated is believed really to state [the rule] ... actually enforced by the courts. The wording of it, however, is not that ordinarily used. The commonest phrase, probably, is that the injury shall be the natural and probable result of the act; a phrase which involves at least a misuse of both adjectives. A more accurate phrase, which is gaining in use, is that the intervening force, unless it is to make the result remote, must be foreseeable."

In People v. Kibbe, 35 N.Y.2d 407, 362 N.Y.S.2d 848, 321 N.E.2d 773 (1974), the defendants stole money from a helplessly drunken victim and left him in near zero temperatures on a rural two-lane highway, having stripped him of his outer clothing with his trousers down around his ankles and shoeless. Sometime later, the victim was killed when he was struck by a vehicle driven by one Blake. Is Blake's act an independent intervening act, cutting the chain of causation? The Court said, "Under the conditions surrounding Blake's operation of his truck (i.e., the fact that he had his low beams on as the two cars approached; that there was no artificial lighting on the highway; and that there was insufficient time in which to react to Stafford's [the victim] presence in his lane), we do not think it may be said that any supervening wrongful act occurred to relieve the defendants from the directly foreseeable consequences of their actions. See also State v. Serebin, 119 Wis.2d 837, 350 N.W.2d 65 (1984) (reversing defendant's conviction for reckless homicide where his conduct was not the cause-in-fact of the victim's death).

2. In Clark v. Commonwealth, 90 Va. 360, 18 S.E. 440 (1893), the court said, "If the prisoner willfully inflicted upon the deceased a dangerous wound, one that was calculated to endanger and destroy life, and death ensued therefrom within a year and a day, the prisoner is none the less responsible for the results although it may appear that the deceased might have recovered but for the aggravation of the wound by skillful or improper treatment.

"But if, on the other hand, a wound or beating was inflicted upon the deceased which was not mortal, and the deceased, while laboring under the effect of the violence, became sick of a disease not caused by such violence, from which disease death ensued within a year and a day, the party charged with the homicide was not criminally responsible for the death, although it also appeared that the symptoms of the disease were aggravated, and the fatal progress quickened, by the enfeebled or irritated condition of the deceased, caused by the violence: Livingston v. Commonwealth, 14 Grat. (55 Va.) 592 (1857)."

Compare the foregoing with the result reached in People v. Flenon, 42 Mich.App. 457, 202 N.W.2d 471 (1972), where the defendant shot his victim in the leg (a non-mortal wound), necessitating amputation above the knee. The victim was discharged from the hospital several weeks later, but within a short time thereafter was readmitted to the hospital. He died from serum hepatitis contracted as a result of exposure to the disease while receiving blood transfusions during the course of the amputation operation. Defendant was convicted of homicide and the Court of Appeals of Michigan affirmed, holding that the defendant could prevail only if it be determined that the contraction of serum hepatitis was due to gross medical negligence. Short of that, it must be considered, said the court, that the consequences of a defendant's attack upon a victim are foreseeable. Since doctors are not infallible, ordinary medical negligence must be considered as foreseeable. See McKinnon v. United States, 550 A.2d 915 (D.C.App.1988), where the defendant slashed his paramour's throat and she died six weeks later as a result of hepatitis caused by her medical treatment. The court held that the defendant was criminally responsible for her death because the medical treatment was not grossly negligent and the infection was reasonably foreseeable.

While the rule that ordinary medical negligence is deemed not to be an independent intervening act sufficient to cut off the chain of causation leading from the initial wrongful act of the defendant to the ultimate death is well established, should the rule be applied where, as in *Flenon,* the original wound inflicted was non-mortal?

Is there a superseding cause where the victim of a gunshot wound dies from vomiting, the vomit having been sucked into the lungs? See Commonwealth v. Green, 477 Pa. 170, 383 A.2d 877 (1978).

3. During a bar holdup, the robbers line up the victims along a wall and proceed to take money from the cash register. While this is going on, a lady among the victims topples over and falls to the floor. The defendants, on seeing this, run out the front of the bar and disappear. It is later determined that the lady suffered cardiac arrest, having had a history of heart disease in the past, due to fright during the holdup. Are the robbers guilty of murder? See State v. McKeiver, 89 N.J.Super. 52, 213 A.2d 320 (1965); State v. Chavers, 294 So.2d 489 (La.1974); Phillips v. State, 289 So.2d 447 (Fla.App.1974).

Defendant snatches the victim's purse, causing her to fall. The fall caused the victim to suffer a broken hip. The broken hip required treatment by surgery. During the surgery, the victim suffered cardiac arrest. Is defendant guilty of murder or any form of homicide? See Adams v. State, 310 So.2d 782 (Fla.App.1975).

4. At common law, when a death occurred after the infliction of a mortal wound, the person inflicting the wound could be charged with the criminal homicide only if death occurred within a year and a day from the infliction of the wound. What is the purpose of such a rule? One possible answer can be found in LaFave & Scott, 2 Substantial Criminal Law § 7.1(c) (1986).

The rule has been modified in some states by statute or court decision.

For instance, in State v. Young, 148 N.J.Super. 405, 372 A.2d 1117 (1977), the New Jersey Superior Court, Appellate Division, ruled that the common law rule does not comport with medical realities, principles of equity or public policy, and rejected it as an anachronism, holding that a defendant could be prosecuted for killing a victim who was rendered a quadriplegic by one of the defendant's bullets and died one year and 63 days after the infliction of the bullet wound from pneumonia secondary to his quadriplegia. The Supreme Court, however, reversed, retaining the year and a day rule. State v. Young, 77 N.J. 245, 390 A.2d 556 (1978). See also Commonwealth v. Lewis, 381 Mass. 411, 409 N.E.2d 771 (1980) (abolishing the year and a day rule).

5. A burglar breaks into a house stealthily, but the occupant, a 65-year old lady living alone, awakes and is frightened. In an attempt to escape the burglar, she jumps out of her bedroom window and falls to her death on the sidewalk. Is defendant-burglar guilty of murder?

For a case in which the defendant was held guilty of second degree murder for the death, by self-administered poison, of a young woman whom defendant had sexually abused, see Stephenson v. State, 205 Ind. 141, 179 N.E. 633 (1932). The issue was whether defendant's conduct had rendered the victim so mentally irresponsible that her own act of taking poison, and the resulting death, could be considered as "caused" by the defendant.

6. The issues discussed above are well discussed in Comment, The Use of the Tort Liability Concept of Proximate Cause in Cases of Criminal Homicide, 56 Nw.U.L.Rev. 791 (1962).

Chapter 5

SEX OFFENSES AND RELATED PROBLEMS

A. RAPE

COMMONWEALTH v. BURKE

Supreme Judicial Court of Massachusetts, 1870.
105 Mass. 376.

GRAY, J. The defendant has been indicted and convicted for aiding and assisting Dennis Green in committing a rape upon Joanna Caton. The single exception taken at the trial was to the refusal of the presiding judge to rule that the evidence introduced was not sufficient to warrant a verdict of guilty. The instructions given were not objected to, and are not reported in the bill of exceptions. The only question before us therefore is, whether, under any instructions applicable to the case, the evidence would support a conviction.

That evidence, which it is unnecessary to state in detail, was sufficient to authorize the jury to find that Green, with the aid and assistance of this defendant, had carnal intercourse with Mrs. Caton, without her previous assent, and while she was, as Green and the defendant both knew, so drunk as to be utterly senseless and incapable of consenting, and with such force as was necessary to effect the purpose.

All the statutes of England and of Massachusetts, and all the text books of authority, which have undertaken to define the crime of rape, have defined it as the having carnal knowledge of a woman by force and against her will. The crime consists in the enforcement of a woman without her consent. The simple question, expressed in the briefest form, is, Was the woman willing or unwilling? The earlier and more weighty authorities show that the words "against her will," in the standard definitions, mean exactly the same thing as "without her consent;" and that the distinction between these phrases, as applied to this crime, which has been suggested in some modern books, is unfounded.

The most ancient statute upon the subject is that of Westm. I. c. 13, making rape (which had been a felony at common law) a misdemeanor, and declaring that no man should "ravish a maiden within age, neither by her own consent, nor without her consent, nor a wife or maiden of full age, nor other woman against her will," on penalty of fine and imprisonment, either at the suit of a party or of the king. The St. of Westm. II, c. 34, ten years later, made rape felony again, and provided that if a man should "ravish a woman, married, maiden, or other woman, where she did not consent, neither before nor after," he should be punished with death, at the appeal of the party; "and likewise, where a man ravisheth a woman, married lady, maiden, or other woman, with force, although she consent afterwards," he should have a similar sentence upon prosecution in behalf of the king.

It is manifest upon the face of the Statutes of Westminster, and is recognized in the oldest commentaries and cases, that the words "without her consent" and "against her will" were used synonymously; and that the second of those statutes was intended to change the punishment only, and not the definition of the crime, upon any indictment for rape—leaving the words "against her will," as used in the first statute, an accurate part of the description. . . .

Coke treats the two phrases as equivalent; for he says: "Rape is felony by the common law declared by parliament, for the unlawful and carnal knowledge and abuse of any woman above the age of ten years against her will, or of a woman child under the age of ten years with her will or against her will;" although in the latter case the words of the St. of Westm. I. (as we have already seen) were "neither by her own consent, nor without her consent." 3 Inst. 60. Coke elsewhere repeatedly defines rape as "the carnal knowledge of a woman by force and against her will." Co.Lit. 123 b. 2 Inst. 180. A similar definition is given by Hale, Hawkins, Comyn, Blackstone, East and Starkie, who wrote while the Statutes of Westminster were in force; as well as by the text writers of most reputation since the St. of 9 Geo. IV, c. 31, repealed the earlier statutes, and assuming the definition of the crime to be well established, provided simply that "every person convicted of the crime of rape shall suffer death as a felon." . . . There is authority for holding that it is not even necessary that an indictment, which alleges that the defendant "feloniously did ravish and carnally know" a woman, should add the words "against her will." . . . However, that may be, the office of those words, if inserted, is simply to negative the woman's previous consent. Stark.Crim.Pl. 431 note.

In the leading modern English case of The Queen v. Camplin, the great majority of the English judges held that a man who gave intoxicating liquor to a girl of thirteen, for the purpose, as the jury found, "of exciting her, not with the intention of rendering her insensible, and then having sexual connection with her," and made her quite drunk, and, while she was in a state of insensibility, took advantage of it, and ravished her, was guilty of rape. It appears indeed by the judgment delivered by Patteson, J., in passing sentence, as reported in 1 Cox Crim.Cas. 220, and 1 C. & K. 746, as well by the contemporaneous notes of Parke, B., printed in a note to 1 Denison, 92, and of Alderson, B., as read by him in The Queen v. Page, 2 Cox Crim.Cas. 133, that the decision was influenced by its having been proved at the trial that, before the girl became insensible the man had attempted to procure her consent, and had failed. But it further appears by those notes that Lord Denman, C.J., Parke, B., and Patteson, J., thought that the violation of any woman without her consent, while she was in a state of insensibility and had no power over her will, by a man knowing at the time that she was in that state, was a rape, whether such state was caused by him or not; for example, as Alderson, B., adds, "in the case of a woman insensibly drunk in the streets, not made so by the prisoner." And in the course of the argument this able judge himself said that it might be considered against the general presumable will of a woman that a man should have unlawful connection with her. The later decisions have established the rule in England that unlawful and forcible connection with a woman in a state of unconsciousness at the time, whether that state has been produced by the act of the prisoner or not, is presumed to be without her consent, and is rape....

The earliest statute of Massachusetts upon the subject was passed in 1642, and, like the English Statutes of Westminster, used "without consent" as synonymous with "against her will," as is apparent upon reading its provisions, which were as follows: 1st. "If any man shall unlawfully have carnal copulation with any woman child under ten years old, he shall be put to death, whether it were with or without the girl's consent." 2d. "If any man shall forcibly and without consent ravish any maid or woman that is lawfully married or contracted, he shall be put to death." 3d. "If any man shall ravish any maid or single woman, committing carnal copulation with her by force, against her will, that is above the age of ten years, he shall be either punished with death, or with some other grievous punishment, according to circumstances, at the discretion of the judges." 2 Mass.Col.Rec. 21. Without dwelling upon the language of the first of these provisions, which related to the abuse of female children, it is manifest that in the second and third, both of which related to the crime of rape, strictly so called, and differed only in the degree of punishment, depending upon the question whether the woman was or was not married or engaged to be married, the legislature used the words "without consent," in the second provision, as precisely equivalent to "against her will," in the third. The later revisions of the statute have abolished the difference in punishment, and therefore omitted the second provision, and thus made the definition of rape in all cases the ravishing and carnally knowing a woman "by force and against her will." ... But they cannot, upon any proper rule of construction of a series of statutes in pari materia, be taken to have changed the description of the offence.

We are therefore unanimously of opinion that the crime, which the evidence in this case tended to prove, of a man's having carnal intercourse with a woman, without her consent, while she was, as he knew, wholly insensible so as to be incapable of consenting, and with such force as was necessary to accomplish the purpose, was rape. If it were otherwise, any woman in a state of utter stupefaction, whether caused by drunkenness, sudden disease, the blow of a third person, or drugs which she had been persuaded to take even by the defendant himself, would be unprotected from personal dishonor. The law is not open to such a reproach.

NOTES

1. Under a first-degree rape statute that pertains to cases where the perpetrator inflicts "suffocation, strangulation, disfigurement, or serious physical injury" upon the victim or another person, or threatens to do so, the loss of virginity by a five-year old rape victim and a 2–3 cm. tear in her perineal area did not qualify to raise the offense to first degree. This did not qualify for "disfigurement" under the statute because such involves an external blemish or scar that impairs one's appearance. Scott v. State, 61 Md.App. 599, 487 A.2d 1204 (1985).

A sexual penetration of a dead body is not a rape. Rape is a crime committed against the will of the victim by force or some other means used to overcome the victim's resistance. As this court noted, "[i]t must be accomplished against a person's will. A dead body cannot consent to or protest a rape, nor can it be in fear of immediate and unlawful bodily injury.... A dead body has no feelings of outrage." Thus, where a trial court ruled that it was irrelevant whether penetration took place before or after the victim had died, reversible error occurred. People v. Sellers, 203 Cal.App.3d 1042, 250 Cal.Rptr. 345 (1988).

2. Many states have enacted so-called "rape-shield" laws designed to negate the common law rule applicable in rape cases that evidence of the complainant's general reputation for morality and chastity can be shown to infer consent and attack the complainant's credibility. Other purposes of these laws are to protect the complainant from embarrassment over intimate affairs normally considered to be private, and encourage rape victims to come forward and report the crime.

Under a state rape shield law that permits evidence of prior sexual conduct between the complainant and defendant to be admitted into evidence "... where it bears on the credibility of the complaining witness or it is material to a fact at issue and its probative value outweighs its private character ...", it was held that "[c]onsensual sexual activity over a period of years, coupled with a claimed consensual act reasonably contemporaneous with the act complained of [four days] is clearly material on the issue of consent.... If believed, the evidence could well have affected the outcome." Thus, such evidence was admissible in spite of the law's strictures. State v. Gonyaw, 146 Vt. 559, 507 A.2d 944 (1985).

A rape shield statute that on its face would prohibit defense use of evidence about the victim's prior sexual activity with other persons was waived—in effect—by a rape victim when she testified that she was a homosexual, because such testimony was equivalent to saying that she *never* consents to sex with men. Consent was the vital issue in the case, and thus defendant's right of confrontation and cross-examination was more important than strict adherence to the statute: not merely the victim's credibility was at stake, but a vital element of the offense. State v. Williams, 21 Ohio St.3d 33, 487 N.E.2d 560 (1986).

Under a rape shield statute that proscribed evidence concerning the "general reputation [...] of the complaining witness's unchaste character or prior sexual conduct," a defendant charged with sexual abuse of his daughter should have been permitted to introduce evidence that she had brought false similar charges against her uncle and grandfather and had falsely claimed to be pregnant on two occasions. The rape shield statute's purpose is to protect against evidence of prior sexual conduct and unchaste character. The defendant, by contrast, sought to impeach the witness's character. The proffered evidence was not "conduct within the purview of the statute." The court went further and said that evidence of prior false accusations should be admissible as substantive evidence that the crime alleged did not take place, if the trial court first finds that there is a reasonable probability of falsity. Clinebell v. Commonwealth, 235 Va. 319, 368 S.E.2d 263 (1988).

A rape shield statute prohibiting evidence of prior sexual conduct by the victim of a rape with persons other than the defendant was not a bar to evidence that the rape victim in this case had provocatively flirted with several male bar patrons in a tavern for several hours before the rape took place. The victim's conduct was in public, thus reducing her privacy interest (a prime concern of such statutes). The evidence was "highly probative" on the defendant's consent defense. Considering the competing interests, the court concluded that application of the statute violated the defendant's constitutional right to defend himself. State v. Colbath, 130 N.H. 316, 540 A.2d 1212 (1988).

Likewise, in People v. Slovinski, 166 Mich.App. 158, 420 N.W.2d 145 (1988), the court ruled that a rape shield statute did not bar evidence that a rape victim was a prostitute. The evidence was probative on the issue of consent, having "a tendency to make [it] more probable that the complainant entered into a financial arrangement with defendant for sexual acts," and the defendant's right of confrontation was simply more important than the State's interest, embodied in the statute, of encouraging rape victims to report their crimes, and Society's belief that unchaste women are no more prone to give untruthful testimony than other witnesses.

A rape shield statute that placed a bar to evidence at a rape trial of "the victim's past sexual conduct with the actor" was held to preclude evidence at trial that the defendant and victim had engaged in consensual sexual relations *after* the date of the alleged offense, as well as *before*. The statute was construed as barring all sexual activity by the victim not incident to the charged rape.

This interpretation was not viewed by the court as violating the defendant's Sixth Amendment right of confrontation, because the defense in this case was that the crime never occurred. Evidence of subsequent consensual sexual activity with the victim was not relevant, or at least, could be said to be only "marginally" relevant. Marginally relevant evidence, the court said, can be barred by a statute on policy grounds.

A dissenter argued that the court had distorted the plain meaning of the statute and that evidence of past consensual sexual activity with the victim had primary impeachment value for a defendant in a rape case. People v. Adair, 207 Mich.App. 287, 524 N.W.2d 256 (1994).

ADAIR

Under a rape shield statute that was interpreted to constitute an absolute ban on evidence relating to a rape victim's chastity, a defendant's attempt to testify that a rape victim had offered him sex in exchange for drugs two weeks before the charged crime was properly barred. The asserted offer was not itself "sexual conduct" which would fit the statutory definition of "specific instances of the victim's prior sexual conduct" that would be allowed in four situations specifically enumerated in the statute.

The court interpreted "sexual conduct" as meaning "physical contact." An "unaccepted and unconsummated verbal offer" to have sex in exchange for drugs was not "sexual conduct." Shand v. State, 103 Md.App. 465, 653 A.2d 1000 (1995).

Although not involving a rape shield law, a recent U.S. Supreme Court case is on point. In Olden v. Kentucky, 488 U.S. 227, 109 S.Ct. 480 (1988), the Court ruled that a trial court's refusal to allow a white rape complainant to be cross-examined about an affair she was having with a black man to whom she first reported her claim of rape (not the defendant), denied the defendant his Sixth Amendment right of confrontation. The defendant's theory was that the complainant made up the story of her rape to divert the suspicions of her boy friend that she was unfaithful. The purpose of the proffered cross-examination was to show the complainant's motivation. The Court ruled this was proper cross-examination material, and outweighed any possible prejudice that might result from revealing an interracial relationship.

3. In order to be guilty of rape, the offender must be at least 14 years of age in some states. This early common law concept, still retained in many jurisdictions, is not based on considerations of physical capacity, but rather on a belief that sexual intercourse by one below that age should not be punished as rape. Accordingly, in Foster v. Commonwealth, 96 Va. 306, 31 S.E. 503 (1898), it was held that a boy under 14 years of age is conclusively presumed to be incapable of committing the crime of rape, or of attempting to commit it, whatever may be the real facts. Therefore, evidence to rebut the presumption is inadmissible. (However, the court added that where the boy assists another in an attempted rape, he may be convicted as a principal in the second degree, and punished the same as the principal in the first degree.)

4. In many jurisdictions today, a man cannot be held criminally liable for the rape of his own wife if she refuses to have sexual relations with him during the marriage and he has forcible intercourse with her. This "spousal exemption" is generally credited to the influence of English common law principles adopted early in this country's history. As Sir Matthew Hale, a seventeenth century English jurist, declared in a treatise often quoted: "[T]he husband cannot be guilty of a rape committed by himself upon his lawful wife, for by their mutual matrimonial consent and contract the wife hath given up herself in this kind unto her husband which she cannot retract." 1 Hale, History of the Pleas of the Crown 629. Contemporary justifications for retaining the spousal exemption include evidentiary problems, tenuous prospects of reconciliation, and availability of other criminal sanctions. In states which have codified the common law elements, then, rape is usually defined as forcible sexual intercourse by the defendant "with a female not his wife."

There is a trend towards modifying this common law rule under more modern views of revocable marriage vows. Wisconsin, for example, has provided that marriage is not a bar to prosecution for rape. W.S.A. § 940.225 (1982–83 Supplement). O.R.S. § 163.375 (1981), provides that "(1) A person who has sexual intercourse with a female commits the crime of rape in the first degree if: (a) The female is subjected to forcible compulsion by the male; ..." In the fall of 1978, Oregon used this statute to prosecute the first man charged with raping his own wife during marriage. A jury of four men and eight women acquitted the defendant. State of Oregon v. Rideout, Marion County Circuit Court, Oregon, December 27, 1978, No. 108,866. (Subsequent to the trial, the Rideouts reconciled; still later, they divorced.)

The Second Circuit Court of Appeals found no violation of equal protection in a New York rape statute that pertained only to men. The gender classification had a rational basis: rapes of males by females are practically non-existent, and the threat of pregnancy poses a unique harm to females that the statute was intended to address. The statute also had a marital exemption, but excluded men living apart from their wives pursuant to court order from the exemption. This, too, would pass constitutional muster (the issue was not squarely before the court) as having a rational basis: men living apart from their wives pursuant to court order present a greater threat of danger to their wives than men living with their wives. Liberta v. Kelly, 839 F.2d 77 (2d Cir.1988). The New York Court of Appeals had previously found the statute to violate state and federal equal protection principles in People v. Liberta, 62 N.Y.2d 651, 476 N.Y.S.2d 1046, 464 N.E.2d 997 (1984), and had put a judicial gloss on the statute to include women and married persons.

Georgia has rejected an implied marital exemption in their rape statutes, noting that women have statutory and constitutional rights not previously recognized under the common law. The Supreme Court of Georgia also rejected such an exemption for its aggravated sodomy statute, noting that consent—express or implied—is not even an element of the offense. Warren v. State, 255 Ga. 151, 336 S.E.2d 221 (1985).

5. The principal case deals with "forcible rape", as distinguished from "statutory rape"—an offense based solely upon the age of the female and without reference to force, consent or chastity. The usual age below which the act is rape is 16.

6. Defendants and prosecutors have sometimes attempted to introduce expert testimony on the issue of whether the defendant's "psychological profile" was indicative of or consistent with that of a sex offender. The courts have usually rejected such evidence as an invasion of the province of the fact-finder. In Pendleton v. Commonwealth, 685 S.W.2d 549 (Ky.1985), the court stated:

> "An opinion as to whether the accused had the ability or propensity to commit such an act is improper because it is an opinion on the ultimate fact, that is, innocence or guilt. Consequently it invades the proper province of the jury. Such an opinion is not evidence of mental condition but is a factual conclusion of the witness on the ultimate issue before the jury which can be reached only by consideration of all the facts."

Another area of expert testimony that has been attempted by prosecutors, is that of demonstrating that a rape victim suffered from "post-traumatic stress syndrome," or "post-rape syndrome." Evidence of this medical condition is said to demonstrate that the victim did not consent to the rape. Some courts have rejected such evidence as an invasion of the province of the jury, or that such evidence has limited probative value that is outweighed by its prejudicial effect. Other courts have accepted such evidence.

Statements made to a doctor by a rape victim a few days before trial that conformed to the doctor's definition of "rape trauma syndrome" were inadmissible hearsay where the victim had not consulted the doctor for treatment or diagnosis, and the doctor had not in fact made a diagnosis. The court did not decide the controversial issue of the admissibility of the rape trauma syndrome, but indicated that if such evidence is to be admissible the testifying expert witness must have made an actual diagnosis. State v. Stafford, 317 N.C. 568, 346 S.E.2d 463 (1986).

Rape trauma syndrome evidence was accepted by the court in Commonwealth v. Gallagher, 353 Pa.Super. 426, 510 A.2d 735 (1986), to explain why the victim had initially given the police the defendant's name as her attacker but could not positively identify him from photographs or face-to-face until four years later.

West Virginia allows evidence of rape trauma syndrome so long as the expert witness does not offer an opinion on whether the victim was raped. "[I]n a prosecution for rape where consent is the defense, qualified expert testimony regarding the existence of symptoms consistent with rape trauma syndrome is relevant and admissible [. . . .] [but] [t]he expert may not give an opinion, expressly or implicitly, as to whether or not the alleged victim was raped." State v. McCoy, 179 W.Va. 223, 366 S.E.2d 731 (1988).

But the State of Washington rejected rape trauma syndrome evidence in rape cases, holding it is inadmissible on the issue of lack of consent. This court labelled such evidence as "unscientific," citing the varieties of experience and reactions of rape victims and the prejudicial impact of the evidence. The evidence was considered as an equivalent to a declaration by an expert witness that a rape had actually taken place, an invasion of the factfinder's role. State v. Black, 109 Wn.2d 336, 745 P.2d 12 (1987).

Expert testimony that a rape victim had suffered from "post traumatic stress disorder," and that the disorder was the result of the rape she complained of, was ruled admissible by Maryland's highest appellate court. The expert, a psychiatrist, did not invade the jury's province of deciding on the credibility of the victim, and he did not use the term "*rape trauma syndrome*." State v. Allewalt, 308 Md. 89, 517 A.2d 741 (1986), rev'g. 61 Md.App. 503, 487 A.2d 664 (1985).

STATE v. WHEELER

Supreme Judicial Court of Maine, 1954.
150 Me. 332, 110 A.2d 578.

TAPLEY, JUSTICE The respondent was indicted for the crime of rape. The case was tried at the October Term, 1953, of the Superior Court for the County of Sagadahoc and State of Maine before a jury. Jury found respondent guilty. Respondent excepted to rulings as to the admissibility of evidence and to the refusal of the presiding Justice to direct a verdict of not guilty at the conclusion of the testimony.

The indictment charged the respondent with rape of a female of the age of sixteen years. The act was alleged to have occurred on September 28, 1953 at Bowdoinham, Maine. The prosecutrix resided in the Town of South Freeport, Maine and on the twenty-seventh day of September, 1953, she went to the Town of Richmond where she was accustomed to spending considerable time. There is much testimony in the record relating to her activities with three boys with whom she was acquainted. It appears that during the evening of September 27th she went to ride with these boys for a distance of one or two miles from Richmond and that during this ride she was submitted to physical violence by being slapped on the face and having her arm twisted in an attempt to remove a portion of her clothing; that she was forcibly ejected from the car and later made her way back to Richmond; that following her return to Richmond she was again approached by the same boys, caused to reenter the car and then taken to a point outside of Richmond where the car was stopped and an attempt made by one of them to rape her. During this attempt, a car passing the parked car of the boys was stopped by one of them. This car was operated by the respondent. The prosecutrix was transferred from the boys' car to that of the respondent. He drove some distance, stopped his automobile on a side road and there committed the act complained of, for which he was indicted, tried and found guilty.

The State must prove beyond a reasonable doubt that the respondent carnally knew the prosecutrix by force, without her consent or against her will.... The element of force and the act against her will are inconsistent with consent. It is obvious, of course, if the prosecutrix willingly consented to the act, there would be no rape.

During the course of the trial the State presented a witness in the person of one Donald Shields, a boy of sixteen years of age, who testified in direct examination that he was a passenger in the back seat of the respondent's car and was present at the time of the alleged rape. The substance of his testimony was that no act of intercourse occurred between the respondent and the prosecutrix. After completion of his direct testimony there was no cross-examination by the defense. Later he was called to the stand by the State and at that time testified that his testimony in direct was false and that he so testified because he was requested and urged to do so by the respondent.

The State's case was predicated on the testimony of the prosecutrix with very little, if any, corroboration. There is no statute in Maine requiring corroboration on the part of the prosecutrix in cases of this nature and it is well settled that a verdict based on the uncorroborated testimony of a complainant will not be disturbed on the mere fact of lack of corroboration. State v. Newcomb, 146 Me. 173, at page 181, 78 A.2d 787. Corroboration, if there is corroboration, must come from sources other than the prosecutrix. Although corroboration is not necessary, it is well for the purpose of this case to analyze the record to determine what corroboration, if any, there is present. The cases hold that where corroboration to any reasonable degree is lacking, it becomes necessary to scrutinize and analyze the testimony of the prosecutrix with great care. Her testimony as to the acts complained of must be such they would be within the realms of probability and credibility.

C.J.S. Rape, § 78, page 560:

> "At common law, and in the absence of a statute requiring corroboration, it is generally held that the unsupported testimony of the prosecutrix, if not contradictory *or incredible, or inherently improbable,* if believed by the jury, is sufficient to sustain a conviction of rape...." (Italics ours.)

The prosecutrix testified that soon after the alleged act occurred she complained to her mother. The mother did not appear as a witness in corroboration of the complainant. There was medical testimony resulting from the examination of the girl but this did not disclose in any way that she had been raped by the defendant.

There is evidence that the complainant suffered some injury to her jaw and she complained of a soreness in the vicinity of her ribs. This condition, according to her own testimony, resulted from the violent physical treatment that she received from the three boys. This fact is further established by the testimony of the boys. The prosecutrix furnishes the only testimony of the actual act of rape.

The testimony of the prosecutrix is of such sordid nature that a detailed account will serve no good purpose. It is suffice to say that the prosecutrix' narration of the rape is inherently improbable and incredible and does not meet the test of common sense....

Reversed.

NOTES

1. For another application of the "implausibility" rule enunciated in the principal case, see Penn v. State, 237 Ind. 374, 146 N.E.2d 240 (1957), in which the defendant was prosecuted for the statutory rape of a "baby sitter," aged 16, who testified that she became pregnant as a result of intercourse with the defendant, Penn. She testified that "when Mr. and Mrs. Penn would return from the evening out, [Penn] would usually go to bed, but that prosecutrix and Mrs. Penn would usually stay up late—popping corn, talking and watching television. They were friends. That, on prior occasions, prosecutrix slept on the davenport in the living room, but that beginning in October she slept in [Penn's] bed with Penn and his wife. Prosecutrix testified that on these occasions the accused would there have intercourse first with one and then the other, with knowledge of both.... Both Penn and his wife flatly denied the entire story of any sexual relations between prosecutrix and appellant." In reversing the defendant's conviction, the Supreme Court of Indiana said:

"Ordinarily reasonable men know that a wife will not knowingly and willingly share the sex life of her husband. Experience teaches that where another woman enters the sex life of her husband a wife does not remain on good terms with the other woman. She does not thereafter invite the other woman to her home to visit, pop corn, and watch television. Especially, she will not share her husband and aid and abet the act by inviting the other woman to her home and accompanying her to the bed of her husband.... We conclude therefore that in this case the uncorroborated testimony of the prosecutrix was so improbable and incredible that no reasonable man could say that the appellant's guilt had been proved beyond a reasonable doubt."

2. In People v. Taylor, 48 Ill.2d 91, 268 N.E.2d 865 (1971), a conviction was reversed where the record showed that the complaining witness had testified that as she was getting out of the defendant's car, where the alleged forcible rape occurred, she kissed him goodbye.

B. THE ISSUE OF HOMOSEXUALITY AND OTHER UNCONVENTIONAL SEXUAL CONDUCT

---

1. STUDIES OF SEXUAL BEHAVIOR

With regard to the extent to which the law should attempt to control deviate sexual conduct, consider the following excerpts from Kinsey, Pomeroy and Martin, Sexual Behavior in the Human Male (1948):

> A. "*Mouth-genital contact.* Mouth-genital contacts of some sort, with the subject as either the active or the passive member in the relationship, occur at some time in the histories of nearly 60 per cent of all males. . . ." (Page 371)
>
> B. "*Animal contacts.* In the total population, only one male in twelve or fourteen (estimated at about 8%) ever has sexual experience with animals. . . . Frequencies of animal contact are similarly low taken as a whole. For most individuals, they do not occur more than once or twice, or a few times in a lifetime." (Page 670)
>
> C. "*Homosexuality.* 37 per cent of the total male population has at least some overt homosexual experience to the point of orgasm between adolescence and old age. This accounts for nearly 2 males out of every 5 that one may meet.
>
> "50 per cent of the males who remain single until age 35 have had overt homosexual experience to the point of orgasm, since the onset of adolescence." (Page 650)

(For the incidence of sexual deviancy in females, see Kinsey, Pomeroy, Martin and Gebhard, Sexual Behavior in the Human Female (1953).)

2. THE LAW ON HOMOSEXUALITY

The Reporters of the Model Penal Code of the American Law Institute (drafted in 1955) proposed that consensual relations between adults in private should be excluded from criminal punishment. Among the stated reasons were:

"As in the case of illicit heterosexual relations, existing law is substantially unenforced, and there is no prospect of real enforcement except against cases of violence, corruption of minors and public solicitation. Statutes that go beyond that permit capricious selection of a very few cases for prosecution and serve primarily the interest of blackmailers. Existence of the criminal threat probably deters some people from seeking psychiatric or other assistance for their emotional problems; certainly conviction and imprisonment are not conducive to cures. Further, there is the fundamental question of the protection to which every individual is entitled against state interference in his personal affairs

when he is not hurting others. Lastly, the practicalities of police administration must be considered. Funds and personnel for police work are limited, and it would appear to be poor policy to use them to any extent in this area when large numbers of atrocious crimes remain unsolved. Even the necessary utilization of police in cases involving minors or public solicitation raises special problems of police morale, because of the entrapment practices that enforcement seems to require, and the temptation to bribery and extortion."

Following the same general views of the A.L.I. Model Penal Code reporters, a number of states have eliminated deviate sexual conduct as a crime except where force is involved, or where it occurs in a public place, or where there is a specified age disparity between the parties. On the other hand, the Texas Penal Code Ann. § 21.06 (Vernon 1974), among others, continues to proscribe deviate sexual intercourse where the genitals of one party are touched to the mouth or anus of another of the same sex, even where it occurs in private. Though objections have been made on the basis of statutory vagueness, rights to privacy and freedom of speech, homosexual "cruising" for sexual partners is often criminally sanctioned through application of statutes prohibiting "solicitation of lewd and lascivious" acts. See the California Penal Code § 647 (West 1982).

Any trend in the caselaw striking down on constitutional grounds sodomy statutes proscribing consensual homosexual acts between adults (see Chapter 2, Sexuality, Note, p. 164), may have been substantially retarded by the decision of the U.S. Supreme Court in Bowers v. Hardwick, 478 U.S. 186, 106 S.Ct. 2841 (1986). In a 5–4 decision and an opinion written by Justice White, the Court laid to rest speculation that its prior decisions recognizing a right of privacy in matters of child rearing, family relationships, procreation, marriage, contraception, and abortion, give homosexual adults a constitutional right to engage in consensual sodomy in private. It approved as not violative of due process a Georgia statute calling for up to 20 years imprisonment for a single act of private, consensual sodomy committed by homosexuals *or* heterosexuals. In a concurrence by Chief Justice Burger, it was noted that a contrary result would "... cast aside millennia of moral teaching."

A sodomy statute that singles out homosexuals by proscribing "deviate sexual intercourse with another person of the same sex" does not violate equal protection principles in light of *Bowers v. Hardwick,* since it is now established that there is no fundamental right to engage in sodomy. The statute also bears a "rational relationship" to the State's permissible goal of protecting public morality and health. State v. Walsh, 713 S.W.2d 508 (Mo.1986).

No constitutional violation was found in a statute that prohibited "deviate sexual intercourse" between consenting homosexuals, but did not apply to consenting adults of the opposite sex. No violation of a constitutionally protected right to privacy was found; homosexuals were not deemed to be a "suspect classification;" and the statute was found to be rationally related to the legitimate state goal of "implementing morality." Baker v. Wade, 769 F.2d 289 (5th Cir.1985), rev'g 553 F.Supp. 1121 (N.D.Tex.1982).

On the other hand, the "natural repugnance" of many in the community notwithstanding, it has been held by one court that there is no overriding compelling state interest to support a state sodomy statute, at least to the extent of barring private acts of oral and anal sex between consenting heterosexual adults. Post v. State, 715 P.2d 1105 (Okl.Cr.1986).

A new issue involving homosexuality centers about the emergence of the disease AIDS, and its prevalence among homosexuals. It is feared by some that legislation pertaining to AIDS may be discriminatory to homosexuals. One recent commentator notes as follows:

> "The Acquired Immunodeficiency Syndrome (AIDS) virus has killed over 33,000 people as of April, 1988. Currently, between one and a half million to two million people are thought to be AIDS carriers. Experts estimate that the death toll will increase tenfold by 1991. Furthermore, resultant patient care by that date will cost between eight and sixteen billion dollars. In response to widespread fear, legislators nation-wide have introduced AIDS-related bills calling for the testing of those "suspected" of infection, and the quarantining of known AIDS carriers under broad-based state police powers over public health.
>
> "The language of these bills is strikingly similar and frequently identical to that of quarantine and testing provisions written nearly a century ago. These antiquated provisions were created in an era when syphilis was considered synonymous with filth, and when some presumed that women carried gonorrhea regardless of whether or not they had ever been exposed. Where medicine and science were lacking, citizens, legislatures, and courts based their actions on cultural stereotypes. The ancient relationship between disease, filth, and taboo naturally oriented the citizenry at the turn of the century to vent their fears upon society's most polluted members—prostitutes.
>
> "This article argues that, in a fruitless and irrational response, the legislatures and courts have placed the blame and unchecked hysteria for AIDS on groups whose behavior is considered to be sexually abnormal. In so doing, we have revived the ancient practice of equating dirt and disease with sexual disorder.
>
> * * *
>
> "With regard to the rights of AIDS carriers and patients, the current disposition of the [U.S. Supreme] Court seems singularly unfavorable. There are several reasons for this omi-

nous prediction, not the least of which includes the Supreme Court's apparently ever-decreasing interest in privacy rights arguments outside the setting of family and procreation since the earlier days of the Burger Court. While it appeared for a time after *Griswold v. Connecticut* and *Roe v. Wade* that the Court was moving toward a more modern and rational approach to individual liberties, every major decision since then, with few exceptions, can only be classified as fitting a trend that brings legal thinking back to a moralistic, traditional viewpoint. This direction has been recently reinforced by the Court's decision in *Bowers v. Hardwick.* The Court, and Burger in particular, relied heavily on tradition and history in denying the right of homosexuals to legally enjoy sexual intimacy in the privacy of a home.

CONCLUSION

"If sexual conduct can be prohibited by the state, as has been shown by the Court's refusal to protect the intimate lives of homosexuals during the thick of the AIDS crisis, then the state will be able to easily defend an assortment of restrictions created to restrict sexual behavior, even if the restrictions fail to narrowly target only unsafe sex practices.

"Hopefully, the quarantining and testing ordinances, like sodomy statutes, will remain vestigial, examples of symbolic legislation. Historically, it has been impossible to regulate or forbid personal choice in sexual behavior, yet society consistently attempts to create illusions of "normalcy." When such illusions interfere with the prevention of a deadly disease, however, they should be subject to the highest scrutiny."

Bergman, "AIDS, Prostitution, and the Use of Historical Stereotypes To Legislate Sexuality", 21 John Marshall Law Rev. 777, 777–778, 828–830, footnotes omitted (1988).

NOTE

Can homosexuality and AIDS (Acquired Immune Deficiency Syndrome) be a basis for a federal civil rights action under 42 U.S.C. § 1985(3), where the plaintiff, a former city firefighter, brought an action against the city and his former union, alleging that the union breached its duty of fair representation and that both the city and union conspired to deprive him of his civil rights? "No," according to the court in David v. Local 801, Danbury Fire Fighters Association, 899 F.Supp. 78 (D.Conn.1995).

The court held that homosexuals and persons sexually affiliated with AIDS do not constitute suspect or quasi-suspect classes entitled to greater than a rational basis scrutiny for purposes of equal protection analysis, and therefore the alleged conspiracy to deprive such class members of their civil rights could not form the basis for a civil rights action.

3. FORNICATION AND ADULTERY

With regard to adultery and fornication, appraise the following statutory provisions, particularly in the light of currently prevailing moral concepts and practices. Also consider that in some jurisdictions such conduct is not criminally proscribed.

Illinois Criminal Code, 720 ILCS (1995):

5/11–7. Adultery

§ 11–7. Adultery. (a) Any person who has sexual intercourse with another not his spouse commits adultery, if the behavior is open and notorious, and

(1) The person is married and the other person involved in such intercourse is not his spouse; or

(2) The person is not married and knows that the other person involved in such intercourse is married.

A person shall be exempt from prosecution under this Section if his liability is based solely on evidence he has given in order to comply with the requirements of Section 4–1.7 of "The Illinois Public Aid Code", approved April 11, 1967, as amended.

(b) Sentence.

Adultery is a Class A misdemeanor.

5/11–8. Fornication

§ 11–8. Fornication. (a) Any person who has sexual intercourse with another not his spouse commits fornication if the behavior is open and notorious.

A person shall be exempt from prosecution under this Section if his liability is based solely on evidence he has given in order to comply with the requirements of Section 4–1.7 of "The Illinois Public Aid Code", approved April 11, 1967, as amended.

(b) Sentence.

Fornication is a Class B misdemeanor.

Some cases have struck down fornication statutes on constitutional privacy grounds and on the basis that they lack a compelling state interest. For example, in Doe v. Duling, 603 F.Supp. 960 (E.D.Va.1985), the court struck down a statute prohibiting the "... non-prostitutional, heterosexual activities of two unmarried consenting adults when such activities occur in the privacy of one's home," as an unconstitutional violation of the right to privacy in the absence of a compelling state interest. The fact that the state was interested in encouraging and regulating marital relationships and moral values, preventing sexual diseases, and minimizing illegitimate births was deemed "laudable" but not "compelling" in the constitutional sense.

Question: In light of the following language from the U.S. Supreme Court's decision in *Bowers v. Hardiwick,* would the *Doe v. Duling* case be decided the same way today:

> "Even if the conduct at issue here is not a fundamental right, respondent asserts that there must be a rational basis for the law and that there is none in this case other than the presumed belief of a majority of the electorate in Georgia that homosexual sodomy is immoral and unacceptable. This is said to be an adequate rationale to support the law. The law, however, is constantly based on notions of morality, and if all laws representing essentially moral choices are to be invalidated under the Due Process Clause, the courts will be very busy indeed. Even respondent makes no such claim, but insists that majority sentiments about the morality of homosexuality should be declared inadequate. We do not agree, and are unpersuaded that the sodomy laws of some 25 States should be invalidated on this basis."

C. MISCELLANEOUS SEX OFFENSES

Other commonly encountered sex offenses include those designed to protect children. They are often titled "child sexual abuse," "contributing to the delinquency" of a minor or taking "indecent liberties" with a child. See Texas Penal Code Ann. § 21.11 (Vernon 1974). In People v. Barron, 57 CrL 1187 (Cal.App.1995), a "resident child molester" law defined the offense in terms of "continuous sexual abuse of a child" over a period of three or more months, mentioning as a basis for a charge either three or more acts of "substantial sexual abuse," or three or more acts of lewd or lascivious conduct. In construing the statute, the court ruled that the three or more acts did not have to be of the same kind to qualify under the statute, but could be different. The court's pragmatic reason for this conclusion was simply that "[t]he problems associated with young children who are the victims of frequent sexual abuse ... do not change simply because the form of sexual abuse varies."

Incest, prostitution, and "public indecency" are also widely proscribed. Regarding public indecency, the California Supreme Court said, in In re Smith, 7 Cal.3d 362, 497 P.2d 807, 102 Cal.Rptr. 335 (1972), that nude sunbathing on an isolated beach, without drawing attention to genitals for sexual purposes, does not satisfy the requirements of the crime prohibiting the willful or lewd exposure of the private parts of the body. The Tenth Circuit Court of Appeals, in United States v. Hymans, 463 F.2d 615 (10th Cir.1972), did not similarly view male and female defendants who had engaged in "skinny dipping" and were arrested while they were sunning themselves on the bank, eating watermelons. The court said it was not "persuaded by such nostalgic authorities as James Whitcomb Riley's 'The Old Swimming Hole', or Mark Twain's 'Adventures of Huckleberry Finn'," and affirmed a conviction for indecent exposure in a national forest. In that case, the court noted that the defendants were near a public campground in an area of concentrated recreation, near posted signs prohibiting nudity.

See also the cases and notes collected in Chapter 2 dealing with First Amendment rights, particularly the section on Obscenity.

A relatively new, related offense is that of "stalking." These statutes are intended to deal with the problem of defendants' following their victims or otherwise pursuing them closely, often for the purpose of committing sexual offenses.

Three recent cases illustrate this type of statute:

A statute, Or.Rev.Stat. §§ 163.735(10)(a), 163.738(3)(a), provided for the issuance of a protective order forbidding "stalking" if there were probable cause to believe that the person against whom the order would be applicable had engaged in stalking "without legitimate purpose." This language was held to be constitutionally vague under federal and state constitutions, because it would not put a person of ordinary intelligence on notice as to what is a "legitimate purpose" within the purview of the statute. Although legislative history might have shed some light on this meaning, the court said that legislative history cannot be used to cure a vagueness problem. State v. Norris–Romine, 134 Or.App. 204 (Or.App.1995.)

In a second case a stalking statute, Mont.Code Ann. § 45–5–220, made it a crime to "purposefully or knowingly cause . . . another person substantial emotional distress or reasonable apprehension of bodily injury or death by repeatedly . . . harassing, threatening, or intimidating the [victim]." The defendant made repeated phone calls to the victim expressing his love for her, a desire to have sex, and later, angry messages when his expressions of love went unheeded. Defendant argued that the statute could not be applied to him because expressions of love are protected under the First Amendment as free speech within the purview of Chaplinsky v. New Hampshire, 315 U.S. 568 (1942).

The court rejected defendant's argument. It said that, "[t]here are several well-defined and narrowly limited classes of speech, the prevention of which have never been thought to raise Constitutional problems. These include the lewd and obscene, the profane, the libelous, and the insulting or 'fighting' words—those which by their very utterance inflict injury or tend to incite an immediate breach of the peace. It has been well observed that such utterances are no essential part of any exposition of ideas, and are of slight social value."

While Chaplinsky dealt with the subject of actual threats, there are other subjects as well that are beyond the pale of First Amendment protections. The defendant's communications to the victim caused injury to her and had no social value cognizable under the First Amendment. State v. Cooney, 271 Mont. 42, 894 P.2d 303 (1995.)

A stalking statute that contained the following presumption was approved in State v. Saunders, 886 P.2d 496 (Okl.App.1994): "Evidence that the defendant continued to engage in a course of conduct involving repeated unconsented contact with the victim after being requested by the victim to discontinue the same or a different form of unconsented contact, and to refrain from any further unconsented contact with the victim, shall give rise to a rebuttable presumption that the continuation of the course of conduct caused the victim to feel terrorized, frightened, intimidated, threatened, harassed, or molested." The defendant argued that the presumption unconstitutionally shifted some of the burden of proof to him.

The court applied the standard test for determining the constitutionality of a presumption, i.e., whether there is a rational connection between the facts proven and the ultimate facts presumed, ruling that the test was satisfied. The court also rejected an argument that the statute was constitutionally void for vagueness because it used the phrase "repeatedly," along with "willfully," and "maliciously" in connection with following and harassing a stalking victim. The phrase, the court ruled, simply refers to the intent element of the crime that must be proven by the state.

D. "SEXUALLY DANGEROUS" PERSONS LEGISLATION

Over a period of years many states have enacted legislation designed to institutionalize potentially dangerous sex offenders "for treatment and cure". The objective has been to institutionalize such persons to prevent their commission of rapes and other serious sexual or sex related offenses.

In some jurisdictions, there can only be a "sexually dangerous persons" proceeding against someone who is already "charged with a criminal offense". Others do not so confine the proceeding.

As a general rule, statutes of this type have been rarely used. Ordinarily the individual only comes to the attention of a prosecutor after he has committed a crime for which he can be sent away on a criminal charge, and perhaps on one that will result in a penitentiary sentence from which he is far less likely to be released on parole than upon release from a mental institution as "cured". There are also a number of constitutional obstacles—e.g., the self-incrimination privilege as regards a compulsory psychiatric examination.

Some scholars feel that the only constructive preventive measures are community level and school programs aimed at seeking out and treating deviational characteristics among children.

Are such proceedings "criminal" within the meaning of the Fifth Amendment's guarantee against compulsory self-incrimination? Under the Illinois Sexually Dangerous Persons Act a prosecutor may seek institutionalization, rather than imprisonment, of a defendant charged with any of certain sex offenses. The proceedings are nonpunitive in purpose and not "criminal." For that reason the U.S. Supreme Court ruled in Allen v. Illinois, 478 U.S. 364, 106 S.Ct. 2988 (1986), that the proceedings do not fall within the meaning of the Fifth Amendment's guarantee against compulsory self-incrimination, even though the Act does not apply until criminal charges have been filed, proceedings under the Act include some safeguards characteristic of criminal trials, and persons adjudged sexually dangerous under the Act are confined with mentally ill convicts in a maximum security institution. The Court also rejected an argument that the Fourteenth Amendment's guarantee of due process required an independent application of the Fifth Amendment privilege to proceedings brought under the Act.

In the recent decision of In re Blodgett, 510 N.W.2d 910 (Minn. 1994), Minnesota's Psychopathic Personality Commitment Act, which originally was ruled constitutional by the United States Supreme Court over 50 years ago in Pearson v. Probate Court of Ramsey County, Minn., 309 U.S. 270 (1940), survived another constitutional challenge based upon due process and equal protection grounds. The Act provides for indefinite civil commitment of persons judged to be "sexual predators." The Minnesota court focused on the state's interest in protecting the public from persons deemed to fall into the category of being mentally ill and dangerous to others. Although the confinee in this case relied upon the decision of Foucha v. Louisiana, 504 U.S. 71, 112 S.Ct. 1780 (1992), for his constitutional challenge, the instant court believed that the Minnesota statute fell within Foucha's identification of the class of mentally ill and dangerous persons who may be constitutionally deprived of liberty indefinitely in civil commitment proceedings.

Similarly, a Tennessee statute providing that all sex offenders were "mentally ill persons" survived a due process challenge in Dean v. McWherter, 70 F.3d 43 (6th Cir.1995). The statute provides that "sex offenders constitute a species of mentally ill persons ... and such persons should be given continued care and treatment so long as their release would constitute a threat to them or the general public."

Chapter 6

MISAPPROPRIATION AND RELATED PROPERTY OFFENSES

A. LARCENY

Larceny, generally speaking, is the crime of stealing. Technically, it consists of several specific elements, namely

a. a taking and

b. a carrying away

c. of the personal property

d. of another

e. with intent to steal.

An act which lacks any one of these elements cannot be larceny.

To understand why the law of larceny is so technical as to require the fulfillment of all of these elements, reference must be made to the history of the offense.

First, larceny was the only form of theft criminally punished under the early common law. The offense was narrowly construed, inasmuch as many forms of deception were not commonly regarded as criminal. The social and economic community lacked the complexity of modern times, and it was thought that with the exercise of ordinary prudence one could protect himself from most sorts of deception. For example, it was held in 1761 that it was not a crime to "make a fool of another" by deliberately delivering fewer goods than were ordered. The civil law was relied upon to correct such a deception; the criminal law would intervene only if the fraud was one which common care could not prevent, such as the use of false weights and measures. As commerce increased, the criminal law expanded to punish new forms of theft; however, the law of larceny had become so fixed that gaps were filled by the addition of new crimes, such as embezzlement and false pretenses, rather than by redefining larceny.

Second, the technicalities surrounding the law of larceny derive to some extent from the fact that grand larceny (larceny of goods having a certain minimum value) was a capital offense. Gradually, as attitudes towards the death penalty changed, judges became reluctant to impose the death penalty upon thieves, especially since the amount which divided grand and petit larceny was very low. Thus, judges would frequently rely upon technicalities to acquit in larceny cases.

The complex nature of the law of theft has little justification today. Some efforts have been made to simplify the law in this area. Notably, several states have abolished the separate offenses of larceny, embezzlement, etc., and combined them in a new crime called "theft." Until such time, however, as reform in this area is complete, it is necessary to understand some of the complexities of the law of larceny, as well as the offenses that have been developed to supplement larceny in the field of theft.

THE ELEMENTS OF LARCENY

1. *The Taking*

It should be stressed at the outset that the "taking" refers to a taking of *possession* of the personal goods of another. Thus, one can take possession of goods over which he has mere *custody,* and such a taking amounts to larceny if the other requirements are present. However, if actual possession is never acquired by the thief, or by one acting at his direction or instigation, larceny has not been committed. Moreover, there is no taking unless the object is first in someone else's possession, either actual or constructive.

The taking can be effected by the hands of the thief, by a mechanical device, or even by an animal trained for that purpose, or by an innocent human being acting under the thief's direction. A "lifting up" of an object by any one of these means is a "taking."

2. *The Carrying Away*

A good illustration of the meaning of the requirement of "carrying away" is the case of a person who took some beaded bags from a show case and put them in the pocket of an overcoat he was carrying on his arm. When a salesman's suspicion was aroused the defendant departed from the store but left his overcoat behind, with the merchandise in it, on a counter about six feet away from the one from which he had taken the objects. This was held to be a "carrying away" within the meaning of the larceny provision of a criminal code then in effect.

Carrying away, without achieving actual possession, however, is insufficient. In a case where the defendant lifted an overcoat from a store dummy and started to walk away with it, but it was secured to the dummy by a chain, which the defendant was unable to break, it was held that the defendant was not guilty of larceny, inasmuch as he never had actual possession of the coat.

3. *Personal Property*

Under common law, only personal property, and not something that might be considered part of the realty, could be the subject of larceny. An illustration of this is a case where a tombstone was taken from a grave in a cemetery. It was held that there could be no larceny of "anything adhering to the soil".

Certain animals were not considered personalty at common law. The theft of a dog, cat, monkey, or fox was not deemed a larceny. However, those animals of a domestic nature that were useful for the sustenance of life came under the umbrella of personalty and could therefore be the subject of a larceny. They included cows, horses, hogs, and chickens.

4. *Another's Property*

According to the common law, one co-owner cannot be guilty of larceny from another co-owner. Thus, a partner who steals partnership property is not guilty of larceny. Likewise, at common law, a spouse does not commit larceny by taking property from the other spouse.

This common law rule is usually abolished by recent theft laws. Even if the person in possession of the property had stolen it, it would be theft to steal it from him or her.

5. *Intent to Steal*

This required element of larceny is not only an historical one, but one of the highest importance today, either under the common law or modern statutory concepts. No one can be guilty of larceny, or of theft as defined under recently enacted statutes or codes, unless he had the intent to permanently deprive the owner of the property that was taken and carried away.

Because of the requirement of an intent to steal, it is often difficult to obtain larceny convictions in cases involving so-called "joy-riding". Where an automobile is taken with the intent to use it for a few hours and then return it to the place where taken, or to leave it in a place where the owner will be likely to recover it, all of the elements of larceny are usually present except for the intent to steal. As a consequence, most states have enacted special legislation concerning this offense.

In shoplifting situations, many merchants are under the impression that the offense is not completed until the goods are taken out of the store, for until then the "intent to steal" cannot be established. But the intent to steal is provable by other factors, such as the carrying of goods from one floor to another. In other words, conduct on the part of the accused that is clearly inconsistent with the ordinary behavior of customers can be used as evidence of intent to steal. According to this test, therefore, a person should not be arrested while he is carrying an unconcealed piece of merchandise in the direction of clerks whom he could conceivably be approaching for an inquiry about the merchandise or where it conceivably appears that he is taking it to a better lighted place for closer inspection. In such instances the accused could reasonably offer such explanations as evidence of no intent to steal. On the other hand, the taking of an object from a counter, placing it in a bag or purse, and walking away from the counter without paying for it, is conduct unbecoming a customer and may reasonably be taken as evidence of intent to steal. One who takes under the honest but erroneous belief the property is his or that he has a right or a permission to take it is not a thief. One who takes without an intent to steal; i.e., mistakenly grabbing another person's coat (and wallet), but later, realizing his error, decides to keep it anyway, is, under modern law, guilty of theft.

NOTES

1. Penal codes or statutes have remedied most of the shortcomings of the common law concepts of larceny, and particularly with respect to the issue as to the meaning of "personal property". For instance, electricity, computer time, and other intangibles are made subject to larceny (or theft), sometimes by the usage of the phrase "anything of value" to the victim. Certain issues remain, however, which must be resolved on a case-by-case basis.

The problems of what constitutes property subject to theft still surface in important cases. Consider the reasoning of the majority in Dowling v. United States, 473 U.S. 207, 105 S.Ct. 3127 (1985).

JUSTICE BLACKMUN delivered the opinion of the Court.

The National Stolen Property Act provides for the imposition of criminal penalties upon any person who "transports in interstate or foreign commerce any goods, wares, merchandise, securities or money, of the value of $5,000 or more, knowing the same to have been stolen, converted or taken by fraud." 18 U.S.C. § 2314. In this case, we must determine whether the statute reaches the interstate transportation of "bootleg" phonorecords, "stolen, converted or taken by fraud" only in the sense that they were manufactured and distributed without the consent of the copyright owners of the musical compositions performed on the records.

... The offenses stemmed from an extensive bootleg record operation involving the manufacture and distribution by mail of recordings of vocal performances by Elvis Presley. The evidence demonstrated that sometime around 1976, Dowling, to that time an avid collector of Presley recordings, began in conjunction with codefendant William Samuel Theaker to manufacture phonorecords of unreleased Presley recordings. They used material from a variety of sources, including studio outtakes, acetates, soundtracks from Presley motion pictures, and tapes of Presley concerts and television appearances.... The bootleg entrepreneurs never obtained authorization from or paid royalties to the owners of the copyrights in the musical compositions.

In the beginning, Dowling, who resided near Baltimore, handled the "artistic" end of the operation, contributing his knowledge of the Presley subculture, seeking out and selecting the musical material, designing the covers and labels, and writing the liner notes, while Theaker, who lived in Los Angeles and had some familiarity with the music industry, took care of the business end, arranging for the record pressings, distributing catalogs, and filling orders. In early 1979, however, having come to suspect that the FBI was investigating the West Coast operation, Theaker began making shipments by commercial trucking companies of large quantities of the albums to Dowling in Maryland. Throughout 1979 and 1980, the venturers did their marketing through Send Service, a labeling and addressing entity, which distributed at least 50,000 copies of their catalog and advertising flyers to addresses on mailing lists provided by Theaker and Dowling. Theaker would collect customers' orders from post office boxes in Glendale, Cal., and mail them to Dowling in Maryland, who would fill the orders. The two did a substantial business: the stipulated testimony establishes that throughout this period Dowling mailed several hundred packages per week and regularly spend $1,000 per week in postage. . . .

. . . Dowling does not contest that he caused the shipment of goods in interstate commerce, or that the shipments had sufficient value to meet the monetary requirement. He argues, instead, that the goods shipped were not "stolen, converted or taken by fraud." In response, the Government does not suggest that Dowling wrongfully came by the phonorecords actually shipped or the physical materials from which they were made; nor does it contend that the objects that Dowling caused to be shipped, the bootleg phonorecords, were "the same" as the copyrights in the musical compositions that he infringed by unauthorized distribution of Presley performances of those compositions. The Government argues, however, that the shipments come within the reach of § 2314 because the phonorecords physically embodied performances of musical compositions that Dowling had no legal right to distribute. According to the Government, the unauthorized use of the musical compositions rendered the phonorecords "stolen, converted or taken by fraud" within the meaning of the statute. We must determine, therefore, whether phonorecords that include the performance of copyrighted musical compositions for the use of which no authorization has been sought nor royalties paid are consequently "stolen, converted or taken by fraud" for purposes of § 2314. We conclude that they are not.

The courts interpreting § 2314 have never required, of course, that the items stolen and transported remain in entirely unaltered form. See, e.g., United States v. Moore, 571 F.2d 154, 158 (CA3) (counterfeit printed Ticketron tickets "the same" as stolen blanks from which they were printed). Nor does it matter that the item owes a major portion of its value to an intangible component. See, e.g., United States v. Seagraves, 265 F.2d 876 (CA3 1959) (geophysical maps identifying possible oil deposits); United States v. Greenwald, 479 F.2d 320 (CA6) (documents bearing secret chemical formulae). But these cases and others prosecuted under § 2314 have always involved physical "goods, wares, [or] merchandise" that have themselves been "stolen, converted or taken by fraud." This basic element comports with the common-sense meaning of the statutory language: by requiring that the "goods, wares, [or] merchandise" be "the same" as those "stolen, converted or taken by fraud," the provision seems clearly to contemplate a physical identity between the items unlawfully obtained and those eventually transported, and hence some prior physical taking of the subject goods.

In contrast, the Government's theory here would make theft, conversion, or fraud equivalent to wrongful appropriation of statutorily protected rights in copyright. The copyright owner, however, holds no ordinary chattel. A copyright, like other intellectual property, comprises a series of carefully defined and carefully delimited interests to which the law affords correspondingly exact protections. "Section 106 of the Copyright Act confers a bundle of exclusive rights to the owner of the copyright," which include the rights "to publish, copy, and distribute the author's work." Harper & Row, Publishers, Inc. v. Nation Enterprises. However, "[t]his protection has never accorded the copyright owner complete control over all possible uses of his work." For example, § 107 of the Copyright Act "codifies the traditional privilege of other authors to make 'fair use' of an earlier writer's work." Likewise, § 115 grants compulsory licenses in nondramatic musical works. Thus, the property rights of a copyright holder have a character distinct from the possessory interest of the owner of simple "goods, wares, [or] merchandise," for the copyright holder's dominion is subjected to precisely defined limits.

It follows that interference with copyright does not easily equate with theft, conversion, or fraud. The Copyright Act even employs a separate term of art to define one who misappropriates a copyright: " 'Anyone who violates any of the exclusive rights of the copyright owner,' that is, anyone who trespasses into his exclusive domain by using or authorizing the use of the copyrighted work in one of the five ways set forth in the statute, 'is an infringer of the copyright.' [17 U.S.C.] § 501(a)." *Sony Corp.*, supra, at ___ (slip op. 15). There is no dispute in this case that Dowling's unauthorized inclusion on his bootleg albums of performances of copyrighted compositions constituted infringement of those copyrights. It is less clear, however, that the taking that occurs when an infringer arrogates the use of another's protected work comfortably fits the terms associated with physical removal employed by § 2314. The infringer invades a statutorily defined province guaranteed to the copyright holder alone. But he does not assume physical control over the copyright; nor does he wholly deprive its owner of its use. While one may colloquially link infringement with some general notion of wrongful appropriation, infringement plainly implicates a more complex set of property interests than does run-of-the-mill theft, conversion, or fraud. As a result, it fits but awkwardly with the language Congress chose—"stolen, converted or taken by fraud"—to describe the sorts of goods whose interstate shipment § 2314 makes criminal. "And, when interpreting a criminal statute that does not explicitly reach the conduct in question, we are reluctant to base an expansive reading on inferences drawn from subjective and variable 'understandings.' " Williams v. United States, 458 U.S., at 286.

The Court also noted that Congress had direct power to enact copyright laws and provide criminal sanctions for their violation, and need not limit their application to interstate commerce cases. Since Congress had always provided lesser penalties for copyright law violations, the Court held that copyrighted performances were not property within the ambit of the National Stolen Property Act. A vigorous dissent characterized the argument of the accused as a "sterile formality."

2. An illustration of one important issue appears in a 1981 decision of the New York Court of Appeals, the highest court of that state, in a consolidation of appeals in three unrelated shoplifting cases—People v. Olivo, People v. Gasparik, and People v. Spatzier, 52 N.Y.2d 309, 438 N.Y.S.2d 242, 420 N.E.2d 40 (1981). In Alivo the defendant was observed taking a set of wrenches, secreting them in his clothes, and walking toward an exit, passing a number of cashiers en route. In Gasparik, the defendant tore off a price tag and a sensormatic device from a jacket which he substituted for his own, after which he walked past several cashiers toward the exit on that floor. In Spatzier, the defendant entered a bookstore carrying an attache case into which he furtively placed a book he removed from a shelf and continued browsing. When he was approached by the store owner and confronted with what had been observed, he struck the owner with the case. The case opened and the book fell out. In all these cases the Court of Appeals sustained the larceny convictions, explicitly holding that "a shoplifter need not leave the store to be guilty of larceny." It noted that the defendant in each case "exercised control over merchandise wholly inconsistent with the store's continued rights."

3. As may well be expected, the monetary value of the stolen property which distinguishes grand larceny from petty larceny in the various statutory provisions has been increased over the years. At the present time the favored

figure seems to be in the vicinity of $100–150. Moreover, in some codes or statutes the terms grand and petty have been eliminated; reference is made only to the degree of punishment based upon the amount of money or the value of the property. Determining the value of stolen property is usually a function of the jury, using the test of "fair cash market value", or "reasonable selling price". Where the evidence is in conflict, the jury's determination will not be disturbed. Many forms of theft carry penalties that apply no matter how large or small the value of the item stolen, e.g., pocket picking, auto theft, robbery.

4. An interesting grand/petty larceny case arises in cases where a person has stolen money or property from the same source over a period of time. Is the delineation to be made on the basis of each theft or the totality of all? Consider the following case:

Defendant, a turnstile maintainer in the New York subway system, was tried for the theft of fares deposited by subway passengers in the station turnstiles. The first larceny involved approximately $1,500, alleged to have been taken over a period of 11 months, while the second charge involved the theft of more than $370 over a period of 10 months. The defendant was convicted of grand larceny, although he had contended at the trial that since the takings occurred over a period of time and in no one instance exceeded $100 (the jurisdiction's statutory dividing line between grand and petty larceny), he was guilty only of a number of petty larcenies. Defendant's conviction was affirmed by the New York Court of Appeals in People v. Cox, 286 N.Y. 137, 36 N.E.2d 84 (1941), holding that there was sufficient evidence to sustain the verdict of the jury that the entire taking was governed by a single intent and a general illegal design.

COMPUTER CRIME

There is no question that widespread use of computers has brought a new appearance to some forms of crime. Employees of a corporation create fictitious consulting companies and then instruct the corporation computer to issue checks to the fictitious companies for non-existent services. Bank clerks (or computer repairmen) cause a computer to transfer funds to accounts they have set up in other banks. Valuable commercial information such as customer mailing lists are drawn without authority from a business computer. A brilliant administrator devises a computer program for scheduling the transport of goods by a nationwide trucking concern—a program worth over a million dollars to the company that buys it; someone then steals the chip on which the program is printed or gets the trucking company's computer to print out the program codes. Executives of an insurance company decide to defraud other companies by selling them phony policies under the guise of reinsurance; knowing they will be audited, the computer program is made to project what the client group would be like if the business grew by 20% ______ i.e., among the new clients how many would be men, women, young, middle-aged, lawyers, salesmen, white, black, how many would renew and how many would die; and the results of this computer projection are then used to adjust the books of the company to make the phony business look real. An employee is fired, becomes vengeful and walks through the company's computer room with a strong electromagnet, causing millions of dollars in damage.

There is no doubt that the computer has brought a colorful new terminology to law enforcement. Consider the following "Data Diddling" (changing data before or during entry into the system); "Trojan Horse" (hiding a short code by improperly instructing the computer into a long program code that is otherwise flawless); "Salami" (taking small amounts such as pennies from each of a hundred thousand savings accounts and putting the sum in the programmer's account); "Superzapping" (bypassing controls by using a program designed to expedite legitimate modifications); "Trap Doors" (points of access deliberately left in otherwise secure systems to permit updates and corrections, which access may be used by a dishonest computer expert who knows where it is or can effectively search for it, or by a dishonest user who accidentally discovers it); "Logic Bomb" (a coded instruction to a computer to perform some act such as transferring funds or information to a perpetrator who has implanted it; the distinct characteristic of the logic bomb is that it is triggered by some event like the occurrence of a date or the use of a specific code; the logic bomb may also serve as a security device as well, since it can be used to destroy a program if improper use is attempted); "Dumpster Diving" (scavanging through discarded printouts to discover computer passwords or data stored in the computer). See Computer Crime, Criminal Justice Resource Manual (United States Department of Justice, 1979). Some of these terms may be colorful descriptions of things that have not and may never occur. There are instances of logic bombs but there may not be any cases of salamis. Taber, A Survey of Computer Crime Studies, 2 Computer L.J. 275, 311–27 (1980).

There are, however, doubts and questions about almost everything else having to do with crime by computer, including the phrase "computer crime" itself. Some prefer the term "computer abuse." First, no one has reliable statistics on its extent and cost. Some states still have no statute specifically defining computer crime. Among those that do there is no uniform definition of computer crime and the oldest of these statutes was passed in 1978 (West's Fla.Stat.Ann. § 815.05), so we are without any historical consensus or general understanding of what constitutes computer crime. Estimates range from $100 million to $3 billion in annual loss. No one agrees on the percentage of computer crime that is reported, but many believe it is small. On the other hand, the American Bar Association's Task Force on Computer Crime conducted a survey in 1984 and reported that annual losses appear "by any measure, to be enormous." There is some disagreement with this assessment, arising from the belief that such enormous losses would be more widely reported by victims.

There are those who believe that effective security measures may inhibit much computer crime. It is at least arguable that the economic incentive to find and implement effective counter measures to computer crime is so strong that in a few years computer crime will not constitute a particularly significant problem for the criminal justice system. Others believe that technological advances will aid the computer criminal.

There is disagreement over the need specially to define computer crime and to enact special statutes to cope with it. One school of thought is that few new laws are needed; theft by computer is still common theft. Unauthorized use of a computer is a theft of services; using a computer to pay a fictitious company set up by an employee is embezzlement; destruction of computer records is vandalism. Perhaps we need better definitions of what exactly constitutes property and how we assess its value, but the law of theft needs little change because of the computer revolution. Others believe that computer crime can be best addressed by laws specifically related to the fact that all computer crime hinges on access to the computer at one of five key points: data input, programming, central processing, output, remote transmission. In short, unauthorized access is the criminal act.

Both points of view may be persuasively argued, but legislative action has tended to favor special statutes. Perhaps this is so because of the reluctance of courts to adopt flexible definitions of property as well as the lack of computer literacy in many judges. Lund v. Commonwealth, 217 Va. 688, 232 S.E.2d 745 (1977) (Unauthorized use of $26,000 worth of computer resources is not larceny). Courts have found it difficult to regard electronic impulses as property capable of theft. United States v. Seidlitz, 589 F.2d 152 (4th Cir.1978) (Former employee used a telephone to gain access to company's valuable and confidential program). In fact, Dowling v. United States, supra, is another example of the difficulty courts have with the misappropriation of non-conventional property. One of the most powerful legal traditions is that for theft to occur tangible property must physically change possession.

In Commonwealth v. Gerulis, 616 A.2d 686 (Pa.Super.1992) a court held that unauthorized accessing of a voice mailbox system was properly prosecuted under a state statute forbidding "unauthorized use of a computer." The key to the court's decision was its finding that a voice mailbox system was a "computer" within the meaning of the statute. "We ... conclude that a voice mailbox is a 'computer, computer system, computer network, computer software, computer program or database, or any part thereof, ...' 18 Pa.C.S. 3933(c). The trial court found that a 'voice mailbox is a computerized hard disk drive electronic message answering system having a digital interface that is accessed, via a password, and through a touch tone telephone.' The mailbox is created by computer software, and the messages are stored on computer disks. There is support in the record for the trial court's finding. The voice mailboxes are 'electronic ... or high speed data processing device[s] ... which perform ... memory functions.' 18 Pa.C.S. 3933(c). As such, the voice mailboxes are 'computers' within the meaning of 18 Pa.C.S. 3933(c)."

Once having decided that a special statute is required, a host of problems arises. What, for example, is a computer? If the definition is too narrow the statute will soon be obsolete. Too broad a definition will place microprocessors now found in typewriters, calculators, watches and automobiles within the ambit of computer crime laws. If all microprocessors are included, however, the case will now be reached of the thief who alters a slot machine computer chip to compel a payoff.

Over twenty states have enacted computer crime laws and there is not enough experience with them to determine if they will be enforceable and effective. One statute enacted by Congress is the Counterfeit Access Device and Computer Fraud Abuse Act of 1984 (18 U.S.C.A. § 1030). Consider its provisions:

FRAUD AND RELATED ACTIVITY IN CONNECTION WITH COMPUTERS

(a) Whoever—

(1) knowingly accesses a computer without authorization or exceeds authorized access, and by means of such conduct obtains information that has been determined by the United States Government pursuant to an Executive order or statute to require protection against unauthorized disclosure for reasons of national defense or foreign relations, or any restricted data, as defined in paragraph r. of section 11 of the Atomic Energy Act of 1954, with the intent or reason to believe that such information so obtained is to be used to the injury of the United States, or to the advantage of any foreign nation;

(2) intentionally accesses a computer without authorization or exceeds authorized access, and thereby obtains information contained in a financial record of a financial institution or of a card issuer as defined in section 1602(n) of title 15, or contained in a file of a consumer reporting agency on a consumer,

(3) intentionally, without authorization to access any computer of a department or agency of the United States, accesses such a computer of that department or agency that is exclusively for the use of the Government of the United States or, in the case of a computer not exclusively for such use, is used by or for the Government of the United States and such conduct affects the use of the Government's operation of such computer;

(4) knowingly and with intent to defraud, accesses a Federal interest computer without authorization, or exceeds authorized access, and by means of such conduct furthers the intended fraud and obtains anything of value, unless the object of the fraud and the thing obtained consists only of the use of the computer;

(5) intentionally accesses a Federal interest computer without authorization, and by means of one or more instances of such conduct alters, damages, or destroys information in any such Federal interest computer, or prevents authorized use of any such computer or information, and thereby—

(A) causes loss to one or more others of a value aggregating $1,000 or more during any one year period; or

(B) modifies or impairs, or potentially modifies or impairs, the medical examination, medical diagnosis, medical treatment, or medical care of one or more individuals; or

(6) knowingly and with intent to defraud traffics in any password or similar information through which a computer may be accessed without authorization, if—

(A) such trafficking affects interstate or foreign commerce; or

(B) such computer is used by or for the Government of the United States; shall be punished as provided in subsection (c) of this section.

(b) Whoever attempts to commit an offense under subsection (a) of this section shall be punished as provided in subsection (c) of this section.

(c) The punishment for an offense under subsection (a) or (b) of this section is—

(1)(A) a fine under this title or imprisonment for not more than ten years, or both, in the case of an offense under subsection (a)(1) of this section which does not occur after a conviction for another offense under such subsection, or an attempt to commit an offense punishable under this subparagraph; and

(B) a fine under this title or imprisonment for not more than twenty years, or both, in the case of an offense under subsection (a)(1) of this section which occurs after a conviction for another offense under such subsection, or an attempt to commit an offense punishable under this subparagraph; and

(2)(A) a fine under this title or imprisonment for not more than one year, or both, in the case of an offense under subsection (a)(2), (a)(3) or (a)(6) of this section which does not occur after a conviction for another offense under such subsection, or an attempt to commit an offense punishable under this subparagraph; and

(B) a fine under this title or imprisonment for not more than ten years, or both, in the case of an offense under subsection (a)(2), (a)(3) or (a)(6) of this section which occurs after a conviction for another offense under such subsection, or an attempt to commit an offense punishable under this subparagraph; and

(3)(A) a fine under this title or imprisonment for not more than five years, or both, in the case of an offense under subsection (a)(4) or (a)(5) of this section which does not occur after a conviction for another offense under such subsection, or an attempt to commit an offense punishable under this subparagraph; and

(B) a fine under this title or imprisonment for not more than ten years, or both, in the case of an offense under subsection (a)(4) or (a)(5) of this section which occurs after a conviction for another offense under such subsection, or an attempt to commit an offense punishable under this subparagraph.

(d) The United States Secret Service shall, in addition to any other agency having such authority, have the authority to investigate offenses under this section. Such authority of the United States Secret Service shall be exercised in accordance with an agreement which shall be entered into by the Secretary of the Treasury and the Attorney General.

(e) As used in this section—

(1) the term "computer" means an electronic, magnetic, optical, electrochemical, or other high speed data processing device performing logical, arithmetic, or storage functions, and includes any data storage facility or communications facility directly related to or operating in conjunction with such device, but such term does not include an automated typewriter or typesetter, a portable hand held calculator, or other similar device;

(2) the term "Federal interest computer" means a computer—

(A) exclusively for the use of a financial institution or the United States Government, or, in the case of a computer not exclusively for such use, used by or for a financial institution or the United States Government and the conduct constituting the offense affects the use of the financial institution's operation or the Government's operation of such computer; or

(B) which is one of two or more computers used in committing the offense, not all of which are located in the same State;

(3) the term "State" includes the District of Columbia, the Commonwealth of Puerto Rico, and any other possession or territory of the United States;

(4) the term "financial institution" means—

(A) a bank with deposits insured by the Federal Deposit Insurance Corporation;

(B) the Federal Reserve or a member of the Federal Reserve including any Federal Reserve Bank;

(C) an institution with accounts insured by the Federal Savings and Loan Insurance Corporation;

(D) a credit union with accounts insured by the National Credit Union Administration;

(E) a member of the Federal home loan bank system and any home loan bank;

(F) any institution of the Farm Credit System under the Farm Credit Act of 1971;

(G) a broker-dealer registered with the Securities and Exchange Commission pursuant to section 15 of the Securities Exchange Act of 1934; and

(H) the Securities Investor Protection Corporation;

(5) the term "financial record" means information derived from any record held by a financial institution pertaining to a customer's relationship with the financial institution;

(6) the term "exceeds authorized access" means to access a computer with authorization and to use such access to obtain or alter information in the computer that the accesser is not entitled so to obtain or alter; and

(7) the term "department of the United States" means the legislative or judicial branch of the Government or one of the executive departments.

(f) This section does not prohibit any lawfully authorized investigative, protective, or intelligence activity of a law enforcement agency of the United States, a State, or a political subdivision of a State, or of an intelligence agency of the United States.

It has been held that the seizure of a computer containing stored electronic mail is not an illegal "intercept" within the meaning of the federal Wiretap Act. During an investigation into allegations of illegal activity by a computer game company, U.S. Secret Service agents obtained a search warrant for the company premises. Pursuant to the search warrant, agents entered the premises and seized a computer used to operate an "electronic bulletin board system." This computer contained private electronic mail which had been sent to (stored on) the computer system, but not yet read (retrieved) by the intended recipients.

The company and users of its electronic mail system filed a lawsuit against the U.S. and Secret Service, alleging that the seizure of such stored electronic mail constituted an unlawful intercept under the Federal Wiretap Act, 18 U.S.C.A. § 2510, as amended by Title I of the Electronic Communications Privacy Act of 1986.

A federal appeals court rejected these claims. It ruled that Congress had not intended to have the term "intercept" in the Act apply to electronic mail which was being stored on a computer system. Steve Jackson Games, Inc. v. U.S. Secret Service, 36 F.3d 457 (5th Cir.1994).

B. EMBEZZLEMENT

WARREN v. STATE

Supreme Court of Indiana 1945.
223 Ind. 552, 62 N.E.2d 624.

RICHMAN, CHIEF JUSTICE. Waiving a jury appellant was tried and convicted of larceny of four cans of Prestone. The only question presented is whether the finding is contrary to law. The evidence leaves no doubt that for more than six months he continued to take property of his employer and convert it to his own use, but he contends that his employment was such as to make his crime embezzlement rather than larceny.

He was employed as a member of a maintenance crew under a foreman in Plant No. 2 of the Allison Division of General Motors Corporation. The plant contained tanks for reception and storage of gasoline, oil and Prestone. To a storage building housing Prestone both the foreman and appellant had keys. "The Chief Engineer ... had exclusive control in Plant No. 2 of this Prestone." Appellant was not authorized to remove Prestone from the building except on requisition from some other person in authority. One of appellant's duties was to receive gasoline. A confederate (who pleaded guilty to the same affidavit upon which appellant was tried) was employed by a trucking company to deliver gasoline to the plant and thus obtained ingress. His truck was used to take away Prestone abstracted by appellant from the storage building. The Prestone was sold and the proceeds divided by appellant and the truck driver. A statement signed by appellant, and admitted in evidence, related numerous such transactions from June through August, 1943. In November they "took out some 30 to 35 drums of Prestone," each containing 55 gallons and sold them for $83 per drum. Appellant's employer became suspicious and early in January, 1944, investigators observed appellant surreptitiously placing four cans in the truck. It was followed away from the plant and the cans, containing Prestone, were recovered. No contention is made by appellant that he had a requisition when he took this Prestone. There was other testimony more favorable to appellant's theory, but upon appeal we look only to the evidence tending to support the finding.

The facts related bring the case within the rule of Colip v. State [1899] ... and cases from other jurisdictions cited in a note in 125 A.L.R. at p. 368, holding that an employe who has "mere custody of personal property, as distinguished from legal possession" and with animo furandi converts same to his own use is guilty of larceny. Here there was no "relation of special trust in regard to the article appropriated" which this court in Colip v. State, supra, said was necessary to an embezzlement. Appellant had access to the storage building but the Prestone therein was in the possession of the employer. We see no essential difference between this case and the hypothetical case of the watchman referred to in the following quotation from Vinnedge v. State [1906]:

"Where there is at most but a naked possession or control—that is, a bare charge—or where the access consists of a mere physical propinquity as an incident of the employment, the felonious appropriation should be regarded as larceny. The reference in the embezzlement statute to officers, agents, attorneys, clerks, servants, and employés is plainly indicative of the intent to limit the denouncement of the statute to cases in which such persons have, as an element of their employment, a special trust concerning the money, article, or thing of value that involves an actual possession thereof or a special right of access to or control over the same. This requirement would not be satisfied, as we may indicate by way of illustration, by the mere control or possession, or physical opportunity of access, which a watchman in charge of a store might have. As before indicated, the relationship contemplated by the statute is one of special trust and confidence; a relationship in which there inheres, either for the particular transaction or for all purposes, a special right of access to, or control or possession of, the money, article, or thing of value which is appropriated."

Usually a watchman carries a key. Appellant's key made access easier but did not give him possession. We regard as immaterial the fact that he was bonded against embezzlement. It perhaps was a circumstance which the court might have taken into consideration in determining the relationship of the parties, but it was in no sense controlling. Appellant's contention that animus furandi was not proved is controverted by the evidence showing that the crime was preceded by similar consummated thefts over a period of many months. Similar transactions may be shown to prove felonious intent, knowledge and other similar states of mind. . . .

The cases relied upon by appellant belong to another category. Davis v. State [1925] recognizes the principle quoted from Colip v. State, supra, but holds that the facts establish the crime of embezzlement. The appellant therein received money as treasurer of an association and later converted it to his own use. He had exclusive possession and control of the fund under a trust to account to his employer. In Jones v. State [1877] a merchant gave his employe some money in an unsealed envelope, directing him to deliver it to other merchants as the purchase price of a load of flour. On the day he succumbed to temptation and fled with the money to another state. State v. Wingo [1883] had similar facts. Each employe was given exclusive possession of the property under a special trust and later formed the felonious intent. . . .

Judgment affirmed.

NOTES

1. There is little or no justification today for the distinction between larceny and embezzlement. Both the offenses of larceny and embezzlement, as

well as many related ones, can be adequately covered under a general statutory offense of "Theft".

2. On the type of employee able to "embezzle" see United States v. Whitlock, 663 F.2d 1094 (D.C.Cir.1980) (assistant cashier); Morgan v. Commonwealth, 242 Ky. 713, 47 S.W.2d 543 (1932) (office manager).

3. In view of the fact that in many instances thefts by employees from their employers are never reported to the law enforcement authorities because of restitution being made by the employee, or someone on his behalf, attorneys should be mindful of the offense known as "compounding a felony" or as "misprision of felony". Consider, for instance, the following provision in the Illinois Criminal Code (720 ILCS 5/32–1):

> A person compounds a crime when he receives or offers to another any consideration for a promise not to prosecute or aid in the prosecution of an offender.

The United States Code (18 U.S.C.A.) contains the following provision:

> § 4. Misprision of felony
>
> Whoever, having knowledge of the actual commission of a felony cognizable by a court of the United States, conceals and does not as soon as possible make known the same to some judge or other person in civil or military authority under the United States, shall be fined not more than $500 or imprisoned not more than three years, or both.

Under the foregoing federal statute, there must be an affirmative act of concealment; mere failure to report an offense does not constitute a violation. United States v. Daddano, 432 F.2d 1119 (7th Cir.1970), cert. denied 402 U.S. 905, 91 S.Ct. 1391 (1971); United States v. Johnson, 546 F.2d 1225 (5th Cir.1977).

The offense of misprision of felony is discussed further in Chapter 8–c, "Parties to Crime."

In a 1948 English case, R. v. Aberg, 32 Crim.App.Reps. 144, Lord Chief Justice Goddard said that "misprision of felony is an offense which is described in the books, but which has been generally regarded nowadays as obsolete or fallen into desuetude". But thirteen years later the House of Lords declared that the offense of misprision of felony still existed in all its vigor. Sykes v. Director of Public Prosecution, [1961] 3 All Eng.L.R. 33, held that if one knows that a felony has been committed and fails to report it, he is guilty of misprision of felony. Concealment, it was held, need not involve a positive act; mere omission is sufficient. Exempted, apparently, are persons within a privileged relationship with the felon (e.g., lawyers, clergymen), for the court in the *Sykes* case referred to "a claim of right made in good faith".

C. FALSE PRETENSES—DECEPTIVE PRACTICES

In the absence of specific statutory language, considerable uncertainty will exist as to what conduct is included in the offense of obtaining money or property by "false pretenses." Modern statutes or criminal code provisions have removed that uncertainty. They usually are patterned after the following recommendation of the American Law Institute's Model Penal Code, § 206.2:

Theft by Deception

(1) *General.* A person commits theft if he obtains property of another by means of deception. A person deceives if he purposely:

(a) creates or reinforces an impression which is false and which he does not believe to be true; or

(b) prevents another from acquiring information which the actor knows would influence the other party in the transaction; or

(c) fails to disclose a lien, adverse claim, or other legal impediment to the enjoyment of property being sold or otherwise transferred or encumbered, regardless of the legal validity of the impediment and regardless of any official record disclosing its existence;

(d) fails to correct a false impression previously created or reinforced by him; or

(e) fails to correct a false impression which he knows to be influencing another to whom he stands in a relationship of special trust and confidence.

(2) *Value, Law, Opinion, Intention; False Promises.* Deception may relate to value, law, opinion, intention or other state of mind. A promise which creates the impression that the promisor intends that the promise shall be performed is deception if he does not have that intention at the time of the promise; but the non-existence of that intention shall not be inferred from the fact alone that the promise was not performed.

(3) *Puffing Excepted.* Exaggerated commendation of wares in communications addressed to the public or to a class or group shall not be deemed deceptive if:

(a) it would be unlikely to mislead the ordinary person of the class or group addressed; and

(b) there is no deception other than as to the actor's belief in the commendation; and

(c) the actor was not in a position of special trust and confidence in relation to the misled party.

"Commendation of wares" includes representation that the price asked is low.

(4) *Non-pecuniary Deception Excepted.* A person does not commit theft by deception where, in a business transaction, the only deception is as to matters having no pecuniary significance.

The Illinois Criminal Code (Ill.Rev.Stats. ch. 38) provides, in § 16–1(b), that a person commits theft when he knowingly "obtains by deception control over property of the owner", and, in § 15–4(e), that "deception" means to knowingly "promise performance which the offender does not intend to perform or knows will not be performed". "Failure to perform", however, "standing alone is not evidence that the offender did not intend to perform" (§ 15–4(e)).

D. RECEIVING STOLEN PROPERTY—THE PRESUMPTION FACTOR

COMMONWEALTH v. OWENS

Supreme Court of Pennsylvania, 1970.
441 Pa. 318, 271 A.2d 230.

ROBERTS, JUSTICE. It has been the law in the criminal courts of Pennsylvania that a defendant's unexplained possession of recently stolen goods is sufficient proof of his guilt of the crime of receiving stolen goods. Although the statute defining that crime provides as an express element that the defendant knew or had reason to know that the goods in question had been stolen, it has been reasoned that such scienter may be presumed from evidence of mere possession. . . .

This case raises a serious question as to the continuing validity of this presumption in light of the United States Supreme Court's recent decisions in Leary v. United States (1969), and Turner v. United States (1970). . . .

At approximately 11:10 P.M. on the evening of January 31, 1967, Dr. Dick Kazin parked and left his automobile on Craft Avenue in the Oakland section of Pittsburgh. Upon returning to the car some twenty minutes later, he discovered one of the car's front windows broken and three handguns and two snow tires missing from within.

On February 19, 1967, Lieutenant O'Connell of the Pittsburgh police force went to the grocery store of one Earl Harris armed with a search warrant seeking contraband moonshine whiskey. Not only did the search for the moonshine prove fruitful, but O'Connell also found one of the pistols that had been stolen from Kazin less than three weeks earlier. At appellant's trial Harris testified that he had purchased the pistol from appellant for a total price of $30, paying $20 in cash with a balance of $10. In partial corroboration of this story Harris' wife Velma testified that appellant had come into the grocery store seeking payment of the $10 balance and attempting to sell a second pistol which he showed to her at that time. Velma Harris admitted, however, that appellant had offered no clue as to how he had come into possession of either of the weapons.

The foregoing is the sum of the prosecution's case.

Appellant testified in his own behalf and admitted having met Harris in prison many years earlier and having seen him on the street several times in the subsequent years. However, he denied any connection with the stolen gun or its sale or attempted sale to Harris. He further denied all of Velma Harris' testimony concerning his supposed demand for a $10 balance and attempt to sell a second gun.

The trier of fact was of course free to credit the testimony of Earl and Velma Harris and to disbelieve that of appellant, but the former established at most only that appellant possessed a stolen pistol at some time less than three weeks after its theft. Thus the presumption of guilty knowledge is the sole basis upon which appellant's conviction can rest, and it is to an assessment of this presumption that we must turn.

The general teaching of *Leary* and *Turner* is that a criminal presumption is unconstitutional "unless it can at least be said with substantial assurance that the presumed fact is more likely than not to flow from the proved fact on which it is made to depend." ...

Leary reversed a conviction for the possession of marihuana knowing the same to have been illegally imported, by invalidating the statutory presumption that such knowledge may be presumed from evidence of mere possession. The Court admitted that information concerning the factual accuracy of the presumption was " 'not within specialized judicial competence or completely commonplace,' " and that significant weight should be accorded to Congress's presumed investigation as to the soundness of the presumption. Nevertheless, in the absence of an actual legislative record documenting the accuracy of the presumption, the Court felt free to and did survey other available data on the subject. From such a survey the Court was willing to assume that the majority of marihuana consumed in the United States was illegally imported but deemed this an insufficient basis for concluding that "a majority of marihuana possessors either are cognizant of the apparently high rate of importation or otherwise have become aware that *their* marihuana was grown abroad." ...

Turner dealt with an almost identical knowledge presumption concerning possession of cocaine and heroin. The Court struck down the presumption as applied to cocaine on the basis of its finding that large amounts of coca leaves, the raw material from which cocaine is derived, are legally imported for medicinal purposes. Respecting heroin, however, the Court sustained the presumption in light of evidence that virtually all domestically consumed heroin is illegally imported and that this fact concerning the source of heroin is not only widely and popularly known but especially known to those who traffic in the drug, "unless they practice a studied ignorance to which they are not entitled." ...

The "more likely than not" test coupled with the examples provided by *Leary* and *Turner* as to how that test should be applied in a given case leave us with little doubt that the knowledge presumption concerning receipt of stolen goods is constitutionally infirm, at least as applied to the circumstances of this case, and we so hold. We reiterate that there is nothing whatever in the record touching upon how appellant originally came into possession of the stolen pistol, and the possibilities of innocent acquisition seem myriad: a gift, payment for services rendered, payment of a debt, purchase from a seemingly reputable dealer in used guns. The only empirical data furnished to us by either party casts considerable doubt upon the probable factual strength of the knowledge presumption. A staff report submitted to the National Commission on the Causes and Prevention of Violence: Firearms and Violence in American Life, ch. 3, at 13–15, estimates that there were 24,000,000 handguns in the United States in 1968, that 54% of all handguns acquired in 1968 were sold used, and that among low income groups 71% of all used firearms were obtained from a friend or a private party. While these figures do not enable us to construct with any degree of accuracy the relative percentages of transfers of stolen and nonstolen guns, they nevertheless do indicate the probability that substantial numbers of used guns are transferred in seemingly innocent circumstances....

* * *

In response, the Commonwealth urges that the wisdom of common experience suffices to demonstrate that a possessor of a recently stolen pistol more likely than not knew or had reason to know that the weapon had been stolen. We fear, however, that the Commonwealth attributes to us and demands of us not merely a sensitivity to the dictates of common experience but a degree of clairvoyance which we do not and shall never possess....

* * *

The order of the Superior Court is reversed and the motion in arrest of judgment is granted and the judgment of sentence is vacated.

EAGEN, J., concurs in the result.

BELL, C.J., filed a dissenting opinion in which COHEN, J., joined.

POMEROY, J., dissents.

BELL, CHIEF JUSTICE (dissenting).

Defendant was tried on June 12, 1967, without a jury, and was found guilty of receiving stolen goods and sentenced to three years' imprisonment. Defendant's motion for arrest of judgment and a discharge, or in the alternative a new trial, was denied by the lower Court. The Superior Court affirmed, per curiam, and we granted allocatur....

* * *

It has been the long and well established law of Pennsylvania that possession of recently stolen property raises a presumption of knowledge that the property had been stolen....

* * *

Many Superior Court cases reiterate (although at times in slightly different language) this well and widely established presumption of guilt from mere possession of recently stolen property....

In a vain attempt to avoid the above-mentioned well established principles of law, the majority base their Opinion upon Leary v. United

States and Turner v. United States. *Leary* and *Turner* are clearly distinguishable on their facts. In *Leary,* the United States Supreme Court held unconstitutional a statutory provision which raised a presumption of knowledge of *illegal importation of marijuana* from the mere possession of marijuana. In *Turner,* the United States Supreme Court held that a statutory presumption of knowledge of *illegal importation of cocaine* from mere possession of cocaine was invalid because much more cocaine is lawfully produced in this country than is smuggled into this country. Furthermore, in *Turner,* a statutory presumption of knowledge of the *illegal importation of heroin* from the mere possession of heroin was upheld because the overwhelming evidence is that the heroin consumed in the United States is *illegally imported.* It is important to note that these two decisions are limited to the particular statutory presumptions in light of the particular circumstances of each case and do not decry or invalidate the Constitutionality of presumptions generally.

The prior decisions of this Court were not written on the sand to be washed away by each wave of new Justices. When crime is running rampant in our cities (and indeed throughout Pennsylvania and our entire Country) and terrifying our law-abiding citizens, this is no time to overrule well settled principles of law to aid criminals and those accused of crime and further jeopardize the safety and security of Society.

For the above reasons, I vigorously dissent.

COHEN, J., joins in this dissenting Opinion.

UNITED STATES v. BROCATO

United States Court of Appeals, 8th Circuit 1971.
437 F.2d 1157, cert. denied 402 U.S. 1010, 91 S.Ct. 2196.

PER CURIAM. In this case, John and Albert Brocato appeal their convictions for knowingly possessing property stolen from an interstate shipment in violation of 18 U.S.C. § 659. They claim that the evidence was insufficient to show possession and that the trial court erred in giving an instruction which permitted the jury to infer defendants' guilty knowledge from their possession of recently stolen property. We find these claims lacking in merit.

The evidence showed that 280 Singer nine-inch portable television sets being transported in interstate commerce disappeared from a truck during the morning of November 6, 1969, at Kansas City, Missouri. Two days later, approximately 100 of the sets were seen in the storage area of a Bertsch and Vegder store located at 9401 Blue Ridge Boulevard, Kansas City, Missouri. This firm did not sell Singer television sets.

The evidence further shows that appellant Albert Brocato leased a Ford Econoline rental truck on November 8, 1969, and that appellant John Brocato drove the truck to the Bertsch and Vegder store that afternoon, where he talked with Anthony LaTore, the store manager. FBI agents placed the store under surveillance that day. The next day,

Sunday, November 9, Anthony LaTore opened the store and he and the two appellants proceeded to load some of the television sets into the leased truck. FBI agents then arrested the three men and found 55 television sets present: 15 in the truck, 5 on the loading dock and 35 in the storage area of the store.

Subsequently, the three arrested persons were indicted for unlawfully possessing chattels of a value in excess of $100.00, that is, 55 Singer nine-inch television sets, which had been stolen from an interstate shipment. The LaTore prosecution was severed from that against these appellants.

The evidence in this case clearly shows that appellants exercised dominion and thus possessed the property in question within the meaning of the statute....

Moreover, we have repeatedly upheld instructions which permit an inference of guilty knowledge from possession of recently stolen property.... See Judge Lay's opinion in United States v. Jones, 418 F.2d 818 (8th Cir.1969), for a detailed discussion of the historical antecedents of these instructions.

The trial court in this case phrased the instruction as follows:

> You are instructed that possession of property recently stolen, if not satisfactorily explained, is a circumstance from which you, the jury, may reasonably draw the inference and find, in the light of the surrounding circumstances shown by the evidence in the case, if you so find, that the person in possession knew the property had been stolen.
>
> * * *
>
> Possession may be satisfactorily explained by facts and circumstances in evidence independent of any testimony or other evidence from any accused.

Pursuant to this instruction, the appellants might have explained the circumstances of their possession of the stolen property in question. John Brocato, however, contends that his prior felony conviction stood in the way of his taking the stand in his own defense. Thus, he argues, the giving of the instruction infringed upon his right against self-incrimination.

Such contention is without merit in this case. Appellants could have presented evidence other than their own testimony to explain the circumstances; yet neither appellant produced any affirmative evidence. Albert Brocato, whose conduct was entwined with that of John Brocato, declined to take the stand, although he apparently possessed no prior criminal record. Thus, appellant John Brocato demonstrates no infringement of his Fifth Amendment right against self-incrimination.

Accordingly, we affirm.

NOTES

1. The Supreme Court of the United States, in Barnes v. United States, 412 U.S. 837, 93 S.Ct. 2357 (1973), upheld the conviction of the defendant for possessing checks stolen from the mails. It approved the trial judge's instruction that possession of recently stolen property, if not satisfactorily explained, is ordinarily a circumstance from which you may reasonably draw an inference and find, in the light of the surrounding circumstances shown by the evidence in the case that the person in possession knew the property had been stolen. In its opinion the Court analyzed its prior decisions involving the validity of presumptions (e.g., the *Leary* and *Turner* cases referred to in the foregoing Commonwealth v. Owens opinion), and stated that what they established was the following principle:

> "... if a statutory inference submitted to the jury as sufficient to support conviction satisfies the reasonable-doubt standard (that is, the evidence necessary to invoke the inference is sufficient for a rational juror to find the inferred fact beyond a reasonable doubt) as well as the more-likely-than-not standard, then it clearly accords with due process."

With regard to the argument that the prosecutor's invocation of a presumption forced the accused to testify in violation of his self-incrimination principle, the Court stated:

> "Introduction of any evidence, direct or circumstantial, tending to implicate the defendant in the alleged crime increases the pressure on him to testify. The mere massing of evidence against a defendant cannot be regarded as a violation of his privilege against self-incrimination."

2. A further and more extensive presentation of the issue of presumptions is contained in the subsequent Chapter 9.

E. ROBBERY*

LEAR v. STATE

Supreme Court of Arizona, 1931.
39 Ariz. 313, 6 P.2d 426.

Ross, J. The appellant was convicted of robbery. He appeals and assigns as error the insufficiency of the evidence to sustain the conviction and the giving of erroneous instructions.

The prosecuting witness, George Gross, testified that around 7 o'clock on the morning of August 12, 1931, he opened the Campbell Quality Shop, located in Buckeye, Maricopa county; that just about that time appellant entered the store and inquired about purchasing some shirts and shoes; that in the meantime he had taken a box of currency and a bag of silver out of the store safe; had placed the currency in the cash register and the bag of silver on the counter; that, while he was in

* Robbery is traditionally classified as a crime against the person; however, since the ultimate purpose of the crime is the misappropriation of property, it is included in this section.

the act of untying or unrolling the bag of silver, and while it was on the counter, appellant grabbed it from his hands and ran out of the back door; that appellant said no word at the time, exhibited no arms, and used no force other than to grab the bag as stated above. Appellant admitted taking the bag of silver and that it contained $33.

It was the contention of appellant at the trial, and is his contention here, that the facts do not show that he committed the crime of robbery. This crime is defined by our statute, section 4602, Revised Code of 1928, as follows: "Robbery is the felonious taking of personal property in the possession of another, from his person or immediate presence and against his will, accomplished by means of force or fear. The fear may be either of an unlawful injury to the person or property of the person robbed, or of a relative or member of his family; or of an immediate and unlawful injury to the person or property of any one in the company of the person robbed at the time of the robbery."

The crimes of robbery and larceny are not the same. The former is classified as a crime against the person and the latter as a crime against property. In robbery there is, in addition to a felonious taking, a violent invasion of the person. If the person is not made to surrender the possession of the personal property by means of force or fear, the dominant element of robbery is not present. The mere taking of property in possession of another, from his person or immediate presence and against his will, is not robbery. Such taking must be accomplished by force or fear to constitute robbery.

The element of fear is not in the case. Appellant made no threat or demonstration. He simply grabbed the bag of silver from the hands of the prosecuting witness and ran away with it. There was no pulling or scrambling for possession of the bag. Was the force employed by appellant the kind of force necessary to constitute robbery? We think not. As we read the cases and textwriters, "the force used must be either before, or at the time of the taking, and must be of such a nature as to shew that it was intended to overpower the party robbed, and prevent his resisting, and not merely to get possession of the property stolen." . . .

NOTES

1. For a note dealing with Lear v. State, see 23 J.Crim.L. & C. 113 (1932).

2. Compare Brown v. Commonwealth, 135 Ky. 635, 117 S.W. 281 (1909), from which the following quotation is taken:

". . . Pearl Wiggins asked Roberts for a dime to buy a bucket of beer. Evidently intending to comply with her request, Roberts drew some money from his pocket, and after he did so the . . . man with Pearl Wiggins suddenly, and with force and violence, snatched or wrenched the money from Roberts' hand, and with equal suddenness swiftly fled and escaped with it. . . . The arrest of the . . . appellants speedily followed. . . . The evidence clearly shows that force was required and used to deprive Roberts of his money, and to constitute robbery the person robbed must be deprived of his property by force, or by putting him in fear. In Davis v. Commonwealth, . . . it was held the fact that the defendant snatched money from the hand of another was evidence of actual violence, which entitled the prosecution to an instruction to the jury to convict if the money was taken against the owner's will, by actual force. And in Jones v. Commonwealth, ... it was also held that, where defendant snatched a pocketbook from the hand of another so quickly that he had no chance to actively resist, there was such a taking by violence as authorized a conviction under an indictment for robbery.

"The trial court did not err in failing to give an instruction under which the jury might have found appellants guilty of larceny. There was indeed no proof of larceny; and it was wholly and altogether to the effect that Roberts' money was taken from him by force and with such violence and suddenness as gave him no opportunity to resist the robbers. The crime was therefore robbery, and the instruction authorizing the jury to find appellants guilty of robbery ... gave the jury all the law of the case."

See also, People v. Campbell, 234 Ill. 391, 84 N.E. 1035 (1908). The defendant in the Campbell case pulled off a diamond pin or stud which was attached by means of a "spiral fastening" to the front part of the shirt of a man while he was waiting to board a street car. The owner testified that he was jostled by several men just before boarding the street car, that as he stepped onto the car he felt a jerk at his diamond pin, and that he then saw the defendant with the pin in his hand. The owner grabbed the defendant's hand and recovered the pin. In sustaining a robbery conviction, the Supreme Court of Illinois said: "In the absence of active opposition, if the article is so attached to the person or clothes as to create resistance, however slight, or if there be a struggle to keep it, the taking is robbery."

Compare Hall v. People, 171 Ill. 540, 49 N.E. 495 (1898) (accused unbuttoned vest and removed pocket book of drunk who did not realize what was happening; held: no robbery). See also, People v. Jones, 290 Ill. 603, 125 N.E. 256 (1919). But see Bell v. State, 167 Tex.Cr.R. 460, 321 S.W.2d 302 (1959) (victim, in a restroom, heard person tiptoeing up behind him, felt a blunt instrument in his back, and then felt the removal of his wallet from his hip pocket (buttonless); held, over strong dissent, to be robbery).

In Commonwealth v. Jones, 362 Mass. 83, 283 N.E.2d 840 (1972), the Massachusetts court, in a case of first impression, decided that the snatching, without additional use of force, can satisfy the requisite element of force to permit a jury verdict of robbery to stand. Nevertheless, it appears to be the general view among American jurisdictions that the sudden taking or snatching of property from another person does not involve that amount of force or violence which is needed to constitute a robbery. See 42 A.L.R.3d 1381 (1972).

3. In Pierce v. Commonwealth, 205 Va. 528, 138 S.E.2d 28 (1964), the court, in following the general common law concept, stated that the crime of robbery includes all of the elements of the crime of larceny. There must be *animus furandi,* in intent to steal. Proof that the defendant in good faith believed he was acting under a claim of right, as where he seeks to enforce payment of a debt, negates the existence of the required mental state even though the taking be accompanied by violence or putting in fear. Contrary to larceny, however, a prosecution for robbery does not require a distinct proof of the specific value of the property taken. As long as the stolen property is described sufficiently so that it may be shown to have some value, a conviction can be sustained.

While *Pierce* appears to represent the majority view in the United States, there is some dissent. In People v. Moseley, 193 Colo. 256, 566 P.2d 331 (1977), the court specifically held that statutory robbery requires no specific intent to permanently deprive the owner of the use or benefit of his property and the decision expressly overruled prior case decisions to the contrary.

4. In Carey v. United States, 296 F.2d 422 (D.C.Cir.1961), appellant sought to have his robbery conviction set aside, arguing that, assuming the intent to take the victim's money did not occur until after she was dead, he could not be guilty of robbery when he removed the money from the victim's blouse. "In other words," said the Court, "he argues that unless the necessary mens rea antedates or at least coincides with, the death of the victim, robbery is legally impossible, a corpse not being a 'person' as that term is understood in the robbery statute." The Court of Appeals rejected the contention, holding that, at the time her money was taken, in the particular circumstances of the case, the victim, "dead or not, was still a 'person'" within the robbery statute of the jurisdiction. "The time interval between the stabbing of [the victim] and the taking of her money was so short that it can hardly be said as a matter of law that the act of asportation was not performed upon a 'person.' ... It is well to note also that appellant himself testified that when he removed [the victim's] money he was under the impression that she was only unconscious, not dead."

In Grigsby v. State, 260 Ark. 499, 542 S.W.2d 275 (1976), the court felt that stealing from a dead body as an afterthought would not constitute a capital felony as armed robbery would be. But, the court emphasized, the jury was not required to believe defendant's testimony. "The sequence of events is unimportant and the killing may precede, coincide with or follow the robbery and still be committed in its perpetration.... It has been aptly said that from the very nature of things it is often impossible for the state to know at just what instant a killing was committed—whether in the commission of a felony, or in attempting to commit a felony, or while withdrawing from the scene of a felony." See also, People v. Pack, 34 Ill.App.3d 894, 341 N.E.2d 4 (1976).

5. Under the common law, obtaining money by a threat to destroy one's home, or by a threat to accuse one of sodomy (whether true or not) constituted robbery. Regina v. Astley, 2 East P.C. 729 (1792).

6. Defendant, after losing a gambling bet, uses force to regain possession of his lost money. Does this constitute robbery? See People v. Rosen, 11 Cal.2d 147, 78 P.2d 727 (1938), and compare Livingston v. State, 214 S.W.2d 119 (Tex.Cr.App.1948). In such cases, of what significance is the fact that a state statute permits (or even compels) the loser (or someone on his behalf) to sue for a recovery of the lost money? See People v. Henry, 202 Mich. 450, 168 N.W. 534 (1918). Consult also 41 J.Crim.L. & C. 467 (1950), and Anno. 75 A.L.R.3d 1000.

7. Considering that robbery is viewed as an offense against the person, is an indictment charging the defendant with robbing a bank properly alleging commission of a robbery? In Crawford v. Commonwealth, 217 Va. 595, 231 S.E.2d 309 (1977), the court said that a corporation could act only through persons—its agents, servants, employees and officers, and that when the indictment read that the defendant robbed The Southland Corporation of $256.39 "it in effect charged that he committed robbery by putting the agents of the corporation in fear and taking its money from their personal protection and in their presence." The court distinguished an earlier decision, Falden v. Commonwealth, 167 Va. 542, 189 S.E. 326 (1937), where it had reversed a judgment convicting the defendant on an indictment which charged conspiracy "to rob a certain United States mail truck," stating that robbery is a crime against the person.

Armed Robbery

1. A sizeable number of jurisdictions provide, by statute, for an aggravated form of robbery, usually called "armed robbery", for which a greater penalty is provided. Typically, some statutes provide that an armed robbery requires the commission of a robbery "while armed with a dangerous weapon". (e.g., Illinois Criminal Code, § 18–2) in Commonwealth v. Blackburn, 354 Mass. 200, 237 N.E.2d 35 (1968), the Supreme Judicial Court of Massachusetts stated that the gist of the offense of armed robbery is the commission of an offense while armed. It is not necessary to show the use of a dangerous weapon in proving the offense. All that need be shown is that the defendant carried a weapon on his person while he committed the robbery. See also, People v. Magby, 37 Ill.2d 197, 226 N.E.2d 33 (1967).

2. Is an unloaded gun a "dangerous weapon"? Most courts seem to hold that any unloaded firearm that can be used as a bludgeon is a dangerous weapon. See 79 A.L.R.2d 1426, and 81 A.L.R.3d 1006. In People v. Roden, 21 N.Y.2d 810, 235 N.E.2d 776 (1968), the Court of Appeals of New York held that an unloaded gun was a dangerous weapon within the meaning of the former Penal Law under which the appellant was charged, even though there was no evidence that the gun had been used as a bludgeon. But see, cf., People v. Richards, 28 Ill.App.3d 505, 328 N.E.2d 692 (1975), and People v. Santucci, 48 A.D.2d 909, 369 N.Y.S.2d 490 (1975).

Where a statute provides that a person charged with exhibiting a pistol during the course of a robbery is guilty in the first degree, unless he shows, as an affirmative defense, that it was not loaded, is the defendant's Fifth Amendment self-incrimination right violated by compelling him to take the stand if he wishes to escape a first degree robbery charge? People v. Felder, 39 A.D.2d 373, 334 N.Y.S.2d 992 (1972), held that there was no violation of right against self-incrimination.

Can toy guns be dangerous weapons? It was stated in Johnson v. Commonwealth, 209 Va. 291, 163 S.E.2d 570 (1968), that the use of a pistol with a blocked barrel, capable of firing blank cartridges only, would sustain a charge of robbery with firearms. This seems to be in line with the majority view, although there are a number of jurisdictions holding differently. See 81 A.L.R.3d 1006. In State v. Dye, 14 Ohio App.2d 7, 235 N.E.2d 250 (1968), the Court of Appeals of Ohio suggested that the gravamen of the crime was the fear induced in the victim and this jury instruction had been given: "Even though you find that one of the revolvers used was a toy cap pistol it would make no difference. If those who were held up had reasonable cause to believe that it was a loaded revolver and such put him or them in fear, then you will say the cap pistol becomes a dangerous weapon." It must be pointed out, however, that the toy pistol used in the case and admitted in evidence was described as "so natural in appearance as to be accepted as real. It was of such weight and size that it could, if used as a blackjack or bludgeon, cause severe harm to the head or face of a victim". Would the same reasoning support a conviction for armed robbery where the toy gun used was a plastic one which, though appearing real, was very light in weight?

3. A man and a woman drove into a gasoline station and directed the attendant to "fill it up all the way." "While the attendant was hanging up the gasoline hose, after filling the tank with gasoline, Richard Hermann [one of the defendants] got out of the car and walked partly around the same. The station attendant then walked near him to inform him as to how much gasoline he had

placed in the tank and what the price of the same was. The attendant testified that during that time 'the woman in the car [the other defendant] slipped over under the wheel.' Richard Hermann opened the car door, and was standing with his head inside of the car in a stooping position, and then 'took a step back and just wheeled with this rifle pointed at my stomach.' Hermann then stated to the attendant, 'Don't try anything,' and when the attendant saw him wheel with the rifle on him, he raised his arms and hands automatically. The attendant testified 'He didn't tell me to throw my hands up, but they just automatically went up.' ... Richard Hermann then got into the car and 'the woman drove the car away.' "

In affirming the conviction of defendants for armed robbery, the Supreme Court of Mississippi, in Hermann v. State, 239 Miss. 523, 123 So.2d 846 (1960), stated: "It will be seen from the foregoing that the crime of stealthily obtaining the gasoline was completed before Richard Hermann pointed the rifle at [the attendant], with the exception that there had been no asportation of the gasoline from the place of business ... at that time. The appellants were able to make their getaway with the gasoline by placing the gasoline station attendant in fear by the exhibition of the deadly weapon, telling him not to start anything, and that 'if you try to follow me, I will hurt you.' The car was driven away while the gasoline station attendant was still standing with his arms and hands raised in the air."

"The appellants rely almost entirely on Register v. State, decided by this Court on November 18, 1957.... The decision in that case followed the general rule as to what was necessary to constitute the crime of armed robbery, this being the offense of which the appellants were convicted in the case at bar. But that which distinguishes the Register case from the case at bar is the fact that in the instant case it was clearly shown, according to the testimony on behalf of the State, that there was no asportation of the gasoline until after the appellant, Richard Hermann, had drawn the deadly weapon on the gasoline station attendant and put him in fear whereas in the Register case there was no proof at all as to whether the intruder in the room of Miss June Flowers took her money out of her billfold prior or subsequent to the time that he choked her and put her in fear....

4. Can a dog be a dangerous weapon within the meaning of the armed robbery statutes? In Commonwealth v. Tarrant, 367 Mass. 411, 326 N.E.2d 710 (1975), the court concluded "that the Commonwealth, in order to prove the crime of armed robbery ... was not actually required to have affirmatively demonstrated that the dog was actually dangerous ... or was in fact used in a harm-inflicting manner, since the proper inquiry is whether the instrumentality is such as to present an objective threat of danger to a person of reasonable and average sensibility." Further, the court said, "[Here] the dog entered the victim's bedroom with the defendant who was carrying a knife; roamed about the room while the defendant searched for goods, moving within close proximity to the victim; and answered to the defendant's orders. A German shepherd is a relatively large and well known breed with the physical capability of inflicting harm...."

For a case holding that a trained German shepherd may be a "dangerous instrument" within the meaning of that phrase as used in a robbery statute, but not a "dangerous weapon" as defined in another statutory provision, see, People v. Torrez, 86 Misc.2d 369, 382 N.Y.S.2d 233 (1976).

F. BURGLARY*

1. The Common Law

At common law the offense of burglary consisted of a *breaking* and *entering* of the *dwelling house* of another, in the *nighttime*, with *intent* to commit a felony. The problems which have arisen over the years with respect to each of these elements are perhaps as complex as those concerning the elements of larceny. Fortunately, many of the early troublesome issues have been obviated by statute. Familiarity with some of the major common law rules is nevertheless helpful to an understanding of the legislation in this area.

a. *Breaking.* The requirement of a "breaking" or "breach" means that the burglar must make a trespassory entry involving the creation of an opening into the dwelling. In State v. Boon, 35 N.C. 244, 246 (1852), the court stated: "Passing an imaginary line is a 'breaking of the close,' and will sustain an action of trespass *quare clausum fregit*. In burglary more is required—there must be a breaking, moving or putting aside of something material, which constitutes a part of the dwelling-house, and is relied on as a security against intrusion."

The breaking may be into any part of a building and need not be a breaking in from the outside. Opening the door of an inner room is therefore sufficient. Davidson v. State, 86 Tex.Cr.R. 243, 216 S.W. 624 (1919).

See Anno., 43 A.L.R.3d 1147.

Constructive breaking occurs under certain circumstances where no force is used to make a way for the entry. The use of a trick or an artifice to gain entry is one type of constructive breaking. In Nichols v. State, 68 Wis. 416, 32 N.W. 543 (1887), for example, the burglar gained entry by concealing himself in a box. In Le Mott's Case, 84 Eng.Rep. 1073 (1650), the burglars merely told a maid that they wanted to speak to the master, and when she opened the door for them they entered and robbed him. Another type of constructive breaking occurs when one who has access to the dwelling, such as a servant, conspires to let another into the house. See Regina v. Johnson, Car. & M. 218, 174 Eng.Rep. 479 (1841).

Entering a dwelling which one has a right to enter at the time entry is made does not constitute a breaking because there is no trespass. Thus, using a key to enter a building which one has an unrestricted right to enter is not a breaking. People v. Kelley, 253 App.Div. 430, 3 N.Y.S.2d 46 (1938); Davis v. Commonwealth, 132 Va. 521, 110 S.E. 356 (1922). However, if the entry by use of a key is made at an unauthorized time, a trespass exists and a breaking occurs. State v. Corcoran,

* The common law crimes of burglary and arson, which are treated in this section, are crimes against the habitation; under modern legislation, however, they have, as here, been grouped with the property offenses.

82 Wash. 44, 143 Pac. 453 (1914). Is it a "breaking" to enter through a partly opened door or window? See cases collected at Anno., 70 A.L.R.3d 881.

b. *Entering.* An entry is made if any part of the body is inside the dwelling, even if only a hand or finger intrudes for the purpose of the breaking. State v. Whitaker, 275 S.W.2d 316 (Mo.1955); Regina v. O'Brien, 4 Cox C.C. 400 (1850); Franco v. State, 42 Tex. 276 (1875). An entry may also be made by inserting an object into the dwelling; however, the object must be inserted for the purpose of carrying out the felonious design, and it is insufficient if the instrument is used only to effect the breach. Walker v. State, 63 Ala. 49 (1879); Rex v. Rust, 1 Mood.C.C. 183 (1828); People v. Williams, 28 Ill.App.3d 402, 328 N.E.2d 682 (1975). The entry must be "consequent upon the breaking," so that if one enters a dwelling through an open door and then opens an inner door but does not go through it, the requirement of entry is lacking. Regina v. Davis, 6 Cox C.C. 369 (1854).

c. *The dwelling house of another.* (1) A dwelling house, under the rules of common law burglary, is a building habitually used as a place to sleep. Rex v. Stock, Russ. & R. 185, 2 Leach C.C. 1015, 7 Taunt. 339 (1810). It may be a store or other place of business, if someone regularly sleeps there, State v. Outlaw, 72 N.C. 598 (1875); but the fact that someone may sleep there from time to time is insufficient, State v. Jenkins, 50 N.C. 430 (1858). If a building is regularly used as a residence during a certain time of the year, for example a summer home, it qualifies as a dwelling house even during the period when it is not occupied. State v. Bair, 112 W.Va. 655, 166 S.E. 369 (1932). The test is whether the occupant intends to return. State v. Meerchouse, 34 Mo. 344 (1864). A building that no one has yet moved into is not considered a dwelling house for purposes of burglary. Woods v. State, 186 Miss. 463, 191 So. 283 (1939); Jones v. State, 532 S.W.2d 596 (Tex.Cr.App. 1976).

Rooms in an inn, hotel, or apartment building are the dwellings of the occupants, unless the occupants are merely transients. People v. Carr, 255 Ill. 203, 99 N.E. 357 (1912). Where the rooms are occupied by transients, however, the rooms are considered the dwelling house of the landlord, whether or not the landlord lives in the building. See Rodgers v. People, 86 N.Y. 360 (1881).

The dwelling house is considered to include not only the dwelling itself but also buildings which are "within the curtilage." The purpose of including buildings used in connection with the dwelling is to protect against the dangers resulting from the likelihood that a dweller who hears a prowler in the nighttime will go forth to protect his family and property. Thus a garage is considered part of the dwelling house where it is in reasonable proximity to the house. Harris v. State, 41 Okl.Cr. 121, 271 P. 957 (1928). A cellar is also within the "curtilage" even though it has no entrance from the dwelling itself and must be entered from the outside. Mitchell v. Commonwealth, 88 Ky. 349, 11 S.W. 209 (1889).

(2) The dwelling house must be that "of another," in the sense that it must be occupied by another. It need not be owned by the victim, inasmuch as burglary at common law is a crime against the habitation and not against property. One may therefore burglarize a building leased to, and occupied by, someone else. Smith v. People, 115 Ill. 17, 3 N.E. 733 (1885). The dweller, however, cannot burglarize his own dwelling, even though it has other occupants. Clarke v. Commonwealth, 66 Va. 908 (1874).

(3) Can a husband burglarize his estranged wife's premises? In a case of first impression for that jurisdiction, the Court of Criminal Appeals of Alabama held that a husband could be found guilty of burglary for a nonconsensual entry of his estranged wife's dwelling where the husband-wife relationship had not yet been dissolved. The court borrowed from this reasoning by the Florida Supreme Court in the 1981 case of Cladd v. State, 398 So.2d 442: "[s]ince burglary is an invasion of the possessory property rights of another, where premises are in the sole possession of the wife, the husband can be guilty of burglary if he makes a nonconsensual entry into her premises with intent to commit an offense, the same as he can be guilty of larceny of his wife's separate property." The Alabama court also ruled that the husband could be found guilty of the capital burglary-murder of his wife. White v. Alabama, 47 CrL 1455 (Ala.App.1990).

d. *Nighttime.* As an element of burglary, nighttime is the period of time between sunset and sunrise, and it is not considered night if there is enough natural daylight so that one can discern the countenance of another man's face. People v. Griffin, 19 Cal. 578 (1862). Both the breaking and entering must occur during the nighttime, but they need not occur on the same night. Rex v. Smith, Russ. & Ry. 417, 168 Eng.Rep. 874 (1820).

e. *With intent to commit a felony.* Although burglary is commonly thought of as an offense committed with intent to steal, the required intent actually includes the intent to commit any felony. It is not necessary that the felony in fact be committed, Wilson v. State, 24 Conn. 56 (1855); however, both the breaking and entering must be made with the necessary intent. Colbert v. State, 91 Ga. 705, 17 S.E. 840 (1893). As noted in the section on larceny, supra at page 551, at common law both grand and petit larceny are felonies. Petit larceny is now frequently made a misdemeanor by statute; however, it is also commonly provided that burglarious intent exists where there is an intent to commit a felony "or to steal."

2. Legislation

Modern legislation on burglary has made a number of changes in the common law, generally broadening the scope of the offense. Following are the various changes, as revealed in an excellent analysis of the modern law of burglary in Note, A Rationale of the Law of Burglary, 57 Colum.L.Rev. 1009 (1951):

(1) All jurisdictions now include virtually all buildings in the scope of the crime, although most jurisdictions attach a more severe penalty to the offense where a dwelling is involved.

(2) A few jurisdictions dispense with the requirement of "entry."

(3) A few jurisdictions dispense with the requirement of "breaking," but some of these require a trespass instead. Others provide a higher penalty where a "breaking" occurs. Where breaking is retained, some jurisdictions provide that absent a "breaking in," a "breaking out" will suffice.

(4) All jurisdictions recognize daytime burglaries, although some provide a more severe penalty for burglaries committed at night.

(5) The jurisdictions define burglarious intent in four principal ways: (a) intent to commit a felony; (b) intent to commit a felony or larceny; (c) intent to commit any crime (with respect to one or more degrees or forms of burglary); and (d) intent to commit certain specified crimes. A few jurisdictions dispense entirely with the requirement of an intent to commit another crime for the lowest degree or form of burglary.

(6) Many jurisdictions have added new elements to the common law crime of burglary. For example, some make special provisions for armed burglary and burglary involving the use of (or attempt or intent to use) explosives, and some require for the offense of first degree burglary that someone be in the building at the time of the offense.

(7) Many jurisdictions have statutes proscribing the possession of tools that can be used in the commission of a burglary. Often, such items are everyday items of personal property. Under a statute defining a "tool, machine or implement" as burglar's tools, a simple pair of gardening gloves did not qualify for inclusion. These were distinguished from items more closely and obviously related to the statutory purpose, such as screwdrivers and boltcutters. "If this Court stretched the phrase 'tool, machine or implement' to include items of personal apparel, we would be in grave danger of destroying both the legislature's intent as to and the common person's understanding of the statutory language." Green v. State, 604 So.2d 471 (Fla.1992).

Modern statutes of "housebreaking," the day-time burglary of a dwelling offense, still require interpretation on what constitutes a dwelling. In Holtman v. State, 12 Md.App. 168, 278 A.2d 82 (1971) a conviction for daytime housebreaking was reversed upon a showing that the defendant had broken into a church. Though it may be the "mansion house of God", the court did not consider it a dwelling within the meaning of the burglary law. On the other hand, an Illinois court construed a "car wash" to be a building falling within the modern Illinois burglary statute above. People v. Blair, 1 Ill.App.3d 6, 272 N.E.2d 404 (1971).

G. RELATED PROPERTY OFFENSES

1. ARSON

1. The Common Law

Arson at common law is the malicious (or, as sometimes stated, wilful and malicious) burning of the dwelling house of another. Like burglary, arson at common law is an offense against habitation, and what has been stated above with respect to "the dwelling house of another" in connection with burglary likewise applies to arson.

a. *Malicious.* The burning must be malicious to constitute arson; consequently, an accidental or negligent burning is not sufficient. Morris v. State, 124 Ala. 44, 27 So. 336 (1900). It is not necessary, however, that destruction of the dwelling be intended, or that the motive be one of ill will. For example, a prisoner in a jail is guilty of arson where he burns a hole in the building solely for the purpose of making an escape. Smith v. State, 23 Tex.App. 357, 5 S.W. 219 (1887); Lockett v. State, 63 Ala. 5 (1879). Contra, State v. Mitchell, 27 N.C. 350 (1845); People v. Cotteral, 18 Johns. 115 (N.Y.1820). An intent to commit an unlawful act the probable consequence of which is a burning is sufficient, where the act is performed without regard to the consequences. State v. Laughlin, 53 N.C. 321 (1861). See also, Regina v. Faulkner, 13 Cox C.C. 550 (1877).

b. *Burning.* Arson is not committed unless some part of the structure of the dwelling house is actually damaged by fire. Blackening or discoloration is insufficient; the fiber of some part of the structural material of the building must be at least slightly damaged. People v. Oliff, 361 Ill. 237, 197 N.E. 777 (1935); State v. Spiegel, 11 Iowa 701, 83 N.W. 722 (1900).

2. The Statutes

As in the case of burglary, the crime of arson has been considerably broadened by modern legislation. The great majority of jurisdictions in the United States have adopted the Model Arson Law. Five principal changes are effected by this law:

(1) The property burned (except in the case of personal property) does not have to be that of another person.

(2) Where a dwelling house is involved, there is no requirement that it be occupied, even occasionally. It may be vacant.

(3) All types of buildings and structures are made the subject of arson.

(4) The intentional burning of the personal property of another, where the property has a value of twenty-five dollars or more, is made arson.

(5) The intentional burning of any property insured against fire damage, where the burning is for the purpose of defrauding the insurer, is made a felony, although it is not called arson.

An example of a modern statutory version of arson is the following from the Illinois Criminal Code, 720 ILCS 5/20–1:

> A person commits arson when, by means of fire or explosive, he knowingly:
>
> (a) Damages any real property, or any personal property having a value of $150 or more, of another without his consent; or
>
> (b) With intent to defraud an insurer, damages any property or any personal property having a value of $150 or more.
>
> Property "of another" means a building or other property, whether real or personal, in which a person other than the offender has an interest which the offender has no authority to defeat or impair, even though the offender may also have an interest in the building or property.

2. MALICIOUS MISCHIEF

The malicious destruction of, or damage to, the property of another is a common law misdemeanor. State v. Watts, 48 Ark. 56, 2 S.W. 342 (1886). In both the United States and England, however, a number of statutes have been enacted to cover most forms of malicious mischief, making some forms felonies and others misdemeanors. Where a particular offense of this character is not covered by statute, it is punishable as a common law offense in those states which retain common law crimes; moreover, the statutes frequently employ a comprehensive section to cover the malicious injury of any real or personal property of another not specifically made criminal by a separate provision.

Consider the following, from the Illinois Criminal Code, 720 ILCS 5/21–1:

> **Criminal Damage to Property**
>
> (1) A person commits an illegal act when he:
>
> (a) knowingly damages any property of another without his consent; or
>
> (b) recklessly by means of fire or explosive damages property of another; or
>
> (c) knowingly starts a fire on the land of another without his consent; or
>
> (d) knowingly injures a domestic animal of another without his consent; or
>
> (e) knowingly deposits on the land or in the building of another, without his consent, any stink bomb or any offensive

smelling compound and thereby intends to interfere with the use by another of the land or building; or

(f) damages any property, other than as described in subsection (b) of Section 20–1, with intent to defraud an insurer; or

(g) knowingly shoots a firearm at any portion of a railroad train.

When the charge of criminal damage to property exceeding a specified value is brought, the extent of the damage is an element of the offense to be resolved by the trier of fact as either exceeding or not exceeding the specified value.

Chapter 7

CRIMINAL RESPONSIBILITY AND THE DEFENSE OF MENTAL IMPAIRMENT

A. THE MENTAL ELEMENT IN CRIME

COMMONWEALTH v. OLSHEFSKI

Pennsylvania District and County Court, 1948.
64 Pa.D. & C. 343.

KREISHER, P.J., September 9, 1948.—On February 6, 1948, John Fisher, a driver for above-named defendant, at the direction of defendant, purchased a load of coal at the Gilberton Coal Company colliery and had the same loaded upon a truck owned by defendant, which had a "U" tag on it, and which, under The Vehicle Code of May 1, 1929, P.L. 905, is permitted to weigh 15,000 pounds plus five percent, or a gross weight of 15,750 pounds. The load was weighed by a licensed weighmaster at the colliery and the weight was given at 15,200 pounds. Fisher drove the truck to the home of defendant, who was out of town at the time and then placed the weigh slip from the colliery in the compartment of the truck. The following day defendant went to the Danville National Bank to do some banking business and observed the Pennsylvania State Police at the northern end of the river bridge checking on trucks. He then returned to his home and drove his truck with the load of coal to the northern end of the river bridge on his way to the borough water department scales for the purpose of having it weighed. He states that he was selling the coal in Danville, and pursuant to the requirements of an ordinance in Danville, he had to have a Danville weigh slip. Before reaching the water department's scales a State policeman stopped him and he was directed to the scales where his load was weighed by the officer and the weigh slip was signed by a licensed weighmaster, showing that his gross weight was 16,015, and that he was, therefore, overloaded 265 pounds. The officer lodged an information for his violation of The Vehicle Code. Defendant waived a hearing and the matter is now before us for disposition....

It is also contended by counsel for defendant that this prosecution should be dismissed for the reason that defendant had in his possession a weigh bill for this particular load by a duly licensed weighmaster, which was weighed the day before, showing that the gross weight of the truck and the load was within the load allowed by law for this particular truck, and that defendant, relying upon this weigh bill, voluntarily drove to where he knew the police were weighing trucks, and was of the belief that his load was a legal load, and therefore, because of this belief, he is not guilty of the crime charged.

In criminal law we have two distinct types of crimes: The one type of crime being the common-law crimes, which are designated as crimes mala in se, which means that they are crimes because the act is bad in and of itself. The other type of crime which did not exist at common law covers those acts which are made criminal by statute, and are termed crimes mala prohibita, and simply means that they are crimes not because they are bad in and of themselves, but merely because the legislative authority makes the act criminal and penal.

In crimes that are mala in se, two elements are necessary for the commission of the crime, viz., the mental element and the physical element. In this type of crime intent is a necessary element, but in statutory crimes, which are simply mala prohibita, the mental element is not necessary for the commission of the crime, and one who does an act in violation of the statute and is caught and prosecuted, is guilty of the crime irrespective of his intent or belief. The power of the legislature to punish an act as a crime, even though it is not bad in and of itself, is an absolute power of the legislature, the only restriction being the constitutional restrictions, and it is the duty of the court to enforce these enactments irrespective of what the court might personally think about the prosecution or the wisdom of the act.

Except for constitutional limitations, the power of the State legislature is absolute. It may punish any act which in its judgment requires punishment, provided it violates no constitutional restriction, and its enactments must be enforced by the courts. The courts cannot review the discretion of the legislature, or pass upon the expediency, wisdom, or propriety of legislative action in matters within its powers. Neither can the courts pass upon the action of a prosecuting officer who prosecutes a person for the violation of a statute which is violated by that person, even though the court might be of the opinion that the officer should have not instituted the prosecution.

If the testimony shows, as in this case, that defendant violated the law, and is prosecuted for that violation, then the court is bound to enforce the legislative enactments, and cannot in good conscience set itself up as the legislature and excuse one person who has violated the law and find another person guilty for the same violation. It is true that this rule of law may seem harsh and unjustifiable, but the court is powerless to correct it, and, therefore, under our duty as judge, we are obliged to hold that this defendant violated The Vehicle Code by having his truck overloaded, and that he is guilty as charged. . . .

PEOPLE v. HUTCHISON

Illinois Appellate Court, 1977.
46 Ill.App.3d 725, 5 Ill.Dec. 189, 361 N.E.2d 328.

MR. PRESIDING JUSTICE CRAVEN delivered the opinion of the court:

Defendant was convicted upon the verdict of a jury of illegal transportation of an alcoholic liquor in violation of section 11–502 of the Illinois Vehicle Code....

The trial court refused defendant's tendered jury instruction which listed knowledge as an element of the offense of illegal transportation....

Without reciting at length the evidence, it appears that defendant was involved in an accident in the city of Champaign. During the police investigation of the accident, a paper bag containing a half-empty bottle of whiskey was found on the transmission hump separating the driver and passenger seats. The bottle belonged to defendant's passenger and defendant had no knowledge it was in the car.

Most crimes require proof of some knowledge or intent on the part of the defendant to support a conviction. Section 4–9 of the Criminal Code of 1961 (Ill.Rev.Stat.1975, ch. 38, par. 4–9) provides that in misdemeanor offenses where there is no possibility of imprisonment and no fine greater than $500 may be imposed no mental state need be proven. Such offenses create an absolute statutory liability. Motor vehicle regulations for the protection of the public safety are generally such offenses....

In these cases, however, absolute liability was established for acts the very nature of which require some conceptualized requirement of knowledge of intent. One cannot, for instance, be arrested for driving without a valid driver's license unless he is knowingly engaged in the act of driving. That is not the case here, as the operator of a motor vehicle, including the defendant here, can never know for certain the possessions of his passenger. To establish absolute liability for such transgressions would be tantamount to punishing a defendant for the sins of his neighbor—sins that he had no knowledge of nor reason to have knowledge of. In this light, "absolute liability" for this offense is contrary to the very basis of our criminal law which requires some knowing omission or commission. We therefore are of the opinion that it was error for the trial court here to refuse defendant's tendered instruction requiring knowledge as an element of the offense and reverse defendant's conviction and remand the case for a new trial.

Reversed and remanded.

REARDON, J., concurs.

MR. JUSTICE MILLS, dissenting:

The somewhat offhand and cavalier dismissal of this issue by the majority is disturbing.

But what is more important, I believe my brothers are wrong.

The majority recognizes the statutory absolute liability provisions of section 4–9 of the Criminal Code of 1961 and that motor vehicle regulations generally fall under its purview. But, they say, the charge at bar of illegal transportation of alcoholic liquor is distinguishable from such cases in that *scienter,* or "knowledge" of the presence of the intoxicant, is an essential element. Such distinction with controlling precedents and Illinois case law escapes me.

In the exercise of police power for the protection of the public at large, the legislature may create offenses *malum prohibitum*—wrong only because they are *prohibited,* not because they are wrong in themselves or are inherently evil. And historically, motor vehicle violations in Illinois have long been considered in this category.

The taproot case is People v. Fernow (1919), 286 Ill. 627, 122 N.E. 155. It was put to us this way:

> "At common law a crime consisted of an unlawful act with evil intent, and in crimes created by statute a specific intent may be required so that the intent and act may constitute the crime, and in such cases the intent must be alleged and proved. Where a specific intent is not an element of the crime it is not always necessary that a criminal intent should exist. In the exercise of the police power for the protection of the public the performance of a specific act may constitute the crime regardless of either knowledge or intent, both of which are immaterial on the question of guilt. For the effective protection of the public the burden is placed upon the individual of ascertaining at his peril whether his act is prohibited by criminal statute. The law in that regard has most frequently arisen in police regulations of the liquor traffic, but it has been applied in precisely the same way in other cases coming within the same rule and reason, such as a sale of imitation butter, a sale of milk below a prescribed quality, the obstruction of a public highway by a railroad corporation for longer than a specified time, the admission of a minor to a pool room, driving an unregistered automobile, killing for sale an animal under a designated age, carriage by an express company for transportation beyond the State line of fish or game, and in prosecutions for bigamy."

* * *

To my view the charge of illegal transportation of liquor is essentially no different from the other Illinois Vehicle Code offenses heretofore found by Illinois courts to be *malum prohibitum* and where knowledge or intent are not required. The police power is the legislature's and violates no constitutional injunction. The purpose is the public good, and therefore, laudible—"the greatest good to the greatest number,". . . .

The statute here—like all absolute liability, *malum prohibitum* offenses—casts a wide net. It drags in the "hotrodder" with five buddies, a couple of opened cold six-packs, a tank full of gas and time on their hands. It *may* also snare the unsuspecting and kind old gentleman who gives a lift from church to the little old lady with the flask of communion wine in her handbag. Well, the kind old gentleman is simply going to have to be more careful in choosing his passengers unless, indeed, he wishes to be punished for the "sins of his neighbors." There are few of us, I wager, who have not had an uneasy moment or two somewhere along the pathway of life. But when you run with the pack and the shotgun is fired, a stray pellet now and then finds an innocent target—or, at least, one without *scienter!*

* * *

I would affirm.

LIPAROTA v. UNITED STATES

Supreme Court of the United States, 1985.
471 U.S. 419, 105 S.Ct. 2084.

JUSTICE BRENNAN delivered the opinion of the Court.

The federal statute governing food stamp fraud provides that "whoever knowingly uses, transfers, acquires, alters, or possesses coupons or authorization cards in any manner not authorized by [the statute] or the regulations" is subject to a fine and imprisonment. 7 U.S.C. § 2024(b). The question presented is whether in a prosecution under this provision the Government must prove that the defendant knew that he was acting in a manner not authorized by statute or regulations.

I

Petitioner Frank Liparota was the co-owner with his brother of Moon's Sandwich Shop in Chicago, Illinois. He was indicted for acquiring and possessing food stamps in violation of § 2024(b). The Department of Agriculture had not authorized petitioner's restaurant to accept food stamps. At trial, the Government proved that petitioner on three occasions purchased food stamps from an undercover Department of Agriculture agent for substantially less than their face value. On the first occasion, the agent informed petitioner that she had $195 worth of food stamps to sell. The agent then accepted petitioner's offer of $150 and consummated the transaction in a back room of the restaurant with petitioner's brother. A similar transaction occurred one week later, in which the agent sold $500 worth of coupons for $350. Approximately one month later, petitioner bought $500 worth of food stamps from the agent for $300.

II

The controversy between the parties concerns the mental state, if any, that the Government must show in proving that petitioner acted "in any manner not authorized by [the statute] or the regulations." The Government argues that petitioner violated the statute if he knew that he acquired or possessed food stamps and if in fact that acquisition or possession was in a manner not authorized by statute or regulations. According to the Government, no *mens rea,* or "evil-meaning mind," *Morissette v. United States,* (1952), is necessary for conviction. Petitioner claims that the Government's interpretation, by dispensing with *mens rea,* dispenses with the only morally blameworthy element in the definition of the crime. To avoid this allegedly untoward result, he claims that an individual violates the statute if he knows that he has acquired or possessed food stamps *and* if he also knows that he has done so in an unauthorized manner.[1] Our task is to determine which meaning Congress intended.

The definition of the elements of a criminal offense is entrusted to the legislature, particularly in the case of federal crimes, which are solely creatures of statute. With respect to the element at issue in this case, however, Congress has not explicitly spelled out the mental state required. Although Congress certainly intended by use of the word "knowingly" to require *some* mental state with respect to *some* element of the crime defined in § 2024(b), the interpretations proffered by both parties accord with congressional intent to this extent. Beyond this, the words themselves provide little guidance. Either interpretation would accord with ordinary usage.[2] The legislative history of the statute contains nothing that would clarify the congressional purpose on this point.

Absent indication of contrary purpose in the language or legislative history of the statute, we believe that § 2024(b) requires a showing that the defendant knew his conduct to be unauthorized by statute or regulations. "The contention that an injury can amount to a crime only when inflicted by intention is no provincial or transient notion. It is as

1. The required mental state may of course be different for different elements of a crime. See generally Robinson & Grail, Element Analysis in Defining Criminal Liability: The Model Penal Code and Beyond, 35 Stan.L.Rev. 681 (1983). In this case, for instance, both parties agree that petitioner must have known that he acquired and possessed food stamps. They disagree over whether any mental element at all is required with respect to the unauthorized nature of that acquisition or possession.

We have also recognized that the mental element in criminal law encompasses more than the two possibilities of "specific" and "general" intent. The Model Penal Code, for instance, recognizes four mental states—purpose, knowledge, recklessness, and negligence. ALI Model Penal Code § 2.02 (Prop.Off. Draft 1962). In this case, petitioner argues that with respect to the element at issue, knowledge is required. The Government contends that *no* mental state is required with respect to that element.

2. One treatise has aptly summed up the ambiguity in an analogous situation:

"Still further difficulty arises from the ambiguity which frequently exists concerning what the words or phrases in question modify. What, for instance, does 'knowingly' modify in a sentence from a 'blue sky' law criminal statute punishing one who 'knowingly sells a security without a permit' from the securities commissioner? To be guilty must the seller of a security without a permit know only that what he is doing constitutes a sale, or must he also know that the thing he sells is a security, or must he also know that he has no permit to sell the security he sells? As a matter of grammar the statute is ambiguous; it is not at all clear how far down the sentence the word 'knowingly' is intended to travel—whether it modifies 'sells,' or 'sells a security,' or 'sells a security without a permit.'" W. LaFave & A. Scott, Criminal Law § 27 (1972).

universal and persistent in mature systems of law as belief in freedom of the human will and a consequent ability and duty of the normal individual to choose between good and evil." Morissette v. United States. Thus, in United States v. United States Gypsum Co., (1978), we noted that "[c]ertainly far more than the simple omission of the appropriate phrase from the statutory definition is necessary to justify dispensing with an intent requirement" and that criminal offenses requiring no *mens rea* have a "generally disfavored status." Similarly, in this case, the failure of Congress explicitly and unambiguously to indicate whether *mens rea* is required does not signal a departure from this background assumption of our criminal law.

This construction is particularly appropriate where, as here, to interpret the statute otherwise would be to criminalize a broad range of apparently innocent conduct. For instance, § 2024(b) declares it criminal to use, transfer, acquire, alter, or possess food stamps in any manner not authorized by statute or regulations. The statute provides further that "[c]oupons issued to eligible households shall be used by them only to purchase food in retail food stores which have been approved for participation in the food stamp program *at prices prevailing in such stores*." 7 U.S.C. § 2016(b) (emphasis added). This seems to be the *only* authorized use. A strict reading of the statute with no knowledge of illegality requirement would thus render criminal a food stamp recipient who, for example, used stamps to purchase food from a store that, unknown to him, charged higher than normal prices to food stamp program participants. Such a reading would also render criminal a nonrecipient of food stamps who "possessed" stamps because he was mistakenly sent them through the mail due to administrative error, "altered" them by tearing them up, and "transferred" them by throwing them away. Of course, Congress *could* have intended that this broad range of conduct be made illegal, perhaps with the understanding that prosecutors would exercise their discretion to avoid such harsh results. However, given the paucity of material suggesting that Congress did so intend, we are reluctant to adopt such a sweeping interpretation.

In addition, requiring *mens rea* is in keeping with our longstanding recognition of the principle that "ambiguity concerning the ambit of criminal statutes should be resolved in favor of lenity." Rewis v. United States. Application of the rule of lenity ensures that criminal statutes will provide fair warning concerning conduct rendered illegal and strikes the appropriate balance between the legislature, the prosecutor, and the court in defining criminal liability. See United States v. Bass, ("because of the seriousness of criminal penalties, and because criminal punishment usually represents the moral condemnation of the community, legislatures and not courts should define criminal activity"). Although the rule of lenity is not to be applied where to do so would conflict with the implied or expressed intent of Congress, it provides a time-honored interpretive guideline when the congressional purpose is unclear. In the instant case, the rule directly supports petitioner's contention that the

Government must prove knowledge of illegality to convict him under § 2024(b).

The Government advances two additional arguments in support of its reading of the statute. First, the Government contends that this Court's decision last Term in United States v. Yermian, (1984), supports its interpretation. *Yermian* involved a prosecution for violation of the federal false statement statute, 18 U.S.C. § 1001.[3] All parties agreed that the statute required proof at least that the defendant "knowingly and willfully" made a false statement. Thus, unlike the instant case, all parties in *Yermian* agreed that the Government had to prove the defendant's *mens rea*. The controversy in *Yermian* centered on whether the Government also had to prove that the defendant knew that the false statement was made in a matter within the jurisdiction of a federal agency. With respect to this element, although the Court held that the Government did not have to prove actual knowledge of federal agency jurisdiction, the Court explicitly reserved the question whether *some* culpability was necessary with respect even to the jurisdictional element. In contrast, the Government in the instant case argues that *no mens rea* is required with respect to any element of the crime. Finally, *Yermian* found that the statutory language was unambiguous and that the legislative history supported its interpretation. The statute at issue in this case differs in both respects.

Second, the Government contends that the § 2024(b) offense is a "public welfare" offense, which the Court defined in United States v. Morissette, to "depend on no mental element but consist only of forbidden acts or omissions." Yet the offense at issue here differs substantially from those "public welfare offenses" we have previously recognized. In most previous instances, Congress has rendered criminal a type of conduct that a reasonable person should know is subject to stringent public regulation and may seriously threaten the community's health or safety. Thus, in United States v. Freed, (1971), we examined the federal statute making it illegal to receive or possess an unregistered firearm. In holding that the Government did not have to prove that the recipient of unregistered hand grenades knew that they were unregistered, we noted that "one would hardly be surprised to learn that possession of hand grenades is not an innocent act." Similarly, in United States v. Dotterweich, (1943), the Court held that a corporate officer could violate the Food and Drug Act when his firm shipped adulterated and misbranded drugs, even "though consciousness of wrongdoing be totally wanting." The distinctions between these cases and the instant case are clear. A food stamp can hardly be compared to a hand grenade, see

3. The statute provides:

"Whoever, in any matter within the jurisdiction of any department or agency of the United States knowingly and willfully falsifies, conceals, or covers up by any trick, scheme, or device a material fact, or makes any false, fictitious or fraudulent statements or representations, or makes or uses any false writing or document knowing the same to contain any false, fictitious or fraudulent statement or entry, shall be fined not more than $10,000 or imprisoned not more than five years, or both."

Freed, nor can the unauthorized acquisition or possession of food stamps be compared to the selling of adulterated drugs, as in *Dotterweich.*

III

We hold that in a prosecution for violation of § 2024(b), the Government must prove that the defendant knew that his acquisition or possession of food stamps was in a manner unauthorized by statute or regulations. This holding does not put an unduly heavy burden on the Government in prosecuting violators of § 2024(b). To prove that petitioner knew that his acquisition or possession of food stamps was unauthorized, for example, the Government need not show that he had knowledge of specific regulations governing food stamp acquisition or possession. Nor must the Government introduce any extraordinary evidence that would conclusively demonstrate petitioner's state of mind. Rather, as in any other criminal prosecution requiring *mens rea,* the Government may prove by reference to facts and circumstances surrounding the case that petitioner knew that his conduct was unauthorized or illegal.[4]

Reversed.

JUSTICE POWELL took no part in the consideration or decision of this case.

JUSTICE WHITE, with whom THE CHIEF JUSTICE joins, dissenting.

Forsaking reliance on either the language or the history of § 2024(b), the majority bases its result on the absence of an explicit rejection of the general principle that criminal liability requires not only an *actus reus,* but a *mens rea.* In my view, the result below is in fact supported by the statute's language and its history, and it is the majority that has ignored general principles of criminal liability.

I

The Court views the statutory problem here as being how far down the sentence the term "knowingly" travels. See ante, n. [2]. Accepting for the moment that if "knowingly" does extend to the "in any manner" language today's holding would be correct—a position with which I take issue below—I doubt that it gets that far. The "in any manner" language is separated from the litany of verbs to which "knowingly" is directly connected by the intervening nouns. We considered an identically phrased statute last Term in United States v. Yermian, (1984). The predecessor to the statute at issue in that case provided: " '[W]hoever shall knowingly and willfully ... make ... any false or fraudulent statements or representations ... in any matter within the jurisdiction of any department or agency of the United States ... shall be fined.' "

4. In this case, for instance, the Government introduced evidence that petitioner bought food stamps at a substantial discount from face value and that he conducted part of the transaction in a back room of his restaurant to avoid the presence of the other patrons. Moreover, the Government asserts that food stamps themselves are stamped "nontransferable." A jury could have inferred from this evidence that petitioner knew that his acquisition and possession of the stamps was unauthorized.

We found that under the "most natural reading" of the statute, "knowingly and willfully" applied only to the making of false or fraudulent statements and not to the fact of jurisdiction. By the same token, the "most natural reading" of § 2024(b) is that knowingly modifies only the verbs to which it is attached.

In any event, I think that the premise of this approach is mistaken. Even accepting that "knowingly" does extend through the sentence, or at least that we should read § 2024(b) as if it does, the statute does not mean what the Court says it does. Rather, it requires only that the defendant be aware of the relevant aspects of his conduct. A requirement that know that he is acting in a particular manner, coupled with the fact that that manner is forbidden, does not establish a defense of ignorance of the law. It creates only a defense of ignorance or mistake of fact. Knowingly to do something that is unauthorized by law is not the same as doing something knowing that it is unauthorized by law.

This point is demonstrated by the hypothetical statute referred to by the majority, which punishes one who "knowingly sells a security without a permit." See ante, at n. [2]. Even if "knowingly" does reach "without a permit," I would think that a defendant who knew that he did not have a permit, though not that a permit was required, could be convicted.

Section 2024(b) is an identical statute, except that instead of detailing the various legal requirements, it incorporates them by proscribing use of coupons "in any manner not authorized" by law. This shorthand approach to drafting does not transform knowledge of illegality into an element of the crime. As written, § 2024(b) is substantively no different than if it had been broken down into a collection of specific provisions making crimes of particular improper uses. For example, food stamps cannot be used to purchase tobacco. 7 CFR §§ 271.2, 274.10(a), 278.2(a) (1985). The statute might have said, *inter alia,* that anyone "who knowingly uses coupons to purchase cigarettes" commits a crime. Under no plausible reading could a defendant then be acquitted because he did not know cigarettes are not "eligible food." But in fact, that is exactly what § 2024(b) does say, it just does not write it out longhand.

The Court's opinion provides another illustration of the general point: someone who used food stamps to purchase groceries at inflated prices without realizing he was overcharged. I agree that such a person may not be convicted, but not for the reason given by the majority. The purchaser did not "knowingly" use the stamps in the proscribed manner, for he was unaware of the circumstances of the transaction that made it illegal.

The majority and I would part company in result as well as rationale if the purchaser knew he was charged higher than normal prices but not that overcharging is prohibited. In such a case, he would have been aware of the nature of his actions, and therefore the purchase would have been "knowing." I would hold that such a mental state satisfies the statute. Under the Court's holding, as I understand it, that person could not be convicted because he did not know that his conduct was illegal.[1]

* * *

I do agree with the Government that when Congress wants to include a knowledge of illegality requirement in a statute it knows how to do so,.... Other provisions of the United States Code explicitly include a requirement of familiarity with the law defining the offense—indeed, in places where, under the majority's analysis, it is entirely superfluous. E.g., 15 U.S.C. §§ 79z–3, 80a–48. Congress could easily have included a similar provision in § 2024(b), but did not.

Finally, the lower court's reading of the statute is consistent with the legislative history. As the majority points out, the history provides little to go on. Significantly, however, the brief discussions of this provision in the relevant congressional Reports do not mention any requirement of knowing illegality. To the contrary, when the Food Stamp Act was rewritten in 1977, the House Report noted that "*[a]ny* unauthorized use, transfer, acquisition, alteration, or possession of food stamps ... may be prosecuted under" § 2024(b). H.R.Rep. No. 95–464, p. 376 (1977).

II

The broad principles of the Court's opinion are easy to live with in a case such as this. But the application of its reasoning might not always be so benign. For example, § 2024(b) is little different from the basic federal prohibition on the manufacture and distribution of controlled substances. 21 U.S.C. § 841(a) provides:

> "Except as authorized by this subchapter, it shall be unlawful for any person knowingly or intentionally—
>
> "(1) to manufacture, distribute, or dispense, or possess with intent to manufacture, distribute or dispense, a controlled substance...."

I am sure that the members of the majority would agree that a defendant charged under this provision could not defend on the ground that he did not realize his manufacture was unauthorized or that the particular substance was controlled. See United States v. Balint, 258 U.S. 250, 42 S.Ct. 301, 66 L.Ed. 604 (1922). On the other hand, it would be a defense if he could prove he thought the substance was something

1. The appropriate prosecutorial target in such a situation would of course be the seller rather than the purchaser. I have no doubt that every prosecutor in the country would agree. The discussion of this hypothetical is wholly academic.

For similar reasons, I am unmoved by the spectre of criminal liability for someone who is mistakenly mailed food stamps and throws them out, and do not think the hypothetical offers much of a guide to congressional intent. We should proceed on the assumption that Congress had in mind the run-of-the-mill situation, not its most bizarre mutation. Arguments that presume wildly unreasonable conduct by government officials are by their nature unconvincing, and reliance on them is likely to do more harm than good. No rule, including that adopted by the Court today, is immune from such contrived defects.

other than what it was. By the same token, I think, someone in petitioner's position should not be heard to say that he did not know his purchase of food stamps was unauthorized, though he may certainly argue that he did not know he was buying food stamps. I would not stretch the term "knowingly" to require awareness of the absence of statutory authority in either of these provisions.

These provisions might be distinguished because of the different placements of the "except as authorized" and the "in any manner not authorized" clauses in the sentences. However, nothing in the majority's opinion indicates that this difference is relevant. Indeed, the logic of the Court's opinion would require knowledge of illegality for conviction under any statute making it a crime to do something "in any manner not authorized by law" or "unlawfully." I suspect that if a case arises in the future where such a result is unacceptable, the Court will manage to distinguish today's decision. But I will be interested to see how it does so.

III

In relying on the "background assumption of our criminal law" that *mens rea* is required, the Court ignores the equally well-founded assumption that ignorance of the law is no excuse. It is "the conventional position that knowledge of the existence, meaning or application of the law determining the elements of an offense is not an element of that offense...." Model Penal Code, at 130.

This Court's prior cases indicate that a statutory requirement of a "knowing violation" does not supersede this principle. For example, under the statute at issue in United States v. International Minerals & Chemical Corp., (1971), the Interstate Commerce Commission was authorized to promulgate regulations regarding the transportation of corrosive liquids, and it was a crime to "knowingly violat[e] any such regulation." Viewing the word "regulations" as "a shorthand designation for specific acts or omissions which violate the Act," we adhered to the traditional rule that ignorance of the law is not a defense. The violation had to be "knowing" in that the defendant had to know that he was transporting corrosive liquids and not, for example, merely water. But there was no requirement that he be aware that he was violating a particular regulation. Similarly, in this case the phrase "in any manner not authorized by" the statute or regulations is a shorthand incorporation of a variety of legal requirements. To be convicted, a defendant must have been aware of what he was doing, but not that it was illegal.

In Boyce Motor Lines, Inc. v. United States, (1952), the Court considered a statute that punished anyone who "knowingly violates" a regulation requiring trucks transporting dangerous items to avoid congested areas where possible. In rejecting a vagueness challenge, the Court read "knowingly" to mean not that the driver had to be aware of the regulation, but that he had to know a safer alternative route was available. Likewise, in construing 18 U.S.C. § 1461, which punishes "[w]hoever knowingly uses the mails for the mailing ... of anything declared by this section or section 3001(e) of Title 39 to be nonmailable," we held that the defendant need not have known that the materials were nonmailable. Hamling v. United States, (1974). "To require proof of a defendant's knowledge of the legal status of the materials would permit the defendant to avoid prosecution by simply claiming that he had not brushed up on the law," and was not required by the statute.

In each of these cases, the statutory language lent itself to the approach adopted today if anything more readily than does § 2024(b).[2] I would read § 2024(b) like those statutes, to require awareness of only the relevant aspects of one's conduct rendering it illegal, not the fact of illegality. This reading does not abandon the "background assumption" of *mens rea* by creating a strict liability offense,[3] and is consistent with the equally important background assumption that ignorance of the law is not a defense.

IV

I wholly agree that "[t]he contention that an injury can amount to a crime only when inflicted by intention is no provincial or transient notion." Morissette v. United States. But the holding of the court below is not at all inconsistent with that longstanding and important principle. Petitioner's conduct was intentional; the jury found that petitioner "realized what he was doing, and was aware of the nature of his conduct, and did not act through ignorance, mistake, or accident." App. 33 (trial court's instructions). Whether he knew which regulation he violated is beside the point.

PEOPLE v. HERNANDEZ

Supreme Court of California, 1964.
61 Cal.2d 529, 39 Cal.Rptr. 361, 393 P.2d 673.

PEEK, JUSTICE.

By information defendant was charged with statutory rape. (Pen. Code, § 261, subd. 1.) Following his plea of not guilty he was convicted

2. The Court distinguishes these as "public welfare offense" cases involving inherently dangerous articles of commerce whose users should have assumed were subject to regulation. Apart from the fact that a reasonable person would also assume food stamps are heavily regulated and not subject to sale and exchange, this distinction is not related to the actual holdings in those cases. The Court's opinion in *Boyce* and the concurrence in *Freed* do not discuss this consideration. And the Court's references to the dangerousness of the goods in *International Minerals* were directed to possible due process challenges to convictions without notice of criminality. As today's majority acknowledges, there is no constitutional defect with the holding of the court below. The only issue here is one of congressional intent.

3. Under a strict liability statute, a defendant can be convicted even though he was unaware of the circumstances of his conduct that made it illegal. To take the example of a statute recently before the Court, a regulation forbidding hunting birds in a "baited" field can be read to have a scienter requirement, in which case it would be a defense to prove that one did not know the field was baited, or not, in which case someone hunting in such a field is guilty even if he did not know and could not have known that it was baited. I do not argue that the latter approach should be taken to this statute, nor would the statutory language allow it.

as charged by the court sitting without a jury and the offense determined to be a misdemeanor.

Section 261 of the Penal Code provides in part as follows: "Rape is an act of sexual intercourse, accomplished with a female not the wife of the perpetrator, under either of the following circumstances: 1. Where the female is under the age of 18 years; . . . ."

The sole contention raised on appeal is that the trial court erred in refusing to permit defendant to present evidence going to his guilt for the purpose of showing that he had in good faith a reasonable belief that the prosecutrix was 18 years or more of age.

The undisputed facts show that the defendant and the prosecuting witness were not married and had been companions for several months prior to January 3, 1961—the date of the commission of the alleged offense. Upon that date the prosecutrix was 17 years and 9 months of age and voluntarily engaged in an act of sexual intercourse with defendant.

In support of his contention defendant relies upon Penal Code § 20, which provides that "there must exist a union, or joint operation of act and intent, or criminal negligence" to constitute the commission of a crime. He further relies upon section 26 of that code which provides that one is not capable of committing a crime who commits an act under an ignorance or mistake of fact which disapproves any criminal intent.

Thus the sole issue relates to the question of intent and knowledge entertained by the defendant at the time of the commission of the crime charged.

Consent of the female is often an unrealistic and unfortunate standard for branding sexual intercourse a crime as serious as forcible rape. Yet the consent standard has been deemed to be required by important policy goals. We are dealing here, of course, with statutory rape where, in one sense, the lack of consent of the female is not an element of the offense. In a broader sense, however, the lack of consent is deemed to remain an element but the law makes a conclusive presumption of the lack thereof because she is presumed too innocent and naive to understand the implications and nature of her act. (People v. Griffen . . .) The law's concern with her capacity or lack thereof to so understand is explained in part by a popular conception of the social, moral and personal values which are preserved by the abstinence from sexual indulgence on the part of a young woman. An unwise disposition of her sexual favor is deemed to do harm both to herself and the social mores by which the community's conduct patterns are established. Hence the law of statutory rape intervenes in an effort to avoid such a disposition. This goal, moreover, is not accomplished by penalizing the naive female but by imposing criminal sanctions against the male, who is conclusively presumed to be responsible for the occurrence. . . .

The assumption that age alone will bring an understanding of the sexual act to a young woman is of doubtful validity. Both learning from the cultural group to which she is a member and her actual sexual experiences will determine her level of comprehension. The sexually experienced 15-year old may be far more acutely aware of the implications of sexual intercourse than her sheltered cousin who is beyond the age of consent. A girl who belongs to a group whose members indulge in sexual intercourse at an early age is likely to rapidly acquire an insight into the rewards and penalties of sexual indulgence. Nevertheless, even in circumstances where a girl's actual comprehension contradicts the law's presumption, the male is deemed criminally responsible for the act, although himself young and naive and responding to advances which may have been made to him.

The law as presently constituted does not concern itself with the relative culpability of the male and female participants in the prohibited sexual act. Even where the young woman is knowledgeable it does not impose sanctions upon her. The knowledgeable young man, on the other hand, is penalized and there are none who would claim that under any construction of the law this should be otherwise. However, the issue raised by the rejected offer of proof in the instant case goes to the culpability of the young man who acts *without* knowledge that an essential factual element exists and has, on the other hand, a positive, reasonable belief that it does not exist.

The primordial concept of *mens rea,* the guilty mind, expresses the principle that it is not conduct alone but conduct accompanied by certain specific mental states which concerns, or should concern the law. In a broad sense the concept may be said to relate to such important doctrines as justification, excuse, mistake, necessity and mental capacity, but in the final analysis it means simply that there must be a "joint operation of act and intent," as expressed in section 20 of the Penal Code, to constitute the commission of a criminal offense. The statutory law, however, furnishes no assistance to the courts beyond that, and the casebooks are filled to overflowing with the courts' struggles to determine just what state of mind should be considered relevant in particular contexts. In numerous instances culpability has been completely eliminated as a necessary element of criminal conduct in spite of the admonition of section 20 to the contrary.... (membership in organizations advocating criminal syndicalism); ... (violation of Corporate Securities Act); ... (sale of liquor).) More recently, however, this court has moved away from the imposition of criminal sanctions in the absence of culpability where the governing statute, by implication or otherwise, expresses no legislative intent or policy to be served by imposing strict liability....

Statutory rape has long furnished a fertile battleground upon which to argue that the lack of knowledgeable conduct is a proper defense. The law in this state now rests, as it did in 1896, with this court's decision in People v. Ratz, ... where it is stated: "The claim here made is not a new one. It has frequently been pressed upon the attention of courts, but in no case, so far as our examination goes, has it met with favor. The object and purpose of the law are too plain to need comment, the crime too infamous to bear discussion. The protection of society, of the family, and of the infant, demand that one who has carnal intercourse under such circumstances shall do so in peril of the fact, and he will not be heard against the evidence to urge his belief that the victim of his outrage had passed the period which would make his act a crime." The age of consent at the time of the Ratz decision was 14 years, and it is noteworthy that the purpose of the rule, as there announced, was to afford protection to young females therein described as "infants." The decision on which the court in Ratz relied was The Queen v. Prince, L.R. 2 Crown Cas. 154. However England has now, by statute, departed from the strict rule, and excludes as a crime an act of sexual intercourse with a female between the ages of 13 and 16 years if the perpetrator is under the age of 24 years, has not previously been charged with a like offense, and believes the female "to be of the age of sixteen or over and has reasonable cause for the belief." ...[1]

The rationale of the Ratz decision, rather than purporting to eliminate intent as an element of the crime, holds that the wrongdoer must assume the risk; that, subjectively, when the act is committed, he consciously intends to proceed regardless of the age of the female and the consequences of his act, and that the circumstances involving the female, whether she be a day or a decade less than the statutory age, are irrelevant. There can be no dispute that a criminal intent exists when the perpetrator proceeds with utter disregard of, or in the lack of grounds for, a belief that the female has reached the age of consent. But if he participates in a mutual act of sexual intercourse, believing his partner to be beyond the age of consent, with reasonable grounds for such belief, where is his criminal intent? In such circumstances he has not consciously taken any risk. Instead he has subjectively eliminated the risk by satisfying himself on reasonable evidence that the crime cannot be committed. If it occurs that he has been misled, we cannot realistically conclude that for such reason alone the intent with which he undertook the act suddenly becomes more heinous.

While the specific contentions herein made have been dealt with and rejected both within and without this state, the courts have uniformly failed to satisfactorily explain the nature of the criminal intent present in the mind of one who in good faith believes he has obtained a lawful consent before engaging in the prohibited act. As in the Ratz case the courts often justify convictions on policy reasons which, in effect, eliminate the element of intent. The Legislature, of course, by making intent an element of the crime, has established the prevailing policy from which it alone can properly advise us to depart.

1. The American Law Institute in its model Penal Code (1962) provides in part as follows at pages 149 and 150:

"Section 213.6. Provisions Generally Applicable (Article 213 [Sexual Offenses].)

"(1) *Mistake as to Age.* Whenever in this Article the criminality of conduct depends upon a child's being below the age of 10, it is no defense that the actor did not know the child's age, or reasonably believed the child to be older than 10. When criminality depends upon the child's being below a critical age other than 10, it is a defense for the actor to prove that he reasonably believed the child to be above the critical age."

We have recently given recognition to the legislative declarations in sections 20 and 26 of the Penal Code, and departed from prior decisional law which had failed to accord full effect to those sections as applied to charges of bigamy. (People v. Vogel,. . . .) We held there that a good faith belief that a former wife had obtained a divorce was a valid defense to a charge of bigamy arising out of a second marriage when the first marriage had not in fact been terminated. Pertinent to the instant contention that defendant's intent did not suddenly become more criminal because it later developed that he had been misled by the prosecutrix, are the following comments appearing in Vogel at page 804 of 46 Cal.2d, at page 854 of 299 P.2d: "Nor would it be reasonable to hold that a person is guilty of bigamy who remarries in good faith in reliance on a judgment of divorce or annulment that is subsequently found not to be the 'judgment of a competent Court'. . . . Since it is often difficult for laymen to know when a judgment is not that of a competent court, we cannot reasonably expect them always to have such knowledge and make them criminals if their bona fide belief proves to be erroneous." Certainly it cannot be a greater wrong to entertain a bona fide but erroneous belief that a valid consent to an act of sexual intercourse has been obtained.

Equally applicable to the instant case are the following remarks, also appearing at page 804 of 46 Cal.2d, at page 855 of 299 P.2d of the Vogel decision: "The severe penalty imposed for bigamy, the serious loss of reputation conviction entails, . . . and the fact that it has been regarded for centuries as a crime involving moral turpitude, make it extremely unlikely that the Legislature meant to include the morally innocent to make sure the guilty did not escape."

We are persuaded that the reluctance to accord to a charge of statutory rape the defense of a lack of criminal intent has no greater justification than in the case of other statutory crimes, where the Legislature has made identical provision with respect to intent. " 'At common law an honest and reasonable belief in the existence of circumstances, which, if true, would make the act for which the person is indicted an innocent act, has always been held to be a good defense. . . . So far as I am aware it has never been suggested that these exceptions do not equally apply to the case of statutory offenses unless they are excluded expressly or by necessary implication.' " . . . Our departure from the views expressed in Ratz is in no manner indicative of a withdrawal from the sound policy that it is in the public interest to protect the sexually naive female from exploitation. No responsible person would hesitate to condemn as untenable a claimed good faith belief in the age of consent of an "infant" female whose obviously tender years preclude the existence of reasonable grounds for that belief. However, the prosecutrix in the instant case was but three months short of 18 years of age and there is nothing in the record to indicate that the purposes of the law as stated in Ratz can be better served by foreclosing the defense of a lack of intent. This is not to say that the granting of consent by even a sexually sophisticated girl known to be less than the statutory age is a defense. We hold only that in the absence of a legislative direction otherwise, a charge of statutory rape is defensible wherein a criminal intent is lacking.

For the foregoing reasons People v. Ratz, supra, and People v. Griffin, supra, are overruled, and People v. Sheffield, 9 Cal.App. 130, 98 P. 67, is disapproved to the extent that such decisions are inconsistent with the views expressed herein....

The judgment is reversed.

NOTES

1. Haddad, The Mental Attitude Requirement in Criminal Law—And Some Exceptions, 59 J.Crim.L., C. & P.S., 4, 15 (1968), suggests, in relation to prosecutions for bigamy:

> Strict liability in these cases is indefensible, whatever be the nature of the underlying mistake of fact. Defendants would not have been engaged in any legal or moral wrong had the facts been as they reasonably believed them to be; hence the principle of substituted intent is unavailable. Penalties from blameless defendants may be heavy, but they are unlikely to deter people who reasonably believe that they are free to marry, so that it makes little sense to say that the stability of the family depends upon a strict-liability standard. Even if such a standard would prevent more bigamous marriages than would a negligence standard, any *in terrorem* effect would also deter people whose marriages would not be bigamous from marrying because they lacked absolute certainty that the first spouse was dead or that a decree existed. This would be a significant deprivation of an important human right. Nor is there proof that juries would be deceived frequently by false claims of reasonable mistake of fact.

Yet, according to LaFave & Scott, I Substantive Criminal Law 579 (1986) a common view of the crime of bigamy is that none of the following constitutes a valid defense: reasonable belief that the first spouse is dead; reasonable belief that the first marriage was illegal; reasonable belief that the decree concerning the first marriage was a divorce decree; or reasonable belief that a foreign divorce would be recognized in the jurisdiction." Perkins, Criminal Law (1957), agrees with this assessment of the "weight of authority," but adds, at p. 840, that "there is much to be said for the 'minority view,' and fortunately the trend is in that direction."

2. The offense of carnal knowledge with a female under the age of consent, commonly called "statutory rape," has been dealt with in the same manner as the offense of bigamy, as far as the mistaken belief of an offender that the girl was above the age of consent is concerned. Most jurisdictions treat the offense as a strict liability crime. A minority of jurisdictions allow the reasonable mistake as to age defense, either by judicial fiat, as in the *Hernandez* case, or by statute. The Illinois Criminal Code, for instance, provides that "It shall be an affirmative defense to indecent liberties with a child [the Illinois equivalent of statutory rape] that: (1) The accused reasonably believed the child was of the age of 16 or upwards at the time of the act giving rise to the charge: ..." 720 ILCS 5/12–17(b).

Section 3–2 provides that after the affirmative defense is raised the prosecution must prove D's guilt beyond a reasonable doubt as to that issue as well as to all the other elements of the defense.

PEOPLE v. YOUNG

Court of Appeals of New York, 1962.
11 N.Y.2d 274, 183 N.E.2d 319.

PER CURIAM. Whether one, who in good faith aggressively intervenes in a struggle between another person and a police officer in civilian dress attempting to effect the lawful arrest of the third person, may be properly convicted of assault in the third degree is a question of law of first impression here.

The opinions in the court below [the Appellate Division of the Supreme Court] in the absence of precedents in this State carefully expound the opposing views found in other jurisdictions. The majority in the Appellate Division have adopted the minority rule in the other States that one who intervenes in a struggle between strangers under the mistaken but reasonable belief that he is protecting another who he assumes is being unlawfully beaten is thereby exonerated from criminal liability.... The weight of authority holds with the dissenters below that one who goes to the aid of a third person does so at his own peril....

While the doctrine espoused by the majority of the court below may have support in some States, we feel that such a policy would not be conducive to an orderly society. We agree with the settled policy of law in most jurisdictions that the right of a person to defend another ordinarily should not be greater than such person's right to defend himself. Subdivision 3 of section 246 of the Penal Law, Consol.Laws, c. 40, does not apply as no offense was being committed on the person of the one resisting the lawful arrest. Whatever may be the public policy where the felony charged requires proof of a specific intent and the issue is justifiable homicide ..., it is not relevant in a prosecution for assault in the third degree where it is only necessary to show that the defendant knowingly struck a blow.

In this case there can be no doubt that the defendant intended to assault the police officer in civilian dress. The resulting assault was forceful. Hence motive or mistake of fact is of no significance as the defendant was not charged with a crime requiring such intent or knowledge. To be guilty of third degree assault "It is sufficient that the defendant voluntarily intended to commit the unlawful act of touching".... Since in these circumstances the aggression was inexcusable the defendant was properly convicted.

Accordingly, the order of the Appellate Division should be reversed and the information reinstated.

FROESSEL, JUDGE (dissenting). [Concurrence by VAN VOORHIS, J.] The law is clear that one may kill in defense of another when there is reasonable, though mistaken, ground for believing that the person slain is about to commit a felony or to do some great personal injury to the apparent victim . . .; yet the majority now hold, for the first time, that in the event of a simple assault under similar circumstances, the mistaken belief, no matter how reasonable, is no defense.

Briefly, the relevant facts are these: On a Friday afternoon at about 3:40, Detectives, Driscoll and Murphy, not in uniform, observed an argument taking place between a motorist and one McGriff in the street in front of premises 64 West 54th Street, in midtown Manhattan. Driscoll attempted to chase McGriff out of the roadway in order to allow traffic to pass, but McGriff refused to move back; his actions caused a crowd to collect. After identifying himself to McGriff, Driscoll placed him under arrest. As McGriff resisted, defendant "came out of the crowd" from Driscoll's rear and struck Murphy about the head with his fist. In the ensuing struggle Driscoll's right kneecap was injured when defendant fell on top of him. At the station house, defendant said he had not known or thought Driscoll and Murphy were police officers.

Defendant testified that while he was proceeding on 54th Street he observed two white men, who appeared to be 45 or 50 years old, pulling on a "colored boy" (McGriff), who appeared to be a lad about 18, whom he did not know. The men had nearly pulled McGriff's pants off, and he was crying. Defendant admitted he knew nothing of what had transpired between the officers and McGriff, and made no inquiry of anyone; he just came there and pulled the officer away from McGriff.

Defendant was convicted of assault third degree. In reversing upon the law and dismissing the information, the Appellate Division held that one is not "criminally liable for assault in the third degree if he goes to the aid of another who he mistakenly, but *reasonably,* believes is being unlawfully beaten, and thereby injures one of the apparent assaulters" (emphasis supplied). While in my opinion the majority below correctly stated the law, I would reverse here and remit so that the Appellate Division may pass on the question of whether or not defendant's conduct was reasonable in light of the circumstances presented at the trial. . . .

As the majority below pointed out, assault is a crime derived from the common law (People v. Katz, 290 N.Y. 361, 365, 49 N.E.2d 482, 484). Basic to the imposition of criminal liability both at common law and under our statutory law is the existence in the one who committed the prohibited act of what has been variously termed a guilty mind, a *mens rea* or a criminal intent. . . .

Criminal intent requires an awareness of wrongdoing. When conduct is based upon mistake of fact reasonably entertained, there can be no such awareness and, therefore, no criminal culpability. In People ex rel. Hegeman v. Corrigan, 195 N.Y. 1, 12, 87 N.E. 792, 796, we stated: "it is very apparent that the innocence or criminality of the intent in a particular act generally depends on the knowledge or belief of the actor at the time. An honest and *reasonable* belief in the existence of circumstances which, if true, would make the act for which the defendant is prosecuted innocent, would be a good defense." (Emphasis supplied.)

It is undisputed that defendant did not know that Driscoll and Murphy were detectives in plain clothes engaged in lawfully apprehending an alleged disorderly person. If, therefore, defendant *reasonably* believed he was lawfully assisting another, he would not have been guilty of a crime. Subdivision 3 of section 246 of the Penal Law provides that it is not unlawful to use force "When committed either by the party about to be injured or *by another person in his aid or defense, in preventing or attempting to prevent an offense against his person,* ... if the force or violence used is not more than sufficient to prevent such offense" (emphasis supplied). The law is thus clear that if defendant entertained an "honest and reasonable belief" ..., that the facts were as he perceived them to be, he would be exonerated from criminal liability.

By ignoring one of the most basic principles of criminal law—that crimes *mala in se* require proof of at least general criminal intent—the majority now hold that the defense of mistake of fact is "of no significance". We are not here dealing with one of "a narrow class of exceptions" ... where the Legislature has created crimes which do not depend on *criminal* intent but which are complete on the mere intentional doing of an act *malum prohibitum*....

There is no need, in my opinion, to consider the law of other States, for New York policy clearly supports the view that one may act on appearances reasonably ascertained, as does New Jersey.... Our Penal Law (§ 1055), to which I have already alluded, is a statement of that policy. The same policy was expressed by this court in People v. Maine,.... There, the defendant observed his brother fighting in the street with two other men; he stepped in and stabbed to death one of the latter. The defense was justifiable homicide under the predecessor of section 1055. The court held it reversible error to admit into evidence the declarations of the defendant's brother, made before defendant happened upon the scene, which tended to show that the brother was the aggressor. We said: "Of course, the acts and conduct of the defendant must be judged solely with reference to the situation as it was when he first and afterwards saw it." Mistake of relevant fact, reasonably entertained, is thus a defense to homicide under section 1055 ... and one who kills in defense of another and proffers this defense of justification is to be judged according to the circumstances as they appeared to him (People v. Maine, ...).

The mistaken belief, however, must be one which is reasonably entertained and the question of reasonableness is for the trier of the facts ... "The question is not, merely, what did the accused believe? but also, what did he have the right to believe?"....

Although the majority of our courts are now purporting to fashion a policy "conducive to an orderly society", by their decision they have defeated their avowed purpose. What public interest is promoted by a principle which would deter one from coming to the aid of a fellow citizen who he has reasonable ground to apprehend is in imminent danger of personal injury at the hands of assailants? Is it reasonable to denominate, as justifiable homicide, a slaying committed under a mistaken but reasonably held belief, and deny this same defense of justification to one using less force? Logic, as well as historical background and related precedent, dictates that the rule and policy expressed by our Legislature in the case of homicide, which is an assault resulting in death, should likewise be applicable to a much less serious assault not resulting in death.

I would reverse the order appealed from and remit the case to the Appellate Division pursuant to section 543–b of the Code of Criminal Procedure "for determination upon the questions of fact raised in that court".

Order reversed, etc.

NOTE

Consider the following from State v. Westlund, 13 Wn.App. 460, 536 P.2d 20 (1975):

"We hold that a bystander may not come to the aid of one being lawfully or unlawfully arrested by a uniformed police officer or one known or who should have been known to the bystander to be a police officer unless the arrestee was in actual danger of serious physical injury. Several elements, therefore, must be present before such a third person's assault of a police officer can be justified on the basis of defense of another. First, a third party may never intervene when the only threat to the arrestee is deprivation of his liberty by an arrest which has no legal justification. Aid is justified only if serious physical injury or death is threatened or inflicted. Second, the serious physical danger threatened or inflicted must be actual. A reasonable but mistaken belief that the arrestee was about to be seriously injured or that the arrestee was entitled to protect himself from such danger is insufficient. The third party acts at his own peril and if it is subsequently determined that the arrestee was not about to be seriously injured, the third party's assault is not justifiable. Third, the physical injury must be serious, the police actions of the type which shock the conscience. Fourth, only force reasonable and necessary to protect the arrestee may be used against the officer."

B. INFANCY

STATE v. MONAHAN

Supreme Court of New Jersey, 1954.
15 N.J. 34, 104 A.2d 21.

JACOBS, J. Prompted by mid-Twentieth Century sociological precepts, our Legislature has directed that children under 16 who commit any offenses which would be criminal if committed by adults, shall not be triable in criminal proceedings but shall be dealt with exclusively by our specialized juvenile courts. The legal issue presented to us is whether this clear statutory mandate may be judicially disregarded to enable a first degree murder trial in the County Court of a 15-year-old boy who participated in a robbery with his father during which his father killed two persons.

In April, 1953 Eugene Monahan and his 15-year-old son Michael were indicted for the murder of William Diskin and Sebastian Weilandics. Eugene Monahan has been tried, convicted and sentenced to death and his appeal is pending before this court. The State concedes that the victims were killed by the father and not the son but asserts that since the homicides occurred during a robbery in which the son participated, the son was equally triable for murder in the first degree, punishable by death unless there is a recommendation of life imprisonment.... A motion was made for transfer of the proceeding against the son to the Juvenile and Domestic Relations Court on the ground that under N.J.S. 2A:85–4 N.J.S.A., and N.J.S. 2A:4–14, N.J.S.A., it was cognizable exclusively in that court. The motion was denied and an appeal was taken....

The principle of removing or mitigating the criminal responsibility of children has ancient origins. In the early case of State v. Aaron, ..., Chief Justice Kirkpatrick restated the settled common law doctrine, adapted from earlier Roman law, that since a child under seven "cannot have discretion to discern between good and evil" he is incapable of committing crime; between the ages of seven and 14 he is subject to a rebuttable presumption of incapacity; and after 14 he is presumptively capable.... Although the common law rule precluded criminal convictions of many young offenders, there are instances in which it failed to do so, with shocking consequences. Blackstone cites cases in which children of very tender age were drastically condemned as adult criminals; he refers to the hanging of an eight-year-old for maliciously burning some barns; to the hanging of a ten-year-old who had killed one of his companions; and to the burning of a girl of 13 who had killed her mistress.... Similar illustrations in our own State are not lacking. In 1818 a boy of 11 was tried for murder ..., and in 1828 a boy of 13 was hanged for an offense which he committed when he was 12.... During most of the Nineteenth Century, child and adult offenders were treated alike although intermittent steps were taken towards their separate confinement. It was not until the turn of the century that modern concepts really began to take form; they embodied the upward movement in the child's age of criminal responsibility, the extended recognition of society's obligation as *parens patriae* to care for delinquent children, and the creation of independent juvenile courts....

The first juvenile court in this country was established in Cook County, Illinois, by an 1899 act which provided that the child offender was to be considered a ward of the state under control of the juvenile court; proceedings were there to be conducted informally with rehabilitative supervision rather than retributive punishment in mind, and without public indictment, trial by jury and other incidents of criminal causes. Thereafter the other states adopted legislation which was comparable though specific provisions varied. Attacks on the legislation based on the absence of indictment, trial by jury and the other constitutional guarantees applicable to criminal proceedings were quickly rejected.... In the Fisher case [213 Pa. 48, 62 A. 200] the Supreme Court of Pennsylvania pointed out that the juvenile court proceeding is not "the trial of a child charged with a crime, but is mercifully to save it from such an ordeal with the prison or penitentiary in its wake, if the child's own good and the best interests of the state justify such salvation." In the Lindsay case [257 Ill. 328, 100 N.E. 894] the Supreme Court of Illinois noted that the "prerogative of the state, arising out of its power and duty, as *parens patriae,* to protect the interest of infants, has always been exercised by courts of chancery" and has not been questioned for generations. In the Lewis case [260 N.Y. 171, 183 N.E. 354] the New York Court of Appeals stated that there is no doubt about the power of the legislature "to say that an act done by a child shall not be a crime." And in the recent Morin case [95 N.H. 518, 68 A.2d 670] the Supreme Court of New Hampshire, in rejecting an attack on its statute relating to delinquent children, said:

> "We think it sufficiently plain that the act in question is designed to permit the exercise of the powers of the state as 'parens patriae,' for the purpose of rehabilitating minor children, and not of punishing them for the commission of a crime. 'It is generally held that the purpose of such statutes is not penal, but protective. It is not that the child shall be punished for breach of a law or regulation, but that he shall have a better chance to become a worthy citizen.' ... Similar statutes have been universally upheld over objections based upon constitutional grounds....

In In re Paniecki [N.J.1935] ..., Vice-Chancellor Backes had occasion to deal with the issue of whether a 15-year-old boy, charged with murder, was triable in the same manner as an adult in the Court of Oyer and Terminer. The vice chancellor held that he was, expressing the sweeping view that the Legislature had no power "to vest jurisdiction in the juvenile court to try the crime of murder (or any other indictable offense) without a jury." He did not consider any of the many cases to the contrary throughout the states and if his view had ultimately prevailed it would have struck a mortal blow to the juvenile court movement in our State....

Immediately after Vice-Chancellor Backes had rendered his decision in the Daniecki case holding that the 15-year-old boy before him was triable for murder in the same manner as an adult, the Legislature took affirmative steps to obviate its effects. It provided in L.1935, c. 285, that a person under the age of 16 shall be deemed incapable of committing a crime under the common law or statute law of this State; and in L.1935, c. 284, in defining delinquency cognizable exclusively in the juvenile court, it included conduct which, if committed by any one 16 or over, would constitute a felony, high misdemeanor, misdemeanor or other offense. The statutory language was unmistakable in design....

In In re Mei ... [N.J.1937], the question was again raised as to whether a 15-year-old was triable for murder in the same manner as an adult; the court held that he was notwithstanding the express terms of L.1935, cc. 284, 285. It did not suggest that the Legislature intended to exclude murder from its comprehensive enactments; nor did it adopt the sweeping view of unconstitutionality expressed in the Daniecki case and later rejected in the Goldberg case. Instead, it rested on the unprecedented ground that since the charge of murder is "so horrible in fact and in the contemplation of society" it must remain "a crime within the purview of the Constitution, whatever name and whatever treatment may be appended to it by the Legislature." ... Viewed strictly as a legal ground it has no supporting basis whatever since the Constitution makes no pertinent mention of murder and the guarantees, when applicable, govern murder and other indictable common law offenses with like force. Viewed strictly as an emotional ground it concededly may not be given any controlling effect.

In approximately half the states the jurisdiction of the juvenile court over children under 16 is exclusive, even where the offense would constitute murder if committed by an adult.... The Standard Juvenile Court Act as revised in 1949 likewise vests exclusive jurisdiction in the juvenile court over all children under 16. It also provides for jurisdiction over children from 16 to 18 but states that if the child is 16 or over and is charged "with an offense which would be a felony if committed by an adult" the juvenile court may in its discretion, certify the child for criminal proceedings. To remove any doubts, it expressly directs that "no child under sixteen years of age shall be so certified." Judicial opinions sustaining such legislation are now legion and the Mei decision stands alone in its notion that a child of seven or over, charged with murder, must be tried in the same manner as an adult regardless of what the Legislature says on the subject. Although the decision is devoid of supporting reason and authority, the suggestion is advanced that since it was rendered many years ago it should be permitted to stand until altered by the Legislature. This approach might have some merit if the Mei decision turned on a matter of statutory construction but the fact is that the court there asserted an absence of constitutional power which no amount of legislation could supply.... In any event, the pertinent legislative enactments after the Mei case clearly reaffirm the plain statutory purpose to vest in the juvenile court, exclusive jurisdiction over children under 16 regardless of the severity of their offenses.... In 1946 the Legislature, in dealing with juvenile court jurisdiction over persons between the ages of 16 and 18, expressly stated that the juvenile court may refer the matter to the prosecutor for criminal trial where the offense was of a "heinous nature." L.1946, c. 77; N.J.S. 2A:4–15, N.J.S.A.... No comparable provision was ever adopted with respect to children under 16, thus evidencing the legislative purpose of preserving the exclusive jurisdiction of the juvenile court in such instances.... When our statutes relating to civil and criminal justice were recently revised, the Legislature re-enacted its comprehensive declarations that a person under the age of 16 shall be deemed incapable of committing a crime, ... and that juvenile delinquency shall include any act which, if committed by an adult, would constitute a felony, high misdemeanor, misdemeanor or other offense....

A majority of the court is satisfied that our present legislation lawfully vests exclusive jurisdiction in the juvenile court over misconduct by children under 16 including misconduct which would constitute murder or other heinous crime if committed by an adult. Accordingly, the order entered below is set aside and the matter is remanded to the Juvenile and Domestic Relations Court of Union County for further proceedings in accordance with the governing statutes and rules of court.

HEHER, J., concurring in result. [The concurring opinion of HEHER, J., is omitted.] For reversal: Justices HEHER, BURLING, JACOBS and BRENNAN—4. For affirmance: Chief Justice VANDERBILT, and Justices OLIPHANT and WACHENFELD—3.

OLIPHANT, J. (dissenting). I find myself compelled to dissent in this case because I differ basically with the approach and reasoning of the majority opinion....

The majority ... have in effect overruled the holding in the Mei case and assert that under the *parens patriae* doctrine, both on psychological and sociological grounds, the State and the Legislature have the power to treat such a crime when committed by an infant on a psychological or sociological basis and bring it within the definition of juvenile delinquency as set forth in the statute....

... [T]he nub of the problem here presented revolves around the statutory provision, N.J.S. 2A:85–4, N.J.S.A., which provides:

> "A person under the age of 16 years is deemed incapable of committing a crime."

This provision seemingly ignores the fundamental fact of the law of nature as applied to man and facts of everyday existence which are of common knowledge and public notice.

I cannot comprehend the reasoning that suggests that marauding gangs of little hoodlums armed with guns, knives, switch knives or other lethal weapons are to be considered as a matter of law incapable of committing the crime of murder. Infants under the age of 21 years, according to statistics, perpetrate a high percentage of the heinous crimes committed throughout the country, and the situation has reached such serious proportions that it is a threat to the public welfare and safety of the law-abiding citizen....

At the common law and in this State, insofar as a crime is concerned, the inability to form a criminal intent is a matter of defense. As to children under the age of seven years there is a conclusive presumption that the child was *doli incapax,* or incapable of entertaining a criminal intent, and no evidence can or should be received to show capacity in fact. Between the ages of seven and 14 the presumption is rebuttable, but the State or prosecution has the burden of showing that the infant has sufficient intelligence to distinguish between right and wrong and to understand the nature and illegality of the particular act. Over the age of 14 children were and are presumed to be *doli capax* and therefore responsible. The presumption is rebuttable but the burden of proof is upon the defendant to establish that he did not have sufficient intelligence to understand the nature and consequences of his act. These rules are consistent with the nature of man and the natural use of his faculties of intellect and will, and his freedom to acquire the necessary knowledge to make the distinction between right and wrong. They are rules to determine the ultimate fact of the ability of an individual to distinguish between right and wrong. The point in life when a person is capable of making this distinction may vary, but once it is reached that person whether it be an adult or a child, is capable of criminal intent....

The views expressed here were of sufficient moment to induce the Legislatures in many states to remove the charge of murder from the field of juvenile delinquency. It is indeed a curious anomaly that in this country, where civilization in some respects has reached its highest peak insofar as the welfare and comfort of an individual is concerned and where the educational opportunities are practically unlimited for a child, we are brought face to face with a statute that in effect denied that the normal child is a rational human being insofar as the highest crime against nature is concerned. I doubt that even in the primitive state of civilization there is any society that subscribes to such a proposition. Bluntly, the statute practically says that a child, within defined age limits, is not a rational being but merely an animal without the will or mind to control its baser animal instincts....

I am unable to subscribe to nor can I find support for the legal theory by which the Legislature can declare that those young in years but old in crime and depravity are incapable of committing the crime of murder. Many such are experienced criminals. A prominent jurist recently said: "The whole problem of juvenile and adolescent delinquency has become worse and is now a scandal." ...

I would affirm the order of the court below in denying the motion for the transfer of the indictments to the Juvenile and Domestic Relations Court.

WACHENFELD, J. (dissenting).

Over the many years our present procedure in reference to these matters has worked out quite satisfactorily. No hue or cry of great injustice has been heard, nor is there a single case the disposition of which has offended the public's sense of essential fairness.

The method of disposing of these cases has now been changed, not by legislative enactment, where the power admittedly resides, but by a new judicial interpretation. In re Mei ..., which has stood for 17 years, is overruled and is no longer the law.

Up until now, all who committed murder, whether old or young, were held strictly accountable to the law. If the offender appreciated the difference between right and wrong, he was answerable in a court of law for the highest crime known, the taking of another's life.

Today's youth is more precocious than yesterday's. His aggressiveness has not been diminished and the record unfortunately shows his propensity for going out of bounds has not decreased. The child who flounts authority is becoming too prevalent, and the seriousness of these infractions is becoming increasingly grim. Juvenile delinquency is still one of our foremost problems, and its solution is being vainly sought by educator, legislator and many public agencies.

How, then, will this change in the law affect the dilemma confronting us? Will it help or hinder? Those of tender age who are likely to commit the crime involved will certainly not be additionally deterred by the knowledge that the punishment for it has practically been abolished and the worse that can befall them for committing a felony murder under the new rule is confinement in a reformatory or correctional institution for the term fixed by the trustees, not to exceed in any case a few years.

Erring youth indeed offers a fertile field for remedial effort, but I doubt if in this instance we are making much of a contribution.

The police now cannot keep track of those they have apprehended and referred to the Juvenile Court. The disposition there is confidential and secret and makes better law enforcement by those responsible for it more difficult. To the classification of the offenses so processed we now add the crime of murder. I have grave fears of its consequences.

I cannot embrace many of the expressions in Justice Oliphant's dissent, but I feel obligated to state briefly the reasons why I would adhere to the decision in In re Mei, supra, and therefore affirm the judgment below.

NOTES

1. In 1978 New Jersey lowered the age of incapacity to commit a crime from the 16 years that prevailed at the time of the *Monahan* decision to 14 years of age.

2. The age of incapacity in Illinois is 13 years of age. In that jurisdiction, as in a number of others, there is concurrent jurisdiction over acts committed by children over the minimum capacity age and 17 years. For instance, in the Illinois Juvenile Court Act (705 ILCS 405/5–4) there is the following provision:

> (6)(a) The definition of delinquent minor under Section 5–3 of this Act shall not apply to any minor who at the time of an offense was at least 15 years of age and who is charged with first degree murder, aggravated criminal sexual assault or armed robbery when the armed robbery was committed with a firearm ... These charges and all other charges arising out of the same incident shall be prosecuted pursuant to the Criminal Code of 1961, as amended.

(b) If before trial or plea an information or indictment is filed which does not charge an offense specified in paragraph (a) of subsection (6) of this Section, the State's Attorney may proceed on the lesser charge or charges but only in Juvenile Court under the provisions of this Act, unless prior to trial the minor defendant knowingly and with advice of counsel waives, in writing, his right to have the matter proceed in Juvenile Court. If before trial or plea an information or indictment is filed which includes one or more charges specified in paragraph (a) of subsection (6) of this Section and additional charges which are not specified in such paragraph, all of the charges arising out of the same incident shall be prosecuted pursuant to the "Criminal Code of 1961".

(c) If after trial or plea the minor is convicted of an offense not covered by paragraph (a) of subsection (6) of this Section, such conviction shall not invalidate the verdict or the prosecution of the minor under the criminal laws of this State.

C. INTOXICATION

PEOPLE v. GUILLETT

Supreme Court of Michigan, 1955.
342 Mich. 1, 69 N.W.2d 140.

BUTZEL, JUSTICE. Lawrence Guillett was informed against for assault with intent to commit rape. He pleaded not guilty and was tried in circuit court where a jury found him guilty of the crime charged. Appellant *in propria persona* has appealed from his conviction on various grounds. The complainant had agreed to spend an evening with him. He, with two other friends, called for her and they visited a tavern where each of them consumed three glasses of beer. She and appellant then went to the home of the latter's parents, and later purchased a bottle of wine out of which she took one glass which she only partially consumed while he apparently finished the bottle. They sat together on a davenport and he made indecent advances which she repulsed. After she arose he then struck her, knocked her down and continued his attempt to commit rape. During a struggle she grabbed a telephone receiver and struck him so many blows on the head that he required hospitalization. She then escaped, ran across the road and the police and an ambulance were summoned. Appellant's mother testified that he had been drinking for several days and that he had come home drunk earlier that day, but she left him to go to work shortly after 3 p.m. His father said that he appeared "dozy."

In view of the testimony the trial judge in his charge to the jury stated:

> "Now, there has been injected here to a great extent, the question of intoxication. I will give you an instruction on that.
>
> "It is a well settled law in this state that voluntary drunkenness is not a defense to crime. A man who puts himself in a

position to have no control over his actions must be held to intend the consequences. The safety of the community requires this rule. Intoxication is so easily counterfeited, and, when real, is so often resorted to as a means of nerving a person up to the commission of some deliberate act and withal is so inexcusable in itself that the law has never recognized it as an excuse for crime.

"In the case of an offense such as the one charged, committed during a period of intoxication, the law presumes the defendant to have intended the obscuration and perversion of his faculties which followed his voluntary intoxication. He must be held to have purposely blinded his moral perception and set his will free from the control of reason—to have suppressed the guards and invited the mutiny; and should therefore be held responsible as well for the vicious excesses of the will thus set free as for the acts done by its prompting."

Defendant has assigned error on the ground that the charge as given was incomplete and therefore misleading because it failed to state that intoxication may serve to negative the existence of the intent required for conviction of the crime charged.

We must conclude that the charge was erroneous. In Roberts v. People, 19 Mich. 401, 418, 420, the defendant was convicted of assault with intent to commit murder. On appeal, after considering the necessity for finding intent in fact, or specific intent, Justice Christiancy discussed the issue of whether drunkenness might negative the existence of that intent. He concluded:

"In determining the question whether the assault was committed with the intent charged, it was therefore material to inquire whether the defendant's mental faculties were so far overcome by the effect of intoxication, as to render him incapable of entertaining the intent. And, for this purpose, it was the right and the duty of the jury—as upon the question of intent of which this forms a part—to take into consideration the nature and the circumstances of the assault, the actions, conduct and demeanor of the defendant, and his declaration before, at the time, and after the assault; and especially to consider the nature of the intent, and what degree of mental capacity was necessary to enable him to entertain the simple intent to kill, under the circumstances of this case—or which is the same thing, how far the mental faculties must be obscured by intoxication to render him incapable of entertaining that particular intent....

"But the Circuit Court held, in effect that no extent of intoxication could have the effect to disprove the intent; treating the intent as an inference of law for the Court, rather than a question of fact for the jury. In this we think there was error."

... A consideration of later Michigan authority reveals that Roberts v. People, supra, remains as the most eloquent and correct statement of law on the subject. Thus in People v. Walker, 38 Mich. 156, Judge Cooley wrote an opinion reversing a conviction of larceny stating:

> "While it is true that drunkenness cannot excuse crime, it is equally true that when a certain intent is a necessary element in a crime, the crime cannot have been committed when the intent did not exist. In larceny the crime does not consist in the wrongful taking of the property, for that might be a mere trespass; but it consists in the wrongful taking with felonious intent; and if the defendant, for any reason whatever, indulged no such intent, the crime cannot have been committed. This was fully explained by Mr. Justice Christiancy in Roberts v. People, 19 Mich. 401, and is familiar law."

... It is to be noted that we are here concerned with intoxication insofar as it might negative the requisite intent, as distinguished from insanity or delirium tremens brought on by intoxication, the latter, if present, being a complete excuse rather than a partial one as here....

It is important in this decision to emphasize that intoxication may only negative the existence of *specific intent*. Examination of the cases reveals that where the rule was applied it was done so in cases where the crime charged also involved a specific intent. Apparently the trial judge in the instant case did not realize this. For the most part his charge was in the exact words of Justice Cooley in People v. Garbutt, 17 Mich. 9. However, it should have been noted that the crime involved in that case was murder, not a specific intent crime, or as was said in Roberts v. People, supra, 19 Mich. at page 417:

> "The correctness of the principle laid down by this Court in People v. Garbutt (17 Mich. 9–19), is not denied; that 'a man who voluntarily puts himself into a condition to have no control of his actions, must be held to intend the consequences.' But this, it is insisted, includes only the consequences which do actually ensue—the crime actually committed; and not in this case the intent charged, if the defendant was at the time incapable of entertaining it, and did not in fact entertain it."
>
> "We think this reasoning is entirely sound, and it is well supported by authority."

The crime of assault with intent to rape involves a specific intent.... The charge was therefore erroneous....

The error here is one of omission. The charge is one of half-truth and misleading. The effect of the instruction given in this case was to instruct the jury that any and all evidence of intoxication had absolutely no bearing on appellant's guilt of the crime charged. It has been said that a charge stating some elements of a crime but omitting others "would have a natural tendency to cause a jury to believe that those stated were exclusive." ... It was therefore prejudicial to the appellant. It was reversible error....

NOTES

1. Consider the following case: Defendant was convicted of murder in the first degree as a result of having beaten his wife to death with a hammer. The trial court charged the jury that even though defendant had been intoxicated and hence easily provoked, the crime would not be manslaughter unless the provocation was sufficient to arouse "sudden passion" in a reasonable, sober man. In affirming the conviction and approving the charge of the trial court, the Court of Appeals, in Bishop v. United States, 107 F.2d 297 (D.C.Cir., 1939), stated:

> "It is only necessary to show that the killing was committed in 'heat of passion' upon sufficient provocation. The test of sufficiency of such provocation is that which would cause an ordinary man, a reasonable man, or an average man, to become so aroused. Such a man can only mean a 'sober man,' and the provocation must be sufficient to create 'heat of passion' in a reasonable, sober man.... If a defendant is intoxicated, there is no requirement that provocation for 'heat of passion' be greater than that which would arouse a reasonable, sober man to act. Certainly, if there be intoxication, a lesser provocation than that which would create 'heat of passion' in a reasonable, sober man cannot be allowed, otherwise, a premium would be granted for voluntary intoxication. The standard of provocation that may create the 'heat of passion' reducing murder to manslaughter is the same for all men, whether drunk or sober. We, therefore, conclude that the court correctly defined manslaughter and the proper standard to be applied when intoxication is pleaded as a defense."

To the same effect with respect to the standard to be applied in considering a plea of self defense by one who killed another while allegedly intoxicated, see Springfield v. State, 96 Ala. 81, 11 So. 250 (1892), where the defendant's conviction of second degree murder was affirmed.

Virginia rejects voluntary intoxication as a defense even as to specific intent crimes, except as to murder where it appears that the accused was too drunk to be capable of deliberation and premeditation. Chittum v. Commonwealth, 211 Va. 12, 174 S.E.2d 779 (1970). To the same effect are McDaniel v. State, 356 So.2d 1151 (Miss.1978); State v. Vaughn, 268 S.C. 119, 232 S.E.2d 328 (1977) Del.Code, tit. 11, Sec. 421, Vernon's Tex.Code Ann.Penal Code, Sec. 8.04.

Courts have held that it is unconstitutional to limit intoxication defenses to specific intent crimes. Commonwealth v. Henson, 394 Mass. 584, 476 N.E.2d 947 (1985); Terry v. State, 465 N.E.2d 1085 (Ind.1984) (also holding the scope of the defense is narrow and may be conclusively refuted by showing the accused drove a car, gave directions and made decisions during the period of the crime). Contra People v. DelGuidice, 199 Colo. 41, 606 P.2d 840 (1979) (constitutional to preclude proof of intoxication where specific intent is not a crime element). And Robinson v. Ponte, 933 F.2d 101 (1st Cir.1991). One large state only recently has allowed intoxication as a defense even in specific intent cases. Commonwealth v. Henson, 394 Mass. 584, 476 N.E.2d 947 (1985). California permits voluntary intoxication to negate a crime committed by reckless disregard. People v. Whitfield, 7 Cal.4th 437, 27 Cal.Rptr.2d 858, 868 P.2d 272 (1994) (thorough opinion).

The standard of intoxication is very high, i.e., severe or extreme intoxication. People v. Savoie, 419 Mich. 118, 349 N.W.2d 139 (1984); State v. Gover, 267 Md. 602, 298 A.2d 378 (1973).

2. Consider also: The defendant believed that an Officer Miller was out to get him. One evening he pulled his girlfriend into a bathroom, closed the door and told her to be quiet because *someone* was out there and *they* were going to get her and him. Her small child, Eric, then walked down the hall. Hearing the steps, defendant said "Here they come". She told him it was just her son but he opened the door and attacked the child with a bedpost. She was able to pick up the child, flee the house and call the police who arrested defendant only after stiff resistance. The Court said, in Norris v. State, 275 Ind. 608, 419 N.E.2d 129 (1981):

> "It appears that the defendant's conduct was both bizarre and out of character, and there was evidence from which the jury could have found that he was acting under a self-administered injection of PCP.
>
> * * *
>
> "The defendant next contends that he was so intoxicated that he could not form any specific intent to commit any of the offenses of which he stands convicted. He assumes incorrectly, however, that all the offenses charged are specific intent crimes; only the attempted murder of Eric Sanford is.
>
> "The acts related above appear to be those of a maniac, however, whether or not the defendant's voluntary intoxication prevented him from forming the specific intent required for attempted murder was a question of fact for the jury and one upon which the defendant bore the burden of proof.
>
> * * *
>
> "... From all the evidence, the jury was entitled to infer that the defendant, suffering from delusions and paranoia, intended to kill whomever was on the other side of the bathroom door, when he opened it and found Eric Sanford. The defendant had been suffering from a fear that *someone* was in the house; that *someone* was trying to get him; and that that *someone* was Officer Miller, whom the defendant believed, rightly or wrongly, was out to get him. Rita Sanford testified that on opening the bathroom door, the defendant looked "... straight ahead, you know, like somebody as big as him." The defendant then used a weapon in a manner which would cause death. Under such circumstances, the jury could find that the defendant intended to use the bedpost to kill someone. See Burkhalter v. State, (1979) Ind., 397 N.E.2d 596, 598. Under the doctrine of transferred intent, the essential element is present if the accused intended to kill someone."

3. For a discussion of the law with respect to involuntary intoxication brought about by duress, see State v. Rice, 379 A.2d 140 (Me.1977), and 73 A.L.R.3d 195 (1976). Also, as regards voluntary as well as involuntary intoxication consider the following provision in the Illinois Criminal Code, 720 ILCS 5/6–3:

> A person who is in an intoxicated or drugged condition is criminally responsible for conduct unless such condition either:

(a) Negatives the existence of a mental state which is an element of the offense; or

(b) Is involuntarily produced and deprives him of substantial capacity either to appreciate the criminality of his conduct or to conform his conduct to the requirements of law.

4. For a discussion of the problem in general, see Paulsen, Intoxication as a Defense to Crime, 1961 U. of Ill.Law Forum 1.

D. THE INSANITY DEFENSE AND INCOMPETENCY TO STAND TRIAL

---

1. THE M'NAGHTEN (RIGHT–WRONG) TEST

DANIEL M'NAGHTEN'S CASE

House of Lords, 1843.
10 Cl. & F. 200, 8 Eng.Reprint 718.

The prisoner had been indicted for [the murder of Edward Drummond, private secretary to Sir Robert Peel.] ... The prisoner pleaded Not guilty.

Evidence having been given of the fact of the shooting of Mr. Drummond, and of his death in consequence thereof, witnesses were called on the part of the prisoner, to prove that he was not, at the time of committing the act, in a sound state of mind....

LORD CHIEF JUSTICE TINDAL (in his charge):—The question to be determined is, whether at the time the act in question was committed, the prisoner had or had not the use of his understanding, so as to know that he was doing a wrong or wicked act. If the jurors should be of opinion that the prisoner was not sensible, at the time he committed it, that he was violating the laws both of God and man, then he would be entitled to a verdict in his favour: but if, on the contrary, they were of opinion that when he committed the act he was in a sound state of mind, then their verdict must be against him.

Verdict, Not guilty, on the ground of insanity.

This verdict, and the question of the nature and extent of the unsoundness of mind which would excuse the commission of a felony of this sort, having been made the subject of debate in the House of Lords, it was determined to take the opinion of the Judges on the law governing such cases....

LORD CHIEF JUSTICE TINDAL.... The first question proposed by your Lordships is this: "What is the law respecting alleged crimes committed by persons afflicted with insane delusion in respect of one or more particular subjects or persons: as, for instance, where at the time of the commission of the alleged crime the accused knew he was acting contrary to law, but did the act complained of with a view, under the influence of insane delusion, of redressing or revenging some supposed grievance or injury, or of producing some supposed public benefit?"

In answer to which question, assuming that your Lordships inquiries are confined to those persons who labour under such partial delusions only, and are not in other respects insane, we are of opinion that, notwithstanding the party accused did the act complained of with a view, under the influence of insane delusion, of redressing or revenging some supposed grievance or injury, or of producing some public benefit, he is nevertheless punishable according to the nature of the crime committed, if he knew at the time of committing such crime that he was acting contrary to law; by which expression we understand your Lordships to mean the law of the land.

Your Lordships are pleased to inquire of us, secondly, "What are the proper questions to be submitted to the jury, where a person alleged to be afflicted with insane delusion respecting one or more particular subjects or persons, is charged with the commission of a crime (murder, for example), and insanity is set up as a defence?" And, thirdly, "In what terms ought the question to be left to the jury as to the prisoner's state of mind at the time when the act was committed?" And as these two questions appear to us to be more conveniently answered together, we have to submit our opinion to be, that the jurors ought to be told in all cases that every man is to be presumed to be sane, and to possess a sufficient degree of reason to be responsible for his crimes, until the contrary be proved to their satisfaction; and that to establish a defence on the ground of insanity, it must be clearly proved that, at the time of the committing of the act, the party accused was labouring under such a defect of reason, from disease of the mind, as not to know the nature and quality of the act he was doing; or, if he did know it, that he did not know he was doing what was wrong. The mode of putting the latter part of the question to the jury on these occasions has generally been, whether the accused at the time of doing the act knew the difference between right and wrong: which mode, though rarely, if ever, leading to any mistake with the jury, is not, as we conceive, so accurate when put generally and in the abstract, as when put with reference to the party's knowledge of right and wrong in respect to the very act with which he is charged. If the question were to be put as to the knowledge of the accused solely and exclusively with reference to the law of the land, it might tend to confound the jury, by inducing them to believe that an actual knowledge of the law of the land was essential in order to lead to a conviction; whereas the law is administered upon the principle that every one must be taken conclusively to know it, without proof that he does know it. If the accused was conscious that the act was one which he ought not to do, and if that act was at the same time contrary to the law of the land, he is punishable; and the usual course therefore has been to leave the question to the jury, whether the party accused had a sufficient degree of reason to know that he was doing an act that was wrong; and this course we think is correct, accompanied with such observations and explanations as the circumstances of each particular case may require.

The fourth question which your Lordships have proposed to us is this:—"If a person under an insane delusion as to existing facts, commits an offence in consequence thereof, is he thereby excused?" To which question the answer must of course depend on the nature of the delusion: but, making the same assumption as we did before, namely, that he labours under such partial delusion only, and is not in other respects insane, we think he must be considered in the same situation as to responsibility as if the facts with respect to which the delusion exists were real. For example, if under the influence of his delusion he supposes another man to be in the act of attempting to take away his life, and he kills that man, as he supposes, in self-defence, he would be exempt from punishment. If his delusion was that the deceased had inflicted a serious injury to his character and fortune, and he killed him in revenge for such supposed injury, he would be liable to punishment....

NOTES

1. There were several rules which antedated the *M'Naghten* test. See the Calendar of Close Rolls, Edward I, 7 Edward I p. 518 (1278) ("Whilst suffering from madness"); Fitz Herbert, New Natura Brevium, 233 B (1794) ("He ... who cannot account or number twenty pence nor can tell who was his father or mother, nor how old he is"); I Hale, Pleas of the Crown, 30 (1847) ("such a person as labouring under melancholy distempers hath yet ordinarily as great understanding, as ordinarily a child of fourteen years hath, is such a person as may be guilty of ... felony").

Consider finally the very old rule commonly called the "Wild Beast Test":

TRIAL OF EDWARD ARNOLD

Kingston Assizes 1724 16 How.St.T.R. 695, 764.

JUSTICE TRACY, charging the jury: ... If a man be deprived of his reason, and consequently of his intention, he cannot be guilty; ... punishment is intended for example, and to deter other persons from wicked designs; but the punishment of a madman, a person that hath no design, can have no example. This is on one side. On the other side, we must be very cautious; it is not every frantic and idle humour of a man, that will exempt him from justice, and the punishment of the law. When a man is guilty of a great offence, it must be very plain and clear, before a man is allowed such an exemption; therefore it is not every kind of frantic humour or something unaccountable in a man's actions, that points him out to be such a madman as is to be exempted from punishment: it must be a man that is totally deprived of his understanding and memory, and doth not know what he is doing, no more than an infant, than a brute, or a wild beast, such a one is never the object of punishment....

A modern use of the same analogy is in State v. Cooper, 286 N.C. 549, 213 S.E.2d 305 (1975):

"We may take judicial notice of the well known fact that a dog, a wild animal or a completely savage, uncivilized man may have the mental capacity to intend to kill and patiently to stalk his prey for that purpose. The law, however, does not impose criminal responsibility upon one who has this level of mental capacity only. For criminal responsibility it requires that the accused have, at the time of the act, the higher mental ability to distinguish between right and wrong with reference to that act. It requires less mental ability to form a purpose to do an act than to determine its moral quality. The jury, by its verdict, has conclusively established that this defendant, at the time he killed his wife and the four little children, had this higher level of mental capacity. It necessarily follows that he had the lesser, included capacity. The jury also determined that he did, in fact, premeditate and deliberate upon the intended killings. It made these determinations in the light of proper instructions as to what constitutes premeditation and deliberation. Premeditation and deliberation do not require a long, sustained period of brooding."

2. As regards the history of the M'Naghten Rules themselves, consider the following from the opinion of Chief Judge Biggs of the Third Circuit Court of Appeals in U.S. v. Currens, 290 F.2d 751 (1961), at pp. 448–449:

"... The M'Naghten Rules ... were engendered by the excitement and fear which grew out of the acquittal of Daniel M'Naghten who had attempted to assassinate Sir Robert Peel, Prime Minister of England, but who instead shot Peel's private secretary, Drummond, because M'Naghten had mistaken Drummond for Peel. The offense against Drummond followed a series of attempted assassinations of members of the English Royal House, including Queen Victoria herself, and attacks on the Queen's ministers. Some of these were considered to have grown out of Anti-Corn-Law League plots. When M'Naghten was acquitted at his trial ... public indignation, led by the Queen, ran so high that the Judges of England were called before the House of Lords to explain their conduct. A series of questions were propounded to them. Their answers, really an advisory opinion which were delivered by Lord Chief Justice Tindal for all fifteen Judges, save Mr. Justice Maule, constitute what are now known as the M'Naghten Rules...."

KNIGHTS v. STATE

Supreme Court of Nebraska, 1899.
58 Neb. 225, 78 N.W. 508.

SULLIVAN, J. In the district court of Washington county, George Knights was convicted of the crime of arson, and sentenced to imprisonment in the penitentiary for a term of 12 years....

In relation to the defense of insanity, upon which the prisoner relied, the court said to the jury, in the twelfth instruction: "You are instructed that the law presumes that every person is sane, and it is not necessary for the state to introduce evidence of sanity in the first instance. When, however, any evidence has been introduced tending to prove insanity of an accused, the burden is then upon the state to establish the fact of the accused's sanity, the same as any other material fact to be established by the state to warrant a conviction. If the testimony introduced in this case tending to prove that the defendant was insane at the time of the alleged burning described in the information raises in your mind a reasonable doubt of his sanity at the time of the alleged burning, then your verdict should be acquittal." It is contended that this instruction gave the jury to understand that the burden of establishing his insanity rested upon the defendant up to a certain point in the trial, and was then shifted from him to the state.... [T]here can be no room to doubt that the court, in the instruction now under consideration, stated the correct doctrine in unmistakable terms. In this case the jury were informed that the law presumes sanity, but that, when the defendant produced evidence tending to prove insanity, the state was charged with a burden which did not previously rest upon it. The court did not say nor imply that the burden of proving insanity was ever on the accused, or that there was a shifting of the burden from him to the state. The substance of what the court did say was that, when the legal presumption of sanity encountered opposing evidence, the law then, for the first time, imposed on the state the onus of showing the prisoner's sanity by the proper measure of proof....

NOTE

It is constitutionally proper to require the defendant to prove his defense of insanity. Leland v. Oregon, 343 U.S. 790, 72 S.Ct. 1002 (1952) (beyond a reasonable doubt); Patterson v. New York, 432 U.S. 197, 97 S.Ct. 2319 (1977) (preponderance of evidence). In recent years an increasing number of states have adopted provisions placing the burden of proof on defendant. In California this was done by public referendum. (Sec. 4 of The Victim's Bill of Rights adopted 1982)

PEOPLE v. WOOD

Court of Appeals of New York, 1962.
12 N.Y.2d 69, 187 N.E.2d 116.

FROESSEL, JUDGE. On July 4, 1960 the bodies of John Rescigno and Frederick Sess, aged 62 and about 77 respectively, were discovered in the "little house" they shared in Astoria, Queens County. In addition to other wounds, Sess had sustained multiple skull fractures. On Rescigno's body were about 16 wounds; his jugular vein had been severed. Defendant, Frederick Charles Wood, aged 50, was convicted of murder first degree (two counts) and sentenced to death.

Wood was taken into custody on July 5th. During the automobile trip to the station house, he told a detective that he had received the cut on his right thumb during a barroom altercation, but when asked the same question later at the police station, he replied that he had been cut by glass fragments while striking Rescigno with a bottle. He thereupon admitted having killed Sess and Rescigno on June 30, 1960, and gave a particularized account of how and why he did so. This statement, recorded in shorthand, transcribed, and signed by defendant, was admitted in evidence at trial without objection.

Defendant made no attempt to controvert the evidence which overwhelmingly established that he killed Rescigno and Sess. His sole defense was insanity. Ordinarily, under these circumstances, we would say little more about the evidence relating to the commission of the crimes. Here, however, since it is indicative of Wood's state of mind on June 30th, we set forth in some detail his statement made to an Assistant District Attorney on July 5th.

Almost at the outset of the interrogation, Wood was asked if he had done something "wrong" in Astoria on the night of June 30th. He replied that he had, that he "knocked off those two guys", "did them in", "killed two men". Defendant then related that at about 3:00 p.m. on June 30th, while he was panhandling on Broadway, New York City, he saw John Rescigno, whom he had never met before, leaving a tavern. Wood had panhandled two dollars, but "was looking for more". He "figured" Rescigno was a "lush" and "might be good for a score". Rescigno purchased a bottle of wine. Defendant obtained an invitation from Rescigno to stay at the latter's house that night. He "figured" he "could make a score" because Rescigno "had been drinking like hell", and defendant "knew what the score was and he didn't".

During the subway ride to Astoria, Rescigno said he was a "pensioner", showed Wood his social security card, and "intimate[d] he has quite a bit of money", at which point defendant "developed an idea I would try to take [rob] him during the evening sometime". When they arrived at the house between 7:00 and 8:00 p.m., the "apartment" was dark, and Rescigno did not turn on the lights. At the time, defendant saw Sess in bed in a bedroom.

They drank some beer; Rescigno took a drink of muscatel "and he gets silly drunk", "mumbles unintelligibly", but Wood finally understood that he suggested they "go to bed together". Continuing: "... I don't like degenerates. I always had a distaste for them.... I knew right then he sealed his fate. I know I'm going to knock him off that night. Not only for his money but for the satisfaction of knocking off a degenerate." But he could not "knock him off right away because [he had] to figure out the angles". Therefore Wood went "along with the gag", gave Rescigno "a mushy kiss", suggested they take it easy, have some more drinks, and told him he was going to stay all night.

Defendant went to the kitchen to find a weapon. Because it was dark and he did not want to turn on the lights, the only weapon he could find was an empty beer bottle. He took the bottle and a package of cigarettes to Rescigno's bedroom, offered Rescigno a cigarette because "just as soon as he reached for the cigarette I had the intention of knocking his brains out, which I did". After rendering the victim unconscious, Wood severed his jugular vein with a piece of jagged glass from the broken bottle. Blood was spurting out, but Wood stood to one side in order to keep from soiling his clothes.

After taking two or three dollars from Rescigno's clothes, Wood remembered a man sleeping in the other room, whom he "figured" he "might as well finish ... off just on the grounds he might be a degenerate also". Defendant returned to the kitchen "figuring out the best weapon to use on this guy". He found a heavy coal shovel, lifted it "to see if it had the right amount of heft", beat Sess on the head with the shovel, then "flailed him unmercifully" with a chair. Wood, in his own language, "was satisfied in my mind he couldn't recover".

Thereupon defendant went to the kitchen, where he washed, and combed his hair—"I could pass for a Sunday school teacher any place on the face of the earth". He then returned to the bedroom, searched Sess' pockets looking for money but "unfortunately" found none. Defendant did not wish to remain long because he felt that Sess' "loud [dying] noise" and the barking of a dog "would tip off the neighbors that something was *wrong*" (emphasis supplied).

Before departing, however, Wood wrote two notes which were found under a cigarette holder on a table in the kitchen. One reads: "And God bless the Parole Board. They're real intelligent people"; the other states: "Now, aren't these two murders a dirty shame. I'm so-o sorry." Wood engaged in this "little caper" to "dress the two knock offs up a bit", and because he has "a flair for the dramatics at times".

The first witness for the *defense* was the Assistant District Attorney, who had testified for the People regarding Wood's statement. He now related what Wood told him during the time the statement was being transcribed. Defendant spoke, among other things, about three murders he had committed in the past. He subsequently described them orally and in writing to the psychiatrists who examined him at Bellevue Hospital prior to trial, and who testified with reference thereto. In 1925 when he was about 15 years old, and because "he couldn't have her", Wood injected arsenic into some cream puffs which he sent to a girl, Cynthia Longo, who died as a result thereof. Thereafter, when he was about 21 years old, he bludgeoned 140 times and stabbed to death a woman he encountered one night. Having contracted syphilis and gonorrhea from another woman, thus becoming angry at women generally, he picked this stranger to kill.

In 1942 defendant murdered John Loman because the latter made a disparaging remark about Wood's girl friend. Wood caused Loman to become very drunk, attempted to asphyxiate him with gas, and when this failed to achieve the desired result, he bashed in Loman's head. With the help of his girl friend, Wood hid the body, planning to dismember it later and dispose of the parts. When arrested, he denied his guilt, and the authorities had a " 'hell of a time' " attempting to prove premeditation. Though convicted of murder second degree, defendant said he was " 'actually guilty of Murder in the First Degree' ". He was sentenced to from 20 years to life, only to be paroled less than a month before the present homicides.

Defendant further told the Assistant District Attorney that after the jury's verdict in the Loman case, but prior to sentence, he slashed his wrists in a suicide "attempt", because he did not want to spend a lot of time in prison, and felt he could obtain better treatment in a hospital. He was sent to Dannemora State Hospital, where he enjoyed himself and was allowed to play cards, but when certain privileges were withdrawn, he became dissatisfied and felt it was time to tell the psychiatrist he was not insane. Defendant boasted that "Anytime I wanted to, I knew I could get out of there because I wasn't insane"; he "could fool anybody", he was "fooling the psychiatrist all along" and "could do it anytime". He succeeded.

After the hospital released him, Wood was transferred to prison, where he determined to and did become a model prisoner as he sorely wanted to gain freedom. Paroled and assigned to Albany district, Wood obtained employment in a laundry. He was not happy there, however, knew that eventually he would begin drinking again, in which event he would lose his job and be returned to prison, and, therefore, decided to lose himself in New York City.

Although the four defense psychiatrists testified in answer to hypothetical questions that on June 30th defendant was laboring under such defect of reason as to know neither the nature nor the quality of his acts nor that they were wrong, their conclusions were largely weakened by lengthy and vigorous cross-examinations. By contrast, the People's two psychiatric experts, who testified that Wood was legally sane, were together asked but six questions on cross-examination, to two of which objections were sustained.

When the defense psychiatrists had testified, defendant, against the advice of his attorneys, took the stand, after having been duly cautioned, and stated that, although he was "very sick" while at Bellevue for examination, "at the time I committed the crime, the two murders, I knew the nature and I knew the quality of my act. I was sane then, perfectly sane, and I am perfectly sane now". He made this statement, he testified, because he had "been living on borrowed time" since 1926, and furthermore he did not "relish the prospect of going back to prison for the rest of my life or to any insane asylum". He was not cross-examined.

Defendant now merely urges that the People failed to establish beyond a reasonable doubt that he knew the acts were wrong. We now consider this contention. In substance, the expert testimony for the defense was that Wood had schizophrenic reaction, an illness from which he had suffered since about 1926, though "not probably an organic illness". In this connection, the defense psychiatrists stated that although defendant's memory was good, his sensorium clear, he was unaware of the full significance and consequences of his acts, though he knew their physical nature and quality, and that his judgment was impaired, his reasoning defective. Further, defendant told the psychiatrists at Bellevue that he considered himself to be "God's emissary" to take and to save life, and that he was presently charged with the duty of seeking out and killing those whom he believed were degenerates. Their cross-examination established beyond peradventure that Wood knew it was against the law to kill a human being.

One of the People's psychiatrists, Dr. Winkler, who first examined Wood in July, 1960 at Kings County Hospital and interviewed him in April, 1961, testified that defendant had a "highly pathological personality . . . a severe personality disorder", which manifested itself early in his life, but had not "deteriorated" since. Dr. Winkler noted that though defendant had been subjected to extensive hospital observation during the course of his lifetime, the diagnosis of schizophrenic reaction was made *for the first time* at Bellevue in the Fall of 1960. The witness further stated that Wood cannot be called "mentally ill or psychotic", and that his moral judgment was not distorted by illness or disease, but had "never developed". Another "peculiarity", Dr. Winkler testified, was defendant's "inability to control his impulses", a pathological sign but not "legal insanity". During three weeks' observation at the hospital in July, 1960, Wood had not shown any evidence of a psychotic condition.

Regarding the "God's emissary" delusion, Dr. Winkler entertained "definite doubts" that this was "a firm, fixed belief" and gave his reasons therefor. It is of some significance that Wood made this assertion for the *first* time in a psychiatric examination during the latter part of January or in February, 1961, seven months after the homicides with which he was charged, and following the administration of sodium amytal, a drug which, according to Dr. Winkler, might induce delusions. The Kings County Hospital report of July, 1960 does not contain a reference to this delusion. Most significant is the fact that Wood did not mention the delusion in his July 5th statement, but admitted he did something "wrong" on June 30th, namely, killed two men. Indeed, he stated then that *he* "always had a distaste" for degenerates, and had killed Rescigno partly "for the satisfaction of" killing a degenerate, and partly to steal money. It may also be noted that the "God's emissary" delusion and degeneracy had nothing to do with his previous three murders.

Moreover, he did not just kill Rescigno when he ascertained the latter was a degenerate, but first had to "figure out the angles", made sure his intended victim was drunk, and then distracted him by offering a cigarette. After the killings, defendant did not tarry long, being apprehensive that Sess' dying noises and the barking of a dog would alert neighbors to the fact "that something was *wrong*" (emphasis supplied). The People's psychiatrist, Dr. D'Angelo, supported Dr. Winkler in his view that defendant knew the nature and quality of his acts and that they were wrong.

In People v. Schmidt, . . . Judge Cardozo, discussing the meaning of the word "wrong" as used in section 1120, Consol.Laws, c. 40 of the Penal Law, held that there are certain circumstances in which the word "ought not to be limited to legal wrong." Continuing: "Knowledge that an act is forbidden by law will in most cases permit the inference of knowledge that, according to the accepted standards of mankind, it is also condemned as an offense against good morals. Obedience to the law is itself a moral duty. If, however, there is an insane delusion that God has appeared to the defendant and ordained the commission of a crime, we think it cannot be said of the offender that he knows the act to be wrong. It is not enough, to relieve from criminal liability, that the prisoner is morally depraved [citation]. It is not enough that he has views of right and wrong at variance with those that find expression in the law. The variance must have its origin in some disease of the mind.... Cases will doubtless arise where criminals will take shelter behind a professed belief that their crime was ordained by God.... We can safely leave such fabrications to the common sense of juries." ...

As defendant concedes in his brief, the Trial Judge correctly charged the jury on the meaning of the word "wrong" when he stated: "When it speaks of the defendant's ignorance of his act as wrong, the law does not mean to permit the individual to be his own judge of what is right or wrong. It says that the individual has sufficient knowledge that an act was wrong if its perpetrator knows that his act is against the law and against the commonly accepted standards of morality and conduct which prevail in the community of mankind. He must know that his act was contrary to the laws of God and man." The Trial Judge then stated an example which is so strikingly parallel to defendant's claim that the jury could not have failed to see the point.

Of course the question as to whether Wood knew it was wrong to kill when he killed Sess and Rescigno was a question of fact for the jury, and, as we stated in People v. Horton, ... "if the record in its entirety presents a fair conflict in the evidence, or if conflicting inferences can properly be drawn from it, '... the determination of the jury will not be interfered with, unless it is clearly against the weight of evidence, or appears to have been influenced by passion, prejudice, mistake or corruption.' ... We see nothing in the record to take the instant case out of this general rule. Of course the fact that a defendant was suffering from some type of mental disorder ..., or that he had a psychopathic personality ..., or that his "moral perceptions were of low order" ..., or that he had an irresistible impulse to commit the crime ..., does not immunize him from criminal responsibility....

There was abundant evidence here upon which the jury reasonably could have rejected entirely the defense that Wood considered himself to be "God's emissary". Moreover, the jury, having been properly instructed, could reasonably have found that defendant was operating under a standard of morality he had set up for himself and which applied only to him. The law does not excuse for such moral depravity or "views of right and wrong at variance with those that find expression in the law" ... While the very nature and circumstances of the present homicides, as well as the expert testimony on both sides, make clear that Wood was not well balanced mentally, the weight of evidence clearly supports the determination, implicit in the verdict, that he knew not only the nature and quality of his acts, but also that they were wrong, as that term was correctly defined and exemplified by the trial court. Under these circumstances we have no right to interfere with the verdict....

Defendant also contends that he was denied a fair trial on the issue of insanity by reason of various rulings of the court and certain conduct and comment of the prosecutor. One of these contentions relates to the remarks of the prosecutor in his summation concerning two of the defense psychiatrists. Specifically he referred to them as "the two happiness boys", as "those two idiots—I am sorry, those two psychiatrists"; he "charged" them with being "ignorant, stupid, incompetent", and scoffed at their titles of "Diplomate". These remarks were clearly improper, and cannot be justified or excused by anything that transpired earlier in the trial. Although we have been disturbed by this aspect of the case, we have concluded that these remarks, now complained of, did not deprive defendant of a fair trial. Only the first of these comments was objected to at the trial, and it was stricken. Counsel did not object to the summation upon the ground that it or any part thereof was inflammatory, nor make a motion for a mistrial. While objection need not be voiced in a capital case to preserve a question for our review, we are of the opinion, on the present record, that the prosecutor's remarks had no influence upon the jury.

We have examined the other contentions of the defendant and find no merit to them.

The judgment appealed from should be affirmed.

FULD, JUDGE (dissenting). I agree with the court that, upon the record before us, the People have established that the defendant was legally sane under the law of this State as it now stands ..., but I cannot refrain from observing that the result demonstrates the unreality, if not the invalidity, of our present standards for determining criminal responsibility. This case serves to confirm the view, frequently expressed over the years, that section 1120 of the Penal Law should be amended and the "right-wrong" test which now controls our decisions changed.

However, since the issue of the defendant's insanity under section 1120 seems to me so extremely close, I do not believe that we may disregard the prosecutor's concededly inexcusable and improper remarks, relating to the defense psychiatrists, as technical error under section 542 of the Code of Criminal Procedure.

DESMOND, C.J., and VAN VOORHIS, J., dissent and vote to reverse and to dismiss the indictment upon the ground that by the clear weight of evidence this defendant is insane under the rule of section 1120 of the Penal Law in which connection we express our strong disapproval of the prosecutor's inexcusable ridicule of the court-appointed psychiatrists.

NOTE

In 1965 New York legislature changed the insanity test to the American Law Institute test discussed later in Section 4.

2. THE IRRESISTIBLE IMPULSE TEST

As a supplement to the M'Naghten test, a number of jurisdictions have adopted the so-called "irresistible impulse" test. Under that test, the jury is instructed that it must acquit the defendant if it finds that the diseased mind of the accused rendered him incapable of exercising the normal governing power of the will so as to control his actions under the compulsion of an insane impulse to act. "The phrase irresistible impulse was rarely used in court—the test was framed in terms of loss, as a result of mental disease, of the power to choose between right and wrong and that loss of power to choose was the cause of the crime." The rule is not a recent one, since an instruction based on the same concept was given as early as 1844 in a Massachusetts case. Chief Justice Shaw's jury instruction in Commonwealth v. Rogers read, in part:

> If then it is proved, to the satisfaction of the jury, that the mind of the accused was in a diseased and unsound state, the question will be, whether the disease existed to so high a degree, that for the time being it overwhelmed the reason, conscience, and judgment, and whether the prisoner, in committing the homicide acted from an irresistible and uncontrollable impulse, if so, then the act was not the act of a voluntary agent, but the involuntary act of the body, without the concurrence of a mind directing it.

Consider the following paragraph from Moenssens, Moses & Inbau, Scientific Evidence in Criminal Cases, (2d ed. 1978), Chapter 3 on "Forensic Psychiatry", § 3.03(2):

> The motivation for formulating the irresistible impulse rule arose from the psychiatrist's difficulty in perceiving the various forms of compulsive behavior within the M'Naghten definition of legal insanity. Compulsive behavior such as kleptomania, pyromania, and dipsomania occurs when the actor does know right from wrong and does contemplate the consequences of his normative violation, knowing it is wrong, but nevertheless persists in the act because of an inner force which he is powerless to resist. Psychiatrists might not categorize this individual as insane in the right-wrong sense; consequently, if such behavior is to be exempted from responsibility, the irresistible impulse is a necessary adjunct to *M'Naghten*.

3. THE DURHAM TEST

In Durham v. United States, 94 U.S.App.D.C. 228, 214 F.2d 862 (1954) defendant Durham, an individual with a long history of mental illness, appealed from his conviction for housebreaking on the grounds that the existing tests in the District of Columbia for determining criminal responsibility (the right-wrong test supplemented by the irresistible impulse test) were not satisfactory criteria for determining criminal responsibility.

The Court of Appeals for the District of Columbia accepted the argument of a large number of medico-legal writers that the right-wrong test is based upon an entirely obsolete and misleading conception of the nature of insanity. It accepted the view of psychiatry that man is an integrated personality of which reason is only one element, not the sole determinant of his conduct. Therefore the right-wrong test, because it considers knowledge or reason alone, is an inadequate guide to mental responsibility for criminal behavior. The fundamental objection to the right-wrong test is that it is made to rest upon any particular symptom. In attempting to define insanity in terms of a symptom, courts have assumed an impossible role.

Turning to the "irresistible impulse test", the court found that test inadequate because based upon the misleading implication that 'diseased mental condition(s)' produce only sudden, momentary or spontaneous inclinations to commit unlawful acts. Such a test gives no recognition to mental illness characterized by brooding and reflection.

Finally, the court concluded that a broader test should be adopted and formulated the rule that an accused is not criminally responsible if his unlawful act was the "product of mental disease or mental defect". It went on to say, "We use 'disease' in the sense of a condition which is considered capable of either improving or deteriorating. We use 'defect' in the sense of a condition which is not considered capable of either improving or deteriorating and which may be either congenital, or the result of injury, or the residual effect of a physical or mental disease".

In essence this test permits a jury to find a defendant not guilty by reason of insanity if it believes beyond a reasonable doubt that the accused suffered from a mental disease or defect and that there was sufficient causal connection between the mental abnormality and the accused's unlawful act to excuse the defendant from criminal responsibility for it.

4. THE AMERICAN LAW INSTITUTE (A.L.I.) TEST, AND THE BRAWNER SUPPLEMENTATION

The response of other jurisdictions to *Durham* was less than enthusiastic. Perhaps this was due in part to the increasing popularity of the A.L.I. test. The American Law Institute, in Tentative Draft No. 4 of its Model Penal Code, proposed the following insanity test:

> (1) A person is not responsible for criminal conduct if at the time of such conduct as a result of mental disease or defect he lacks substantial capacity either to appreciate the criminality of his conduct or to conform his conduct to the requirements of law.
>
> (2) The terms "mental disease or defect" do not include an abnormality manifested only by repeated criminal or otherwise anti-social conduct.

As the A.L.I. test became adopted in more jurisdictions, the *Durham* rule lost what little stature it had achieved. Then on June 23, 1972, the Court of Appeals for the District of Columbia, in United States v. Brawner, 471 F.2d 969 (D.C.Cir.1972), abandoned *Durham* and accepted the A.L.I. test. The court continued to adhere, however, to the definition of "mental disease or defect" it had earlier articulated in McDonald v. United States, 114 U.S.App.D.C. 120, 312 F.2d 847 (1962): "mental disease or defect includes any abnormal condition of the mind which substantially affects mental or emotional processes and substantially impairs behavior controls." The principal reason for the *Brawner* departure from *Durham* was the undue dominance gained by experts giving testimony on insanity. This dominance occurred because of the broad area of relevance encompassed by the *Durham's* "product" concept which "did not signify a reasonably identifiable common ground that was also shared by the nonlegal experts, and the laymen serving on the jury as the representatives of the community." Accordingly, the court decided:

> The experts have meaningful information to impart, not only to the existence of mental illness or not, but also on its relationship to the incident charged as an offense. In the interest of justice this valued information should be available, and should not be lost or blocked by requirements that unnaturally restrict communication between the experts and the jury. The more we have pondered the problem the more convinced we have become that the sound solution lies not in further shaping of the *Durham* "product" approach in more refined molds, but in adopting the ALI's formulation as the linchpin of our jurisprudence.
>
> The ALI's formulation retains the core requirement of a meaningful relationship between the mental illness and the incident charged. The language in the ALI rule is sufficiently in the common ken that its use in the courtroom, or in preparation for trial, permits a reasonable three-way communication—between (a) the law-trained, judges and lawyers; (b) the experts and (c) the jurymen—without insisting on a vocabulary that is either stilted or stultified, or conducive to a testimonial mystique permitting expert dominance and encroachment on the jury's function. There is no indication in the available literature that any such untoward development has attended the reasonably widespread adoption of the ALI rule in the Federal courts and a substantial number of state courts.

With respect to the caveat paragraph in subsection (2) of the Model Penal Code test, which excludes from the concept of mental disease or defect abnormalities that are manifested only by repeated criminal or otherwise anti-social conduct, the *Brawner* court took notice of the fact that there was a split among the jurisdiction which had adopted the ALI test concerning this provision. Some courts had concluded to adopt the caveat, which excluded the defense of insanity for the so-called psychopathic personalities or sociopaths, while other jurisdictions had specifically decided to omit it from the test. The *Brawner* case pragmatically adopted the caveat paragraph as a rule for application by the judge, to avoid miscarriage of justice, but not for inclusion in instructions to the jury.

NOTES

1. The court's opinion in the 1972 case of United States v. Brawner was written by Circuit Judge Leventhal. Chief Judge Bazelon, who had written the Durham v. United States opinion in 1954 wrote a separate opinion in *Brawner,* concurring in part and dissenting in part. He stated in part: "We are unanimous in our decision today to abandon the formulation of criminal responsibility adopted eighteen years ago in Durham.... But the adoption of this new test [ALI] is largely an anticlimax, for even though *Durham's* language survived until today's decision, the significant differences between our approach and the approach of the ALI test vanished many years ago". Chief Judge Bazelon then proceeds to dispel the notion that the court's action achieved "uniformity" in the federal courts and also expresses the pessimistic view that the ALI test will not produce significantly better results than those obtained under *Durham.* The two opinions, read together (and some 70 pages long) provide an excellent analysis of the insanity defense problem.

2. Virtually all federal courts adopted and used the ALI test until 1984 when Congress eliminated the defense insofar as it interfered with one's ability to conform conduct to the requirements of law. 18 U.S.C. 17.

Many states, too, have adopted the A.L.I. formulation, whether by statute (e.g., Illinois, Maryland, Montana, Vermont), or by judicial decision, as in State v. White, 93 Idaho 153, 456 P.2d 797 (1969), Hill v. State, 252 Ind. 601, 251 N.E.2d 429 (1969), Terry v. Commonwealth, 371 S.W.2d 862 (Ky.1963); and Commonwealth v. McHoul, 352 Mass. 544, 226 N.E.2d 556 (1967). Some courts, on the other hand, have rejected the A.L.I. test and retained M'Naghten, (e.g., State v. White, 60 Wn.2d 551, 374 P.2d 942 (1962)). Compare: State v. Griffin, 99 Ariz. 43, 406 P.2d 397 (1965); State v. Lucas, 30 N.J. 37, 152 A.2d 50 (1959); State v. Harkness, 160 N.W.2d 324 (Iowa 1968); Kuk v. State, 80 Nev. 291, 392 P.2d 630 (1964); People v. Drew, 22 Cal.3d 333, 149 Cal.Rptr. 275, 583 P.2d 1318 (1978).

3. A few states have enacted statutory or code provisions adopting slightly modified versions of the A.L.I. text.

The Illinois Criminal Code (720 ILCS 5/6–2) provides as follows:

> (a) A person is not criminally responsible for conduct if at the time of such conduct, as a result of mental disease or mental defect, he lacks substantial capacity either to appreciate the criminality of his conduct or to conform his conduct to the requirements of law.
>
> (b) The terms "mental disease or mental defect" do not include an abnormality manifested only by repeated criminal or otherwise antisocial conduct.

The New York Penal Law (§ 30.05) reads as follows:

> 1. A person is not criminally responsible for conduct if at the time of such conduct, as a result of mental disease or defect, he lacks substantial capacity to know or appreciate either:

(a) The nature and consequence of such conduct; or

(b) That such conduct was wrong.

HOLLOWAY v. UNITED STATES

United States Court of Appeals, District of Columbia Circuit, 1945.
80 U.S.App.D.C. 3, 148 F.2d 665.

[Defendant was convicted of rape. He appealed on the sole ground that the record disclosed such substantial doubt of his sanity that the verdict should be set aside. The record disclosed that in 1940 the defendant was held in Gallinger Hospital for mental observation. Later he was confined in a federal hospital as a mental patient. And, in 1943, he was again committed to Gallinger Hospital as a mental patient. He was later released, not as recovered, in the custody of his mother, with further directions for the treatment of his mental disorders. Some months after this release he raped two women on the same day. Following is the Court of Appeals' opinion affirming the defendant's conviction.]

ARNOLD, J. The application of [the tests for insanity], however they are phrased, to a borderline case can be nothing more than a moral judgment that it is just or unjust to blame the defendant for what he did. Legal tests of criminal insanity are not and cannot be the result of scientific analysis or objective judgment. There is no objective standard by which such a judgment of an admittedly abnormal offender can be measured. They must be based on the instinctive sense of justice of ordinary men....

[W]hen psychiatrists attempt on the witness stand to reconcile the therapeutic standards of their own art with the moral judgment of the criminal law they become confused. Thus it is common to find groups of distinguished scientists of the mind testifying on both sides and in all directions with positiveness and conviction. This is not because they are unreliable or because those who testify on one side are more skillful or learned than those who testify on the other. It is rather because to the psychiatrist mental cases are a series of imperceptible gradations from the mild psychopath to the extreme psychotic, whereas criminal law allows for no gradations. It requires a final decisive moral judgment of the culpability of the accused. For purposes of conviction there is no twilight zone between abnormality and insanity. An offender is wholly sane or wholly insane.

A complete reconciliation between the medical tests of insanity and the moral tests of criminal responsibility is impossible. The purposes are different; the assumptions behind the two standards are different. For that reason the principal function of a psychiatrist who testifies on the mental state of an abnormal offender is to inform the jury of the character of his mental disease. The psychiatrist's moral judgment reached on the basis of his observations is relevant. But it cannot bind the jury except within broad limits. To command respect criminal law must not offend against the common belief that men who talk rationally are in most cases morally responsible for what they do.

The institution which applies our inherited ideas of moral responsibility to individuals prosecuted for crime is a jury of ordinary men. These men must be told that in order to convict they should have no reasonable doubt of the defendant's sanity. After they have declared by their verdict that they have no such doubt their judgment should not be disturbed on the ground it is contrary to expert psychiatric opinion. Psychiatry offers us no standard for measuring the validity of the jury's moral judgment as to culpability. To justify a reversal circumstances must be such that the verdict shocks the conscience of the court.

NOTES

There occasionally arise attempted defenses based upon the assumption that a person cannot stop himself from crime because of certain physical or mental conditions which may not be mental diseases. Three examples suffice:

1. Involuntary Subliminal Television Intoxication

In the case of Zamora v. State, 361 So.2d 776 (Fla.App.1978), counsel for the defendant, a 15 year old boy charged with murder in the course of a burglary and robbery, had sought to prove that the crime was the result of violence he had often watched on television. The appellate court upheld the trial judge's ruling in which he refused to allow a college psychology professor to testify as to the effect of such television viewing on children, and that such TV shows could have affected the defendant's ability to distinguish right from wrong.

2. Automatism

The contention has been made that a person should not be considered guilty of a crime if at the time of the act he was not conscious of what he was doing even though he was capable of action. This may occur in persons with epilepsy, concussions, hypoglycemia, or sleepwalking. While courts recognize the defense as valid in theory, it rarely succeeds. See Fulcher v. State, 633 P.2d 142 (Wyo.1981); People v. Grant, 71 Ill.2d 551, 17 Ill.Dec. 814, 377 N.E.2d 4 (1978).

3. Multiple Personality

The very rare and quite serious mental problem of multiple personalities surfaces in criminal cases when the accused claims another one of his personalities, not the one presently before the Court, committed the offense. Though this defense is not often made and, when made, rarely believed by juries, some courts have found a novel resolution. They hold that if the personality which committed the crime was legally sane then the accused is liable whether or not the personality in court is the same as the one committing the crime. See State v. Rodrigues, 67 Hawaii 70, 679 P.2d 615 (1984); State v. Grimsley, 3 Ohio App.3d 265, 444 N.E.2d 1071 (1982); Kirkland v. State, 166 Ga.App. 478, 304 S.E.2d 561 (1983).

5. DIMINISHED RESPONSIBILITY

For a number of years, in a few jurisdictions, a defense of partial insanity or diminished responsibility was permitted. It was offered when an accused was not legally insane but was sufficiently deranged so that he might not be able to form a specific intent required for conviction under a particular statute. For example, an accused may claim he was mentally unable to form a premeditated intent to kill and thus unable to commit murder, although still capable of manslaughter. Like intoxication, diminished responsibility could, in some places, be used to defeat a charge of a crime requiring specific intent. Unlike an insanity defense, diminished responsibility leads to freedom or a lesser sentence and not to commitment to a mental institution. Many states simply reject the defense. See State v. Wilcox, 70 Ohio St.2d 182, 436 N.E.2d 523 (1982). The only state in which it was widely used has abolished it, Cal.Penal Code § 25(a) (West's 1982). Some states have narrow statutory diminished capacity defenses. See State v. Breakiron, 108 N.J. 591, 532 A.2d 199 (1987). It is available in federal cases, United States v. Twine, 853 F.2d 676 (9th Cir.1988).

6. THE FUTURE OF THE INSANITY DEFENSE

There has been a great deal of controversy over the scope of the insanity defense in recent years. Some, but not all of it, was generated by the insanity verdict in United States v. Hinckley (Attempted assassination of President Reagan). A strong argument is made in favor of the defense on its merits along with suggestions that improved administration of the defense in court would resolve the admitted deficits of the defense, all in Goldstein. The Insanity Defense, 222–25 (1967).

One idea of many years standing is to abolish the defense and allow evidence of mental disease to be heard only on the question of appropriate sentence. See Wigmore, "The Deranged or Defective Delinquent," in Illinois Crime Survey (1929); Morris, Psychiatry and the Dangerous Criminal, 41 So.Cal.L.Rev. 514 (1968). Psychiatrists have also doubted the validity of the defense. Perr, "Is the Insanity Defense Unconscionable," 20 J.For.Sci. 169 (1975); Clanon, et al. "Less Insanity in the Courts," 68 A.B.A.J. 824 (1982). It is an open question whether this course of action would be constitutional. One court found it constitutional. State v. Korell, 213 Mont. 316, 690 P.2d 992 (1984).

Another idea is to place the burden of proof upon the defendant, which notion was discussed in the Note after Knights v. State, supra, p. 438.

A third suggestion is to reject the A.L.I. test and return to a form of the M'Naghten test of insanity, i.e., whether the defendant, as a result of mental disease or defect, was unable to appreciate the wrongfulness of his or her conduct at the time of the offense. The American Bar Association supports this test. Similarly, California has changed its rule to approve the defense "when the accused person proves by a preponderance of the evidence that he or she was incapable of knowing or understanding the nature and quality of his or her act and of distinguishing right from wrong at the time of the commission of the offense,"

West's Ann.Cal.Penal Code § 25(b). Congress adopted this course of action in 1984 by amending 18 U.S.C.A. § 20 to read

> (a) *Affirmative Defense*—It is an affirmative defense to a prosecution under any federal statute that, at the time of the commission of the acts constituting the offense, the defendant, as the result of severe mental disease or defect, was unable to appreciate the nature and quality or the wrongfulness of his acts. Mental disease or defect does not otherwise constitute a defense.
>
> (b) *Burden of Proof*—The defendant has the burden of proving the defense of insanity by clear and convincing evidence.

A fourth proposal is to provide a judge or jury with the option of finding a defendant "Guilty but Mentally Ill" (G.M.I.) instead of "Not Guilty by Reason of Insanity" (N.G.I.) One found to be G.M.I. is sentenced just as though he was convicted outright, but the state is obligated to provide mental treatment until he recovers, at which time he serves the remainder of his sentence. Such statutes are criticized on the grounds that there is no way a reasonable person can judge between "insanity" which excuses conduct, and some lesser but still significant degree of "mental illness" which does not. Such attacks have failed in court. See, Taylor v. State, 440 N.E.2d 1109 (Ind.1982); People v. Rone, 109 Mich.App. 702, 311 N.W.2d 835 (1981).

7. INCOMPETENCY

1. *Incompetency to Stand Trial.* A person cannot be brought to trial if his mental condition at that time is such that he is "unable to understand the nature and purpose of the proceedings against him, or to assist in his defense". Whenever that condition is found to exist (by a judge or jury), he will be committed to a mental institution and can only be tried thereafter if and when he improves sufficiently to satisfy the above stated requirements.

2. *Incompetency at Time of Scheduled Execution.* In death penalty cases there can be no execution if prior to the time of the scheduled event the sentenced person develops a mental condition that will not permit him "to understand the nature and purpose" of the sentence of death.

Chapter 8

UNCOMPLETED CRIMINAL CONDUCT AND CRIMINAL COMBINATIONS

A. UNCOMPLETED CRIMINAL CONDUCT

1. ATTEMPT

PEOPLE v. PALUCH

Appellate Court of Illinois, Second District, 1966.
78 Ill.App.2d 356, 222 N.E.2d 508.

DAVIS, JUSTICE. The defendant, Michael Paluch, was charged, in the Circuit Court of the 18th Judicial Circuit, DuPage County, with attempting to practice barbering without a certificate of registration as a barber in violation of Ill.Rev.Stat.1965, ch. 16¾, par. 14.92(b)(1). The case was tried before the court without a jury and the defendant was found guilty as charged and a fine in the sum of $25 was imposed. The defendant contends that the evidence was not sufficient to sustain the judgment.

On November 5, 1965, Ernie Pinkston, an agent of the barber's union, went to a barber shop located in Glen Ellyn. It was 9:00 A.M. and the shop was not yet open. He then saw the defendant unlock the rear door and enter the shop. Shortly thereafter, he went to the front door and asked the defendant if the shop was open. The defendant unlocked the door, admitted Pinkston, walked over to the barber chair, put on his smock and offered the chair to Pinkston. The defendant had his own barber tools—clipping shears, razors and combs.

Pinkston then showed the defendant his business card and asked to see his license. The defendant twice motioned to a particular license which, in fact, was not his. No one else was in the shop at the time. When later asked if he worked at the shop, the defendant answered "yes" and admitted that he had no license.

Both the defendant and the State refer to the Criminal Code of 1961, ... with reference to the elements necessary to establish the offense of an "attempt," which provides:

> "A person commits an attempt when, with intent to commit a specific offense, he does any act which constitutes a substantial step toward the commission of that offense."

Two elements must be present to constitute an attempt: (1) an intent to commit a specific offense, and (2) an act which is a substantial step towards its commission. The defendant contends that all that can be shown by the record in this case is a mere preparation to do something, but that no act constituting a substantial step toward barbering was committed....

As pointed out in the Committee Comments to par. 8–4 of the Criminal Code ... the determination of when the preparation to commit an offense ceases and the perpetration of the offense begins, is a troublesome problem. The distinction between the preparation and the attempt is largely a matter of degree, and whether certain given conduct constitutes an actual attempt is a question unique to each particular case.

In order to constitute an attempt, it is not requisite that the act of the defendant is necessarily the last deed immediately preceding that which would render the substantive crime complete.... In Commonwealth v. Peaslee, 177 Mass. 267, 59 N.E. 55 (1901), Mr. Justice Holmes, as Chief Justice of the Supreme Judicial Court of Massachusetts, discussed the considerations necessary in determining whether there were sufficient acts to constitute an attempt to commit an offense under circumstances where further acts were required to perpetrate the offense. He there noted that the acts may then be nothing more than preparation to commit an offense which is not punishable, but also stated that given preparations may constitute an attempt, the determining factor being a matter of degree. As illustrative of this comment, his opinion states:

> "If the preparation comes very near to the accomplishment of the act, the intent to complete it renders the crime so probable that the act will be a misdemeanor, although there is still a locus poenitentiae, in the need of a further exertion of the will to complete the crime. As was observed in a recent case, the degree of proximity held sufficient may vary with circumstances, including, among other things, the apprehension which the particular crime is calculated to excite."

The crux of the determination of whether the acts are sufficient to constitute an attempt really is whether, when given the specific intent to commit an offense, the acts taken in furtherance thereof are such that there is a dangerous proximity to success in carrying out the intent. In Hyde v. United States, 225 U.S. 347, 32 S.Ct. 793 (1911), Mr. Justice Holmes, in his dissenting opinion, ... adequately delineates the distinction between the mere preparation to commit an offense and an attempt to perpetrate the offense, in these words:

> "But combination, intention and overt act may all be present without amounting to a criminal attempt—as if all that were done should be an agreement to murder a man fifty miles away, and the purchase of a pistol for the purpose. There must be

dangerous proximity to success. But when that exists the overt act is the essence of the offense."

The language of par. 8–4 of the Criminal Code, stating that there must be a substantial step toward the commission of the offense indicates that it is not necessary for an "attempt" that the last proximate act to the completion of the offense be done. In addition, the Illinois Supreme Court has likewise considered this problem. In People v. Woods, 24 Ill.2d at page 158, 180 N.E.2d at page 478, [cert. denied 371 U.S. 819, 83 S.Ct. 34 (1962)] it stated:

> "Mere preparation to commit a crime, of course, does not constitute an attempt to commit it. We feel however that an attempt does exist where a person, with intent to commit a specific offense, performs acts which constitute substantial steps toward the commission of that offense."

The defendant, who conceded that he worked at the barber shop, was the only person there. He had a key and unlocked the shop. He had barber tools. He had a fraudulent license which was posted near the barber chair. He admitted Pinkston to the shop, put on his smock—as it was referred to by the witness—and motioned him to the chair. At this point the defendant was precluded from barbering without a certification of registration, only by the fact that the witness showed the defendant his business card and did not get into the chair. These facts are sufficient to establish the defendant's attempt to violate the statute, as charged.

The defendant argues that barber tools need not be used exclusively for barbering, and that there is nothing to establish that he had a specific intent to practice barbering. In view of the foregoing facts, we find it unbelievable that the defendant had any intent other than to barber and to use the barbering tools, chair and shop for that purpose.

The acts of the defendant were not of such serious character and consequence that he could be expected to feel genuinely apprehensive about what he was doing. The degree of proximity to the actual commission of a crime necessary for there to be an attempt is, in part, determined by the apprehension which the particular crime is calculated to excite. The greater the apprehension, the greater the likelihood that a would-be offender will not follow through with his intended plans. Inasmuch as the offense involved was only a misdemeanor and the penalty inconsequential, there was no cause for serious apprehension on the part of the defendant in connection with the commission of this particular offense, and it was inconceivable that at this late moment he would repent and alter his course of conduct out of fear or concern. He had then taken substantial steps toward the commission of the act of barbering without a certificate of registration. His intention and overt acts resulted in conduct in the very close proximity to the commission of the offense and constituted an attempt. . . .

Judgment affirmed.

MORAN, PRESIDING JUSTICE (dissenting).

I agree with the majority opinion up to the point where it holds that the defendant was guilty of certain acts which constituted a substantial step toward the commission of the offense charged. It is this facet of the case alone with which I disagree.

While it is true that the distinction between the preparation and the substantial step toward the commission of an act, is one of degree, and must be determined by the circumstances of each case; nevertheless, I believe the facts in the case at bar are insufficient to establish the act which constitutes a substantial step toward the commission of the offense.

The majority opinion relies upon, among others, People v. Woods, 24 Ill.2d 154, 158, 180 N.E.2d 475 (1962) [, cert. denied 371 U.S. 819, 83 S.Ct. 34 (1962)]; however, in that case the defendant commenced toward performance of the act by giving the complaining witness a sedative, although not taken by her, nevertheless it was directed toward her. There was, in addition, the fact that the defendant had received a fee for services to be rendered; the fact that instruments needed to perform the operation were in a pan on the stove; and the fact that the complaining witness stated she was ready and began to remove her clothing.

In the case at bar, while there is no doubt that the necessary intent was present, still there is no evidence that the defendant took a "first step" toward commission of the intended crime against Pinkston, the complaining witness. Pinkston, the only one present other than the defendant at the time of the alleged "act", testified that the defendant unlocked the barbershop door, walked back to the barber chair and put on his smock. He further testified that he, Pinkston, walked over and set his briefcase down and the defendant "offered me to get into the chair; at that, I handed him my business card." Thereafter, Pinkston looked around to see where his license was but did not see it. In addition, the defendant had his own barber tools present.

This is the only evidence offered to establish the act which together with the intent is a necessary element to constitute the offense of an "attempt." I would concede that if Pinkston had sat in the barber chair, as offered, and an over-garment placed upon him, then it could be said that a substantial step toward the commission of the offense charged had taken place—even though not one hair was clipped from his head. However, this is not the evidence. The best that can be said of the evidence adduced in this case toward the charge of attempting to practice barbering without a certificate of registration as a barber, is that the defendant started preparing himself but never got to the point of preparing the person against whom the attempt was to have been made. Therefore, I must, and do, dissent from my learned colleagues.

NOTES

1. In Martin v. Commonwealth, 195 Va. 1107, 81 S.E.2d 574 (1954), defendant was charged with attempt to commit pandering by feloniously placing

a female in his dwelling house for the purpose of causing her "to cohabit" with male persons. It appeared that after taking the girl to his apartment, the defendant solicited three young men to have sexual intercourse with the girl upon payment of money to him. He took the boys to his room, where the girl was lying in bed nude. One of the boys said he would go get the necessary money, but when he returned shortly thereafter the defendant had already been arrested by the police. The question arose whether the attempt to commit pandering had occurred when the girl had not yet commenced any preparation to have sexual relations with the boys nor had the defendant received the money. In that regard, the court stated:

> It is well settled in this jurisdiction that in criminal law an attempt is an unfinished crime, and is compounded of two elements, the intent to commit the crime and the doing of some direct act towards its consummation, but falling short of the execution of the ultimate design; that it need not be the last proximate act towards the consummation of the crime in contemplation, but is sufficient if it be an act apparently adopted to produce the result intended; mere preparation is not sufficient....
>
> The defendant contends that the acts charged amounted to nothing more than a mere preparation to commit a crime, and that the allegations do not show any overt act towards its accomplishment....
>
> The undisputed evidence shows that the defendant did everything but receive money in the pursuance of his plans. He placed the female in his room, exhibited her lying in bed nude to three male persons, and solicited money from those persons for the purpose of causing her to have sexual intercourse with them. One of the males went to get the money to be paid to Martin, but the intervention of the police prevented payment and the final consummation of the intended crime. This was not due to any fault or change of plans on Martin's part. He performed direct ineffectual acts towards the commission of the offense of pandering, and when he did this, the attempt to commit the offense was complete....

2. In People v. Rizzo, 246 N.Y. 334, 158 N.E. 888 (1927), the defendant and others planned to hold up a man carrying money for a payroll from the bank to a company. Armed with firearms, they started out in an automobile looking for the carrier of the money, whom Rizzo claimed to be able to identify. They drove from the bank to the company and back in an attempt to spot the carrier, but failed to find him. Meanwhile they were watched and followed by police officers who moved in and arrested the defendant and his cohorts. In reversing the conviction of attempt to commit robbery the court held that the acts of the defendant and his friends had not progressed to the point of nearness to commission of the act as is required for a conviction for attempt. They were looking for the man who was transporting the money, but they had not seen nor discovered him at the time they were arrested. The court said: "In a word, these defendants had planned to commit a crime, and were looking around the city for an opportunity to commit it, but the opportunity fortunately never came. Men would not be guilty of an attempt at burglary if they had planned to break into a building and were arrested while they were hunting about the streets for the building not knowing where it was. Neither would a man be guilty of an attempt to commit murder if he armed himself and started out to find the person whom he had planned to kill but could not find him."

Conviction of an attempt to commit a crime requires proof of intent to commit the crime, plus a substantial step toward commission of the crime. In this case defendants were found to be "casing" a bank and having disguises and weapons that could be used to rob the bank. They were arrested when one of the defendants entered a store near the bank and the other two defendants were leaning against their car facing the bank. At that point they had made "no move toward the bank." The arrest was ruled premature. U.S. v. Buffington, 815 F.2d 1292 (9th Cir.1987).

3. What is the status of one who intends to commit a crime and takes certain steps toward its perpetration but who voluntarily abandons the project prior to its completion? It seems clear that if the requisite elements of an attempt are present, abandonment due to some extrinsic cause, such as the unexpected arrival of police officers or the intended victim, will be of no effect. See, e.g., People v. Carter, 73 Cal.App. 495, 238 P. 1059 (1925). However, as stated in People v. Von Hecht, 133 Cal.App.2d 25, 283 P.2d 764 (1955), "Abandonment is a defense if the attempt to commit a crime is freely and voluntarily abandoned before the act is put in process of final execution and where there is no outside cause prompting such abandonment."

If the plans of a would-be offender are abandoned before the "act is put in process of final execution", is this really a defense of abandonment, or should we rather say that the offense of attempt had not yet been committed because the defendant's act, though preparation for an offense, had not yet reached the stage of a "substantial step" needed to constitute the offense of attempt?

4. Consider the following statutory provisions regarding the general definition of the offense of attempt in the Illinois Criminal Code, 720 ILCS 5/8–4:

§ 8–4(a) *Elements of the Offense.* A person commits an attempt when, with intent to commit a specific offense, he does any act which constitutes a substantial step toward the commission of that offense.

§ 8–4(b) *Impossibility.* It shall not be a defense to a charge of attempt that because of a misapprehension of the circumstances it would have been impossible for the accused to commit the offense attempted.

5. Consider Waters v. State, 2 Md.App. 216, 234 A.2d 147 (1967), in which an 80 year old man was convicted of assault with intent to commit rape. He contended that physical inability to engage in "sexual activity" precluded a conviction of an offense based upon "intent to rape". In affirming defendant's conviction the court said: "While there can be no attempt in a case involving legal impossibility, as attempting to do what is not a crime is not attempting to commit a crime, factual impossibility of success does not prevent the attempt from being made. Physical incapacity to commit a crime does not affect the capacity of one to be guilty of an attempt. Thus a man who is physically impotent may be guilty of an attempt to commit rape."

Since at common law an accused under the age of fourteen is conclusively presumed to be incapable of committing the crime of rape, whatever the real facts may be, "it logically follows, as a plain legal deduction, that he was also incapable in law of an attempt to commit it. . . ." Foster v. Commonwealth, 96 Va. 306, 31 S.E. 503 (1898). But in Preddy v. Commonwealth, 184 Va. 765, 36 S.E.2d 549 (1946), the court held that a 67-year old man was properly convicted of attempting to rape a ten-year old girl, even though the defendant might have been impotent. See, in this connection, the excellent note on impossibility of consummation of substantive crime as a defense to conspiracy or attempt prosecutions at 37 A.L.R.3d 375 (1971). On the question of impotency as a defense to a charge of rape, attempted rape, or assault with intent to commit rape, see Annot., 23 A.L.R.3d 1351 (1969).

6. In People v. Krovarz, 697 P.2d 378 (Colo.1985), the Supreme Court of Colorado ruled that a general culpable mental state of knowledge supports a conviction for attempted aggravated robbery. It rejected an argument that proof of specific intent to commit aggravated robbery is required to convict for an attempted offense. The court stated that, "[T]he culpability for criminal attempt rests primarily upon the actor's purpose to cause harmful consequences," and noted that punishment for attempt is justified on the basis that although the defendant's underlying purpose may have been frustrated, there was a probability of future dangerousness that could have been fulfilled at any time. "The probability of future dangerousness, however, is not confined to actors whose conscious purpose is to perform the proscribed acts or achieve the proscribed results, i.e., those possessing the culpable mental state of specific intent.... We believe that this danger is equally present when one acts knowingly."

7. Related in part to the law of attempt (although it also relates to the law of conspiracy, *infra*), is the concept of aiding and abetting. This can be a separate crime.

It has been held that where there was a statute specifically making it a crime for a person to fail to protect a child from an abuser, a father who simply stood by while his wife abused their child could not be convicted under a separate aiding and abetting statute on the theory that his inaction contributed to his wife's abuse of the child.

The court said that in an aiding and abetting case the state must show that the defendant (1) undertook *conduct* (overt or "verbal," as the Court called it) that objectively aided another person to commit a crime, and (2) had the intent or "conscious desire" to assist the main actor in committing the crime. There was no evidence in the case that the father-defendant had ever done anything to affirmatively harm the child. An aiding and abetting theory, the Court noted, would make the active child abuse statute ("protecting a child from an abuser") "redundant and meaningless." The state had either selected the wrong statute or had miscalculated the sufficiency of its evidence to establish aiding and abetting. State v. Rundle, 176 Wis.2d 985, 500 N.W.2d 916 (1993).

2. SOLICITATION

PEOPLE v. LUBOW

New York Court of Appeals, 1971.
29 N.Y.2d 58, 323 N.Y.S.2d 829, 272 N.E.2d 331.

BERGAN, JUDGE.

The revised Penal Law creates a new kind of offense, simpler in structure than an attempt or a conspiracy, and resting solely on communication without need for any resulting action (art. 100, Criminal Solicitation, part of tit. G, Anticipatory Offenses, L.1965, ch. 1030) Consol.Laws, c. 40. Attempts to commit crimes and conspiracies are continued with some changes as crimes and these, too, are grouped within title G as "Anticipatory Offenses" (art. 105, Conspiracies; art. 110, Attempts).

The basic statutory definition of criminal solicitation is that with intent that another person shall "engage in conduct constituting a crime" the accused "solicits, requests, commands, importunes or otherwise attempts to cause such other person to engage in such conduct". This basic definitory language is continued through three grades of solicitation, the gravity depending on what crime the conduct sought to be induced would effectuate.

If the conduct would be "a crime" it is criminal solicitation in the third degree, a "violation" (§ 100.00); if the conduct would be "a felony" it is criminal solicitation in the second degree, a class A misdemeanor (§ 100.05); and if the conduct would be murder or kidnapping in the first degree it is criminal solicitation in the first degree, a class D felony (§ 100.10).

As it has been noted, nothing need be done under the statute in furtherance of the communication ("solicits, commands, importunes") to constitute the offense. The communication itself with intent the other person engage in the unlawful conduct is enough. It needs no corroboration.

And an attempt at communication which fails to reach the other person may also constitute the offense for the concluding clause "or otherwise attempts to cause such other person to engage in such conduct" would seem literally to embrace as an attempt an undelivered letter or message initiated with the necessary intent.

Appellants have been convicted after a trial by a three-Judge panel in the Criminal Court of the City of New York of violation of section 100.05 which describes solicitation to commit a felony. The information on which the prosecution is based is made by complainant Max Silverman. It describes the charge as criminal solicitation and states that "defendants attempted to cause deponent to commit the crime of grand larceny" in that they "attempted to induce the deponent to obtain precious stones on partial credit with a view towards appropriating the property to their own use and not paying the creditors, said conduct constituting the crime of larceny by false promise".

Although the Penal Law section number is not stated in the information, it was clearly stated in court before the opening of the trial that the charge was a violation of section 100.05 and the facts alleged that the inducement was to commit grand larceny, a felony, which gave adequate notice of the nature of the offense involved.

The proof in support of the charge, if factually accepted by the trial court, as it was by a majority of the Judges (one dissenting), was sufficient to warrant conviction. The Appellate Term affirmed unanimously.

The evidence showed that complainant Silverman and both defendants were engaged in the jewelry business. It could be found that defendant Lubow owed Silverman $30,000 for diamonds on notes which were unpaid; that Lubow had told Silverman he was associated with a big operator interested in buying diamonds and introduced him to defendant Gissinger.

It could also be found that in October, 1967, Silverman met the two defendants together at their office, demanded his money, and said that because of the amount owed him he was being forced into bankruptcy.

Silverman testified in response to this Lubow said "Well, let's make it a big one, a big bankruptcy", and Gissinger said this was a good idea. When Silverman asked "how it is done" he testified that Lubow, with Gissinger participating, outlined a method by which diamonds would be purchased partly on credit, sold for less than cost, with the proceeds pyramided to boost Silverman's credit rating until very substantial amounts came in, when there was to be a bankruptcy with Silverman explaining that he had lost the cash gambling in Puerto Rico and Las Vegas. The cash would be divided among the three men. The gambling explanation for the disappearance of cash would be made to seem believable by producing credit cards for Puerto Rico and Las Vegas. Silverman testified that Lubow said "we would eventually wind up with a quarter of a million dollars each" and that Gissinger said "maybe millions".

Silverman reported this proposal to the District Attorney in October, 1967 and the following month a police detective equipped Silverman with a tape recorder concealed on his person which was in operation during conversations with defendants on November 16 and which tends to substantiate the charge. The reel was received in evidence on concession that it was taken from the machine Silverman wore November 16.

A police detective testified as an expert that a "bust out operation" is a "pyramiding of credit by rapid purchasing of merchandise, and the rapid selling of the same merchandise sometimes 10 and 20 per cent the cost of the merchandise itself, and they keep selling and buying until they establish such a credit rating that they are able to purchase a large order at the end of their operation, and at this time they go into bankruptcy or they just leave".

There thus seems sufficient evidence in the record to find that defendants intended Silverman to engage in conduct constituting a felony by defrauding creditors of amounts making out grand larceny and that they importuned Silverman to engage in such conduct. Thus the proof meets the actual terms of the statute.

The statute itself is a valid exercise of legislative power. Commentators closely associated with the drafting of the Model Penal Code of the American Law Institute, from which the New York solicitation statute stems, have observed: "Purposeful solicitation presents dangers calling for preventive intervention and is sufficiently indicative of a disposition towards criminal activity to call for liability. Moreover, the fortuity that the person solicited does not agree to commit or attempt to commit the incited crime plainly should not relieve the solicitor of liability, when otherwise he would be a conspirator or an accomplice."

Solicitation to commit a felony was a misdemeanor at common law. (People v. Bush, 4 Hill 133, 135; Rex v. Higgins, 2 East 5). Summarizing this historical fact Judge Cardozo observed: "So at common law, incitement to a felony, when it did not reach the stage of an attempt, was itself a separate crime, and like conspiracy, which it resembled, was a misdemeanor, not a felony" (People v. Werblow, 241 N.Y. 55, 66, 148 N.E. 786, 791, citing Higgins and Rex v. Gregory, L.R. 1 C.C.R. 77).

But as People v. Bush demonstrates, the solicitation in early New York cases was treated as closely related to an attempt. There defendant asked another to burn a barn and gave him a match for that purpose. This principle was followed to some extent but there were fundamental difficulties with it under the concept of attempt and it seems not to have been followed after *Bloom.*

Although this Penal Law provision is the first statutory enactment in New York, there have been statutes aimed at criminal solicitation in some other States, notably California.

In commenting on the criminal solicitation enactment of article 100, two lawyers who were active in the work of the State Commission on Revision of the Penal Law and Criminal Code which prepared the present statute observed that article 100 "closes that gap" for those who believe, as apparently the commission and the American Law Institute did, that "solicitation to commit a crime involves sufficient culpability to warrant criminal sanctions".

There are, however, potential difficulties inherent in this penal provision which should be looked at, even though all of them are not decisive in this present case. One, of course, is the absence of any need for corroboration. The tape recording here tends to give some independent support to the testimony of Silverman, but there are types of criminal conduct which might be solicited where there would be a heavy thrust placed on the credibility of a single witness testifying to a conversation. Extraordinary care might be required in deciding when to prosecute; in determining the truth; and in appellate review of the factual decision.

One example would be the suggestion of one person to another that he commit a sexual offense; another is the suggestion that he commit perjury. The Model Penal Code did not require corroboration; but aside from the need for corroboration which is traditional in some sexual offenses, there are dangers in the misinterpretation of innuendos or remarks which could be taken as invitations to commit sexual offenses. These are discussed by Wechsler-Jones-Korn (61 Col.L.Rev., p. 623, supra) with the comment that "it is a risk implicit in the punishment of almost all inchoate crimes".

In two opinions for the California Supreme Court, Justice Traynor has analyzed that State's criminal solicitations statute (Penal Code, § 653f; Benson v. Superior Ct. of Los Angeles County, and People v. Burt).

The first case was for solicitation to commit perjury and the second for solicitation to commit extortion.

The California statute is based on a specific list of serious crimes to which criminal solicitation expressly applies; but as to all of them the statute requires that the offense "must be proved by the testimony of two witnesses, or of one witness and corroborating circumstances".

The basic public justification for legislative enactment is, however, very similar to New York's and was developed in the *Burt* opinion: "Legislative concern with the proscribed soliciting is demonstrated not only by the gravity of the crimes specified but by the fact that the crime, unlike conspiracy, does not require the commission of any overt act. It is complete when the solicitation is made, and it is immaterial that the object of the solicitation is never consummated, or that no steps are taken toward its consummation." The California Legislature was concerned "not only with the prevention of the harm that would result should the inducements prove successful, but with protecting inhabitants of this state from being exposed to inducements to commit or join in the commission of the crimes specified."

Another potential problem with the statute is that it includes an attempt to commit unlawful solicitation, i.e., solicits, etc., "or otherwise attempts to cause" the conduct. This has the same effect as the Model Penal Code, but the language there is different. The code spells the purpose out more specifically that: "It is immaterial ... that the actor fails to communicate with the person he solicits to commit a crime if his conduct was designed to effect such communication". This could be an attempt in the classic sense and might be committed by a telephone message initiated but never delivered. The present Penal Law, stated in different language, has the same effect.

Appellants raise a point based on the reduplicative overplay of section 100.00 which is a "violation" and section 100.05, of which they have been convicted, a "class A misdemeanor".

Literally, the same act could fall within either section; and specifically the acts charged to appellants could come within either.

Section 100.00 relates to solicitation of another person to "engage in conduct constituting a crime" and section 100.05 to "engage in conduct constituting a felony".

Since a felony is a crime, whenever a charge is made based on solicitation to commit felony, it would come within both sections. It is not entirely clear why the statute was drawn this way. The commentators Denzer and McQuillan observe that although section 100.00 "embraces solicitation to commit any crime from a class B misdemeanor up to a class A felony, its principal application would normally be to those solicitation offenses not covered by the higher degrees".

Whatever may be said of the abstract merits of a choice of prosecution based on the same act between a higher or lesser degree of crime, it seems to have been decided that prosecution for the higher degree is permissible.

* * *

PEOPLE v. SPENCER

Criminal Court of the City of New York, Queens County, 1971.
66 Misc.2d 658, 322 N.Y.S.2d 266.

M. MARVIN BERGER, JUDGE:

At a preliminary hearing, held before this Court, the defendant was charged with the felony of attempted sodomy and endangering the welfare of a minor, a misdemeanor.

The charges, contained in the affidavit of the mother of an 8-year old boy, state that the defendant, seated in an automobile, called the child to the car and offered him money to commit an act of sodomy. The boy rejected the offer and reported the incident to his mother the same day.

At the preliminary hearing, the sworn testimony of the arresting officer supported some details of the boy's unsworn account.

The child's evidence, both in chief and under cross-examination, made it clear that the defendant remained in his automobile, drove past the child without stopping or changing the direction of the vehicle, that he kept his hands on the steering wheel and did not expose himself.

The threshold question is whether a verbal solicitation to commit a crime constitutes an attempt to commit the crime.

Section 110 of the Penal Law defines an attempt as follows:

> "A person is guilty of an attempt to commit a crime when, with intent to commit a crime, he engages in conduct which tends to effect the commission of such crime. . . ."

It derives from Section 2 of the old Penal Law which defined an attempt as "an act done, with intent to commit a crime, and tending but failing to effect its commission."

According to the annotations in the McKinney's Edition of the Penal Law (Vol. 39, p. 180), the attempt had to proceed beyond mere preparation and approach consummation of the forbidden act.

The People assert that the defendant, by slowing down his vehicle to keep pace with the infant's gait and by offering him money to commit fellatio on him, engaged in a direct effort to commit sodomy. By focusing his solicitation on a specific person, the defendant had progressed from preparation—the search for a likely victim of his advances—to an attempt.

People v. Ditchik, (N.Y.1942), frequently cited in decisions dealing with attempts, states:

> "Acts in furtherance of a criminal project do not reach the stage of an attempt, unless they carry the project forward within dangerous proximity to the criminal end to be attained."

Other cases, principally People v. Rizzo (N.Y.1927), make it clear that the purpose or intent must be linked to an overt act tending to the commission of the crime albeit not "the last proximate one for the completion of the offense."

In short, in the words of the Official Draft of the Model Penal Code (Sec. 5.01) the "substantial step in a course of conduct planned to culminate in ... commission of a crime" must be "... strongly corroborative of the actor's criminal purpose."

The court's inquiry must then focus on whether verbal solicitation of another to engage in criminal conduct is an attempt to commit a crime.

In the absence of any reported New York case on this point, we must rely on other sources.

The general proposition stated in 21 Am.Jur.2d § 113, is as follows:

> "Though solicitation may constitute an element in some attempts, the usual view seems to be that soliciting another to commit a crime is not, by itself, sufficient to constitute an attempt to commit that crime. This has been explained on the ground that the offenses of solicitation and attempt are analytically distinct in their elements, and that there is no overt act, since solicitation is in the nature of preparation rather than perpetration. Some cases however take the view that even though a solicitation to commit a misdemeanor does not constitute an attempt to commit the misdemeanor, a solicitation to commit a felony may be punished as an attempt."

The majority view is set forth in Gervin v. State, 212 Tenn. 653, 656, 657, 371 S.W.2d 449, 450–451 (1963) as follows:

> "The weight of American authority holds, as a general proposition, that mere criminal solicitation of another to commit a crime does not constitute an attempt...."

To the same effect is State v. Blechman (N.J.1946), in which the court states:

> "The solicitation constitutes a substantive crime in itself, and not an abortive attempt to perpetrate the crime solicited. It falls short of an attempt, in the legal sense, to commit the offense solicited."

In the area of what the Penal Law collectively describes as "Sex Offenses" (Art. 130), there appears to be no New York precedent spelling out the distinction between solicitation and attempt.

In the article dealing with adultery, in 2 Am.Jur.2d 966, the following is stated:

> "The weight of authority also is that solicitation is not an overt act leading up to the commission of the crime and accordingly solicitation to commit adultery is not an attempt to commit the offense and is not indictable as such."

In State v. Butler (Wash.1894), the Supreme Court of Washington reviewed a conviction for attempted adultery based on defendant's efforts "by means of promises of the payment of money, and by direct invitation by word of mouth ... to persuade and procure" the complainant, a married woman, to have sexual intercourse with the defendant.

In writing the unanimous opinion of the Court, sustaining the granting of defendant's motion in arrest of judgment, Scott, J. said:

> "Now, it seems to us that solicitation to commit adultery is no part of the act of adultery itself, and consequently cannot be held to be an attempt. What is it? It involves the expression of a desire and a willingness on the part of one person to commit the act of adultery with another, and an attempt to get that person's consent, but no more."

And in another early case, Smith v. Commonwealth (Pa.1867), the Supreme Court of Pennsylvania said:

> "... a rule of law which should make mere solicitation to fornication or adultery indictable would be an impractical rule—one that in the present usages and manners of society would lead to great abuses and oppressions.... In a high moral sense, it may be true that solicitation is an attempt, but in a legal sense it is not."

To the same effect is Cole v. State (1917) and State v. Bowles (Kans.1905).

Very close to the fact situation in the instant case is State v. Harney (Mo.1890), in which the defendant on a public street asked a girl under 12 years of age to accompany him to a wooden shed to engage in sexual intercourse. The state appealed from a judgment quashing the defendant's indictment on a charge of attempted rape. (The Missouri statute defined sexual intercourse with a female child under 12 as rape.) Likewise, the statutes provided that "every person who shall attempt to commit an offense prohibited by law, and in such attempt shall do any act towards the commission of such offense, but shall fail in the perpetration thereof, shall be punished."

Brace, J., for a unanimous Supreme Court wrote in *Harney,* supra:

"The only charge that can be evolved from the verbose reiterations of this indictment is that the defendant, by verbal solicitations, tried to obtain the consent of a child under the age of 12 years to have sexual intercourse with him and failed. However despicable and deserving of punishment such conduct may be, it falls short of the criminal offense attempted to be charged, to constitute which there must be an actual attempt to have intercourse with such child. So long as the evil purpose dwells in contemplation only, it is beyond the grasp of these provisions of the law. The indictment, failing to charge any actual attempt upon the part of the defendant to have sexual intercourse with the child, was properly quashed, and the judgment is affirmed."

Accordingly the defendant cannot be charged with attempted sodomy and that portion of the charge is dismissed.

The People urge that the testimony was sufficient to spell out a charge of endangering the welfare of a minor in violation of section 260.10 of the Penal Law.

Since the defendant is not the complainant's parent or guardian, the charge must fall within subdivision 1 of the section which makes it a crime to act in a manner likely to be injurious to the physical, mental or moral welfare of a child less than 16 years of age.

The defendant urges that in the absence of physical acts performed to the complainant or in a situation which would impair a child's morals the charge cannot be supported.

However, under the predecessor statute, sec. 483 of the Penal Law which punishes a person who wilfully causes a child under 16 to be placed in a situation "that its life or limb is endangered, or its health is likely to be injured, or its morals likely to be impaired", the courts have gone beyond the limited construction urged by defendant.

First, it is made clear by People on Complaint of Barber v. Caminiti (N.Y.1941) that there need be no specific intent to injure or impair the child's morals or proof of actual impairment of morals.

And in People v. Bergerson (N.Y.1966) it was held that the defendant, in affording minors with the facilities for a beer party in his home, had violated the statute.

Similarly in People v. Ammirati (N.Y.1964), the conviction was sustained on evidence that the defendant furnished pills known as "goof balls" to the complaining witness.

The defendant in this case submits that the child was "flippant, composed and did not display the effects of having been shocked by what took place, if such took place as he states."

The court questions the implication that a complainant must react to an offer to commit sodomy with manifestations of shock, disgust or revulsion in order to spell out sufficient cause to hold the defendant to answer to the charge of endangering a minor's welfare.

Perhaps in time society will develop an appropriate response to an invitation to engage in pederasty. However, it may well be doubted that a child of eight will be required to adopt an accepted form of acquiescence or refusal.

The court feels that the solicitation in question is well within the parameters of the activity forbidden by sec. 260.10 of the Penal Law as endangering the welfare of a child.

We now come to the question of whether the alleged conduct of the defendant, failing to constitute an attempt to commit sodomy, but clearly spelling out the crime of endangering the welfare of a minor, also comprised criminal solicitation in the second degree.

By the terms of sec. 100.05 of the Penal Law, "a person is guilty of criminal solicitation in the second degree when, with intent that another person engage in conduct constituting a felony, he solicits, requests, commands, or importunes or otherwise attempts to cause such other person to engage in such conduct."

The People contend that if the charges of attempted sodomy and endangering a minor's welfare have not been supported by the People's evidence, the court, in the alternative, should hold the defendant to answer to the crime of criminal solicitation.

The court holds that the solicitation is a separate, additional and not alternative offense, independent of and not necessarily incidental to the commission of the crime solicited, so as to escape the exempting effects of sec. 100.20 of the Penal Law.

That section states that a person is not guilty of criminal solicitation when his solicitation is the kind of conduct necessarily incidental to perpetration of the crime. Under such circumstances, according to the statute, when the solicitation "is related to but separate from the crime solicited," the actor is guilty of the related and separate offense only and not of criminal solicitation.

By way of illustration, the commentary to the McKinney's edition of the Penal Law (Sec. 100.20) posits the situation in which a public servant, A, seeks a bribe from B, in return for favorable official action. Such conduct is bribe receiving within the prohibition of sec. 200.10, as well as solicitation to commit bribery. According to the commentators, A may be convicted of bribe receiving only and not of criminal solicitation.

Here the crime solicited was sodomy. The solicitation was not necessarily incidental to the crime sought to be perpetrated. The crime charged was an effort to engage in deviate sexual intercourse with a child under eleven. (Sec. 130.50) Seeking the child's consent is an independent offense. True, if the invitation had resulted in deviate intercourse, the solicitation would have merged into the completed crime of sodomy.

By its very language sec. 100.20 implies that the solicitation bore fruit in the form of a completed crime. Unless this is the correct interpretation of the language of the statute, an unsuccessful effort to commit a crime falling short of an attempt may escape the condemnation of the law.

In any event the Court feels that this is a case in which "that solicitation to commit a crime involves sufficient culpability to warrant criminal sanctions" (39 McKinney's Penal Law p. 169).

* * *

In summary, the defendant will stand trial on charges of criminal solicitation and endangering the welfare of a child. The charge of attempted sodomy is dismissed.

NOTE

Also illustrative of solicitation statutes is Ill.Rev.Stat. 720 ILCS 5/8–1:

> A person commits solicitation when, with intent that an offense be committed, other than first degree murder, he commands, encourages or requests another to commit that offense.

B. CRIMINAL COMBINATIONS—CONSPIRACIES

The various elements that comprise the offense of "conspiracy" and the evidentiary problems encountered in its prosecution are of considerably less concern to police officers than to criminal law practitioners and the courts. Nevertheless, it is an offense with which the police must be familiar and there are a few of its aspects that are of practical concern to them. The following proposed statutory provisions, and the note material thereafter, should suffice.

The Proposed Official Draft of the Model Penal Code of the American Law Institute, 1962

Section 5.03. Criminal Conspiracy

(1) *Definition of Conspiracy.* A person is guilty of conspiracy with another person or persons to commit a crime if with the purpose of promoting or facilitating its commission he:

> (a) agrees with such other person or persons that they or one or more of them will engage in conduct which constitutes such crime or an attempt or solicitation to commit such crime; or
>
> (b) agrees to aid such other person or persons in the planning or commission of such crime or of an attempt or solicitation to commit such crime.

(2) *Scope of Conspiratorial Relationship.* If a person guilty of conspiracy, as defined by Subsection (1) of this Section, knows that a person with whom he conspires to commit a crime has conspired with

another person or persons to commit the same crime, he is guilty of conspiring with such other person or persons, whether or not he knows their identity, to commit such crime.

(3) *Conspiracy With Multiple Criminal Objectives.* If a person conspires to commit a number of crimes, he is guilty of only one conspiracy so long as such multiple crimes are the object of the same agreement or continuous conspiratorial relationship.

* * *

(5) *Overt Act.* No person may be convicted of conspiracy to commit a crime, other than a felony of the first or second degree, unless an overt act in pursuance of such conspiracy is alleged and proved to have been done by him or by a person with whom he conspired.

(6) *Renunciation of Criminal Purpose.* It is an affirmative defense that the actor, after conspiring to commit a crime, thwarted the success of the conspiracy, under circumstances manifesting a complete and voluntary renunciation of his criminal purpose.

(7) *Duration of Conspiracy.* [: . . .]

> (a) conspiracy is a continuing course of conduct which terminates when the crime or crimes which are its object are committed or the agreement that they be committed is abandoned by the defendant and by those with whom he conspired; and
>
> (b) such abandonment is presumed if neither the defendant nor anyone with whom he conspired does any overt act in pursuance of the conspiracy during the applicable period of limitation; and
>
> (c) if an individual abandons the agreement, the conspiracy is terminated as to him only if and when he advises those with whom he conspired of his abandonment or he informs the law enforcement authorities of the existence of the conspiracy and of his participation therein.

Section 5.04. Incapacity, Irresponsibility or Immunity of Party to Solicitation or Conspiracy

(1) Except as provided in Subsection (2) of this Section, it is immaterial to the liability of a person who solicits or conspires with another to commit a crime that:

> (a) he or the person whom he solicits or with whom he conspires does not occupy a particular position or have a particular characteristic which is an element of such crime, if he believes that one of them does; or
>
> (b) the person whom he solicits or with whom he conspires is irresponsible or has an immunity to prosecution or conviction for the commission of the crime.

(2) It is a defense to a charge of solicitation or conspiracy to commit a crime that if the criminal object were achieved, the actor would not be guilty of a crime under the law defining the offense....

The Final Report of the National Commission on Reform of Federal Criminal Laws (1971)

§ 1004. Criminal Conspiracy

(1) Offense. A person is guilty of conspiracy if he agrees with one or more persons to engage in or cause the performance of conduct which, in fact, constitutes a crime or crimes, and any one or more of such persons does an act to effect an objective of the conspiracy. The agreement need not be explicit but may be implicit in the fact of collaboration or existence of other circumstances.

(2) Parties to Conspiracy. If a person knows or could expect that one with whom he agrees has agreed or will agree with another to effect the same objective, he shall be deemed to have agreed with the other, whether or not he knows the other's identity.

(3) Duration of Conspiracy. A conspiracy shall be deemed to continue until its objectives are accomplished, frustrated or abandoned. "Objectives" includes escape from the scene of the crime, distribution of booty, and measures, other than silence, for concealing the crime or obstructing justice in relation to it. A conspiracy shall be deemed to have been abandoned if no overt act to effect its objectives has been committed by any conspirator during the applicable period of limitations.

(4) Defense Precluded. It is no defense to a prosecution under this section that the person with whom such person is alleged to have conspired has been acquitted, has not been prosecuted or convicted, has been convicted of a different offense, is immune from prosecution, or is otherwise not subject to justice.

* * *

NOTES

1. Concerning the underlying concept of the conspiracy offense, as well as the common law definition and requirements, consider the following from State v. Carbone, 10 N.J. 329, 91 A.2d 571 (1952):

"At common law, a conspiracy consists not merely in the intention but in the agreement of two or more persons (not being husband and wife) to do an unlawful act, or to do a lawful act by unlawful means. So long as such a design rests in intention only, it is not indictable. When two agree to carry it into effect, the very plot is an act in itself, and the act of each of the parties, promise against promise, *actus contra actum,* capable of being enforced if lawful, punishable if for a criminal object or for the use of criminal means. The agreement is an advancement of the intention which each has conceived in his mind; the mind proceeds from a secret intention to the overt act of mutual consultation and agreement.... It is not requisite, in order to constitute a conspiracy at common law, that the acts agreed to be done be such as would be criminal if done; it is enough if the acts agreed to be done, although not criminal, be wrongful, i.e., amount to a civil wrong. The gist of the offense of conspiracy lies, not in doing the act, nor effecting the purpose for which the conspiracy is formed, nor in attempting to do them, nor in inciting others to do them, but in the forming of the scheme or agreement between the parties.... The offense depends on the unlawful agreement and not on the act which follows it; the latter is not evidence of the former.... The combination itself is vicious and gives the public an interest to interfere by indictment.... The external or overt act of the crime is concert by which initial consent to a common purpose is exchanged.... In order to render one criminally liable for conspiracy at common law, it must be shown that he entered into an agreement as thus defined with one or more persons, whether charged with him in the indictment or not, and whether known or unknown....

"But it is not essential that there be direct contact between the parties, or that all enter into the conspiratorial agreement at one and the same time. 'It may be that the alleged conspirators have never seen each other, and have never corresponded. One may have never heard the name of the other, and yet by the law they may be parties to the same common criminal agreement.' ... 'What has to be ascertained is always the same matter: is it true to say, ... that the acts of the accused were done in pursuance of a criminal purpose held in common between them?' One who joins a conspiracy after its formation is equally guilty with the original conspirators....

"... an agreement or combination between two or more persons to commit a crime constitutes a conspiracy punishable as a misdemeanor, if with certain exceptions there be an overt act in furtherance of the object of the agreement by one or more of the parties.... The union is invested with a potentiality for evil that renders the plan criminal in itself, and punishable as such if an act be done to effect its object....

"... Overt acts proved against one or more of the prisoners may be looked to as against all of them to show the nature and object of the conspiracy....

"Where two or more persons have entered into a conspiracy to perpetrate a crime, the acts and declarations of one of the conspirators in furtherance of the common object are deemed in law the facts and declarations of all. This on the theory of a joint or mutual agency *ad hoc* for the prosecution of the common plan...."

Can an agreement between a defendant and a federal agent acting in an undercover capacity to commit a crime be a conspiracy? "No," according to United States v. de Bright, 742 F.2d 1196 (9th Cir.1984), because a criminal conspiracy requires at least two persons who genuinely intend to carry out a criminal objective. Thus, if a defendant introduces evidence at trial from which the jury can reasonably believe that he conspired only with a government agent, the defendant is entitled to a jury instruction that it takes more to constitute a conspiracy.

2. The "overt act" requirement specified in the preceding note, as well as in the American Law Institute's proposed statute, was defined by Justice Holmes in Hyde v. United States, 225 U.S. 347, 388, 32 S.Ct. 793, 810 (1912), in the following manner: "The overt act is simply evidence that the conspiracy has passed beyond words and is on foot when the act is done."

Under the doctrine of Pinkerton v. United States, 328 U.S. 640, 66 S.Ct. 1180 (1946), which held that each member of a conspiracy is criminally liable for any crime committed by coconspirators during the course of and in furtherance of the conspiracy, several coconspirators in a cocaine selling ring could be convicted of the murder of an undercover agent committed by other members of the conspiracy, even though they did not personally participate in the killing. United States v. Alvarez, 755 F.2d 830 (11th Cir.1985).

Every defendant who joins in concerted criminal activity to commit the felony of robbery is vicariously responsible for the use of force in the commission of the crime by a codefendant, even if they do not know that the codefendant possesses a firearm or that he intends to use it. Carter v. Commonwealth, 232 Va. 122, 348 S.E.2d 265 (1986).

3. One of the most advantageous features of a conspiracy case, insofar as the prosecution is concerned, and one of which the police should be mindful, is the fact that whatever any one conspirator says or does in *furtherance of the conspiracy* is usable as evidence against all of the other conspirators. In other words, each one acts as an agent of the others in effectuating their objective. See Hanger v. United States, 398 F.2d 91, 100 (8th Cir.1968), cert. denied 393 U.S. 1119, 89 S.Ct. 995 (1969) and United States v. Bazinet, 462 F.2d 982, 991 (8th Cir.), cert. denied 409 U.S. 1010, 93 S.Ct. 453 (1972).

Concealment efforts may or may not be considered "in furtherance" of the conspiracy, depending upon the circumstances of the particular case. The following language from the Supreme Court decision in Grunewald v. United States, 353 U.S. 391, at 405–06, 77 S.Ct. 963, at 974 (1957), should be helpful in making the delineation:

"... a vital distinction must be made between acts of concealment done in furtherance of the *main* criminal objectives of the conspiracy, and acts of concealment done after these central objectives have been attained, for the purpose only of covering up after the crime. Thus the Government argues in its brief that 'in the crime of kidnapping, the acts of conspirators in hiding while waiting for ransom would clearly be planned acts of concealment which would be in aid of the conspiracy to kidnap. So here, there can be no doubt that ... all acts of concealment, whether to hide the identity of the conspirators or the action theretofore taken, were unquestionably in furtherance of the initial conspiracy....' We do not think the analogy is valid. Kidnapers in hiding, waiting for ransom, commit acts of concealment in furtherance of the objectives of the conspiracy itself, just as repainting a stolen car would be in furtherance of a conspiracy to steal; in both cases the successful accomplishment of the crime necessitates concealment. More closely analogous to our case would be conspiring kidnapers who cover their traces after the main conspiracy is finally ended—i.e., after they have abandoned the kidnaped person and then take care to escape detection. In the latter case, as here, the acts of covering up can by themselves indicate nothing more than that the conspirators do not wish to be apprehended—a concomitant, certainly, of every crime since Cain attempted to conceal the murder of Abel from the Lord."

In United States v. Inadi, 475 U.S. 387, 106 S.Ct. 1121 (1986), the U.S. Supreme Court ruled that an out-of-court statement of a non-testifying coconspirator is admissible at trial, and the witness's unavailability need not first be demonstrated, as would be generally true of the use of a witness's prior recorded testimony in order to avoid a Sixth Amendment Confrontation Clause problem. The Court applied a cost-benefit approach: requiring a demonstration of unavailability in coconspirator cases would necessitate the expenditure of considerable judicial time, while doing little to enhance the quality of the overall truth-seeking process.

4. Although the federal drug conspiracy statute, 21 U.S.C.A. § 846, would not cover a spot sale between a drug wholesaler and drug dealer, where there was an implicit agreement between the defendant, a drug dealer, that he would buy most if not all of his drugs from the wholesaler, and it appeared that he knew the intimate workings of the wholesaler's business and was attempting to improve his relationship with the wholesaler, a conspiracy was made out under the statute. The conspiracy statute assumes a "jointness" of operation which presents special dangers of new and increased criminal activity not found in a spot sale between two parties. A conspiracy need not be founded on a formal agreement; an implicit agreement and appropriate facts also suffice under the conspiracy statute.

The court said: "We think that a realistic appraisal of Moran's [defendant/retailer] and Willis' [wholesaler] relationship would permit a jury to find that it amounts to an implicit agreement and comprehends the continuing supply by one to the other of drugs for resale to customers.... Even though Moran was not an employee nor did Willis and Moran formally divide the profits, in this case a jury could conclude that both Willis and Moran had an ongoing stake in the success of Moran's own sales of the drugs Moran acquired from Willis.... From those sales Moran could profit directly and Willis indirectly through the maintenance of the drug distribution channel crucial for a drug network. *See generally* Direct Sales Co. v. United States, 319 U.S. 703, 717 (1943). Such an arrangement, we think, is not only an agreement within the ordinary conspiracy-law ambit but is one that unites two participants in seeking to accomplish the crime of distribution and involves *both* of the dangers of conspiracy—increased likelihood of success and extension to other crimes—to which the cases advert. We think that the pragmatic approach of *Direct Sales* in defining conspiracy foreshadows the result in this case and, given Congress' intent to stamp out drug transactions, it certainly did not mean to narrow the conspiracy concept when it enacted 21 U.S.C.A. § 846, the statute involved in this case." United States v. Moran, 984 F.2d 1299 (1st Cir.1993).

5. Many jurisdictions have spousal privilege statutes that prevent one spouse from testifying against the other about criminal conduct. Such statutes may not be invoked by the defendant-spouse if the spouses have been engaged in what constitutes conspiratorial activity.

For example, one court ruled that when a spouse is willing to testify, a spousal privilege statute should not prevent him or her from doing so if the spouses have been engaged in a "partnership in crime." This court notes, "greater public good will result from permitting the spouse of an accused to testify willingly concerning their joint criminal activities than would come from permitting the accused to erect a roadblock against the search for truth." United States v. Estes, 793 F.2d 465 (2d Cir.1986).

The result was the same where the spouses had been "joint participants" in a crime. "[W]hen the witness-spouse and defendant-spouse are engaged in joint criminal activity, the public's interest in discovering the truth about criminal activity outweighs the public's interest in protecting the privacy of such a communication ... [but] the testifying spouse must be more than a simple receptor of a statement by the defendant-spouse that he committed a crime.... Active participation in, or furtherance of, patently criminal activity by the witness-spouse must be shown." State v. Witchey, 388 N.W.2d 893 (S.D.1986).

Pennsylvania's spousal privilege statute has an exception for "criminal proceeding[s] against either for bodily injury or violence attempted, done or threatened upon the other [...]" In a narrow reading, a lower Pennsylvania court restricted the exception to intentional crimes committed against the witness spouse. The exception did not apply in this case where the defendant was charged with several counts of vehicular homicide; his wife was badly injured in the accident, but the defendant was not charged with her injuries. The wife should not have been permitted to testify against her husband, the court ruled. "[N]o charges whatsoever were filed against appellant for any alleged criminal activity toward his wife. [...] We believe the statute was not enacted to apply to the facts of this case, an automobile accident resulting in serious injury to a spouse, but instead are persuaded the exception to the incompetency rule was designed to protect those spouses victimized by an act of intentional violence committed upon them by an accused spouse." Commonwealth v. Dungan, 372 Pa.Super. 323, 539 A.2d 817 (1988).

C. PARTIES TO THE CRIME—ACCESSORIES BEFORE AND AFTER THE FACT

Normally, criminal liability is predicated upon the doing of an act, usually by the defendant. Early in the development of the common law, however, the courts recognized that criminal liability could be predicated upon conduct done by a party other than the defendant, for whose conduct the defendant would be held responsible. Consider, in this connection, the following excerpt from Usselton v. People, 149 Ill. 612, 36 N.E. 952 (1894):

"By the ancient common law, existing prior to the reign of Henry IV,—the latter part of the fourteenth and beginning of the fifteenth centuries,—those persons only were considered principals who committed the overt act, while those who were present, aiding and abetting, were deemed accessories at the fact, and those who, not being present had advised or encouraged the perpetration of the crime, were deemed accessories before the fact. During that reign it seems to have been settled as the law that he who was present, aiding and abetting in the perpetration of the crime, was to be considered as a principal, the courts holding that all who were actually or constructively present, but not actively participating in the crime, were principals of the second degree. (1 Russell on Crimes, (Greenl. ed.) 26; 1 Bishop on Crim.Law, 648.) And this continued to be the common law as it was adopted in this State.

"An accessory before the fact, at common law, is defined by Sir Mathew Hale to be 'one who, being absent at the time of the commission of the offense, doth yet procure, counsel or command another to commit it.' And absence, it is said, is indispensably necessary to constitute one an accessory, for if he be actually or constructively present when the felony is committed, he is an aider and abettor, and not an accessory before the fact, (1 Hale's P.C. 615; 4 Blackstone's Com. 36, 37; 1 Archbold on Crim.Pl. and Pr. 14;) or, as defined by Bishop, (1 Crim.Law, 673): 'An accessory before the fact is one whose will contributes to another's felonious act, committed while too far himself from the act to be a principal.' No distinction was made in the punishment of a principal and of an accessory before the fact by the common law, the principle that what one does by the agency of another he does by himself, applying equally in criminal and civil cases. Broom's Legal Maxims, (2d ed.) 643. At common law, an accessory before the fact, without his consent, could only be tried after the conviction of the principal. While the principal remained amenable to indictment and conviction, the accessory had the right to insist upon the conviction of the principal offender before he was put upon trial, for, as said by Blackstone, (book 4, 323), '*non constitit* whether any felony was committed or no, till the principal was attainted, and it might so happen that the accessory be convicted one day and the principal acquitted the next, which would be absurd.' And this absurdity might happen wherever the trial of the principal might occur subsequently to that of the accessory. This was subject to the exception, that where the accessory was indicted with the principal he might waive the right, and thereupon they might be put upon trial jointly.

"It seems that the distinction between accessories before the fact and principals, up to a late date, at least, has been retained in England. By Statute 7, Geo. IV, chap. 64, sec. 9, it is provided that persons who shall counsel, procure or command any other person to commit a felony shall be deemed guilty of a felony, and may be indicted and convicted, either as accessory before the fact to the principal felony, together with the principal felon, or after his conviction, or may be indicted and convicted of a substantive felony, whether the principal felon shall have been convicted or not, etc. (See 11 and 12 Vic. 46, sec. 1.) And such seems to be the rule in some of the States which have adopted, in substance, Statute 7, Geo. IV. In this State, however, the distinction between accessories before the fact and principals has been abolished. By section 2, division 2, of the Criminal Code, (par. 331, Starr & Curtis,) it is provided: 'An accessory is he who stands by and aids, abets or assists, or who, not being present aiding, abetting or assisting, hath advised, encouraged, aided or abetted the perpetration of the crime. He who thus aids, abets, assists, advises or encourages shall be considered as principal, and punished accordingly.' It is to be observed that in the definition of accessories are included those who were principals in the second degree at common law,—that is, those standing by, aiding and abetting,—as well as those who, not being present, had advised and encouraged the perpetration of the crime, and it is expressly provided that all persons who are thus defined to be accessories shall be deemed principals, and punished accordingly. It necessarily follows, that none of the rights of the defendant incident to the prosecution of the defendant as an accessory,—such as, that he may insist upon the conviction of the principal before his arraignment and trial,—can inhere, for the reason that he is himself to be considered and regarded as a principal in the crime charged. All stand before the law as principals in the perpetration of the crime. By the express provision of the succeeding section of the Code, every person falling within the definition of an accessory thus given may be put upon trial with the principal actor in the perpetration of the crime, or before or after the latter's conviction, or whether he is amenable to justice or not, and 'punished as principal.'

"It is observable, that the advising or encouraging of another to commit a felony is not created into a substantive felony, of itself, but is made to so connect the offender with the principal felony that he becomes a principal in its commission. There is, in the nature of things, no difference in the degree of moral turpitude between the man whose will has procured the commission of a crime, and the one who willfully carries out his malignant purpose. . . ."

In defining the relationships and responsibilities of the parties to criminal offenses, modern statutory treatment has, in general, obliterated the common law distinctions between "principals" and "accessories before the fact".

SYKES v. DIRECTOR OF PUBLIC PROSECUTIONS

House of Lords, 1961.
3 W.L.R. 371.

LORD DENNING. My Lords, this case raises the question whether there is today such an offense as misprision of felony. Mr. Edward Clarke says that there has never been such an offense known to our law; or if there has, he says, it has ceased to be an offense by becoming obsolete. The Solicitor-General says that there always has been such an offense and the present case is a good example of its continuing usefulness. The facts giving rise to the question were as follows:

About March 18, 1960, thieves got into the weapon armoury at a United States Air Force station in Norfolk. They stole 100 pistols, 4 submachine-guns and about 1,960 rounds of ammunition. They hired a taxi and took the stolen goods to Manchester. They took them into the house of a man named Kenny. A day or two later a man named Whittle brought a van to Kenny's house and took the "stuff" to the house of a man named Black.

On March 23, 1960, Sykes comes into the story. We do not know how he came to know about the guns and ammunition but we know that he went up to an Irishman named Kerwin who was a waiter in a Manchester club and asked him: "Have you any contacts with the I.R.A.?" Kerwin said: "I don't want to talk about it in the club." They talked about it later: and they went to a hotel where they met two men. One of them was Kenny (the man who first received the guns in Manchester) and the other was a man named Tucker (who has not appeared in the story before). Kenny said they had 100 revolvers, some submachine-guns and ammunition for sale. Kerwin led them to think that he had contacts with the I.R.A. and would have to go to London to see them. But instead of going to London, he went to the police and acted under their instructions.

On March 27, 1960, Kerwin (prompted thereto by the police) told Sykes that he had arranged to dispose of the guns but he needed a sample to convince the organisation that the guns were there. Kerwin that night asked Sykes what he expected to gain financially and he said: "Half of what Tucker gets for his share."

On March 28, 1960, Kenny took a sample of one of the pistols and gave it to Kerwin (who gave it to the police). Later the police disguised themselves as would-be purchasers of the guns. They were taken to Black's house and shown the goods. Whereupon the police officers disclosed their identity, and arrested Kenny, Whittle and Black. They took possession of the stolen property. Afterwards they arrested Tucker and Sykes.

In the early morning of March 29, 1960, at the police station, the superintendent said to Sykes: "I have reason to believe that you were the man who first got into touch with an Irishman and asked him to contact the I.R.A. so that they could buy the guns and that you have been actively helping Kenny and Tucker in arranging for the sale of these guns during the past week." Sykes said: "Look, Inspector, that can't be possible. I don't know this man Kenny and I haven't seen Tucker for four months."

All five men were taken before the magistrates. Kenny, Tucker, Whittle and Black were charged with receiving the goods, knowing them to have been stolen. Sykes was charged as being accessory after the fact. After the evidence was taken, counsel for Sykes urged strongly that he ought not to be committed for trial on the charge of being accessory: there was no evidence that he had taken any active steps to conceal the felony or had done any act for *the purpose* of assisting the others to escape conviction.... But the magistrates committed all five men for trial.

When counsel was instructed to draft the indictment, he was so impressed by the argument which had been urged before the magistrates that he did not put in a count charging Sykes with being an accessory after the fact but charged him with misprision of felony....

There remains the ... point whether active concealment is an essential ingredient of [misprision of felony]. Now the ingredients of the offense can best be seen by comparing it with offenses of like degree which have other ingredients.

First: *Accessory after the fact.* The classic definition of an accessory after the fact is when a person, knowing a felony to have been committed, receives, relieves, comforts, or assists the felon, see 1 Hale P.C. 618, 4 Black. 37. These are all *active* acts of assistance from which it can be inferred that he assented to the felon going free, in contrast to misprision which consists of concealment only, from which no inference of assent need be drawn. It might be thought that the acts of assistance given by Sykes in the present case would be such as to make him an accessory after the fact. But it has been said that, to make a man an accessory, the assistance must be given to the felon *personally,* in order to prevent or hinder him from being apprehended or tried or suffering punishment ... so that if the assistance was not given the felon personally, but only indirectly by persuading witnesses not to give evidence against him ... or if the acts of assistance were done, not to hinder the arrest of the felon, but with another motive, such as to avoid arrest himself ... or to make money for himself without regard to what happened to the felon (as in the present case), he would not be guilty as an accessory after the fact. It was these limitations on the offense of being an accessory that led to Sykes being charged with misprision of felony....

This review of the authorities shows that the essential ingredients of misprision of felony are:

1. *Knowledge.* The accused man must know that a felony has been committed by someone else. His knowledge must be proved in the way in which the prosecution have been accustomed in other crimes when knowledge is an ingredient, such as receiving, accessory after the fact, compounding a felony, and so forth. That is to say, there must be evidence that a reasonable man in his place, with such facts and information before him as the accused had, would have known that a felony had been committed. From such evidence the jury may infer that the accused man himself had knowledge of it. He need not know the difference between felony and misdemeanour—many a lawyer has to look in the books for the purpose—but he must at least know that a serious offense has been committed: or, as the commissioners of 1840 put it, an offense of an "aggravated complexion": for after all, that is still, broadly speaking, the difference between a felony and misdemeanour. Felonies are the serious offenses. Misdemeanours are the less serious. If he knows that a serious offense has been committed—and a lawyer on turning up the books sees it is a felony—that will suffice. This requirement that it must be a serious offense disposes of many of the supposed absurdities, such as boys stealing apples, which many laymen would rank as a misdemeanour and no one would think he was bound to report to the police. It means that misprision comprehends an offense which is of so serious a character that an ordinary law-abiding citizen would realise he ought to report it to the police.

2. *Concealment.* The accused man must have "concealed or kept secret" his knowledge. He need not have done anything active: but it is his duty by law to disclose to proper authority all material facts known to him relative to the offence. It is not sufficient to tell the police that a felony has been committed. He must tell the name of the man who did it, if he knows it; the place, and so forth. All material facts known to him.... If he fails or refuses to perform this duty when there is a reasonable opportunity available to him to do so, then he is guilty of misprision. He can perform this duty by reporting to the police or a magistrate or anyone else in lawful authority. Failure to do so is a misprision of felony.

Misprision of felony is itself a misdemeanour and is punishable by fine and imprisonment. Whatever limitations may have existed in olden days on the period of imprisonment that might be imposed, the only limitation now is that it must not be an inordinately heavy sentence.

My Lords, it was said that this offence is out of date. I do not think so. The arm of the law would be too short if it was powerless to reach those who are "contact" men for thieves or assist them to gather in the fruits of their crime; or those who indulge in gang warfare and refuse to help in its suppression. There is no other offence of which such persons are guilty save that of misprision of felony.

I am not dismayed by the suggestion that the offence of misprision is impossibly wide: for I think it is subject to just limitations. Non-disclosure may be due to a claim of right made in good faith. For instance, if a lawyer is told by his client that he has committed a felony, it would be no misprision in the lawyer not to report it to the police, for he might in good faith claim that he was under a duty to keep it confidential. Likewise with doctor and patient, and clergyman and parishioner. There are other relationships which may give rise to a claim in good faith that it is in the public interest not to disclose it. For instance, if an employer discovers that his servant has been stealing from the till, he might well be justified in giving him another chance rather than reporting him to the police. Likewise with the master of a college and a student. But close family or personal ties will not suffice where the offence is of so serious a character that it ought to be reported. In 1315 it was held that it was the duty of a brother to raise hue and cry against his own brother and he was fined for not doing so ... and in 1938 a mistress was found guilty of misprision for shielding her lover.... The judges have not been called upon further to define the just limitations to misprision, but I do not doubt their ability to do so, if called upon.

My Lords, there was some discussion before us whether a man was bound to disclose a contemplated felony which comes to his knowledge, such as a planned raid on a bank. There is a striking passage in Lambard's Eirenarcha (1614), p. 289, which says that failure to do so is misprision of felony ... and the commissioners who reported on the Criminal Law in 1843 were clearly in favour of it. They said: "The necessity for making such disclosures extends, perhaps, with greater force, to the knowledge of a meditated crime, the perpetration of which may, by means of such a disclosure, be prevented, than it does to the knowledge of one already committed." This is good sense and may well be good law. I would therefore reserve this point which does not arise in the present case....

Lord Goddard....

Though in my opinion the offence should be sparingly prosecuted, I am by no means prepared to say that it has no use in our criminal law at the present day; it may well be used when there is technical difficulty in framing a charge of being an accessory after the fact to a felony, and counsel who had acted for the prosecution told us that was the reason for using it in the instant case. Moreover, it is almost a common-place in these days to find the police appealing for persons whom they think must be able to throw light on some serious crime to come forward and give their assistance. And there have been instances quite recently in wounding cases arising out of gang warfare of refusing to assist the police as to the identity of the attackers, whether from fear of reprisals or from a mistaken sense of loyalty. It is very easy to poke ridicule at the offence and say that it obliges people to inform against a boy stealing an apple. The law is nowadays administered with dignity and common sense. And if it is said it obliges a father to inform against his son, or vice versa, I would answer that in the case of a really heinous crime be it so.

In my opinion, therefore, misprision of felony is today an indictable misdemeanour at common law, and a person is guilty of the crime if knowing that a felony has been committed he conceals his knowledge from those responsible for the preservation of the peace, be they constables or justices, within a reasonable time and having a reasonable opportunity for so doing. What is a reasonable time and opportunity is a question of fact for a jury, and also whether the knowledge that he has is so definite that it ought to be disclosed. A man is neither bound nor would he be wise to disclose rumours or mere gossip, but if facts are within his knowledge that would materially assist in the detection and arrest of a felon he must disclose them as it is a duty he owes to the State. The gist of the offence is concealment which may be passive, that is mere non-disclosure, or active in destroying or hiding evidence, though in the latter case it would probably often amount to being an accessory after the fact, and I would add that where it is thought possible and proper to charge a person as an accessory it is preferable to do so rather than have recourse to the offence of misprision....

Appeal Dismissed.

NOTES

1. Parliament, in its Criminal Law Act of 1967, abolished the crime of misprision of felony except for treason. It substituted the offense of "compounding a crime."

2. In the United States there is generally lacking any obligation upon the part of anyone to report a criminal offense or reveal the identity of its perpetrator. The closest we have come in this country are the offenses of "compounding a felony" or "misprision of felony" (previously discussed, in Ch. 6–B), and prohibitions upon the concealment of fugitives.

A good discussion of the general subject is contained in Pope v. State, 284 Md. 309, 396 A.2d 1054, 1 A.L.R.4th 1 (1979), which ruled that there is no misprision of felony in Maryland and discussed the development of the offense under the common law.

3. A somewhat related offense is "complicity." Such statutes usually require a finding that the defendant had a duty to prevent the underlying crime. A Kentucky statute, KRS 502.020(1)(c), makes a person liable for the crime of

another when, with intent of promoting or facilitating the commission of a crime, the person "[h]aving a legal duty to prevent the commission of the offense, fails to make a proper effort to do so." In Knox v. Commonwealth, 735 S.W.2d 711 (Ky.1987), the court dealt with this question: If a mother fails to prevent her husband from raping her daughter, even though the daughter has previously complained of assaults by the husband upon the daughter, can the mother be convicted under the complicity statute? The court said "no," at least not where the complicity statute required a finding that the defendant had a legal duty to prevent the crime. The court declined to find a legal duty on the mother's part to prevent her daughter's rape. The State had a child abuse *reporting* statute, but the court declined to find this as creating a duty to *prevent* such abuse.

4. Another related concept is that of being an accomplice. Applying the principle that an accomplice is liable for the unlawful conduct of others that he aids and abets, a defendant who stood guard over a victim's parents while the victim was raped by his two companions was properly convicted of two separate crimes of accomplice rape ("rape in concert" under California law). "California, applying this principle as embodied in its law, quite properly punished [defendant] for each of the two acts of rape in concert that he aided and abetted when he guarded the parents. Nothing in the Constitution prevents this; indeed, in applying federal law, this court routinely has upheld convictions for multiple crimes aided and abetted by a single course of conduct. [...] Although [defendant] stood guard only once, he enabled his accomplices to commit two rapes in concert. This is more culpable than enabling them to commit only one. Each rape was a separate wrongful act." Watts v. Bonneville, 879 F.2d 685 (9th Cir.1989). The prosecution may prove inconsistent facts at the separate trials of accomplices without running afoul of the Double Jeopardy Clause. Nichols v. Scott, 69 F.2d 1255 (5th Cir.1995), *reversing* 802 F.Supp. 66 (S.D.Tex.1992).

*

PART 2

BASIC LEGAL CONCEPTS REGARDING PROOF OF GUILT

Chapter 9

REASONABLE DOUBT AND PRESUMPTIONS OF FACT

A. THE REQUIREMENT OF PROOF BEYOND A REASONABLE DOUBT

MULLANEY v. WILBUR

Supreme Court of the United States, 1975.
421 U.S. 684, 95 S.Ct. 1881.

MR. JUSTICE POWELL delivered the opinion of the Court.

The State of Maine requires a defendant charged with murder to prove that he acted "in the heat of passion on sudden provocation" in order to reduce the homicide to manslaughter. We must decide whether this rule comports with the due process requirement, as defined in In re Winship, 397 U.S. 358, 364, 90 S.Ct. 1068, 1072 (1970), that the prosecution prove beyond a reasonable doubt every fact necessary to constitute the crime charged.

I

In June 1966 a jury found respondent Stillman E. Wilbur, Jr., guilty of murder. The case against him rested on his own pretrial statement and on circumstantial evidence showing that he fatally assaulted Claude Hebert in the latter's hotel room. Respondent's statement, introduced by the prosecution, claimed that he had attacked Hebert in a frenzy provoked by Hebert's homosexual advance. The defense offered no evidence, but argued that the homicide was not unlawful since respondent lacked criminal intent. Alternatively, Wilbur's counsel asserted that at most the homicide was manslaughter rather than murder, since it occurred in the heat of passion provoked by the homosexual assault.

The trial court instructed the jury that Maine law recognizes only two kinds of homicide, murder and manslaughter, and that these offenses are not subdivided into different degrees. The common elements of both are that the homicide be unlawful—i.e., neither justifiable nor excusable—and that it be intentional. The prosecution is required to prove these elements by proof beyond a reasonable doubt, and only if they are so proved is the jury to consider the distinction between murder and manslaughter.

In view of the evidence the trial court drew particular attention to the difference between murder and manslaughter. After reading the statutory definitions of both offenses,[1] the court charged that "malice aforethought is an essential and indispensable element of the crime of murder," without which the homicide would be manslaughter. The jury was further instructed, however, that if the prosecution established that the homicide was both intentional and unlawful, malice aforethought was to be conclusively implied unless the defendant proved by a fair preponderance of the evidence that he acted in the heat of passion on sudden provocation. The court emphasized that "malice aforethought and heat of passion on sudden provocation are inconsistent things," thus, by proving the latter the defendant would negate the former and reduce the homicide from murder to manslaughter. The court then concluded its charge with elaborate definitions of "heat of passion" and "sudden provocation."

The Maine law of homicide, as it bears on this case, can be stated succinctly: Absent justification or excuse, all intentional or criminally reckless killings are felonious homicides. Felonious homicide is punished as murder—i.e., by life imprisonment—unless the defendant proves by a fair preponderance of the evidence that it was committed in the heat of passion on sudden provocation, in which case it is punished as manslaughter—i.e., by a fine not to exceed $1,000 or by imprisonment not to exceed 20 years. The issue is whether the Maine rule requiring the defendant to prove that he acted in the heat of passion on sudden provocation accords with due process.

A

Our analysis may be illuminated if this issue is placed in historical context.

At early common law only those homicides committed in the enforcement of justice were considered justifiable; all others were deemed unlawful and were punished by death. Gradually, however, the severity of the common-law punishment for homicide abated. Between the 13th

1. The Maine murder statute, Me.Rev. Stat., Tit. 17, § 2651, provides:

> "Whoever unlawfully kills a human being with malice aforethought, either express or implied, is guilty of murder and shall be punished by imprisonment for life."

The manslaughter statute, Tit. 17, § 2551, in relevant part provides:

> "Whoever unlawfully kills a human being in the heat of passion, on sudden provocation, without express or implied malice aforethought . . . shall be punished by a fine of not more than $1,000 or by imprisonment for not more than 20 years. . . ."

and 16th centuries the class of justifiable homicides expanded to include, for example, accidental homicides and those committed in self-defense.... It was said that "manslaughter (when voluntary) arises from the sudden heat of passions, murder from the wickedness of the heart." 4 Blackstone's Commentaries 190. Malice aforethought was designated as the element that distinguished the two crimes, but it was recognized that such malice could be implied by law as well as proved by evidence. Absent proof that an unlawful homicide resulted from "sudden and sufficiently violent provocation," the homicide was "presumed to be malicious." In view of this presumption, the early English authorities, relying on the case of The King v. Onerby, 92 Eng.Rep. 465 (KB 1727), held that once the prosecution proved that the accused had committed the homicide, it was "incumbent on the prisoner to make out ... all ... circumstances of justification, excuse or alleviation ... to the satisfaction of the court and jury." 4 Blackstone's Commentaries 201. Thus, at common law the burden of proving heat of passion on sudden provocation appears to have rested on the defendant.

In this country the concept of malice aforethought took on two distinct meanings: in some jurisdictions it came to signify a substantive element of intent, requiring the prosecution to prove that the defendant intended to kill or to inflict great bodily harm; in other jurisdictions it remained a policy presumption, indicating only that absent proof to the contrary a homicide was presumed not to have occurred in the heat of passion. In a landmark case, Commonwealth v. York, 9 Met. (50 Mass.) 93 (1845), Chief Justice Shaw of the Massachusetts Supreme Judicial Court held that the defendant was required to negate malice aforethought by proving by a preponderance of the evidence that he acted in the heat of passion. Initially, *York* was adopted in Maine as well as several other jurisdictions. In 1895, however, in the context of deciding a question of federal criminal procedure, this Court explicitly considered and unanimously rejected the general approach articulated in *York*. Davis v. United States, 160 U.S. 469, 16 S.Ct. 353.[2] And, in the past half century, the large majority of States have abandoned *York* and now require the prosecution to prove the absence of the heat of passion on sudden provocation beyond a reasonable doubt. See LaFave & Austin, Criminal Law 539–540 (1972).

This historical review establishes two important points. First, the fact at issue here—the presence or absence of the heat of passion on sudden provocation—has been, almost from the inception of the common law of homicide, the single most important factor in determining the degree of culpability attaching to an unlawful homicide. And, second, the clear trend has been toward requiring the prosecution to bear the ultimate burden of proving this fact.

2. In Leland v. Oregon, 343 U.S. 790, 72 S.Ct. 1002 (1952), the Court declined to apply the specific holding of *Davis*—that the prosecution must prove sanity beyond a reasonable doubt—to the States.

B

Petitioners, the warden of the Maine Prison and the State of Maine argue that despite these considerations *Winship* should not be extended to the present case. They note that as a formal matter the absence of the heat of passion on sudden provocation is not a "fact necessary to constitute the *crime*" of felonious homicide in Maine. In re Winship (emphasis supplied). This distinction is relevant, according to petitioners, because in *Winship* the facts at issue were essential to establish criminality in the first instance whereas the fact in question here does not come into play until the jury already has determined that the defendant is guilty and may be punished at least for manslaughter. In this situation, petitioners maintain, the defendant's critical interests in liberty and reputation are no longer of paramount concern since, irrespective of the presence or absence of the heat of passion on sudden provocation, he is likely to lose his liberty and certain to be stigmatized. In short, petitioners would limit *Winship* to those facts which, if not proved, would wholly exonerate the defendant.

This analysis fails to recognize that the criminal law of Maine, like that of other jurisdictions, is concerned not only with guilt or innocence in the abstract but also with the degree of criminal culpability. Maine has chosen to distinguish those who kill in the heat of passion from those who kill in the absence of this factor. Because the former are less "blameworth[y]," State v. Lafferty, 309 A.2d, at 671, 673 (concurring opinion), they are subject to substantially less severe penalties. By drawing this distinction, while refusing to require the prosecution to establish beyond a reasonable doubt the fact upon which it turns, Maine denigrates the interests found critical in *Winship*.

The safeguards of due process are not rendered unavailing simply because a determination may already have been reached that would stigmatize the defendant and that might lead to a significant impairment of personal liberty. The fact remains that the consequences resulting from a verdict of murder, as compared with a verdict of manslaughter, differ significantly. Indeed, when viewed in terms of the potential difference in restrictions of personal liberty attendant to each conviction, the distinction established by Maine between murder and manslaughter may be of greater importance than the difference between guilt or innocence for many lesser crimes.

Moreover, if *Winship* were limited to those facts that constitute a crime as defined by state law, a State could undermine many of the interests that decision sought to protect without effecting any substantive change in its law. It would only be necessary to redefine the elements that comprise different crimes, characterizing them as factors that bear solely on the extent of punishment. An extreme example of this approach can be fashioned from the law challenged in this case. Maine divides the single generic offense of felonious homicide into three distinct punishment categories—murder, voluntary manslaughter, and involuntary manslaughter. Only the first two of these categories require that the homicidal act either be intentional or the result of criminally reckless conduct. But under Maine law these facts of intent are not general elements of the crime of felonious homicide. Instead, they bear only on the appropriate punishment category. Thus, if petitioners' argument were accepted, Maine could impose a life sentence for any felonious homicide—even those that traditionally might be considered involuntary manslaughter—unless the *defendant* was able to prove that his act was neither intentional nor criminally reckless.

Winship is concerned with substance rather than this kind of formalism. The rationale of that case requires an analysis that looks to the "operation and effect of the law as applied and enforced by the state," and to the interests of both the State and the defendant as affected by the allocation of the burden of proof.

In *Winship* the court emphasized the societal interests in the reliability of jury verdicts:

> "The requirement of proof beyond a reasonable doubt has [a] vital role in our criminal procedure for cogent reasons. The accused during a criminal prosecution has at stake interests of immense importance, both because of the possibility that he may lose his liberty upon conviction and because of the certainty that he would be stigmatized by the conviction.
>
> * * *
>
> "Moreover, use of the reasonable-doubt standard is indispensable to command the respect and confidence of the community in applications of the criminal law. It is critical that the moral force of the criminal law not be diluted by a standard of proof that leaves people in doubt whether innocent men are being condemned."

* * *

... In *Winship* the ultimate burden of persuasion remained with the prosecution, although the standard had been reduced to proof by a fair preponderance of the evidence. In this case, by contrast, the State has affirmatively shifted the burden of proof to the defendant. The result, in a case such as this one where the defendant is required to prove the critical fact in dispute, is to increase further the likelihood of an erroneous murder conviction. Such a result directly contravenes the principle articulated in Speiser v. Randall, 357 U.S. 513, 525–526, 78 S.Ct. 1332, 1342 (1958):

> "[W]here one party has at stake an interest of transcending value—as a criminal defendant his liberty—th[e] margin of error is reduced as to him by the process of placing on the [prosecution] the burden ... of persuading the factfinder at the conclusion of the trial...."

C

It has been suggested that because of the difficulties in negating an argument that the homicide was committed in the heat of passion the burden of proving this fact should rest on the defendant. No doubt this is often a heavy burden for the prosecution to satisfy. The same may be said of the requirement of proof beyond a reasonable doubt of many controverted facts in a criminal trial. But this is the traditional burden which our system of criminal justice deems essential.

Indeed ... most States require the prosecution to prove the absence of passion beyond a reasonable doubt. Moreover, the difficulty of meeting such an exacting burden is mitigated in Maine where the fact at issue is largely an "objective, rather than a subjective, behavioral criterion." State v. Rollins, 295 A.2d, at 920. In this respect, proving that the defendant did not act in the heat of passion on sudden provocation is similar to proving any other element of intent; it may be established by adducing evidence of the factual circumstances surrounding the commission of the homicide. And although intent is typically considered a fact peculiarly within the knowledge of the defendant, this does not, as the Court has long recognized, justify shifting the burden to him.

Nor is the requirement of proving a negative unique in our system of criminal jurisprudence. Maine itself requires the prosecution to prove the absence of self-defense beyond a reasonable doubt. Satisfying this burden imposes an obligation that, in all practical effect, is identical to the burden involved in negating the heat of passion on sudden provocation. Thus, we discern no unique hardship on the prosecution that would justify requiring the defendant to carry the burden of proving a fact so critical to criminal culpability.[3]

Maine law requires a defendant to establish by a preponderance of the evidence that he acted in the heat of passion on sudden provocation in order to reduce murder to manslaughter. Under this burden of proof a defendant can be given a life sentence when the evidence indicates that

3. This conclusion is supported by consideration of a related line of cases. Generally in a criminal case the prosecution bears both the production burden and the persuasion burden. In some instances, however, it is aided by a presumption, see Davis v. United States, 160 U.S. 469, 16 S.Ct. 353 (1895) (presumption of sanity), or a permissible inference, see United States v. Gainey, 380 U.S. 63, 85 S.Ct. 754 (1965) (inference of knowledge from presence at an illegal still). These procedural devices require (in the case of a presumption) or permit (in the case of an inference) the trier of fact to conclude that the prosecution has met its burden of proof with respect to the presumed or inferred fact by having satisfactorily established other facts. Thus, in effect they require the defendant to present some evidence contesting the otherwise presumed or inferred fact. See Barnes v. United States, 412 U.S. 837, 846 n. 11, 93 S.Ct. 2357, 2363 (1973). Since they shift the production burden to the defendant, these devices must satisfy certain due process requirements.

In each of these cases, however, the ultimate burden of persuasion by proof beyond a reasonable doubt remained on the prosecution. Shifting the burden of persuasion to the defendant obviously places an even greater strain upon him since he no longer need only present some evidence with respect to the fact at issue; he must affirmatively establish that fact. Accordingly, the Due Process Clause demands more exacting standards before the State may require a defendant to bear this ultimate burden of persuasion. See generally Ashford & Risinger, Presumptions, Assumptions and Due Process in Criminal Cases: A Theoretical Overview, 78 Yale L.J. 165 (1969).

it is *as likely as not* that he deserves a significantly lesser sentence. This is an intolerable result in a society where, to paraphrase Mr. Justice Harlan, it is far worse to sentence one guilty only of manslaughter as a murderer than to sentence a murderer for the lesser crime of manslaughter. We therefore hold that the Due Process Clause requires the prosecution to prove beyond a reasonable doubt the absence of the heat of passion on sudden provocation when the issue is properly presented in a homicide case.

MR. JUSTICE REHNQUIST, with whom THE CHIEF JUSTICE joins, concurring.

While I join in the Court's opinion, the somewhat peculiar posture of the case as it comes to us leads me to add these observations.

* * *

I agree with the Court that In re Winship, does require that the prosecution prove beyond a reasonable doubt every element which constitutes the crime charged against a defendant. I see no inconsistency between that holding and the holding of Leland v. Oregon, 343 U.S. 790, 72 S.Ct. 1002 (1952). In the latter case this Court held that there was no constitutional requirement that the State shoulder the burden of proving the sanity of the defendant.

The Court noted in *Leland* that the issue of insanity as a defense to a criminal charge was considered by the jury only after it had found that all elements of the offense, including the *mens rea* if any required by state law, had been proven beyond a reasonable doubt. Although as the state court's instructions in *Leland* recognized, evidence relevant to insanity as defined by state law may also be relevant to whether the required *mens rea* was present, the existence or nonexistence of legal insanity bears no necessary relationship to the existence or nonexistence of the required mental elements of the crime. For this reason, Oregon's placement of the burden of proof on insanity on Leland, unlike Maine's redefinition of homicide in the instant case, did not effect an unconstitutional shift in the State's traditional burden of proof beyond a reasonable doubt of all necessary elements of the offense. Both the Court's opinion and the concurring opinion of Mr. Justice Harlan in In re Winship, supra, stress the importance of proof beyond a reasonable doubt in a criminal case as "bottomed on a fundamental value determination of our society that it is far worse to convict an innocent man than to let a guilty man go free." Having once met that rigorous burden of proof that, for example, in a case such as this, the defendant not only killed a fellow human being, but did it with malice aforethought, the State could quite consistently with such a constitutional principle conclude that a defendant who sought to establish the defense of insanity, and thereby escape any punishment whatever for a heinous crime, should bear the laboring oar on such an issue.

NOTES

1. In In re Winship, 397 U.S. 358, 90 S.Ct. 1068 (1970), the Court said: "... we explicitly hold that the Due Process Clause protects the accused against

conviction except upon proof of guilt beyond a reasonable doubt of every fact necessary to constitute the crime with which he is charged". The Court then went on to hold that the reasonable doubt standard was a constitutional requirement in the adjudicatory stage of state juvenile court proceedings where the allegation underlying the delinquency petition is the alleged violation of a criminal statute.

Justice Harlan, in his concurring opinion viewed the reasonable doubt standard as "bottomed on a fundamental value determination of our society that it is far worse to convict an innocent man than to let a guilty man go free". He relied upon two propositions which he thought could not be fairly disputed:

> First, in a judicial proceeding in which there is a dispute about the facts of some earlier event, the factfinder cannot acquire unassailably accurate knowledge of what happened. Instead, all the factfinder can acquire is a belief of what *probably* happened. The intensity of this belief—the degree to which a factfinder is convinced that a given act actually occurred—can, of course, vary. In this regard, a standard of proof represents an attempt to instruct the factfinder concerning the degree of confidence our society thinks he should have in the correctness of factual conclusions for a particular type of adjudication. Although the phrases "preponderance of the evidence" and "proof beyond a reasonable doubt" are quantitatively imprecise, they do communicate to the finder of fact different notions concerning the degree of confidence he is expected to have in the correctness of his factual conclusions.
>
> A second proposition, which is really nothing more than a corollary of the first, is that the trier of fact will sometimes, despite his best efforts, be wrong in his factual conclusions. In a lawsuit between two parties, a factual error can make a difference in one of two ways. First, it can result in a judgment in favor of the plaintiff when the true facts warrant a judgment for the defendant. The analogue in a criminal case would be the conviction of an innocent man. On the other hand, an erroneous factual determination can result in a judgment for the defendant when the true facts justify a judgment in plaintiff's favor. The criminal analogue would be the acquittal of a guilty man.
>
> The standard of proof influences the relative frequency of these two types of erroneous outcomes. If, for example, the standard of proof for a criminal trial were a preponderance of the evidence rather than proof beyond a reasonable doubt, there would be a smaller risk of factual errors that result in freeing guilty persons, but a far greater risk of factual errors that result in convicting the innocent. Because the standard of proof affects the comparative frequency of these two types of erroneous outcomes, the choice of the standard to be applied in a particular kind of litigation should, in a rational world, reflect an assessment of the comparative social disutility of each.
>
> When one makes such an assessment, the reason for different standards of proof in civil as opposed to criminal litigation becomes apparent. In a civil suit between two private parties for money damages, for example, we view it as no more serious in general for there to be an erroneous verdict in the defendant's favor than for there to be an erroneous verdict in the plaintiff's favor. A preponderance of the evidence standard therefore seems peculiarly appropriate for, as explained most sensibly, it simply requires the trier of fact "to believe that

the existence of a fact is more probable than its nonexistence before [he] may find in favor of the party who has the burden to persuade the [judge] of the fact's existence."

In a criminal case, on the other hand, we do not view the social disutility of convicting an innocent man as equivalent to the disutility of acquitting someone who is guilty. As Mr. Justice Brennan wrote for the Court in Speiser v. Randall (1958):

> "There is always in litigation a margin of error, representing error in factfinding, which both parties must take into account. Where one party has at stake an interest of transcending value—as a criminal defendant his liberty—this margin of error is reduced as to him by the process of placing on the other party the burden ... of persuading the fact-finder at the conclusion of the trial of his guilt beyond a reasonable doubt."

In this context, I view the requirement of proof beyond a reasonable doubt in a criminal case as bottomed on a fundamental value determination of our society that it is far worse to convict an innocent man than to let a guilty man go free. It is only because of the nearly complete and long-standing acceptance of the reasonable-doubt standard by the States in criminal trials that the Court has not before today had to hold explicitly that due process, as an expression of fundamental procedural fairness requires a more stringent standard for criminal trials than for ordinary civil litigation.

Justice Black dissented in *Winship* from the Court's declaration that the reasonable doubt standard is constitutionally mandated in criminal cases. Chief Justice Burger, joined by Justice Stewart, dissented from the requirement as applied to juvenile court proceedings and deplored the transformation of juvenile courts "into criminal courts, which is what we are well on the way to accomplishing".

Compare the statement of the Court in *In re Winship* in the first paragraph of this note 1 with the following statement of the plurality of the Court in Apodaca v. Oregon, 406 U.S. 404, 92 S.Ct. 1628 (1972):

> "We are quite sure, however, that the Sixth Amendment itself has never been held to require proof beyond a reasonable doubt in criminal cases. The reasonable doubt standard developed separately from both the jury trial and the unanimous verdict ... the rule requiring proof of crime beyond a reasonable doubt did not crystallize in this country until after the Constitution was adopted."

2. In Patterson v. New York, 432 U.S. 197, 97 S.Ct. 2319 (1977), the Supreme Court held that *Mullaney* does not prohibit placing the burden of proof as to an *affirmative defense* on the defendant, where that affirmative defense (even if it merely reduces the grade of the offense) bears no relationship to the elements of the crime (such as death, causation, and intent). In the case in question, the New York statute provided that "extreme emotion disturbance" reduced murder to manslaughter. It placed upon the defendant the burden of persuasion on the "emotion disturbance" issue. The Court upheld the statutory scheme. Apparently *Patterson* would be sound precedent for a holding that a statute could require the accused to prove that he acted under "serious provocation" in order to reduce murder to voluntary manslaughter. In People v. Kohl, 72 N.Y.2d 191, 527 N.E.2d 1182 (1988) the Court upheld a statute placing the burden of proving insanity upon the defendant but also required the jury be told

the state must prove beyond a reasonable doubt that defendant had a "conscious objective" to kill the victim.

In Martin v. Ohio, 480 U.S. 228, 107 S.Ct. 1098 (1987) the Court sustained an Ohio law which required an accused to prove self-defense by a preponderance of the evidence. The Court regarded *Patterson* as a controlling precedent and approved the Ohio rule despite the fact that it was law only in Ohio and South Carolina.

BORUM v. UNITED STATES

United States Court of Appeals, 1967.
127 U.S.App.D.C. 48, 380 F.2d 595.

BAZELON, CHIEF JUDGE. Borum appeals from a jury conviction for housebreaking. In another appeal, decided today, we affirmed Borum's conviction for housebreaking and robbery committed one month after the alleged crime in the instant case. [Stevenson and Borum v. United States, 380 F.2d 590.] In that case, as in this one, the Government's fingerprint evidence proved that at some time the defendants touched objects found at the scene of the crime. But there the Government introduced additional evidence indicating that these objects were generally inaccessible to the defendants and that therefore the objects were probably touched during the commission of the crime. Here, the Government introduced no evidence indicating that the objects were generally inaccessible to Borum. Therefore, we reverse.

The Government's evidence showed that complainant's home was entered and ransacked in his absence between 11:45 a.m. and 3:00 p.m. on June 2, 1965. Four fingerprints, taken from one or two empty jars, were identified as Borum's. Other fingerprints, found on different jars and on a metal box, had not been identified by the time of trial. Complainant testified that the jars had contained a valuable coin collection and that the coin collection was stolen along with other items of personal property. However, Borum was tried for, but not convicted of, grand larceny. On cross-examination and rebuttal the Government elicited testimony which, when all inferences are made in favor of the Government placed Borum within a mile and a half of complainant's home at about 1:00 p.m. Borum's principal contention is that the trial court erred in denying his motions for acquittal at the conclusion of the Government's case and at the conclusion of all the testimony. [According to the court's footnote 1, "The motion must be granted 'if there is no evidence upon which a reasonable mind might fairly conclude guilt beyond a reasonable doubt' ", citing supporting cases.]

The Government's evidence shows that Borum touched the one or two jars in question. But there is no evidence, *either direct or circumstantial,* which indicates that he touched the jars in the course of a housebreaking on June 2, 1965. Indeed, one of the Government's own witnesses testified that Borum's fingerprints could have been on the jars "indefinitely." And another agreed that the fingerprints could have been on the jars "for a period of ... years."[1] The Government introduced no evidence which could account for, or even suggest an inference about, the custody or location of the jars during that period.

Of course, the jury may have thought that Borum could not have touched the jars at any other time or in any other place. The jury may have thought that Borum never had any opportunity to touch the jars outside the house either before or after complainant bought them.[2] But that conclusion would have been based on speculation alone. The jury had no way to determine where the complainant purchased the jars, or how long he had them before June 2, or whether complainant ever removed them from his home, or how long the prints were on the jars. The Government need not negate all inferences consistent with innocence which could arise from the fingerprints. It negated none.[3]

With evidence so inconclusive, a reasonable person must have a reasonable doubt about Borum's guilt. The case should not have been submitted to the jury, for the Government produced no evidence, *either direct or circumstantial,* which could support an inference that the fingerprints were placed on the jars during commission of the crime. Fingerprint evidence is very reliable. It is a kind of evidence courts should encourage police to obtain. But to allow this conviction to stand would be to hold that anyone who touches anything which is found later at the scene of a crime may be convicted, provided he was within a mile and a half of the scene when the crime may have been committed. We decline to adopt such a rule.

Reversed with directions to enter a judgment of acquittal.

J. SKELLY WRIGHT, CIRCUIT JUDGE (concurring) [opinion omitted].

BURGER, CIRCUIT JUDGE (dissenting):

1. There can be no dispute in this case (1) that in order to make the fingerprints support Borum's conviction of housebreaking the Government was required to show that he touched the jars on June 2, in the course of the housebreaking; and (2) that the Government relied on the fingerprint evidence alone. The trial judge charged the jury as follows:

> The Court charges you, members of the jury, because of the fact that two of the Government's expert fingerprint witnesses testified that latent fingerprints on certain objects may last indefinitely, unless the Government has proved beyond a reasonable doubt that the fingerprints the Government relies on were left by the defendant on June 2nd, 1965 at the time of the alleged housebreaking on the objects referred to in the expert's testimony, you must find the defendant not guilty. Now the Government rests its case in this matter of expert testimony on what it called circumstantial evidence. In criminal cases there are two types of evidence. One type is known as direct evidence, and another type of evidence is known as circumstantial evidence. By direct evidence is meant evidence of eye witnesses who saw the act perpetrated.
>
> Now there was no one who testified here that they saw the defendant commit the housebreaking or grand larceny. The Government relies, as I said before, upon the circumstantial evidence of the fingerprints.

In fact, the only "direct" evidence in the case was the testimony of an eye witness who said that Borum was not the man he saw on the complainant's porch around the time of the crime.

2. It is at least reasonable to suppose that Borum touched the jars in question outside the house, since the police did not find Borum's fingerprints on any of the other jars or on anything else in the house, even though the house was forcibly entered and thoroughly ransacked.

3. Borum made no attempt to explain the existence of his fingerprints, but under our law he was not obliged to do so.

The majority sets a new record of usurpation of the jury's fact finding function.... The majority justifies the holding with no more than the astonishing statement that "if we allow this conviction to stand, anyone who touches anything which is found later at the scene of a crime could be convicted...." If there are any "predictions of gloom and doom" in what is said today, I suggest they are to be found in that statement.

No one questions that a court is required to grant a motion for acquittal if the evidence is such that a reasonable juror *must* have a reasonable doubt as to the defendant's guilt. But today's holding blandly ignores the corollary to this proposition, which we have stated in our leading case on the subject, that

> if a reasonable mind *might* fairly have a reasonable doubt or *might not* have one, *the case is for the jury,* and the decision is for the jurors to make.[4]

Moreover, this court has made it plain that the mere existence of other possible hypotheses is not enough to remove the case from the jury:

> If the judge were to direct acquittal whenever in his opinion the evidence failed to exclude every hypothesis but that of guilt, he would preempt the functions of the jury. Under such a rule, the judge would have to be convinced of guilt beyond peradventure of doubt before the jury would be permitted to consider the case. That is not the place of the jury in criminal procedure. They are the judges of facts and of guilt or innocence, not merely a device for checking upon the conclusions of the judge.

Law enforcement agencies have been given frequent judicial lectures that they should rely on "scientific" evidence rather than on confessions and recent Supreme Court decisions in criminal cases reflect this point of view. Here we have a conviction resting on one of the highest forms of scientific evidence.

The undisputed evidence before the jury in this case established that 300 pounds of coins were stolen, that four separate fingerprints of Appellant were found on glass jars in which the coin collection was kept, and that these jars were stored in the second floor closet of a private home to which Appellant had no lawful access.

Many cases have found fingerprint evidence alone to be sufficient to support conviction.... The majority in the instant case considers four fingerprints so inconclusive that reasonable persons must necessarily have a reasonable doubt about Appellant's guilt. The majority seems to assume that the prosecution's case must answer *all* questions and remove *all* doubts, which, of course, is not the law because that would be impossible; the proof need only satisfy reasonable doubt.

4. Curley v. United States, 81 U.S.App. D.C. 389, 392, 160 F.2d 229, 233 (1947). Emphasis added.

Judge Bazelon solemnly states the obvious, that we must not let juries speculate. But it is surely equally obvious law that on appeal all inferences from the evidence must be made *against,* not for, Appellant, and that a reviewing court may not indulge in speculation. Judge Bazelon ignores these very basic rules and embarks on an excursion of appellate speculation wholly outside the record. To me, the problems which the majority sees in this case are to be resolved—as they were here—by allowing the jurors to perform their traditional duty, applying their collective experience in weighing probabilities, to determine whether it was reasonable to draw an inference that Appellant entered the complainant's home and, alone or with others, committed a crime.

Nevertheless, Judge Bazelon frets:

> The jury had no way to determine [1] where the complainant purchased the jars, or [2] how long he had them before June 2, or [3] whether complainant ever removed them from his home, or [4] how long the prints were on the jars.

Here we have not one judicial speculation but *four* in a transparent effort to create an illusion of doubt. We surely can assume that Appellant's experienced trial lawyer made those arguments to the jury if she thought they had any validity. But when judges do this they take on the partisan role of advocates, especially in making contentions rejected by the lawful fact finders. Judge Bazelon goes on to state

> there is no evidence *either direct or circumstantial* which indicates that he touched the jars in the course of a housebreaking on June 2, 1965. (Emphasis original.)

Under this novel and remarkable standard the majority denies the jury its right to draw reasonable inferences from facts in evidence.

Having conjured up their own speculative explanation and "bootstrapped" themselves into doubt and confusion, my colleagues conclude:

> The Government need not negate all inferences consistent with innocence which could arise from the fingerprints. It negated none. (Footnotes omitted).

Resolving factual and credibility issues contrary to the decision of the trial judge and 12 jurors is a favorite sport of some appellate judges, but that function is not lawfully ours. Judge Youngdahl, the trial judge, after hearing all the evidence, and against his background of more than 30 years as a trial and appellate judge, was fully satisfied that a rational inference of guilt could be drawn by the jury from the evidence. Judge Youngdahl examined this aspect of the case first on a motion for acquittal, second on a motion for a directed verdict, and for a third time on a motion for judgment N.O.V. His memorandum on denial of that motion is included as an appendix to this dissent; it reflects his scrupulous care in evaluating the evidence.

To the already vast array of safeguards fashioned for the protection of an accused, including the ancient presumption of innocence, the requirements for proof beyond reasonable doubt, and a unanimous verdict, my colleagues would add a new dimension: that guilt must be established beyond *all* and every *doubt.* Happily that effort falls on the same day it is launched. But it is only a fortuity that Borum is not to be released today to renew his career of crime, since he stands convicted of *three* crimes all committed within a relatively short space of time. My colleagues set him free as to the conviction in this case but his conviction in *Stevenson and Borum* is affirmed today on evidence essentially the same, i.e., fingerprints, which the majority finds insufficient in this appeal. Borum's appeal in his third case is awaiting briefs.

It should be clear from Judge Danaher's excellent opinion in *Stevenson and Borum* that the result in the instant appeal cannot be regarded as changing the basic rule on the respective roles of judge and jury. At best, it is an isolated instance of judges dabbling in the jury function of dispensing mercy and exercising the executive function of dispensing clemency.

I suggest that the kind of nit-picking appellate review exhibited by reversal of this conviction may help explain why the public is losing confidence in the administration of justice. I suggest also that if we continue on this course we may well come to be known as a society incapable of defending itself—the impotent society.

NOTE

For cases holding contrary to the foregoing main case, and for a discussion generally of the presumptions based upon fingerprint evidence, consult Moenssens, Inbau, and Starrs Scientific Evidence in Criminal Cases (3d ed. 1986), Ch. 7.

B. THE MEANING OF "REASONABLE DOUBT"

VICTOR v. NEBRASKA

Supreme Court of the United States, 1994.
511 U.S. 1, 114 S.Ct. 1239.

JUSTICE O'CONNOR delivered the opinion of the Court.*

The government must prove beyond a reasonable doubt every element of a charged offense. *In re Winship,* (1970). Although this standard is an ancient and honored aspect of our criminal justice system, it defies easy explication. In these cases, we consider the constitutionality of two attempts to define "reasonable doubt."

I

The beyond a reasonable doubt standard is a requirement of due process, but the Constitution neither prohibits trial courts from defining

* Justices Blackmun and Souter join only Part II of this opinion. Justice Ginsburg joins only Parts II, III–B, and IV.

reasonable doubt nor requires them to do so as a matter of course. Indeed, so long as the court instructs the jury on the necessity that the defendant's guilt be proven beyond a reasonable doubt, the Constitution does not require that any particular form of words be used in advising the jury of the government's burden of proof. Rather, "taken as a whole, the instructions [must] correctly conve[y] the concept of reasonable doubt to the jury." *Holland v. United States* (1954).

In only one case have we held that a definition of reasonable doubt violated the Due Process Clause. *Cage v. Louisiana* (1990) (*per curiam*). There, the jurors were told:

> " '[A reasonable doubt] is one that is founded upon a real tangible substantial basis and not upon mere caprice and conjecture. *It must be such doubt as would give rise to a grave uncertainty,* raised in your mind by reasons of the unsatisfactory character of the evidence or lack thereof. A reasonable doubt is not a mere possible doubt. *It is an actual substantial doubt.* It is a doubt that a reasonable man can seriously entertain. What is required is not an absolute or mathematical certainty, but a *moral certainty.*' "

We held that the highlighted portions of the instruction rendered it unconstitutional:

> "It is plain to us that the words 'substantial' and 'grave,' as they are commonly understood, suggest a higher degree of doubt than is required for acquittal under the reasonable doubt standard. When those statements are then considered with the reference to 'moral certainty,' rather than evidentiary certainty, it becomes clear that a reasonable juror could have interpreted the instruction to allow a finding of guilt based on a degree of proof below that required by the Due Process Clause."

In a subsequent case, we made clear that the proper inquiry is not whether the instruction "could have" been applied in unconstitutional manner, but whether there is a reasonable likelihood that the jury *did* so apply it. *Estelle v. McGuire,* (1991). The constitutional question in the present cases, therefore, is whether there is a reasonable likelihood that the jury understood the instructions to allow conviction based on proof insufficient to meet the *Winship* standard.

* * *

II

On October 14, 1984, petitioner Sandoval shot three men, two of them fatally, in a gang-related incident in Los Angeles. About two weeks later, he entered the home of a man who had given information to the police about the murders and shot him dead; Sandoval then killed the man's wife because she had seen him murder her husband. Sandoval was convicted on four counts of first degree murder. The jury found that Sandoval personally used a firearm in the commission of each offense, and found the special circumstance of multiple murder. He was sentenced to death for murdering the woman and to life in prison without possibility of parole for the other three murders. The California Supreme Court affirmed the convictions and sentences.

The jury in Sandoval's case was given the following instruction on the government's burden of proof:

> "A defendant in a criminal action is presumed to be innocent until the contrary is proved, and in case of a reasonable doubt whether his guilt is satisfactorily shown, he is entitled to a verdict of not guilty. This presumption places upon the State the burden of proving him guilty beyond a reasonable doubt.
>
> "Reasonable doubt is defined as follows: It is *not a mere possible doubt;* because everything relating to human affairs, and *depending on moral evidence,* is open to some possible or imaginary doubt. It is that state of the case which, after the entire comparison and consideration of all the evidence, leaves the minds of the jurors in that condition that they cannot say they feel an abiding conviction, *to a moral certainty,* of the truth of the charge."

The California Supreme Court rejected Sandoval's claim that the instruction, particularly the highlighted passages, violated the Due Process Clause.

The instruction given in Sandoval's case has its genesis in a charge given by Chief Justice Shaw of the Massachusetts Supreme Judicial Court more than a century ago:

> "[W]hat is reasonable doubt? It is a term often used, probably pretty well understood, but not easily defined. It is not mere possible doubt; because every thing relating to human affairs, and depending on moral evidence, is open to some possible or imaginary doubt. It is that state of the case, which, after the entire comparison and consideration of all the evidence, leaves the minds of jurors in that condition that they cannot say they feel an abiding conviction, to a moral certainty, of the truth of the charge. The burden of proof is upon the prosecutor. All the presumptions of law independent of evidence are in favor of innocence; and every person is presumed to be innocent until he is proved guilty. If upon such proof there is reasonable doubt remaining, the accused is entitled to the benefit of it by an acquittal. For it is not sufficient to establish a probability, though a strong one arising from the doctrine of chances, that the fact charged is more likely to be true than the contrary; but the evidence must establish the truth of the fact to a reasonable and moral certainty; a certainty that convinces and directs the understanding, and satisfies the reason and judgment, of those who are bound to act consci-

entiously upon it. This we take to be proof beyond reasonable doubt." Commonwealth v. Webster, 59 Mass. 295, 320 (1850).

The *Webster* charge is representative of the time when "American courts began applying [the beyond a reasonable doubt standard] in its modern form in criminal cases." In [1866], the California Supreme Court characterized the *Webster* instruction as "probably the most satisfactory definition ever given to the words 'reasonable doubt' in any case known to criminal jurisprudence." And in 1927, the state legislature adopted the bulk of the *Webster* instruction as a statutory definition of reasonable doubt.

* * *

A

Sandoval's primary objection is to the use of the phrases "moral evidence" and "moral certainty" in the instruction. This part of the charge was lifted verbatim from Chief Justice Shaw's *Webster* decision; some understanding of the historical context in which that instruction was written is accordingly helpful in evaluating its continuing validity.

* * *

When Chief Justice Shaw penned the *Webster* instruction in 1850, moral certainty meant a state of subjective certitude about some event or occurrence. As the Massachusetts Supreme Judicial Court subsequently explained:

> "Proof 'beyond a reasonable doubt' ... is proof 'to a moral certainty,' as distinguished from an absolute certainty. As applied to a judicial trial for crime, the two phrases are synonymous and equivalent; each has been used by eminent judges to explain the other; and each signifies such proof as satisfies the judgment and consciences of the jury, as reasonable men, and applying their reason to the evidence before them, that the crime charged has been committed by the defendant, and so satisfies them as to leave no other reasonable conclusion possible." Commonwealth v. Costley, 118 Mass. 1, 24 (1875).

* * *

We recognize that the phrase "moral evidence" is not a mainstay of the modern lexicon, though we do not think it means anything different today than it did in the 19th century. The few contemporary dictionaries that define moral evidence do so consistently with its original meaning. * * *

Moreover, the instruction itself gives a definition of the phrase. The jury was told that "everything relating to human affairs, and depending on moral evidence, is open to some possible or imaginary doubt"—in other words, that absolute certainty is unattainable in matters relating to human affairs. Moral evidence, in this sentence, can only mean empirical evidence offered to prove such matters—the proof introduced at trial.

This conclusion is reinforced by other instructions given in Sandoval's case. The judge informed the jurors that their duty was "to determine the facts of the case from the evidence received in the trial and not from any other source." The judge continued: "Evidence consists of testimony of witnesses, writings, material objects, or anything presented to the senses and offered to prove the existence or nonexistence of a fact." The judge also told the jurors that "you must not be influenced by pity for a defendant or by prejudice against him," and that "[y]ou must not be swayed by mere sentiment, conjecture, sympathy, passion, prejudice, public opinion or public feeling." These instructions correctly pointed the jurors' attention to the facts of the case before them, not (as Sandoval contends) the ethics or morality of Sandoval's criminal acts. Accordingly, we find the reference to moral evidence unproblematic.

We are somewhat more concerned with Sandoval's argument that the phrase "moral certainty" has lost its historical meaning, and that a modern jury would understand it to allow conviction on proof that does not meet the beyond a reasonable doubt standard. Words and phrases can change meaning over time: a passage generally understood in 1850 may be incomprehensible or confusing to a modern juror. And although some contemporary dictionaries contain definitions of moral certainty similar to the 19th century understanding of the phrase, ... we are willing to accept Sandoval's premise that "moral certainty," standing alone, might not be recognized by modern jurors as a synonym for "proof beyond a reasonable doubt." But it does not necessarily follow that the California instruction is unconstitutional.

Sandoval first argues that moral certainty would be understood by modern jurors to mean a standard of proof lower than beyond a reasonable doubt. In support of this proposition, Sandoval points to contemporary dictionaries that define moral certainty in terms of probability. But the beyond a reasonable doubt standard is itself probabilistic. "[I]n a judicial proceeding in which there is a dispute about the facts of some earlier event, the factfinder cannot acquire unassailably accurate knowledge of what happened. Instead, all the factfinder can acquire is a belief of what *probably* happened." *In re Winship,* (Harlan, J., concurring). The problem is not that moral certainty may be understood in terms of probability, but that a jury might understand the phrase to mean something less than the very high level of probability required by the Constitution in criminal cases.

Although in this respect moral certainty is ambiguous in the abstract, the rest of the instruction given in Sandoval's case lends content to the phrase. The jurors were told that they must have "an abiding conviction, to a moral certainty, of the truth of the charge." An instruction cast in terms of an abiding conviction as to guilt, without reference to moral certainty, correctly states the government's burden of proof. And the judge had already informed the jury that matters relating to human affairs are proven by moral evidence, giving the same meaning to the word moral in this part of the instruction, moral certainty can only mean certainty with respect to human affairs. As used in this instruction, therefore, we are satisfied that the reference to moral certainty, in conjunction with the abiding conviction language, "impress[ed] upon the factfinder the need to reach a subjective state of near certitude of the guilt of the accused." Accordingly, we reject Sandoval's contention that the moral certainty element of the California instruction invited the jury to convict him on proof below that required by the Due Process Clause.

Sandoval's second argument is a variant of the first. Accepting that the instruction requires a high level of confidence in the defendant's guilt, Sandoval argues that a juror might be convinced to a moral certainty that the defendant is guilty even though the government has failed to *prove* his guilt beyond a reasonable doubt.

[T]he moral certainty language cannot be sequestered from its surroundings. The jury in Sandoval's case was told that a reasonable doubt is "that state of the case which, *after the entire comparison and consideration of all the evidence,* leaves the minds of the jurors in that condition that they cannot say they feel an abiding conviction, to a moral certainty, of the truth of the charge." The instruction thus explicitly told the jurors that their conclusion had to be based on the evidence in the case. Other instructions reinforced this message. The jury was told "to determine the facts of the case from the evidence received in the trial and not from any other source." The judge continued that "you must not be influenced by pity for a defendant or by prejudice against him.... You must not be swayed by mere sentiment, conjecture, sympathy, passion, prejudice, public opinion or public feeling." Accordingly, there is no reasonable likelihood that the jury would have understood moral certainty to be disassociated from the evidence in the case.

We do not think it reasonably likely that the jury understood the words moral certainty either as suggesting a standard of proof lower than due process requires or as allowing conviction on factors other than the government's proof. At the same time, however, we do not condone the use of the phrase. As modern dictionary definitions of moral certainty attest, the common meaning of the phrase has changed since it was used in the *Webster* instruction, and it may continue to do so to the point that it conflicts with the *Winship* standard. Indeed, the definitions of reasonable doubt most widely used in the federal courts do not contain any reference to moral certainty. But we have no supervisory power over the state courts, and in the context of the instructions as a whole we cannot say that the use of the phrase rendered the instruction given in Sandoval's case unconstitutional.

B

Finally, Sandoval objects to the portion of the charge in which the judge instructed the jury that a reasonable doubt is "not a mere possible doubt." * * * "[A] 'reasonable doubt,' at a minimum, is one based upon 'reason.' " A fanciful doubt is not a reasonable doubt. As Sandoval's defense attorney told the jury: "[A]nything can be possible.... [A] planet could be made out of blue cheese. But that's really not in the realm of what we're talking about." That this is the sense in which the instruction uses "possible" is made clear from the final phrase of the sentence, which notes that everything "is open to some possible or imaginary doubt." We therefore reject Sandoval's challenge to this portion of the instruction as well.

III

On December 26, 1987, petitioner Victor went to the Omaha home of an 82-year-old woman for whom he occasionally did gardening work. Once inside, he beat her with a pipe and cut her throat with a knife, killing her. Victor was convicted of first degree murder. A three-judge panel found the statutory aggravating circumstances that Victor had previously been convicted of murder, and that the murder in this case was especially heinous, atrocious, and cruel. Finding none of the statutory mitigating circumstances, the panel sentenced Victor to death. The Nebraska Supreme Court affirmed the conviction and sentence.

At Victor's trial, the judge instructed the jury that "[t]he burden is always on the State to prove beyond a reasonable doubt all of the material elements of the crime charged, and this burden never shifts." The charge continued:

> " 'Reasonable doubt' is such a doubt as would cause a reasonable and prudent person, in one of the graver and more important transactions of life, to pause and hesitate before taking the represented facts as true and relying and acting thereon. It is such a doubt as will not permit you, after full, fair, and impartial consideration of all the evidence, to have an abiding conviction, *to a moral certainty,* of the guilt of the accused. At the same time, absolute or mathematical certainty is not required. You may be convinced of the truth of a fact beyond a reasonable doubt and yet be fully aware that possibly you may be mistaken. You may find an accused guilty upon the *strong probabilities of the case,* provided such probabilities are strong enough to exclude any doubt of his guilt that is reasonable. A reasonable doubt is an *actual and substantial doubt* arising from the evidence, from the facts or circumstances shown by the evidence, or from the lack of evidence on the part of the state, as distinguished from a doubt arising from mere possibility, from bare imagination, or from fanciful conjecture."

* * *

The instruction given in Victor's case can be traced to two separate lines of cases. Much of the charge is taken from Chief Justice Shaw's *Webster* instruction. The rest derives from a series of decisions approving instructions cast in terms of an "actual doubt" that would cause a reasonable person to hesitate to act.

* * *

Victor's primary argument is that equating a reasonable doubt with a "substantial doubt" overstated the degree of doubt necessary for acquittal. We agree that this construction is somewhat problematic. On the one hand, "substantial" means "not seeming or imaginary"; on the other, it means "that specified to a large degree." The former is unexceptionable, as it informs the jury only that a reasonable doubt is something more than a speculative one; but the latter could imply a doubt greater than required for acquittal under *Winship*. Any ambiguity, however, is removed by reading the phrase in the context of the sentence in which it appears: "A reasonable doubt is an actual and substantial doubt ... *as distinguished from* a doubt arising from mere possibility, from bare imagination, or from fanciful conjecture."

* * *

In any event, the instruction provided an alternative definition of reasonable doubt: a doubt that would cause a reasonable person to hesitate to act. This is a formulation we have repeatedly approved, and to the extent the word substantial denotes the quantum of doubt necessary for acquittal, the hesitate to act standard gives a common-sense benchmark for just how substantial such a doubt must be. We therefore do not think it reasonably likely that the jury would have interpreted this instruction to indicate that the doubt must be anything other than a reasonable one.

* * *

Finally, Victor argues that the reference to "strong probabilities" in the instruction unconstitutionally understated the government's burden. But in the same sentence, the instruction informs the jury that the probabilities must be strong enough to prove the defendant's guilt beyond a reasonable doubt. We upheld a nearly identical instruction in *Dunbar v. United States,* (1895): "While it is true that [the challenged instruction] used the words 'probabilities' and 'strong probabilities,' yet it emphasized the fact that those probabilities must be so strong as to exclude any reasonable doubt, and that is unquestionably the law". That conclusion has lost no force in the course of a century, and we therefore consider *Dunbar* controlling on this point.

AFFIRMED

JUSTICE KENNEDY, concurring. [OPINION OMITTED]

JUSTICE GINSBURG, concurring in part and concurring in the judgment. [OPINION OMITTED]

JUSTICE BLACKMUN, with whom JUSTICE SOUTER joins in all but Part II, concurring in part and dissenting in part.

Our democracy rests in no small part on our faith in the ability of the criminal justice system to separate those who are guilty from those who are not. This is a faith which springs fundamentally from the requirement that unless guilt is established beyond all reasonable doubt, the accused shall go free.

Despite the inherent appeal of the reasonable-doubt standard, it provides protection to the innocent only to the extent that the standard, in reality, is an enforceable rule of law. To be a meaningful safeguard, the reasonable-doubt standard must have a tangible meaning that is capable of being understood by those who are required to apply it. It must be stated accurately and with the precision owed to those whose liberty or life is at risk. Because of the extraordinarily high stakes in criminal trials, "[i]t is critical that the moral force of the criminal law not be diluted by a standard of proof that leaves people in doubt whether innocent men are being condemned."

When reviewing a jury instruction that defines "reasonable doubt," it is necessary to consider the instruction as a whole and to give the words their common and ordinary meaning. It is not sufficient for the jury instruction merely to be susceptible to an interpretation that is technically correct. The important question is whether there is a "reasonable likelihood" that the jury was misled or confused by the instruction, and therefore applied it in a way that violated the Constitution. Any jury instruction defining "reasonable doubt" that suggests an improperly high degree of doubt for acquittal or an improperly low degree of certainty for conviction, offends due process. Either misstatement of the reasonable-doubt standard is prejudicial to the defendant, as it "vitiates all of the jury's findings," and removes the only constitutionally appropriate predicate for the jury's verdict.

* * *

In my view, the predominance of potentially misleading language in Victor's instruction made it likely that the jury interpreted the phrase "substantial doubt" to mean that a "large" doubt, as opposed to a merely reasonable doubt, is required to acquit a defendant. It seems that a central purpose of the instruction is to minimize the jury's sense of responsibility for the conviction of those who may be innocent. The instruction goes out of its way to assure jurors that "[y]ou may be convinced of the truth of a fact beyond a reasonable doubt and yet be fully aware that possibly you may be mistaken"; and then, after acquainting jurors with the possibility that their consciences will be unsettled after convicting the defendant, the instruction states that the jurors should feel free to convict based on the "strong probabilities of the case." Viewed as a whole, the instruction is geared toward assuring jurors that although they may be mistaken, they are to make their decision on those "strong probabilities," and only a "substantial doubt" of a defendant's guilt should deter them from convicting.

The majority dismisses the potentially harmful effects of the "strong probabilities" language on the grounds that a "nearly identical instruction" was upheld by the Court a century ago. *Dunbar v. United States,* (1895). But the instruction in *Dunbar* did not equate reasonable doubt with "substantial doubt," nor did it contain the phrase "moral certainty." As the majority appreciates elsewhere in its opinion, challenged jury instructions must be considered in their entirety. Rather than examining the jury instruction as a whole, the majority parses it, ignoring the relationship between the challenged phrases as well as their cumulative effect.

Considering the instruction in its entirety, it seems fairly obvious to me that the "strong probabilities" language increased the likelihood that the jury understood "substantial doubt" to mean "to a large degree." Indeed, the jury could have a reasonable doubt about a defendant's guilt but still find that the "strong probabilities" are in favor of conviction. Only when a reasonable doubt is understood to be a doubt "to a large degree" does the "strong probabilities" language begin to make sense. * * * A jury could have a large and reasonable doubt about a defendant's guilt but still find the defendant guilty on "the strong probabilities of the case," believing it "likely" that the defendant committed the crime for which he was charged.

To be sure, the instruction does qualify the "strong probabilities" language by noting that "the strong probabilities of the case" should be "strong enough to exclude any doubt of his guilt that is reasonable." But this qualification is useless since a "doubt of his guilt that is reasonable" is immediately defined, in the very next sentence, as a "substantial doubt." Thus, the supposed clarification only compounds the confusion, by referring the jury to the "substantial doubt" phrase as a means of defining the "strong probabilities" language.

Finally, the instruction issued in Victor's case states that a reasonable doubt "is such a doubt as will not permit you, after full, fair, and impartial consideration of all the evidence, to have an abiding conviction, *to a moral certainty,* of the guilt of the accused." * * * The risk that jurors would understand "moral certainty" to authorize convictions based in part on value judgments regarding the defendant's behavior is particularly high in cases where the defendant is alleged to have committed a repugnant or brutal crime. [The] "moral certainty" phrase in Victor's instruction is particularly dangerous because it is used in conjunction with language that overstates the degree of doubt necessary to convict. This relationship between the "moral certainty" language, which potentially understates the degree of certainty required to convict, and the "substantial doubt," "strong probabilities," and "possibly you may be mistaken" language which, especially when taken together, overstates the degree of doubt necessary to acquit,....

* * * [A]ll of the misleading language is mutually reinforcing, both overstating the degree of doubt necessary to acquit and understating the degree of certainty required to convict.

This confusing and misleading state of affairs leads me ineluctably to the conclusion that, in Victor's case, there exists a reasonable likelihood that the jury believed that a lesser burden of proof rested with the prosecution. * * * Where, as here, a jury instruction attempts but fails to convey with clarity and accuracy the meaning of reasonable doubt, the reviewing court should reverse the conviction and remand for a new trial. * * *

NOTE

In State v. Portillo, 182 Ariz. 592, 898 P.2d 970 (1995) the Court approved this instruction.

The state has the burden of proving the defendant guilty beyond a reasonable doubt. In civil cases, it is only necessary to prove that a fact is more likely true than not or that its truth is highly probable. In criminal cases such as this, the state's proof must be more powerful than that. It must be beyond a reasonable doubt.

Proof beyond a reasonable doubt is proof that leaves you firmly convinced of the defendant's guilt. There are very few things in this world that we know with absolute certainty, and in criminal cases the law does not require proof that overcomes every doubt. If, based on your consideration of the evidence, you are firmly convinced that the defendant is guilty of the crime charged, you must find him/her guilty. If, on the other hand, you think there is a real possibility that he/she is not guilty, you must give him/her the benefit of the doubt and find him/her not guilty.

C. SPECIFIC PRESUMPTIONS AND INFERENCES

PEOPLE v. TERRA

Court of Appeals of New York, 1951.
303 N.Y. 332, 102 N.E.2d 576.

FULD, JUDGE. On July 19, 1949, a machine gun and ammunition for it were found in a one-room store, occupied—or so the jury could have concluded—by the brothers Terra and used by them in connection with their business of distributing and servicing pinball machines. They were indicted, accused of illegally possessing a machine gun in violation of subdivision 1–a of section 1897 of the Penal Law, Consol. Laws, c. 40. Adjudged guilty after trial, they seek a reversal upon the ground that the jury was permitted, by virtue of the court's charge, to rest its verdict upon that clause of subdivision 1–a, which provides that "The presence of such machine-gun in any room, dwelling, structure or vehicle shall be presumptive evidence of its illegal possession by all the persons occupying the place where such machine-gun is found." It is urged that the statute, insofar as it creates the presumption, is unconstitutional.

The presumption provision, broad in scope, applies not only where, as here, the machine gun is found in a "room," but also where it is discovered in a "dwelling," "structure" or "vehicle". Mindful of the policy that courts decide only those constitutional questions necessary for determination of the case as presented, ... we consider the statute only insofar as it relates to the presumption based upon occupancy of a "room"....

Presumptions are no innovation in the field of criminal law. For many years legislatures have been enacting statutes providing that certain facts, which in themselves would be insufficient to justify a conviction, shall, when proved, constitute presumptive or prima facie evidence of the existence of the principal fact in issue. Although such provisions undoubtedly facilitate proof of guilt and the task of the prosecution, they are not, for that reason, to be condemned. However, the presumptive device provided for may not be employed in such manner as to impair the right to trial by jury, relieve the prosecution of its burden of proving guilt beyond a reasonable doubt or otherwise deny to persons accused of crime, "those fundamental rights and immutable principles of justice which are embraced within the conception of due process of law." ... And, since a defendant is presumed to be innocent until the contrary is proved, due process, it has been said, demands that "a verdict against [him] ... be preceded by the introduction of some evidence which tends to prove the elements of the crime charged." Tot v. United States ... [319 U.S. 463, 63 S.Ct. 1241].

The validity of a presumption statute, the permissibility of the presumption created, depend, therefore, upon whether, based on life and life's experiences, a rational connection between the fact proved and the ultimate fact presumed may be said to exist.... "... the fact upon which the presumption is to rest must have some fair relation to, or natural connection with, the main fact." ... "What is proved must be so related to what is inferred ... as to be at least a warning signal ... experience must teach that the evidence held to be inculpatory has at least a sinister significance"....

Turning to the case before us, there can be no doubt about the "sinister significance" of proof of a machine gun in a room occupied by an accused or about the reasonableness of the connection between its illegal possession and occupancy of the room where it is kept. Persons who occupy a room who either reside in it or use it in the conduct and operation of a business or other venture—and that is what in its present context the statutory term "occupying" signifies ...—normally know what is in it; and, certainly, when the object is as large and uncommon as a machine gun, it is neither unreasonable nor unfair to presume that the room's occupants are aware of its presence. That being so, the legislature may not be considered arbitrary if it acts upon the presumption and erects it into evidence of a possession that is "conscious" and "knowing".

On the basis of somewhat similar reasoning, the Supreme Court of the United States has upheld the validity of a statute providing that the existence of a liquor still upon "real estate" constitutes prima facie evidence that those "in actual possession" of the land knew of the location of the still and may, on the strength of that presumption, be held guilty of the crime of permitting a still to be operated upon their property.... And this court has today reaffirmed the constitutionality of section 1898–a of the Penal Law, which recites that the "presence in an automobile" of any gun or other designated weapon "shall be presumptive evidence of its illegal possession by all the persons ... in such automobile at the time such weapon ... is found." ... If such statutes are constitutional—one presuming knowledge of a still from possession of perhaps a large area of land and the other presuming possession of a gun from mere presence in an automobile—then, a fortiori, a provision declaring possession of a gun inferable from occupancy of the room where it is found, is reasonable and valid.

Except for law enforcement officials and the few other groups expressly exempted from the application of subdivision 1–a of section 1897, a machine gun is never permissible equipment or standard stock in trade of any legitimate business or profession, and rarely, if ever, is its possessor either law-abiding or engaged upon a lawful task. If, therefore, it is reasonable—and we have shown that it is—to presume possession of a machine gun from evidence that defendants were occupying the room in which it was kept, it follows almost as matter of course that it is rational further to infer an *illegal* possession, since a machine gun is property "not likely ... to be found in the possession of innocent parties." ...

The section 1897 presumption, with which we are concerned, is to be contrasted with subdivision (f) of section 2 of the Federal Firearms Act, 15 U.S.C.A. § 902(f), declared unconstitutional in Tot v. United States, supra,.... That provision prescribed that the possession of a firearm by any person who has been convicted of a crime of violence or is a fugitive from justice shall be presumptive evidence that the article was received by him *in* interstate commerce *after* the effective date of the statute. Absence of a rational basis for such an inference is as patent as is existence of a reasonable connection between actual possession of a machine gun and its illegal, guilty possession.

The statute here challenged visits no oppressive burden upon an accused. It gives him every opportunity to rebut the presumption—for which, as we have seen, there is fair and reasonable basis—merely calling upon him to explain the highly sinister and suspicious proof that a deathdealing machine gun was found in a room occupied by him. And, even if he offers no explanation, the jury may still refuse to convict. The burden of proof upon the entire case, the duty of establishing guilt beyond a reasonable doubt, remains as ever with the prosecution. Defendant's right to a fair trial continues undiminished; no hardship is imposed, no constitutional right or safeguard impaired.

The judgment should be affirmed.

Judgment affirmed.

NOTE

With regard to the contention that even though a presumption may meet the standard adopted in this case, the defendant is in effect forced to take the witness stand in his own behalf, in violation of his self-incrimination privilege, consider the fact that he may well be able, if innocent, to produce evidence to that effect from sources other than his own lips. Moreover, as was stated earlier in a note in Ch. 6, there is the following from Barnes v. United States, 412 U.S. 837, 93 S.Ct. 2357 (1973):

> "Introduction of any evidence, direct or circumstantial, tending to implicate the defendant in the alleged crime increases the pressure on him to testify. The mere massing of evidence against a defendant cannot be regarded as a violation of his privilege against self-incrimination."

LEARY v. UNITED STATES

Supreme Court of the United States, 1969.
395 U.S. 6, 89 S.Ct. 1532, appeal after remand 431 F.2d 85 (Fifth Circuit 1970).

MR. JUSTICE HARLAN delivered the opinion of the Court.

This case presents constitutional questions arising out of the conviction of the petitioner, Dr. Timothy Leary, for violation of two federal statutes governing traffic in marihuana.

The circumstances surrounding petitioner's conviction were as follows. On December 20, 1965, petitioner left New York by automobile, intending a vacation trip to Yucatan, Mexico. He was accompanied by his daughter and son, both teenagers, and two other persons. On December 22, 1965, the party drove across the International Bridge between the United States and Mexico at Laredo, Texas. They stopped at the Mexican customs station and, after apparently being denied entry, drove back across the bridge. They halted at the American secondary inspection area, explained the situation to a customs inspector, and stated that they had nothing from Mexico to declare. The inspector asked them to alight, examined the interior of the car, and saw what appeared to be marihuana seeds on the floor. The inspector then received permission to search the car and passengers. Small amounts of marihuana were found on the car floor and in the glove compartment. A personal search of petitioner's daughter revealed a silver snuff box containing semi-refined marihuana and three partially smoked marihuana cigarettes.

* * *

We granted certiorari to consider ... whether petitioner was denied due process by the application of the part of 21 U.S.C.A. § 176a which provides that a defendant's possession of marihuana shall be deemed sufficient evidence that the marihuana was illegally imported or brought into the United States, and that the defendant knew of the illegal importation or bringing in, unless the defendant explains his possession to the satisfaction of the jury. For reasons which follow, we hold in favor of the petitioner ... and reverse the judgment of the Court of Appeals.

So far as here relevant, the presumption ... authorizes the jury to infer from a defendant's possession of marihuana two necessary elements of the crime: (1) that the marihuana was imported or brought into the United States illegally; and (2) that the defendant knew of the unlawful importation or bringing in. Petitioner argues that neither inference is valid, citing undisputed testimony at his trial to the effect that marihuana will grow anywhere in the United States, and that some actually is grown here. The Government contends, on the other hand, that both inferences are permissible. For reasons that follow, we hold unconstitutional that part of the presumption which relates to a defendant's knowledge of illegal importation. Consequently, we do not reach the question of the validity of the "illegal importation" inference.

* * *

Once it is established that a significant percentage of domestically consumed marihuana may not have been imported at all, then it can no longer be postulated, without proof, that possessors will be even roughly aware of the proportion actually imported. We conclude that in order to sustain the inference of knowledge we must find on the basis of the available materials that a majority of marihuana possessors either are cognizant of the apparently high rate of importation or otherwise have become aware that *their* marihuana was grown abroad.

We can imagine five ways in which a possessor might acquire such knowledge: (1) he might be aware of the proportion of domestically consumed marihuana which is smuggled from abroad and deduce that his was illegally imported; (2) he might have smuggled the marihuana himself; (3) he might have learned by indirect means that the marihuana consumed in his locality or furnished by his supplier was smuggled from abroad; (4) he might have specified foreign marihuana when making his "buy," or might have been told the source of the marihuana by his supplier; (5) he might be able to tell the source from the appearance, packaging, or taste of the marihuana itself.

* * *

... the materials at our disposal leave us at large to estimate even roughly the proportion of marihuana possessors who have learned in one way or another the origin of their marihuana. It must also be recognized that a not inconsiderable proportion of domestically consumed marihuana appears to have been grown in this country, and that its possessors must be taken to have "known," if anything, that their marihuana was *not* illegally imported. In short, it would be no more than speculation were we to say that even as much as a majority of possessors "knew" the source of their marihuana.

Nor are these deficiencies in the foundation for the "knowledge" presumption overcome by paying, as we do, the utmost deference to the congressional determination that this presumption was warranted. For Congress, no less than we, is subject to constitutional requirements, and in this instance the legislative record falls even shorter of furnishing an adequate foundation for the "knowledge" presumption than do the more extensive materials we have examined.

We thus cannot escape the duty of setting aside petitioner's conviction....

* * *

NOTES

1. Is the presumption that possession shows knowledge of illegal importation valid with regard to other narcotic substances? The Supreme Court in Turner v. United States, 396 U.S. 398, 90 S.Ct. 642 (1970) answered that question in the affirmative for heroin but in the negative for cocaine. This distinction was drawn because a sizeable quantity of cocaine is lawfully produced in this country for medicinal purposes, and, consequently, there is the very real possibility that cocaine in a defendant's possession may have been stolen from a legal source. That possibility is sufficient to negate either the presumption that all cocaine was illegally imported or that the accused knew of its importation.

For presumption validity purposes, may a distinction be made between users of the drug and sellers of it?

2. The Supreme Court recently upheld a statutory presumption of possession of a firearm in County Court of Ulster County, N.Y. v. Allen, 442 U.S. 140, 99 S.Ct. 2213 (1979):

Mr. Justice Stevens, speaking for the court said:

"A New York statute provides that, with certain exceptions, the presence of a firearm in an automobile is presumptive evidence of its illegal possession by all persons then occupying the vehicle. The United States Court of Appeals for the Second Circuit held that ... the statute is 'unconstitutional on its face.'

"Four persons, three adult males (respondents) and a 16-year-old girl (Jane Doe, who is not a respondent here), were jointly tried on charges that they possessed two loaded handguns, a loaded machinegun, and over a pound of heroin found in a Chevrolet in which they were riding when it was stopped for speeding on the New York Thruway shortly after noon on March 28, 1973. The two large-caliber handguns, which together with their ammunition weighed approximately six pounds, were seen through the window of the car by the investigating police officer. They were positioned crosswise in an open handbag on either the front floor or the front seat of the car on the passenger side where Jane Doe was sitting. Jane Doe admitted that the handbag was hers. The machinegun and the heroin were discovered in the trunk after the police pried it open. The car had been borrowed from the driver's brother earlier that day; the key to the trunk could not be found in the car or on the person of any of its occupants, although there was testimony that two of the occupants had placed something in the trunk before embarking in the borrowed car. The jury convicted all four of possession of the handguns and acquitted them of possession of the contents of the trunk.

"Counsel for all four defendants objected to the introduction into evidence of the two handguns, the machinegun, and the drugs, arguing that the State had not adequately demonstrated a connection between their clients and the contraband. The trial court overruled the objection, relying on the presumption of possession created by the New York statute. Because that presumption does not apply if a weapon is found 'upon the person' of one of the occupants of the car, the three male defendants also moved to dismiss the charges relating to the handguns on the ground that the guns were found on the person of Jane Doe. Respondents made this motion both at the close of the prosecution's case and at the close of all evidence. The trial judge twice denied it, concluding that the applicability of the 'on the person' exception was a question of fact for the jury.

"At the close of the trial, the judge instructed the jurors that they were entitled to infer possession from the defendants' presence in the car. He did not make any reference to the 'upon the person' exception in his explanation of the statutory presumption, nor did any of the defendants object to this omission or request alternative or additional instructions on the subject.

"As applied to the facts of this case, the presumption of possession is entirely rational.... The argument against possession by any of the respondents was predicated solely on the fact that the guns were in Jane Doe's pocketbook. But several circumstances ... made it highly improbable that she was the sole custodian of those weapons.

"Even if it was reasonable to conclude that she had placed the guns in her purse before the car was stopped by police, the facts strongly suggest that Jane Doe was not the only person able to exercise dominion over them. The two guns were too large to be concealed in her handbag. The bag was consequently open, and part of one of the guns was in plain view, within easy access of the driver of the car and even, perhaps, of the other two respondents who were riding in the rear seat.

"Moreover, it is highly improbable that the loaded guns belonged to Jane Doe or that she was solely responsible for their being in her purse. As a 16-year-old girl in the company of three adult men she was the least likely of the four to be carrying one, let alone two, heavy handguns. It is far more probable that she relied on the pocketknife found in her brassiere for any necessary self-protection. Under these circumstances, it was not unreasonable for her counsel to argue and for the jury to infer that when the car was halted for speeding, the other passengers in the car anticipated the risk of a search and attempted to conceal their weapons in a pocketbook in the front seat. The inference is surely more likely than the notion that these weapons were the sole property of the 16-year-old girl.

"Under these circumstances, the jury would have been entirely reasonable in rejecting the suggestion—which, incidentally, defense counsel did not even advance in their closing arguments to the jury—that the handguns were in the sole possession of Jane Doe. Assuming that the jury did reject it, the case is tantamount to one in which the guns were lying on the floor or the seat of the car in the plain view of the three other occupants of the automobile. In such a case it is surely rational to infer that each of the respondents was fully aware of the presence of the guns and had both the ability and the intent to exercise dominion and control over the weapons. The application of the statutory presumption in this case therefore comports with the standard laid down in Tot v. United States, 319 U.S. 463, 467, and restated in Leary v. United States [520]. For there is a 'rational connection' between the basic facts that the prosecution proved and the ultimate fact presumed, and the latter is 'more likely than not to flow from' the former.

"Respondents argue, however, that the validity of the New York presumption must be judged by a 'reasonable doubt' test rather than the 'more likely than not' standard employed in Leary. Under the more stringent test, it is argued that a statutory presumption must be rejected unless the evidence necessary to invoke the inference is sufficient for a rational jury to find the inferred fact beyond a reasonable doubt. Respondents' argument again overlooks the distinction between a permissive presumption on which the prosecution is entitled to rely as one not-necessarily-sufficient part of its proof and a mandatory presumption which the jury must accept even if it is the sole evidence of an element of the offense.

"In the latter situation, since the prosecution bears the burden of establishing guilt, it may not rest its case entirely on a presumption unless the fact proved is sufficient to support the inference of guilt beyond a reasonable doubt. But in the former situation, the prosecution may rely on all of the evidence in the record to meet the reasonable doubt standard. There is no more reason to require a permissive statutory presumption to meet a reasonable doubt standard before it may be permitted to play any part in a trial than there is to require that degree of probative force for other relevant evidence before it may be admitted. As long as it is clear that the presumption is not the sole and sufficient basis for a finding of guilt, it need only satisfy the test described in *Leary*.

"The permissive presumption, as used in this case, satisfied the *Leary* test. . . ."

3. Where an automobile is involved in a speeding violation and the driver escapes apprehension, may a court indulge in a presumption that the owner is the violator? What about a parking violation?

One of the early cases upon the subject is People v. Hildebrandt, 308 N.Y. 397, 126 N.E.2d 377 (1955), in which a "photo-traffic camera" (which took two photos, at a set time interval apart, of the moving vehicle) ascertained that the automobile belonging to the defendant was speeding. The driver was not identified or arrested. Two weeks later the defendant was charged with the offense. Relying upon a prior parking violation case, the prosecutor urged the court to presume that the driver was the owner. A majority of the court refused to do so. Judge Fuld, in his dissent, said that there should be no distinction made between the two types of situations; a presumption was warranted in both, and it could be established by the court without benefit of legislative authorization. He further commented:

> The test of the validity of a presumption has often been formulated. It requires that the fact proved, that is, the fact from which the inference proceeds, be rationally connected to the fact inferred. We have said, quite recently and in a serious criminal case, that a presumption is good or bad depending "upon whether, based on life and life's experiences, a rational connection between the fact proved and the ultimate fact presumed may be said to exist." . . .
>
> The inference is, of course, rebuttable, and, to satisfy the demands of due process, it is not essential that the inferred fact follow as an inevitable conclusion from the proposition which has been proved. Here, for example, the circumstance that it is not always the owner of a speeding car who is at the wheel does not *ipso facto* invalidate the presumption. The basic test is whether common experience supports *the probability, not the certainty,* that, if the first fact is true, the second is also true. . . .
>
> The balance between the rights of the individual and the interests of society may at times be a delicate one, but here the court, in my view, is going far beyond the necessities of the case. The body of the offense, speeding, has been proved, and only the question of identity remains. It

does not strike me as harsh, or as imposing any but the lightest burden, to require a defendant in a case such as this to offer evidence upon a fact peculiarly within his own knowledge, particularly since it may be done through the testimony of others....

The general case law rule is in accord with the majority view in the previous case. A few jurisdictions, however, have statutes which establish such a presumption. The Connecticut Motor Vehicle Law (§ 14–107) is one example, and its constitutionality was upheld in State v. Knudsen, 3 Conn.Cir. 458, 217 A.2d 236 (1965). The presumption, however, seems to hinge upon the existence of a legislative enactment. See 18 Traffic Digest and Review (April issue, 21; May issue, 21, of 1970); Annot., 49 A.L.R.2d 456 (1956). One such statute in Pennsylvania was struck down as violative of federal and state constitutional protections against self-incrimination. Commonwealth v. Slaybaugh, 468 Pa. 618, 364 A.2d 687 (1976).

Even without legislative authorization, a jurisdiction which may disallow the presumption in moving violation cases will relax its guard with respect to parking violations. For instance, the New York Court of Appeals which decided the aforementioned *Hildebrandt* case upheld a court established presumption in a parking violation case. In discussing the earlier case of People v. Rubin, 284 N.Y. 392, 31 N.E.2d 501 (1940), the *Hildebrandt* court said: "After all, parking violations are of a special sort. The car is left unattended, there is usually no one present to be arrested, and it is not unreasonable to charge to the owner an illegal storage of his vehicle in a public street". 308 N.Y. 397, 402, 126 N.E.2d 377, 379 (1955).

Typical of many ordinances resolving the parking problem issue is the following from the Municipal Code of Chicago (27–364): "Whenever any vehicle shall have been parked in violation of any of the provisions of any ordinance prohibiting or restricting parking, the person in whose name such vehicle is registered shall be prima facie responsible for such violations and subject to the penalty therefor". The constitutionality of this ordinance was upheld in City of Chicago v. Hertz Commercial Leasing Corp., 71 Ill.2d 333, 17 Ill.Dec. 1, 375 N.E.2d 1285 (1978), cert. denied 439 U.S. 929, 99 S.Ct. 315 (1978).

4. Occasionally courts and commentators phrase permissible presumptions in terms of a "logical inference." For example, in Donigan, et al., The Evidence Handbook 23 (4th ed. 1980), it is noted:

"In the absence of satisfactory explanation, exclusive possession of stolen goods permits the logical inference either that he was the thief or that he received the stolen goods ... [citing] 29 Am.Jur.2d, Evidence, sec. 229; Decennial Digest, Burglary, sec. 42, Larceny, sec. 64, Receiving Stolen Goods, sec. 8; Note 15 A.L.R.Fed. 856; 'Presumptions and inferences arising in prosecution under National Motor Vehicle Theft Act (Dyer Act) 18 U.S.C.S., secs. 2312, 2313, from unexplained possession of motor vehicle'; Barnes v. United States, 412 U.S. 837, 93 S.Ct. 2357, 37 L.Ed.2d 380 (1970), quoted in sec. 4–1, n. 14, supra; Rugendorf v. United States, 376 U.S. 528, 84 S.Ct. 825, 11 L.Ed.2d 887 (1964): '(P)ossession of the fruits of crime, recently after its commission, justifies the inference that the possession is guilty possession, and, though only *prima facie* evidence of guilt, may be of controlling weight, unless explained by the circumstances or accounted for in some way consistent with innocence,' quoting from Wilson v. United States, 162 U.S. 613, 16 S.Ct. 895, 40 L.Ed. 1090 (1896).... Possession of goods with an obliterated serial number likewise permits the inference that the possessor was either the thief or knew the goods to be stolen when he received them ... [citing] People v. Gallagher, 241 N.W.2d 759 (Mich.Ct.App.1979)."

The same source points out, however, that inferences should be distinguished from presumptions:

"Inferences have many qualities in common with presumptions but they are not the same thing. The distinction is that a presumption is a deduction which the law requires, while an inference is one which the fact finder may or may not draw according to his own conclusions. Inferences are sometimes called 'presumptions of fact' and distinguished from 'presumptions of law' but this terminology is confusing and should be avoided."

Donigan, et al., The Evidence Handbook 22 (4th ed. 1980) (footnotes omitted) (emphasis in original).

5. One of the most venerable presumptions in criminal law was expressed in a traditional instruction to the jury that a person "is presumed to intend the natural and probable consequences of his acts." This type of instruction was held unconstitutional in 1979 because it relieved the prosecution entirely of its burden to prove the mental state of the accused. Sandstrom v. Montana, 442 U.S. 510, 99 S.Ct. 2450 (1979) In 1985 the Court faced the issue again. The accused, an escaping prisoner, shot and killed the resident of a house who slammed the door in his face when the accused demanded keys to a car. The shot was fired through the door and the defense claimed the shooting was accidental and without intent to kill. The trial judge told the jury about the presumption of innocence, and the state's burden of proof. He further said, "Acts of a person of sound mind and discretion are presumed to be the product of the person's will, but the presumption may be rebutted. A person of sound mind and discretion is presumed to intend the natural and probable consequences of his acts, but the presumption may be rebutted. A person will not be presumed to act with criminal intention but the trier of fact, that is, the Jury may find criminal intention upon a consideration of words, conduct, demeanor, motive and all other circumstances connected with the act for which the accused is prosecuted." The Court held that reasonable jurors could believe they had been told they must presume the accused acted intentionally unless the accused rebutted this presumption. Under the *Sandstrom* opinion this is forbidden although the jury could be told that it was permissible to infer intentional action from the actions of the accused. The majority of the Court found the instruction to the jury as a whole did not sufficiently insure that the jury would not presume intent. Francis v. Franklin, 471 U.S. 307, 105 S.Ct. 1965 (1985).

6. In Carella v. California, 491 U.S. 263, 109 S.Ct. 2419 (1989), the Court held that jury instructions, given at a trial of grand theft based on the defendant's failure to return a rental car, that required the jury to presume that the defendant intended to commit theft by fraud upon a finding that the car was not returned within 20 days of a written demand by the owner of the car after the expiration of the lease agreement, violated due process principles. The same conclusion was reached with respect to a presumption that the defendant had embezzled the car upon a finding that he failed to return it within five days after the lease agreement had expired.

*

PART 3

LEGAL LIMITATIONS UPON LAW ENFORCEMENT PRACTICES AND PROCEDURES

Chapter 10

THE LIMITS OF UNDERCOVER WORK

A. ENTRAPMENT—DID THE POLICE CREATE THE CRIME?

1. THE BASIC RULES

UNITED STATES v. RUSSELL

Supreme Court of the United States, 1973.
411 U.S. 423, 93 S.Ct. 1637.

MR. JUSTICE REHNQUIST delivered the opinion of the Court.

* * *

... On December 7, 1969, Joe Shapiro, an undercover agent for the Federal Bureau of Narcotics and Dangerous Drugs, went to respondent's home on Whidbey Island in the State of Washington where he met with respondent and his two codefendants, John and Patrick Connolly. Shapiro's assignment was to locate a laboratory where it was believed that methamphetamine was being manufactured illicitly. He told the respondent and the Connollys that he represented an organization in the Pacific Northwest that was interested in controlling the manufacture and distribution of methamphetamine. He then made an offer to supply the defendants with the chemical phenyl-2-propanone, an essential ingredient in the manufacture of methamphetamine, in return for one-half of the drug produced. This offer was made on the condition that Agent Shapiro be shown a sample of the drug which they were making and the laboratory where it was being produced.

During the conversation Patrick Connolly revealed that he had been making the drug since May 1969 and since then had produced three pounds of it. John Connolly gave the agent a bag containing a quantity of methamphetamine that he represented as being from "the last batch that we made." Shortly thereafter, Shapiro and Patrick Connolly left respondent's house to view the laboratory which was located in the Connolly house on Whidbey Island. At the house Shapiro observed an empty bottle bearing the chemical label phenyl-2-propanone.

By prearrangement Shapiro returned to the Connolly house on December 9, 1969, to supply 100 grams of propanone and observe the chemical reaction. When he arrived he observed Patrick Connolly and the respondent cutting up pieces of aluminum foil and placing them in a large flask. There was testimony that some of the foil pieces accidentally fell on the floor and were picked up by the respondent and Shapiro and put into the flask.[1] Thereafter Patrick Connolly added all of the necessary chemicals, including the propanone brought by Shapiro, to make two batches of methamphetamine. The manufacturing process having been completed the following morning, Shapiro was given one-half of the drug and respondent kept the remainder. Shapiro offered to buy, and the respondent agreed to sell, part of the remainder for $60.

About a month later Shapiro returned to the Connolly house and met with Patrick Connolly to ask if he was still interested in their "business arrangement." Connolly replied that he was interested but that he had recently obtained two additional bottles of phenyl-2-propanone and would not be finished with them for a couple of days. He provided some additional methamphetamine to Shapiro at that time. Three days later Shapiro returned to the Connolly house with a search warrant and, among other items, seized an empty 500-gram bottle of propanone and a 100-gram bottle, not the one he had provided, that was partially filled with the chemical.

There was testimony at the trial of respondent and Patrick Connolly that phenyl-2-propanone was generally difficult to obtain. At the request of the Bureau of Narcotics and Dangerous Drugs, some chemical supply firms had voluntarily ceased selling the chemical.

At the close of the evidence, and after receiving the District Judge's standard entrapment instruction,[2] the jury found the respondent guilty on all counts charged. On appeal the respondent conceded that the jury could have found him predisposed to commit the offenses, but argued that on the facts presented there was entrapment as a matter of law. The Court of Appeals agreed, although it did not find the District Court had misconstrued or misapplied the traditional standards governing the

1. Agent Shapiro did not otherwise participate in the manufacture of the drug or direct any of the work.

2. The District Judge stated the governing law on entrapment as follows:

"Where a person has the willingness and the readiness to break the law, the mere fact that the government agent provides what appears to be a favorable opportunity is not entrapment." He then instructed the jury to acquit respondent if it had a "reasonable doubt whether the defendant had the previous intent or purpose to commit the offense ... and did so only because he was induced or persuaded by some officer or agent of the government." No exception was taken by respondent to this instruction.

entrapment defense. Rather, the court in effect expanded the traditional notion of entrapment, which focuses on the predisposition of the defendant, to mandate dismissal of a criminal prosecution whenever the court determines that there has been "an intolerable degree of governmental participation in the criminal enterprise." In this case the court decided that the conduct of the agent in supplying a scarce ingredient essential for the manufacture of a controlled substance established that defense.

This Court first recognized and applied the entrapment defense in Sorrells v. United States, 287 U.S. 435, 53 S.Ct. 210, (1932). In *Sorrells*, a federal prohibition agent visited the defendant while posing as a tourist and engaged him in conversation about their common war experiences. After gaining the defendant's confidence, the agent asked for some liquor, was twice refused, but upon asking a third time the defendant finally capitulated, and was subsequently prosecuted for violating the National Prohibition Act.

Mr. Chief Justice Hughes, speaking for the Court, held that as a matter of statutory construction the defense of entrapment should have been available to the defendant. Under the theory propounded by the Chief Justice, the entrapment defense prohibits law enforcement officers from instigating a criminal act by persons "otherwise innocent in order to lure them to its commission and to punish them." Thus, the thrust of the entrapment defense was held to focus on the intent or predisposition of the defendant to commit the crime. "[I]f the defendant seeks acquittal by reason of entrapment he cannot complain of an appropriate and searching inquiry into his own conduct and predisposition as bearing upon that issue."

Mr. Justice Roberts concurred but was of the view "that courts must be closed to the trial of a crime instigated by the government's own agents." The difference in the view of the majority and the concurring opinions is that in the former the inquiry focuses on the predisposition of the defendant, whereas in the latter the inquiry focuses on whether the government "instigated the crime."

In 1958 the Court again considered the theory underlying the entrapment defense and expressly reaffirmed the view expressed by the *Sorrells* majority. Sherman v. United States, supra. In *Sherman* the defendant was convicted of selling narcotics to a Government informer. As in *Sorrells*, it appears that the Government agent gained the confidence of the defendant and, despite initial reluctance, the defendant finally acceded to the repeated importunings of the agent to commit the criminal act. On the basis of *Sorrells*, this Court reversed the affirmance of the defendant's conviction.

In affirming the theory underlying *Sorrells*, Mr. Chief Justice Warren for the Court, held that "[t]o determine whether entrapment has been established, a line must be drawn between the trap for the unwary innocent and the trap for the unwary criminal." Mr. Justice Frankfurter stated in an opinion concurring in the result that he believed Mr.

Justice Roberts had the better view in *Sorrells* and would have framed the question to be asked in an entrapment defense in terms of "whether the police conduct revealed in the particular case falls below standards ... for the proper use of governmental power."

In the instant case respondent asks us to reconsider the theory of the entrapment defense as it is set forth in the majority opinions in *Sorrells* and *Sherman*. His principal contention is that the defense should rest on constitutional grounds. He argues that the level of Shapiro's involvement in the manufacture of the methamphetamine was so high that a criminal prosecution for the drug's manufacture violates the fundamental principles of due process. The respondent contends that the same factors that led this Court to apply the exclusionary rule to illegal searches and seizures and confessions should be considered here. But he would have the Court go further in deterring undesirable official conduct by requiring that any prosecution be barred absolutely because of the police involvement in criminal activity. The analogy is imperfect in any event, for the principal reason behind the adoption of the exclusionary rule was the government's "failure to observe its own laws." ... the government's conduct here violated no independent constitutional right of the respondent. Nor did Shapiro violate any federal statute or rule or commit any crime in infiltrating the respondent's drug enterprise.

Respondent would overcome this basic weakness in his analogy to the exclusionary rule cases by having the Court adopt a rigid constitutional rule that would preclude any prosecution when it is shown that the criminal conduct would not have been possible had not an undercover agent "supplied an indispensable means to the commission of the crime that could not have been obtained otherwise, through legal or illegal channels." Even if we were to surmount the difficulties attending the notion that due process of law can be embodied in fixed rules, and those attending respondent's particular formulation, the rule he proposes would not appear to be of significant benefit to him. For on the record presented it appears that he cannot fit within the terms of the very rule he proposes.

The record discloses that although the propanone was difficult to obtain it was by no means impossible. The defendants admitted making the drug both before and after those batches made with the propanone supplied by Shapiro. Shapiro testified that he saw an empty bottle labeled phenyl-2-propanone on his first visit to the laboratory on December 7, 1969. And when the laboratory was searched pursuant to a search warrant on January 10, 1970, two additional bottles labeled phenyl-2-propanone were seized. Thus, the facts in the record amply demonstrate that the propanone used in the illicit manufacture of methamphetamine not only *could* have been obtained without the intervention of Shapiro but was in fact obtained by these defendants.

While we may some day be presented with a situation in which the conduct of law enforcement agents is so outrageous that due process principles would absolutely bar the government from invoking judicial processes to obtain a conviction, the instant case is distinctly not of that breed. Shapiro's contribution of propanone to the criminal enterprise already in process was scarcely objectionable. The chemical is by itself a harmless substance and its possession is legal. While the government may have been seeking to make it more difficult for drug rings, such as that of which respondent was a member, to obtain the chemical, the evidence described above shows that it nonetheless was obtainable. The law enforcement conduct here stops far short of violating that "fundamental fairness, shocking to the universal sense of justice," mandated by the Due Process Clause of the Fifth Amendment.

The illicit manufacture of drugs is not a sporadic, isolated criminal incident, but a continuing, though illegal, business enterprise. In order to obtain convictions for illegally manufacturing drugs, the gathering of evidence of past unlawful conduct frequently proves to be an all but impossible task. Thus in drug-related offenses law enforcement personnel have turned to one of the only practicable means of detection: the infiltration of drug rings and a limited participation in their unlawful present practices. Such infiltration is a recognized and permissible means of apprehension; if that be so, then the supply of some item of value that the drug ring requires must, as a general rule, also be permissible. For an agent will not be taken into the confidence of the illegal entrepreneurs unless he has something of value to offer them. Law enforcement tactics such as this can hardly be said to violate "fundamental fairness" or "shocking to the universal sense of justice."

Respondent also urges, as an alternative to his constitutional argument, that we broaden the nonconstitutional defense of entrapment in order to sustain the judgment of the Court of Appeals. This Court's opinions in Sorrells v. United States, supra, and Sherman v. United States, supra, held that the principal element in the defense of entrapment was the defendant's predisposition to commit the crime. Respondent conceded in the Court of Appeals, as well he might, "that he may have harbored a predisposition to commit the charged offenses." Yet he argues that the jury's refusal to find entrapment under the charge submitted to it by the trial court should be overturned and the views of Justices Roberts and Frankfurter, concurring in *Sorrells* and *Sherman*, respectively, which make the essential element of the defense turn on the type and degree of governmental conduct, be adopted as the law.

We decline to overrule these cases. *Sorrells* is a precedent of long standing that has already been once reexamined in *Sherman* and implicitly there reaffirmed. Since the defense is not of a constitutional dimension, Congress may address itself to the question and adopt any substantive definition of the defense that it may find desirable.

Several decisions of the United States district courts and courts of appeals have undoubtedly gone beyond this Court's opinions in *Sorrells* and *Sherman* in order to bar prosecutions because of what they thought to be, for want of a better term, "overzealous law enforcement." But the defense of entrapment enunciated in those opinions was not intended to give the federal judiciary a "chancellor's foot" veto over law enforcement practices of which it did not approve. The execution of the federal laws under our Constitution is confided primarily to the Executive Branch of the Government, subject to applicable constitutional and statutory limitations and to judicially fashioned rules to enforce those limitations. We think that the decision of the Court of Appeals in this case quite unnecessarily introduces an unmanageably subjective standard which is contrary to the holdings of this Court in *Sorrells* and *Sherman.*

Those cases establish that entrapment is a relatively limited defense. It is rooted, not in any authority of the Judicial Branch to dismiss prosecutions for what it feels to have been "overzealous law enforcement," but instead in the notion that Congress could not have intended criminal punishment for a defendant who has committed all the elements of a proscribed offense but was induced to commit them by the Government.

Sorrells and *Sherman* both recognize "that the fact that officers or employees of the Government merely afford opportunities or facilities for the commission of the offense does not defeat the prosecution." Nor will the mere fact of deceit defeat a prosecution, for there are circumstances when the use of deceit is the only practicable law enforcement technique available. It is only when the Government's deception actually implants the criminal design in the mind of the defendant that the defense of entrapment comes into play.

Respondent's concession in the Court of Appeals that the jury finding as to predisposition was supported by the evidence is, therefore, fatal to his claim of entrapment. He was an active participant in an illegal drug manufacturing enterprise which began before the government agent appeared on the scene, and continued after the government agent had left the scene. He was, in the words of *Sherman,* supra, not an "unwary innocent" but an "unwary criminal." The Court of Appeals was wrong, we believe, when it sought to broaden the principle laid down in *Sorrells* and *Sherman.* Its judgment is therefore

Reversed.

MR. JUSTICE DOUGLAS, with whom MR. JUSTICE BRENNAN concurs, dissenting. [Opinion omitted]

MR. JUSTICE STEWART, with whom MR. JUSTICE BRENNAN and MR. JUSTICE MARSHALL join, dissenting.

In my view, this objective approach to entrapment advanced by [Justice Roberts and by Justice Frankfurter] is the only one truly consistent with the underlying rationale of the defense. Indeed, the very basis of the entrapment defense itself demands adherence to an approach that focuses on the conduct of the governmental agents, rather than on whether the defendant was "predisposed" or "otherwise innocent." I find it impossible to believe that the purpose of the defense is to effectuate some unexpressed congressional intent to exclude from its criminal statutes persons who committed a prohibited act, but would not have done so except for the Government's inducements. For, as Mr. Justice Frankfurter put it, "the only legislative intention that can with any show of reason be extracted from the statute is the intention to make criminal precisely the conduct in which the defendant has engaged." Since, by definition, the entrapment defense cannot arise unless the defendant actually committed the proscribed act, that defendant is manifestly covered by the terms of the criminal statute involved.

Furthermore, to say that such a defendant is "otherwise innocent" or not "predisposed" to commit the crime is misleading, at best. The very fact that he has committed an act that Congress has determined to be illegal demonstrates conclusively that he is not innocent of the offense. He may not have originated the precise plan or the precise details, but he was "predisposed" in the sense that he has proved to be quite capable of committing the crime. That he was induced, provoked, or tempted to do so by government agents does not make him any more innocent or any less predisposed than he would be if he had been induced, provoked, or tempted by a private person—which, of course, would not entitle him to cry "entrapment." Since the only difference between these situations is the identity of the tempter, it follows that the significant focus must be on the conduct of the government agents, and not on the predisposition of the defendant.

The purpose of the entrapment defense, then, cannot be to protect persons who are "otherwise innocent." Rather, it must be to prohibit unlawful governmental activity in instigating crime. As Mr. Justice Brandeis stated in Casey v. United States, "This prosecution should be stopped, not because some right of Casey's has been denied, but in order to protect the government. To protect it from illegal conduct of its officers. To preserve the purity of its courts." If that is so, then whether the particular defendant was "predisposed" or "otherwise innocent" is irrelevant; and the important question becomes whether the Government's conduct in inducing the crime was beyond judicial toleration.

Moreover, a test that makes the entrapment defense depend on whether the defendant had the requisite predisposition permits the introduction into evidence of all kinds of hearsay, suspicion, and rumor—all of which would be inadmissible in any other context—in order to prove the defendant's predisposition. It allows the prosecution, in offering such proof, to rely on the defendant's bad reputation or past criminal activities, including even rumored activities of which the prosecution may have insufficient evidence to obtain an indictment, and to present the agent's suspicions as to why they chose to tempt this defendant. This sort of evidence is not only unreliable, as the hearsay rule recognizes; but it is also highly prejudicial, especially if the matter is submitted to the jury, for, despite instructions to the contrary, the jury may well consider such evidence as probative not simply of the defendant's predisposition, but of his guilt of the offense with which he stands charged.

More fundamentally, focusing on the defendant's innocence or predisposition has the direct effect of making what is permissible or impermissible police conduct depend upon the past record and propensities of the particular defendant involved. Stated another way, this subjective test means that the Government is permitted to entrap a person with a criminal record or bad reputation, and then to prosecute him for the manufactured crime, confident that his record or reputation itself will be enough to show that he was predisposed to commit the offense anyway.

* * *

This does not mean, of course, that the Government's use of undercover activity, strategy, or deception is necessarily unlawful. Indeed, many crimes, especially so-called victimless crimes, could not otherwise be detected. Thus, government agents may engage in conduct that is likely, when objectively considered, to afford a person ready and willing to commit the crime an opportunity to do so.

But when the agents' involvement in criminal activities goes beyond the mere offering of such an opportunity and when their conduct is of a kind that could induce or instigate the commission of a crime by one not ready and willing to commit it, then—regardless of the character or propensities of the particular person induced—I think entrapment has occurred. For in that situation, the Government has engaged in the impermissible manufacturing of crime, and the federal courts should bar the prosecution in order to preserve the institutional integrity of the system of federal criminal justice.

* * *

II

* * *

It cannot be doubted that if phenyl-2-propanone had been wholly unobtainable from other sources, the agent's undercover offer to supply it to the respondent in return for part of the illicit methamphetamine produced therewith—an offer initiated and carried out by the agent for the purpose of prosecuting the respondent for producing methamphetamine—would be precisely the type of governmental conduct that constitutes entrapment under any definition. For the agent's conduct in that situation would make possible the commission of an otherwise totally impossible crime, and, I should suppose, would thus be a textbook example of instigating the commission of a criminal offense in order to prosecute someone for committing it.

But assuming in this case that the phenyl-2-propanone was obtainable through independent sources, the fact remains that that used for the particular batch of methamphetamine involved in all three counts of the indictment with which the respondent was charged—i.e., that produced on December 10, 1969—was supplied by the Government. This essential ingredient was indisputably difficult to obtain, and yet what was used in committing the offenses of which the respondent was convicted was offered to the respondent by the Government agent on the agent's own initiative, and was readily supplied to the respondent in needed amounts. If the chemical was so easily available elsewhere, then why did not the agent simply wait until the respondent had himself obtained the ingredients and produced the drug, and then buy it from him? The very fact that the agent felt it incumbent upon him to offer to supply phenyl-2-propanone in return for the drug casts considerable doubt on the theory that the chemical could easily have been procured without the agent's intervention, and that therefore the agent merely afforded an opportunity for the commission of a criminal offense.

In this case, the chemical ingredient was available only to licensed persons, and the Government itself had requested suppliers not to sell that ingredient even to people with a license. Yet the Government agent readily offered, and supplied, that ingredient to an unlicensed person and asked him to make a certain illegal drug with it. The Government then prosecuted that person for making the drug produced *with the very ingredient* which its agent had so helpfully supplied. This strikes me as the very pattern of conduct that should be held to constitute entrapment as a matter of law.

It is the Government's duty to prevent crime, not to promote it. Here, the Government's agent asked that the illegal drug be produced for him, solved his quarry's practical problems with the assurance that he could provide the one essential ingredient that was difficult to obtain, furnished that element as he had promised, and bought the finished product from the respondent—all so that the respondent could be prosecuted for producing and selling the very drug for which the agent had asked and for which he had provided the necessary component. Under the objective approach that I would follow, this respondent was entrapped, regardless of his predisposition or "innocence."

* * *

I would affirm the judgment of the Court of Appeals.

NOTE

1. Traditionally entrapment is a mental state defense like insanity or intoxication. The accused may admit to delivering narcotics but claims to have done so without intent to commit a crime, but, for example, to put an end to endlessly repeated requests for narcotics from an undercover officer. Indeed the accused may claim entrapment even while denying that he delivered contraband. Mathews v. United States, 485 U.S. 58, 108 S.Ct. 883 (1988). To determine the validity of this claim courts have directed attention to two factors:

a. *Inducements:* In Sherman v. United States, 356 U.S. 369, 78 S.Ct. 819 (1958), the Court found entrapment when an informer met Sherman at a doctor's office where both were being treated for narcotics addiction. The two met several times and had become acquainted and discussed the problems of addiction. Eventually the informer said he was not responding to treatment and required narcotics. Sherman first refused and then tried to avoid the issue but, after several repeated requests, each predicated on the claim that the informer was suffering, Sherman agreed to get narcotics and share them with the informer. He did this on several occasions and the informer paid his share of the cost. After several such times, the informer told police he had a seller for them.

The decision in *Sherman* is not typical. Entrapment defenses are presented at trial and usually rejected by triers of fact. On appeal a guilty verdict of the judge or jury is almost always sustained even when there was considerable evidence of inducement.

In In re Toler, 26 Ill.2d 100, 185 N.E.2d 874 (1962) an undercover officer told defendant that he worked for a dentist whose son was an addict and who, because of a change in law, could no longer prescribe narcotics for his son. The officer said his boss needed to get good heroin off the street because the son "was in pretty bad shape, we didn't think he would live very long." After some twenty requests, defendant purchased narcotics and resold them at no profit to the officer. A majority of the Court sustained the conviction. See also, United States v. Struyf, 701 F.2d 875 (11th Cir.1983). (Defendant's friend and former brother-in-law, an informer, persuaded defendant over a period of time to go in on a drug deal, partly by his claim that he desperately needed money to care for himself and his family.) United States v. Citro, 842 F.2d 1149 (9th Cir.1988) (repeated inducements do not entrap if there are merely money and dinners).

b. *Predisposition:* Even when the government's inducements for illegal acts are compelling, entrapment will not occur if the accused was already predisposed to commit the crime. Predisposition may be proved by showing that the accused had prior convictions for similar offenses, that he committed or indicated willingness to commit a similar, but uncharged, offense, that he displayed some criminal expertise in carrying out the offense, that he was readily able to commit the offense, i.e., the accused had quick access to a quantity of illegal drugs and so forth.

Jennifer Skarie lived on an isolated ranch with her three sons and several women who she had taken in. At one time Bear had lived there, he was violent and often armed and was forced out by Skarie because of his drug use. He threatened Skarie. He was also a government informer and some months after he was booted out of the house, he pressured Skarie to put him in touch with drug sellers. He sometimes called her ten times a day. He impaled one of her chickens on a stick and left it outside her door. He remarked that what happened to chickens could happen to people. He told Skarie he could slit the throat of her horses and threatened to kidnap her six-year-old son. Eventually she did what Bear asked. After she finally yielded she did participate more actively in the drug trade. The Court found entrapment as a matter of law because her predisposition, i.e. her apparent willingness after she started to assist Bear, could not be counted against her; "predisposition is tested at a time 'prior to the Government acts intended to create predisposition.'" United States v. Skarie, 971 F.2d 317 (9th Cir.1992).

Under traditional entrapment rules, the police do not have to show any evidence of predisposition in order to approach an individual to ask him, say, to sell narcotics or accept a wager. Kadis v. United States, 373 F.2d 370 (1st Cir.1967). Predisposition is considered in connection with inducement to arrive at a judgment of whether there was entrapment. Consider United States v. Tobias, 662 F.2d 381 (5th Cir.1981) where the DEA established a chemical supply company and placed advertisements in High Times Magazine to sell various chemicals and equipment used in the manufacture of illegal drugs. Tobias requested and received more information from the company. Tobias then telephoned the company on numerous occasions to order supplies and to check on his orders. Within one month of placing his first order, Tobias called the company to cancel his orders because he had discovered he did not possess the knowledge or the equipment to manufacture cocaine. Before he could cancel his orders, however, a DEA agent asked him what he was trying to do. Tobias admitted his desire to manufacture cocaine and related his difficulties in trying to do so. The agent pretended to sympathize with Tobias, and stated that he too found cocaine difficult to manufacture. In response, Tobias stated that he was not interested in manufacturing cocaine per se, but that he just wanted to make some money. The agent then suggested that a number of drugs were easier to manufacture than cocaine, including amphetamines and phencyclidine (PCP). The agent explained that making PCP was as easy as "baking a cake" and offered to send Tobias everything he would need to make PCP for $500. Tobias agreed. After receiving the chemicals, Tobias called the company thirteen times for advice on how to make PCP. [His claim of entrapment was rejected because of his predisposition to commit the offense evidenced by his answering the advertisement, his expressed desire to make money, and the fact that he placed all of the thirteen calls to DEA on his own initiative.]

A discussion of the interplay of concepts of inducement and predisposition is found in United States v. Evans, 924 F.2d 714 (7th Cir.1991):

> POSNER, J.
>
> A high school classmate of Evans, who was working as a government informant and who believed Evans to be a drug dealer, approached Evans (who was managing a furniture store) and asked him whether he was interested in buying a large quantity of marijuana. According to the informant, he was, and a month later Evans produced $20,000 in cash to buy one hundred pounds of marijuana—at which point he was arrested. Evans was a purchaser of marijuana for personal use, not a dealer, was reluctant to become a dealer, and rebuffed the informant's solicitations the first five times that the informant visited him at the store. Finally on the sixth visit he yielded and he admits that from then on he was a willing participant in the scheme to buy a large quantity of marijuana. But he insists that the defense of entrapment does not require that the defendant have been reluctant throughout the entire course of the criminal conduct. He is right. If he was indeed entrapped, it is irrelevant that the entrapment was so effective as to make him not only a willing but an eager participant, United States v. Rodriguez, 858 F.2d 809, 816 (1st Cir.1988), just as, in the converse case, second thoughts following initial enthusiasm do not establish entrapment. United States v. Marren, 890 F.2d 924, 931 (7th Cir.1989).
>
> The weakness in Evans's position is his belief that the defense of entrapment requires only that the defendant have been induced, in the sense of successfully solicited, by a government agent to commit the crime and that he have yielded to the solicitation with reluctance. That is an eccentric formulation. As usually formulated, the defense requires the defendant to prove that he was (1) induced by someone working for or on behalf of the government to commit a crime that he was (2) not predisposed to commit. The First Circuit doesn't like the "inducement" part of the formula and has reformulated the defense as the

single question whether the government corrupted the defendant. Kadis v. United States, 373 F.2d 370, 373 (1st Cir.1967). The Supreme Court's decision in *United States v. Russell* (1973) seems to reformulate the defense as the single question whether the defendant was induced. But most of the recent cases require proof of both inducement, in the sense merely of successful solicitation, and lack of predisposition. Some cases, it is true, say that "solicitation and inducement are not the same thing." But they mean either that solicitation is not entrapment or that solicitation that fails to induce is not inducement. Or else as in *Russell* they expand "inducement" to make it synonymous with entrapment.

All this suggests a certain semantic disarray. But when we go behind words to policy, we can see that something like predisposition, in the sense of inordinate willingness to participate in criminal activity, must be the key inquiry, though as a verbal matter it could be folded into inducement viewed as the government's really having *caused,* in some rich sense, the criminal activity to occur, as distinct from merely providing a convenient occasion for it to occur. The centrality of predisposition can be seen by considering the purpose of the doctrine of entrapment. It is to prevent the police from turning a law-abiding person into a criminal. A law-abiding person is one who resists the temptations, which abound in our society today, to commit crimes. Such a person can be induced to commit a crime only by grave threats, by fraud (the police might persuade him that the act they want him to commit is not criminal), or, in the usual case in which entrapment is pleaded, by extraordinary promises—the sorts of promises that would blind the ordinary person to his legal duties. So if the police offered a derelict $100,000 to commit a minor crime that he wouldn't have dreamed of committing for the usual gain that such a crime could be expected to yield, and he accepted the offer and committed the crime, that would be entrapment.

* * *

... The police did not offer Evans a cent. They offered him a source of supply, in wholesale quantities, at market prices. They offered him, in other words, an opportunity to enter the drug trade (assuming improbably that he was not already in it, as the informant suspected) on the usual terms. A person who takes advantage of an ordinary opportunity to commit criminal acts—not an extraordinary opportunity, the sort of thing that might entice an otherwise law-abiding person—is not entrapped. Such a person is predisposed to crime in the sense that the ordinary profits of crime are incentive enough to him to commit crimes; he is ready and waiting; all that is wanting is the opportunity. It is a detail that the police create the opportunity before a real drug dealer does. The fact that he may not have jumped at the chance—that he may therefore have been willing rather than eager to commit the crime that the government solicited him to commit—does not by itself establish lack of criminal predisposition. Yet it is the only fact to which he appeals as evidence on this essential issue.

Probably the caution, the hesitation, that Evans showed (always assuming that his testimony is believed) were just simple prudence in an illegal activity. It was also prudent of him to show up heavily armed at the rendezvous at which he was to turn over the $20,000 and receive in exchange the marijuana. Our explanation for his hesitation may be debatable, but at most—giving him the benefit of every favorable inference possible—that initial hesitation was a sting of conscience too quickly pulled to allow a reasonable jury to conclude that Evans lacked criminal predisposition. It is no doubt unfortunate that issues of disposition and character should be injected into a criminal case, but we do not see how else the defense of entrapment can be kept within the bounds indicated by its rationale.

2. Some jurisdictions follow the "objective" approach favored by Justice Stewart in his dissent in *Russell* and do not consider the question of predisposition. See People v. Barraza, 23 Cal.3d 675, 153 Cal.Rptr. 459, 591 P.2d 947 (1979):

> "MOSK, J.
>
> The success of an entrapment defense should not turn on differences among defendants; we are not concerned with who first conceived or who willingly, or reluctantly, acquiesced in a criminal project. What we do care about is how much and what manner of persuasion, pressure, and cajoling are brought to bear by law enforcement officials to induce persons to commit crimes.
>
> * * *
>
> "We hold that the proper test of entrapment in California is the following: was the conduct of the law enforcement agent likely to induce a normally law-abiding person to commit the offense? For the purposes of this test, we presume that such a person would normally resist the temptation to commit a crime presented by the simple opportunity to act unlawfully. Official conduct that does no more than offer that opportunity to the suspect—for example, a decoy program—is therefore permissible; but it is impermissible for the police or their agents to pressure the suspect by overbearing conduct such as badgering, cajoling, importuning, or other affirmative acts likely to induce a normally law-abiding person to commit the crime.
>
> "Although the determination of what police conduct is impermissible must to some extent proceed on an ad hoc basis, guidance will generally be found in the application of one or both of two principles. First, if the actions of the law enforcement agent would generate in a normally law-abiding person a motive for the crime other than ordinary criminal intent, entrapment will be established. An example of such conduct would be an appeal by the police that would induce such a person to commit the act because of friendship or sympathy, instead of a desire for personal gain or other typical criminal purpose. Second, affirmative police conduct that would make commission of the crime unusually attractive to a normally law-abiding person will likewise constitute entrapment. Such conduct would include, for example, a guarantee that the act is not illegal or the offense will go undetected, an offer of exorbitant consideration or any similar enticement.
>
> "Finally, while the inquiry must focus primarily on the conduct of the law enforcement agent, that conduct is not to be viewed in a vacuum; it should also be judged by the effect it would have on a normally law-abiding person situated in the circumstances of the case at hand. Among the circumstances that may be relevant for this purpose, for example, are the transactions preceding the offense, the suspect's response to the inducements of the officer, the gravity of the crime, and

the difficulty of detecting instances of its commission. We reiterate, however, that under this test such matters as the character of the suspect, his predisposition to commit the offense, and his subjective intent are irrelevant.

"Richardson, J.

"I respectfully dissent, . . .

"The majority now proposes to ban consideration of the particular defendant and replace him with a hypothetical 'normally law-abiding person' who is described as 'a person [who] would normally resist the temptation to commit a crime presented by the simple opportunity to act unlawfully.' The briefest reflection reveals the difficulties inherent in this definition. The individual who has *never* committed a criminal act can safely be categorized as a 'normally law-abiding person' since presumably his unblemished record is proof of his ability to resist temptation. However, what of the individual who has transgressed in the past either once or several times? Is he no longer '*normally* law-abiding'? Is 'normally' synonymous with 'generally'? If it may be drawn at all, the line between 'normally law-abiding' individuals and 'others' is not so easily fixed as the majority suggests.

"The fallacy underlying the majority's thesis, of course, is that in the very real world of criminal conduct there are no hypothetical people. To attempt to judge police conduct in a vacuum is to engage in a futile and meaningless exercise in semantics. The majority abandons the actual for the hypothetical. It thereby substitutes the unreal for the real, with unnecessary complications that inevitably result therefrom.

* * *

3. Some statutes require the defendant to prove *both* that the police conduct exceeded permissible limits *and* that defendant had no predisposition. See State v. Rockholt, 96 N.J. 570, 476 A.2d 1236 (1984). Even where the state must prove the absence of entrapment, it will win if it disproves *either* improper inducement *or* lack of predisposition. United States v. El-Gawli, 837 F.2d 142 (3d Cir.1988).

4. One judge has explained the theory underlying the entrapment defense in a novel way. See United States v. Kaminski, 703 F.2d 1004 (7th Cir.1983):

POSNER, CIRCUIT JUDGE, concurring.

I join Judge Pell's opinion for the court without any reservations, and write separately merely to float a suggestion for giving practical content to the elusive concept, which is fundamental to the entrapment doctrine, of predisposition to commit a crime.

If the police entice someone to commit a crime who would not have done so without their blandishments, and then arrest him and he is prosecuted, convicted, and punished, law enforcement resources are squandered in the following sense: resources that could and should have been used in an effort to reduce the nation's unacceptably high crime rate are used instead in the entirely sterile activity of first inciting and then punishing a crime. However, if the police are just inducing someone to commit sooner a crime he would have committed eventually, but to do so in controlled circumstances where the costs to the criminal justice system of apprehension and conviction are minimized, the police are economizing on resources. It is particularly difficult to catch arsonists, so if all the police were doing here was making it easier to catch an arsonist—not inducing someone to become an arsonist—they were using law enforcement resources properly and there is no occasion for judicial intervention. And I am persuaded that that is the situation in this case.

Thus in my view "entrapment" is merely the name we give to a particularly unproductive use of law enforcement resources, which our system properly condemns. If this is right, the implementing concept of "predisposition to crime" calls less for psychological conjecture than for a common-sense assessment of whether it is likely that the defendant would have committed the crime anyway—without the blandishments the police used on him—but at a time and place where it would have been more difficult for them to apprehend him and the state to convict him, or whether the police used threats or promises so powerful that a law-abiding individual was induced to commit a crime. If the latter is the case, the police tactics do not merely affect the timing and location of a crime; they cause crime.

Nevada recently condemned as entrapment a decoy operation in which undercover officers, with money hanging from their pockets, posed as drunkards passed out in public areas. The Court was, for reasons not apparent to the reader, especially critical of young prosecutors and police officers. But the Court also used a form of economic analysis to sustain its holding, e.g. for healthy, energetic people in the prime of life—during balmy summer months when the sidewalks are warm—perhaps few pastimes could seem more enticing than to go fishing for "suckers," who succumb to their artificial bait. Few such tyros will pause to weigh the social costs of entrapping young underclass males into manufactured crime, to-wit:

(1) the loss to the entrapped person's employer of a trained, apparently acceptable employee, as was the case here;

(2) the loss to society in general of the entrapped person's productivity;

(3) the cost to society for the services of publicly paid prosecution and defense counsel, and support personnel;

(4) the expenditure of the court system's time;

(5) the overhead cost of imprisoning a person who previously was self-supporting, at an annual expenditure in the neighborhood of $14,000 per year;

(6) the lost use of a prison cell with a replacement value of perhaps $60,000 (generating what economists call an "opportunity cost" of an additional number of thousands of dollars per year), which might otherwise be used to incarcerate a real criminal;

(7) the cost to any family and dependents of the entrapped person, who lose their breadwinner;

(8) finally, the cost to society of maintaining a larger-than-necessary parole and probation system in order to supervise entrapped persons after their release, even though no supervision would foreseeably have been necessary if the entrapped persons had been left in peace to begin with.

Washoe County Sheriff v. Hawkins, 104 Nev. 70, 752 P.2d 769 (1988). The same Court later approved a decoy operation where the money was not dangling from a pocket and its possessor was not feigning sleep. De Pasquale v. State, 104 Nev. 338, 757 P.2d 367 (1988).

5. In some situations, an undercover agent deals with Target A but has no direct contact with B. A and B engage in joint criminal activity. Even if the police have improperly induced A to commit the crime so that A has an entrapment defense, B will have no such defense where A induced B to participate in the crime. Courts have rejected concepts of "derivative entrapment." The inducements offered by a private citizen who has not agreed to assist efforts to gather evidence cannot constitute entrapment. The government has engaged in no wrongdoing as to B if agents did nothing to induce B to participate in the crime. According to United States v. Emmert, 829 F.2d 805 (9th Cir.1987), this is so even when government agents contemplate that Target A will pass on word of the inducements to Target B. Does this extension of the limitation upon entrapment make sense? What is its rationale?

2. PREDISPOSITION REVISITED

JACOBSON v. UNITED STATES

Supreme Court of the United States, 1992.
503 U.S. 540, 112 S.Ct. 1535.

JUSTICE WHITE delivered the opinion of the Court.

On September 24, 1987, petitioner Keith Jacobson was indicted for violating a provision of the Child Protection Act of 1984, which criminalizes the knowing receipt through the mails of a "visual depiction [that] involves the use of a minor engaging in sexually explicit conduct...." Petitioner was found guilty after a jury trial.

I

In February 1984, petitioner, a 56–year–old veteran-turned-farmer who supported his elderly father in Nebraska, ordered two magazines and a brochure from a California adult bookstore. The magazines, entitled Bare Boys I and Bare Boys II, contained photographs of nude preteen and teenage boys. The contents of the magazines startled petitioner, who testified that he had expected to receive photographs of "young men 18 years or older." On cross-examination, he explained his response to the magazines:

> "[PROSECUTOR]: [Y]ou were shocked and surprised that there were pictures of very young boys without clothes on, is that correct?
>
> "[JACOBSON]: Yes, I was.
>
> "[PROSECUTOR]: Were you offended?

* * *

> "[JACOBSON]: I was not offended because I thought these were a nudist type publication. Many of the pictures were out in a rural or outdoor setting. There was—I didn't draw any sexual connotation or connection with that."

The young men depicted in the magazines were not engaged in sexual activity, and petitioner's receipt of the magazines was legal under both federal and Nebraska law. Within three months, the law with respect to child pornography changed; Congress passed the Act illegalizing the receipt through the mails of sexually explicit depictions of children. In the very month that the new provision became law, postal inspectors found petitioner's name on the mailing list of the California bookstore that had mailed him Bare Boys I and II. There followed over the next 2½ years, repeated efforts by two Government agencies, through five fictitious organizations and a bogus pen pal, to explore petitioner's willingness to break the new law by ordering sexually explicit photographs of children through the mail.

The Government began its efforts in January 1985 when a postal inspector sent petitioner a letter supposedly from the American Hedonist Society, which in fact was a fictitious organization. The letter included a membership application and stated the Society's doctrine: that members had the "right to read what we desire, the right to discuss similar interests with those who share our philosophy, and finally that we have the right to seek pleasure without restrictions being placed on us by outdated puritan morality." Petitioner enrolled in the organization and returned a sexual attitude questionnaire that asked him to rank on a scale of one to four his enjoyment of various sexual materials, with one being "really enjoy," two being "enjoy," three being "somewhat enjoy," and four being "do not enjoy." Petitioner ranked the entry "[p]reteen sex" as a two, but indicated that he was opposed to pedophilia.

For a time, the Government left petitioner alone. But then a new "prohibited mail specialist" in the Postal Service found petitioner's name in a file, and in May 1986, petitioner received a solicitation from a second fictitious consumer research company, "Midlands Data Research," seeking a response from those who "believe in the joys of sex and the complete awareness of those lusty and youthful lads and lasses of the neophite [*sic*] age." The letter never explained whether "neophite" referred to minors or young adults. Petitioner responded: "Please feel free to send me more information, I am interested in teenage sexuality. Please keep my name confidential."

Petitioner then heard from yet another Government creation, "Heartland Institute for a New Tomorrow" (HINT), which proclaimed that it was "an organization founded to protect and promote sexual freedom and freedom of choice. We believe that arbitrarily imposed legislative sanctions restricting *your* sexual freedom should be rescinded through the legislative process." The letter also enclosed a second survey. Petitioner indicated that his interest in "[p]reteen sex-homosexual" material was above average, but not high. In response to another question, petitioner wrote: "Not only sexual expression but freedom of the press is under attack. We must be ever vigilant to counter attack right wing fundamentalists who are determined to curtail our freedoms."

"HINT" replied, portraying itself as a lobbying organization seeking to repeal "all statutes which regulate sexual activities, except those laws which deal with violent behavior, such as rape. HINT is also lobbying to eliminate any legal definition of 'the age of consent'." These lobbying efforts were to be funded by sales from a catalog to be published in the future "offering the sale of various items which we believe you will find to be both interesting and stimulating." HINT also provided computer matching of group members with similar survey responses; and, although petitioner was supplied with a list of potential "pen pals," he did not initiate any correspondence.

Nevertheless, the Government's "prohibited mail specialist" began writing to petitioner, using the pseudonym "Carl Long." The letters employed a tactic known as "mirroring," which the inspector described as "reflect[ing] whatever the interests are of the person we are writing to." Petitioner responded at first, indicating that his interest was primarily in "male-male items." Inspector "Long" wrote back:

> "My interests too are primarily male-male items. Are you satisfied with the type of VCR tapes available? Personally, I like the amateur stuff better if its [sic] well produced as it can get more kinky and also seems more real. I think the actors enjoy it more."

Petitioner responded:

> "As far as my likes are concerned, I like good looking young guys (in their late teens and early 20's) doing their thing together."

Petitioner's letters to "Long" made no reference to child pornography. After writing two letters, petitioner discontinued the correspondence.

By March 1987, 34 months had passed since the Government obtained petitioner's name from the mailing list of the California bookstore, and 26 months had passed since the Postal Service had commenced its mailings to petitioner. Although petitioner had responded to surveys and letters, the Government had no evidence that petitioner had ever intentionally possessed or been exposed to child pornography. The Postal Service had not checked petitioner's mail to determine whether he was receiving questionable mailings from persons—other than the Government—involved in the child pornography industry.

At this point, a second Government agency, the Customs Service, included petitioner in its own child pornography sting, "Operation Borderline," after receiving his name on lists submitted by the Postal Service. Using the name of a fictitious Canadian company called "Produit Outaouais," the Customs Service mailed petitioner a brochure advertising photographs of young boys engaging in sex. Petitioner placed an order that was never filled.

The Postal Service also continued its efforts in the Jacobson case, writing to petitioner as the "Far Eastern Trading Company Ltd." The letter began:

> "As many of you know, much hysterical nonsense has appeared in the American media concerning 'pornography' and what must be done to stop it from coming across your borders. This brief letter does not allow us to give much comments; however, why is your government spending millions of dollars to exercise international censorship while tons of drugs, which makes yours the world's most crime ridden country are passed through easily."

The letter went on to say:

> "[W]e have devised a method of getting these to you without prying eyes of U.S. Customs seizing your mail.... After consultations with American solicitors, we have been advised that once we have posted our material through your system, it cannot be opened for any inspection without authorization of a judge."

The letter invited petitioner to send for more information. It also asked petitioner to sign an affirmation that he was "not a law enforcement officer or agent of the U.S. Government acting in an undercover capacity for the purpose of entrapping Far Eastern Trading Company, its agents or customers." Petitioner responded. A catalogue was sent, and petitioner ordered Boys Who Love Boys, a pornographic magazine depicting young boys engaged in various sexual activities. Petitioner was arrested after a controlled delivery of a photocopy of the magazine.

When petitioner was asked at trial why he placed such an order, he explained that the Government had succeeded in piquing his curiosity:

> "Well, the statement was made of all the trouble and the hysteria over pornography and I wanted to see what the material was. It didn't describe the—I didn't know for sure what kind of sexual action they were referring to in the Canadian letter...."

In petitioner's home, the Government found the Bare Boys magazines and materials that the Government had sent to him in the course of its protracted investigation, but no other materials that would indicate that petitioner collected or was actively interested in child pornography.

II

There can be no dispute about the evils of child pornography or the difficulties that laws and law enforcement have encountered in eliminating it. Likewise, there can be no dispute that the Government may use undercover agents to enforce the law. "It is well settled that the fact that officers or employees of the Government merely afford opportunities or facilities for the commission of the offense does not defeat the prosecution. Artifice and stratagem may be employed to catch those engaged in criminal enterprises." *Sorrells v. United States,* (1932).

In their zeal to enforce the law, however, Government agents may not originate a criminal design, implant in an innocent person's mind the disposition to commit a criminal act, and then induce commission of the crime so that the Government may prosecute. Where the Government has induced an individual to break the law and the defense of entrapment is at issue, as it was in this case, the prosecution must prove beyond reasonable doubt that the defendant was disposed to commit the criminal act prior to first being approached by Government agents.[1]

Thus, an agent deployed to stop the traffic in illegal drugs may offer the opportunity to buy or sell drugs, and, if the offer is accepted, make an arrest on the spot or later. In such a typical case, or in a more elaborate "sting" operation involving government-sponsored fencing where the defendant is simply provided with the opportunity to commit a crime, the entrapment defense is of little use because the ready commission of the criminal act amply demonstrates the defendant's predisposition. Had the agents in this case simply offered petitioner the opportunity to order child pornography through the mails, and petitioner—who must be presumed to know the law—had promptly availed himself of this criminal opportunity, it is unlikely that his entrapment defense would have warranted a jury instruction.

But that is not what happened here. By the time petitioner finally placed his order, he had already been the target of 26 months of repeated mailings and communications from Government agents and fictitious organizations. Therefore, although he had become predisposed to break the law by May 1987, it is our view that the Government did not prove

1. Inducement is not at issue in this case. The Government does not dispute that it induced petitioner to commit the crime. The sole issue is whether the Government carried its burden of proving that petitioner was predisposed to violate the law before the Government intervened. The dissent is mistaken in claiming that this is an innovation in entrapment law and in suggesting that the Government's conduct prior to the moment of solicitation is irrelevant. The Court rejected these arguments five decades ago in Sorrells, when the Court wrote that the Government may not punish an individual "for an alleged offense which is the product of the creative activity of its own officials". Indeed, the proposition that the accused must be predisposed prior to contact with law enforcement officers is so firmly established that the Government conceded the point at oral argument, submitting that the evidence it developed during the course of its investigation was probative because it indicated petitioner's state of mind prior to the commencement of the Government's investigation.

This long-established standard in no way encroaches upon Government investigatory activities. Indeed, the Government's internal guidelines for undercover operations provide that an inducement to commit a crime should not be offered unless:

"(a) there is a reasonable indication, based on information developed through informants or other means, that the subject is engaging, has engaged, or is likely to engage in illegal activity of a similar type; or

"(b) The opportunity for illegal activity has been structured so that there is reason for believing that persons drawn to the opportunity, or brought to it, are predisposed to engage in the contemplated illegal activity." Attorney General's Guidelines on FBI Undercover Operations (Dec. 31, 1980), reprinted in S.Rep. No. 97–682, p. 551 (1982).

that this predisposition was independent and not the product of the attention that the Government had directed at petitioner since January 1985.

The prosecution's evidence of predisposition falls into two categories: evidence developed prior to the Postal Service's mail campaign, and that developed during the course of the investigation. The sole piece of preinvestigation evidence is petitioner's 1984 order and receipt of the Bare Boys magazines. But this is scant if any proof of petitioner's predisposition to commit an illegal act, the criminal character of which a defendant is presumed to know. It may indicate a predisposition to view sexually-oriented photographs that are responsive to his sexual tastes; but evidence that merely indicates a generic inclination to act within a broad range, not all of which is criminal, is of little probative value in establishing predisposition.

Furthermore, petitioner was acting within the law at the time he received these magazines. Receipt through the mails of sexually explicit depictions of children for noncommercial use did not become illegal under federal law until May 1984, and Nebraska had no law that forbade petitioner's possession of such material until 1988. Neb.Rev.Stat. § 28–813.01 (1989). Evidence of predisposition to do what once was lawful is not, by itself, sufficient to show predisposition to do what is now illegal, for there is a common understanding that most people obey the law even when they disapprove of it. This obedience may reflect a generalized respect for legality or the fear of prosecution, but for whatever reason, the law's prohibitions are matters of consequence. Hence, the fact that petitioner legally ordered and received the Bare Boys magazines does little to further the Government's burden of proving that petitioner was predisposed to commit a criminal act. This is particularly true given petitioner's unchallenged testimony was that he did not know until they arrived that the magazines would depict minors.

The prosecution's evidence gathered during the investigation also fails to carry the Government's burden. Petitioner's responses to the many communications prior to the ultimate criminal act were at most indicative of certain personal inclinations, including a predisposition to view photographs of preteen sex and a willingness to promote a given agenda by supporting lobbying organizations. Even so, petitioner's responses hardly support an inference that he would commit the crime of receiving child pornography through the mails.[2] Furthermore, a person's inclinations and "fantasies ... are his own and beyond the reach of government...." *Paris Adult Theatre I v. Slaton,* (1973).

On the other hand, the strong arguable inference is that, by waving the banner of individual rights and disparaging the legitimacy and

2. We do not hold, as the dissent suggests, that the Government was required to prove that petitioner knowingly violated the law. We simply conclude that proof that petitioner engaged in legal conduct and possessed certain generalized personal inclinations is not sufficient evidence to prove beyond a reasonable doubt that he would have been predisposed to commit the crime charged independent of the Government's coaxing.

constitutionality of efforts to restrict the availability of sexually explicit materials, the Government not only excited petitioner's interest in sexually explicit materials banned by law but also exerted substantial pressure on petitioner to obtain and read such material as part of a fight against censorship and the infringement of individual rights. For instance, HINT described itself as "an organization founded to protect and promote sexual freedom and freedom of choice" and stated that "the most appropriate means to accomplish [its] objectives is to promote honest dialogue among concerned individuals and to continue its lobbying efforts with State Legislators." These lobbying efforts were to be financed through catalogue sales. Mailings from the equally fictitious American Hedonist Society, and the correspondence from the nonexistent Carl Long, endorsed these themes.

Similarly, the two solicitations in the spring of 1987 raised the spectre of censorship while suggesting that petitioner ought to be allowed to do what he had been solicited to do. The mailing from the Customs Service referred to "the worldwide ban and intense enforcement on this type of material," observed that "what was legal and commonplace is now an 'underground' and secretive service," and emphasized that "[t]his environment forces us to take extreme measures" to insure delivery. The Postal Service solicitation described the concern about child pornography as "hysterical nonsense," decried "international censorship," and assured petitioner, based on consultation with "American solicitors" that an order that had been posted could not be opened for inspection without authorization of a judge. It further asked petitioner to affirm that he was not a government agent attempting to entrap the mail order company or its customers. In these particulars, both government solicitations suggested that receiving this material was something that petitioner ought to be allowed to do.

Petitioner's ready response to these solicitations cannot be enough to establish beyond reasonable doubt that he was predisposed, prior to the Government acts intended to create predisposition, to commit the crime of receiving child pornography through the mails. The evidence that petitioner was ready and willing to commit the offense came only after the Government had devoted 2½ years to convincing him that he had or should have the right to engage in the very behavior proscribed by law. Rational jurors could not say beyond a reasonable doubt that petitioner possessed the requisite predisposition prior to the Government's investigation and that it existed independent of the Government's many and varied approaches to petitioner. As was explained in *Sherman,* where entrapment was found as a matter of law, "the Government [may not] pla[y] on the weaknesses of an innocent party and beguil[e] him into committing crimes which he otherwise would not have attempted."

When the Government's quest for convictions leads to the apprehension of an otherwise law-abiding citizen who, if left to his own devices, likely would have never run afoul of the law, the courts should intervene.

Because we conclude that this is such a case and that the prosecution failed, as a matter of law, to adduce evidence to support the jury verdict that petitioner was predisposed, independent of the Government's acts and beyond a reasonable doubt, to violate the law by receiving child pornography through the mails, we reverse the Court of Appeals' judgment affirming the conviction of Keith Jacobson.

It is so ordered.

JUSTICE O'CONNOR, with whom THE CHIEF JUSTICE and JUSTICE KENNEDY join, and with whom JUSTICE SCALIA joins except as to Part II, dissenting.

Keith Jacobson was offered only two opportunities to buy child pornography through the mail. Both times, he ordered. Both times, he asked for opportunities to buy more. He needed no Government agent to coax, threaten, or persuade him; no one played on his sympathies, friendship, or suggested that his committing the crime would further a greater good. In fact, no Government agent even contacted him face-to-face. The Government contends that from the enthusiasm with which Mr. Jacobson responded to the chance to commit a crime, a reasonable jury could permissibly infer beyond a reasonable doubt that he was predisposed to commit the crime. I agree.

The first time the Government sent Mr. Jacobson a catalog of illegal materials, he ordered a set of photographs advertised as picturing "young boys in sex action fun." He enclosed the following note with his order: "I received your brochure and decided to place an order. If I like your product, I will order more later." For reasons undisclosed in the record, Mr. Jacobson's order was never delivered.

The second time the Government sent a catalog of illegal materials, Mr. Jacobson ordered a magazine called "Boys Who Love Boys," described as: "11 year old and 14 year old boys get it on in every way possible. Oral, anal sex and heavy masturbation. If you love boys, you will be delighted with this." Along with his order, Mr. Jacobson sent the following note: "Will order other items later. I want to be discreet in order to protect you and me."

Government agents admittedly did not offer Mr. Jacobson the chance to buy child pornography right away. Instead, they first sent questionnaires in order to make sure that he was generally interested in the subject matter. Indeed, a "cold call" in such a business would not only risk rebuff and suspicion, but might also shock and offend the uninitiated, or expose minors to suggestive materials. Mr. Jacobson's responses to the questionnaires gave the investigators reason to think he would be interested in photographs depicting preteen sex.

I believe the Court fails to acknowledge the reasonableness of the jury's inference from the evidence, redefines "predisposition," and introduces a new requirement that Government sting operations have a reasonable suspicion of illegal activity before contacting a suspect.

I

This Court has held previously that a defendant's predisposition is to be assessed as of the time the Government agent first suggested the crime, not when the Government agent first became involved. *Sherman v. United States,* (1958). Until the Government actually makes a suggestion of criminal conduct, it could not be said to have "implant[ed] in the mind of an innocent person the disposition to commit the alleged offense and induce its commission...." *Sorrells v. United States,* (1932). Even in *Sherman v. United States,* in which the Court held that the defendant had been entrapped as a matter of law, the Government agent had repeatedly and unsuccessfully coaxed the defendant to buy drugs, ultimately succeeding only by playing on the defendant's sympathy. The Court found lack of predisposition based on the Government's numerous unsuccessful attempts to induce the crime, not on the basis of preliminary contacts with the defendant.

Today, the Court holds that Government conduct may be considered to create a predisposition to commit a crime, even before any Government action to induce the commission of the crime. In my view, this holding changes entrapment doctrine. Generally, the inquiry is whether a suspect is predisposed before the Government induces the commission of the crime, not before the Government makes initial contact with him. There is no dispute here that the Government's questionnaires and letters were not sufficient to establish inducement; they did not even suggest that Mr. Jacobson should engage in any illegal activity. If all the Government had done was to send these materials, Mr. Jacobson's entrapment defense would fail. Yet the Court holds that the Government must prove not only that a suspect was predisposed to commit the crime before the opportunity to commit it arose, but also before the Government came on the scene.

The rule that preliminary Government contact can create a predisposition has the potential to be misread by lower courts as well as criminal investigators as requiring that the Government must have sufficient evidence of a defendant's predisposition *before it ever seeks to contact him.* Surely the Court cannot intend to impose such a requirement, for it would mean that the Government must have a reasonable suspicion of criminal activity before it begins an investigation, a condition that we have never before imposed. The Court denies that its new rule will affect run-of-the-mill sting operations, and one hopes that it means what it says. Nonetheless, after this case, every defendant will claim that something the Government agent did before soliciting the crime "created" a predisposition that was not there before. For example, a bribe taker will claim that the description of the amount of money available was so enticing that it implanted a disposition to accept the bribe later offered. A drug buyer will claim that the description of the drug's purity and effects was so tempting that it created the urge to try it for the first time. In short, the Court's opinion could be read to prohibit the Government from advertising the seductions of criminal activity as part of its sting operation, for fear of creating a predisposition in its suspects. That limitation would be especially likely to hamper sting operations such as this one, which mimic the advertising done by genuine purveyors of pornography. No doubt the Court would protest that its opinion does not stand for so broad a proposition, but the apparent lack of a principled basis for distinguishing these scenarios exposes a flaw in the more limited rule the Court today adopts.

The Court's rule is all the more troubling because it does not distinguish between Government conduct that merely highlights the temptation of the crime itself, and Government conduct that threatens, coerces, or leads a suspect to commit a crime in order to fulfill some other obligation. For example, in *Sorrells,* the Government agent repeatedly asked for illegal liquor, coaxing the defendant to accede on the ground that "one former war buddy would get liquor for another." In *Sherman,* the Government agent played on the defendant's sympathies, pretending to be going through drug withdrawal and begging the defendant to relieve his distress by helping him buy drugs.

The Government conduct in this case is not comparable. While the Court states that the Government "exerted substantial pressure on petitioner to obtain and read such material as part of a fight against censorship and the infringement of individual rights," one looks at the record in vain for evidence of such "substantial pressure." The most one finds is letters advocating legislative action to liberalize obscenity laws, letters which could easily be ignored or thrown away. Much later, the Government sent separate mailings of catalogs of illegal materials. Nowhere did the Government suggest that the proceeds of the sale of the illegal materials would be used to support legislative reforms. While one of the HINT letters suggested that lobbying efforts would be funded by sales from a catalog, Record, the catalogs actually sent, nearly a year later, were from different fictitious entities (Produit Outaouais and Far Eastern Trading Company), and gave no suggestion that money would be used for any political purposes. Nor did the Government claim to be organizing a civil disobedience movement, which would protest the pornography laws by breaking them. Contrary to the gloss given the evidence by the Court, the Government's suggestions of illegality may also have made buyers beware, and increased the mystique of the materials offered: "[f]or those of you who have enjoyed youthful material ... we have devised a method of getting these to you without prying eyes of U.S. Customs seizing your mail." Mr. Jacobson's curiosity to see what " 'all the trouble and the hysteria' " was about, is certainly susceptible of more than one interpretation. And it is the jury that is charged with the obligation of interpreting it. In sum, the Court fails to construe the evidence in the light most favorable to the Government, and fails to draw all reasonable inferences in the Government's favor. It was surely reasonable for the jury to infer that Mr. Jacobson was predisposed beyond a reasonable doubt, even if other inferences from the evidence were also possible.

II

The second puzzling thing about the Court's opinion is its redefinition of predisposition. The Court acknowledges that "[p]etitioner's responses to the many communications prior to the ultimate criminal act were ... indicative of certain personal inclinations, including a predisposition to view photographs of preteen sex...." If true, this should have settled the matter; Mr. Jacobson was predisposed to engage in the illegal conduct. Yet, the Court concludes, "petitioner's responses hardly support an inference that he would commit the crime of receiving child pornography through the mails."

The Court seems to add something new to the burden of proving predisposition. Not only must the Government show that a defendant was predisposed to engage in the illegal conduct, here, receiving photographs of minors engaged in sex, but also that the defendant was predisposed to break the law knowingly in order to do so. The statute violated here, however, does not "require proof of specific intent to break the law; it requires only knowing receipt of visual depictions produced by using minors engaged in sexually explicit conduct. See 18 U.S.C. § 2252(a)(2). Under the Court's analysis, however, the Government must prove *more* to show predisposition than it need prove in order to convict.

The Court ignores the judgment of Congress that specific intent is not an element of the crime of receiving sexually explicit photographs of minors. The elements of predisposition should track the elements of the crime. The predisposition requirement is meant to eliminate the entrapment defense for those defendants who would have committed the crime anyway, even absent Government inducement. Because a defendant might very well be convicted of the crime here absent Government inducement even though he did not know his conduct was illegal, a specific intent requirement does little to distinguish between those who would commit the crime without the inducement and those who would not. In sum, although the fact that Mr. Jacobson's purchases of *Bare Boys I* and *Bare Boys II* were legal at the time may have some relevance to the question of predisposition, it is not, as the Court suggests, dispositive.

It was, however, the jury's task, as the conscience of the community, to decide whether or not Mr. Jacobson was a willing participant in the criminal activity here or an innocent dupe. The jury is the traditional "defense against arbitrary law enforcement." *Duncan v. Louisiana,* (1968). There is no dispute that the jury in this case was fully and accurately instructed on the law of entrapment, and nonetheless found Mr. Jacobson guilty. Because I believe there was sufficient evidence to uphold the jury's verdict, I respectfully dissent.

NOTE

Courts have recognized that *Jacobson* has changed the entrapment defense. On the strength of *Jacobson,* a sharply divided en banc Court of Appeals reversed a money laundering conviction in United States v. Hollingsworth, 27 F.3d 1196,

1198 (7th Cir.1994) (en banc) (6–5). In *Hollingsworth,* an orthodontist and farmer in Arkansas were convicted of laundering money for what turned out to be a government agent. The venture began when the two defendants (Hollingsworth and Pickard) started an international banking business by buying two foreign banking licenses. Although they advertised, the two never found any customers. Finally they decided to sell one of the banking licenses and advertised it in U.S.A. Today. A U.S. customs agent saw the ad and decided to investigate the defendants' activities. During their first negotiations, the agent explained that his organization had a lot of cash and needed to deposit it somewhere. Defendant Pickard pointed out that the money could be deposited abroad, or divided into lots of $10,000 and deposited in the U.S. Pickard later retracted the suggestion of depositing the cash abroad, remarking that that would violate the law. (There was no evidence Pickard knew his other suggestion was also illegal). Pickard asked the agent to assure him that the cash was not from drug sales and that the agent was not a federal agent or informer. In another conversation, Pickard asked the agent whether he wanted them to "clean and polish" funds or for "extended services." Later, Pickard indicated he was interested only in a long-term banking relationship.

Nearly six months after the last unfruitful contact, at a time when the defendant's "business" was still customerless and on the verge of collapsing, the agent called Pickard again. He said he was "overwhelmed" and arranged to meet Pickard with $20,000 in sting money. The agent explained the money was from gun smuggling into South Africa. Pickard was to arrange a wire transfer of $20,000 to the agent's bank account, and then take possession of the cash for a fee of $2,405. Subsequent transactions of this sort, one carried out by Hollingsworth, brought the total transferred to $20,000. Finally, the defendants were arrested. When arrested, they were carrying false-name passports issued by the mythical "Dominion of Melchizedek." They had no other customers.

Judge Posner, writing for the majority, said that the circuits had been "drifting" toward the view that predisposition was shown by a "willingness" to commit the crime, but *Jacobson* now requires something more:

> Predisposition is not a purely mental state, the state of being willing to swallow the government's bait.... The defendant must be so situated by reason of previous training or experience or occupation or acquaintances that it is likely that if the government had not induced him to commit the crime some criminal would have done so; only then does a sting or other arranged crime take a dangerous person out of circulation. A public official is in a position to take bribes; a drug addict to deal drugs; a gun dealer to engage in illegal gun sales. For these and other traditional targets of stings all that must be shown to establish predisposition and thus defeat the defense of entrapment is willingness to violate the law without extraordinary inducements; ability can be presumed. It is different when the defendant is not in a position without the government's help to become involved in illegal activity. *Id.* at 1199.

Posner based his analysis on the language in *Jacobson* that entrapment doctrine protected against "the apprehension of an otherwise law-abiding citizen who, if left to his own devices, likely would have never run afoul of the law." The dissenters, Judges Coffey, Easterbrook, Ripple, Bauer, and Kanne, argued that Posner had read too much into the *Jacobson* opinion. Instead, they emphasized the defendants' lack of reluctance to engage in the money laundering, and pointed to Pickard's familiarity with money laundering terminology, his caution as to the agent's identity but lack of reservation about the illegality of the conduct, and the fact that Pickard often initiated contact with the agent. The entrapment doctrine should not protect the willing, though inept or disorganized criminal, regardless of his harmlessness, the dissent argued. Judge Ripple also disagreed with the majority's holding that Hollingsworth, who had not been directly contacted by the government agent but had heard of the scheme only through Pickard, could still take advantage of the entrapment doctrine.

While eager acceptance of criminal opportunity *may* still be sufficient to prove predisposition, *Jacobson* has encouraged circuit courts to reject that inference where significant and persistent government encouragement was required to induce the crime. See United States v. Sandoval, 20 F.3d 134 (5th Cir.1994) (predisposition not shown where agent asked the target ten times for a bribe before the target reluctantly acceded).

The First Circuit interpreted *Jacobson* to mean that the government may not, in trying to induce the target of a sting to commit a crime, confront her with circumstances that are different from the ordinary or typical circumstances of a private inducement. United States v. Gendron, 18 F.3d 955, 962 (1st Cir.1994).

B. DUE PROCESS—WAS THE POLICE CONDUCT "OUTRAGEOUS"?

1. DO CRIMINAL ACTS BY THE POLICE EXCUSE CRIMINAL ACTS BY OTHERS?

HAMPTON v. UNITED STATES

Supreme Court of the United States, 1976.
425 U.S. 484, 96 S.Ct. 1646.

MR. JUSTICE REHNQUIST announced the judgment of the Court in an opinion in which THE CHIEF JUSTICE and MR. JUSTICE WHITE join.

This case presents the question of whether a defendant may be convicted for the sale of contraband which he procured from a government informer or agent. The Court of Appeals for the Eighth Circuit held he could be, and we agree.

I

* * *

... The case arose from two sales of heroin by petitioner to agents of the Federal Drug Enforcement Administration (DEA) in St. Louis on February 25 and 26, 1974. The sales were arranged by one Hutton, who was a pool-playing acquaintance of petitioner at the Pud bar in St. Louis and also a DEA informant.

According to the Government's witnesses, in late February 1974, Hutton and petitioner were shooting pool at the Pud when petitioner, after observing "track" (needle) marks on Hutton's arms told Hutton that he needed money and knew where he could get some heroin. Hutton responded that he could find a buyer and petitioner suggested that he "get in touch with those people." Hutton then called DEA agent Terry Sawyer and arranged a sale for 10 p.m. on February 25.

At the appointed time, Hutton and petitioner went to a pre-arranged meeting place and were met by Agent Sawyer and DEA Agent McDowell, posing as narcotics dealers. Petitioner produced a tinfoil packet from his cap and turned it over to the agents who tested it, pronounced it "okay," and negotiated a price of $145 which was paid to petitioner. Before they parted, petitioner told Sawyer that he could obtain larger quantities of heroin and gave Sawyer a phone number where he could be reached.

The next day Sawyer called petitioner and arranged for another "buy" that afternoon. Petitioner got Hutton to go along and they met the agents again near where they had been the previous night.

They all entered the agents' car, and petitioner again produced a tinfoil packet from his cap. The agents again field-tested it and pronounced it satisfactory. Petitioner then asked for $500 which Agent Sawyer said he would get from the trunk. Sawyer got out and opened the trunk which was a signal to other agents to move in and arrest petitioner, which they did.

Petitioner's version of events was quite different. According to him, in response to petitioner's statement that he was short of cash, Hutton said that he had a friend who was a pharmacist who could produce a non-narcotic counterfeit drug which would give the same reaction as heroin. Hutton proposed selling this drug to gullible acquaintances who would be led to believe they were buying heroin. Petitioner testified that they successfully duped one buyer with this fake drug and that the sale which led to the arrest was solicited by petitioner in an effort to profit further from this ploy.

Petitioner contended that he neither intended to sell, nor knew that he was dealing in heroin and that all of the drugs he sold were supplied by Hutton. His account was at least partially disbelieved by the jury which was instructed that in order to convict petitioner they had to find that the Government proved "that the defendant knowingly did an act which the law forbids, purposely intending to violate the law." Thus the guilty verdict necessarily implies that the jury rejected petitioner's claim that he did not know the substance was heroin, and petitioner himself admitted both soliciting and carrying out sales. The only relevance of his version of the facts, then, lies in his having requested an instruction embodying that version. He did not request a standard entrapment instruction but he did request the following:

> "The defendant asserts that he was the victim of entrapment as to the crimes charged in the indictment.
>
> "If you find that the defendant's sales of narcotics were sales of narcotics supplied to him by an informer in the employ

of or acting on behalf of the government, then you must acquit the defendant because the law as a matter of policy forbids his conviction in such a case.

"Furthermore, under this particular defense, you need not consider the predisposition of the defendant to commit the offense charged, because if the governmental involvement through its informer reached the point that I have just defined in your own minds, then the predisposition of the defendant would not matter."

The trial court refused the instruction.

II

In *Russell* we held that the statutory defense of entrapment was not available where it was conceded that a government agent supplied a necessary ingredient in the manufacture of an illicit drug. We reaffirmed the principle of Sorrells v. United States, ... and Sherman v. United States ..., that the entrapment defense "focus[es] on the intent or predisposition of the defendant to commit the crime," ... rather than upon the conduct of the Government's agents. We ruled out the possibility that the defense of entrapment could ever be based upon governmental misconduct in a case, such as this one, where the predisposition of the defendant to commit the crime was established.

... In view of these holdings, petitioner correctly recognizes that his case does not qualify as one involving "entrapment" at all. He instead relies on the language in *Russell* that "we may some day be presented with a situation in which the conduct of law enforcement agents is so outrageous that due process principles would absolutely bar the government from invoking judicial processes to obtain a conviction.... ["]

In urging that this case involves a violation of his due process rights, petitioner misapprehends the meaning of the quoted language in *Russell*, supra. Admittedly petitioner's case is different from Russell's but the difference is one of degree, not of kind. In *Russell* the ingredient supplied by the Government agent was a legal drug which the defendants demonstrably could have obtained from other sources besides the Government. Here the drug which the government informant allegedly supplied to petitioner was both illegal and constituted the *corpus delicti* for the sale of which the petitioner was convicted. The Government obviously played a more significant role in enabling petitioner to sell contraband in this case than it did in *Russell*.

But in each case the Government agents were acting in concert with the defendant, and in each case either the jury found or the defendant conceded that he was predisposed to commit the crime for which he was convicted. The remedy of the criminal defendant with respect to the acts of Government agents, which, far from being resisted, are encouraged by him, lies solely in the defense of entrapment. But, as noted, petitioner's conceded predisposition rendered this defense unavailable to him.

* * *

The limitations of the Due Process Clause of the Fifth Amendment come into play only when the Government activity in question violates some protected right of the *defendant*. Here, as we have noted, the police, the Government informant, and the defendant acted in concert with one another. If the result of the governmental activity is to "implant in the mind of an innocent person the disposition to commit the alleged offense and induce its commission . . . ," . . . the defendant is protected by the defense of entrapment. If the police engage in illegal activity in concert with a defendant beyond the scope of their duties the remedy lies, not in freeing the equally culpable defendant, but in prosecuting the police under the applicable provisions of state or federal law. . . . But the police conduct here no more deprived defendant of any right secured to him by the United States Constitution than did the police conduct in *Russell* deprive Russell of any rights.

Affirmed.

MR. JUSTICE POWELL, with whom MR. JUSTICE BLACKMUN joins, concurring in the judgment.

I concur in the judgment of the Court and much of the plurality opinion directed specifically to Hampton's contention. I am not able to join the remainder of the plurality opinion, as it would unnecessarily reach and decide difficult questions not before us.

In discussing Hampton's due process contention, it enunciates a *per se* rule:

> "[In *Russell,*] [w]e ruled out the possibility that the defense of entrapment could *ever* be based upon governmental misconduct in a case, such as this one, where the predisposition of the defendant to commit the crime was established."
>
> * * *
>
> "The remedy of the criminal defendant with respect to the acts of Government agents, which . . . are encouraged by him, lies *solely* in the defense of entrapment."

The plurality thus says that the concept of fundamental fairness inherent in the guarantee of due process would never prevent the conviction of a predisposed defendant, regardless of the outrageousness of police behavior in light of the surrounding circumstances.

I do not understand *Russell* or earlier cases delineating the predisposition-focused defense of entrapment to have gone so far, and there was no need for them to do so. In those cases the Court was confronted with specific claims of police "overinvolvement" in criminal activity involving contraband. Disposition of those claims did not require the Court to consider whether overinvolvement of Government agents in contraband offenses could ever reach such proportions as to bar conviction of a predisposed defendant as a matter of due process. Nor have we had occasion yet to confront Government overinvolvement in areas outside the realm of contraband offenses. In these circumstances, I am unwilling to conclude that an analysis other than one limited to predisposition would never be appropriate under due process principles.

* * *

I am not unmindful of the doctrinal and practical difficulties of delineating limits to police involvement in crime that do not focus on predisposition, as Government participation ordinarily will be fully justified in society's "war with the criminal classes." This undoubtedly is the concern that prompts the plurality to embrace an absolute rule. But we left these questions open in *Russell*, and this case is controlled completely by *Russell*. I therefore am unwilling to join the plurality in concluding that, no matter what the circumstances, neither due process principles nor our supervisory power could support a bar to conviction in any case where the Government is able to prove predisposition.

* * *

MR. JUSTICE BRENNAN, with whom MR. JUSTICE STEWART and MR. JUSTICE MARSHALL concur, dissenting.

I think that reversal of petitioner's conviction is also compelled for those who follow the "subjective" approach to the defense of entrapment. I agree with Mr. Justice Powell that *Russell* does not foreclose imposition of a bar to conviction—based upon our supervisory power or due process principles—where the conduct of law enforcement authorities is sufficiently offensive, even though the individuals entitled to invoke such a defense might be "predisposed." ... In my view, the police activity in this case was beyond permissible limits.

Two facts significantly distinguish this case from *Russell*. First, the chemical supplied in that case was not contraband. In contrast, petitioner claims that the very narcotic he is accused of selling was supplied by an agent of the Government....

Second, the defendant in *Russell* "was an active participant in an illegal drug manufacturing enterprise which began before the Government agent appeared on the scene, and continued after the Government agent had left the scene." ... Russell was charged with unlawfully manufacturing and processing methamphetamine, ... and his crime was participation in an ongoing operation. In contrast, the two sales for which petitioner was convicted were allegedly instigated by Government agents and completed by the Government's purchase. The beginning and end of this crime thus coincided exactly with the Government's entry into and withdrawal from the criminal activity involved in this case, while the Government was not similarly involved in Russell's crime....

... Where the Government's agent deliberately sets up the accused by supplying him with contraband and then bringing him to another agent as a potential purchaser, the Government's role has passed the point of toleration.... The Government is doing nothing less than buying contraband from itself through an intermediary and jailing the intermediary.... There is little, if any, law enforcement interest promoted by such conduct; plainly it is not designed to discover ongoing drug traffic. Rather, such conduct deliberately entices an individual to commit a crime. That the accused is "predisposed" cannot possibly justify the action of government officials in purposefully creating the crime. No one would suggest that the police could round up and jail all "predisposed" individuals, yet that is precisely what set-ups like the instant one are intended to accomplish.... Thus, this case is nothing less than an instance of "the Government ... seeking to punish for an alleged offense which is the product of the creative activity of its own officials." ...

... For the reasons stated I would at a minimum hold that conviction is barred as a matter of law where the subject of the criminal charge is the sale of contraband provided to the defendant by a Government agent....

NOTES

1. In People v. Strong, 21 Ill.2d 320, 172 N.E.2d 765 (1961), the Illinois Supreme Court made the following ruling:

> While we are sympathetic to the problems of enforcement agencies in controlling the narcotics traffic, and their use of informers to that end, we cannot condone the action of one acting for the government in supplying the very narcotics that gave rise to the alleged offense.... This is more than mere inducement. In reality the government is supplying the *sine qua non* of the offense.

Cases like *Hampton* and *Strong* frequently involve maneuvers designed to require the prosecution to produce an informer at trial. Typically, after introduction to the defendant by an informer, an undercover agent makes a hand-to-hand purchase from the defendant in the absence of the informer. The prosecution thus hopes to try the case without producing the informer at trial; but the defendant testifies that the informer, out of the presence of the undercover agent, originally left the packet of narcotics with the defendant. If this is a good defense, then the prosecution will have to produce the informer at trial to rebut the allegation.

Even after *Russell* and *Hampton*, some jurisdictions, as a matter of state law, continue to apply a rule like that announced in *Strong:* a defendant cannot be convicted of a narcotics offense if the government informer originally supplied the substance in question to the defendant. See State v. Talbot, 71 N.J. 160, 364 A.2d 9 (1976); People v. Stanley, 68 Mich.App. 559, 243 N.W.2d 684 (1976). However, Illinois has reversed its position and rejected the rule that it had announced in *Strong*. See People v. Cross, 77 Ill.2d 396, 33 Ill.Dec. 285, 396 N.E.2d 812 (1979).

The DEA believed Santana was running (from prison) a large scale heroin network through Fuentes and others. Fuentes knew an undercover agent posing as a heroin supplier and asked the agent for a sample and the agent delivered 13 grams of 92% pure heroin (which equals 2,500 street sale doses). The DEA never recovered the sample and the defendants in the criminal cases asked for dismissal because the government acted outrageously in fronting so much heroin and then losing track of it so it presumably wound up in the hands of persons who were damaged by its use. Is the defense argument sound? The matter was well analyzed on both trial and appeal. United States v. Santana, 808 F.Supp. 77 (D.Mass.1992), reversed 6 F.3d 1 (1st Cir.1993).

2. A paid F.B.I. informant penetrated an interstate burglary ring and worked with them for over sixteen months while reporting daily to the F.B.I. During this period, he went with two ring members on forty burglaries and took part in the sale of stolen goods to fences. A claim that the police conduct was outrageous was rejected. In United States v. Brown, 635 F.2d 1207, 1212 (6th Cir.1980) the Court said:

> . . . [W]e begin our analysis with the basic proposition that the use of paid informants to infiltrate criminal enterprises is a "recognized and permissible means of investigation."
>
> This proposition remains true even though the informant or government agent engages in some criminal activity or supplies something of value to the criminal enterprise. The informant or government agent must be allowed to further the interests of the criminal enterprise in some manner to gain the confidence of the criminal elements with which he must deal.
>
> The type of criminal activity under investigation is also a relevant consideration regarding the scope of permissible government conduct. For example, the need to use paid informants to infiltrate criminal enterprises is regarded as especially necessary in the investigation of drug-related crimes. . . .
>
> Another pertinent inquiry is whether the government instigates the criminal activity in question, or whether it infiltrates a preexisting criminal enterprise. A related consideration is whether the government directs or controls the activities of the criminal enterprise or whether it merely acquiesces in its criminality. . . .
>
> We also note that the strength of the connection, or causal relationship, between the challenged government conduct and the commission of the acts for which the defendant stands convicted is an important consideration. We agree with the Tenth Circuit that "the more immediate the impact of the government's conduct upon a particular defendant, the more vigorously would be applied *Russell's* test for constitutional impropriety."
>
> On the facts presented by this record, the court finds no violation of due process. Although the individual burglars and fences might be detectable without infiltration, certainly the use of this investigative technique facilitated a more expeditious and thorough investigation. The burglary ring under investigation, like many drug rings, would have been extremely difficult to thwart without the use of Miller as an undercover agent.
>
> There is no showing of any kind that Miller, or any of the FBI agents involved in this case, instigated any criminal activity. The burglary ring was fully operative when Miller "joined" it. Even after

Miller joined the ring, it appears that his participation in its criminal endeavors was limited to following the members' instructions. Miller was instructed by the FBI to participate in criminal activity only if failure to do so would endanger his life. Nothing in the record suggests that he departed from these instructions....

We find that, in its use of Miller, the government in no way increased the number of burglaries, or the likelihood of their success. Miller reported to the FBI on a daily basis. He revealed the location of burglaries and sometimes provided an inventory of the things taken, thus facilitating the recovery of stolen items such as those that form the basis of Brown's conviction. Although it did not materialize, Miller's presence also provided the FBI with a possible source of advance notice of burglaries. Miller also could have prevented personal injury to surprised occupants if the need had arisen. The only effect Miller's presence had on the activities of the ring was that the FBI was informed of the illegal activity in which the ring was engaged. Nothing in the facts convinces us in the least that Miller's conduct was "shocking to the universal sense of justice." *Russell*, supra, 411 U.S. at 432, 93 S.Ct. at 1643.

Brown attempts to bootstrap Miller's involvement in the burglaries to the level of demonstrably outrageous conduct by dramatically emphasizing the danger of loss of property and the possibility of personal harm occasioned by the burglaries. Brown contends that after Miller accompanied Frazier and Campbell on the first burglary, they should have been arrested. If this course had been followed, argues Brown, "39 ... burglaries would have been prevented; 39 fewer homes would have been violated; 39 fewer families endangered." We find this argument unpersuasive.

Law enforcement officials are often presented with a formidable problem when they become aware of the criminal activity of individuals who are involved in a large criminal enterprise. The alternatives presented to those officials are exceedingly poor. They may arrest known criminals, thus ceasing their particular harmful effect on society; or they may allow them to continue in their violation of the law with the hope that further investigation will reveal a greater number of those involved in the criminal enterprise, the exposure and arrest of whom may effectively eliminate a much broader range and degree of criminal activity.

This is the dilemma confronted by the FBI agents in charge of the HAMFAT investigation. They were compelled to decide whether to arrest Frazier and Campbell when their criminality became known, or to delay those arrests with the prospect of casting a much larger net, and of eliminating a much broader range of criminality. This problem reasserted itself periodically as evidence accumulated sufficient to arrest and convict other members of the ring.

The difficulty of the problem was exacerbated by the fact that either alternative chosen would result in some harm to society, for the choice of either alternative results in the continuing criminality of some members of the ring. Once the burglary ring began its criminal operations, an event the government had nothing whatsoever to do with, a certain amount of harm to society was an inevitable result. Faced with this situation, the government was forced to choose an alternative that, in its judgment, would result in the least amount of harm. This type of decision is affected by a multitude of varied and subtle considerations, with which law enforcement personnel are only too familiar. Nothing in the record before us indicates that the FBI erred so dramatically in their decision in the instant case that the fundamental canons of due process were violated.

3. The Courts have generally refused to sustain claims for dismissal of charges based upon the fact that a police officer or agent engaged in acts prohibited by criminal law. The recent use by narcotics officers of "reverses" in which police sell narcotics and then arrest the buyers clearly raises the issue. Courts have approved reverses. See United States v. Savage, 701 F.2d 867 (11th Cir.1983). Such operations have been approved even when arrests were not made after every delivery of contraband. In United States v. Rogers, 701 F.2d 871 (11th Cir.1983) the Court observed:

> Appellants also point out that a DEA agent testified that some marijuana under the DEA's control may have left the DEA's warehouse in the form of samples given to brokers and prospective purchasers. Appellants argue it is intolerable that the government would allow marijuana out on the streets in violation of the law. It is apparent, however, that if the DEA's operation was to succeed, the agents had to conduct themselves as normal marijuana sellers so as not to arouse suspicion. Such conduct included distributing small samples of marijuana to potential buyers. This conduct is not even close to being outrageous and shocking. The appellants would have us believe that the government must forego confiscating huge amounts of illicit drug money and arresting numerous persons involved in illegal drug smuggling because on occasion it must provide a handful of marijuana as a sample to prospective buyers. We find this argument without logical support. Thus, we reject it.

4. At least two cases placed heavy reliance on evidence of predisposition or its absence in determining whether a defendant's due process rights were violated. See United States v. Tobias, 662 F.2d 381 (5th Cir.1981) ("Tobias was a predisposed active participant, motivated solely by a desire to make money"), and United States v. Batres-Santolino, 521 F.Supp. 744 (N.D.Cal.1981) ("As obvious novices it is inconceivable [defendants] could have entered the secretive world of international drug smuggling on their own. Established drug exporters would have spotted them instantly as amateurs and dismissed their efforts as ludicrous").

5. Compare People ex rel. Difanis v. Boston, 92 Ill.App.3d 962, 48 Ill.Dec. 302, 416 N.E.2d 333 (1981) (no due process violation where individuals working for the prosecutor engaged in sexual acts as part of an effort to prove the existence of a prostitution operation), and Anchorage v. Flanagan, 649 P.2d 957 (Alaska App.1982) (officer engaged in sexual contact with prostitute before effecting the arrest does not violate due process), with People v. Wisneski, 96 Mich.App. 299, 292 N.W.2d 196 (1980) (improper for government informer to use sex to get a physician illegally to dispense drugs).

In United States v. Simpson, 813 F.2d 1462 (9th Cir.1987), an undercover agent for the F.B.I., with the knowledge of federal agents, developed a sexual relationship with a target before she asked him to sell drugs to some friends. The friends turned out to be F.B.I. agents. The court held that these circumstances were not so outrageous as to have violated due process. The court said that it saw "no principled way to identify a fixed point along the continuum from casual physical contact to intense physical bonding beyond which the relationship becomes 'shocking' when entertained by an informant." It added that the police have been allowed to recruit family members as informers, citing a case where agents offered a five-year-old child five dollars to tell where mommy hid her heroin. The court also emphasized that the F.B.I. had not encouraged the sexual relationship, but rather had merely closed its eyes to the relationship after telling the informer not to continue with it. It concluded that the government sometimes can use methods that may not be judged moral if judged by "abstract" notions of decency, conceding that "many people in our society may find the deceptive use of sex in law enforcement to be morally offensive." See U.S. v. Yater, 756 F.2d 1058 (5th Cir.1985) (defendant ill with cancer; government informers allegedly promised him that his eighteen month old child would be cared for by an informer after defendant's death); United States v. Shoffner, 826 F.2d 619 (7th Cir.1987) (No overreach where informant slept with defendant, government paid for an abortion and informant turned in family members).

6. An excellent overview of entrapment theories is found in Park, The Entrapment Controversy, 60 Minn.L.Rev. 163 (1976).

2. DID THE POLICE OVERREACH?

UNITED STATES v. KELLY

United States Court of Appeals, District of Columbia Circuit, 1983.
707 F.2d 1460.

PER CURIAM:

Judge MacKinnon files an opinion in Parts I, II, III(A) and IV of which Chief Judge Robinson concurs. Judge Ginsburg files an opinion in which Chief Judge Robinson concurs. Thus Parts I, II, III(A) and IV of Judge MacKinnon's opinion together with Judge Ginsburg's opinion constitute the opinion of the court. The judgment appealed from is reversed, and the case is remanded to the District Court with instructions to reinstate the indictment and the verdict of the jury, and for further proceedings.

MACKINNON, CIRCUIT JUDGE.

* * *

Kelly and two other individuals, Eugene Ciuzio and Stanley Weisz, were charged with conspiracy to commit bribery and interstate travel to commit bribery. A jury found each defendant guilty on all counts. However, the district court granted Kelly's motion to dismiss the indictment, entering a judgment of acquittal in his favor, because it concluded that the FBI's actions in furtherance of Abscam were so outrageous that prosecution of Kelly was barred by principles of due process.

* * *

I. Facts

A. *The Abscam Investigation*

In the spring of 1978, the FBI's Long Island office began an undercover investigation with the initial goal of recovering stolen art and securities. The code name for this investigation was "Abscam," a name derived from Abdul Enterprises, the name of a fictitious FBI-created organization which ostensibly represented two Arabs of considerable wealth interested in "investing" in the United States. Convicted confidence man Melvin Weinberg was enlisted by the FBI to assist in the creation and operation of Abscam.[1] Weinberg played the role of financial advisor to Abdul Enterprises, while FBI agents "held" other positions in that organization. Beginning in January 1979, Anthony Amoroso, a special agent for the FBI, assumed the role of president of Abdul Enterprises.

Initially, the FBI made it known on the streets that Abdul Enterprises had money to invest and waited to be approached with proposals.[2] Abdul Enterprises turned away individuals offering legitimate transactions, but maintained contact with those suggesting illegal activity. In November 1978 Abdul Enterprises was approached by two businessmen, William Rosenberg and William Eden, concerning the possibility of financing certain equipment to be leased to the City of Camden, New Jersey. It appeared that the transaction would require payment of a bribe to Angelo Errichetti, then Mayor of Camden. Thereafter the focus of Abscam shifted to political corruption and organized crime.[3]

On July 26, 1979, Mayor Errichetti, who had since been introduced to the Abscam agents by Eden and Rosenberg, and Howard Criden, a Philadelphia lawyer and associate of Errichetti, met with Weinberg and Amoroso on a yacht in Florida to discuss financing for a proposed casino that a client of Criden wished to build. During the day Amoroso and Errichetti discussed the problems that might face the wealthy Arabs who controlled Abdul Enterprises should an Iranian-type revolution occur in their country and they sought to come to the United States as perma-

1. From 1968 until 1976, Weinberg had operated an illegitimate business known as London Investors. Weinberg, claiming to represent wealthy investors, promised to arrange loans in exchange for "loan origination fees" *paid in advance*. Of course, Weinberg never arranged the loans, but rather absconded with the fees.

Weinberg was arrested by the FBI in 1976 for his London Investors activities and, in 1977, pled guilty to mail and wire fraud charges brought in the United States District Court. In exchange for his cooperation in four organized crime cases, the FBI interceded on Weinberg's behalf before the district court. As a result, Weinberg was sentenced to three years probation and permitted to return to New York to assist the FBI. Thereafter, Weinberg assisted the FBI in Abscam, which was modeled after his successful London Investors scheme. Beginning in August 1978, Weinberg received $1000 per month—raised in 1979 to $3000 per month—for his Abscam work.

2. As Weinberg explained, "we had a big honey pot and all the flies came to it." Tr. at 1691.

3. In December 1979 Mayor Errichetti met with the representatives of Abdul Enterprises and boasted that "he could control" Atlantic City. He later indicated that a bribe of $300,000 to $400,000 would guarantee a gambling license. Errichetti ultimately *led Abscam* to a number of other corrupt public officials. In March 1979 Abscam uncovered corruption in the Immigration and Naturalization Service.

nent residents. Amoroso enlisted Errichetti's assistance in obtaining the "cooperation" of public officials and suggested that money would be no problem. Errichetti and Criden agreed and, on August 22, 1979, introduced the Abscam agents to Congressman Michael Myers, who accepted $50,000 in exchange for his promise to assist the wealthy Arabs. Thus was introduced the "asylum scenario"—whereby members of Congress were paid bribes to ensure that they would introduce private immigration legislation on behalf of the wealthy Arabs if and when necessary—which ultimately caught Kelly.

B. *Abscam's Introduction to Kelly*

On September 10, 1979, Weinberg met with Rosenberg and sought his aid in locating politicians willing to assist his Arab employers to become permanent residents of the United States. Weinberg outlined the assistance required, indicating that the Arabs would pay $25,000 to a member of the House of Representatives and $50,000 to a member of the Senate for their promise of future assistance. Weinberg suggested that Amoroso would "talk one and one and make the guy safe" at the time of the payoff. In October 1979 Rosenberg related the proposal to a business associate and accountant, Stanley Weisz. Rosenberg told Weisz that the Arabs needed immigration assistance and that Weisz would receive a fee for the proper introductions.

On November 20, 1979, Weisz, while on vacation in Boynton Beach, Florida, met with his longtime business associate, Eugene Ciuzio. During their conversation, Weisz related the Arabs' need for immigration assistance to Ciuzio. Ciuzio replied that he knew a congressman who might be willing to help the Arabs and indicated he would check with him and get back to Weisz. In fact, Ciuzio had never discussed immigration matters with Kelly, having first met Kelly on October 1, 1979, in an Orlando restaurant.

Ciuzio promptly arranged to meet with Kelly at the Tampa airport on November 23, 1979. At that meeting Ciuzio told Kelly that he had some Arab clients with immigration difficulties and asked Kelly if he could help them. Kelly indicated that his office handled such matters routinely and that he would be glad to assist the Arabs, particularly since Ciuzio indicated they might invest in his district. Ciuzio informed Kelly that he—Ciuzio—would receive a large fee if Kelly helped the Arabs; Kelly told Ciuzio that the fee would cause no difficulties. Ciuzio promptly called Weisz from the Tampa airport and indicated that Kelly would be happy to help the Arabs.

In mid-December 1979 Weisz informed Rosenberg of Ciuzio's friendship with a Florida congressman who was willing to help the Arabs. On December 16, 1979, Rosenberg called Weinberg and told him that he had a "candidate" who would assist with the Arabs' immigration problems. Rosenberg indicated that the individual was a congressman from Florida, that he wanted $250,000, and that payment would have to be on "an escrow basis." Weinberg suggested that the Congressman be paid $25,000 down, with the balance paid when legislation was required.

Rosenberg agreed to set up a meeting with the Congressman at Abdul Enterprises' Washington, D.C., townhouse on January 8, 1980. Rosenberg called Weisz and told him of Weinberg's positive response. Weisz gave Rosenberg Ciuzio's telephone number and agreed to call Ciuzio to ask him to contact Weinberg. On December 17, 1979, Rosenberg again called Weinberg and explained that Weinberg would be contacted by "a fellow by the name of Gino [Ciuzio] who will handle all the arrangements for you and who will give you the person."

On December 19, 1979, Amoroso and Weinberg met with Ciuzio in Hollywood, Florida, and explained the assistance that would be expected of the Congressman. *Ciuzio indicated that the individual was Congressman Richard Kelly and intimated that he and Kelly had had previous dealings of a similar nature.*[4] Ciuzio suggested that he told Kelly of the offer and claimed that Kelly left the arrangements to him. Ciuzio opposed direct payment to Kelly and suggested that the money instead be escrowed through Weisz. Amoroso assured him that a private meeting between Amoroso and Kelly would protect the Congressman, and that the wealthy Arabs would invest in Kelly's district to provide an explanation for Kelly's assistance. Weinberg made it clear that the meeting and payment of $25,000 was to assure the Arabs that Kelly

> got the money [and] when we're ready to move that he is gonna be with us.

Ciuzio agreed to "lay out the story" for Kelly.

On December 21, 1979, Ciuzio telephoned Weinberg and suggested a January 8, 1980, meeting with Kelly. Ciuzio reiterated that he and Weisz did not want to have the money handed directly to the Congressman. Weinberg insisted that Kelly be directly involved in the transaction, but indicated that

> [a]ll he [Amoroso] wants the Congressman [to do] is to tell him what he's gonna do for him for the money.

Ciuzio agreed, but requested that they use "the right script, nice and soft."

On December 23, 1979, Ciuzio met Kelly at a restaurant in Alexandria, Virginia, and explained the proposal. *Kelly testified* that Ciuzio told him that

> there were two Arabs that were going to come into the United States and there was concern that they would have an immigration problem, and that if they did, they wanted to be assured that they would have some assistance from a person with some authority and that in this connection, a representative of these Arabs was prepared to pay a half a million dollars for this assistance. And that the arrangements would be that the two

4. Referring to Kelly, Ciuzio asserted:

Not that I'll ever use it on em, of course, but I'm just saying uh umm. *He's in.* Ya know, we were holdin' hands for a long time, now he's pregnant, ya understand. *He's already takin' money* so we're married and thats all. (emphasis added).

> Arabs may not come into the country, but that their representatives wanted to have a meeting.
>
> They wanted to be sure that in the event they needed something, that they would have established a relationship, a contact that would cause this assistance to be available. And in this connection, that they would pay $25,000 just as earnest money.... *I would receive $25,000 just for going to the meeting*, and nothing would be expected of me, and then if at a later time there developed that there would be some need, then I would be expected to render this assistance and that *I would receive at that time an additional $100,000*, and the rest of the money was to be paid to [Ciuzio, Rosenberg, and Weisz]....

Ciuzio also told Kelly of the Arabs' intention of investing substantial sums in the districts of cooperative congressmen.

Kelly agreed to go to the meeting and give his assurances that he would help the Arabs, despite the fact that Ciuzio, Rosenberg, and Weisz would be paid as a result. However, Kelly testified that he refused to accept money for doing so:

> I would be glad to do it. But as far as my receiving any money for doing it, I just simply didn't want to do that. There wasn't any need to.
>
> There was no problem. It was a standard procedure and that I would not accept any money.... I said, ... I will do that. You can depend on me, I will go to the [h]ouse and we will give these assurances to the representatives....
>
> I am glad to do this as a favor to you. If you want to do something for me ... I have got some real estate that I want to sell and perhaps you can help me find a buyer for that.

C. *Abscam's Payoff to Kelly*

Shortly after 10:00 p.m. on January 8, 1980, Kelly, Ciuzio, Rosenberg, and Weisz arrived at Abdul Enterprises' Washington, D.C., townhouse to meet with Weinberg and Amoroso. Initially Weinberg met with Ciuzio, who vigorously sought to disuade Amoroso from attempting to bribe Kelly directly. The two ultimately agreed that Kelly would acknowledge that the money was in exchange for his agreement to assist the Arabs, but that Ciuzio would actually take the money from the meeting:

> WEINBERG: You can be in with him, all right?
>
> CIUZIO: Well I think I should be here to, ahh steer the f____ing thing ...
>
> WEINBERG: Let him, let, just put the money on the table and say here, take it ... here Congressman, here's the twenty-five thousand and that's it, you pick it up.
>
> CIUZIO: Go along with that, he knows the answers too.

WEINBERG: All right, so....

CIUZIO: I rehearsed with him.

After this conversation Kelly and Amoroso met privately. Amoroso explained the Arabs' immigration difficulties and their willingness to pay to have "friends" in Congress when required. He also indicated that the Arabs would invest in their "friends'" districts in order to protect them from pressure. Kelly's response revealed that he was aware of the purpose for the investments:

> AMOROSO: Now I realize that ahh there's a possibility that ahh if, if you were to introduce something like this, that ahh, people would ask, well why is he doing it, ya known, well what's the reason, now....
>
> KELLY: I've got the reason.
>
> AMOROSO: OK, what ... would that be ... investing?
>
> KELLY: Sure.

Kelly agreed to assist the Arabs, and, as recorded on the video tape, indicated that Amoroso's arrangement with Ciuzio was fine:

> All of this stuff that you've been talking about ... *I don't know anything about that, I'm not involved with it* ... Gino and these guys are my friend[s] ... what you said makes a lot of sense to me ... I'm gonna stick with ya ... *and you can put me out there on the hill, and when you come back in the morning, I'll still be there*.... So this ... will be helpful to me and ... maybe ... down the road sometime, you can do me a favor. *But in the meantime, whatever these guys are doing is all right, but I got no part in that*.... In other words, ... your arrangement with these people is ... all fine.... [Y]ou have my assurance that what you have told me here, sounds like a good thing and ... I will ... stick by these people.

After Amoroso received a call from Assistant United States Attorney Jacobs who was monitoring the meeting and who thought Kelly was being "cute," and after Kelly conferred with Ciuzio, Amoroso sought to clarify Kelly's position. Kelly made it clear that he wanted the money given to Ciuzio:

> KELLY: [Y]ou and I gotta ... learn to talk to each other.
>
> AMOROSO: Well I know ...
>
> KELLY: [D]on't stumble around, jump in there ...
>
> AMOROSO: Jump in there and give it to you?
>
> KELLY: Sure.
>
> AMOROSO: Ok. I was under the impression ... when this thing was set up ... that I was gonna give you something ... tonight....
>
> KELLY: Yeah.

AMOROSO: Ok, and that the rest was gonna come....

KELLY: Yeah.

AMOROSO: when you introduce that.

KELLY: That's right.

AMOROSO: Ok, is that, is that still....

KELLY: Yeah. Here's ... what the thing is. Umm ahh just simply deal with Gino [Ciuzio] about it.

AMOROSO: Ok. You want me to give him the money ... here?

KELLY: Sure.

However, when Amoroso indicated that all of the money was intended to go to Kelly, and that Ciuzio would be separately compensated, Kelly was confused:

> I understood that what you were talking about was ... all there was as far as Tony [sic, should be Ciuzio] was concerned and so as far as I'm concerned, he takes that.... [B]ut I see I didn't know ... about this other arrangement.... It's ... all right but I didn't know about that. So lets talk about it some.

Amoroso explained that he thought that giving the money directly to Kelly would avoid witnesses, thus protecting him. Kelly agreed:

AMOROSO: I thought that the best way of doing it was ... a one on one between you and I. Now to me that sounds like ... if you're looking for security ... the best way of doing it.

KELLY: I think so too.

Amoroso then gave Kelly $25,000 in cash and Kelly stuffed the money into the pockets of his suit.

II. The District Court Decision

In ruling on Kelly's motion to dismiss the indictment and to set aside the verdict of the jury, the district court acknowledged the need for undercover investigative techniques to detect "diabolical criminal conduct so sophisticated as to be nearly impossible to detect," but concluded that

> as Abscam affected Kelly, it was not the type of carefully devised and supervised covert operation generally accepted by the courts. In many respects it differed sharply from traditionally accepted types of operations.

The district court complained that the asylum scenario was not triggered by any suspicion of corruption in government and that, unlike ordinary, passive sting operations, it utilized legal and illegal bait promoted by a "recruiting agent" "to persuade the Congressman to become a sting patron." The district court concluded that the sole purpose of the asylum scenario was to test the virtue of members of Congress.

The district court admitted its personal distaste for the concept of law enforcement agencies testing the virtue of congressmen, but held, assuming that such activities were proper,

> the application of the testing procedures in this case patently exceeds the outer limits of any concept of fundamental fairness.
>
> The litmus test—or temptation—should be one which the individual is likely to encounter in the ordinary course. To offer any other type of temptation does not serve the function of preventing crime by apprehending those who, when faced with actual opportunity, would become criminals. Instead, it creates a whole new type of crime that would not exist but for the government's actions.
>
> When improper proposals are rejected in these virtue-testing ventures, the guinea pig should be left alone. *In ordinary real life situations, anyone who would seek to corrupt a Congressman would certainly not continue to press in the face of a rejection for fear of being reported and arrested.* The FBI of course had no such restraints in this case. (emphasis added).

The district court found that Kelly rejected the bribe offer at his meeting with Ciuzio on December 23, that Ciuzio informed the Abscam agents of that fact at the townhouse on January 8, and that Kelly initially rejected the bribe in his meeting with Amoroso.... Accordingly, the district court concluded

> that in the circumstances of this case, any further pursuit and pressure on the part of government agents was nothing short of outrageous.... If the government had no knowledge of Kelly doing anything wrong up to his rejection of illicit money, its continuing role as the third man in a fight between his conscience and temptation rises above the level of mere offensiveness to that of being "outrageous." *No concept of fundamental fairness can accommodate what happened to Kelly in this case.* (Emphasis added).

III. Analysis

A. *The Due Process Defense*

The district court concluded that the FBI's conduct in furtherance of Abscam was so outrageous that prosecution of Kelly was barred by principles of due process.

* * *

Our task in this case, therefore, is to assess whether the FBI's conduct in Abscam reached a "demonstrable level of outrageousness," while keeping in mind the difficulties inherent in detecting corrupt public officials. United States v. Russell. Measured against this standard, the FBI's conduct did not violate due process.

B. *Abscam*

Abscam was indeed an elaborate hoax, involving a fictitious, FBI-created corporation purportedly representing Arabs of enormous wealth, as well as the limousines, yachts, and lavishly appointed residences necessary to make the hoax believable. Yet stripped of these trappings of wealth, Abscam was no more than an "opportunity for the commission of crime by those willing to do so." United States v. Myers (2d Cir.1982). Amoroso and Weinberg let it be known that they would pay substantial sums of money to congressmen willing to promise to assist the wealthy Arabs with their immigration difficulties. Thereafter, the FBI operatives simply waited for the grapevine to work and to see who appeared to take bribes. No congressmen were targeted for investigation; rather, Abscam pursued all who were brought to the operation by the grapevine. In essence, then, Abscam was *not* significantly different from an undercover drug or fencing operation offering to buy from all who appear at its door.[5] Instead of buying stolen goods or contraband

5. The district court concluded that Abscam was unlike ordinary, "passive" undercover operations because it used "recruiting agents" to spread the word that bribes were available. I disagree. I seriously doubt that the government would establish an undercover drug or fencing operation without spreading the word, through informants and criminal elements (labeled "recruiting agents" by the district court), that its services were available. The Abscam investigators did no more.

My colleagues term Abscam an extraordinary operation. It was extraordinary only in the positions of some of the individuals involved and in the intangible nature of the "commodity" purchased. Otherwise, it is strikingly similar to ordinary undercover operations. To conclude otherwise suggests lack of familiarity with changes in the law enforcement activities of the FBI since the death of J. Edgar Hoover in 1972. Final Report of the Select Committee to Study Undercover Activities of Components of the Department of Justice, S.Rep. No. 682, 97th Cong., 2d Sess. 39 (1982). Hoover was an advocate of keeping FBI activities "of an open character not in any manner subject to criticism." He resisted efforts to get the FBI into drug enforcement because it would have required that FBI agents become involved in "unsavory" undercover operations, but was forced by presidential directive to allow undercover FBI activities in defense intelligence matters during World War II. Following Hoover's death his successor, Clarence M. Kelly, with the support of Congress, and pursuant to widespread public demand, began to move the FBI into "big cases" involving *white-collar* and organized crime.

Initially, the FBI, in cooperation with local law enforcement authorities, established undercover fencing operations, gaining valuable experience in undercover techniques "that avoided claims of entrapment." Thereafter, the FBI's undercover activities have expanded to include "investigations of white-collar crimes, political corruption, personal and property crimes, and racketeering crimes." The FBI now also has responsibility to investigate violations of the criminal drug laws of the United States. 28 C.F.R. § 0.85(a) (1982). Unfortunately, the government cannot select the nature of the crimes that will be committed and the detection of many of these "big" crimes require highly sophisticated undercover operations. Congressional appropriations for such undercover activity have increased substantially, from $1 million for 53 operations in 1977 to $4.5 million for 463 operations in 1981. Thus, although large FBI undercover operations might once have been characterized as extraordinary, such operations are now clearly part of the FBI's routine activities and their legality is not destroyed by their imaginative character.

My colleagues also criticize the failure of the FBI to closely supervise the Abscam operation. To the extent that this criticism extends to the non-FBI middlemen, such as Ciuzio, Rosenberg and Weisz, involved in Abscam, their activities could hardly be "supervised" because they did not know Abscam was an undercover investigation. The FBI took considerable precautions to compensate for its inability to control the representations of the middlemen.

Finally, my colleagues appear to criticize the amount of money and other benefits offered by Abscam to Kelly. In my view the

drugs, Abscam bought corrupt official influence in Congress. Such government involvement in crime does not violate principles of due process.

We need not determine the exact limits on government involvement in crime imposed by the due process clause for it is clear that the FBI's involvement in Abscam was less than that government involvement found unobjectionable by the Supreme Court.[6] ...

In each of these cases [Russell and Hampton] the government not only provided an *opportunity* to commit a crime, but also provided the *means* to commit that crime. Nevertheless, in each case the Supreme Court concluded that the government's conduct did not violate due process. Where, as in Abscam, the government simply provides the opportunity to commit a crime, prosecution of a defendant does not violate principles of due process. This conclusion is in accord with decisions of the Second and Third Circuits upholding Abscam convictions challenged on due process grounds. United States v. Williams, 705 F.2d 603 (2d Cir.1983); United States v. Myers, 692 F.2d 823 (2d Cir.1982); United States v. Alexandro, 675 F.2d 34 (2d Cir.); United States v. Jannotti, 673 F.2d 578 (3d Cir.) (en banc).

C. *Specific Claims*

1. *Reasonable Suspicion*

Nor do any of the specifically challenged FBI actions in furtherance of Abscam reach that "demonstrable level of outrageousness" which would bar Kelly's prosecution. The district court stressed that Abscam's asylum scenario was not triggered by any suspicion of corruption in government. Yet prior to setting the asylum scenario in motion, Abscam had uncovered evidence of official corruption in New Jersey and in the Immigration and Naturalization Service. Prior to enlisting Rosenberg's

sums offered were not unreasonable or "outrageous," particularly if it is remembered that Abscam was dealing with corruption of high government officials and historically in such cases substantial payments are made. Examples are legion: United States v. Jannotti, (3d Cir.) (en banc), (1982) (bribery of member of Philadelphia City Council; payments in range of $10,000 to $30,000 not excessive); United States v. Manton, 107 F.2d 834, 840–44 (2d Cir. 1938), (bribery of circuit judge of United States Court of Appeals for the Second Circuit; payment in Depression dollars totaling over $188,000; payments ranged from $11,500 to $60,000); Fall v. United States, 49 F.2d 506, 512 (D.C.Cir.), (Tea Pot Dome scandal; bribery of cabinet officer; payments of large amounts of government bonds and "loan" of $100,000, worth at least $1 million today); United States v. Williams, No. 81 CR 269 (N.D.Ill. May 1981) (conspiracy to bribe United States Senator from Nevada; offered Las Vegas property valued at approximately $1.6 million at $200,000 discount; see N.Y. Times, Oct. 22, 1982, at A18, col. 1). Many other cases could be cited but no more are necessary to establish that the sums offered Kelly were not "in excess of real-world opportunities" even though that is not the test. Had they been Kelly would have become suspicious and would have shied away. That the bait was taken here is the best evidence that it was within the "real world" of the Congressman, i.e., that his "price" was estimated correctly.

6. For this reason, we need not decide the validity of the due process test formulated by the district court—whether the temptation offered is "one which the individual is likely to encounter in the ordinary course." It is suggested, however, that criminal conduct being as highly varied as it is that such test is unduly speculative.

aid in the asylum scenario, the Abscam operatives had seen at least one congressman accept a bribe for immigration assistance. Finally, prior to the January 8 meeting with Kelly, the Abscam operatives had evidence from which they could conclude that Kelly was, in fact, corrupt. Ciuzio stated as much in his meeting with Amoroso and Weinberg on December 19. Furthermore, *Ciuzio told Weinberg on December 20 that he asked Kelly to call him from a "safe" phone booth to discuss the transaction; that Kelly did so was strong evidence for the Abscam operatives that Kelly was fully aware that he was participating in an illicit transaction.*[7] Thus, the FBI had ample suspicion of corruption to justify pursuing the asylum scenario and Kelly, if such suspicion was necessary.[8] In asserting the contrary, my colleagues, without explanation, fail to give a common sense interpretation to the uncontradicted evidence in the record. Members of the federal judiciary have no power to veto law enforcement practices merely because such practices offend their personal tastes.

2. *Utilization of Weinberg*

It is submitted that Kelly's argument that the FBI violated due process by utilizing the services of an admitted confidence man, Melvin Weinberg, in Abscam should likewise be rejected. Successful creation of an "elaborate hoax" such as Abscam may well *require* employment of "experts" such as Weinberg to give the operation an aura of "credibility" and "contacts" with criminal elements. The employment of a convicted confidence man in Abscam is analogous to the entirely proper employment of a convicted seller of drugs to purchase drugs from a suspected distributor. As the Second Circuit stated:

> [U]se of dishonest and deceitful informants like Weinberg creates risks to which the attention of juries must be forcefully called, but the Due Process Clause does not forbid their employment, detail their supervision, nor specify their compensation.

United States v. Myers. In this case, Weinberg's checkered background and dubious credibility were brought before the jury through vigorous cross-examination. The jury was entitled to consider Weinberg's testimony and give it such weight as it found appropriate. In my view there was no error of constitutional dimension in the FBI's use of Weinberg's services in Abscam.

3. *Failure to Memorialize Conversations*

Similarly, Kelly's claim that the FBI violated due process by failing to record or memorialize every conversation between Weinberg and Kelly's codefendants is without merit. At trial, only *Weisz* seriously challenged Weinberg's version of an unrecorded conversation—a five

7. *Kelly admitted* calling Ciuzio from a public phone booth at Ciuzio's request.

8. Although we need not decide the question, both the Second and Third Circuits have rejected the argument that the government must have reasonable suspicion of wrongdoing before proceeding with an undercover operation such as Abscam. United States v. Jannotti; United States v. Myers.

minute telephone conversation with Weisz on December 21, 1979. Kelly had the benefit of Weisz' "exculpatory" version of this conversation at trial and has failed to explain how any of the other unrecorded conversations would have added anything of significance to his defense. The FBI operatives successfully recorded the vast majority of their communications with Kelly and his codefendants, including all but one of their critical conversations. The FBI's occasional failure to record Abscam conversations does not constitute a due process violation.

4. *Multiple Bribe Offers*

Finally, Kelly contends that the FBI operatives violated due process when they persisted in offering a bribe after what he characterizes as his initial rejection. Kelly asserts that he rejected the bribe at his meeting with Ciuzio on December 23, that Ciuzio informed Amoroso and Weinberg of that fact at the townhouse on January 8, and that he rejected the bribe several times in his meeting with Amoroso. Kelly argues, and the district court agreed, that under these circumstances Amoroso's several bribe offers to Kelly were outrageous and violated due process. I cannot agree.

The evidence in this case clearly demonstrates that at no time did Kelly reject Abscam's corrupt immigration proposal. On both December 23 and January 8, Kelly agreed to assure the wealthy Arabs that he would help them with their immigration problems as a favor to Ciuzio, despite the fact that Kelly knew that in return the Arabs would pay substantial sums to Ciuzio, Rosenberg, and Weisz. It is also clear that Kelly understood that part of the arrangement was that the Arabs would make substantial investments in his district. Such agreements, which would benefit Kelly indirectly, constitute violations of the bribery statute. Furthermore, the discussions between Ciuzio, Kelly, and the Abscam operatives at the townhouse of January 8 focused on the *manner* in which the bribe would be paid, not on whether it would be paid. Ciuzio told Weinberg not to bribe Kelly directly, but agreed that he would take the money for Kelly. After agreeing that Amoroso was going to give him some money at the meeting, Kelly asked Amoroso to pay the bribe to Ciuzio—to "deal with [Ciuzio] about it." In my view, Congressman Kelly "did not reject a bribe, he [initially] rejected its payment under circumstances he feared would be incriminating." United States v. Myers.[9]

I likewise reject Kelly's characterization of his conversation with Amoroso on January 8 as a *series* of bribe offers. Although the terms of

9. In *Myers*, the Second Circuit considered the appeal of Congressman Frank Thompson, who first met Amoroso and Weinberg on the morning of October 9, 1979. At that meeting Thompson rejected Amoroso's offer of money and left. After further discussions with an intermediary, Howard Criden, Thompson again met with Amoroso, agreed to assist the wealthy Arabs, and asked Criden to "look after" the $50,000 offered by Amoroso. Criden carried the money from the meeting. On these facts, which in many respects are more favorable to a due process defense than those in Kelly's case, the Second Circuit rejected Thompson's claim that the FBI violated due process by offering a bribe after his initial rejection of the bribe at the first meeting.

the corrupt Abscam proposal were mentioned several times during that conversation, Amoroso's discussion reflects the evasive and circumspect negotiation to be expected of a person seeking to corrupt a public official. In my view, Amoroso's conversation with Kelly on January 8 can be fairly characterized only as a *single offer* of a corrupt proposal to Kelly. For these reasons I reject Kelly's contention that he initially rejected a bribe, that the Abscam agents persisted in offering him a bribe, and that they thus violated due process.

IV. CONCLUSION

Like the district court,

> we like to think, and we hope, that our Congressmen and Senators, and indeed all public servants, are strong enough to withstand any imaginable pressure and reject any type of temptation no matter how attractive, and walk away.... But in reality, *the hard fact is that our public servants* are not recruited from the seminaries and monasteries across the land and that they *are plagued by the frailties of human nature.*

(Emphasis added). Because of this fact and because dishonest public officials, responsive more to money than to their obligations to the nation, may cause grave harm to our society, we recognize the need for law enforcement efforts to detect official corruption. Furthermore, such corruption is "that type of elusive, difficult to detect, covert crime which may justify Government infiltration and undercover activities." United States v. Alexandro.

The Supreme Court has made it clear that "a successful due process defense must be predicated on *intolerable government conduct* which goes beyond that necessary to sustain an entrapment defense." United States v. Jannotti, (emphasis added). Considering the genuine need to detect corrupt public officials, as well as the difficulties inherent in doing so, we conclude that the FBI's conduct in furtherance of its Abscam operation, insofar as it involved Kelly, simply did not reach intolerable levels. Accordingly, having carefully considered all of Kelly's claims that the government's conduct violated due process, we reverse the district court's dismissal of the indictment, as well as its entry of the judgment of acquittal, and direct the district court to reinstate the indictment and the verdict of the jury.

Judgment accordingly.

GINSBURG, CIRCUIT JUDGE:

"Abscam," as the District Court's thoughtful opinion details, was an extraordinary operation. The investigation was steered in large part by a convicted swindler; it relied upon con men to identify and attract targets, to whom legitimate as well as illegitimate inducements were offered; it proceeded without close supervision by responsible officials.[1]

1. We do not share Judge MacKinnon's view that, apart from "trappings of wealth," Abscam "was *not* significantly different from" run-of-the-mine "passive" un-

The District Court allowed the jury to determine whether defendant Kelly was "predisposed" to commit the crime charged, and therefore not "entrapped" under the current definition of that defense. After the jury returned a guilty verdict, however, the District Court dismissed the indictment against Kelly on the ground that the government's conduct of the investigation was fundamentally unfair, and therefore incompatible with due process. The sole issue properly before us for review is the correctness of the due process ruling.

The District Court stated and attempted to apply an objective test to determine when government investigation exceeds tolerable limits: Was the crime-inducing conduct in which the government engaged, the temptation presented to the target, modeled on reality? This test, the District Court indicated, should apply when the government had no knowledge of prior wrongdoing by the target and no reason to believe the target was about to commit a crime; it would serve as a check against government creation (rather than apprehension) of criminals by offers or importuning that would never occur in the real world.

The real-world test, as applied by the District Court, is speculative. The District Judge assumed that a person who offers a bribe would retreat upon encountering an initial rejection and would not "have the audacity" to press on "for fear of being reported."[2] But the first overture renders the party offering the bribe vulnerable to prosecution. "In for a calf," such a person might press on if he perceives any chance of ultimate success.[3] Nonetheless, were the slate clean, we might be attracted to an approach similar to the District Court's, and would perhaps ask whether, in real-world circumstances, the person snared would ever encounter bait as alluring as the offer the government tendered.[4]

dercover operations. See Judge MacKinnon's opinion. As the District Court's opinion sets out in painstaking detail, the Abscam actors did a good deal more than simply "spread the word." Nor can we agree with Judge MacKinnon that the FBI "had ample suspicion of corruption to justify pursuing ... Kelly." That suspicion, as Judge MacKinnon recites, was based on Ciuzio's report to Amoroso and Weinberg that "Kelly was, in fact, corrupt." But as the District Court observed:

> Ciuzio went to great lengths to make it appear that he had virtual control over the Congressman, indicating at the time that Kelly was dishonest and was already taking money and had various other weaknesses. He indicated that he had known and cultivated Kelly for about 2½ years. None of this was true. No attempt was made to verify it; and there is no indication that Weinberg and Amoroso believed it.

2. As the District Judge finally phrased his application of the real-world test: "If after an illegal offer is made, the subject rejects it in any fashion, the government cannot press on."

3. As the government points out, Brief for Appellant at 68, parties to real-world transactions could readily adjust to a one-refusal rule: the bribe taker would always resist the first overture.

4. The inquiry might extend to the nature of the reward and quid pro quo authorized by responsible officials of the Department of Justice and the FBI, the efforts made to assure that those who carried out the scam adhered to the approved script, and the nature of the transaction in fact proposed to the target. The tolerable limit would be crossed if the opportunity offered differed qualitatively from, and therefore was more difficult to resist than, those the target would otherwise encounter.

Exchanges such as this one between an FBI agent and Ciuzio, the unwitting middle-man who conveyed the FBI's offer to Kelly, would invite particular scrutiny:

However, our slate contains references that lower courts are not positioned to erase. We may not alter the contours of the entrapment defense under a due process cloak, and we lack authority, where no *specific* constitutional right of the defendant has been violated, to dismiss indictments as an exercise of supervisory power over the conduct of federal law enforcement agents. Precedent dictates that we refrain from applying the general due process constraint to bar a conviction except in the rare instance of "[p]olice overinvolvement in crime" that reaches "a demonstrable level of outrageousness." Hampton v. United States, (Powell, J., concurring) (cases, "if any," in which a "predisposed" defendant can successfully invoke a due process defense "will be rare").

The requisite level of outrageousness, the Supreme Court has indicated, is not established merely upon a showing of obnoxious behavior or even flagrant misconduct on the part of the police; the broad "fundamental fairness" guarantee, it appears from High Court decisions, is not transgressed absent "coercion, violence or brutality to the person." See Irvine v. California, (1952).

The importuning of Congressman Kelly and the offers made to him, extraordinary and in excess of real-world opportunities as they appear to have been, did not involve the infliction of pain or physical or psychological coercion. We are therefore constrained to reverse, although we share the District Court's grave concern that the Abscam drama, both in its general tenor, and in "the [particular] manner in which Kelly was handled," unfolded as "an unwholesome spectacle."

NOTE

1. A general history of the "Abscam" cases is found in "Gershman, Abscam, The Judiciary and the Ethics of Entrapment," 91 Yale L.J. 1565 (1982). Also see United States v. Williams, 705 F.2d 603 (2d Cir.1983) where the conviction of Senator Harrison Williams was upheld even though the inducement might have had a value of millions of dollars of business profit.

2. Consider the decision in People v. Isaacson, 44 N.Y.2d 511, 406 N.Y.S.2d 714, 378 N.E.2d 78 (1978). In *Isaacson* police in New York arrested J.D.B., a man with a history of inveterate drug use and sales. While under arrest for sale of drugs he was physically beaten by the police and threatened with further harm. He was eventually released on bail. In the interim the police learned the drugs he sold them most recently were not amphetamines but caffeine pills. Upon the advice of his attorney—but still believing he still faced punishment for amphetamine sale—he agreed to act as an informer. Later J.D.B. stated he received no promises other than an improved bargaining position and that the physical violence and threats did not influence his decision to cooperate. However, he would not have aided the police if they had not deceived him about the gravity of the charges he faced. J.D.B. began his work as an informant by

[Ciuzio] Now, you you're saying ya gonna give em twenty-five thousand

[FBI Agent] Right

[Ciuzio] For doin nothin

[FBI Agent] For doin nothin

[Ciuzio] To stand by

[FBI Agent] To stand by. And if the guy comes, when the guy comes....

* * *

calling people he knew for the purpose of setting up drug sales. He reached Isaacson whom he had known for two years at State College, Pa.

Isaacson was a graduate student and teacher at Penn State, soon to receive a doctoral degree in botany. He admitted a small amount of drug use but had no criminal record. J.D.B. told Isaacson that he was facing 15 years to life, was abandoned by his parents, had been beaten by the police and needed to make a "score" or "deal" to pay a lawyer. Isaacson said, and J.D.B. denied, that J.D.B. was crying and sobbing during this talk.

Over a two week period J.D.B. made seven calls to Isaacson before arranging a sale. J.D.B. first sought heroin but Isaacson refused. As to cocaine, Isaacson first sought to put J.D.B. off by saying there was nothing worthwhile.

At the time of J.D.B.'s calls, Isaacson was living in State College with a woman who was a daily user of drugs. She said Isaacson had made two one gram sales of cocaine to J.D.B. two months before J.D.B. became an informant. Isaacson worked 12 to 14 hours a day and had no access to someone who could provide the two ounces of cocaine J.D.B. wanted, but his girl friend did and the transaction was arranged. The deal was worth $1,000 to Isaacson and his girl, but Isaacson's principal motive was to help J.D.B.

Isaacson and J.D.B. then scheduled a meeting. J.D.B. conferred with the New York police about the sale. He was advised to ask for two ounces to be sure of getting one—a statutory predicate for a higher sentence. He was told the sale must occur in New York despite the fact that Isaacson feared New York drug laws and did not want to enter the state. Isaacson chose an elaborate method of delivery of the cocaine in order, he said, to avoid a rip off. The method was suggested by the supplier his girl friend found. J.D.B. used a ruse to get Isaacson to New York—gradually negotiating to get their meeting to Lawrenceville, Pa. just south of the state boundary. Then J.D.B. designated a tavern which he said was in Lawrenceville but was, in fact, in Lindley, N.Y. Isaacson was fooled because the state line marker was damaged and hidden by vegetation. A large "Welcome to New York" sign was placed on a bridge several hundred yards past the tavern. The sale from Isaacson to J.D.B. occurred at the tavern. Isaacson was arrested and eventually sentenced to fifteen years to life.

The majority found that entrapment did not occur, as a matter of law, because Isaacson was predisposed to commit the offense. There was a due process violation arising from the police conduct at least under the due process clause of the state constitution. First, Isaacson's prior small, casual sales and lack of access to a large supplier show the more serious offense here would not have occurred without persistent instigation. Second, the abuse and deception of J.D.B., despite the fact it was directed against someone other than defendant, shows police misconduct. Third, J.D.B.'s persistence, appeals to sympathy in the face of Isaacson's refusal, goes too far. Fourth, the geographical shell game and the insistence on a specified amount display a police goal—not of cutting off a source of narcotics—but simply creating a statistic, one more conviction. "In sum this case exposes the ugliness of police brutality, upon which was imposed a cunning subterfuge employed to enlist the services of an informant who, deceived into thinking he was facing a stiff prison sentence desperately sought out any individual he could to satisfy the police thirst for conviction, even of a resident of another State possessed of no intention to enter our confines. Separately considered, the items of conduct may not rise to a level justifying dismissal but viewed in totality they reveal a brazen and continuing pattern in disregard of fundamental rights."

The dissenters argued the record showed Isaacson did deal extensively in cocaine and other drugs and used scales in his college laboratory to assist him in these sales. The police abuse of J.D.B. was not a violation of *defendant's* rights. The luring of Isaacson to New York was not misconduct especially since Isaacson knew J.D.B. intended to resell the cocaine in New York. The delay and reluctance of Isaacson was not due to his innocence but to a disruption in his line of supply and his unwillingness to go to New York.

Isaacson represents a fairly unique application of due process theory to police conduct in arranging the commission of crime.

Courts have found few occasions to rely upon the *Isaacson* decision. One court has rejected due process claim based upon threatened legal consequences to an informer which caused him to turn against the accused. People v. Harris, 165 Cal.App.3d 324, 211 Cal.Rptr. 493 (1985). Another court relied on *Isaacson* to overturn convictions based on the conduct and testimony of an informer whose fee payments were contingent upon positive results. State v. Glosson, 462 So.2d 1082 (Fla.1985). The holding in *Glosson* is not widely accepted. United States v. Grimes, 438 F.2d 391 (6th Cir.1971); People v. Mills, 40 Ill.2d 4, 237 N.E.2d 697 (1968).

Defense lawyers frequently cite United States v. Archer, 486 F.2d 670 (2d Cir.1973), for the proposition that government agents, working undercover, cannot be allowed to manufacture federal jurisdiction. There it was because of the stratagems of the agents that the illegal activities of the defendants took upon an interstate character. The court held that no federal crime occurred. Noting that *Archer* has rarely if ever been applied as precedent to reverse a conviction, the Seventh Circuit in a thoughtful opinion in United States v. Podolsky, 798 F.2d 177 (7th Cir.1986), observed:

> What the government actually did in *Archer* was like the purchase of illegal drugs by an undercover agent of the Drug Enforcement Administration—also a sham transaction designed to induce a crime to be committed at a time and in a place convenient to the government.

The desire of officers to select the place of a transaction can arise for a variety of reasons. Suppose that a sale of a small quantity of cocaine is ordinarily a Class 3, probationable felony. Suppose that, from a concern for school children, the legislature makes the sale of such a substance a Class 1 felony, with a mandatory minimum sentence of ten years, if done within one thousand feet of a school. Compare Title 21, § 845(a), of the United States Code, and see United States v. Lewin, 900 F.2d 145 (8th Cir.1990) (defendant's knowledge that school is within 1,000 feet not an element of the offense). Suppose further that, in arranging a controlled purchase of cocaine, the undercover officer arranges to meet the target at a place he knows to be 950 feet from a school, although the target's prior suspected dealings have had no nexus to schools. Some defense attorneys claim that such alleged "misuse" of the enhanced penalty statutes are the rule rather than the exception. Nevertheless, an entrapment defense is not likely to succeed under these circumstances. See generally State v. Burch, 545 So.2d 279 (Fla.App.1989).

Other courts have rejected "outrageous conduct" challenges to governmental tactics designed to obtain a favorable venue. See United States v. Padilla, 869 F.2d 372 (8th Cir.1989), involving efforts to create venue in the Eastern District of Missouri rather than in the more "indulgent" Southern District of Florida. There an unsympathetic court ruled, "If it was convenient for Chappas to agree to come to St. Louis to deliver cocaine, it is convenient for him to stand trial in St. Louis on federal cocaine charges."

In United States v. Ford, 918 F.2d 1343 (8th Cir.1990), the court rejected an "outrageous conduct" claim where the police allegedly supplied a targeted seller with small amounts of drugs for his own use. The court said that it was reluctant to establish a flat rule that the police cannot do X. They feared that would-be wrongdoers would test to see whether their business associates were really police agents by insisting that they do X before the targets would commit themselves to criminal activity.

For one decision concerning the limits on the use of informers, see United States v. Gonzales, 927 F.2d 139 (3d Cir.1991) (no Due Process violation where the compensation of the informer depended upon the amount of money that the target would forfeit when caught in the criminal activity of buying drugs).

3. Consider United States v. Twigg, 588 F.2d 373 (3d Cir.1978), another case reversing a conviction on due process grounds:

ROSENN, CIRCUIT JUDGE

* * *

At the behest of the Drug Enforcement Agency, Kubica, a convicted felon striving to reduce the severity of his sentence, communicated with Neville and suggested the establishment of a speed laboratory. The Government gratuitously supplied about 20 percent of the glassware and the indispensable ingredient, phenyl-2-propanone. It is unclear whether the parties had the means or the money to obtain the chemical on their own. The DEA made arrangements with chemical supply houses to facilitate the purchase of the rest of the materials. Kubica, operating under the business name "Chem Kleen" supplied by the DEA, actually purchased all of the supplies with the exception of a separatory funnel. (The funnel was secured by Twigg at the direction of Kubica who was engaged in operating the laboratory.) When problems were encountered in locating an adequate production site, the Government found the solution by providing an isolated farmhouse well-suited for the location of an illegally operated laboratory. Again, there was no cost to the defendants. At all times during the production process, Kubica was completely in charge and furnished all of the laboratory expertise. Neither defendant had the know-how with which to actually manufacture methamphetamine. The assistance they provided was minimal and then at the specific direction of Kubica.

These instances of police involvement must be evaluated against the following backdrop. The only evidence that Neville was predisposed to commit the crime was his receptivity to Kubica's proposal to engage in the venture and the testimony of Kubica that he had worked with Neville in a similar laboratory four years earlier. Unlike other cases rejecting this defense, the police investigation here was not concerned with an existing laboratory, the illicit plan did not originate with the criminal defendants, and neither of the defendants were chemists—an indispensable requisite to this criminal enterprise.[1]

* * *

1. We also find it baffling that the Government would urge the reduction of the jail sentence for a man who may have run as many as 50 or 100 speed laboratories in the past in exchange for the convictions of two men with no apparent criminal designs and without the expertise required to set up a single laboratory.

When Kubica, at the instance of the DEA, reestablished contact with Neville, the latter was not engaged in any illicit drug activity. Using Kubica, and actively participating with him, the DEA agents deceptively implanted the criminal design in Neville's mind. They set him up, encouraged him, provided the essential supplies and technical expertise, and when he and Kubica encountered difficulties in consummating the crime, they assisted in finding solutions. This egregious conduct on the part of government agents generated new crimes by the defendant merely for the sake of pressing criminal charges against him when, as far as the record reveals, he was lawfully and peacefully minding his own affairs. Fundamental fairness does not permit us to countenance such actions by law enforcement officials and prosecution for a crime so fomented by them will be barred.

* * *

Twigg did not become involved in this criminal enterprise until March 1, 1977—the day the laboratory went into operation. His reason for becoming involved was to repay a debt owed to Neville. Neville introduced Twigg to Kubica, and then Twigg and Kubica went shopping for additional supplies, which Kubica purchased. There is no evidence to suggest that Twigg was aware of the ultimate purpose of these errands until informed by Kubica after returning to the farmhouse. All actions taken by Twigg from that time until his arrest were at the specific direction of Kubica, the government agent. Twigg contributed nothing in terms of expertise, money, supplies, or ideas. It also appears that Twigg would not even have shared in the proceeds from the sale of the drug. In light of these facts, we hold that Twigg's conviction is also tainted by the conduct of the DEA agents and that fundamental fairness requires its reversal.

ADAMS, CIRCUIT JUDGE, dissenting.

Under these circumstances, I am unable to join the Court in relying on the government's "instigation" of this conspiracy as support for the conclusion that the government involvement here was "outrageous." [2]

It is true, of course, that the government did more here than "suggest" the operation. Through Kubica it provided chemicals, some laboratory equipment, money, and chemical expertise. But it must be remembered that Kubica was recreating the partnership he had had with Neville a few years earlier. He would inevitably be expected to perform the same duties he had undertaken then. If the government were unable to do as much as it in fact did, the entire operation directed against Neville would have been impossible.

Why the government was willing to use Kubica in this way in order to reach Neville is unclear. The majority appears to be of the view that Kubica, with his chemical expertise, was the more valuable catch and the more logical target for hard nosed prosecution. This may well be the case. But I am reluctant to second-guess the DEA choice of target. Neville, after all, was able to provide both money and "contacts." It cannot be said with any certainty that such a

2. Moreover, even if I were persuaded by the majority's argument as to defendant Neville, I would reject their conclusion as to defendant Twigg. There was no government inducement of Twigg at all. He was brought into the crime by Neville. Instigation by a private person has never been a defense to criminal charges. Nor have the other facts stressed by the majority, Twigg's relative unimportance to the overall scheme, the likelihood that he would not share in the proceeds and his motives for undertaking the crime, traditionally been thought to constitute defenses to charges of criminal activity. On these facts I cannot believe that Twigg has even a colorable claim of either entrapment or overinvolvement.

person may not ultimately prove more important than a chemist in breaking up the network of drug manufacturers and suppliers in this country.

Whatever our judgment of their wisdom may be, DEA officials chose to utilize Kubica to pursue Neville. Given this decision, as a practical matter, they had to furnish through Kubica the same skills and materials Kubica had provided in the earlier conspiracy. This they did; and Neville, and through Neville, Twigg, willingly participated in the conspiracy. Although there is reason to question this sort of law enforcement, I cannot say that it shocks my conscience or that it reaches a demonstrable level of outrageousness beyond my toleration. This is so in part because I recognize the difficulties faced by the DEA in combatting the spread of illegal drugs. But, more importantly, I am particularly mindful of *Russell's* warning that the federal judiciary is not to exercise " 'a Chancellor's foot' veto over law enforcement practices of which it [does] not approve." To broaden the limited exception fashioned by Mr. Justice Powell in *Hampton* may well have just such an effect. Because I believe that that opinion authorizes judicial intervention under the due process clause only in extreme cases, I must respectfully dissent from the majority's reversal of the convictions of both Neville and Twigg.

Courts have found few occasions to rely upon the *Isaacson* decision. One court has rejected a due process claim based upon threatened legal consequences to an informer which caused him to turn against the accused. People v. Harris, 165 Cal.App.3d 324, 211 Cal.Rptr. 493 (1985). Another court relied on *Isaacson* to overturn convictions based on the conduct and testimony of an informer whose fee payments were contingent upon positive results. State v. Glosson, 462 So.2d 1082 (Fla.1985). Hunter v. State, 531 So.2d 239 (Fla.App.1988) (improper to use informant who needed to purchase one more kilo of drugs to gain freedom from a 15 year sentence). The holding in *Glosson* is not widely accepted. United States v. Grimes, 438 F.2d 391 (6th Cir.1971); People v. Mills, 40 Ill.2d 4, 237 N.E.2d 697 (1968). Compare United States v. Cresta, 825 F.2d 538 (1th Cir.1987) (details of fee were told in open court; witness was corroborated).

Chapter 11

EYE-WITNESS IDENTIFICATION PROCEDURES

A. THE RIGHT TO PRESENCE OF COUNSEL

UNITED STATES v. WADE

Supreme Court of the United States, 1967.
388 U.S. 218, 87 S.Ct. 1926.

MR. JUSTICE BRENNAN delivered the opinion of the Court.

The question here is whether courtroom identifications of an accused at trial are to be excluded from evidence because the accused was exhibited to the witnesses before trial at a post-indictment lineup conducted for identification purposes without notice to and in the absence of the accused's appointed counsel.

The federally insured bank in Eustace, Texas, was robbed on September 21, 1964. A man with a small strip of tape on each side of his face entered the bank, pointed a pistol at the female cashier and the vice president, the only persons in the bank at the time, and forced them to fill a pillowcase with the bank's money. The man then drove away with an accomplice waiting in a stolen car outside the bank. On March 23, 1965, an indictment was returned against respondent Wade and two others for conspiring to rob the bank, and against Wade and the accomplice for the robbery itself. Wade was arrested on April 2, and counsel was appointed to represent him on April 26. Fifteen days later an FBI agent, without notice to Wade's lawyer, arranged to have the two bank employees observe a lineup made up of Wade and five or six other prisoners and conducted in a courtroom of the local county courthouse. Each person in the line wore strips of tape such as allegedly worn by the robber and upon direction each said something like "put the money in the bag," the words allegedly uttered by the robber. Both bank employees identified Wade in the lineup as the bank robber.

At trial the two employees, when asked on direct examination if the robber was in the courtroom, pointed to Wade. The prior lineup identification was then elicited from both employees on cross-examination. At the close of testimony, Wade's counsel moved for a judgment of acquittal or, alternatively, to strike the bank officials' courtroom identifications on the ground that conduct of the lineup, without notice to and in the absence of his appointed counsel, violated his Fifth Amendment privilege against self-incrimination and his Sixth Amendment right to the assistance of counsel. The motion was denied, and Wade was convicted. The Court of Appeals for the Fifth Circuit reversed the conviction and ordered a new trial at which the in-court identification evidence was to be excluded, holding that, though the lineup did not violate Wade's Fifth Amendment rights, "the lineup, held as it was, in the absence of counsel, already chosen to represent appellant, was a violation of his Sixth Amendment rights. . . ." We granted certiorari and set the case for oral argument with Gilbert v. State of California, and Stovall v. Denno, which present similar questions. We reverse the judgment of the Court of Appeals and remand to that court with direction to enter a new judgment vacating the conviction and remanding the case to the District Court for further proceedings consistent with this opinion.

I.

Neither the lineup itself nor anything shown by this record that Wade was required to do in the lineup violated his privilege against self-incrimination. We have only recently reaffirmed that the privilege "protects an accused only from being compelled to testify against himself, or otherwise provide the State with evidence of a testimonial or communicative nature. . . ." Schmerber v. California, 384 U.S. 757, 86 S.Ct. 1826. We there held that compelling a suspect to submit to a withdrawal of a sample of his blood for analysis for alcohol content and the admission in evidence of the analysis report was not compulsion to those ends. That holding was supported by the opinion in Holt v. United States ... in which case a question arose as to whether a blouse belonged to the defendant. A witness testified at trial that the defendant put on the blouse and it had fit him. The defendant argued that the admission of the testimony was error because compelling him to put on the blouse was a violation of his privilege. The Court rejected the claim as "an extravagant extension of the Fifth Amendment," Mr. Justice Holmes saying for the Court:

> "[T]he prohibition of compelling a man in a criminal court to be witness against himself is a prohibition of the use of physical or moral compulsion to extort communications from him, not an exclusion of his body as evidence when it may be material."

* * *

We have no doubt that compelling the accused merely to exhibit his person for observation by a prosecution witness prior to trial involves no compulsion of the accused to give evidence having testimonial significance. It is compulsion of the accused to exhibit his physical characteristics, not compulsion to disclose any knowledge he might have. It is no different from compelling Schmerber to provide a blood sample or Holt to wear the blouse, and, as in those instances, is not within the cover of the privilege. Similarly, compelling Wade to speak within hearing distance of the witnesses, even to utter words purportedly uttered by the robber, was not compulsion to utter statements of a "testimonial" nature; he was required to use his voice as an identifying physical characteristic, not to speak his guilt. We held in *Schmerber,* supra, that the distinction to be drawn under the Fifth Amendment privilege against self-incrimination is one between an accused's "communications" in whatever form, vocal or physical, and "compulsion which makes a suspect or accused the source of 'real or physical evidence,' ". We recognized that "both federal and state courts have usually held that . . . [the privilege] offers no protection against compulsion to submit to fingerprinting, photography, or measurements, to write or speak for identification, to appear in court, to stand, to assume a stance, to walk, or to make a particular gesture." None of these activities becomes testimonial within the scope of the privilege because required of the accused in a pretrial lineup.

Moreover, it deserves emphasis, that this case presents no question of the admissibility in evidence of anything Wade said or did at the lineup which implicates his privilege. The Government offered no such evidence as part of its case, and what came out about the lineup proceedings on Wade's cross-examination of the bank employees involved no violation of Wade's privilege.

II.

The fact that the lineup involved no violation of Wade's privilege against self-incrimination does not, however, dispose of his contention that the court room identifications should have been excluded because the lineup was conducted without notice to and in the absence of his counsel. Our rejection of the right to counsel claim in *Schmerber* rested on our conclusion in that case that "no issue of counsel's ability to assist petitioner in respect of any rights he did possess is presented." In contrast, in this case it is urged that the assistance of counsel at the lineup was indispensable to protect Wade's most basic right as a criminal defendant—his right to a fair trial at which the witnesses against him might be meaningfully cross-examined.

. . . When the Bill of Rights was adopted, there were no organized police forces as we know them today. The accused confronted the prosecutor and the witnesses against him, and the evidence was marshalled, largely at the trial itself. In contrast, today's law enforcement machinery involves critical confrontations of the accused by the prosecution at pretrial proceedings where the results might well settle the accused's fate and reduce the trial itself to a mere formality. In recognition of these realities of modern criminal prosecution, our cases have construed the Sixth Amendment guarantee to apply to "critical" stages of the proceedings. . . .

. . . It is central to that principle that in addition to counsel's presence at trial, the accused is guaranteed that he need not stand alone against the State at any stage of the prosecution, formal or informal, in court or out, where counsel's absence might derogate the accused's right to a fair trial.... The presence of counsel at such critical confrontations, as at the trial itself, operates to assure that the accused's interests will be protected consistently with our adversary theory of criminal prosecution.

In sum, the principle of Powell v. Alabama and succeeding cases requires that we scrutinize *any* pretrial confrontation of the accused to determine whether the presence of his counsel is necessary to preserve the defendant's basic right to a fair trial as affected by his right meaningfully to cross-examine the witnesses against him and to have effective assistance of counsel at the trial itself. It calls upon us to analyze whether potential substantial prejudice to defendant's rights inheres in the particular confrontation and the ability of counsel to help avoid that prejudice.

III.

The Government characterizes the lineup as a mere preparatory step in the gathering of the prosecution's evidence, not different—for Sixth Amendment purposes—from various other preparatory steps, such as systematized or scientific analyses of the accused's fingerprints, blood sample, clothing, hair, and the like. We think there are differences which preclude such stages being characterized as critical stages at which the accused has the right to the presence of his counsel. Knowledge of the techniques of science and technology is sufficiently available, and the variables in techniques few enough, that the accused has the opportunity for a meaningful confrontation of the Government's case at trial through the ordinary processes of cross-examination of the Government's expert witnesses and the presentation of the evidence of his own experts. The denial of a right to have his counsel present at such analyses does not therefore violate the Sixth Amendment; they are not critical stages since there is minimal risk that his counsel's absence at such stages might derogate his right to a fair trial.

IV.

But the confrontation compelled by the State between the accused and the victim or witnesses to a crime to elicit identification evidence is peculiarly riddled with innumerable dangers and variable factors which might seriously, even crucially, derogate from a fair trial. The vagaries of eyewitness identification are well-known; the annals of criminal law are rife with instances of mistaken identification.[1] Mr. Justice Frankfurter once said: "What is the worth of identification testimony even when uncontradicted? The identification of strangers is proverbially untrustworthy. The hazards of such testimony are established by a formidable number of instances in the records of English and American trials. These instances are recent—not due to the brutalities of ancient

1. Borchard, Convicting the Innocent; Frank & Frank, Not Guilty; Wall, Eyewitness Identification in Criminal Cases, 3 Wigmore, Evidence § 786(a) (3d ed. 1940); Rolph, Personal Identity; Gross, Criminal Investigation 47–54 (Jackson ed. 1962); Williams, Proof of Guilt 83–98 (1952); Wills, Circumstantial Evidence 192–205 (7th ed. 1937); Wigmore, The Science of Judicial Proof §§ 250–253.

criminal procedure." The Case of Sacco and Vanzetti 30 (1927). A major factor contributing to the high incidence of miscarriage of justice from mistaken identification has been the degree of suggestion inherent in the manner in which the prosecution presents the suspect to witnesses for pretrial identification. A commentator has observed that "the influence of improper suggestion upon identifying witnesses probably accounts for more miscarriages of justice than any other single factor—perhaps it is responsible for more such errors than all other factors combined." Wall, Eyewitness Identification in Criminal Cases 26. Suggestion can be created intentionally or unintentionally in many subtle ways. And the dangers for the suspect are particularly grave when the witness' opportunity for observation was insubstantial, and thus his susceptibility to suggestion the greatest.

Moreover, "it is a matter of common experience that, once a witness has picked out the accused at the line-up, he is not likely to go back on his word later on, so that in practice the issue of identity may (in the absence of other relevant evidence) for all practical purposes be determined there and then, before the trial." [2]

The pretrial confrontation for purpose of identification may take the form of a lineup, also known as an "identification parade" or "showup," as in the present case, or presentation of the suspect alone to the witness, as in Stovall v. Denno, post. It is obvious that risks of suggestion attend either form of confrontation and increase the dangers inhering in eyewitness identification. But as is the case with secret interrogations, there is serious difficulty in depicting what transpires at lineups and other forms of identification confrontations. "Privacy results in secrecy and this in turn results in a gap in our knowledge as to what in fact goes on...." Miranda v. State of Arizona, supra. For the same reasons, the defense can seldom reconstruct the manner and mode of lineup identification for judge or jury at trial. Those participating in a lineup with the accused may often be police officers; in any event, the participants' names are rarely recorded or divulged at trial.[3] The impediments to an objective observation are increased when the victim is the witness. Lineups are prevalent in rape and robbery prosecutions and present a particular hazard that a victim's understandable outrage may excite vengeful or spiteful motives. In any event, neither witnesses nor lineup participants are apt to be alert for conditions prejudicial to the suspect. And if they were, it would likely be of scant benefit to the suspect since neither witnesses nor lineup participants are likely to be schooled in the detection of suggestive influences.[4] Improper influences

2. Williams & Hammelmann, Identification Parades, Part I, [1963] Crim.L.Rev. 479, 482.

3. See Rolph, Personal Identity 50; "The bright burden of identity, at these parades, is lifted from the innocent participants to hover about the suspects, leaving the rest featureless and unknown and without interest."

4. An additional impediment to the detection of such influences by participants, including the suspect, is the physical conditions often surrounding the conduct of the lineup. In many, lights shine on the stage in such a way that the suspect cannot see the witness. In some a one-way mirror is used and what is said on the witness' side cannot be heard.

may go undetected by a suspect, guilty or not, who experiences the emotional tension which we might expect in one being confronted with potential accusers. Even when he does observe abuse, if he has a criminal record he may be reluctant to take the stand and open up the admission of prior convictions. Moreover any protestations by the suspect of the fairness of the lineup made at trial are likely to be in vain;[5] the jury's choice is between the accused's unsupported version and that of the police officers present.[6] In short, the accused's inability effectively to reconstruct at trial any unfairness that occurred at the lineup may deprive him of his only opportunity meaningfully to attack the credibility of the witness' courtroom identification.

What facts have been disclosed in specific cases about the conduct of pretrial confrontations for identification illustrate both the potential for substantial prejudice to the accused at that stage and the need for its revelation at trial. A commentator provides some striking examples:

> "In a Canadian case ... the defendant had been picked out of a lineup of six men, of which he was the only Oriental. In other cases, a blackhaired suspect was placed upon a group of light-haired persons, tall suspects have been made to stand with short nonsuspects, and, in a case where the perpetrator of the crime was known to be a youth, a suspect under twenty was placed in a lineup with five other persons, all of whom were forty or over."

Similarly state reports, in the course of describing prior identifications admitted as evidence of guilt, reveal numerous instances of suggestive procedures, for example, that all in the lineup but the suspect were known to the identifying witness, that the other participants in a lineup were grossly dissimilar in appearance from the suspect, that only the suspect was required to wear distinctive clothing which the culprit

5. See In re Groban, 352 U.S. 330, 340, 77 S.Ct. 510, 516 (Black, J., dissenting). The difficult position of defendants in attempting to protest the manner of pretrial identification is illustrated by the many state court cases in which contentions of blatant abuse rested on their unsupportable allegations, usually controverted by the police officers present.... For a striking case in which hardly anyone agreed upon what occurred at the lineup, including who identified whom, see Johnson v. State, 237 Md. 283, 206 A.2d 138 (1965).

6. An instructive example of the defendant's predicament may be found in Proctor v. State, 223 Md. 394, 164 A.2d 708 (1960). A prior identification is admissible in Maryland only under the salutary rule that it cannot have been made "under conditions of unfairness or unreliability." Against the defendant's contention that these conditions had not been met, the Court stated:

"In the instant case, there are no such facts as, in our judgment, would call for a finding that the identification ... was made under conditions of unfairness or unreliability. The relatively large number of persons put into the room together for [the victim] to look at is one circumstance indicating fairness, and the fact that the police officer was unable to remember the appearances of the others and could not recall if they had physical characteristics similar to [the defendant's] or not is at least suggestive that they were not of any one type or that they all differed markedly in looks from the defendant. There is no evidence that the Police Sergeant gave the complaining witness any indication as to which of the thirteen men was the defendant; the Sergeant's testimony is simply that he asked [the victim] if he could identify [the defendant] after having put the thirteen men in the courtroom."

allegedly wore, that the witness is told by the police that they have caught the culprit after which the defendant is brought before the witness alone or is viewed in jail, that the suspect is pointed out before or during a lineup, and that the participants in the lineup are asked to try on an article of clothing which fits only the suspect.[7]

The potential for improper influence is illustrated by the circumstances, insofar as they appear, surrounding the prior identifications in the three cases we decide today. In the present case, the testimony of the identifying witnesses elicited on cross-examination revealed that those witnesses were taken to the courthouse and seated in the courtroom to await assembly of the lineup. The courtroom faced on a hallway observable to the witnesses through an open door. The cashier testified that she saw Wade "standing in the hall" within sight of an FBI agent. Five or six other prisoners later appeared in the hall. The vice president testified that he saw a person in the hall in the custody of the agent who "resembled the person that we identified as the one that entered the bank." [8]

The lineup in *Gilbert* was conducted in an auditorium in which some 100 witnesses to several alleged state and federal robberies charged to Gilbert made wholesale identifications of Gilbert as the robber in each others' presence, a procedure said to run counter to the most elemental precepts of the psychology of suggestion. And the vice of suggestion created by the identification in *Stovall* was the presentation to the witness of the suspect alone handcuffed to police officers. It is hard to imagine a situation more clearly conveying the suggestion to the witness that the one presented is believed guilty by the police.

The few cases that have surfaced therefore reveal the existence of a process attended with hazards of serious unfairness to the criminal accused and strongly suggest the plight of the more numerous defendants who are unable to ferret out suggestive influences in the secrecy of the confrontation. We do not assume that these risks are the result of police procedures intentionally designed to prejudice an accused. Rather we assume they derive from the dangers inherent in eyewitness identification and the suggestibility inherent in the context of the pretrial identification. Glanville Williams, in one of the most comprehensive studies of such forms of identification, said "[T]he fact that the police themselves have, in a given case, little or no doubt that the man put up for identification has committed the offense, and that their chief preoccupation is with the problem of getting sufficient proof, because he has not 'come clean,' involves a danger that this persuasion may communicate itself even in a doubtful case to the witness in some way...."

7. [For case citations supporting the foregoing statements, consult original footnotes 18 through 21.]

8. See Wall, supra, n. 7, at 48; Napley, Problems of Effecting the Presentation of the Case for a Defendant, 66 Col.L.Rev. 94, 99 (1966): "[W]hile many identification parades are conducted by the police with scrupulous regard for fairness, it is not unknown for the identifying witness to be placed in a position where he can see the suspect before the parade forms...."

Williams & Hammelmann, Identification Parades, Part I, [1963] Crim. L.Rev. 479, 483.

Insofar as the accused's conviction may rest on a courtroom identification in fact the fruit of a suspect pretrial identification which the accused is helpless to subject to effective scrutiny at trial, the accused is deprived of that right of cross-examination which is an essential safeguard to his right to confront the witnesses against him.... And even though cross-examination is a precious safeguard to a fair trial, it cannot be viewed as an absolute assurance of accuracy and reliability. Thus in the present context, where so many variables and pitfalls exist, the first line of defense must be the prevention of unfairness and the lessening of the hazards of eyewitness identification at the lineup itself. The trial which might determine the accused's fate may well not be that in the courtroom but that at the pretrial confrontation, with the State aligned against the accused, the witness the sole jury, and the accused unprotected against the overreaching, intentional or unintentional, and with little or no effective appeal from the judgment there rendered by the witness—"that's the man."

Since it appears that there is grave potential for prejudice, intentional or not, in the pretrial lineup, which may not be capable of reconstruction at trial, and since presence of counsel itself can often avert prejudice and assure a meaningful confrontation at trial,[9] there can be little doubt

9. One commentator proposes a model statute providing not only for counsel, but other safeguards as well:

"Most if not all, of the attacks on the lineup process could be averted by a uniform statute modeled upon the best features of the civilian codes. Any proposed statute should provide for the right to counsel during any lineup or during any confrontation. Provision should be made that any person, whether a victim or a witness, must give a description of the suspect before he views any arrested person. A written record of this description should be required, and the witness should be made to sign it. This written record would be available for inspection by defense counsel for copying before the trial and for use at the trial in testing the accuracy of the identification made during the lineup and during the trial.

"This ideal statute would require at least six persons in addition to the accused in a lineup, and these persons would have to be of approximately the same height, weight, coloration of hair and skin, and bodily types as the suspect. In addition, all of these men should, as nearly as possible, be dressed alike. If distinctive garb was used during the crime, the suspect should not be forced to wear similar clothing in the lineup unless all of the other persons are similarly garbed. A complete written report of the names, addresses, descriptive details of the other persons in the lineup, and of everything which transpired during the identification would be mandatory. This report would include everything stated by the identifying witness during this step, including any reasons given by him as to what features, etc., have sparked his recognition.

"This statute should permit voice identification tests by having each person in the lineup repeat identical innocuous phrases, and it would be impermissible to force the use of words allegedly used during a criminal act.

"The statute would enjoin the police from suggesting to any viewer that one or more persons in the lineup had been arrested as a suspect. If more than one witness is to make an identification, each witness should be required to do so separately and should be forbidden to speak to another witness until all of them have completed the process.

"The statute could require the use of movie cameras and tape recorders to record the lineup process in those states which are financially able to afford these devices. Finally, the statute should provide that any evidence obtained as the result of a violation of this statute would

that for Wade the post-indictment lineup was a critical stage of the prosecution at which he was "as much entitled to such aid [of counsel] ... as at the trial itself." ... Thus both Wade and his counsel should have been notified of the impending lineup, and counsel's presence should have been a requisite to conduct of the lineup, absent an "intelligent waiver." ... No substantial countervailing policy considerations have been advanced against the requirement of the presence of counsel. Concern is expressed that the requirement will forestall prompt identifications and result in obstruction of the confrontations. As for the first, we note that in the two cases in which the right to counsel is today held to apply, counsel had already been appointed and no argument is made in either case that notice to counsel would have prejudicially delayed the confrontations. Moreover, we leave open the question whether the presence of substitute counsel might not suffice where notification and presence of the suspect's own counsel would result in prejudicial delay.[10] And to refuse to recognize the right to counsel for fear that counsel will obstruct the course of justice is contrary to the basic assumptions upon which this Court has operated in Sixth Amendment cases. We rejected similar logic in Miranda v. State of Arizona, concerning presence of counsel during custodial interrogation:

> "[A]n attorney is merely exercising the good professional judgment he has been taught. This is not cause for considering the attorney a menace to law enforcement. He is merely carrying out what he is sworn to do under his oath—to protect to the extent of his ability the rights of his client. In fulfilling this responsibility the attorney plays a vital role in the administration of criminal justice under our Constitution."

In our view counsel can hardly impede legitimate law enforcement; on the contrary, for the reasons expressed, law enforcement may be assisted by preventing the infiltration of taint in the prosecution's identification evidence.[11] That result cannot help the guilty avoid conviction but can only help assure that the right man has been brought to justice.[12]

be inadmissible." Murray, The Criminal Lineup at Home and Abroad, 1966 Utah L.Rev. 610, 627–628.

10. Although the right to counsel usually means a right to the suspect's own counsel, provision for substitute counsel may be justified on the ground that the substitute counsel's presence may eliminate the hazards which render the lineup a critical stage for the presence of the suspect's *own* counsel.

11. Concern is also expressed that the presence of counsel will force divulgence of the identity of government witnesses whose identity the Government may want to conceal. To the extent that this is a valid or significant state interest there are police practices commonly used to effect concealment, for example, masking the face.

12. Most other nations surround the lineup with safeguards against prejudice to the suspect. In England the suspect must be allowed the presence of his solicitor or a friend, Napley, supra, at 98–99; Germany requires the presence of retained counsel; France forbids the confrontation of the suspect in the absence of his counsel; Spain, Mexico, and Italy provide detailed procedures prescribing the conditions under which confrontation must occur under the supervision of a judicial officer who sees to it that the proceedings are officially recorded to assure adequate scrutiny at trial. Murray, The Criminal Lineup at Home and Abroad, 1966 Utah L.Rev. 610, 621–627.

Legislative or other regulations, such as those of local police departments, which eliminate the risks of abuse and unintentional suggestion at lineup proceedings and the impediments to meaningful confrontation at trial may also remove the basis for regarding the stage as "critical." [13] But neither Congress nor the federal authorities has seen fit to provide a solution. What we hold today "in no way creates a constitutional straitjacket which will handicap sound efforts at reform, nor is it intended to have this effect." ...

V.

We come now to the question whether the denial of Wade's motion to strike the courtroom identification by the bank witnesses at trial because of the absence of his counsel at the lineup required, as the Court of Appeals held, the grant of a new trial at which such evidence is to be excluded. We do not think this disposition can be justified without first giving the Government the opportunity to establish by clear and convincing evidence that the in-court identifications were based upon observations of the suspect other than the lineup identification.... Where, as here, the admissibility of evidence of the lineup identification itself is not involved, a per se rule of exclusion of courtroom identification would be unjustified.... A rule limited solely to the exclusion of testimony concerning identification at the lineup itself, without regard to admissibility of the courtroom identification, would render the right to counsel an empty one. The lineup is most often used, as in the present case, to crystallize the witnesses' identification of the defendant for future reference. We have already noted that the lineup identification will have that effect. The State may then rest upon the witnesses' unequivocal courtroom identification, and not mention the pretrial identification as part of the State's case at trial. Counsel is then in the predicament in which Wade's counsel found himself—realizing that possible unfairness at the lineup may be the sole means of attack upon the unequivocal courtroom identification, and having to probe in the dark in an attempt to discover and reveal unfairness, while bolstering the government witness' courtroom identification by bringing out and dwelling upon his prior identification. Since counsel's presence at the lineup would equip him to attack not only the lineup identification but the courtroom identification as well, limiting the impact of violation of the right to

13. Thirty years ago Wigmore suggested a "scientific method" of pretrial identification "to reduce the risk of error hitherto inherent in such proceedings." Wigmore, The Science of Judicial Proof 541 (3d ed. 1937). Under this approach, at least 100 talking films would be prepared of men from various occupations, races, etc. Each would be photographed in a number of stock movements, with and without hat and coat, and would read aloud a standard passage. The suspect would be filmed in the same manner. Some 25 of the films would be shown in succession in a special projection room in which each witness would be provided an electric button which would activate a board backstage when pressed to indicate that the witness had identified a given person. Provision would be made for the degree of hesitancy in the identification to be indicated by the number of presses. Of course, the more systematic and scientific a process or proceeding, including one for purposes of identification, the less the impediment to reconstruction of the conditions bearing upon the reliability of that process or proceeding at trial....

counsel to exclusion of evidence only of identification at the lineup itself disregards a critical element of that right.

We think it follows that the proper test to be applied in these situations is that quoted in Wong Sun v. United States, 371 U.S. 471, 488, 83 S.Ct. 407, 417, "Whether, granting establishment of the primary illegality, the evidence to which instant objection is made has been come at by exploitation of that illegality or instead by means sufficiently distinguishable to be purged of the primary taint." ... Application of this test in the present context requires consideration of various factors; for example, the prior opportunity to observe the alleged criminal act, the existence of any discrepancy between any pre-lineup description and the defendant's actual description, any identification prior to lineup of another person, the identification by picture of the defendant prior to the lineup, failure to identify the defendant on a prior occasion, and the lapse of time between the alleged act and the lineup identification. It is also relevant to consider those facts which, despite the absence of counsel, are disclosed concerning the conduct of the lineup.

We doubt that the Court of Appeals applied the proper test for exclusion of the in-court identification of the two witnesses. The court stated that "it cannot be said with any certainty that they would have recognized appellant at the time of trial if this intervening lineup had not occurred," and that the testimony of the two witnesses "may well have been colored by the illegal procedure [and] was prejudicial." Moreover, the court was persuaded, in part, by the "compulsory verbal responses made by Wade at the instance of the Special Agent." This implies the erroneous holding that Wade's privilege against self-incrimination was violated so that the denial of counsel required exclusion.

On the record now before us we cannot make the determination whether the in-court identifications had an independent origin. This was not an issue at trial, although there is some evidence relevant to a determination. That inquiry is most properly made in the District Court. We therefore think the appropriate procedure to be followed is to vacate the conviction pending a hearing to determine whether the in-court identifications had an independent source, or whether, in any event, the introduction of the evidence was harmless error, and for the District Court to reinstate the conviction or order a new trial, as may be proper. See United States v. Shotwell Mfg. Co., 355 U.S. 233, 245–246, 78 S.Ct. 245, 253.

The judgment of the Court of Appeals is vacated and the case is remanded to that court with direction to enter a new judgment vacating the conviction and remanding the case to the District Court for further proceedings consistent with this opinion. It is so ordered.

Judgment of Court of Appeals vacated and case remanded with direction.

MR. JUSTICE BLACK, dissenting in part and concurring in part.

* * *

The Court in Part I of its opinion rejects Wade's Fifth Amendment contention. From that I dissent. In Parts II–IV of its opinion, the Court sustains Wade's claim of denial of right to counsel in the out-of-court lineup, and in that I concur. In Part V, the Court remands the case to the District Court to consider whether the courtroom identification of Wade was the fruit of the illegal lineup, and if it were, to grant him a new trial unless the court concludes that the courtroom identification was harmless error. I would reverse the Court of Appeals' reversal of Wade's conviction, but I would not remand for further proceedings since the prosecution not having used the out-of-court lineup identification against Wade at his trial, I believe the conviction should be affirmed.

I.

In rejecting Wade's claim that his privilege against self-incrimination was violated by compelling him to appear in the lineup wearing the tape and uttering the words given him by the police, the Court relies on the recent holding in Schmerber v. State of California. In that case the Court held that taking blood from a man's body against his will in order to convict him of a crime did not compel him to be a witness against himself. I dissented from that holding, and still dissent. The Court's reason for its holding was that the sample of Schmerber's blood taken in order to convict him of crime was neither "testimonial" nor "communicative" evidence. I think it was both. It seems quite plain to me that the Fifth Amendment's Self-incrimination Clause was designed to bar the Government from forcing any person to supply proof of his own crime, precisely what Schmerber was forced to do when he was forced to supply his blood. The Government simply took his blood against his will and over his counsel's protest for the purpose of convicting him of crime. So here, having Wade in its custody awaiting trial to see if he could or would be convicted of crime, the Government forced him to stand in a lineup, wear strips on his face, and speak certain words, in order to make it possible for government witnesses to identify him as a criminal. Had Wade been compelled to utter these or any other words in open court, it is plain that he would have been entitled to a new trial because of having been compelled to be a witness against himself. Being forced by Government to help convict himself and to supply evidence against himself by talking outside the courtroom is equally violative of his constitutional right not to be compelled to be a witness against himself. Consequently, because of this violation of the Fifth Amendment, and not because of my own personal view that the Government's conduct was "unfair," "prejudicial," or "improper," I would prohibit the prosecution's use of lineup identification at trial.

II.

I agree with the Court, in large part because of the reasons it gives, that failure to notify Wade's counsel that Wade was to be put in a lineup by government officers and to be forced to talk and wear tape on his face denied Wade the right to counsel in violation of the Sixth Amendment. Once again, my reason for this conclusion is solely the Sixth Amendment's guarantee that "the accused shall enjoy the right . . . to have the assistance of counsel for his defence." As this Court's opinion points out, "[t]he plain wording of this guarantee thus encompasses counsel's assistance whenever necessary to assure a meaningful 'defence.' "

But there are implications in the Court's opinion that by a "fair trial" the Court means a trial which a majority of this Court deems to be "fair" and that a lineup is a "critical stage" only because the Court, now assessing the "innumerable dangers" which inhere in it, thinks it is such. That these implications are justified is evidenced by the Court's suggestion that "legislative or other regulations . . . which eliminate the abuse . . . at lineup proceedings . . . may also remove the basis for regarding the stage as 'critical.' " . . . I am wholly unwilling to make the specific constitutional right of counsel dependent on judges' vague and transitory notions of fairness and their equally transitory, though "practical," assessment of the "risk that . . . counsel's absence . . . might derogate from a fair trial." . . .

III.

I would reverse Wade's conviction without further ado had the prosecution at trial made use of his lineup identification either in place of courtroom identification or to bolster in a harmful manner crucial courtroom identification. But the prosecution here did neither of these things. After prosecution witnesses under oath identified Wade in the courtroom, it was the defense, and not the prosecution, which brought out the prior lineup identification. While stating that "a *per se* rule of exclusion of courtroom identification would be unjustified," the Court, nevertheless remands this case for "a hearing to determine whether the in-court identifications had an independent source," or were the tainted fruits of the invalidly conducted lineup. From this holding I dissent.

In the first place, even if this Court has power to establish such a rule of evidence I think the rule fashioned by the Court is unsound. The "taint"-"fruit" determination required by the Court involves more than considerable difficulty. I think it is practically impossible. How is a witness capable of probing the recesses of his mind to draw a sharp line between a courtroom identification due exclusively to an earlier lineup and a courtroom identification due to memory not based on the lineup? What kind of "clear and convincing evidence" can the prosecution offer to prove upon what particular events memories resulting in an in-court identification rest? How long will trials be delayed while judges turn psychologists to probe the subconscious minds of witnesses? All these questions are posed but not answered by the Court's opinion. In my view, the Fifth and Sixth Amendments are satisfied if the prosecution is precluded from using lineup identification as either an alternative to or corroboration of courtroom identification. If the prosecution does neither and its witnesses under oath identify the defendant in the courtroom, then I can find no justification for stopping the trial in midstream to hold a lengthy "taint"-"fruit" hearing. The fact of and circumstances surrounding a prior lineup identification might be used by the defense to impeach the credibility of the in-court identifications, but not to exclude them completely.

But more important, there is no constitutional provision upon which I can rely that directly or by implication gives this Court power to establish what amounts to a constitutional rule of evidence to govern, not only the Federal Government, but the States in their trial of state crimes under state laws in state courts. See Gilbert v. California, post. The Constitution deliberately reposed in States very broad power to create and to try crimes according to their own rules and policies.... Before being deprived of this power, the least that they can ask is that we should be able to point to a federal constitutional provision that either by express language or by necessary implication grants us the power to fashion this novel rule of evidence to govern their criminal trials....

Perhaps the Court presumes to write this constitutional rule of evidence on the Fourteenth Amendment's Due Process Clause. This is not the time or place to consider that claim. Suffice it for me to say briefly that I find no such authority in the Due Process Clause. It undoubtedly provides that a person must be tried in accordance with the "Law of the Land." Consequently, it violates due process to try a person in a way prohibited by the Fourth, Fifth, or Sixth Amendments of our written Constitution. But I have never been able to subscribe to the dogma that the Due Process Clause empowers this Court to declare any law, including a rule of evidence, unconstitutional which it believes is contrary to tradition, decency, fundamental justice, or any of the other wide-meaning words used by judges to claim power under the Due Process Clause.... I have an abiding idea that if the Framers had wanted to let judges write the Constitution on any such day-to-day beliefs of theirs, they would have said so instead of so carefully defining their grants and prohibitions in a written constitution. With no more authority than the Due Process Clause I am wholly unwilling to tell the state or federal courts that the United States Constitution forbids them to allow courtroom identification without the prosecution first proving that the identification does not rest in whole or in part on an illegal lineup. Should I do so, I would feel that we are deciding what the Constitution is, not from what it says, but from what we think it would have been wise for the Framers to put in it. That to me would be "judicial activism" at its worst. I would leave the States and Federal Government free to decide their own rules of evidence. That, I believe, is their constitutional prerogative.

I would affirm Wade's conviction.

MR. JUSTICE WHITE, whom MR. JUSTICE HARLAN and MR. JUSTICE STEWART join, dissenting in part and concurring in part.

The Court's opinion is far reaching. It proceeds first by creating a new *per se* rule of constitutional law: a criminal suspect cannot be subjected to a pretrial identification process in the absence of his counsel without violating the Sixth Amendment. If he is, the State may not buttress a later courtroom identification of the witness by any reference to the previous identification. Furthermore, the courtroom identification is not admissible at all unless the State can establish by clear and convincing proof that the testimony is not the fruit of the earlier identification made in the absence of defendant's counsel—admittedly a heavy burden for the State and probably an impossible one. For all intents and purposes, courtroom identifications are barred if pretrial identifications have occurred without counsel being present.

The rule applies to any lineup, to any other techniques employed to produce an identification and *a fortiori* to a face-to-face encounter between the witness and the suspect alone, regardless of when the identification occurs, in time or place, and whether before or after indictment or information. It matters not how well the witness knows the suspect, whether the witness is the suspect's mother, brother, or long-time associate, and no matter how long or well the witness observed the perpetrator at the scene of the crime. The kidnap victim who has lived for days with his abductor is in the same category as the witness who had had only a fleeting glimpse of the criminal. Neither may identify the suspect without defendant's counsel being present. The same strictures apply regardless of the number of other witnesses who positively identify the defendant and regardless of the corroborative evidence showing that it was the defendant who has committed the crime.

The premise for the Court's rule is not the general unreliability of eyewitness identifications nor the difficulties inherent in observation, recall, and recognition. The Court assumes a narrower evil as the basis for its rule—improper police suggestion which contributes to erroneous identifications. The Court apparently believes that improper police procedures are so widespread that a broad prophylactic rule must be laid down, requiring the presence of counsel at all pretrial identifications, in order to detect recurring instances of police misconduct.[1] I do not share this pervasive distrust of all official investigations. None of the materials the Court relies upon supports it.[2] Certainly, I would bow to solid fact, but the Court quite obviously does not have before it any reliable, comprehensive survey of current police practices on which to base its

1. Yet in Stovall v. Denno, 388 U.S. 293, 87 S.Ct. 1967, the Court recognizes that improper police conduct in the identification process has not been so widespread as to justify full retroactivity for its new rule.

2. In Miranda v. State of Arizona, the Court noted that O'Hara, Fundamentals of Criminal Investigation (1956) is a text that has enjoyed extensive use among law enforcement agencies and among students of police science. The quality of the work was said to rest on the author's long service as observer, lecturer in police science, and work as a federal crime investigator. O'Hara does not suggest that the police should or do use identification machinery improperly; instead he argues for techniques that would increase the reliability of eyewitness identifications, and there is no reason to suggest that O'Hara's views are not shared and practiced by the majority of police departments throughout the land.

new rule. Until it does, the Court should avoid excluding relevant evidence from state criminal trials.

The Court goes beyond assuming that a great majority of the country's police departments are following improper practices at pretrial identifications. To find the lineup a "critical" stage of the proceeding and to exclude identifications made in the absence of counsel, the Court must also assume that police "suggestion," if it occurs at all, leads to erroneous rather than accurate identifications and that reprehensible police conduct will have an unavoidable and largely undiscoverable impact on the trial. This in turn assumes that there is now no adequate source from which defense counsel can learn about the circumstances of the pretrial identification in order to place before the jury all of the considerations which should enter into an appraisal of courtroom identification evidence. But these are treacherous and unsupported assumptions resting as they do on the notion that the defendant will not be aware, that the police and the witnesses will forget or prevaricate, that defense counsel will be unable to bring out the truth and that neither jury, judge, nor appellate court is a sufficient safeguard against unacceptable police conduct occurring at a pretrial identification procedure. I am unable to share the Court's view of the willingness of the police and the ordinary citizen-witness to dissemble, either with respect to the identification of the defendant or with respect to the circumstances surrounding a pretrial identification.

There are several striking aspects to the Court's holding. First, the rule does not bar courtroom identifications where there have been no previous identifications in the presence of the police, although when identified in the courtroom, the defendant is known to be in custody and charged with the commission of a crime. Second, the Court seems to say that if suitable legislative standards were adopted for the conduct of pretrial identifications, thereby lessening the hazards in such confrontations, it would not insist on the presence of counsel. But if this is true, why does not the Court simply fashion what it deems to be constitutionally acceptable procedures for the authorities to follow? Certainly the Court is correct in suggesting that the new rule will be wholly inapplicable where police departments themselves have established suitable safeguards.

Third, courtroom identification may be barred, absent counsel at a prior identification, regardless of the extent of counsel's information concerning the circumstances of the previous confrontation between witness and defendant—apparently even if there were recordings or sound-movies of the events as they occurred. But if the rule is premised on the defendant's right to have his counsel know, there seems little basis for not accepting other means to inform. A disinterested observer, recordings, photographs—any one of them would seem adequate to furnish the basis for a meaningful cross-examination of the eyewitness who identifies the defendant in the courtroom.

I share the Court's view that the criminal trial, at the very least, should aim at truthful factfinding, including accurate eyewitness identifications. I doubt, however, on the basis of our present information, that the tragic mistakes which have occurred in criminal trials are as much the product of improper police conduct as they are the consequence of the difficulties inherent in eyewitness testimony and in resolving evidentiary conflicts by court or jury. I doubt that the Court's new rule will obviate these difficulties, or that the situation will be measurably improved by inserting defense counsel into the investigative processes of police departments everywhere.

But, it may be asked, what possible state interest militates against requiring the presence of defense counsel at lineups? After all, the argument goes, he *may* do some good, he *may* upgrade the quality of identification evidence in state courts and he can scarcely do any harm. Even if true, this is a feeble foundation for fastening an ironclad constitutional rule upon state criminal procedures. Absent some reliably established constitutional violation, the processes by which the States enforce their criminal laws are their own prerogative. The States *do* have an interest in conducting their own affairs, an interest which cannot be displaced simply by saying that there are no valid arguments with respect to the merits of a federal rule emanating from this Court.

Beyond this, however, requiring counsel at pretrial identifications as an invariable rule trenches on other valid state interests. One of them is its concern with the prompt and efficient enforcement of its criminal laws. Identifications frequently take place after arrest but before indictment or information is filed. The police may have arrested a suspect on probable cause but may still have the wrong man. Both the suspect and the State have every interest in a prompt identification at that stage, the suspect in order to secure his immediate release and the State because prompt and early identification enhances *accurate* identification and because it must know whether it is on the right investigative track. Unavoidably, however, the absolute rule requiring the presence of counsel will cause significant delay and it may very well result in no pretrial identification at all. Counsel must be appointed and a time arranged convenient for him and the witnesses. Meanwhile, it may be necessary to file charges against the suspect who may then be released on bail, in the federal system very often on his own recognizance, with neither the State nor the defendant having the benefit of a properly conducted identification procedure.

Nor do I think the witnesses themselves can be ignored. They will now be required to be present at the convenience of counsel rather than their own. Many may be much less willing to participate if the identification stage is transformed into an adversary proceeding not under the control of a judge. Others may fear for their own safety if their identity is known at an early date, especially when there is no way of knowing until the lineup occurs whether or not the police really have the right man.[3]

Finally, I think the Court's new rule is vulnerable in terms of its own unimpeachable purpose of increasing the reliability of identification testimony.

Law enforcement officers have the obligation to convict the guilty and to make sure they do not convict the innocent. They must be dedicated to making the criminal trial a procedure for the ascertainment of the true facts surrounding the commission of the crime. To this extent, our so-called adversary system is not adversary at all; nor should it be. But defense counsel has no comparable obligation to ascertain or present the truth. Our system assigns him a different mission. He must be and is interested in not convicting the innocent, but, absent a voluntary plea of guilty, we also insist that he defend his client whether he is innocent or guilty. The State has the obligation to present the evidence. Defense counsel need present nothing, even if he knows what the truth is. He need furnish no witnesses to the police, reveal any confidences of his client, nor furnish any other information to help the prosecution's case. If he can confuse a witness, even a truthful one, or make him appear at a disadvantage, unsure or indecisive, that will be his normal course. Our interest in not convicting the innocent permits counsel to put the State to its proof, to put the State's case in the worst possible light regardless of what he thinks or knows to be the truth. Undoubtedly there are some limits which defense counsel must observe but more often than not, defense counsel will cross-examine a prosecution witness, and impeach him if he can, even if he thinks the witness is telling the truth, just as he will attempt to destroy a witness who he thinks is lying. In this respect, as part of our modified adversary system and as part of the duty imposed on the most honorable defense counsel, we countenance or require conduct which in many instances has little, if any, relation to the search for truth.

I would not extend this system, at least as it presently operates, to police investigations and would not require counsel's presence at pretrial identification procedures. Counsel's interest is in not having his client placed at the scene of the crime, regardless of his whereabouts. Some counsel may advise their clients to refuse to make any movements or to speak any words in a lineup or even to appear in one. To that extent the impact on truthful factfinding is quite obvious. Others will not only observe what occurs and develop possibilities for later cross-examination but will hover over witnesses and begin their cross-examination then, menacing truthful factfinding as thoroughly as the Court fears the police now do. Certainly there is an implicit invitation to counsel to suggest rules for the lineup and to manage and produce it as best he can. I therefore doubt that the Court's new rule, at least absent some clearly defined limits on counsel's role, will measurably contribute to more reliable pretrial identifications. My fears are that it will have precisely

3. I would not have thought that the State's interest regarding its sources of identification is any less than its interest in protecting informants, especially those who may aid in identification but who will not be used as witnesses.

the opposite result. It may well produce fewer convictions, but that is hardly a proper measure of its long-run acceptability. In my view, the State is entitled to investigate and develop its case outside the presence of defense counsel. This includes the right to have private conversations with identification witnesses, just as defense counsel may have his own consultations with these and other witnesses without having the prosecutor present.

Whether today's judgment would be an acceptable exercise of supervisory power over federal courts is another question. But as a constitutional matter, the judgment in this case is erroneous and although I concur in Parts I and III of the Court's opinion I respectfully register this dissent.

MR. JUSTICE FORTAS, with whom THE CHIEF JUSTICE and MR. JUSTICE DOUGLAS join, concurring in part and dissenting in part.

1. I agree with the Court that the exhibition of the person of the accused at a lineup is not itself a violation of the privilege against self-incrimination. In itself, it is no more subject to constitutional objection than the exhibition of the person of the accused in the courtroom for identification purposes. It is an incident of the State's power to arrest, and a reasonable and justifiable aspect of the State's custody resulting from arrest. It does not require that the accused take affirmative, volitional action, but only that, having been duly arrested he may be seen for identification purposes. It is, however, a "critical stage" in the prosecution, and I agree with the Court that the opportunity to have counsel present must be made available.

2. In my view, however, the accused may not be compelled in a lineup to speak the words uttered by the person who committed the crime. I am confident that it could not be compelled in court. It cannot be compelled in a lineup. It is more than passive, mute assistance to the eyes of the victim or of witnesses. It is the kind of volitional act—the kind of forced cooperation by the accused—which is within the historical perimeter of the privilege against compelled self-incrimination.

Our history and tradition teach and command that an accused may stand mute. The privilege means just that; not less than that. According to the Court, an accused may be jailed—indefinitely—until he is willing to say, for an identifying audience, whatever was said in the course of the commission of the crime. Presumably this would include, "Your money or your life"—or perhaps, words of assault in a rape case. This is intolerable under our constitutional system.

I completely agree that the accused must be advised of and given the right to counsel before a lineup—and I join in that part of the Court's opinion; but this is an empty right unless we mean to insist upon the accused's fundamental constitutional immunities. One of these is that the accused may not be compelled to speak. To compel him to speak would violate the privilege against self-incrimination, which is incorporated in the Fifth Amendment.

* * *

An accused cannot be compelled to utter the words spoken by the criminal in the course of the crime. I thoroughly disagree with the Court's statement that such compulsion does not violate the Fifth Amendment. The Court relies upon Schmerber v. State of California to support this.... But *Schmerber* which authorized the forced extraction of blood from the veins of an unwilling human being, did not compel the person actively to cooperate—to accuse himself by a volitional act which differs only in degree from compelling him to act out the crime, which, I assume, would be rebuffed by the Court....

To permit *Schmerber* to apply in any respect beyond its holding is, in my opinion, indefensible. To permit its insidious doctrine to extend beyond the invasion of the body, which it permits, to compulsion of the will of a man, is to deny and defy a precious part of our historical faith and to discard one of the most profoundly cherished instruments by which we have established the freedom and dignity of the individual. We should not so alter the balance between the rights of the individual and of the state, achieved over centuries of conflict.

3. While the Court holds that the accused must be advised of and given the right to counsel at the lineup, it makes the privilege meaningless in this important respect. Unless counsel has been waived or, being present, has not objected to the accused's utterance of words used in the course of committing the crime, to compel such an utterance is constitutional error.*

Accordingly, while I join the Court in requiring vacating of the judgment below for a determination as to whether the identification of respondent was based upon factors independent of the lineup, I would do so not only because of the failure to offer counsel before the lineup but also because of the violation of respondent's Fifth Amendment rights.

NOTES

1. In Gilbert v. California, 388 U.S. 263, 87 S.Ct. 1951 (1967), the Court elaborated on its several holdings in *Wade.* The Court held that requiring a suspect to give handwriting exemplars in the absence of counsel violated neither Fifth nor Sixth Amendment rights. The Court further held that a lineup conducted without notice to Gilbert's counsel some sixteen days after indictment violated Gilbert's right to counsel. With respect to those witnesses who identified Gilbert at trial, the Court held that Gilbert was entitled to a hearing whether their courtroom identification was untainted by their observations of Gilbert at the illegal lineup. The Court finally held that testimony concerning the pre-trial confrontation introduced by the prosecution was erroneously admitted. Such testimony, according to the Court, was the direct product of illegal law-enforcement conduct and "only a per se exclusionary rule as to such testimony can be an effective sanction to assure that law enforcement authorities will respect the accused's constitutional right to the presence of his counsel at the critical lineup."

* While it is conceivable that legislation might provide a meticulous lineup procedure which would *satisfy* constitutional requirements, I do not agree with the Court that this would "remove the basis for regarding the [lineup] stage as 'critical.' "

2. Can the right to counsel at lineups be waived? Every court that has considered the question has answered in the affirmative. See State v. Taylor, 456 S.W.2d 9 (Mo.1970); Hayes v. State, 46 Wis.2d 93, 175 N.W.2d 625 (1970); Compare State v. Bass, 280 N.C. 435, 186 S.E.2d 384 (1972) with State v. Mems, 281 N.C. 658, 190 S.E.2d 164 (1972). A waiver must be voluntary. Compare Redding v. State, 10 Md.App. 601, 272 A.2d 70 (1971) with Chambers v. State, 46 Ala.App. 247, 240 So.2d 370 (1970) (waiver voluntary when suspect was told he could go home if he was not identified). Warnings of the right to counsel *at the lineup* must be given. The mere giving of Miranda warnings is not sufficient (United States v. Ayers, 426 F.2d 524 (2nd Cir.1970)) but such warnings may be considered as supplementing other warnings specifically concerning the lineup. See People v. Evans, 16 Cal.App.3d 510, 94 Cal.Rptr. 88 (1971).

KIRBY v. ILLINOIS

Supreme Court of the United States, 1972.
406 U.S. 682, 92 S.Ct. 1877.

MR. JUSTICE STEWART announced the judgment of the Court in an opinion in which THE CHIEF JUSTICE, MR. JUSTICE BLACKMUN, and MR. JUSTICE REHNQUIST join.

... In the present case we are asked to extend the *Wade-Gilbert per se* exclusionary rule to identification testimony based upon a police station showup that took place *before* the defendant had been indicted or otherwise formally charged with any criminal offense.

On February 21, 1968, a man named Willie Shard reported to the Chicago police that the previous day two men had robbed him on a Chicago street of a wallet containing, among other things, travellers checks and a Social Security card. On February 22, two police officers stopped the petitioner and a companion, Ralph Bean, on West Madison Street in Chicago. When asked for identification, the petitioner produced a wallet that contained three travellers checks and a Social Security card, all bearing the name of Willie Shard. Papers with Shard's name on them were also found in Bean's possession. When asked to explain his possession of Shard's property, the petitioner first said that the travellers checks were "play money," and then told the officers that he had won them in a crap game. The officers then arrested the petitioner and Bean and took them to a police station.

Only after arriving at the police station, and checking the records there, did the arresting officers learn of the Shard robbery. A police car was then dispatched to Shard's place of employment, where it picked up Shard and brought him to the police station. Immediately upon entering the room in the police station where the petitioner and Bean were seated at a table, Shard positively identified them as the men who had robbed him two days earlier. No lawyer was present in the room, and neither the petitioner nor Bean had asked for legal assistance, or been advised of any right to the presence of counsel.

... A pretrial motion to suppress Shard's identification testimony was denied, and at the trial Shard testified as a witness for the prosecution. In his testimony he described his identification of the two men at the police station on February 22, and identified them again in the courtroom as the men who had robbed him on February 20. He was cross-examined at length regarding the circumstances of his identification of the two defendants. The jury found both defendants guilty.

I

We note at the outset that the constitutional privilege against compulsory self-incrimination is in no way implicated here....

It follows that the doctrine of Miranda v. Arizona has no applicability whatever to the issue before us. For the *Miranda* decision was based exclusively upon the Fifth and Fourteenth Amendment privilege against compulsory self-incrimination, upon the theory that custodial *interrogation* is inherently coercive.

The *Wade-Gilbert* exclusionary rule, by contrast, stems from a quite different constitutional guarantee—the guarantee of the right to counsel contained in the Sixth and Fourteenth Amendments. Unless all semblance of principled constitutional adjudication is to be abandoned, therefore, it is to the decisions construing that guarantee that we must look in determining the present controversy.

In a line of constitutional cases in this Court stemming back to the Court's landmark opinion in Powell v. Alabama, 287 U.S. 45, 53 S.Ct. 55, it has been firmly established that a person's Sixth and Fourteenth Amendment right to counsel attaches only at or after the time that adversary judicial proceedings have been initiated against him.

This is not to say that a defendant in a criminal case has a constitutional right to counsel only at the trial itself. The *Powell* case makes clear that the right attaches at the time of arraignment, and the Court has recently held that it exists also at the time of a preliminary hearing. But the point is that, while members of the Court have differed as to existence of the right to counsel in the contexts of some of the above cases, *all* of those cases have involved points of time at or after the initiation of adversary judicial criminal proceedings—whether by way of formal charge, preliminary hearing, indictment, information, or arraignment.

The initiation of judicial criminal proceedings is far from a mere formalism. It is the starting point of our whole system of adversary criminal justice. For it is only then that the Government has committed itself to prosecute, and only then that the adverse positions of Government and defendant have solidified. It is then that a defendant finds himself faced with the prosecutorial forces of organized society, and immersed in the intricacies of substantive and procedural criminal law. It is this point, therefore, that marks the commencement of the "criminal prosecutions" to which alone the explicit guarantees of the Sixth Amendment are applicable.

In this case we are asked to import into a routine police investigation an absolute constitutional guarantee historically and rationally applicable only after the onset of formal prosecutorial proceedings. We decline to do so. Less than a year after *Wade* and *Gilbert* were decided, the Court explained the rule of those decisions as follows: "The rationale of those cases was that an accused is entitled to counsel at any 'critical stage of the *prosecution,*' and that a post-indictment lineup is such a 'critical stage.'" (Emphasis supplied.) Simmons v. United States, 390 U.S. 377, 382–383, 88 S.Ct. 967, 970. We decline to depart from that rationale today by imposing a *per se* exclusionary rule upon testimony concerning an identification that took place long before the commencement of any prosecution whatever.

II

What has been said is not to suggest that there may not be occasions during the course of a criminal investigation when the police do abuse identification procedures. Such abuses are not beyond the reach of the Constitution. As the Court pointed out in *Wade* itself, it is always necessary to "scrutinize *any* pretrial confrontation...." The Due Process Clause of the Fifth and Fourteenth Amendments forbids a lineup that is unnecessarily suggestive and conducive to irreparable mistaken identification. When a person has not been formally charged with a criminal offense, *Stovall* strikes the appropriate constitutional balance between the right of a suspect to be protected from prejudicial procedures and the interest of society in the prompt and purposeful investigation of an unsolved crime.

The judgment is affirmed.

MR. CHIEF JUSTICE BURGER, concurring. [OMITTED]

MR. JUSTICE POWELL, concurring in the result. [OMITTED]

MR. JUSTICE BRENNAN, with whom MR. JUSTICE DOUGLAS and MR. JUSTICE MARSHALL join, dissenting....

In view of *Wade,* it is plain, and the plurality today does not attempt to dispute it, that there inhere in a confrontation for identification conducted after arrest * the identical hazards to a fair trial that inhere in such a confrontation conducted "after the onset of formal prosecutorial proceedings." The plurality apparently considers an arrest, which for present purposes we must assume to be based upon probable cause to be nothing more than part of "a routine police investigation," ibid., and thus not "the starting point of our whole system of adversary criminal justice,". An arrest, according to the plurality, does not face the accused "with the prosecutorial forces of organized society," nor immerse him "in the intricacies of substantive and procedural criminal law." Those consequences ensue, says the plurality, only with "[t]he initiation of judicial criminal proceedings," "[f]or it is only then that the Government

* This case does not require me to consider confrontations that take place before custody, see e.g., Bratten v. Delaware, 307 F.Supp. 643 (Del.1969); nor accidental confrontations not arranged by the police, see, e.g., United States v. Pollack, 427 F.2d 1168 (CA5 1970); nor on-the-scene encounters shortly after the crime, see, e.g. Russell v. United States, 408 F.2d 1280 (D.C.Cir. 1969).

has committed itself to prosecute, and only then that the adverse positions of Government and defendant have solidified." If these propositions do not amount to "mere formalism," ibid., it is difficult to know how to characterize them. An arrest evidences the belief of the police that the perpetrator of a crime has been caught. A post-arrest confrontation for identification is not "a mere preparatory step in the gathering of the prosecution's evidence." A primary, and frequently sole, purpose of the confrontation for identification at that stage is to accumulate proof to buttress the conclusion of the police that they have the offender in hand. The plurality offers no reason, and I can think of none, for concluding that a post-arrest confrontation for identification, unlike a post-charge confrontation, is not among those "critical confrontations of the accused by the prosecution at pretrial proceedings where the results might well settle the accused's fate and reduce the trial itself to a mere formality."

The highly suggestive form of confrontation employed in this case underscores the point. This showup was particularly fraught with the peril of mistaken identification. In the setting of a police station squad room where all present except petitioner and Bean were police officers, the danger was quite real that Shard's understandable resentment might lead him too readily to agree with the police that the pair under arrest, and the only persons exhibited to him, were indeed the robbers.... Shard's testimony itself demonstrates the necessity for such safeguards. On direct examination, Shard identified petitioner and Bean not as the alleged robbers on trial in the courtroom, but as the pair he saw at the police station....

* * *

Wade and *Gilbert,* of course, happened to involve post-indictment confrontations. Yet even a cursory perusal of the opinions in those cases reveals that nothing at all turned upon that particular circumstance. In short, it is fair to conclude that rather than "declin[ing] to depart from [the] rationale" of *Wade* and *Gilbert,* the plurality today, albeit purporting to be engaged in "principled constitutional adjudication," refuses even to recognize that "rationale." For my part, I do not agree that we "extend" *Wade* and *Gilbert,* by holding that the principles of those cases apply to confrontations for identification conducted after arrest. Because Shard testified at trial about his identification of petitioner at the police station showup, the exclusionary rule of *Gilbert,* requires reversal.

MR. JUSTICE WHITE, dissenting. [OMITTED]

NOTES

1. Two serious questions arise with reference to the scope of *Kirby.* First, in some jurisdictions a suspect is brought to a "bond" court shortly after arrest. Does this court appearance, which is limited solely to the setting of bail, represent the onset of formal prosecutorial proceedings? Does it make a difference whether a prosecutor appears at the hearing or the police appear without a prosecutor? Second, if the police get an arrest warrant from a court does this signify the commencement of prosecution? Some courts have answered in the

affirmative. United States ex rel. Robinson v. Zelker, 468 F.2d 159 (2d Cir. 1972), the court said:

> "The first question we have is whether 'adversary judicial proceedings' had been 'initiated' within Kirby v. Illinois....
>
> * * *
>
> "Here the arrest warrant itself commanded that appellant be brought forthwith before the Criminal Court 'to answer the said charge, and to be dealt with according to law.' These were formal criminal proceedings, for the warrant had been signed by a judge based on an 'information upon oath' that appellant did commit the crimes of assault, robbery and possession of a dangerous weapon. This being true, *Wade* required counsel at the show-up, for we see no distinction based on the chance fact that the identifying witness was also a police officer. Time was not of the essence, a lineup could have been arranged and there appeared to be no 'substantial countervailing policy considerations' against requiring the presence of counsel as suggested in *Wade.*"

In dissent Judge Hayes said:

> "I cannot agree with the majority's conclusion that 'adversary judicial criminal proceedings,' within the meaning of Kirby v. Illinois, had been begun in this case at the time of the pre-trial show-up, entitling Robinson to counsel at that show-up. In *Kirby* the Court said:
>
>> 'The initiation of judicial criminal proceedings is far from a mere formalism. It is the starting point of our whole system of adversary criminal justice. *For it is only then that the Government has committed itself to prosecute, and only then that the adverse positions of Government and defendant have solidified.* It is this point, therefore, that marks the commencement of the "criminal prosecutions" to which alone the explicit guarantees of the Sixth Amendment are applicable.'
>>
>> "Here the only judicial action taken against Robinson was the issuance of a warrant of arrest. He was not even arraigned until the day after the show-up.... It seems clear that such a warrant is not a point at which 'the Government has committed itself to prosecute, and ... the adverse positions of Government and defendant have solidified' ".

See Arnold v. State, 484 S.W.2d 248 (Mo.1972). See also State v. Earle, 60 N.J. 550, 292 A.2d 2 (1972) and People v. Agee, 100 Ill.App.3d 878, 56 Ill.Dec. 164, 427 N.E.2d 244 (1981) (rule does not apply when suspect is in custody on an unrelated charge). Does the answer to the question depend on whether, under local law, a complaint for an arrest warrant, which may only state the facts showing probable cause, is sufficient to meet the formal requirements for complaints charging a crime, i.e., affirmative allegations of each of the elements of the crime, citation to the statute violated, etc.?

Consider the following comments in United States v. Duvall, 537 F.2d 15, at 21–22 (2d Cir.1976):

> "We see no reason in principle why the filing of a complaint should be deemed to give rise to a right to counsel immediately upon arrest pursuant to warrant. As said in 8 Moore, Federal Practice ¶ 3.02 (Cipes, 1975 rev.), 'The principal function of a complaint "is as a basis

for an application for an arrest warrant."' See Gaither v. United States, 134 U.S.App.D.C. 154, 413 F.2d 1061, 1076 (1969). There is no reason in the nature of things why an arrest warrant should need to be predicated on a complaint rather than simply an affidavit as in the case of a search warrant, F.R.Cr.P. 41; indeed Rule 4 permits the showing of probable cause for arrest to be made either in the complaint or in an affidavit or affidavits filed with the complaint. The requirements of Rule 5 bear equally on 'an officer making an arrest under a warrant issued upon a complaint or any person making an arrest without a warrant.' We perceive no reason why Sixth Amendment rights should accrue sooner in the former instance than in the latter. Furthermore to hold that the accrual of the right to counsel is accelerated by use of the warrant procedure would tend to discourage this whereas the policy should be to encourage it."

Another decision holding that the issuance of an arrest warrant gives rise to the right to counsel, at a subsequent lineup is People v. Hinton, 23 Ill.App.3d 369, 319 N.E.2d 313 (1974). See also State v. Mitchell, 593 S.W.2d 280 (Tenn.1980). The argument that fewer arrest warrants will be issued if the issuance of a warrant creates a right to counsel is not merely puff in an appellate brief. This is precisely what has happened in Cook County, Illinois, where prosecutors are most reluctant to seek an arrest warrant if they know that a lineup will be held after the suspect is captured and if they believe that the suspect will be apprehended within a short period of time.

The issue is of increasing importance because of the more frequent use of arrest warrants mandated by Payton v. New York (infra Ch. 14 of this text), and by earlier state and federal decisions which before *Payton* had reached the "*Payton* result." See also Tarpley v. Estelle, 703 F.2d 157 (5th Cir.1983), which indicates that an arrest followed by a judicial appearance may not always trigger the right to counsel. Citing McGee v. Estelle, 625 F.2d 1206 (5th Cir.1980), the Court reasoned that the taking of a suspect before a judge or magistrate does not always signify a commitment to prosecution. See also Lomax v. Alabama, 629 F.2d 413 (5th Cir.1980).

Can the authorities prevent attachment of the right to counsel by declaring on the face of the arrest warrant that issuance of the warrant does not commit the district attorney to going forward with a criminal prosecution? Consider the propriety of this use of an arrest warrant. Such declarations are made on the face of arrest warrants in some California jurisdictions. See footnote 1 of Edwards v. Arizona in Chapter 12 of this text.

In People v. Blake, 35 N.Y.2d 331, 361 N.Y.S.2d 881, 320 N.E.2d 625 (1974), the Court held that undue delay between arrest and filing of a formal charge is a suspect circumstance but found a two hour delay to be reasonable. Holland v. Perini, 512 F.2d 99 (6th Cir.1975), approved a delay of twenty-four hours even though the delay appeared deliberate.

A discussion of when the Sixth Amendment applies is also found at Chapter 12 of this text.

3. An accused who is represented by counsel on another charge does not, for that reason alone, have the right to the presence of that attorney at a lineup conducted for another offense. See Boyd v. Henderson, 555 F.2d 56 (2d Cir.1977) (general review of precedents).

4. The question of right to counsel has also arisen in connection with identification from photographs. Without exception every court considering the

question has held that there is no right to counsel when police show photographs of suspects who are not in custody. What is the basis for this holding? The same result has been reached by the majority of courts when the Sixth Amendment claim was made on behalf of a suspect in custody.

In United States v. Ash, 413 U.S. 300, 93 S.Ct. 2568 (1973), the Court resolved the question, as appears in the following excerpts from the opinion:

"MR. JUSTICE BLACKMUN delivered the opinion of the Court.

"On the morning of August 26, 1965, a man with a stocking mask entered a bank in Washington, D.C., and began waving a pistol. He ordered an employee to hang up the telephone and instructed all others present not to move. Seconds later a second man, also wearing a stocking mask, entered the bank, scooped up money from tellers' drawers into a bag, and left. The gunman followed, and both men escaped through an alley. The robbery lasted three or four minutes.

"A Government informer, Clarence McFarland, told authorities that he had discussed the robbery with Charles J. Ash, Jr., the respondent here. Acting on this information, an FBI agent, in February 1966, showed five black-and-white mug shots, of Negro males of generally the same age, height, and weight, one of which was of Ash, to four witnesses. All four made uncertain identifications of Ash's picture. At this time Ash was not in custody and had not been charged. On April 1, 1966, an indictment was returned charging Ash and a codefendant, John L. Bailey, in five counts related to this bank robbery.

"Trial was finally set for May 1968, almost three years after the crime. In preparing for trial, the prosecutor decided to use a photographic display to determine whether the witnesses he planned to call would be able to make in-court identifications. Shortly before the trial, an FBI agent and the prosecutor showed five color photographs to the four witnesses who previously had tentatively identified the black-and-white photograph of Ash. Three of the witnesses selected the picture of Ash, but one was unable to make any selection. None of the witnesses selected the picture of Bailey which was in the group. This post-indictment identification provides the basis for respondent Ash's claim that he was denied the right to counsel at a 'critical stage' of the prosecution....

"At trial, the three witnesses who had been inside the bank identified Ash as the gunman, but they were unwilling to state that they were certain of their identifications. None of these made an in-court identification of Bailey. The fourth witness, who had been in a car outside the bank and who had seen the fleeing robbers after they had removed their masks, made positive in-court identifications of both Ash and Bailey. Bailey's counsel then sought to impeach this in-court identification by calling the FBI agent who had shown the color photographs to the witnesses immediately before trial. Bailey's counsel demonstrated that the witness who had identified Bailey in court had failed to identify a color photograph of Bailey. During the course of the examination, Bailey's counsel also, before the jury, brought out the fact that this witness had selected another man as one of the robbers. At this point the prosecutor became concerned that the jury might believe that the witness had selected a third person when, in fact, the witness had selected a photograph of Ash. After a conference at the bench, the trial judge ruled that all five color photographs would be admitted into evidence. The Court of Appeals held that this constituted the introduction of a post-indictment identification at the prosecutor's request and over the objection of defense counsel.

"McFarland testified as a Government witness. He said he had discussed plans for the robbery with Ash before the event and, later, had discussed the results of the robbery with Ash in the presence of Bailey. McFarland was shown to possess an extensive criminal record and a history as an informer.

"The jury convicted Ash on all counts. It was unable to reach a verdict on the charges against Bailey, and his motion for acquittal was granted....

"[A] review of the history and expansion of the Sixth Amendment counsel guarantee demonstrates that the test utilized by the Court has called for examination of the event in order to determine whether the accused required aid in coping with legal problems or assistance in meeting his adversary.

"The structure of *Wade,* viewed in light of the careful limitation of the Court's language to 'confrontations,' makes it clear that lack of scientific precision and inability to reconstruct an event are not the tests for requiring counsel in the first instance. These are, instead, the tests to determine whether confrontation with counsel at trial can serve as a substitute for counsel at the pretrial confrontation. If accurate reconstruction is possible, the risks inherent in any confrontation still remain, but the opportunity to cure defects at trial causes the confrontation to cease to be 'critical.' ...

"A substantial departure from the historical test would be necessary if the Sixth Amendment were interpreted to give Ash a right to counsel at the photographic identification in this case. Since the accused himself is not present at the time of the photographic display, and asserts no right to be present, Brief for the Respondent 40, no possibility arises that the accused might be misled by his lack of familiarity with the law or overpowered by his professional adversary. Similarly, the counsel guarantee would not be used to produce equality in a trial-like adversary confrontation.

"Even if we were willing to view the counsel guarantee in broad terms as a generalized protection of the adversary process, we would be unwilling to go so far as to extend the right to a portion of the prosecutor's trial-preparation interviews with witnesses. Although photography is relatively new, the interviewing of witnesses before trial is a procedure that predates the Sixth Amendment. In England in the 16th and 17th centuries counsel regularly interviewed witnesses before trial. The traditional counterbalance in the American adversary system for these interviews arises from the equal ability of defense counsel to seek and interview witnesses himself.

"That adversary mechanism remains as effective for a photographic display as for other parts of pretrial interviews. No greater limitations are placed on defense counsel in constructing displays, seeking witnesses, and conducting photographic identifications than those applicable to the prosecution. Selection of the picture of a person other than the accused, or the inability of a witness to make any selection, will be useful to the defense in precisely the same manner that the selection of a picture of the defendant would be useful to the prosecution. In this very case, for example, the initial tender of the photographic display was by Bailey's counsel, who sought to demonstrate that the witness had failed to make a photographic identification. Although we do not suggest that equality of access to photographs removes all potential for abuse, it does remove any inequality in the adversary process itself and thereby fully satisfies the historical spirit of the Sixth Amendment's counsel guarantee.

"Pretrial photographic identifications, however, are hardly unique in offering possibilities for the actions of the prosecutor unfairly to prejudice the accused. Evidence favorable to the accused may be withheld; testimony of witnesses may be manipulated; the results of laboratory tests may be contrived. In many ways the prosecutor, by accident or by design, may improperly subvert the trial. The primary safeguard against abuses of this kind is the ethical responsibility of the prosecutor, who, as so often has been said, may 'strike hard blows' but not 'foul ones.' If that safeguard fails, review remains available under due process standards. These same safeguards apply to misuse of photographs.

"We are not persuaded that the risks inherent in the use of photographic displays are so pernicious that an extraordinary system of safeguards is required.

"We hold, then, that the Sixth Amendment does not grant the right to counsel at photographic displays conducted by the Government for the purpose of allowing a witness to attempt an identification of the offender....

"MR. JUSTICE STEWART, concurring in the judgment.

* * *

"A photographic identification is quite different from a lineup, for there are substantially fewer possibilities of impermissible suggestion when photographs are used, and those unfair influences can be readily reconstructed at trial. It is true that the defendant's photograph may be markedly different from the others displayed, but this unfairness can be demonstrated at trial from an actual comparison of the photographs used or from the witness' description of the display. Similarly, it is possible that the photographs could be arranged in a suggestive manner, or that by comment or gesture the prosecuting authorities might single out the defendant's picture. But these are the kinds of overt influence that a witness can easily recount and that would serve to impeach the identification testimony. In short, there are few possibilities for unfair suggestiveness—and those rather blatant and easily reconstructed. Accordingly, an accused would not be foreclosed from an effective cross-examination of an identification witness simply because his counsel was not present at the photographic display. For this reason, a photographic display cannot fairly be considered a 'critical stage' of the prosecution....

"Preparing witnesses for trial by checking their identification testimony against a photographic display is little different, in my view, from the prosecutor's other interviews with the victim or other witnesses before trial. While these procedures can be improperly conducted, the possibility of irretrievable prejudice is remote, since any unfairness that does occur can usually be flushed out at trial through cross-examination of the prosecution witnesses.

"MR. JUSTICE BRENNAN, with whom MR. JUSTICE DOUGLAS and MR. JUSTICE MARSHALL join, dissenting.

Indeed, in reality, preservation of the photographs affords little protection to the unrepresented accused. For although retention of the photographs may mitigate the dangers of misidentification due to the suggestiveness of the photographs themselves, it cannot in any sense reveal to defense counsel the more subtle, and therefore more dangerous, suggestiveness that might derive from the manner in which the photographs were displayed or any accompanying comments or gestures. Moreover, the accused cannot rely upon the witnesses themselves to expose these latter sources of suggestion, for the witnesses are not 'apt to be alert for conditions prejudicial to the suspect. And if they were, it would be of scant benefit to the suspect' since the witnesses are hardly 'likely to be schooled in the detection of suggestive influences.'

"Finally, and *unlike* the lineup situation, the accused himself is not even present at the photographic identification, thereby reducing the likelihood that irregularities in the procedures will ever come to light....

* * *

"The fundamental premise underlying *all* of this Court's decisions holding the right to counsel applicable at 'critical' pretrial proceedings, is that a 'stage' of the prosecution must be deemed 'critical' for the purposes of the Sixth Amendment if it is one at which the presence of counsel is necessary to protect the fairness of *the trial itself.*

"This established conception of the Sixth Amendment guarantee is, of course, in no sense dependent upon the physical 'presence of the accused,' at a 'trial-like confrontation' with the Government, at which the accused requires the 'guiding hand of counsel.'

"There is something ironic about the Court's conclusion today that a pretrial lineup identification is a 'critical stage' of the prosecution because counsel's presence can help to compensate for the accused's deficiencies as an observer, but that a pretrial photographic identification is not a 'critical stage' of the prosecution because the accused is not able to observe at all. In my view, there simply is no meaningful difference, in terms of the need for attendance of counsel, between corporeal and photographic identifications.

5. After the decision in *Ash,* one court, the Supreme Court of Michigan, held that the right to counsel at a photographic identification was required under its own state constitution. People v. Jackson, 391 Mich. 323, 217 N.W.2d 22 (1974). Other state courts have not. For example: State v. Malani, 59 Hawaii 167, 578 P.2d 236 (1978).

6. Assuming that counsel has no right to be present when the police talk to a witness shortly before a lineup, must counsel be permitted to be present when the police interview the witness immediately after the witness views the lineup? Consider United States v. Tolliver, 569 F.2d 724 (2d Cir.1978):

"The Line-Up Procedure

The issue posed is whether the exclusion of counsel from the room where Zima made his identification was an unconstitutional deprivation of appellant's right to counsel at a 'crucial stage of the proceeding'.

In *Wade,* the Court held that a post-indictment line-up was a 'critical' stage in a criminal proceeding and that the Sixth Amendment right of confrontation required the presence of counsel at the line-up. The Court said nothing about when a line-up ends, so that counsel need no longer be present. It can be argued that a line-up is not finished until the witness has declared whether or not he can identify a particular person as the perpetrator of the crime. People v. Williams, 3 Cal.3d 853, 856, 92 Cal.Rptr. 6, 8–9, 478 P.2d 942, 944–45 (1971) (4 to 3). On the other hand, it can be maintained that the purpose for which counsel must be present is essentially to see that the line-up procedure is itself adequate to avoid improper suggestion, such as the wearing of differentiating clothes, or a disparity in appearance between the other persons in the line-up and the suspect himself.

"The Fourth, Fifth and Ninth Circuits have held that the 'confrontation' ends when the defendant is no longer in the presence of the identifying witness, and that his identification may, therefore, be revealed in private to the prosecution, at least in the first instance, without the presence of defense counsel.

"In [the Fourth Circuit case of United States v. Cunningham, 423 F.2d 1269 (1970)], Judge Winter reasoned that '[t]he rationale of these cases is the potential intentional or unintentional suggestion inherent in the actual confrontation and the difficulty of establishing at trial by objective evidence the circumstances under which the line-up proceeded.'

"We now join our sister circuits in holding that the actual identification from a *line-up* (as well as a photographic spread), if made outside the presence of the defendant, is constitutionally valid, since the actual confrontation is the only 'critical stage' requiring the presence of counsel.

"We note, however, that the verbatim recording of the identification or failure of identification is so easy to achieve that it should be considered as an extension of the line-up, even though the 'confrontation' feature ends when the defendant no longer faces the witness. There is no reason why the statement of the witness, even if not made immediately available to the defendant, should not be preserved and made available to defense counsel in time for a pretrial suppression hearing. See ALI, *A Model Code of Pre-Arraignment Procedures* § 160.4 (May 20, 1975). And even when videotape is not available, a tape recording machine is generally procurable without difficulty.

"No recording was made here. We think this was error, but, in the circumstances of this case, harmless error.

"Our problem on this appeal goes beyond the problem faced by the Fourth, Fifth and Ninth Circuits. Those cases did not deal with a refusal by the prosecution to let the defense know who the identifying witness was, nor did they involve a denial of access to him for pretrial interview, as was the case here.

"On the contrary, part of the rationale for holding that defense counsel need not be present at the moment of identification has been thought to be that the witness was made available to defense counsel for interview thereafter and, in any event, before the trial began. In this case, the opposite procedure was followed. The witness was told not to say anything during the line-up while defense counsel was present, and defense counsel was not permitted to learn the identity of the witness until it was flushed out by means of the motion to suppress.

"Discovery of evidence in criminal prosecutions is, inevitably, more restricted than discovery in civil cases.... In strict logic one may, of course, ask why, if the object of discovery is truth, it is not even more important to allow full discovery to a criminal defendant whose liberty is at stake. The conventional answers, which have stood the test of time, are that there is more likelihood of the subornation of perjury by bribery or threat in criminal cases, and that where certain defendants who have been committed to a life of violence are involved, the danger to the safety of the witness outweighs total discovery as a *preliminary* requirement of fair trial. Cross-examination at the trial assisted by such modern aids as the Jencks Act, 18 U.S.C. § 3500, and the limited discovery provided by the Federal Rules of Criminal Procedure, have been thought to be weapons strong enough to prevent miscarriages of justice.

"There is, to be sure, no way to prove the thesis. We may in fact, admit that the prevalence of violence in our social order has led to some weakening of the procedures available to defendants charged with crimes. In consequence, the pervasive fear for the safety of witnesses must, in some respects, adversely affect even the docile type of criminal defendant who would harm no one by physical violence....

* * *

"Even if a constitutional principle were involved, however, we could hardly suggest a neutral principle that separates the potentially violent defendant from others. It has always been the burden of the non-violent criminal to suffer from some of the restrictions imposed for fear of harm from the violent. Here the defendant was a participant in an armed robbery and escape. The third man was unapprehended and at large. We can make no special rule for such a case, but the wisdom, indeed the necessity, for protecting identifying witnesses from harm must be a paramount consideration. We, accordingly, hold that the prosecution may withhold the identity of witnesses on identification, subject to the rules applicable to disclosure of prosecutorial evidence, and, generally, only if the interview after the line-up is recorded and preserved. We believe, moreover, that, before such withholding of identity by the prosecution upon a post-indictment line-up, a direction to permit such procedure should be obtained from the judge *ex parte* as a means of resolving the conflict between a defendant's need for evidence and the Government's claim of privilege based on a finding that the public security requires the withholding. While such a direction was not obtained from Judge Dooling, and the identification interviews were not recorded, the error was harmless here. There can be no doubt that Tolliver was, indeed, the driver of the Cadillac, and the only exculpating evidence presented was defendant's pretrial statement that he was not involved in the robbery, which the jury declined to credit. There was no constitutional or other error in the line-up procedure followed, and even if the refusal to disclose the identity of Zima should be held to be error of constitutional magnitude, it would be 'harmless constitutional error.' "

7. The cases decided after *Wade* and *Gilbert* have held the essential purpose served by counsel at the lineup is that of a witness or observer. Counsel cannot stop a lineup simply by walking away. See Vernon v. State, 12 Md.App. 430, 278 A.2d 609 (1971). There are some inherent problems for defense counsel who appears at a lineup for his client. Does he have a duty to make suggestions about how to make the lineup fairer? If he does make suggestions, should they be designed to produce a fair lineup or one weighted as heavily as possible in favor of his client? A searching criticism of the use of counsel to correct lineup abuses is found in Read, Lawyers at Lineups, Constitutional Necessity or Avoidable Extravagance?, 17 U.C.L.A.L.Rev. 339 (1969). Consider these excerpts:

> "(a) *Those participating may be police officers.*
>
> How will a lawyer's presence change this and is this an evil in and of itself? It must be remembered that the purpose of a lineup is to aid the police in investigating a crime. Certainly it must be conceded that police should be able to participate in their own investigative techniques.
>
> "(b) *The participants' names are rarely divulged.*
>
> The obvious remedy is to require the names to be divulged. In the District of Columbia a 'sheet' is routinely kept, listing the names of those participating in the lineup and the names of the conducting officers. The sheet is available to the defense.

"(c) *The victim is not an effective witness as to what occurred.*

Neither is the defendant's lawyer. Audio and visual recording devices, photographs, and the like are much more effective. Even a lay observer, in the absence of such devices, would probably make a better witness than the defendant's lawyer. It is my view the jury would be much more likely to believe an independent observer than an accused's own attorney testifying on behalf of his client.

"(d) *The victim's outrage may excite 'vengeful or spiteful motives' and the victim will not be alert to conditions prejudicial to the suspect.*

A lawyer's presence will not change this. Only regularized lineup procedures that are faithfully followed can minimize suggestive procedures that may point the victim's outrage at the wrong person.

"(e) *Neither witnesses nor lineup participants are alert for conditions 'prejudicial' to the suspect or schooled in the detection of suggestive influence.*

A lawyer is not necessarily 'schooled' in detecting suggestive influences either. A psychologist might be better equipped for the task. Even assuming the lawyer spots such conditions, what can he do about them except prepare himself to be a witness at trial? Certainly any impartial observer, acquainted with the problem and given examples of what to look for, could do as well as any lawyer. Better yet, since the purpose of a lawyer's presence is to acquaint judge and jury with what occurred, photographs, videotapes, or recordings would do this much more vividly. And adoption of regularized procedures might avoid suggestive conditions in the first place.

"(f) *Jury will not believe a suspect's version of what occurred.*

Will it be much more likely to believe the suspect's lawyer's version of what occurred? Probably not. Therefore, objective reproduction by mechanical devices again will better counter this evil."

Professor Read studied one jurisdiction (District of Columbia) in which efforts were made to provide counsel at lineups. His finding:

"Legal Aid seems to concede that under present conditions there is no real reason for defense counsel to appear at the lineup. First, except for minor alterations, the police will not change their set procedures. Second, there is no one there to record any objection that might be made. Legal Aid personnel seem generally to be of the opinion that the presence of an attorney at a lineup is simply not necessary if the attorney is to take a limited role.

* * *

"Experienced police officers and prosecuting attorneys are convinced that any discovery of a witness' name by some defense attorneys is tantamount to disclosure of that name to that lawyer's client. These same police officers and prosecuting attorneys feel that many prospective witnesses are refusing to participate in lineup procedures because of real fear of retaliation from the accused or friends of the accused once a witness' identity is discovered. A particularly sensitive situation evidently exists in the District of Columbia. It was reported that fear of physical intimidation seems especially acute among many Negro witnesses and victims of crime who are asked to cooperate with the police. Police officers charged that the real problem with the lineups is not that witnesses are too susceptible to suggestion but, on the contrary, witnesses are too reluctant to participate freely in the process. Several defense attorneys conceded that a serious problem of witness intimidation does exist and that Wade's command that a lawyer be present at lineups may have exacerbated the situation.

"Another vigorously raised complaint of police and prosecution attorneys relates to the conduct of defense counsel in altering the appearance of their clients prior to their client's participation in a lineup. For example, a young defendant may be arrested while sporting a mustache, an 'Afro haircut' and very bright clothing. When he shows up for the lineup, his Afro haircut is removed, his mustache is shaved off, and he is wearing a suit and tie. An extreme example of this occurred when a female impersonator was arrested in his feminine disguise and then showed up for the lineup in typical male attire. The United States Attorney's Office thus feels that intimidation and disguise of suspects by defense lawyers is the 'other side of the coin' from the suggestive influence problem."

[Ed. Note. The incident of changed appearance cited by Professor Read is quite similar to that which occurred in United States v. Jackson, 476 F.2d 249 (7th Cir.1973)]:

"My observations and conversations with police, prosecuting attorneys and defense attorneys have convinced me that the lineup is a necessary tool in the arsenal of investigatory techniques available to the police. However, it is also my view that the presence of defense counsel at a lineup is simply not necessary to insure the fairness of the procedure. His passive role renders him basically impotent; he is unable to change the slightest detail in any way unless the police decide to cooperate; he is unable to make and have recorded any objections he may have; and he has no way of preserving what occurred except through his own notes and memory.

"Not only is the defense lawyer's presence only minimally effective in preventing unfairness and preserving a record of what occurred, his presence, in certain cases, can actually hinder the administration of criminal justice. Some lawyers have turned the lineup, a police investigatory technique, into a discovery proceeding. A serious danger of intimidation exists in many cases when the identity of witnesses is discovered and disclosed to defendants. Furthermore, by drastically altering the appearance of defendants, defense counsel can actually nullify the usefulness of the lineup process as an investigatory tool. Wade was intended to protect an accused from suggestive lineup procedures; however, in certain cases, the real effect of the Wade remedy is to destroy the utility of the lineup procedure and to make intimidation of witnesses easier."

8. In *Wade* it was suggested that "Legislative or other regulations, such as those of local police departments, which eliminate the risk of abuse and unintentional suggestion at lineup proceedings and the impediments to meaningful confrontation at trial may also remove the basis for regarding the stage as 'critical' ", United States v. Wade, 388 U.S. at 239, 87 S.Ct. 1938. Yet, that language was explicitly disavowed by four of six Justices joining in the opinion.

(Black, J. and Fortas, J. joined by Warren, C.J. and Douglas J.). A fifth Justice implicitly rejected the proposition. (Clark, J.).

The only attempt to rely on the suggestion that regulations might obviate the right to counsel has been rebuffed with the reasoning that such regulations would be adequate only if they succeeded in elevating eyewitness identification procedures to the level of reliability present in procedures for analyzing fingerprints, blood samples and hair. See People v. Fowler, 1 Cal.3d 355, 82 Cal.Rptr. 363, 372, 461 P.2d 643, 652 (1969). If this is the standard to be met by legislation or regulation, then is acceptable regulation possible? Is this the appropriate standard by which to judge lineup regulations?

B. SUGGESTIVENESS IN IDENTIFICATION PROCEDURES

MANSON v. BRATHWAITE

Supreme Court of the United States, 1977.
432 U.S. 98, 97 S.Ct. 2243.

MR. JUSTICE BLACKMUN delivered the opinion of the Court.

This case presents the issue as to whether the Due Process Clause of the Fourteenth Amendment compels the exclusion, in a state criminal trial, apart from any consideration of reliability, of pretrial identification evidence obtained by a police procedure that was both suggestive and unnecessary.

I

Jimmy D. Glover, a full-time trooper of the Connecticut State Police, in 1970 was assigned to the Narcotics Division in an undercover capacity. On May 5 of that year, about 7:45 p.m. E.D.T. and while there was still daylight, Glover and Henry Alton Brown, an informant, went to an apartment building at 201 Westland, in Hartford, for the purpose of purchasing narcotics from "Dickie Boy" Cicero, a known narcotics dealer. Cicero, it was thought, lived on the third floor of that apartment building. Glover and Brown entered the building, observed by back-up Officers D'Onofrio and Gaffey, and proceeded by stairs to the third floor. Glover knocked at the door of one of the two apartments served by the stairway. The area was illuminated by natural light from a window in the third floor hallway. The door was opened 12 to 18 inches in response to the knock. Glover observed a man standing at the door and, behind him, a woman. Brown identified himself. Glover then asked for "two things" of narcotics. The man at the door held out his hand, and Glover gave him two $10 bills. The door closed. Soon the man returned and handed Glover two glassine bags. While the door was open, Glover stood within two feet of the person from whom he made the purchase and observed his face. Five to seven minutes elapsed from the time the door first opened until it closed the second time.

Glover and Brown then left the building. This was about eight minutes after their arrival. Glover drove to headquarters where he described the seller to D'Onofrio and Gaffey. Glover at that time did not know the identity of the seller. He described him as being "a colored man, approximately five feet eleven inches tall, dark complexion, black hair, short Afro style, and having high cheekbones, and of heavy build. He was wearing at the time blue pants and a plaid shirt." D'Onofrio, suspecting from this description that respondent might be the seller, obtained a photograph of respondent from the Records Division of the Hartford Police Department. He left it at Glover's office. D'Onofrio was not acquainted with respondent personally, but did know him by sight and had seen him "[s]everal times" prior to May 5. Glover, when alone, viewed the photograph for the first time upon his return to headquarters on May 7; he identified the person shown as the one from whom he had purchased the narcotics.

The toxicological report on the contents of the glassine bags revealed the presence of heroin. The report was dated July 16, 1970.

Respondent was arrested on July 27 while visiting at the apartment of a Mrs. Ramsey on the third floor of 201 Westland. This was the apartment at which the narcotics sale had taken place on May 5.

Respondent was charged, in a two-count information, with possession and sale of heroin. At his trial in January 1971, the photograph from which Glover had identified respondent was received in evidence without objection on the part of the defense. Glover also testified that, although he had not seen respondent in the eight months that had elapsed since the sale, "there [was] no doubt whatsoever" in his mind that the person shown on the photograph was respondent. Glover also made a positive in-court identification without objection.

No explanation was offered by the prosecution for the failure to utilize a photographic array or to conduct a lineup....

The jury found respondent guilty on both counts of the information.

II

Stovall v. Denno, [1967], concerned a petitioner who had been convicted in a New York court of murder. He was arrested the day following the crime and was taken by the police to a hospital where the victim's wife, also wounded in the assault, was a patient. After observing Stovall and hearing him speak, she identified him as the murderer. She later made an in-court identification. This Court affirmed. On the identification issue, the Court reviewed the practice of showing a suspect singly for purposes of identification, and the claim that this was so unnecessarily suggestive and conducive to irreparable mistaken identification that it constituted a denial of due process of law. The Court noted that the practice "has been widely condemned," but it concluded that "a claimed violation of due process of law in the conduct of a confrontation depends on the totality of the circumstances surrounding it." In that case, showing Stovall to the victim's spouse "was imperative." The Court then [OBSERVED] that the spouse was the only person who could possibly exonerate the accused; that the hospital was not far from the courthouse and jail; that no one knew how long she might live; that she was not able to visit the jail; and that taking Stovall to the hospital room was the only feasible procedure, and, under the circumstances, " 'the usual police station line-up ... was out of the question.' "

Neil v. Biggers, [1972], concerned a respondent who had been convicted in a Tennessee court of rape, on evidence consisting in part of the victim's visual and voice identification of Biggers at a station-house showup seven months after the crime. The victim had been in her assailant's presence for some time and had directly observed him indoors and under a full moon outdoors. She testified that she had "no doubt" that Biggers was her assailant. She previously had given the police a description of the assailant. She had made no identification of others presented at previous showups, lineups, or through photographs. This Court held that the evidence properly had been allowed to go to the jury. The Court reviewed Stovall and certain later cases where it had considered the scope of due process protection against the admission of evidence derived from suggestive identification procedures, namely, Simmons v. United States (1968); Foster v. California (1969); and Coleman v. Alabama (1970).[2] The Court concluded that general guidelines emerged from these cases "as to the relationship between suggestiveness and misidentification." The "admission of evidence of a showup without more does not violate due process." The Court expressed concern about the lapse of seven months between the crime and the confrontation and observed that this "would be a seriously negative factor in most cases." The "central question," however, was "whether under the 'totality of the circumstances' the identification was reliable even though the confrontation procedure was suggestive." Applying that test, the Court found "no substantial likelihood of misidentification. The evidence was properly allowed to go to the jury."

* * *

2. Simmons involved photographs, mostly group ones, shown to bankteller victims who made in-court identifications. The Court discussed the "chance of misidentification," declined to prohibit the procedure "either in the exercise of our supervisory power or, still less, as a matter of constitutional requirement," and held that each case must be considered on its facts and that a conviction would be set aside only if the identification procedure "was so impermissibly suggestive as to give rise to a very substantial likelihood of irreparable misidentification." The out-of-court identification was not offered. Mr. Justice Black would have denied Simmons' due process claim as frivolous.

Foster concerned repeated confrontations between a suspect and the manager of an office that had been robbed. At a second lineup, but not at the first and not at a personal one-to-one confrontation, the manager identified the suspect. At trial he testified as to this and made an in-court identification. The Court reaffirmed the Stovall standard and then concluded that the repeated confrontations were so suggestive as to violate due process. The case was remanded for the state courts to consider the question of harmless error.

In Coleman a plurality of the Court was of the view that the trial court did not err when it found that the victim's in-court identifications did not stem from a lineup procedure so impermissibly suggestive as to give rise to a substantial likelihood of misidentification.

Biggers well might be seen to provide an unambiguous answer to the question before us: the admission of testimony concerning a suggestive and unnecessary identification procedure does not violate due process so long as the identification possesses sufficient aspects of reliability.[3] In one passage, however, the Court observed that the challenged procedure occurred pre-*Stovall* and that a strict rule would make little sense with regard to a confrontation that preceded the Court's first indication that a suggestive procedure might lead to the exclusion of evidence. One perhaps might argue that, by implication, the Court suggested that a different rule could apply post-*Stovall.* The question before us, then, is simply whether the *Biggers* analysis applies to post-*Stovall* confrontations as well as to those pre-*Stovall.*

III

In the present case the "sole evidence tying Brathwaite to the possession and sale of the heroin consisted in his identifications by the police undercover agent, Jimmy Glover."

* * *

IV

The State at the outset acknowledges that "the procedure in the instant case was suggestive [because only one photograph was used] and unnecessary" [because there was no emergency or exigent circumstance]. The respondent proposes a *per se* rule of exclusion that he claims is dictated by the demands of the Fourteenth Amendment's guarantee of due process. He rightly observes that this is the first case in which this Court has had occasion to rule upon strictly post-*Stovall* out-of-court identification evidence of the challenged kind.

Since the decision in *Biggers,* the courts of appeals appear to have developed at least two approaches to such evidence. The first, or *per se* approach, employed by the Second Circuit in the present case, focuses on

3. Mr. Justice Marshall argues in dissent that our cases have "established two different due process tests for two very different situations." Pretrial identifications are to be covered by Stovall, which is said to require exclusion of evidence concerning unnecessarily suggestive pretrial identifications without regard to reliability. In-court identifications, on the other hand, are to be governed by Simmons and admissibility turns on reliability. The Court's cases are sorted into one category or the other. Biggers, which clearly adopts the reliability of the identification as the guiding factor in the admissibility of both pretrial and in-court identifications, is condemned for mixing the two lines and for adopting a uniform rule.

Although it must be acknowledged that our cases are not uniform in their emphasis, they hardly suggest the formal structure the dissent would impose on them. If our cases truly established two different rules, one might expect at some point at least passing reference to the fact. There is none. And if Biggers departed so grievously from the past cases, it is surprising that there was not at least some mention of the point in Mr. Justice Brennan's dissent. In fact, the cases are not so readily sorted as the dissent suggests. Although Foster involved both in-court and out-of-court identifications, the Court seemed to apply only a single standard for both. And although Coleman involved only an in-court identification, the plurality cited Stovall for the guiding rule that the claim was to be assessed on the "totality of the surrounding circumstances." Thus, Biggers is not properly seen as a departure from the past cases, but as a synthesis of them.

the procedures employed and requires exclusion of the out-of-court identification evidence, without regard to reliability, whenever it has been obtained through unnecessarily suggested confrontation procedures.[4] The justifications advanced are the elimination of evidence of uncertain reliability, deterrence of the police and prosecutors, and the stated "fair assurance against the awful risks of misidentification."

The second, or more lenient, approach is one that continues to rely on the totality of the circumstances. It permits the admission of the confrontation evidence if, despite the suggestive aspect, the out-of-court identification possesses certain features of reliability. Its adherents feel that the *per se* approach is not mandated by the Due Process Clause of the Fourteenth Amendment. This second approach, in contrast to the other, is *ad hoc* and serves to limit the societal costs imposed by a sanction that excludes relevant evidence from consideration and evaluation by the trier of fact.

The respondent here stresses the need for deterrence of improper identification practice, a factor he regards as pre-eminent. Photographic identification, it is said, continues to be needlessly employed. He notes that the legislative regulation "the Court hoped *Wade* would engender" has not been forthcoming. He argues that a totality rule cannot be expected to have a significant deterrent impact; only a strict rule of exclusion will have direct and immediate impact on law enforcement agents. Identification evidence is so convincing to the jury that sweeping exclusionary rules are required. Fairness of the trial is threatened by suggestive confrontation evidence, and thus, it is said, an exclusionary rule has an established constitutional predicate.

There are, of course, several interests to be considered and taken into account.... *Wade* and its companion cases reflect the concern that the jury not hear eyewitness testimony unless that evidence has aspects of reliability. It must be observed that both approaches before us are responsive to this concern. The *per se* rule, however, goes too far since its application automatically and peremptorily, and without consideration of alleviating factors, keeps evidence from the jury that is reliable and relevant.

The second factor is deterrence. Although the *per se* approach has the more significant deterrent effect, the totality approach also has an influence on police behavior. The police will guard against unnecessarily suggestive procedures under the totality rule, as well as the *per se* one, for fear that their actions will lead to the exclusion of identifications as unreliable.

The third factor is the effect on the administration of justice. Here the *per se* approach suffers serious drawbacks. Since it denies the trier

4. Although the *per se* approach demands the exclusion of testimony concerning unnecessarily suggestive identifications, it does permit the admission of testimony concerning a subsequent identification, including an in-court identification, if the subsequent identification is determined to be reliable. The totality approach, in contrast, is simpler: if the challenged identification is reliable, then testimony as to it and any identification in its wake is admissible.

reliable evidence, it may result, on occasion, in the guilty going free. Also, because of its rigidity, the *per se* approach may make error by the trial judge more likely than the totality approach. And in those cases in which the admission of identification evidence is error under the *per se* approach but not under the totality approach—cases in which the identification is reliable despite an unnecessarily suggestive identification procedure—reversal is a draconian sanction. Certainly, inflexible rules of exclusion, that may frustrate rather than promote justice, have not been viewed recently by this Court with unlimited enthusiasm.

* * *

The standard, after all, is that of fairness as required by the Due Process Clause of the Fourteenth Amendment.

We therefore conclude that reliability is the linchpin in determining the admissibility of identification testimony for both pre- and post-*Stovall* confrontations. The factors to be considered are set out in *Biggers*. These include the opportunity of the witness to view the criminal at the time of the crime, the witness' degree of attention, the accuracy of his prior description of the criminal, the level of certainty demonstrated at the confrontation, and the time between the crime and the confrontation. Against these factors is to be weighed the corrupting effect of the suggestive identification itself.

V

We turn, then, to the facts of this case and apply the analysis:

1. The opportunity to view. Glover testified that for two to three minutes he stood at the apartment door, within two feet of the respondent. The door opened twice, and each time the man stood at the door. The moments passed, the conversation took place, and payment was made. Glover looked directly at his vendor. It was near sunset, to be sure, but the sun had not yet set, so it was not dark or even dusk or twilight. Natural light from outside entered the hallway through a window. There was natural light, as well, from inside the apartment.

2. The degree of attention. Glover was not a casual or passing observer, as is so often the case with eyewitness identification. Trooper Glover was a trained police officer on duty—and specialized and dangerous duty—when he called at the third floor of 201 Westland in Hartford on May 5, 1970. Glover himself was a Negro and unlikely to perceive only general features of "hundreds of Hartford black males," as the Court of Appeals stated. It is true that Glover's duty was that of ferreting out narcotics offenders and that he would be expected in his work to produce results. But it is also true that, as a specially trained, assigned, and experienced officer, he could be expected to pay scrupulous attention to detail, for he knew that subsequently he would have to find and arrest his vendor. In addition, he knew that his claimed observations would be subject later to close scrutiny and examination at any trial.

3. The accuracy of the description. Glover's description was given to D'Onofrio within minutes after the transaction. It included the vendor's race, his height, his build, the color and style of his hair, and the high cheekbone facial feature. It also included clothing the vendor wore. No claim has been made that respondent did not possess the physical characteristics so described. D'Onofrio reacted positively at once. Two days later, when Glover was alone, he viewed the photograph D'Onofrio produced and identified its subject as the narcotics seller.

4. The witness' level of certainty. There is no dispute that the photograph in question was that of respondent. Glover, in response to a question whether the photograph was that of the person from whom he made the purchase, testified: "There is no question whatsoever." This positive assurance was repeated.

5. The time between the crime and the confrontation. Glover's description of his vendor was given to D'Onofrio within minutes of the crime. The photographic identification took place only two days later. We do not have here the passage of weeks or months between the crime and the viewing of the photograph.

These indicators of Glover's ability to make an accurate identification are hardly outweighed by the corrupting effect of the challenged identification itself. Although identifications arising from single-photograph displays may be viewed in general with suspicion, we find in the instant case little pressure on the witness to acquiesce in the suggestion that such a display entails. D'Onofrio had left the photograph at Glover's office and was not present when Glover first viewed it two days after the event. There thus was little urgency and Glover could view the photograph at his leisure. And since Glover examined the photograph alone, there was no coercive pressure to make an identification arising from the presence of another. The identification was made in circumstances allowing care and reflection.

* * *

Surely, we cannot say that under all the circumstances of this case there is "a very substantial likelihood of irreparable misidentification." Simmons v. United States. Short of that point, such evidence is for the jury to weigh. We are content to rely upon the good sense and judgment of American juries, for evidence with some element of untrustworthiness is customary grist for the jury mill. Juries are not so susceptible that they cannot measure intelligently the weight of identification testimony that has some questionable feature.

We conclude that the criteria laid down in *Biggers* are to be applied in determining the admissibility of evidence offered by the prosecution concerning a post-*Stovall* identification, and that those criteria are satisfactorily met and complied with here.

MR. JUSTICE STEVENS, concurring.

While I join the Court's opinion, I would emphasize two points.

First, as I indicated in my opinion in United States ex rel. Kirby v. Sturges, 510 F.2d 397, 405–406 (7th Cir.1975), the arguments in favor of fashioning new rules to minimize the danger of convicting the innocent on the basis of unreliable eyewitness testimony carry substantial force. Nevertheless, for the reasons stated in that opinion, as well as those stated by the Court today, I am persuaded that this rulemaking function can be performed "more effectively by the legislative process than by a somewhat clumsy judicial fiat," and that the Federal Constitution does not foreclose experimentation by the States in the development of such rules.

Second, in evaluating the admissibility of particular identification testimony it is sometimes difficult to put other evidence of guilt entirely to one side.[5]

MR. JUSTICE BLACKMUN'S opinion for the Court carefully avoids this pitfall and correctly relies only on appropriate indicia of the reliability of the identification itself. Although I consider the factual question in this case extremely close, I am persuaded that the Court has resolved it properly.

MR. JUSTICE MARSHALL, with whom MR. JUSTICE BRENNAN joins, dissenting.

Today's decision can come as no surprise to those who have been watching the Court dismantle the protections against mistaken eyewitness testimony erected a decade ago in *Wade, Gilbert,* and Stovall v. Denno. But it is still distressing to see the Court virtually ignore the teaching of experience embodied in those decisions and blindly uphold the conviction of a defendant who may well be innocent.

The development of due process protections against mistaken identification evidence, begun in *Stovall,* was continued in Simmons v. United States (1968). There, the Court developed a different rule to deal with the admission of in-court identification testimony that the accused claimed had been fatally tainted by a previous suggestive confrontation. In *Simmons,* the exclusionary effect of *Stovall* had already been accomplished, since the prosecution made no use of the suggestive confrontation. *Simmons,* therefore, did not deal with the constitutionality of the pretrial identification procedure. The only question was the impact of the Due Process Clause on an in-court identification that was not itself unnecessarily suggestive. *Simmons* held that due process was violated by the later identification if the pretrial procedure had been "so impermissibly suggestive as to give rise to a very substantial likelihood of irreparable misidentification." This test focused not on the necessity for

5. In this case, for example, the fact that the defendant was a regular visitor to the apartment where the drug transaction occurred tends to confirm his guilt. In the *Kirby* case, supra, where the conviction was for robbery, the fact that papers from the victim's wallet were found in the possession of the defendant made it difficult to question the reliability of the identification. These facts should not, however, be considered to support the admissibility of eyewitness testimony when applying the criteria identified in *Biggers.* Properly analyzed, however, such facts would be relevant to a question whether error, if any, in admitting identification testimony was harmless.

the challenged pretrial procedure, but on the degree of suggestiveness that it entailed. In applying this test, the Court understandably considered the circumstances surrounding the witnesses' initial opportunity to view the crime. Finding that any suggestion in the pretrial confrontation had not affected the fairness of the in-court identification, *Simmons* rejected petitioner's due process attack on his conviction.

Again, comparison with the *Wade* cases is instructive. The inquiry mandated by *Simmons* is similar to the independent source test used in *Wade* where an in-court identification is sought following an uncounseled lineup. In both cases, the issue is whether the witness is identifying the defendant solely on the basis of his memory of events at the time of the crime, or whether he is merely remembering the person he picked out in a pretrial procedure. Accordingly, in both situations, the relevant inquiry includes factors bearing on the accuracy of the witness' identification, including his opportunity to view the crime.

Thus, *Stovall* and *Simmons* established two different due process tests for two very different situations. Where the prosecution sought to use evidence of a questionable pretrial identification, *Stovall* required its exclusion, because due process had been violated by the confrontation, unless the necessity for the unduly suggestive procedure outweighed its potential for generating an irreparably mistaken identification. The *Simmons* test, on the other hand, was directed to ascertaining due process violations in the introduction of in-court identification testimony that the defendant claimed was tainted by pretrial procedures. In the latter situation, a court could consider the reliability of the identification under all the circumstances.

* * *

The Court inexplicably seemed to erase the distinction between *Stovall* and *Simmons* situations in Neil v. Biggers.

* * *

Apparently, the Court does not consider *Biggers* controlling in this case. I entirely agree, since I believe that *Biggers* was wrongly decided. The Court, however, concludes that *Biggers* is distinguishable because it, like the identification decisions that preceded it, involved a pre-*Stovall* confrontation, and because a paragraph in *Biggers* itself seems to distinguish between pre- and post-*Stovall* confrontations. Accordingly, in determining the admissibility of the post-*Stovall* identification in this case, the Court considers two alternatives, a *per se* exclusionary rule and a totality of the circumstances approach. The Court weighs three factors in deciding that the totality approach, which is essentially the test used in *Biggers,* should be applied. In my view, the Court wrongly evaluates the impact of these factors.

First, the Court acknowledges that one of the factors, deterrence of police use of unnecessarily suggestive identification procedures, favors the *per se* rule. Indeed, it does so heavily, for such a rule would make it unquestionably clear to the police they must never use a suggestive procedure when a fairer alternative is available. I have no doubt that conduct would quickly conform to the rule.

Second, the Court gives passing consideration to the dangers of eyewitness identification recognized in the *Wade* trilogy. It concludes, however, that the grave risk of error does not justify adoption of the *per se* approach because that would too often result in exclusion of relevant evidence. In my view, this conclusion totally ignores the lessons of *Wade*. The dangers of mistaken identification are, as *Stovall* held, simply too great to permit unnecessarily suggestive identifications. Neither *Biggers* nor the Court's opinion today point to any contrary empirical evidence. Studies since *Wade* have only reinforced the validity of its assessment of the dangers of identification testimony. While the Court is "content to rely on the good sense and judgment of American juries," the impetus for *Stovall* and *Wade* was repeated miscarriages of justice resulting from juries' willingness to credit inaccurate eyewitness testimony.

Finally, the Court errs in its assessment of the relative impact of the two approaches on the administration of justice. The Court relies most heavily on this factor finding that "reversal is a draconian sanction" in cases where the identification is reliable despite an unnecessarily suggestive procedure used to obtain it. Relying on little more than a strong distaste for "inflexible rules of exclusion," the Court rejects the *per se* test. In so doing, the Court disregards two significant distinctions between the *per se* rule advocated in this case and the exclusionary remedies for certain other constitutional violations.

First, the *per se* rule here is not "inflexible." Where evidence is suppressed, for example, as the fruit of an unlawful search, it may well be forever lost to the prosecution. Identification evidence, however, can by its very nature be readily and effectively reproduced. The in-court identification, permitted under *Wade* and *Simmons* if it has a source independent of an uncounseled or suggestive procedure, is one example. Similarly, when a prosecuting attorney learns that there has been a suggestive confrontation, he can easily arrange another lineup conducted under scrupulously fair conditions. Since the same factors are evaluated in applying both the Court's totality test and the *Wade-Simmons* independent source inquiry, any identification which is "reliable" under the Court's test will support admission of evidence concerning such a fairly conducted lineup. The evidence of an additional, properly conducted confrontation will be more persuasive to a jury, thereby increasing the chance of a justified conviction where a reliable identification was tainted by a suggestive confrontation. At the same time, however, the effect of an unnecessarily suggestive identification—which has no value whatsoever in the law enforcement process—will be completely eliminated.

Second, other exclusionary rules have been criticized for preventing jury consideration of relevant and usually reliable evidence in order to serve interests unrelated to guilt or innocence, such as discouraging illegal searches or denial of counsel. Suggestively obtained eyewitness testimony is excluded, in contrast, precisely because of its unreliability and concomitant irrelevance. Its exclusion both protects the integrity of the truth-seeking function of the trial and discourages police use of needlessly inaccurate and ineffective investigatory methods.

Indeed, impermissibly suggestive identifications are not merely worthless law enforcement tools. They pose a grave threat to society at large in a more direct way than most governmental disobedience of the law. For if the police and the public erroneously conclude, on the basis of an unnecessarily suggestive confrontation, that the right man has been caught and convicted, the real outlaw must still remain at large. Law enforcement has failed in its primary function and has left society unprotected from the depredations of an active criminal.

For these reasons, I conclude that adoption of the *per se* rule would enhance, rather than detract from, the effective administration of justice. In my view, the Court's totality test will allow seriously unreliable and misleading evidence to be put before juries. Equally important, it will allow dangerous criminals to remain on the streets while citizens assume that police action has given them protection. According to my calculus, all three of the factors upon which the Court relies point to acceptance of the *per se* approach.

Even more disturbing than the Court's reliance on the totality test, however, is the analysis it uses, which suggests a reinterpretation of the concept of due process of law in criminal cases. The decision suggests that due process violations in identification procedures may not be measured by whether the Government employed procedures violating standards of fundamental fairness. By relying on the probable accuracy of a challenged identification, instead of the necessity for its use, the Court seems to be ascertaining whether the defendant was probably guilty. Until today, I had thought that "Equal justice under law" meant that the existence of constitutional violations did not depend on the race, sex, religion, nationality or likely guilt of the accused. The Due Process Clause requires adherence to the same high standard of fundamental fairness in dealing with every criminal defendant, whatever his personal characteristics and irrespective of the strength of the State's case against him. Strong evidence that the defendant is guilty should be relevant only to the determination whether an error of constitutional magnitude was nevertheless harmless beyond a reasonable doubt. See Chapman v. California (1967). By importing the question of guilt into the initial determination of whether there was a constitutional violation, the apparent effect of the Court's decision is to undermine the protection afforded by the Due Process Clause. It is therefore important to note that the state courts remain free, in interpreting state constitutions, to guard against the evil clearly identified by this case.

* * *

Despite my strong disagreement with the Court over the proper standards to be applied in this case, I am pleased that its application of the totality test does recognize the continuing vitality of *Stovall.* In assessing the reliability of the identification, the Court mandates weighing "the corrupting effect of the challenged identification itself" against the "indicators of [a witness'] ability to make an accurate identification." The Court holds, as Neil v. Biggers failed to, that a due process identification inquiry must take account of the suggestiveness of a confrontation and the likelihood that it led to misidentification, as recognized in *Stovall* and *Wade.* Thus, even if a witness did have an otherwise adequate opportunity to view a criminal, the later use of a highly suggestive identification procedure can render his testimony inadmissible. Indeed, it is my view that, assuming applicability of the totality test enunciated by the Court, the facts of the present case require that result.

* * *

NOTES

1. The testimony of an eyewitness is subject to a complex set of exclusionary rules. Evidence of pre-trial identification (testimony by the witness on direct examination that he attended a lineup and picked out the defendant as the offender) is subject to one per se rule of exclusion. If the pre-trial confrontation is conducted in violation of the right to counsel (Wade-Gilbert), evidence of the pre-trial confrontation is excluded. A similar per se rule of exclusion for cases involving unnecessarily suggestive confrontations was rejected in Manson v. Brathwaite, but it was adopted as a matter of state law in People v. Adams, 53 N.Y.2d 241, 440 N.Y.S.2d 902, 423 N.E.2d 379 (1981) and in Commonwealth v. Johnson, 420 Mass. 458, 650 N.E.2d 1257 (1995) (under state constitution suggestive procedures lead to suppression of evidence even if identification at the procedure was reliable). In *Manson* the Court adopted a rule admitting evidence of suggestive confrontations if the identification possesses sufficient aspects of reliability; to exclude there must be "a very substantial likelihood of irreparable mistaken identification." Evidence of in-court identification (i.e. testimony by the witness that the offender is the defendant sitting in the courtroom) is subject to derivative exclusionary rules. If, and only if, the Court has found that the pre-trial confrontation violates one (or both) of the per se exclusionary rules, will there be suppression of evidence of in-court identification. People v. Rodriguez, 10 Cal.App.3d 18, 88 Cal.Rptr. 789 (1970). However, if the prosecution can prove by clear and convincing evidence that the in-court identification has a source independent of the illegal pre-trial confrontation, then evidence of the in-court identification is admissible.

In determining whether there was an independent source of an in-court identification, several factors are considered. The most common of these are:

> (1) prior opportunity of witnesses to observe the criminal act, (2) existence of a discrepancy between any pre-lineup description and the actual appearance of the accused, (3) any identification of another person prior to the lineup, (4) failure to identify the accused on a prior occasion, (5) lapse of time between the criminal act and the lineup identification, (6) prior photographic identification from a large group of photographs, (7) the presence of distinctive physical characteristics in defendant, (8) prior acquaintance of witness with the suspect, (9) ability

and training at identification, (10) the exercise of unusual care to make observations, (11) prompt identification at first confrontation.

See United States ex rel. Geralds v. Deegan, 292 F.Supp. 968 (S.D.N.Y.1968) and 307 F.Supp. 56 (S.D.N.Y.1969), and People v. Kachar, 400 Mich. 78, 252 N.W.2d 807 (1977).

If the trial court decides to suppress evidence of pre-trial confrontation but refuses to suppress evidence of in-court identification, the defense has the option to bring the pre-trial confrontation out at trial if it is thought helpful to a defense attack on the courtroom identification. Davis v. State, 467 P.2d 521 (Okl.Cr.1970). If the defense brings out some of the facts concerning the pre-trial confrontation, the state may bring out the rest of the circumstances. Commonwealth v. Redmond, 357 Mass. 333, 258 N.E.2d 287 (1970).

An error in the admission of identification evidence does not constitute automatic reversible error. Such errors may be harmless. See Gilbert v. California, 388 U.S. 263, 274, 87 S.Ct. 1951 (1967); United States v. Wade, 388 U.S. 218, 242, 87 S.Ct. 1926 (1967).

2. The due process clause condemns confrontations which are "unnecessarily suggestive and conducive to irreparable mistaken identification." Stovall v. Denno, supra, which announced this rule also upheld a confrontation with a witness thought to be near death because the procedure was *necessarily* suggestive.

Are there any other forms of necessarily suggestive confrontations? Consider the 6′ 10″ or the 4′ 10″ suspect, or the suspect with prominent scars or tattoos. See State v. Mallette, 159 Conn. 143, 267 A.2d 438 (1970); People v. Faulkner, 28 Cal.App.3d 384, 104 Cal.Rptr. 625 (1972). Consider also the suspect who engages in conduct which attracts attention, i.e., protests his arrest, buries his head in his hands, etc. See United States v. Holsey, 437 F.2d 250 (10th Cir.1970); People v. Nelson, 40 Ill.2d 146, 238 N.E.2d 378 (1968). What value has the notion that in difficult cases the police ought to use photographic identification procedures? Is the notion based on the assumption that eyewitness identification is based exclusively on facial characteristics? If so, is that a valid assumption? Is photographic identification as reliable as corporeal identification? In the last analysis does the presence of unusual physical characteristics make identification more or less reliable? If a suspect is so unusual that he cannot be placed in an adequate line-up, is it fairer to use a one to one "showup"?

The question of when a flawed procedure is necessary is addressed in Commonwealth v. Austin, 421 Mass. 357, 657 N.E.2d 458 (1995):

GREANEY, JUSTICE.

On February 20, 1990, an armed man entered the First Federal Savings Bank in Somerset and attempted to rob it. Laurie Gervasio and Jeanie Mizher, employees of the bank, witnessed the attempted robbery. They described the gunman as approximately six feet tall, slender, fair skinned, wearing a knit cap and a tan or gold overcoat. They described his face as long and thin and stated that he had an extremely large nose and very distinctive nervous mannerisms. The man fled the bank after seeing a police officer through the bank window. The officer pursued the robber, who fired shots at his pursuer at least twice. Several minutes later, while making his escape in a waiting vehicle, the robber also fired his gun at some bystanders.

Gervasio testified that the robber walked within three feet of her desk as he approached the teller. She had a clear view of him and observed him throughout the robbery. Mizher also had an unobstructed view of the robber. Her attention was drawn to him when he yelled instructions to the teller. Mizher watched him until he left the bank, approximately three minutes later.

After the robbery, Gervasio went to the East Providence police station to view two lineups of eight men each. She did not see the robber among these individuals. She then went to the Somerset police station and assisted an officer in making a composite drawing of the robber. The day following the attempted robbery, Mizher and Gervasio separately viewed about 200 color photographs. Neither witness selected a photograph from this array. Both women stated that they were positive they could identify the robber if they saw him again.

Two days later, on February 23, the two women were shown another photographic array consisting of eight photographs. Neither identified the robber from this array. However, Mizher selected a photograph from this array as a picture which might give the police some idea of the robber's appearance. She was sure the person depicted in this photograph was not the robber.[1]

On February 23, there was an armed bank robbery in Rhode Island. The robber was not apprehended, but the robbery was recorded by the bank's surveillance camera. The police watched the videotape of the robbery and noticed that the individual on the videotape (Rhode Island robber) resembled Gervasio's composite drawing of the Somerset robber. The mannerisms displayed by the Rhode Island robber, and the similar modus operandi, led the police to believe that the two banks had been robbed by the same individual. Also on February 23, a Somerset detective learned from a colleague of a recent armed bank robbery in Salem, New Hampshire, having characteristics similar to the Somerset and Rhode Island robberies.

On February 24, the police showed the videotape to Gervasio. She was warned to remain unbiased as she watched it. Within seconds of observing the man on the videotape, Gervasio stated that he was the man who robbed the Somerset bank. The police later showed the videotape to Mizher who also identified the man, without hesitation, as the Somerset bank robber.

On February 26, the East Providence police department began showing the surveillance videotape to its officers as they came on duty. Two police officers who were former correction officers recognized the man in the videotape as Thomas Austin, who had previously been incarcerated. The police obtained two photographs of the defendant and placed one of them in a photographic array consisting of twelve photographs. This array was shown to both witnesses. Mizher chose the defendant's photograph immediately. Gervasio stated that the defendant's photograph resembled the robber but that the man in the photograph had skin that was darker than the robber's skin. An officer then showed the second photograph of the defendant to Gervasio. This photograph was of a better quality and depicted the defendant with a lighter complexion. Gervasio identified him as the Somerset robber.

The defendant was arrested, pursuant to a warrant, and placed in a lineup with four other men. Gervasio and Mizher viewed the lineup separately and

1. The defendant's photograph was not included in either of these arrays, nor was he present in the lineups.

both immediately identified the defendant as the man who robbed the Somerset bank.[2]

The police had extremely good justification in this case for not resorting to a different identification procedure. Three armed bank robberies (in New Hampshire, Massachusetts, and Rhode Island) had occurred within a few days of each other. Two percipient bank managers had confronted the Somerset robber, and these witnesses had examined over 200 photographs and failed to make an identification. The witnesses were certain, however, that they could identify the Somerset robber if they saw him again, and one of them had assisted in the preparation of a composite drawing of the criminal. The police could take into consideration that the percipient witnesses appeared unusually reliable and nonsuggestible.

The Rhode Island and New Hampshire robberies bore a high degree of similarity to the modus operandi of the Somerset robbery, and the man who appeared in the videotape of the Rhode Island robbery resembled the man depicted in the composite drawing. The police were keenly aware that at least one dangerous bank robber was at large, and that whoever was involved could either escape altogether or strike again with possible injury to, or loss of, human life.[3] The police acted responsibly in concluding that a prompt viewing by the witnesses of the surveillance tape from the Rhode Island robbery was needed. Specifically, the police needed to determine, as quickly as possible, whether the robberies were committed by a single individual. Based on the identification by the witnesses (or the lack thereof), the police in these communities would know whether they were dealing with one bank robber or more, and could focus their investigation accordingly. If the witnesses identified the man in the videotape as the Somerset robber, the Somerset police would have access to a photographic representation of the man, in addition to the composite drawing on which they were relying.

The defendant does not suggest that an alternate identification procedure was available and should have been employed. He argues instead that the police should have forgone attempting to establish a connection between these three crimes until such time as the perpetrator of the Rhode Island robbery had been identified or apprehended, opening the possibility of identification by lineup or traditional photographic array. This suggestion appears feasible only in hindsight. At the time the videotape was shown to Gervasio and Mizher, the police could not have known that the man in the videotape would be recognized promptly by members of the East Providence police department. Facing robberies in three States, the police departments involved could not make effective determinations on how to proceed in attempting to locate what might have been several perpetrators.

The identification made from the surveillance videotape confirmed that one man had robbed the Somerset and Rhode Island banks, and strengthened the inference that he had also been responsible for the New Hampshire robbery. That valuable information in turn led to the identity of a suspect in the Somerset

2. The defendant does not argue that either the photographic array or the lineup from which he was identified was suggestive.

3. At the hearing on the defendant's motion to suppress, a Somerset police officer testified to the urgency and concern felt by the police department:

"I was concerned there was a guy that fired shots at police and at citizens that was holding up banks. The [modus operandi] fit the description of bank robberies throughout the area, as far away as Salem, New Hampshire, and we believed we had a guy out there that was going to rob a bank a day until somebody was killed."

robbery and caused the police promptly to arrange further pretrial identifications by the witnesses of the defendant through a photographic array and a lineup which are not challenged as improper in any respect. We conclude that, in the circumstances, which included a serious risk to public safety posed by a series of crimes having a similar modus operandi and eyewitnesses who appeared exceptionally nonsuggestible, the police had good reason for what they did, and the surveillance videotape identification was not, as a result, unnecessarily suggestive.

O'CONNOR, JUSTICE (dissenting, with whom LIACOS, C.J., joins).

One-on-one confrontations are inherently suggestive, but their suggestiveness pales in comparison to the suggestiveness in this case in which the police showed the witnesses to a bank robbery a videotape of the suspect in the act of robbing a bank. The message to the witnesses was not only the usual message presented by a one-on-one showup, which is that the police had reason to believe that the man being shown to the witnesses was the man who had committed the crime they had witnessed. Here, the additional powerful message to the witnesses to a recent bank robbery was that the police were undoubtedly right because the man being shown to them was unquestionably a bank robber; if he would rob one bank, he would rob other banks. It is impossible to imagine a more suggestive "confrontation" than the one that occurred in this case, and that suggestiveness was not diminished one iota by the witnesses' opportunities to observe the robber of the Somerset bank.

Basic fairness requires that, in considering the admissibility in this case of the videotape identification, the court recognize not only that the procedure was suggestive but also that the suggestiveness was enormous.

It cannot be said with confidence that the procedure was not "conducive to irreparable misidentification." To the contrary, the procedure invited irreparable misidentification. Therefore, the videotape identification evidence should have been excluded. It should have been excluded even if one were to concede, which I do not, that the procedure, which apparently was designed only to determine whether the police should look for one bank robber or two, qualifies as having been "necessary" or based on "good reason." The admission of the videotape identification evidence was erroneous and the error cannot properly be viewed as harmless. Therefore, the conviction should be reversed.

3. The first test by which a line-up or a photographic display is judged is whether it is suggestive (the question of necessity need be reached only if there is suggestiveness).

Suggestiveness is tested by looking at what the witness sees and then asking which of the persons in the line-up stands out. A line-up must also be weighed in terms of the individual witnesses. For example, a line-up may include several fairly similar men all wearing eyeglasses only one of which has horn rim frames. If the witness described the criminal as wearing eyeglasses, the line-up may be perfectly valid. If the witness specifically described the criminal's glasses as hornrimmed, a different view of the line-up might be taken. Generally speaking, a few objective standards for fair line-ups can be definitely established but the courts have not had great difficulty making the determination on a case by case basis. Sometimes, however, the judgment is difficult to make at the trial level. Both court and counsel are familiar with what the defendant looks like, and in a line-up photograph, the defendant will stand out. Whether the defendant would stand out to the eyes of a witness who had observed only the crime is another question and, of course, the only question that has to be answered.

One interesting method to test suggestiveness would be to form a street corner poll, by presenting a picture of a line-up to a group of strangers and inquiring whether they can tell which person is the one suspected by the police. This was tried in People v. Suleski, 58 A.D.2d 1023, 397 N.Y.S.2d 280 (1977), but the results (seven out of ten picked the defendant) did not persuade the court to condemn the line-up.

See Reed, Eyewitness Identification of an Armed Robber Within A Biased Police Lineup, 12 J.Pol.Sci. 310 (1984).

4. Suggestiveness may also inhere in circumstances occurring outside the limited sphere of what the witness sees at a line-up. The police may indirectly tell a witness that a particular man is their candidate for prosecution, i.e., "Take a good look at the third man from the left." The fact that the police say that they have a suspect in custody does not constitute a suggestive practice so long as no particular suspect is pointed out by police. See People v. Wooley, 127 Ill.App.2d 249, 262 N.E.2d 237 (1970); State v. McClure, 107 Ariz. 351, 488 P.2d 971 (1971). The reasoning of these courts is that any witness who is asked to view a line-up will obviously conclude that the police have a suspect. See Coleman v. Alabama, 399 U.S. 1, 6, 90 S.Ct. 1999, 2001 (1970).

In Commonwealth v. Bonnoyer, 25 Mass.App.Ct. 444, 519 N.E.2d 791 (1988) a witness had identified the defendant before trial. She was troubled by doubt. She had, in fact, a poor chance to see the offender, gave a very general description and hesitated a long while before identification. To relieve her anxiety, a police officer told her the accomplice had confessed and implicated defendant. The trial judge found that her present recognition of defendant was based upon her subsequent encounters with defendant in the courtroom. The court refused to permit her to testify. On appeal the Court said

> The Commonwealth, convinced of Bonnoyer's guilt, views as disproportionate a remedy that may enable him to escape prosecution. There is no certainty, however, that he was in fact the second robber, as there sometimes is when a perpetrator is apprehended at the scene, or is known to an eyewitness, or is found shortly thereafter with identifiable stolen articles. It does not threaten the integrity of the truthfinding process to force the prosecution to rely (to the extent that it can) on what so far as now appears is the only genuinely solid evidence that it has implicating Bonnoyer: namely, the testimony of Jensen, the confessed robber.
>
> In affirming the judge's ruling as a proper exercise of his discretion, we stress the unique configuration of facts this case presents. Surely there will be many instances in which a witness to a crime will identify a perpetrator and then learn of facts confirming the correctness of his identification: that the person he had identified has confessed, for example, or has been found in possession of loot or a distinctive weapon, or has been independently identified by another witness. No problem of admissibility will arise, either under the independent source test of *Commonwealth v. Botelho,* or the reliability test of *Neil v. Biggers* (1972), so long as the initial identification and its later repetitions are found to be based on the witness's observations at the scene of the crime. The factors which make this case distinctive are that Haber's initial identification was unreliable; her ability to identify Bonnoyer now is the product not of her observations at the time of the robbery but of the confirmatory evidence of an accomplice's confession; the confes-

sion, insofar as it implicates Bonnoyer, is not self-evidently reliable; it will not be admissible (unless Jensen testifies); Haber learned of it only after expressing her doubts as to the correctness of her identification; and the source of her information was a police officer who divulged it for the purpose of putting her doubts to rest.

Order allowing motion to suppress affirmed.

5. In *Stovall* the Supreme Court specifically noted that "The practice of showing suspects singly to persons for the purpose of identification, and not as part of a line-up has been widely condemned." Yet an exception to this rule has been found in cases involving confrontations occurring shortly after the crime. A discussion of one-man showups is contained in Bates v. United States, 405 F.2d 1104 (D.C.Cir.1968), which involved a pre-*Wade* confrontation. In affirming, the Court (Burger, C.J.) said:

> "There is no prohibition against a view of a suspect alone in what is called a 'one-man show-up' when this occurs near the time of the alleged criminal act; such a course does not tend to bring about misidentification but rather tends under some circumstances to insure accuracy. The rationale underlying this is in some respects not unlike that which the law relies on to make an exception to the hearsay rule, allowing spontaneous utterances a standing which they would not be given if uttered at a later point in time. An early identification is not in error. Of course, proof of infirmities and subjective factors, such as hysteria of a witness, can be explored on cross-examination and in argument. Prudent police work would confine these on-the-spot identifications to situations in which possible doubts as to identification needed to be resolved promptly; absent such need the conventional line-up viewing is the appropriate procedure.
>
> "... [T]he police action in returning the suspect to the vicinity of the crime for immediate identification fosters the desirable objective of fresh, accurate identification which in some instances may lead to the immediate release of an innocent suspect and at the same time enable the police to resume the search for the fleeing culprit while the trial is fresh".

How prompt must a confrontation be in order to come within this exception? The usual case involves an identification made no more than two or three hours after the offense. See Virgin Islands v. Callwood, 440 F.2d 1206 (3d Cir.1971); State v. Sears, 182 Neb. 384, 155 N.W.2d 332 (1967).

Some courts find all stationhouse showups to be inherently suggestive and not to be used in the absence of emergency. People v. Riley, 70 N.Y.2d 523, 522 N.Y.S.2d 842, 517 N.E.2d 520 (1987).

A similar doctrine has arisen when a witness accidentally encounters a suspect as in the case where both are injured and brought to the same emergency room. In such a case *Stovall* is not likely to affect admissibility. This conclusion rests on two factors: (a) there is no deliberate misconduct by the police, see Coleman v. Alabama, 399 U.S. 1, 90 S.Ct. 1999 (1970), and, (b) if the confrontation is truly accidental then there is likely to have been no suggestive aspect leading to an unreliable identification. See United States v. Jackson, 448 F.2d 963 (9th Cir.1971); United States v. Pollack, 427 F.2d 1168 (5th Cir.1970) (court building); State v. Dutton, 112 N.J.Super. 402, 271 A.2d 593 (1970) (at hospital—victim on a stretcher); Commonwealth v. Leaster, 362 Mass. 407, 287 N.E.2d 122 (1972). Accidental encounters may, however, be shown to be clearly suggestive and, if so, may result in suppression of the identification. United States v. Emanuele, 51 F.3d 1123 (3d Cir.1995) (Defendant in shackles being escorted past witnesses who then discussed his identity among themselves.)

6. In Thigpen v. Cory, 804 F.2d 893 (6th Cir.1986), over a dissent, the majority of the court held that because *Manson* is concerned with reliability and not deterrence of police misconduct, the Constitution may require the suppression of unreliable identification evidence even when the police have not engaged in misconduct. There the police had arrested the suspect and his brother and had placed them in a lineup. The victim identified the brother but did not identify William Thigpen. The police then released William Thigpen, who later appeared at his brother's preliminary hearing and at the brother's trial. After seeing William Thigpen on these occasions, the victim told authorities, some two months after the robbery, that he believed that William had been the second robber. The majority determined that the whole course of encounters was unduly suggestive. Then, applying the *Manson* factors, it found the in-court identification of William Thigpen to be unreliable. As the dissent noted, this was a "hard case," in part because other evidence suggested that the second offender had been a third Thigpen brother and not William. It is probably fair to say that many courts would disagree with the majority's analysis in *Thigpen*, and would instead hold that police misconduct is a necessary but not a sufficient basis for suppression of identification testimony after *Manson*.

7. Several works by psychologists concern eye-witness identification. See E. Loftus, Eye–Witness Testimony (1979); A.D. Yarmee, The Psychology of Eye Witness Testimony (1980). There is disagreement among psychologists about the validity of such studies. The conflict of views is aired in McCloskey & Egeth, Eyewitness Identification: What Can A Psychologist Tell A Jury, 38 Am.Psych. 550 (1983) and Loftus, Silence is Not Golden, 38 Am.Psych. 564 (1983). Generally it is within the discretion of the trial judge whether to permit expert psychological testimony concerning eye-witness identification to be presented to the jury which is deciding innocence or guilt. For a review of the cases, see State v. Helterbridle, 301 N.W.2d 545 (Minn.1980). The Arizona Supreme Court in State v. Chapple, 135 Ariz. 281, 660 P.2d 1208 (1983), became the first court to hold that a trial judge, on the particular facts of a case, abused his discretion in failing to admit expert testimony bearing on eye-witness testimony. See also United States v. Downing, 753 F.2d 1224 (3d Cir.1985); State v. Buell, 22 Ohio St.3d 124, 489 N.E.2d 795 (1986) (expert may testify generally about the factors which may lead to eyewitness error but may not testify as to why the specific witnesses in the case may have erred); Comment, Eyewitness Identification: Should Psychologists Be Permitted to Address The Jury, 75 J.Crim.L. & Criminology 1321 (1984).

Recent decisions limiting the use of expert witnesses in eye-witness identification cases include State v. Johnson, 49 Wn.App. 432, 743 P.2d 290 (1987), and United States v. Christophe, 833 F.2d 1296 (9th Cir.1987) (skillful cross-examination and an appeal to jury experience and common sense will suffice.)

8. In Johnson v. Ross, 955 F.2d 178 (2d Cir.1992) a witness identified defendant and his clothing. A trial court found the identification procedure to be suggestive and suppressed the identification of the defendant while permitting the witness to say the hat and jacket were those worn by the robber after which it was proven that the hat and jacket were worn by defendant when he was arrested. The Court said:

Johnson's claim is flawed because the special dangers attendant to the identification of suspects do not exist with equal strength where the identification of clothing is concerned. Of course, the procedures used to obtain an identification of clothing can be suggestive. But it is the notorious inaccuracy of eyewitness identifications of *suspects* that gave the initial impetus to scholarly concern and judicial remedies. *See* Felice J. Levine, *The Psychology of Criminal Identification: The Gap From* Wade *to* Kirby, 121 U.Pa.L.Rev. 1079, 1081 (1973) ("Erroneous identification of suspects has long been recognized by commentators as a crucial problem in the administration of justice."); *United States v. Wade* (1967) ("The identification of strangers is proverbially untrustworthy.") Moreover, the unfairness that results from a potentially inaccurate, confrontational identification of a suspect is compounded by the persuasiveness with which juries regard this evidence. Levine, *supra,* at 1081–82. As the Supreme Court explained in *Wade:* "The trial which might determine the accused's fate may well not be that in the courtroom but that at the pretrial confrontation, with ... the witness the sole jury ... and with little or no effective appeal from the judgment there rendered by the witness—'that's the man.' " We have no basis to believe that a witness's identification of clothing is either as susceptible to error or as persuasive to a jury as a witness's identification of a suspect. Indeed, a clothing identification is—particularly in this day and age of mass-marketing—often open to the argument that someone other than the perpetrator may have worn the same clothing. Thus, we find that identification of clothing is not a procedure so inherently "conducive to irreparable mistaken identification," as to provide the basis for a denial of due process. Any suggestiveness is of course a proper matter for cross-examination as well as argument. Therefore, Johnson's claim must fail.

Chapter 12

CRIMINAL INTERROGATIONS AND CONFESSIONS

A. THE REQUIREMENT OF VOLUNTARINESS

1. EFFECT OF FORCE OR THREAT OF FORCE

BROWN v. MISSISSIPPI

Supreme Court of the United States, 1936.
297 U.S. 278, 56 S.Ct. 461.

MR. CHIEF JUSTICE HUGHES delivered the opinion of the Court.

The question in this case is whether convictions, which rest solely upon confessions shown to have been extorted by officers of the state by brutality and violence, are consistent with the due process of law required by the Fourteenth Amendment of the Constitution of the United States.

Petitioners were indicted for the murder of one Raymond Stewart, whose death occurred on March 30, 1934. They were indicted on April 4, 1934, and were then arraigned and pleaded not guilty. Counsel were appointed by the court to defend them. Trial was begun the next morning and was concluded on the following day, when they were found guilty and sentenced to death.

Aside from the confessions, there was no evidence sufficient to warrant the submission of the case to the jury. After a preliminary inquiry, testimony as to the confessions was received over the objection of defendants' counsel. Defendants then testified that the confessions were false and had been procured by physical torture. The case went to the jury with instructions, upon the request of defendants' counsel, that if the jury had reasonable doubt as to the confessions having resulted from coercion, and that they were not true, they were not to be considered as evidence. On their appeal to the Supreme Court of the State, defendants assigned as error the inadmissibility of the confessions. The judgment was affirmed....

Defendants then moved in the Supreme Court of the State to arrest the judgment and for a new trial on the ground that all the evidence against them was obtained by coercion and brutality known to the court and to the district attorney, and that defendants had been denied the benefit of counsel or opportunity to confer with counsel in a reasonable manner. The motion was supported by affidavits. At about the same time, defendants filed in the Supreme Court a "suggestion of error" explicitly challenging the proceedings of the trial, in the use of the confessions and with respect to the alleged denial of representation by counsel, as violating the due process clause of the Fourteenth Amendment of the Constitution of the United States. The state court entertained the suggestion of error, considered the federal question, and decided it against defendants' contentions.... Two judges dissented.... We granted a writ of certiorari....

The grounds of the decision were (1) that immunity from self-incrimination is not essential to due process of law; and (2) that the failure of the trial court to exclude the confessions after the introduction of evidence showing their incompetency, in the absence of a request for such exclusion, did not deprive the defendants of life or liberty without due process of law; and that even if the trial court had erroneously overruled a motion to exclude the confessions, the ruling would have been mere error reversible on appeal, but not a violation of constitutional right....

The opinion of the state court did not set forth the evidence as to the circumstances in which the confessions were procured. That the evidence established that they were procured by coercion was not questioned. The state court said: "After the state closed its case on the merits, the appellants, for the first time, introduced evidence from which it appears that the confessions were not made voluntarily but were coerced." ... There is no dispute as to the facts upon this point, and as they are clearly and adequately stated in the dissenting opinion of Judge Griffith (with whom Judge Anderson concurred), showing both the extreme brutality of the measures to extort the confessions and the participation of the state authorities, we quote this part of his opinion in full, as follows ...:

"The crime with which these defendants, all ignorant negroes, are charged, was discovered about 1 o'clock p.m. on Friday, March 30, 1934. On that night one Dial, a deputy sheriff, accompanied by others, came to the home of Ellington, one of the defendants, and requested him to accompany them to the house of the deceased, and there a number of white men were gathered, who began to accuse the defendant of the crime. Upon his denial they seized him, and with the participation of the deputy they hanged him by a rope to the limb of a tree, and, having let him down, they hung him again, and when he was let down the second time, and he still protested his innocence, he was tied to a tree and whipped, and, still declining to accede to the demands that he confess, he was finally released, and he returned with some difficulty to his home, suffering intense pain and agony. The record of the testimony shows that the signs of the rope on his neck were plainly visible during the so-called trial. A day or two thereafter the said deputy, accompanied by another, returned to the home of the said defendant and arrested him, and departed with the prisoner towards the jail in an adjoining county, but went by a route which led into the state of Alabama; and while on the way, in that state, the deputy stopped and again severely whipped the defendant, declaring that he would continue the whipping until he confessed, and the defendant then agreed to confess to such a statement as the deputy would dictate, and he did so, after which he was delivered to jail.

"The other two defendants, Ed Brown and Henry Shields, were also arrested and taken to the same jail. On Sunday night, April 1, 1934, the same deputy, accompanied by a number of white men, one of whom was also an officer, and by the jailer, came to the jail, and the two last named defendants were made to strip and they were laid over chairs and their backs were cut to pieces with a leather strap with buckles on it, and they were likewise made by the said deputy definitely to understand that the whipping would be continued unless and until they confessed, and not only confessed, but confessed in every matter of detail as demanded by those present; and in this manner the defendants confessed the crime, and, as the whippings progressed and were repeated, they changed or adjusted their confession in all particulars of detail so as to conform to the demands of their torturers. When the confessions had been obtained in the exact form and contents as desired by the mob, they left with the parting admonition and warning that, if the defendants changed their story at any time in any respect from that last stated, the perpetrators of the outrage would administer the same or equally effective treatment.

"Further details of the brutal treatment to which these helpless prisoners were subjected need not be pursued. It is sufficient to say that in pertinent respects the transcript reads more like pages torn from some medieval account than a record made within the confines of a modern civilization which aspires to an enlightened constitutional government.

"All this having been accomplished, on the next day, that is, on Monday, April 2, when the defendants had been given time to recuperate somewhat from the tortures to which they had been subjected, the two sheriffs, one of the county where the crime was committed, and the other of the county of the jail in which the prisoners were confined, came to the jail, accompanied by eight other persons, some of them deputies, there to hear the free and voluntary confession of these miserable and abject defendants. The sheriff of the county of the crime admitted that he had heard of the whipping, but averred that he had no personal knowledge of it. He admitted that one of the defendants, when brought before him to confess, was limping and did not sit down, and that this particular defendant then and there stated that he had been strapped so severely that he could not sit down, and, as already stated, the signs of the rope on the neck of another of the defendants were plainly visible to all. Nevertheless the solemn farce of hearing the free and voluntary confessions was gone through with, and these two sheriffs and one other person then present were the three witnesses used in court to establish the so-called confessions, which were received by the court and admitted in evidence over the objections of the defendants duly entered of record as each of the said three witnesses delivered their alleged testimony. There was thus enough before the court when these confessions were first offered to make known to the court that they were not, beyond all reasonable doubt, free and voluntary; and the failure of the court then to exclude the confessions is sufficient to reverse the judgment, under every rule of procedure that has heretofore been prescribed, and hence it was not necessary subsequently to renew the objections by motion or otherwise.

"The spurious confessions having been obtained—and the farce last mentioned having been gone through with on Monday, April 2d—the court, then in session, on the following day, Tuesday, April 3, 1934, ordered the grand jury to reassemble on the succeeding day, April 4, 1934, at 9 o'clock, and on the morning of the day last mentioned the grand jury returned an indictment against the defendants for murder. Late that afternoon the defendants were brought from the jail in the adjoining county and arraigned, when one or more of them offered to plead guilty, which the court declined to accept, and, upon inquiry whether they had or desired counsel, they stated that they had none, and did not suppose that counsel could be of any assistance to them. The court thereupon appointed counsel, and set the case for trial for the following morning at 9 o'clock, and the defendants were returned to the jail in the adjoining county about thirty miles away.

"The defendants were brought to the courthouse of the county on the following morning, April 5th, and the so-called trial was opened, and was concluded on the next day, April 6, 1934, and resulted in a pretended conviction with death sentences. The evidence upon which the conviction was obtained was the so-called confessions. Without this evidence, a peremptory instruction to find for the defendants would have been inescapable. The defendants were put on the stand, and by their testimony the facts and the details thereof as to the manner by which the confessions were extorted from them were fully developed, and it is further disclosed by the record that the same deputy, Dial, under whose guiding hand and active participation the tortures to coerce the confessions were administered, was actively in the performance of the supposed duties of a court deputy in the courthouse and in the presence of the prisoners during what is denominated, in complimentary terms, the trial of these defendants. This deputy was put on the stand by the state in rebuttal, and admitted the whippings. It is interesting to note that in his testimony with reference to the whipping of the defendant Ellington, and in response to the inquiry as to how severely he was whipped, the deputy stated, 'Not too much for a negro; not as much as I would have done if it were left to me.' Two others who had participated in these whippings were introduced and admitted it—not a single witness was introduced who denied it. The facts are not only undisputed, they are admitted, and admitted to have been done by officers of the state, in conjunction with other participants, and all this was definitely well known to everybody connected with the trial, and during the trial, including the state's prosecuting attorney and the trial judge presiding."

* * *

The state is free to regulate the procedure of its courts in accordance with its own conceptions of policy, unless in so doing it "offends some principle of justice so rooted in the traditions and conscience of our people as to be ranked as fundamental." Snyder v. Massachusetts, 291 U.S. 97, 105, 54 S.Ct. 330, 332; Rogers v. Peck, 199 U.S. 425, 434, 26 S.Ct. 87. The state may abolish trial by jury. It may dispense with indictment by a grand jury and substitute complaint or information. Walker v. Sauvinet, 92 U.S. 90; Hurtado v. California, 110 U.S. 516, 4 S.Ct. 111, 292; Snyder v. Massachusetts, supra. But the freedom of the state in establishing its policy is the freedom of constitutional government and is limited by the requirement of due process of law. Because a state may dispense with a jury trial, it does not follow that it may substitute trial by ordeal. The rack and torture chamber may not be substituted for the witness stand. The state may not permit an accused to be hurried to conviction under mob domination—where the whole proceeding is but a mask—without supplying corrective process. Moore v. Dempsey, 261 U.S. 86, 91, 43 S.Ct. 265. The state may not deny to the accused the aid of counsel. Powell v. Alabama, 287 U.S. 45, 53 S.Ct. 55. Nor may a state, through the action of its officers, contrive a conviction through the pretense of a trial which in truth is "but used as a means of depriving a defendant of liberty through a deliberate deception of court and jury by the presentation of testimony known to be perjured." Mooney v. Holohan, 294 U.S. 103, 112, 55 S.Ct. 340. And the trial equally is a mere pretense where the state authorities have contrived a conviction resting solely upon confessions obtained by violence. The due process clause requires "that state action, whether through one agency or another, shall be consistent with the fundamental principles of liberty and justice which lie at the base of all our civil and political institutions." Hebert v. Louisiana, 272 U.S. 312, 316, 47 S.Ct. 103, 104. It would be difficult to conceive of methods more revolting to the sense of justice than those taken to procure the confessions of these petitioners, and the use of the confessions thus obtained as the basis for conviction and sentence was a clear denial of due process.

It is in this view that the further contention of the State must be considered. That contention rests upon the failure of counsel for the accused, who had objected to the admissibility of the confessions, to move for their exclusion after they had been introduced and the fact of coercion had been proved. It is a contention which proceeds upon a misconception of the nature of petitioners' complaint. That complaint is not of the commission of mere error, but of a wrong so fundamental that it made the whole proceeding a mere pretense of a trial and rendered the conviction and sentence wholly void. Moore v. Dempsey, supra. We are not concerned with a mere question of state practice, or whether counsel assigned to petitioners were competent or mistakenly assumed that their first objections were sufficient. In an earlier case the Supreme Court of the State had recognized the duty of the court to supply corrective process where due process of law had been denied. In Fisher v. State, 145 Miss. 116, 134, 110 So. 361, 365, the court said: "Coercing the supposed state's criminals into confessions and using such confessions so coerced from them against them in trials has been the curse of all countries. It was the chief iniquity, the crowning infamy of the Star Chamber, and the Inquisition, and other similar institutions. The Constitution recognized the evils that lay behind these practices and prohibited them in this country.... The duty of maintaining constitutional rights of a person on trial for his life rises above mere rules of procedure, and wherever the court is clearly satisfied that such violations exist, it will refuse to sanction such violations and will apply the corrective."

In the instant case, the trial court was fully advised by the undisputed evidence of the way in which the confessions had been procured. The trial court knew that there was no other evidence upon which conviction and sentence could be based. Yet it proceeded to permit conviction and to pronounce sentence. The conviction and sentence were void for want of the essential elements of due process, and the proceeding thus vitiated could be challenged in any appropriate manner. Mooney v. Holohan, supra. It was challenged before the Supreme Court of the State by the express invocation of the Fourteenth Amendment. That court entertained the challenge, considered the federal question thus presented, but declined to enforce petitioners' constitutional right. The court thus denied a federal right fully established and specially set up and claimed, and the judgment must be reversed.

It is so ordered.

NOTE

In the Middle Ages in Europe, and at times in many other parts of the world, a confession was a prerequisite to a finding of guilty. A confession was called "the queen of evidence," and the necessity of obtaining confessions in order to convict led to the development of many forms of torture. For a description of some of the torture practices of times past, and for an excellent source of reference material upon the subject, see Abe, Self-Incrimination—Japan and the United States, 46 J.Crim.L., C. & P.S. 613 (1956).

2. INHERENT COERCION

ASHCRAFT v. TENNESSEE

Supreme Court of the United States, 1944.
322 U.S. 143, 64 S.Ct. 921.

[The essential facts of the case, as they appear in the Court's opinion, are as follows: The defendant had been taken late one afternoon to a morgue where he identified as his wife the body of a woman who had been beaten to death. From the morgue Ashcraft was escorted to the county jail and questioned for several hours, after which he was released without having been placed under formal arrest. Nine days later he was arrested and taken to jail for further questioning. He was interrogated intermittently for 28 hours, whereupon he told the officers a man named Ware had killed his wife. Ware, who had not been suspected previously, was arrested and he promptly admitted the killing, stating further that Ashcraft had hired him to do it. Ashcraft was confronted with Ware's confession and the interrogation continued for another 8 hours, at the end of which time Ashcraft admitted his guilt but refused to sign a written confession. He repeated his admission of guilt to two business men and to his own family physician, who were called in to witness the confession. The doctor also examined Ashcraft and found him free from any signs of physical abuse. His oral confession was admitted in evidence and his conviction in the trial court was affirmed by the Supreme Court of Tennessee.]

MR. JUSTICE BLACK delivered the opinion of the Court.

... Our conclusion is that if Ashcraft made a confession it was not voluntary but compelled. We reach this conclusion from facts which are not in dispute at all. Ashcraft, a citizen of excellent reputation, was taken into custody by police officers. Ten days' examination of the Ashcrafts' maid, and of several others, in jail where they were held, had revealed nothing whatever against Ashcraft. Inquiries among his neighbors and business associates likewise had failed to unearth one single tangible clue pointing to his guilt. For thirty-six hours after Ashcraft's seizure during which period he was held incommunicado, without sleep or rest, relays of officers, experienced investigators, and highly trained lawyers questioned him without respite. From the beginning of the questioning at 7 o'clock on Saturday evening until 6 o'clock on Monday morning Ashcraft denied that he had anything to do with the murder of his wife. And at a hearing before a magistrate about 8:30 Monday morning Ashcraft pleaded not guilty to the charge of murder which the officers had sought to make him confess during the previous thirty-six hours.

We think a situation such as that here shown by uncontradicted evidence is so inherently coercive that its very existence is irreconcilable with the possession of mental freedom by a lone suspect against whom its full coercive force is brought to bear. It is inconceivable that any court of justice in the land, conducted as our courts are, open to the public, would permit prosecutors serving in relays to keep a defendant witness under continuous cross examination for thirty-six hours without rest or sleep in an effort to extract a "voluntary" confession. Nor can we, consistently with Constitutional due process of law, hold voluntary a confession where prosecutors do the same thing away from the restraining influences of a public trial in an open court room....

The Constitution of the United States stands as a bar against the conviction of any individual in an American court by means of a coerced confession. There have been, and are now, certain foreign nations with governments dedicated to an opposite policy: governments which convict individuals with testimony obtained by police organizations possessed of an unrestrained power to seize persons suspected of crimes against the state, hold them in secret custody, and wring from them confessions by physical or mental torture. So long as the Constitution remains the basic law of our Republic, America will not have that kind of government.

... The judgment affirming Ashcraft's conviction is reversed and the cause is remanded to the Supreme Court of Tennessee for proceedings not inconsistent with this opinion. It is so ordered....

MR. JUSTICE JACKSON, dissenting.

A sovereign state is now before us, summoned on the charge that it has obtained convictions by methods so unfair that a federal court must set aside what the state courts have done. Heretofore the state has had the benefit of a presumption of regularity and legality. A confession made by one in custody heretofore has been admissible in evidence unless it was proved and found that it was obtained by pressures so strong that it was in fact involuntarily made, that the individual will of the particular confessor had been overcome by torture, mob violence, fraud, trickery, threats, or promises. Even where there was excess and abuse of power on the part of officers, the State still was entitled to use the confession if upon examination of the whole evidence it was found to negative the view that the accused had "so lost his freedom of action that the statements made were not his but were the result of the deprivation of his free choice to admit, to deny, or to refuse to answer." Lisenba v. California, 314 U.S. 219, 241, 62 S.Ct. 280, 292.

In determining these issues of fact, respect for the sovereign character of the several states always has constrained this Court to give great weight to findings of fact of state courts. While we have sometimes gone back of state court determinations to make sure whether the guaranties of the Fourteenth Amendment have or have not been violated, in close cases the decisions of state courts have often been sufficient to tip the scales in favor of affirmance....

As we read the present decision the Court in effect declines to apply these well-established principles. Instead, it: (1) substitutes for determination on conflicting evidence the question whether this confession was actually produced by coercion, a presumption that it was, on a new doctrine that examination in custody of this duration is "inherently coercive"; (2) it makes that presumption irrebuttable—i.e., a rule of law—because, while it goes back of the State decisions to find certain facts, it refuses to resolve conflicts in evidence to determine whether other of the State's proof is sufficient to overcome such presumption; and, in so doing, (3) it sets aside the findings by the courts of Tennessee that on all the facts this confession did not result from coercion, either giving those findings no weight or regarding them as immaterial.

We must bear in mind that this case does not come here from a lower federal court over whose conduct we may assert a general supervisory power. If it did, we should be at liberty to apply rules as to the admissibility of confessions, based on our own conception of permissible procedure, and in which we may embody restrictions even greater than those imposed upon the states by the Fourteenth Amendment.... But we have no such supervisory power over state courts. We may not lay down rules of evidence for them nor revise their decisions merely because we feel more confidence in our own wisdom and rectitude. We have no power to discipline the police or law-enforcement officers of the State of Tennessee nor to reverse its convictions in retribution for conduct which we may personally disapprove.

The burden of protecting society from most crimes against persons and property falls upon the state. Different states have different crime problems and some freedom to vary procedures according to their own ideas. Here, a state was forced by an unwitnessed and baffling murder to vindicate its law and protect its society. To nullify its conviction in this particular case upon a consideration of all the facts would be a delicate exercise of federal judicial power. But to go beyond this, as the Court does today, and divine in the due process clause of the Fourteenth Amendment an exclusion of confessions on an irrebuttable presumption that custody and examination are "inherently coercive" if of some unspecified duration within thirty-six hours, requires us to make more than a passing expression of our doubts and disagreements.

The claim of a suspect to immunity from questioning creates one of the most vexing problems in criminal law—that branch of the law which does the courts and the legal profession least credit. The consequences upon society of limiting examination of persons out of court cannot fairly be appraised without recognition of the advantage criminals already enjoy in immunity from compulsory examination in court. Of this latter Mr. Justice Cardozo, for an all but unanimous Court, said: "This too might be lost, and justice still be done. Indeed, today as in the past there are students of our penal system who look upon the immunity as a mischief rather than a benefit, and who would limit its scope, or destroy it altogether. No doubt there would remain the need to give protection against torture, physical or mental." Palko v. Connecticut, 302 U.S. 319, 325, 326, 58 S.Ct. 149, 151, 152.

This Court never yet has held that the Constitution denies a State the right to use a confession just because the confessor was questioned in custody where it did not also find other circumstances that deprived him of a "free choice to admit, to deny, or to refuse to answer." ... The Constitution requires that a conviction rest on a fair trial. Forced confessions are ruled out of a fair trial. They are ruled out because they have been wrung from a prisoner by measures which are offensive to concepts of fundamental fairness. Different courts have used different terms to express the test by which to judge the inadmissibility of a confession, such as "forced," "coerced," "involuntary," "extorted," "loss of freedom of will." But always where we have professed to speak with the voice of the due process clause, the test, in whatever words stated, has been applied to the particular confessor at the time of confession.

It is for this reason that American courts hold almost universally and very properly that a confession obtained during or shortly after the confessor has been subjected to brutality, torture, beating, starvation, or physical pain of any kind is prima facie "involuntary." The effect of threats alone may depend more on individual susceptibility to fear. But men are so constituted that many will risk the postponed consequences of yielding to a demand for a confession in order to be rid of present or imminent physical suffering. Actual or threatened violence have no place in eliciting truth and it is fair to assume that no officer of the law will resort to cruelty if truth is what he is seeking. We need not be too exacting about proof of the effects of such violence on the individual involved, for their effect on the human personality is invariably and seriously demoralizing.

When, however, we consider a confession obtained by questioning, even if persistent and prolonged, we are in a different field. Interrogation per se is not, while violence per se is, an outlaw. Questioning is an indispensable instrumentality of justice. It may be abused, of course, as cross-examination in court may be abused, but the principles by which we may adjudge when it passes constitutional limits are quite different from those that condemn police brutality, and are far more difficult to apply. And they call for a more responsible and cautious exercise of our office. For we may err on the side of hostility to violence without doing injury to legitimate prosecution of crime; we cannot read an undiscriminating hostility to mere interrogation into the Constitution without unduly fettering the States in protecting society from the criminal.

It probably is the normal instinct to deny and conceal any shameful or guilty act. Even a "voluntary confession" is not likely to be the product of the same motives with which one may volunteer information that does not incriminate or concern him. The term "voluntary" confession does not mean voluntary in the sense of a confession to a priest merely to rid one's soul of a sense of guilt. "Voluntary confessions" in criminal law are the product of calculations of a different order, and usually proceed from a belief that further denial is useless and perhaps prejudicial. To speak of any confessions of crime made after arrest as being "voluntary" or "uncoerced" is somewhat inaccurate, although traditional.

A confession is wholly and incontestably voluntary only if a guilty person gives himself up to the law and becomes his own accuser. The Court bases its decision on the premise that custody and examination of a prisoner for thirty-six hours is "inherently coercive." Of course it is. And so is custody and examination for one hour. Arrest itself is inherently coercive, and so is detention. When not justified, infliction of such indignities upon the person is actionable as a tort. Of course such acts put pressure upon the prisoner to answer questions, to answer them truthfully, and to confess if guilty.

But does the Constitution prohibit use of all confessions made after arrest because questioning, while one is deprived of freedom, is "inherently coercive"? The Court does not quite say so, but it is moving far and fast in that direction. The step it now takes is to hold this confession inadmissible because of the time taken in getting it.

The duration and intensity of an examination or inquisition always have been regarded as one of the relevant and important considerations in estimating its effect on the will of the individual involved. Thirty-six hours is a long stretch of questioning. That the inquiry was prolonged and persistent is a factor that in any calculation of its effect on Ashcraft would count heavily against the confession. But some men would withstand for days pressures that would destroy the will of another in hours. Always heretofore the ultimate question has been whether the confessor was in possession of his own will and self-control at the time of confession. For its bearing on this question the Court always has considered the confessor's strength or weakness, whether he was educated or illiterate, intelligent or moronic, well or ill, Negro or white.

But the Court refuses in this case to be guided by this test. It rejects the finding of the Tennessee courts and says it must make an "independent examination" of the circumstances. Then it says that it will not "resolve any of the disputed questions of fact" relating to the circumstances of the confession. Instead of finding as a fact that Ashcraft's freedom of will was impaired, it substitutes the doctrine that the situation was "inherently coercive." It thus reaches on a *part* of the evidence in the case a conclusion which I shall demonstrate it could not properly reach on *all* the evidence. And it refuses to resolve the conflicts in the other evidence to determine whether it rebuts the presumption thus reached that the confession is a coerced one.

If the constitutional admissibility of a confession is no longer to be measured by the mental state of the individual confessor but by a general doctrine dependent on the clock, it should be capable of statement in definite terms. If thirty-six hours is more than is permissible, what about 24? or 12? or 6? or 1? All are "inherently coercive." Of course questions of law like this often turn on matters of degree. But are not the states entitled to know, if this Court is able to state, what the considerations are which make any particular degree decisive? How else may state courts apply our tests? . . .

MR. JUSTICE ROBERTS and MR. JUSTICE FRANKFURTER join in this opinion.

NOTE

The year prior to the Supreme Court decision in the *Ashcraft* case, the Court, by invoking its supervisory power over lower federal courts, held, in McNabb v. United States, 318 U.S. 332, 63 S.Ct. 608 (1943), that not only must a confession be a voluntary one, but it also must have been obtained by "civilized" interrogation procedures. Specifically, the Court ruled that where federal officers interrogated an arrested person, instead of taking him without unnecessary delay before a federal magistrate (for a preliminary hearing), as required by law, any confession obtained during the period of delay was inadmissible in evidence, regardless of its voluntariness or trustworthiness.

Although the federal statute used the words "without unnecessary delay," some lower federal courts after the *McNabb* case applied the statute as though this meant "immediately." That presented a severe curtailment upon the opportunities for interrogations conducted by federal officers and particularly in Washington, D.C., with its street crime problems similar to many other large cities. It also augmented the initial resentment toward the *McNabb* decision in Congress as well as from other groups. Moreover, the *McNabb* rule narrowly survived a 1948 Supreme Court decision in Upshaw v. United States, 335 U.S. 410. Nevertheless, the Court unanimously reaffirmed the *McNabb* rule in the 1957 case of Mallory v. United States, 354 U.S. 449. Thereafter it was referred to as the *McNabb–Mallory rule.*

After repeated attempts by members of Congress to enact a bill abolishing the *McNabb–Mallory* rule (as it was privileged to do because the rule was not of constitutional dimension), and after a Presidential veto of one that was enacted in 1966, Congress did succeed in effecting its demise 2 years later. The life-span of the *McNabb–Mallory* rule as a federal rule was 25 years, until it was abolished in the 1968 Omnibus Crime Act, 18 U.S.C.A. 3501 (1969). (In 1978 Arizona enacted a similar statute, § 13–3988, Ariz.Rev.Stats.)

Very few state supreme courts adopted the *McNabb–Mallory* rule; most exercised the option of rejecting it. Even some of the adopting ones diluted its effect in application. Moreover, the legislature in one of the adopting states (Maryland) nullified the rule in 1982. Thus, few of its traces remain. As one legal scholar described the fate of the *McNabb–Mallory* rule (even in 1978), it was a "grenade that fizzled."

The *McNabb–Mallory* rule has lost its vitality, but interrogators must be mindful of the fact that an undue detention delay, or one exceeding the specified state statutory time limitation, may be considered in determining confession voluntariness.

3. PROOF OF VOLUNTARINESS

PEOPLE v. MARKHAM

Supreme Court of California, 1989.
49 Cal.3d 63, 775 P.2d 1042.

Opinion by Eagleson, J., with Lucas, C.J., Panelli, Kaufman and Kennard, JJ., concurring. Separate concurring opinions by Mosk and Broussard, JJ., concurring in the judgment.

In People v. Jimenez (1978) 21 Cal.3d 595, 580 P.2d 672, this court adopted as a judicially declared rule of criminal procedure "the requirement that at trial the People prove the voluntariness of a defendant's confession beyond a reasonable doubt." The United States Supreme Court had earlier held that the federal Constitution required only that the prosecution prove a confession voluntary by a preponderance of the evidence. Lego v. Twomey (1972) 404 U.S. 477, 489.

We granted review in this case to determine whether article I, section 28, subdivision (d) of the California Constitution (hereafter section 28(d))—commonly referred to as the "truth-in-evidence law" and adopted in 1982 as part-and-parcel of the ballot initiative popularly known as Proposition 8—has abrogated the Jimenez rule requiring a greater degree of proof of voluntariness than its federal counterpart....

* * *

The Constitution of the United States requires no more than that the voluntariness of confessions or admissions be proved by a preponderance of the evidence at trial. (Lego v. Twomey, supra). Section 28(d) establishes that standard as the rule in California.

The decision of the Court of Appeal upholding defendant's judgment of conviction is affirmed.

[Concurring opinions of Mosk, J. and Brass.]

With the utmost reluctance, I concur in the judgment ... I join in that conclusion, yielding as I must to the mandate of the retrogressive Proposition 8.

* * *

I must observe that in Asia, Latin America, and other areas of this troubled world courageous men and women are striving, and some are dying, *to establish and expand* individual rights. It is ironic that in California our existing individual rights are being *curtailed.*

We cannot blame the United States Constitution or the United States Supreme Court for this situation.

* * *

... the blame ... must be placed squarely on Proposition 8. That ill-conceived measure has struck down California precedents on individual rights as it has encountered them in its path of destruction.

Broussard, J.

I concur in the judgment under compulsion ...

4. EFFECT UPON ADMISSIBILITY BY UNLAWFUL ARREST AND THE ILLEGAL SEIZURE OF INCRIMINATING EVIDENCE

DUNAWAY v. NEW YORK

Supreme Court of the United States, 1979.
442 U.S. 200, 99 S.Ct. 2248.

[The relevant facts and statements for consideration of the issue of confession admissibility in this case are in the U.S. Reporter syllabus that follows:]

A Rochester, N.Y., police detective questioned a jail inmate, the supposed source of a lead implicating petitioner in an attempted robbery and homicide, but learned nothing that supplied "enough information to get a warrant" for petitioner's arrest. Nevertheless, the detective ordered other detectives to "pick up" petitioner and "bring him in." Petitioner was then taken into custody, and although not told that he was under arrest, he would have been physically restrained if he had attempted to leave. He was driven to police headquarters and placed in an interrogation room, where he was questioned by officers after being given the warnings required by Miranda v. Arizona, *384 U.S. 436.* He waived counsel and eventually made statements and drew sketches that incriminated him in the crime. At his state-court trial, his motions to suppress the statements and sketches were denied, and he was convicted. The New York appellate courts affirmed the conviction, but this Court vacated the judgment, and remanded for further consideration in light of the supervening decision in Brown v. Illinois, *422 U.S. 590,* which held that there is no per se rule that Miranda warnings in and of themselves suffice to cure a Fourth Amendment violation involved in obtaining inculpatory statements during custodial interrogation following a formal arrest on less than probable cause, and that in order to use such statements, the prosecution must show not only that the statements meet the Fifth Amendment voluntariness standard, but also that the causal connection between the statements and the illegal arrest is broken sufficiently to purge the primary taint of the illegal arrest in light of the distinct policies and interests of the Fourth Amendment. On remand from the New York Court of Appeals, the trial court granted petitioner's motion to suppress, but the Appellate Division of the New York Supreme Court reversed, holding that although the police lacked probable cause to arrest petitioner, law enforcement officials may detain an individual upon reasonable suspicion for questioning for a reasonable period of time under carefully controlled conditions which are ample to protect the individual's Fifth and Sixth Amendment rights, and that even if petitioner's detention were illegal, the taint of such detention was sufficiently attenuated to allow the admission of his statements and sketches.

Held:

1. The Rochester police violated the Fourth and Fourteenth Amendments when, without probable cause to arrest, they seized petitioner and transported him to the police station for interrogation.

(a) Petitioner was "seized" in the Fourth Amendment sense when he was taken involuntarily to the police station, and the State concedes that the police lacked probable cause to arrest him before his incriminating statement during interrogation.

(b) Terry v. Ohio, *392 U.S. 1,* which held that limited "stop and frisk" searches for weapons are so substantially less intrusive than arrests that the general rule requiring probable cause to make Fourth Amendment "seizures" reasonable can be replaced by a test balancing the limited violation of individual privacy against the opposing interests in crime prevention and detection and in the police officer's safety, and the Terry case's progeny, do not support the application of a balancing test so as to hold that "seizures" such as that in this case may be justified by mere "reasonable suspicion." The narrow intrusions in Terry and its progeny were judged by a balancing test rather than the general rule requiring probable cause only because those intrusions fell so far short of the kind of intrusion associated with an arrest. For all but those narrowly defined intrusions, the requisite balancing has been performed in centuries of precedent and is embodied in the principle that seizures are reasonable only if supported by probable cause.

(c) The treatment of petitioner, whether or not technically characterized as an arrest, was in important respects indistinguishable from a traditional arrest and must be supported by probable cause. Detention for custodial interrogation—regardless of its label—intrudes so severely on interests protected by the Fourth Amendment as necessarily to trigger the traditional safeguards against illegal arrest....

2. The connection between the unconstitutional police conduct and the incriminating statements and sketches obtained during petitioner's illegal detention was not sufficiently attenuated to permit the use at trial of the statements and sketches.

(a) Even though proper Miranda warnings may have been given and petitioner's statements may have been "voluntary" for purposes of the Fifth Amendment, "[the] exclusionary rule, ... when utilized to effectuate the Fourth Amendment, serves interests and policies that are distinct from those it serves under the Fifth." *Brown v. Illinois, supra, at 601.* While a confession after proper Miranda warnings may be found "voluntary" for Fifth Amendment purposes, this type of "voluntariness" is merely a threshold requirement for Fourth Amendment analysis.

(b) Under Fourth Amendment analysis, which focuses on "the causal connection between the illegality and the confession," *Brown v. Illinois, supra,* factors to be considered in determining whether the confession is obtained by exploitation of an illegal arrest include: the temporal proximity of the arrest and the confession, the presence of intervening circumstances, and, particularly, the purpose and flagrancy of the official misconduct. Here, petitioner was admittedly seized without probable cause in the hope that something might turn up, and confessed without any intervening event of significance....

BRENNAN, J., delivered the opinion of the Court, in which STEWART, WHITE, MARSHALL, BLACKMUN, and STEVENS, JJ., joined. WHITE, J., and STEVENS, J., filed concurring opinions. REHNQUIST, J., filed a dissenting opinion in which BURGER, C.J., joined. POWELL, J., took no part in the consideration or decision of the case.

* * *

DISSENT: MR. JUSTICE REHNQUIST, with whom the CHIEF JUSTICE (BURGER) joins, dissenting.

If the Court did no more in this case than it announced in the opening sentence of its opinion—"decide ... the question reserved 10 years ago in Morales v. New York, *396 U.S. 102 (1969),* namely, 'the question of the legality of custodial questioning on less than probable cause for a full-fledged arrest' "—I would have little difficulty joining its opinion. The decision of this question, however, does not, contrary to the implication in the Court's opening sentence, decide this case. For the Court goes on to conclude that petitioner Dunaway was in fact "seized" within the meaning of the Fourth Amendment, and that the connection between Dunaway's purported detention and the evidence obtained therefrom was not sufficiently attenuated as to dissipate the taint of the alleged unlawful police conduct. I cannot agree with either conclusion, and accordingly, I dissent.

There is obviously nothing in the Fourth Amendment that prohibits police from calling from their vehicle to a particular individual on the street and asking him to come over and talk with them; nor is there anything in the Fourth Amendment that prevents the police from knocking on the door of a person's house and when the person answers the door, inquiring whether he is willing to answer questions that they wish to put to him. "Obviously, not all personal intercourse between policemen and citizens involves 'seizures' of persons." Terry v. Ohio, *392 U.S. 1, 19 n. 16 (1968).* Voluntary questioning not involving any "seizure" for Fourth Amendment purposes may take place under any number of varying circumstances. And the occasions will not be few when a particular individual agrees voluntarily to answer questions that the police wish to put to him either on the street, at the station, or in his house, and later regrets his willingness to answer those questions. However, such morning-after regrets do not render involuntary responses that were voluntary at the time they were made. In my view, this is a case where the defendant voluntarily accompanied the police to the station to answer their questions.

* * *

... No involuntary detention for questioning was shown to have taken place. The Fourth Amendment, accordingly, does not require suppression of petitioner's statements.

PEOPLE v. TURNER

Appellate Court of Illinois, 1994.
259 Ill.App.3d 979, 631 N.E.2d 1236;
Cert. denied, ___ U.S. ___, 115 S.Ct. 956 (1995).

Justice McNamara delivered the opinion of the court:

Following a bench trial, defendant, Gregory Turner, was convicted of armed violence (Ill.Rev.Stat.1988, ch. 38, par. 33A–1(b)) and the first degree murder of S.T. (Ill.Rev.Stat.1988, ch. 38, par. 9–1), and was sentenced to a prison term of 30 years. Defendant appeals, contending that the trial court committed reversible error in denying his motion to suppress inculpatory statements he made to police two days after the murder, which he argues were induced by virtue of having been confronted with evidence illegally seized from his home shortly before he confessed. In addition, defendant argues that the statements should have been suppressed because they were brought about by the exploitation of an unlawful arrest.

The relevant facts are as follows. On June 10, 1988, defendant gave a confession which may be summarized as follows: On June 8, 1988, after he and the deceased had sex, she demanded $30. They continued to quarrel, and defendant hit her with his fist. When she tried to hit him back, defendant stabbed her.

Defendant filed a motion to quash arrest and suppress evidence, contesting his arrest, the search of his parents' house, the seizure of a pair of blood-stained shoes and a sketch, and the admission of his inculpatory statements. At the hearing on the motion, the State called Detective James Boylan. Boylan testified that at approximately 4:30 p.m. on June 9, he and his partner, Detective Michael Cummings, went to the deceased's home where they interviewed several individuals including a friend named Vetta Cole. Cole informed the detectives that the deceased at one time told her she was afraid of defendant. At approximately 6:30 p.m., Cole accompanied the detectives in their vehicle to defendant's house. They knocked on the door, and defendant's mother answered. Defendant was not at home so they left a business card with her and asked her to tell defendant to contact them. They did not enter the house at that time.

* * *

At approximately 2:30 a.m., the detectives went to defendant's house. They knocked on the door, and defendant's parents answered and invited them in. Boylan told them that defendant was cooperating with the police in the investigation of the deceased's murder and that they were questioning him about his whereabouts on the night in question. They asked defendant's mother if she had seen defendant on that particular night. She stated that she heard him come home around 1:30 a.m., go down to the basement where he slept, and leave sometime thereafter. The detectives asked her if they could see where defendant slept, and she and defendant's father took them to the basement. Boylan could not recall whether they told them that defendant said they could search his room.

The detectives noticed a pair of shoes lying on the floor, and they asked defendant's mother if they belonged to defendant. She responded that they did, and Boylan picked them up and noticed what appeared to be blood stains on the bottom. The detectives asked defendant's mother if they could take the shoes with them, and she said yes....

* * *

Defendant's father stated that defendant paid rent to live in the basement, and he considered defendant's area to be private. He stated that he would not go into defendant's area without his permission.

* * *

Defendant contends that his inculpatory statements should have been suppressed because they were brought about by exploiting the illegal search of his house and seizure of his gym shoes. Defendant argues that the police induced his confession by confronting him with their knowledge of the shoes, which they told him were stained with human blood. The trial court disagreed, holding that defendant's confession was a product of his own free will and was sufficiently attenuated from the illegal search and seizure so as to be purged of its taint. In so holding, the trial court placed almost exclusive reliance on the fact that defendant first learned of the bloody shoes at 3:30 a.m. and did not confess at that time. The court reasoned that defendant's failure to confess when first confronted with the knowledge of the illegally-seized evidence at 3:30 ruled out any possibility that it induced him to later confess at 8:00 a.m. In its order, the court concluded:

> "We know that the defendant knew of the seizure before Boylan and Cummings spoke to him around 3:30 A.M. And if [defendant] had confessed at that time, no other reasonable interpretation could be made except that the confession came about because of confronting the defendant with the knowledge gained by the illegal search and seizure. But, that did not happen. [Defendant] did not confess then.

* * *

After carefully reviewing the record, we must conclude that the trial court manifestly erred in denying defendant's motion to suppress his confession statements because the factors underlying its ruling are not supported by the evidence. That defendant, as the trial court found, had an opportunity to confess at 3:30 a.m. after learning of the shoes, but did not, is not borne out by the record. Accordingly, the trial court's reasoning that "since knowledge of the gym shoes didn't induce a confession at 3:30, it was not the inducement that brought about the confession at 8:00 A.M." must be rejected.

* * *

In view of the foregoing, we conclude that defendant's inculpatory statements were not obtained by means sufficiently distinguishable from the illegal search of his house and seizure of his shoes as to be purged of the taint arising from that illegality.... The totality of the evidence indicates that the police exploited the "fruits" of the illegal search and seizure to force a confession from defendant. Under these circumstances, we hold that the State has failed to meet its burden of proving, by clear and convincing evidence, that defendant's confession was a product of his free will, independent of the taint of the illegal search and seizure.

* * *

UNITED STATES v. VARELA

United States Court of Appeals, Second Circuit 1992.
968 F.2d 259.

OAKES, Chief Judge:

This appeal concerns the scope of the exclusionary rule. Following arrest on narcotics charges on March 16, 1990, Carlos Varela made incriminating statements concerning himself and others who were allegedly involved in cocaine trafficking. These statements were subsequently suppressed as the fruit of an arrest without probable cause and, in response to a government motion, the indictment against Varela was dismissed. Later that year, Varela, testifying before a grand jury under a grant of immunity, contradicted these suppressed statements. Varela was charged with attempting to influence and impede a grand jury investigation and with making false declarations to a grand jury, in violation of 18 U.S.C. §§ 1503, 1623(a) (1988); and the previously suppressed statements were adduced at trial—over Varela's objection—to prove the government's case. Varela appeals from a judgment of the United States District Court for the Eastern District of New York, Reena Raggi, Judge, convicting him on both counts, following a jury trial.

We must decide in this appeal whether the exclusionary rule bars the use of unlawfully obtained post-arrest statements—statements that were suppressed for the purpose of proving that Varela committed one crime—to prove that Varela subsequently committed another crime, perjury. The deterrence theory of the exclusionary rule, which now holds sway, requires us, before suppressing evidence in a particular proceeding, to balance the deterrent effect of applying the exclusionary rule against the cost to society of excluding relevant information. ... We join the First, Fifth, and Ninth Circuits in concluding that the exclusionary rule does not apply in such a case, see United States v. Finucan, 708 F.2d 838, 845 (1st Cir.1983) ...

* * *

... if law enforcement officials already are prohibited from using unlawfully seized evidence to convict a defendant of the offenses under investigation, then, in theory, the officials already have been deterred from engaging in such activities; thus, the relevant question becomes whether any incremental deterrence results from excluding the same evidence in a subsequent proceeding....

Applying this teaching to the case at hand, we are forced to conclude that the addition marginal deterrence achieved by excluding Varela's March 16, 1990 statement in his perjury trial does not outweigh the societal benefit from permitting the use of the statement in this context....

B. PERMISSIBLE INTERROGATION TACTICS AND TECHNIQUES

1. TRICKERY AND DECEIT

FRAZIER v. CUPP

Supreme Court of the United States, 1969.
394 U.S. 731, 89 S.Ct. 1420.

MR. JUSTICE MARSHALL delivered the opinion of the Court.

* * *

Petitioner's second argument concerns the admission into evidence of his own confession. The circumstances under which the confession was obtained can be summarized briefly. Petitioner was arrested about 4:15 p.m. on September 24, 1964. He was taken to headquarters where questioning began at about 5 p.m. The interrogation, which was tape-recorded, ended slightly more than an hour later, and by 6:45 p.m. petitioner had signed a written version of his confession.

[The interrogation and trial of this case occurred prior to Miranda v. Arizona, which follows later in this chapter; consequently, the warnings of constitutional rights were not required.]

After the questioning had begun and after a few routine facts were ascertained, petitioner was questioned briefly about the location of his Marine uniform. He was next asked where he was on the night in question. Although he admitted that he was with his cousin Rawls, he denied being with any third person. Then petitioner was given a somewhat abbreviated description of his constitutional rights. He was told that he could have an attorney if he wanted one and that anything he said could be used against him at trial. Questioning thereafter became somewhat more vigorous, but petitioner continued to deny being with anyone but Rawls. At this point, the officer questioning petitioner told him, falsely, that Rawls had been brought in and that he had confessed. Petitioner still was reluctant to talk, but after the officer sympathetically suggested that the victim had started a fight by making homosexual advances, petitioner began to spill out his story. Shortly after he began he again showed signs of reluctance and said, "I think I had better get a lawyer before I talk any more. I am going to get into trouble more than I am in now." The officer replied simply, "You can't be in any more trouble than you are in now," and the questioning session proceeded. A full confession was obtained and, after further warnings, a written version was signed.

* * *

Petitioner also presses the alternative argument that his confession was involuntary and that it should have been excluded for that reason. The trial judge, after an evidentiary hearing during which the tape recording was played, could not agree with this contention, and our reading of the record does not lead us to a contrary conclusion. Before petitioner made any incriminating statements, he received partial warnings of his constitutional rights; this is, of course, a circumstance quite relevant to a finding of voluntariness. Davis v. North Carolina, 384 U.S. 737, 740, 741 (1966). The questioning was of short duration, and petitioner was a mature individual of normal intelligence. The fact that the police misrepresented the statements that Rawls had made is, while relevant, insufficient in our view to make this otherwise voluntary confession inadmissible. These cases must be decided by viewing the "totality of the circumstances," see, e.g., Clewis v. Texas, 386 U.S. 707, 708 (1967), and on the facts of this case we can find no error in the admission of petitioner's confession.

* * *

Because we find none of petitioner's contentions meritorious, we affirm the judgment of the Court of Appeals.

Affirmed.

MR. CHIEF JUSTICE WARREN and MR. JUSTICE DOUGLAS concur in the result.

MR. JUSTICE FORTAS took no part in the consideration or decision of this case.

NOTES

1. In People v. Lee, 111 Ill.2d 454, 490 N.E.2d 688 (1986), an assistant prosecutor falsely told the arrestee (defendant) that his fingerprints "were found all over" the apartment of the rape victim. He then admitted being in the apartment, which he had previously denied, and then confessed to the rape. Following are excerpts from the majority opinion of the Illinois Supreme Court:

"This court's recent decision in People v. Martin, 102 Ill.2d 412, 466 N.E.2d 228, *cert. denied* (1984), 469 U.S. 935, 105 S.Ct. 334, 270, is dispositive on this issue. There, both the police and the State's Attorney knowingly and falsely told the defendant that his codefendant had named him as the "triggerman" in a homicide. The defendant then made incriminating statements. This court found under the totality of the circumstances, that defendant's incriminating statements were given freely, voluntarily, and without any coercion overbearing his will despite the deliberate and false misrepresentation.

"*Martin* holds that inculpatory statements which are voluntary are not necessarily vitiated by misrepresentations by authorities. A misrepresentation which prompts inculpatory statements is only one factor to be considered in determining the voluntariness of the resulting statements. Other factors must be considered as well, such as, the 'age, education and intelligence of the accused, the duration of questioning, and whether he received his constitutional rights or was subjected to any physical punishment.' On the record before us, we find no indication that defendant's will was overborne such that any inculpatory statements were involuntary."

Two members of the court briefly expressed their disapproval of the deceptive practice employed in the interrogation.

2. In the Hawaiian Supreme Court case of State v. Kelekolio, 849 P.2d 58 (1993), the court, at p. 73, adopted a rule "to measure the legitimacy of the use of 'deception' by the police in eliciting confessions or inculpatory statements from suspects and arrestees." The rule said the court, "is that employment by the police of deliberate falsehoods *intrinsic* to the facts of the alleged offense in question will be treated as one of the totality of circumstances surrounding the confession or statement to be considered in assessing its voluntariness; on the other hand, deliberate falsehoods *extrinsic* to the facts of the alleged offense, which are of a type reasonably likely to procure an untrue statement or to influence an accused to make a confession regardless of guilt, will be regarded as coercive per se, thus obviating the need for a "totality of circumstances" analysis of voluntariness.

The court offered examples of the type of "intrinsic falsehoods" that would include "misrepresentations regarding the existence of incriminating evidence such as "(1) placement of the defendant's vehicle at the crime scene ... (2) physical evidence linked to the victim found in the defendant's car, ... (3) discovery of the murder weapon, ... (4) a claim that the murder victim is still alive, ... (5) presence of the defendant's fingerprints on the getaway car or at the crime scene.... (6) positive identification of the defendant by reliable witnesses, ... and (7) discovery of a nonexistent witness ...

"Some examples of *extrinsic* falsehoods—of a type reasonably likely to procure an untrue statement or to influence an accused to make a confession regardless of guilt—would include (1) assurances of divine salvation upon confession, ... (2) promises of mental health treatment in exchange for a confession, ... (3) assurances of treatment in a 'nice hospital' (in which the defendant could have his personal belongings and be visited by his girlfriend) in lieu of incarceration, in exchange for a confession ... (4) promises of more favorable treatment in the event of a confession, ... (5) misrepresentations of legal principles, such as (a) suggesting that the defendant would have the burden of convincing a judge and jury at trial that he was 'perfectly innocent' and had nothing to do with the offense, ... (b) misrepresenting the consequences of a 'habitual offender' conviction, ... and (c) holding out that the defendant's confession cannot be used against him at a trial, ... and (6) misrepresentations by an interrogating police officer, who is a close friend of the defendant, that the defendant's failure to confess will get the officer into trouble with his superiors and jeopardize the well-being of the officer's pregnant wife and children, ...

* * *

"Notwithstanding our holding, we emphasize that we are not purporting to enunciate a bright line per se rule that the use of intrinsic factual deception cannot, given the totality of circumstances surrounding any given statement, result in an involuntary confession. Rather, the rule that we formulate today merely declines to foreclose the admissibility of confessions, as a per se matter, procured in part through the use of this kind of deception. Such confessions remain subject to 'totality of circumstances' ... and may still be the product of interrogation techniques that are ' "so offensive to a civilized system of justice" ' that ' "they must be condemned" ' under principles of due process, ..."

Compare the foregoing test of deception legitimacy with the suggested test in *Criminal Interrogation and Confessions* (3d ed. 1986), by Inbau, Reid, and Buckley, at p. 217:

"A guideline that an interrogator may use in any case situation where he may be in doubt as to the permissibility of any particular type of trickery or deceit, is to ask himself the following question: 'Is what I am about to do, or say, apt to make an innocent person confess'? If the answer to the question is 'no,' the interrogator should go ahead and do or say what was contemplated. On the other hand, if the answer is 'yes,' the interrogator should refrain from doing or saying what he had in mind. This is the only understandable test of any practical value for interrogators to follow. Moreover, it is the only test that is fair both to the public and to the accused or suspected individual."

STATE v. CAYWARD

District Court of Appeals of Florida, 1989.
552 So.2d 971.

SCHEB, Acting Chief Judge.

The state appeals the trial court's order suppressing the defendant's confession. The trial court ruled the confession was involuntary because the police intentionally fabricated laboratory reports and exhibited them to the defendant during an interrogation in an attempt to secure a confession. The trial court found that the police tactics violated the defendant's constitutional right to due process of law. We affirm.

The relevant facts are undisputed. The defendant is a nineteen-year-old male suspected by the police of sexually assaulting and smothering his five-year-old niece. The police had focused their investigation on the defendant. They conducted an extensive interview of the defendant in three stages. Although they suspected the defendant, they did not think they had sufficient evidence with which to charge him. With the knowledge of the state attorney's office, the police fabricated two scientific reports which they intended to use as ploys in interrogating the defendant. One false report was prepared on stationery of the Florida Department of Criminal Law Enforcement; another was prepared on stationery of Life Codes, Inc., a testing organization. These false reports indicated that a scientific test established that the semen stains on the victim's underwear came from the defendant. The police showed the reports to the defendant as a device to induce a confession. Some time later during the interview, the defendant confessed.

After an evidentiary hearing, the trial court found that the defendant's attendance at the interview in response to a request by the police was voluntary, that he was advised of his rights under Miranda v. Arizona, 384 U.S. 436, 86 S.Ct. 1602 (1966), and that he signed a form waiving those rights. The interview, conducted by a police detective and an investigator from the state attorney's office, lasted approximately two hours. The defendant repeatedly denied his involvement. Eventually he was shown the false reports the police had manufactured. The reports were presented as genuine, and their significance was explained to the defendant. After the interview concluded, the defendant asked, "What happens now?" The investigator told him, "We are going to the grand jury," and indicated that the state would seek the death penalty. The defendant then indicated his involvement, first unrecorded and later on tape.

The trial judge did not find any evidence of physical coercion. The court concluded, however, that the fabrication and exhibition of documents purporting to be laboratory reports from reputable organizations is police conduct which cannot be sanctioned. The court ordered that the "portion of the defendant's statement taken on April 13, 1988 that was given after he was either shown the fabricated reports or advised of their contents or of their incriminating nature or of their existence, whichever be first, is suppressed and shall not be used in evidence against him."

The state appeals, contending that the trial court erred in suppressing the defendant's statements....

We begin our discussion with a recognition that a trial court's ruling concerning voluntariness of a confession comes to this court cloaked in the same presumption of correctness which attends jury verdicts and final judgments....

We recognize the basic principle that when conduct of law enforcement is outrageous, due process bars the government from invoking judicial process to obtain a conviction. United States v. Russell, 411 U.S. 423, 93 S.Ct. 1637 (1973). That the Florida Supreme Court is wedded to this principle is evidenced by its quotation with approval from Justice Stevens' dissent in Moran v. Burbine, 475 U.S. 412, 106 S.Ct. 1135 (1986). "[D]ue process requires fairness, integrity and honor in the operation of the criminal justice system, and in its treatment of the citizen's cardinal constitutional protections." ...

It has become well established that physical coercion by the police invalidates a confession on due process grounds. Colorado v. Connelly, 479 U.S. 157, 107 S.Ct. 515 (1986). For many years, however, the courts have focused on the more common and subtle form of coercion—psychological inducement. *See Miranda.* Since the coercion here was psychological and not physical, the state cites Wasko v. State, 505 So.2d 1314 (Fla.1987), to support its argument that the per se involuntariness rule does not apply in Florida and voluntariness must be determined by the totality of the evidence. Roman v. State, 475 So.2d 1228 (Fla.1985). The state argues that the trial judge erred in isolating the state's use of fabricated reports because he incorrectly elevated that one factor to a per se violation of due process.

We agree with the state that police deception does not render a confession involuntary per se. Frazier v. Cupp, 394 U.S. 731, 89 S.Ct. 1420 (1969). While Florida courts have frequently condemned the articulation by the police of incorrect, misleading statements to suspects, they have upheld the resulting confessions. ... Police deception does not automatically invalidate a confession especially where there is no doubt that the defendant was read and understood his *Miranda* rights. Halliwell v. State, 323 So.2d 557 (Fla.1975); Miller v. Fenton, 796 F.2d 598 (3d Cir.1986).

* * *

The instant case, however, presents a different question and one which appears to be one of first impression not only in Florida but in the United States. The reporters are filled with examples of the police making false *verbal* assertions to a suspect, but counsel has not indicated nor has our research revealed any case in which the police actually manufactured false documents and used them precisely as the police did in this case. Our inquiry then is whether there is a qualitative difference between the verbal artifices deemed acceptable and the presentation of the falsely contrived scientific documents challenged here. We think there is, and we agree with the trial judge that the police overstepped the line of permitted deception.

It admittedly is difficult for us to draw a distinction purely on legal grounds in light of the sometimes egregious verbal misrepresentations which have previously been allowed. Our opinion, therefore, is the result not only of prior case law, but of a careful examination of traditional constitutional protections as well as practical considerations. Based on what we perceive as an intrinsic distinction between verbal assertions and manufactured documentation, we draw what we hope will be a bright line by saying that the type of deception engaged in here has no place in our criminal justice system.

It may well be that a suspect is more impressed and thereby more easily induced to confess when presented with tangible, official-looking reports as opposed to merely being told that some tests have implicated him. If one perceives such a difference, it probably originates in the notion that a document which purports to be authoritative impresses one as being inherently more permanent and facially reliable than a simple verbal statement.

The very fact that our law insists that a suspect be advised of his *Miranda* rights and indicate that he understands them is almost an acknowledgment that individuals questioned by the police are entering an uncertain arena. *See Miranda,* 384 U.S. 436 at 458, 86 S.Ct. 1602 at 1619, 16 L.Ed.2d 694 at 714 (police interrogation is inherently coercive, and unless adequate protective devices are employed, no statement can truly be voluntarily given). Realistically, suspects given *Miranda* rights recognize that the object of a police inquiry is to confirm the suspicions held by the police. Police interrogations, even those of the least aggressive nature, are imbued with an atmosphere of confrontation. Thus, a suspect reasonably expects that police will make assertions and disclose or not disclose certain information in an attempt to observe the suspect's reactions.

We think, however, that both the suspect's and the public's expectations concerning the built-in adversariness of police interrogations do not encompass the notion that the police will knowingly fabricate tangible documentation or physical evidence against an individual. Such an idea brings to mind the horrors of less advanced centuries in our civilization when magistrates at times schemed with sovereigns to frame political rivals. This is precisely one of the parade of horrors civics teachers have long taught their pupils that our modern judicial system was designed to correct. Thus we think the manufacturing of false documents by police officials offends our traditional notions of due process of law under both the federal and state constitutions. . . .

In addition to our spontaneous distaste for the conduct we have reviewed in this matter, we have practical concerns regarding use of the false reports beyond the inducement of a confession. Unlike oral misrepresentations, manufactured documents have the potential of indefinite life and the facial appearance of authenticity. A report falsified for interrogation purposes might well be retained and filed in police paperwork. Such reports have the potential of finding their way into the courtroom.

Several factors make such a possibility realistic. First, police departments are involved in thousands of investigations each year. Second, many of these investigations result in criminal trials which swell the already staggering caseloads of the criminal justice system. Third, we must consider the long periods of time which often elapse between an investigation and the trial. During this time, those officials involved in the manufacturing of the false reports could leave for other jobs, die, or simply forget the circumstances under which the reports were obtained. This dangerous possibility is exacerbated by the common availability of photo reproduction processes, conducive to the widespread dissemination of documents. Paperwork is an inherent necessity of modern law enforcement, and multiple copies of documents are made and filed in different departments according to various filing systems. Even if some copies were properly marked as false or even destroyed, other copies might remain and cause dangerous confusion.

We are further concerned that false documents retained in police or state attorney's files might be disclosed to the media as a result of the public records law. A suspect's reputation could be unwittingly yet unfairly and permanently marred and his right to a fair trial jeopardized by the media's innocent reporting of falsified documents.

We can also conceive of an unintended scenario where a manufactured document, initially designed only for use in interrogation, might be admitted as substantive evidence against a defendant. Although one hopes that such an error would be discovered in preparation for trial, the reality of our courts' heavy caseloads is that counsel and trial judges routinely accept as true documents which appear to be reliable reports from known government and private agencies. Section 90.902, Florida Statutes (1987), a part of the evidence code, makes it unnecessary to authenticate with extrinsic evidence documents which purport to be from any state department, officer, or agency. We note that one of the two manufactured reports in issue here could be classified as a self-authenticating document.

We shudder to think of the impact that questionable authenticity of court records might have not only on the trial level, but on the appellate level. We are routinely presented with documents in court files which we must assume to be genuine. To sanction the manufacturing of false documents, which have the potential of being admitted as substantive evidence, would severely diminish our confidence in relying upon facially valid documents in court files.

Additionally, were we to approve the conduct taken in this case, we might be opening the door for police to fabricate court documents, including warrants, orders, and judgments. We think that such a step would drastically erode and perhaps eliminate the public's recognition of the authority of court orders, and without the citizenry's respect, our judicial system cannot long survive.

A final factor, which weighs heavily in our decision, concerns the increased confidence the public generally feels toward the police. This feeling of assurance has been earned over the course of several decades by increased professionalism of law enforcement agencies, education, and community involvement. We recognize that law enforcement officers must be allowed a degree of latitude in interrogating suspects, and we acknowledge the role of confessions in the administration of the criminal justice system. We must, however, decline to undermine the rapport the police have developed with the public by approving participation of law enforcement officers in practices which most citizens would consider highly inappropriate. We think that for us to sanction the manufacturing of false documents by the police would greatly lessen the respect the public has for the criminal justice system and for those sworn to uphold and enforce the law. In a word, in administration of the criminal law, we simply cannot allow the end of securing a confession to justify the means employed in this case.

We certify the following question to the Supreme Court of Florida as a question of great public importance:

Does the fabrication and exhibition of false documents to a suspect by police in an attempt to induce a confession violate due process rights under federal and state constitutions?

Affirmed.

HALL and THREADGILL, JJ., concur.

[Florida Supreme Court review of this case was dismissed in State v. Cayward, 562 So.2d 347 (1990).]

2. PROMISES

1. In United States v. Rutledge, 900 F.2d 1127 (7th Cir.1990), the suspect-defendant, while being interrogated for drug dealing, was told that his cooperation would be brought to the attention of the sentencing

judge. The resulting confession was held admissible. See, however, United States v. Baldwin, 60 F.3d 369 (7th Cir.1995), in which the full circuit court was divided as to whether an en banc hearing should be granted regarding the "cooperation" issue. The majority prevailed in denying a review.

2. Consider the following provision in § 60.45 of New York's Criminal Procedure Law, and particularly, the "substantial risk" test in 2(i):

Rules of evidence; admissibility of statements of defendants

> 1. Evidence of a written or oral confession, admission, or other statement made by a defendant with respect to his participation or lack of participation in the offense charged, may not be received in evidence against him in a criminal proceeding if such statement was involuntarily made.
>
> 2. A confession, admission or other statement is "involuntarily made" by a defendant when it is obtained from him:
>
> (a) By any person by the use or threatened use of physical force upon the defendant or another person, or by means of any other improper conduct or undue pressure which impaired the defendant's physical or mental condition to the extent of undermining his ability to make a choice whether or not to make a statement; or
>
> (b) By a public servant engaged in law enforcement activity or by a person then acting under his direction or in cooperation with him:
>
> (i) by means of any promise or statement of fact, which promise or statement creates a substantial risk that the defendant might falsely incriminate himself; or
>
> (ii) in violation of such rights as the defendant may derive from the constitution of this state or of the United States.

C. THE PRACTICAL NECESSITY FOR INTERROGATIONS AND THE MORALITY OF DECEIVING SUSPECTS

1. THE NECESSITY

1. Consider the following viewpoint expressed in *Criminal Interrogation and Confessions* (3d ed. 1986), by Inbau, Reid, and Buckley at xiii:

> "There is a gross misconception, generated and perpetuated by fiction writers, movies, and TV, that if criminal investigators carefully examine a crime scene, they will almost always find a clue that will lead them to the offender; and that, furthermore, once the criminal is located, he will readily confess or otherwise

reveal guilt, as by attempting to escape. This, however, is pure fiction. As a matter of fact, the art and science of criminal investigation have not developed to a point where the search for and the examination of physical evidence will always, or even in most cases, reveal a clue to the identity of the perpetrator or provide the necessary legal proof of guilt. In criminal investigations, even the most efficient type, there are many, many instances where physical clues are entirely absent, and the only approach to a possible solution of the crime is the interrogation of the criminal suspect himself, as well as of others who may possess significant information. . . ."

The text presents the various tactics and techniques for the interrogations of criminal suspects, all of which, state the authors, measure up to the requirements of the law.

The authors submit the following guideline for interrogators in ascertaining the legal permissibility of their conduct: "Is what I am about to do, or say, apt to make an innocent person confess?: If the answer is 'no,' the interrogator should go ahead and do or say what was contemplated. On the other hand, if the answer is 'yes,' the interrogator should refrain from doing or saying what was on his mind." They assert that this is the only understandable test of any practical value for interrogators to follow. Moreover, they urge that this is the only test that is fair both to the public and to the accused or suspected individual." (P. 217)

2. In the Canadian Supreme Court case of Rothman v. The Queen, 59 C.C.C.2d 30 (1981), the following appeared in the concurring opinion of Justice Lamar:

"It must also be borne in mind that the investigation of crime and the detection of criminals is not a game to be governed by the Marquess of Queensbury rules. The authorities, in dealing with shrewd and often sophisticated criminals, must sometimes of necessity resort to tricks or other forms of deceit and should not ... be hampered in their work. What should be repressed vigorously is conduct on their part that shocks the community. That a police officer pretend to be a lock-up chaplain and hear a suspect's confession is conduct that shocks the community; so is pretending to be the duty legal aid lawyer eliciting in that way incriminating statements from suspects or accused; injecting pentothal into a diabetic suspect pretending it is his daily shot of insulin and using his statement in evidence would also shock the community; but generally speaking, pretending to be a hard drug addict to break a drug ring would not shock the community; nor would, as in this case, pretending to be a truck driver to secure the conviction of a trafficker; in fact, what would shock the community would be preventing the police from resorting to such a trick."

3. Chef Justice Weintraub of the New Jersey Supreme court expressed the following viewpoint in State v. McKnight, 52 N.J. 35, 243 A.2d 240 (1968):

> "When the guilty go undetected, or, if detected, are nonetheless set free because plain evidence of guilt is suppressed, the price is exacted from what might be the first right of the individual, the right to be protected from criminal attack in his home, in his work, and in the street. Government is constituted to provide law and order. The Bill of Rights must be understood in light of that mission.
>
> "There is no right to escape detection. There is no right to commit a perfect crime or to an equal opportunity to that end. The Constitution is not at all offended when a guilty man stubs his toe. On the contrary, it is decent to hope that he will. Nor is it dirty business to use evidence a defendant himself may furnish in the detectional stage. Voluntary confessions accord with high moral values, and as to the culprit who reveals his guilt unwittingly with no intent to shed his inner burden, it is no more unfair to use the evidence he thereby reveals than it is to turn against him clues at the scene of the crime which a brighter, better-informed, or more gifted criminal would not have left. Thus the Fifth Amendment does not say that a man shall not be permitted to incriminate himself, or that he shall not be persuaded to do so. It says no more than that a man shall not be 'compelled' to give evidence against himself."

4. Consider, with respect to the "practical necessity" issue, the possible advantage to a convicted defendant—in a federal court—of a compliance with § 3 E 1.1 of the United States Sentencing Commission Guidelines Manual. It provides as follows: "*Acceptance of Responsibility:* (a) If a defendant clearly demonstrates a recognition and affirmative acceptance of personal responsibility for his criminal conduct, reduce the offense level by 2 levels." The Commentary to § 3 E 1.1 provides, that in determining whether a defendant qualifies for that provision, appropriate consideration may be given to the "voluntary and truthful admission to authorities of involvement in the offense and related conduct."

2. THE MORALITY FACTOR

Some writers upon the subject of the morality of the interrogator's conduct involving tactics of trickery and deceit contend that such practices are not only unfair to suspects but are also demoralizing to the interrogators themselves.

1. In a 1992 article entitled "The Ethics of Deceptive Interrogation" appearing in *The Criminal Justice Ethics Journal* (Winter/Spring 1992), Professor of Law Jerome H. Skolnick and a graduate student, Richard A. Leo, of the University of California (Berkeley) state at p. 3, the following: "Contemporary police interrogation is routinely decep-

tive," and "is shot through with deception. Police are instructed to—and do—trick, lie, and cajole to elicit so-called 'voluntary' confessions." Some examples that the authors mention are "police may misrepresent the nature and seriousness of the offense . . . or tell a suspect that a murder victim is still alive, hoping that this will compel the suspect to talk, or police may exaggerate the seriousness of the offense—overstating, for example, the amount of money embezzled—so that the suspect feels compelled to confess to a smaller role in the offense." (Pp. 5 & 6.)

Skolnick and Leo also commented: "Although affirmed in the interest of crime control values by its advocates like Fred Inbau—who, along with his co-author John Reid, has exerted a major influence on generations of police interrogators—it may generate quite unanticipated consequences" such as "the effects of systematic lying on law enforcement's reputation for veracity." (P. 9.)

In one of his separate articles, Leo contended that "trickery may be the functional equivalent of coercion, since both strategies may induce involuntary behavior." See Leo, "From Coercion to Deception: The Changing Nature of Police Interrogation in America," 18 *Crime, Law and Social Change.* 35, 54 (1992).

2. In a 1995 article entitled "Trust, Lies and Interrogation," by Professor of Law Margaret L. Paris of the University of Oregon, in 3 *Virginia Journal of Social Policy & the Law* 3, she stated, in the Introduction, that she owes much to the clients with whom she worked as a criminal defense attorney for six years. "Almost all of them," she stated, "were guilty of having committed crimes, and many, though by no means all, impressed me with their remorse, humanity, and overwhelming desire to reenter relationships of trust." She proposed that "communities urge their deliberative bodies make rules authorizing certain interrogation techniques." However, "among the techniques prohibited should be interrogations' lies." She added that "a rule prohibiting interrogators from lying to suspects will facilitate trusts between suspects and government." (Pp. 7, 9.)

D. REMEDIES FOR ABUSIVE INTERROGATIONS

1. CIVIL REMEDIES

Under recent case law, a federal civil rights action may be available to a person who has been the victim of a coerced confession or even an abusive interrogation. The pertinent federal statute (42 U.S.C.A. § 1983) reads:

> "Every person who, under color of any statute, ordinance, regulation, custom, or usage, of any State or Territory, subjects, or causes to be subjected, any citizen of the United States or other person within the jurisdiction thereof to the deprivation of any rights, privileges, or immunities secured by the Constitu-

tion and the laws, shall be liable to the party injured in an action at law, suit in equity, or other proper proceeding for redress."

A clear and disturbing example of the type of police interrogation that qualifies for the application of Section 1983 is the following 1992 case, reported here in considerably condensed form:

COOPER v. DUPNIK

United States Circuit Court of Appeals, Ninth Circuit, 1992.
963 F.2d 1220.

Trott, Circuit Judge (for the majority).

Cooper sued employees of the Pima County Sheriff's Department and the Tucson Police Department, as well as the agencies and municipalities for which they worked. Cooper alleged a violation of 42 U.S.C. § 1983 (1988), and various state laws; he also included a count for defamation. All of the defendants moved for summary judgment based on the doctrine of qualified immunity; the district court denied the motion. On appeal, a panel of this court reversed on all counts except the defamation claim. Cooper v. Dupnik, 924 F.2d 1520 (9th Cir.1991). Cooper successfully petitioned for a rehearing en banc. 933 F.2d 798 (9th Cir.1991).

* * *

Our review of the denial of appellants' motion for summary judgment is de novo, and in conducting this review, we contemplate the evidence presented to the district court in the light most favorable to Cooper, the nonmoving party. As to the issue of qualified immunity, we look to see whether the police "acted reasonably under settled law in the circumstances." ... We note that in the main, the facts on which Cooper's complaint is based are not contested.

We affirm the district court on all counts.

* * *

On May 7, 1986, an identification technician for the Tucson Police Department named Timothy O'Sullivan, whose primary responsibility was to produce color photographs for the police laboratory, decided with no input from the Task Force that Michael Cooper might be a suspect of its investigation. The record shows that O'Sullivan had not done any substantial fingerprint work for at least six (and possibly nine) years. He previously had failed the state's fingerprint examination. Nevertheless, he obtained Cooper's known fingerprints and compared them—hastily and without following proper procedure—with latent fingerprints lifted as evidence from the scene of one of the Prime Time Rapist's attacks, ...

O'Sullivan concluded he had a match, and he asked the supervisor of the lab, Mr. Scott, to verify his conclusions. Scott, who also was not a certified latent fingerprint examiner, confirmed O'Sullivan's match; O'Sullivan called Detective Wright and reported the finding.

* * *

Wright came to the lab and asked O'Sullivan to check Cooper's known prints against latent prints lifted at the scene of another attack. O'Sullivan had some difficulty making a match, but Scott looked at the prints and concluded he had a positive comparison. When Sergeant Taylor was informed of this development, he ordered the immediate arrest of Michael Cooper.

O'Sullivan and Scott were mistaken: the latent prints at the crime scenes did not belong to Michael Cooper. These mistakes, however, were not discovered until it was too late to avoid some of their consequences.

At approximately 3:00 P.M. of the same day, Barkman and Wright located Cooper in the office of the Pima County Probation Department [Cooper was on probation for a fraud conviction] where Cooper was initially interviewed for twenty to thirty minutes. Barkman's plan to undermine Cooper's right to remain silent was in effect from the moment he and Detective Wright walked through the door. At the outset of the interview, which was tape-recorded, Barkman fully advised Cooper of his Miranda rights, but deliberately turned the advisement into what he hoped Cooper would perceive as a joke. Barkman's psychological ploy was designed to make Cooper ignore the warnings, and begin to talk. Barkman intended to undercut Cooper's Constitutional right not to talk to the Task Force by complying with Miranda's safeguards in form only, not in spirit or in substance. For example, after he first jokingly asked Cooper if Cooper had a rights card, Barkman said, "I could read you my driver's license if you like."

* * *

. . . At the end of this interview, during which Cooper denied he was the Prime Time Rapist, he formally was arrested. Cooper then made the first of two unequivocal requests for an attorney, a request which Barkman and Wright expected, and which they deliberately ignored, in conformity with their plan.

* * *

Wright and Barkman both participated in Cooper's interrogation. Wright went first, and Barkman acknowledged that when he took over, he intended to "go in there and hammer him." In accord with the plan, the record amply demonstrates that Cooper was subjected to Barkman's interrogation techniques designed to instill stress, hopelessness, and fear, and to break his resistance.

* * *

Cooper was reduced to a state of agitation and anxiety marked by tears and sobbing as he persistently maintained his innocence in the face of Barkman's onslaught. He repeated his request for an attorney, stating, "I want to talk to my lawyer, Nancy Pastero, as soon as possible, sir, and I will not give you any more of my honesty because you're not buying it." This request, which contains a statement of unwillingness to talk, as well as a desire to consult an attorney, was disregarded.

* * *

There came a time well into the interrogation, however, when Barkman concluded that Cooper was innocent. Barkman exited the interrogation room and reported his conclusion to Sergeant Taylor. When he did so, the scene (which we piece together from different parts of Barkman's deposition) was dramatic....

* * *

... At about 9:00 P.M. that evening, with Cooper still maintaining his innocence, the interrogation ceased. He was then booked in the Pima County Jail where he may have had access to a telephone. The plan, although implemented with great intensity, had failed to yield a confession.

... After more examination of the fingerprint evidence ... the persons working on the fingerprint comparisons concluded that they did not have a match after all. They found sufficient discrepancies to cancel the points of comparison, and they reported their findings to Sergeant Taylor.

* * *

... the Task Force met with the local prosecuting attorney. Sergeant Taylor argued to keep Cooper in jail, but Barkman at this point insisted Cooper was innocent. The prosecuting attorney was not persuaded by Sergeant Taylor, and Cooper finally was released during the afternoon of that day, May 8, 1986, nearly twenty-four hours after his arrest. During his incarceration, and despite two attempts to contact an attorney, Cooper apparently had no contact with the outside world—including his family.

* * *

On January 8, 1987, Cooper and his wife filed a civil action in the United States District Court for the District of Arizona. The lawsuit named the following defendants: [members of various county agencies and the participating investigating police and interrogators.]

* * *

We note that Cooper sues in connection with the interrogation for the alleged violation of his substantive Constitutional rights, not merely for violations of the procedural safeguards provided by Miranda. He now concedes, however, that the Sixth Amendment right to counsel is inapposite because he never formally was charged in court with a crime....

Cooper's suit in connection with this appeal hinges on whether the appellants deprived him of a Constitutional right.

* * *

The panel rejected Cooper's claim on four additional grounds. First, it concluded Cooper's Fourteenth Amendment rights were not violated because Cooper did not confess to any crime. Second, it overlooked Miranda's primary holding that the Constitutional right against compulsory self-incrimination, known as the right to remain silent, is applicable to suspects in police custody; as a result, it rejected Cooper's Fifth Amendment claim. Third, the panel determined Cooper's substantive due process rights were not violated because the Task Force's conduct did not " 'shock[ ] the conscious' [sic]." ... Fourth, the panel decided that all appellants were protected from suit by the doctrine of qualified immunity, because "[t]here are simply no section 1983 substantive due process cases with similar facts." ...

We respectfully disagree with the majority of the original panel on each of these issues. First, the record reveals Cooper made statements which could and probably would have been used against him had he gone to trial. Detective Wright was asked if she believed the interrogation produced information that substantiated Cooper's involvement in two of the cases. Her answer was: "There was information from my interview with him that, yes, I thought it could." Cooper's statements were the product of impermissible conduct by the Task Force; the fact that they did not technically qualify as a "confession" is irrelevant.

By the same reasoning, Cooper's Fourteenth Amendment rights also were violated. It is irrelevant that Cooper's coerced statements were never introduced against him at trial. The Task Force's wrongdoing was complete at the moment it forced Cooper to speak. This case does not involve an inchoate Constitutional violation.

Second, to characterize the Task Force's conduct as a mere violation of Miranda's prophylactic advisement requirements is to see a hurricane as but a movement of air. The appellants in this case engaged in the premeditated elimination of Mr. Cooper's substantive Fifth Amendment rights, not merely the disposal of the procedural safeguards designed to protect those rights. Thus, Cooper's statements were "compelled" and "coerced."

* * *

Third, the Task Force's conduct unquestionably shocks the conscience, and thus violates substantive due process. The original panel conceded that "the question is a close one," Cooper, 924 F.2d at 1530, but then concluded there was no violation. With all respect, we do not think the question is close: the Task Force's conduct was iniquitous, and surely does "more than offend some fastidious squeamishness or private sentimentalism about combatting crime too energetically." Rochin, 342 U.S. at 172, 72 S.Ct. at 209.

Fourth and finally, the appellants are not protected by the doctrine of qualified (good-faith) immunity. Qualified immunity protects officials from suits under § 1983 for violations of rights which are not "clearly established at the time of the challenged actions...." Mitchell, 472 U.S. at 528, 105 S.Ct. at 2816. But this case does not involve any borderline Constitutional rights. There is no question that the Constitutional holding in Miranda is "clearly established" law; similarly, there is no question that the appellants' conduct violates both the Fifth Amendment itself (as opposed to just the Miranda rules designed to protect it), and the Fourteenth Amendment. Appellants knew they were violating the Constitution. See Malley v. Briggs, 475 U.S. 335 (1986) (qualified immunity is not available to officials who "knowingly violate the law").

For these reasons, we believe that Cooper, relying on multiple theories, has made out a prima facie case under § 1983 against the appellants. Accordingly, we affirm the district court on all counts and remand the case for trial. Our analysis follows.

* * *

Can the coercing by police of a statement from a suspect in custody ripen into a full-blown Constitutional violation only if and when the statement is tendered and used against the declarant in court? We think not. The Supreme Court in 1936 established clearly and beyond anyone's misapprehension the proposition that the Constitution, as a limit on the behavior of government officials, flatly prohibits coercion in the pursuit of a statement from a person suspected of a crime.

* * *

There is a second Fourteenth Amendment substantive due process yardstick available to Cooper as a theory of § 1983 liability. The test is whether the Task Force's conduct "shocks the conscience." Rochin, 342 U.S. at 172, 72 S.Ct. at 209. Rochin outlawed all police conduct that "offend[s] those canons of decency and fairness which express the notions of justice of English-speaking peoples even toward those charged with the most heinous offenses." ... We address this issue last not because it is less significant than the Fifth Amendment compulsion and due process coercion claims already discussed, but because an explication of the facts in connection with those claims is necessary to determine whether the "canons of fairness and decency," referred to in Rochin, were violated by the activities of the Task Force in dealing with Cooper.

[Three of the judges dissented. The basic objection appears in Judge Brunetti's dissent, in which two other judges concurred:]

The interrogation of Cooper was not accomplished in such an outrageous fashion as to shock the conscience and thus deprive Cooper of his substantive due process rights. The police used interrogation methods that were harsh but which have been held to satisfy the requirements of due process. Their techniques, employed during four hours of questioning, involved no physical abuse or threats of physical abuse.

Because their conduct did not violate the Fifth Amendment and thus would not provide a § 1983 cause of action under that amendment, it would be anomalous to bootstrap the claim through a due process analysis when the amendment on point was not violated.

[In a dissent by Judge Leavy, with the concurrence of two of the other dissenters, the following appears in the concluding paragraph:]

Whatever the holding of the majority may be, it comes in a case in which whatever was "coerced" from the accused convinced his interrogators of his innocence and was apparently totally consistent with the truth. In my view, no privilege against self-incrimination is lost until a court erroneously admits into evidence an involuntary or otherwise infirm statement.

2. CRIMINAL REMEDIES

A civil rights violation, which gives rise to a civil suit under 42 U.S.C.A. § 1983, may also precipitate a criminal indictment against the offending officer(s) under 18 U.S.C.A. § 242. That provision reads as follows:

> Whoever, under color of any law, statute, ordinance, regulation, or custom, willfully subjects any inhabitant of any State, Territory, or District to the deprivation of any rights, privileges, or immunities secured or protected by the constitution or laws of the United States, or to different punishments, pains, or penalties, on account of such inhabitant being an alien, or by reason of his color, or race, than are prescribed for the punishment of citizens, shall be fined not more than $1,000 or imprisoned not more than one year, or both; and if death results shall be subject to imprisonment for any term of years or for life.

If two or more persons are involved, the civil rights conspiracy statute may be invoked (18 U.S.C.A. § 241). That statute provides for a 10 year penalty and a $10,000 fine.

A criminal sanction specifically drafted to encompass the problems under discussion here is the Illinois statutory provision in ILCS, § 720, 5/12, which reads as follows:

Compelling Confession or Information by Force or Threat

(a) A person who, with intent to obtain a confession, statement or information regarding any offense, inflicts or threatens to inflict physical harm upon the person threatened or upon any other person commits the offense of compelling a confession or information by force or threat.

(b) Sentence. Compelling a confession or information is a felony.

E. WARNINGS OF CONSTITUTIONAL RIGHTS—MIRANDA v. ARIZONA AND THE INTERPRETATION OF ITS REQUIREMENTS

1. THE MIRANDA MANDATE

MIRANDA v. ARIZONA; VIGNERA v. NEW YORK; WESTOVER v. UNITED STATES; CALIFORNIA v. STEWART

Supreme Court of the United States, 1966.
384 U.S. 436, 86 S.Ct. 1602.

MR. CHIEF JUSTICE WARREN delivered the opinion of the Court [with the concurrence of Justices Black, Douglas, Brennan, and Fortas].

The cases before us raise questions which go to the roots of our concepts of American criminal jurisprudence; the restraints society must observe consistent with the Federal Constitution in prosecuting individuals for crime. More specifically, we deal with the admissibility of statements obtained from an individual who is subjected to custodial police interrogation and the necessity for procedures which assure that the individual is accorded his privilege under the Fifth Amendment to the Constitution not to be compelled to incriminate himself.

We dealt with certain phases of this problem recently in Escobedo v. State of Illinois, 378 U.S. 478, 84 S.Ct. 1758 (1964).

There, as in the four cases before us, law enforcement officials took the defendant into custody and interrogated him in a police station for the purpose of obtaining a confession. The police did not effectively advise him of his right to remain silent or of his right to consult with his attorney. Rather, they confronted him with an alleged accomplice who accused him of having perpetrated a murder. When the defendant denied the accusation and said "I didn't shoot Manuel, you did it," they handcuffed him and took him to an interrogation room. There, while handcuffed and standing, he was questioned for four hours until he confessed. During this interrogation, the police denied his request to speak to his attorney, and they prevented his retained attorney, who had come to the police station, from consulting with him. At his trial, the State, over his objection, introduced the confession against him. We held that the statements thus made were constitutionally inadmissible.

* * *

Our holding will be spelled out with some specificity in the pages which follow but briefly stated it is this: the prosecution may not use statements, whether exculpatory or inculpatory, stemming from custodial interrogation of the defendant unless it demonstrates the use of procedural safeguards effective to secure the privilege against self-incrimination. By custodial interrogation, we mean questioning initiated by law enforcement officers after a person has been taken into custody or otherwise deprived of his freedom of action in any significant way.[1] As for the procedural safeguards to be employed, unless other fully effective means are devised to inform accused persons of their right of silence and to assure a continuous opportunity to exercise it, the following measures are required. Prior to any questioning, the person must be warned that he has a right to remain silent, that any statement he does make may be used as evidence against him, and that he has a right to the presence of an attorney, either retained or appointed. The defendant may waive effectuation of these rights, provided the waiver is made voluntarily, knowingly and intelligently. If, however, he indicates in any manner and at any stage of the process that he wishes to consult with an attorney before speaking there can be no questioning. Likewise, if the individual is alone and indicates in any manner that he does not wish to be interrogated, the police may not question him. The mere fact that he may have answered some questions or volunteered some statements on his own does not deprive him of the right to refrain from answering any further inquiries until he has consulted with an attorney and thereafter consents to be questioned.

I.

The constitutional issue we decide in each of these cases is the admissibility of statements obtained from a defendant questioned while in custody or otherwise deprived of his freedom of action in any significant way. In each, the defendant was questioned by police officers, detectives, or a prosecuting attorney in a room in which he was cut off from the outside world. In none of these cases was the defendant given a full and effective warning of his rights at the outset of the interrogation process. In all the cases, the questioning elicited oral admissions, and in three of them, signed statements as well which were admitted at their trials. They all thus share salient features—incommunicado interrogation of individuals in a police-dominated atmosphere, resulting in self-incriminating statements without full warnings of constitutional rights.

An understanding of the nature and setting of this in-custody interrogation is essential to our decisions today. The difficulty in depicting what transpires at such interrogations stems from the fact that in this country they have largely taken place incommunicado. From extensive factual studies undertaken in the early 1930's, ... it is clear that police violence and the "third degree" flourished at that time. In a series of cases decided by this Court long after these studies, the police resorted to physical brutality—beatings, hanging, whipping—and to sustained and protracted questioning incommunicado in order to extort confessions. The Commission on Civil Rights in 1961 found much

1. This is what we meant in *Escobedo* when we spoke of an investigation which had focused on an accused.

evidence to indicate that "some policemen still resort to physical force to obtain confessions." The use of physical brutality and violence is not, unfortunately, relegated to the past or to any part of the country. Only recently in Kings County, New York, the police brutally beat, kicked and placed lighted cigarette butts on the back of a potential witness under interrogation for the purpose of securing a statement incriminating a third party.

The examples given above are undoubtedly the exception now, but they are sufficiently widespread to be the object of concern. Unless a proper limitation upon custodial interrogation is achieved—such as these decisions will advance—there can be no assurance that practices of this nature will be eradicated in the foreseeable future....

* * *

Again we stress that the modern practice of in-custody interrogation is psychologically rather than physically oriented. As we have stated before, ... "this Court has recognized that coercion can be mental as well as physical, and that the blood of the accused is not the only hallmark of an unconstitutional inquisition." Interrogation still takes place in privacy. Privacy results in secrecy and this in turn results in a gap in our knowledge as to what in fact goes on in the interrogation rooms. A valuable source of information about present police practices, however, may be found in various police manuals and texts which document procedures employed with success in the past, and which recommended various other effective tactics. These texts are used by law enforcement agencies themselves as guides.[2] It should be noted that these texts professedly present the most enlightened and effective means presently used to obtain statements through custodial interrogation. By considering these texts and other data, it is possible to describe procedures observed and noted around the country.

The officers are told by the manuals that the "principal psychological factor contributing to a successful interrogation is privacy—being alone with the person under interrogation." [Inbau and Reid] The efficacy of this tactic has been explained as follows:

2. The methods described in Inbau & Reid, Criminal Interrogation and Confessions (1962), are a revision and enlargement of material presented in three prior editions of a predecessor text, Lie Detection and Criminal Interrogation (3d ed. 1953). The authors and their associates are officers of the Chicago Police Scientific Crime Detection Laboratory and have had extensive experience in writing, lecturing and speaking to law enforcement authorities over a 20–year period. They say that the techniques portrayed in their manuals reflect their experiences and are the most effective psychological stratagems to employ during interrogations. Similarly, the techniques described in O'Hara, Fundamentals of Criminal Investigation (1956), were gleaned from long service as observer, lecturer in police science, and work as a federal criminal investigator. All these texts have had rather extensive use among law enforcement agencies and among students of police science, with total sales and circulation of over 44,000.

[Editors' note: Inbau was Director of the Laboratory from 1938–1941; he has had no official connection with it since then. Reid was on the Laboratory staff from 1938 to 1947; he too had no official connection with it since that time. Moreover, at the time of the Miranda decision in 1966 Inbau had been a *full time* Professor of Law at Northwestern University School of Law for *21 years.*]

"If at all practicable, the interrogation should take place in the investigator's office or at least in a room of his own choice. The subject should be deprived of every psychological advantage. In his own home he may be confident, indignant, or recalcitrant. He is more keenly aware of his rights and more reluctant to tell of his indiscretions or criminal behavior within the walls of his home. Moreover his family and other friends are nearby, their presence lending moral support. In his office, the investigator possesses all the advantages. The atmosphere suggests the invincibility of the forces of the law." [O'Hara]

To highlight the isolation and unfamiliar surroundings, the manuals instruct the police to display an air of confidence in the suspect's guilt and from outward appearance to maintain only an interest in confirming certain details. The guilt of the subject is to be posited as a fact. The interrogator should direct his comments toward the reasons why the subject committed the act, rather than court failure by asking the subject whether he did it. Like other men, perhaps the subject has had a bad family life, had an unhappy childhood, had too much to drink, had an unrequited desire for women. The officers are instructed to minimize the moral seriousness of the offense, to cast blame on the victim or on society. These tactics are designed to put the subject in a psychological state where his story is but an elaboration of what the police purport to know already—that he is guilty. Explanations to the contrary are dismissed and discouraged.

The texts thus stress that the major qualities an interrogator should possess are patience and perseverance. One writer describes the efficacy of these characteristics in this manner:

"In the preceding paragraphs emphasis has been placed on kindness and strategems. The investigator will, however, encounter many situations where the sheer weight of his personality will be the deciding factor. Where emotional appeals and tricks are employed to no avail, he must rely on an oppressive atmosphere of dogged persistence. He must interrogate steadily and without relent, leaving the subject no prospect of surcease. He must dominate his subject and overwhelm him with his inexorable will to obtain the truth. He should interrogate for a spell of several hours pausing only for the subject's necessities in acknowledgement of the need to avoid a charge of duress that can be technically substantiated. In a serious case, the interrogation may continue for days, with the required intervals for food and sleep, but with no respite from the atmosphere of domination. It is possible in this way to induce the subject to talk without resorting to duress or coercion. The method should be used only when the guilt of the subject appears highly probable." [O'Hara]

The manuals suggest that the suspect be offered legal excuses for his actions in order to obtain an initial admission of guilt. Where there is a suspected revenge-killing, for example, the interrogator may say:

> "Joe, you probably didn't go out looking for this fellow with the purpose of shooting him. My guess is, however, that you expected something from him and that's why you carried a gun—for your own protection. You knew him for what he was, no good. Then when you met him he probably started using foul, abusive language and he gave some indication that he was about to pull a gun on you, and that's when you had to act to save your own life. That's about it, isn't it, Joe?" [Inbau & Reid]

Having then obtained the admission of shooting, the interrogator is advised to refer to circumstantial evidence which negates the self-defense explanation. This should enable him to secure the entire story. One text notes that "Even if he fails to do so, the inconsistency between the subject's original denial of the shooting and his present admission of at least doing the shooting will serve to deprive him of a self-defense 'out' at the time of trial." [Inbau & Reid]

When the techniques described above prove unavailing, the texts recommend they be alternated with a show of some hostility. One ploy often used has been termed the "friendly-unfriendly" or the "Mutt and Jeff" act:

> ". . . In this technique, two agents are employed. Mutt, the relentless investigator, who knows the subject is guilty and is not going to waste any time. He's sent a dozen men away for this crime and he's going to send the subject away for the full term. Jeff, on the other hand, is obviously a kindhearted man. He has a family himself. He has a brother who was involved in a little scrape like this. He disapproves of Mutt and his tactics and will arrange to get him off the case if the subject will cooperate. He can't hold Mutt off for very long. The subject would be wise to make a quick decision. The technique is applied by having both investigators present while Mutt acts out his role. Jeff may stand by quietly and demur at some of Mutt's tactics. When Jeff makes his plea for cooperation, Mutt is not present in the room." [O'Hara]

The interrogators sometimes are instructed to induce a confession out of trickery. The technique here is quite effective in crimes which require identification or which run in series. In the identification situation, the interrogator may take a break in his questioning to place the subject among a group of men in a line-up. "The witness or complainant (previously coached, if necessary) studies the line-up and confidently points out the subject as the guilty party." [O'Hara] Then the questioning resumes "as though there were now no doubt about the guilt of the subject." A variation on this technique is called the "reverse line-up":

> "The accused is placed in a line-up, but this time he is identified by several fictitious witnesses or victims who associated him with different offenses. It is expected that the subject will become desperate and confess to the offense under investigation in order to escape from the false accusations." [O'Hara]

The manuals also contain instructions for police on how to handle the individual who refuses to discuss the matter entirely, or who asks for an attorney or relatives. The examiner is to concede him the right to remain silent. "This usually has a very undermining effect. First of all, he is disappointed in his expectation of an unfavorable reaction on the part of the interrogator. Secondly, a concession of this right to remain silent impresses the subject with the apparent fairness of his interrogator." [Inbau & Reid] After this psychological conditioning, however, the officer is told to point out the incriminating significance of the suspect's refusal to talk:

> "Joe, you have a right to remain silent. That's your privilege and I'm the last person in the world who'll try to take it away from you. If that's the way you want to leave this, O.K. But let me ask you this. Suppose you were in my shoes and I were in yours and you called me in to ask me about this and I told you, 'I don't want to answer any of your questions.' You'd think I had something to hide, and you'd probably be right in thinking that. That's exactly what I'll have to think about you, and so will everybody else. So let's sit here and talk this whole thing over." [Inbau & Reid]

Few will persist in their initial refusal to talk, it is said, if this monologue is employed correctly.

In the event that the subject wishes to speak to a relative or an attorney, the following advice is tendered:

> "[T]he interrogator should respond by suggesting that the subject first tell the truth to the interrogator himself rather than get anyone else involved in the matter. If the request is for an attorney, the interrogator may suggest that the subject save himself or his family the expense of any such professional service, particularly if he is innocent of the offense under investigation. The interrogator may also add, 'Joe, I'm only looking for the truth, and if you're telling the truth, that's it. You can handle this by yourself.' " [Inbau & Reid]

From these representative samples of interrogation techniques, the setting prescribed by the manuals and observed in practice becomes clear. In essence, it is this: To be alone with the subject is essential to prevent distraction and to deprive him of any outside support. The aura of confidence in his guilt undermines his will to resist. He merely confirms the preconceived story the police seek to have him describe. Patience and persistence, at times relentless questioning, are employed. To obtain a confession, the interrogator must "patiently maneuver himself or his quarry into a position from which the desired objective may be attained." When normal procedures fail to produce the needed result, the police may resort to deceptive stratagems such as giving false legal advice. It is important to keep the subject off balance, for example, by trading on his insecurity about himself or his surroundings. The police then persuade, trick, or cajole him out of exercising his constitutional rights.

* * *

In the cases before us today, given this background, we concern ourselves primarily with this interrogation atmosphere and the evils it can bring. In No. 759, Miranda v. Arizona, the police arrested the defendant and took him to a special interrogation room where they secured a confession. In No. 760, Vignera v. New York, the defendant made oral admissions to the police after interrogation in the afternoon, and then signed an inculpatory statement upon being questioned by an assistant district attorney later the same evening. In No. 761, Westover v. United States, the defendant was handed over to the Federal Bureau of Investigation by local authorities after they had detained and interrogated him for a lengthy period, both at night and the following morning. After some two hours of questioning, the federal officers had obtained signed statements from the defendant. Lastly, in No. 584, California v. Stewart, the local police held the defendant five days in the station and interrogated him on nine separate occasions before they secured his inculpatory statement.

In these cases, we might not find the defendants' statements to have been involuntary in traditional terms. Our concern for adequate safeguards to protect precious Fifth Amendment rights is, of course, not lessened in the slightest. In each of the cases, the defendant was thrust into an unfamiliar atmosphere and run through menacing police interrogation procedures. The potentiality for compulsion is forcefully apparent, for example, in *Miranda,* where the indigent Mexican defendant was a seriously disturbed individual with pronounced sexual fantasies, and in *Stewart,* in which the defendant was an indigent Los Angeles Negro who had dropped out of school in the sixth grade. To be sure, the records do not evince over physical coercion or patent psychological ploys. The fact remains that in none of these cases did the officers undertake to afford appropriate safeguards at the outset of the interrogation to insure that the statements were truly the product of free choice.

It is obvious that such an interrogation environment is created for no purpose other than to subjugate the individual to the will of his examiner. This atmosphere carries its own badge of intimidation. To be sure, this is not physical intimidation, but it is equally destructive of human dignity. The current practice of incommunicado interrogation is at odds with one of our Nation's most cherished principles—that the individual may not be compelled to incriminate himself. Unless adequate protective devices are employed to dispel the compulsion inherent in custodial surroundings, no statement obtained from the defendant can truly be the product of his free choice.

From the foregoing, we can readily perceive an intimate connection between the privilege against self-incrimination and police custodial questioning. It is fitting to turn to the Self–Incrimination Clause to determine its applicability in this situation.

II.

* * *

The question in these cases is whether the privilege is fully applicable during a period of custodial interrogation. In this Court, the privilege has consistently been accorded a liberal construction.... We are satisfied that all the principles embodied in the privilege apply to informal compulsion exerted by law-enforcement officers during in-custody questioning. An individual swept from familiar surroundings into police custody, surrounded by antagonistic forces, and subjected to the techniques of persuasion described above cannot be otherwise than under compulsion to speak. As a practical matter, the compulsion to speak in the isolated setting of the police station may well be greater than in courts or other official investigations, where there are often impartial observers to guard against intimidation or trickery.

* * *

III.

Today, then, there can be no doubt that the Fifth Amendment privilege is available outside of criminal court proceedings and serves to protect persons in all settings in which their freedom of action is curtailed in any significant way from being compelled to incriminate themselves....

It is impossible for us to foresee the potential alternatives for protecting the privilege which might be devised by Congress or the States in the exercise of their creative rule-making capacities. Therefore we cannot say that the Constitution necessarily requires adherence to any particular solution for the inherent compulsions of the interrogation process as it is presently conducted. Our decision in no way creates a constitutional strait-jacket which will handicap sound efforts at reform, nor is it intended to have this effect. We encourage Congress and the States to continue their laudable search for increasingly effective ways of protecting the rights of the individual while promoting efficient enforcement of our criminal laws. However, unless we are shown other procedures which are at least as effective in apprising accused persons of their right of silence and in assuring a continuous opportunity to exercise it, the following safeguards must be observed.

At the outset, if a person in custody is to be subjected to interrogation, he must first be informed in clear and unequivocal terms that he has the right to remain silent. For those unaware of the privilege, the warning is needed simply to make them aware of it—the threshold requirement for an intelligent decision as to its exercise. More important, such a warning is an absolute prerequisite in overcoming the inherent pressures of the interrogation atmosphere. It is not just the subnormal or woefully ignorant who succumb to an interrogator's imprecations, whether implied or expressly stated, that the interrogation will continue until a confession is obtained or that silence in the face of accusation is itself damning and will bode ill when presented to a jury. Further, the warning will show the individual that his interrogators are prepared to recognize his privilege should he choose to exercise it.

The Fifth Amendment privilege is so fundamental to our system of constitutional rule and the expedient of giving an adequate warning as to the availability of the privilege so simple, we will not pause to inquire in individual cases whether the defendant was aware of his rights without a warning being given. Assessments of the knowledge the defendant possessed, based on information as to his age, education, intelligence, or prior contact with authorities, can never be more than speculation; a warning is a clearcut fact. More important, whatever the background of the person interrogated, a warning at the time of the interrogation is indispensable to overcome its pressures and to insure that the individual knows he is free to exercise the privilege at that point in time.

The warning of the right to remain silent must be accompanied by the explanation that anything said can and will be used against the individual in court. This warning is needed in order to make him aware not only of the privilege, but also of the consequences of foregoing it. It is only through an awareness of these consequences that there can be any assurance of real understanding and intelligent exercise of the privilege. Moreover, this warning may serve to make the individual more acutely aware that he is faced with a phase of the adversary system—that he is not in the presence of persons acting solely in his interest.

The circumstances surrounding in-custody interrogation can operate very quickly to overbear the will of one merely made aware of his privilege by his interrogators. Therefore, the right to have counsel present at the interrogation is indispensable to the protection of the Fifth Amendment privilege under the system we delineate today. Our aim is to assure that the individual's right to choose between silence and speech remains unfettered throughout the interrogation process. A once-stated warning, delivered by those who will conduct the interrogation, cannot itself suffice to that end among those who most require knowledge of their rights. A mere warning given by the interrogators is not alone sufficient to accomplish that end. Prosecutors themselves claim that the admonishment of the right to remain silent without more "will benefit only the recidivist and the professional." Brief for the National District Attorneys Association as *amicus curiae,* p. 14. Even preliminary advice given to the accused by his own attorney can be swiftly overcome by the secret interrogation process. Thus, the need for counsel to protect the Fifth Amendment privilege comprehends not merely a right to consult with counsel prior to questioning, but also to have counsel present during any questioning if the defendant so desires.

The presence of counsel at the interrogation may serve several significant subsidiary functions as well. If the accused decides to talk to his interrogators, the assistance of counsel can mitigate the dangers of untrustworthiness. With a lawyer present the likelihood that the police will practice coercion is reduced, and if coercion is nevertheless exercised the lawyer can testify to it in court. The presence of a lawyer can also help to guarantee that the accused gives a fully accurate statement to the police and that the statement is rightly reported by the prosecution at trial....

An individual need not make a pre-interrogation request for a lawyer. While such request affirmatively secures his right to have one, his failure to ask for a lawyer does not constitute a waiver. No effective waiver of the right to counsel during interrogation can be recognized unless specifically made after the warnings we here delineate have been given. The accused who does not know his rights and therefore does not make a request may be the person who most needs counsel....

* * *

Accordingly we hold that an individual held for interrogation must be clearly informed that he has the right to consult with a lawyer and to have the lawyer with him during interrogation under the system for protecting the privilege we delineate today. As with the warnings of the right to remain silent and that anything stated can be used in evidence against him, this warning is an absolute prerequisite to interrogation. No amount of circumstantial evidence that the person may have been aware of this right will suffice to stand in its stead. Only through such a warning is there ascertainable assurance that the accused was aware of this right.

If an individual indicates that he wishes the assistance of counsel before any interrogation occurs, the authorities cannot rationally ignore or deny his request on the basis that the individual does not have or cannot afford a retained attorney. The financial ability of the individual has no relationship to the scope of the rights involved here....

In order fully to apprise a person interrogated of the extent of his rights under this system then, it is necessary to warn him not only that he has the right to consult with an attorney, but also that if he is indigent a lawyer will be appointed to represent him....

Once warnings have been given, the subsequent procedure is clear. If the individual indicates in any manner, at any time prior to or during questioning, that he wishes to remain silent, the interrogation must cease. At this point he has shown that he intends to exercise his Fifth Amendment privilege; any statement taken after the person invokes his privilege cannot be other than the product of compulsion, subtle or otherwise. Without the right to cut off questioning, the setting of in-custody interrogation operates on the individual to overcome free choice in producing a statement after the privilege has been once invoked. If the individual states that he wants an attorney, the interrogation must cease until an attorney is present. At that time, the individual must have an opportunity to confer with the attorney and to have him present during any subsequent questioning. If the individual cannot obtain an attorney and he indicates that he wants one before speaking to police, they must respect his decision to remain silent.

This does not mean, as some have suggested, that each police station must have a "station house lawyer" present at all times to advise prisoners. It does mean, however, that if police propose to interrogate a person they must make known to him that he is entitled to a lawyer and that if he cannot afford one, a lawyer will be provided for him prior to any interrogation. If authorities conclude that they will not provide counsel during a reasonable period of time in which investigation in the field is carried out, they may refrain from doing so without violating the person's Fifth Amendment privilege so long as they do not question him during that time.

If the interrogation continues without the presence of an attorney and a statement is taken, a heavy burden rests on the government to demonstrate that the defendant knowingly and intelligently waived his privilege against self-incrimination and his right to retained or appointed counsel.... Since the State is responsible for establishing the isolated circumstances under which the interrogation takes place and has the only means of making available corroborated evidence of warnings given during incommunicado interrogation, the burden is rightly on its shoulders.

An express statement that the individual is willing to make a statement and does not want an attorney followed closely by a statement could constitute a waiver. But a valid waiver will not be presumed simply from the silence of the accused after warnings are given or simply from the fact that a confession was in fact eventually obtained.... Moreover, where in-custody interrogation is involved, there is no room for the contention that the privilege is waived if the individual answers some questions or gives some information on his own prior to invoking his right to remain silent when interrogated....

Whatever the testimony of the authorities as to waiver of rights by an accused, the fact of lengthy interrogation or incommunicado incarceration before a statement is made is strong evidence that the accused did not validly waive his rights. In these circumstances the fact that the individual eventually made a statement is consistent with the conclusion that the compelling influence of the interrogation finally forced him to do so. It is inconsistent with any notion of a voluntary relinquishment of the privilege. Moreover, any evidence that the accused was threatened, tricked, or cajoled into a waiver will, of course, show that the defendant did not voluntarily waive his privilege. The requirement of warnings and waiver of rights is a fundamental with respect to the Fifth Amendment privilege and not simply a preliminary ritual to existing methods of interrogation.

The warnings required and the waiver necessary in accordance with our opinion today are, in the absence of a fully effective equivalent, prerequisites to the admissibility of any statement made by a defendant. No distinction can be drawn between statements which are direct confessions and statements which amount to "admissions" of part or all of an offense.... Similarly, for precisely the same reason, no distinction may be drawn between inculpatory statements and statements alleged to be merely "exculpatory." If a statement made were in fact truly exculpatory it would, of course, never be used by the prosecution. In fact, statements merely intended to be exculpatory by the defendant are often used to impeach his testimony at trial or to demonstrate untruths in the statement given under interrogation and thus to prove guilt by implication. These statements are incriminating in any meaningful sense of the word and may not be used without the full warnings and effective waiver required for any other statement....

The principles announced today deal with the protection which must be given to the privilege against self-incrimination when the individual is first subjected to police interrogation while in custody at the station or otherwise deprived of his freedom of action in any significant way. It is at this point that our adversary system of criminal proceedings commences, distinguishing itself at the outset from the inquisitorial system recognized in some countries. Under the system of warnings we delineate today or under any other system which may be devised and found effective, the safeguards to be erected about the privilege must come into play at this point.

Our decision is not intended to hamper the traditional function of police officers in investigating crime. When an individual is in custody on probable cause, the police may, of course, seek out evidence in the field to be used at trial against him. Such investigation may include inquiry of persons not under restraint. General on-the-scene questioning as to facts surrounding a crime or other general questioning of citizens in the fact-finding process is not affected by our holding. It is an act of responsible citizenship for individuals to give whatever information they may have to aid in law enforcement. In such situations the compelling atmosphere inherent in the process of in-custody interrogation is not necessarily present.[3]

In dealing with statements obtained through interrogation, we do not purport to find all confessions inadmissible. Confessions remain a proper element in law enforcement. Any statement given freely and voluntarily without any compelling influences is, of course, admissible in evidence. The fundamental import of the privilege while an individual is in custody is not whether he is allowed to talk to the police without the

3. The distinction and its significance has been aptly described in the opinion of a Scottish court:

"In former times such questioning, if undertaken, would be conducted by police officers visiting the house or place of business of the suspect and there questioning him, probably in the presence of a relation or friend. However convenient the modern practice may be, it must normally create a situation very unfavourable to the suspect." Chalmers v. H.M. Advocate, [1954] Sess. Cas. 66, 78 (J.C.).

benefit of warnings and counsel, but whether he can be interrogated. There is no requirement that police stop a person who enters a police station and states that he wishes to confess to a crime, or a person who calls the police to offer a confession or any other statement he desires to make. Volunteered statements of any kind are not barred by the Fifth Amendment and their admissibility is not affected by our holding today.

To summarize, we hold that when an individual is taken into custody or otherwise deprived of his freedom by the authorities in any significant way and is subjected to questioning, the privilege against self-incrimination is jeopardized. Procedural safeguards must be employed to protect the privilege and unless other fully effective means are adopted to notify the person of his right of silence and to assure that the exercise of the right will be scrupulously honored, the following measures are required. He must be warned prior to any questioning that he has the right to remain silent, that anything he says can be used against him in a court of law, that he has the right to the presence of an attorney, and that if he cannot afford an attorney one will be appointed for him prior to any questioning if he so desires. Opportunity to exercise these rights must be afforded to him throughout the interrogation. After such warnings have been given, and such opportunity afforded him, the individual may knowingly and intelligently waive these rights and agree to answer questions or make a statement. But unless and until such warnings and waiver are demonstrated by the prosecution at trial, no evidence obtained as a result of interrogation can be used against him.

IV.

A recurrent argument made in these cases is that society's need for interrogation outweighs the privilege....

* * *

In announcing these principles, we are not unmindful of the burdens which law enforcement officials must bear, often under trying circumstances. We also fully recognize the obligation of all citizens to aid in enforcing the criminal laws. This Court, while protecting individual rights, has always given ample latitude to law enforcement agencies in the legitimate exercise of their duties. The limits we have placed on the interrogation process should not constitute an undue interference with a proper system of law enforcement. As we have noted, our decision does not in any way preclude police from carrying out their traditional investigatory functions. Although confessions may play an important role in some convictions, the cases before us present graphic examples of the overstatement of the "need" for confessions. In each case authorities conducted interrogations ranging up to five days in duration despite the presence, through standard investigating practices, of considerable evidence against each defendant.[4]

* * *

4. Miranda, Vignera, and Westover were identified by eyewitnesses. Marked bills from the bank robbed were found in Westover's car. Articles stolen from the victim

Over the years the Federal Bureau of Investigation has compiled an exemplary record of effective law enforcement while advising any suspect or arrested person at the outset of an interview, that he is not required to make a statement, that any statement may be used against him in court, that the individual may obtain the services of an attorney of his own choice and, more recently, that he has a right to free counsel if he is unable to pay....

The practice of the FBI can readily be emulated by state and local enforcement agencies. The argument that the FBI deals with different crimes than are dealt with by state authorities does not mitigate the significance of the FBI experience.

The experience in some other countries also suggests that the danger to law enforcement in curbs on interrogation is overplayed....

The English procedure since 1912 under the Judges' Rules is significant. As recently strengthened, the Rules require that a cautionary warning be given an accused by a police officer as soon as he has evidence that affords reasonable grounds for suspicion; they also require that any statement made be given by the accused without questioning by police.

The right of the individual to consult with an attorney during this period is expressly recognized.

The safeguards present under Scottish law may be even greater than in England. Scottish judicial decisions bar use in evidence of most confessions obtained through police interrogation. In India, confessions made to police not in the presence of a magistrate have been excluded by rule of evidence since 1872, at a time when it operated under British law. Identical provisions appear in the Evidence Ordinance of Ceylon, enacted in 1895.... There appears to have been no marked detrimental effect on criminal law enforcement in these jurisdictions as a result of these rules. Conditions of law enforcement in our country are sufficiently similar to permit reference to this experience as assurance that lawlessness will not result from warning an individual of his rights or allowing him to exercise them. Moreover, it is consistent with our legal system that we give at least as much protection to these rights as is given in the jurisdictions described. We deal in our country with rights grounded in a specific requirement of the Fifth Amendment of the Constitution, whereas other jurisdictions arrived at their conclusions on the basis of principles of justice not so specifically defined.

It is also urged upon us that we withhold decision on this issue until state legislative bodies and advisory groups have had an opportunity to deal with these problems by rule making.... We have already pointed out that the Constitution does not require any specific code of procedures for protecting the privilege against self-incrimination during custodial interrogation. Congress and the States are free to develop their

as well as from several other robbery victims were found in Stewart's home at the outset of the investigation.

own safeguards for the privilege, so long as they are fully as effective as those described above in informing accused persons of their right of silence and in affording a continuous opportunity to exercise it. In any event, however, the issues presented are of constitutional dimensions and must be determined by the courts. The admissibility of a statement in the face of a claim that it was obtained in violation of the defendant's constitutional rights is an issue the resolution of which has long since been undertaken by this Court.... Where rights secured by the Constitution are involved, there can be no rule making or legislation which would abrogate them.

* * *

[Miranda reversed; Vignera reversed; Westover reversed; Stewart (state appellate court reversal of conviction) affirmed.]

MR. JUSTICE CLARK, dissenting in Nos. 759, 760, and 761, and concurring in the result in No. 584.

* * *

The *ipse dixit* of the majority has no support in our cases. Indeed, the Court admits that "we might not find the defendants' statements [here] to have been involuntary in traditional terms." ... The Court holds that failure to follow the new procedures requires inexorably the exclusion of any statement by the accused, as well as the fruits thereof. Such a strict constitutional specific inserted at the nerve center of crime detection may well kill the patient.[5] Since there is at this time a paucity of information and an almost total lack of empirical knowledge on the practical operation of requirements truly comparable to those announced by the majority, I would be more restrained lest we go too far too fast.

* * *

The rule prior to today ... depended upon "a totality of circumstances evidencing an involuntary ... admission of guilt." ...

I would continue to follow that rule. Under the "totality of circumstances" rule ... I would consider in each case whether the police officer prior to custodial interrogation added the warning that the suspect might have counsel present at the interrogation and, further, that a court would appoint one at his request if he was too poor to employ counsel. In the absence of warnings, the burden would be on the State to prove that counsel was knowingly and intelligently waived or that in

5. The Court points to England, Scotland, Ceylon and India as having equally rigid rules. As my Brother Harlan points out, post, ... the Court is mistaken in this regard, for it overlooks counterbalancing prosecutorial advantages. Moreover, the requirements of the Federal Bureau of Investigation do not appear ... to be as strict as those imposed today in at least two respects: (1) The offer of counsel is articulated only as "a right to counsel"; nothing is said about a right to have counsel present at the custodial interrogation ...; [and (2) the warning issued by the FBI does not indicate that the agent "will secure counsel"].

the totality of the circumstances, including the failure to give the necessary warnings, the confession was clearly voluntary.

* * *

In this way we would not be acting in the dark nor in one full sweep changing the traditional rules of custodial interrogation which this Court has for so long recognized as a justifiable and proper tool in balancing individual rights against the rights of society. It will be soon enough to go further when we are able to appraise with somewhat better accuracy the effect of such a holding.

* * *

MR. JUSTICE HARLAN, whom MR. JUSTICE STEWART and MR. JUSTICE WHITE join, dissenting.

I believe the decision of the Court represents poor constitutional law and entails harmful consequences for the country at large. How serious these consequences may prove to be only time can tell. But the basic flaws in the Court's justification seem to me readily apparent now once all sides of the problem are considered.

I. INTRODUCTION

* * *

... The new rules are not designed to guard against police brutality or other unmistakably banned forms of coercion. Those who use third-degree tactics and deny them in court are equally able and destined to lie as skillfully about warnings and waivers. Rather, the thrust of the new rules is to negate all pressures, to reinforce the nervous or ignorant suspect, and ultimately to discourage any confession at all. The aim in short is toward "voluntariness" in a utopian sense, or to view it from a different angle, voluntariness with a vengeance.

To incorporate this notion into the Constitution requires a strained reading of history and precedent and a disregard of the very pragmatic concerns that alone may on occasion justify such strains....

II. CONSTITUTIONAL PREMISES

It is most fitting to begin an inquiry into the constitutional precedents by surveying the limits on confessions the Court has evolved under the Due Process Clause ... because these cases show that there exists a workable and effective means of dealing with confessions in a judicial manner; because the cases are the baseline from which the Court now departs and so serve to measure the actual as opposed to the professed distance it travels; and because examination of them helps reveal how the Court has coasted into its present position.

The earliest confession cases in this Court emerged from federal prosecutions and were settled on a nonconstitutional basis, the Court adopting the common-law rule that the absence of inducements, promises, and threats made a confession voluntary and admissible. ...

* * *

The Court's opening contention, that the Fifth Amendment governs police station confessions, is perhaps not an impermissible extension of the law but it has little to commend itself in the present circumstances. Historically, the privilege against self-incrimination did not bear at all on the use of extra-legal confessions, for which distinct standards evolved; indeed, "the *history* of the two principles is wide apart, differing by one hundred years in origin, and derived through separate lines of precedents...." ... Even those who would readily enlarge the privilege must concede some linguistic difficulties since the Fifth Amendment in terms proscribes only compelling any person "in any criminal case to be a witness against himself." ...

... Certainly the privilege does represent a protective concern for the accused and an emphasis upon accusatorial rather than inquisitorial values in law enforcement, although this is similarly true of other limitations such as the grand jury requirement and the reasonable doubt standard. Accusatorial values, however, have openly been absorbed into the due process standard governing confessions; this indeed is why at present "the kinship of the two rules [governing confessions and self-incrimination] is too apparent for denial." ... Since extension of the general principle has already occurred, to insist that the privilege applies as such serves only to carry over inapposite historical details and engaging rhetoric and to obscure the policy choices to be made in regulating confessions.

Having decided that the Fifth Amendment privilege does apply in the police station, the Court reveals that the privilege imposes more exacting restrictions than does the Fourteenth Amendment's voluntariness test. It then emerges ... that the Fifth Amendment requires for an admissible confession that it be given by one distinctly aware of his right not to speak and shielded from "the compelling atmosphere" of interrogation. From these key premises, the Court finally develops the safeguards of warning, counsel, and so forth. I do not believe these premises are sustained by precedents under the Fifth Amendment.

The more important premise is that pressure on the suspect must be eliminated though it be only the subtle influence of the atmosphere and surroundings. The Fifth Amendment, however, has never been thought to forbid *all* pressure to incriminate one's self in the situations covered by it. On the contrary, it has been held that failure to incriminate one's self can result in denial of removal of one's case from state to federal court; in refusal of a military commission; in denial of a discharge in bankruptcy; and in numerous other adverse consequences. This is not to say that short of jail or torture any sanction is permissible in any case; policy and history alike may impose sharp limits. However, the Court's unspoken assumption that *any* pressure violates the privilege is not supported by the precedents and it has failed to show why the Fifth

Amendment prohibits that relatively mild pressure the Due Process Clause permits.

The Court appears similarly wrong in thinking that precise knowledge of one's rights is a settled prerequisite under the Fifth Amendment to the loss of its protections. A number of lower federal court cases have held that grand jury witnesses need not always be warned of their privilege, ... and Wigmore states this to be the better rule for trial witnesses.... No Fifth Amendment precedent is cited for the Court's contrary view....

A closing word must be said about the Assistance of Counsel Clause of the Sixth Amendment, which is never expressly relied on by the Court but whose judicial precedents turn out to be linchpins of the confession rules announced today. To support its requirement of a knowing and intelligent waiver, the Court cites [a number of cases which] concerned counsel at trial or on appeal. While the Court finds no pertinent difference between judicial proceedings and police interrogation, I believe the differences are vast....

The only attempt in this Court to carry the right to counsel into the station house occurred in *Escobedo,* the Court repeating several times that that stage was no less "critical" than trial itself. This is hardly persuasive when we consider that a grand jury inquiry, the filing of a certiorari petition, and certainly the purchase of narcotics by an undercover agent from a prospective defendant may all be equally "critical" yet provision of counsel and advice on the score have never been thought compelled by the Constitution in such cases. The sound reason why this right is so freely extended for a criminal trial is the severe injustice risked by confronting an untrained defendant with a range of technical points of law, evidence, and tactics familiar to the prosecutor but not to himself. This danger shrinks markedly in the police station where indeed the lawyer in fulfilling his professional responsibilities of necessity may become an obstacle to truthfinding.

* * *

III. Policy Considerations

... Legal history has been stretched before to satisfy deep needs of society. In this instance, however, the Court has not and cannot make the powerful showing that its new rules are plainly desirable in the context of our society, something which is surely demanded before those rules are engrafted onto the Constitution and imposed on every State and county in the land.

Without at all subscribing to the generally black picture of police conduct painted by the Court, I think it must be frankly recognized at the outset that police questioning allowable under due process precedents may inherently entail some pressure on the suspect and may seek advantage in his ignorance or weaknesses. The atmosphere and questioning techniques, proper and fair though they be, can in themselves exert a tug on the suspect to confess, and in this light "[t]o speak of any confessions of crime made after arrest as being 'voluntary' or 'uncoerced' is somewhat inaccurate, although traditional. A confession is wholly and incontestably voluntary only if a guilty person gives himself up to the law and become his own accuser." ... Until today, the role of the Constitution has been only to sift out *undue* pressure, not to assure spontaneous confessions....

The Court's new rules aim to offset these minor pressures and disadvantages intrinsic to any kind of police interrogation. The rules do not serve due process interests in preventing blatant coercion since, as I noted earlier, they do nothing to contain the policeman who is prepared to lie from the start. The rules work for reliability in confessions almost only in the Pickwickian sense that they can prevent some from being given at all.[6] ...

What the Court largely ignores is that its rules impair, if they will not eventually serve wholly to frustrate, an instrument of law enforcement that has long and quite reasonably been thought worth the price paid for it. There can be little doubt that the Court's new code would markedly decrease the number of confessions. To warn the suspect that he may remain silent and remind him that his confession may be used in court are minor obstructions. To require also an express waiver by the suspect and an end to questioning whenever he demurs must heavily handicap questioning. And to suggest or provide counsel for the suspect simply invites the end of the interrogation.

How much harm this decision will inflict on law enforcement cannot fairly be predicted with accuracy. Evidence on the role of confessions is notoriously incomplete, and little is added by the Court's reference to the FBI experience and the resources believed wasted in interrogation. We do know that some crimes cannot be solved without confessions, that ample expert testimony attests to their importance in crime control, and that the Court is taking a real risk with society's welfare in imposing its new regime on the country. The social costs of crime are too great to call the new rules anything but a hazardous experimentation.

While passing over the costs and risks of its experiment, the Court portrays the evils of normal police questioning in terms which I think are exaggerated. Albeit stringently confined by the due process standards interrogation is no doubt often inconvenient and unpleasant for the suspect. However, it is no less so for a man to be arrested and jailed, to have his house searched, or to stand trial in court, yet all this may properly happen to the most innocent given probable cause, a warrant, or an indictment. Society has always paid a stiff price for law and order, and peaceful interrogation is not one of the dark moments of the law.

6. The Court's vision of a lawyer "mitigat[ing] the dangers of untrustworthiness" by witnessing coercion and assisting accuracy in the confession is largely a fancy; for if counsel arrives, there is rarely going to be a police station confession. Watts v. State of Indiana, [1949] (separate opinion of Jackson, J.): "[A]ny lawyer worth his salt will tell the suspect in no uncertain terms to make no statement to police under any circumstances." ...

... it may make the analysis more graphic to consider the actual facts of one of the four cases reversed by the Court. Miranda v. Arizona serves best, being neither the hardest nor easiest of the four under the Court's standards.

On March 3, 1963, an 18–year–old girl was kidnapped and forcibly raped near Phoenix, Arizona. Ten days later, on the morning of March 13, petitioner Miranda was arrested and taken to the police station. At this time Miranda was 23 years old, indigent, and educated to the extent of completing half the ninth grade. He had "an emotional illness" of the schizophrenic type, according to the doctor who eventually examined him; the doctor's report also stated that Miranda was "alert and oriented as to time, place, and person," intelligent within normal limits, competent to stand trial, and came within the legal definition. At the police station, the victim picked Miranda out of a lineup, and two officers then took him into a separate room to interrogate him, starting about 11:30 a.m. Though at first denying his guilt, within a short time Miranda gave a detailed oral confession and then wrote out in his own hand and signed a brief statement admitting and describing the crime. All this was accomplished in two hours or less without any force, threats or promises and—I will assume this though the record is uncertain, without any effective warnings at all.

Miranda's oral and written confessions are now held inadmissible under the Court's new rules. One is entitled to feel astonished that the Constitution can be read to produce this result. These confessions were obtained during brief, daytime questioning conducted by two officers and unmarked by any of the traditional indicia of coercion. They assured a conviction for a brutal and unsettling crime, for which the police had and quite possibly could obtain little evidence other than the victim's identifications, evidence which is frequently unreliable. There was, in sum, a legitimate purpose, no perceptible unfairness, and certainly little risk of injustice in the interrogation. Yet the resulting confessions, and the responsible course of police practice they represent, are to be sacrificed to the Court's own fine-spun conception of fairness which I seriously doubt is shared by many thinking citizens in this country.

* * *

The Court in closing its general discussion invokes the practice in federal and foreign jurisdictions as lending weight to its new curbs on confessions for all the States. A brief résumé will suffice to show that none of these jurisdictions has struck so one-sided a balance as the Court does today. Heaviest reliance is placed on the FBI practice. Differing circumstances may make this comparison quite untrustworthy, but in any event the FBI falls sensibly short of the Court's formalistic rules. For example, there is no indication that FBI agents must obtain an affirmative "waiver" before they pursue their questioning. Nor is it clear that one invoking his right to silence may not be prevailed upon to change his mind. And the warning as to appointed counsel apparently indicates only that one will be assigned by the judge when the suspect appears before him; the thrust of the Court's rules is to induce the suspect to obtain appointed counsel before continuing the interview. Apparently American military practice, briefly mentioned by the Court, has these same limits and is still less favorable to the suspect than the FBI warning, making no mention of appointed counsel.

The law of the foreign countries described by the Court also reflects a more moderate conception of the rights of the accused as against those of society when other data are considered. Concededly, the English experience is most relevant. In that country, a caution as to silence but not counsel has long been mandated by the "Judges' Rules," which also place other somewhat imprecise limits on police cross-examination of suspects. However, in the court's discretion confessions can be and apparently quite frequently are admitted in evidence despite disregard of the Judges' Rules, so long as they are found voluntary under the common-law test. Moreover, the check that exists on the use of pretrial statements is counterbalanced by the evident admissibility of fruits of an illegal confession and by the judge's often-used authority to comment adversely on the defendant's failure to testify.

India, Ceylon and Scotland are the other examples chosen by the Court. In India and Ceylon the general ban on police-adduced confessions cited by the Court is subject to a major exception: if evidence is uncovered by police questioning, it is fully admissible at trial along with the confession itself, so far as it relates to the evidence and is not blatantly coerced. Scotland's limits on interrogation do measure up to the Court's; however, restrained comment at trial on the defendant's failure to take the stand is allowed the judge, and in many other respects Scotch law redresses the prosecutor's disadvantage in ways not permitted in this country. The Court ends its survey by inputing added strength to our privilege against self-incrimination since, by contrast to other countries, it is embodied in a written Constitution. Considering the liberties the Court has today taken with constitutional history and precedent, few will find this emphasis persuasive.

* * *

... Despite the Court's disclaimer, the practical effect of the decision made today must inevitably be to handicap seriously sound efforts at reform, not least by removing options necessary to a just compromise of competing interests. Of course legislative reform is rarely speedy or unanimous, though this Court has been more patient in the past. But the legislative reforms when they come would have the vast advantage of empirical data and comprehensive study, they would allow experimentation and use of solutions not open to the courts, and they would restore the initiative in criminal law reform to those forums where it truly belongs.

* * *

In conclusion: Nothing in the letter or the spirit of the Constitution or in the precedents squares with the heavy-handed and one-sided action that is so precipitously taken by the Court in the name of fulfiling its constitutional responsibilities. The foray which the Court makes today brings to mind the wise and far-sighted words of Mr. Justice Jackson: "This Court is forever adding new stories to the temples of constitutional law, and the temples have a way of collapsing when one story too many is added."

MR. JUSTICE WHITE, with whom MR. JUSTICE HARLAN and MR. JUSTICE STEWART join, dissenting.

* * *

That the Court's holding today is neither compelled nor even strongly suggested by the language of the Fifth Amendment, is at odds with American and English legal history, and involves a departure from a long line of precedent does not prove either that the Court has exceeded its powers or that the Court is wrong or unwise in its present reinterpretation of the Fifth Amendment. It does, however, underscore the obvious—that the Court has not discovered or found the law in making today's decision, nor has it derived it from some irrefutable sources; what it has done is to make new law and new public policy in much the same way that it has in the course of interpreting other great clauses of the Constitution. This is what the Court historically has done. Indeed, it is what it must do and will continue to do until and unless there is some fundamental change in the constitutional distribution of governmental powers.

But if the Court is here and now to announce new and fundamental policy to govern certain aspects of our affairs, it is wholly legitimate to examine the mode of this or any other constitutional decision in this Court and to inquire into the advisability of its end product in terms of the long-range interest of the country. At the very least, the Court's text and reasoning should withstand analysis and be a fair exposition of the constitutional provision which its opinion interprets. Decisions like these cannot rest alone on syllogism, metaphysics or some ill-defined notions of natural justice, although each will perhaps play its part. In proceeding to such constructions as it now announces, the Court should also duly consider all the factors and interests bearing upon the cases, at least insofar as the relevant materials are available; and if the necessary considerations are not treated in the record or obtainable from some other reliable source, the Court should not proceed to formulate fundamental policies based on speculation alone.

First, we may inquire what are the textual and factual bases of this new fundamental rule. To reach the result announced on the grounds it does, the Court must stay within the confines of the Fifth Amendment, which forbids self-incrimination only if *compelled*. Hence the core of the Court's opinion is that because of the "compulsion inherent in custodial surroundings, no statement obtained from [a] defendant [in custody] can truly be the product of his free choice," absent the use of adequate protective devices as described by the Court. However, the Court does not point to any sudden in-rush of new knowledge requiring the rejection of 70 years' experience. Nor does it assert that its novel conclusion reflects a changing consensus among state courts, or that a succession of cases had steadily eroded the old rule and proved it unworkable,.... Rather than asserting new knowledge, the Court concedes that it cannot truly know what occurs during custodial questioning, because of the innate secrecy of such proceedings. It extrapolates a picture of what it conceives to be the norm from police investigatorial manuals, published in 1959 and 1962 or earlier, without any attempt to allow for adjustments in police practices that may have occurred in the wake of more recent decisions of state appellate tribunals or this Court. But even if the relentless application of the described procedures could lead to involuntary confessions, it most assuredly does not follow that each and every case will disclose this kind of interrogation or this kind of consequence.[7] Insofar as appears from the Court's opinion, it has not examined a single transcript of any police interrogation, let alone the interrogation that took place in any one of these cases which it decides today. Judged by any of the standards for empirical investigation utilized in the social sciences the factual basis for the Court's premise is patently inadequate.

Although in the Court's view in-custody interrogation is inherently coercive, the Court says that the spontaneous product of the coercion of arrest and detention is still to be deemed voluntary. An accused, arrested on probable cause, may blurt out a confession which will be admissible despite the fact that he is alone and in custody, without any showing that he had any notion of his right to remain silent or of the consequences of his admission. Yet, under the Court's rule, if the police ask him a single question such as "Do you have anything to say?" or "Did you kill your wife?" his response, if there is one, has somehow been compelled, even if the accused has been clearly warned of his right to remain silent. Common sense informs us to the contrary. While one may say that the response was "involuntary" in the sense the question provoked or was the occasion for the response and thus the defendant was induced to speak out when he might have remained silent if not arrested and not questioned, it is patently unsound to say the response is compelled.

* * *

The obvious underpinning of the Court's decision is a deep-seated distrust of all confessions. As the Court declares that the accused may not be interrogated without counsel present, absent a waiver of the right to counsel, and as the Court all but admonishes the lawyer to advise the

7. In fact, the type of sustained interrogation described by the Court appears to be the exception rather than the rule. A survey of 399 cases in one city found that in almost half of the cases the interrogation lasted less than 30 minutes. Barrett, Police Practices and the Law—From Arrest to Release or Charge, 50 Calif.L.Rev. 11, 41–45 (1962). Questioning tends to be confused and sporadic and is usually concentrated on confrontations with witnesses or new items of evidence, as these are obtained by officers conducting the investigation....

accused to remain silent, the result adds up to a judicial judgment that evidence from the accused should not be used against him in any way, whether compelled or not....

* * *

The most basic function of any government is to provide for the security of the individual and of his property. These ends of society are served by the criminal laws which for the most part are aimed at the prevention of crime. Without the reasonably effective performance of the task of preventing private violence and retaliation it is idle to talk about human dignity and civilized values.

* * *

The rule announced today will measurably weaken the ability of the criminal law to perform these tasks. It is a deliberate calculus to prevent interrogations, to reduce the incidence of confessions and pleas of guilty and to increase the number of trials. Criminal trials, no matter how efficient the police are, are not sure bets for the prosecution, nor should they be if the evidence is not forthcoming. Under the present law, the prosecution fails to prove its case in about 30% of the criminal cases actually tried in the federal courts. But it is something else again to remove from the ordinary criminal case all those confessions which heretofore have been held to be free and voluntary acts of the accused and to thus establish a new constitutional barrier to the ascertainment of truth by the judicial process. There is, in my view, every reason to believe that a good many criminal defendants who otherwise would have been convicted on what this Court has previously thought to be the most satisfactory kind of evidence will now under this new version of the Fifth Amendment, either not be tried at all or will be acquitted if the State's evidence, minus the confession, is put to the test of litigation.

I have no desire whatsoever to share the responsibility for any such impact on the present criminal process.

* * *

There is another aspect to the effect of the Court's rule on the person whom the police have arrested on probable cause. The fact is that he may not be guilty at all and may be able to extricate himself quickly and simply if he were told the circumstances of his arrest and were asked to explain. This effort, and his release, must now await the hiring of a lawyer or his appointment by the court, consultation with counsel and then a session with the police or the prosecutor. Similarly, where probable cause exists to arrest several suspects, as where the body of the victim is discovered in a house having several residents, it will often be true that a suspect may be cleared only through the results of interrogation of other suspects. Here too the release of the innocent may be delayed by the Court's rule.

Much of the trouble with the Court's new rule is that it will operate indiscriminately in all criminal cases, regardless of the severity of the crime or the circumstances involved. It applies to every defendant, whether the professional criminal or one committing a crime of momentary passion who is not part and parcel of organized crime. It will slow down the investigation and the apprehension of confederates in those cases where time is of the essence, such as kidnapping, ... those involving national security ... and some of those involving organized crime. In the latter context the lawyer who arrives may also be the lawyer for the defendant's colleagues and can be relied upon to insure that no breach of the organization's security takes place even though the accused may feel that the best thing he can do is to cooperate.

* * *

NOTES

1. Louisiana, by a constitutional provision (art. 1, § 13) and also by statute (art. 218.1, Code of Criminal Procedure), has extended the *Miranda* concept to require the warnings at the time of all arrests.

* * *

2. On the question of the costs of Miranda rule, see:

(a) Inbau and Manak, "Miranda v. Arizona—Is It Worth The Cost? (A Sample Survey With Commentary of the Expenditure of Court Time and Effort)" 24 Cal.West.L.Rev. 185 (1988):

> "... Our only objective was to demonstrate, without resort to comparisons, that a 'considerable' amount of court time and effort has been expended, not only upon *Miranda* itself, but also upon its progeny ever since that decision in 1966.

* * *

"It was once thought that after the initial impact of *Miranda,* the various issues that might arise from it would soon be resolved by the Supreme Court in other cases. The prediction was that there would be an eventual diminution of litigation over *Miranda's* requirements not only in the Supreme Court, but also in lower federal appellate courts, and in the state appellate courts as well. As reasonable as that assumption may have been, the facts are to the contrary. [Our figures] demonstrate that the number of *Miranda* issue cases decided by the Supreme Court has actually increased during the twenty year period since its inception, along with substantial increases in the number of pages and words in the opinions disposing of them.

"In the United States Circuit Courts of Appeals, *Miranda* issues were discussed in 980 cases decided during the period 1966–1986. The opinions consisted of 2,155 pages and approximately 1,200,000 words. The prosecution prevailed in 803 cases, the defense in 177.

"The California courts of appeal decided 363 cases from 1966 through 1986, for a total of 905 pages and approximately 450,000 words, dealing solely with substantive *Miranda* issues. The prosecution prevailed in 281 cases, the defense in 82.

"No attempt was made, nor did we think it was even possible, to ascertain the extent to which *Miranda* issues have encroached upon the time and efforts of the *trial courts* on either the federal or state level. We submit that the results of any such survey, if feasible, would have produced staggering figures, especially in view of the fact that defense counsel in confession cases almost invariably inject the *Miranda* element into their objections to the admissibility of confessions. Furthermore, the number of appellate court cases is some indication, of course, of what has been occurring in the trial courts.

"As is true with regard to the trial court expenditure of time and effort, there is no way by which the overall *monetary costs* produced by *Miranda* could be assessed. Without doubt, however, such costs must be very substantial."

The authors also state in clear, summary form the arguments against Miranda. 24 Cal.West.L.Rev. at 193–98.

(b) A response to Inbau and Manak appeared in a subsequent issue of the California Western Law Review (vol. 25, pp. 88–97), by Matthew Lippman:

". . . the number of Supreme Court cases addressing *Miranda* issues hardly constitutes a huge expenditure of effort. From 1966 through 1986, the Supreme Court decided forty-four such cases, an average of slightly more than two per year.

"Inbau and Manak also contend that there has been a 'substantial increase' in the number of words and pages in the *Miranda* decisions. The number of words and pages in a *Miranda* decision results from a number of variables, most of which are unrelated to the complexity of the *Miranda* issues in a case (e.g., which justice or judge wrote the opinion). Scrutiny of the authors' data does not suggest that the *Miranda* rule is burdensome. From 1966 through 1986, substantive *Miranda* issues were considered in forty-four cases, comprising a total of 606 pages and 160,000 words in the official United States Reports. This is an average of roughly thirteen pages per case, a rather modest total for a Supreme Court decision. In the same period, the United States circuit courts decided 980 *Miranda* issue cases consisting of 2,155 pages, or an average of slightly over two pages per case.

"It is true that the number of pages in the Supreme Court *Miranda* decisions increased in the 1984–1986 period. However, there was a decline in the average number of pages contained in the three cases that were decided between 1986 and June 1987. The earlier increase thus must be viewed over time before any reliable figure can be derived. In addition, a comparative analysis of decisions in other areas might reveal that an ideological conflict on the Court has increased the length of other civil liberties and criminal procedure rulings.

"Thus, judging by the authors' indicators, it is not certain whether an inordinate amount of time and effort is being consumed on *Miranda* issues. . . .

* * *

2. INTERPRETATION OF THE MIRANDA REQUIREMENTS

(A) MEANINGS OF "CUSTODY" AND "DEPRIVATION OF FREEDOM OF ACTION IN ANY SIGNIFICANT WAY"

UNITED STATES v. MESA

United States Court of Appeals, Third Circuit, 1980.
638 F.2d 582.

SEITZ, Chief Judge. This is an appeal by the government from an interlocutory order of the district court, 487 F.Supp. 562, granting the motion of the defendant, Rigoberto Mesa, to suppress a tape-recorded conversation between Mesa and an FBI agent. Jurisdiction is based on 18 U.S.C. s 3731 (1976).

I.

The facts are undisputed. On January 28, 1980, Karin Little, Mesa's "common-law" wife, and Sonia Mesa, his daughter, were shot and wounded. Later that day, the victims, both of whom survived, informed the FBI that Mesa had inflicted their injuries. The FBI was unable to locate Mesa on January 28 and obtained a warrant for his arrest from a United States Magistrate the next morning. At approximately 2:00 p.m. on January 29, three FBI agents went to the El Sombrero Motel in Brown Mills, New Jersey and inquired about Mesa. They learned that Mesa had barricaded himself in his room sometime before 10:00 a.m. that day. The agents evacuated the rooms on each side of Mesa's room and blocked off traffic in the vicinity.

The agents then called to Mesa through a bullhorn, informed him that they were FBI agents, that they had a warrant for his arrest, and that he should come out with his hands raised. Mesa did not respond. The agents repeated their statement between ten and twelve times over the course of approximately one hour, but Mesa still did not respond. During this period, additional law enforcement officials arrived at the scene. Eventually, between twenty-five and thirty officers surrounded the motel.

The agents believed that Mesa was armed, and they did not know whether he had hostages. Because they deemed it inadvisable to forcibly take Mesa into their custody, the agents requested the assistance of Special Agent Theodore Viater, the FBI's hostage negotiator for the area.

When Agent Viater arrived, the agents decided that because there was no commercial telephone in Mesa's room it would be necessary to use a mobile telephone to talk with Mesa. An FBI agent then used the bullhorn to ask Mesa if he would take a telephone receiver into the room to talk with Viater. Mesa indicated by hand signals that he would take the phone.

* * *

Viater and Mesa then conversed over the mobile phone for approximately three and one half hours. This conversation primarily involved long narrative monologues by Mesa, with Viater passively listening. Viater had been informed that Mesa had been under psychiatric care and that he might have suicidal tendencies. The comments Viater made during the conversation were supportive and seemed designed to keep Mesa talking in order to establish a relationship of trust. The following comment is representative:

> I'm concerned about you Rigoberto, I'm concerned about your welfare, and I'm concerned about your health and I want to make absolutely certain that you and I trust each other and we can bring this problem to a successful solution.

During this conversation, Mesa discussed his experiences in Vietnam, his relationship with his family during his childhood in Cuba, his relationship with his "common-law" wife and children, other events of his life, and the events surrounding the shooting on January 28. Viater generally limited his interjections into this narrative to comments such as "Umhum" and "I understand," with an occasional question concerning Mesa's most recent statement or a longer comment evidencing understanding for Mesa's situation. Viater hoped that by establishing this atmosphere of trust he could convince Mesa to surrender without harming himself or any of the officials in the area.

Mesa finally surrendered peacefully at approximately 6:30 p.m. At this point, the FBI agents gave Mesa the warnings specified in Miranda v. Arizona. After he had surrendered, Mesa thanked Viater for listening to him and stated that he would have killed himself had it not been for Viater.

At no time during the taped conversation did Viater give Mesa Miranda warnings. Mesa argues that the contents of the conversation should be suppressed because of the failure to give these warnings. The district court conducted a hearing on Mesa's motion to suppress on April 3, 1980. It held that the taped conversation must be suppressed because Viater's conversation with Mesa constituted "custodial interrogation" within the meaning of Miranda. I now will consider whether the FBI's conduct was "custodial interrogation" as contemplated by the Miranda Court.

II.

Miranda held that when the government conducts a "custodial interrogation," it may not introduce statements made by the defendant at this interrogation unless he first had been given the now-familiar Miranda warnings. This court has recognized that "custodial interrogation" is not susceptible of an exact definition; thus the determination whether statements are the product of such "custodial interrogation" must be made on a case-by-case basis....

Miranda warnings are designed to protect against the evils of "custodial interrogation," and they are not intended to unduly interfere with a proper system of law enforcement or to hamper the police's traditional investigatory functions....

... Since Miranda, the Court has indicated that to determine whether there has been a "custodial interrogation," a court must make two discrete inquiries. First, it must determine whether the suspect was in "custody." ... If the suspect was in "custody", the court then must decide whether the police interrogated him....

* * *

Because Mesa, by barricading himself in his motel room with a gun, successfully prevented the FBI from exercising any control over his immediate actions or forcing him to be subjected to their questioning, he was not in custody within the meaning of Miranda....

... If the police compel an armed, barricaded suspect to incriminate himself ..., the suspect can attack the admissibility of his statements on the ground that they were not voluntary, but compelled by the police in violation of his fifth amendment rights....

* * *

I conclude that where an armed suspect who possibly has hostages barricades himself away from the police, he is not in custody and therefore Miranda warnings need not be given as a prerequisite to the admission of his statements into evidence. Because a suspect who places himself in this position is not in "custody" within the meaning of the Miranda rule, I need not address the difficult issue whether Viater's conversation with Mesa constituted "interrogation" under such rule.

The order of the district court suppressing the taped conversation will be reversed.

ADAMS, Circuit Judge, concurring.

I concur in the result reached by Chief Judge Seitz because, in my view, Mesa's statements were made in the course of a colloquy that is not an "interrogation," as that term was recently defined by the Supreme Court in Rhode Island v. Innis, 446 U.S. 291 (1980).

Several factors lead me to conclude that Agent Viater was not interrogating Mesa. Viater spoke with Mesa in an attempt to defuse an admittedly delicate and volatile situation, which presented a tangible danger of suicide or other violence. Mesa indicated that he wished to talk to the agent, because he was in need of a sympathetic listener to whom he could vent his confused and tortured mind. Viater acted not as a questioner, but primarily as a listener. The conversation between Viater and Mesa was nonadversarial and noninquisitive in nature, and Viater's empathetic tone conveyed little of the subtle compulsion that characterizes police interrogation. The concern expressed in Miranda that a defendant might be "subjugated to the will of the examiner" is not present here. The comments interjected by the agent were not designed to elicit an incriminating response from Mesa, but were calculated to convey sympathy and understanding, to indicate that Viater was still listening, and to keep Mesa from dwelling on thoughts of suicide. The agent's prime motivation was to achieve a peaceful resolution of the confrontation, and it was only by talking to Mesa about his fears and recent events that Viater could hope to bring about this goal. Indeed, when Viater asked Mesa to elaborate on his contention that he was provoked, he did so not to lure him into a confession, but to encourage him to continue expressing his concerns. This was necessary to allay Mesa's feeling that his life was over.

* * *

Admittedly, in light of the lower court's finding that Viater had a secondary purpose of gathering possible evidence, the question of whether Mesa was subjected to interrogation is an extremely close one. My conclusion that the statements are admissible is compelled by the realization that it would be impractical and counterproductive to require Miranda warnings to be given in such a sensitive situation fraught with a potential for tragedy. The success of a negotiating mission such as the one undertaken by Agent Viater is ultimately dependent on establishing an atmosphere of trust and understanding. It was crucial for Viater to convince Mesa that his aim was to provide help and a sympathetic ear. If the agent had been required to commence the conversation with the Miranda warnings, he would have created an adversarial atmosphere from the outset. The reading of the warnings would no doubt have eradicated any possibility for establishing trust and understanding. In attempting to negotiate the peaceful surrender of a suspect or hostages, law enforcement personnel should not be forced to make a pressured judgment as to whether reading the Miranda warnings would deter the suspect from talking, when it is the chance to engage the suspect in a dialogue that holds the main hope for saving lives. The delicacy of the position in which an agent might find himself is amply demonstrated by this case, where Mesa stressed that he would have killed himself if he had not talked to Viater.

Because I conclude that the exchange between Viater and the agent did not constitute an interrogation for the purpose of the Miranda rule, I do not find it necessary to address the difficult issue whether Mesa was "in custody," although I concede that this is a proposition not free from doubt....

WEINER, District Judge, dissenting.

* * *

Because I agree with the District Court that Mesa was subject to custodial interrogation and differ with Chief Judge Seitz's conclusion that Mesa was not in custody for purposes of a Miranda warning while barricaded in his motel room and surrounded by federal, military, and local law enforcement officers, and with the conclusion of Judge Adams that no interrogation took place, I would affirm the District Court's order and must therefore respectfully dissent.

(B) Specificity of the Warnings

CALIFORNIA v. PRYSOCK

Supreme Court of the United States, 1981.
453 U.S. 355, 101 S.Ct. 2806.

Per Curiam.

This case presents the question whether the warnings given to respondent prior to a recorded conversation with a police officer satisfied the requirements of Miranda v. Arizona. Although ordinarily this Court would not be inclined to review a case involving application of that precedent to a particular set of facts, ... the opinion of the California Court of Appeal essentially laid down a flat rule requiring that the content of *Miranda* warnings be a virtual incantation of the precise language contained in the *Miranda* opinion. Because such a rigid rule was not mandated by *Miranda* or any other decision of this Court, and is not required to serve the purposes of *Miranda,* we ... reverse.

On January 30, 1978, Mrs. Donna Iris Erickson was brutally murdered. Later that evening respondent and a codefendant were apprehended for commission of the offense. Respondent was brought to a substation of the Tulare County Sheriff's Department and advised of his *Miranda* rights. He declined to talk and, since he was a minor, his parents were notified. Respondent's parents arrived and after meeting with them respondent decided to answer police questions. An officer questioned respondent, on tape, with respondent's parents present. The tape reflects that the following warnings were given prior to any questioning:

> "Sgt. Byrd: ... Mr. Randall James Prysock, earlier today I advised you of your legal rights and at that time you advised me you did not wish to talk to me, is that correct?
>
> "Randall P.: Yeh.
>
> "Sgt. Byrd: And, uh, during, at the first interview your folks were not present, they are now present. I want to go through your legal rights again with you and after each legal right I would like for you to answer whether you understand it or not.... Your legal rights, Mr. Prysock, is [*sic*] follows: Number One, you have the right to remain silent. This means you don't have to talk to me at all unless you so desire. Do you understand this?
>
> "Randall P.: Yeh.

"Sgt. Byrd: If you give up your right to remain silent, anything you say can and will be used as evidence against you in a court of law. Do you understand this?

"Randall P.: Yes.

"Sgt. Byrd: You have the right to talk to a lawyer before you are questioned, have him present with you while you are being questioned, and all during the questioning. Do you understand this?

"Randall P.: Yes.

"Sgt. Byrd: You also, being a juvenile, you have the right to have your parents present, which they are. Do you understand this?

"Randall P.: Yes.

"Sgt. Byrd: Even if they weren't here, you'd have this right. Do you understand this?

"Randall P.: Yes.

"Sgt. Byrd: You all, uh, if,—you have the right to have a lawyer appointed to represent you at no cost to yourself. Do you understand this?

"Randall P.: Yes.

"Sgt. Byrd: Now, having all these legal rights in mind, do you wish to talk to me at this time?

"Randall P.: Yes." ...

At this point, at the request of Mrs. Prysock, a conversation took place with the tape recorder turned off. According to Sgt. Byrd, Mrs. Prysock asked if respondent could still have an attorney at a later time if he gave a statement now without one. Sgt. Byrd assured Mrs. Prysock that respondent would have an attorney when he went to court and that "he could have one at this time if he wished one." ... At trial in the Superior Court of Tulare County the court denied respondent's motion to suppress the taped statement. Respondent was convicted by a jury of first-degree murder with two special circumstances—torture and robbery....

... The Court of Appeal ruled that respondent's recorded incriminating statements, given with his parents present, had to be excluded from consideration by the jury because respondent was not properly advised of his right to the services of a free attorney before and during interrogation. Although respondent was indisputably informed that he had "the right to talk to a lawyer before you are questioned, have him present with you while you are being questioned, and all during the questioning," and further informed that he had "the right to have a lawyer appointed to represent you at no cost to yourself," the Court of Appeal ruled that these warnings were inadequate because respondent was not explicitly informed of his right to have an attorney appointed before further questioning. The Court of Appeal stated that "[o]ne of [*Miranda's*] virtues is its precise requirements which are so easily met," and quoted from Harryman v. Estelle, 616 F.2d 870, 873–874 (CA5), that " 'the rigidity of the *Miranda* rules and the way in which they are to be applied was conceived of and continues to be recognized as the decision's greatest strength.' " Relying on two previous decisions of the California Court of Appeal, the court ruled that the requirements of *Miranda* were not met in this case. The California Supreme Court denied a petition for hearing, with two justices dissenting.

This Court has never indicated that the "rigidity" of *Miranda* extends to the precise formulation of the warnings given a criminal defendant. See, e.g., United States v. Lamia, 429 F.2d 373, 375–376 (CA2) (1970). This Court and others *have* stressed as one virtue of *Miranda* the fact that the giving of the warnings obviates the need for a case-by-case inquiry into the actual voluntariness of the admissions of the accused. Nothing in these observations suggests any desirable rigidity in the *form* of the required warnings.

Quite the contrary, *Miranda* itself indicated that no talismanic incantation was required to satisfy its strictures. The Court in that case stated that "[t]he warnings required and the waiver necessary in accordance with our opinion today are, *in the absence of a fully effective equivalent,* prerequisites to the admissibility of any statement made by a defendant." (emphasis supplied). Just last Term in considering when *Miranda* applied we noted that that decision announced procedural safeguards including "the now familiar *Miranda* warnings ... *or their equivalent.*" Rhode Island v. Innis, (1980) (emphasis supplied).

Other courts considering the precise question presented by this case—whether a criminal defendant was adequately informed of his right to the presence of appointed counsel prior to and during interrogation—have not required a verbatim recital of the words of the *Miranda* opinion but rather have examined the warnings given to determine if the reference to the right to appointed counsel was linked with some future point in time after the police interrogation. In United States v. Garcia, 431 F.2d 134 (CA9 1970) ... for example, the court found inadequate advice to the defendant that she could "have an attorney appointed to represent you when you first appear before the U.S. Commissioner or the Court." People v. Bolinski, relied upon by the court below, is a case of this type. Two separate sets of warnings were ruled inadequate. In the first, the defendant was advised that "*if he was charged* ... he would be appointed counsel." (emphasis supplied). In the second, the defendant, then in Illinois and about to be moved to California, was advised that " 'the court would appoint [an attorney] *in Riverside County* [, California].' " (emphasis supplied). In both instances the reference to appointed counsel was linked to a future point in time after police interrogation, and therefore did not fully advise the suspect of his right to appointed counsel before such interrogation.

Here, in contrast, nothing in the warnings given respondent suggested any limitation on the right to the presence of appointed counsel different from the clearly conveyed rights to a lawyer in general, including the right "to a lawyer before you are questioned, . . . while you are being questioned, and all during the questioning." Like United States v. Noa, 443 F.2d 144 (CA9 1971), where the warnings given were substantially similar to those given here and defendant's argument was the same as that adopted by the Court of Appeal, "[t]his is not a case in which the defendant was not informed of his right to the presence of an attorney during questioning . . . or in which the offer of an appointed attorney was associated with a future time in court. . . ."

It is clear that the police in this case fully conveyed to respondent his rights as required by *Miranda.* He was told of his right to have a lawyer present prior to and during interrogation, and his right to have a lawyer appointed at no cost if he could not afford one. These warnings conveyed to respondent his right to have a lawyer appointed if he could not afford one prior to and during interrogation. The Court of Appeal erred in holding that the warnings were inadequate simply because of the order in which they were given.

Because respondent was given the warnings required by *Miranda,* the decision of the California Court of Appeal to the contrary is reversed.

It is so ordered.

JUSTICE STEVENS, with whom JUSTICE BRENNAN and JUSTICE MARSHALL join, dissenting.

A juvenile informed by police that he has a right to counsel may understand that right to include one or more of three options: (1) that he has a right to have a lawyer represent him if he or his parents are able and willing to hire one; (2) that, if he cannot afford to hire an attorney, he has a right to have a lawyer represent him without charge *at trial,* even if his parents are unwilling to spend money on his behalf; or (3) that, if he is unable to afford an attorney, he has a right to consult a lawyer without charge before he decides whether to talk to the police, even if his parents decline to pay for such legal representation. All three of these options are encompassed within the right to counsel possessed by a juvenile charged with a crime. In this case, the first two options were explained to respondent, but the third was not.

This Court held that . . . an individual taken into police custody and subjected to questioning must be given the *Miranda* warnings:

> "He must be warned prior to any questioning that he has the right to remain silent, that anything he says can be used against him in a court of law, that he has the right to the presence of an attorney, and that if he cannot afford an attorney one will be appointed for him prior to any questioning if he so desires."

This formulation makes it clear beyond any doubt that an indigent accused has the right to the presence of an attorney and the right to have that attorney appointed to represent him prior to any questioning.

While it is certainly true, as the Court emphasizes today, that the Federal Constitution does not require a "talismanic incantation" of the language of the *Miranda* opinion, it is also indisputable that it requires that an accused be adequately informed of his right to have counsel appointed prior to any police questioning.

The California Court of Appeal in this case analyzed the warning given respondent, and concluded that he had not been adequately informed of this crucial right. The police sergeant informed respondent that he had the right to have counsel present during questioning and, after a brief interlude, informed him that he had the right to appointed counsel. The Court of Appeal concluded that this warning was constitutionally inadequate, not because it deviated from the precise language of *Miranda,* but because

> "[u]nfortunately, the minor was not given the crucial information that the services of the free attorney were available *prior to the impending questioning.*" There can be no question that *Miranda* requires, as a matter of federal constitutional law, that an accused effectively be provided with this "crucial information" in some form. The Court's demonstration that the Constitution does not require that the precise language of *Miranda* be recited to an accused simply fails to come to terms with the express finding of the California Court of Appeal that respondent was not given this information. The warning recited by the police sergeant is sufficiently ambiguous on its face to provide adequate support for the California court's finding. That court's conclusion is at least reasonable, and is clearly not so patently erroneous as to warrant summary reversal.

The ambiguity in the warning given respondent is further demonstrated by the colloquy between the police sergeant and respondent's parents that occurred *after* respondent was told that he had the "right to have a lawyer appointed to represent you at no cost to yourself." Because lawyers are normally "appointed" by judges, and not by law enforcement officers, the reference to appointed counsel could reasonably have been understood to refer to trial counsel.... That is what respondent's parents must have assumed, because their ensuing colloquy with the sergeant related to their option "to *hire* a lawyer."

The judges on the California Court of Appeal and on the California Supreme Court, all of whom are presumably more familiar with the procedures followed by California police officers than we are, concluded that respondent was not adequately informed of his right to have a lawyer present without charge during the questioning. This Court is not at all fair to those judges when it construes their conscientious appraisal of a somewhat ambiguous record as requiring "a virtual incantation of the precise language contained in the *Miranda* opinion." It seems clear to me that it is this Court, rather than the state courts, that is guilty of attaching greater importance to the form of the *Miranda* ritual than to the substance of the message it is intended to convey.

I respectfully dissent.

NOTE

Some law enforcement agencies (pursuant to the directives of prosecutors or other legal advisors) go beyond the requirements of *Miranda* by adding to the four necessary admonitions, specifying, for example, the right to cut off questioning at any time. Even "standard" *Miranda* cards in some jurisdictions go beyond the four warnings required by the Supreme Court. Some officers also repeat the litany of warnings several times over a short period, another practice not mandated by *Miranda.*

These practices are exemplified by reference to specific cases, including the interrogation of John Hinckley regarding the shooting of President Ronald Reagan in 1981. The events are described as follows, in The Mischief of Miranda v. Arizona, 73 J.C.L. & Crim. 101 (1982), by Inbau:

Immediately after the attempted assassination, the District of Columbia police and Secret Service agents arrested Hinckley and took him to the local police headquarters, arriving there at 2:40 p.m. They wanted to question Hinckley not only as to his motive but also about the possible involvement of accomplices. Before doing so, however, they dutifully read to him the warnings of constitutional rights that the Supreme Court mandated in *Miranda.* Moreover, the warnings given to Hinckley, as we shall see, contained embellishments of the court prescribed ones, and they were read to him on *three separate occasions* within a *two hour period.* After receiving the third set of warnings Hinckley was presented with a "waiver of rights" form on which he responded "yes" to the questions whether he had read his rights and understood them. Then he was asked whether he "wished to answer any questions." At this point Hinckley answered, "I don't know. I'm not sure; I think I ought to talk to Joe Bates [his father's lawyer in Dallas]." Hinckley added: "I want to talk to you, but first I want to talk to Joe Bates."

Following the D.C. police "booking procedure" (identification data and fingerprints), and while the police were attempting to contact Joe Bates, two FBI agents arrived and arrested Hinckley for violation of the Presidential Assassination Statute. They were informed of all that had transpired and then took Hinckley to the FBI field office at approximately 5:15 p.m. He received the *Miranda* warnings for the *fourth time,* at the field office. He was also presented with another waiver form, supplied by the FBI. Hinckley signed his name to it; however, "it was clearly understood that he did not waive his right not to answer questions before consulting counsel." Nevertheless, he did answer various "background" questions asked by FBI agents.

The "background" information was suppressed by the D.C. District Court. It reasoned that the information was elicited from Hinckley in violation of *Miranda,* which prohibits the interrogation of a custodial suspect after he announces or indicates he wants to have a lawyer present. As already quoted, Hinckley had said he wanted one, although he did so rather hesitatingly.

The district court ruling was affirmed by the Court of Appeals for the D.C. Circuit. Both courts rejected the government's contention that the questioning of Hinckley at the FBI office was merely "standard processing procedure" of an "essentially administrative nature." The courts concluded that Hinckley had, in fact, been interrogated and that the purpose of the questioning was to obtain personal background information from Hinckley which would negate an anticipated insanity plea at the time of trial. It was obvious that Hinckley could not deny he did the shooting, so the only conceivable defense would be that of insanity. That was, in fact, the plea at his trial, which began on April 26, 1982.

In view of the court rulings declaring the "background information" inadmissible at trial, whatever value that information may have been to the prosecution was irretrievably lost. The government decided not to seek Supreme Court review of the appellate court's decision. Reliance had to be placed, therefore, upon independent evidence of Hinckley's sanity, including the testimony of the prosecution's psychiatrists that he was sane at the time of the shooting. Their testimony was contradicted, however, by several defense psychiatrists. Hinckley was found not guilty by reason of insanity.

(c) The Meaning of "Waiver"

PEOPLE v. BRAESEKE

Supreme Court of California, 1979.
159 Cal.Rptr. 684, 602 P.2d 384.

Defendant was convicted in the Superior Court ... of first-degree murder of his mother, father and grandfather, and defendant appealed. The Supreme Court, Manuel, J., held that: (1) the People may, on appeal by defendant and pursuant to statute governing decisions on rulings adverse to State, obtain review of allegedly erroneous rulings by trial court in order to secure affirmance of judgment of conviction; (2) defendant's request to speak "off the record" cannot constitute knowing and intelligent waiver of Miranda rights; and (3) trial court erred in not suppressing defendant's subsequent statements and certain physical evidence as products of first unlawfully obtained confession.

Reversed.

On August 24, 1976, at approximately 1 a.m., defendant, who was then 20 years old, summoned Alameda County Sheriff's deputies to his home. There the deputies found the bodies of defendant's mother, father and grandfather; all were dead as the result of multiple gunshot wounds.

In response to questioning by the deputies, defendant said he had last seen his parents and grandfather alive at 9 p.m. when he left the house to go to a movie with his friend David Barker. The deputies noticed that although the master bedroom appeared to have been ransacked, there was no sign of forced entry; also, a number of items that would normally have been taken in a burglary were left untouched.

Defendant was taken to the sheriff's substation where he was interviewed by Sergeants Cervi and Seher shortly after 4 a.m. He related the same version of events he had earlier recounted. The interview ended about 5:15 a.m. Sergeants Cervi and Seher then discussed the case out of defendant's presence. They noted that defendant had blood splattered on his pants leg and that there were inconsistencies between defendant's story and that of his friend David Barker whom the officers had interviewed earlier. The officers therefore decided to conduct a further interview of defendant.

The second interview began about 6 a.m. It was not tape recorded, but defendant was fully advised of his Miranda rights. Defendant said he understood his rights and was willing to talk with the officers. When asked about the blood on his pants, defendant stated that it must have been acquired when he was checking the bodies. The officers replied that "splattered" blood would not be the result of having rubbed against a bloody object and that they believed defendant had committed the homicides. At this point defendant said he did not want to discuss the matter further without an attorney present. The questioning ceased, and Sergeant Cervi told defendant that if he wanted to talk at some later time he would have to contact the officers. Defendant was then arrested and booked.

During the booking procedure, Cervi asked defendant for his name, address and date of birth. When he asked defendant the name of his next of kin, defendant fell silent and asked if he could speak with Cervi alone and "off the record" (hereafter referred to as the "off the record statement"). Cervi agreed, and defendant began asking him hypothetical questions: "What if I tell you the rifle was somewhere where some kids may find it?" What would happen to him if he had done all the things the officers had accused him of doing? Cervi replied that he would appreciate any information defendant could give him but that defendant would have to go to jail. Defendant testified that Cervi also told him that "it would be better for (him)" if he gave a statement but that he would have to go to jail anyway.

Cervi then asked defendant, "(C)an I turn the tape recorder on; and can we get a statement from you to that effect?" Defendant said yes, and Cervi turned on the tape recorder at 7:25 a.m., from memory attempted to readmonish defendant of his Miranda rights, and recorded his statement (hereinafter referred to as Confession No. 1). In response to leading questions by Cervi, which omitted reference to the "off the record" request, defendant acknowledged that he had come forward during the booking procedure and asked to talk to Cervi ... about the incident. In response to further questions, defendant stated that he was acting voluntarily and was willing to waive his right to have an attorney present. Cervi concentrated on defendant's understanding of his right to counsel and neglected to include in his readmonishment the right to remain silent.

* * *

During the formal statement defendant confessed that he and David Barker had murdered his mother, father and grandfather with a .22 caliber rifle. At the conclusion of the formal statement (Confession No. 1) defendant led the officers to the spot where he had hidden the rifle.

About 1 p.m. the same day defendant gave a tape-recorded statement to Deputy District Attorney Michael Cardoza (hereafter referred to as Confession No. 2). Cardoza began by advising defendant of his Miranda rights. Defendant said he understood them and was willing to talk. He confirmed the prior sequence of events and stated that he was aware of his Miranda rights and understood them at the time he asked to talk to Sergeant Cervi. Defendant was again asked whether he was willing to waive his rights and talk; he said he was and again gave a full confession (Confession No. 2). This interview ended at 2:09 p.m.

* * *

Defendant made a pretrial motion to suppress his off the record statement to Sergeant Cervi, the two tape-recorded confessions (Confessions No. 1 and 2), the rifle and various items of physical evidence which were allegedly products of the confessions. He also moved to suppress a statement made two days after his arrest on the ground that it too was a product of the earlier confessions. The trial court ruled that the confession to Cervi (Confession No. 1) must be suppressed because it had not been preceded by an adequate Miranda warning. The rest of the items defendant sought to have suppressed were ruled admissible.

* * *

The warnings given appear sufficient There remains, however, the question whether defendant knowingly and intelligently waived his Miranda rights.

It is beyond dispute that once a defendant has asserted his right to counsel the interrogation must cease.... It may not be resumed without counsel unless compelling evidence of a waiver of the suspect's rights appears.... Even when the defendant has not asserted his right to counsel, a "heavy burden rests on the Government to demonstrate that the defendant knowingly and intelligently waived his privilege against self-incrimination and his right to retained or appointed counsel."

* * *

In view of the lack of any credible evidence that defendant's initiation of the conversation with Sergeant Cervi constituted a knowing and intelligent waiver of his Miranda rights, we must conclude that the continued interrogation of defendant was in violation of Miranda and that the confession resulting therefrom is inadmissible....

Defendant contends that the trial court erred in not suppressing his subsequent statements and certain physical evidence as products of the first confession. "The fruits of an illegally conducted interrogation are no less inadmissible during the trial of the declarant than his statements themselves."

... Absent prosecution evidence showing a break in the causative chain between Seriatim confessions, there is a presumption that the subsequent confessions were the product of the same improper police conduct which induced the first confession.

* * *

The improper introduction of a confession constitutes reversible error.

The judgment is reversed.

BIRD, C.J., and TOBRINER and NEWMAN, JJ., concur.

CLARK, Justice, dissenting.

How did the constable blunder? What did the officers do that they should not have done? What should have been done that was left undone?

The conduct of the police was irreproachable. Therefore, the lesson ("prophylactic effect") derived from today's decision can only be that this court no longer accepts convictions based on voluntary confessions. This despite the fact that many convicted criminals (few criminals, of course, are convicted) would go free but for confessions. Worse, recognition that some desire to tell the truth and should be permitted to do so escapes the majority of our court.

* * *

It would be difficult to imagine more compelling evidence of waiver of one's privilege to sit silent. Conversely, defendant's desire to describe his conduct to those charged with its solution is clear and should not be frustrated by our court.

Defendant's conviction for these grave crimes, cold-blooded murder of his father, mother and grandfather to secure his inheritance should be affirmed.

MOSK and RICHARDSON, JJ., concur.

NOTES

1. The prosecution filed a petition for certiorari in the United States Supreme Court. After a grant of the petition, the case was remanded to the California Supreme Court "to consider whether its judgment was based on federal or state grounds, or both." The California Supreme Court certified that its judgment was "based upon *Miranda v. Arizona* and the fifth amendment to the United States Constitution." Further review was denied by the United States Supreme Court.

Braeske was retried and convicted upon evidence obtained (after some initial resistance from a TV network) of incriminating statements Braeseke made while in jail after his first conviction during an interview with Mike Wallace on CBS's "60 Minutes" TV program. Braeseke's unsuccessful defense at his second trial was the influence of an hallucinogenic drug ("angel dust") at the time of the killings.

[From 24 California Western Law Review at p. 193 (1988).]

2. As the validity of the required "knowing and intelligent waiver" by a person of subnormal intelligence, see People v. Bernasco, 138 Ill.2d 349, 562

N.E.2d 958 (1990). The Illinois Supreme Court held invalid a *Miranda* waiver by a 17 year old burglary suspect with a low I.Q. of 80.

For a report on an empirical study to determine the ability of juveniles to comprehend the meaning and significance of *Miranda* rights, see Holtz, Miranda in a Juvenile Setting; a Child's Right to Silence, 78 J.Cr.L. & Crim. 534 (1987). It reports that only 20% of the youths tested had an adequate understanding of the entire set of warnings. The author submits an extensive "Youth Rights Form," to be signed by both the juvenile and parent of guardian, as a substitute for the regular waiver.

In another study, a psychology professor concludes that the comprehension of the *Miranda* rights by juveniles is "so deficient as to mandate a per se exclusion of waivers made without legal counsel." Grisso, Juveniles Capacities to Waive Miranda Rights: An Empirical Analysis, 68 Calif.L.Rev. 1134 (1980).

A number of states have statutes requiring the presence of a parent or other interested adult at the time of an interrogation of a suspected juvenile. See, for example: Colo.Rev.Stat., Sec. 19–2–210 (West Supp.1993); Conn.Gen.Stat.Ann. 46b–137(a) (West Supp.1979); N.M.Stat.Ann. § 32–1–27(a) 1978; Okla.Stat. Ann., Tit. 10, § 1109(a) (West Supp. 1979–80).

(D) Exceptions to the Requirements of Miranda

1. A "public safety" exception has been made to the *Miranda* mandate, based upon the reasoning that the underlying principle of *Miranda* contemplates case situations in which a critical time factor is not present, in contrast to a case in which immediate police action may be required. An example is the Supreme Court case of New York v. Quarles, 467 U.S. 649 (1984), in which the Court ruled that a "public safety" exception was warranted to justify a police officer's failure to advise a handcuffed suspect of the warnings before asking him of the location of a discarded gun in a public place.

2. Private protective security officers are generally exempted from issuing the warnings even when an arrest is made in the area where they are accorded such powers. A leading case is People v. Deborah C., a Minor, 177 Cal.Rptr. 852, 635 P.2d 446 (1981); another is People v. Ray, 65 N.Y.2d 282, 480 N.E.2d 1065 (1985). Also see Protective Security Law (2d ed. 1996) by Inbau, Farber, and Arnold, at 72–75.

(E) Impeachment of Defendant's Testimony With Statements Obtained in Violation of *Miranda*

The Supreme Court has held, in two cases, that a person's statements obtained without proper *Miranda* warnings or prescribed procedures may nevertheless be used to attack his credibility if he testifies at trial that he did not commit the charged offense. In one of the cases, Harris v. New York, 401 U.S. 222, 91 S.Ct. 643 (1971), the interrogation omitted the *Miranda* required warning of right to appointed counsel. Chief Justice Burger, speaking for a majority of the Court, gave the following reason for the decision:

> "Every criminal defendant is privileged to testify in his own defense, or to refuse to do so. But that privilege cannot be

construed to include the right to commit perjury. Having voluntarily taken the stand, petitioner was under an obligation to speak truthfully and accurately, and the prosecution here did no more than utilize the traditional truth-testing devices of the adversary process. Had inconsistent statements been made by the accused to some third person, it could hardly be contended that the conflict could not be laid before the jury by way of cross-examination and impeachment.

"The shield provided by *Miranda* cannot be perverted into a license to use perjury by way of a defense, free from the risk of confrontation with prior inconsistent utterances. We hold, therefore, that petitioner's credibility was appropriately impeached by use of his earlier conflicting statements."

In the second of the two cases, Oregon v. Hass, 420 U.S. 714, 95 S.Ct. 1215 (1975), the accused, while in a patrol car after having received the *Miranda* warnings, stated he would like to call an attorney. He was told he could do so "as soon as we got to the office." Thereafter he admitted the theft and disclosed the location of the stolen property. At his trial he denied committing the offense, whereupon the prosecution offered the incriminating evidence to impeach him. A majority of the Court approved of this impeachment, for the following reasons:

"As in *Harris,* it does not follow from *Miranda* that evidence inadmissible against Hass in the prosecution's case in chief is barred for all purposes, always provided that 'the trustworthiness of the evidence satisfies legal standards.' Again, the impeaching material would provide valuable aid to the jury in assessing the defendant's credibility; again, 'the benefits of this process should not be lost'; and again, making the deterrent effect assumption, there is sufficient deterrence when the evidence in question is made unavailable to the prosecution in its case in chief. If all this sufficed for the result in *Harris,* it supports and demands a like result in Hass' case. Here, too, the shield provided by *Miranda* is not to be perverted to a license to testify inconsistently, or even perjuriously, free from the risk of confrontation with prior inconsistent utterances."

The dissenting Justices expressed their concern as follows: "Under today's holding, once the warnings are given, police have almost no incentive for following Miranda's requirement that if the individual states that he wants an attorney, the interrogation must cease until an attorney is present."

3. THE FUTURE OF MIRANDA?

In *Miranda* the court invited Congress and the state legislatures to devise some suitable alternative to *Miranda,* although the court was not explicit as to what would be acceptable to it. In accordance with the perceived invitation, Congress in the 1968 Omnibus Crime Bill provided an alternative, and so did the Arizona legislature in 1969. 18 U.S.C.A. § 3501; Ariz.Rev.Stat. § 13–3988. Essentially this legislation declared that voluntariness was the test of confession admissibility, but that in determining the issue of voluntariness, consideration should be given to whether the suspect had been advised of his right to silence and to a lawyer. However, the presence or absence of those factors would not be conclusive with respect to voluntariness.

No case has been presented to the Supreme Court, or to any other court of review, that would test the validity of either the congressional or Arizona enactment. Moreover, on a number of occasions, the suggestion has been offered that an appropriate case should be presented to the Supreme Court for a review of either the federal or state enactment. See the following from "Miranda v. Arizona—Is It Worth the Cost?", by Inbau and Manak, 24 Calif. Western Law Rev. 185, at 199 (1988):

"The Court should extricate itself from this self-inflicted burden of time and effort, which could be better devoted to cases involving matters of far greater importance than the prophylactic rules of *Miranda's* mandate. An auxiliary benefit would be an end to the mischief created by *Miranda* for the police and prosecutors as well as for the many trial and appellate courts.

"There should be no further delay in remedial action by the Supreme Court ... an appropriate circumstance would be a case pertaining to the constitutional validity of the relevant provision of the 1968 Congressional Omnibus Crime Act or its 1969 Arizona counterpart. Direct action toward *Miranda's* demise would be far preferable to the slower 'erosion' process about which a few of the Justices have complained. The erosion route would only perpetuate further erosion of valuable court time and effort."

In the 1994 case of Davis v. United States, 114 S.Ct. 2350, Justice Scalia, in his concurring opinion, raised the question as to why the Government had not raised the issue of § 3501 in its brief, and during the oral arguments he and two other Justices presented the same question to the Government's attorney. No satisfactory explanation was given. Justice Scalia also commented in his concurring opinion in Davis, at p. 2357 that "This is not the first case in which the United States has declined to invoke § 3501 before us—nor even the first case in which that failure has been called to its attention ... in fact, with limited exceptions the provision has been studiously avoided by every administration, not only in this court but in the lower courts, since its enactment more than 25 years ago."

On March 14, 1996, the student editors of the Northwestern University Law Review sponsored a "Dump Miranda?" program with eight panelists evenly divided upon the issue. Prepared papers from two of them were published in the Review: Cassell, Paul G., "Miranda's Social Costs: An Empirical Reassessment," 90 Nw.L.Rev. 387 (1996); and Shulhofer, Stephen J., "Miranda's Practical Effect: Substantial Benefits and Vanishingly Small Social Costs, 90 Nw.L.Rev. 500 (1996).

Chapter 13

THE LAW OF ARREST

A. HISTORICAL BACKGROUND *

Origin of the Police Department

The conditions in England during the centuries in which the law of arrest was being cast into its present shape, the seventeenth and eighteenth, were very different from those prevailing today in either England or the United States. Police departments were unknown, for it was not until 1829 that Sir Robert Peel persuaded the English Parliament to pass an act creating a police force for the city of London. In his honor the policemen were called "Bobbies", a nickname which London policemen still bear. Of course, Peel's idea was not entirely new; if it had been, Parliament would probably not have enacted it. For some years previously, various experiments had been tried and different sections of London had attempted to maintain groups of watchmen, but these men were usually ill-trained and always too few in number to provide satisfactory police protection. Outside of London, there were virtually no police officers, though in some places small groups of men undertook without compensation to keep the peace. There was thus nothing at all comparable to police departments, as we know them, before 1829. . . .

Up to the time of Sir Robert Peel, the methods of policing England differed little from those used in the days of the Norman kings. The Crown appointed sheriffs and constables among whose manifold duties was that of arresting wrongdoers, but the principal burden of keeping the peace lay on the community as a whole. Hence arose the institutions of the posse comitatus and the hue and cry. When a serious crime was committed and the offender could be tracked, the hue and cry was raised. It was then the duty of all the neighbors to seize their weapons and aid in the pursuit, which continued from county to county until the offender was captured or had escaped. Furthermore, sheriffs and constables often called upon ordinary citizens to form a posse comitatus and assist in making arrests. . . . This practice is still common in the more sparsely settled parts of this country where police officers are few and

* From an article by the late Professor Sam Bass Warner, which was published in 26 A.B.A.J. 151 (1940) and in 31 J.Crim.L. & C. 111 (1940). The historical information it reveals should receive consideration when an analysis is made of present day cases involving arrest and detention procedures.

hundreds of citizens sometimes take part in man-hunts, the modern equivalent of the hue and cry.

Right of Private Persons to Make Arrests

For the most part, however, victims of crimes were supposed, with the aid of their relatives and neighbors, to do their own detective work and themselves to arrest and prosecute offenders.... In fact, the right of private persons to make arrests was in nearly all respects equal to that of sheriffs and constables. So adequate did it seem, that when the "Bobbies" were created they were given no additional powers. They differed from private persons only in being employed to do that which the latter could do if so inclined....

When a suspect was apprehended, he found himself in a sorry plight. Persons charged with serious offenses were rarely granted their freedom on bail. For example, even as late as 1800, the highly respectable Mrs. Leigh Perrot, aunt of Jane Austen, was unable to persuade the judges to admit her to bail, though she was accused merely of shoplifting. She had to spend the winter in jail in spite of her wealth, the absurdity of the charge, and the special trip her husband took to London in an effort to persuade the Court of King's Bench to release her on bail....

In 1823, Sir Robert Peel also started the great reform which transformed prisons from business enterprises operated for the benefit of the keepers into liabilities of the taxpayers. Everywhere prior to that date and in some places until recently, jailers had been able to make a profit out of their unfortunate charges. Dickens' account of Mr. Pickwick's experiences in prison indicates some of the more legitimate ways in which this was done. Every incident of prison life, from admission to discharge, was made the occasion for levying fees. Fees were charged for the privilege of detention in this or that part of the prison, for a separate room, for a bed, for a mattress, for the use of bedclothes, etc., etc. When a prisoner was acquitted, he was not released until he paid all the fees due, including a fee for discharge.... What happened to prisoners unable to pay their fees depended upon the century and the humanitarian instincts of the jailer. In Massachusetts at the end of the seventeenth century such unfortunates might be sold for life or a period of years into the service of anybody willing to pay their fees....

Sufferings of Persons in Jail Awaiting Trial

Since jailers were held responsible for escapes and many jails were constructed for some other purpose and hence easy to break out of, prisoners were often kept in irons. Those without means to buy better accommodations were frequently huddled together in dark, filthy rooms, in close proximity to depravity and disease. Under such conditions imprisonment until the next term of court was often equivalent to a death sentence, especially during the frequent periods when the prisons were swept by a malignant form of typhus known as "gaol fever". In 1759 an English authority estimated that each year a fourth of the people in prison died there....

These misfortunes awaited persons thrown into prison pending trial, but an even worse fate, if that were possible, might result from arrest. During the centuries when the law of arrest was developing, kidnaping was much more prevalent than at present. As arrests were commonly made by private persons, the victim must often have been in doubt whether he was being arrested for crime, seized for ransom, or perhaps shanghaied for service as an English seaman or even as a slave on a foreign galley.

Arrests With and Without a Warrant

Such a state of affairs naturally developed a law strictly circumscribing the right to arrest and prescribing the disposition of the prisoner after arrest, with little distinction between the right of private citizens and public officials to make arrests. It was expected that most arrests would be made after the issuance of a warrant, whereas today the vast majority of arrests are made without a warrant. Hence, the right to arrest for a misdemeanor was with a few exceptions limited to misdemeanors amounting to a breach of the peace and then only when committed in the presence of the person making the arrest. This is still the law in many states, but in the majority police officers, and sometimes even private citizens, have been given the right to arrest for any misdemeanor committed in their presence....

Either an officer or a private person could, and still can, arrest for a felony actually committed either when it was committed in his presence or he has reasonable cause to believe that the person to be arrested committed it. There also developed at the beginning of the nineteenth century the rule prevailing in many American states, that an officer may arrest whenever he has reasonable cause to believe that the person to be arrested has committed a felony, even though no felony has in fact been committed.... [1]

B. DEFINITION, LEGISLATIVE PROVISIONS, AND COURT PRESCRIBED RULES

1. DEFINITION OF ARREST

"An arrest is the taking of another into custody for the actual or purported purpose of bringing the other before a court, body or official, or of otherwise securing the administration of the law....

"Mere words will not constitute an arrest, while on the other hand no actual physical touching is essential.... an assertion of authority and purpose to arrest followed by submission of the arrestee constitutes an arrest. There can be no arrest without either touching or submission." Perkins, Elements of Police Science 223, 227 (1942).

1. Also with regard to the historical background of the law of arrest, see the interesting article entitled The First Urban Policeman, by Martin A. Kelly, 1 J. Police Sci. & Adm. 56 (1973).

"Arrest is the taking of a person into custody in order that he may be forthcoming to answer for the commission of an offense." Sec. 18, Code of Criminal Procedure, American Law Institute.

"'Arrest' means the taking of a person into custody." 725 ILCS 5/102–5 of the 1992 Illinois Code of Criminal Procedure. "An arrest is made by an actual restraint of the person or by his submission to custody." 725 ILCS 5/107–5 (1992).

2. ARREST (SEIZURE OF THE PERSON) UNDER THE FOURTH AMENDMENT

UNITED STATES v. MENDENHALL

Supreme Court of the United States, 1980.
446 U.S. 544, 100 S.Ct. 1870.

MR. JUSTICE STEWART announced the judgment of the Court and delivered an opinion, in which MR. JUSTICE REHNQUIST joined.**

The respondent was brought to trial in the United States District Court for the Eastern District of Michigan on a charge of possessing heroin with intent to distribute it. She moved to suppress the introduction at trial of the heroin as evidence against her on the ground that it had been acquired from her through an unconstitutional search and seizure by agents of the Drug Enforcement Administration (DEA). The District Court denied the respondent's motion, and she was convicted after a trial upon stipulated facts. The Court of Appeals, 596 F.2d 706, reversed, finding the search of the respondent's person to have been unlawful. We granted certiorari to consider whether any right of the respondent guaranteed by the Fourth Amendment was violated in the circumstances presented by this case. 444 U.S. 822, 100 S.Ct. 42.

I

At the hearing in the trial court on the respondent's motion to suppress, it was established how the heroin she was charged with possessing had been obtained from her. The respondent arrived at the Detroit Metropolitan Airport on a commercial airline flight from Los Angeles early in the morning on February 10, 1976. As she disembarked from the airplane, she was observed by two agents of the DEA, who were present at the airport for the purpose of detecting unlawful

** THE CHIEF JUSTICE, MR. JUSTICE BLACKMUN, and MR. JUSTICE POWELL also join all but Part II–A of this opinion.

traffic in narcotics. After observing the respondent's conduct, which appeared to the agents to be characteristic of persons unlawfully carrying narcotics,[1] the agents approached her as she was walking through the concourse, identified themselves as federal agents, and asked to see her identification and airline ticket. The respondent produced her driver's license, which was in the name of Sylvia Mendenhall, and, in answer to a question of one of the agents, stated that she resided at the address appearing on the license. The airline ticket was issued in the name of "Annette Ford." When asked why the ticket bore a name different from her own, the respondent stated that she "just felt like using that name." In response to a further question, the respondent indicated that she had been in California only two days. Agent Anderson then specifically identified himself as a federal narcotics agent and, according to his testimony, the respondent "became quite shaken, extremely nervous. She had a hard time speaking."

After returning the airline ticket and driver's license to her, Agent Anderson asked the respondent if she would accompany him to the airport DEA office for further questions. She did so, although the record does not indicate a verbal response to the request. The office, which was located up one flight of stairs about 50 feet from where the respondent had first been approached, consisted of a reception area adjoined by three other rooms. At the office the agent asked the respondent if she would allow a search of her person and handbag and told her that she had the right to decline the search if she desired. She responded: "Go ahead." She then handed Agent Anderson her purse, which contained a receipt for an airline ticket that had been issued to "F. Bush" three days earlier for a flight from Pittsburgh through Chicago to Los Angeles. The agent asked whether this was the ticket that she had used for her flight to California, and the respondent stated that it was.

A female police officer then arrived to conduct the search of the respondent's person. She asked the agents if the respondent had consented to be searched. The agents said that she had, and the respondent followed the policewoman into a private room. There the policewoman again asked the respondent if she consented to the search, and the respondent replied that she did. The policewoman explained that the search would require that the respondent remove her clothing. The respondent stated that she had a plane to catch and was assured by the policewoman that if she were carrying no narcotics, there would be no problem. The respondent then began to disrobe without further comment. As the respondent removed her clothing, she took from her

1. The agent testified that the respondent's behavior fit the so-called "drug courier profile"—an informally compiled abstract of characteristics thought typical of persons carrying illicit drugs. In this case the agents thought it relevant that (1) the respondent was arriving on a flight from Los Angeles, a city believed by the agents to be the place of origin for much of the heroin brought to Detroit; (2) the respondent was the last person to leave the plane, "appeared to be very nervous," and "completely scanned the whole area where [the agents] were standing"; (3) after leaving the plane the respondent proceeded past the baggage area without claiming any luggage; and (4) the respondent changed airlines for her flight out of Detroit.

undergarments two small packages, one of which appeared to contain heroin, and handed both to the policewoman. The agents then arrested the respondent for possessing heroin.

It was on the basis of this evidence that the District Court denied the respondent's motion to suppress. The court concluded that the agents' conduct in initially approaching the respondent and asking to see her ticket and identification was a permissible investigative stop under the standards of Terry v. Ohio, 392 U.S. 1, 88 S.Ct. 1868, and United States v. Brignoni-Ponce, 422 U.S. 873, 95 S.Ct. 2574, finding that this conduct was based on specific and articulable facts that justified a suspicion of criminal activity. The court also found that the respondent had not been placed under arrest or otherwise detained when she was asked to accompany the agents to the DEA office, but had accompanied the agents " 'voluntarily in a spirit of apparent cooperation.' " It was the court's view that no arrest occurred until after the heroin had been found. Finally, the trial court found that the respondent "gave her consent to the search [in the DEA office] and . . . such consent was freely and voluntarily given."

The Court of Appeals reversed the respondent's subsequent conviction, stating only that "the court concludes that this case is indistinguishable from United States v. McCaleb," 552 F.2d 717 (CA6 1977). In *McCaleb* the Court of Appeals had suppressed heroin seized by DEA agents at the Detroit Airport in circumstances substantially similar to those in the present case. The Court of Appeals there disapproved the Government's reliance on the so-called "drug courier profile," and held that the agents could not reasonably have suspected criminal activity in that case, for the reason that "the activities of the [persons] observed by DEA agents, were consistent with innocent behavior." The Court of Appeals further concluded in *McCaleb* that, even if the initial approach had been permissible, asking the suspects to accompany the agents to a private room for further questioning constituted an arrest requiring probable cause. Finally, the court in *McCaleb* held that the consent to the search in that case had not been voluntarily given, principally because it was the fruit of what the court believed to have been an unconstitutional detention.

On rehearing en banc of the present case, the Court of Appeals reaffirmed its original decision, stating simply that the respondent had not validly consented to the search "within the meaning of [*McCaleb*]."

II

The Fourth Amendment provides that "the right of the people to be secure in their persons, houses, papers, and effects, against unreasonable searches and seizures, shall not be violated. . . ." There is no question in this case that the respondent possessed this constitutional right of personal security as she walked through the Detroit Airport, for "the Fourth Amendment protects people, not places," Katz v. United States, 389 U.S. 347, 351, 88 S.Ct. 507, 511. Here the Government concedes that its agents had neither a warrant nor probable cause to believe that the respondent was carrying narcotics when the agents conducted a search of the respondent's person. It is the Government's position, however, that the search was conducted pursuant to the respondent's consent, and thus was excepted from the requirements of both a warrant and probable cause. See Schneckloth v. Bustamonte, 412 U.S. 218, 93 S.Ct. 2041. Evidently, the Court of Appeals concluded that the respondent's apparent consent to the search was in fact not voluntarily given and was in any event the product of earlier official conduct violative of the Fourth Amendment. We must first consider, therefore, whether such conduct occurred, either on the concourse or in the DEA office at the airport.

A

The Fourth Amendment's requirement that searches and seizures be founded upon an objective justification, governs all seizures of the person, "including seizures that involve only a brief detention short of traditional arrest. Davis v. Mississippi, 394 U.S. 721 [89 S.Ct. 1394] (1969); Terry v. Ohio, 392 U.S. 1, 16–19 [88 S.Ct. 1868, 1877] (1968)." United States v. Brignoni-Ponce, supra, at 878, 95 S.Ct., at 2578.[2] Accordingly, if the respondent was "seized" when the DEA agents approached her on the concourse and asked questions of her, the agents' conduct in doing so was constitutional only if they reasonably suspected the respondent of wrongdoing. But "[o]bviously, not all personal intercourse between policemen and citizens involves 'seizures' of persons. Only when the officer, by means of physical force or show of authority, has in some way restrained the liberty of a citizen may we conclude that

2. In the District Court and the Court of Appeals, the parties evidently assumed that the respondent was seized when she was approached on the airport concourse and was asked if she would show her identification and airline ticket. In its brief on the merits and oral argument in this Court, however, the Government has argued that no seizure occurred, and the respondent has joined the argument. While the Court ordinarily does not consider matters neither raised before nor decided by the courts below, see Adickes v. Kress & Co., 398 U.S. 144, 147, n. 2, 90 S.Ct. 1598, 1602, n. 2, it has done so in exceptional circumstances. See Youakim v. Miller, 425 U.S. 231, 234, 96 S.Ct. 1399, 1401; Duignan v. United States, 274 U.S. 195, 200, 47 S.Ct. 566, 568. We consider the Government's contention that there was no seizure of the respondent in this case, because the contrary assumption, embraced by the trial court and the Court of Appeals, rests on a serious misapprehension of federal constitutional law. And because the determination of the question is essential to the correct disposition of the other issues in the case, we shall treat it as "fairly comprised" by the questions presented in the petition for certiorari. This Court's Rule 23(1)(c). See Procunier v. Navarette, 434 U.S. 555, 559–560, n. 6, 98 S.Ct. 855, 858–859, n. 6; Blonder-Tongue Laboratories, Inc. v. University of Illinois Foundation, 402 U.S. 313, 320–321, n. 6, 91 S.Ct. 1434, 1438–1439, n. 6.

The evidentiary record in the trial court is adequate to permit consideration of the contention. The material facts are not disputed. A major question throughout the controversy has been whether the respondent was at any time detained by the DEA agents. Counsel for the respondent has argued that she was arrested while proceeding through the concourse. The trial court and the Court of Appeals characterized the incident as an "investigatory stop." But the correctness of the legal characterization of the facts appearing in the record is a matter for this Court to determine. See Schneckloth v. Bustamonte, 412 U.S. 218, 226, 93 S.Ct. 2041, 2047; Bumper v. North Carolina, 391 U.S. 543, 548–550, 88 S.Ct. 1788, 1791–1792.

a 'seizure' has occurred." Terry v. Ohio, 392 U.S., at 19, n. 16, 88 S.Ct., at 1879, n. 16.

The distinction between an intrusion amounting to a "seizure" of the person and an encounter that intrudes upon no constitutionally protected interest is illustrated by the facts of Terry v. Ohio, which the Court recounted as follows: "Officer McFadden approached the three men, identified himself as a police officer and asked for their names.... When the men 'mumbled something' in response to his inquiries, Officer McFadden grabbed petitioner Terry, spun him around so that they were facing the other two, with Terry between McFadden and the others, and patted down the outside of his clothing." Obviously the officer "seized" Terry and subjected him to a "search" when he took hold of him, spun him around, and patted down the outer surfaces of his clothing. What was not determined in that case, however, was that a seizure had taken place before the officer physically restrained Terry for purposes of searching his person for weapons. The Court "assume[d] that up to that point no intrusion upon constitutionally protected rights had occurred." The Court's assumption appears entirely correct in view of the fact, noted in the concurring opinion of Mr. Justice White, that "[t]here is nothing in the Constitution which prevents a policeman from addressing questions to anyone on the streets." Police officers enjoy "the liberty (again, possessed by every citizen) to address questions to other persons," although "ordinarily the person addressed has an equal right to ignore his interrogator and walk away."

Similarly, the Court in Sibron v. New York, 392 U.S. 40, 88 S.Ct. 1889, a case decided the same day as Terry v. Ohio, indicated that not every encounter between a police officer and a citizen is an intrusion requiring an objective justification. In that case, a police officer, before conducting what was later found to have been an unlawful search, approached Sibron in a restaurant and told him to come outside, which Sibron did. The Court had no occasion to decide whether there was a "seizure" of Sibron inside the restaurant antecedent to the seizure that accompanied the search. The record was "barren of any indication whether Sibron accompanied [the officer] outside in submission to a show of force or authority which left him no choice, or *whether he went voluntarily in a spirit of apparent cooperation* with the officer's investigation." (Emphasis added). Plainly, in the latter event, there was no seizure until the police officer in some way demonstrably curtailed Sibron's liberty.

We adhere to the view that a person is "seized" only when, by means of physical force or a show of authority, his freedom of movement is restrained. Only when such restraint is imposed is there any foundation whatever for invoking constitutional safeguards. The purpose of the Fourth Amendment is not to eliminate all contact between the police and the citizenry, but "to prevent arbitrary and oppressive interference by enforcement officials with the privacy and personal security of individuals." United States v. Martinez-Fuerte, 428 U.S. 543, 554, 96 S.Ct. 3074, 3081. As long as the person to whom questions are put remains free to disregard the questions and walk away, there has been no intrusion upon that person's liberty or privacy as would under the Constitution require some particularized and objective justification.

Moreover, characterizing every street encounter between a citizen and the police as a "seizure," while not enhancing any interest secured by the Fourth Amendment, would impose wholly unrealistic restrictions upon a wide variety of legitimate law enforcement practices. The Court has on other occasions referred to the acknowledged need for police questioning as a tool in the effective enforcement of the criminal laws. "Without such investigation, those who were innocent might be falsely accused, those who were guilty might wholly escape prosecution, and many crimes would go unsolved. In short, the security of all would be diminished. Haynes v. Washington, 373 U.S. 503, 515 [83 S.Ct. 1336, 1344]." Schneckloth v. Bustamonte, 412 U.S., at 225, 93 S.Ct., at 2046.

We conclude that a person has been "seized" within the meaning of the Fourth Amendment only if, in view of all of the circumstances surrounding the incident, a reasonable person would have believed that he was not free to leave.[3] Examples of circumstances that might indicate a seizure, even where the person did not attempt to leave, would be the threatening presence of several officers, the display of a weapon by an officer, some physical touching of the person of the citizen, or the use of language or tone of voice indicating that compliance with the officer's request might be compelled. See Terry v. Ohio, supra, 392 U.S. at 19, n. 16, 88 S.Ct., at 1879, n. 16; Dunaway v. New York, 442 U.S. 200, 207, and n. 6, 99 S.Ct. 2248, 2253; 3 W. LaFave, Search and Seizure 53–55 (1978). In the absence of some such evidence, otherwise inoffensive contact between a member of the public and the police cannot, as a matter of law, amount to a seizure of that person.

On the facts of this case, no "seizure" of the respondent occurred. The events took place in the public concourse. The agents wore no uniforms and displayed no weapons. They did not summon the respondent to their presence, but instead approached her and identified themselves as federal agents. They requested, but did not demand to see the respondent's identification and ticket. Such conduct without more, did not amount to an intrusion upon any constitutionally protected interest. The respondent was not seized simply by reason of the fact that the agents approached her, asked her if she would show them her ticket and identification, and posed to her a few questions. Nor was it enough to establish a seizure that the person asking the questions was a law enforcement official. See Terry v. Ohio, 392 U.S., at 31, 32–33, 88 S.Ct., at 1885–1886 (Harlan, J., concurring). See also ALI, Model Code of Pre-Arraignment Procedure § 110.1(1) and commentary, at 257–261 (1975). In short, nothing in the record suggests that the respondent had any objective reason to believe that she was not free to end the conversation

3. We agree with the District Court that the subjective intention of the DEA agent in this case to detain the respondent, had she attempted to leave, is irrelevant except insofar as that may have been conveyed to the respondent.

in the concourse and proceed on her way, and for that reason we conclude that the agents' initial approach to her was not a seizure.

Our conclusion that no seizure occurred is not affected by the fact that the respondent was not expressly told by the agents that she was free to decline to cooperate with their inquiry, for the voluntariness of her responses does not depend upon her having been so informed. See Schneckloth v. Bustamonte, supra. We also reject the argument that the only inference to be drawn from the fact that the respondent acted in a manner so contrary to her self-interest is that she was compelled to answer the agents' questions. It may happen that a person makes statements to law enforcement officials that he later regrets, but the issue in such cases is not whether the statement was self-protective, but rather whether it was made voluntarily.

The Court's decision last Term in Brown v. Texas, 443 U.S. 47, 99 S.Ct. 2637, on which the respondent relies, is not apposite. It could not have been plainer under the circumstances there presented that Brown was forcibly detained by the officers. In that case, two police officers approached Brown in an alley, and asked him to identify himself and to explain his reason for being there. Brown "refused to identify himself and angrily asserted that the officers had no right to stop him." Up to this point there was no seizure. But after continuing to protest the officers' power to interrogate him, Brown was first frisked, and then arrested for violation of a state statute making it a criminal offense for a person to refuse to give his name and address to an officer "who has lawfully stopped him and requested the information." The Court simply held in that case that because the officers had no reason to suspect Brown of wrongdoing, there was no basis for detaining him, and therefore no permissible foundation for applying the state statute in the circumstances there presented.

The Court's decisions involving investigatory stops of automobiles do not point in any different direction. In United States v. Brignoni-Ponce, 422 U.S. 873, 95 S.Ct. 2574, the Court held that a roving patrol of law enforcement officers could stop motorists in the general area of an international border for brief inquiry into their residence status only if the officers reasonably suspected that the vehicle might contain aliens who were illegally in the country. The Government did not contend in that case that the persons whose automobiles were detained were not seized. Indeed, the Government acknowledged that the occupants of a detained vehicle were required to respond to the officers' questions and on some occasions to produce documents evidencing their eligibility to be in the United States. Moreover, stopping or diverting an automobile in transit, with the attendant opportunity for a visual inspection of areas of the passenger compartment not otherwise observable, is materially more intrusive than a question put to a passing pedestrian, and the fact that the former amounts to a seizure tells very little about the constitutional status of the latter. See also Delaware v. Prouse, 440 U.S. 648, 99 S.Ct.

1391; United States v. Martinez-Fuerte, 428 U.S., at 556–559, 96 S.Ct., at 3082–3083.

* * *

III

We conclude that the District Court's determination that the respondent consented to the search of her person "freely and voluntarily" was sustained by the evidence and that the Court of Appeals was, therefore, in error in setting it aside. Accordingly, the judgment of the Court of Appeals is reversed, and the case is remanded to that court for further proceedings.

It is so ordered.

MR. JUSTICE POWELL, with whom THE CHIEF JUSTICE and MR. JUSTICE BLACKMUN join, concurring in part and concurring in the judgment.

I join Parts I, II–B, II–C, and III of the Court's opinion. Because neither of the courts below considered the question, I do not reach the Government's contention that the agents did not "seize" the respondent within the meaning of the Fourth Amendment. In my view, we may assume for present purposes that the stop did constitute a seizure.[1] I would hold—as did the District Court—that the federal agents had reasonable suspicion that the respondent was engaging in criminal activity, and, therefore, that they did not violate the Fourth Amendment by stopping the respondent for routine questioning.

* * *

MR. JUSTICE WHITE, with whom MR. JUSTICE BRENNAN, MR. JUSTICE MARSHALL, and MR. JUSTICE STEVENS join, dissenting.

The Court today concludes that agents of the Drug Enforcement Administration (DEA) acted lawfully in stopping a traveler changing planes in an airport terminal and escorting her to a DEA office for a strip-search of her person. This result is particularly curious because a majority of the Members of the Court refuse to reject the conclusion that Ms. Mendenhall was "seized," while a separate majority decline to hold that there were reasonable grounds to justify a seizure. Mr. Justice Stewart concludes that the DEA agents acted lawfully, regardless of whether there were any reasonable grounds for suspecting Ms. Mendenhall of criminal activity, because he finds that Ms. Mendenhall was not

1. Mr. Justice Stewart concludes in Part II–A that there was no "seizure" within the meaning of the Fourth Amendment. He reasons that such a seizure occurs "only if, in view of all of the circumstances surrounding the incident, a reasonable person would have believed that he was not free to leave." *Ante,* at 1877. Mr. Justice Stewart also notes that " '[t]here is nothing in the Constitution which prevents a policeman from addressing questions to anyone on the streets.' " Ante, at 1876, quoting Terry v. Ohio, 392 U.S. 1, 34, 88 S.Ct. 1868, 1886, 20 L.Ed.2d 889 (1968) (White, J., concurring). I do not necessarily disagree with the views expressed in Part II–A. For me, the question whether the respondent in this case reasonably could have thought she was free to "walk away" when asked by two Government agents for her driver's license and ticket is extremely close.

"seized" by the DEA agents, even though throughout the proceedings below the Government never questioned the fact that a seizure had occurred necessitating a showing of antecedent reasonable suspicion. Mr. Justice Powell's opinion concludes that even though Ms. Mendenhall may have been "seized," the seizure was lawful because her behavior while changing planes in the airport provided reasonable suspicion that she was engaging in criminal activity. The Court then concludes, based on the absence of evidence that Ms. Mendenhall resisted her detention, that she voluntarily consented to being taken to the DEA office, even though she in fact had no choice in the matter. This conclusion is inconsistent with our recognition that consent cannot be presumed from a showing of acquiescence to authority, and it cannot be reconciled with our decision last Term in Dunaway v. New York, 442 U.S. 200, 99 S.Ct. 2248 (1979).

I

Beginning with Terry v. Ohio, 392 U.S. 1, 16, 88 S.Ct. 1868, 1877, 20 L.Ed.2d 889 (1968), the Court has recognized repeatedly that the Fourth Amendment's proscription of unreasonable "seizures" protects individuals during encounters with police that do not give rise to an arrest. United States v. Brignoni-Ponce, 422 U.S. 873, 878, 95 S.Ct. 2574, 2578; United States v. Martinez-Fuerte, 428 U.S. 543, 556, 96 S.Ct. 3074, 3082 (1976); Delaware v. Prouse, 440 U.S. 648, 653, 99 S.Ct. 1391, 1396 (1979). In *Terry* we "emphatically reject[ed]" the notion that a "stop" "is outside the purview of the Fourth Amendment because ... [it is not a] 'seizure' within the meaning of the Constitution." 392 U.S., at 16, 88 S.Ct., at 1877. We concluded that "the sounder course is to recognize that the Fourth Amendment governs all intrusions by agents of the public upon personal security, and to make the scope of the particular intrusion, in light of all the exigencies of the case, a central element in the analysis of reasonableness." Id., at 18, n. 15, 88 S.Ct., at 1878. Applying this principle,

> "[w]e have recognized that in some circumstances an officer may detain a suspect briefly for questioning although he does not have 'probable cause' to believe that the suspect is involved in criminal activity, as is required for a traditional arrest. However, we have required the officers to have a reasonable suspicion, based on objective facts, that the individual is involved in criminal activity." Brown v. Texas, 443 U.S. 47, 51, 99 S.Ct. 2637, 2641 (1979) (citations omitted).

Throughout the lower court proceedings in this case, the Government never questioned that the initial stop of Ms. Mendenhall was a "seizure" that required reasonable suspicion. Rather, the Government sought to justify the stop by arguing that Ms. Mendenhall's behavior had given rise to reasonable suspicion because it was consistent with portions of the so-called "drug courier profile," an informal amalgam of characteristics thought to be associated with persons carrying illegal drugs. Having failed to convince the Court of Appeals that the DEA agents had reasonable suspicion for the stop, the Government seeks reversal here by arguing for the first time that no "seizure" occurred, an argument that Mr. Justice Stewart now accepts, thereby pretermitting the question whether there was reasonable suspicion to stop Ms. Mendenhall. Mr. Justice Stewart's opinion not only is inconsistent with our usual refusal to reverse judgments on grounds not raised below, but it also addresses a fact-bound question with a totality-of-circumstances assessment that is best left in the first instance to the trial court, particularly since the question was not litigated below and hence we cannot be sure is adequately addressed by the record before us.

Mr. Justice Stewart believes that a "seizure" within the meaning of the Fourth Amendment occurs when an individual's freedom of movement is restrained by means of physical force or a show of authority. Although it is undisputed that Ms. Mendenhall was not free to leave after the DEA agents stopped her and inspected her identification, App. 19, Mr. Justice Stewart concludes that she was not "seized" because he finds that, under the totality of the circumstances, a reasonable person would have believed that she was free to leave. While basing this finding on an alleged absence from the record of objective evidence indicating that Ms. Mendenhall was not free to ignore the officer's inquiries and continue on her way, Mr. Justice Stewart's opinion brushes off the fact that this asserted evidentiary deficiency may be largely attributable to the fact that the "seizure" question was never raised below. In assessing what the record does reveal, the opinion discounts certain objective factors that would tend to support a "seizure" finding, while relying on contrary factors inconclusive even under its own illustrations of how a "seizure" may be established. Moreover, although Mr. Justice Stewart's opinion purports to make its "seizure" finding turn on objective factors known to the person accosted, in distinguishing prior decisions holding that investigatory stops constitute "seizures," it does not rely on differences in the extent to which persons accosted could reasonably believe that they were free to leave. Even if one believes the Government should be permitted to raise the "seizure" question in this Court, the proper course would be to direct a remand to the District Court for an evidentiary hearing on the question, rather than to decide it in the first instance in this Court.

II

Assuming, as we should, that Ms. Mendenhall was "seized" within the meaning of the Fourth Amendment when she was stopped by the DEA agents, the legality of that stop turns on whether there were reasonable grounds for suspecting her of criminal activity at the time of the stop. Brown v. Texas, 443 U.S., at 51, 99 S.Ct., at 2641. To establish that there was reasonable suspicion for the stop, it was necessary for the police at least to "be able to point to specific and articulable facts which, taken together with rational inferences from those facts, reasonably warrant that intrusion." Terry v. Ohio, 392 U.S., at 21, 88 S.Ct., at 1880.

At the time they stopped Ms. Mendenhall, the DEA agents' suspicion that she was engaged in criminal activity was based solely on their brief observations of her conduct at the airport. The officers had no advance information that Ms. Mendenhall, or anyone on her flight, would be carrying drugs. What the agents observed Ms. Mendenhall do in the airport was not "unusual conduct" which would lead an experienced officer reasonably to conclude that criminal activity was afoot, id., at 30, 88 S.Ct., at 1884, but rather the kind of behavior that could reasonably be expected of anyone changing planes in an airport terminal.

None of the aspects of Ms. Mendenhall's conduct, either alone or in combination, were sufficient to provide reasonable suspicion that she was engaged in criminal activity. The fact that Ms. Mendenhall was the last person to alight from a flight originating in Los Angeles was plainly insufficient to provide a basis for stopping her. Nor was the fact that her flight originated from a "major source city," for the mere proximity of a person to areas with a high incidence of drug activity or to persons known to be drug addicts, does not provide the necessary reasonable suspicion for an investigatory stop. Ybarra v. Illinois, 444 U.S. 85, 100 S.Ct. 338 (1979); Brown v. Texas, supra; Sibron v. New York, 392 U.S. 40, 62, 88 S.Ct. 1889, 1902 (1968). Under the circumstances of this case, the DEA agents' observations that Ms. Mendenhall claimed no luggage and changed airlines were also insufficient to provide reasonable suspicion. Unlike the situation in Terry v. Ohio, 392 U.S., at 28, 88 S.Ct., at 1883, where "nothing in [the suspects'] conduct from the time [the officer] first noticed them until the time he confronted them and identified himself as a police officer gave him sufficient reason to negate [his] hypothesis" of criminal behavior, Ms. Mendenhall's subsequent conduct negated any reasonable inference that she was traveling a long distance without luggage or changing her ticket to a different airline to avoid detection. Agent Anderson testified that he heard the ticket agent tell Ms. Mendenhall that her ticket to Pittsburgh already was in order and that all she needed was a boarding pass for the flight. Thus it should have been plain to an experienced observer that Ms. Mendenhall's failure to claim luggage was attributable to the fact that she was already ticketed through to Pittsburgh on a different airline. Because Agent Anderson's suspicion that Ms. Mendenhall was transporting narcotics could be based only on "his inchoate and unparticularized suspicion or 'hunch,'" rather than "specific reasonable inferences which he is entitled to draw from the facts in light of his experience," id., at 27, 88 S.Ct., at 1883, he was not justified in "seizing" Ms. Mendenhall.

III

Whatever doubt there may be concerning whether Ms. Mendenhall's Fourth Amendment interests were implicated during the initial stages of her confrontation with the DEA agents, she undoubtedly was "seized" within the meaning of the Fourth Amendment when the agents escorted her from the public area of the terminal to the DEA office for questioning and a strip-search of her person. In Dunaway v. New York, 442 U.S.

200, 99 S.Ct. 2248 (1979), we held that a person who accompanied police officers to a police station for purposes of interrogation undoubtedly "was 'seized' in the Fourth Amendment sense," even though "he was not told he was under arrest." We found it significant that the suspect was taken to a police station, "was never informed that he was 'free to go,'" and "would have been physically restrained if he had refused to accompany the officers or had tried to escape their custody." Like the "seizure" in *Dunaway,* the nature of the intrusion to which Ms. Mendenhall was subjected when she was escorted by DEA agents to their office and detained there for questioning and a strip-search was so great that it "was in important respects indistinguishable from a traditional arrest." Ibid. Although Ms. Mendenhall was not told that she was under arrest, she in fact was not free to refuse to go to the DEA office and was not told that she was. Furthermore, once inside the office, Ms. Mendenhall would not have been permitted to leave without submitting to a strip-search. Thus, as in *Dunaway,*

> "[t]he mere facts that [the suspect] was not told he was under arrest, was not 'booked,' and would not have had an arrest record if the interrogation had proved fruitless, while not insignificant for all purposes, ... obviously do not make [the suspect's] seizure even roughly analogous to the narrowly defined intrusions involved in *Terry* and its progeny." Id., at 212–213, 99 S.Ct., at 2256 (citation omitted).

Because the intrusion to which Ms. Mendenhall was subjected when she was escorted to the DEA office is of the same character as that involved in *Dunaway,* probable cause, which concededly was absent, was required to support the intrusion.

The Court's suggestion that no Fourth Amendment interest possessed by Ms. Mendenhall was implicated because she consented to go to the DEA office is inconsistent with *Dunaway* and unsupported in the record. There was no evidence in the record to support the District Court's speculation, made before *Dunaway* was decided, that Ms. Mendenhall accompanied "Agent Anderson to the airport DEA Office 'voluntarily in a spirit of apparent cooperation with the [agent's] investigation,' Sibron v. New York, 392 U.S. 40, 63 [88 S.Ct. 1889, 1902] (1968)." Ms. Mendenhall did not testify at the suppression hearing and the officers presented no testimony concerning what she said, if anything, when informed that the officers wanted her to come with them to the DEA office. Indeed, the only testimony concerning what occurred between Agent Anderson's "request" and Ms. Mendenhall's arrival at the DEA office is the agent's testimony that if Ms. Mendenhall had wanted to leave at that point she would have been forcibly restrained. The evidence of consent here is even flimsier than that we rejected in *Dunaway* where it was claimed that the suspect made an affirmative response when asked if he would accompany the officers to the police station. Dunaway v. New York, supra, at 223, 99 S.Ct., at 2261 (Rehnquist, J., dissenting). Also in Sibron v. New York, from which the District Court culled its description of Ms. Mendenhall's "consent," we described a record in a similar state as "totally barren of any indication whether Sibron accompanied Patrolman Martin outside in submission to a show of force or authority which left him no choice, or whether he went voluntarily in a spirit of apparent cooperation with the officer's investigation."

The Court recognizes that the Government has the burden of proving that Ms. Mendenhall consented to accompany the officers, but it nevertheless holds that the "totality of evidence was plainly adequate" to support a finding of consent. On the record before us, the Court's conclusion can only be based on the notion that consent can be assumed from the absence of proof that a suspect resisted police authority. This is a notion that we have squarely rejected. In Bumper v. North Carolina, 391 U.S. 543, 548–549, 88 S.Ct. 1788, 1792 (1968), the Court held that the prosecution's "burden of proving that the consent was, in fact, freely and voluntarily given . . . cannot be discharged by showing no more than acquiescence to a claim of lawful authority." (Footnotes omitted.) Johnson v. United States, 333 U.S. 10, 68 S.Ct. 367, 92 L.Ed. 436 (1948); Amos v. United States, 255 U.S. 313, 41 S.Ct. 266 (1921). While the Government need not prove that Ms. Mendenhall knew that she had a right to refuse to accompany the officers, Schneckloth v. Bustamonte, 412 U.S. 218, 93 S.Ct. 2041 (1973), it cannot rely solely on acquiescence to the officers' wishes to establish the requisite consent. The Court of Appeals properly understood this in rejecting the District Court's "findings" of consent.

Since the defendant was not present to testify at the suppression hearing, we can only speculate about her state of mind as her encounter with the DEA agents progressed from surveillance, to detention, to questioning, to seclusion in a private office, to the female officer's command to remove her clothing. Nevertheless, it is unbelievable that this sequence of events involved no invasion of a citizen's constitutionally protected interest in privacy. The rule of law requires a different conclusion.

Because Ms. Mendenhall was being illegally detained at the time of the search of her person, her suppression motion should have been granted in the absence of evidence to dissipate the taint.

DUNAWAY v. NEW YORK

Supreme Court of the United States, 1979.
442 U.S. 200, 99 S.Ct. 2248.

MR. JUSTICE BRENNAN delivered the opinion of the Court.

We decide in this case the question reserved 10 years ago in Morales v. New York, 396 U.S. 102, 90 S.Ct. 291 (1969), namely, "the question of the legality of custodial questioning on less than probable cause for a full-fledged arrest." Id., at 106.

I

On March 26, 1971, the proprietor of a pizza parlor in Rochester, N.Y., was killed during an attempted robbery. On August 10, 1971,

Detective Anthony Fantigrossi of the Rochester Police was told by another officer that an informant had supplied a possible lead implicating petitioner in the crime. Fantigrossi questioned the supposed source of the lead—a jail inmate awaiting trial for burglary—but learned nothing that supplied "enough information to get a warrant" for petitioner's arrest. Nevertheless, Fantigrossi ordered other detectives to "pick up" petitioner and "bring him in." Three detectives located petitioner at a neighbor's house on the morning of August 11. Petitioner was taken into custody; although he was not told he was under arrest, he would have been physically restrained if he had attempted to leave. He was driven to police headquarters in a police car and placed in an interrogation room, where he was questioned by officers after being given the warnings required by Miranda v. Arizona, 384 U.S. 436, 86 S.Ct. 1602 (1966). Petitioner waived counsel and eventually made statements and drew sketches that incriminated him in the crime.

At petitioner's jury trial for attempted robbery and felony murder, his motions to suppress the statements and sketches were denied, and he was convicted.

* * *

II

We first consider whether the Rochester police violated the Fourth and Fourteenth Amendments when, without probable cause to arrest, they took petitioner into custody, transported him to the police station, and detained him there for interrogation.

The Fourth Amendment, applicable to the States through the Fourteenth Amendment, Mapp v. Ohio, 367 U.S. 643, 81 S.Ct. 1684 (1961), provides: "The right of the people to be secure in their persons ... against unreasonable searches and seizures, shall not be violated, and no Warrants shall issue but upon probable cause...." There can be little doubt that petitioner was "seized" in the Fourth Amendment sense when he was taken involuntarily to the police station. And respondent State concedes that the police lacked probable cause to arrest petitioner before his incriminating statement during interrogation. Nevertheless respondent contends that the seizure of petitioner did not amount to an arrest and was therefore permissible under the Fourth Amendment because the police had a "reasonable suspicion" that petitioner possessed "intimate knowledge about a serious and unsolved crime." We disagree.

Before Terry v. Ohio, 392 U.S. 1, 88 S.Ct. 1868 (1968), the Fourth Amendment's guarantee against unreasonable seizures of persons was analyzed in terms of arrest, probable cause for arrest, and warrants based on such probable cause. The basic principles were relatively simple and straightforward: The term "arrest" was synonymous with those seizures governed by the Fourth Amendment. While warrants were not required in all circumstances, the requirement of probable cause, as elaborated in numerous precedents, was treated as absolute.

The "long-prevailing standards" of probable cause embodied "the best compromise that has been found for accommodating [the] often opposing interests" in "safeguard[ing] citizens from rash and unreasonable interferences with privacy" and in "seek[ing] to give fair leeway for enforcing the law in the community's protection." Brinegar v. United States, 338 U.S. 160, 176, 69 S.Ct. 1302, 1311 (1949). The standard of probable cause thus represented the accumulated wisdom of precedent and experience as to the minimum justification necessary to make the kind of intrusion involved in an arrest "reasonable" under the Fourth Amendment. The standard applied to all arrests, without the need to "balance" the interests and circumstances involved in particular situations. Cf. Camara v. Municipal Court, 387 U.S. 523, 87 S.Ct. 1727 (1967).

Terry for the first time recognized an exception to the requirement that Fourth Amendment seizures of persons must be based on probable cause. That case involved a brief, on-the-spot stop on the street and a frisk for weapons, a situation that did not fit comfortably within the traditional concept of an "arrest." Nevertheless, the Court held that even this type of "necessarily swift action predicated upon the on-the-spot observations of the officer on the beat" constituted a "serious intrusion upon the sanctity of the person, which may inflict great indignity and arouse strong resentment," and therefore "must be tested by the Fourth Amendment's general proscription against unreasonable searches and seizures." However, since the intrusion involved in a "stop and frisk" was so much less severe than that involved in traditional "arrests," the Court declined to stretch the concept of "arrest"—and the general rule requiring probable cause to make arrests "reasonable" under the Fourth Amendment—to cover such intrusions. Instead, the Court treated the stop-and-frisk intrusion as a *sui generis* "rubric of police conduct." And to determine the justification necessary to make this specially limited intrusion "reasonable" under the Fourth Amendment, the Court balanced the limited violation of individual privacy involved against the opposing interests in crime prevention and detection and in the police officer's safety. As a consequence, the Court established "a narrowly drawn authority to permit a reasonable search for weapons for the protection of the police officer, where he has reason to believe that he is dealing with an armed and dangerous individual, regardless of whether he has probable cause to arrest the individual for a crime." Thus, *Terry* departed from traditional Fourth Amendment analysis in two respects. First, it defined a special category of Fourth Amendment "seizures" so substantially less intrusive than arrests that the general rule requiring probable cause to make Fourth Amendment "seizures" reasonable could be replaced by a balancing test. Second, the application of this balancing test led the Court to approve this narrowly defined less intrusive seizure on grounds less rigorous than probable cause, but only for the purpose of a pat-down for weapons.

Because *Terry* involved an exception to the general rule requiring probable cause, this Court has been careful to maintain its narrow scope.

Terry itself involved a limited, on-the-street frisk for weapons.[1] Two subsequent cases which applied *Terry* also involved limited weapons frisks. See Adams v. Williams, 407 U.S. 143, 92 S.Ct. 1921 (1972) (frisk for weapons on basis of reasonable suspicion); Pennsylvania v. Mimms, 434 U.S. 106, 98 S.Ct. 330 (1977) (order to get out of car is permissible *"de minimis"* intrusion after car is lawfully detained for traffic violations; frisk for weapons justified after "bulge" observed in jacket). United States v. Brignoni-Ponce, 422 U.S. 873, 95 S.Ct. 2574 (1975), applied *Terry* in the special context of roving border patrols stopping automobiles to check for illegal immigrants. The investigative stops usually consumed less than a minute and involved "a brief question or two." 422 U.S., at 880, 95 S.Ct., at 2579. The Court stated that "[b]ecause of the limited nature of the intrusion, stops of this sort may be justified on facts that do not amount to the probable cause required for an arrest."[2] See also United States v. Martinez-Fuerte, 428 U.S. 543, 96 S.Ct. 3074 (1976) (fixed checkpoint to stop and check vehicles for aliens); Delaware v. Prouse, 440 U.S. 648, 99 S.Ct. 1391 (1979) (random checks for drivers' licenses and proper vehicle registration not permitted on less than articulable reasonable suspicion).

Respondent State now urges the Court to apply a balancing test, rather than the general rule, to custodial interrogations, and to hold that "seizures" such as that in this case may be justified by mere "reasonable suspicion."[3] *Terry* and its progeny clearly do not support such a result.

1. *Terry* specifically declined to address "the constitutional propriety of an investigative 'seizure' upon less than probable cause for purposes of 'detention' and/or interrogation." Id., at 19 n. 16, 88 S.Ct., at 1879. Mr. Justice White, in a concurring opinion, made these observations on the matter of interrogation during an investigative stop:

> "There is nothing in the Constitution which prevents a policeman from addressing questions to anyone on the streets. Absent special circumstances, the person approached may not be detained or frisked but may refuse to cooperate and go on his way. However, given the proper circumstances, such as those in this case, it seems to me the person may be briefly detained against his will while pertinent questions are directed to him. Of course, the person stopped is not obliged to answer, answers may not be compelled, and refusal to answer furnishes no basis for an arrest, although it may alert the officer to the need for continued observation." Id., at 34, 88 S.Ct., at 1886.

2. "[B]ecause of the importance of the governmental interest at stake, the minimal intrusion of a brief stop, and the absence of practical alternatives for policing the border, we hold that when an officer's observations lead him reasonably to suspect that a particular vehicle may contain aliens who are illegally in the country, he may stop the car briefly and investigate the circumstances that provoke suspicion." 422 U.S., at 881, 95 S.Ct., at 2580.

3. The factors that respondent would consider relevant in its balancing test, and the scope of the rule the test would produce, are not completely clear. The Appellate Division quoted two apparently different tests from the Court of Appeals opinion in People v. Morales, 42 N.Y.2d 129, 397 N.Y.S.2d 587, 366 N.E.2d 248 (1977):

> " '[L]aw enforcement officials may detain an individual upon reasonable suspicion for questioning for a reasonable and brief period of time under carefully controlled conditions which are ample to protect the individual's Fifth and Sixth Amendment rights' (42 N.Y.2d, at p. 135, 397 N.Y.S.2d, at p. 590, 366 N.E.2d, at p. 251). ' "[A] policeman's right to request information while discharging his law enforcement duties will hinge on the manner and intensity of the interference, the gravity of the crime involved and the circumstances attending the encounter" ' (42 N.Y.2d, at p. 137, 397 N.Y.S.2d, at p. 591, 366 N.E.2d, at p. 251, quoting from People v. De Bour, 40 N.Y.2d 210, 219,

The narrow intrusions involved in those cases were judged by a balancing test rather than by the general principle that Fourth Amendment seizures must be supported by the "long-prevailing standards" of probable cause, only because these intrusions fell far short of the kind of intrusion associated with an arrest. Indeed, *Brignoni-Ponce* expressly refused to extend *Terry* in the manner respondent now urges. The Court there stated: "The officer may question the driver and passengers about their citizenship and immigration status, and he may ask them to explain suspicious circumstances, *but any further detention or search must be based on consent or probable cause*" (emphasis added). Accord, United States v. Martinez-Fuerte, supra, 428 U.S., at 567, 96 S.Ct., at 3087.

In contrast to the brief and narrowly circumscribed intrusions involved in those cases, the detention of petitioner was in important respects indistinguishable from a traditional arrest. Petitioner was not questioned briefly where he was found. Instead, he was taken from a neighbor's home to a police car, transported to a police station, and placed in an interrogation room. He was never informed that he was "free to go"; indeed, he would have been physically restrained if he had refused to accompany the officers or had tried to escape their custody. The application of the Fourth Amendment's requirement of probable cause does not depend on whether an intrusion of this magnitude is termed an "arrest" under state law. The mere facts that petitioner was not told he was under arrest, was not "booked," and would not have had an arrest record if the interrogation had proved fruitless, while not insignificant for all purposes, see Cupp v. Murphy, 412 U.S. 291, 93 S.Ct. 2000 (1973), obviously do not make petitioner's seizure even roughly analogous to the narrowly defined intrusions involved in *Terry* and its progeny. Indeed, any "exception" that could cover a seizure as intrusive as that in this case would threaten to swallow the general rule that Fourth Amendment seizures are "reasonable" only if based on probable cause.

The central importance of the probable-cause requirement to the protection of a citizen's privacy afforded by the Fourth Amendment's guarantees cannot be compromised in this fashion. "The requirement of probable cause has roots that are deep in our history." Henry v. United States, 361 U.S. 98, 100, 80 S.Ct. 168, 170 (1959). Hostility to seizures based on mere suspicion was a prime motivation for the adoption of the Fourth Amendment, and decisions immediately after its adoption affirmed that "common rumor or report, suspicion, or even 'strong reason to suspect' was not adequate to support a warrant for

386 N.Y.S.2d 375, 382, 352 N.E.2d 562, 569)."

Then, in characterizing the case before it, the Appellate Division suggested yet a third "test":

"[T]his case involves a brief detention for interrogation based upon reasonable suspicion, where there was no formal accusation filed against defendant and where great public interest existed in solving a brutal crime which had remained unsolved for a period of almost five months."

arrest." The familiar threshold standard of probable cause for Fourth Amendment seizures reflects the benefit of extensive experience accommodating the factors relevant to the "reasonableness" requirement of the Fourth Amendment, and provides the relative simplicity and clarity necessary to the implementation of a workable rule. See Brinegar v. United States, supra, 388 U.S., at 175–176, 69 S.Ct., at 1310–1311.

In effect, respondent urges us to adopt a multifactor balancing test of "reasonable police conduct under the circumstances" to cover all seizures that do not amount to technical arrests. But the protections intended by the Framers could all too easily disappear in the consideration and balancing of the multifarious circumstances presented by different cases, especially when that balancing may be done in the first instance by police officers engaged in the "often competitive enterprise of ferreting out crime." Johnson v. United States, 333 U.S. 10, 14, 68 S.Ct. 367, 369 (1948). A single, familiar standard is essential to guide police officers, who have only limited time and expertise to reflect on and balance the social and individual interests involved in the specific circumstances they confront.[4] Indeed, our recognition of these dangers, and our consequent reluctance to depart from the proved protections afforded by the general rule, are reflected in the narrow limitations emphasized in the cases employing the balancing test. For all but those narrowly defined intrusions, the requisite "balancing" has been performed in centuries of precedent and is embodied in the principle that seizures are "reasonable" only if supported by probable cause.

Moreover, two important decisions since *Terry* confirm the conclusion that the treatment of petitioner, whether or not it is technically characterized as an arrest, must be supported by probable cause. Davis v. Mississippi, 394 U.S. 721, 89 S.Ct. 1394 (1969), decided the Term after *Terry,* considered whether fingerprints taken from a suspect detained without probable cause must be excluded from evidence. The State argued that the detention "was of a type which does not require probable cause," because it occurred during an investigative, rather than accusatory, stage, and because it was for the sole purpose of taking fingerprints. Rejecting the State's first argument, the Court warned:

> "[T]o argue that the Fourth Amendment does not apply to the investigatory stage is fundamentally to misconceive the purposes of the Fourth Amendment. Investigatory seizures would subject unlimited numbers of innocent persons to the harassment and ignominy incident to involuntary detention. Nothing is more clear than that the Fourth Amendment was meant to prevent wholesale intrusions upon the personal security of our citizenry, whether these intrusions be termed 'arrests' or 'investigatory detentions.' "

4. While the rule proposed by respondent is not entirely clear, the Appellate Division cited with approval a test that would require an officer to weigh before any custodial interrogation "the manner and intensity of the interference, the gravity of the crime involved and the circumstances attending the encounter."

The State's second argument in *Davis* was more substantial, largely because of the *distinctions* between taking fingerprints and interrogation:

> "Fingerprinting involves none of the probing into an individual's private life and thoughts that marks an interrogation or search. Nor can fingerprint detention be employed repeatedly to harass any individual, since the police need only one set of each person's prints. Furthermore, fingerprinting is an inherently more reliable and effective crime-solving tool than eyewitness identifications or confessions and is not subject to such abuses as the improper line-up and the 'third degree.' Finally, because there is no danger of destruction of fingerprints, the limited detention need not come unexpectedly or at an inconvenient time."

In *Davis,* however, the Court found it unnecessary to decide the validity of a "narrowly circumscribed procedure for obtaining" the fingerprints of suspects without probable cause—in part because, as the Court emphasized, "petitioner was not merely fingerprinted during the ... detention but *also subjected to interrogation*" (emphasis added). The detention therefore violated the Fourth Amendment.

Brown v. Illinois, 422 U.S. 590, 95 S.Ct. 2254 (1975), similarly disapproved arrests made for "investigatory" purposes on less than probable cause. Although Brown's arrest had more of the trappings of a technical formal arrest than petitioner's, such differences in form must not be exalted over substance.[5] Once in the police station, Brown was taken to an interrogation room, and his experience was indistinguishable from petitioner's. Our condemnation of the police conduct in *Brown* fits equally the police conduct in this case:

> "The impropriety of the arrest was obvious; awareness of the fact was virtually conceded by the two detectives when they repeatedly acknowledged, in their testimony, that the purpose of their action was 'for investigation' or for 'questioning.' ... The arrest, both in design and in execution, was investigatory. The detectives embarked upon this expedition for evidence in the hope that something might turn up."

These passages from *Davis* and *Brown* reflect the conclusion that detention for custodial interrogation—regardless of its label—intrudes so severely on interests protected by the Fourth Amendment as necessarily to trigger the traditional safeguards against illegal arrest. We accordingly hold that the Rochester police violated the Fourth and Fourteenth Amendments when, without probable cause, they seized petitioner and transported him to the police station for interrogation.

* * *

5. The officers drew their guns, informed Brown that he was under arrest, and handcuffed him. But Brown, unlike petitioner, was not a teenager; and the police had a report that he possessed a pistol and had used it on occasion, 422 U.S., at 594, 95 S.Ct., at 2257. The police in this case would have resorted to similar measures if petitioner had resisted being taken into custody.

MICHIGAN v. CHESTERNUT

Supreme Court of the United States, 1988.
486 U.S. 567, 108 S.Ct. 1975.

JUSTICE BLACKMUN delivered the opinion of the Court.

In this case we review a determination by the Michigan Court of Appeals that any "investigatory pursuit" of a person undertaken by the police necessarily constitutes a seizure under the Fourth Amendment of the Constitution. We conclude that the police conduct in this case did not amount to a seizure, for it would not have communicated to a reasonable person that he was not at liberty to ignore the police presence and go about his business.

I

Early on the afternoon of December 19, 1984, four officers riding in a marked police cruiser were engaged in routine patrol duties in metropolitan Detroit. As the cruiser came to an intersection, one of the officers observed a car pull over to the curb. A man got out of the car and approached respondent Michael Mose Chesternut, who was standing alone on the corner. When respondent saw the patrol car nearing the corner where he stood, he turned and began to run. As Officer Peltier, one of those in the car, later testified, the patrol car followed respondent around the corner "to see where he was going." App. 25. The cruiser quickly caught up with respondent and drove alongside him for a short distance. As they drove beside him, the officers observed respondent discard a number of packets he pulled from his right-hand pocket. Officer Peltier got out of the cruiser to examine the packets. He discovered that they contained pills. While Peltier was engaged in this inspection, respondent, who had run only a few paces farther, stopped. Surmising on the basis of his experience as a paramedic that the pills contained codeine, Officer Peltier arrested respondent for the possession of narcotics and took him to the stationhouse. During an ensuing search, the police discovered in respondent's hatband another packet of pills, a packet containing heroin, and a hypodermic needle. Respondent was charged with knowingly and intentionally possessing heroin, tablets containing codeine, and tablets containing diazapam, all in violation of Mich.Comp.Laws § 333.7403(2) (1980).

At a preliminary hearing, at which Officer Peltier was the only witness, respondent moved to dismiss the charges on the ground that he had been unlawfully seized during the police pursuit preceding his disposal of the packets. The presiding magistrate granted the motion and dismissed the complaint.[1] Relying on People v. Terrell, 77 Mich.

1. The magistrate did not independently consider whether the codeine pills, if lawfully seized, established probable cause justifying respondent's arrest. The Fourth Amendment issue before us is therefore limited to the police conduct preceding and including respondent's disposal of the packets.

App. 676, 259 N.W.2d 187 (1977),[2] the magistrate ruled from the bench that a police "chase" like the one involved in this case implicated Fourth Amendment protections and could not be justified by the mere fact that the suspect ran at the sight of the police. App. 31–35. Applying a clearly erroneous standard to the magistrate's ruling, the trial court upheld the dismissal order. Id., at 2–10.

The Michigan Court of Appeals "reluctantly" affirmed, 157 Mich. App. 181, 184, 403 N.W.2d 74, 76 (1986), noting that "although we find the result unfortunate, we cannot say that the lower court's ruling was clearly erroneous under the present law or the facts presented." Id., at 183, 403 N.W.2d, at 75. Like the courts below it, the Court of Appeals rested its ruling on state precedents interpreting the Fourth Amendment.[3] The court determined, first, that any "investigatory pursuit" amounts to a seizure under Terry v. Ohio, 392 U.S. 1, 88 S.Ct. 1868 (1968). "As soon as the officers began their pursuit," the court explained, "defendant's freedom was restricted." 157 Mich.App., at 183, 403 N.W.2d, at 75. The court went on to conclude that respondent's flight from the police was insufficient, by itself, to give rise to the particularized suspicion necessary to justify this kind of seizure. Because "the police saw [respondent] do absolutely nothing illegal nor did they observe other suspicious activity," the court determined that the investigatory pursuit had violated the Fourth Amendment's prohibition against unreasonable seizures. Id., at 184, 403 N.W.2d, at 76.

2. In *Terrell,* a police officer got out of his unmarked car and "gave chase" on foot after allegedly observing the defendant stick his hand in his pocket and run at the sight of the officer. 77 Mich.App., at 678, 259 N.W.2d, at 188. According to the officer, the defendant ran into an apartment building where the officer observed him drop a clear envelope containing a brown powdery substance. Having determined that the package might contain heroin, the officer arrested the defendant. At a pretrial hearing, the trial court granted the defendant's motion to suppress the envelope and its contents. The Michigan Court of Appeals affirmed, finding that the police "investigatory pursuit" constituted a seizure that was unjustified by any particularized suspicion that the defendant was engaged in criminal activity. Id., at 679–680, 259 N.W.2d, at 188–189.

3. The Michigan Court of Appeals rested its holding on *People v. Terrell,* supra, and People v. Shabaz, 424 Mich. 42, 378 N.W.2d 451 (1985), cert. dismissed (in view of that respondent's death), ___ U.S. ___, [106 S.Ct. 3326] (1986), both of which were to the effect that the defendant in question had been seized in violation of the Fourth Amendment of the United States Constitution. In *Shabaz,* the Michigan Supreme Court quoted "Michigan's analogous [constitutional] provision," without elaboration, in a footnote following a recitation of the Fourth Amendment. Id., 424 Mich., at 52, n. 4, 378 N.W.2d, at 455, n. 4. The Supreme Court said nothing to suggest that the Michigan Constitution's seizure provision provided an independent source of relief, and the court's entire analysis rested expressly on the Fourth Amendment and federal cases. Similarly, in *Terrell,* the Michigan Court of Appeals stated that the suppression of evidence and dismissal of charges against the defendant "was soundly based on existing law, state and Federal," but made clear that the scope of the right in question was defined "by the Fourth Amendment's general proscription against unreasonable searches and seizures." 77 Mich.App., at 679, 259 N.W.2d, at 188, citing Terry v. Ohio, 392 U.S. 1, 20, 88 S.Ct. 1868, 1879 (1968). In light of the bases for the courts' decisions in *Shabaz* and *Terrell,* we readily conclude that the decision below likewise rests on the Michigan courts' interpretation of the Federal Constitution and not on any adequate and independent state ground. See Michigan v. Long, 463 U.S. 1032, 103 S.Ct. 3469 (1983). The defense in effect concedes this. See Tr. of Oral Arg. 38–39.

After the Michigan Supreme Court denied petitioner leave to appeal,[4] App. to Pet. for Cert. 9a, petitioner sought review here. We granted a writ of certiorari, ___ U.S. ___, 108 S.Ct. 226 (1987), to consider whether the officers' pursuit of respondent constituted a seizure implicating Fourth Amendment protections, and, if so, whether the act of fleeing, by itself, was sufficient to constitute reasonable suspicion justifying that seizure. Because we conclude that the officers' conduct did not constitute a seizure, we need not reach the second question.

II

A

Petitioner argues that the Fourth Amendment is never implicated until an individual stops in response to the police's show of authority. Thus, petitioner would have us rule that a lack of objective and particularized suspicion would not poison police conduct, no matter how coercive, as long as the police did not succeed in actually apprehending the individual. Respondent contends, in sharp contrast, that any and all police "chases" are Fourth Amendment seizures. Respondent would have us rule that the police may never pursue an individual absent a particularized and objective basis for suspecting that he is engaged in criminal activity.

Both petitioner and respondent, it seems to us, in their attempts to fashion a brightline rule applicable to all investigatory pursuits, have failed to heed this Court's clear direction that any assessment as to whether police conduct amounts to a seizure implicating the Fourth Amendment must take into account " 'all the circumstances surrounding the incident' " in each individual case. INS v. Delgado, 466 U.S. 210, 215, 104 S.Ct. 1758, 1762 (1984), quoting United States v. Mendenhall, 446 U.S. 544, 554, 100 S.Ct. 1870, 1877 (1980) (opinion of Stewart, J.). Rather than adopting either rule proposed by the parties and determining that an investigatory pursuit is or is not *necessarily* a seizure under the Fourth Amendment, we adhere to our traditional contextual approach, and determine only that, in this particular case, the police conduct in question did not amount to a seizure.

B

In Terry v. Ohio, 392 U.S. 1, 88 S.Ct. 1868 (1968), the Court noted:

> "Obviously, not all personal intercourse between policemen and citizens involves 'seizures' of persons. Only when the officer, by means of physical force or show of authority, has in some way restrained the liberty of a citizen may we conclude that a 'seizure' has occurred." Id., at 19, n. 16, 88 S.Ct., at 1879, n. 16.

4. Two Justices of the Michigan Supreme Court would have granted leave to appeal. See App. to Pet. for Cert. 10a.

A decade later in *United States v. Mendenhall,* Justice Stewart, writing for himself and then Justice Rehnquist, first transposed this analysis into a test to be applied in determining whether "a person has been 'seized' within the meaning of the Fourth Amendment." 446 U.S., at 554, 100 S.Ct., at 1877.[5] The test provides that the police can be said to have seized an individual "only if, in view of all of the circumstances surrounding the incident, a reasonable person would have believed that he was not free to leave." Ibid. The Court has since embraced this test. See INS v. Delgado, 466 U.S., at 215, 104 S.Ct., at 1762. See also Florida v. Royer, 460 U.S. 491, 502, 103 S.Ct. 1319, 1326–27 (1983) (plurality opinion); id., at 514 (Blackmun, J., dissenting).

The test is necessarily imprecise, because it is designed to assess the coercive effect of police conduct, taken as a whole, rather than to focus on particular details of that conduct in isolation. Moreover, what constitutes a restraint on liberty prompting a person to conclude that he is not free to "leave" will vary, not only with the particular police conduct at issue, but also with the setting in which the conduct occurs. Compare *United States v. Mendenhall,* supra (considering whether police request to see identification and ticket of individual who stopped upon police's approach constituted seizure), with *INS v. Delgado,* supra (considering whether INS "factory survey" conducted while employees continued to move about constituted seizure of entire work force).

While the test is flexible enough to be applied to the whole range of police conduct in an equally broad range of settings, it calls for consistent application from one police encounter to the next, regardless of the particular individual's response to the actions of the police. The test's objective standard—looking to the reasonable man's interpretation of the conduct in question—allows the police to determine in advance whether the conduct contemplated will implicate the Fourth Amendment. 3 W. LaFave, Search and Seizure § 9.2(h), pp. 407–408 (2d ed. 1987). This "reasonable person" standard also ensures that the scope of Fourth Amendment protection does not vary with the state of mind of the particular individual being approached.

C

Applying the Court's test to the facts of this case, we conclude that respondent was not seized by the police before he discarded the packets containing the controlled substance. Although Officer Peltier referred to the police conduct as a "chase," and the magistrate who originally dismissed the complaint was impressed by this description,[6] the charac-

5. Three other Justices, otherwise in the majority, chose not to reach the question whether the federal officers had seized respondent. United States v. Mendenhall, 446 U.S. 544, 560, 100 S.Ct. 1870, 1880 (1980) (opinion concurring in part and concurring in the judgment).

6. At the preliminary hearing, the magistrate interrupted the State's attorney, who was asserting that the police were simply performing routine patrolling duties, with the following:

"That would be fine until the Officer said we were chasing him in the car, otherwise I would agree with you. My ears picked up when the Officer said that, you know. He said we went around. I

terization is not enough, standing alone, to implicate Fourth Amendment protections. Contrary to respondent's assertion that a chase necessarily communicates that detention is intended and imminent, Brief for Respondent 9, the police conduct involved here would not have communicated to the reasonable person an attempt to capture or otherwise intrude upon respondent's freedom of movement.[7] The record does not reflect that the police activated a siren or flashers; or that they commanded respondent to halt, or displayed any weapons; or that they operated the car in an aggressive manner to block respondent's course or otherwise control the direction or speed of his movement. Tr. of Oral Arg. 2, 11, 20.[8] While the very presence of a police car driving parallel to a running pedestrian could be somewhat intimidating, this kind of police presence does not, standing alone, constitute a seizure.[9] Cf. United States v. Knotts, 460 U.S. 276, 103 S.Ct. 1081, (1983) (holding that continuous surveillance on public thoroughfares by visual observation and electronic "beeper" does not constitute seizure); Florida v. Royer, 460 U.S., at 497, 103 S.Ct., at 1323–24 (plurality opinion) (noting that mere approach by law enforcement officers, identified as such, does not constitute seizure). Without more, the police conduct here—a brief acceleration to catch up with respondent, followed by a short drive alongside him—was not "so intimidating" that respondent could reasonably have believed that he was not free to disregard the police presence and go about his business. INS v. Delgado, 466 U.S., at 216, 104 S.Ct., at 1762–63. The police therefore were not required to have "a particularized and objective basis for suspecting [respondent] of criminal activity," in order to pursue him. United States v. Cortez, 449 U.S. 411, 417–418, 101 S.Ct. 690, 694–695 (1981).

asked him why were you chasing him in the car, why were you chasing him and he said because he was running and we wanted to see where he was going." App. 29–30.

7. As Officer Peltier explained, the goal of the "chase" was not to capture respondent, but "to see where he was going." *Id.,* at 25. Of course, the subjective intent of the officers is relevant to an assessment of the Fourth Amendment implications of police conduct only to the extent that that intent has been conveyed to the person confronted. United States v. Mendenhall, 446 U.S., at 554, n. 6, 100 S.Ct., at 1877, n. 6 (opinion of Stewart, J.). See also 3 W. LaFave, Search and Seizure § 9.2(h), p. 407 (2d ed. 1987) (uncommunicated intent of police irrelevant to determination of whether seizure occurred).

8. The facts of this case are not identical to the facts involved in both *Terrell* and *Shabaz,* upon which the Michigan courts relied in finding a seizure in this case. In both *Terrell* and *Shabaz,* a police officer got out of the car to chase the pedestrian suspect on foot, after which the defendant abandoned the inculpatory evidence. People v. Terrell, 77 Mich.App., at 678, 259 N.W.2d, at 188; People v. Shabaz, 424 Mich., at 47–48, 378 N.W.2d, at 453. In *Shabaz,* the State appears to have stipulated that the chase, whose clear object was to apprehend the defendant, constituted a seizure. Id., at 52, 378 N.W.2d, at 455. While no similar stipulation was entered in *Terrell,* the goal of that chase appears to have been equally clear. We, of course, intimate no view as to the federal constitutional correctness of either of those Michigan state-court cases.

9. The United States, which has submitted a brief as *amicus curiae,* suggests that, in some circumstances, police pursuit "will amount to a stop from the outset or from an early point in the chase, if the police command the person to halt and indicate that he is not free to go." Brief for United States as *Amicus Curiae* 13. Of course, such circumstances are not before us in this case. We therefore leave to another day the determination of the circumstances in which police pursuit could amount to a seizure under the Fourth Amendment.

III

Because respondent was not unlawfully seized during the initial police pursuit, we conclude that charges against him were improperly dismissed. Accordingly, we reverse the judgment of the Michigan Court of Appeals, and remand the case to that court for further proceedings not inconsistent with this opinion.

It is so ordered.

JUSTICE KENNEDY, with whom JUSTICE SCALIA joins, concurring.

It is no bold step to conclude, as the Court does, that the evidence should have been admitted, for respondent's unprovoked flight gave the police ample cause to stop him. The Court instead concentrates on the significance of the chase; and as to that it is fair to interpret its opinion as finding no more than an absence of improper conduct. We would do well to add that, barring the need to inquire about hot pursuit, which is not at issue here, neither "chase" nor "investigative pursuit" need be included in the lexicon of the Fourth Amendment.

A Fourth Amendment seizure occurs when an individual remains in the control of law enforcement officials because he reasonably believes, on the basis of their conduct toward him, that he is not free to go. See, e.g., INS v. Delgado, 466 U.S. 210, 215, 104 S.Ct. 1758, 1762 (1984); United States v. Mendenhall, 446 U.S. 544, 554, 100 S.Ct. 1870, 1877 (1980) (opinion of Stewart, J.). The case before us presented an opportunity to consider whether even an unmistakable show of authority can result in the seizure of a person who attempts to elude apprehension and who discloses contraband or other incriminating evidence before he is ultimately detained. It is at least plausible to say that whether or not the officers' conduct communicates to a person a reasonable belief that they intend to apprehend him, such conduct does not implicate Fourth Amendment protections until it achieves a restraining effect. The Court's opinion does not foreclose this holding, and I concur.

3. ILLUSTRATIVE LEGISLATIVE PROVISIONS REGARDING ARRESTS BY THE POLICE AS WELL AS BY PRIVATE CITIZENS

At the present time, the arrest rights of police officers and of private citizens are usually prescribed by legislative enactments, and they vary to a considerable extent, from jurisdiction to jurisdiction, as will be observed from the following selections:

Statutes and Code Provisions

California

Penal Code (West, 1985 & 1988 Supp.):

§ 836. A peace officer may make an arrest in obedience to a warrant, or may . . . without a warrant, arrest a person:

1. Whenever he has reasonable cause to believe that the person to be arrested has committed a public offense in his presence.

2. When a person arrested has committed a felony, although not in his presence.

3. Whenever he has reasonable cause to believe that the person to be arrested has committed a felony, whether or not a felony has in fact been committed.

§ 836.5. (a) A public officer or employee, when authorized by ordinance, may arrest a person without a warrant whenever he has reasonable cause to believe the person to be arrested has committed a misdemeanor in his presence which is a violation of a statute or ordinance which the officer or employee has the duty to enforce.

§ 837. A private person may arrest another:

1. For a public offense committed or attempted in his presence.

2. When the person arrested has committed a felony, although not in his presence.

3. When a felony has been in fact committed, and he has reasonable cause for believing the person arrested to have committed it.

(According to § 16, "crimes and public offenses" include "felonies", "misdemeanors", and "infractions". § 17(a) provides: "A felony is a crime which is punishable with death or by imprisonment in the state prison. Every other crime or public offense is a misdemeanor except those offenses that are classified as infractions.")

Illinois

Code of Criminal Procedure, 725 ILCS 5/107–2 (1992):

Arrest by Peace Officer. A peace officer may arrest a person when:

(a) He has a warrant commanding that such person be arrested; or

(b) He has reasonable grounds to believe that a warrant for the person's arrest has been issued in this State or in another jurisdiction; or

(c) He has reasonable grounds to believe that the person is committing or has committed an offense [defined in § 102–15 as "a violation of any penal statute of this State"].

* * *

725 ILCS 5/107–3. Arrest by Private Person. Any person may arrest another when he has reasonable grounds to believe that an offense other than an ordinance violation is being committed.

725 ILCS 5/107–4. Arrest by Peace Officer From Other Jurisdiction. (a) As used in this Section:

(1) "State" means any State of the United States and the District of Columbia.

(2) "Peace Officer" means any peace officer or member of any duly organized State, County, or Municipal peace unit or police force of another State.

(3) "Fresh pursuit" means the immediate pursuit of a person who is endeavoring to avoid arrest.

(b) Any peace officer of another State who enters this State in fresh pursuit and continues within this State in fresh pursuit of a person in order to arrest him on the ground that he has committed an offense in the other State has the same authority to arrest and hold the person in custody as peace officers of this State have to arrest and hold a person in custody on the ground that he has committed an offense in this State.

(c) If an arrest is made in this State by a peace officer of another State in accordance with the provisions of this Section he shall without unnecessary delay take the person arrested before the circuit court of the county in which the arrest was made. Such court shall conduct a hearing for the purpose of determining the lawfulness of the arrest. If the court determines that the arrest was lawful it shall commit the person arrested, to await for a reasonable time the issuance of an extradition warrant by the Governor of this State, or admit him to bail for such purpose. If the court determines that the arrest was unlawful it shall discharge the person arrested.

New York

Criminal Procedure Law (McKinney 1981):

§ 140.10.

1. Subject to the provisions of subdivision two, a police officer may arrest a person for:

(a) Any offense when he has reasonable cause to believe that such person has committed such offense in his presence; and

(b) A crime when he has reasonable cause to believe that such person has committed such crime, whether in his presence or otherwise.

2. A police officer may arrest a person for a petty offense, pursuant to subdivision one, only when:

(a) Such offense was committed or believed by him to have been committed within the geographical area of such police officer's employment; and

(b) Such arrest is made in the county in which such offense was committed or believed to have been committed or in an adjoining county; except that the police officer may follow such person in continuous close pursuit, commencing either in the county in which the offense was or is believed to have been committed or in an adjoining county, in and through any county of the state, and may arrest him in any county in which he apprehends him.

3. A police officer may arrest a person for a crime, pursuant to subdivision one, whether or not such crime was committed within the geographical area of such police officer's employment, and he may make such arrest within the state, regardless of the situs of the commission of the crime. In addition, he may, if necessary, pursue such person outside the state and may arrest him in any state the laws of which contain provisions equivalent [to New York law].

§ 140.30.

1. Subject to the provisions of subdivision two, any person may arrest another person (a) for a felony when the latter has in fact committed such felony, and (b) for any offense when the latter has in fact committed such offense in his presence.

2. Such an arrest, if for a felony, may be made anywhere in the state. If the arrest is for an offense other than a felony, it may be made only in the county in which such offense was committed.

[When an arrest is made in accordance with this provision, according to § 140.35, the arrester "must inform the person whom he is arresting of the reason for such arrest unless he encounters physical resistance, flight or other factors rendering such procedure impractical".]

According to § 10.00 of the Penal Law of New York (McKinney 1987), the words "offense" and "crime" are differentiated as follows:

> "Offense" means conduct for which a sentence to a term of imprisonment or to a fine is provided by any law of this state or by any law, local law or ordinance of a political subdivision of this state, or by any order, rule or regulation of any governmental instrumentality authorized by law to adopt the same.
>
> "Crime" means a misdemeanor or a felony.

And in New York (also in § 10.00), the distinction between "misdemeanor" and "felony" is set out in the following terms:

> "Misdemeanor" means an offense, other than a "traffic infraction," for which a sentence to a term of imprisonment in excess of fifteen days may be imposed, but for which a sentence to a term of imprisonment in excess of one year cannot be imposed.
>
> "Felony" means an offense for which a sentence to a term of imprisonment in excess of one year may be imposed.

Federal

There is no single act regarding the arrest powers of federal officers generally. The matter is dealt with by separate statutes pertaining to particular groups of officers. For instance, there is a separate provision for FBI agents, and it authorizes an arrest, without warrant, for "any offense against the United States committed in their presence, or for any felony cognizable under the laws of the United States if they have reasonable grounds to believe that the person to be arrested has committed or is committing such felony." 18 U.S.C. § 3052 (1985). Another statute confers a similar power upon marshals and their deputies. 18 U.S.C. § 3053 (1985).

Separate statutes provide similar arrest powers for offenses that are the province of the Secret Service, 18 U.S.C. § 3056, the Bureau of Narcotics and Dangerous Drugs, 21 U.S.C. § 878(a)(3), the Postal Inspectors, 18 U.S.C. § 3061(a)(2)–(3) (1985), Officers of the Customs Service, 19 U.S.C. §§ 1589 and 1589(a) (1988), and the I.R.S. enforcement agents (26 U.S.C. § 7608(b)(2)(B) (1985)). Bureau of Prisons enforcement personnel may make warrantless arrests for specified offenses only if they have "reasonable grounds to believe that the arrested person is guilty of such offense, and if there is likelihood of his escaping before an arrest warrant can be obtained." 18 U.S.C. § 3050 (1985 § 1988 Supp.).

Arrest Warrants

Warrants for Arrest. Fairly typical of the legislative conditions for the issuance of court orders—warrants—for arrest is the following provision of the Illinois Criminal Code, 725 ILCS 5/107–9 (1992):

(a) When a complaint is presented to a court charging that an offense has been committed it shall examine upon oath or affirmation the complainant or any witnesses.

(b) The complaint shall be in writing and shall:

(1) State the name of the accused if known, and if not known the accused may be designated by any name or description by which he can be identified with reasonable certainty;

(2) State the offense with which the accused is charged;

(3) State the time and place of the offense as definitely as can be done by the complainant; and

(4) Be subscribed and sworn to by the complainant.

(c) A warrant shall be issued by the court for the arrest of the person complained against if it appears from the contents of the complaint and the examination of the complainant or other witnesses, if any, that the person against whom the complaint was made has committed an offense.

(d) The warrant of arrest shall:

(1) Be in writing;

(2) Specify the name, sex and birth date of the person to be arrested or if his name, sex or birth date is unknown, shall designate such person by any name or description by which he can be identified with reasonable certainty;

(3) Set forth the nature of the offense;

(4) State the date when issued and the municipality or county where issued;

(5) Be signed by the judge of the court with the title of his office;

(6) Command that the person against whom the complaint was made be arrested and brought before the court issuing the warrant or if he is absent or unable to act before the nearest or most accessible court in the same county;

(7) Specify the amount of bail; and

(8) Specify any geographical limitation placed on the execution of the warrant, but such limitation shall not be expressed in mileage.

(e) The warrant shall be directed to all peace officers in the State. It shall be executed by the peace officer, or by a private person specially named therein, at any location within the geographic limitation for execution placed on the warrant. If no geographic limitation is placed on the warrant, then it may be executed anywhere in the State.

(f) The warrant may be issued electronically or electromagnetically by use of a facsimile transmission machine and any such warrant shall have the same validity as a written warrant.

4. ARREST IMMUNITY

Certain individuals may be exempt from arrest on a temporary or permanent basis, depending upon the nature of the arrest, and the person's occupation and activities. The exemption in some cases is common law, but generally it is pursuant to statute. The exemption from civil arrest is far more common than one for criminal arrest.

The broadest arrest immunity is conferred upon diplomats of a foreign nation, their families and staffs. These individuals are not subject to the criminal laws of the host country. See the Foreign Sovereign Immunities Act of 1976, 28 U.S.C.A. §§ 1602–1631 (1976).

Statutory immunity from civil arrest has been conferred upon public officials in the performance of their official duties, military personnel, and officers of the court while attending or traveling to and from court. See e.g., N.Y. Legislative Law § 2 (McKinney 1952). This latter privilege arose from the common law.

Article 1, § 6 of the United States Constitution provides that Senators and Representatives "shall in all cases, except Treason, Felony and Breach of the Peace, be privileged from arrest during their attendance at the session of their respective Houses, and in going to and returning from the same". This phrase removes criminal offenses from the Congressional arrest immunity.

5. DETENTION SHORT OF ARREST

In addition to the power of arrest, law enforcement officers, and also private persons, have the right, under certain conditions, to detain persons short of an actual arrest. The police, for instance, have the right to stop a motorist who has violated a traffic law and issue to him a notice or citation to appear in court at a designated time on the charge filed by the officer who observed the violation. This has not been viewed as an arrest because, according to the definitions previously discussed, there is no intention on the part of the officer to take the motorist into "custody" to answer the charge. Such a detention has been sanctioned on the theory that the use of the highways by motorists is a privilege and not an absolute right, and the privilege may be subjected to various conditions, including the stopping to check upon driver licenses and car registrations.

However, in Delaware v. Prouse, 440 U.S. 648, 99 S.Ct. 1391 (1979), the U.S. Supreme Court held that, except where there is at least articulable and reasonable suspicion that a motorist is unlicensed or that an automobile is not registered, or that either the vehicle or an occupant is otherwise subject to seizure for violation of law, stopping an automobile and detaining the driver in order to check his driver's license and the registration of the automobile are unreasonable under the Fourth Amendment. All vehicle stops must be based upon founded suspicion of law violation. Such a stop may now be considered an "arrest" or "seizure" within the definitions articulated in United States v. Mendenhall, 446 U.S. 544, 100 S.Ct. 1870 (1980), discussed earlier in this chapter.

Also, as will be discussed in detail later on in this casebook, there is the right of the police to "stop-and-frisk", under reasonable circumstances, persons whom they reasonably suspect of criminality.

A property owner, merchant, or an agent of either one, may, under certain circumstances detain a person on the premises whom they reasonably believe to be in wrongful possession of property belonging to the property owner or merchant. Such a detention, however, is permissible only when done in a reasonable manner and only for the time reasonably necessary to investigate the facts. Although this right has a common law foundation, there are many state statutes which specifically recognize it and delineate its extent and limitations. See Ill.Rev.Stat., ch. 38 § 16A–5 (1988) and N.Y. General Business Law § 218 (McKinney 1988).

6. THE RIGHT TO RESIST ARREST

The following summary of the right to resist arrest is taken from the Law Enforcement Legal Defense Manual of Americans for Effective Law Enforcement (January, 1978, pp. 3–4):

"Although it is well settled, both by case law and statute, that no person has the right to resist a police officer making a lawful arrest, several questions may still arise when, for instance, force is used in accomplishing an arrest or where the arrest itself is possibly unlawful. The problem, then, is when and to what extent an arrestee is justified in resisting a peace officer? How much force may be used in resisting the arrest or assault?

"Every citizen has the duty to submit to the authority of police officers making lawful arrests, and any resistance amounts to an obstruction of the officer in the performance of his duties. A person may be excused for resisting arrest if he acts under reasonable mistake of fact, or if the officer is using excessive force in performing his duties, whether the arrest is lawful or not. The basic rules of self-defense still apply, i.e., when a person is being attacked, and in good faith and with reasonable grounds believes that his life is in danger, or that he is likely to suffer great bodily harm, he has a right to meet that force with such force as he believes reasonably necessary to defend himself under the circumstances.

"The principles of self-defense apply where an arresting officer has used excessive force in attempting to effect a lawful arrest. When the use of excessive force by an officer amounts to an assault, the arrestee may use reasonable force to resist the officer. Similarly, where an officer, without provocation, assaults an arrestee, the arrestee may use reasonable force to defend himself. It is noteworthy, however, that at no time can anyone use any more force than is reasonable under the circumstances; this may extend to the use of deadly force in extreme cases.

"There are qualifications on how much force can be used in resisting a lawful arrest: (1) an arrestee cannot continue to use force after the officer has ceased using excessive force; (2) a person must stop using force if he believes that the officer will also stop the use of his excessive force, if the arrestee ceases to resist; and (3) the use of self-defense is not available to one whose own actions prompted the officer to use excessive force in the first place.

"The situation is only slightly different in the case of an unlawful arrest. Under the common law theory, an officer making an unlawful arrest is not discharging the duties of his office. Thus an arrestee is privileged in using reasonable force to prevent the unlawful deprivation of his liberty. Jails, and the criminal justice system in general, at the time this common law rule was developed, were quite different than they are today. It was not unreasonable to expect a person to resist vigorously to being unlawfully thrown into the kind of pit that the jails were in the Middle Ages.

"This common law rule has been abolished either by statute or case law in many states today. The modern theory is that citizens must submit to the authority of peace officers and leave it to the courts to determine the legality of the arrest.* Again, however, the law recognizes that no court can remedy bodily injury suffered as a result of undue force used during an arrest. Therefore, if, in making an arrest, the officer uses excessive force, the arrestee is justified in using the force reasonably necessary to defend himself, with the same qualifications as set out above for lawful arrests.

"This problem is one of concern to all law enforcement agencies for the following reasons:

> 1. *An officer who illegally uses force to overcome the resistance of a citizen placed under arrest subjects himself and his department to a claim or lawsuit for assault and battery. If the action is brought in federal court under 42 U.S.Code § 1983, the complaint will allege a civil rights violation.*
>
> 2. *If a criminal court dismisses charges placed against a citizen for resisting arrest or assaulting an officer, a civil suit for false arrest might ensue. In federal court, this might also be a civil rights violation.*
>
> 3. *If an officer is assaulted and injured by a citizen who lawfully resists the arrest with force, the officer's opportunity to successfully sue the citizen for damages is limited or nonexistent.*"

7. POST-ARREST REQUIREMENTS AND INITIAL JUDICIAL INQUIRY

Illustrative of the obligations imposed upon a person who has effected an arrest are the following:

* Among the cases cited in the foregoing article regarding the right to self-defense against an assault in the face of a threat of serious bodily harm are: State v. Wright, 1 N.C.App. 479, 162 S.E.2d 56 (1968); Randall v. State, 447 S.W.2d 912 (Tex. 1968); State v. Westlund, 13 Wn.App. 460, 536 P.2d 20 (1975); People v. Henderson, 58 Cal.App.3d 349, 129 Cal.Rptr. 844 (1976).

Of the cited cases which deal with the degree of force allowable on the part of the person upon whom an arresting officer has used excessive force, one which states the general rule is State v. Mulvihill, 57 N.J. 151, 270 A.2d 277 (1970):

"If the officer employs excessive and unnecessary force, the citizen may respond or counter with the use of reasonable force to protect himself, and if in doing so the officer is injured no criminal offense has been committed."

The right to resist excessive police force is qualified, however, by the principle that once the officer ceases using excessive force, or the arrestee knows that if he stops resisting the officer will cease using excessive force, the arrestee can no longer use force and claim the right to defend himself from the assault. In support of this principle the previously cited case of State v. Mulvihill.

Illinois Code of Criminal Procedure, 725 ILCS 5/109–1 (1992):

Person arrested. (a) A person arrested with or without a warrant shall be taken without unnecessary delay before the nearest and most accessible judge in that county, except when such county is a participant in a regional jail authority, in which event such person may be taken to the nearest and most accessible judge, irrespective of the county where such judge presides, and a charge shall be filed. Whenever a person arrested either with or without a warrant is required to be taken before a judge, and such person is in a different building than the building in which the judge is located, a charge may be filed against such person by way of a two-way closed circuit television system, except that a hearing to deny bail to the defendant may not be conducted by way of closed circuit television.

(b) The judge shall:

(1) Inform the defendant of the charge against him and shall provide him with a copy of the charge.

(2) Advise the defendant of his right to counsel and if indigent shall appoint a public defender or licensed attorney at law of this State to represent him in accordance with the provisions of Section 113–3 of this Code.

(3) Schedule a preliminary hearing in appropriate cases; and

(4) Admit the defendant to bail in accordance with the provisions of Article 110 of this Code.

(c) The court may issue an order of protection in accordance with the provisions of Article 112A of this Code.

Rule 5(a) of the Federal Rules of Criminal Procedure:

An officer making an arrest under a warrant issued upon a complaint or any person making an arrest without a warrant shall take the arrested person without unnecessary delay before the nearest available federal magistrate or, in the event that a federal magistrate is not reasonably available, before a state or local judicial officer authorized by 18 U.S.C. § 3041. If a person arrested without a warrant is brought before a magistrate, a complaint shall be filed forthwith which shall comply with the requirements of Rule 4(a) with respect to the showing of probable cause. When a person, arrested with or without a warrant or given a summons, appears initially before the magistrate, the magistrate shall proceed in accordance with the applicable subdivisions of this rule.

Arrest statutes generally make no provision for the release of an arrestee by the police themselves, even after it becomes apparent that the person arrested is innocent of the offense for which he has been arrested. Accordingly, such a person is held in custody until he can be brought before a magistrate, as required by a literal interpretation of arrest statute provisions. Some courts hold that a police release is unlawful and may be the basis for a civil action on the part of the arrestee. When an arrestee of this type is taken before a magistrate he is, in some localities, charged with "disorderly conduct," found guilty, and sentence suspended. All this is done with court cooperation, and it is supposed to "protect" the police from false arrest suits. As a practical matter it does have that effect; legally, speaking, however, it does not.

Some police departments have developed a practice, without actual legal authorization, however, of permitting a commanding officer to release innocent arrestees. Seldom, of course, does a person who is released in this manner resort to legal action on the theory that his police release was not legally authorized.

Section 134(a), comment f of the Restatement 2d of Torts (1965) states that whenever a police officer or private person ascertains beyond a reasonable doubt that he was mistaken in making the arrest without a warrant he is no longer privileged to keep the person in custody and must release him, unless the person desires to be taken before a court to have the stigma officially removed. The section also provides for release in cases of mistaken identity.

The 1963 Illinois Code of Criminal Procedure, Ill.Rev.Stat. ch. 38 § 107–6 (1981) contains the following provision:

> A peace officer who arrests a person without a warrant is authorized to release the person without requiring him to appear before a court when the officer is satisfied that there are no grounds for criminal complaint against the person arrested.

The reasons for the insistence in a democratic society that the police take arrested persons before a judicial officer are obvious; to follow any other practice would deprive the arrestee of an impartial evaluation of the reasonableness for holding him for further proceedings. This evaluation is known as a "preliminary hearing".

Preliminary Hearing

A preliminary hearing is a relatively informal proceeding by means of which a determination is made as to whether there are reasonable grounds for believing the accused committed the offense—as to whether it is fair, under the circumstances, to require the accused to stand a regular trial. If after such a hearing the judge or magistrate decides that the accusation is without probable cause, the accused will be discharged. This discharge, however, will not bar a grand jury indictment if subsequently developed evidence (or the same evidence presented at the preliminary hearing) satisfies the grand jury that the accusation is well founded.

In the event an arrested person is not formally charged with an offense and is not taken before a judge or other magistrate "without unnecessary delay" he, or rather someone on his behalf, may petition a judge for a "writ of habeas corpus" and thereby attempt to secure his release or at least compel the police to file a specific charge against him, in which latter event he may seek his release on bond. If the court issues the writ, the police or other custodians of the arrested person are required, either immediately or at an early designated time, to bring him into court (that is, "you have the body," which is the literal meaning of the term "habeas corpus"), and to explain to the court the reason or justification for holding the accused person in custody.

Upon the police showing adequate cause, a court may continue the hearing in order to give the police a little more time to conduct a further investigation before making the formal charge against the arrestee. Many times, however, the police are required to file their charges immediately or release the prisoner.

NOTE

In Gerstein v. Pugh, 420 U.S. 103, 95 S.Ct. 854 (1975), the United States Supreme Court held:

* * *

"As framed by the proceedings below, this case presents two issues: whether a person arrested and held for trial on [a prosecutor's] information is entitled to a judicial determination of probable cause for detention, and if so, whether the adversary hearing ordered by the District Court and approved by the Court of Appeals is required by the Constitution.

* * *

"To implement the Fourth Amendment's protection against unfounded invasions of liberty and privacy, the Court has required that the existence of probable cause be decided by a neutral and detached magistrate whenever possible....

"Maximum protection of individual rights could be assured by requiring a magistrate's review of the factual justification prior to any arrest, but such a requirement would constitute an intolerable handicap for legitimate law enforcement. Thus, while the Court has expressed a preference for the use of arrest warrants when feasible, it has never invalidated an arrest supported by probable cause solely because the officers failed to secure a warrant.

"Under this practical compromise, a policeman's on-the-scene assessment of probable cause provides legal justification for arresting a person suspected of crime, and for a brief period of detention to take the administrative steps incident to arrest. Once the suspect is in custody, however, the reasons that justify dispensing with the magistrate's neutral judgment evaporate. There no longer is any danger that the suspect will escape or commit further crimes while the police submit their evidence to a magistrate. And, while the State's reasons for taking summary action subside, the suspect's need for a neutral determination of probable cause increases significantly. The consequences of prolonged detention may be more serious than the interference occasioned by arrest. Pretrial confinement may imperil the suspect's job, interrupt his source of income, and impair his family relationships. Even pretrial release may be accompanied by burdensome conditions that effect a significant restraint on liberty. When the stakes are this high, the detached judgment of a neutral magistrate is essential if the Fourth Amendment is to furnish meaningful protection from unfounded interference with liberty. Accordingly, we hold that the Fourth Amendment requires a judicial determination of probable cause as a prerequisite to extended restraint on liberty following arrest.

* * *

"Under the Florida procedures challenged here, a person arrested without a warrant and charged by information may be jailed or subjected to other restraints pending trial without any opportunity for a probable cause determination.[1] Petitioner defends this practice on the ground that the prosecutor's decision to file an information is itself a determination of probable cause that furnishes sufficient reason to detain a defendant pending trial. Although a conscientious decision that the evidence warrants prosecution affords a measure of protection against unfounded detention, we do not think prosecutorial judgment standing alone meets the requirements of the Fourth Amendment.[2]

* * *

"In holding that the prosecutor's assessment of probable cause is not sufficient alone to justify restraint on liberty pending trial, we do not imply that the accused is entitled to judicial oversight or review of the decision to prosecute. Instead, we adhere to the Court's prior holding that a judicial hearing is not prerequisite to prosecution by information.... Thus, as the Court of Appeals noted below, although a suspect who is presently detained may challenge the probable cause for that confinement, a conviction will not be vacated on the ground that the defendant was detained pending trial without a determination of probable cause.

"Both the District Court and the Court of Appeals held that the determination of probable cause must be accompanied by the full panoply of adversary safeguards—counsel, confrontation, cross-examination, and compulsory process for witnesses. A full preliminary hearing of this sort is modeled after the procedure used in many States to determine whether the evidence justifies going to trial under an information or presenting the case to a grand jury. The standard of proof required of the prosecution is usually referred to as 'probable cause,' but in some jurisdictions it may approach a prima facie case of guilt. When the hearing takes this form, adversary procedures are customarily employed. The importance of the issue to both the State and the accused justifies the presentation of witnesses and full exploration of their testimony on cross-examination. This kind of hearing also requires appointment of counsel for indigent defendants. And, as the hearing assumes increased importance and the procedures become more complex, the likelihood that it can be held promptly after arrest diminishes.

"These adversary safeguards are not essential for the probable cause determination required by the Fourth Amendment. The sole issue is whether there is

1. A person arrested under a warrant would have received a prior judicial determination of probable cause. Under Fla. Rule Crim.Proc. 3.120 (West 1975), a warrant may be issued upon a sworn complaint that states facts showing that the suspect has committed a crime. The magistrate may also take testimony under oath to determine if there is reasonable ground to believe the complaint is true.

2. By contrast, the Court has held that an indictment, "fair upon its face," and returned by a "properly constituted grand jury" conclusively determines the existence of probable cause and requires issuance of an arrest warrant without further inquiry. Ex parte United States, 287 U.S. 241, 250, 53 S.Ct. 129 (1932). The willingness to let a grand jury's judgment substitute for that of a neutral and detached magistrate is attributable to the grand jury's relationship to the courts and its historical role of protecting individuals from unjust prosecution. See United States v. Calandra, 414 U.S. 338, 342–346, 94 S.Ct. 613, 617–619 (1974).

probable cause for detaining the arrested person pending further proceedings. This issue can be determined reliably without an adversary hearing. The standard is the same as that for arrest. That standard—probable cause to believe the suspect has committed a crime—traditionally has been decided by a magistrate in a nonadversary proceeding on hearsay and written testimony, and the Court has approved these informal modes of proof.

"The use of an informal procedure is justified not only by the lesser consequences of a probable cause determination but also by the nature of the determination itself. It does not require the fine resolution of conflicting evidence that a reasonable-doubt or even a preponderance standard demands, and credibility determinations are seldom crucial in deciding whether the evidence supports a reasonable belief in guilt. This is not to say that confrontation and cross-examination might not enhance the reliability of probable cause determinations in some cases. In most cases, however, their value would be too slight to justify holding, as a matter of constitutional principle, that these formalities and safeguards designed for trial must also be employed in making the Fourth Amendment determination of probable cause.

"Because of its limited function and its nonadversary character, the probable cause determination is not a 'critical stage' in the prosecution that would require appointed counsel....

"Although we conclude that the Constitution does not require an adversary determination of probable cause, we recognize that state systems of criminal procedure vary widely. There is no single preferred pretrial procedure, and the nature of the probable cause determination usually will be shaped to accord with a State's pretrial procedure viewed as a whole. While we limit our holding to the precise requirement of the Fourth Amendment, we recognize the desirability of flexibility and experimentation by the States. It may be found desirable, for example, to make the probable cause determination at the suspect's first appearance before a judicial officer, or the determination may be incorporated into the procedure for setting bail or fixing other conditions of pretrial release. In some States, existing procedures may satisfy the requirement of the Fourth Amendment. Others may require only minor adjustment, such as acceleration of existing preliminary hearings. Whatever procedure a State may adopt, it must provide a fair and reliable determination of probable cause as a condition for any significant pretrial restraint on liberty, and this determination must be made by a judicial officer either before or promptly after arrest."

C. THE NEED FOR ARREST WARRANT

UNITED STATES v. WATSON

Supreme Court of the United States, 1976.
423 U.S. 411, 96 S.Ct. 820.

[On August 17, 1972, an informant of proven reliability delivered a stolen credit card to federal postal inspectors, alleging that he had received the card from Henry Watson, who had instructed the informant to purchase airline tickets with it. Although authorities had probable cause to arrest Watson, they neither arrested him immediately nor applied for an arrest warrant. Instead they arranged for a meeting between the informant and Watson to be held on August 22. The meeting was postponed until August 23, at which time the informant signalled to postal inspectors that Watson had indicated that he presently had additional stolen credit cards in his possession. The inspectors entered the restaurant where the meeting had taken place, arrested Watson without a warrant, and searched his person, finding nothing. Watson, however, consented to a search of his near-by car; that search yielded stolen credit cards. These cards were admitted at trial, at which Watson was acquitted of the August 17 charge and convicted of August 23 charges. The United States Court of Appeals for the Ninth Circuit reversed the convictions, holding that the arrest was illegal for want of a warrant, and that the illegal arrest fatally tainted the consent to search. The Ninth Circuit held that an arrest warrant must be obtained even for a felony arrest in a public place, unless emergency circumstances necessitate an immediate arrest.]

MR. JUSTICE WHITE delivered the opinion of the Court.

* * *

Contrary to the Court of Appeals' view, Watson's arrest was not invalid because executed without a warrant. Section 3061(a) of Title 18 U.S.C. expressly empowers the Board of Governors of the Postal Service to authorize Postal Service officers and employees "performing duties related to the inspection of postal matters" to

> "(3) make arrests without warrant for felonies cognizable under the laws of the United States if they have reasonable grounds to believe that the person to be arrested has committed or is committing such a felony."

... [T]he Board of Governors has exercised that power and authorized warrantless arrests. There being probable cause in this case to believe that Watson had violated § 1708, the inspector and his subordinates, in arresting Watson, were acting strictly in accordance with the governing statute and regulations. The effect of the judgment of the Court of Appeals was to invalidate the statute as applied in this case and as applied to all the situations where a court fails to find exigent circumstances justifying a warrantless arrest. We reverse that judgment.

Under the Fourth Amendment, the people are to be "secure in their persons, houses, papers, and effects, against unreasonable searches and seizures, ... and no Warrants shall issue, but upon probable cause...." Section 3061 represents a judgment by Congress that it is not unreasonable under the Fourth Amendment for postal inspectors to arrest without a warrant provided they have probable cause to do so. This was not an isolated or quixotic judgment of the legislative branch. Other federal law enforcement officers have been expressly authorized by statute for many years to make felony arrests on probable cause but without a warrant. This is true of United States Marshals, 18 U.S.C. § 3053, and of agents of the Federal Bureau of Investigation, 18 U.S.C. § 3052; the Drug Enforcement Administration, 84 Stat. 1273, 21 U.S.C. § 878; the

Secret Service, 18 U.S.C. § 3056(a); and the Customs Service, 26 U.S.C. § 7607.

... Moreover, there is nothing in the Court's prior cases indicating that under the Fourth Amendment a warrant is required to make a valid arrest for a felony. Indeed, the relevant prior decisions are uniformly to the contrary.

"The usual rule is that a police officer may arrest without warrant one believed by the officer upon reasonable cause to have been guilty of a felony...." Carroll v. United States, 267 U.S. 132, 156, 45 S.Ct. 280, 286 (1925). In Henry v. United States, 361 U.S. 98, 80 S.Ct. 168 (1959), the Court dealt with an FBI agent's warrantless arrest under 18 U.S.C. § 3052 which authorizes a warrantless arrest where there are reasonable grounds to believe that the person to be arrested has committed a felony. The Court declared that "[t]he statute states the constitutional standard...." ... The necessary inquiry, therefore, was not whether there was a warrant or whether there was time to get one but whether there was probable cause for the arrest.... Just last Term, while recognizing that maximum protection of individual rights could be assured by requiring a magistrate's review of the factual justification prior to any arrest, we stated that "such a requirement would constitute an intolerable handicap for legitimate law enforcement" and noted that the Court "has never invalidated an arrest supported by probable cause solely because the officers failed to secure a warrant." Gerstein v. Pugh,....

The cases construing the Fourth Amendment thus reflect the ancient common-law rule that a peace officer was permitted to arrest without a warrant for a misdemeanor or felony committed in his presence as well as for a felony not committed in his presence if there was reasonable grounds for making the arrest. 10 Halsbury's Laws of England 344–345 (3d ed. 1955); 4 Blackstone's Commentaries 292–293 (Lewis ed. 1902); 1 J. Stephen, A History of the Criminal Law of England 193 (1883).... This has also been the prevailing rule under state constitutions and statutes....

In Rohan v. Sawin, 59 Mass. (5 Cush.) 281 (1851), a false-arrest case, the Supreme Judicial Court of Massachusetts held that the common-law rule obtained in that State. Given probable cause to arrest, "[t]he authority of the constable to arrest without warrant, in cases of felony, is most fully established by the elementary books, and adjudicated cases." ... In reaching this judgment the court observed:

> "It has been sometimes contended, that an arrest of this character, without a warrant, was a violation of the great fundamental principles of our national and state constitutions, forbidding unreasonable searches and arrests, except by warrant founded upon a complaint made under oath. Those provisions doubtless had another and different purpose, being in restraint of general warrants to make searches, and requiring warrants to issue only upon a complaint made under oath. They do not conflict with the authority of constables or other

> peace-officers, or private persons under proper limitations, to arrest without warrant those who have committed felonies. The public safety, and the due apprehension of criminals, charged with heinous offenses, imperiously require that such arrests should be made without warrant by officers of the law."
>
> . . .

Also rejected . . . was the trial court's view that to justify a warrantless arrest, the State must show "an immediate necessity therefor, arising from the danger, that the plaintiff would otherwise escape, or secrete the stolen property, before a warrant could be procured against him." The Supreme Judicial Court ruled that there was no "authority for thus restricting a constable in the exercise of his authority to arrest for a felony without a warrant." . . .

* * *

The balance struck by the common law in generally authorizing felony arrests on probable cause, but without warrant, has survived substantially intact. It appears in almost all of the States in the form of express statutory authorization. . . .

This is the rule Congress has long directed its principal law enforcement officers to follow. Congress has plainly decided against conditioning warrantless arrest power on proof of exigent circumstances. Law enforcement officers may find it wise to seek arrest warrants where practicable to do so, and their judgments about probable cause may be more readily accepted where backed by a warrant issued by a magistrate. See United States v. Ventresca, 380 U.S. 102, 106, 85 S.Ct. 741, 744–745 (1965). . . . But we decline to transform this judicial preference into a constitutional rule when the judgment of the Nation and the Congress has for so long been to authorize warrantless public arrests on probable cause rather than to encumber criminal prosecutions with endless litigation with respect to the existence of exigent circumstances, whether it was practicable to get a warrant, whether the suspect was about to flee, and the like.

Watson's arrest did not violate the Fourth Amendment, and the Court of Appeals erred in holding to the contrary.

* * *

MR. JUSTICE POWELL, concurring.

On its face, our decision today creates a certain anomaly. There is no more basic constitutional rule in the Fourth Amendment area than that which makes a warrantless search unreasonable except in a few "jealously and carefully drawn" exceptional circumstances. . . . On more than one occasion this Court has rejected an argument that a law enforcement officer's own probable cause to search a private place for contraband or evidence of crime should excuse his otherwise unexplained failure to procure a warrant beforehand. . . .

Since the Fourth Amendment speaks equally to both searches and seizures, and since an arrest, the taking hold of one's person is quintessentially, a seizure, it would seem that the constitutional provision should impose the same limitations upon arrests that it does upon searches. Indeed, as an abstract matter an argument can be made that the restrictions upon arrest perhaps should be greater. A search may cause only annoyance and temporary inconvenience to the law-abiding citizen, assuming more serious dimension only when it turns up evidence of criminality. An arrest, however, is a serious personal intrusion regardless of whether the person seized is guilty or innocent. Although an arrestee cannot be held for a significant period without some neutral determination that there are grounds to do so, no decision that he should go free can come quickly enough to erase the invasion of his privacy that already will have occurred.... Logic therefore would seem to dictate that arrests be subject to the warrant requirement at least to the same extent as searches.

But logic sometimes must defer to history and experience. The Court's opinion emphasizes the historical sanction accorded warrantless felony arrests....

The historical momentum for acceptance of warrantless arrests, already strong at the adoption of the Fourth Amendment, has gained strength during the ensuing two centuries. Both the judiciary and the legislative bodies of this Nation repeatedly have placed their imprimaturs upon the practice and, as the Government emphasizes, law enforcement agencies have developed their investigative and arrest procedures upon an assumption that warrantless arrests were valid so long as based upon probable cause. The decision of the Court of Appeals in this case was virtually unprecedented. Of course, no practice that is inconsistent with constitutional protections can be saved merely by appeal to previous uncritical acceptance. But the warrantless felony arrest, long preferred at common law and unimpeached at the passage of the Fourth Amendment, is not such a practice. Given the revolutionary implications of such a holding, a declaration at this late date that warrantless felony arrests are constitutionally infirm would have to rest upon reasons more substantial than a desire to harmonize the rules for arrest with those governing searches.

Moreover, a constitutional rule permitting felony arrests only with a warrant or in exigent circumstances could severely hamper effective law enforcement. Good police practice often requires postponing an arrest, even after probable cause has been established, in order to place the suspect under surveillance or otherwise develop further evidence necessary to prove guilt to a jury. Under the holding of the Court of Appeals such additional investigative work could imperil the entire prosecution. Should the officers fail to obtain a warrant initially, and later be required by unforeseen circumstances to arrest immediately with no chance to procure a last-minute warrant, they would ask a court decision that the subsequent exigency did not excuse their failure to get a warrant in the interim since they first developed probable cause. If the officers attempted to meet such a contingency by procuring a warrant as soon as they had probable cause and then merely held it during their subsequent investigation, they would risk a court decision that the warrant had grown stale by the time it was used. Law enforcement personnel caught in this squeeze could ensure validity of their arrests only by obtaining a warrant and arresting as soon as probable cause existed, thereby foreclosing the possibility of gathering vital additional evidence from the suspect's continued actions.

In sum, the historical and policy reasons sketched above fully justify the Court's sustaining of a warrantless arrest upon probable cause, despite the resulting divergence between the constitutional rule governing searches and that now held applicable to seizures of the person.

* * *

[STEWART, J., concurring.]

The arrest in this case was made upon probable cause in a public place in broad daylight. The Court holds that this arrest did not violate the Fourth Amendment, and I agree. The Court does *not* decide, nor could it decide in this case, whether or under what circumstances an officer must obtain a warrant before he may lawfully enter a private place to effect an arrest.* . . .

* * *

[MR. JUSTICE MARSHALL, dissenting.]

* * *

. . . The Court reaches its conclusion that a warrant is not necessary for a police officer to make an arrest in a public place, so long as he has probable cause to believe a felony has been committed, on the basis of its views of precedent and history. . . . None of the cases cited by the Court squarely confronted the issue decided today. Moreover, an examination of the history relied on by the Court shows that it does not support the conclusion laid upon it.

* * *

[MR. JUSTICE MARSHALL then engaged in a thorough analysis of historical developments, from which he concluded that at common law only the most serious offenses were called "felonies," and that many crimes presently deemed felonies were considered misdemeanors at common law.]

* * *

Thus the lesson of the common law, and those courts in this country that have accepted its rule, is an ambiguous one. Applied in its original context, the common-law rule would allow the warrantless arrest of

* [On the issue of entry upon private premises to effect an arrest, see the discussion of Payton v. New York, 445 U.S. 573, 100 S.Ct. 1371 (1980), and Steagald v. United States, 451 U.S. 204, 101 S.Ct. 1642 (1981), in Chapter 14–D, infra.]

some, but not all, of those we call felons today. Accordingly, the Court is simply historically wrong when it tells us that "[t]he balance struck by the common law in generally authorizing felony arrests on probable cause, but without a warrant, has survived substantially intact." ... Indeed, the only clear lesson of history is contrary to the one the Court draws: the common law considered the arrest warrant far more important than today's decision leaves it.

I do not mean by this that a modern warrant requirement should apply only to arrests precisely analogous to common-law misdemeanors, and be inapplicable to analogues of common-law felonies. Rather, the point is simply that the Court's unblinking literalism cannot replace analysis of the constitutional interests involved. While we can learn from the common law, the ancient rule does not provide a simple answer directly transferable to our system. Thus, in considering the applicability of the common-law rule to our present constitutional scheme, we must consider *both* of the rule's two opposing constructs: the presumption favoring warrants, as well as the exception allowing immediate arrests of the most dangerous criminals. The Court's failure to do so, indeed its failure to recognize any tension in the common-law rule at all, drains all validity from its historical analysis.

* * *

The Court has typically engaged in a two-part analysis in deciding whether the presumption favoring a warrant should be given effect in situations where a warrant has not previously been clearly required. Utilizing that approach we must now consider (1) whether the privacy of our citizens will be better protected by ordinarily requiring a warrant to be issued before they may be arrested; and (2) whether a warrant requirement would unduly burden legitimate governmental interests....

The first question is easily answered. Of course the privacy of our citizens will be better protected by a warrant requirement. We have recognized that "the Fourth Amendment protects people, not places." Katz v. United States ... [Casebook, ch. 14–F]. Indeed, the privacy guaranteed by the Fourth Amendment is quintessentially personal.... Thus a warrant is required in search situations not because of some high regard for property, but because of our regard for the individual, and *his* interest in his possessions and person....

Not only is the Fourth Amendment directly addressed to the privacy of our citizens, but it speaks in indistinguishable terms about the freedom of both persons and property from unreasonable seizures. A warrant is required in the search situation to protect the privacy of the individual, but there can be no less invasion of privacy when the individual himself, rather than his property, is searched and seized. Indeed, an unjustified arrest that forces the individual temporarily to forfeit his right to control his person and movements and interrupts the course of his daily business may be more intrusive than an unjustified search....

A warrant requirement for arrests would, of course, minimize the possibility that such an intrusion into the individual's sacred sphere of personal privacy would occur on less than probable cause. Primarily for this reason, a warrant is required for searches. Surely there is no reason to place greater trust in the partisan assessment of a police officer that there is probable cause for an arrest than in his determination that probable cause exists for a search....

We come then to the second part of the warrant test: whether a warrant requirement would unduly burden legitimate law enforcement interests....

The Government's assertion that a warrant requirement would impose an intolerable burden stems, in large part, from the specious supposition that procurement of an arrest warrant would be necessary as soon as probable cause ripens. Brief for the United States, 22–24. There is no requirement that a search warrant be obtained the moment police have probable cause to search. The rule is only that present probable cause be shown and a warrant obtained before a search is undertaken. Fed.Rule Crim.Proc. 41. ... The same rule should obtain for arrest warrants, where it may even make more sense. Certainly, there is less need for prompt procurement of a warrant in the arrest situation. Unlike probable cause to search, probable cause to arrest, once formed will continue to exist for the indefinite future, at least if no intervening exculpatory facts come to light....

This sensible approach obviates most of the difficulties that have been suggested with an arrest warrant rule. Police would not have to cut their investigation short the moment they obtain probable cause to arrest, nor would undercover agents be forced suddenly to terminate their work and forfeit their covers.... Moreover, if in the course of the continued police investigation exigent circumstances develop that demand an immediate arrest, the arrest may be made without fear of unconstitutionality, so long as the exigency was unanticipated and not used to avoid the arrest warrant requirement.... Likewise, if in the course of the continued investigation police uncover evidence tying the suspect to another crime, they may immediately arrest him for that crime if exigency demands it, and still be in full conformity with the warrant rule.... Other than where police attempt to evade the warrant requirement, the rule would invalidate an arrest only in the obvious situation: where police, with probable cause but without exigent circumstances, set out to arrest a suspect. Such an arrest must be void, even if exigency develops in the course of the arrest that would ordinarily validate it; otherwise the warrant requirement would be reduced to a toothless prescription.

In sum, the requirement that officers about to arrest a suspect ordinarily obtain a warrant before they do so does not seem unduly burdensome, at least no more burdensome than any other requirement that law enforcement officials undertake a new procedure in order to comply with the dictates of the Constitution....

It is suggested, however, that even if application of this rule does not require police to secure a warrant as soon as they obtain probable cause, the confused officer would nonetheless be prone to do so. If so, police "would risk a court decision that the warrant had grown stale by the time it was used." ... (Powell, J., concurring) .... This fear is groundless. First, as suggested above, the requirement that police procure a warrant before an arrest is made is rather simple of application. Thus, there is no need for the police to find themselves in this "squeeze." Second, the "squeeze" is nonexistent. Just as it is virtually impossible for probable cause for an arrest to grow stale between the time of formation and the time a warrant is procured, it is virtually impossible for probable cause to become stale between procurement and arrest. Delay by law enforcement officers in executing an arrest warrant does not ordinarily affect the legality of the arrest....

* * *

NOTES

1. The "failure" to obtain an arrest warrant for Henry Watson between August 17 and August 23 may be readily explained. The purpose of an arrest warrant is to initiate prosecution. An Assistant United States Attorney should not permit application for a warrant unless he or she has a prosecutable case. Until August 23, when the informant signalled that additional evidence was at hand, the only evidence authorities had linking Watson to the August 17 possession of a stolen credit card was the uncorroborated word of the informant. This was adequate for probable cause to arrest, but was hardly sufficient to persuade a federal prosecutor to bring a charge. Even after the August 23 corroborative evidence was presented to the jury, Watson was acquitted of the August 17 charge. He was convicted of the August 23 charges on the basis of the federal inspectors' testimony concerning the discovery of cards in Watson's glove compartment on August 23.

2. Five months after *Watson,* the Supreme Court decided United States v. Santana, 427 U.S. 38, 96 S.Ct. 2406 (1976). Police officers had probable cause to arrest Santana. As they approached her home, they observed her on its threshold. The police entered onto her property. Santana retreated into her home. The police followed her through the open door. They arrested her within, and discovered incriminating evidence incident to the arrest. In a 7–2 decision, the Court found the warrantless arrest valid and offered the following rationale:

> "While it may be true that under the common law of property the threshold of one's dwelling is 'private,' as is the yard surrounding the house, it is nonetheless clear that under the cases interpreting the Fourth Amendment Santana was in a 'public' place. She was not in an area where she had any expectation of privacy. 'What a person knowingly exposes to the public, even in his own house or office, is not a subject of Fourth Amendment protection.' Katz v. United States (1967). She was not merely visible to the public but as exposed to public view, speech, hearing and touch as if she had been standing completely outside her house. Hester v. United States, 265 U.S. 57, 59, 44 S.Ct. 445, 446 (1924). Thus, when the police, who concededly had

probable cause to do so, sought to arrest her, they merely intended to perform a function which we have approved in *Watson.*

"The only remaining question is whether her act of retreating into her house could thwart an otherwise proper arrest. We hold that it could not. In Warden v. Hayden, 387 U.S. 294, 87 S.Ct. 1642 (1967), we recognized the right of police, who had probable cause to believe that an armed robber had entered a house a few minutes before, to make a warrantless entry to arrest the robber and to search for weapons. This case, involving a true 'hot pursuit,' is clearly governed by *Warden;* the need to act quickly here is even greater than in that case while the intrusion is much less.... The fact that the pursuit here ended almost as soon as it began did not render it any the less a 'hot pursuit' sufficient to justify the warrantless entry into Santana's house. Once Santana saw the police, there was likewise a realistic expectation that any delay would result in destruction of evidence. See Vale v. Louisiana, 399 U.S. 30, 35, 90 S.Ct. 1969, 1972 (1970). Once she had been arrested the search, incident to that arrest, which produced the drugs and money was clearly justified....

"We thus conclude that a suspect may not defeat an arrest which has been set in motion in a public place, and is therefore proper under *Watson,* by the expedient of escaping to a private place...."

* * *

In United States v. Vaneaton, 49 F.3d 1423 (9th Cir.1995), the court held that officers could step across a threshold to complete an arrest if a suspect opens the door for the officers and stands just inside. The dissenting judge in *Vaneaton* argued that the majority's reliance on *United States v. Santana* was misplaced, because there the suspect stood "on" the threshold, whereas Vaneaton stood just inside the threshold, hence within the home in the language of *Payton.*

3. In Payton v. New York, 445 U.S. 573, 100 S.Ct. 1371 (1980), the U.S. Supreme Court held that the Fourth Amendment prohibits the police from making a warrantless and non-consensual entry into a suspect's home to make a routine felony arrest. In Steagald v. United States, 451 U.S. 204, 101 S.Ct. 1642 (1981), the Court held that in the absence of exigent circumstances or consent, the police can not legally search for the subject of an arrest warrant in the house of a third party without first obtaining a search warrant. These cases are discussed in chapter 14–D, infra.

4. In view of the significant role that the *Watson* court gave to the common law in interpreting Fourth Amendment limits upon arrest powers, there are serious constitutional questions about the validity of statutes in some states which permit an officer, upon probable cause, to make a warrantless arrest for a misdemeanor offense *not* committed in his or her presence. See, e.g., Ill.Rev. Stat. 725 ILCS 5/107–2 (1992).

According to one recent decision, despite the common law history, the Fourth Amendment does not mandate use of an arrest warrant where the arrest is for a misdemeanor not committed in the officer's presence. Fields v. City of South Houston, Texas, 922 F.2d 1183 (5th Cir.1991).

5. Even if an arrest warrant were never required by the Fourth Amendment, there still could be concern about whether a particular arrest warrant were valid for purposes of the Fourth Amendment. Suppose that a federal agent

obtains an arrest warrant and then makes the arrest in a public place and finds evidence on the arrestee's person in a search incident to arrest. If in order to justify the arrest, the prosecutor relies solely upon the arrest warrant and makes no effort to prove through live testimony that there was probable cause for the arrest, then the validity of the arrest (and of the search incident to arrest) will depend upon the validity of the arrest warrant. This is true even though the Fourth Amendment did not mandate that an arrest warrant be obtained.

As with search warrants, arrest warrants, to pass the test of the Fourth Amendment, must be supported by sworn data establishing probable cause and presented to the magistrate before issuance. Whiteley v. Warden, 401 U.S. 560, 91 S.Ct. 1031 (1971); Giordenello v. United States, 357 U.S. 480, 78 S.Ct. 1245 (1958). (In many jurisdictions sworn oral testimony rather than affidavits are used to support applications for arrest warrants.) Only a neutral judicial officer can issue a constitutionally valid arrest warrant. The arrestee must be named or described with particularity. In other words, many of the doctrines discussed earlier in this chapter are applicable in arrest warrant cases.

In many jurisdictions arrest warrants were frequently issued upon the basis of conclusory allegations that a particular person has committed a crime. These warrants were invalid for Fourth Amendment purposes. The significance of their invalidity often was not great, however. As *Watson* and the other previous material indicates, frequently arrest warrants are not constitutionally required. Faced with an invalid warrant, a prosecutor can proceed as if no warrant existed at all. If the arrest is challenged in such a case, the prosecutor need only prove through live testimony that there was probable cause for arrest. Then, too, if the arrest yielded no evidence, ordinarily the legality of the arrest will be irrelevant to the outcome of the criminal case.

D. EXTRADITION OF ACCUSED PERSONS LOCATED IN OTHER JURISDICTIONS

There are instances where a person charged with a crime is located in another jurisdiction or country. To effect his return from another country there must exist a treaty providing for mutual extradition of fugitives; in the absence of a treaty there is no legal right to the return of a fugitive. With regard to interstate situations there is a provision in the Constitution (Art. IV, § 2, d. 2), commonly referred to as the Extradition Clause, which reads as follows:

> A Person charged in any State with Treason, Felony, or other Crime, who shall flee from Justice, and be found in another State, shall on Demand of the executive Authority of the State from which he fled, be delivered up, to be removed to the State having Jurisdiction of the Crime.

In implementation of this constitutional authorization, practically all of the states have adopted the Uniform Extradition Act. It sets forth the procedures which must be followed, and it even covers case situations where the wanted person has not actually fled from, nor was he physically present in the demanding state at the time of the offense; all that is required is a charge that the wanted person committed an act within the host state or in a third state "intentionally resulting in a crime in the state whose executive authority is making the demand".*

NOTES

1. The fact that a fugitive may have been illegally arrested, or even kidnapped, for return to the state where the crime was committed does not affect the court's jurisdiction to try the case. Frisbie v. Collins, 342 U.S. 519, 72 S.Ct. 509 (1952); United States v. Sobell, 142 F.Supp. 515 (S.D.N.Y.1956), affirmed 244 F.2d 520 (2d Cir.), cert. denied 355 U.S. 873, 78 S.Ct. 120 (1957); People v. Griffith, 130 Colo. 475, 276 P.2d 559 (1954).

In the case of Adolph Eichmann, the chief executioner of millions of Jews during the Nazi regime in Germany, the Supreme Court of Israel relied heavily upon American case law to justify its right to try Eichmann, who had been kidnapped in Argentina and flown to Israel for trial. See Pearlman, The Capture and Trial of Adolph Eichmann (1963) 112.

In United States v. Alvarez–Machain, 504 U.S. 655, 112 S.Ct. 2188 (1992), the United States Supreme Court held that an extradition treaty between Mexico and the United States did not bar kidnapping as a method of securing jurisdiction and thus no treaty violation occurred when Alvarez–Machain was kidnapped in Mexico and brought to trial in the United States.

United States v. Toscanino, 500 F.2d 267 (2d Cir. 1974), held that torture, drugging, and kidnapping of a suspect by United States agents in foreign countries, if proved, would deprive the United States District Court of jurisdiction over the defendant. The Second Circuit read recent expansion of general Due Process notions to undermine the principle that the methods by which the defendant has been brought before the court are irrelevant to the court's jurisdiction. However, in United States ex rel. Lujan v. Gengler, 510 F.2d 62 (2d Cir.), cert. denied 421 U.S. 1001, 95 S.Ct. 2400 (1975), the same court acknowledged that not every irregularity in bringing a defendant into the jurisdiction would require his release. One month later, in Gerstein v. Pugh, 420 U.S. 103, 95 S.Ct. 854 (1975), the United States Supreme Court cited with approval Frisbie v. Collins and stated: "Nor do we retreat from the established rule that illegal arrest or detention does not void a subsequent conviction."

2. In Pacileo v. Walker, 449 U.S. 86, 101 S.Ct. 308 (1980), the U.S. Supreme Court held that Art. IV, § 2, cl. 2, and its implementing statute, 18 U.S.C.A. § 3182, do not give courts of "asylum" or "sending" states authority to inquire into prison conditions of a "demanding" state. Therefore, once the governor of California had issued a warrant for the arrest and rendition in response to a request from the governor of Arkansas, any claims concerning alleged constitutional defects in the Arkansas penal system could only be heard in the courts of Arkansas, not in California. Reluctantly, relying upon *Pacileo*, the Supreme Court of Michigan held in Brown v. Sheriff of Wayne County, 415 Mich. 658, 330 N.W.2d 335 (1982), that it could not inquire into the constitutionality of prison conditions in Alabama in evaluating a fugitive's habeas corpus challenge to an Alabama request for extradition, even though such an inquiry would not require extensive hearings in Michigan, since federal litigation in Alabama had already demonstrated constitutional flaws in Alabama's prison

* For information regarding extradition as well as other aspects of the interstate crime control problem see: The Handbook on Interstate Crime Control (1978) (prepared by the Council of State Governments, 203 N. Wabash St., Chicago, Ill. 60605).

system. Expressing its dissatisfaction with the result it felt compelled to reach in applying *Pacileo's* application of Art. IV, § 2, cl. 2, the Michigan court stated:

> "This Court thus rests squarely on the horns of a moral dilemma. Are we compelled by our role as a part of the federal system to adhere to a rule which we perceive to have been articulated without exception by the federal courts, although the concerns underlying that rule apply with less force in this case and its application will almost certainly result in deprivations of constitutional rights? Can considerations of comity and efficiency lead this Court to act when Alabama's noncompliance with the Constitution has already been determined by a United States district court sitting in that state?
>
> "We conclude that we are obliged by *Pacileo* to hold that a habeas corpus court in the asylum state is limited to the minimal review described therein, and that the petitions for habeas corpus filed by Blount and Brown must therefore be denied. *Pacileo* reaffirms in a context parallel to the present one [*Michigan v.*] *Doran's* [439 U.S. 282, 99 S.Ct. 530 (1979)] prescription of an extremely narrow role for the courts of the asylum state, a role which in effect reserves to the demanding state adjudication of all of a petitioner's claims that his legal or constitutional rights have been violated or will be violated by his return. The United States Supreme Court appears resolved to construe the Extradition Clause in accordance with the principles sketched in *Doran,* supra, 439 U.S. 287–288, 99 S.Ct. at 534–35:
>
>> The purpose of the Clause was to preclude any state from becoming a sanctuary for fugitives from justice of another state and thus "balkanize" the administration of criminal justice among the several states. It articulated, in mandatory language, the concepts of comity and full faith and credit, found in the immediately preceding clause of Art IV. The Extradition Clause, like the Commerce Clause, served important national objectives of a newly developing country striving to foster national unity.... In the administration of justice, no less than in trade and commerce, national unity was thought to be served by de-emphasizing state lines for certain purposes, without impinging on essential state autonomy.
>
> "Recognizing the importance of comity and full faith and credit and of avoiding 'balkanization' of the administration of criminal justice, we regret that those important interests cannot, in an appropriate case, be outweighed by the right of an individual human being to be free from cruel and unusual punishment.
>
> "Our reading of *Pacileo* indicates that the United States Supreme Court is not disposed to allow an asylum state court even to consider a present finding of unconstitutionality made by a court domiciled in the demanding state, but will require a fugitive named in an extradition warrant and charged with a crime in the demanding state to pursue his tenuous remedy in courts located in the demanding state."

3. The Seventh Circuit Court of Appeals has held in Re Extradition of Burt, 737 F.2d 1477 (7th Cir.1984), that even though early case law appears to restrict habeas corpus review in extradition cases to an examination of jurisdictional defects, the U.S. Supreme Court has, in effect, redefined the scope of review to include evaluation of due process and speedy trial claims. This view, however,

has been repudiated by the U.S. Supreme Court in California v. Superior Court of California (Smolin), 482 U.S. 400, 107 S.Ct. 2433 (1987). In a 7–2 decision, the Court held that the scope of judicial inquiry in an asylum state under the federal extradition statute is limited and does not include whether the defendant committed the crime alleged by the requesting state or has various defenses. The Court stressed that proceedings under the statute are summary in nature and the asylum state court must confine itself to whether the requisites of the statute have been met, such as, in this case, whether a crime was charged under the laws of the requesting state. In the case at bar the extradition papers correctly set forth each element of the crime of kidnapping under the laws of the requesting state. It was error for the asylum state to deny extradition on the ground that it was legally impossible for the defendant to have committed the offense in the requesting state. That issue could only be dealt with in the requesting state. The Court thus reaffirms the narrow scope of the issues under the statute and this may end the practice of some asylum state courts of turning extradition hearings into "mini-trials" replete with consideration of substantive defenses, constitutional issues, and questions of guilt or innocence. In Puerto Rico v. Branstad, 483 U.S. 219, 107 S.Ct. 2802 (1987), the Court went on to overrule precedent that had stood for over 125 years, Kentucky v. Dennison, 65 U.S. (24 How.) 66 (1860), and held that a federal court can order a state governor to comply with a valid demand for extradition under constitutional and statutory provisions. The Court noted that *Dennison* was the product of an era where the power of the federal government was at its lowest ebb since adoption of the Constitution. Today, on the other hand, it is routine for federal courts to order state officials to comply with federal constitutional duties.

In Ramirez v. United States, 470 U.S. 1058, 105 S.Ct. 1771 (1985), the Court split 4–4 (Mr. Justice Powell took no part in the case) and affirmed a decision of the Indiana Court of Appeals that a Michigan inmate who agreed to be returned to Indiana to stand trial on relatively minor charges could be prosecuted for more serious offenses that did not arise out of the same transaction and that were not covered by Indiana's request for custody under the Interstate Agreement on Detainers.

The "knowing and intelligent" standard for waiving constitutional rights is not necessary for a waiver of the rights guaranteed by the Interstate Agreement on Detainers. While the higher standard is appropriate for constitutional rights that guarantee a fair trial or the integrity of the truth-seeking process, the purpose behind the Agreement has nothing to do with ensuring a fair trial, but only to facilitate the trial of outstanding charges. United States v. Lawson, 736 F.2d 835 (2d Cir.1984).

It has been held that the same standard set forth in Dusky v. United States, 362 U.S. 402, 80 S.Ct. 788 (1960), for determining a defendant's competency to stand trial should be used for "determining whether a petitioner is sufficiently competent that a court may proceed to resolve the questions presented by a writ of habeas corpus issued in connection with a pending extradition request." *Dusky* held that "it must appear that the accused has [sufficient] present ability to consult with his attorney with a reasonable degree of rational understanding, and that he has a rational as well as a factual understanding of the proceedings against him." Pruett v. Barry, 696 P.2d 789 (Colo.1985).

Denying presentence confinement credit for time spent fighting extradition in another state does not deny due process by "chilling" a defendant's right to challenge extradition or unfairly punish him for exercising it. It also does not deny the defendant equal protection, because while a state may not treat defendants differently while "within its jurisdiction," here the defendant was not in the jurisdiction denying credit while he was in the other state fighting extradition. Johnson v. Manson, 196 Conn. 309, 493 A.2d 846 (1985).

In Carchman v. Nash, 473 U.S. 716, 105 S.Ct. 3401 (1985), the U.S. Supreme Court ruled on the basis of statutory construction and legislative history, that Article III of the Interstate Agreement on Detainers, which gives the prisoner the right to demand the speedy disposition of "any untried indictment, information or complaint" that is the basis of a detainer lodged against him by another state, does not apply to detainers based on probation violation charges. The Court noted that the various references in Article III and elsewhere in the Agreement referred to pending criminal charges exclusively, and observed that application of Article III to probation charges would not carry out the legislative purpose. "[*T*]he uncertainties in the underlying charge, in the likelihood of the prisoner's receiving an additional sentence, and in the length of incarceration generally are less in the case of probation-violation detainers than in the case of criminal-charge detainers."

Chapter 14

SEARCHES AND SEIZURES

A. PROBABLE CAUSE TO ARREST PRIOR TO SEARCH FOR AND SEIZURE OF EVIDENCE FROM ARRESTEE

DRAPER v. UNITED STATES

Supreme Court of the United States, 1959.
358 U.S. 307, 79 S.Ct. 329.

MR. JUSTICE WHITTAKER delivered the opinion of the Court.

* * *

The evidence offered at the hearing on the motion to suppress was not substantially disputed. It established that one Marsh, a federal narcotic agent with 29 years' experience, was stationed at Denver; that one Hereford had been engaged as a "special employee" of the Bureau of Narcotics at Denver for about six months, and from time to time gave information to Marsh regarding violations of the narcotic laws, for which Hereford was paid small sums of money, and that Marsh had always found the information given by Hereford to be accurate and reliable. On September 3, 1956, Hereford told Marsh that James Draper (petitioner) recently had taken up abode at a stated address in Denver and "was peddling narcotics to several addicts" in that city. Four days later, on September 7, Hereford told Marsh "that Draper had gone to Chicago the day before [September 6] by train [and] that he was going to bring back three ounces of heroin [and] that he would return to Denver either on the morning of the 8th of September or the morning of the 9th of September also by train." Hereford also gave Marsh a detailed physical description of Draper and of the clothing he was wearing, and said that he would be carrying "a tan zipper bag," and habitually "walked real fast."

On the morning of September 8, Marsh and a Denver police officer went to the Denver Union Station and kept watch over all incoming trains from Chicago, but they did not see anyone fitting the description that Hereford had given. Repeating the process on the morning of September 9, they saw a person, having the exact physical attributes and wearing the precise clothing described by Hereford, alight from an incoming Chicago train and start walking "fast" toward the exit. He was carrying a tan zipper bag in his right hand and the left was thrust in his raincoat pocket. Marsh, accompanied by the police officer, overtook, stopped and arrested him. They then searched him and found the two "envelopes containing heroin" clutched in his left hand in his raincoat pocket, and found the syringe in the tan zipper bag. Marsh then took him (petitioner) into custody. Hereford died four days after the arrest and therefore did not testify at the hearing on the motion.

26 U.S.C. (Supp. V) § 7607, added by § 104(a) of the Narcotic Control Act of 1956, 70 Stat. 570, 26 U.S.C.A. § 7607, provides, in pertinent part:

> "The Commissioner ... and agents, of the Bureau of Narcotics ... may—
>
> * * *
>
> "(2) Make arrests without warrant for violations of any law of the United States relating to narcotic drugs ... where the violation is committed in the presence of the person making the arrest or where such person has reasonable grounds to believe that the person to be arrested has committed or is committing such violation."

The crucial question for us then is whether knowledge of the related facts and circumstances gave Marsh "probable cause" within the meaning of the Fourth Amendment, and "reasonable grounds" within the meaning of § 104(a), supra, to believe that petitioner had committed or was committing a violation of the narcotic laws. If it did, the arrest, though without a warrant, was lawful....

Petitioner ... contends (1) that the information given by Hereford to Marsh was "hearsay" and, because hearsay is not legally competent evidence in a criminal trial, could not legally have been considered, but should have been put out of mind, by Marsh in assessing whether he had "probable cause" and "reasonable grounds" to arrest petitioner without a warrant, and (2) that, even if hearsay could lawfully have been considered, Marsh's information should be held insufficient to show "probable cause" and "reasonable grounds" to believe that petitioner had violated or was violating the narcotic laws and to justify his arrest without a warrant.

Considering the first contention, we find petitioner entirely in error. Brinegar v. United States, 338 U.S. 160, 172–173, 69 S.Ct. 1302, 1309, has settled the question the other way. There, in a similar situation, the convict contended "that the factors relating to inadmissibility of the evidence [for] *purposes of proving guilt at the trial,* deprive[d] the evidence as a whole of sufficiency to show probable cause for the search...." (Emphasis added.) But this Court rejecting that contention, said: "[T]he so-called distinction places a wholly unwarranted emphasis upon the criterion of admissibility in evidence, to prove the accused's guilt, of facts relied upon to show probable cause. The emphasis, we think, goes much too far in confusing and disregarding the difference between what is required to prove guilt in a criminal case and what is required to show probable cause for arrest or search. It approaches requiring (if it does not in practical effect require) proof sufficient to establish guilt in order to substantiate the existence of probable cause. There is a large difference between the two things to be proved [guilt and probable cause], as well as between the tribunals which determine them, and therefore a like difference in the *quanta* and modes of proof required to establish them." ...

Nor can we agree with petitioner's second contention that Marsh's information was insufficient to show probable cause and reasonable grounds to believe that petitioner had violated or was violating the narcotic laws and to justify his arrest without a warrant. The information given to narcotic agent Marsh by "special employee" Hereford may have been hearsay to Marsh, but coming from one employed for that purpose and whose information had always been found accurate and reliable, it is clear that Marsh would have been derelict in his duties had he not pursued it. And when, in pursuing that information, he saw a man, having the exact physical attributes and wearing the precise clothing and carrying the tan zipper bag that Hereford had described, alight from one of the very trains from the very place stated by Hereford and start to walk at a "fast" pace toward the station exit, Marsh had personally verified every facet of the information given him by Hereford except whether petitioner had accomplished his mission and had the three ounces of heroin on his person or in his bag. And surely, with every other bit of Hereford's information being thus personally verified, Marsh had "reasonable grounds" to believe that the remaining unverified bit of Hereford's information—that Draper would have the heroin with him—was likewise true.

"In dealing with probable cause ... as the very name implies, we deal with probabilities. These are not technical; they are the factual and practical considerations of everyday life on which reasonable and prudent men, not legal technicians, act." Brinegar v. United States. Probable cause exists where "the facts and circumstances within their [the arresting officer's] knowledge and of which they had reasonably trustworthy information [are] sufficient in themselves to warrant a man of reasonable caution in the belief that" an offense has been or is being committed. Carroll v. United States, 267 U.S. 132, 162, 45 S.Ct. 280, 288....

We believe that, under the facts and circumstances here, Marsh had probable cause and reasonable grounds to believe that petitioner was committing a violation of the laws of the United States relating to narcotic drugs at the time he arrested him. The arrest was therefore lawful, and the subsequent search and seizure, having been made incident to that lawful arrest, were likewise valid. It follows that petitioner's motion to suppress was properly denied and that the seized heroin was competent evidence lawfully received at the trial.

Affirmed.

THE CHIEF JUSTICE and MR. JUSTICE FRANKFURTER took no part in the consideration or decision of this case.

MR. JUSTICE DOUGLAS, dissenting.

Of course, the education we receive from mystery stories and television shows teaches that what happened in this case is efficient police work. The police are tipped off that a man carrying narcotics will step off the morning train. A man meeting the precise description does alight from the train. No warrant for his arrest has been—or as I see it, could then be—obtained. Yet he is arrested; and narcotics are found in his pocket and a syringe in the bag he carried. This is the familiar pattern of crime detection which has been dinned into public consciousness as the correct and efficient one. It is however, a distorted reflection of the constitutional system under which we are supposed to live.

With all due deference, the arrest made here on the mere word of an informer violated the spirit of the Fourth Amendment and the requirement of the law, . . . governing arrests in narcotics cases. If an arrest is made without a warrant, the offense must be committed in the presence of the officer or the officer must have "reasonable grounds to believe that the person to be arrested has committed or is committing" a violation of the narcotics law. The arresting officers did not have a bit of evidence, known to them and as to which they could take an oath had they gone to a magistrate for a warrant, that petitioner had committed any crime. The arresting officers did not know the grounds on which the informer based his conclusion; nor did they seek to find out what they were. They acted solely on the informer's word. In my view that was not enough.

The rule which permits arrest for felonies, as distinguished from misdemeanors, if there are reasonable grounds for believing a crime has been or is being committed . . . grew out of the need to protect the public safety by making prompt arrests. Yet, apart from those cases where the crime is committed in the presence of the officer, arrests without warrants, like searches without warrants, are the exception, not the rule in our society. Lord Chief Justice Pratt in Wilkes v. Wood, condemned not only the odious general warrant, in which the name of the citizen to be arrested was left blank, but the whole scheme of seizures and searches under "a discretionary power" of law officers to act "wherever their suspicions may chance to fall"—a practice which he denounced as "totally subversive of the liberty of the subject." See III May, Constitutional History of England, c. XI. Wilkes had written in 1762, "To take any man into custody, and deprive him of his liberty, without having some seeming foundation at least, on which to justify such a step, is inconsistent with wisdom and sound policy." The Life and Political Writings of John Wilkes, p. 372.

George III in 1777 pressed for a bill which would allow arrests on suspicion of treason committed in America. The words were "suspected of" treason and it was to these words that Wilkes addressed himself in Parliament. "There is not a syllable in the Bill of the degree of probability attending the suspicion.... Is it possible, Sir, to give more despotic powers to a bashaw of the Turkish empire? What security is left for the devoted objects of this Bill against the malice of a prejudiced individual, a wicked magistrate ... ?" The Speeches of Mr. Wilkes, p. 102.

These words and the complaints against which they were directed were well known on this side of the water. Hamilton wrote about "the practice of arbitrary imprisonments" which he denounced as "the favorite and most formidable instruments of tyranny." Federalist No. 84. The writs of assistance, against which James Otis proclaimed, were vicious in the same way as the general warrants, since they required no showing of "probable cause" before a magistrate, and since they allowed the police to search on suspicion and without "reasonable grounds" for believing that a crime had been or was being committed. Otis' protest was eloquent; but he lost the case. His speech, however, rallied public opinion. "Then and there," wrote John Adams, "the child Independence was born." 10 Life and Works of John Adams (1856), p. 248. ...

The Court is quite correct in saying that proof of "reasonable grounds" for believing a crime was being committed need not be proof admissible at the trial. It could be inferences from suspicious acts, e.g., consort with known peddlers, the surreptitious passing of a package, an intercepted message suggesting criminal activities, or any number of such events coming to the knowledge of the officer.... But, if he takes the law into his own hands and does not seek the protection of a warrant, he must act on some evidence known to him. This important requirement should be strictly enforced, lest the whole process of arrest revert once more to whispered accusations by people. When we lower the guards as we do today, we risk making the role of the informer—odious in our history—once more supreme....

Here the officers had no evidence—apart from the mere word of an informer—that petitioner was committing a crime. The fact that petitioner walked fast and carried a tan zipper bag was not evidence of any crime. The officers knew nothing except what they had been told by the informer. If they went to a magistrate to get a warrant of arrest and relied solely on the report of the informer, it is not conceivable to me that one would be granted. For they could not present to the magistrate any of the facts which the informer may have had. They could swear only to the fact that the informer had made the accusation. They could swear to no evidence that lay in their own knowledge. They could present, on information and belief, no facts which the informer disclosed. No magistrate could issue a warrant on the mere word of an officer, without more. We are not justified in lowering the standard when an arrest is made without a warrant and allowing the officers more leeway than we grant the magistrate.

With all deference I think we break with tradition when we sustain this arrest....

BECK v. OHIO

Supreme Court of the United States, 1964.
379 U.S. 89, 85 S.Ct. 223.

MR. JUSTICE STEWART delivered the opinion of the Court.

On the afternoon of November 10, 1961, the petitioner, William Beck, was driving his automobile in the vicinity of East 115th Street and Beulah Avenue in Cleveland, Ohio. Cleveland police officers accosted him, identified themselves, and ordered him to pull over to the curb. The officers possessed neither an arrest warrant nor a search warrant. Placing him under arrest, they searched his car but found nothing of interest. They then took him to a nearby police station where they searched his person and found an envelope containing a number of clearing house slips "beneath the sock of his leg." The petitioner was subsequently charged in the Cleveland Municipal Court with possession of clearing house slips in violation of a state criminal statute. He filed a motion to suppress as evidence the clearing house slips in question, upon the ground that the police had obtained them by means of an unreasonable search and seizure in violation of the Fourth and Fourteenth Amendments. After a hearing the motion was overruled, the clearing house slips were admitted in evidence, and the petitioner was convicted. His conviction was affirmed by an Ohio Court of Appeals, and ultimately by the Supreme Court of Ohio, with two judges dissenting. We granted certiorari to consider the petitioner's claim that, under the rule of Mapp v. Ohio, the clearing house slips were wrongly admitted in evidence against him because they had been seized by the Cleveland police in violation of the Fourth and Fourteenth Amendments.

Although the police officers did not obtain a warrant before arresting the petitioner and searching his automobile and his person, the Supreme Court of Ohio found the search nonetheless constitutionally valid as a search incident to a lawful arrest. And it is upon that basis that the Ohio decision has been supported by the respondent here. See Draper v. United States; Ker v. California, 374 U.S. 23, 83 S.Ct. 1623.

There are limits to the permissible scope of a warrantless search incident to a lawful arrest, but we proceed on the premise that, if the arrest itself was lawful, those limits were not exceeded here. The constitutional validity of the search in this case, then, must depend upon the constitutional validity of the petitioner's arrest. Whether that arrest was constitutionally valid depends in turn upon whether, at the moment the arrest was made, the officers had probable cause to make it—whether at that moment the facts and circumstances within their knowledge and of which they had reasonably trustworthy information were sufficient to warrant a prudent man in believing that the petitioner had committed or was committing an offense. Brinegar v. United States, 338 U.S. 160, 175–176, 69 S.Ct. 1302, 1310–1311; Henry v. United States, 361 U.S. 98, 102, 80 S.Ct. 168, 171. "The rule of probable cause is a practical, nontechnical conception affording the best compromise that has been found for accommodating . . . often opposing interests. Requiring more would unduly hamper law enforcement. To allow less would be to leave law-abiding citizens at the mercy of the officers' whim or caprice." Brinegar v. United States, supra. . . .

The trial court made no findings of fact in this case. The trial judge simply made a conclusory statement: "A lawful arrest has been made, and this was a search incidental to that lawful arrest." The Court of Appeals merely found "no error prejudicial to the appellant." In the Supreme Court of Ohio, Judge Zimmerman's opinion contained a narrative recital which is accurately excerpted in the dissenting opinions filed today. But, putting aside the question of whether this opinion can fairly be called the opinion of the court, such a recital in an appellate opinion is hardly the equivalent of findings made by the trier of the facts. In any event, after giving full scope to the flexibility demanded by "a recognition that conditions and circumstances vary just as do investigative and enforcement techniques," we hold that the arrest of the petitioner cannot on the record before us be squared with the demands of the Fourth and Fourteenth Amendments.

The record is meager, consisting only of the testimony of one of the arresting officers, given at the hearing on the motion to suppress. As to the officer's own knowledge of the petitioner before the arrest, the record shows no more than that the officer "had a police picture of him and knew what he looked like," and that the officer knew that the petitioner had "a record in connection with clearing house and scheme of chance." Beyond that, the officer testified only that he had "information" that he had "heard reports," that "someone specifically did relate that information," and that he "knew who that person was." There is nowhere in the record any indication of what "information" or "reports" the officer had received, or, beyond what has been set out above, from what source the "information" and "reports" had come. The officer testified that when he left the station house, "I had in mind looking for [the petitioner] in the area of East 115th Street and Beulah, stopping him if I did see him make a stop in that area." But the officer testified to nothing that would indicate that any informer had said that the petitioner could be found at that time and place. Cf. Draper v. United States. And the record does not show that the officers saw the petitioner "stop" before they arrested him, or that they saw, heard, smelled, or otherwise perceived anything else to give them ground for belief that the petitioner had acted or was then acting unlawfully.

No decision of this Court has upheld the constitutional validity of a warrantless arrest with support so scant as this record presents. The respondent relies upon Draper v. United States. But in that case the record showed that a named special employee of narcotics agents who had on numerous occasions given reliable information had told the arresting officer that the defendant, whom he described minutely, had taken up residence at a stated address and was selling narcotics to addicts in Denver. The informer further had told the officer that the defendant was going to Chicago to obtain narcotics and would be returning to Denver on one of two trains from Chicago, which event in fact took place. In complete contrast, the record in this case does not contain a single objective fact to support a belief by the officers that the petitioner was engaged in criminal activity at the time they arrested him.

An arrest without a warrant bypasses the safeguards provided by an objective predetermination of probable cause, and substitutes instead the far less reliable procedure of an after-the-event justification for the arrest or search, too likely to be subtly influenced by the familiar shortcomings of hindsight judgment. "Whether or not the requirements of reliability and particularity of the information on which an officer may act are more stringent where an arrest warrant is absent, they surely cannot be less stringent than where an arrest warrant is obtained. Otherwise, a principal incentive now existing for the procurement of arrest warrants would be destroyed." Wong Sun v. United States, 371 U.S. 471, 479–480, 83 S.Ct. 407, 413. Yet even in cases where warrants were obtained, the Court has held that the Constitution demands a greater showing of probable cause than can be found in the present record.

When the constitutional validity of an arrest is challenged, it is the function of a court to determine whether the facts available to the officers at the moment of the arrest would "warrant a man of reasonable caution in the belief" that an offense has been committed. Carroll v. United States, 267 U.S. 132, 162, 45 S.Ct. 280, 288. If the court is not informed of the facts upon which the arresting officers acted, it cannot properly discharge that function. All that the trial court was told in this case was that the officers knew what the petitioner looked like and knew that he had a previous record of arrests or convictions for violations of the clearing house law. Beyond that, the arresting officer who testified said no more than that someone (he did not say who) had told him something (he did not say what) about the petitioner. We do not hold that the officer's knowledge of the petitioner's physical appearance and previous record was either inadmissible or entirely irrelevant upon the issue of probable cause. See Brinegar v. United States, 338 U.S. 160, 172–174, 69 S.Ct. 1302, 1309–1310. But to hold that knowledge of either or both of these facts constituted probable cause would be to hold that anyone with a previous criminal record could be arrested at will.

It is possible that an informer did in fact relate information to the police officer in this case which constituted probable cause for the petitioner's arrest. But when the constitutional validity of that arrest was challenged, it was incumbent upon the prosecution to show with considerably more specificity than was shown in this case what the informer actually said, and why the officer thought the information was credible. We may assume that the officers acted in good faith in arresting the petitioner. But "good faith on the part of the arresting officers is not enough." Henry v. United States. If subjective good faith alone were the test, the protections of the Fourth Amendment would evaporate, and the people would be "secure in their persons, houses, papers, and effects," only in the discretion of the police.

Reversed....

[The dissenting opinions of Justices Black, Clark and Harlan have been omitted. They were of the view that the facts found by the Ohio Supreme Court, and the inferences drawn from the testimony of the prosecution's witnesses satisfied the probable cause element.]

NOTES

1. In *Draper,* the officers relied upon the word of a proven informer. Suppose an officer is approached by an ordinary citizen who claims to have witnessed or suffered the commission of a crime. Since the officer has no prior experience with the alleged victim or witness, may he give credence to their statements? Consider the following:

(a) United States ex rel. Cardaio v. Casscles, 446 F.2d 632, 635–37 (2nd Cir.1971):

> "On June 1, 1964, the Manhattan police received information that narcotics could be found in an apartment at 31 Bedford Street, Manhattan. Lieutenant Mulligan and other officers went to that address. While they were waiting at the door of the apartment, Tod Konrad appeared. In answer to the officer's inquiry, Konrad said that he had marijuana in his apartment. He further remarked that he was 'a nervous wreck' because the night before he had been 'stuck up' and robbed of approximately eight pounds of marijuana. He said that one of his assailants was armed with a gun. He characterized this man as a 'beatnik type of kid,' with long hair, about twenty years old, whose name was Nick. He gave the officers Nick's telephone number. It was a Queens number....
>
> "Detective King ascertained that the telephone number was that of Nicholas Cardaio of 43–10 Auburndale Lane, Queens. Petitioner lived at that address, a two-family house. The other apartment in the house was occupied by petitioner's father, also named Nicholas Cardaio. It is not entirely clear whether the telephone number was that of the father or the son.
>
> "[The police then effected a warrantless arrest of petitioner] ... Konrad's information was first hand. It was based on his personal knowledge. He said that the marijuana had been taken from him by a robber at gunpoint. He gave the police a description of his assailant as a young man, about twenty, 'a beatnik type' with long hair. He furnished his name, 'Nick,' and his telephone number. Investigation confirmed that the telephone was listed under the name of a 'Nick', i.e., Nicholas Cardaio. When the officers arrived at the Auburndale Lane house, they inquired if 'Nick' was there and were told that he was. Upon entering, they observed petitioner, who presumably conformed to Konrad's description. The fact that there was another Nicholas Cardaio, petitioner's father, at that address, is immaterial. The description obviously could not apply to the father. There is no doubt that Konrad's information led the police directly to petitioner. It was

sufficient to induce a reasonable belief on their part that petitioner was the man who had committed the crime.

* * *

"... We have found no case in which evidence of previous reliability of the informant has been thought necessary where the information comes from the person who is himself the victim of the crime about which he complains. To require such proof would create a standard impossible of attainment, as a practical matter, for, as has been pointed out:

> 'Most victims of crime are total strangers to arresting officers as are most of the persons they arrest.'

"In United States ex rel. Walls v. Mancusi, 406 F.2d 505 (2d Cir.1969), this court found probable cause where the victim of a holdup, previously unknown to the police, told a nearby policeman of the attack and gave a description of the assailants. To be sure, the culprits were still in sight and were observed running away, thereby tending to corroborate the victim's accusation. We do not regard that fact, however, as such a vital distinction as to require a different result in the present case. In *Pendergrast,* the victim picked out the defendant from a crowd of onlookers, and defendant stoutly denied the accusation prior to his arrest. In Brown v. United States, 125 U.S.App.D.C. 43, 365 F.2d 976 (1966), information broadcast over a police radio which came from an unknown victim, reporting a robbery and giving a somewhat inaccurate description of the defendant and his automobile, was held sufficient. The court pointed out that 'the victim's report has the virtue of being based on personal observation,' and 'is less likely to be colored by self-interest than is that of an informant.'

"We hold that the police were entitled to rely upon Konrad's information and that it afforded them probable cause to arrest petitioner."

(b) A different rationale exists for establishing the reliability of named "citizen-informers" as opposed to the traditional idea of unnamed police contacts or informers who usually themselves are criminals. Information supplied to officers by the traditional police informer is not given in the spirit of a concerned citizen, but often is given in exchange for some concession, payment, or simply out of revenge against the subject. The nature of these persons and the information which they supply convey a certain impression of unreliability, and it is proper to demand that some evidence of their credibility and reliability be shown. One practical way of making such a showing is to point to accurate information which they have supplied in the past.

However, an ordinary citizen who reports a crime which has been committed in his presence, or that a crime is being or will be committed, stands on much different ground than a police informer. He is a witness to criminal activity who is assumed to act with an intent to aid the police in law enforcement because of his concern for society or for his own safety. He does not expect any gain or concession in exchange for his information. An informer of this type usually would not have more than one opportunity to supply information to the police, thereby precluding proof of his reliability by pointing to previous accurate information which he has supplied.

It would be unreasonable to demand the same showing of prior reliability in the case of such an informer as in the case of a "traditional police informer." Rather, the reliability of such a person should be evaluated from the nature of his report, his opportunity to hear and see the matters reported, and the extent to which it can be verified by independent police investigation. State v. Paszek, 50 Wis.2d 619, 184 N.W.2d 836 (1971). See also United States v. Mahler, 442 F.2d 1172, 1174–75 (9th Cir.), cert. denied 404 U.S. 993, 92 S.Ct. 541 (1971) (crime victim is presumed reliable); Brooks v. United States, 416 F.2d 1044, 1049 (5th Cir.1969), cert. denied 397 U.S. 1048, 90 S.Ct. 1378 (1970) (local law enforcement officers are reliable informants).

Consult Thompson and Starkman, The Citizen Informant Rule, 64 J.Crim.L. & C. 163 (1973).

(c) The same rule of presumed reliability applies to accomplices. See United States v. Long, 449 F.2d 288, 292–93 (8th Cir.1971), cert. denied 405 U.S. 974 (1972). The reason for the rule is somewhat different in accomplice cases. The courts rely on personal knowledge of the accomplice and upon the fact that he is not anonymous. The courts also consider the fact that he is making an admission against his own interest by declaring his own involvement in illegal conduct. Such an admission has been thought to be likely to be true. See United States v. Harris, 403 U.S. 573, 91 S.Ct. 2075 (1971).

2. The source of information given to officers is not limited to identified citizens and anonymous police informers. In recent years the use of computer information and credit card checks have become significant. With respect to computer reports, it has been held that the police may rely upon computer reports to make arrests but that the ultimate validity of the arrest will be determined by the sufficiency of the information on which the computer report was based, i.e. whether the officer originating the report had enough information to justify an arrest. United States v. Williams, 459 F.2d 44 (9th Cir.1972).

3. It is fairly common for several officers to participate in an investigation in such a manner that no single officer knows enough about the case to establish probable cause although the collective knowledge of the officers establishes probable cause. In this connection consider the following from State v. Stark, 288 Minn. 286, 290–91, 179 N.W.2d 597, 600, cert. denied 402 U.S. 930, 91 S.Ct. 1529 (1971):

> "The arresting officer was a patrolman who did not personally know all these facts but, as a matter of police routine, he had been told that defendant was wanted for robbery and he had been given the defendant's photograph. When he was given the order to arrest the defendant, it appeared that the defendant was about to flee. Defendant argues that because the arresting officer did not have sufficient knowledge or information to establish probable cause, the arrest was illegal. This is not the correct test. The test is whether the law-enforcement agency as a corporate body possessed sufficient information to establish probable cause. Smith v. United States, 123 App.D.C. 202, 358 F.2d 833; Farrow v. State, 233 Md. 526, 197 A.2d 434. In this case probable cause was established by all information possessed by police as a unit and therefore the arrest was lawful." See also United States v. Stratton, 453 F.2d 36, 37 (8th Cir.), cert. denied 405 U.S. 1069, 92 S.Ct. 1515 (1972); Stassi v. United States, 410 F.2d 946, 952 (5th Cir.1969) ("The officers were working in close concert with each other and the knowledge of one of them was the knowledge of all").

4. Must the police know exactly the crime for which they arrest? Consider the following from People v. Georgev, 38 Ill.2d 165, 230 N.E.2d 851 (1967):

> "We deem that the circumstances here reasonably indicated to the lone officer who stopped the defendant's car that he had probable cause to believe he was confronted with a crime other than the simple automobile regulatory violations. The auto the accused occupied was 'running with fictitious plates,' as the officer testified. The defendant and Cantu each claimed to have been the driver of the auto. The defendant did not have any driver's license and Cantu did not have a valid one. The officer observed rolls of coins on the floor of the auto and an adding machine on the rear seat of the car, partially covered by a coat. It was 2:00 A.M. Considering all of the circumstances surrounding the officer's encounter with the defendant and Cantu, the officer as a reasonably prudent person was justified in the belief that a crime, such as auto theft, burglary or knowing possession of stolen property, had been committed and that evidence confirming such belief could be found in the auto occupied by the defendant and Cantu. The search's validity was not impaired by the fact that the officer did not know of the specific offense that the search might disclose."

B. PROBABLE CAUSE FOR A WARRANT

ILLINOIS v. GATES

Supreme Court of the United States, 1983.
462 U.S. 213, 103 S.Ct. 2317.

JUSTICE REHNQUIST delivered the opinion of the Court.

Respondents Lance and Susan Gates were indicted for violation of state drug laws after police officers, executing a search warrant, discovered marijuana and other contraband in their automobile and home. Prior to trial the Gates' moved to suppress evidence seized during this search. The Illinois Supreme Court, 85 Ill.2d 376, 423 N.E.2d 887 (1981) affirmed the decisions of lower state courts, 82 Ill.App.3d 749, 403 N.E.2d 77 (1980) granting the motion. It held that the affidavit submitted in support of the State's application for a warrant to search the Gates' property was inadequate under this Court's decisions in Aguilar v. Texas, 378 U.S. 108, 84 S.Ct. 1509 (1964) and Spinelli v. United States, 393 U.S. 410, 89 S.Ct. 584 (1969).

We granted certiorari to consider the application of the Fourth Amendment to a magistrate's issuance of a search warrant on the basis of a partially corroborated anonymous informant's tip. After receiving briefs and hearing oral argument on this question, however, we requested the parties to address an additional question:

> "Whether the rule requiring the exclusion at a criminal trial of evidence obtained in violation of the Fourth Amendment, Mapp v. Ohio, 367 U.S. 643, 81 S.Ct. 1684 (1961); Weeks v. United States, 232 U.S. 383, 34 S.Ct. 341 (1914), should to any extent be modified, so as, for example, not to require the exclusion of

evidence obtained in the reasonable belief that the search and seizure at issue was consistent with the Fourth Amendment."

We decide today, with apologies to all, that the issue we framed for the parties was not presented to the Illinois courts and, accordingly, do not address it. Rather, we consider the question originally presented in the petition for certiorari, and conclude that the Illinois Supreme Court read the requirements of our Fourth Amendment decisions too restrictively. Initially, however, we set forth our reasons for not addressing the question regarding modification of the exclusionary rule framed in our order of November 29, 1982, ___ U.S. ___, 103 S.Ct. 436.

* * *

II

We now turn to the question presented in the State's original petition for certiorari, which requires us to decide whether respondents' rights under the Fourth and Fourteenth Amendments were violated by the search of their car and house. A chronological statement of events usefully introduces the issues at stake. Bloomingdale, Ill., is a suburb of Chicago located in DuPage County. On May 3, 1978, the Bloomingdale Police Department received by mail an anonymous handwritten letter which read as follows:

> "This letter is to inform you that you have a couple in your town who strictly make their living on selling drugs. They are Sue and Lance Gates, they live on Greenway, off Bloomingdale Rd. in the condominiums. Most of their buys are done in Florida. Sue his wife drives their car to Florida, where she leaves it to be loaded up with drugs, then Lance flys down and drives it back. Sue flys back after she drops the car off in Florida. May 3 she is driving down there again and Lance will be flying down in a few days to drive it back. At the time Lance drives the car back he has the trunk loaded with over $100,-000.00 in drugs. Presently they have over $100,000.00 worth of drugs in their basement.
>
> They brag about the fact they never have to work, and make their entire living on pushers.
>
> I guarantee if you watch them carefully you will make a big catch. They are friends with some big drugs dealers, who visit their house often.
>
> Lance & Susan Gates
> Greenway
> in Condominiums"

The letter was referred by the Chief of Police of the Bloomingdale Police Department to Detective Mader, who decided to pursue the tip. Mader learned, from the office of the Illinois Secretary of State, that an Illinois driver's license had been issued to one Lance Gates, residing at a stated address in Bloomingdale. He contacted a confidential informant, whose examination of certain financial records revealed a more recent address for the Gates, and he also learned from a police officer assigned to O'Hare Airport that "L. Gates" had made a reservation on Eastern Airlines flight 245 to West Palm Beach, Fla., scheduled to depart from Chicago on May 5 at 4:15 p.m.

Mader then made arrangements with an agent of the Drug Enforcement Administration for surveillance of the May 5 Eastern Airlines flight. The agent later reported to Mader that Gates had boarded the flight, and that federal agents in Florida had observed him arrive in West Palm Beach and take a taxi to the nearby Holiday Inn. They also reported that Gates went to a room registered to one Susan Gates and that, at 7:00 a.m. the next morning, Gates and an unidentified woman left the motel in a Mercury bearing Illinois license plates and drove northbound on an interstate frequently used by travelers to the Chicago area. In addition, the DEA agent informed Mader that the license plate number on the Mercury registered to a Hornet station wagon owned by Gates. The agent also advised Mader that the driving time between West Palm Beach and Bloomingdale was approximately 22 to 24 hours.

Mader signed an affidavit setting forth the foregoing facts, and submitted it to a judge of the Circuit Court of DuPage County, together with a copy of the anonymous letter. The judge of that court thereupon issued a search warrant for the Gates' residence and for their automobile. The judge, in deciding to issue the warrant, could have determined that the *modus operandi* of the Gates had been substantially corroborated. As the anonymous letter predicted, Lance Gates had flown from Chicago to West Palm Beach late in the afternoon of May 5th, had checked into a hotel room registered in the name of his wife, and, at 7:00 a.m. the following morning, had headed north, accompanied by an unidentified woman, out of West Palm Beach on an interstate highway used by travelers from South Florida to Chicago in an automobile bearing a license plate issued to him.

At 5:15 a.m. on March 7th, only 36 hours after he had flown out of Chicago, Lance Gates, and his wife, returned to their home in Bloomingdale, driving the car in which they had left West Palm Beach some 22 hours earlier. The Bloomingdale police were awaiting them, searched the trunk of the Mercury, and uncovered approximately 350 pounds of marijuana. A search of the Gates' home revealed marijuana, weapons, and other contraband. The Illinois Circuit Court ordered suppression of all these items, on the ground that the affidavit submitted to the Circuit Judge failed to support the necessary determination of probable cause to believe that the Gates' automobile and home contained the contraband in question. This decision was affirmed in turn by the Illinois Appellate Court and by a divided vote of the Supreme Court of Illinois.

The Illinois Supreme Court concluded—and we are inclined to agree—that, standing alone, the anonymous letter sent to the Bloomingdale Police Department would not provide the basis for a magistrate's determination that there was probable cause to believe contraband would be found in the Gates' car and home. The letter provides virtually nothing from which one might conclude that its author is either honest or his information reliable; likewise, the letter gives absolutely no indication of the basis for the writer's predictions regarding the Gates' criminal activities. Something more was required, then, before a magistrate could conclude that there was probable cause to believe that contraband would be found in the Gates' home and car.

The Illinois Supreme Court also properly recognized that Detective Mader's affidavit might be capable of supplementing the anonymous letter with information sufficient to permit a determination of probable cause. See Whiteley v. Warden, 401 U.S. 560, 567, 91 S.Ct. 1031, 1036 (1971). In holding that the affidavit in fact did not contain sufficient additional information to sustain a determination of probable cause, the Illinois court applied a "two-pronged test," derived from our decision in Spinelli v. United States, 393 U.S. 410, 89 S.Ct. 584 (1969).[1] The Illinois Supreme Court, like some others, apparently understood *Spinelli* as requiring that the anonymous letter satisfy each of two independent requirements before it could be relied on. According to this view, the letter, as supplemented by Mader's affidavit, first had to adequately reveal the "basis of knowledge" of the letter writer—the particular means by which he came by the information given in his report. Second, it had to provide facts sufficiently establishing either the "veracity" of the affiant's informant, or, alternatively, the "reliability" of the informant's report in this particular case.

The Illinois court, alluding to an elaborate set of legal rules that have developed among various lower courts to enforce the "two-pronged test,"[2] found that the test had not been satisfied. First, the "veracity"

1. In *Spinelli,* police officers observed Mr. Spinelli going to and from a particular apartment, which the telephone company said contained two telephones with stated numbers. The officers also were "informed by a confidential reliable informant that William Spinelli [was engaging in illegal gambling activities]" at the apartment, and that he used two phones, with numbers corresponding to those possessed by the police. The officers submitted an affidavit with this information to a magistrate and obtained a warrant to search Spinelli's apartment. We held that the magistrate could have made his determination of probable cause only by "abdicating his constitutional function," id., at 416, 89 S.Ct., at 589. The Government's affidavit contained absolutely no information regarding the informant's reliability. Thus, it did not satisfy *Aguilar*'s requirement that such affidavits contain "some of the underlying circumstances" indicating that "the informant ... was 'credible'" or that "his information [was] 'reliable.'" *Aguilar,* supra, 378 U.S., at 114, 84 S.Ct., at 1514. In addition, the tip failed to satisfy *Aguilar*'s requirement that it detail "some of the underlying circumstances from which the informant concluded that ... narcotics were where he claimed they were. We also held that if the tip concerning Spinelli had contained "sufficient detail" to permit the magistrate to conclude "that he [was] relying on something more substantial than a casual rumor circulating in the underworld or an accusation based merely on an individual's general reputation," 393 U.S., at 416, 89 S.Ct., at 589, then he properly could have relied on it; we thought, however, that the tip lacked the requisite detail to permit this "self-verifying detail" analysis.

2. See, e.g., Stanley v. State, 19 Md.App. 507, 313 A.2d 847 (Md.App.1974). In summary, these rules posit that the "veracity" prong of the *Spinelli* test has two "spurs"—the informant's "credibility" and the "reliability" of his information. Various interpretations are advanced for the

prong was not satisfied because, "there was simply no basis [for] ... conclud[ing] that the anonymous person [who wrote the letter to the Bloomingdale Police Department] was credible." The court indicated that corroboration by police of details contained in the letter might never satisfy the "veracity" prong, and in any event, could not do so if, as in the present case, only "innocent" details are corroborated. In addition, the letter gave no indication of the basis of its writer's knowledge of the Gates' activities. The Illinois court understood *Spinelli* as permitting the detail contained in a tip to be used to infer that the informant had a reliable basis for his statements, but it thought that the anonymous letter failed to provide sufficient detail to permit such an inference. Thus, it concluded that no showing of probable cause had been made.

We agree with the Illinois Supreme Court that an informant's "veracity," "reliability" and "basis of knowledge" are all highly relevant in determining the value of his report. We do not agree, however, that these elements should be understood as entirely separate and independent requirements to be rigidly exacted in every case,[3] which the opinion of the Supreme Court of Illinois would imply. Rather, as detailed below, they should be understood simply as closely intertwined issues that may usefully illuminate the commonsense, practical question whether there is "probable cause" to believe that contraband or evidence is located in a particular place.

III

This totality of the circumstances approach is far more consistent with our prior treatment of probable cause[4] than is any rigid demand

meaning of the "reliability" spur of the "veracity" prong. Both the "basis of knowledge" prong and the "veracity" prong are treated as entirely separate requirements, which must be independently satisfied in every case in order to sustain a determination of probable cause. Some ancillary doctrines are relied on to satisfy certain of the foregoing requirements. For example, the "self-verifying detail" of a tip may satisfy the "basis of knowledge" requirement, although not the "credibility" spur of the "veracity" prong. Conversely, corroboration would seem not capable of supporting the "basis of knowledge" prong, but only the "veracity" prong.

The decision in *Stanley,* while expressly approving and conscientiously attempting to apply the "two-pronged test" observes that "[t]he built-in subtleties [of the test] are such, however, that a slipshod application calls down upon us the fury of Murphy's Law." The decision also suggested that it is necessary "to evolve analogous guidelines [to hearsay rules employed in trial settings] for the reception of hearsay in a probable cause setting."

3. The entirely independent character that the *Spinelli* prongs have assumed is indicated both by the opinion of the Illinois Supreme Court in this case, and by decisions of other courts. One frequently cited decision, Stanley v. State, 19 Md.App. 507, 313 A.2d 847, 861 (Md.App.1974), remarks that "the dual requirements represented by the 'two-pronged test' are 'analytically severable' and an 'overkill' on one prong will not carry over to make up for a deficit on the other prong."

4. Our original phrasing of the so-called "two-pronged test" in Aguilar v. Texas, supra, suggests that the two prongs were intended simply as guides to a magistrate's determination of probable cause, not as inflexible, independent requirements applicable in every case. In *Aguilar,* we required only that:

> "... the magistrate must be informed of *some of the underlying circumstances* from which the informant concluded that ... narcotics were where he claimed they were, and *some of the underlying circumstances* from which the officer concluded that the informant ... was 'credible' or

that specific "tests" be satisfied by every informant's tip. Perhaps the central teaching of our decisions bearing on the probable cause standard is that it is a "practical, nontechnical conception." Brinegar v. United States, 338 U.S. 160, 176, 69 S.Ct. 1302, 1311 (1949). "In dealing with probable cause, ... as the very name implies, we deal with probabilities. These are not technical; they are the factual and practical considerations of everyday life on which reasonable and prudent men, not legal technicians, act." Our observation in United States v. Cortez, 449 U.S. 411, 418, 101 S.Ct. 690, 695 (1981), regarding "particularized suspicion," is also applicable to the probable cause standard:

> The process does not deal with hard certainties, but with probabilities. Long before the law of probabilities was articulated as such, practical people formulated certain common-sense conclusions about human behavior; jurors as factfinders are permitted to do the same—and so are law enforcement officers. Finally, the evidence thus collected must be seen and weighed not in terms of library analysis by scholars, but as understood by those versed in the field of law enforcement.

As these comments illustrate, probable cause is a fluid concept—turning on the assessment of probabilities in particular factual contexts—not readily, or even usefully, reduced to a neat set of legal rules. Informants' tips doubtless come in many shapes and sizes from many different types of persons. As we said in Adams v. Williams, 407 U.S. 143, 147, 92 S.Ct. 1921, 1924 (1972), "Informants' tips, like all other clues and evidence coming to a policeman on the scene may vary greatly in their value and reliability." Rigid legal rules are ill-suited to an area of such diversity. "One simple rule will not cover every situation." [5]

his information 'reliable.'" (Emphasis added.)

As our language indicates, we intended neither a rigid compartmentalization of the inquiries into an informant's "veracity," "reliability" and "basis of knowledge," nor that these inquiries be elaborate exegeses of an informant's tip. Rather, we required only that *some* facts bearing on two particular issues be provided to the magistrate. Our decision in Jaben v. United States, 381 U.S. 214, 85 S.Ct. 1365 (1965), demonstrated this latter point. We held there that a criminal complaint showed probable cause to believe the defendant had attempted to evade the payment of income taxes. We commented that:

> "Obviously any reliance upon factual allegations necessarily entails some degree of reliability upon the credibility of the source.... Nor does it indicate that each factual allegation which the affiant puts forth must be independently documented, or that each and every fact which contributed to his conclusions be spelled out in the complaint.... *It simply requires that enough information be presented to the Commissioner to enable him to make the judgment that the charges are not capricious and are sufficiently supported to justify bringing into play the further steps of the criminal process.*" (Emphasis added).

5. The diversity of informants' tips, as well as the usefulness of the totality of the circumstances approach to probable cause, is reflected in our prior decisions on the subject. In Jones v. United States, 362 U.S. 257, 271, 80 S.Ct. 725, 736 (1960), we held that probable cause to search petitioners' apartment was established by an affidavit based principally on an informant's tip. The unnamed informant claimed to have purchased narcotics from petitioners at their apartment; the affiant stated that he had been given correct information from the informant on a prior occasion. This, and the fact that petitioners had admitted to police officers on another occasion that they were narcotics users, sufficed to support the magistrate's determination of probable cause.

Moreover, the "two-pronged test" directs analysis into two largely independent channels—the informant's "veracity" or "reliability" and his "basis of knowledge." There are persuasive arguments against according these two elements such independent status. Instead, they are better understood as relevant considerations in the totality of circumstances analysis that traditionally has guided probable cause determinations: a deficiency in one may be compensated for, in determining the overall reliability of a tip, by a strong showing as to the other, or by some other indicia of reliability. See, e.g., Adams v. Williams, supra, 407 U.S., at 146–147, 92 S.Ct., at 1923–1924; Harris v. United States, 403 U.S. 573, 91 S.Ct. 2075 (1971).

If, for example, a particular informant is known for the unusual reliability of his predictions of certain types of criminal activities in a locality, his failure, in a particular case, to thoroughly set forth the basis of his knowledge surely should not serve as an absolute bar to a finding of probable cause based on his tip. See United States v. Sellers, 483 F.2d 37 (CA5 1973).[6] Likewise, if an unquestionably honest citizen comes forward with a report of criminal activity—which if fabricated would subject him to criminal liability—we have found rigorous scrutiny of the basis of his knowledge unnecessary. Conversely, even if we entertain some doubt as to an informant's motives, his explicit and detailed description of alleged wrongdoing, along with a statement that the event was observed first-hand, entitles his tip to greater weight than might otherwise be the case. Unlike a totality of circumstances analysis, which permits a balanced assessment of the relative weights of all the various indicia of reliability (and unreliability) attending an informant's tip, the "two-pronged test" has encouraged an excessively technical

Likewise, in Rugendorf v. United States, 376 U.S. 528, 84 S.Ct. 825 (1964), the Court upheld a magistrate's determination that there was probable cause to believe that certain stolen property would be found in petitioner's apartment. The affidavit submitted to the magistrate stated that certain furs had been stolen, and that a confidential informant, who previously had furnished confidential information, said that he saw the furs in petitioner's home. Moreover, another confidential informant, also claimed to be reliable, stated that one Schweihs had stolen the furs. Police reports indicated that petitioner had been seen in Schweihs' company and a third informant stated that petitioner was a fence for Schweihs.

Finally, in Ker v. California, 374 U.S. 23, 83 S.Ct. 1623 (1963), we held that information within the knowledge of officers who searched the Ker's apartment provided them with probable cause to believe drugs would be found there. The officers were aware that one Murphy had previously sold marijuana to a police officer; the transaction had occurred in an isolated area, to which Murphy had led the police. The night after this transaction, police observed Ker and Murphy meet in the same location. Murphy approached Ker's car, and, although police could see nothing change hands, Murphy's *modus operandi* was identical to what it had been the night before. Moreover, when police followed Ker from the scene of the meeting with Murphy he managed to lose them after performing an abrupt U-turn. Finally, the police had a statement from an informant who had provided reliable information previously, that Ker was engaged in selling marijuana, and that his source was Murphy. We concluded that "To say that this coincidence of information was sufficient to support a reasonable belief of the officers that Ker was illegally in possession of marijuana is to indulge in understatement."

6. Compare Stanley v. State, 19 Md. App. 507, 313 A.2d 847, 861 (Md.App.1974), reasoning that "Even assuming 'credibility' amounting to sainthood, the judge still may not accept the bare conclusion of a sworn and known and trusted police-affiant."

dissection of informants' tips,[7] with undue attention being focused on isolated issues that cannot sensibly be divorced from the other facts presented to the magistrate.

As early as Locke v. United States, 7 Cranch. 339, 348 (1813), Chief Justice Marshall observed, in a closely related context, that "the term 'probable cause,' according to its usual acceptation, means less than evidence which would justify condemnation.... It imports a seizure made under circumstances which warrant suspicion." More recently, we said that "the *quanta* ... of proof" appropriate in ordinary judicial proceedings are inapplicable to the decision to issue a warrant. *Brinegar,* supra, at 173, 1309. Finely-tuned standards such as proof beyond a reasonable doubt or by a preponderance of the evidence, useful in formal trials, have no place in the magistrate's decision. While an effort to fix some general, numerically precise degree of certainty corresponding to "probable cause" may not be helpful, it is clear that "only the probability, and not a prima facie showing, of criminal activity is the standard of probable cause." *Spinelli,* supra, at 419, 590. See Model Code of Pre-Arraignment Procedure § 210.1(7) (Proposed Off. Draft 1972); W. LaFave, Search and Seizure, § 3.2(3) (1978).

We also have recognized that affidavits "are normally drafted by nonlawyers in the midst and haste of a criminal investigation. Technical requirements of elaborate specificity once exacted under common law pleading have no proper place in this area." Likewise, search and arrest warrants long have been issued by persons who are neither lawyers nor judges, and who certainly do not remain abreast of each judicial refinement of the nature of "probable cause." See Shadwick v. City of Tampa, 407 U.S. 345, 348–350, 92 S.Ct. 2119, 2121–2122 (1972). The rigorous inquiry into the *Spinelli* prongs and the complex superstructure of evidentiary and analytical rules that some have seen implicit in our

7. Some lower court decisions, brought to our attention by the State, reflect a rigid application of such rules. In Bridger v. State, 503 S.W.2d 801 (Tex.Cr.App.1974), the affiant had received a confession of armed robbery from one of two suspects in the robbery; in addition, the suspect had given the officer $800 in cash stolen during the robbery. The suspect also told the officer that the gun used in the robbery was hidden in the other suspect's apartment. A warrant issued on the basis of this was invalidated on the ground that the affidavit did not satisfactorily describe how the accomplice had obtained his information regarding the gun.

Likewise, in People v. Palanza, 55 Ill. App.3d 1028, 371 N.E.2d 687 (Ill.App.1978), the affidavit submitted in support of an application for a search warrant stated that an informant of proven and uncontested reliability had seen, in specifically described premises, "a quantity of a white crystalline substance which was represented to the informant by a white male occupant of the premises to be cocaine. Informant has observed cocaine on numerous occasions in the past and is thoroughly familiar with its appearance. The informant states that the white crystalline powder he observed in the above described premises appeared to him to be cocaine." The warrant issued on the basis of the affidavit was invalidated because "There is no indication as to how the informant or for that matter any other person could tell whether a white substance was cocaine and not some other substance such as sugar or salt."

Finally, in People v. Brethauer, 174 Colo. 29, 482 P.2d 369 (Colo.1971), an informant, stated to have supplied reliable information in the past, claimed that L.S.D. and marijuana were located on certain premises. The affiant supplied police with drugs, which were tested by police and confirmed to be illegal substances. The affidavit setting forth these, and other, facts was found defective under both prongs of *Spinelli.*

Spinelli decision, cannot be reconciled with the fact that many warrants are—quite properly, ibid.—issued on the basis of nontechnical, commonsense judgments of laymen applying a standard less demanding than those used in more formal legal proceedings. Likewise, given the informal, often hurried context in which it must be applied, the "built-in subtleties," Stanley v. State, 19 Md.App. 507, 313 A.2d 847, 860 (Md. App.1974), of the "two-pronged test" are particularly unlikely to assist magistrates in determining probable cause.

Similarly, we have repeatedly said that after-the-fact scrutiny by courts of the sufficiency of an affidavit should not take the form of *de novo* review. A magistrate's "determination of probable cause should be paid great deference by reviewing courts." *Spinelli,* supra. "A grudging or negative attitude by reviewing courts toward warrants," *Ventresca,* supra, is inconsistent with the Fourth Amendment's strong preference for searches conducted pursuant to a warrant "courts should not invalidate ... warrant[s] by interpreting affidavit[s] in a hypertechnical, rather than a commonsense, manner."

If the affidavits submitted by police officers are subjected to the type of scrutiny some courts have deemed appropriate, police might well resort to warrantless searches, with the hope of relying on consent or some other exception to the warrant clause that might develop at the time of the search. In addition, the possession of a warrant by officers conducting an arrest or search greatly reduces the perception of unlawful or intrusive police conduct, by assuring "the individual whose property is searched or seized of the lawful authority of the executing officer, his need to search, and the limits of his power to search." United States v. Chadwick, 433 U.S. 1, 9, 97 S.Ct. 2476, 2482 (1977). Reflecting this preference for the warrant process, the traditional standard for review of an issuing magistrate's probable cause determination has been that so long as the magistrate had a "substantial basis for ... conclud[ing]" that a search would uncover evidence of wrongdoing, the Fourth Amendment requires no more. Jones v. United States, 362 U.S. 257, 271, 80 S.Ct. 725, 736 (1960).[8] We think reaffirmation of this standard better serves the purpose of encouraging recourse to the warrant procedure and is more consistent with our traditional deference to the probable cause determinations of magistrates than is the "two-pronged test."

Finally, the direction taken by decisions following *Spinelli* poorly serves "the most basic function of any government": "to provide for the security of the individual and of his property." The strictures that

8. We also have said that "Although in a particular case it may not be easy to determine when an affidavit demonstrates the existence of probable cause, the resolution of doubtful or marginal cases in this area should be largely determined by the preference to be accorded to warrants." This reflects both a desire to encourage use of the warrant process by police officers and a recognition that once a warrant has been obtained, intrusion upon interests protected by the Fourth Amendment is less severe than otherwise may be the case. Even if we were to accept the premise that the accurate assessment of probable cause would be furthered by the "two-pronged test," which we do not, these Fourth Amendment policies would require a less rigorous standard than that which appears to have been read into *Aguilar* and *Spinelli.*

inevitably accompany the "two-pronged test" cannot avoid seriously impeding the task of law enforcement. If, as the Illinois Supreme Court apparently thought, that test must be rigorously applied in every case, anonymous tips seldom would be of greatly diminished [sic] value in police work. Ordinary citizens, like ordinary witnesses, see Federal Rules of Evidence 701, Advisory Committee Note (1976), generally do not provide extensive recitations of the basis of their everyday observations. Likewise, as the Illinois Supreme Court observed in this case, the veracity of persons supplying anonymous tips is by hypothesis largely unknown, and unknowable. As a result, anonymous tips seldom could survive a rigorous application of either of the *Spinelli* prongs. Yet, such tips, particularly when supplemented by independent police investigation, frequently contribute to the solution of otherwise "perfect crimes." While a conscientious assessment of the basis for crediting such tips is required by the Fourth Amendment, a standard that leaves virtually no place for anonymous citizen informants is not.

For all these reasons, we conclude that it is wiser to abandon the "two-pronged test" established by our decisions in *Aguilar* and *Spinelli.*[9] In its place we reaffirm the totality of the circumstances analysis that traditionally has informed probable cause determinations. The task of the issuing magistrate is simply to make a practical, common-sense decision whether, given all the circumstances set forth in the affidavit before him, including the "veracity" and "basis of knowledge" of persons supplying hearsay information, there is a fair probability that contraband or evidence of a crime will be found in a particular place. And the duty of a reviewing court is simply to ensure that the magistrate had a "substantial basis for ... conclud[ing]" that probable cause existed. Jones v. United States, supra. We are convinced that this flexible, easily applied standard will better achieve the accommodation of public and private interests that the Fourth Amendment requires than does the approach that has developed from *Aguilar* and *Spinelli.*

Our earlier cases illustrate the limits beyond which a magistrate may not venture in issuing a warrant. A sworn statement of an affiant that "he has cause to suspect and does believe that" liquor illegally brought into the United States is located on certain premises will not do. Nathanson v. United States, 290 U.S. 41, 54 S.Ct. 11, 78 L.Ed. 159

9. The Court's decision in *Spinelli* has been the subject of considerable criticism, both by members of this Court and others. Justice BLACKMUN, concurring in United States v. Harris, supra, noted his long-held view "that *Spinelli* ... was wrongly decided" by this Court. Justice Black similarly would have overruled that decision. Likewise, a noted commentator has observed that "[t]he *Aguilar-Spinelli* formulation has provoked apparently ceaseless litigation."

Whether the allegations submitted to the magistrate in *Spinelli* would, under the view we now take, have supported a finding of probable cause, we think it would not be profitable to decide. There are so many variables in the probable cause equation that one determination will seldom be a useful "precedent" for another. Suffice it to say that while we in no way abandon *Spinelli*'s concern for the trustworthiness of informers and for the principle that it is the magistrate who must ultimately make a finding of probable cause, we reject the rigid categorization suggested by some of its language.

(1933). An affidavit must provide the magistrate with a substantial basis for determining the existence of probable cause, and the wholly conclusory statement at issue in *Nathanson* failed to meet this requirement. An officer's statement that "affiants have received reliable information from a credible person and believe" that heroin is stored in a home, is likewise inadequate. Aguilar v. Texas (1964). As in *Nathanson,* this is a mere conclusory statement that gives the magistrate virtually no basis at all for making a judgment regarding probable cause. Sufficient information must be presented to the magistrate to allow that official to determine probable cause; his action cannot be a mere ratification of the bare conclusions of others. In order to ensure that such an abdication of the magistrate's duty does not occur, courts must continue to conscientiously review the sufficiency of affidavits on which warrants are issued. But when we move beyond the "bare bones" affidavits present in cases such as *Nathanson* and *Aguilar,* this area simply does not lend itself to a prescribed set of rules, like that which had developed from *Spinelli.* Instead, the flexible, common-sense standard articulated in *Jones, Ventresca,* and *Brinegar* better serves the purposes of the Fourth Amendment's probable cause requirement.

Justice Brennan's dissent suggests in several places that the approach we take today somehow downgrades the role of the neutral magistrate, because *Aguilar* and *Spinelli* "preserve the role of magistrates as independent arbiters of probable cause. . . . " Quite the contrary, we believe, is the case. The essential protection of the warrant requirement of the Fourth Amendment, as stated in Johnson v. United States, 333 U.S. 10, 68 S.Ct. 367 (1948), is in "requiring that [the usual inferences which reasonable men draw from evidence] be drawn by a neutral and detached magistrate instead of being judged by the officer engaged in the often competitive enterprise of ferreting out crime." Nothing in our opinion in any way lessens the authority of the magistrate to draw such reasonable inferences as he will from the material supplied to him by applicants for a warrant; indeed, he is freer than under the regime of *Aguilar* and *Spinelli* to draw such inferences, or to refuse to draw them if he is so minded.

The real gist of Justice Brennan's criticism seems to be a second argument, somewhat at odds with the first, that magistrates should be restricted in their authority to make probable cause determinations by the standards laid down in *Aguilar* and *Spinelli,* and that such findings "should not be authorized unless there is some assurance that the information on which they are based has been obtained in a reliable way by an honest or credible person." However, under our opinion magistrates remain perfectly free to exact such assurances as they deem necessary, as well as those required by this opinion, in making probable cause determinations. Justice Brennan would apparently prefer that magistrates be restricted in their findings of probable cause by the development of an elaborate body of case law dealing with the "veracity" prong of the *Spinelli* test, which in turn is broken down into two "spurs"—the informant's "credibility" and the "reliability" of his information, together with the "basis of knowledge" prong of the *Spinelli* test. See n. 4, supra. That such a labyrinthine body of judicial refinement bears any relationship to familiar definitions of probable cause is hard to imagine. Probable cause deals "with probabilities. These are not technical; they are the factual and practical considerations of everyday life on which reasonable and prudent men, not legal technicians, act," Brinegar v. United States, supra.

Justice Brennan's dissent also suggests that "words such as 'practical,' 'nontechnical,' and 'common sense,' as used in the Court's opinion, are but code words for an overly-permissive attitude towards police practices in derogation of the rights secured by the Fourth Amendment." An easy, but not a complete, answer to this rather florid statement would be that nothing we know about Justice Rutledge suggests that he would have used the words he chose in *Brinegar* in such a manner. More fundamentally, no one doubts that "under our Constitution only measures consistent with the Fourth Amendment may be employed by government to cure [the horrors of drug trafficking];" but this agreement does not advance the inquiry as to which measures are, and which measures are not, consistent with the Fourth Amendment. "Fidelity" to the commands of the Constitution suggests balanced judgment rather than exhortation. The highest "fidelity" is achieved neither by the judge who instinctively goes furthest in upholding even the most bizzare claim of individual constitutional rights, any more than it is achieved by a judge who instinctively goes furthest in accepting the most restrictive claims of governmental authorities. The task of this Court, as of other courts, is to "hold the balance true," and we think we have done that in this case.

IV

Our decisions applying the totality of circumstances analysis outlined above have consistently recognized the value of corroboration of details of an informant's tip by independent police work. In Jones v. United States, supra, we held that an affidavit relying on hearsay "is not to be deemed insufficient on that score, so long as a substantial basis for crediting the hearsay is presented." We went on to say that even in making a warrantless arrest an officer "may rely upon information received through an informant, rather than upon his direct observations, so long as the informant's statement is reasonably corroborated by other matters within the officer's knowledge." Likewise, we recognized the probative value of corroborative efforts of police officials in *Aguilar* —the source of the "two-pronged test"—by observing that if the police had made some effort to corroborate the informant's report at issue, "an entirely different case" would have been presented.

Our decision in Draper v. United States, 358 U.S. 307, 79 S.Ct. 329 (1959), however, is the classic case on the value of corroborative efforts of police officials. There, an informant named Hereford reported that Draper would arrive in Denver on a train from Chicago on one of two days, and that he would be carrying a quantity of heroin. The informant also supplied a fairly detailed physical description of Draper, and predicted that he would be wearing a light colored raincoat, brown slacks and black shoes, and would be walking "real fast." Hereford gave no indication of the basis for his information.[10]

On one of the stated dates police officers observed a man matching this description exit a train arriving from Chicago; his attire and luggage matched Hereford's report and he was walking rapidly. We explained in *Draper* that, by this point in his investigation, the arresting officer "had personally verified every facet of the information given him by Hereford except whether petitioner had accomplished his mission and had the three ounces of heroin on his person or in his bag. And surely, with every other bit of Hereford's information being thus personally verified, [the officer] had 'reasonable grounds' to believe that the remaining unverified bit of Hereford's information—that Draper would have the heroin with him—was likewise true."

The showing of probable cause in the present case was fully as compelling as that in *Draper*. Even standing alone, the facts obtained through the independent investigation of Mader and the DEA at least suggested that the Gates were involved in drug trafficking. In addition to being a popular vacation site, Florida is well-known as a source of narcotics and other illegal drugs. See United States v. Mendenhall, 446 U.S. 544, 562, 100 S.Ct. 1870, 1881 (1980) (Powell, J., concurring); DEA, Narcotics Intelligence Estimate, The Supply of Drugs to the U.S. Illicit Market From Foreign and Domestic Sources 10 (1979). Lance Gates' flight to Palm Beach, his brief, overnight stay in a motel, and apparent immediate return north to Chicago in the family car, conveniently awaiting him in West Palm Beach, is as suggestive of a pre-arranged drug run, as it is of an ordinary vacation trip.

In addition, the magistrate could rely on the anonymous letter, which had been corroborated in major part by Mader's efforts—just as had occurred in *Draper*.[11] The Supreme Court of Illinois reasoned that

10. The tip in *Draper* might well not have survived the rigid application of the "two-pronged test" that developed following *Spinelli*. The only reference to Hereford's reliability was that he had "been engaged as a 'special employee' of the Bureau of Narcotics at Denver for about six months, and from time to time gave information to [the police] for small sums of money, and that [the officer] had always found the information given by Hereford to be accurate and reliable." Likewise, the tip gave no indication of how Hereford came by his information. At most, the detailed and accurate predictions in the tip indicated that, however Hereford obtained his information, it was reliable.

11. The Illinois Supreme Court thought that the verification of details contained in the anonymous letter in this case amounted only to "the corroboration of innocent activity," J.A. 12a, and that this was insufficient to support a finding of probable cause. We are inclined to agree, however, with the observation of Justice Moran in his dissenting opinion that "In this case, just as in *Draper*, seemingly innocent activity became suspicious in the light of the initial tip." J.A. 18a. And it bears noting that *all* of the corroborating detail established in *Draper*, supra, was of entirely innocent activity—a fact later pointed out by the Court in both Jones v. United States, 362 U.S. 257, 269–270, 80 S.Ct. 725, 735–736 (1960), and Ker v. California, 374 U.S. 23, 36, 83 S.Ct. 1623, 1631 (1963).

This is perfectly reasonable. As discussed previously, probable cause requires only a probability or substantial chance of criminal activity, not an actual showing of such activity. By hypothesis, therefore, in-

Draper involved an informant who had given reliable information on previous occasions, while the honesty and reliability of the anonymous informant in this case were unknown to the Bloomingdale police. While this distinction might be an apt one at the time the police department received the anonymous letter, it became far less significant after Mader's independent investigative work occurred. The corroboration of the letter's predictions that the Gates' car would be in Florida, that Lance Gates would fly to Florida in the next day or so, and that he would drive the car north toward Bloomingdale all indicated, albeit not with certainty, that the informant's other assertions also were true. "Because an informant is right about some things, he is more probably right about other facts," *Spinelli,* supra, including the claim regarding the Gates' illegal activity. This may well not be the type of "reliability" or "veracity" necessary to satisfy some views of the "veracity prong" of *Spinelli,* but we think it suffices for the practical, common-sense judgment called for in making a probable cause determination. It is enough, for purposes of assessing probable cause, that "corroboration through other sources of information reduced the chances of a reckless or prevaricating tale," thus providing "a substantial basis for crediting the hearsay."

Finally, the anonymous letter contained a range of details relating not just to easily obtained facts and conditions existing at the time of the tip, but to future actions of third parties ordinarily not easily predicted. The letter writer's accurate information as to the travel plans of each of the Gates was of a character likely obtained only from the Gates themselves, or from someone familiar with their not entirely ordinary travel plans. If the informant had access to accurate information of this type a magistrate could properly conclude that it was not unlikely that he also had access to reliable information of the Gates' alleged illegal activities.[12] Of course, the Gates' travel plans might have been learned

nocent behavior frequently will provide the basis for a showing of probable cause; to require otherwise would be to *sub silentio* impose a drastically more rigorous definition of probable cause than the security of our citizens demands. We think the Illinois court attempted a too rigid classification of the types of conduct that may be relied upon in seeking to demonstrate probable cause. See Brown v. Texas, 443 U.S. 47, 52, n. 2, 99 S.Ct. 2637, 2641, n. 2 (1979). In making a determination of probable cause the relevant inquiry is not whether particular conduct is "innocent" or "guilty," but the degree of suspicion that attaches to particular types of non-criminal acts.

12. The dissent seizes on one inaccuracy in the anonymous informant's letter—its statement that Sue Gates would fly from Florida to Illinois, when in fact she drove—and argues that the probative value of the entire tip was undermined by this allegedly "material mistake." We have never required that informants used by the police be infallible, and can see no reason to impose such a requirement in this case. Probable cause, particularly when police have obtained a warrant, simply does not require the perfection the dissent finds necessary.

Likewise, there is no force to the dissent's argument that the Gates' action in leaving their home unguarded undercut the informant's claim that drugs were hidden there. Indeed, the line-by-line scrutiny that the dissent applies to the anonymous letter is akin to that we find inappropriate in reviewing magistrate's decisions. The dissent apparently attributes to the magistrate who issued the warrant in this case the rather implausible notion that persons dealing in drugs always stay at home, apparently out of fear that to leave might risk intrusion by criminals. If accurate, one could not help

from a talkative neighbor or travel agent; under the "two-pronged test" developed from *Spinelli,* the character of the details in the anonymous letter might well not permit a sufficiently clear inference regarding the letter writer's "basis of knowledge." But, as discussed previously, supra, 2332, probable cause does not demand the certainty we associate with formal trials. It is enough that there was a fair probability that the writer of the anonymous letter had obtained his entire story either from the Gates or someone they trusted. And corroboration of major portions of the letter's predictions provides just this probability. It is apparent, therefore, that the judge issuing the warrant had a "substantial basis for ... conclud[ing]" that probable cause to search the Gates' home and car existed. The judgment of the Supreme Court of Illinois therefore must be

Reversed.

JUSTICE WHITE, concurring in the judgment.

In my view, the question regarding modification of the exclusionary rule framed in our order of November 29, 1982, is properly before us and should be addressed. I continue to believe that the exclusionary rule is an inappropriate remedy where law enforcement officials act in the reasonable belief that a search and seizure was consistent with the Fourth Amendment—a position I set forth in Stone v. Powell, 428 U.S. 465, 537–539, 96 S.Ct. 3027, 3032–3033 (1976). In this case, it was fully reasonable for the Bloomingdale, Illinois police to believe that their search of respondents' house and automobile comported with the Fourth Amendment as the search was conducted pursuant to a judicially-issued warrant. The exclusion of probative evidence where the constable has *not* blundered not only sets the criminal free but also fails to serve any constitutional interest in securing compliance with the important requirements of the Fourth Amendment. On this basis, I concur in the Court's judgment that the decision of the Illinois Supreme Court must be reversed.

III

Since a majority of the Court deems it inappropriate to address the good faith issue, I briefly address the question that the Court does reach—whether the warrant authorizing the search and seizure of respondents' car and home was constitutionally valid. Abandoning the "two-pronged test" of *Aguilar* and *Spinelli,* the Court upholds the validity of the warrant under a new "totality of the circumstances"

sympathizing with the self-imposed isolation of people so situated. In reality, however, it is scarcely likely that the magistrate ever thought that the anonymous tip "kept one spouse" at home, much less that he relied on the theory advanced by the dissent. The letter simply says that Sue would fly from Florida to Illinois, without indicating whether the Gates made the bitter choice of leaving the drugs in their house, or those in their car, unguarded. The magistrate's determination that there might be drugs or evidence of criminal activity in the Gates' home was well-supported by the less speculative theory, noted in text, that if the informant could predict with considerable accuracy the somewhat unusual travel plans of the Gates, he probably also had a reliable basis for his statements that the Gates kept a large quantity of drugs in their home and frequently were visited by other drug traffickers there.

approach. Although I agree that the warrant should be upheld, I reach this conclusion in accordance with the *Aguilar-Spinelli* framework.

A

For present purposes, the *Aguilar-Spinelli* rules can be summed up as follows. First, an affidavit based on an informer's tip, standing alone, cannot provide probable cause for issuance of a warrant unless the tip includes information that apprises the magistrate of the informant's basis for concluding that the contraband is where he claims it is (the "basis of knowledge" prong), *and* the affiant informs the magistrate of his basis for believing that the informant is credible (the "veracity" prong).[13] Second, if a tip fails under either or both of the two prongs, probable cause may yet be established by independent police investigatory work that corroborates the tip to such an extent that it supports "both the inference that the informer was generally trustworthy and that he made his charge on the basis of information obtained in a reliable way." *Spinelli,* supra. In instances where the officers rely on corroboration, the ultimate question is whether the corroborated tip "is as trustworthy as a tip which would pass *Aguilar's* tests without independent corroboration."

In the present case, it is undisputed that the anonymous tip, by itself, did not furnish probable cause. The question is whether those portions of the affidavit describing the results of the police investigation of the respondents, when considered in light of the tip, "would permit the suspicions engendered by the informant's report to ripen into a judgment that a crime was probably being committed." *Spinelli,* supra. The Illinois Supreme Court concluded that the corroboration was insufficient to permit such a ripening. The court reasoned as follows:

> "[T]he nature of the corroborating evidence in this case would satisfy neither the 'basis of knowledge' nor the 'veracity' prong of *Aguilar.* Looking to the affidavit submitted as support for Detective Mader's request that a search warrant issue, we note that the corroborative evidence here was only of innocent activity. Mader's independent investigation revealed only that Lance and Sue Gates lived on Greenway Drive; that Lance Gates booked passage on a flight to Florida; that upon arriving he entered a room registered to his wife; and that he and his wife left the hotel together by car. The corroboration of innocent activity is insufficient to support a finding of probable cause."

13. The "veracity" prong is satisfied by a recitation in the affidavit that the informant previously supplied accurate information to the police, or by proof that the informant gave his information against his penal interest. The "basis of knowledge" prong is satisfied by a statement from the informant that he personally observed the criminal activity, or, if he came by the information indirectly, by a satisfactory explanation of why his sources were reliable, or, in the absence of a statement detailing the manner in which the information was gathered, by a description of the accused's criminal activity in sufficient detail that the magistrate may infer that the informant is relying on something more substantial than casual rumor or an individual's general reputation.

In my view, the lower court's characterization of the Gates' activity here as totally "innocent" is dubious. In fact, the behavior was quite suspicious. I agree with the Court that Lance Gates' flight to Palm Beach, an area known to be a source of narcotics, the brief overnight stay in a motel, and apparent immediate return North, suggest a pattern that trained law-enforcement officers have recognized as indicative of illicit drug-dealing activity.

Even, however, had the corroboration related only to completely innocuous activities, this fact alone would not preclude the issuance of a valid warrant. The critical issue is not whether the activities observed by the police are innocent or suspicious. Instead, the proper focus should be on whether the actions of the suspects, whatever their nature, give rise to an inference that the informant is credible and that he obtained his information in a reliable manner.

Thus, in Draper v. United States, supra, an informant stated on Sept. 7 that Draper would be carrying narcotics when he arrived by train in Denver on the morning of Sept. 8 or Sept. 9. The informant also provided the police with a detailed physical description of the clothes Draper would be wearing when he alighted from the train. The police observed Draper leaving a train on the morning of Sept. 9, and he was wearing the precise clothing described by the informant. The Court held that the police had probable cause to arrest Draper at this point, even though the police had seen nothing more than the totally innocent act of a man getting off a train carrying a briefcase. As we later explained in *Spinelli,* the important point was that the corroboration showed both that the informant was credible, i.e. that he "had not been fabricating his report out of whole cloth," *Spinelli,* supra, 393 U.S., at 417, 89 S.Ct., at 589, and that he had an adequate basis of knowledge for his allegations, "since the report was of the sort which in common experience may be recognized as having been obtained in a reliable way." The fact that the informer was able to predict, two days in advance, the exact clothing Draper would be wearing dispelled the possibility that his tip was just based on rumor or "an off-hand remark heard at a neighborhood bar." Probably Draper had planned in advance to wear these specific clothes so that an accomplice could identify him. A clear inference could therefore be drawn that the informant was either involved in the criminal scheme himself or that he otherwise had access to reliable, inside information.[14]

14. Thus, as interpreted in *Spinelli,* the Court in *Draper* held that there was probable cause because "the kind of information related by the informant [was] not generally sent ahead of a person's arrival in a city except to those who are intimately connected with making careful arrangements for meeting him." *Spinelli,* supra, 393 U.S., at 426, 89 S.Ct., at 594 (White, J., concurring). As I said in *Spinelli,* the conclusion that *Draper* itself was based on this fact is far from inescapable. Prior to *Spinelli, Draper* was susceptible to the interpretation that it stood for the proposition that "the existence of the tenth and critical fact is made sufficiently probable to justify the issuance of a warrant by verifying nine other facts coming from the same source." *Spinelli,* supra, at 426–427, 89 S.Ct., at 594–595 (White, J., concurring). But it now seems clear that the Court in *Spinelli* rejected this reading of *Draper.*

Justice Brennan, post, at 2354–2355, erroneously interprets my *Spinelli* concur-

As in *Draper,* the police investigation in the present case satisfactorily demonstrated that the informant's tip was as trustworthy as one that would alone satisfy the *Aguilar* tests. The tip predicted that Sue Gates would drive to Florida, that Lance Gates would fly there a few days after May 3, and that Lance would then drive the car back. After the police corroborated these facts,[15] the magistrate could reasonably have inferred, as he apparently did, that the informant, who had specific knowledge of these unusual travel plans, did not make up his story and that he obtained his information in a reliable way. It is theoretically possible, as respondents insist, that the tip could have been supplied by a "vindictive travel agent" and that the Gates' activities, although unusual, might not have been unlawful.[16] But *Aguilar* and *Spinelli,* like our other cases, do not require that certain guilt be established before a warrant may properly be issued. "[O]nly the probability, and not a prima facie showing, of criminal activity is the standard of probable cause." *Spinelli,* supra, at 419, 89 S.Ct., at 590 (citing Beck v. Ohio, 379 U.S. 89, 96, 85 S.Ct. 223, 228, 13 L.Ed.2d 142 (1964)). I therefore conclude that the judgment of the Illinois Supreme Court invalidating the warrant must be reversed.

B

The Court agrees that the warrant was valid, but, in the process of reaching this conclusion, it overrules the *Aguilar-Spinelli* tests and replaces them with a "totality of the circumstances" standard. As shown above, it is not at all necessary to overrule *Aguilar-Spinelli* in order to reverse the judgment below. Therefore, because I am inclined to believe that, when applied properly, the *Aguilar-Spinelli* rules play an appropriate role in probable cause determinations, and because the Court's holding may foretell an evisceration of the probable cause standard, I do not join the Court's holding.

The Court reasons, that the "veracity" and "basis of knowledge" tests are not independent, and that a deficiency as to one can be compensated for by a strong showing as to the other. Thus, a finding of

rence as espousing the view that "corroboration of certain details in a tip may be sufficient to satisfy the veracity, but not the basis of knowledge, prong of *Aguilar.*" Others have made the same mistake. See, e.g., Comment, 20 Am.Crim.L.Rev. 99, 105 (1982). I did not say that corroboration could *never* satisfy the basis of knowledge prong. My concern was, and still is, that the prong might be deemed satisfied on the basis of corroboration of information that does not in any way suggest that the informant had an adequate basis of knowledge for his report. If, however, as in *Draper,* the police corroborate information from which it can be inferred that the informant's tip was grounded on inside information, this corroboration is sufficient to satisfy the basis of knowledge prong. *Spinelli,* supra, at 426, 89 S.Ct., at 594 (White, J., concurring). The rules would indeed be strange if, as Justice Brennan suggests, post, at 2356, the basis of knowledge prong could be satisfied by detail in the tip alone, but not by independent police work.

15. Justice Stevens is correct, post, at 2360, that one of the informant's predictions proved to be inaccurate. However, I agree with the Court, ante, at 2335, n. 14, that an informant need not be infallible.

16. It is also true, as Justice Stevens points out, post, at 2360, n. 3, that the fact that respondents were last seen leaving West Palm Beach on a northbound interstate highway is far from conclusive proof that they were heading directly to Bloomingdale.

probable cause may be based on a tip from an informant "known for the unusual reliability of his predictions" or from "an unquestionably honest citizen," even if the report fails thoroughly to set forth the basis upon which the information was obtained. If this is so, then it must follow *a fortiori* that "the affidavit of an officer, known by the magistrate to be honest and experienced, stating that [contraband] is located in a certain building" must be acceptable. It would be "quixotic" if a similar statement from an honest informant, but not one from an honest officer, could furnish probable cause. But we have repeatedly held that the unsupported assertion or belief of an officer does not satisfy the probable cause requirement. Thus, this portion of today's holding can be read as implicitly rejecting the teachings of these prior holdings.

The Court may not intend so drastic a result. Indeed, the Court expressly reaffirms the validity of cases such as *Nathanson* that have held that, no matter how reliable the affiant-officer may be, a warrant should not be issued unless the affidavit discloses supporting facts and circumstances. The Court limits these cases to situations involving affidavits containing only "bare conclusions" and holds that, if an affidavit contains anything more, it should be left to the issuing magistrate to decide, based solely on "practical[ity]" and "common-sense," whether there is a fair probability that contraband will be found in a particular place.

Thus, as I read the majority opinion, it appears that the question whether the probable cause standard is to be diluted is left to the common-sense judgments of issuing magistrates. I am reluctant to approve any standard that does not expressly require, as a prerequisite to issuance of a warrant, some showing of facts from which an inference may be drawn that the informant is credible and that his information was obtained in a reliable way. The Court is correctly concerned with the fact that some lower courts have been applying *Aguilar-Spinelli* in an unduly rigid manner. I believe, however, that with clarification of the rule of corroborating information, the lower courts are fully able to properly interpret *Aguilar-Spinelli* and avoid such unduly-rigid applications. I may be wrong; it ultimately may prove to be the case that the only profitable instruction we can provide to magistrates is to rely on common sense. But the question whether a particular anonymous tip provides the basis for issuance of a warrant will often be a difficult one, and I would at least attempt to provide more precise guidance by clarifying *Aguilar-Spinelli* and the relationship of those cases with *Draper* before totally abdicating our responsibility in this area. Hence, I do not join the Court's opinion rejecting the *Aguilar-Spinelli* rules.

JUSTICE BRENNAN, with whom JUSTICE MARSHALL joins, dissenting.

Although I join JUSTICE STEVENS' dissenting opinion and agree with him that the warrant is invalid even under the Court's newly announced "totality of the circumstances" test, see post, at 2361–2362, and n. 8, I write separately to dissent from the Court's unjustified and ill-advised rejection of the two-prong test for evaluating the validity of a warrant based on hearsay announced in Aguilar v. Texas and refined in Spinelli v. United States (1969).

I

The Court's current Fourth Amendment jurisprudence, as reflected by today's unfortunate decision, patently disregards Justice Jackson's admonition in Brinegar v. United States (1949):

> "[Fourth Amendment rights] ... are not mere second-class rights but belong in the catalog of indispensable freedoms. Among deprivations of rights, none is so effective in cowing a population, crushing the spirit of the individual and putting terror in every heart. Uncontrolled search and seizure is one of the first and most effective weapons in the arsenal of every arbitrary government....
>
> "But the right to be secure against searches and seizures is one of the most difficult to protect. Since the officers are themselves the chief invaders, there is no enforcement outside of court."

In recognition of the judiciary's role as the only effective guardian of Fourth Amendment rights, this Court has developed over the last half century a set of coherent rules governing a magistrate's consideration of a warrant application and the showings that are necessary to support a finding of probable cause. We start with the proposition that a neutral and detached magistrate, and not the police, should determine whether there is probable cause to support the issuance of a warrant.

* * *

In order to emphasize the magistrate's role as an independent arbiter of probable cause and to insure that searches or seizures are not effected on less than probable cause, the Court has insisted that police officers provide magistrates with the underlying facts and circumstances that support the officers' conclusions. In Nathanson v. United States (1933), the Court held invalid a search warrant that was based on a customs agent's "mere affirmation of suspicion and belief without any statement of adequate supporting facts." The Court stated that "[u]nder the Fourth Amendment, an officer may not properly issue a warrant to search a private dwelling unless he can find probable cause therefor from facts or circumstances presented to him under oath or affirmation. Mere affirmance of belief or suspicion is not enough."

In Giordenello v. United States, supra, the Court reviewed an arrest warrant issued under the Federal Rules of Criminal Procedure based on a complaint sworn to by a Federal Bureau of Narcotics agent. Based on the agent's testimony at the suppression hearing, the Court noted that "until the warrant was issued ... [the agent's] suspicions of petitioner's guilt derived entirely from information given him by law enforcement officers and other persons in Houston, none of whom either appeared before the Commissioner or submitted affidavits." The Court found it unnecessary to decide whether a warrant could be based solely on hearsay information, for the complaint was "defective in not providing a sufficient basis upon which a finding of probable cause could be made." In particular, the complaint contained no affirmative allegation that the agent spoke with personal knowledge nor did it indicate any sources for the agent's conclusion. The Court expressly rejected the argument that these deficiencies could be cured by "the Commissioner's reliance upon a presumption that the complaint was made on the personal knowledge of the complaining officer."

As noted, the Court did not decide the hearsay question lurking in *Giordenello.* The use of hearsay to support the issuance of a warrant presents special problems because informants, unlike police officers, are not regarded as presumptively reliable or honest. Moreover, the basis for an informant's conclusions is not always clear from an affidavit that merely reports those conclusions. If the conclusory allegations of a police officer are insufficient to support a finding of probable cause, surely the conclusory allegations of an informant should *a fortiori* be insufficient.

In Jones v. United States, supra, the Court considered "whether an affidavit which sets out personal observations relating to the existence of cause to search is to be deemed insufficient by virtue of the fact that it sets out not the affiant's observations but those of another." The Court held that hearsay information can support the issuance of a warrant "so long as a substantial basis for crediting the hearsay is presented." The Court found that there was a substantial basis for crediting the hearsay involved in *Jones.* The informant's report was based on the informant's personal knowledge, and the informant previously had provided accurate information. Moreover, the informant's story was corroborated by other sources. Finally, the defendant was known to the police to be a narcotics user.

Aguilar v. Texas merely made explicit what was implicit in *Jones.* In considering a search warrant based on hearsay, the Court reviewed *Nathanson* and *Giordenello* and noted the requirement established by those cases that an officer provide the magistrate with the underlying facts or circumstances that support the officer's conclusion that there is probable cause to justify the issuance of a warrant.

* * *

While recognizing that a warrant may be based on hearsay, the Court established the following standard [in *Aguilar*]:

> "[T]he magistrate must be informed of some of the underlying circumstances from which the informant concluded that the narcotics were where he claimed they were, and some of the underlying circumstances from which the officer concluded that the informant, whose identity need not be disclosed ... was 'credible' or his information 'reliable.' Otherwise, 'the inferences from the facts which lead to the complaint' will be drawn

not 'by a neutral and detached magistrate,' as the Constitution requires, but instead, by a police officer 'engaged in the often competitive enterprise of ferreting out crime' ... or, as in this case, by an unidentified informant."

The *Aguilar* standard was refined in Spinelli v. United States (1969). In *Spinelli,* the Court reviewed a search warrant based on an affidavit that was "more ample," id., at 413, than the one in *Aguilar.* The affidavit in *Spinelli* contained not only a tip from an informant, but also a report of an independent police investigation that allegedly corroborated the informant's tip. Ibid. Under these circumstances, the Court stated that it was "required to delineate the manner in which *Aguilar*'s two-pronged test should be applied...."

The Court held that the *Aguilar* test should be applied to the tip, and approved two additional ways of satisfying that test. First, the Court suggested that if the tip contained sufficient detail describing the accused's criminal activity it might satisfy *Aguilar*'s basis of knowledge prong. Such detail might assure the magistrate that he is "relying on something more substantial than a casual rumor circulating in the underworld or an accusation based merely on an individual's general reputation." Although the tip in the case before it did not meet this standard, "[t]he detail provided by the informant in Draper v. United States, 358 U.S. 307, 79 S.Ct. 329 (1959), provide[d] a suitable benchmark," because "[a] magistrate, when confronted with such detail, could reasonably infer that the informant had gained his information in a reliable way."

Second, the Court stated that police corroboration of the details of a tip could provide a basis for satisfying *Aguilar.* The Court's opinion is not a model of clarity on this issue since it appears to suggest that corroboration can satisfy both the basis of knowledge and veracity prongs of *Aguilar.* Justice WHITE'S concurring opinion, however, points the way to a proper reading of the Court's opinion. After reviewing the Court's decision in Draper v. United States, supra, Justice WHITE concluded that "[t]he thrust of *Draper* is not that the verified facts have independent significance with respect to proof of [another unverified fact.]" In his view, "[t]he argument instead relates to the reliability of the source: because an informant is right about some things, he is more probably right about other facts, usually the critical, unverified facts." Justice White then pointed out that prior cases had rejected "the notion that the past reliability of an officer is sufficient reason for believing his current assertions." Justice White went on to state:

> "Nor would it suffice, I suppose, if a reliable informant states there is gambling equipment in Apartment 607 and then proceeds to describe in detail Apartment 201, a description which is verified before applying for the warrant. He was right about 201, but that hardly makes him more believable about the equipment in 607. But what if he states that there are narcot-

ics locked in a safe in Apartment 300, which is described in detail, and the apartment manager verifies everything but the contents of the safe? I doubt that the report about the narcotics is made appreciably more believable by the verification. The informant could still have gotten his information concerning the safe from others about whom nothing is known or could have inferred the presence of narcotics from circumstances which a magistrate would find unacceptable."

I find this reasoning persuasive. Properly understood, therefore, *Spinelli* stands for the proposition that corroboration of certain details in a tip may be sufficient to satisfy the veracity, but not the basis of knowledge, prong of *Aguilar.* As noted, *Spinelli* also suggests that in some limited circumstances considerable detail in an informant's tip may be adequate to satisfy the basis of knowledge prong of *Aguilar.*

Although the rules drawn from the cases discussed above are cast in procedural terms, they advance an important underlying substantive value: Findings of probable cause, and attendant intrusions, should not be authorized unless there is some assurance that the information on which they are based has been obtained in a reliable way by an honest or credible person. As applied to police officers, the rules focus on the way in which the information was acquired. As applied to informants, the rules focus both on the honesty or credibility of the informant and on the reliability of the way in which the information was acquired. Insofar as it is more complicated, an evaluation of affidavits based on hearsay involves a more difficult inquiry. This suggests a need to structure the inquiry in an effort to insure greater accuracy. The standards announced in *Aguilar,* as refined by *Spinelli,* fulfill that need. The standards inform the police of what information they have to provide and magistrates of what information they should demand. The standards also inform magistrates of the subsidiary findings they must make in order to arrive at an ultimate finding of probable cause. *Spinelli,* properly understood, directs the magistrate's attention to the possibility that the presence of self-verifying detail might satisfy *Aguilar*'s basis of knowledge prong and that corroboration of the details of a tip might satisfy *Aguilar*'s veracity prong. By requiring police to provide certain crucial information to magistrates and by structuring magistrates' probable cause inquiries, *Aguilar* and *Spinelli* assure the magistrate's role as an independent arbiter of probable cause, insure greater accuracy in probable cause determinations, and advance the substantive value identified above.

At the heart of the Court's decision to abandon *Aguilar* and *Spinelli* appears to be its belief that "the direction taken by decisions following *Spinelli* poorly serves 'the most basic function of any government: to provide for the security of the individual and of his property.' " Ante, at 2331. This conclusion rests on the judgment that *Aguilar* and *Spinelli* "seriously imped[e] the task of law enforcement," ibid., and render anonymous tips valueless in police work. Ibid. Surely, the Court overstates its case. See supra, at 2331. But of particular concern to all

Americans must be that the Court gives virtually no consideration to the value of insuring that findings of probable cause are based on information that a magistrate can reasonably say has been obtained in a reliable way by an honest or credible person. I share Justice WHITE'S fear that the Court's rejection of *Aguilar* and *Spinelli* and its adoption of a new totality of the circumstances test "may foretell an evisceration of the probable cause standard. . . ."

III

The Court's complete failure to provide any persuasive reason for rejecting *Aguilar* and *Spinelli* doubtlessly reflects impatience with what it perceives to be "overly technical" rules governing searches and seizures under the Fourth Amendment. Words such as "practical," "nontechnical," and "commonsense," as used in the Court's opinion, are but code words for an overly permissive attitude towards police practices in derogation of the rights secured by the Fourth Amendment. Everyone shares the Court's concern over the horrors of drug trafficking, but under our Constitution only measures consistent with the Fourth Amendment may be employed by government to cure this evil. We must be ever mindful of Justice Stewart's admonition in Coolidge v. New Hampshire, 403 U.S. 443, 91 S.Ct. 2022 (1971), that "[i]n times of unrest, whether caused by crime or racial conflict or fear of internal subversion, this basic law and the values that it represents may appear unrealistic or 'extravagant' to some. But the values were those of the authors of our fundamental constitutional concepts." In the same vein, Glasser v. United States, 315 U.S. 60, 62 S.Ct. 457 (1942), warned that "[s]teps innocently taken may, one by one, lead to the irretrievable impairment of substantial liberties."

Rights secured by the Fourth Amendment are particularly difficult to protect because their "advocates are usually criminals." By replacing *Aguilar* and *Spinelli* with a test that provides no assurance that magistrates, rather than the police, or informants, will make determinations of probable cause; imposes no structure on magistrates' probable cause inquiries; and invites the possibility that intrusions may be justified on less than reliable information from an honest or credible person, today's decision threatens to "obliterate one of the most fundamental distinctions between our form of government, where officers are under the law, and the police-state where they are the law." Johnson v. United States (1948).

JUSTICE STEVENS, with whom JUSTICE BRENNAN joins, dissenting.

The fact that Lance and Sue Gates made a 22-hour nonstop drive from West Palm Beach, Florida, to Bloomingdale, Illinois, only a few hours after Lance had flown to Florida provided persuasive evidence that they were engaged in illicit activity. That fact, however, was not known to the magistrate when he issued the warrant to search their home.

What the magistrate did know at that time was that the anonymous informant had not been completely accurate in his or her predictions.

The informant had indicated that "Sue drives their car to Florida *where she leaves it to be loaded up with drugs.... Sue flies back after she drops the car off in Florida.*" Yet Detective Mader's affidavit reported that she "left the West Palm Beach area driving the Mercury northbound."

The discrepancy between the informant's predictions and the facts known to Detective Mader is significant for three reasons. First, it cast doubt on the informant's hypothesis that the Gates already had "over $100,000 worth of drugs in their basement," The informant had predicted an itinerary that always kept one spouse in Bloomingdale, suggesting that the Gates did not want to leave their home unguarded because something valuable was hidden within. That inference obviously could not be drawn when it was known that the pair was actually together over a thousand miles from home.

Second, the discrepancy made the Gates' conduct seem substantially less unusual than the informant had predicted it would be. It would have been odd if, as predicted, Sue had driven down to Florida on Wednesday, left the car, and flown right back to Illinois. But the mere facts that Sue was in West Palm Beach with the car, that she was joined by her husband at the Holiday Inn on Friday, and that the couple drove north together the next morning are neither unusual nor probative of criminal activity.

Third, the fact that the anonymous letter contained a material mistake undermines the reasonableness of relying on it as a basis for making a forcible entry into a private home.

Of course, the activities in this case did not stop when the magistrate issued the warrant. The Gates drove all night to Bloomingdale, the officers searched the car and found 400 pounds of marijuana, and then they searched the house. However, none of these subsequent events may be considered in evaluating the warrant, and the search of the house was legal only if the warrant was valid. Vale v. Louisiana, 399 U.S. 30, 33–35, 90 S.Ct. 1969, 1971–1972 (1970). I cannot accept the Court's casual conclusion that, *before the Gates arrived in Bloomingdale,* there was probable cause to justify a valid entry and search of a private home. No one knows who the informant in this case was, or what motivated him or her to write the note. Given that the note's predictions were faulty in one significant respect, and were corroborated by nothing except ordinary innocent activity, I must surmise that the Court's evaluation of the warrant's validity has been colored by subsequent events.

* * *

... When the Court discusses the merits, however, it attaches no weight to the conclusions of the Circuit Judge of DuPage County, Illinois, of the three judges of the Second District of the Illinois Appellate Court, or of the five justices of the Illinois Supreme Court, all of whom concluded that the warrant was not based on probable cause. In a fact-bound inquiry of this sort, the judgment of three levels of state courts, all of whom are better able to evaluate the probable reliability of anonymous informants in Bloomingdale, Illinois, than we are, should be entitled to at least a presumption of accuracy....

NOTES

1. In Massachusetts v. Upton, 466 U.S. 727, 104 S.Ct. 2085 (1984) the U. S. Supreme Court dealt with a decision of a state court that had also adopted a narrow application of *Gates*. In a brief per curiam opinion the Court stated:

> "The Massachusetts court apparently viewed *Gates* as merely adding a new wrinkle to this two-pronged test: where an informant's veracity and/or basis of knowledge are not sufficiently clear, substantial corroboration of the tip may save an otherwise invalid warrant.
>
> "We think that the Supreme Judicial Court of Massachusetts misunderstood our decision in *Gates*. We did not merely refine or qualify the 'two-pronged test.' We rejected it as hypertechnical and divorced from 'the factual and practical considerations of everyday life on which reasonable and prudent men, not legal technicians, act.' Brinegar v. United States, 338 U.S. 160 (1949). Our statement on that score was explicit. '[W]e conclude that it is wiser to abandon the "two-pronged test" established by our decisions in *Aguilar* and *Spinelli*. In its place we reaffirm the totality of the circumstances analysis that traditionally has informed probable cause determinations.' *Gates*. This 'totality of the circumstances' analysis is more in keeping with the 'practical, common-sense decision' demanded of the magistrate."

2. Frequently, police officers may have probable cause to believe that A committed a burglary, that several valuable pieces of jewelry were taken and that A resides at a certain address. Do they have probable cause to believe that the stolen articles are hidden or kept in A's *home*? Most courts adopt the principle that a suspect's own home may be searched, and also accept the principle that "evidence of [a suspect's] continued presence or, at least, of frequent visits [will mark] the premises as a logical target for a search warrant, despite ... lack of a possessory interest in the premises" Commonwealth v. DeMasi, 362 Mass. 53, 283 N.E.2d 845 (1972). Some courts reject this principle. See United States v. Flanagan, 423 F.2d 745 (5th Cir.1970). The issue is not fully settled. In United States v. Bailey, 458 F.2d 408 (9th Cir.1972) the court was faced with this problem: In writing for the majority, Judge Hufstedler held:

> "The affidavit in support of the search of the house is no better than the affidavit for the automobile warrant. The affidavit simply discloses that Bailey had been seen at the house and that Cochran was arrested there. No facts are recited from which it could be inferred that Bailey and Cochran were other than casual social guests at the residence. At the trial, there was no evidence that Bailey and Cochran had leased the house, but that fact was not before the issuing magistrate.
>
>> '[A]ll data necessary to show probable cause for the issuance of a search warrant must be contained within the four corners of a written affidavit given under oath.'
>
> "In short, there is nothing but conjecture to sustain the conclusion that the house contained the objects of the search. As we observed in United States v. Lucarz (9th Cir.1970) 430 F.2d 1051, 1055:

'[S]imply from the existence of probable cause to believe a suspect guilty, [it does not follow in all cases] that there is also probable cause to search his residence. If that were so, there would be no reason to distinguish search warrants from arrest warrants, and cases like Chimel v. California, ... would make little sense.'"

In dissent, Judge Kilkenny wrote:

"The affidavit supporting the issuance of the warrant for the search of the home reveals that appellant's female co-conspirator in the bank robbery, the lady who used the large brown manila envelope to carry the money obtained in the robbery, was arrested at 2256 E. Prince Road, Tucson, Arizona. The affidavit reveals that the home had been under surveillance for some time and that appellant was observed in the premises on April 23, 1971, and at other subsequent times prior to the arrest. The affidavit clearly sets forth the joint activities of appellant and the female co-conspirator immediately prior to and at the time of the robbery. From the facts stated in the affidavit, the Magistrate could reasonably infer: (1) that appellant or his co-conspirator, or both, were occupying the premises; (2) that as occupants, they might well have concealed on the premises a portion of the fruits of the robbery or the clothing which they wore at the time; and (3) probable cause existed for the issuance of the warrant. The logic employed by our court in *Lucarz,* supra, is here of particular significance. I quote from the opinion:

" 'The affidavit demonstrated the theft of the sort of materials that one would expect to be hidden at appellant's place of residence, both because of their value and bulk.'

"The affidavit should be interpreted in a common sense and realistic manner, United States v. Ventresca, and the warrant should issue when a man of reasonable caution would be of the belief that the items to be seized were in a particular location."

3. The law of probable cause has, since *Aguilar–Spinelli* (and even after *Gates*), given rise to the practice of using tried and true formulations to establish probable cause. Some police departments have put standard warrant language on computers and word processors from which an officer can select appropriate formulae. Should this practice affect the validity of the warrant? See Coleman v. State, 308 Ark. 631, 826 S.W.2d 273 (1992) (Practice unwise where officer knew more than was implied by the verbal formula he selected from the word processor memory bank).

C. SPECIFIC WARRANT REQUIREMENTS

1. ISSUANCE OF THE WARRANT

Warrants may be issued only by neutral, detached judicial officers. Neither prosecutors nor police officers may issue warrants.[1] Moreover, the "judicial" title of the person who issues the warrant is not altogether controlling. In one case the Court invalidated a warrant issued by a justice of the peace who received five dollars for every warrant which he

1. Coolidge v. New Hampshire, 403 U.S. 443, 91 S.Ct. 2022 (1971).

issued and nothing for considering and rejecting a warrant application. The justice of the peace had issued over 5,000 warrants and acknowledged that he depended upon the fee system as his chief source of income.[2] However, under some circumstances a court clerk may issue an arrest warrant.[3]

Generally speaking, only law enforcement officers may execute a warrant.

2. FORM AND NATURE OF THE WARRANT

The warrant is usually applied for on a pre-printed form containing blanks for names, addresses, items to be seized, etc., and a space for setting out the facts establishing probable cause. The warrant and the affidavit (or complaint or petition) for the warrant are usually prepared on separate pieces of paper. The process of preparing papers and presenting them to a magistrate is time-consuming. In rural areas or at odd hours of the night, there may be substantial delay before a warrant can be secured.

3. SPECIFICATION AS TO THE PLACE TO BE SEARCHED

The place to be searched must be described with particularity. In the case of a single family residence this is usually done by giving the street address. In rural areas a rural route address may be given. In some cases a map may be incorporated into the warrant or a legal description (which is the surveyor's official description) of the property may be given. Problems arise in cases involving multiple dwellings at a specific address. Often apartments do not have numbers and they should be described by location. Even this technique presents problems, for the police may not be able to secure an accurate description of the manner in which apartments are distributed. It may be advisable for officers to identify apartments by the name of the occupant if it is known, as well as apartment number or location.

Occasionally deficiencies occur in warrant descriptions. When the affidavit or complaint for the warrant contains a complete description the courts will construe the warrant and the affidavit together as one document and sustain the warrant. Some law enforcement officers will draft a warrant adding the specific statement that the material contained in the affidavit is incorporated in the warrant and made a part of the warrant.

Minor errors in street address are not always fatal, if the court can conclude that only one particular place is obviously referred to in the warrant and that the officers (who may well have conducted a surveillance of the place) could not have possibly been confused about the place to be searched.

2. Connally v. Georgia, 429 U.S. 245, 97 S.Ct. 546 (1977).

3. Shadwick v. City of Tampa, 407 U.S. 345, 92 S.Ct. 2119 (1972).

If a search warrant is overbroad in its description of the place to be searched can the error be cured by a "reasonable mistake of fact" on the part of the procuring police officers? In Maryland v. Garrison, 480 U.S. 79, 107 S.Ct. 1013 (1987), the U.S. Supreme Court held that where the police made a reasonable mistake of fact to the effect that the third floor of a building was composed of one living unit, and they obtained a search warrant for "the premises known as 2036 Park Avenue third floor apartment ...," but, at the time of execution of the warrant, it turned out that there were two living units on the third floor, one occupied by the defendant who was not the original suspect, and this mistaken belief continued until the time of the search when incriminating evidence involving the defendant was uncovered, the search did not violate the Fourth Amendment. The court ruled that a search warrant that has an overbroad description of the premises to be searched is not invalid if the mistake of fact by the police was reasonable under the circumstances. The particularity requirement of the Fourth Amendment is subject to an objective reasonableness standard, just as is the probable cause requirement. The Court relied in part upon Hill v. California, 401 U.S. 797, 91 S.Ct. 1106 (1971), where the police reasonably arrested and searched the wrong person. That case's "underlying rationale that an officer's reasonable misidentification of a person does not invalidate a valid arrest is equally applicable to an officer's reasonable failure to appreciate that a valid warrant describes too broadly the premises to be searched." Here, the objective facts available to the police at the time they executed the search warrant did not indicate that the warrant was overbroad or that they were in an apartment other than that described in the warrant. The police did not realize the mistake until the search had been completed and the incriminating evidence had been found.

4. PREMISES OTHER THAN THOSE OF CRIMINAL SUSPECT

In 1978 the Supreme Court rejected claims that a warrant could not issue if the premises to be searched were (1) owned or occupied by a person who was not himself reasonably suspected of involvement in the crime being investigated, or (2) occupied by a newspaper that is not involved in the crime.[4]

5. SPECIFICATION OF ITEMS TO BE SEIZED

A warrant must specifically describe the items to be seized. A general warrant is constitutionally prohibited and a warrant which simply authorizes a search of a certain premises without specifying what is to be seized is invalid.[5]

There is no restriction on the number and kind of items that can be seized. Contraband, fruits, instrumentalities and evidence of a crime are all subject to seizure pursuant to warrant. There are some state statutes which preclude the seizure of "mere evidence" but this restric-

4. Zurcher v. Stanford Daily, 436 U.S. 547, 98 S.Ct. 1970 (1978).

5. Commonwealth v. Sheppard, 387 Mass. 488, 441 N.E.2d 725 (1982); reversed on the grounds that although the warrant was invalid, the officer acted in good faith, Massachusetts v. Sheppard, 468 U.S. 981, 104 S.Ct. 3424 (1984), see Chapter 15, infra.

tive rule is declining since the Supreme Court held it was not constitutionally required and would not be applied to federal officers.

It is clear that if, during the course of lawfully executing a warrant, the police discover seizable items not named in the warrant they may seize the items. This sort of police practice is usually justified under the "plain view" doctrine. However, once all the named items are found the search must stop.

In determining what kind of description is sufficient, a rule of reason applies. "Gaming apparatus" may be sufficient, while "stolen tires" may be insufficient, because the tires clearly can be described by reference to a brand name or perhaps even serial number. "Narcotics paraphernalia" is generally good enough. Contraband generally need not be described in great detail.

6. SPECIFICATION AS TO WHEN THE WARRANT IS TO BE EXECUTED

The warrant itself will usually not contain specific requirements that a warrant be executed at any particular time. There are time limits applicable to warrants but these limits are usually prescribed by statute or court rule and vary from jurisdiction to jurisdiction. A delay in executing a warrant even when the statutory time limit is met may render the search unreasonable. This occurs when the delay in execution makes it likely that the evidence may no longer be at the place to be searched. A delay in execution of a warrant may be required where the police secure a warrant before the items to be seized have arrived at the place to be searched, i.e., the "anticipatory" warrant.

Some jurisdictions require that warrants be executed only in daylight hours unless special procedures are followed and the warrant specifies that nighttime execution is permissible. Among the special procedures are requirements of securing the signatures of two magistrates, of showing a need for prompt execution of the warrant, or of producing "positive" affidavits. The restrictive nighttime search rule is purely a matter of local or statutory law. It has no constitutional basis.

7. SPECIFICATION OF THE PERSON TO BE SEARCHED OR ARRESTED

The warrant must describe the person as well as the premises, if a person is to be searched or arrested. Ordinarily the person is identified by his name. If a person's name is not known, his physical appearance, nickname, and place of residence or place he frequents may be used to satisfy the specificity requirement.

D. POLICE ENTRY TO EXECUTE WARRANTS OR EFFECT ARRESTS

PAYTON v. NEW YORK

Supreme Court of the United States, 1980.
445 U.S. 573, 100 S.Ct. 1371.

Mr. JUSTICE STEVENS delivered the opinion of the Court.

These appeals challenge the constitutionality of New York statutes that authorize police officers to enter a private residence without a warrant and with force, if necessary, to make a routine felony arrest.

* * *

On January 14, 1970, after two days of intensive investigation, New York detectives had assembled evidence sufficient to establish probable cause to believe that Theodore Payton had murdered the manager of a gas station two days earlier. At about 7:30 a.m. on January 15, six officers went to Payton's apartment in the Bronx, intending to arrest him. They had not obtained a warrant. Although light and music emanated from the apartment, there was no response to their knock on the metal door. They summoned emergency assistance and, about 30 minutes later, used crowbars to break open the door and enter the apartment. No one was there. In plain view, however, was a 30-caliber shell casing that was seized and later admitted into evidence at Payton's murder trial.

In due course Payton surrendered to the police, was indicted for murder, and moved to suppress the evidence taken from his apartment. The trial judge held that the warrantless and forcible entry was authorized by the New York Code of Criminal Procedure, and that the evidence in plain view was properly seized. He found that exigent circumstances justified the officers' failure to announce their purpose before entering the apartment as required by the statute. He had no occasion, however, to decide whether those circumstances also would have justified the failure to obtain a warrant, because he concluded that the warrantless entry was adequately supported by the statute without regard to the circumstances. The Appellate Division, First Department, summarily affirmed.

On March 14, 1974, Obie Riddick was arrested for the commission of two armed robberies that had occurred in 1971. He had been identified by the victims in June of 1973 and in January 1974 the police had learned his address. They did not obtain a warrant for his arrest. At about noon on March 14, a detective, accompanied by three other officers, knocked on the door of the Queens house where Riddick was living. When his young son opened the door, they could see Riddick sitting in bed covered by a sheet. They entered the house and placed him under arrest. Before permitting him to dress, they opened a chest of drawers two feet from the bed in search of weapons and found narcotics and related paraphernalia. Riddick was subsequently indicted on narcotics charges. At a suppression hearing, the trial judge held that the warrantless entry into his home was authorized by the revised New York statute,[1] and that the search of the immediate area was reasonable under Chimel v. California (1969). The Appellate Division, Second Department, affirmed the denial of the suppression motion.

The New York Court of Appeals, in a single opinion, affirmed the convictions of both Payton and Riddick.

* * *

Although it is arguable that the warrantless entry to effect Payton's arrest might have been justified by exigent circumstances, none of the New York courts relied on any such justification. The Court of Appeals majority treated both *Payton's* and *Riddick's* cases as involving routine arrests in which there was ample time to obtain a warrant, and we will do the same. Accordingly, we have no occasion to consider the sort of emergency or dangerous situation, described in our cases as "exigent circumstances," that would justify a warrantless entry into a home for the purpose of either arrest or search.

Nor do these cases raise any question concerning the authority of the police, without either a search or arrest warrant, to enter a third party's home to arrest a suspect. The police broke into Payton's apartment intending to arrest Payton and they arrested Riddick in his own dwelling. We also note that in neither case is it argued that the police lacked probable cause to believe that the suspect was at home when they entered. Finally, in both cases we are dealing with entries into homes made without the consent of any occupant. In *Payton,* the police used crowbars to break down the door and in *Riddick,* although his three-year-old son answered the door, the police entered before Riddick had an opportunity either to object or to consent.

1. New York Criminal Procedure Law § 140.15(4) provides, with respect to arrest without a warrant:

> "In order to effect such an arrest, a police officer may enter premises in which he reasonably believes such person to be present, under the same circumstances and in the same manner as would be authorized, by the provisions of subdivisions four and five of section 120.80, if he were attempting to make such arrest pursuant to a warrant of arrest."

Section 120.80, governing execution of arrest warrants, provides in relevant part:

> "4. In order to effect the arrest, the police officer may, under the circumstances and in a manner prescribed in this subdivision, enter any premises in which he reasonably believes defendant to be present. Before such entry, he must give, or make reasonable effort to give, notice of his authority and purpose to an occupant thereof, unless there is reasonable cause to believe that the giving of such notice will:
>
> "(a) Result in the defendant escaping or attempting to escape; or
>
> "(b) Endanger the life or safety of the officer or another person; or
>
> "(c) Result in the destruction, damaging or secretion of material evidence.
>
> "5. If the officer is authorized to enter premises without giving notice of his authority and purpose, or if after giving such notice he is not admitted, he may enter such premises, and by a breaking if necessary."

It is familiar history that indiscriminate searches and seizures conducted under the authority of "general warrants" were the immediate evils that motivated the framing and adoption of the Fourth Amendment. Indeed, as originally proposed in the House of Representatives, the draft contained only one clause, which directly imposed limitations on the issuance of warrants, but imposed no express restrictions on warrantless searches or seizures. As it was ultimately adopted, however, the Amendment contained two separate clauses, the first protecting the basic right to be free from unreasonable searches and seizures and the second requiring that warrants be particular and supported by probable cause.

* * *

It is thus perfectly clear that the evil the Amendment was designed to prevent was broader than the abuse of a general warrant. Unreasonable searches or seizures conducted without any warrant at all are condemned by the plain language of the first clause of the Amendment.

* * *

The simple language of the Amendment applies equally to seizures of persons and to seizures of property. Our analysis in this case may therefore properly commence with rules that have been well established in Fourth Amendment litigation involving tangible items. As the Court unanimously reiterated just a few years ago, the "physical entry of the home is the chief evil against which the wording of the Fourth Amendment is directed." United States v. United States District Court (1970). And we have long adhered to the view that the warrant procedure minimizes the danger of needless intrusions of that sort.

It is a "basic principle of Fourth Amendment law" that searches and seizures inside a home without a warrant are presumptively unreasonable. Yet it is also well-settled that objects such as weapons or contraband found in a public place may be seized by the police without a warrant. The seizure of property in plain view involves no invasion of privacy and is presumptively reasonable, assuming that there is probable cause to associate the property with criminal activity. The distinction between a warrantless seizure in an open area and such a seizure on private premises was plainly stated in G.M. Leasing Corp. v. United States (1977):

> "It is one thing to seize without a warrant property resting in an open area or seizable by levy without an intrusion into privacy, and it is quite another thing to effect a warrantless seizure of property, even that owned by a corporation, situated on private premises to which access is not otherwise available for the seizing officer."

As the late Judge Leventhal recognized, this distinction has equal force when the seizure of a person is involved. Writing on the constitutional issue now before us for the United States Court of Appeals for the District of Columbia Circuit sitting en banc, Dorman v. United States,

140 U.S.App.D.C. 313, 435 F.2d 385 (1969), Judge Leventhal first noted the settled rule that warrantless arrests in public places are valid. He immediately recognized, however, that

> "[a] greater burden is placed [ ] on officials who enter a home or dwelling without consent. Freedom from intrusion into the home or dwelling is the archetype of the privacy protection secured by the Fourth Amendment."

His analysis of this question then focused on the long-settled premise that, absent exigent circumstances, a warrantless entry to search for weapons or contraband is unconstitutional even when a felony has been committed and there is probable cause to believe that incriminating evidence will be found within. He reasoned that the constitutional protection afforded to the individual's interest in the privacy of his own home is equally applicable to a warrantless entry for the purpose of arresting a resident of the house; for it is inherent in such an entry that a search for the suspect may be required before he can be apprehended. Judge Leventhal concluded that an entry to arrest and an entry to search for and to seize property implicate the same interest in preserving the privacy and the sanctity of the home, and justify the same level of constitutional protection.

* * *

We find this reasoning to be persuasive and in accord with this Court's Fourth Amendment decisions.

The majority of the New York Court of Appeals, however, suggested that there is a substantial difference in the relative intrusiveness of an entry to search for property and an entry to search for a person. It is true that the area that may legally be searched is broader when executing a search warrant than when executing an arrest warrant in the home. See Chimel v. California, supra. This difference may be more theoretical than real, however, because the police may need to check the entire premises for safety reasons, and sometimes they ignore the restrictions on searches incident to arrest.

But the critical point is that any differences in the intrusiveness of entries to search and entries to arrest are merely ones of degree rather than kind. The two intrusions share this fundamental characteristic: the breach of the entrance to an individual's home. The Fourth Amendment protects the individual's privacy in a variety of settings. In none is the zone of privacy more clearly defined than when bounded by the unambiguous physical dimensions of an individual's home—a zone that finds its roots in clear and specific constitutional terms: "The right of the people to be secure in their ... houses ... shall not be violated." That language unequivocally establishes the proposition that "[a]t the very core [of the Fourth Amendment] stands the right of a man to retreat into his own home and there be free from unreasonable government intrusion." Silverman v. United States (1961). In terms that apply equally to seizures of property and to seizures of persons, the

Fourth Amendment has drawn a firm line at the entrance to the house. Absent exigent circumstances, that threshold may not reasonably be crossed without a warrant.

* * *

An examination of the common law understanding of an officer's authority to arrest sheds light on the obviously relevant, if not entirely dispositive,[2] consideration of what the Framers of the Amendment might have thought to be reasonable.

* * *

Thus, our study of the relevant common law does not provide the same guidance that was present in *Watson.* Whereas the rule concerning the validity of an arrest in a public place was supported by cases directly in point and by the unanimous views of the commentators, we have found no direct authority supporting forcible entries into a home to make a routine arrest and the weight of the scholarly opinion is somewhat to the contrary. Indeed, the absence of any Seventeenth or Eighteenth Century English cases directly in point, together with the unequivocal endorsement of the tenet that "a man's house is his castle," strongly suggest that the prevailing practice was not to make such arrests except in hot pursuit or when authorized by a warrant. In all events, the issue is not one that can be said to have been definitively settled by the common law at the time the Fourth Amendment was adopted.

* * *

A longstanding, widespread practice is not immune from constitutional scrutiny. But neither is it to be lightly brushed aside. This is particularly so when the constitutional standard is as amorphous as the word "reasonable," and when custom and contemporary norms necessarily play such a large role in the constitutional analysis. In this case, although the weight of state-law authority is clear, there is by no means the kind of virtual unanimity on this question that was present in United States v. Watson with regard to warrantless arrests in public places. Only 24 of the 50 States currently sanction warrantless entries into the home to arrest and there is an obvious declining trend. Fur-

2. There are important differences between the common-law rules relating to searches and seizures and those that have evolved through the process of interpreting the Fourth Amendment in light of contemporary norms and conditions. For example, whereas the kinds of property subject to seizure under warrants had been limited to contraband and the fruits or instrumentalities of crime, see Gouled v. United States, 255 U.S. 298, 309, 41 S.Ct. 261, 265, the category of property that may be seized, consistent with the Fourth Amendment, has been expanded to include mere evidence. Warden v. Hayden, 387 U.S. 294, 87 S.Ct. 1642. Also, the prohibitions of the Amendment have been extended to protect against invasion by electronic eavesdropping of an individual's privacy in a phone booth not owned by him, Katz v. United States, 389 U.S. 347, 88 S.Ct. 507, even though the earlier law had focused on the physical invasion of the individual's person or property interests in the course of a seizure of tangible objects. See Olmstead v. United States, 277 U.S. 438, 466, 48 S.Ct. 564.

ther, the strength of the trend is greater than the numbers alone indicate. Seven state courts have recently held that warrantless home arrests violate their respective *state* constitutions. That is significant because by invoking a state constitutional provision, a state court immunizes its decision from review by this Court. This heightened degree of immutability underscores the depth of the principle underlying the result.

No congressional determination that warrantless entries into the home are "reasonable" has been called to our attention. None of the federal statutes cited in the *Watson* opinion reflects any such legislative judgment. Thus, that support for the *Watson* holding finds no counterpart in this case.

* * *

In this case, however, neither history nor this Nation's experience requires us to disregard the overriding respect for the sanctity of the home that has been embedded in our traditions since the origins of the Republic.[3]

The parties have argued at some length about the practical consequences of a warrant requirement as a precondition to a felony arrest in the home. In the absence of any evidence that effective law enforcement has suffered in those States that already have such a requirement, we are inclined to view such arguments with skepticism. More fundamentally, however, such arguments of policy must give way to a constitutional command that we consider to be unequivocal.

Finally, we note the State's suggestion that only a search warrant based on probable cause to believe the suspect is at home at a given time can adequately protect the privacy interests at stake, and since such a warrant requirement is manifestly impractical, there need be no warrant of any kind. We find this ingenious argument unpersuasive. It is true that an arrest warrant requirement may afford less protection than a search warrant requirement, but it will suffice to interpose the magistrate's determination of probable cause between the zealous officer and the citizen. If there is sufficient evidence of a citizen's participation in a felony to persuade a judicial officer that his arrest is justified, it is constitutionally reasonable to require him to open his doors to the officers of the law. Thus, for Fourth Amendment purposes, an arrest warrant founded on probable cause implicitly carries with it the limited authority to enter a dwelling in which the suspect lives when there is reason to believe the suspect is within.

3. There can be no doubt that Pitt's address in the House of Commons in March of 1763 echoed and re-echoed throughout the Colonies:

"'The poorest man may in his cottage bid defiance to all the forces of the Crown. It may be frail; its roof may shake; the wind may blow through it; the storm may enter; the rain may enter; but the King of England cannot enter—all his force dares not cross the threshold of the ruined tenement!'" Miller v. United States, 357 U.S., at 307, 78 S.Ct., at 1195.

Because no arrest warrant was obtained in either of these cases, the judgments must be reversed and the cases remanded to the New York Court of Appeals for further proceedings not inconsistent with this opinion.

MR. JUSTICE BLACKMUN, concurring.

[Opinion omitted]

MR. JUSTICE WHITE, with whom THE CHIEF JUSTICE and MR. JUSTICE REHNQUIST join, dissenting.

* * *

In sum, the background, text, and legislative history of the Fourth Amendment demonstrate that the purpose was to restrict the abuses that had developed with respect to warrants; the Amendment preserved common-law rules of arrest. Because it was not considered generally unreasonable at common law for officers to break doors to effect a warrantless felony arrest, I do not believe that the Fourth Amendment was intended to outlaw the types of police conduct at issue in the present case.

* * *

Today's decision rests, in large measure, on the premise that warrantless arrest entries constitute a particularly severe invasion of personal privacy. I do not dispute that the home is generally a very private area or that the common law displayed a special "reverence . . . for the individual's right of privacy in his house." Miller v. United States (1958).

* * *

Yet we settled in *Watson* that the intrusiveness of a public arrest is not enough to mandate the obtaining of a warrant. The inquiry in the present case, therefore, is whether the incremental intrusiveness that results from an arrest's being made *in the dwelling* is enough to support an inflexible constitutional rule requiring warrants for such arrests whenever exigent circumstances are not present.

Today's decision ignores the carefully crafted restrictions on the common-law power of arrest entry and thereby overestimates the dangers inherent in that practice. At common law, absent exigent circumstances, entries to arrest could be made only for felony. Even in cases of felony, the officers were required to announce their presence, demand admission, and be refused entry before they were entitled to break doors. Further, it seems generally accepted that entries could be made only during daylight hours. And, in my view, the officer entering to arrest must have reasonable grounds to believe, not only that the arrestee has committed a crime, but also that the person suspected is present in the house at the time of the entry.[4]

4. I do not necessarily disagree with the Court's discussion of the quantum of probable cause necessary to make a valid home arrest. The Court indicates that only an

These four restrictions on home arrests—felony, knock and announce, daytime, and stringent probable cause—constitute powerful and complementary protections for the privacy interests associated with the home. The felony requirement guards against abusive or arbitrary enforcement and ensures that invasions of the home occur only in case of the most serious crimes. The knock and announce and daytime requirement protect individuals against the fear, humiliation and embarrassment of being aroused from the beds in states of partial or complete undress. And these requirements allow the arrestee to surrender at his front door, thereby maintaining his dignity and preventing the officers from entering other rooms of the dwelling. The stringent probable cause requirement would help ensure against the possibility that the police would enter when the suspect was not home, and, in searching for him, frighten members of the family or ransack parts of the house, seizing items in plain view. In short, these requirements, taken together, permit an individual suspected of a serious crime to surrender at the front door of his dwelling and thereby avoid most of the humiliation and indignity that the Court seems to believe necessarily accompany a house arrest entry. Such a front door arrest, in my view, is no more intrusive on personal privacy than the public warrantless arrests which we found to pass constitutional muster in *Watson.*[5]

All of these limitations on warrantless arrest entries are satisfied on the facts of the present cases. The arrests here were for serious felonies—murder and armed robbery—and both occurred during daylight hours. The authorizing statutes required that the police announce their business and demand entry; neither Payton nor Riddick makes any contention that these statutory requirements were not fulfilled. And it is not argued that the police had no probable cause to believe that both Payton and Riddick were in their dwellings at the time of the entries. Today's decision, therefore, sweeps away any possibility that warrantless home entries might be permitted in some limited situations other than those in which exigent circumstances are present. The Court substitutes, in one sweeping decision, a rigid constitutional rule in place of the common-law approach, evolved over hundreds of years, which achieved a flexible accommodation between the demands of personal privacy and the legitimate needs of law enforcement.

A rule permitting warrantless arrest entries would not pose a danger that officers would use their entry power as a pretext to justify an otherwise invalid warrantless search. A search pursuant to a warrantless arrest entry will rarely, if ever, be as complete as one under

arrest warrant, and not a search warrant, is required. To obtain the warrant, therefore, the officers need only show probable cause that a crime has been committed and that the suspect committed it. However, under today's decision, the officers apparently need an extra increment of probable cause when executing the arrest warrant, namely grounds to believe that the suspect is within the dwelling.

5. If the suspect flees or hides, of course, the intrusiveness of the entry will be somewhat greater; but the policeman's hands should not be tied merely because of the possibility that the suspect will fail to cooperate with legitimate actions by law enforcement personnel.

authority of a search warrant. If the suspect surrenders at the door, the officers may not enter other rooms. Of course, the suspect may flee or hide, or may not be at home, but the officers cannot anticipate the first two of these possibilities and the last is unlikely given the requirement of probable cause to believe that the suspect is at home. Even when officers are justified in searching other rooms, they may seize only items within the arrestee's position or immediate control or items in plain view discovered during the course of a search reasonably directed at discovering a hiding suspect. Hence a warrantless home entry is likely to uncover far less evidence than a search conducted under authority of a search warrant. Furthermore, an arrest entry will inevitably tip off the suspects and likely result in destruction or removal of evidence not uncovered during the arrest. I therefore cannot believe that the police would take the risk of losing valuable evidence through a pretextual arrest entry rather than applying to a magistrate for a search warrant.

While exaggerating the invasion of personal privacy involved in home arrests, the Court fails to account for the danger that its rule will "severely hamper effective law enforcement," United States v. Watson (Powell, J., concurring). The policeman on his beat must now make subtle discriminations that perplex even judges in their chambers. As Mr. Justice Powell noted, concurring in *Watson,* police will sometimes delay making an arrest, even after probable cause is established, in order to be sure that they have enough evidence to convict. Then, if they suddenly have to arrest, they run the risk that the subsequent exigency will not excuse their prior failure to obtain a warrant. This problem cannot effectively be cured by obtaining a warrant as soon as probable cause is established because of the chance that the warrant will go stale before the arrest is made.

Further, police officers will often face the difficult task of deciding whether the circumstances are sufficiently exigent to justify their entry to arrest without a warrant. This is a decision that must be made quickly in the most trying of circumstances. If the officers mistakenly decide that the circumstances are exigent, the arrest will be invalid and any evidence seized incident to the arrest or in plain view will be excluded at trial. On the other hand, if the officers mistakenly determine that exigent circumstances are lacking, they may refrain from making the arrest, thus creating the possibility that a dangerous criminal will escape into the community. The police could reduce the likelihood of escape by staking out all possible exits until the circumstances become clearly exigent or a warrant is obtained. But the costs of such a stakeout seem excessive in an era of rising crime and scarce police resources.

The uncertainty inherent in the exigent circumstances determination burdens the judicial system as well. In the case of searches, exigent circumstances are sufficiently unusual that this Court has determined that the benefits of a warrant outweigh the burdens imposed, including the burdens on the judicial system. In contrast, arrests recurringly involve exigent circumstances, and this Court has heretofore held that a warrant can be dispensed with without undue sacrifice in Fourth Amendment values. The situation should be no different with respect to arrests in the home. Under today's decision, whenever the police have made a warrantless home arrest there will be the possibility of "endless litigation with respect to the existence of exigent circumstances, whether it was practicable to get a warrant, whether the suspect was about to flee, and the like," United States v. Watson.

Our cases establish that the ultimate test under the Fourth Amendment is one of "reasonableness." I cannot join the Court in declaring unreasonable a practice which has been thought entirely reasonable by so many for so long. It would be far preferable to adopt a clear and simple rule: after knocking and announcing their presence, police may enter the home to make a daytime arrest without a warrant when there is probable cause to believe that the person to be arrested committed a felony and is present in the house. This rule would best comport with the commonlaw background, with the traditional practice in the States, and with the history and policies of the Fourth Amendment. Accordingly, I respectfully dissent.

MR. JUSTICE REHNQUIST, dissenting.

[Opinion Omitted]

NOTES

1. *Payton* did not decide what type of special or exigent circumstances would justify a warrantless, non-consensual entry into a suspect's home for the purpose of arrest. Many of the federal and state cases which reached the "*Payton* rule" before *Payton* spelled out factors to be considered. Among the most important such early decisions were Dorman v. United States, 435 F.2d 385 (D.C.Cir.1970), and Vance v. North Carolina, 432 F.2d 984 (4th Cir.1970).

Some commentators have observed that, after the *Payton* decision, many courts have been quick to find exigent circumstances and to excuse the absence of an arrest warrant. Nevertheless, there have been a few decisions which have rejected exigent circumstances claims. See, e.g., United States v. Minick, 438 A.2d 205 (D.C.App.1981) (warrantless arrest of rape suspect in his home four hours after alleged offense).

2. Would the analysis in *Payton* require any different result if the suspect appeared at his door in response to a police knock and the officer merely stepped across the threshold to make the arrest? Can the police validly use the tactic of tricking the suspect out of his home by, for example, telling him that his parked car has been damaged by another vehicle? If not, why not, considering that in such a case, the police would make an arrest in a public place without intruding against the privacy of the home? One court has approved use of such a tactic. See People v. Moore, 102 Ill.App.3d 651, 57 Ill.Dec. 949, 429 N.E.2d 1312 (1981).

3. In Welsh v. Wisconsin, 466 U.S. 740, 104 S.Ct. 2091 (1984), the U. S. Supreme Court held that *Payton* applied to a warrantless arrest of a drunk driving suspect who was asleep in his home. The State of Wisconsin had made the offense a nonjailable civil matter. The mere fact that evidence of intoxication would dissipate before the police could obtain a warrant did not create an exigency that would excuse compliance with *Payton.* The Court stated, "it is

difficult to conceive of a warrantless home arrest that would not be unreasonable under the Fourth Amendment when the underlying offense is extremely minor".

Payton is generally read to require an arrest warrant to enter a suspect's home without consent, for the purposes of a non-emergency arrest, although a few jurisdictions utilize search warrants. When the home which is entered is not the suspect's however, a different issue is presented as is seen in the case which follows.

4. Police entries to observe allegedly obscene materials and to make arrests for possession, continue to raise special problems because of the unique First Amendment issues involved (see Chapter 2, B. Freedom of the Press—The Obscenity Issue). In Maryland v. Macon, 472 U.S. 463, 105 S.Ct. 2778 (1985), the U.S. Supreme Court ruled that where police entered a store without a warrant during regular business hours—just like any other potential patron—no violation of the store owner's right of privacy occurred and purchase by the police of allegedly obscene magazines was not a Fourth Amendment seizure. In *Macon* a police officer entered an adult bookstore, looked over the magazines offered for sale and purchased two of the magazines with a $50 bill, receiving $38 in change. After looking over the magazines the officer concluded that they were obscene and then arrested the clerk, retrieving the $50 bill, but not returning the change. He made the determination of obscenity without consulting a judge. The magazine, but not the $50 bill, was introduced at trial. The Court ruled that the officer's entry into the store and examination of the magazines, which were on public display, was not a search within the purview of the Fourth Amendment. "The mere expectation that the possibly illegal nature of a product will not come to the attention of the authorities ... is not one that society is prepared to recognize as reasonable." Nor was this a "seizure" under the Fourth Amendment, since the clerk voluntarily transferred title to the magazines upon tender of the purchase price. Since only two magazines were taken, there was no risk of a "prior restraint" under the First Amendment. Even though the officer later retrieved his purchase money, this did not retrospectively transform the transfer into a warrantless seizure. The remedy for this tactic was restitution or suppression of the $50 bill, if it had been offered as evidence, not suppression of the magazines. Even if the warrantless arrest was an unreasonable "seizure" of the clerk, an issue not decided by the Court, it had no effect on the evidence which was already in the lawful possession of the police.

STEAGALD v. UNITED STATES

Supreme Court of the United States, 1981.
451 U.S. 204, 101 S.Ct. 1642.

JUSTICE MARSHALL delivered the opinion of the Court.

The issue in this case is whether, under the Fourth Amendment, a law enforcement officer may legally search for the subject of an arrest warrant in the home of a third party without first obtaining a search warrant. Concluding that a search warrant must be obtained absent exigent circumstances or consent, we reverse the judgment of the United States Court of Appeals for the Fifth Circuit affirming petitioner's conviction.

In early January 1978, an agent of the Drug Enforcement Administration (DEA) was contacted in Detroit, Mich., by a confidential informant who suggested that he might be able to locate Ricky Lyons, a federal fugitive wanted on drug charges. On January 14, 1978, the informant called the agent again, and gave him a telephone number in the Atlanta, Ga., area where, according to the informant, Ricky Lyons could be reached during the next 24 hours. On January 16, 1978, the agent called fellow DEA Agent Kelly Goodowens in Atlanta and relayed the information he had obtained from the informant. Goodowens contacted Southern Bell Telephone Company, and secured the address corresponding to the telephone number obtained by the informant. Goodowens also discovered that Lyons was the subject of a six-month-old arrest warrant.

Two days later, Goodowens and 11 other officers drove to the address supplied by the telephone company to search for Lyons. The officers observed two men standing outside the house to be searched. These men were Hoyt Gaultney and petitioner Gary Steagald. The officers approached with guns drawn, frisked both men, and, after demanding identification, determined that neither man was Lyons. Several agents proceeded to the house. Gaultney's wife answered the door, and informed the agents that she was alone in the house. She was told to place her hands against the wall and was guarded in that position while one agent searched the house. Ricky Lyons was not found, but during the search of the house the agent observed what he believed to be cocaine. Upon being informed of this discovery, Agent Goodowens sent an officer to obtain a search warrant and in the meantime conducted a second search of the house, which uncovered additional incriminating evidence. During a third search conducted pursuant to a search warrant, the agents uncovered 43 pounds of cocaine. Petitioner was arrested and indicted on federal drug charges.

Prior to trial, petitioner moved to suppress all evidence uncovered during the various searches on the ground that it was illegally obtained because the agents had failed to secure a search warrant before entering the house. Agent Goodowens testified at the suppression hearing that there had been no "physical hinderance" preventing him from obtaining a search warrant and that he did not do so because he believed that the arrest warrant for Ricky Lyons was sufficient to justify the entry and search. The District Court agreed with this view, and denied the suppression motion. Petitioner was convicted, and renewed his challenge to the search in his appeal. A divided Court of Appeals for the Fifth Circuit affirmed the District Court's denial of petitioner's suppression motion.

The Government initially seeks to avert our consideration of the Fifth Circuit's decision by suggesting that petitioner may, regardless of the merits of that decision, lack an expectation of privacy in the house sufficient to prevail on his Fourth Amendment claim. This argument was never raised by the Government in the courts below. Moreover, in its brief in opposition to certiorari the Government represented to this Court that the house in question was "petitioner's residence" and was "occupied by petitioner, Gaultney, and Gaultney's wife." However, the

Government now contends that the record does not clearly show that petitioner had a reasonable expectation of privacy in the house, and hence urges us to remand the case to the District Court for re-examination of this factual question.

We decline to follow the suggested disposition. Aside from arguing that a search warrant was not constitutionally required, the Government was initially entitled to defend against petitioner's charge of an unlawful search by asserting that petitioner lacked a reasonable expectation of privacy in the searched home, or that he consented to the search, or that exigent circumstances justified the entry. The Government, however, may lose its right to raise factual issues of this sort before this Court when it has made contrary assertions in the courts below, when it has acquiesced in contrary findings by those courts, or when it has failed to raise such questions in a timely fashion during the litigation.

* * *

The question before us is a narrow one.[1] The search at issue here took place in the absence of consent or exigent circumstances. Except in such special situations, we have consistently held that the entry into a home to conduct a search or make an arrest is unreasonable under the Fourth Amendment unless done pursuant to a warrant.

* * *

Here, of course, the agents had a warrant—one authorizing the arrest of Ricky Lyons. However, the Fourth Amendment claim here is not being raised by Ricky Lyons. Instead, the challenge to the search is asserted by a person not named in the warrant who was convicted on the basis of evidence uncovered during a search of his residence for Ricky Lyons. Thus, the narrow issue before us is whether an arrest warrant—as opposed to a search warrant—is adequate to protect the Fourth Amendment interests of persons not named in the warrant, when their homes are searched without their consent and in the absence of exigent circumstances.

* * *

[W]hile an arrest warrant and a search warrant both serve to subject the probable cause determination of the police to judicial review, the interests protected by the two warrants differ. An arrest warrant is issued by a magistrate upon a showing that probable cause exists to believe that the subject of the warrant has committed an offense and thus the warrant primarily serves to protect an individual from an unreasonable seizure. A search warrant, in contrast, is issued upon a showing of probable cause to believe that the legitimate object of a search is located in a particular place, and therefore safeguards an

1. Initially, we assume without deciding that the information relayed to Agent Goodowens concerning the whereabouts of Ricky Lyons would have been sufficient to establish probable cause to believe that Lyons was at the house searched by the agents.

individual's interest in the privacy of his home and possessions against the unjustified intrusion of the police.

Thus, whether the arrest warrant issued in this case adequately safeguarded the interests protected by the Fourth Amendment depends upon what the warrant authorized the agents to do. To be sure, the warrant embodied a judicial finding that there was probable cause to believe that Ricky Lyons had committed a felony, and the warrant therefore authorized the officers to seize Lyons. However, the agents sought to do more than use the warrant to arrest Lyons in a public place or in his home; instead, they relied on the warrant as legal authority to enter the home of a third person based on their belief that Ricky Lyons might be a guest there. Regardless of how reasonable this belief might have been, it was never subjected to the detached scrutiny of a judicial officer. Thus, while the warrant in this case may have protected Lyons from an unreasonable seizure, it did absolutely nothing to protect petitioner's privacy interest in being free from an unreasonable invasion and search of his home. Instead, petitioner's only protection from an illegal entry and search was the agent's personal determination of probable cause. In the absence of exigent circumstances, we have consistently held that such judicially untested determinations are not reliable enough to justify an entry into a person's home to arrest him without a warrant, or a search of a home for objects in the absence of a search warrant. We see no reason to depart from this settled course when the search of a home is for a person rather than an object.

A contrary conclusion—that the police, acting alone and in the absence of exigent circumstances, may decide when there is sufficient justification for searching the home of a third party for the subject of an arrest warrant—would create a significant potential for abuse. Armed solely with an arrest warrant for a single person, the police could search all the homes of that individual's friends and acquaintances. See, e.g., Lankford v. Galston, 364 F.2d 197 (C.A.4, 1966) (enjoining police practice under which 300 homes searched pursuant to arrest warrants for two fugitives). Moreover, an arrest warrant may serve as the pretext for entering a home in which the police have a suspicion, but not probable cause to believe, that illegal activity is taking place. The Government recognizes the potential for such abuses, but contends that existing remedies—such as motions to suppress illegally procured evidence and damage actions for Fourth Amendment violations—provide adequate means of redress. We do not agree. As we observed on a previous occasion, "[t]he [Fourth] Amendment is designed to prevent, not simply to redress, unlawful police action." Chimel v. California, supra. Indeed, if suppression motions and damage actions were sufficient to implement the Fourth Amendment's prohibition against unreasonable searches and seizures, there would be no need for the constitutional requirement that in the absence of exigent circumstances a warrant must be obtained for a home arrest or a search of a home for objects. We have instead concluded that in such cases the participation of a detached magistrate in the probable cause determination is an essential element of a reasonable search or seizure, and we believe that the same conclusion should apply here.

In sum, two distinct interests were implicated by the search at issue here—Ricky Lyon's interest in being free from an unreasonable seizure and petitioner's interest in being free from an unreasonable search of his home. Because the arrest warrant for Lyons addressed only the former interest, the search of petitioner's home was no more reasonable from petitioner's perspective than it would have been if conducted in the absence of any warrant. Since warrantless searches of a home are impermissible absent consent or exigent circumstances, we conclude that the instant search violated the Fourth Amendment.

The Government concedes that this view is "apparently logical," that it furthers the general policies underlying the Fourth Amendment, and that it "has the virtue of producing symmetry between the law of entry to conduct a search for things to be seized and the law of entry to conduct a search for persons to be seized." Yet we are informed that this conclusion is "not without its flaws" in that it is contrary to common law precedent and creates some practical problems of law enforcement. We treat these contentions in turn.

* * *

While the common law thus sheds relatively little light on the narrow question before us, the history of the Fourth Amendment strongly suggests that its Framers would not have sanctioned the instant search. The Fourth Amendment was intended partly to protect against the abuses of the general warrants that had occurred in England and of the writs of assistance used in the Colonies. The general warrant specified only an offense—typically seditious libel—and left to the discretion of the executing officials the decision as to which persons should be arrested and which places should be searched. Similarly, the writs of assistance used in the Colonies noted only the object of the search—any uncustomed goods—and thus left customs officials completely free to search any place where they believed such goods might be. The central objectionable feature of both warrants was that they provided no judicial check on the determination of the executing officials that the evidence available justified an intrusion into any particular home. An arrest warrant, to the extent that it is invoked as authority to enter the homes of third parties, suffers from the same infirmity. Like a writ of assistance, it specifies only the object of a search—in this case, Ricky Lyons—and leaves to the unfettered discretion of the police the decision as to which particular homes should be searched. We do not believe that the Framers of the Fourth Amendment would have condoned such a result.

The Government also suggests that practical problems might arise if law enforcement officers are required to obtain a search warrant before entering the home of a third party to make an arrest. The basis of this concern is that persons, as opposed to objects, are inherently mobile, and thus officers seeking to effect an arrest may be forced to return to the magistrate several times as the subject of the arrest warrant moves from place to place. We are convinced, however, that a search warrant requirement will not significantly impede effective law enforcement efforts.

First, the situations in which a search warrant will be necessary are few. As noted in Payton v. New York, an arrest warrant alone will suffice to enter a suspect's own residence to effect his arrest. Furthermore, if probable cause exists, no warrant is required to apprehend a suspected felon in a public place. Thus, the subject of an arrest warrant can be readily seized before entering or after leaving the home of a third party. Finally, the exigent circumstances doctrine significantly limits the situations in which a search warrant would be needed. For example, a warrantless entry of a home would be justified if the police were in "hot pursuit" of a fugitive. Thus, to the extent that searches for persons pose special problems, we believe that the exigent circumstances doctrine is adequate to accommodate legitimate law enforcement needs.

Moreover, in those situations in which a search warrant is necessary, the inconvenience incurred by the police is simply not that significant. First, if the police know of the location of the felon when they obtain an arrest warrant, the additional burden of obtaining a search warrant at the same time is miniscule. The inconvenience of obtaining such a warrant does not increase significantly when an outstanding arrest warrant already exists. In this case, for example, Agent Goodowens knew the address of the house to be searched two days in advance, and planned the raid from the federal courthouse in Atlanta where, we are informed, three full time magistrates were on duty. In routine search cases such as this, the short time required to obtain a search warrant from a magistrate will seldom hinder efforts to apprehend a felon. Finally, if a magistrate is not nearby, a telephonic search warrant can usually be obtained. See Fed.Rule Crim.Proc. 41(c)(1), (2).

Whatever practical problems remain, however, cannot outweigh the constitutional interests at stake. Any warrant requirement impedes to some extent the vigor with which the Government can seek to enforce its laws, yet the Fourth Amendment recognizes that this restraint is necessary in some cases to protect against unreasonable searches and seizures. We conclude that this is such a case. The additional burden imposed on the police by a warrant requirement is minimal. In contrast, the right protected—that of presumptively innocent people to be secure in their homes from unjustified, forcible intrusions by the Government—is weighty. Thus, in order to render the instant search reasonable under the Fourth Amendment, a search warrant was required.

Accordingly, the judgment of the Court of Appeals is reversed and the case is remanded to that court for further proceedings consistent with this opinion.

The Chief Justice concurs in the judgment.

JUSTICE REHNQUIST, with whom JUSTICE WHITE joins, dissenting.

* * *

While I cannot subscribe to the Court's decision today, I will not falsely cry "wolf" in this dissent. The decision rests on a very special set of facts, and with a change in one or more of them it is clear that no separate search warrant would be required even under the reasoning of the Court.

On the one side *Payton* makes clear that an arrest warrant is all that is needed to enter the suspect's "home" to effect the arrest. 445 U.S., at 602–603. If a suspect has been living in a particular dwelling for any significant period, say a few days, it can certainly be considered his "home" for Fourth Amendment purposes, even if the premises are owned by a third party and others are living there, and even if the suspect concurrently maintains a residence elsewhere as well. In such a case the police could enter the premises with only an arrest warrant. On the other side, the more fleeting a suspect's connection with the premises, such as when he is a mere visitor, the more likely that exigent circumstances will exist justifying immediate police action without departing to obtain a search warrant. The practical damage done to effective law enforcement by today's decision, without any basis in the Constitution, may well be minimal if courts carefully consider the various conjuries of facts in the actual case before them.

The genuinely unfortunate aspect of today's ruling is not that fewer fugitives will be brought to book, or fewer criminals apprehended, though both of these consequences will undoubtedly occur; the greater misfortune is the increased uncertainty imposed on police officers in the field, committing magistrates, and trial judges, who must confront variations and permutations of this factual situation on a day-to-day basis. They will, in their various capacities, have to weigh the time during which a suspect for whom there is an outstanding arrest warrant has been in the building, whether the dwelling is the suspect's home, how long he has lived there, whether he is likely to leave immediately, and a number of related and equally imponderable questions. Certainty and repose, as Justice Holmes said, may not be the destiny of man, but one might have hoped for a higher degree of certainty in this one narrow but important area of the law than is offered by today's decision.

NOTES

1. The Supreme Court decided in Wilson v. Arkansas, ___ U.S. ___, 115 S.Ct. 1914 (1995) that the Fourth Amendment requires police officers to knock and announce themselves before entering to execute a warrant, unless "law enforcement interests ... establish the reasonableness of an unannounced entry."

2. A warrant to search the "person" of a drug suspect is not sufficiently specific to authorize a body cavity search, the Eighth Circuit held. United States v. Nelson, 36 F.3d 758 (8th Cir.1994). Police, with a search warrant, detained a suspected drug courier, made a visual inspection of his rectum, had a doctor

attempt a rectal examination, x-rayed him, and then used an endoscopic procedure to remove an object from his stomach.

3. A search warrant also does not give police the right to invite the media. The Second Circuit held that the warrant to search the home of credit card fraud suspects did not authorize police to invite along a CBS television news crew from "Street Stories," a weekly news magazine program. Ayeni v. Mottola, 35 F.3d 680 (2d Cir.1994), cert. denied ___ U.S. ___, 115 S.Ct. 1689 (1995).

E. WARRANTLESS SEARCHES

1. SEARCH INCIDENT TO ARREST

(A) SEARCH OF THE ARRESTEE

UNITED STATES v. ROBINSON

Supreme Court of the United States, 1973.
414 U.S. 218, 94 S.Ct. 467.

MR. JUSTICE REHNQUIST delivered the opinion of the Court.

Respondent Robinson was convicted in United States District Court for the District of Columbia of the possession and facilitation of concealment of heroin.... On his appeal ... the Court of Appeals *en banc* reversed the judgment of conviction, holding that the heroin introduced in evidence against respondent had been obtained as a result of a search which violated the Fourth Amendment to the United States Constitution....

On April 23, 1968, at approximately 11 o'clock p.m., Officer Richard Jenks, a 15-year veteran of the District of Columbia Metropolitan Police Department, observed the respondent driving a 1965 Cadillac near the intersection of 8th and C Streets, Southeast, in the District of Columbia. Jenks, as a result of previous investigation following a check of respondent's operator's permit four days earlier, determined there was reason to believe that respondent was operating a motor vehicle after the revocation of his operator's permit. This is an offense defined by statute in the District of Columbia which carries a mandatory minimum jail term, a mandatory minimum fine, or both.

Jenks signaled respondent to stop the automobile, which respondent did, and all three of the occupants emerged from the car. At that point Jenks informed respondent that he was under arrest for "operating after revocation and obtaining a permit by misrepresentation." It was assumed by the majority of the Court of Appeals, and is conceded by the respondent here, that Jenks had probable cause to arrest respondent, and that he effected a full custody arrest.

In accordance with procedures prescribed in Police Department instructions. Jenks then began to search respondent. He explained at a subsequent hearing that he was "face to face" with the respondent, and "placed [his] hands on [the respondent], my right hand to his left breast like this (demonstrating) and proceeded to pat him down thus (with the right hand)." During this patdown, Jenks felt an object in the left breast pocket of the heavy coat respondent was wearing, but testified that he "couldn't tell what it was" and also that he "couldn't actually tell the size of it." Jenks then reached into the pocket and pulled out the object, which turned out to be a "crumpled up cigarette package." Jenks testified that at this point he still did not know what was in the package:

> "As I felt the package I could feel objects in the package but I couldn't tell what they were.... I knew they weren't cigarettes."

The officer then opened the cigarette pack and found 14 gelatin capsules of white powder which he thought to be, and which later analysis proved to be, heroin. Jenks then continued his search of respondent to completion, feeling around his waist and trouser legs, and examining the remaining pockets. The heroin seized from the respondent was admitted into evidence at the trial which resulted in his conviction in the District Court....

It is well settled that a search incident to a lawful arrest is a traditional exception to the warrant requirement of the Fourth Amendment. This general exception has historically been formulated into two distinct propositions. The first is that a search may be made of the *person* of the arrestee by virtue of the lawful arrest. The second is that a search may be made of the area within the control of the arrestee.

Examination of this Court's decisions in the area show that these two propositions have been treated quite differently. The validity of the search of a person incident to a lawful arrest has been regarded as settled from its first enunciation, and has remained virtually unchallenged until the present case. The validity of the second proposition, while likewise conceded in principle, has been subject to differing interpretations as to the extent of the area which may be searched.

Because the rule requiring exclusion of evidence obtained in violation of the Fourth Amendment was first enunciated in Weeks v. United States, 232 U.S. 383 (1914), it is understandable that virtually all of this Court's search and seizure law has been developed since that time....

* * *

In its decision of this case, the majority of the Court of Appeals decided that even after a police officer lawfully places a suspect under arrest for the purpose of taking him into custody, he may not ordinarily proceed to fully search the prisoner. He must instead conduct a limited frisk of the outer clothing and remove such weapons that he may, as a result of that limited frisk, reasonably believe the suspect has in his possession. While recognizing that Terry v. Ohio, 392 U.S. 1 (1968) [reported subsequently in Section G of this chapter], dealt with a permissible "frisk" incident to an investigative stop based on less than probable cause to arrest, the Court of Appeals felt that the principles of that case should be carried over to this probable cause arrest for driving while one's license is revoked. Since there would be no further evidence of such a crime to be obtained in a search of the arrestee, the Court held that only a search for weapons could be justified.

Terry v. Ohio did not involve an arrest for probable cause, and it made quite clear that the "protective frisk" for weapons which it approved might be conducted without probable cause. The Court's opinion explicitly recognized that there is a "distinction in purpose, character, and extent between a search incident to an arrest and a limited search for weapons". . . .

* * *

[Although] earlier authorities are sketchy, they tend to support the broad statement of the authority to search incident to arrest found in the successive decisions of this Court, rather than the restrictive one which was applied by the Court of Appeals in this case. The scarcity of case law before *Weeks* is doubtless due in part to the fact that the exclusionary rule there enunciated had been first adopted only 11 years earlier in Iowa; but it would seem to be also due in part to the fact that the issue was regarded as well-settled.

The Court of Appeals in effect determined that the *only* reason supporting the authority for a *full* search incident to lawful arrest was the possibility of discovery of evidence or fruits. Concluding that there could be no evidence or fruits in the case of an offense such as that with which respondent was charged, it held that any protective search would have to be limited by the conditions laid down in *Terry* for a search upon less than probable cause to arrest. Quite apart from the fact that *Terry* clearly recognized the distinction between the two types of searches, and that a different rule governed one than governed the other, we find additional reason to disagree with the Court of Appeals.

The justification or reason for the authority to search incident to a lawful arrest rests quite as much on the need to disarm the suspect in order to take him into custody as it does on the need to preserve evidence on his person for later use at trial. The standards traditionally governing a search incident to lawful arrest are not, therefore, commuted to the stricter *Terry* standards by the absence of probable fruits or further evidence of the particular crime for which the arrest is made.

Nor are we inclined, on the basis of what seems to us to be a rather speculative judgment, to qualify the breadth of the general authority to search incident to a lawful custodial arrest on an assumption that persons arrested for the offense of driving while their license has been revoked are less likely to be possessed of dangerous weapons than are those arrested for other crimes.[1] It is scarcely open to doubt that the danger to an officer is far greater in the case of the extended exposure which follows the taking of a suspect into custody and transporting him to the police station than in the case of the relatively fleeting contact resulting from the typical *Terry*-type stop. This is an adequate basis for treating all custodial arrests alike for purposes of search justification.

But quite apart from these distinctions, our more fundamental disagreement with the Court of Appeals arises from its suggestion that there must be litigated in each case the issue of whether or not there was present one of the reasons supporting the authority for a search of the person incident to a lawful arrest. We do not think the long line of authorities of this Court dating back to *Weeks,* nor what we can glean from the history of practice in this country and in England, requires such a case by case adjudication. A police officer's determination as to how and where to search the person of a suspect whom he has arrested is necessarily a quick *ad hoc* judgment which the Fourth Amendment does not require to be broken down in each instance into an analysis of each step in the search. The authority to search the person incident to a lawful custodial arrest while based upon the need to disarm and to discover evidence, does not depend on what a court may later decide was the probability in a particular arrest situation that weapons or evidence would in fact be found upon the person of the suspect. A custodial arrest of a suspect based on probable cause is a reasonable intrusion under the Fourth Amendment; that intrusion being lawful, a search incident to the arrest requires no additional justification. It is the fact of the lawful arrest which establishes the authority to search, and we hold that in the case of a lawful custodial arrest a full search of the person is not only an exception to the warrant requirement of the Fourth Amendment, but is also a "reasonable" search under that Amendment.

* * *

[MR. JUSTICE POWELL's concurring opinion is omitted.]

MR. JUSTICE MARSHALL, with whom MR. JUSTICE DOUGLAS and MR. JUSTICE BRENNAN join, dissenting.

Certain fundamental principles have characterized this Court's Fourth Amendment jurisprudence over the years. Perhaps the most basic of these was expressed by Mr. Justice Butler, speaking for a

1. Such an assumption appears at least questionable in light of the available statistical data concerning assaults on police officers who are in the course of making arrests. The danger to the police officer flows from the fact of the arrest, and its attendant proximity, stress and uncertainty, and not from the grounds for arrest. One study concludes that approximately 30% of the shootings of police officers occur when the officer approaches a person seated in a car. Bristow Police Officer Shootings—A Factual Evaluation, 54 J.Crim.L.C. & P.S. 93 (1963), cited in Adams v. Williams, 407 U.S. 143, 148 (1972). The Government in its brief notes that the Uniform Crime Reports, prepared by the Federal Bureau of Investigation, indicate that a significant percentage of police officer murders occur when the officers are making traffic stops. Those reports indicate that during January-March, 1973, 35 police officers were murdered; 11 of those officers were killed while engaged in traffic stops.

unanimous Court in Go-Bart Co. v. United States, 282 U.S. 344, 51 S.Ct. 153 (1931): "There is no formula for the determination of reasonableness. Each case is to be decided on its own facts and circumstances." As we recently held, "The constitutional validity of a warrantless search is preeminently the sort of question which can only be decided in the concrete factual context of the individual case." Sibron v. New York, 392 U.S. 40, 59 (1968). And the intensive, at times painstaking, case by case analysis characteristic of our Fourth Amendment decisions bespeaks our "jealous regard for maintaining the integrity of individual rights." Mapp v. Ohio, 367 U.S. 643, 647, 81 S.Ct. 1684, 1687 (1961).

In the present case, however, the majority turns its back on these principles, holding that "the fact of the lawful arrest" always establishes the authority to conduct a full search of the arrestee's person, regardless of whether in a particular case "there was present one of the reasons supporting the authority for a search of the person incident to a lawful arrest." The majority's approach represents a clear and marked departure from our long tradition of case-by-case adjudication of the reasonableness of searches and seizures under the Fourth Amendment. I continue to believe that "[t]he scheme of the Fourth Amendment becomes meaningful only when it is assured that at some point the conduct of those charged with enforcing the laws can be subjected to the more detached, neutral scrutiny of a judge who must evaluate the reasonableness of a particular search or seizure in light of the particular circumstances." Terry v. Ohio. Because I find the majority's reasoning to be at odds with these fundamental principles, I must respectfully dissent.

* * *

The majority's attempt to avoid case-by-case adjudication of Fourth Amendment issues is not only misguided as a matter of principle, but is also doomed to fail as a matter of practical application. As the majority itself is well aware, the powers granted the police in this case are strong ones, subject to potential abuse. Although, in this particular case, Officer Jenks was required by Police Department regulation to make an in-custody arrest rather than to issue a citation, in most jurisdictions and for most traffic offenses the determination of whether to issue a citation or effect a full arrest is discretionary with the officer. There is always the possibility that a police officer, lacking probable cause to obtain a search warrant, will use a traffic arrest as a pretext to conduct a search. I suggest this possibility not to impugn the integrity of our police, but merely to point out that case-by-case adjudication will always be necessary to determine whether a full arrest was effected for purely legitimate reasons or, rather, as a pretext for searching the arrestee....

* * *

NOTES

1. In the companion case of Gustafson v. Florida, 414 U.S. 260, 94 S.Ct. 488 (1973), the Supreme Court issued the following ruling (with the same three Justices dissenting as in *Robinson*):

> We hold that upon arresting petitioner for the offense of driving his automobile without a valid operator's license, and taking him into custody, Smith was entitled to make a full search of petitioner's person incident to that lawful arrest. Since it is the fact of custodial arrest which gives rise to the authority to search, it is of no moment that Smith did not indicate any subjective fear of the petitioner or that he did not himself suspect that the petitioner was armed. Having in the course of his lawful search come upon the box of cigarettes, Smith was entitled to inspect it; and when his inspection revealed the homemade cigarettes which he believed to contain an unlawful substance, he was entitled to seize them as "fruits, instrumentalities or contraband" probative of criminal conduct.

2. In Fuller v. M.G. Jewelry, 950 F.2d 1437 (9th Cir.1991) the police department had a policy requiring strip and body cavity searches of all persons arrested for a felony. The court followed its own precedent in holding such a policy unconstitutional and then further held such searches permissible only where officials have reasonable suspicion that the arrestee harbors weapons or dangerous contraband. Reasonable suspicion that stolen goods are concealed on the arrestee is not a justification for a warrantless strip or body cavity search.

(B) Searches of Arrest Area and of Persons Therein

CHIMEL v. CALIFORNIA

Supreme Court of the United States, 1969.
395 U.S. 752, 89 S.Ct. 2034.

Mr. Justice Stewart delivered the opinion of the Court.

This case raises basic questions concerning the permissible scope under the Fourth Amendment of a search incident to a lawful arrest.

The relevant facts are essentially undisputed. Late in the afternoon of September 13, 1965, three police officers arrived at the Santa Ana, California, home of the petitioner with a warrant authorizing his arrest for the burglary of a coin shop. The officers knocked on the door, identified themselves to the petitioner's wife and asked if they might come inside. She ushered them into the house, where they waited 10 or 15 minutes until the petitioner returned home from work. When the petitioner entered the house, one of the officers handed him the arrest warrant and asked for permission to "look around." The petitioner objected, but was advised that "on the basis of the lawful arrest," the officers would nonetheless conduct a search. No search warrant had been issued.

Accompanied by the petitioner's wife, the officers then looked through the entire three-bedroom house, including the attic, the garage, and a small workshop. In some rooms the search was relatively cursory. In the master bedroom and sewing room, however, the officers directed the petitioner's wife to open drawers and "to physically move contents of the drawers from side to side so that [they] might view any items that would have come from [the] burglary." After completing the search, they seized numerous items—primarily coins, but also several medals, tokens, and a few other objects. The entire search took between 45 minutes and an hour.

At the petitioner's subsequent state trial on two charges of burglary, the items taken from his house were admitted into evidence against him, over his objection that they had been unconstitutionally seized. He was convicted, and the judgments of conviction were affirmed by both the California District Court of Appeal and the California Supreme Court. Both courts accepted the petitioner's contention that the arrest warrant was invalid because the supporting affidavit was set out in conclusory terms, but held that since the arresting officers had procured the warrant "in good faith," and since in any event they had had sufficient information to constitute probable cause for the petitioner's arrest, that arrest had been lawful. From this conclusion the appellate courts went on to hold that the search of the petitioner's home had been justified, despite the absence of a search warrant, on the ground that it had been incident to a valid arrest. We granted certiorari in order to consider the petitioner's substantial constitutional claims.

Without deciding the question, we proceed on the hypothesis that the California courts were correct in holding that the arrest of the petitioner was valid under the Constitution. This brings us directly to the question whether the warrantless search of the petitioner's entire house can be constitutionally justified as incident to that arrest. The decisions of this Court bearing upon that question have been far from consistent, as even the most cursory review makes evident.

Approval of a warrantless search incident to a lawful arrest seems first to have been articulated by the Court in 1914 as dictum in Weeks v. United States, 232 U.S. 383, 34 S.Ct. 341, in which the Court stated:

> "What then is the present case? Before answering that inquiry specifically, it may be well by a process of exclusion to state what it is not. It is not an assertion of the right on the part of the Government, always recognized under English and American law, to search the person of the accused when legally arrested to discover and seize the fruits or evidences of crime."

That statement made no reference to any right to search the *place* where an arrest occurs, but was limited to a right to search the "person." Eleven years later the case of Carroll v. United States, 267 U.S. 132, 45 S.Ct. 280, brought the following embellishment of the *Weeks* statement:

> "When a man is legally arrested for an offense, whatever is found upon his person *or in his control* which it is unlawful for him to have and which may be used to prove the offense may be seized and held as evidence in the prosecution." (Emphasis added.)

Still, that assertion too was far from a claim that the "place" where one is arrested may be searched so long as the arrest is valid. Without explanation, however, the principle emerged in expanded form a few months later in Agnello v. United States, 269 U.S. 20, 46 S.Ct. 4—although still by way of dictum:

> "The right without a search warrant contemporaneously to search persons lawfully arrested while committing crime and to search the place where the arrest is made in order to find and seize things connected with the crime as its fruits or as the means by which it was committed, as well as weapons and other things to effect an escape from custody, is not to be doubted. See Carroll v. United States, 267 U.S. 132, 158, 45 S.Ct. 280; Weeks v. United States, 232 U.S. 383, 392, 34 S.Ct. 341."

And in Marron v. United States, 275 U.S. 192, 48 S.Ct. 74, two years later, the dictum of *Agnello* appeared to be the foundation of the Court's decision. In that case federal agents had secured a search warrant authorizing the seizure of liquor and certain articles used in its manufacture. When they arrived at the premises to be searched, they saw "that the place was used for retailing and drinking intoxicating liquors." They proceeded to arrest the person in charge and to execute the warrant. In searching a closet for the items listed in the warrant they came across an incriminating ledger, concededly not covered by the warrant, which they also seized. The Court upheld the seizure of the ledger by holding that since the agents had made a lawful arrest, "[t]hey had a right without a warrant contemporaneously to search the place in order to find and seize the things used to carry on the criminal enterprise."

That the *Marron* opinion did not mean all that it seemed to say became evident, however, a few years later in Go-Bart Importing Co. v. United States, 282 U.S. 344, 51 S.Ct. 153, and United States v. Lefkowitz, 285 U.S. 452, 52 S.Ct. 420. In each of those cases the opinion of the Court was written by Mr. Justice Butler, who had authored the opinion in *Marron.* In *Go-Bart,* agents had searched the office of persons whom they had lawfully arrested, and had taken several papers from a desk, a safe, and other parts of the office. The Court noted that no crime had been committed in the agents' presence, and that although the agent in charge "had an abundance of information and time to swear out a valid [search] warrant, he failed to do so." In holding the search and seizure unlawful, the Court stated:

> "Plainly the case before us is essentially different from Marron v. United States, 275 U.S. 192, 48 S.Ct. 74. There, officers executing a valid search warrant for intoxicating liquors found and arrested one Birdsall who in pursuance of a conspiracy was actually engaged in running a saloon. As an incident to the arrest they seized a ledger in a closet where the liquor or some of it was kept and some bills beside the cash register. These things were visible and accessible and in the offender's immediate custody. There was no threat of force or general search or rummaging of the place."

This limited characterization of *Marron* was reiterated in *Lefkowitz,* a case in which the Court held unlawful a search of desk drawers and a cabinet despite the fact that the search had accompanied a lawful arrest.

The limiting views expressed in *Go-Bart* and *Lefkowitz* were thrown to the winds, however, in Harris v. United States, 331 U.S. 145, 67 S.Ct. 1098, decided in 1947. In that case, officers had obtained a warrant for Harris' arrest on the basis of his alleged involvement with the cashing and interstate transportation of a forged check. He was arrested in the living room of his four-room apartment, and in an attempt to recover two canceled checks thought to have been used in effecting the forgery, the officers undertook a thorough search of the entire apartment. Inside a desk drawer they found a sealed envelope marked "George Harris, personal papers." The envelope, which was then torn open, was found to contain altered selective service documents, and those documents were used to secure Harris' conviction for violating the Selective Training and Service Act of 1940. The Court rejected Harris' Fourth Amendment claim, sustaining the search as "incident to arrest."

Only a year after *Harris,* however, the pendulum swung again. In Trupiano v. United States, 334 U.S. 699, 68 S.Ct. 1229, agents raided the site of an illicit distillery, saw one of several conspirators operating the still, and arrested him, contemporaneously "seiz[ing] the illicit distillery." The Court held that the arrest and others made subsequently had been valid, but that the unexplained failure of the agents to procure a search warrant—in spite of the fact that they had had more than enough time before the raid to do so—rendered the search unlawful. The opinion stated:

> "It is a cardinal rule that, in seizing goods and articles, law enforcement agents must secure and use search warrants wherever reasonably practicable.... This rule rests upon the desirability of having magistrates rather than police officers determine when searches and seizures are permissible and what limitations should be placed upon such activities.... To provide the necessary security against unreasonable intrusions upon the private lives of individuals, the framers of the Fourth Amendment required adherence to judicial processes wherever possible. And subsequent history has confirmed the wisdom of that requirement.
>
> * * *
>
> "A search or seizure without a warrant as an incident to a lawful arrest has always been considered to be a strictly limited right. It grows out of the inherent necessities of the situation at the time of the arrest. But there must be something more in the way of necessity than merely a lawful arrest."

In 1950, two years after *Trupiano,* came United States v. Rabinowitz, 339 U.S. 56, 70 S.Ct. 430, the decision upon which California primarily relies in the case now before us. In *Rabinowitz,* federal authorities had been informed that the defendant was dealing in stamps bearing forged overprints. On the basis of that information they secured a warrant for his arrest, which they executed at his one-room business office. At the time of the arrest, the officers "searched the desk, safe, and file cabinets in the office for about an hour and a half," and seized 573 stamps with forged overprints. The stamps were admitted into evidence at the defendant's trial and this Court affirmed his conviction, rejecting the contention that the warrantless search had been unlawful. The Court held that the search in its entirety fell within the principle giving law enforcement authorities "[t]he right 'to search the place where the arrest is made in order to find and seize things connected with the crime....' " *Harris* was regarded as "ample authority" for that conclusion. The opinion rejected the rule of *Trupiano* that "in seizing goods and articles, law enforcement agents must secure and use search warrants wherever reasonably practicable." The test, said the Court, "is not whether it is reasonable to procure a search warrant, but whether the search was reasonable."

Rabinowitz has come to stand for the proposition, *inter alia,* that a warrantless search "incident to a lawful arrest" may generally extend to the area that is considered to be in the "possession" or under the "control" of the person arrested. And it was on the basis of that proposition that the California courts upheld the search of the petitioner's entire house in this case. That doctrine, however, at least in the broad sense in which it was applied by the California courts in this case, can withstand neither historical nor rational analysis.

Even limited to its own facts, the *Rabinowitz* decision was, as we have seen, hardly founded on an unimpeachable line of authority. As Mr. Justice Frankfurter commented in dissent in that case, the "hint" contained in *Weeks* was, without persuasive justification, "loosely turned into dictum and finally elevated to a decision." And the approach taken in cases such as *Go-Bart, Lefkowitz,* and *Trupiano* was essentially disregarded by the *Rabinowitz* Court.

Nor is the rationale by which the State seeks here to sustain the search of the petitioner's house supported by a reasoned view of the background and purpose of the Fourth Amendment. Mr. Justice Frankfurter wisely pointed out in his *Rabinowitz* dissent that the Amendment's proscription of "unreasonable searches and seizures" must be read in light of "the history that gave rise to the words"—a history of "abuses so deeply felt by the Colonies as to be one of the potent causes of the Revolution...." The Amendment was in large part a reaction to the general warrants and warrantless searches that had so alienated the colonists and had helped speed the movement for independence. In the scheme of the Amendment, therefore, the requirement that "no Warrants shall issue, but upon probable cause," plays a crucial part....

* * *

Only last Term in Terry v. Ohio, 392 U.S. 1, 88 S.Ct. 1868, we emphasized that "the police must, whenever practicable, obtain advance judicial approval of searches and seizures through the warrant procedure," and that "[t]he scope of [a] search must be 'strictly tied to and justified by' the circumstances which rendered its initiation permissible." The search undertaken by the officer in that "stop and frisk" case was sustained under that test, because it was no more than a "protective ... search for weapons." But in a companion case, Sibron v. New York, 392 U.S. 40, 88 S.Ct. 1889, we applied the same standard to another set of facts and reached a contrary result, holding that a policeman's action in thrusting his hand into a suspect's pocket had been neither motivated by nor limited to the objective of protection. Rather, the search had been made in order to find narcotics, which were in fact found.

A similar analysis underlies the "search incident to arrest" principle, and marks its proper extent. When an arrest is made, it is reasonable for the arresting officer to search the person arrested in order to remove any weapons that the latter might seek to use in order to resist arrest or effect his escape. Otherwise, the officer's safety might well be endangered, and the arrest itself frustrated. In addition, it is entirely reasonable for the arresting officer to search for and seize any evidence on the arrestee's person in order to prevent its concealment or destruction. And the area into which an arrestee might reach in order to grab a weapon or evidentiary items must, of course, be governed by a like rule. A gun on a table or in a drawer in front of one who is arrested can be as dangerous to the arresting officer as one concealed in the clothing of the person arrested. There is ample justification, therefore, for a search of the arrestee's person and the area "within his immediate control"—construing that phrase to mean the area from within which he might gain possession of a weapon or destructible evidence.

There is no comparable justification, however, for routinely searching rooms other than that in which an arrest occurs—or, for that matter, for searching through all the desk drawers or other closed or concealed areas in that room itself. Such searches, in the absence of well-recognized exceptions, may be made only under the authority of a search warrant. The "adherence to judicial processes" mandated by the Fourth Amendment requires no less.

* * *

It is argued in the present case that it is "reasonable" to search a man's house when he is arrested in it. But that argument is founded on little more than a subjective view regarding the acceptability of certain sorts of police conduct, and not on considerations relevant to Fourth Amendment interests. Under such an unconfined analysis, Fourth Amendment protection in this area would approach the evaporation point. It is not easy to explain why, for instance, it is less subjectively "reasonable" to search a man's house when he is arrested on his front lawn—or just down the street—than it is when he happens to be in the house at the time of arrest.

* * *

It would be possible, of course, to draw a line between *Rabinowitz* and *Harris* on the one hand, and this case on the other. For *Rabinowitz* involved a single room, and *Harris* a four-room apartment, while in the case before us an entire house was searched. But such a distinction would be highly artificial. The rationale that allowed the searches and seizures in *Rabinowitz* and *Harris* would allow the searches and seizures in this case. No consideration relevant to the Fourth Amendment suggests any point of rational limitation, once the search is allowed to go beyond the area from which the person arrested might obtain weapons or evidentiary items. The only reasoned distinction is one between a search of the person arrested and the area within his reach on the one hand, and more extensive searches on the other.

The petitioner correctly points out that one result of decisions such as *Rabinowitz* and *Harris* is to give law enforcement officials the opportunity to engage in searches not justified by probable cause, by the simple expedient of arranging to arrest suspects at home rather than elsewhere. We do not suggest that the petitioner is necessarily correct in his assertion that such a strategy was utilized here, but the fact remains that had he been arrested earlier in the day, at his place of employment rather than at home, no search of his house could have been made without a search warrant. In any event, even apart from the possibility of such police tactics, the general point so forcefully made by Judge Learned Hand in United States v. Kirschenblatt, 2d Cir., 16 F.2d 202, remains:

> "After arresting a man in his house, to rummage at will among his papers in search of whatever will convict him, appears to us to be indistinguishable from what might be done under a general warrant; indeed, the warrant would give more protection, for presumably it must be issued by a magistrate. True, by hypothesis the power would not exist, if the supposed offender were not found on the premises; but it is small consolation to know that one's papers are safe only so long as one is not at home."

Rabinowitz and *Harris* have been the subject of critical commentary for many years, and have been relied upon less and less in our own decisions. It is time, for the reasons we have stated, to hold that on their own facts, and insofar as the principles they stand for are inconsistent with those that we have endorsed today, they are no longer to be followed.

Application of sound Fourth Amendment principles to the facts of this case produces a clear result. The search here went far beyond the petitioner's person and the area from within which he might have obtained either a weapon or something that could have been used as evidence against him. There was no constitutional justification, in the absence of a search warrant, for extending the search beyond that area. The scope of the search was, therefore, "unreasonable" under the

Fourth and Fourteenth Amendments, and the petitioner's conviction cannot stand.

Reversed.

[Omitted is the dissenting opinion of Justices White and Black. The concurring opinion of Justice Harlan is also omitted.]

NOTES

1. In *Chimel,* the Court thought that the police should get a warrant before searching the home of an arrestee and implied that the police could watch the home in the interim. Would the use of the telephone search warrant solve the police problem of maintaining security over the premises while a warrant is secured?

2. Normally a search incident to an arrest occurs after the arrest is made. Is it necessary that the arrest be made *before* the search? As was said in Holt v. Simpson, 340 F.2d 853, 856 (7th Cir.1965):

"When probable cause for an arrest exists independently of what the search produces, the fact that the search precedes the formal arrest is immaterial when the search and arrest are nearly simultaneous and constitute for all practical purposes but one transaction. To hold differently would be to allow a technical formality of time to control when there had been no real interference with the substantive rights of a defendant."

3. Under *Chimel* the right to search the person who is arrested is clear. See Ricehill v. Brewer, 459 F.2d 537 (8th Cir.1972). How extensive may this search be? The following cases all approved extensive searches. State v. Wood, 262 La. 259, 263 So.2d 28 (1972) (suspect's mouth); Gaddis v. State, 497 P.2d 1087 (Okl.Crim.1972) (pubic hairs taken from clothes of arrestee); People v. Pinette, 42 Mich.App. 250, 201 N.W.2d 692 (1972) (shoes of arrestee). See generally State v. Swartsfager, 11 Or.App. 69, 501 P.2d 1321 (1972).

In United States v. Simpson, 453 F.2d 1028 (10th Cir.1972), the defendant was properly arrested by state officers for unlawful possession of explosives. Simpson's person was searched and the contents of his wallet examined. These contents included the selective service cards of another person and Simpson was prosecuted for illegal possession of those cards in federal court. He challenged the legality of the search. The Court held:

"The general rule is that incident to a lawful arrest, a search without a warrant may be made of portable personal effects in the immediate possession of the person arrested. The discovery during a search of a totally unrelated object which provides grounds for prosecution of a crime different than that which the accused was arrested for does not render the search invalid. Thus when Simpson's wallet was searched it was done incident to a lawful arrest and even though incriminating objects unrelated to the offense for which he was arrested were discovered, the search was valid. The incriminating Selective Service Certificate and Classification Card were admissible in evidence in the instant prosecution. We observe that although the general rule approved here does not require specific justification on a case-to-case basis, we take notice that knives and other small weapons can be secreted in wallets and that cards and addresses may disclose names of those who may have conspired with the person searched in the commission of the crime charged."

4. In Cupp v. Murphy, 412 U.S. 291, 93 S.Ct. 2000 (1973), in which the police were investigating the murder of the defendant's wife, who had lacerations

on her throat, he was detained long enough to obtain scrapings of his fingernails. This was held constitutionally permissible, the Court saying:

"Where there is no formal arrest, as in the case before us, a person might well be less hostile to the police and less likely to take conspicuous, immediate steps to destroy incriminating evidence on his person. Since he knows he is going to be released, he might be likely instead to be concerned with diverting attention away from himself. Accordingly, we do not hold that a full *Chimel* search would have been justified in this case without a formal arrest and without a warrant. But the respondent was not subjected to such a search.

"At the time Murphy was being detained at the station house, he was obviously aware of the detectives' suspicions. Though he did not have the full warning of official suspicion that a formal arrest provides, Murphy was sufficiently apprised of his suspected role in the crime to motivate him to attempt to destroy what evidence he could without attracting further attention. Testimony at trial indicated that after he refused to consent to the taking of fingernail samples, he put his hands behind his back and appeared to rub them together. He then put his hands in his pockets, and a 'metallic sound, such as keys or change rattling' was heard. The rationale of *Chimel,* in these circumstances, justified the police in subjecting him to the very limited search necessary to preserve the highly evanescent evidence they found under his fingernails,....

"On the facts of this case, considering the existence of probable cause, the very limited intrusion undertaken incident to the station house detention, and the ready destructibility of the evidence, we cannot say that this search violated the Fourth and Fourteenth Amendments."

5. May an officer conduct a search of the companion of someone he arrests, at least to the extent of determining whether or not the companion is armed? Consider the following from United States v. Berryhill, 445 F.2d 1189 (9th Cir.1971):

"The postal inspectors had obtained a warrant for the arrest of defendant for the Kawa check theft and were looking for him. The arresting officers had knowledge of defendant's prior arrest history, including information that he usually had weapons close to him. Defendant and his wife, the former driving, the latter a front-seat passenger, were located in an automobile and were stopped to effectuate the arrest at a busy intersection. The arrest was made with drawn pistols covering both occupants of the car, defendant was required to disembark and spread-eagle against the car where he was searched for weapons, handcuffed and taken to the officer's car by Inspector Loffler. Inspector Michaelson observed that Mrs. Berryhill was clutching a handbag with a paper sack protruding from the top. The paper sack was too small for its contents and in the top of the sack, the officer saw what appeared to be several envelopes. Michaelson, covering Mrs. Berryhill with his firearm, searched the handbag for weapons and found the mail matter which is the subject of Counts VI and XIII. On interrogation, defendant said, 'Look here, officer, the mail in her purse is mine. I told her to put it in there and she does what I say because she is my wife.'

"We are here concerned with the right to search another occupant of the vehicle, Mrs. Clarice Berryhill, who was clutching the handbag in which the stolen mail matter described in Counts VI and XIII was found. The fact that envelopes were observed protruding from the top of the paper sack might arguably have supported the reasonableness of the search, but the arresting officer described it as purely a search for weapons. And the lawful arrest of Berryhill cannot legalize a personal search of a companion for evidence against her simply because she was there. United States v. Di Re, 332 U.S. 581, 68 S.Ct. 222 (1948). The Supreme Court, however, has clarified the right of peace officers to protect themselves from the reasonably anticipated possibility of assault. In Terry v. Ohio, 393 U.S. 1, 88 S.Ct. 1868 (1967), the Court affirmed the right of a limited search 'to assure ... that the person with whom he is dealing is not armed with a weapon that could unexpectedly and fatally be used against him' despite the absence of probable cause for an arrest. We think that *Terry* recognizes and common sense dictates that the legality of such a limited intrusion into a citizen's personal privacy extends to a criminal's companions at the time of arrest. It is inconceivable that a peace officer effecting a lawful arrest of an occupant of a vehicle must expose himself to a shot in the back from defendant's associate because he cannot, on the spot, make the nice distinction between whether the other is a companion in crime or a social acquaintance. All companions of the arrestee within the immediate vicinity, capable of accomplishing a harmful assault on the officer, are constitutionally subjected to the cursory 'pat-down' reasonably necessary to give assurance that they are unarmed."

6. The Massachusetts Supreme Judicial Court rejected the analysis of *Berryhill,* holding that frisks of an arrestee's companions must satisfy the "reasonable suspicion" standard of Terry v. Ohio. Commonwealth v. Ng, 420 Mass. 236, 649 N.E.2d 157 (1995).

ILLINOIS v. LAFAYETTE

Supreme Court of the United States, 1983.
462 U.S. 640, 103 S.Ct. 2605.

CHIEF JUSTICE BURGER delivered the opinion of the Court.

The question presented is whether, at the time an arrested person arrives at a police station, the police may, without obtaining a warrant, search a shoulder bag carried by that person.

I

On September 1, 1980, at about 10 p.m., Officer Maurice Mietzner of the Kankakee City Police arrived at the Town Cinema in Kankakee, Illinois, in response to a call about a disturbance. There he found respondent involved in an altercation with the theatre manager. He arrested respondent for disturbing the peace, handcuffed him, and took him to the police station. Respondent carried a purse-type shoulder bag on the trip to the station.

At the police station respondent was taken to the booking room; there, Officer Mietzner removed the handcuffs from respondent and ordered him to empty his pockets and place the contents on the counter. After doing so, respondent took a package of cigarettes from his shoulder bag and placed the bag on the counter. Mietzner then removed the contents of the bag, and found ten amphetamine pills inside a cigarette case package.

Respondent was subsequently charged with violating Section 402(b) of the Illinois Controlled Substances Act, Ill.Rev.Stat., ch. 56½, ¶ 1402(b), on the basis of the controlled substances found in his shoulder bag. A pretrial suppression hearing was held at which the State argued that the search of the shoulder bag was a valid inventory search under South Dakota v. Opperman, 428 U.S. 364, 96 S.Ct. 3092 (1976). Officer Mietzner testified that he examined the bag's contents because it was standard procedure to inventory "everything" in the possession of an arrested person. He testified that he was not seeking and did not expect to find drugs or weapons when he searched the bag and he conceded that the shoulder bag was small enough that it could have been placed and sealed in a bag, container or locker for protective purposes. After the hearing, but before any ruling, the State submitted a brief in which it argued for the first time that the search was valid as a delayed search incident to arrest. Thereafter, the trial court ordered the suppression of the amphetamine pills.

On appeal, the Illinois Appellate Court affirmed. It first held that the State had waived the argument that the search was incident to a valid arrest by failing to raise that argument at the suppression hearing. However, the court went on to discuss and reject the State's argument: "[E]ven assuming, *arguendo,* that the State has not waived this argument, the stationhouse search of the shoulder bag did not constitute a valid search incident to a lawful arrest."

The State court also held that the search was not a valid inventory of respondent's belongings. It purported to distinguish South Dakota v. Opperman, supra, on the basis that there is a greater privacy interest in a purse-type shoulder bag than in an automobile, and that the State's legitimate interests could have been met in a less intrusive manner, by "sealing [the shoulder bag] within a plastic bag or box and placing it in a secured locker." The Illinois court concluded:

> "Therefore, the postponed warrantless search of the [respondent's] shoulder bag was neither incident to his lawful arrest nor a valid inventory of his belongings, and thus, violated the fourth amendment."

The Illinois Supreme Court denied discretionary review. We granted certiorari, because of the frequency with which this question confronts police and courts, and we reverse.

II

The question here is whether, consistent with the Fourth Amendment, it is reasonable for police to search the personal effects of a person under lawful arrest as part of the routine administrative procedure at a police stationhouse incident to booking and jailing the suspect. The justification for such searches does not rest on probable cause, and hence the absence of a warrant is immaterial to the reasonableness of the search. Indeed, we have previously established that the inventory search constitutes a well-defined exception to the warrant requirement. See South Dakota v. Opperman, supra. The Illinois court and respondent rely on United States v. Chadwick, 433 U.S. 1, 97 S.Ct. 2476 (1977), and Arkansa v. Sanders, 442 U.S. 753, 99 S.Ct. 2586 (1979); in the former, we noted that "probable cause to search is irrelevant" in inventory searches and went on to state:

> "This is so because the salutary functions of a warrant simply have no application in that context; the constitutional reasonableness of inventory searches must be determined on other bases."

A so-called inventory search is not an independent legal concept but rather an incidental administrative step following arrest and preceding incarceration. To determine whether the search of respondent's shoulder bag was unreasonable we must "balanc[e] its intrusion on the individual's Fourth Amendment interests against its promotion of legitimate governmental interests." Delaware v. Prouse, 440 U.S. 648, 654, 99 S.Ct. 1391, 1396 (1979).

In order to see an inventory search in proper perspective, it is necessary to study the evolution of interests along the continuum from arrest to incarceration. We have held that immediately upon arrest an officer may lawfully search the person of an arrestee, United States v. Robinson, 414 U.S. 218, 94 S.Ct. 467 (1973); he may also search the area within the arrestee's immediate control, Chimel v. California, 395 U.S. 752, 89 S.Ct. 2034 (1969). We explained the basis for this doctrine in United States v. Robinson, supra, where we said:

> "A police officer's determination as to how and where to search the person of a suspect whom he has arrested is necessarily a quick *ad hoc* judgment which the Fourth Amendment does not require to be broken down in each instance into an analysis of each step in the search. The authority to search the person incident to a lawful custodial arrest, while based upon the need to disarm and to discover evidence, does not depend on what a court may later decide was the probability in a particular arrest situation that weapons or evidence would in fact be found upon the person of the suspect. A custodial arrest of a suspect based on probable cause is a reasonable intrusion under the Fourth Amendment; that intrusion being lawful, a search incident to the arrest requires no additional justification. *It is the fact of the lawful arrest which establishes the authority to search, and we hold that in the case of a lawful custodial arrest a full search of the person is not only an exception to the warrant requirement of the Fourth Amendment, but is also a 'reasonable' search under that Amendment.*" 414 U.S., at 235, 94 S.Ct., at 477 (emphasis added).

An arrested person is not invariably taken to a police station or confined; if an arrestee is taken to the police station, that is no more than a continuation of the custody inherent in the arrest status. Nonetheless, the factors justifying a search of the person and personal effects of an arrestee upon reaching a police station but prior to being placed in confinement are somewhat different from the factors justifying an immediate search at the time and place of arrest.

The governmental interests underlying a stationhouse search of the arrestee's person and possessions may in some circumstances be even greater than those supporting a search immediately following arrest. Consequently, the scope of a stationhouse search will often vary from that made at the time of arrest. Police conduct that would be impractical or unreasonable—or embarrassingly intrusive—on the street can more readily—and privately—be performed at the station. For example, the interests supporting a search incident to arrest would hardly justify disrobing an arrestee on the street, but the practical necessities of routine jail administration may even justify taking a prisoner's clothes before confining him, although that step would be rare. This was made clear in United States v. Edwards, supra, 415 U.S., at 804, 94 S.Ct., at 1237–1238: "With or without probable cause, the authorities were entitled [at the stationhouse] not only to search [the arrestee's] clothing but also to take it from him and keep it in official custody."

At the stationhouse, it is entirely proper for police to remove and list or inventory property found on the person or in the possession of an arrested person who is to be jailed. A range of governmental interests support an inventory process. It is not unheard of for persons employed in police activities to steal property taken from arrested persons; similarly, arrested persons have been known to make false claims regarding what was taken from their possession at the stationhouse. A standardized procedure for making a list or inventory as soon as reasonable after reaching the stationhouse not only deters false claims but also inhibits theft or careless handling of articles taken from the arrested person. Arrested persons have also been known to injure themselves—or others—with belts, knives, drugs or other items on their person while being detained. Dangerous instrumentalities—such as razor blades, bombs, or weapons—can be concealed in innocent-looking articles taken from the arrestee's possession. The bare recital of these mundane realities justifies reasonable measures by police to limit these risks—either while the items are in police possession or at the time they are returned to the arrestee upon his release. Examining all the items removed from the arrestee's person or possession and listing or inventorying them is an entirely reasonable administrative procedure. It is immaterial whether the police actually fear any particular package or container; the need to protect against such risks arises independent of a particular officer's subjective concerns. See United States v. Robinson, supra. Finally, inspection of an arrestee's personal property may assist the police in ascertaining or verifying his identity. See 2 W. LaFave, Search and Seizure § 5.3, at 306–307 (1978). In short, every consideration of orderly police administration benefiting both police and the public points toward the appropriateness of the examination of respondent's shoulder bag prior to his incarceration.

Our prior cases amply support this conclusion. In South Dakota v. Opperman, supra, we upheld a search of the contents of the glove compartment of an abandoned automobile lawfully impounded by the police. We held that the search was reasonable because it served legitimate governmental interests that outweighed the individual's privacy interests in the contents of his car. Those measures protected the owner's property while it was in the custody of the police and protected police against possible false claims of theft. We found no need to consider the existence of less intrusive means of protecting the police and the property in their custody—such as locking the car and impounding it in safe storage under guard. Similarly, standardized inventory procedures are appropriate to serve legitimate governmental interests at stake here.

The Illinois court held that the search of respondent's shoulder bag was unreasonable because "preservation of the defendant's property and protection of police from claims of lost or stolen property, 'could have been achieved in a less intrusive manner.' For example, . . . the defendant's shoulder bag could easily have been secured by sealing it within a plastic bag or box and placing it in a secured locker." Perhaps so, but the real question is not what "could have been achieved," but whether the Fourth Amendment *requires* such steps; it is not our function to write a manual on administering routine, neutral procedures of the stationhouse. Our role is to assure against violations of the Constitution.

The reasonableness of any particular governmental activity does not necessarily or invariably turn on the existence of alternative "less intrusive" means. In Cady v. Dombrowski, 413 U.S. 433, 93 S.Ct. 2523 (1973), for example, we upheld the search of the trunk of a car to find a revolver suspected of being there. We rejected the contention that the public could equally well have been protected by the posting of a guard over the automobile. In language equally applicable to this case, we held, "[t]he fact that the protection of the public might, in the abstract, have been accomplished by 'less intrusive' means does not, by itself, render the search unreasonable." We are hardly in a position to second-guess police departments as to what practical administrative method will best deter theft by and false claims against its employees and preserve the security of the stationhouse. It is evident that a stationhouse search of every item carried on or by a person who has lawfully been taken into custody by the police will amply serve the important and legitimate governmental interests involved.

Even if less intrusive means existed of protecting some particular types of property, it would be unreasonable to expect police officers in the everyday course of business to make fine and subtle distinctions in deciding which containers or items may be searched and which must be sealed as a unit. Only recently in New York v. Belton, 453 U.S. 454, 101 S.Ct. 2860 (1981), we stated: " '[a] single familiar standard is essential to guide police officers, who have only limited time and expertise to reflect on and balance the social and individual interests involved in the specific circumstances they confront.' "

Applying these principles, we hold that it is not "unreasonable" for police, as part of the routine procedure incident to incarcerating an arrested person, to search any container or article in his possession, in accordance with established inventory procedures.

The judgment of the Illinois Appellate Court is reversed and the case is remanded for proceedings not inconsistent with this opinion.

It is so ordered.

JUSTICE MARSHALL, with whom JUSTICE BRENNAN joins, concurring in the judgment.

I agree that the police do not need a warrant or probable cause to conduct an inventory search prior to incarcerating a suspect, and I therefore concur in the judgment. The practical necessities of securing persons and property in a jailhouse setting justify an inventory search as part of the standard procedure incident to incarceration.

A very different case would be presented if the State had relied solely on the fact of arrest to justify the search of respondent's shoulder bag. A warrantless search incident to arrest must be justified by a need to remove weapons or prevent the destruction of evidence. Officer Mietzner did not in fact deem it necessary to search the bag when he arrested respondent, and I seriously doubt that such a search would have been lawful. A search at the time of respondent's arrest could not have been justified by a need to prevent the destruction of evidence, for there is no evidence or fruits of the offense—disturbing the peace—of which respondent was suspected. Moreover, although a concern about weapons might have justified seizure of the bag, such a concern could not have justified the further step of searching the bag following its seizure.

NOTE

Even before the foregoing principal case, the courts recognized that the right to search a person lawfully arrested is related to the established right of the police to inventory the property of a person about to be incarcerated. Charles v. United States, 278 F.2d 386 (9th Cir.1960); Westover v. United States, 394 F.2d 164 (9th Cir.1968); People v. Glaubman, 175 Colo. 41, 485 P.2d 711 (1971); State v. Hohensee, 473 S.W.2d 379 (Mo.1971). Some cases suggest that if the arrestee may be released on bail or recognizance before any period of incarceration, inventory search cannot be justified. People v. Overlee, 174 Colo. 202, 483 P.2d 222 (1971).

2. PLAIN VIEW SEIZURES

UNITED STATES v. WRIGHT

United States Court of Appeals, District of Columbia, 1971.
146 U.S.App.D.C. 126, 449 F.2d 1355.

PER CURIAM.

Appellant was convicted of grand larceny of a Chevrolet Corvette transmission, found by police in appellant's garage immediately before and at the time of his arrest. . . .

I. *Facts Relevant to the Issue Presented*

All the events took place on 18 May 1968, beginning at 5:00 a.m. when the police were notified that a 1967 Chevrolet Corvette had been stolen. By 4:20 p.m. Police Officers Huffstutler and Howard had located the Corvette, stripped of its transmission, engine, radiator, hood and steering wheel. From various pieces of evidence in and around the car Officer Huffstutler concluded that the Corvette had been stripped elsewhere, and by an examination of the terrain deduced the probable locale of the stripping within a three-block area. In a systematic survey of all streets and alleys they observed tell-tale sweepings of nuts and bolts in front of a three-car garage, and in addition several red rags of the type previously noted on the stripped Corvette. A comparison of the rags found at the two locations showed they were identical. The officers returned to the garage.

The three sliding doors of the garage were not completely closed because of their construction and age, leaving an opening of approximately eight or nine inches. Inside it was "relatively dark," so the officer employed his flashlight to look in through the gap. Lying ten feet away he noticed a transmission shaft. On his knees for a better view, he identified it as a Chevrolet product, and observed that the speedometer cable had been clipped. After returning to the stripped Corvette, a check of its speedometer cable showed it, too, had been clipped.

On notifying the Auto Squad of his discoveries, Officer Huffstutler was advised to go to the garage and recover the stolen transmission. Instead, he returned to his precinct and began to type an application for a search warrant. On reflection, he decided it was better then to return to the garage, interview its owner, and set in motion the procedure to take fingerprints from the Corvette.

On arrival at the garage Officer Huffstutler and his partner noted an automobile with its trunk open, parked so the trunk could be loaded from a little alleyway which led to the side door of the garage. Inside the open trunk were a steering wheel, clutch plate, and pressure plate, all 1967 Corvette equipment, and each of which corresponded to items stripped from the stolen car. With guns drawn the officers moved toward the open side door of the garage, and as they did appellant Wright and two others emerged. The three were arrested for possession of stolen property. Leaving them in custody, Officer Huffstutler entered the open door of the garage and located the Corvette transmission which had been moved to another place inside....

II. *Legality of the Officer's First Look*

Appellant contends strenuously that his rights under the Fourth Amendment were violated not once but twice by illegal search of the garage. He argues that the officer's action in peering through the eight or nine-inch crack was a search, particularly since it was aided by artificial light; that such search was illegal; that this illegal search tainted the seizure thereafter of the auto transmission at the time of the arrest. As in Dorsey v. United States [125 U.S.App.D.C. 355, 372 F.2d 928 (1967)], "the Government argues there can be no question of an illegal search since there was no search at all."

There was no search here. There are at least two doctrines or perhaps two different characterizations of the same doctrine, which we have enunciated in previous decisions on which the officer's conduct was legally justified. For convenience they might be termed the "challenging situation" and "plain view" doctrines.

A. *A closer look at a challenging situation.*

In *Dorsey,* supra, two officers approached a parked car occupied by two recognized, known narcotics violators. Although it was 11:00 p.m. the officers could see the driver and the passenger were turned facing each other as though examining something on the seat. The officer on the driver's side directed his flashlight into the car and illuminated in Dorsey's hand a cellophane bag filled with white-powdered, gelatin capsules. When Dorsey placed the bag on the ledge of the glove compartment, the other officer reached through the open window, seized the bag, and placed Dorsey under arrest. As the driver complained of the officer flashing his light inside the car, the officer noticed that the driver was dropping heroin capsules on the floor. He, too, was arrested and nine heroin capsules were picked up off the floor.

Without either characterizing the officer's action as a search or attempting to justify it as a search, we held that

> "The essential inquiry, as is customarily the case in Fourth Amendment claims, is the reasonableness of the police conduct under the circumstances.... Reasonableness involves consideration of the nature of the police conduct as well as the occasion of its exercise. We think the evidence supported a view of that conduct as not transgressing the constitutional standard.
>
> "... When the officers suddenly saw [the appellants] situated as they were at the time and place in question, the former were entitled to extend their preventive patrolling mission to the extent of approaching the car and observing what was going on inside.... We do not think the need to employ a visual aid at night in the form of a flashlight converts this form lawful into unlawful conduct. A car parked at 14th and U Streets at eleven o'clock at night, occupied by known narcotics offenders, bears little resemblance to a home or dwelling. If policemen are to serve any purpose of detecting and preventing crime by being out on the streets at all, *they must be able to take a closer look at challenging situations as they encounter them.* All we hold here is that this was one of those situations, and that the police response to it was a justifiable one which did not project their law enforcement responsibilities beyond permissible constitutional limits."

We think the facts and holding in *Dorsey,* supra, are comparable and decisive of appellant's contentions in regard to his first alleged illegal search.

B. *Plain view.*

James v. United States [135 U.S.App.D.C. 314, 418 F.2d 1150 (1969)] is equally dispositive of appellant's first claim and is closer on the operative facts. In *James* a police officer observed a partially stripped-down new Pontiac, and three days later observed that the stripping job had been completed. When he saw the new Pontiac the second time, completely stripped, the police officer entered the premises to investigate further, and in so doing secured the license number from the rear tag, the front license plate being missing.

On a pre-trial motion to suppress the District Court did exclude the rear license plate and the owner's manual found through the officer's entry on the unoccupied garage premises, but appellant also contended that all the stolen property discovered pursuant to a later issued search warrant should be suppressed, because this was the fruit of illegal observations by the officer from outside the garage which preceded his entry on the premises, and those observations violated his Fourth Amendment rights. The garage door was ajar and the officer was able to look under and observe parts and tools thrown about. In *James* we held that

> "The police are free to observe circumstances in evidence that are in 'plain view' to the public ... the plain view doctrine was reaffirmed in Harris v. United States, 390 U.S. 234, 88 S.Ct. 992, 19 L.Ed.2d 1067 (1968). That the policeman may have to crane his neck, or bend over, or squat, does not render the doctrine inapplicable, so long as what he saw would have been visible to any curious passerby...."

Whether it be considered that the transmission was in "plain view" to start with, or whether the officer took "a closer look at a challenging situation," we conclude that no rights of appellant protected by the Fourth Amendment were violated by Officer Huffstutler peering through the gap between the garage doors.

III. *Legality of the Seizure of the Transmission in the Garage*

Appellant contends with equal vigor that the seizure of the auto transmission was illegal as being the product of an illegal search either if the entry of Officer Huffstutler into the garage is considered independently, or if his entry is considered as the product of his previously illegal search by peering through the gap in the garage doors....

A. *Plain view.*

All the authorities cited above in our discussion of the doctrine of "plain view" are equally applicable to Officer Huffstutler's seizure of the auto transmission. Obviously the doctrine of "plain view" would be a rather sterile doctrine if it extended only so far as police officers' looking. In all of the "plain view" cases, the viewing has been followed by a seizure of evidence.

We do not ignore that Officer Huffstutler had spotted the stolen auto transmission within ten feet of him, had noted the cut speedometer cable, had gone the few blocks to the stripped Corvette to see if its speedometer cable was cut (it was), then returned to the garage for a final look before going to his precinct. After a short time there he returned to the garage, made the arrests, and seized the auto transmission. All of the events from the time the two officers first came upon the stripped Corvette, searched the neighborhood, made their observations in the garage, went back to the stripped Corvette, went back to the garage, went to the precinct, returned to the garage for the third time—all took place in exactly two hours. The time interval from when Officer Huffstutler first spotted the stolen transmission is not certain, but it probably was more than an hour and not more than an hour and a half.

What appellant is contending for here is to write into the doctrine of "plain view" a continuous observation requirement. Is the officer required to keep his eye glued to the knothole while he motions for help with a free hand? If the officer had known the additional fact of the Corvette's speedometer cable being cut at the time he first saw the transmission, and had left his point of observation to return to his car to radio his headquarters, and then returned to the gap in the garage doors only to find the transmission had been moved out of his vision, would he then have been barred from moving inside the garage to seize what he was certain was stolen property? If an interruption of the officer's plain view of stolen property is allowed, how long an interruption is permitted?

In Creighton [v. United States, 132 U.S.App.D.C. 115, 406 F.2d 651 (1968)], the police had observed various items of property openly displayed in appellant's car, after he had been arrested for a traffic violation. Learning of a burglary later while appellant was still at the station house, police went to appellant's car and seized the stolen property. We held that the goods were in plain view, and that there was no search, hence no warrant was required. In *Creighton,* as in the case at bar, the original "plain view" of the stolen property by the officers occurred at a time when the officers did not *know* the items were stolen. In *Creighton* there was an interval after the sighting, during which a phone call turned up a report of a burglary; in *Wright* here there was an interval after the officer's first look, during which he checked the cut speedometer cable. In each case, after the clinching piece of information had been secured, the officer returned to the stolen property and seized it. No search was involved in either case.

In the circumstances of this case we believe that on the doctrine of "plain view" Officer Huffstutler was authorized to carry that doctrine to its logical conclusion, seize the stolen property he had observed, and that the one-hour to hour-and-a-half interval in which the other events connected with his investigation transpired did not preclude him from doing this. On his return to the garage at the time the arrests were made it was the officer's duty to follow up, see if the transmission was still there, and recover the stolen property if he could. Whether he could see the transmission through the open door is in our judgment immaterial. He had seen it in the garage no more than an hour and a half before; it was not an unreasonable seizure under the Fourth Amendment for him to step inside, identify it again, and have it moved out along with the other stolen automobile parts that were already in the process of being spirited away.

Our holding on this point finds support in the American Law Institute Tentative Draft No. 3 of A Model Code of Pre-Arraignment Procedure (1970), Part II, Search and Seizure. Section 6.06, Seizure Independent of Search, provides:

> An officer who, in the course of otherwise lawful activity, observes or otherwise becomes aware of the nature and location of things which he reasonably believes to be subject to seizure under Section SS 1.03, and which therefore can be seized without a search, may seize such things.

Section SS 1.03(b) lists as subject to search and seizure "contraband, the fruits of crime, or things otherwise criminally possessed."

It was not necessary for Officer Huffstutler to make a search to discover the auto transmission when he seized it at the time of the arrest. He had already observed the transmission and become aware that it was located inside the garage. He had carefully checked it to be the fruit of the crime he was investigating and, in the language of the American Law Institute draft, it was "subject to seizure (as fruits of crime) . . . and . . . therefore can be seized without a search."

The Commentary on this draft Section is illuminating:

> "The authorization with respect to the seizure of things plainly observable in private premises does raise some questions under Johnson v. United States, 333 U.S. 10 [68 S.Ct. 367, 92 L.Ed. 436] (1948). There the opium was not visible but it was plainly observable by odor perceptible off the premises. Nevertheless entrance and seizure without a warrant was held unlawful. . . . However, although the *presence* of opium was observable, its location was not evident, and a search was in fact necessary; the authorization in the draft does not cover a search, but *only an entry for things already perceived and ready to hand.*" (Last emphasis supplied.) . . .

B. *Seizure to prevent removal of evidence.*

The police officer had seen the auto transmission shortly before, the other missing parts from the Corvette he was at the moment viewing in the trunk of another car, obviously in preparation to be hauled away. He was obligated to recover the stolen transmission without giving the miscreants a chance to spirit this away, too. The officers had no idea how many persons other than those visible were involved, hence

> "On the basis of such a plain view discovery of the fruits of a crime which were identified both by description and label, it was not only reasonable for the officers to seize them notwithstanding the absence of a search warrant, but it would have been a dereliction of their duty for them not to do so. To say that the police must leave evidence which they find (without engaging in an improper search) in order to go after a search warrant, on the assumption that the items will remain in the same place until they return with the warrant, is to ignore reality." [citing from United States v. Thweatt, 140 U.S.App.D.C. 120, 433 F.2d 1226, 1231 (1970)]

The officers were confronted with a situation which called for immediate action. The action which they took, the seizure of the stolen transmission, was the reasonable action to satisfy the exigent circumstances present.

* * *

[The dissenting opinion of Judge Wright is omitted.]

NOTES

1. Many plain view cases turn upon whether an officer has a right to be in the place from which vantage point he made his observations. Sometimes the law says he has a right to be there even if the property owner objects—for example, (1) a place which he has entered to search under a valid search warrant, or (2) the home of a suspect he has entered to make a valid arrest, with or without a warrant.

Sometimes the officer will be on private property with the express consent of the owner of the property or of someone with an interest in the property. At other times the officer will be on property which has been opened to the general public, for instance a pool room or gambling hall which welcomes the trade of all who enter. The officer's failure to affirmatively identify himself does not make his entry illegal even where knowledge of his identity would lead to his exclusion. See People v. Walker, 30 Ill.2d 213, 195 N.E.2d 654 (1964); People v. Abrams, 48 Ill.2d 446, 271 N.E.2d 37 (1971) (antiwar gathering, officer lawfully present on private property until announcement that officers are not welcome).

Affirmative misrepresentations as a means of entering a home where there is no other lawful justification for such entry will make the entry illegal and render inadmissible plain view seizures and observations within. If posing as a gas company meter reader is clearly impermissible, must a vice officer use his true name in making a date with a prostitute in order to make lawful his entry into her apartment? See People v. St. Ives, 110 Ill.App.2d 37, 249 N.E.2d 97 (1969).

It should be noted that open fields, even if privately owned, are not "protected" areas except within the relatively narrow limits of the curtilage. See Air Pollution Variance Board v. Western Alfalfa Corp., 416 U.S. 861, 94 S.Ct. 2114 (1974); United States ex rel. Saiken v. Bensinger, 546 F.2d 1292 (7th Cir.1976), on appeal following remand in 489 F.2d 865 (7th Cir.1973). See also

Conrad v. State, 63 Wis.2d 616, 218 N.W.2d 252 (1974). Both *Saiken* and *Conrad* involved successful quests for buried bodies, which were upheld under the "open field" doctrine.

2. Katz v. United States, 389 U.S. 347, 88 S.Ct. 507 (1967), has modified plain view doctrines in some jurisdictions so that even absent a trespass, a reasonable expectation of privacy may prevent seizure of plain view evidence. Of course under *Katz* what a person knowingly exposes to the public is not protected by the Fourth Amendment since there is no reasonable expectation of privacy. See United States v. Hanahan, 442 F.2d 649 (7th Cir.1971) (looking from sidewalk through open garage door); People v. Colvin, 19 Cal.App.3d 14, 96 Cal.Rptr. 397 (1971) (standing on guardrail of street looking into open window); Gil v. Beto, 440 F.2d 666 (5th Cir.1971) (looking into open motel room window from parking lot); State v. Kaaheena, 59 Hawaii 23, 575 P.2d 462 (1978) (plain view not applicable where police had to climb up to look through one inch hole in closed blinds).

Some courts have refused to find a reasonable expectation of privacy where the evidence can be seen from a vantage point where the officer has a right to be so long as no mechanical device is used to enhance the officer's senses. People v. Wright, 41 Ill.2d 170, 242 N.E.2d 180 (1968). Certainly the less sophisticated the device, the more likely a court will be to find no *Katz* violation. Commonwealth v. Hernley, 216 Pa.Super. 177, 263 A.2d 904 (1970) (use of binoculars by officer mounted on ladder to get "plain view" of activities behind undraped windows). Numerous cases have upheld the use of flashlights, Walker v. Beto, 437 F.2d 1018 (5th Cir.1971); United States v. Wright, 449 F.2d 1355 (D.C.Cir. 1971). Compare United States v. Kim, 415 F.Supp. 1252 (D.Hawaii 1976) (disapproving use of special military scopes).

Another aspect of *Katz* may actually broaden plain view doctrines. If a person exposes to the public evidence of a crime by leaving it on his land visible from the public way, he may be said to have no expectation of privacy in the item. He thus may subject such an item to a warrantless seizure, even if the object is within the curtilage of his dwelling, at least where the seizure requires no entry into the dwelling. See City of Decatur v. Kushmer, 43 Ill.2d 334, 253 N.E.2d 425 (1969); People v. George, 49 Ill.2d 372, 274 N.E.2d 26 (1971). United States v. Santana, 427 U.S. 38, 96 S.Ct. 2406 (1976), supports this reading of *Katz*.

In California v. Ciraolo, 476 U.S. 207, 106 S.Ct. 1809 (1986), the U.S. Supreme Court ruled that police warrantless aerial surveillance of a defendant's backyard garden, undertaken *specifically* to determine whether he was growing marijuana in his backyard, was not a violation of the defendant's Fourth Amendment expectation of privacy, even though the defendant had completely enclosed his backyard with two tall fences, and even though the garden was technically within the curtilage of the house under the "open fields" doctrine. The defendant may have retained a subjective expectation of privacy in his backyard, but, under the circumstances of the modern reality of aircraft overflights, such an expectation was not *reasonable* under *Katz.*

The Chief Justice, writing for a 5–4 Court, concluded, "The Fourth Amendment simply does not require the police traveling in the public airways at this altitude [1,000 feet] to obtain a warrant in order to observe what is visible to the naked eye." In the companion case of Dow Chemical Co. v. United States, 476 U.S. 227, 106 S.Ct. 1819 (1986), the same majority of the Court concluded that aerial photography by the federal Environmental Protection Agency of a 2,000 acre industrial site did not violate the Fourth Amendment. Such property would not even enjoy the curtilage protection of the open fields doctrine. "[A]n industrial complex is more comparable to an open field and as such it is open to the view and observation of persons in aircraft lawfully in the public airspace immediately above or sufficiently near the area for the reach of cameras." Moreover, in the case of warrantless inspection of commercial property "... the expectation of privacy ... differs significantly from the sanctity accorded an individual's home." Any lack of specific statutory authority of the EPA to make such observations was not a factor, since the observations could have been made by any members of the public by use of the public airways.

No violation of a defendant's reasonable expectation of privacy took place when a police helicopter flew over his fenced-in backyard at an altitude of 500 feet in a helicopter and officers saw marijuana growing in the backyard. The altitude was legal for helicopters, the craft did not hover, and the contraband was visible to the naked eye from the craft. The court relied upon *Ciraolo* and found no reason to distinguish *Ciraolo* from the instant case merely because *Ciraolo* involved an aerial overflight by fixed-wing aircraft and the altitude in the instant case would have been unlawful for fixed-wing craft. People v. Romo, 198 Cal.App.3d 581, 243 Cal.Rptr. 801 (1988). On February 22, 1988, the U.S. Supreme Court granted certiorari in Riley v. Florida, 511 So.2d 282 (Fla.1987), to consider the identical issue involved in the *Romo* case. On January 23, 1989, the Court ruled 5–4 in *Riley,* 488 U.S. 445, 109 S.Ct. 693 (1989), that prosecutors could use evidence obtained by the police hovering 400 feet above the defendant's greenhouse. Marijuana was sighted through a hole in the roof of the greenhouse. Although five Justices agreed that this was not a violation of the defendant's Fourth Amendment rights, they could not agree on a majority opinion.

Questions of reasonable expectation of privacy and abandonment of property frequently arise in the context of garbage and trash disposed of by householders. In California v. Greenwood, 486 U.S. 35, 108 S.Ct. 1625 (1988), the defendant placed evidence of his drug trafficking in opaque plastic garbage bags and put the bags at curbside (beyond the curtilage of his house) for pickup by the garbage collector. The garbage collector cooperated with the police by turning the bags over to them; they then sorted through the contents of the bags, found evidence of drug violations, and used the evidence to obtain a search warrant for defendant's house.

In a 6–2 decision the Court found no violation of the Fourth Amendment. There could be no reasonable expectation of privacy in the contents of the bags under the circumstances. "[P]lastic garbage bags left on or at the side of a public street are readily accessible to animals, children, scavengers, snoops, and other members of the public. [...] Moreover, respondents placed their refuse at the curb for the express purpose of conveying it to a third party, the trash collector, who might himself have sorted through respondents' trash or permitted others, such as the police, to do so."

The Court's decision is similar to the caselaw in all of the federal circuits and state appellate courts that have considered the right to privacy in trash. The fact that the State Supreme Court in this case, People v. Krivda, 5 Cal.3d 357, 96 Cal.Rptr. 62, 486 P.2d 1262 (1971), had recognized a state constitutional basis for finding a right to privacy in defendant's trash was meaningless for the federal Fourth Amendment analysis, nor did it create a federally protected due process right.

3. In Oliver v. United States, 466 U.S. 170, 104 S.Ct. 1735 (1984), the court considered whether *Katz* modified the holding of Hester v. United States, 265 U.S. 57, 44 S.Ct. 445 (1924), to the extent of requiring warrants for the search of highly secluded fields. The court re-affirmed the vitality of *Hester*, holding that there is no reasonable expectation of privacy in "open fields." The police, therefore, may conduct a warrantless search of such areas outside the curtilage of dwellings, even though they must traverse fences and ignore "No Trespassing" signs, and thereby become technical "trespassers" under traditional property law.

The residential curtilage rules were further clarified in United States v. Dunn, 480 U.S. 294, 107 S.Ct. 1134 (1987). The Court ruled that a barn on a 198 acre farm, which was located 60 yards from the defendant's house and 50 yards from a fence surrounding the house, and which was itself surrounded by a fence, was not within the curtilage of the house and thus lacked the protection of the Fourth Amendment. In an attempt to clarify the often confusing rules on "residential curtilage," the Court adopted a four-point analysis to determine the existence of such curtilage. All these factors are to be considered in resolving the issue: "[1] the proximity of the area claimed to be curtilage to the home, [2] whether the area is included within an enclosure surrounding the home, [3] the nature of the uses to which the area is put, and [4] the steps taken by the resident to protect the area from observation by people passing by." The defendant lost his argument for curtilage primarily on the basis of the third point—the police had "objective information" in this case that the barn was being used as a drug laboratory rather than devoted to the ordinary pursuits of homestead, which is the primary basis for the residential curtilage protection.

4. In Horton v. California, 496 U.S. 128, 110 S.Ct. 2301 (1990), the United States Supreme Court ruled that in order to qualify as a plain view seizure, an officer's observation of contraband or evidence need not be "inadvertent."

NORTH v. SUPERIOR COURT

Supreme Court of California, 1972.
8 Cal.3d 301, 104 Cal.Rptr. 833, 502 P.2d 1305.

BURKE, JUSTICE.

According to evidence presented at the preliminary hearing, the victim, a school girl, told Detective Neesan, the arresting officer, that on October 4, 1971, as she was walking home from school, she was pulled into a car at knifepoint by the driver. According to Neesan, the victim described the car as "a light blue two-door car. She thought it was a Ford fastback...." The victim indicated that the car was "higher" than ordinary, had two front bucket seats separated by a center console containing a gear shift and glove box, and was equipped with what appeared to be custom carpeting of a "shag type, with long pile, possibly multicolored yellow and brown."

Following the alleged incident, the officers showed the victim a series of 13 photographs, from which she selected two persons as possible suspects; petitioner was one of the suspects she chose. Detective Neesan had known petitioner and was aware that he had been arrested on two prior occasions involving female victims "picked up in a vehicle while they were on the street." Neesan obtained and drove to petitioner's address where he observed a vehicle (a light blue two-door 1964 Ford) matching the description given by the victim. Neesan then determined that the vehicle was registered to a "female subject" but that a transfer notice was on file dated July 29, 1971. Neesan next asked the victim to review a police "mug book" containing photographs of automobiles and to try and pick out the suspect vehicle. She picked out a 1964 Ford as the car within which she had been abducted.

On October 5, at 8:30 p.m., Neesan drove back to petitioner's residence and arrested petitioner inside his apartment. Petitioner's wife was also present in the apartment. Petitioner asked Neesan if he could give his car keys to her, but Neesan refused since the car was to be towed to the police station. Later that night, the car was examined for fingerprints and various tests made and measurements taken. Although the fingerprints taken at this time were "negative," subsequent tests made on October 7, disclosed "positive" prints of the victim. The October 5 tests did indicate that the left rear tire was similar in design to the impression left at the crime scene, and that the car's "wheel span" matched measurements taken at the scene. Apparently, examination of the vehicle turned up additional evidence linking petitioner with the crime. No search warrant was obtained by the officers who seized and examined petitioner's car.

* * *

1. *The Seizure and Subsequent Examination of Petitioner's Car*

* * *

We [have previously set] forth the following principle "distilled" from the foregoing cases: "When officers, incidental to a lawful arrest, seize an automobile or other object in the reasonable belief that such object *is itself evidence* of the commission of the crime for which such arrest is made, any subsequent examination of said object undertaken for the purpose of determining its evidentiary value does not constitute a 'search' within the meaning of the Fourth Amendment.

* * *

Here, petitioner's car was seized contemporaneous with petitioner's arrest, as evidence of the alleged kidnapping; the car was believed to be the very instrumentality used to commit the kidnapping. Of course, since petitioner was arrested in his apartment, a *search* of the car could not have been made as "incident to arrest"; such searches must be limited to the area within the suspect's immediate control. (E.g., Chimel v. California, 395 U.S. 752, 89 S.Ct. 2034.) We are concerned, however, with a *seizure* of evidence in plain sight of arresting officers rather than a search for such evidence.... [T]his court has recognized an important exception to the rule announced in the *Chimel* case, supra, namely, that " 'objects falling in the plain view of an officer who has a right to be in a position to have that view are subject to seizure and may be introduced in evidence.' " Thus, in [an earlier case], we upheld the seizure of contraband found in plain view of officers conducting a post-arrest house search for additional suspects. Although the instant case involves the seizure of evidence of an offense rather than contraband itself, the cases no longer recognize a distinction between contraband and "mere evidence" for purposes of applying the Fourth Amendment. Petitioner's car was parked on a public street, in plain view of the arresting officers. Under [the] authorities cited above, the officers properly seized the car as evidence of the alleged kidnapping.

Petitioner contends, however, that our [rule] must be reexamined and modified in the light of the subsequent decision of the United States Supreme Court in Coolidge v. New Hampshire. *Coolidge,* properly understood, leaves [our holding] undisturbed.

In *Coolidge,* the police arrested a murder suspect in his house and thereupon seized his automobile and searched it later at the police station, finding physical evidence that the victim had been inside the vehicle. The record disclosed that the police had known for some time of the probable role of the car in the crime, and there were no "exigent circumstances" to justify a warrantless search. Accordingly, the plurality opinion of Justice Stewart concluded that the seizure could not be justified on the theory that the vehicle was itself the "instrumentality" of the crime and was discovered "in plain view" of the officers. Justice Stewart was of the opinion that the "plain view" doctrine is applicable only to the *inadvertent* discovery of incriminating evidence.

If the plurality opinion in *Coolidge* were entitled to binding effect as precedent, we would have difficulty distinguishing its holding from the instant case, for the discovery of petitioner's car was no more "inadvertent" than in *Coolidge.* However, that portion of Justice Stewart's plurality opinion which proposed the adoption of new restrictions to the "plain view" rule was signed by only four members of the court (Stewart, J., Douglas, J., Brennan, J., and Marshall, J.). Although concurring in the judgment, Justice Harlan declined to join in that portion of the opinion and the four remaining justices expressly disagreed with Justice Stewart on this point....

It follows that the "plain view" issue raised by the plurality opinion was in fact considered by an equally divided court, and hence was not actually decided in *Coolidge.* As stated in [one of our earlier cases] involving a different aspect of the *Coolidge* plurality opinion, "under settled doctrine, the judgment of an equally divided United States Supreme Court 'is without force as precedent.' Thus we are bound to apply the [vehicle search] rule according to our present understanding of its scope."

We conclude that our decision in *Teale* correctly sets forth the present law regarding warrantless seizures of evidentiary items in plain view of arresting officers, and that the superior court in the instant case properly denied petitioner's motion to suppress evidence derived from the subsequent police examination of petitioner's vehicle.

[The remainder of the opinion concerning admissibility of defendant's conversations with his wife is omitted.]

[The concurring and dissenting opinion of CHIEF JUSTICE WRIGHT joined by JUSTICE MCCOMB is omitted.]

TOBRINER, JUSTICE, dissenting.

* * *

On the issue of the evidence acquired through examination of the automobile, I agree with the conclusion and reasoning of Justice Sullivan. In my opinion, the suppression of this evidence is required by the decision of the United States Supreme Court in Coolidge v. New Hampshire (1971) 403 U.S. 443, 91 S.Ct. 2022. Despite the divergent views expressed by the justices in that case, and the absence of a single majority opinion, the fact remains that the United States Supreme Court ordered suppression of the evidence obtained by examination of Coolidge's car. Unless we can find and articulate some reasonable distinction between the facts of *Coolidge* and of the present case, we must conclude that the Supreme Court would also exclude the evidence at issue in the present case.

In both *Coolidge* and the instant case the crime was committed inside the defendant's automobile. In both cases the defendant was arrested inside his home; his car was parked outside the residence and in plain sight from the public streets. In *Coolidge* the police had an invalid search warrant; here they had no warrant at all. In both cases the police impounded the cars, examined them meticulously, and through this examination discovered evidence introduced against defendant. In both cases the defendant objected to the introduction of the evidence, and in both the state sought to uphold the evidence on the ground that the automobile was evidence of the crime in plain sight from public vantage.

Justice Burke contends, in effect, that because *Coolidge* did not yield a clear majority opinion, that the decision of the Supreme Court in that case may be disregarded by this court. I would maintain to the contrary, that when a case comes before us which is in all material facts identical to *Coolidge,* we must treat *the result* reached in *Coolidge* as controlling, and exclude the evidence in question. I have stated briefly the material facts of his case and of *Coolidge* and can find no reasonable basis to distinguish the two cases.

PETERS, J., concurs.

SULLIVAN, JUSTICE (dissenting).

* * *

. . . the simple fact is that there is no support in *Coolidge* or other decisions of the high court for the seizure of the car on the mere basis that it is in plain view. . . .

As is well stated by Mr. Justice Stewart in Coolidge v. New Hampshire, "plain view *alone* is never enough to justify the warrantless seizure of evidence." The "plain view" doctrine merely allows an officer with a *prior justification* for a search to seize evidence which he inadvertently discovers. After all, "in the vast majority of cases, *any* evidence seized by the police will be in plain view, at least at the moment of seizure." Probable cause alone is not enough. If this exception to the requirement of a warrant were not so limited it would erode entirely the guarantee of the Fourth Amendment.

Detective Neesan discovered the automobile in plain view and had probable cause to believe it was connected with the crime under investigation; what he lacked, however, was either a warrant or exigent circumstances. Since he had seen the car the day before he seized it, it cannot be argued that he found it inadvertently when he went to arrest defendant. The seizure is not lawful simply because the automobile was in plain view on the street.

UNITED STATES v. JACOBSEN

Supreme Court of the United States, 1984.
466 U.S. 109, 104 S.Ct. 1652.

JUSTICE STEVENS delivered the opinion of the Court.

During their examination of a damaged package, the employees of a private freight carrier observed a white powdery substance, originally concealed within eight layers of wrappings. They summoned a federal agent, who removed a trace of the powder, subjected it to a chemical test and determined that it was cocaine. The question presented is whether the Fourth Amendment required the agent to obtain a warrant before he did so.

The relevant facts are not in dispute. Early in the morning of May 1, 1981, a supervisor at the Minneapolis-St. Paul airport Federal Express office asked the office manager to look at a package that had been damaged and torn by a forklift. They then opened the package in order to examine its contents pursuant to a written company policy regarding insurance claims.

The container was an ordinary cardboard box wrapped in brown paper. Inside the box five or six pieces of crumpled newspaper covered a tube about 10 inches long; the tube was made of the silver tape used on basement ducts. The supervisor and office manager cut open the tube, and found a series of four zip-lock plastic bags, the outermost enclosing the other three and the innermost containing about six and a half ounces of white powder. When they observed the white powder in the innermost bag, they notified the Drug Enforcement Administration. Before the first DEA agent arrived, they replaced the plastic bags in the tube and put the tube and the newspapers back into the box.

When the first federal agent arrived, the box, still wrapped in brown paper, but with a hole punched in its side and the top open, was placed on a desk. The agent saw that one end of the tube had been slit open; he removed the four plastic bags from the tube and saw the white powder. He then opened each of the four bags and removed a trace of the white substance with a knife blade. A field test made on the spot identified the substance as cocaine.[1]

In due course, other agents arrived, made a second field test, rewrapped the package, obtained a warrant to search the place to which it was addressed, executed the warrant, and arrested respondents. After they were indicted for the crime of possessing an illegal substance with intent to distribute, their motion to suppress the evidence on the ground that the warrant was the product of an illegal search and seizure was denied; they were tried and convicted, and appealed. The Court of Appeals reversed. It held that the validity of the search warrant depended on the validity of the agents' warrantless test of the white powder,[2] that the testing constituted a significant expansion of the earlier private search, and that a warrant was required. 683 F.2d 296 (CA8 1982).

As the Court of Appeals recognized, its decision conflicted with a decision of another court of appeals on comparable facts, United States v. Barry, 673 F.2d 912 (CA6), cert. denied, 459 U.S. ___, 103 S.Ct. 238, 74 L.Ed.2d 188 (1982). For that reason, and because field tests play an important role in the enforcement of the narcotics laws, we granted certiorari, 460 U.S. ___, 103 S.Ct. 1271, 75 L.Ed.2d 493 (1983).

I

The first clause of the Fourth Amendment provides that the "right of the people to be secure in their persons, houses, papers and effects, against unreasonable searches and seizures, shall not be violated...." This text protects two types of expectations, one involving "searches," the other "seizures." A "search" occurs when an expectation of privacy that society is prepared to consider reasonable is infringed.[3] A "seizure" of property occurs when there is some meaningful interference with an

1. As the test is described in the evidence, it involved the use of three test tubes. When a substance containing cocaine is placed in one test tube after another, it will cause liquids to take on a certain sequence of colors. Such a test discloses whether or not the substance is cocaine, but there is no evidence that it would identify any other substances.

2. The Court of Appeals did not hold that the facts would not have justified the issuance of a warrant without reference to the test results; the court merely held that the facts recited in the warrant application, which relied almost entirely on the results of the field tests, would not support the issuance of the warrant if the field test was itself unlawful. "It is elementary that in passing on the validity of a warrant, the reviewing court may consider *only* information brought to the magistrate's attention." Spinelli v. United States, 393 U.S. 410, 413, n. 3, 89 S.Ct. 584, 587 n. 3, 21 L.Ed.2d 637 (1969) (emphasis in original) (quoting Aguilar v. Texas, 378 U.S. 108, 109, n. 1, 84 S.Ct. 1509, 1511 n. 1, 12 L.Ed.2d 723 (1964)). See Illinois v. Gates, 462 U.S. ___, ___, 103 S.Ct. 2317, 2331, 76 L.Ed.2d 527 (1983).

3. See Illinois v. Andreas, 463 U.S. ___, ___, 103 S.Ct. 3319, 3323, 77 L.Ed.2d 1003 (1983); United States v. Knotts, 460 U.S. ___, ___, 103 S.Ct. 1081, 1085, 75 L.Ed.2d 55 (1983); Smith v. Maryland, 442 U.S. 735, 739–741, 99 S.Ct. 2577, 2579–2580, 61 L.Ed.2d 220 (1979); Terry v. Ohio, 392 U.S. 1, 9, 88 S.Ct. 1868, 1873, 20 L.Ed.2d 889 (1968).

individual's possessory interests in that property.[4] This Court has also consistently construed this protection as proscribing only governmental action; it is wholly inapplicable "to a search or seizure, even an unreasonable one, effected by a private individual not acting as an agent of the Government or with the participation or knowledge of any governmental official." Walter v. United States, 447 U.S. 649, 662, 100 S.Ct. 2395, 2404, 65 L.Ed.2d 410 (1980) (BLACKMUN, J., dissenting).

When the wrapped parcel involved in this case was delivered to the private freight carrier, it was unquestionably an "effect" within the meaning of the Fourth Amendment. Letters and other sealed packages are in the general class of effects in which the public at large has a legitimate expectation of privacy; warrantless searches of such effects are presumptively unreasonable. Even when government agents may lawfully seize such a package to prevent loss or destruction of suspected contraband, the Fourth Amendment requires that they obtain a warrant before examining the contents of such a package.[5] Such a warrantless search could not be characterized as reasonable simply because, after the official invasion of privacy occurred, contraband is discovered. Conversely, in this case the fact that agents of the private carrier independently opened the package and made an examination that might have been impermissible for a government agent cannot render otherwise reasonable official conduct unreasonable. The reasonableness of an official invasion of the citizen's privacy must be appraised on the basis of the facts as they existed at the time that invasion occurred.

The initial invasions of respondents' package were occasioned by private action. Those invasions revealed that the package contained

4. See United States v. Place, 462 U.S. ___, 103 S.Ct. 2637, 77 L.Ed.2d 110 (1983); id., at ___, 103 S.Ct., at 2649 (BRENNAN, J., concurring in the result); Texas v. Brown, 460 U.S. ___, ___, 103 S.Ct. 1535, 1547, 75 L.Ed.2d 502 (1983) (STEVENS, J., concurring in the judgment); see also United States v. Chadwick, 433 U.S. 1, 13–14, n. 8, 97 S.Ct. 2476, 2484–2485, n. 8, 53 L.Ed.2d 538 (1977); Hale v. Henkel, 201 U.S. 43, 76, 26 S.Ct. 370, 379, 50 L.Ed. 652 (1906). While the concept of a "seizure" of property is not much discussed in our cases, this definition follows from our oft-repeated definition of the "seizure" of a person within the meaning of the Fourth Amendment—meaningful interference, however brief, with an individual's freedom of movement. See Michigan v. Summers, 452 U.S. 692, 696, 101 S.Ct. 2587, 2590, 69 L.Ed.2d 340 (1981); Reid v. Georgia, 448 U.S. 438, 440, n. *, 100 S.Ct. 2752, 2753, n. *, 65 L.Ed.2d 890 (1980) (per curiam); United States v. Mendenhall, 446 U.S. 544, 551–554, 100 S.Ct. 1870, 1875–1877, 64 L.Ed.2d 497 (1980) (opinion of Stewart, J.); Brown v. Texas, 443 U.S. 47, 50, 99 S.Ct. 2637, 2640, 61 L.Ed.2d 357 (1979); United States v. Brignoni-Ponce, 422 U.S. 873, 878, 95 S.Ct. 2574, 2578, 45 L.Ed.2d 607 (1975); Cupp v. Murphy, 412 U.S. 291, 294–295, 93 S.Ct. 2000, 2003–2004, 36 L.Ed.2d 900 (1973); Davis v. Mississippi, 394 U.S. 721, 726–727, 89 S.Ct. 1394, 1397–1398, 22 L.Ed.2d 676 (1969); Terry v. Ohio, 392 U.S. 1, 16, 19, n. 16, 88 S.Ct. 1868, 1879, n. 16, 20 L.Ed.2d 889 (1968).

5. See, e.g., United States v. Place, 462 U.S. ___, ___, 103 S.Ct. 2637, 2641, 77 L.Ed.2d 110 (1983); United States v. Ross, 456 U.S. 798, 809–812, 102 S.Ct. 2157, 2164–2166, 72 L.Ed.2d 572 (1982); Robbins v. California, 453 U.S. 420, 426, 101 S.Ct. 2841, 2845, 69 L.Ed.2d 744 (1981) (plurality opinion); Arkansas v. Sanders, 442 U.S. 753, 762, 99 S.Ct. 2586, 2592, 61 L.Ed.2d 235 (1979); United States v. Chadwick, 433 U.S. 1, 13 and n. 8, 97 S.Ct. 2476, 2485 and n. 8, 53 L.Ed.2d 538 (1977); United States v. Van Leeuwen, 397 U.S. 249, 90 S.Ct. 1029, 25 L.Ed.2d 282 (1970). There is, of course, a well recognized exception for customs searches; but that exception is not involved in this case.

only one significant item, a suspicious looking tape tube. Cutting the end of the tube and extracting its contents revealed a suspicious looking plastic bag of white powder. Whether those invasions were accidental or deliberate,[6] and whether they were reasonable or unreasonable, they did not violate the Fourth Amendment because of their private character.

The additional invasions of respondents' privacy by the government agent must be tested by the degree to which they exceeded the scope of the private search. That standard was adopted by a majority of the Court in Walter v. United States, 447 U.S. 649, 100 S.Ct. 2395, 65 L.Ed.2d 410 (1980). In *Walter* a private party had opened a misdirected carton, found rolls of motion picture films that appeared to be contraband, and turned the carton over to the Federal Bureau of Investigation. Later, without obtaining a warrant, FBI agents obtained a projector and viewed the films. While there was no single opinion of the Court, a majority did agree on the appropriate analysis of a governmental search which follows on the heels of a private one. Two Justices took the position:

> "If a properly authorized official search is limited by the particular terms of its authorization, at least the same kind of strict limitation must be applied to any official use of a private party's invasion of another person's privacy. Even though some circumstances—for example, if the results of the private search are in plain view when materials are turned over to the Government—may justify the Government's reexamination of the materials, surely the Government may not exceed the scope of the private search unless it has the right to make an independent search. In these cases, the private party had not actually viewed the films. Prior to the Government's screening one could only draw inferences about what was on the films. The projection of the films was a significant expansion of the search that had been conducted previously by a private party and therefore must be characterized as a separate search." Id., at 657, 100 S.Ct., at 2401 (opinion of STEVENS, J., joined by STEWART, J.) (footnote omitted).[7]

Four additional Justices, while disagreeing with this characterization of the scope of the private search, were also of the view that the legality of the governmental search must be tested by the scope of the antecedent private search.

6. A post-trial affidavit indicates that an agent of Federal Express may have opened the package because he was suspicious about its contents, and not because of damage from a forklift. However, the lower courts found no governmental involvement in the private search, a finding not challenged by respondents. The affidavit thus is of no relevance to the issue we decide.

7. See also id., 447 U.S., at 658–659, 100 S.Ct., at 2402–2403 (footnotes omitted) ("The fact that the cartons were unexpectedly opened by a third party before the shipment was delivered to its intended consignee does not alter the consignor's legitimate expectation of privacy. The private search merely frustrated that expectation in part. It did not simply strip the remaining unfrustrated portion of that expectation of all Fourth Amendment protection.").

"Under these circumstances, since the L'Eggs employees so fully ascertained the nature of the films before contacting the authorities, we find that the FBI's subsequent viewing of the movies on a projector did not 'change the nature of the search' and was not an additional search subject to the warrant requirement." ... Walter v. United States, 447 U.S. 649, 100 S.Ct. 2395, 65 L.Ed.2d 410 (1980).[8]

This standard follows from the analysis applicable when private parties reveal other kinds of private information to the authorities. It is well-settled that when an individual reveals private information to another, he assumes the risk that his confidant will reveal that information to the authorities, and if that occurs the Fourth Amendment does not prohibit governmental use of that information. Once frustration of the original expectation of privacy occurs, the Fourth Amendment does not prohibit governmental use of the now-nonprivate information: "This Court has held repeatedly that the Fourth Amendment does not prohibit the obtaining of information revealed to a third party and conveyed by him to Government authorities, even if the information is revealed on the assumption that it will be used only for a limited purpose and the confidence placed in a third party will not be betrayed." United States v. Miller, 425 U.S. 435, 443, 96 S.Ct. 1619, 1624, 48 L.Ed.2d 71 (1976). The Fourth Amendment is implicated only if the authorities use information with respect to which the expectation of privacy has not already been frustrated. In such a case the authorities have not relied on what is in effect a private search, and therefore presumptively violate the Fourth Amendment if they act without a warrant.[9]

In this case, the federal agents' invasions of respondents' privacy involved two steps: first, they removed the tube from the box, the plastic bags from the tube and a trace of powder from the innermost bag; second, they made a chemical test of the powder. Although we ultimately conclude that both actions were reasonable for essentially the same reason, it is useful to discuss them separately.

II

When the first federal agent on the scene initially saw the package, he knew it contained nothing of significance except a tube containing plastic bags and, ultimately, white powder. It is not entirely clear that the powder was visible to him before he removed the tube from the box.[10]

8. In *Walter*, a majority of the Court found a violation of the Fourth Amendment. For present purposes, the disagreement between the majority and the dissenters in that case with respect to the comparison between the private search and the official search is less significant than the agreement on the standard to be applied in evaluating the relationship between the two searches.

9. See Katz v. United States, 389 U.S. 347, 88 S.Ct. 507, 19 L.Ed.2d 576 (1967); Berger v. New York, 388 U.S. 41, 87 S.Ct. 1873, 18 L.Ed.2d 1040 (1967); Silverman v. United States, 365 U.S. 505, 81 S.Ct. 679, 5 L.Ed.2d 734 (1961).

10. Daniel Stegemoller, the Federal Express office manager, testified at the suppression hearing that the white substance was not visible without reentering the package at the time the first agent arrived.

Even if the white powder was not itself in "plain view" because it was still enclosed in so many containers and covered with papers, there was a virtual certainty that nothing else of significance was in the package and that a manual inspection of the tube and its contents would not tell him anything more than he already had been told. Respondents do not dispute that the Government could utilize the Federal Express employees' testimony concerning the contents of the package. If that is the case, it hardly infringed respondents' privacy for the agents to reexamine the contents of the open package by brushing aside a crumpled newspaper and picking up the tube. The advantage the Government gained thereby was merely avoiding the risk of a flaw in the employees' recollection, rather than in further infringing respondents' privacy. Protecting the risk of misdescription hardly enhances any legitimate privacy interest, and is not protected by the Fourth Amendment. Respondents could have no privacy interest in the contents of the package, since it remained unsealed and since the Federal Express employees had just examined the package and had, of their own accord, invited the federal agent to their offices for the express purpose of viewing its contents. The agent's viewing of what a private party had freely made available for his inspection did not violate the Fourth Amendment....

Similarly, the removal of the plastic bags from the tube and the agent's visual inspection of their contents enabled the agent to learn nothing that had not previously been learned during the private search.[11]

App. 42–43; 58. As JUSTICE WHITE points out, the magistrate found that the "tube was in plain view in the box and the bags of white powder were visible from the end of the tube." App. to Pet. for Cert. 18a. The bags were, however, only visible if one picked up the tube and peered inside through a small aperture; even then, what was visible was only the translucent bag that contained the white powder. The powder itself was barely visible, and surely was not so plainly in view that the agents did "no more than fail to avert their eyes," post, at 1665. In any event, respondents filed objections to the magistrate's report with the District Court. The District Court declined to resolve respondents' objection, ruling that fact immaterial and assuming for purposes of its decision "that the newspaper in the box covered the gray tube and that neither the gray tube nor the contraband could be seen when the box was turned over to the DEA agents." App. to Pet. for Cert. 12a–13a. At trial, the federal agent first on the scene testified that the powder was not visible until after he pulled the plastic bags out of the tube. App. 71–72. Respondents continue to argue this case on the assumption that the Magistrate's report is incorrect. Brief for Respondents 2–3. As our discussion will make clear, we agree with the District Court that it does not matter whether the loose piece of newspaper covered the tube at the time the agent first saw the box.

11. We reject JUSTICE WHITE'S suggestion that this case is indistinguishable from one in which the police simply learn from a private party that a container contains contraband, seize it from its owner, and conduct a warrantless search which, as JUSTICE WHITE properly observes, would be unconstitutional. Here, the Federal Express employees who were lawfully in possession of the package invited the agent to examine its contents; the governmental conduct was made possible only because private parties had compromised the integrity of this container. JUSTICE WHITE would have this case turn on the fortuity of whether the Federal Express agents placed the tube back into the box. But in the context of their previous examination of the package, their communication of what they had learned to the agent, and their offer to have the agent inspect it, that act surely could not create any privacy interest with respect to the package that would not otherwise exist. See Illinois v. Andreas, 463 U.S. ___, ___, 103 S.Ct. 3319, 3323, 77 L.Ed.2d 1003 (1983). Thus the precise character of the white powder's visibility to the naked eye is far less significant than the facts that the container could no longer support any ex-

It infringed no legitimate expectation of privacy and hence was not a "search" within the meaning of the Fourth Amendment.

While the agents' assertion of dominion and control over the package and its contents did constitute a "seizure,"[12] that seizure was not unreasonable. The fact that, prior to the field test, respondents' privacy interest in the contents of the package had been largely compromised, is highly relevant to the reasonableness of the agents' conduct in this respect. The agents had already learned a great deal about the contents of the package from the Federal Express employees, all of which was consistent with what they could see. The package itself, which had previously been opened, remained unsealed, and the Federal Express employees had invited the agents to examine its contents. Under these circumstances, the package could no longer support any expectation of privacy; it was just like a balloon "the distinctive character [of which] spoke volumes as to its contents, particularly to the trained eye of the officer," Texas v. Brown, 460 U.S. ___, ___, 103 S.Ct. 1535, 1545, 75 L.Ed.2d 502 (1983) (plurality opinion); see also id., at ___, 103 S.Ct., at 1543 (POWELL, J., concurring in the judgment); or the hypothetical gun case in Arkansas v. Sanders, 442 U.S. 753, 764–765, n. 13, 99 S.Ct. 2586, 2593–2594, n. 13, 61 L.Ed.2d 235 (1979). Such containers may be seized, at least temporarily, without a warrant. Accordingly, since it was apparent that the tube and plastic bags contained contraband and little else, this warrantless seizure was reasonable,[13] for it is well-settled that it is constitutionally reasonable for law enforcement officials to seize "effects" that cannot support a justifiable expectation of privacy without a warrant, based on probable cause to believe they contain contraband.

III

The question remains whether the additional intrusion occasioned by the field test, which had not been conducted by the Federal Express

pectation of privacy, and that it was virtually certain that it contained nothing but contraband. Contrary to JUSTICE WHITE'S suggestion, we do not "sanction[ ] warrantless searches of closed or covered containers or packages whenever probable cause exists as a result of a prior private search." Post, at 1665. A container which can support a reasonable expectation of privacy may not be searched, even on probable cause, without a warrant. See United States v. Ross, 456 U.S. 798, 809–812, 102 S.Ct. 2157, 2164–2166, 72 L.Ed.2d 572 (1982); Robbins v. California, 453 U.S. 420, 426–427, 101 S.Ct. 2841, 2845–2846, 69 L.Ed.2d 744 (1981) (plurality opinion); Arkansas v. Sanders, 442 U.S. 753, 764–765, 99 S.Ct. 2586, 2593–2594, 61 L.Ed.2d 235 (1979); United States v. Chadwick, 433 U.S. 1, 97 S.Ct. 2476, 53 L.Ed.2d 538 (1977).

12. Both the Magistrate and the District Court found that the agents took custody of the package from Federal Express after they arrived. Although respondents had entrusted possession of the items to Federal Express, the decision by governmental authorities to exert dominion and control over the package for their own purposes clearly constituted a "seizure," though not necessarily an unreasonable one. See United States v. Van Leeuwen, 397 U.S. 249, 90 S.Ct. 1029, 25 L.Ed.2d 282 (1970). Indeed, this is one thing on which the entire Court appeared to agree in *Walter*.

13. Respondents concede that the agents had probable cause to believe the package contained contraband. Therefore we need not decide whether the agents could have seized the package based on something less than probable cause. Some seizures can be justified by an articulable suspicion of criminal activity. See United States v. Place, 462 U.S. ___, 103 S.Ct. 2637, 77 L.Ed.2d 110 (1983).

agents and therefore exceeded the scope of the private search, was an unlawful "search" or "seizure" within the meaning of the Fourth Amendment.

The field test at issue could disclose only one fact previously unknown to the agent—whether or not a suspicious white powder was cocaine. It could tell him nothing more, not even whether the substance was sugar or talcum powder. We must first determine whether this can be considered a "search" subject to the Fourth Amendment—did it infringe an expectation of privacy that society is prepared to consider reasonable?

The concept of an interest in privacy that society is prepared to recognize as reasonable is, by its very nature, critically different from the mere expectation, however well justified, that certain facts will not come to the attention of the authorities.[14] Indeed, this distinction underlies the rule that Government may utilize information voluntarily disclosed to a governmental informant, despite the criminal's reasonable expectation that his associates would not disclose confidential information to the authorities. See United States v. White, 401 U.S. 745, 751–752, 91 S.Ct. 1122, 1125–1126, 28 L.Ed.2d 453 (1971) (plurality opinion).

A chemical test that merely discloses whether or not a particular substance is cocaine does not compromise any legitimate interest in privacy. This conclusion is not dependent on the result of any particular test. It is probably safe to assume that virtually all of the tests conducted under circumstances comparable to those disclosed by this record would result in a positive finding; in such cases, no legitimate interest has been compromised. But even if the results are negative—merely disclosing that the substance is something other than cocaine—such a result reveals nothing of special interest. Congress has decided—and there is no question about its power to do so—to treat the interest in "privately" possessing cocaine as illegitimate; thus governmental conduct that can reveal whether a substance is cocaine, and no other arguably "private" fact, compromises no legitimate privacy interest.[15]

14. "Obviously, however, a 'legitimate' expectation of privacy by definition means more than a subjective expectation of not being discovered. A burglar plying his trade in a summer cabin during the off season may have a thoroughly justified subjective expectation of privacy, but it is not one which the law recognizes as 'legitimate.' His presence, in the words of Jones [v. United States, 362 U.S. 257, 267, 80 S.Ct. 725, 734, 4 L.Ed.2d 697 (1960)], is 'wrongful,' his expectation of privacy is not one that society is prepared to recognize as 'reasonable.' Katz v. United States, 389 U.S., at 361, 88 S.Ct., at 516 (Harlan, J., concurring). And it would, of course, be merely tautological to fall back on the notion that those expectations of privacy which are legitimate depend primarily on cases deciding exclusionary-rule issues in criminal cases. Legitimation of expectations of privacy by law must have a source outside of the Fourth Amendment, either by reference to concepts of real or personal property law or to understandings that are recognized and permitted by society." Rakas v. Illinois, 439 U.S. 128, 143–144, n. 12, 99 S.Ct. 421, 430–431, n. 12, 58 L.Ed.2d 387 (1978).

15. See Loewy, The Fourth Amendment as a Device for Protecting the Innocent, 81 Mich.L.Rev. 1229 (1983). Our discussion, of course, is confined to possession of contraband. It is not necessarily the case that the purely "private" possession of an article that cannot be distributed in commerce is itself illegitimate. See Stanley v. Georgia, 394 U.S. 557, 89 S.Ct. 1243, 22 L.Ed.2d 542 (1969).

This conclusion is dictated by United States v. Place, 462 U.S. ___, 103 S.Ct. 2637, 77 L.Ed.2d 110 (1983), in which the Court held that subjecting luggage to a "sniff test" by a trained narcotics detection dog was not a "search" within the meaning of the Fourth Amendment:

> "A 'canine sniff' by a well-trained narcotics detection dog, however, does not require opening of the luggage. It does not expose noncontraband items that otherwise would remain hidden from public view, as does, for example, an officer's rummaging through the contents of the luggage. Thus, the manner in which information is obtained through this investigative technique is much less intrusive than a typical search. Moreover, the sniff discloses only the presence or absence of narcotics, a contraband item. Thus, despite the fact that the sniff tells the authorities something about the contents of the luggage, the information obtained is limited." Id., at ___, 103 S.Ct., at 2644.[16]

Here, as in *Place,* the likelihood that official conduct of the kind disclosed by the record will actually compromise any legitimate interest in privacy seems much too remote to characterize the testing as a search subject to the Fourth Amendment.

We have concluded, in Part II, supra, that the initial "seizure" of the package and its contents was reasonable. Nevertheless, as *Place* also holds, a seizure lawful at its inception can nevertheless violate the Fourth Amendment because its manner of execution unreasonably infringes possessory interests protected by the Fourth Amendment's prohibition on "unreasonable seizures."[17] Here, the field test did affect respondents' possessory interests protected by the Amendment, since by destroying a quantity of the powder it converted what had been only a temporary deprivation of possessory interests into a permanent one. To assess the reasonableness of this conduct, "[w]e must balance the nature and quality of the intrusion on the individual's Fourth Amendment interests against the importance of the governmental interests alleged to justify the intrusion." Id., at ___, 103 S.Ct., at 2642.[18]

Applying this test, we conclude that the destruction of the powder during the course of the field test was reasonable. The law enforcement

16. Respondents attempt to distinguish *Place* arguing that it involved no physical invasion of Place's effects, unlike the conduct at issue here. However, as the quotation makes clear, the *reason* this did not intrude upon any legitimate privacy interest was that the governmental conduct could reveal nothing about noncontraband items. That rationale is fully applicable here.

17. In *Place,* the Court held that while the initial seizure of luggage for the purpose of subjecting it to a "dog sniff" test was reasonable, the seizure became unreasonable because its length unduly intruded upon constitutionally protected interests. See id., 462 U.S., at ___, 103 S.Ct., at 2645.

18. See, e.g., Michigan v. Long, 463 U.S. ___, ___, 103 S.Ct. 3469, 3479, 77 L.Ed.2d 1201 (1983); Delaware v. Prouse, 440 U.S. 648, 654, 99 S.Ct. 1391, 1396, 59 L.Ed.2d 660 (1979); United States v. Brignoni-Ponce, 422 U.S. 873, 878, 95 S.Ct. 2574, 2578, 45 L.Ed.2d 607 (1975); Terry v. Ohio, 392 U.S. 1, 20–21, 88 S.Ct. 1868, 1879–1880, 20 L.Ed.2d 889 (1968); Camara v. Municipal Court, 387 U.S. 523, 536–537, 87 S.Ct. 1727, 1734–1735, 18 L.Ed.2d 930 (1967).

interests justifying the procedure were substantial; the suspicious nature of the material made it virtually certain that the substance tested was in fact contraband. Conversely, because only a trace amount of material was involved, the loss of which appears to have gone unnoticed by respondents, and since the property had already been lawfully detained, the "seizure" could, at most, have only a de minimis impact on any protected property interest. Cf. Cardwell v. Lewis, 417 U.S. 583, 591–592, 94 S.Ct. 2464, 2469–2470, 41 L.Ed.2d 325 (1974) (plurality opinion) (examination of automobile's tires and taking of paint scrapings was a *de minimis* invasion of constitutional interests).[19] Under these circumstances, the safeguards of a warrant would only minimally advance Fourth Amendment interests. This warrantless "seizure" was reasonable.[20]

In sum, the federal agents did not infringe any constitutionally protected privacy interest that had not already been frustrated as the result of private conduct. To the extent that a protected possessory interest was infringed, the infringement was de minimis and constitutionally reasonable. The judgment of the Court of Appeals is

Reversed.

[Omitted is the concurring opinion of Justice White and the dissenting opinion of Justices Brennan and Marshall.]

* * *

NOTES

1. In a plurality opinion of only four Justices in Texas v. Brown, 460 U.S. 730, 103 S.Ct. 1535 (1983), the Supreme Court stated that a police officer could seize without a warrant a tied-off, opaque balloon lying on the seat of a lawfully stopped car, because the officer knew from past experience that balloons are commonly used to package and transport drugs. The entire Court agreed that this was a "plain view" seizure, but could not agree on a definition of the doctrine, particularly the requirement that the incriminating nature of the evidence be "immediately apparent." The plurality Justices took the position that a police officer does not have to "know" that the items are evidence. He

19. In fact, respondents do not contend that the amount of material tested was large enough to make it possible for them to have detected its loss. The only description in the record of the amount of cocaine seized is that "[i]t was a trace amount." App. 75.

20. See Cupp v. Murphy, 412 U.S. 291, 296, 93 S.Ct. 2000, 2004, 36 L.Ed.2d 900 (1973) (warrantless search and seizure limited to scraping suspect's fingernails justified even when full search may not be). Cf. Place, 462 U.S., at ___, 103 S.Ct., at 2644–2645 (approving brief warrantless seizure of luggage for purposes of "sniff test" based on its minimal intrusiveness and reasonable belief that the luggage contained contraband); Van Leeuwen v. United States, 397 U.S. 249, 252–253, 90 S.Ct. 1029, 1032–1033, 25 L.Ed.2d 282 (1970) (detention of package on reasonable suspicion was justified since detention infringed no "significant Fourth Amendment interest"). Of course, where more substantial invasions of constitutionally protected interests are involved, a warrantless search or seizure is unreasonable in the absence of exigent circumstances.... We do not suggest, however, that any seizure of a small amount of material is necessarily reasonable. An agent's arbitrary decision to take the "white powder" he finds in a neighbor's sugar bowl, or his medicine cabinet, and subject it to a field test for cocaine, might well work an unreasonable seizure.

only needs "probable cause to associate the property with criminal activity," which was clearly present when the officer saw balloons in the glove compartment as the defendant was going through it looking for his license, and saw another balloon on the seat. The plurality opinion was written by Justice Rehnquist, with various concurrences and dissents by Justices White, Powell, Blackmun, Stevens, Brennan and Marshall.

In Arizona v. Hicks, 480 U.S. 321, 107 S.Ct. 1149 (1987), the Court finally made it clear that "probable cause" is all that is necessary in order to support a plain view seizure of evidence under the plain view exception to the warrant requirement, rather than a finding that the contraband nature of the evidence be "immediately apparent." However, an "inspection" of an object may be a "search" under the Fourth Amendment, not a "plain view seizure." Here the police were lawfully in an apartment to investigate a shot fired from the apartment that wounded someone in a unit below the apartment. While in the apartment, which was filled with litter, trash, weapons and drug paraphernalia, they saw some expensive stereo equipment that seemed "out of place" and that they thought might be stolen. They moved the components to see the serial numbers and then called the numbers into a police station to confirm that they were stolen. This moving of the components was a "search" under the Fourth Amendment, not a "plain view seizure," and at any rate, took place before the police had probable cause to believe that the components had been stolen. Thus, although the Court settles once and for all that a plain view seizure can be based on only probable cause, the Court declines to find an "inspection" exception to the probable cause requirement. An interesting concurrence by Justice White, which may form the basis of subsequent Court action, argued that the "inadvertent discovery" aspect of the plain view doctrine is not constitutionally required. The Chief Justice and Justices Powell and O'Connor dissented. They agreed that probable cause is all that is required to support a plain view seizure, not the "immediately apparent" formula, but argued that a "cursory inspection" of an object similar to moving the stereo components to see their serial numbers, could be constitutionally supported by "reasonable suspicion," rather than probable cause.

2. Omitted from the materials on plain view seizures is the Supreme Court case of Coolidge v. New Hampshire, 403 U.S. 443, 91 S.Ct. 2022 (1971). Space considerations precluded its inclusion in the present casebook edition. Moreover, it is discussed in the California court's opinion in the preceding principal case of North v. Superior Court. However, we direct attention to it for the benefit of readers who may wish to make the effort to analyze the various lengthy opinions contained in the full report of the case. As previously stated, the case also deals at length with the general subject of automobile searches. See also Horton v. California, 496 U.S. 128, 110 S.Ct. 2301 (1990).

3. Recently police have used thermal imaging devices to detect abnormal heating pattern inside a home which may confirm use of the home to grow marijuana in a hothouse. The device is usually used after checking for high electricity usage and blacked out windows. Several circuits have held that thermal imaging is not a search because it does not penetrate walls or reveal human conversations or activities. United States v. Ford, 34 F.3d 992 (11th Cir.1994); United States v. Pinson, 24 F.3d 1056 (8th Cir.1994), cert. denied ___ U.S. ___, 115 S.Ct. 664 (1994); United States v. Myers, 46 F.3d 668 (7th Cir.1995). See also, United States v. Ishmael, 48 F.3d 850 (5th Cir.1995) (thermal imaging is a search, but reasonable and nonintrusive). But the Supreme Court of Washington found its use without a warrant to be a particular-

ly intrusive means of observation of activities occurring within the home and which a person is entitled to keep private under the Fourth Amendment absent a warrant. State v. Young, 123 Wash.2d 173, 867 P.2d 593 (1994).

4. There are cases in which a police stop or search is clearly within the law but the officer's purpose may not coincide with the legal justification for search. Commonly it is argued that a traffic stop (or an inventory) was conducted by an officer who had no interest in traffic offenses (or inventory) but merely used lawful authority as a pretext to enable the officer to pursue a narcotics or gun investigation. Most courts have entertained challenges to searches on the grounds that they were pretextual. But the standard is not the actual motive of the officer (which is assumed to be pretextual); the issue is whether a reasonable officer "would" have acted anyway (minority rule) or whether a reasonable officer "could" have acted as this officer did. A recent opinion reviewed the law and effectively wrote the pretext objection out of the law holding "traffic stops based on probable cause, even if other motivations existed, are not illegal." United States v. Ferguson, 8 F.3d 385 (6th Cir.1993) en banc (11–2).

5. A doctrine analogous to plain view is a "plain feel" rule which permits an officer who feels something incriminating during a frisk authority to seize it without a warrant. See United States v. Williams, 822 F.2d 1174 (D.C.Cir.1987); United States v. Buchannon, 878 F.2d 1065 (8th Cir.1989).

In Minnesota v. Dickerson, 508 U.S. 366, 113 S.Ct. 2130 (1993) the Court approved a "plain feel" rule. It first noted that contraband that comes into the plain view of an officer during a frisk may be seized and then reasoned:

> "The same can be said of tactile discoveries of contraband. If a police officer lawfully pats down a suspect's outer clothing and feels an object whose contour or mass makes its identity immediately apparent, there has been no invasion of the suspect's privacy beyond that already authorized by the officer's search for weapons; if the object is contraband, its warrantless seizure would be justified by the same practical considerations that inhere in the plain view context.
>
> The Minnesota Supreme Court rejected an analogy to the plain-view doctrine on two grounds: first, its belief that 'the sense of touch is inherently less immediate and less reliable than the sense of sight,' and second, that 'the sense of touch is far more intrusive into the personal privacy that is at the core of the [F]ourth [A]mendment.' ... We have a somewhat different view. First *Terry* itself demonstrates that the sense of touch is capable of revealing the nature of an object with sufficient reliability to support a seizure. The very premise of *Terry* itself demonstrates that the sense of touch is capable of revealing the nature of an object with sufficient reliability to support a seizure. The very premise of *Terry,* after all, is that officers will be able to detect the presence of weapons through the sense of touch and *Terry* upheld precisely such a seizure. Even if it were true that the sense of touch is generally less reliable than the sense of sight, that only suggests that officers will less often be able to justify seizures of unseen contraband. Regardless of whether the officer detects the contraband by sight or by touch, however, the Fourth Amendment's requirement that the officer have probable cause to believe that the item is contraband before seizing it ensures against excessively speculative seizures. The court's second concern—that touch is more intrusive into privacy than is sight—is inapposite in light of the fact that the intrusion the court fears has

already been authorized by the lawful search for weapons. The seizure of an item whose identity is already known occasions no further invasion of privacy...."

The Court went on to hold that "plain feel" could not be used to justify seizure of crack cocaine when the officer did not immediately detect what it was, but had to manipulate the plastic wrapped object several times before realizing it was cocaine.

6. Interception of a telephone conversation when one party uses a cordless phone is not a search, since users of cordless phones know that their conversations may be intercepted and thus have no reasonable expectation of privacy. In re Askin, 47 F.3d 100 (4th Cir.1995).

3. CONSENT SEARCHES

PEOPLE v. GONZALEZ

Court of Appeals of New York, 1976.
39 N.Y.2d 122, 383 N.Y.S.2d 215, 347 N.E.2d 575.

BREITEL, CHIEF JUDGE.

The exclusive issue is whether in a criminal action defendants' written consents to search their apartment were involuntary as a matter of law....

On September 17, 1973, Agent Michael Horn of the United States Drug Enforcement Administration, while negotiating a prospective drug sale, received a "sample" of cocaine from Joseph Gonzalez in the bedroom of his small, three-room Castle Hill apartment in the northern part of New York County. Gonzalez took the cocaine from a clear plastic bag on top of the bedroom dresser. Present in the bedroom at the time of the transaction was Mr. Gonzalez' bride of three days, Tracy. Both Gonzalezes were under 20 years of age.

A few minutes after leaving the apartment, Agent Horn returned with another Federal agent, Hochman, to arrest Mr. Gonzalez for the initial sale and for possession of drugs and Mrs. Gonzalez only for possession. The agents came upon Mr. Gonzalez in the hallway outside his apartment. They identified themselves and Agent Hochman drew his weapon. When they tried to arrest him, Gonzalez resisted and a brief struggle ensued. During the struggle, Agent Hochman and Gonzalez fell down a flight of stairs and the agent's gun was dropped. Also during the struggle, Gonzalez shouted to his wife to "lock the door [or] something like that". Gonzalez was finally subdued by the agents, now assisted by a third agent, and his arms were handcuffed behind his back.

Agents Horn and Hochman then knocked on the apartment door and identified themselves. When no immediate response was forthcoming, the agents banged and kicked the door. At this point, six other agents arrived, now an aggregate of nine. After about five minutes Mrs. Gonzalez opened the door and was immediately handcuffed and placed in the bedroom by the agents. (At the suppression hearing she admitted that, during the interval, she had been disposing of drugs.) Mr. Gonzalez was brought in by Agent Jenkins and placed in the living room.

Nine Federal agents were now in the small apartment with the handcuffed and separated Gonzalezes. Some of the agents began their "standard procedure" of checking closets for possible other occupants of the apartment. No otherwise full-scale search for contraband was conducted. After the visual search, two agents left to check the area below the apartment windows, and two others went outside the apartment to reassure neighbors who had been disturbed by the fracas. Three agents were clustered about Mr. Gonzalez, "conversing" with him. At least one agent was guarding Mrs. Gonzalez in the bedroom. None of the agents had their weapons drawn while they were in the apartment.

Without described preliminary conversation, Agent Horn read Mr. Gonzalez the now standard preinterrogation warnings. On question, Gonzalez responded that he understood them. Agent Horn and two other agents then went into the guarded bedroom and read Mrs. Gonzalez the same warnings, and she too said that she understood them.

About five minutes after the agents had entered the apartment, Mrs. Gonzalez' mother and grandfather came in. Mrs. Gonzalez' mother immediately went into the bedroom to talk with her daughter. Mrs. Gonzalez' grandfather berated her for having married Joseph. After being in the apartment for approximately five minutes, they were "required to leave" by the agents. Agent Jenkins explained that Mrs. Gonzalez' mother "could say what she had to say and it was time to leave". These events consumed a period of approximately one-half hour.

The bare description of what had occurred thus far is the version of the Federal agents. As might be expected, a quite different narration was given by the defense witnesses, who described threats to expose the defendants to State prosecution under the severe State sentencing laws, threats to separate the newlyweds forever, and the desirability of defendants signing consents to a full-blown search of the apartment induced further by the comment about how a search warrant was "on the way". Interestingly, when asked whether he had threatened Mr. Gonzalez with State prosecution with its well-advertised severe penalties, rather than Federal prosecution, Agent Horn replied with negative pregnant in classic form "Not in the apartment". True, after the arrest, Mr. Gonzalez averred that he had been so threatened in seeking his cooperation with the Federal agents. This is now explained to have occurred in a different "context" and at a different time.

Agent Horn then returned to the living room and asked Mr. Gonzalez whether he now wished to "waive his rights". Gonzalez said that he did. The Federal agent then asked him whether he was willing to sign a statement consenting to a search. Agent Horn read a printed consent form to Gonzalez and had him read it. Having agreed to sign the consent form, Gonzalez was unbound and signed the form. At the suppression hearing, Mr. Gonzalez testified that, when he signed the consent, he did not know whether his wife had disposed of all the drugs before she let the agents enter the apartment.

Returning now to the bedroom, Agent Horn told Mrs. Gonzalez that her husband had signed a consent form and asked her if she would. After seeing her husband's signature to the consent form, she said that she would sign it too. The Federal agent read a consent form to her and then handed it to her to read and sign.

At the suppression hearing, Mrs. Gonzalez was asked whether "there were other drugs in the apartment other than the ones that you had flushed down the toilet bowl?" She responded "No". She was then asked whether she thought she had gotten rid of everything. She responded "Pretty much". She was asked "So, when you signed the consent you figured you had gotten rid of everything?" She responded "No". She testified that she knew some cocaine had been found in the bathroom before she had signed the consent. When finally asked "Did you know there were any others [drugs] in the apartment?" She responded "I wasn't sure."

After the Gonzalezes were taken away, a full-blown search discovered a commercial quantity of drugs. The significance of a rummage search after the Gonzalezes had been removed indicated again the critical need for the consent, if there were no warrant.

* * *

One of the limited exceptions to the warrant requirement and, indeed, to the requirement of probable cause, is voluntary consent to the search. In the instant case, the People concede that the legality of the search of the Gonzalez apartment turns entirely upon the validity of either of the Gonzalez' consents. (Indeed, the agents by obtaining and relying on the signed consents indicated unequivocally that they recognized the doubtfulness of a right to a rummage search without a warrant.) Of course, the People also recognize that theirs is the heavy burden of proving the voluntariness of the purported consents.

Consent to search is voluntary when it is a true act of the will, an unequivocal product of an essentially free and unconstrained choice. Voluntariness is incompatible with official coercion, actual or implicit, overt or subtle.

No one circumstance is determinative of the voluntariness of consent. Whether consent has been voluntarily given or is only a yielding to overbearing official pressure must be determined from the circumstances.

An important, although not dispositive, factor in determining the voluntariness of an apparent consent is whether the consenter is in custody or under arrest, and the circumstances surrounding the custody or arrest. True, custody or arrest alone does not necessarily preclude voluntariness. Custody, or, more compellingly, the immediate events of an arrest, especially a resisted arrest, do, however, engender an atmosphere of authority ordinarily contradictory of a capacity to exercise a free and unconstrained will. This is especially true when the individual in custody or under arrest is confronted by a large number of police agents. Moreover, the fact that a defendant was handcuffed has been considered a significant factor in determining whether his apparent consent was but a capitulation to authority. Submission to authority is not consent.

In the instant case, the Gonzalezes were arrested, separated from each other and their arms were handcuffed behind their backs. As many as nine armed Federal agents had swarmed about the small apartment and, about one-half hour after their entry, each defendant was asked to sign the consent to search in the immediate presence of at least three agents. Mrs. Gonzalez' mother and grandfather had been excluded from the premises. Thus, the atmosphere, as inferred from the testimony of the agents and interpreted on the objective facts, in which the "consents" were obtained could hardly have been more coercive, short of direct police testimony of actual duress.

Another factor to be considered in determining the voluntariness of an apparent consent is the background of the consenter. A consent to search by a case-hardened sophisticate in crime, calloused in dealing with police, is more likely to be the product of calculation than awe. Here, the Gonzalezes were both under 20 years of age and were newly-weds of three days. They had had very limited prior contact with the police. Under these circumstances, the ineluctable inference, except to the jaded, is that the consents could not be, on any creditable view of the agents' testimony, the product of a free and unconstrained choice.

Another factor to be considered is whether the consenter has been, previously to the giving of the consents, or for that matter even later, evasive or un-co-operative with the law enforcement authorities. Of course, if defendants had assisted the Federal agents in their search, this would be evidence of a voluntary consent. But, to the contrary, Mr. Gonzalez had previously forcibly resisted arrest by the Federal agents, one of whom had his weapon drawn. Mrs. Gonzalez, too, did not open the apartment door immediately upon request, she delayed approximately six minutes. She then opened the door only when the banging and kicking at the door indicated that the agents would enter in any event. If Mrs. Gonzalez had been trying to dispose of contraband, it was now obvious, she was not to be left free to complete the task. Such determined resistance and evasion is hardly compatible with a suddenly voluntary consent, which consent in all likelihood would be recognized as self-destructive. Instead, the circumstances are evidence that the consents were a yielding of overbearing official pressure.

A final factor is whether a defendant was advised of his right to refuse to consent. Such advice is not mandatory. Failure to advise, however, may be considered in determining whether a consent was voluntary. In the instant case, the Gonzalezes were informed of their right to refuse to consent to the search. It must be noted that such advice was contained in a printed form read to and signed by them, hardly an amelioration of the coercive atmosphere in the apartment.

In taking the composite of the facts: the number of agents present in the small apartment; the youth of the Gonzalezes; the separation and handcuffing of these newlyweds; the removal of parent and grandparent from the scene; the circumstances of the arrests; and the sudden acquiescence of the segregated couple, handcuffed, and without further ado, in the signing of the printed consents, negates totally the idea of a free act of will, or else the pious language of the cases is only a gloss on an unacknowledged ugly reality. Under these circumstances, as a matter of law, the apparent consent was induced by overbearing official conduct and was not a free exercise of the will.

What has been said thus far is enough, or should be enough. But there are two aspects of the narrated events, always giving the police version alone, which for some purposes merit elaboration, if only to see that the facts in cases involving constitutional limitations are not clinically dissected with the body fluids drained and the network of nerves dead.

The removal of the mother and the grandfather, hardly done in the almost Chesterfieldian manner described by the police, but even so, relieved these two young people of the only persons at hand, perhaps at that point better than a lawyer, to advise them and offer moral and material support in making a choice which would affect their liberty and undoubtedly the course of their lives. Of course, these persons of the blood need not have been permitted to remain, but surely their removal first before the consents were obtained, makes the almost wordless obtaining of the consents a mockery.

The second aspect is the swarming of armed Federal agents in the small apartment, hardly a backdrop for a voluntary act, again with an almost wordless preamble, in signing a printed consent to a necessarily fateful full-blown search. The worst of it is that all this was unnecessary once defendants had been arrested and the agents and the defendants remained long enough in the premises for a search warrant to be obtained, a warrant that must have been granted, and with a time interval involved which made impossible the removal of any hidden contraband pending the obtaining of the warrant. None of the permitted exceptions to a warrantless search were present. This was offensive official conduct more suitable to a police society than to a policed society.

* * *

JASEN, JUDGE (dissenting).

I take no issue with Chief Judge Breitel's exquisite analysis of the law of consent. My difficulty is, rather, with the application of the law to the particular circumstances of this case and with the conclusion reached by the majority that "on no view of the evidentiary facts was there an exercise of free will in the giving of the consents."

* * *

... As I view the facts before us, there is evidence upon which the court could find, as the trial court did, that the defendants willingly consented to a search of their apartment. The record discloses that the consent was not given until after Tracy Gonzalez disposed of the drugs that she and the police had known to be in the apartment. The defendants do not contend that the agents actually abused them, either physically or verbally. A careful reading of the transcript of the suppression hearing discloses that the testimony of the various officers is consistent and credible, while the versions proffered by the defendants vary and are cluttered with contradictions and asserted lapses of memory. Thus, there is support in the record that at the time the consent was executed, the atmosphere in the apartment was relaxed and the defendants were cool and rational. The Appellate Division did not question the veracity of the agents. Nor did the court find any evidence of overbearing police conduct. Rather, that court refused to accept, as a matter of law, the fact that defendants, faced with the possibility of a mandatory life sentence, would voluntarily consent to a search of their apartment. I cannot accept this reasoning. Defendants, caught with the goods, might well imagine that co-operation with authorities might earn them at least a small measure of leniency, whereas an obstinate refusal in the face of harsh reality would serve little purpose. Moreover, the defendants offered several conflicting claims at the hearing as to why they had signed the consent form. One of their claims was that they had signed the form because the agents told them that they would obtain a search warrant if the defendants had refused to sign the form. Assuming that the statement was made, it would not affect the voluntariness of the consent since there was sufficient evidence to justify the issuance of a warrant.

Upon this evidence, I believe that the trial court could properly find that the defendants did voluntarily consent to the search of their apartment, and that it cannot be said, as a matter of law, that there is no view of the evidence to sustain such a finding.

NOTES

1. In United States v. Smith, 308 F.2d 657 (2d Cir.1962), the court stated that "if the defendant permits a warrantless search of his home or establishment in the mistaken belief that he has nothing there which will incriminate him, it has been held that the search has been voluntarily consented to ... if the defendant admits his guilt to the officer, instead of denying it to him, and then allows a search without a warrant, this strongly implies voluntary consent on his part ... the degree of affirmative assistance given to the police by the suspect is often relevant in determining whether consent exists."

Where the police indicate they have a warrant but no warrant is produced at trial or the warrant turns out to be invalid, consent is vitiated. Bumper v. North Carolina, 391 U.S. 543, 88 S.Ct. 1788 (1968). The mere threat to get a warrant, however, has been held insufficient to negate voluntariness of consent. Barlow v. State, 280 A.2d 703 (Del.1971); State v. Douglas, 488 P.2d 1366 (Or.1971). Deception may vitiate consent. Commonwealth v. Brown, 437 Pa. 1, 261 A.2d 879 (1970) (officer told defendant he would sell gun and instead had a ballistics test run); Graves v. Beto, 424 F.2d 524 (5th Cir.1970) (defendant told blood sample was for alcohol test but it was used to type his blood for comparison with blood stains in rape case); United States v. J. B. Kramer Grocery, 418 F.2d 987 (9th Cir.1969) (false assertion of right to search without a warrant). In cases where an officer gains entry into premises, there is some issue as to whether consent to enter is necessarily vitiated. Thus an officer may not pose as a gas man to gain entry, but perhaps using a false name he gains entry into a room by making an appointment with a prostitute over the telephone is permissible. People v. St. Ives, 110 Ill.App.2d 37, 249 N.E.2d 97 (1969). Threats of force will make consent involuntary. Weed v. United States, 340 F.2d 827 (10th Cir.1965) (officers with drawn guns said they could get warrant); Waldron v. United States, 219 F.2d 37 (D.C.Cir.1955) (police told pregnant girl they could not be responsible for the conditions of the house if they had to get a warrant). Consider, State v. Redford, 27 Utah 2d 379, 496 P.2d 884 (1972) (police officer bought an automobile solely to acquire the right to search it).

2. A person who consents to a search may limit the scope of the search and those limitations must be respected. United States v. Dichiarinte, 445 F.2d 126 (7th Cir.1971) (consent to search for narcotics does not confer authority to search for papers); State v. Koucoules, 343 A.2d 860 (Me.1974) (thorough review of the rule).

3. A consent may be invalid if the party giving the consent is mentally incompetent. See United States v. Elrod, 441 F.2d 353 (5th Cir.1971).

4. With regard to the issue as to who has the right to give consent for a search that results in the procurement of incriminating evidence against a defendant, it has been held that a hotel owner, clerk, or other employee may not grant permission to the police to search the room of a guest, despite the management's right to enter guest rooms for hotel related purposes. Stoner v. California, 376 U.S. 483, 84 S.Ct. 889 (1964). Suppose, however, that a landlord rents a garage to a tenant who uses it to store stolen property. When suspicion falls upon the landlord, may he "exculpate" himself with the authorities by opening the garage and letting them search with his consent? This problem was presented in United States v. Botsch, 364 F.2d 542 (2d Cir.1966), and the court sustained such a search. See, e.g., Stoner v. California, 376 U.S. 483, 84 S.Ct. 889 (1964) (hotel clerk can't consent to search of guest's room); Frazier v. Cupp, 394 U.S. 731, 89 S.Ct. 1420 (1969) (where duffle bag left in cousin's home and cousin was joint user of bag, consent of cousin was sufficient for search); and United States v. Matlock, 415 U.S. 164, 94 S.Ct. 988 (1974) (a third party who possesses common authority over area can consent to search, woman who cohabited with roomer able to consent to search of bedroom she sometimes occupied).

5. Numerous consent case situations have arisen, such as those involving the power of consent on the part of a co-tenant, a spouse (or "live-in" companion), a parent, an employer as regards an employer's desk or locker, etc. Usually the key factor is the nature and the extent of control possessed by the consenting individual, either over the premises or the container in the premises that has been subjected to the search.

6. Must the person who consents to search be given a warning of his right to refuse? In Schneckloth v. Bustamonte, 412 U.S. 218, 93 S.Ct. 2041 (1973), the Court said that "voluntariness is a question of fact to be determined from all the circumstances, and while the subject's knowledge of a right to refuse is a factor to be taken into account, the prosecution is not required to demonstrate

such knowledge as a prerequisite to establishing a voluntary consent." And in the more recent case of United States v. Watson, 423 U.S. 411, 96 S.Ct. 820 (1976), the Supreme Court held that Fourth Amendment warnings were not essential even where the consenting party was in police custody.

In State v. Robinette, 73 Ohio St.3d 650, 653 N.E.2d 695 (Ohio 1995), the Supreme Court of Ohio ruled that an officer must warn a motorist when an investigative detention has ended, before attempting to obtain a consent to search the motorist's car. Certiorari was granted by the United States Supreme Court on March 4, 1996, 58 CrL 3179, limited to the issue: "Does Fourth Amendment require police officers to inform motorists, lawfully stopped for traffic violations, that legal detention has concluded before any subsequent interrogation or search will be found to be consensual?" A decision by the Court was expected by Fall, 1996.

7. Frequently a consent issue arises when a defendant claims that a statement which he gave while under arrest should be suppressed because the arrest was unlawful for want of probable cause. See Brown v. Illinois, 422 U.S. 590, 95 S.Ct. 2254 (1975). Often the prosecution responds by asserting that the defendant had voluntarily accompanied authorities to the place of detention and was not under arrest. The issue then is whether the suspect merely acquiesced to a show of authority or instead voluntarily agreed to accompany the authorities. Varying factual situations have led to some victories for the prosecution and some for the defense in state and federal reviewing courts. The prosecution's consent theory prevailed in United States v. Mendenhall, 446 U.S. 544, 100 S.Ct. 1870 (1980), but not in Dunaway v. New York, 442 U.S. 200, 99 S.Ct. 2248 (1979).

8. In Florida v. Royer, 460 U.S. 491, 103 S.Ct. 1319 (1983), the defendant was a nervous young man paying cash for an airline ticket from Miami to New York under an assumed name and carrying heavy American Tourister bags. The Court said that the police had sufficient grounds to temporarily detain him and his luggage while they attempted to verify or dispel their suspicions that he was a drug courier; however, they exceeded the limits of an investigative stop where they asked defendant to accompany them to a small police room, and retained his ticket and driver's license and indicated in no way that he was free to depart. When the validity of a search rests on consent, the state has the burden of proving that the necessary consent was obtained and that it was freely and voluntarily given, a burden not satisfied by showing mere submission to claim of lawful authority. This was a burden not met in this case. For excerpts of the opinion in *Royer* see p. 964, supra.

9. In Illinois v. Rodriguez, 497 U.S. 177, 110 S.Ct. 2793 (1990), the Court validated the concept of a consent search based upon "apparent authority." The majority stated that a search is not unreasonable, within the meaning of the Fourth Amendment, "when officers enter without a warrant because they reasonably (though erroneously) believe that the person who has consented to their entry is a resident of the premises . . ." It added:

> Even when the invitation is accompanied by an explicit assertion that the person lives there, the surrounding circumstances could conceivably be such that a reasonable person would doubt its truth and not act upon it without further inquiry. As with other factual determinations bearing upon search and seizure, determination of consent to enter must "be judged against an objective standard: would the facts available to the officer at the moment . . . 'warrant a man of reasonable

> caution in the belief' " that the consenting party had authority over the premises? Terry v. Ohio (1968). If not, then warrantless entry without further inquiry is unlawful unless authority actually exists. But if so, the search is valid.

Three dissenters objected, saying:

> Our cases demonstrate that third-party consent searches are free from constitutional challenge only to the extent that they rest on consent by a party empowered to do so. The majority's conclusion to the contrary ignores the legitimate expectations of privacy on which individuals are entitled to rely. That a person who allows another joint access over his property thereby limits his expectation of privacy does not justify trampling the rights of a person who has not similarly relinquished any of his privacy expectations.

10. In Florida v. Jimeno, 500 U.S. 248, 111 S.Ct. 1801 (1991), following a traffic stop, an officer told the driver that he believed the driver was carrying narcotics in his car. He said he was looking for narcotics and obtained consent to search the vehicle after admonishing the suspect of his right not to consent. Supposedly the suspect said he had nothing to hide. Apparently this statement was not altogether accurate: the officer found a kilogram of cocaine inside a brown paper bag on the floorboard of the car.

The Florida Supreme Court upheld a trial judge's decision to exclude the cocaine, holding that the consent to search the car did not authorize a search of the paper bag found in the car. The United States Supreme Court disagreed and overturned the suppression order. It declared:

> A reasonable person may be expected to know that narcotics are generally carried in some form of a container. "Contraband goods rarely are strewn across the trunk or floor of a car." United States v. Ross (1982) (Casebook p. 451). The authorization to search in this case, therefore, extended beyond the surface of the car's interior to the paper bag lying on the floor's interior.
>
> The dissent responded:
>
> By the same logic a person who consents to a search of the car ... could also be deemed to consent to a search of his person or indeed of his body cavities, since a reasonable person may be expected to know that drug carriers frequently store their contraband on their persons or in their body cavities.... The majority ... never identifies a reason for conflating distinct privacy expectations that a person has in cars and in closed containers.

4. ABANDONED PROPERTY

ABEL v. UNITED STATES

Supreme Court of the United States, 1960.
362 U.S. 217, 80 S.Ct. 683.

MR. JUSTICE FRANKFURTER delivered the opinion of the Court.

The question in this case is whether [certain] items were properly admitted into evidence at the petitioner's trial for conspiracy to commit espionage. All ... items were seized by officers of the Government without a search warrant. The seizures did not occur in connection with the exertion of the criminal process against petitioner. They arose out of his administrative arrest by the United States Immigration and Naturalization Service as a preliminary to his deportation. A motion to suppress these items as evidence, duly made in the District Court, was denied after a full hearing. 155 F.Supp. 8. Petitioner was tried, convicted and sentenced to thirty years' imprisonment and to the payment of a fine of $3,000. . . .

The ... items, all in petitioner's possession at the time of his administrative arrest, the admissibility of which is in question were the following:

* * *

[A] a hollowed-out pencil containing 18 microfilms; and

[B] a block of wood, wrapped in sandpaper, and containing within it a small booklet with a series of numbers on each page, a so-called "cipher pad."

* * *

Petitioner was arrested by officers of the Immigration and Naturalization Service (hereafter abbreviated as I.N.S.) on June 21, 1957, in a single room in the Hotel Latham in New York City, his then abode.

* * *

After placing petitioner under arrest, the four I.N.S. agents undertook a search of his person and of all of his belongings in the room, and the adjoining bathroom, which lasted for from fifteen to twenty minutes. Petitioner did not give consent to this search; his consent was not sought. The F.B.I. agents observed this search but took no part in it. It was Schoenenberger's testimony to the District Court that the purpose of this search was to discover weapons and documentary evidence of petitioner's "alienage"—that is, documents to substantiate the information regarding petitioner's status as an alien which the I.N.S. had received from the F.B.I. During this search one of the challenged items of evidence, the one we have designated (2), a birth certificate for "Martin Collins," was seized. Weapons were not found, nor was any other evidence regarding petitioner's "alienage."

When the search was completed, petitioner was told to dress himself, to assemble his things and to choose what he wished to take with him. With the help of the I.N.S. agents almost everything in the room was packed into petitioner's baggage. A few things petitioner deliberately left on a window sill, indicating that he did not want to take them, and several other things which he chose not to pack up into his luggage he put into the room's wastepaper basket.

* * *

When petitioner's belongings had been completely packed, petitioner agreed to check out of the hotel. One of the F.B.I. agents obtained his bill from the hotel and petitioner paid it. Petitioner was then handcuffed and taken, along with his baggage, to a waiting automobile and thence to the headquarters of the I.N.S. in New York.

As soon as petitioner had been taken from the hotel an F.B.I. agent, Kehoe, who had been in the room adjoining petitioner's during the arrest and search and who, like the I.N.S. agents, had no search warrant, received permission from the hotel management to search the room just vacated by petitioner. Although the bill which petitioner had paid entitled him to occupy the room until 3 p.m. of that day, the hotel's practice was to consider a room vacated whenever a guest removed his baggage and turned in his key. Kehoe conducted a search of petitioner's room which lasted for about three hours. Among other things, he seized the contents of the wastepaper basket into which petitioner had put some things while packing his belongings. Two of the items thus seized were the challenged items of evidence we have designated [A] and [B]: a hollow pencil containing microfilm and a block of wood containing a "cipher pad."

* * *

We have left to the last the admissibility of the hollowed-out pencil and the block of wood containing a "cipher pad," because their admissibility is founded upon an entirely different set of considerations. These two items were found by an agent of the F.B.I. in the course of a search he undertook of petitioner's hotel room, immediately after petitioner had paid his bill and vacated the room. They were found in the room's wastepaper basket, where petitioner had put them while packing his belongings and preparing to leave. No pretense is made that this search by the F.B.I. was for any purpose other than to gather evidence of crime, that is, evidence of petitioner's espionage. As such, however, it was entirely lawful, although undertaken without a warrant. This is so for the reason that at the time of the search petitioner had vacated the room. The hotel then had the exclusive right to its possession, and the hotel management freely gave its consent that the search be made. Nor was it unlawful to seize the entire contents of the wastepaper basket, even though some of its contents had no connection with crime. So far as the record shows, petitioner had abandoned these articles. He had thrown them away. So far as he was concerned, they were *bona vacantia*. There can be nothing unlawful in the Government's appropriation of such abandoned property. The two items which were eventually introduced in evidence were assertedly means for the commission of espionage and were themselves seizable as such. These two items having been lawfully seized by the Government in connection with an investigation of crime, we encounter no basis for discussing further their admissibility as evidence.

Affirmed.

[The dissenting opinions of JUSTICE DOUGLAS and JUSTICE BRENNAN are omitted.]

NOTES

1. The doctrine of abandoned property is sometimes applied when a suspect arrested by the police drops or throws some contraband to the ground. When a person discards incriminating evidence before an arrest occurs, then the property is generally seizable as abandoned property. See People v. Harris, 15 Cal.App.3d 498, 93 Cal.Rptr. 285 (1971); State v. Ryan, 358 So.2d 1274 (La.1978) (true abandonment occurred when a police car stopped a block away and an officer got out of the car).

2. In Venner v. State, 30 Md.App. 599, 354 A.2d 483 (1976), the court approved a search which had been conducted of a prisoner's excrement.

3. Consider the facts of United States v. Hall, 47 F.3d 1091 (11th Cir.1995). There, the defendant had run discarded documents through a shredder, sealed them in opaque green garbage bags, placed the bag inside an enclosed garbage dumpster located adjacent to the company's offices 40 yards up a private road, to be picked up by a private trash collection service. The court held the company had no reasonable expectation of privacy in the garbage, because there was no barrier preventing access to the dumpster and the immediate vicinities of commercial buildings are treated differently for privacy purposes than are residences.

5. AUTOMOBILE SEARCHES

CHAMBERS v. MARONEY

Supreme Court of the United States, 1970.
399 U.S. 42, 90 S.Ct. 1975.

MR. JUSTICE WHITE delivered the opinion of the Court.

The principal question in this case concerns the admissibility of evidence seized from an automobile, in which petitioner was riding at the time of his arrest, after the automobile was taken to a police station and was there thoroughly searched without a warrant. The Court of Appeals for the Third Circuit found no violation of petitioner's Fourth Amendment rights. We affirm.

I

During the night of May 20, 1963, a Gulf service station in North Braddock, Pennsylvania, was robbed by two men each of whom carried and displayed a gun. The robbers took the currency from the cash register; the service station attendant, one Stephen Kovacich, was directed to place the coins in his right hand glove, which was then taken by the robbers. Two teen-agers, who had earlier noticed a blue compact station wagon circling the block in the vicinity of the Gulf station, then saw the station wagon speed away from a parking lot close to the Gulf station; about the same time, they learned that the Gulf station had been robbed. They reported to police, who arrived immediately, that four men were in the station wagon and one was wearing a green sweater. Kovacich told the police that one of the men who robbed him was wearing a green sweater and the other was wearing a trench coat.

A description of the car and the two robbers was broadcast over the police radio. Within an hour, a light blue compact station wagon answering the description and carrying four men was stopped by the police about two miles from the Gulf station. Petitioner was one of the men in the station wagon. He was wearing a green sweater and there was a trench coat in the car. The occupants were arrested and the car was driven to the police station. In the course of a thorough search of the car at the station, the police found concealed in a compartment under the dashboard two .38 caliber revolvers (one loaded with dumdum bullets), a right hand glove containing small change, and certain cards bearing the name of Raymond Havicon, the attendant at a Boron service station in McKeesport, Pennsylvania, who had been robbed at gun point on May 13, 1963. In the course of a warrant-authorized search of petitioner's home the day after petitioner's arrest, police found and seized certain .38 caliber ammunition, including some dumdum bullets similar to those found in one of the guns taken from the station wagon.

Petitioner was indicted for both robberies. His first trial ended in a mistrial but he was convicted of both robberies at the second trial. Both Kovacich and Havicon identified petitioner as one of the robbers. The materials taken from the station wagon were introduced into evidence, Kovacich identifying his glove and Havicon the cards taken in the May 13 robbery. The bullets seized at petitioner's house were also introduced over objections of petitioner's counsel. Petitioner was sentenced to a term of four to eight years' imprisonment for the May 13 robbery and to a term of two to seven years' imprisonment for the May 20 robbery, the sentences to run consecutively. Petitioner did not take a direct appeal from these convictions. In 1965, petitioner sought a writ of habeas corpus in the state court, which denied the writ after a brief evidentiary hearing; the denial of the writ was affirmed on appeal in the Pennsylvania appellate courts. Habeas corpus proceedings were then commenced in the United States District Court for the Western District of Pennsylvania. An order to show cause was issued. Based on the State's response and the state court record, the petition for habeas corpus was denied without a hearing. The Court of Appeals for the Third Circuit affirmed, . . . and we granted certiorari.

II

We pass quickly the claim that the search of the automobile was the fruit of an unlawful arrest. Both the courts below thought the arresting officers had probable cause to make the arrest. We agree. Having talked to the teen-age observers and to the victim Kovacich, the police had ample cause to stop a light blue compact station wagon carrying four men and to arrest the occupants, one of whom was wearing a green sweater and one of whom had a trench coat with him in the car.[1]

1. In any event, as we point out below, the validity of an arrest is not necessarily determinative of the right to search a car if there is probable cause to make the search. Here, as will be true in many cases, the circumstances justifying the arrest are also those furnishing probable cause for the search.

Even so, the search which produced the incriminating evidence was made at the police station some time after the arrest and cannot be justified as a search incident to an arrest: "Once an accused is under arrest and in custody, then a search made at another place, without a warrant, is simply not incident to the arrest." Preston v. United States, 376 U.S. 364, 367, 84 S.Ct. 881, 883 (1964). Dyke v. Taylor Implement Mfg. Co., 391 U.S. 216, 88 S.Ct. 1472 (1968), is to the same effect; the reasons which have been thought sufficient to justify warrantless searches carried out in connection with an arrest no longer obtain when the accused is safely in custody at the station house.

There are, however, alternative grounds arguably justifying the search of the car in this case. In *Preston,* supra, the arrest was for vagrancy; it was apparent that the officers had no cause to believe that evidence of crime was concealed in the auto. In *Dyke,* supra, the Court expressly rejected the suggestion that there was probable cause to search the car. Here the situation is different, for the police had probable cause to believe that the robbers, carrying guns and the fruits of the crime, had fled the scene in a light blue compact station wagon which would be carrying four men, one wearing a green sweater and another wearing a trench coat. As the state courts correctly held, there was probable cause to arrest the occupants of the station wagon that the officers stopped; just as obviously was there probable cause to search the car for guns and stolen money.

In terms of the circumstances justifying a warrantless search, the Court has long distinguished between an automobile and a home or office. In Carroll v. United States, 267 U.S. 132, 45 S.Ct. 280 (1925), the issue was the admissibility in evidence of contraband liquor seized in a warrantless search of a car on the highway. After surveying the law from the time of the adoption of the Fourth Amendment onward, the Court held that automobiles and other conveyances may be searched without a warrant in circumstances which would not justify the search without a warrant of a house or an office, provided that there is probable cause to believe that the car contains articles that the officers are entitled to seize. The Court expressed its holding as follows:

"We have made a somewhat extended reference to these statutes to show that the guaranty of freedom from unreasonable searches and seizures by the Fourth Amendment has been construed, practically since the beginning of the government, as recognizing a necessary difference between a search of a store, dwelling house, or other structure in respect of which a proper official warrant readily may be obtained and a search of a ship, motor boat, wagon, or automobile for contraband goods, where it is not practicable to secure a warrant, because the vehicle can be quickly moved out of the locality or jurisdiction in which the warrant must be sought.

"Having thus established that contraband goods concealed and illegally transported in an automobile or other vehicle may be searched for without a warrant, we come now to consider under what circumstances such search may be made.... [T]hose lawfully within the country, entitled to use the public highways, have a right to free passage without interruption or search unless there is known to a competent official, authorized to search, probable cause for believing that their vehicles are carrying contraband or illegal merchandise.

* * *

"The measure of legality of such a seizure is, therefore, that the seizing officer shall have reasonable or probable cause for believing that the automobile which he stops and seizes has contraband liquor therein which is being illegally transported." 267 U.S., at 153–154, 155–156, 45 S.Ct. at 285–286.

The Court also noted that the search of an auto on probable cause proceeds on a theory wholly different from that justifying the search incident to an arrest:

"The right to search and the validity of the seizure are not dependent on the right to arrest. They are dependent on the reasonable cause the seizing officer has for belief that the contents of the automobile offend against the law." 267 U.S., at 158–159, 45 S.Ct. at 287.

Finding that there was probable cause for the search and seizure at issue before it, the Court affirmed the convictions.

Carroll was followed and applied in Husty v. United States, 282 U.S. 694, 51 S.Ct. 240 (1931), and Scher v. United States, 305 U.S. 251, 59 S.Ct. 174 (1938). It was reaffirmed and followed in Brinegar v. United States, 338 U.S. 160, 69 S.Ct. 1302 (1949). In 1964, the opinion in *Preston,* supra, cited both *Brinegar* and *Carroll* with approval. In Cooper v. California, 386 U.S. 58, 87 S.Ct. 788 (1967),[2] the Court read *Preston* as dealing primarily with a search incident to arrest and cited that case for the proposition that the mobility of a car may make the search of a car without a warrant reasonable "although the result might be the opposite in a search of a home, a store, or other fixed piece of property." The Court's opinion in *Dyke,* recognized that "[a]utomobiles, because of their mobility, may be searched without a warrant upon facts not justifying a warrantless search of a residence or office," citing *Brinegar* and *Carroll,* supra. However, because there was insufficient reason to search the car involved in the *Dyke* case, the Court did not reach the question of whether those cases "extend to a warrantless search, based upon probable cause, of an automobile which, having been stopped originally on a highway, is parked outside a courthouse." 391 U.S., at 222, 88 S.Ct. at 1476.[3]

2. *Cooper* involved the warrantless search of a car held for forfeiture under state law. Evidence seized from the car in that search was held admissible. In the case before us no claim is made that state law authorized that the station wagon be held as evidence or as an instrumentality of the crime; nor was the station wagon an abandoned or stolen vehicle. The question here is whether probable cause justifies a warrantless search in the circumstances presented.

3. Nothing said last term in Chimel v. California, 395 U.S. 752, 89 S.Ct. 2034 (1969), purported to modify or affect the rationale of *Carroll.* As the Court noted:

Neither *Carroll,* supra, nor other cases in this Court require or suggest that in every conceivable circumstance the search of an auto even with probable cause may be made without the extra protection for privacy which a warrant affords. But the circumstances which furnish probable cause to search a particular auto for particular articles are most often unforeseeable; moreover, the opportunity to search is fleeting since a car is readily movable. Where this is true, as in *Carroll* and the case before us now, if an effective search is to be made at any time, either the search must be made immediately without a warrant or the car itself must be seized and held without a warrant for whatever period is necessary to obtain a warrant for the search.[4]

In enforcing the Fourth Amendment's prohibition against unreasonable searches and seizures, the Court has insisted upon probable cause as a minimum requirement for a reasonable search permitted by the Constitution. As a general rule, it has also required the judgment of a magistrate on the probable cause issue and the issuance of a warrant before a search is made. Only in exigent circumstances will the judgment of the police as to probable cause serve as a sufficient authorization for a search. *Carroll,* supra, holds a search warrant unnecessary where there is probable cause to search an automobile stopped on the highway; the car is movable, the occupants are alerted, and the car's contents may never be found again if a warrant must be obtained. Hence, an immediate search is constitutionally permissible.

Arguably, because of the preference for a magistrate's judgment, only the immobilization of the car should be permitted until a search warrant is obtained; arguably, only the "lesser" intrusion is permissible until the magistrate authorizes the "greater." But which is the "greater" and which the "lesser" intrusion is itself a debatable question and the answer may depend on a variety of circumstances. For constitutional purposes, we see no difference between on the one hand seizing and holding a car before presenting the probable cause issue to a magistrate and on the other hand carrying out an immediate search without a warrant. Given probable cause to search, either course is reasonable under the Fourth Amendment.

On the facts before us, the blue station wagon could have been searched on the spot when it was stopped since there was probable cause to search and it was a fleeting target for a search. The probable cause factor still obtained at the station house and so did the mobility of the

"Our holding today is of course entirely consistent with the recognized principle that, assuming the existence of probable cause, automobiles and other vehicles may be searched without warrants 'where it is not practicable to secure a warrant, because the vehicle can be quickly moved out of the locality or jurisdiction in which the warrant must be sought.' Carroll v. United States, 267 U.S. 132, 153, 45 S.Ct. 280, 285, 69 L.Ed. 543; see Brinegar v. United States, 338 U.S. 160, 69 S.Ct. 1302, 93 L.Ed. 1879." 395 U.S., at 764 n. 9, 89 S.Ct. at 2040.

4. Following the car until a warrant can be obtained seems an impractical alternative since, among other things, the car may be taken out of the jurisdiction. Tracing the car and searching it hours or days later would of course permit instruments or fruits of crime to be removed from the car before the search.

car unless the Fourth Amendment permits a warrantless seizure of the car and the denial of its use to anyone until a warrant is secured. In that event there is little to choose in terms of practical consequences between an immediate search without a warrant and the car's immobilization until a warrant is obtained.[5] The same consequences may not follow where there is unforeseeable cause to search a house. But as *Carroll,* supra, held, for the purposes of the Fourth Amendment there is a constitutional difference between houses and cars....

Affirmed.

MR. JUSTICE BLACKMUN took no part in the consideration or decision of this case.

(The concurring opinion of MR. JUSTICE STEWART is omitted.)

[MR. JUSTICE HARLAN concurred in part and dissented in part. Opinion omitted.]

NOTES

1. Despite *Chambers* a number of state and federal courts held that where the car had been taken to the police station and removed from the possession of the vehicle's occupants (as where the occupants were arrested), a warrantless search was impermissible. The courts reasoned that under such circumstances no emergency existed to justify action without the intervention of a neutral judicial officer. See State v. Massey, 310 So.2d 557 (La.1975).

In Texas v. White, 423 U.S. 67, 96 S.Ct. 304 (1975), in a brief per curiam opinion, the Supreme Court upheld a warrantless search, upon probable cause, in a situation where there was no apparent need for emergency action. *White* rejected the suggestion that the holding in *Chambers* was limited to factual situations where there is need for prompt action following the stop of the vehicle in transit. In a per curiam opinion handed down on July 2, 1982, the United States Supreme Court again adhered to its decision in Texas v. White. It declared "that the justification to conduct such a warrantless search does not vanish once the car has been immobilized; nor does it depend upon ... assessment of the likelihood in each particular case that the car would have been driven away, or that its contents would have been tampered with, during the period required for the police to obtain a warrant." Michigan v. Thomas, 458 U.S. 259, 102 S.Ct. 3079 (1982).

In United States v. Johns, 469 U.S. 478, 105 S.Ct. 881 (1985), the U.S. Supreme Court all but eliminated the contemporaneity requirement for the automobile exception. It held that where customs officers had probable cause to believe that vehicles used by defendant and packages therein contained narcotics, the officers could enter the truck and seize the packages. The fact that they put the packages of narcotics in storage and did not open them for three days was not unreasonable. The Court went so far as to say that a delay of "several" days would not in itself be unreasonable, although it did indicate that if a defendant could show specific prejudice resulting from the delay, the warrantless search would not be approved under the automobile exception.

5. It was not unreasonable in this case to take the car to the station house. All occupants in the car were arrested in a dark parking lot in the middle of the night. A careful search at that point was impractical and perhaps not safe for the officers, and it would serve the owner's convenience and the safety of his car to have the vehicle and the keys together at the station house.

Under the automobile exception to the warrant requirement of *Carroll* and *Chambers,* two ingredients must be present: (1) probable cause, and (2) exigent circumstances. On the second requirement, the mere "ability" of the automobile to "become mobile" is sufficient to satisfy the exception. The court in the instant case found exigency in two circumstances: (1) the car in question which was parked at defendant's apartment belonged to someone other than the defendant—who could have easily moved the car before a warrant could be obtained; (2) the defendant's roommate was his brother and the brother could easily have gained access to the car to destroy evidence that might be used against the defendant. This court disagrees with some courts that have indicated that exigency is no longer required under the automobile exception. United States v. Alexander, 835 F.2d 1406 (11th Cir.1988).

2. On July 1, 1981, the Supreme Court decided two cases that involved the seizure and the search of items in an automobile. The two decisions serve as a reminder of the importance of keeping distinct various exceptions to the warrant requirement even though different exceptions may have possible application in a single factual setting.

In New York v. Belton, 453 U.S. 454, 101 S.Ct. 2860 (1981), the Court upheld the search of the interior of a vehicle and of a jacket found therein, using the doctrine of search incident to arrest. In effect the Court declared that where a person in an automobile is validly arrested, Chimel v. California, 395 U.S. 752, 89 S.Ct. 2034 (1969), permits the search of the vehicle's interior, even if the arrestee has been removed from the car. The search apparently can extend to closed containers and, under United States v. Robinson, 414 U.S. 218, 94 S.Ct. 467 (1973), does not depend upon the probability that the search will yield evidence. The Court distinguished Arkansas v. Sanders, 442 U.S. 753, 99 S.Ct. 2586 (1979), noting that *Sanders* did not involve the doctrine of search incident to arrest.

In Robbins v. California, 453 U.S. 420, 101 S.Ct. 2841 (1981), the prosecution sought to justify the search of a wrapped package found in the luggage compartment of a vehicle. It did not rely on the doctrine of search incident to arrest. Instead the Court considered the applicability of the automobile exception. It held that this exception cannot justify the warrantless search of a closed container found in a vehicle, even if the vehicle has been stopped in transit, and even if there is probable cause to believe that the container contains contraband or evidence of a crime. A year later the Court would reconsider the holdings of *Robbins* in United States v. Ross, infra.

Excerpts from *Robbins* and *Belton* follow:

Justice Stewart announced the judgment of the Court in *Robbins* and delivered an opinion, in which Justice Brennan, Justice White, and Justice Marshall joined.

On the early morning of January 5, 1975, California Highway Patrol officers stopped the petitioner's car—a 1966 Chevrolet station wagon—because he had been driving erratically. He got out of his vehicle and walked towards the patrol car. When one of the officers asked him for his driver's license and the station wagon's registration, he fumbled with his wallet. When the petitioner opened the car door to get out the registration, the officers smelled marihuana smoke. One of the officers patted the petitioner down, and discovered a vial of liquid. The officer then searched the passenger compartment of the car, and found marihuana as well as equipment for using it.

After putting the petitioner in the patrol car, the officers opened the tailgate of the station wagon, located a handle set flush in the deck, and lifted it up to uncover a recessed luggage compartment. In the compartment were a tote bag and two packages wrapped in green opaque plastic. The police unwrapped the packages; each one contained 15 pounds of marihuana.

* * *

In the present case, the Court once again encounters the argument—made in the Government's brief *amicus curiae*—that the contents of a closed container carried in a vehicle are somehow not fully protected by the Fourth Amendment. But this argument is inconsistent with the Court's decisions in *Chadwick* and *Sanders*. Those cases made clear, if it was not clear before, that a closed piece of luggage found in a lawfully searched car is constitutionally protected to the same extent as are closed pieces of luggage found anywhere else.

The respondent, however, proposes that the *nature* of a container may diminish the constitutional protection to which it otherwise would be entitled—that the Fourth Amendment protects only containers commonly used to transport "personal effects." By personal effects the respondent means property worn on or carried about the person or having some intimate relation to the person. In taking this position, the respondent relies on numerous opinions that have drawn a distinction between pieces of sturdy luggage, like suitcases, and flimsier containers, like cardboard boxes.

* * *

The respondent's argument cannot prevail for at least two reasons. First, it has no basis in the language or meaning of the Fourth Amendment. That Amendment protects people and their effects, and it protects those effects whether they are "personal" or "impersonal." The contents of Chadwick's footlocker and Sanders' suitcase were immune from a warrantless search because they had been placed within a closed, opaque container and because Chadwick and Sanders had thereby reasonably "manifested an expectation that the contents would remain free from public examination." United States v. Chadwick. Once placed within such a container, a diary and a dishpan are equally protected by the Fourth Amendment.

Second, even if one wished to import such a distinction into the Fourth Amendment, it is difficult if not impossible to perceive any objective criteria by which that task might be accomplished. What one person may put into a suitcase, another may put into a paper bag. And as the disparate results in the decided cases indicate, no court, no constable, no citizen, can sensibly be asked to distinguish the relative "privacy interests" in a closed suitcase, briefcase, portfolio, duffle bag, or box.

The respondent protests that footnote 13 of the *Sanders* opinion says that "[n]ot all containers and packages found by police during the course of a search will deserve the full protection of the Fourth Amendment." But the exceptions listed in the succeeding sentences of the footnote are the very model of exceptions which prove the rule: "Thus, some containers (for example a kit of burglar tools or a gun case) by their very nature cannot support any reasonable expectation of privacy because their contents can be inferred from their outward appearance. Similarly, in some cases the contents of a package will be open to 'plain view,' thereby obviating the need for a warrant." The second of these exceptions obviously refers to items in a container that is not closed. The first exception is likewise little more than another variation of the "plain view" exception, since, if the distinctive configuration of a container proclaims its contents, the contents cannot fairly be said to have been removed from a searching officer's view. The same would be true, of course, if the container were transparent, or otherwise clearly revealed its contents. In short, the negative implication of footnote 13 of the *Sanders* opinion is that, unless the container is such that its contents may be said to be in plain view, those contents are fully protected by the Fourth Amendment.

The California Court of Appeal believed that the packages in the present case fell directly within the second exception described in this footnote, since "[a]ny experienced observer could have inferred from the appearance of the packages that they contained bricks of marijuana." The only evidence the Court cited to support this proposition was the testimony of one of the officers who arrested the petitioner. When asked whether there was anything about "these two plastic wrapped green blocks which attracted your attention," the officer replied, somewhat obscurely,

> "A. I had previous knowledge of transportation of such blocks. Normally contraband is wrapped this way, merely hearsay. I had never seen them before.
>
> "Q. You had heard contraband was packaged this way?
>
> "A. Yes."

This vague testimony certainly did not establish that marihuana is ordinarily "packaged this way." Expectations of privacy are established by general social norms, and to fall within the second exception of the footnote in question a container must so clearly announce its contents, whether by its distinctive configuration, its transparency, or otherwise, that its contents are obvious to an observer. If indeed a green plastic wrapping reliably indicates that a package could only contain marihuana, that fact was not shown by the evidence of record in this case.

Although the two bricks of marihuana were discovered during a lawful search of the petitioner's car, they were inside a closed, opaque container. We reaffirm today that such a container may not be opened without a warrant, even if it is found during the course of the lawful search of an automobile. Since the respondent does not allege the presence of any circumstances that would constitute a valid exception to this general rule [†] it is clear that the opening of the closed containers without a search warrant violated the Fourth and Fourteenth Amendments. Accordingly, the judgment of the California Court of Appeal is reversed.

THE CHIEF JUSTICE concurs in the judgment.

JUSTICE POWELL concurring in the judgment.

* * *

As the plurality today goes well beyond *Sanders* or any other prior case to establish a new "bright line" rule, I cannot join its opinion. It would require officers to obtain warrants in order to examine the contents of insubstantial

† In particular, it is not argued that the opening of the packages was incident to a lawful custodial arrest. Further, the respondent does not argue that the petitioner consented to the opening of the packages.

containers in which no one had a reasonable expectation of privacy. The plurality's approach strains the rationales of our prior cases and imposes substantial burdens on law enforcement without vindicating any significant values of privacy. I nevertheless concur in the judgment because the manner in which the package at issue was carefully wrapped and sealed evidenced petitioner's expectation of privacy in its contents. As we have stressed in prior decisions, a central purpose of the Fourth Amendment is to safeguard reasonable expectations of privacy.

* * *

This case and New York v. Belton, 453 U.S. 454, 101 S.Ct. 2860 (1981), decided today, involve three different Fourth Amendment questions that arise in automobile cases: (A) the scope of the search incident to arrest on the public highway; (B) whether officers must obtain a warrant when they have probable cause to search a particular container in which the suspect has a reasonable expectation of privacy; and (C), the scope of the "automobile exception" to the warrant requirement, which potentially includes all areas of the car and containers found therein. These issues frequently are intertwined, as the similar facts of these cases suggest: both involve the stop of an automobile upon probable cause, the arrest of the occupants, the search of the automobile, and the search of a personal container found therein. Nonetheless, the cases have been litigated and presented to us under entirely different theories. Intelligent analysis cannot proceed unless the issues are addressed separately. Viewing similar facts from entirely different perspectives need not lead to identical results.

* * *

I have joined the Court's opinion in *Belton* because I concluded that a "bright line" rule was necessary in the quite different circumstances addressed there. *Belton,* unlike this case, concerns only the exception to the warrant requirement for a search incident to arrest; contrary to Justice Stevens' implication, the courts below never found that the officer had probable cause to search the automobile. *Belton* presents the volatile and fluid situation of an encounter between an arresting officer and a suspect apprehended on the public highway. While Chimel v. California (1969), determines in principle the scope of a warrantless search incident to arrest, practical necessity requires that we allow an officer in these circumstances to secure thoroughly the automobile without requiring him in haste and under pressure to make close calculations about danger to himself or the vulnerability of evidence.

Any "bright line" rule does involve costs. *Belton* trades marginal privacy of containers within the passenger area of an automobile for protection of the officer and of destructible evidence. The balance of these interests strongly favors the Court's rule. The occupants of an automobile enjoy only a limited expectation of privacy in the interior of the automobile itself. This limited interest is diminished further when the occupants are placed under custodial arrest. Immediately preceding the arrest, the passengers have complete control over the entire interior of the automobile, and can place weapons or contraband into pockets or other containers as the officer approaches. Thus, practically speaking, it is difficult to justify varying degrees of protection for the general interior of the car and for the various containers found within. These considerations do not apply to the trunk of the car, which is not within the control of the passengers either immediately before or during the process of arrest.

Although petitioner Robbins was arrested, this case was litigated only on the question whether the officers needed a warrant to open a sealed, opaquely wrapped container in the rear compartment of a station wagon.

[Separate dissenting opinions of Justice Blackmun, Justice Rehnquist, and Justice Stevens are omitted.]

JUSTICE STEWART delivered the opinion of the Court in *Belton.*

When the occupant of an automobile is subjected to a lawful custodial arrest, does the constitutionally permissible scope of a search incident to his arrest include the passenger compartment of the automobile in which he was riding? That is the question at issue in the present case.

On April 9, 1978, Trooper Douglas Nicot, a New York State policeman driving an unmarked car on the New York Thruway, was passed by another automobile travelling at an excessive rate of speed. Nicot gave chase, overtook the speeding vehicle, and ordered its driver to pull it over to the side of the road and stop. There were four men in the car, one of whom was Roger Belton, the respondent in this case. The policeman asked to see the driver's license and automobile registration, and discovered that none of the men owned the vehicle or was related to its owner. Meanwhile, the policeman had smelled burnt marihuana and had seen on the floor of the car an envelope marked "Supergold" that he associated with marihuana. He therefore directed the men to get out of the car, and placed them under arrest for the unlawful possession of marihuana. He patted down each of the men and "split them up into four separate areas of the Thruway at this time so they would not be in physical touching area of each other." He then picked up the envelope marked "Supergold" and found that it contained marihuana. After giving the arrestees the warnings required by *Miranda,* the state policeman searched each one of them. He then searched the passenger compartment of the car. On the back seat he found a black leather jacket belonging to Belton. He unzipped one of the pockets of the jacket and discovered cocaine. Placing the jacket in his automobile, he drove the four arrestees to a nearby police station.

* * *

The Court's opinion in *Chimel* emphasized the principle that, as the Court had said in Terry v. Ohio, infra, at p. 1071, "The scope of [a] search must be 'strictly tied to and justified by' the circumstances which rendered its initiation permissible." Thus while the Court in *Chimel* found "ample justification" for a search of "the area from within which [an arrestee] might gain possession of a weapon or destructible evidence,' the Court found "no comparable justification . . . for routinely searching any room other than that in which an arrest occurs—or, for that matter, for searching through all the desk drawers or other closed or concealed areas in that room itself."

Although the principle that limits a search incident to a lawful custodial arrest may be stated clearly enough, courts have discovered the principle difficult to apply in specific cases. Yet, as one commentator has pointed out, the protection of the Fourth and Fourteenth Amendments "can only be realized if the police are acting under a set of rules which, in most instances, makes it possible to reach a correct determination beforehand as to whether an invasion of privacy is justified in the interest of law enforcement." LaFave, "Case-by-Case Adjudication" versus "Standardized Procedures": The Robinson Dilemma, 1974 Sup.Ct.Rev. 127, 142. This is because

> "Fourth Amendment doctrine, given force and effect by the exclusionary rule, is primarily intended to regulate the police in their day-to-day activities and thus ought to be expressed in terms that are readily applicable by the police in the context of the law enforcement activities in which they are necessarily engaged. A highly sophisticated set of rules, qualified by all sorts of ifs, ands, and buts and requiring the drawing of subtle nuances and hairline distinctions, may be the sort of heady stuff upon which the facile minds of lawyers and judges eagerly feed, but they may be 'literally impossible of application by the officer in the field.' "

In short, "A single, familiar standard is essential to guide police officers, who have only limited time and expertise to reflect on and balance the social and individual interests involved in the specific circumstances they confront." Dunaway v. New York.

* * *

Our reading of the cases suggests the generalization that articles inside the relatively narrow compass of the passenger compartment of an automobile are in fact generally, even if not inevitably, within "the area into which an arrestee might reach in order to grab a weapon or evidentiary item." *Chimel.* In order to establish the workable rule this category of cases requires, we read *Chimel's* definition of the limits of the area that may be searched in light of that generalization. Accordingly, we hold that when a policeman has made a lawful custodial arrest of the occupant of an automobile, he may, as a contemporaneous incident of that arrest, search the passenger compartment of that automobile.

It follows from this conclusion that the police may also examine the contents of any containers found within the passenger compartment, for if the passenger compartment is within reach of the arrestee, so also will containers in it be within his reach. Such a container may, of course, be searched whether it is open or closed, since the justification for the search is not that the arrestee has no privacy interest in the container, but that the lawful custodial arrest justifies the infringement of any privacy interest the arrestee may have. Thus, while the Court in *Chimel* held that the police could not search all the drawers in an arrestee's house simply because the police had arrested him at home, the Court noted that drawers within an arrestee's reach could be searched because of the danger their contents might pose to the police.

It is true, of course, that these containers will sometimes be such that they could hold neither a weapon nor evidence of the criminal conduct for which the suspect was arrested. However, in United States v. Robinson, the Court rejected the argument that such a container—there a "crumpled up cigarette package"—located during a search of Robinson incident to his arrest could not be searched: "The authority to search the person incident to a lawful custodial arrest, while based upon the need to disarm and to discover evidence, does not depend on what a court may later decide was the probability in a particular arrest situation that weapons or evidence would in fact be found upon the person of the suspect. A custodial arrest of a suspect based on probable cause is a reasonable intrusion under the Fourth Amendment; that intrusion being lawful, a search incident to the arrest requires no additional justification."

The New York Court of Appeals relied upon *Chadwick* and *Sanders* in concluding that the search and seizure in the present case were constitutionally invalid. But neither of those cases involved an arguably valid search incident to a lawful custodial arrest. As the Court pointed out in the *Chadwick* case, "Here the search was conducted more than an hour after federal agents had gained exclusive control of the footlocker and long after respondents were securely in custody; the search therefore cannot be viewed as incidental to the arrest or as justified by any other exigency." And in the *Sanders* case, the Court explicitly stated that it did not "consider the constitutionality of searches of luggage incident to the arrest of its possessor.

* * *

It is not questioned that the respondent was the subject of a lawful custodial arrest on a charge of possessing marihuana. The search of the respondent's jacket followed immediately upon that arrest. The jacket was located inside the passenger compartment of the car in which the respondent had been a passenger just before he was arrested. The jacket was thus within the area which we have concluded was "within the arrestee's immediate control" within the meaning of the *Chimel* case. The search of the jacket, therefore, was a search incident to a lawful custodial arrest, and it did not violate the Fourth and Fourteenth Amendments. Accordingly, the judgment is reversed.

JUSTICE REHNQUIST, concurring.

[Opinion Omitted.]

JUSTICE STEVENS, concurring in the judgment.

[Opinion Omitted.]

JUSTICE BRENNAN, with whom JUSTICE MARSHALL joins, dissenting.

In Chimel v. California, 395 U.S. 752, 89 S.Ct. 2034 (1969), this Court carefully analyzed more than 50 years of conflicting precedent governing the permissible scope of warrantless searches incident to custodial arrest. The Court today turns its back on the product of that analysis, formulating an arbitrary "bright line" rule applicable to "recent" occupants of automobiles that fails to reflect *Chimel*'s underlying policy justifications. While the Court claims to leave *Chimel* intact, I fear that its unwarranted abandonment of the principles underlying that decision may signal a wholesale retreat from our carefully developed search-incident-to-arrest analysis. I dissent.

* * *

The *Chimel* exception to the warrant requirement was designed with two principal concerns in mind: the safety of the arresting officer and the preservation of easily concealed or destructible evidence. Recognizing that a suspect might have access to weapons or contraband at the time of arrest, the Court declared:

> "When an arrest is made, it is reasonable for the arresting officer to search the person arrested in order to remove any weapons that the latter might seek to use in order to resist arrest or effect his escape. Otherwise, the officer's safety might well be endangered, and the arrest itself frustrated. In addition, it is entirely reasonable for the arresting officer to search for and seize any evidence on the arrestee's person in order to prevent its concealment or destruction. And the area into which an arrestee might reach in order to grab a weapon or evidentiary items must, of course, be governed by a like rule."

The *Chimel* standard was narrowly tailored to address these concerns: it permits police officers who have effected a custodial arrest to conduct a warrantless search "of the arrestee's person and the area 'within his immediate control'—construing that phrase to mean the area from within which he might gain possession of a weapon or destructible evidence."

* * *

As the facts of this case make clear, the Court today substantially expands the permissible scope of searches incident to arrest by permitting police officers to search areas and containers the arrestee could not possibly reach at the time of arrest. These facts demonstrate that at the time Belton and his three companions were placed under custodial arrest—which was *after* they had been removed from the car, patted down, and separated—none of them could have reached the jackets that had been left on the back seat of the car.

* * *

The Court seeks to justify its departure from the principles underlying *Chimel* by proclaiming the need for a new bright line rule to guide the officer in the field. As we pointed out in Mincey v. Arizona, however, "the mere fact that law enforcement may be made more efficient can never by itself justify disregard of the Fourth Amendment." Moreover, the Court's attempt to forge a "bright line" rule fails on its own terms. While the "interior/trunk" distinction may provide a workable guide in certain routine cases—for example, where the officer arrests the driver of a car and then immediately searches the seats and floor—in the long run, I suspect it will create far more problems than it solves. The Court's new approach leaves open too many questions and, more important, it provides the police and the courts with too few tools with which to find the answers.

Thus, although the Court concludes that a warrantless search of a car may take place even though the suspect was arrested outside the car, it does not indicate how long after the suspect's arrest that search may validly be conducted. Would a warrantless search incident to arrest be valid if conducted five minutes after the suspect left his car? Thirty minutes? Three hours? Does it matter whether the suspect is standing in close proximity to the car when the search is conducted? Does it matter whether the police formed probable cause to arrest before or after the suspect left his car? And *why* is the rule announced today necessarily limited to searches of cars? What if a suspect is seen walking out of a house where the police, peering in from outside, had formed probable cause to believe a crime was being committed? Could the police then arrest that suspect and enter the house to conduct a search incident to arrest? Even assuming today's rule is limited to searches of the "interior" of cars—an assumption not demanded by logic—what is meant by "interior"? Does it include locked glove compartments, the interior of door panels, or the area under the floorboards? Are special rules necessary for station wagons and hatchbacks, where the luggage compartment may be reached through the interior, or taxicabs, where a glass panel might separate the driver's compartment from the rest of the car? Are the only containers that may be searched those that are large enough to be "capable of holding another object"? Or does the new rule apply to any container, even if it "could hold neither a weapon nor evidence of the criminal conduct for which the suspect was arrested"?

The Court does not give the police any "bright line" answers to these questions. More important, because the Court's new rule abandons the justifications underlying *Chimel, it offers no guidance to the police officer seeking to work out these answers for himself.* As we warned in *Chimel,* "No consideration relevant to the Fourth Amendment suggests any point of rational limitation, once the search is allowed to go beyond the area from which the person arrested might obtain weapons or evidentiary items."

* * *

3. Under the "bright line" rule of *Belton* the police can search the passenger compartment of a vehicle (including closed containers) after the custodial arrest of an occupant. What if the occupant has been totally immobilized, removed from the vehicle, and the search takes place 30–40 minutes after the arrest; does *Belton* apply? "No," according to the Ninth Circuit in United States v. Vasey, 834 F.2d 782 (9th Cir.1987). If the occupant has been rendered "absolutely incapable" of getting into the passenger compartment (the defendant/driver was handcuffed and in a patrol car at the time of the search) and the delay in the search is "insignificant" (30–40 minutes in this case), the search can no longer be considered as "incident to the arrest."

On the other hand, a 10–minute delay from the time a driver was arrested to the time his vehicle was searched while he was in handcuffs, did *not* negate the search as incident to arrest under *Belton.* "Contemporaneous" under *Belton,* this court says, is not the same as "simultaneous." All that is required is that the search of the vehicle take place during "the same time period" as the arrest. The "time period" is measured by the time reasonably necessary to perform a law enforcement officer's duties attendant upon an arrest. Here the officer arrested the driver, handcuffed him, placed him in the police car, and then went back to search the car—all part of a continuous sequence. State v. Williams, 516 So.2d 1081 (Fla.App.1987).

4. What is the scope of the "passenger compartment" of an automobile? One court allowed a search of a hatch area of a hatchback incident to arrest of the driver. United States v. Doward, 41 F.3d 789 (1st Cir.1994), cert. denied ___ U.S. ___, 115 S.Ct. 1716 (1995).

5. The New Jersey Supreme Court has rejected Belton on state constitutional grounds, holding that a warrantless search of the passenger compartment of a vehicle may not be made solely because the driver has been arrested for a minor traffic violation. State v. Pierce, 136 N.J. 184, 642 A.2d 947 (1994). The Supreme Court of Pennsylvania has also ruled to the same effect. Commonwealth v. White, 669 A.2d 896 (Pa.1995).

UNITED STATES v. ROSS

Supreme Court of the United States, 1982.
456 U.S. 798, 102 S.Ct. 2157.

JUSTICE STEVENS delivered the opinion of the Court.

In Carroll v. United States, 267 U.S. 132, 45 S.Ct. 280 (1925), the Court held that a warrantless search of an automobile stopped by police officers who had probable cause to believe the vehicle contained contraband was not unreasonable within the meaning of the Fourth Amendment. The Court in *Carroll* did not explicitly address the scope of the search that is permissible. In this case, we consider the extent to which police officers—who have legitimately stopped an automobile and who have probable cause to believe that contraband is concealed somewhere within it—may conduct a probing search of compartments and containers within the vehicle whose contents are not in plain view. We hold that they may conduct a search of the vehicle that is as thorough as a magistrate could authorize in a warrant "particularly describing the place to be searched."

In the evening of November 27, 1978, an informant who had previously proved to be reliable telephoned Detective Marcum of the District of Columbia Police Department and told him that an individual known as "Bandit" was selling narcotics kept in the trunk of a car parked at 439 Ridge Street. The informant stated that he had just observed "Bandit" complete a sale and that "Bandit" had told him that additional narcotics were in the trunk. The informant gave Marcum a detailed description of "Bandit" and stated that the car was a "purplish maroon" Chevrolet Malibu with District of Columbia license plates.

Accompanied by Detective Cassidy and Sergeant Gonzales, Marcum immediately drove to the area and found a maroon Malibu parked in front of 439 Ridge Street. A license check disclosed that the car was registered to Albert Ross; a computer check on Ross revealed that he fit the informant's description and used the alias "Bandit." In two passes through the neighborhood the officers did not observe anyone matching the informant's description. To avoid alerting persons on the street, they left the area.

The officers returned five minutes later and observed the maroon Malibu turning off Ridge Street onto Fourth Street. They pulled alongside the Malibu, noticed that the driver matched the informant's description, and stopped the car. Marcum and Cassidy told the driver—later identified as Albert Ross, the respondent in this action—to get out of the vehicle. While they searched Ross, Sergeant Gonzales discovered a bullet on the car's front seat. He searched the interior of the car and found a pistol in the glove compartment. Ross then was arrested and handcuffed. Detective Cassidy took Ross' keys and opened the trunk, where he found a closed brown paper bag. He opened the bag and discovered a number of glassine bags containing a white powder. Cassidy replaced the bag, closed the trunk, and drove the car to Headquarters.

At the police station Cassidy thoroughly searched the car. In addition to the "lunch-type" brown paper bag, Cassidy found in the trunk a zippered red leather pouch. He unzipped the pouch and discovered $3,200 in cash. The police laboratory later determined that the powder in the paper bag was heroin. No warrant was obtained.

Ross was charged with possession of heroin with intent to distribute, in violation of 21 U.S.C. § 841(a). Prior to trial, he moved to suppress the heroin found in the paper bag and the currency found in the leather pouch. After an evidentiary hearing, the District Court denied the motion to suppress. The heroin and currency were introduced in evidence at trial and Ross was convicted.

A three-judge panel of the Court of Appeals reversed the conviction. It held that the police had probable cause to stop and search Ross' car and that, under Carroll v. United States, supra, and Chambers v. Maroney, 399 U.S. 42, 90 S.Ct. 1975 (1970), the officers lawfully could search the automobile—including its trunk—without a warrant. The court considered separately, however, the warrantless search of the two containers found in the trunk. On the basis of Arkansas v. Sanders, 442 U.S. 753, 99 S.Ct. 2586 (1979), the court concluded that the constitutionality of a warrantless search of a container found in an automobile depends on whether the owner possesses a reasonable expectation of privacy in its contents. Applying that test, the court held that the warrantless search of the paper bag was valid but the search of the leather pouch was not. The court remanded for a new trial at which the items taken from the paper bag, but not those from the leather pouch, could be admitted.[1]

The entire Court of Appeals then voted to rehear the case en banc. A majority of the court rejected the panel's conclusion that a distinction of constitutional significance existed between the two containers found in respondent's trunk; it held that the police should not have opened either container without first obtaining a warrant. The en banc Court of Appeals considered, and rejected, the argument that it was reasonable for the police to open both the paper bag and the leather pouch because they were entitled to conduct a warrantless search of the entire vehicle in which the two containers were found. The majority concluded that this argument was foreclosed by *Sanders.*

Three dissenting judges interpreted *Sanders* differently.

* * *

There is, however, no dispute among judges about the importance of striving for clarification in this area of the law. For countless vehicles are stopped on highways and public streets every day and our cases demonstrate that it is not uncommon for police officers to have probable cause to believe that contraband may be found in a stopped vehicle. In every such case a conflict is presented between the individual's constitutionally protected interest in privacy and the public interest in effective law enforcement. No single rule of law can resolve every conflict, but our conviction that clarification is feasible led us to grant the Government's petition for certiorari in this case and to invite the parties to address the question whether the decision in *Robbins* should be reconsidered.

We begin with a review of the decision in *Carroll* itself. In the fall of 1921, federal prohibition agents obtained evidence that George Carroll and John Kiro were "bootleggers" who frequently traveled between Grand Rapids and Detroit in an Oldsmobile Roadster.[2] On December

1. The court rejected the Government's argument that the warrantless search of the leather pouch was justified as incident to respondent's arrest. The Government has not challenged this holding.

2. On September 29, 1921, Carroll and Kiro met the agents in Grand Rapids and agreed to sell them three cases of whiskey. The sale was not consummated, however, possibly because Carroll learned the agents' true identity. In October, the agents discovered Carroll and Kiro driving the Oldsmobile Roadster on the road to Detroit, which was known as an active center for the introduction of illegal liquor into this country. The agents followed the roadster as far as East Lansing, but there abandoned the chase.

15, 1921, the agents unexpectedly encountered Carroll and Kiro driving west on that route in that car. The officers gave pursuit, stopped the roadster on the highway, and directed Carroll and Kiro to get out of the car.

No contraband was visible in the front seat of the Oldsmobile and the rear portion of the roadster was closed. One of the agents raised the rumble seat but found no liquor. He raised the seat cushion and again found nothing. The officer then struck at the "lazyback" of the seat and noticed that it was "harder than upholstery ordinarily is in those backs." 267 U.S., at 174. He tore open the seat cushion and discovered 68 bottles of gin and whiskey concealed inside. No warrant had been obtained for the search.

Carroll and Kiro were convicted of transporting intoxicating liquor in violation of the National Prohibition Act. On review of those convictions, this Court ruled that the warrantless search of the roadster was reasonable within the meaning of the Fourth Amendment. In an extensive opinion written by Chief Justice Taft, the Court held:

> "On reason and authority the true rule is that if the search and seizure without a warrant are made upon probable cause, that is, upon a belief, reasonably arising out of circumstances known to the seizing officer, that an automobile or other vehicle contains that which by law is subject to seizure and destruction, the search and seizure are valid. The Fourth Amendment is to be construed in the light of what was deemed an unreasonable search and seizure when it was adopted, and in a manner which will conserve public interests as well as the interests and rights of individual citizens."

The Court explained at length the basis for this rule. The Court noted that historically warrantless searches of vessels, wagons, and carriages—as opposed to fixed premises such as a home or other building—had been considered reasonable by Congress.

* * *

Thus, since its earliest days Congress had recognized the impracticability of securing a warrant in cases involving the transportation of contraband goods. It is this impracticability, viewed in historical perspective, that provided the basis for the *Carroll* decision. Given the nature of an automobile in transit, the Court recognized that an immediate intrusion is necessary if police officers are to secure the illicit substance. In this class of cases, the Court held that a warrantless search of an automobile is not unreasonable.[3]

3. Subsequent cases make clear that the decision in *Carroll* was not based on the fact that the only course available to the police was an immediate search. As Justice Harlan later recognized, although a failure to *seize* a moving automobile believed to contain contraband might deprive officers of the illicit goods, once a vehicle itself has been stopped the exigency does not necessarily justify a warrantless *search.* Chambers v. Maroney (opinion of Harlan, J.). The Court in *Chambers,* however—

In defining the nature of this "exception" to the general rule that "[i]n cases where the securing of a warrant is reasonably practicable, it must be used," the Court in *Carroll* emphasized the importance of the requirement that officers have probable cause to believe that the vehicle contains contraband.

... Moreover, the probable cause determination must be based on objective facts that could justify the issuance of a warrant by a magistrate and not merely on the subjective good faith of the police officers. " '[A]s we have seen, good faith is not enough to constitute probable cause. That faith must be grounded on facts within knowledge of the [officer], which in the judgment of the court would make his faith reasonable.' " Id., at 161–162 (quoting Director General v. Kastenbaum, 263 U.S. 25, 28, 44 S.Ct. 52, 53 (1923)).

In short, the exception to the warrant requirement established in *Carroll*—the scope of which we consider in this case—applies only to searches of vehicles that are supported by probable cause. In this class of cases, a search is not unreasonable if based on facts that would justify the issuance of a warrant, even though a warrant has not actually been obtained.

The rationale justifying a warrantless search of an automobile that is believed to be transporting contraband arguably applies with equal force to any movable container that is believed to be carrying an illicit substance. That argument, however, was squarely rejected in United States v. Chadwick, 433 U.S. 1, 97 S.Ct. 2476 (1977).

Chadwick involved the warrantless search of a 200-pound footlocker secured with two padlocks. Federal railroad officials in San Diego became suspicious when they noticed that a brown footlocker loaded onto a train bound for Boston was unusually heavy and leaking talcum

with only Justice Harlan dissenting—refused to adopt a rule that would permit a warrantless seizure but prohibit a warrantless search. The Court held that if police officers have probable cause to justify a warrantless seizure of an automobile on a public roadway, they may conduct an immediate search of the contents of that vehicle. "For constitutional purposes, we see no difference between on the one hand seizing and holding a car before presenting the probable cause issue to a magistrate and on the other hand carrying out an immediate search without a warrant. Given probable cause to search, either course is reasonable under the Fourth Amendment." Chambers v. Maroney.

The Court also has held that if an immediate search on the street is permissible without a warrant, a search soon thereafter at the police station is permissible if the vehicle is impounded. *Chambers,* supra; Texas v. White, 423 U.S. 67, 96 S.Ct. 304 (1975). These decisions are based on the practicalities of the situations presented and a realistic appraisal of the relatively minor protection that a contrary rule would provide for privacy interests. Given the scope of the initial intrusion caused by a seizure of an automobile—which often could leave the occupants stranded on the highway—the Court rejected an inflexible rule that would force police officers in every case either to post guard at the vehicle while a warrant is obtained or to tow the vehicle itself to the station. Similarly, if an immediate search on the scene could be conducted, but not one at the station if the vehicle is impounded, police often simply would search the vehicle on the street—at no advantage to the occupants, yet possibly at certain cost to the police. The rules as applied in particular cases may appear unsatisfactory. They reflect, however, a reasoned application of the more general rule that if an individual gives the police probable cause to believe a vehicle is transporting contraband, he loses the right to proceed on his way without official interference.

powder, a substance often used to mask the odor of marijuana. Narcotics agents met the train in Boston and a trained police dog signaled the presence of a controlled substance inside the footlocker. The agents did not seize the footlocker, however, at this time; they waited until respondent Chadwick arrived and the footlocker was placed in the trunk of Chadwick's automobile. Before the engine was started, the officers arrested Chadwick and his two companions. The agents then removed the footlocker to a secured place, opened it without a warrant, and discovered a large quantity of marijuana.

In a subsequent criminal proceeding, Chadwick claimed that the warrantless search of the footlocker violated the Fourth Amendment. In the District Court, the Government argued that as soon as the footlocker was placed in the automobile a warrantless search was permissible under *Carroll.* The District Court rejected that argument, and the Government did not pursue it on appeal.[4] Rather, the Government contended in this Court that the warrant requirement of the Fourth Amendment applied only to searches of homes and other "core" areas of privacy. The Court unanimously rejected that contention. Writing for the Court, The Chief Justice stated:

> "[I]f there is little evidence that the Framers intended the Warrant Clause to operate outside the home, there is no evidence at all that they intended to exclude from protection of the Clause all searches occurring outside the home. The absence of a contemporary outcry against warrantless searches in public places was because, aside from searches incident to arrest, such warrantless searches were not a large issue in colonial America. Thus, silence in the historical record tells us little about the Framers' attitude toward application of the Warrant Clause to the search of respondents' footlocker. What we do know is that the Framers were men who focused on the wrongs of that day but who intended the Fourth Amendment to safeguard fundamental values which would far outlast the specific abuses which gave it birth."

The Court in *Chadwick* specifically rejected the argument that the warrantless search was "reasonable" because a footlocker has some of the mobile characteristics that support warrantless searches of automobiles. The Court recognized that "a person's expectations of privacy in personal luggage are substantially greater than in an automobile," and noted that the practical problems associated with the temporary detention of a piece of luggage during the period of time necessary to obtain a warrant are significantly less than those associated with the detention of an automobile. In ruling that the warrantless search of the footlocker was unjustified, the Court reaffirmed the general principle that closed

4. This Court specifically noted "The Government does not contend that the footlocker's brief contact with Chadwick's car makes this an automobile search, but it is argued that the rationale of our automobile search cases demonstrates the reasonableness of permitting warrantless searches of luggage; the Government views such luggage as analogous to motor vehicles for Fourth Amendment purposes."

packages and containers may not be searched without a warrant. In sum, the Court in *Chadwick* declined to extend the rationale of the "automobile exception" to permit a warrantless search of any movable container found in a public place.

The facts in Arkansas v. Sanders, 442 U.S. 753, 99 S.Ct. 2586 (1979), were similar to those in *Chadwick.* In *Sanders,* a Little Rock police officer received information from a reliable informant that Sanders would arrive at the local airport on a specified flight that afternoon carrying a green suitcase containing marijuana. The officer went to the airport. Sanders arrived on schedule and retrieved a green suitcase from the airline baggage service. Sanders gave the suitcase to a waiting companion who placed it in the trunk of a taxi. Sanders and his companion drove off in the cab; police officers followed and stopped the taxi several blocks from the airport. The officers opened the trunk, seized the suitcase, and searched it on the scene without a warrant. As predicted, the suitcase contained marijuana.

The Arkansas Supreme Court ruled that the warrantless search of the suitcase was impermissible under the Fourth Amendment, and this Court affirmed. As in *Chadwick,* the mere fact that the suitcase had been placed in the trunk of the vehicle did not render the automobile exception of *Carroll* applicable; the police had probable cause to seize the suitcase before it was placed in the trunk of the cab and did not have probable cause to search the taxi itself. Since the suitcase had been placed in the trunk, no danger existed that its contents could have been secreted elsewhere in the vehicle.... In rejecting the State's argument that the warrantless search of the suitcase was justified on the ground that it had been taken from an automobile lawfully stopped on the street, the Court broadly suggested that a warrantless search of a container found in an automobile could never be sustained as part of a warrantless search of the automobile itself. The Court did not suggest that it mattered whether probable cause existed to search the entire vehicle. It is clear, however, that in neither *Chadwick* nor *Sanders* did the police have probable cause to search the vehicle or anything within it except the footlocker in the former case and the green suitcase in the latter.

Robbins v. California, 453 U.S. 420, 101 S.Ct. 2841 (1981), however, was a case in which suspicion was not directed at a specific container. In that case the Court for the first time was forced to consider whether police officers who are entitled to conduct a warrantless search of an automobile stopped on a public roadway may open a container found within the vehicle. In the early morning of January 5, 1975, police officers stopped Robbins' station wagon because he was driving erratically. Robbins got out of the car, but later returned to obtain the vehicle's registration papers. When he opened the car door, the officers smelled marijuana smoke. One of the officers searched Robbins and discovered a vial of liquid; in a search of the interior of the car the officer found marijuana. The police officers then opened the tailgate of the station wagon and raised the cover of a recessed luggage compartment. In the compartment they found two packages wrapped in green opaque plastic. The police unwrapped the packages and discovered a large amount of marijuana in each.

Robbins was charged with various drug offenses and moved to suppress the contents of the plastic packages. The California Court of Appeal held that "[s]earch of the automobile was proper when the officers learned that appellant was smoking marijuana when they stopped him" and that the warrantless search of the packages was justified because "the contents of the packages could have been inferred from their outward appearance, so that appellant could not have held a reasonable expectation of privacy with respect to the contents."

This Court reversed. Writing for a plurality, Justice Stewart rejected the argument that the outward appearance of the packages precluded Robbins from having a reasonable expectation of privacy in their contents. He also squarely rejected the argument that there is a constitutional distinction between searches of luggage and searches of "less worthy" containers. Justice Stewart reasoned that all containers are equally protected by the Fourth Amendment unless their contents are in plain view. The plurality concluded that the warrantless search was impermissible because *Chadwick* and *Sanders* had established that "a closed piece of luggage found in a lawfully searched car is constitutionally protected to the same extent as are closed pieces of luggage found anywhere else."

In a concurring opinion, Justice Powell, the author of the Court's opinion in *Sanders,* stated that "[t]he plurality's approach strains the rationales of our prior cases and imposes substantial burdens on law enforcement without vindicating any significant values of privacy." He noted that possibly "the controlling question should be the scope of the automobile exception to the warrant requirement," and explained that under that view

> "when the police have probable cause to search an automobile, rather than only to search a particular container that fortuitously is located in it, the exigencies that allow the police to search the entire automobile without a warrant support the warrantless search of every container found therein. This analysis is entirely consistent with the holdings in *Chadwick* and *Sanders,* neither of which is an 'automobile case,' because the police there had probable cause to search the double-locked footlocker and the suitcase respectively before either came near an automobile."

The parties in *Robbins* had not pressed that argument, however, and Justice Powell concluded that institutional constraints made it inappropriate to re-examine basic doctrine without full adversary presentation. He concurred in the judgment, since it was supported—although not compelled—by the Court's opinion in *Sanders,* and stated that a future case might present a better opportunity for thorough consideration of the basic principles in this troubled area.

That case has arrived. Unlike *Chadwick* and *Sanders,* in this case police officers had probable cause to search respondent's entire vehicle.[5] Unlike *Robbins,* in this case the parties have squarely addressed the question whether, in the course of a legitimate warrantless search of an automobile, police are entitled to open containers found within the vehicle. We now address that question. Its answer is determined by the scope of the search that is authorized by the exception to the warrant requirement set forth in *Carroll.*

In *Carroll* itself, the whiskey that the prohibition agents seized was not in plain view. It was discovered only after an officer opened the rumble seat and tore open the upholstery of the lazyback. The Court did not find the scope of the search unreasonable. Having stopped Carroll and Kiro on a public road and subjected them to the indignity of a vehicle search—which the Court found to be a reasonable intrusion on their privacy because it was based on probable cause that their vehicle was transporting contraband—prohibition agents were entitled to tear open a portion of the roadster itself. The scope of the search was no greater than a magistrate could have authorized by issuing a warrant based on the probable cause that justified the search. Since such a warrant could have authorized the agents to open the rear portion of the roadster and to rip the upholstery in their search for concealed whiskey, the search was constitutionally permissible.

In Chambers v. Maroney the police found weapons and stolen property "concealed in a compartment under the dashboard." No suggestion was made that the scope of the search was impermissible. It would be illogical to assume that the outcome of *Chambers*—or the outcome of *Carroll* itself—would have been different if the police had found the secreted contraband enclosed within a secondary container and had opened that container without a warrant. If it was reasonable for prohibition agents to rip open the upholstery in *Carroll,* it certainly would have been reasonable for them to look into a burlap sack stashed inside; if it was reasonable to open the concealed compartment in *Chambers,* it would have been equally reasonable to open a paper bag crumpled within it. A contrary rule could produce absurd results inconsistent with the decision in *Carroll* itself.

In its application of *Carroll,* this Court in fact has sustained warrantless searches of containers found during a lawful search of an automobile.

* * *

5. The en banc Court of Appeals stated that "[b]ased on the tip the police received, Ross's car was properly stopped and searched, and the pouch and bag were properly seized." 655 F.2d, at 1168 (footnote omitted). The court explained:

"[W]e believe it clear that the police had ample and reasonable cause to stop Ross and to search his car. The informer had supplied accurate information on prior occasions, and he was an eyewitness to sales of narcotics by Ross. He said he had just seen Ross take narcotics from the trunk of his car in making a sale and heard him say he possessed additional narcotics."

The court further noted that "[i]n this case, the informant told the police that Ross had narcotics in the trunk of his car. No specific container was identified."

In these cases it was not contended that police officers needed a warrant to open the whiskey bags or to unwrap the brown paper packages. These decisions nevertheless "have much weight, as they show that this point neither occurred to the bar nor the bench." Bank of the United States v. Deveaux, 5 Cranch 61, 88 (Marshall, C. J.). The fact that no such argument was even made illuminates the profession's understanding of the scope of the search permitted under *Carroll.* Indeed, prior to the decisions in *Chadwick* and *Sanders,* courts routinely had held that containers and packages found during a legitimate warrantless search of an automobile also could be searched without a warrant.

As we have stated the decision in *Carroll* was based on the Court's appraisal of practical considerations viewed in the perspective of history. It is therefore significant that the practical consequences of the *Carroll* decision would be largely nullified if the permissible scope of a warrantless search of an automobile did not include containers and packages found inside the vehicle. Contraband goods rarely are strewn across the trunk or floor of a car, since by their very nature such goods must be withheld from public view, they rarely can be placed in an automobile unless they are enclosed within some form of container. The Court in *Carroll* held that "contraband goods *concealed* and illegally transported in an automobile or other vehicle may be searched for without a warrant." As we noted in Henry v. United States, 361 U.S. 98, 104, 80 S.Ct. 168 (1959), the decision in *Carroll* "merely relaxed the requirements for a warrant on grounds of impracticability." It neither broadened nor limited the scope of a lawful search based on probable cause.

A lawful search of fixed premises generally extends to the entire area in which the object of the search may be found and is not limited by the possibility that separate acts of entry or opening may be required to complete the search. Thus, a warrant that authorizes an officer to search a home for illegal weapons also provides authority to open closets, chests, drawers, and containers in which the weapon might be found. A warrant to open a footlocker to search for marijuana would also authorize the opening of packages found inside. A warrant to search a vehicle would support a search of every part of the vehicle that might contain the object of the search. When a legitimate search is under way, and when its purpose and its limits have been precisely defined, nice distinctions between closets, drawers, and containers, in the case of a home, or between glove compartments, upholstered seats, trunks, and wrapped packages, in the case of a vehicle, must give way to the interest in the prompt and efficient completion of the task at hand.[6]

6. The practical considerations that justify a warrantless search of an automobile continue to apply until the entire search of the automobile and its contents has been completed. Arguably, the entire vehicle itself (including its upholstery) could be searched without a warrant, with all wrapped articles and containers found during that search then taken to a magistrate. But prohibiting police from opening immediately a container in which the object of the search is most likely to be found and instead forcing them first to comb the entire vehicle would actually exacerbate the intrusion on privacy interests. Moreover, until the container itself was opened the

This rule applies equally to all containers, as indeed we believe it must. One point on which the Court was in virtually unanimous agreement in *Robbins* was that a constitutional distinction between "worthy" and "unworthy" containers would be improper. Even though such a distinction perhaps could evolve in a series of cases in which paper bags, locked trunks, lunch buckets, and orange crates were placed on one side of the line or the other,[7] the central purpose of the Fourth Amendment forecloses such a distinction. For just as the most frail cottage in the kingdom is absolutely entitled to the same guarantees of privacy as the most majestic mansion, so also may a traveler who carries a toothbrush and a few articles of clothing in a paper bag or knotted scarf claim an equal right to conceal his possessions from official inspection as the sophisticated executive with the locked attaché case.

As Justice Stewart stated in *Robbins,* the Fourth Amendment provides protection to the owner of every container that conceals its contents from plain view. But the protection afforded by the Amendment varies in different settings. The luggage carried by a traveler entering the country may be searched at random by a customs officer; the luggage may be searched no matter how great the traveler's desire to conceal the contents may be. A container carried at the time of arrest often may be searched without a warrant and even without any specific suspicion concerning its contents. A container that may conceal the object of a search authorized by a warrant may be opened immediately; the individual's interest in privacy must give way to the magistrate's official determination of probable cause.

In the same manner, an individual's expectation of privacy in a vehicle and its contents may not survive if probable cause is given to believe that the vehicle is transporting contraband. Certainly the privacy interests in a car's trunk or glove compartment may be no less than those in a movable container. An individual undoubtedly has a significant interest that the upholstery of his automobile will not be ripped or a hidden compartment within it opened. These interests must yield to the authority of a search, however, which—in light of *Carroll*—does not itself require the prior approval of a magistrate. The scope of a warrantless search based on probable cause is no narrower—and no broader—than the scope of a search authorized by a warrant supported

police could never be certain that the contraband was not secreted in a yet undiscovered portion of the vehicle; thus in every case in which a container was found, the vehicle would need to be secured while a warrant was obtained. Such a requirement would be directly inconsistent with the rationale supporting the decisions in *Carroll* and *Chambers*.

7. If the distinction is based on the proposition that the Fourth Amendment protects only those containers that objectively manifest an individual's reasonable expectation of privacy, however, the propriety of a warrantless search necessarily would turn on much more than the fabric of the container. A paper bag stapled shut and marked "private" might be found to manifest a reasonable expectation of privacy, as could a cardboard box stacked on top of two pieces of heavy luggage. The propriety of the warrantless search seemingly would turn on an objective appraisal of all the surrounding circumstances.

by probable cause. Only the prior approval of the magistrate is waived; the search otherwise is as the magistrate could authorize.[8]

The scope of a warrantless search of an automobile thus is not defined by the nature of the container in which the contraband is secreted. Rather, it is defined by the object of the search and the places in which there is probable cause to believe that it may be found. Just as probable cause to believe that a stolen lawnmower may be found in a garage will not support a warrant to search an upstairs bedroom, probable cause to believe that undocumented aliens are being transported in a van will not justify a warrantless search of a suitcase. Probable cause to believe that a container placed in the trunk of a taxi contains contraband or evidence does not justify a search of the entire cab.

Our decision today is inconsistent with the disposition in Robbins v. California and with the portion of the opinion in Arkansas v. Sanders on which the plurality in *Robbins* relied. Nevertheless, the doctrine of *stare decisis* does not preclude this action. Although we have rejected some of the reasoning in *Sanders,* we adhere to our holding in that case; although we reject the precise holding in *Robbins,* there was no Court opinion supporting a single rationale for its judgment and the reasoning we adopt today was not presented by the parties in that case. Moreover, it is clear that no legitimate reliance interest can be frustrated by our decision today.[9] ... The exception recognized in *Carroll* is unquestionably one that is "specifically established and well-delineated." We hold that the scope of the warrantless search authorized by that exception is no broader and no narrower than a magistrate could legitimately authorize by warrant. If probable cause justifies the search of a lawfully stopped vehicle, it justifies the search of every part of the vehicle and its contents that may conceal the object of the search.

[Concurring opinions of JUSTICES BLACKMUN and POWELL omitted.]

[Dissenting opinion of JUSTICE WHITE omitted.]

JUSTICE MARSHALL, with whom JUSTICE BRENNAN joins, dissenting.

The majority today not only repeals all realistic limits on warrantless automobile searches, it repeals the Fourth Amendment warrant requirement itself. By equating a police officer's estimation of probable cause with a magistrate's, the Court utterly disregards the value of a neutral and detached magistrate....

* * *

8. In choosing to search without a warrant on their own assessment of probable cause, police officers of course lose the protection that a warrant would provide to them in an action for damages brought by an individual claiming that the search was unconstitutional. Although an officer may establish that he acted in good faith in conducting the search by other evidence, a warrant issued by a magistrate normally suffices to establish it.

9. Any interest in maintaining the status quo that might be asserted by persons who may have structured their business of distributing narcotics or other illicit substances on the basis of judicial precedents clearly would not be legitimate.

According to the majority, whenever police have probable cause to believe that contraband may be found within an automobile that they have stopped on the highway, they may search not only the automobile but also any container found inside it, without obtaining a warrant. The scope of the search, we are told, is as broad as a magistrate could authorize in a warrant to search the automobile. The majority makes little attempt to justify this rule in terms of recognized Fourth Amendment values. The Court simply ignores the critical function that a magistrate serves. And although the Court purports to rely on the mobility of an automobile and the impracticability of obtaining a warrant, it never explains why these concerns permit the warrantless search of a *container,* which can easily be seized and immobilized while police are obtaining a warrant.

* * *

This "mobility" rationale is something of a misnomer, since the police ordinarily can remove the car's occupants and secure the vehicle on the spot. However, the inherent mobility of the vehicle often creates situations in which the police's only alternative to an immediate search may be to release the automobile from their possession. This alternative creates an unacceptably high risk of losing the contents of the vehicle, and is a principal basis for the Court's automobile exception to the warrant requirement.

In many cases, however, the police will, prior to searching the car, have cause to arrest the occupants and bring them to the station for booking. In this situation, the police can ordinarily seize the automobile and bring it to the station. Because the vehicle is now in the exclusive control of the authorities, any subsequent search cannot be justified by the mobility of the car. Rather, an immediate warrantless search of the vehicle is permitted because of the second major justification for the automobile exception: the diminished expectation of privacy in an automobile.

* * *

[Ed. Note: Justice Marshall then argued that there is not the same diminished expectation of privacy in containers as there is in vehicles.]

Finally, the majority's new rule is theoretically unsound and will create anomalous and unwarranted results. These consequences are readily apparent from the Court's attempt to reconcile its new rule with the holdings of *Chadwick* and *Sanders.* The Court suggests that probable cause to search only a container does not justify a warrantless search of an automobile in which it is placed, absent reason to believe that the contents could be secreted elsewhere in the vehicle. This, the majority asserts, is an indication that the new rule is carefully limited to its justification, and is not inconsistent with *Chadwick* and *Sanders.* But why is such a container more private, less difficult for police to seize and store, or in any other relevant respect more properly subject to the warrant requirement, than a container that police discover in a probable cause search of an entire automobile? This rule plainly has peculiar and unworkable consequences: the Government "must show that the investigating officer knew enough but not too much, that he had sufficient knowledge to establish probable cause but insufficient knowledge to know exactly where the contraband was located." United States v. Ross, 655 F.2d 1159, 1202 (CADC 1981) (en banc) (Wilkey, J., dissenting).

Alternatively, the majority may be suggesting that *Chadwick* and *Sanders* may be explained because the connection of the container to the vehicle was incidental in these two cases. That is, because police had preexisting probable cause to seize and search the containers, they were not entitled to wait until the item was placed in a vehicle to take advantage of the automobile exception. Cf. I wholeheartedly agree that police cannot employ a pretext to escape Fourth Amendment prohibitions and cannot rely on an exigency that they could easily have avoided. This interpretation, however, might well be an exception that swallows up the majority's rule. In neither *Chadwick* nor *Sanders* did the Court suggest that the delay of the police was a pretext for taking advantage of the automobile exception. For all that appears, the Government may have had legitimate reasons for not searching as soon as they had probable cause.[10]

* * *

This case will have profound implications for the privacy of citizens traveling in automobiles, as the Court well understands. "For countless vehicles are stopped on highways and public streets every day and our cases demonstrate that it is not uncommon for police officers to have probable cause to believe that contraband may be found in a stopped vehicle." A closed paper bag, a tool box, a knapsack, a suitcase, and an attache case can alike be searched without the protection of the judgment of a neutral magistrate, based only on the rarely disturbed decision of a police officer that he has probable cause to search for contraband in the vehicle. The Court derives satisfaction from the fact that its rule does not exalt the rights of the wealthy over the rights of the poor. A rule so broad that all citizens lose vital Fourth Amendment protection is no cause for celebration.

NOTES

1. In California v. Carney, 471 U.S. 386, 105 S.Ct. 2066 (1985), the U.S. Supreme Court held that the warrantless search of a motor home was proper under the "automobile exception." The Court took the position that the two

10. The Court purports to restrict its rule to areas that the police have probable cause to search, as "defined by the object of the search and the places in which there is probable cause to believe that it may be found." Ante, at 25. I agree, of course, that the probable cause component of the automobile exception must be strictly construed. I fear, however, that the restriction that the Court emphasizes may have little practical value. See United States v. Ross, 655 F.2d 1159, 1168, n. 21 (CADC 1981) (en banc). If police open a container within a car and find contraband, they may acquire probable cause to believe that other portions of the car, and other containers within it, will contain contraband. In practice, the Court's rule may amount to a wholesale authorization for police to search any car from top to bottom when they have suspicion, whether localized or general, that it contains contraband.

factors justifying the automobile exception—probable cause and exigent circumstances (mobility)—come into play when a vehicle capable of being used on the highway is found stationary in a place not regularly used for residential purposes. If such a vehicle is readily mobile, there is a reduced expectation of privacy, a factor that *Ross* focused on in reaffirming the *Carroll* rule. To create an exception to *Carroll* merely because the vehicle could also be used as a dwelling "would require that we apply the exception depending upon the size of a vehicle and the quality of its appointments...." The Court noted that a motor home "lends itself easily to use as an instrument of illicit drug traffic and other illegal activity." It also noted that it was *not* ruling on whether the *Carroll* rule would apply where a mobile home is elevated on blocks or connected to utilities, a question left for another day and another case.

In Oklahoma v. Castleberry, 471 U.S. 146, 105 S.Ct. 1859 (1985), because of Justice Powell's illness, the U.S. Supreme Court deadlocked 4–4 and affirmed a ruling of the Oklahoma Court of Criminal Appeals that police officers who had probable cause to believe that defendants were carrying narcotics in certain suitcases should have obtained a warrant before searching the suitcases found in the trunk of a car after they confronted the defendants and defendants threw the suitcases into the car and slammed the trunk shut. At issue was a portion of the holding in *Ross* where the Supreme Court held that where the police know in advance that particular closed containers in an automobile have contraband in them, they must have a warrant to search the containers. That part of *Ross* remains intact, at least for the time being.

2. In California v. Acevedo, 500 U.S. 565, 111 S.Ct. 1982 (1991), the Court revisited one of the exceptions recognized in Ross: the prohibition of a warrantless search of a closed container where the probable cause data is limited to the container and where there is no probable cause to believe that a search of the vehicle itself would yield evidence or contraband. The majority wrote:

> To the extent that the Chadwick–Sanders rule protects privacy, its protection is minimal. Law enforcement officers may seize a container and hold it until they obtain a search warrant. And the police often will be able to search containers without a warrant, despite the Chadwick–Sanders rule, as a search incident to a lawful arrest. New York v. Belton (1981).

* * *

Finally, the search of a paper bag intrudes far less on individual privacy than does the incursion sanctioned long ago in Carroll. In that case, prohibition agents slashed the upholstery of the automobile. This Court nonetheless found their search to be reasonable under the Fourth Amendment. If destroying the interior of an automobile is not unreasonable, we cannot conclude that looking inside a closed container is. In light of the minimal protection to privacy afforded by the Chadwick–Sanders rule, and our serious doubt whether that rule substantially serves privacy interests, we now hold that the Fourth Amendment does not compel separate treatment for an automobile search that extends only to a container within the vehicle.

The Chadwick–Sanders rule not only has failed to protect privacy but it has also confused courts and police officers and impeded effective law enforcement.

* * *

JUSTICE SCALIA concurring:

The Fourth Amendment does not by its terms require a prior warrant for searches and seizures; it merely prohibits searches and seizures that are "unreasonable." What it explicitly states regarding warrants is by way of limitation upon their issuance rather than requirement of their use. See Wakely v. Hart, 6 Binney 316, 318 (Pa.1814). For the warrant was a means of insulating officials from personal liability assessed by colonial juries. An officer who searched or seized without a warrant did so at his own risk; he would be liable for trespass, including exemplary damages, unless the jury found that his action was "reasonable." Amar, The Bill of Rights as a Constitution, 100 Yale L.J. 1131, 1178–1180 (1991); Huckle v. Money, 95 Eng.Rep. 768 (K.B.1763). If, however, the officer acted pursuant to a proper warrant, he would be absolutely immune. See Bell v. Clapp, 10 Johns. 263 (N.Y.1813); 4 W. Blackstone, Commentaries 288 (1769). By restricting the issuance of warrants, the Framers endeavored to preserve the jury's role in regulating searches and seizures. Amar, supra; Posner, Rethinking the Fourth Amendment, 1981 S.Ct.Rev., 49, 72–73; see also T. Taylor, Two Studies in Constitutional Interpretation 41 (1969).

Although the Fourth Amendment does not explicitly impose the requirement of a warrant, it is of course textually possible to consider that implicit within the requirement of reasonableness. For some years after the (still continuing) explosion in Fourth Amendment litigation that followed our announcement of the exclusionary rule in Weeks v. United States (1914), our jurisprudence lurched back and forth between imposing a categorical warrant requirement and looking to reasonableness alone. (The opinions preferring a warrant involved searches of structures.)

* * *

See Chimel v. California (1969); Coolidge v. New Hampshire (1971).

The victory was illusory. Even before today's decision, the "warrant requirement" had become so riddled with exceptions that it was basically unrecognizable. In 1985, one commentator cataloged nearly 20 such exceptions, including "searches incident to arrest ... automobile searches ... border searches ... administrative searches of regulated businesses ... exigent circumstances ... search[es] incident to nonarrest when there is probable cause to arrest ... boat boarding for document checks ... welfare searches ... inventory searches ... airport searches ... school search[es]...." Bradley, Two Models of the Fourth Amendment, 83 Mich.L.Rev. 1468, 1473–1474 (1985). Since then, we have added at least two more. California v. Carney (1985) (searches of mobile homes); O'Connor v. Ortega (1987) (searches of offices of government employees). Our intricate body of law regarding "reasonable expectation of privacy" has been developed largely as a means of creating these exceptions, enabling a search to be denominated not a Fourth Amendment "search" and therefore not subject to the general warrant requirement.

* * *

There can be no clarity in this area unless we make up our minds, and unless the principles we express comport with the actions we take.

In my view, the path out of this confusion should be sought by returning to the first principle that the "reasonableness" requirement of the Fourth Amendment affords the protection that the common law afforded. I have no difficulty with the proposition that that includes the requirement of a warrant, where the common law required a warrant; and it may even be that changes in the surrounding legal rules (for example, elimination of the common-law rule that reasonable, good-faith belief was no defense to absolute liability for trespass, Little v. Barreme, 2 Cranch 170, 2 L.Ed. 243 (1804) (Marshall, C.J.); see generally Amar, Of Sovereignty and Federalism, 96 Yale L.J. 1425, 1486–1487 (1987)), may make a warrant indispensable to reasonableness where it once was not. But the supposed "general rule" that a warrant is always required does not appear to have any basis in the common law and confuses rather than facilitates any attempt to develop rules of reasonableness in light of changed legal circumstances, as the anomaly eliminated and the anomaly created by today's holding both demonstrate.

Three Justices dissented. JUSTICE STEVENS wrote:

In the nine years since *Ross* was decided, the Court has considered three cases in which the police had probable cause to search a particular container and one in which they had probable cause to search two vehicles. The decisions in all four of those cases were perfectly straightforward and provide no evidence of confusion in the state or lower federal courts.

* * *

The Court's statement that *Chadwick* and *Sanders* provide only "minimal protection to privacy," is also unpersuasive. Every citizen clearly has an interest in the privacy of the contents of his or her luggage, briefcase, handbag or any other container that conceals private papers and effects from public scrutiny. That privacy interest has been recognized repeatedly in cases spanning more than a century.

* * *

Under the Court's holding today, the privacy interest that protects the contents of a suitcase or a briefcase from a warrantless search when it is in public view simply vanishes when its owner climbs into a taxicab. Unquestionably the rejection of the *Sanders* line of cases by today's decision will result in a significant loss of individual privacy.

To support its argument that today's holding works only a minimal intrusion on privacy, the Court suggests that "[i]f the police know that they may open a bag only if they are actually searching the entire car, they may search more extensively than they otherwise would in order to establish the general probable cause required by *Ross*." As I have already noted, this fear is unexplained and inexplicable. Neither evidence uncovered in the course of a search nor the scope of the search conducted can be used to provide *post hoc* justification for a search unsupported by probable cause at its inception.

The Court also justifies its claim that its holding inflicts only minor damage by suggesting that, under *New York v. Belton* (1981), the police could have arrested respondent and searched his bag if respondent had placed the bag in the passenger compartment of the automobile instead of the trunk. In *Belton,* however, the justification for stopping the car and arresting the driver had nothing to do with the subsequent search, which was based on the potential danger to the arresting officer.... I would not extend *Belton* 's holding to this case, in which the container—which was protected from a warrantless search before it was placed in the car—provided the only justification for the arrest. Even accepting *Belton* 's application to a case like this one, however, the Court's logic extends its holding to a container placed in the *trunk* of a vehicle, rather than in the passenger compartment. And the Court makes this extension without any justification whatsoever other than convenience to law enforcement.

6. THE CRIME SCENE SEARCH

MINCEY v. ARIZONA

Supreme Court of the United States, 1977.
434 U.S. 1343, 98 S.Ct. 23.

MR. JUSTICE STEWART delivered the opinion of the Court.

On the afternoon of October 28, 1974, undercover police officer Barry Headricks of the Metropolitan Area Narcotics Squad knocked on the door of an apartment in Tucson, Ariz., occupied by the petitioner, Rufus Mincey. Earlier in the day, Officer Headricks had allegedly arranged to purchase a quantity of heroin from Mincey and had left, ostensibly to obtain money. On his return he was accompanied by nine other plainclothes policemen and a deputy county attorney. The door was opened by John Hodgman, one of three acquaintances of Mincey who were in the living room of the apartment. Officer Headricks slipped inside and moved quickly into the bedroom. Hodgman attempted to slam the door in order to keep the other officers from entering, but was pushed back against the wall. As the police entered the apartment, a rapid volley of shots was heard from the bedroom. Officer Headricks emerged and collapsed on the floor. When other officers entered the bedroom they found Mincey lying on the floor, wounded and semiconscious. Officer Headricks died a few hours later in the hospital.

The question presented is whether the search of Mincey's apartment was constitutionally permissible. After the shooting, the narcotics agents, thinking that other persons in the apartment might have been injured, looked about quickly for other victims. They found a young woman wounded in the bedroom closet and Mincey apparently unconscious in the bedroom, as well as Mincey's three acquaintances (one of whom had been wounded in the head) in the living room. Emergency assistance was requested and some medical aid administered to Officer Headricks. But the agents refrained from further investigation, pursuant to a Tucson Police Department directive that police officers should not investigate incidents in which they are involved. They neither searched further nor seized any evidence; they merely guarded the suspects and the premises.

Within 10 minutes, however, homicide detectives who had heard a radio report of the shooting arrived and took charge of the investigation. They supervised the removal of Officer Headricks and the suspects, trying to make sure that the scene was disturbed as little as possible, and then proceeded to gather evidence. Their search lasted four days, during which period the entire apartment was searched, photographed, and diagrammed. The officers opened drawers, closets and cupboards, and inspected their contents; they emptied clothing pockets; they dug bullet fragments out of the walls and floors; they pulled up sections of the carpet and removed them for examination. Every item in the apartment was closely examined and inventoried, and two to three hundred objects were seized. In short, Mincey's apartment was subjected to an exhaustive and intrusive search. No warrant was ever obtained.

The petitioner's pretrial motion, to suppress the fruits of this search was denied after a hearing. Much of the evidence introduced against him at trial (including photographs and diagrams, bullets and shell casings, guns, narcotics, and narcotics paraphernalia) was the product of the four-day search of his apartment. On appeal the Arizona Supreme Court reaffirmed previous decisions in which it had held that the warrantless search of the scene of a homicide is constitutionally permissible. It stated its ruling as follows:

> "We hold a reasonable, warrantless search of the scene of a homicide—or of a serious personal injury with likelihood of death where there is reason to suspect foul play—does not violate the Fourth Amendment to the United States Constitution where the law enforcement officers were legally on the premises in the first instance.... For the search to be reasonable, the purpose must be limited to determining the circumstances of death and the scope must not exceed that purpose. The search must also begin within a reasonable period following the time when the officials first learn of the murder (or potential murder)."

Since the investigating homicide detectives knew that Officer Headricks was seriously injured, began the search promptly upon their arrival at the apartment, and searched only for evidence either establishing the circumstances of death or "relevant to motive and intent or knowledge (narcotics, e.g.)," the court found that the warrantless search of the petitioner's apartment had not violated the Fourth and Fourteenth Amendments.

We cannot agree. The Fourth Amendment proscribes all unreasonable searches and seizures, and it is a cardinal principle that "searches conducted outside the judicial process, without prior approval by judge or magistrate, are per se unreasonable under the Fourth Amendment—subject only to a few specifically established and well-delineated exceptions." The Arizona Supreme Court did not hold that the search of the petitioner's apartment fell within any of the exceptions to the warrant requirement previously recognized by this Court, but rather that the search of a homicide scene should be recognized as an additional exception.

Several reasons are advanced by the State to meet its "burden ... to show the existence of such an exceptional situation" as to justify creating a new exception to the warrant requirement. None of these reasons, however, persuades us of the validity of the generic exception delineated by the Arizona Supreme Court.

The first contention is that the search of the petitioner's apartment did not invade any constitutionally protected right of privacy. This argument appears to have two prongs. On the one hand, the State urges that by shooting Officer Headricks, Mincey forfeited any reasonable expectation of privacy in his apartment. We have recently rejected a similar waiver argument in Michigan v. Tyler; it suffices here to say that this reasoning would impermissibly convict the suspect even before the evidence against him was gathered.[1] On the other hand, the State contends that the police entry to arrest Mincey was so great an invasion of his privacy that the additional intrusion caused by the search was constitutionally irrelevant. But this claim is hardly tenable in light of the extensive nature of this search. It is one thing to say that one who is legally taken into police custody has a lessened right of privacy in his person. See United States v. Edwards. It is quite another to argue that he also has a lessened right of privacy in his entire house. Indeed this very argument was rejected when it was advanced to support the warrantless search of a dwelling where an arrest occurred as "incident" to the arrest of its occupant. Chimel v. California. Thus, this search cannot be justified on the ground that no constitutionally protected right of privacy was invaded.

The State's second argument in support of Arizona's categorical exception to the warrant requirement is that a possible homicide presents an emergency situation demanding immediate action. We do not question the right of the police to respond to emergency situations. Numerous state and federal cases have recognized that the Fourth Amendment does not bar police officers from making warrantless entries and searches when they reasonably believe that a person within is in need of immediate aid. Similarly, when the police come upon the scene of a homicide they may make a prompt warrantless search of the area to see if there are other victims or if a killer is still on the premises. "The need to protect or preserve life or avoid serious injury is justification for what would otherwise be illegal absent an exigency or emergency." Wayne v. United States, 318 F.2d 205, 212 (opinion of Burger, J.). And the police may seize any evidence that is in plain view during the course of their legitimate emergency activities. But a warrantless search must be "strictly circumscribed by the exigencies which justify its initiation," and it simply cannot be contended that this search was justified by any emergency threatening life or limb. All the persons in Mincey's apartment had been located before the investigating homicide officers arrived there and began their search. And a four-day search that included opening dresser drawers and ripping up carpets can hardly be rationalized in terms of the legitimate concerns that justify an emergency search.

Third, the State points to the vital public interest in the prompt investigation of the extremely serious crime of murder. No one can

1. Moreover, this rationale would be inapplicable if a homicide occurred at the home of the victim, or of a stranger, yet the Arizona cases indicate that a warrantless search in such a case would also be permissible under the "murder scene exception."

doubt the importance of this goal. But the public interest in the investigation of other serious crimes is comparable. If the warrantless search of a homicide scene is reasonable, why not the warrantless search of the scene of a rape, a robbery, or a burglary? "No consideration relevant to the Fourth Amendment suggests any point of rational limitation" of such a doctrine.

Moreover, the mere fact that law enforcement may be made more efficient can never by itself justify disregard of the Fourth Amendment. The investigation of crime would always be simplified if warrants were unnecessary. But the Fourth Amendment reflects the view of those who wrote the Bill of Rights that the privacy of a person's home and property may not be totally sacrificed in the name of maximum simplicity in enforcement of the criminal law. For this reason, warrants are generally required to search a person's home or his person unless "the exigencies of the situation" make the needs of law enforcement so compelling that the warrantless search is objectively reasonable under the Fourth Amendment.

Except for the fact that the offense under investigation was a homicide, there were no exigent circumstances in this case, as, indeed, the Arizona Supreme Court recognized. There was no indication that evidence would be lost, destroyed or removed during the time required to obtain a search warrant. Indeed, the police guard at the apartment minimized that possibility. And there is no suggestion that a search warrant could not easily and conveniently have been obtained. We decline to hold that the seriousness of the offense under investigation itself creates exigent circumstances of the kind that under the Fourth Amendment justify a warrantless search.

Finally, the State argues that the "murder scene exception" is constitutionally permissible because it is narrowly confined by the guidelines set forth in the decision of the Arizona Supreme Court. In light of the extensive search that took place in this case it may be questioned what protection the guidelines afford a person in whose home a homicide or assault occurs. Indeed, these so-called guidelines are hardly so rigidly confining as the State seems to assert. They confer unbridled discretion upon the individual officer to interpret such terms as "reasonable … search," "serious personal injury with likelihood of death where there is reason to suspect foul play," and "reasonable period." It is precisely this kind of judgmental assessment of the reasonableness and scope of a proposed search that the Fourth Amendment requires be made by a neutral and objective magistrate, not a police officer.

* * *

In sum, we hold that the "murder scene exception" created by the Arizona Supreme Court is inconsistent with the Fourth and Fourteenth Amendments—that the warrantless search of Mincey's apartment was not constitutionally permissible simply because a homicide had recently occurred there.

[The opinions of Justices Marshall and Brennan, concurring, and the opinion of Justice Rehnquist, concurring in part and dissenting in part, are omitted.]

THOMPSON v. LOUISIANA

Supreme Court of the United States, 1984.
469 U.S. 17, 105 S.Ct. 409.

Per curiam.

In this case, the Louisiana Supreme Court upheld the validity of a warrantless "murder scene" search of petitioner's home. Because this holding is in direct conflict with our opinion in Mincey v. Arizona, 437 U.S. 385, 98 S.Ct. 2408, 57 L.Ed.2d 290 (1978), we reverse.

I

The Louisiana Supreme Court states the facts as follows:

> "On May 18, 1982, several deputies from the Jefferson Parish Sheriff's Department arrived at [petitioner's] home in response to a report by the [petitioner's] daughter of a homicide. The deputies entered the house, made a cursory search and discovered [petitioner's] husband dead of a gunshot wound in a bedroom and the [petitioner] lying unconscious in another bedroom due to an apparent drug overdose. According to the [petitioner's] daughter, the [petitioner] had shot her husband, then ingested a quantity of pills in a suicide attempt, and then, changing her mind, called her daughter, informed her of the situation and requested help. The daughter then contacted the police. Upon their arrival, the daughter admitted them into the house and directed them to the rooms containing the [petitioner] and the victim. The deputies immediately transported the then unconscious [petitioner] to a hospital and secured the scene. Thirty-five minutes later two members of the homicide unit of the Jefferson Parish Sheriff's Office arrived and conducted a follow-up investigation of the homicide and attempted suicide.
>
> "The homicide investigators entered the residence and commenced what they described at the motion to suppress hearing as a 'general exploratory search for evidence of a crime.' During their search, which lasted approximately two hours, the detectives examined each room of the house." State v. Thompson, 448 So.2d 666, 668 (La.1984).

Petitioner was subsequently indicted for the second degree murder of her husband. She moved to suppress three items of evidence discovered during the search, including a pistol found inside a chest of drawers in the same room as the deceased's body, a torn up note found in a wastepaper basket in an adjoining bathroom, and another letter (alleged to be a suicide note) found folded up inside an envelope containing a Christmas card on the top of a chest of drawers. All of this evidence was found in the "general exploratory search for evidence" conducted by two homicide investigators who arrived at the scene approximately 35 minutes after petitioner was sent to the hospital. See ibid. By the time those investigators arrived, the officers who originally arrived at the scene had already searched the premises for other victims or suspects. See Mincey, supra, 437 U.S., at 392, 98 S.Ct., at 2413. The investigators testified that they had time to secure a warrant before commencing the search, see State v. Thompson, supra, at 668, and that no one had given consent to the search, see Petition for Certiorari App. A, at 8, 19–20 (transcript of testimony of Detectives Zinna and Masson at suppression hearing).

The trial court originally denied petitioner's motion to suppress. However, the trial court then granted petitioner's motion for reconsideration and partially reversed its former decision, holding that the gun and the suicide letter found in the Christmas card were obtained in violation of the Fourth Amendment and therefore must be suppressed. The Louisiana Court of Appeal denied the State's application for a writ of review. A sharply divided Louisiana Supreme Court subsequently held all of the evidence seized to be admissible.

II

As we stated in United States v. Chadwick, 433 U.S. 1, 9, 97 S.Ct. 2476, 2482, 53 L.Ed.2d 538 (1977), "in this area we do not write on a clean slate." In a long line of cases, this Court has stressed that "searches conducted outside the judicial process, without prior approval by judge or magistrate, are *per se* unreasonable under the Fourth Amendment—subject only to a few specifically established and well delineated exceptions." Katz v. United States, 389 U.S. 347, 357, 88 S.Ct. 507, 514, 19 L.Ed.2d 576 (1967) (footnotes omitted). This was not a principle freshly coined for the occasion in *Katz,* but rather represented this Court's long-standing understanding of the relationship between the two clauses of the Fourth Amendment.[1] See Katz, supra, at 357 n. 18 and 19, 88 S.Ct., at 514 n. 18 and 19. Since the time of *Katz,* this Court has recognized the existence of additional exceptions.... However, we have consistently reaffirmed our understanding that in all cases outside the exceptions to the warrant requirement the Fourth Amendment requires the interposition of a neutral and detached magistrate between the police and the "persons, houses, papers and effects" of the citizen....

A

Although the homicide investigators in this case may well have had probable cause to search the premises, it is undisputed that they did not

1. "The right of the people to be secure in their persons, houses, papers and effects against unreasonable searches and seizures, shall not be violated and no warrants shall issue, but upon probable cause, supported by oath or affirmation, and particularly describing the place to be searched, and persons or things to be seized." U.S. Const. amend. 4.

obtain a warrant. Therefore, for the search to be valid, it must fall within one of the narrow and specifically delineated exceptions to the warrant requirement. In Mincey v. Arizona, 437 U.S. 385, 98 S.Ct. 2408, 57 L.Ed.2d 290 (1978), we unanimously rejected the contention that one of the exceptions to the warrant clause is a "murder scene exception." Although we noted that police may make warrantless entries on premises where "they reasonably believe that a person within is in need of immediate aid," id., at 392, 98 S.Ct., at 2413, and that "they may make a prompt warrantless search of the area to see if there are other victims or if a killer is still on the premises," ibid., we held that "the 'murder scene exception' ... is inconsistent with the Fourth and Fourteenth Amendments—that the warrantless search of Mincey's apartment was not constitutionally permissible simply because a homicide had recently occurred there." Id., at 395, 98 S.Ct., at 2414. *Mincey* is squarely on point in the instant case.

B

The Louisiana Supreme Court attempted to distinguish *Mincey* in several ways. The court noted that *Mincey* involved a four-day search of the premises, while the search in this case took only two hours and was conducted on the same day as the murder. See State v. Thompson, supra, at 671. Although we agree that the scope of the intrusion was certainly greater in *Mincey* than here, nothing in *Mincey* turned on the length of time taken in the search or the date on which it was conducted. A two-hour general search remains a significant intrusion on petitioner's privacy and therefore may only be conducted subject to the constraints—including the warrant requirement—of the Fourth Amendment.

The Louisiana Court also believed that petitioner had a "diminished" expectation of privacy in her home, thus validating a search that otherwise would have been unconstitutional. Ibid. The court noted that petitioner telephoned her daughter to request assistance. The daughter then called the police and let them in to the residence. These facts, according to the court, demonstrated a diminished expectation of privacy in petitioner's dwelling and therefore legitimated the warrantless search.[2]

Petitioner's attempt to get medical assistance does not evidence a diminished expectation of privacy on her part. To be sure, this action would have justified the authorities in seizing evidence under the plain view doctrine while they were in petitioner's house to offer her assistance. In addition, the same doctrine may justify seizure of evidence obtained in the limited "victim-or-suspect" search discussed in *Mincey*. However, the evidence at issue here was not discovered in plain view while the police were assisting petitioner to the hospital, nor was it

2. The Louisiana Supreme Court seemed to believe that the fact that "both parties with authority over the premises [petitioner and her husband] were either dead or unconscious and in an apparently grave condition," State v. Thompson, supra, at 671, in some way diminished petitioner's expectation of privacy in the premises. Yet neither petitioner's unavailability nor the death of her husband have any bearing on petitioner's continuing privacy interests.

discovered during the "victim-or-suspect" search that had been completed by the time the homicide investigators arrived. Petitioner's call for help can hardly be seen as an invitation to the general public that would have converted her home into the sort of public place for which no warrant to search would be necessary. Therefore, the Louisiana Supreme Court's diminished expectation of privacy argument fails to distinguish this case from *Mincey.*

The State contends that there was a sufficient element of consent in this case to distinguish it from the facts of *Mincey.* The Louisiana Supreme Court's decision does not attempt to validate the search as consensual, although it attempts to support its diminished expectation of privacy argument by reference to the daughter's "apparent authority" over the premises when she originally permitted the police to enter. State v. Thompson, supra, at 671. Because the issue of consent is ordinarily a factual issue unsuitable for our consideration in the first instance, we express no opinion as to whether the search at issue here might be justified as consensual. However, we note that both homicide investigators explicitly testified that they had received no consent to search. Any claim of valid consent in this case would have to be measured against the standards of United States v. Matlock, 415 U.S. 164, 94 S.Ct. 988, 39 L.Ed.2d 242 (1974) and Schneckcloth v. Bustamonte, 412 U.S. 218, 93 S.Ct. 2041, 36 L.Ed.2d 854 (1973).

III

For the reasons stated above, petitioner's motion for leave to proceed *in forma pauperis* is granted, the petition for writ of certiorari is granted, the judgment of the Louisiana Supreme Court is reversed, and the cause is remanded for further proceedings not inconsistent with this opinion.

It is so ordered.

NOTES

1. Prior to *Mincey,* some courts found a crime scene exception to the warrant requirement. People v. King, 54 Ill.2d 291, 296 N.E.2d 731 (1973) "setting of immediate violence"; United States v. Birrell, 470 F.2d 113 (2d Cir.1972) (dictum); Thomas v. State, 118 Ga.App. 359, 163 S.E.2d 850 (1968); Palmore v. State, 283 Ala. 501, 218 So.2d 830 (1969). The Supreme Judicial Court of Maine concurred:

> "We are satisfied that if the police cannot after lawful entry make the sort of prompt, orderly and methodical investigation of the scene of a violent death that is here shown the protection of the legitimate interests of society will be seriously weakened." State v. Chapman, 250 A.2d 203, 207–12 (Me. 1969).

Is it possible to conceive a case where police would not have probable cause for a warrant to search a crime scene?

2. In Michigan v. Tyler, 436 U.S. 499, 98 S.Ct. 1942 (1978), the Court held that an entry onto premises to fight a fire requires no warrant, and once officials are in the building they may remain there for a reasonable time to investigate the cause of the fire, but any subsequent investigation must be made pursuant to

the warrant procedures governing administrative searches. If the investigating officials develop probable cause to believe that arson was committed, they would need a search warrant based upon traditional probable cause to regain entry to the premises. More recently, in Michigan v. Clifford, 464 U.S. 287, 104 S.Ct. 641 (1984), a four Justice plurality stated that an administrative warrant would be permissible if the object of the subsequent search were primarily to determine the cause of the fire, but a criminal search warrant would be required if the objective were to gain evidence of a crime.

F. WIRETAPPING AND EAVESDROPPING

BERGER v. NEW YORK

Supreme Court of the United States, 1967.
388 U.S. 41, 87 S.Ct. 1873.

MR. JUSTICE CLARK delivered the opinion of the Court.

This writ tests the validity of New York's permissive eavesdrop statute[1] under the Fourth, Fifth, Ninth, and Fourteenth Amendments. The claim is that the statute sets up a system of surveillance which involves trespassory intrusions into private, constitutionally protected premises, and is an invasion of the privilege against self-incrimination....

Berger, the petitioner, was convicted on two counts of conspiracy to bribe the Chairman of the New York State Liquor Authority. The case arose out of the complaint of one Ralph Pansini to the District Attorney's office that agents of the State Liquor Authority had entered his bar and grill and without cause seized his books and records. Pansini

1. "§ 813–a. Ex parte order for eavesdropping.

"An ex parte order for eavesdropping as defined in subdivisions one and two of section seven hundred thirty-eight of the penal law may be issued by any justice of the supreme court or judge of a county court or of the court of general sessions of the county of New York upon oath or affirmation of a district attorney, or of the attorney-general or of an officer above the rank of sergeant of any police department of the state or of any political subdivision thereof, that there is reasonable ground to believe that evidence of crime may be thus obtained, and particularly describing the person or persons whose communications, conversations or discussions are to be overheard or recorded and the purpose thereof, and, in the case of a telegraphic or telephonic communication, identifying the particular telephone number or telegraph line involved. In connection with the issuance of such an order the justice or judge may examine on oath the applicant and any other witness he may produce and shall satisfy himself of the existence of reasonable grounds for the granting of such application. Any such order shall be effective for the time specified therein but not for a period of more than two months unless extended or renewed by the justice or judge who signed and issued the original order upon satisfying himself that such extension or renewal is in the public interest. Any such order together with the papers upon which the application was based, shall be delivered to and retained by the applicant as authority for the eavesdropping authorized therein. A true copy of such order shall at all times be retained in his possession by the judge or justice issuing the same, and, in the event of the denial of an application for such an order, a true copy of the papers upon which the application was based shall in like manner be retained by the judge or justice denying the same.

asserted that the raid was in reprisal for his failure to pay a bribe for a liquor license. Numerous complaints had been filed with the District Attorney's office charging the payment of bribes by applicants for liquor licenses. On the direction of that office, Pansini, while equipped with a minifon recording device, interviewed an employee of the Authority. The employee advised Pansini that the price for a license was $10,000 and suggested that he contact attorney Harry Neyer. Neyer subsequently told Pansini that he worked with the Authority employee before and that the latter was aware of the going rate on liquor licenses downtown.

On the basis of this evidence an eavesdrop order was obtained from a Justice of the State Supreme Court, as provided by § 813–a. The order permitted the installation, for a period of 60 days, of a recording device in Neyer's office. On the basis of leads obtained from this eavesdrop a second order permitting the installation, for a like period, of a recording device in the office of one Harry Steinman was obtained. After some two weeks of eavesdropping a conspiracy was uncovered involving the issuance of liquor licenses for the Playboy and Tenement Clubs, both of New York City. Petitioner was indicted as "a go-between" for the principal conspirators, who though not named in the indictment were disclosed in a bill of particulars. Relevant portions of the recordings were received in evidence at the trial and were played to the jury, all over the objection of the petitioner. The parties have stipulated that the District Attorney "had no information upon which to proceed to present a case to the Grand Jury, or on the basis of which to prosecute" the petitioner except by the use of the eavesdrop evidence.

Eavesdropping is an ancient practice which at common law was condemned as a nuisance. IV Blackstone, Commentaries § 168.

The telephone brought on a new and more modern eavesdropper known as the "wiretapper."

Sophisticated electronic devices have now been developed (commonly known as "bugging") which are capable of eavesdropping on anyone in most any given situation. They are to be distinguished from "wiretapping" which is confined to the interception of telegraphic and telephonic communications. Miniature in size—no larger than a postage stamp (⅜″ ×] ⅜″ ×] ⅛″)—these gadgets pick up whispers within a room and broadcast them half a block away to a receiver. It is said that certain types of electronic rays beamed at walls or glass windows are capable of catching voice vibrations as they are bounced off the latter. Since 1940 eavesdropping has become a big business. Manufacturing concerns offer complete detection systems which automatically record voices under most any conditions by remote control. A microphone concealed in a book, a lamp, or other unsuspecting place in a room, or made into a fountain pen, tie clasp, lapel button, or cuff link increases the range of these powerful wireless transmitters to a half mile. Receivers pick up the transmission with interference-free reception on a special wave frequency. And, of late, a combination mirror transmitter has been developed which permits not only sight but voice transmission up to 300 feet. Likewise, parabolic microphones, which can overhear conversations without being placed within the premises monitored, have been developed. See Westin, Science, Privacy and Freedom, 66 Col.L.Rev. 1003, 1005–1010.

As science developed these detection techniques, law makers, sensing the resulting invasion of individual privacy, have provided some statutory protection for the public. Seven states, California, Illinois, Maryland, Massachusetts, Nevada, New York, and Oregon, prohibit surreptitious eavesdropping by mechanical or electronic device. However, all, save Illinois, permit official court-ordered eavesdropping. Some 36 states prohibit wiretapping. But of these, 27 permit "authorized" interception of some type. Federal law prohibits interception and divulging or publishing of the content of wiretaps without exception. In sum, it is fair to say that wiretapping on the whole is outlawed, except for permissive use by law enforcement officials in some states; while electronic eavesdropping is—save for seven states—permitted both officially and privately. And, in six of the seven states, electronic eavesdropping ("bugging") is permissible on court order. . . .

The Court was faced with its first wiretap case in 1928, Olmstead v. United States, 277 U.S. 438, 48 S.Ct. 564. There the interception of Olmstead's telephone line was accomplished without entry upon his premises and was, therefore, found not to be proscribed by the Fourth Amendment. The basis of the decision was that the Constitution did not forbid the obtaining of evidence by wiretapping unless it involved actual unlawful entry into the house. Statements in the opinion that "a conversation passing over a telephone wire" cannot be said to come within the Fourth Amendment's enumeration of "persons, houses, papers, and effects" have been negated by our subsequent cases as hereinafter noted. They found "conversation" was within the Fourth Amendment's protections, and that the use of electronic devices to capture it was a "search" within the meaning of the Amendment, and we so hold. In any event, Congress soon thereafter, and some say in answer to *Olmstead,* specifically prohibited the interception without authorization and the divulging or publishing of the contents of telephonic communications. And the *Nardone* cases (Nardone v. United States), 302 U.S. 379, 58 S.Ct. 275 (1937) and 308 U.S. 338, 60 S.Ct. 266 (1939), extended the exclusionary rule to wiretap evidence offered in federal prosecutions.

The first "bugging" case reached the Court in 1942 in Goldman v. United States, 316 U.S. 129, 62 S.Ct. 993. There the Court found that the use of a detectaphone placed against an office wall in order to hear private conversations in the office next door did not violate the Fourth Amendment because there was no physical trespass in connection with the relevant interception. And in On Lee v. United States, 343 U.S. 747, 72 S.Ct. 967 (1952), we found that since "no trespass was committed" a conversation between Lee and a federal agent, occurring in the former's laundry and electronically recorded, was not condemned by the Fourth Amendment. Thereafter in Silverman v. United States, 365 U.S. 505, 81

S.Ct. 679 (1961), the Court found "that the eavesdropping was accomplished by means of an unauthorized physical penetration into the premises occupied by the petitioners." A spike a foot long with a microphone attached to it was inserted under a baseboard into a party wall until it made contact with the heating duct that ran through the entire house occupied by Silverman, making a perfect sounding board through which the conversations in question were overheard. Significantly, the Court held that its decision did "not turn upon the technicality of a trespass upon a party wall as a matter of local law. It is based upon the reality of an actual intrusion into a constitutionally protected area." ... The Fourth Amendment commands that a warrant issue not only upon probable cause supported by oath or affirmation, but also "particularly describing the place to be searched, and the persons or things to be seized." New York's statute lacks this particularization. It merely says that a warrant may issue on reasonable ground to believe that evidence of crime may be obtained by the eavesdrop. It lays down no requirement for particularity in the warrant as to what specific crime has been or is being committed, nor "the place to be searched," or "the persons or things to be seized" as specifically required by the Fourth Amendment. The need for particularity and evidence of reliability in the showing required when judicial authorization of a search is sought is especially great in the case of eavesdropping. By its very nature eavesdropping involves an intrusion on privacy that is broad in scope. As was said in Osborn v. United States, 385 U.S. 323, 87 S.Ct. 429 (1966), the "indiscriminate use of such devices in law enforcement raises grave constitutional questions under the Fourth and Fifth Amendments," and imposes "a heavier responsibility on this Court in its supervision of the fairness of procedures...." There, two judges acting jointly authorized the installation of a device on the person of a prospective witness to record conversations between him and an attorney for a defendant then on trial in the United States District Court. The judicial authorization was based on an affidavit of the witness setting out in detail previous conversations between the witness and the attorney concerning the bribery of jurors in the case. The recording device was, as the Court said, authorized "under the most precise and discriminate circumstances, circumstances which fully met the 'requirement of particularity'" of the Fourth Amendment. The Court was asked to exclude the evidence of the recording of the conversations. The Court refused to do so, finding that the recording, although an invasion of the privacy protected by the Fourth Amendment, was admissible because of the authorization of the judges, based upon "a detailed factual affidavit alleging the commission of a specific criminal offense directly and immediately affecting the administration of justice ... for the narrow and particularized purpose of ascertaining the truth of the affidavit's allegations." The invasion was lawful because there was sufficient proof to obtain a search warrant to make the search for the limited purpose outlined in the order of the judges. Through these "precise and discriminate" procedures the order authorizing the use of the electronic device afforded similar protections to those that are present in the use of conventional warrants authorizing the seizure of tangible evidence. Among other safeguards, the order described the type of conversation sought with particularity, thus indicating the specific objective of the Government in entering the constitutionally protected area and the limitations placed upon the officer executing the warrant. Under it the officer could not search unauthorized areas; likewise, once the property sought, and for which the order was issued, was found the officer could not use the order as a passkey to further search. In addition, the order authorized one limited intrusion rather than a series or a continuous surveillance. And, we note that a new order was issued when the officer sought to resume the search and probable cause was shown for the succeeding one. Moreover, the order was executed by the officer with dispatch, not over a prolonged and extended period. In this manner no greater invasion of privacy was permitted than was necessary under the circumstances. Finally the officer was required to and did make a return on the order showing how it was executed and what was seized. Through these strict precautions the danger of an unlawful search and seizure was minimized.

On the contrary, New York's statute lays down no such "precise and discriminate" requirements.... New York's broadside authorization rather than being "carefully circumscribed" so as to prevent unauthorized invasions of privacy actually permits general searches by electronic devices.... The Fourth Amendment's requirement that a warrant "particularly describ[e] the place to be searched, and the persons or things to be seized," repudiated these general warrants and "makes general searches ... impossible and prevents the seizure of one thing under a warrant describing another. As to what is to be taken, nothing is left to the discretion of the officer executing the warrant."

We believe the statute here is equally offensive. First, as we have mentioned, eavesdropping is authorized without requiring belief that any particular offense has been or is being committed; nor that the property sought, the conversations, be particularly described. The purpose of the probable cause requirement of the Fourth Amendment to keep the state out of constitutionally protected areas until it has reason to believe that a specific crime has been or is being committed is thereby wholly aborted. Likewise the statute's failure to describe with particularity the conversations sought gives the officer a roving commission to seize any and all conversations. It is true that the statute requires the naming of "the person or persons whose communications, conversations or discussions are to be overheard or recorded...." But this does no more than identify the person whose constitutionally protected area is to be invaded rather than "particularly describing" the communications, conversations, or discussions to be seized. As with general warrants this leaves too much to the discretion of the officer executing the order. Secondly, authorization of eavesdropping for a two-month period is the equivalent of a series of intrusions, searches, and seizures pursuant to a single showing of probable cause. Prompt execution is also avoided. During such a long and continuous (24 hours a day) period the conversations of any and all persons coming into the area covered by the device will be seized indiscriminately and without regard to their connection to the crime under investigation. Moreover, the statute permits, as was done here, extensions of the original two-month period—presumedly for two months each—on a mere showing that such extension is "in the public interest." Apparently the original grounds on which the eavesdrop order was initially issued also form the basis of the renewal. This we believe insufficient without a showing of present probable cause for the continuance of the eavesdrop. Third, the statute places no termination date on the eavesdrop once the conversation sought is seized. This is left entirely in the discretion of the officer. Finally, the statute's procedure, necessarily because its success depends on secrecy, has no requirement for notice as do conventional warrants, nor does it overcome this defect by requiring some showing of special facts. On the contrary, it permits uncontested entry without any showing of exigent circumstances. Such a showing of exigency, in order to avoid notice would appear more important in eavesdropping, with its inherent dangers, than that required when conventional procedures of search and seizure are utilized. Nor does the statute provide for a return on the warrant thereby leaving full discretion in the officer as to the use of seized conversations of innocent as well as guilty parties. In short, the statute's blanket grant of permission to eavesdrop is without adequate judicial supervision or protective procedures.

It is said with fervor that electronic eavesdropping is a most important technique of law enforcement and that outlawing it will severely cripple crime detection. The monumental report of the President's Crime Commission entitled "The Challenge of Crime in a Free Society" informs us that the majority of law enforcement officials say that this is especially true in the detection of organized crime. As the Commission reports, there can be no question about the serious proportions of professional criminal activity in this country. However, we have found no empirical statistics on the use of electronic devices (bugging) in the fight against organized crime. Indeed, there are even figures available in the wiretap category which indicate to the contrary. See, Dash, Schwartz, and Knowlton. The Eavesdroppers (1959), District Attorney Silver's poll, 105, 117–119.... Brooklyn's District Attorney Silver's poll of the State of New York indicates that during the 12-year period (1942–1954) duly authorized wiretaps in bribery and corruption cases constituted only a small percentage of the whole. It indicates that this category only involved 10% of the total wiretaps. The overwhelming majority were in the categories of larceny, extortion, coercion, and blackmail, accounting for almost 50%. Organized gambling was about 11%. Statistics are not available on subsequent years. Dash, supra, p. 40.

An often repeated statement of District Attorney Hogan of New York County was made at a hearing before the Senate Judiciary Committee at which he advocated the amendment of the Federal Communications Act of 1934, supra, so as to permit "telephonic interception" of conversations. As he testified, "Federal statutory law [the 1934 Act] has been interpreted in such a way as to bar us from divulging wiretap evidence, even in the courtroom in the course of criminal prosecution". Mr. Hogan then said that "without it [wiretaps] my own office could not have convicted ... top figures in the underworld." He then named nine persons his office had convicted and one on whom he had furnished "leads" secured from wiretaps to the authorities of New Jersey. Evidence secured from wiretaps, as Mr. Hogan said, was not admissible in "criminal prosecutions." He was advocating that the Congress adopt a measure that would make it admissible; Hearings on S. 2813 and S. 1495, before the Committee on the Judiciary of the United States Senate, 87th Cong., 2d Sess., pp. 173, 174 (1962). The President's Crime Commission also emphasizes in its report the need for wiretapping in the investigation of organized crime because of the telephone's "relatively free use" by those engaged in the business and the difficulty of infiltrating their organizations. The Congress, though long importuned, has not amended the 1934 Act to permit it.

We are also advised by the Solicitor General of the United States that the Federal Government has abandoned the use of electronic eavesdropping for "prosecutorial purposes." Despite these actions of the Federal Government there has been no failure of law enforcement in that field.

In any event we cannot forgive the requirements of the Fourth Amendment in the name of law enforcement. This is no formality that we require today but a fundamental rule that has long been recognized as basic to the privacy of every home in America. While "[t]he requirements of the Fourth Amendment are not inflexible, or obtusely unyielding to the legitimate needs of law enforcement," Lopez v. United States, supra, at 464, 83 S.Ct. at 1404, dissenting opinion of Brennan, J., it is not asking too much that officers be required to comply with the basic command of the Fourth Amendment before the innermost secrets of one's home or office are invaded. Few threats to liberty exist which are greater than that posed by the use of eavesdropping devices. Some may claim that without the use of such devices crime detection in certain areas may suffer some delays since eavesdropping is quicker, easier, and more certain. However, techniques and practices may well be developed that will operate just as speedily and certain—and what is more important—without attending illegality.

It is said that neither a warrant nor a statute authorizing eavesdropping can be drawn so as to meet the Fourth Amendment's requirements. If that be true then the "fruits" of eavesdropping devices are barred under the Amendment. On the other hand this Court has in the past, under specific conditions and circumstances, sustained the use of eavesdropping devices. In the latter case the eavesdropping device was permitted where the "commission of a specific offense" was charged, its use was "under the most precise and discriminating circumstances" and the effective administration of justice in a federal court was at stake. The States are under no greater restrictions. The Fourth Amendment does not make the "precincts of the home or office ... sanctuaries where the law can never reach." but it does prescribe a constitutional standard that must be met before official invasion is permissible. Our concern with the statute here is whether its language permits a trespassory invasion of the home, by general warrant, contrary to the command of the Fourth Amendment. As it is written, we believe that it does.

Reversed.

[MR. JUSTICE DOUGLAS' concurring opinion is omitted.]

MR. JUSTICE STEWART, concurring in the result.

I fully agree with Mr. Justice Black, Mr. Justice Harlan, and Mr. Justice White, that this New York law is entirely constitutional. In short, I think that "electronic eavesdropping, *as such* or as it is permitted by this statute, is not an unreasonable search and seizure." The statute contains many provisions more stringent than the Fourth Amendment generally requires, as Mr. Justice Black has so forcefully pointed out....

The issue before us, as Mr. Justice White says, is "whether *this* search complied with Fourth Amendment standards." For me that issue is an extremely close one in the circumstances of this case. It certainly cannot be resolved by incantation of ritual phrases like "general warrant." Its resolution involves "the unavoidable task in any search and seizure case: was the particular search and seizure reasonable or not?"

I would hold that the affidavits on which the judicial order issued in this case did not constitute a showing of probable cause adequate to justify the authorizing order. The need for particularity and evidence of reliability in the showing required when judicial authorization is sought for the kind of electronic eavesdropping involved in this case is especially great. The standard of reasonableness embodied in the Fourth Amendment demands that the showing of justification match the degree of intrusion. By its very nature electronic eavesdropping for a 60-day period, even of a specified office, involves a broad invasion of a constitutionally protected area. Only the most precise and rigorous standard of probable cause should justify an intrusion of this sort. I think the affidavits presented to the judge who authorized the electronic surveillance of the Steinman office failed to meet such a standard.

So far as the record shows, the only basis for the Steinman order consisted of two affidavits. One of them contained factual allegations supported only by bare, unexplained references to "evidence" in the district attorney's office and "evidence" obtained by the Neyer eavesdrop. No underlying facts were presented on the basis of which the judge could evaluate these general allegations. The second affidavit was no more than a statement of another assistant district attorney that he had read his associate's affidavit and was satisfied on that basis alone that proper grounds were presented for the issuance of an authorizing order.

This might be enough to satisfy the standards of the Fourth Amendment for a conventional search or arrest. But I think it was constitutionally insufficient to constitute probable cause to justify an intrusion of the scope and duration that was permitted in this case.

Accordingly, I would reverse the judgment.

MR. JUSTICE BLACK, dissenting.... Evidence obtained by electronic eavesdropping was used to convict the petitioner here of conspiracy to bribe the chairman of the State Liquor Authority which controls the issuance of liquor licenses in New York. It is stipulated that without this evidence a conviction could not have been obtained and it seems apparent that use of that evidence showed petitioner to be a briber beyond all reasonable doubt. Notwithstanding petitioner's obvious guilt, however, the Court now strikes down his conviction in a way that plainly makes it impossible ever to convict him again. This is true because the Court not only holds that the judicial orders which were the basis of the authority to eavesdrop were insufficient, but holds that the New York eavesdropping statute is *on its face* violative of the Fourth Amendment. And while the Court faintly intimates to the contrary, it seems obvious to me that its holding, by creating obstacles that cannot be overcome, makes it completely impossible for the State or the Federal Government ever to have a valid eavesdropping statute. All of this is done, it seems to me, in part because of the Court's hostility to eavesdropping as "ignoble" and "dirty business" and in part because of fear that rapidly advancing science and technology is making eavesdropping more and more effective. Neither of these, nor any other grounds that I can think of, are sufficient in my judgment to justify a holding that the use of evidence secured by eavesdropping is barred by the Constitution.

* * *

MR. JUSTICE HARLAN, dissenting....

I turn to what properly is the central issue in this case: the validity under the Warrants Clause of the Fourth Amendment of the eavesdropping order under which the recordings employed at petitioner's trial were obtained. It is essential first to set out certain of the pertinent facts.

The disputed recordings were made under the authority of a § 813–a order, dated June 12, 1962, permitting the installation of an eavesdropping device in the business office of one Harry Steinman; the order, in turn, was, so far as this record shows, issued solely upon the basis of information contained in affidavits submitted to the issuing judge by two assistant district attorneys. The first affidavit, signed by Assistant District Attorney Goldstein, indicated that the Rackets Bureau of the District Attorney's Office of New York County was then conducting an investigation of alleged corruption in the State Liquor Authority, and that the Bureau had received information that persons desiring to obtain or retain liquor licenses were obliged to pay large sums to officials of the Authority. It described the methods by which the bribe money was transmitted through certain attorneys to the officials. The affidavit asserted that one Harry Neyer, a former employee of the Authority, served as a "conduit." It indicated that evidence had been obtained "over a duly authorized eavesdropping device installed in the office of the aforesaid Harry Neyer," that conferences "relative to the payment of unlawful fees" occurred in Steinman's office. The number and street address of the office were provided. The affidavit specified that the "evidence indicates that the said Harry Steinman has agreed to pay, through the aforesaid Harry Neyer, $30,000" in order to secure a license for the Palladium Ballroom, an establishment within New York City. The Palladium, it was noted, had been the subject of hearings before the Authority "because of narcotic arrests therein." On the basis of this information, the affidavit sought an order to install a recording device in Steinman's business office.

The second affidavit, signed by Assistant District Attorney Scotti, averred that Scotti, as the Chief of the Bureau to which Goldstein was assigned, had read Goldstein's affidavit, and had concluded that the order might properly issue under § 813–a.

The order as issued permitted the recording of "any and all conversations, communications and discussions" in Steinman's business office for a period of 60 days.

The central objections mounted to this order by petitioner, and repeated as to the statute itself by the Court, are three: first, that it fails to specify with adequate particularity the conversations to be seized; second, that it permits a general and indiscriminate search and seizure; and third, that the order was issued without a showing of probable cause.

Each of the first two objections depends principally upon a problem of definition: the meaning in this context of the constitutional distinction between "search" and "seizure." If listening alone completes a "seizure," it would be virtually impossible for state authorities at a probable cause hearing to describe with particularity the seizures which would later be made during extended eavesdropping; correspondingly, seizures would unavoidably be made which lacked any sufficient nexus with the offenses for which the order was first issued. There is no need for present purposes to explore at length the question's subtleties; it suffices to indicate that, in my view, conversations are not "seized" either by eavesdropping alone, or by their recording so that they may later be heard at the eavesdropper's convenience. Just as some exercise of dominion, beyond mere perception, is necessary for the seizure of tangibles so some use of the conversation beyond the initial listening process is required for the seizure of the spoken word. With this premise, I turn to these three objections.

The "particularity" demanded by the Fourth Amendment has never been thought by this Court to be reducible "to formula"; it has instead been made plain that its measurement must take fully into account the character both of the materials to be seized and of the purposes of the seizures. Accordingly, where the materials "are books, and the basis for their seizure is the ideas which they contain," the most "scrupulous exactitude" is demanded in the warrant's description; but where the special problems associated with the First Amendment are not involved, as they are not here, a more "reasonable particularity," is permissible. The degree of particularity necessary is best measured by that requirement's purposes. The central purpose of the particularity requirement is to leave "nothing ... to the discretion of the officer executing the warrant," by describing the materials to be seized with precision sufficient to prevent "the seizure of one thing under a warrant describing another." The state authorities are not compelled at the probable cause hearing to wager, upon penalty of a subsequent reversal, that they can successfully predict each of the characteristics of the materials which they will later seize, such a demand would, by discouraging the use of the judicial process, defeat the Amendment's central purpose.

The materials to be seized are instead described with sufficient particularity if the warrant readily permits their identification both by those entrusted with the warrant's execution and by the court in any subsequent judicial proceeding. "It is," the Court has said with reference to the particularity of the place to be searched, "enough if the description is such that the officer ... can, with reasonable effort ascertain and identify" the warrant's objects.

These standards must be equally applicable to the seizure of words, and, under them, this order did not lack the requisite particularity. The order here permitted the interception, or search, of any and all conversations occurring within the order's time limitations at the specified location; but this direction must be read in light of the terms of the affidavits, which, under § 813, form part of the authority for the eavesdropping. The affidavits make plain that, among the intercepted conversations, the police were authorized to seize only those "relative to the payment of unlawful fees to obtain liquor licenses." These directions sufficed to provide a standard which left nothing in the choice of materials to be seized to the "whim," of the state authorities. There could be no difficulty, either in the course of the search or in any subsequent judicial proceeding, in determining whether specific conversations were among those authorized for seizure by the order. The Fourth and Fourteenth Amendments do not demand more.

Nor was the order invalid because it permitted the search of any and all conversations occurring at the specified location; if the requisite papers have identified the materials to be seized with sufficient particularity, as they did here, and if the search was confined to an appropriate area, the order is not invalidated by the examination of all within that area reasonably necessary for discovery of the materials to be seized. I do not doubt that searches by eavesdrop must be confined in time precisely as the search for tangibles is confined in space, but the actual duration of the intrusion here, or for that matter the total period authorized by the order, was not, given the character of the offenses involved, excessive. All the disputed evidence was obtained within 13 days, scarcely unreasonable in light of an alleged conspiracy involving many individuals and a lengthy series of transactions.

The question therefore remains only whether, as petitioner suggests, the order was issued without an adequate showing of probable cause.... it suffices now simply to emphasize that the information presented to the magistrate or commissioner must permit him to "judge for himself the persuasiveness of the facts relied on by a complaining officer." The magistrate must "assess independently the probability" that the facts are as the complainant has alleged; he may not "accept without question the complainant's mere conclusion."

As measured by the terms of the affidavits here, the issuing judge could properly have concluded that probable cause existed for the order.... the judge was provided the evidence which supported the affiants' conclusions; he was not compelled to rely merely on their "affirmation of suspicion and belief." In my opinion, taking the Steinman affidavits on their face, the constitutional requirements of probable cause were fully satisfied....

[JUSTICE WHITE'S dissenting opinion omitted.]

KATZ v. UNITED STATES

Supreme Court of the United States, 1967.
389 U.S. 347, 88 S.Ct. 507.

MR. JUSTICE STEWART delivered the opinion of the Court.

The petitioner was convicted in the District Court for the Southern District of California under an eight-count indictment charging him with transmitting wagering information by telephone from Los Angeles to Miami and Boston in violation of a federal statute. At trial the Government was permitted, over the petitioner's objection, to introduce evidence of the petitioner's end of telephone conversations, overheard by FBI agents who had attached an electronic listening and recording device to the outside of the public telephone booth from which he had placed his calls. In affirming his conviction, the Court of Appeals rejected the contention that the recordings had been obtained in violation of the Fourth Amendment, because "[t]here was no physical entrance into the area occupied by, [the petitioner]." We granted certiorari in order to consider the constitutional questions thus presented.

The petitioner has phrased those questions as follows:

> "A. Whether a public telephone booth is a constitutionally protected area so that evidence obtained by attaching an electronic listening recording device to the top of such a booth is obtained in violation of the right to privacy of the user of the booth.
>
> "B. Whether physical penetration of a constitutionally protected area is necessary before a search and seizure can be said to

be violative of the Fourth Amendment to the United States Constitution."

We decline to adopt this formulation of the issues. In the first place the correct solution of Fourth Amendment problems is not necessarily promoted by incantation of the phrase "constitutionally protected area." Secondly, the Fourth Amendment cannot be translated into a general constitutional "right to privacy." That Amendment protects individual privacy against certain kinds of governmental intrusion, but its protections go further, and often have nothing to do with privacy at all. Other provisions of the Constitution protect personal privacy from other forms of governmental invasion. But the protection of a person's *general* right to privacy—his right to be let alone by other people—is, like the protection of his property and of his very life, left largely to the law of the individual States.

Because of the misleading way the issues have been formulated, the parties have attached great significance to the characterization of the telephone booth from which the petitioner placed his calls. The petitioner has strenuously argued that the booth was a "constitutionally protected area." The Government has maintained with equal vigor that it was not. But this effort to decide whether or not a given "area," viewed in the abstract, is "constitutionally protected" deflects attention from the problem presented by this case. For the Fourth Amendment protects people, not places. What a person knowingly exposes to the public, even in his own home or office, is not a subject of Fourth Amendment protection. But what he seeks to preserve as private, even in an area accessible to the public may be constitutionally protected.

The Government stresses the fact that the telephone booth from which the petitioner made his calls was constructed partly of glass, so that he was as visible after he entered it as he would have been if he had remained outside. But what he sought to exclude when he entered the booth was not the intruding eye—it was the uninvited ear. He did not shed his right to do so simply because he made his calls from a place where he might be seen. No less than an individual in a business office, in a friend's apartment, or in a taxicab, a person in a telephone booth may rely upon the protection of the Fourth Amendment. One who occupies it, shuts the door behind him, and pays the toll that permits him to place a call, is surely entitled to assume that the words he utters into the mouthpiece will not be broadcast to the world. To read the Constitution more narrowly is to ignore the vital role that the public telephone has come to play in private communication.

The Government contends, however, that the activities of its agents in this case should not be tested by Fourth Amendment requirements, for the surveillance technique they employed involved no physical penetration of the telephone booth from which the petitioner placed his calls. It is true that the absence of such penetration was at one time thought to foreclose further Fourth Amendment inquiry, although a closely divided Court supposed in *Olmstead* that surveillance without any trespass and without the seizure of any material object fell outside the ambit of the Constitution, we have since departed from the narrow view on which that decision rested. Indeed, we have expressly held that the Fourth Amendment governs not only the seizure of tangible items, but extends as well to the recording of oral statements overheard without any "technical trespass under ... local property law." Once this much is acknowledged, and once it is recognized that the Fourth Amendment protects people—and not simply "areas"—against unreasonable searches and seizures it becomes clear that the reach of that Amendment cannot turn upon the presence or absence of a physical intrusion into any given enclosure.

We conclude that the underpinnings of *Olmstead* and *Goldman* have been so eroded by our subsequent decisions that the "trespass" doctrine there enunciated can no longer be regarded as controlling. The Government's activities in electronically listening to and recording the petitioner's words violated the privacy upon which he justifiably relied while using the telephone booth and thus constituted a "search and seizure" within the meaning of the Fourth Amendment. The fact that the electronic device employed to achieve that end did not happen to penetrate the wall of the booth can have no constitutional significance.

The question remaining for decision, then, is whether the search and seizure conducted in this case complied with constitutional standards. In that regard, the Government's position is that its agents acted in an entirely defensible manner: They did not begin their electronic surveillance until investigation of the petitioner's activities had established a strong probability that he was using the telephone in question to transmit gambling information to persons in other States, in violation of federal law. Moreover, the surveillance was limited, both in scope and in duration, to the specific purpose of establishing the contents of the petitioner's unlawful telephonic communications. The agents confined their surveillance to the brief periods during which he used the telephone booth, and they took great care to overhear only the conversations of the petitioner himself.

Accepting this account of the Government's actions as accurate, it is clear that this surveillance was so narrowly circumscribed that a duly authorized magistrate, properly notified of the need for such investigation, specifically informed of the basis on which it was to proceed, and clearly apprised of the precise intrusion it would entail, could constitutionally have authorized, with appropriate safeguards, the very limited search and seizure that the Government asserts in fact took place....

The Government urges that, because its agents relied upon the decisions in *Olmstead* and *Goldman,* and because they did no more here than they might properly have done with prior judicial sanction, we should retroactively validate their conduct. That we cannot do. It is apparent that the agents in this case acted with restraint. Yet the inescapable fact is that this restraint was imposed by the agents themselves, not by a judicial officer. They were not required, before commencing the search, to present their estimate of probable cause for detached scrutiny by a neutral magistrate. They were not compelled, during the conduct of the search itself, to observe precise limits established in advance by a specific court order. Nor were they directed, after the search had been completed, to notify the authorizing magistrate in detail of all that had been seized. In the absence of such safeguards, this Court has never sustained a search upon the sole ground that officers reasonably expected to find evidence of a particular crime and voluntarily confined their activities to the least intrusive means consistent with that end....

[The government argues that] that surveillance of a telephone booth should be exempted from the usual requirement of advance authorization by a magistrate upon a showing of probable cause. We cannot agree. Omission of such authorization

> "bypasses the safeguards provided by an objective predetermination of probable cause, and substitutes instead the far less reliable procedure of an after-the-event justification for the ... search, too likely to be subtly influenced by the familiar shortcomings of hindsight judgment."

And bypassing a neutral predetermination of the *scope* of a search leaves individuals secure from Fourth Amendment violations "only in the discretion of the police."

These considerations do not vanish when the search in question is transferred from the setting of a home, an office, or a hotel room, to that of a telephone booth. Wherever a man may be, he is entitled to know that he will remain free from unreasonable searches and seizures. The government agents here ignored "the procedure of antecedent justification ... that is central to the Fourth Amendment," a procedure that we hold to be a constitutional precondition of the kind of electronic surveillance involved in this case. Because the surveillance here failed to meet that condition, and because it led to the petitioner's conviction, the judgment must be reversed.

It is so ordered.

Judgment reversed.

MR. JUSTICE MARSHALL took no part in the consideration or decision of this case.

[The concurring opinion of JUSTICES DOUGLAS and BRENNAN is omitted.]

MR. JUSTICE HARLAN, concurring.

I join the opinion of the Court, which I read to hold only (a) that an enclosed telephone booth is an area where, like a home, a person has a constitutionally protected reasonable expectation of privacy; (b) that electronic as well as physical intrusion into a place that is in this sense private may constitute a violation of the Fourth Amendment; and (c) that the invasion of a constitutionally protected area by federal authorities is, as the Court has long held, presumptively unreasonable in the absence of a search warrant.

As the Court's opinion states, "The Fourth Amendment protects people, not places." The question, however, is what protection it affords to those people. Generally, as here, the answer to that question requires reference to a "place." My understanding of the rule that has emerged from prior decisions is that there is a twofold requirement, first that a person have exhibited an actual (subjective) expectation of privacy and, second, that the expectation be one that society is prepared to recognize as "reasonable." Thus a man's home is, for most purposes, a place where he expects privacy, but objects, activities, or statements that he exposes to the "plain view" of outsiders are not "protected" because no intention to keep them to himself has been exhibited. On the other hand, conversations in the open would not be protected against being overheard, for the expectation of privacy under the circumstances would be unreasonable.

The critical fact in this case is that "[o]ne who occupies it, [a telephone booth] shuts the door behind him, and pays the toll that permits him to place a call, is surely entitled to assume" that his conversation is not being intercepted. The point is not that the booth is "accessible to the public" at other times, but that it is a temporarily private place whose momentary occupants' expectations of freedom from intrusion are recognized as reasonable....

Finally, I do not read the Court's opinion to declare that no interception of a conversation one-half of which occurs in a public telephone booth can be reasonable in the absence of a warrant. As elsewhere under the Fourth Amendment, warrants are the general rule, to which the legitimate needs of law enforcement may demand specific exceptions. It will be time enough to consider any such exceptions when an appropriate occasion presents itself, and I agree with the Court that this is not one.

[The concurring opinion of Justice White and the dissenting opinion of Justice Black are omitted.]

NOTES

1. In order to comply with the constitutional mandates enunciated by the Supreme Court, in the 1968 Omnibus Crime Control and Safe Streets Act, Congress, after expressing its awareness of law enforcement needs to engage in wiretapping and eavesdropping, particularly in organized crime cases, set forth a number of safeguards against abusive law enforcement practices. The Act itself is too lengthy for reproduction in this casebook. For the reader interested in all of the details, the Act may be found in Title 18 of the United States Code, in Sections 2510 through 2520.

Basically, the Act requires a court order for the use of any electronic, mechanical, or other device to tap a telephone or to intercept other oral conversations that "affect interstate commerce," which, of course, as previously demonstrated in Chapter 3, includes practically any kind of "business operation." One notable exception is the situation where one party to the conversation gives consent to the telephone tapping or to the interception of any other of his conversations. There is also an "emergency" condition provision, subject to certain restrictive conditions. A failure to comply with the requirements of the Act subjects the violator to a criminal prosecution as well as a civil suit, along with the exclusion in court of improperly obtained evidence.

2. The Act has been upheld and construed in several federal cases. Two of the more recent ones are United States v. Donovan, 429 U.S. 413, 97 S.Ct. 658 (1977), and Scott v. United States, 436 U.S. 128, 98 S.Ct. 1717 (1978). In the first case (involving organized gambling), the issue was whether the Government need only disclose to the court authorizing the wiretap the names of the "principal targets" of the intercept, and also whether other persons whose conversations were overheard need be served with notice of the fact their conversations were overheard, as is required with respect to the "principal targets." The second case (involving narcotic operations) concerned the interpretation of the requirement that the wiretap "be conducted in such a way as to minimize the interception of communications not otherwise subject to interception." As with the Act itself, space considerations do not allow for their inclusion in this book. The reference is offered, however, for readers with a special interest in the particular problems of interpretation which the two cases involve.

3. State wiretap and electronic surveillance statutes similar to the federal one have been construed and upheld by several state courts. See Commonwealth v. Vitello, 367 Mass. 224, 327 N.E.2d 819 (1975). Many states, however, have not adopted laws in conformity with the federal legislation. Moreover, a few prohibit all electronic interceptions of communications. Others require the consent of one party.

State statutes allowing court-ordered wiretaps must conform to the federal statute. For example, wiretap orders must be based upon probable cause related to certain categories of offenses enumerated in Section 2516 of the federal statute. A state statute cannot authorize a wiretap in search of evidence for a less serious offense. See People v. Shapiro, 50 N.Y.2d 747, 431 N.Y.S.2d 422, 409 N.E.2d 897 (1980) (New York statute invalidated when it provided for tap in connection with non-forceful sexual crime against a child).

During the last several years, federal legislation was proposed to limit electronic surveillance in national security matters, even when foreign agents are suspected of engaging in efforts to undermine United States security by engaging in criminal activities within the United States. Both the Ford administration and the Carter administration have endorsed the concept of requiring warrants to authorize any non-emergency national security wiretapping conducted within the United States. In 1978 such legislation was enacted. Foreign Intelligence Surveillance Act of 1978, 50 U.S.C.A. §§1801–1811 (Supp. V. 1981).

4. In 1970 Congress added a section to the Omnibus Crime bill (§ 2518(4)), which permitted court orders to compel telephone companies "to furnish ... all information, facilities and technical assistance necessary to accomplish the interception unobtrusively." In United States v. New York Telephone Company, 434 U.S. 159, 98 S.Ct. 364 (1977), the Supreme Court found that District Courts possessed this power even without § 2518(4), and held that a United States District Court may properly direct a telephone company "to provide federal law enforcement officials the facilities and technical assistance necessary for the implementation of its order authorizing the use of pen registers to investigate

offenses which there was probable cause to believe were being committed by means of the telephone."

5. Although law enforcement officers are not constitutionally required to obtain a traditional wiretap order or a search warrant to use pen registers or trap and trace devices, under recent federal legislation judicial authorization must now be obtained in non-emergency situations. The application for authorization must state that information sought is relevant to an ongoing criminal investigation. 18 United States Code Sections 3121–3126. All states were required to conform to this federal legislation by October 2, 1988.

G. SEARCHES AND SEIZURES UPON LESS THAN PROBABLE CAUSE

1. STOP AND FRISK

TERRY v. OHIO

Supreme Court of the United States, 1968.
392 U.S. 1, 88 S.Ct. 1868.

MR. CHIEF JUSTICE WARREN delivered the opinion of the Court.

This case presents serious questions concerning the role of the Fourth Amendment in the confrontation on the street between the citizen and the policeman investigating suspicious circumstances.

Petitioner Terry was convicted of carrying a concealed weapon. Following the denial of a pretrial motion to suppress, the prosecution introduced in evidence two revolvers and a number of bullets seized from Terry and a codefendant, Richard Chilton, by Cleveland Police Detective Martin McFadden. At the hearing on the motion to suppress this evidence, Officer McFadden testified that while he was patrolling in plain clothes in downtown Cleveland at approximately 2:30 in the afternoon of October 31, 1963, his attention was attracted by two men, Chilton and Terry, standing on the corner of Huron Road and Euclid Avenue. He had never seen the two men before, and he was unable to say precisely what first drew his eye to them. However, he testified that he had been a policeman for 39 years and a detective for 35 and that he had been assigned to patrol this vicinity of downtown Cleveland for shoplifters and pickpockets for 30 years. He explained that he had developed routine habits of observation over the years and that he would "stand and watch people or walk and watch people at many intervals of the day." He added: "Now, in this case when I looked over they didn't look right to me at the time."

His interest aroused, Officer McFadden took up a post of observation in the entrance to a store 300 to 400 feet away from the two men. "I get more purpose to watch them when I seen their movements," he testified. He saw one of the men leave the other one and walk south-west on Huron Road, past some stores. The man paused for a moment and looked in a store window, then walked on a short distance, turned around and walked back toward the corner, pausing once again to look in the same store window. He rejoined his companion at the corner, and the two conferred briefly. Then the second man went through the same series of motions, strolling down Huron Road, looking in the same window, walking on a short distance, turning back, peering in the store window again, and returning to confer with the first man at the corner. The two men repeated this ritual alternately between five and six times apiece—in all, roughly a dozen trips. At one point, while the two were standing together on the corner, a third man approached them and engaged them briefly in conversation. This man then left the two others and walked west on Euclid Avenue. Chilton and Terry resumed their measured pacing, peering, and conferring. After this had gone on for 10 to 12 minutes, the two men walked off together, heading west on Euclid Avenue, following the path taken earlier by the third man.

By this time Officer McFadden had become thoroughly suspicious. He testified that after observing their elaborately casual and oft-repeated reconnaissance of the store window on Huron Road, he suspected the two men of "casing a job, a stick-up," and that he considered it his duty as a police officer to investigate further. He added that he feared "they may have a gun." Thus, Officer McFadden followed Chilton and Terry and saw them stop in front of Zucker's store to talk to the same man who had conferred with them earlier on the street corner. Deciding that the situation was ripe for direct action, Officer McFadden approached the three men, identified himself as a police officer and asked for their names. At this point his knowledge was confined to what he had observed. He was not acquainted with any of the three men by name or by sight, and he had received no information concerning them from any other source. When the men "mumbled something" in response to his inquiries, Officer McFadden grabbed petitioner Terry, spun him around so that they were facing the other two, with Terry between McFadden and the others, and patted down the outside of his clothing. In the left breast pocket of Terry's overcoat Officer McFadden felt a pistol. He reached inside the overcoat pocket, but was unable to remove the gun. At this point, keeping Terry between himself and the others, the officer ordered all three men to enter Zucker's store. As they went in, he removed Terry's overcoat completely, retrieved a .38 caliber revolver from the pocket and ordered all three men to face the wall with their hands raised. Officer McFadden proceeded to pat down the outer clothing of Chilton and the third man, Katz. He discovered another revolver in the outer pocket of Chilton's overcoat, but no weapons were found on Katz. The officer testified that he only patted the men down to see whether they had weapons, and that he did not put his hands beneath the outer garments of either Terry or Chilton until he felt their guns. So far as appears from the record, he never placed his hands beneath Katz's outer garments. Officer McFadden seized Chilton's gun, asked the proprietor of the store to call a police wagon, and took all three

men to the station, where Chilton and Terry were formally charged with carrying concealed weapons.

On the motion to suppress the guns the prosecution took the position that they had been seized following a search incident to a lawful arrest. The trial court rejected this theory, stating that it "would be stretching the facts beyond reasonable comprehension" to find that Officer McFadden had had probable cause to arrest the men before he patted them down for weapons. However, the court denied the defendant's motion on the ground that Officer McFadden, on the basis of his experience, "had reasonable cause to believe ... that the defendants were conducting themselves suspiciously, and some interrogation should be made of their action." Purely for his own protection, the court held, the officer had the right to pat down the outer clothing of these men, whom he had reasonable cause to believe might be armed. The court distinguished between an investigatory "stop" and an arrest, and between a "frisk" of the outer clothing for weapons and a full-blown search for evidence of crime. The frisk, it held, was essential to the proper performance of the officer's investigatory duties, for without it "the answer to the police officer may be a bullet, and a loaded pistol discovered during the frisk is admissible."

After the court denied their motion to suppress, Chilton and Terry waived jury trial and pleaded not guilty. The court adjudged them guilty....

I.

The Fourth Amendment provides that "the right of the people to be secure in their persons, houses, papers, and effects, against unreasonable searches and seizures, shall not be violated...." This inestimable right of personal security belongs as much to the citizen on the streets of our great cities as to the homeowner closeted in his study to dispose of his secret affairs....

Unquestionably petitioner was entitled to the protection of the Fourth Amendment as he walked down the street in Cleveland. The question is whether in all the circumstances of this on-the-street encounter, his right to personal security was violated by an unreasonable search and seizure.

We would be less than candid if we did not acknowledge that this question thrusts to the fore difficult and troublesome issues regarding a sensitive area of police activity—issues which have never before been squarely presented to this Court. Reflective of the tensions involved are the practical and constitutional arguments pressed with great vigor on both sides of the public debate over the power of the police to "stop and frisk"—as it is sometimes euphemistically termed—suspicious persons.

On the one hand, it is frequently argued that in dealing with the rapidly unfolding and often dangerous situations on city streets the police are in need of an escalating set of flexible responses, graduated in relation to the amount of information they possess. For this purpose it is urged that distinctions should be made between a "stop" and an "arrest" (or a "seizure" of a person), and between a "frisk" and a "search." Thus, it is argued, the police should be allowed to "stop" a person and detain him briefly for questioning upon suspicion that he may be connected with criminal activity. Upon suspicion that the person may be armed, the police should have the power to "frisk" him for weapons. If the "stop" and the "frisk" give rise to probable cause to believe that the suspect has committed a crime, then the police should be empowered to make a formal "arrest," and a full incident "search" of the person. This scheme is justified in part upon the notion that a "stop" and a "frisk" amount to a mere "minor inconvenience and petty indignity," which can properly be imposed upon the citizen in the interest of effective law enforcement on the basis of a police officer's suspicion.[1]

On the other side the argument is made that the authority of the police must be strictly circumscribed by the law of arrest and search as it has developed to date in the traditional jurisprudence of the Fourth Amendment. It is contended with some force that there is not—and cannot be—a variety of police activity which does not depend solely upon the voluntary cooperation of the citizen and yet which stops short of an arrest based upon probable cause to make such an arrest. The heart of the Fourth Amendment, the argument runs, is a severe requirement of specific justification for any intrusion upon protected personal security, coupled with a highly developed system of judicial controls to enforce upon the agents of the State the commands of the Constitution. Acquiescence by the courts in the compulsion inherent in the field interrogation practices at issue here, it is urged, would constitute an abdication of judicial control over, and indeed an encouragement of, substantial interference with liberty and personal security by police officers whose judgment is necessarily colored by their primary involvement in "the often competitive enterprise of ferreting out crime." Johnson v. United States, 333 U.S. 10, 14, 68 S.Ct. 367, 369 (1948). This, it is argued, can only serve to exacerbate police-community tensions in the crowded centers of our Nation's cities.

In this context we approach the issues in this case mindful of the limitations of the judicial function in controlling the myriad daily situations in which policemen and citizens confront each other on the street.

1. "... [T]he evidence needed to make the inquiry is not of the same degree or conclusiveness as that required for an arrest. The stopping of the individual to inquire is not an arrest and the ground upon which the police may make the inquiry may be less incriminating than the ground for an arrest for a crime known to have been committed....

"And as the right to stop and inquire is to be justified for a cause less conclusive than that which would sustain an arrest, so the right to frisk may be justified as an incident to inquiry upon grounds of elemental safety and precaution which might not initially sustain a search. Ultimately the validity of the frisk narrows down to whether there is or is not a right by the police to touch the person questioned. The sense of exterior touch here involved is not very far different from the sense of sight or hearing—senses upon which police customarily act." People v. Rivera, 14 N.Y.2d 441, 445, 447, 201 N.E.2d 32, 34, 35, 252 N.Y.S.2d 458, 461, 463 (1964), cert. denied, 379 U.S. 978, 85 S.Ct. 679 (1965).

The State has characterized the issue here as "the right of a police officer ... to make an on-the-street stop, interrogate and pat down for weapons (known in the street vernacular as 'stop and frisk')." But this is only partly accurate. For the issue is not the abstract propriety of the police conduct, but the admissibility against petitioner of the evidence uncovered by the search and seizure. Ever since its inception, the rule excluding evidence seized in violation of the Fourth Amendment has been recognized as a principal mode of discouraging lawless police conduct. Thus its major thrust is a deterrent one, and experience has taught that it is the only effective deterrent to police misconduct in the criminal context, and that without it the constitutional guarantee against unreasonable searches and seizures would be a mere "form of words." The rule also serves another vital function—"the imperative of judicial integrity." Courts which sit under our Constitution cannot and will not be made party to lawless invasions of the constitutional rights of citizens by permitting unhindered governmental use of the fruits of such invasions. Thus in our system evidentiary rulings provide the context in which the judicial process of inclusion and exclusion approves some conduct as comporting with constitutional guarantees and disapproves other actions by state agents. A ruling admitting evidence in a criminal trial, we recognize, has the necessary effect of legitimizing the conduct which produced the evidence, while an application of the exclusionary rule withholds the constitutional imprimatur.

The exclusionary rule has its limitations, however, as a tool of judicial control. It cannot properly be invoked to exclude the products of legitimate police investigative techniques on the ground that much conduct which is closely similar involves unwarranted intrusions upon constitutional protections. Moreover, in some contexts the rule is ineffective as a deterrent. Street encounters between citizens and police officers are incredibly rich in diversity. They range from wholly friendly exchanges of pleasantries or mutually useful information to hostile confrontations of armed men involving arrests, or injuries, or loss of life. Moreover, hostile confrontations are not all of a piece. Some of them begin in a friendly enough manner, only to take a different turn upon the injection of some unexpected element into the conversation. Encounters are initiated by the police for a wide variety of purposes, some of which are wholly unrelated to a desire to prosecute for crime.[2] Doubtless some police "field interrogation" conduct violates the Fourth Amendment. But a stern refusal by this Court to condone such activity does not necessarily render it responsive to the exclusionary rule. Re-

2. See Tiffany, McIntyre & Rotenberg, Detection of Crime: Stopping and Questioning, Search and Seizure, Encouragement and Entrapment 18–56 (1967). This sort of police conduct may, for example, be designed simply to help an intoxicated person find his way home, with no intention of arresting him unless he becomes obstreperous. Or the police may be seeking to mediate a domestic quarrel which threatens to erupt into violence. They may accost a woman in an area known for prostitution as part of a harassment campaign designed to drive prostitutes away without the considerable difficulty involved in prosecuting them. Or they may be conducting a dragnet search of all teenagers in a particular section of the city for weapons because they have heard rumors of an impending gang fight.

gardless of how effective the rule may be where obtaining convictions is an important objective of the police, it is powerless to deter invasions of constitutionally guaranteed rights where the police either have no interest in prosecuting or are willing to forego successful prosecution in the interest of serving some other goal.

Proper adjudication of cases in which the exclusionary rule is invoked demands a constant awareness of these limitations. The wholesale harassment by certain elements of the police community, of which minority groups, particularly Negroes, frequently complain,[3] will not be stopped by the exclusion of any evidence from any criminal trial. Yet a rigid and unthinking application of the exclusionary rule, in futile protest against practices which it can never be used effectively to control, may exact a high toll in human injury and frustration of efforts to prevent crime. No judicial opinion can comprehend the protean variety of the street encounter, and we can only judge the facts of the case before us. Nothing we say today is to be taken as indicating approval of police conduct outside the legitimate investigative sphere. Under our decision, courts still retain their traditional responsibility to guard against police conduct which is overbearing or harassing, or which trenches upon personal security without the objective evidentiary justification which the Constitution requires. When such conduct is identified, it must be condemned by the judiciary and its fruits must be excluded from evidence in criminal trials. And, of course, our approval of legitimate and restrained investigative conduct undertaken on the basis of ample factual justification should in no way discourage the employment of other remedies than the exclusionary rule to curtail abuses for which that sanction may prove inappropriate.

Having thus roughly sketched the perimeters of the constitutional debate over the limits on police investigative conduct in general and the background against which this case presents itself, we turn our attention to the quite narrow question posed by the facts before us: whether it is always unreasonable for a policeman to seize a person and subject him to a limited search for weapons unless there is probable cause for an arrest. Given the narrowness of this question, we have no occasion to canvass in

3. The President's Commission on Law Enforcement and Administration of Justice found that "in many communities, field interrogations are a major source of friction between the police and minority groups." President's Commission on Law Enforcement and Administration of Justice, Task Force Report: The Police 183 (1967). It was reported that the friction caused by "misuse of field interrogations" increases "as more police departments adopt 'aggressive patrol' in which officers are encouraged routinely to stop and question persons on the street who are unknown to them, who are suspicious, or whose purpose for being abroad is not readily evident." Id., at 184. While the frequency with which "frisking" forms a part of field interrogation practice varies tremendously with the locale, the objective of the interrogation, and the particular officer, see Tiffany, McIntyre & Rotenberg, supra, n. 9, at 47–48, it cannot help but be a severely exacerbating factor in police-community tensions. This is particularly true in situations where the "stop and frisk" of youths or minority group members is "motivated by the officers' perceived need to maintain the power image of the beat officer, an aim sometimes accomplished by humiliating anyone who attempts to undermine police control of the streets." Id., at 47–48.

detail the constitutional limitations upon the scope of a policeman's power when he confronts a citizen without probable cause to arrest him.

II.

Our first task is to establish at what point in this encounter the Fourth Amendment becomes relevant. That is, we must decide whether and when Officer McFadden "seized" Terry and whether and when he conducted a "search." There is some suggestion in the use of such terms as "stop" and "frisk" that such police conduct is outside the purview of the Fourth Amendment because neither action rises to the level of a "search" or "seizure" within the meaning of the Constitution. We emphatically reject this notion. It is quite plain that the Fourth Amendment governs "seizures" of the person which do not eventuate in a trip to the station house and prosecution for crime—"arrests" in traditional terminology. It must be recognized that whenever a police officer accosts an individual and restrains his freedom to walk away, he has "seized" that person. And it is nothing less than sheer torture of the English language to suggest that a careful exploration of the outer surfaces of a person's clothing all over his or her body in an attempt to find weapons is not a "search." Moreover, it is simply fantastic to urge that such a procedure performed in public by a policeman while the citizen stands helpless, perhaps facing a wall with his hands raised, is a "petty indignity."[4] It is a serious intrusion upon the sanctity of the person, which may inflict great indignity and arouse strong resentment, and it is not to be undertaken lightly.[5]

The danger in the logic which proceeds upon distinctions between a "stop" and an "arrest," or "seizure" of the person, and between a "frisk" and a "search" is two-fold. It seeks to isolate from constitutional scrutiny the initial stages of the contact between the policeman and the citizen. And by suggesting a rigid all-or-nothing model of justification and regulation under the Amendment, it obscures the utility of limitations upon the scope, as well as the initiation, of police action as a means of constitutional regulation. This Court has held in the past that a search which is reasonable at its inception may violate the Fourth Amendment by virtue of its intolerable intensity and scope. The scope of the search must be "strictly tied to and justified by" the circumstances which rendered its initiation permissible. Warden v. Hayden,

4. Consider the following apt description:

> "[T]he officer must feel with sensitive fingers every portion of the prisoner's body. A thorough search must be made of the prisoner's arms and armpits, waistline and back, the groin and area about the testicles, and entire surface of the legs down to the feet." Priar & Martin, Searching and Disarming Criminals, 45 J.Crim., L.C. & P.S. 481 (1954).

5. We have noted that the abusive practices which play a major, though by no means exclusive, role in creating this friction are not susceptible of control by means of the exclusionary rule, and cannot properly dictate our decision with respect to the powers of the police in genuine investigative and preventive situations. However, the degree of community resentment aroused by particular practices is clearly relevant to an assessment of the quality of the intrusion upon reasonable expectations of personal security caused by those practices.

387 U.S. 294, 310, 87 S.Ct. 1642, 1651, 1652 (1967) (Mr. Justice Fortas, concurring).

The distinctions of classical "stop-and-frisk" theory thus serve to divert attention from the central inquiry under the Fourth Amendment—the reasonableness in all the circumstances of the particular governmental invasion of a citizen's personal security. "Search" and "seizure" are not talismans. We therefore reject the notions that the Fourth Amendment does not come into play at all as a limitation upon police conduct if the officers stop short of something called a "technical arrest" or a "full-blown search."

In this case there can be no question, then, that Officer McFadden "seized" petitioner and subjected him to a "search" when he took hold of him and patted down the outer surfaces of his clothing. We must decide whether at that point it was reasonable for Officer McFadden to have interfered with petitioner's personal security as he did.[6] And in determining whether the seizure and search were "unreasonable" our inquiry is a dual one—whether the officer's action was justified at its inception, and whether it was reasonably related in scope to the circumstances which justified the interference in the first place.

III.

If this case involved police conduct subject to the Warrant Clause of the Fourth Amendment, we would have to ascertain whether "probable cause" existed to justify the search and seizure which took place. However, that is not the case. We do not retreat from our holdings that the police must, whenever practicable, obtain advance judicial approval of searches and seizures through the warrant procedure ... or that in most instances failure to comply with the warrant requirement can only be excused by exigent circumstances. But we deal here with an entire rubric of police conduct—necessarily swift action predicated upon the on-the-spot observations of the officer on the beat—which historically has not been, and as a practical matter could not be, subjected to the warrant procedure. Instead, the conduct involved in this case must be tested by the Fourth Amendment's general proscription against unreasonable searches and seizures.

Nonetheless, the notions which underlie both the warrant procedure and the requirement of probable cause remain fully relevant in this context. In order to assess the reasonableness of Officer McFadden's conduct as a general proposition, it is necessary "first to focus upon the

6. We thus decide nothing today concerning the constitutional propriety of an investigative "seizure" upon less than probable cause for purposes of "detention" and/or interrogation. Obviously, not all personal intercourse between policemen and citizens involves "seizures" of persons. Only when the officer, by means of physical force or show of authority, has in some way restrained the liberty of a citizen may we conclude that a "seizure" has occurred. We cannot tell with any certainty upon this record whether any such "seizure" took place here prior to Officer McFadden's initiation of physical contact for purposes of searching Terry for weapons, and we thus may assume that up to that point no intrusion upon constitutionally protected rights had occurred.

governmental interest which allegedly justifies official intrusion upon the constitutionally protected interests of the private citizen," for there is "no ready test for determining reasonableness other than by balancing the need to search [or seize] against the invasion which the search [or seizure] entails." Camara v. Municipal Court, 387 U.S. 523, 534, 536–537, 87 S.Ct. 1727, 1733–1735 (1967). And in justifying the particular intrusion the police officer must be able to point to specific and articulable facts which, taken together with rational inferences from those facts, reasonably warrant that intrusion. The scheme of the Fourth Amendment becomes meaningful only when it is assured that at some point the conduct of those charged with enforcing the laws can be subjected to the more detached, neutral scrutiny of a judge who must evaluate the reasonableness of a particular search or seizure in light of the particular circumstances. And in making that assessment it is imperative that the facts be judged against an objective standard: would the facts available to the officer at the moment of the seizure or the search "warrant a man of reasonable caution in the belief" that the action taken was appropriate? Anything less would invite intrusions upon constitutionally guaranteed rights based on nothing more substantial than inarticulate hunches, a result this Court has consistently refused to sanction. And simple " 'good faith on the part of the arresting officer is not enough.' ... If subjective good faith alone were the test, the protections of the Fourth Amendment would evaporate, and the people would be 'secure in their persons, houses, papers, and effects,' only in the discretion of the police."

Applying these principles to this case, we consider first the nature and extent of the governmental interests involved. One general interest is of course that of effective crime prevention and detection; it is this interest which underlies the recognition that a police officer may in appropriate circumstances and in an appropriate manner approach a person for purposes of investigating possibly criminal behavior even though there is no probable cause to make an arrest. It was this legitimate investigative function Officer McFadden was discharging when he decided to approach petitioner and his companions. He had observed Terry, Chilton, and Katz go through a series of acts, each of them perhaps innocent in itself, but which taken together warranted further investigation. There is nothing unusual in two men standing together on a street corner, perhaps waiting for someone. Nor is there anything suspicious about people in such circumstances strolling up and down the street, singly or in pairs. Store windows, moreover, are made to be looked in. But the story is quite different where, as here, two men hover about a street corner for an extended period of time, at the end of which it becomes apparent that they are not waiting for anyone or anything; where these men pace alternately along an identical route, pausing to stare in the same store window roughly 24 times; where each completion of this route is followed immediately by a conference between the two men on the corner; where they are joined in one of these conferences by a third man who leaves swiftly; and where the two men finally follow the third and rejoin him a couple of blocks away. It would have been poor police work indeed for an officer of 30 years' experience in the detection of thievery from stores in this same neighborhood to have failed to investigate this behavior further.

The crux of this case, however, is not the propriety of Officer McFadden's taking steps to investigate petitioner's suspicious behavior, but rather, whether there was justification for McFadden's invasion of Terry's personal security by searching him for weapons in the course of that investigation. We are now concerned with more than the governmental interest in investigating crime; in addition, there is the more immediate interest of the police officer in taking steps to assure himself that the person with whom he is dealing is not armed with a weapon that could unexpectedly and fatally be used against him. Certainly it would be unreasonable to require that police officers take unnecessary risks in the performance of their duties. American criminals have a long tradition of armed violence, and every year in this country many law enforcement officers are killed in the line of duty, and thousands more are wounded. Virtually all of these deaths and a substantial portion of the injuries are inflicted with guns and knives.

In view of these facts, we cannot blind ourselves to the need for law enforcement officers to protect themselves and other prospective victims of violence in situations where they may lack probable cause for an arrest. When an officer is justified in believing that the individual whose suspicious behavior he is investigating at close range is armed and presently dangerous to the officer or to others, it would appear to be clearly unreasonable to deny the officer the power to take necessary measures to determine whether the person is in fact carrying a weapon and to neutralize the threat of physical harm.

We must still consider, however, the nature and quality of the intrusion on individual rights which must be accepted if police officers are to be conceded the right to search for weapons in situations where probable cause to arrest for crime is lacking. Even a limited search of the outer clothing for weapons constitutes a severe, though brief, intrusion upon cherished personal security, and it must surely be an annoying, frightening, and perhaps humiliating experience. Petitioner contends that such an intrusion is permissible only incident to a lawful arrest, either for a crime involving the possession of weapons or for a crime the commission of which led the officer to investigate in the first place. However, this argument must be closely examined.

Petitioner does not argue that a police officer should refrain from making any investigation of suspicious circumstances until such time as he has probable cause to make an arrest; nor does he deny that police officers in properly discharging their investigative function may find themselves confronting persons who might well be armed and dangerous. Moreover, he does not say that an officer is always unjustified in searching a suspect to discover weapons. Rather, he says it is unreasonable for the policeman to take that step until such time as the situation evolves to a point where there is probable cause to make an arrest. When that point has been reached, petitioner would concede the officer's right to conduct a search of the suspect for weapons, fruits or instrumentalities of the crime, or "mere" evidence, incident to the arrest.

There are two weaknesses in this line of reasoning, however. First, it fails to take account of traditional limitations upon the scope of searches, and thus recognizes no distinction in purpose, character, and extent between a search incident to an arrest and a limited search for weapons. The former, although justified in part by the acknowledged necessity to protect the arresting officer from assault with a concealed weapon, Preston v. United States, 376 U.S. 364, 367, 84 S.Ct. 881, 883 (1964), is also justified on other grounds, ibid., and can therefore involve a relatively extensive exploration of the person. A search for weapons in the absence of probable cause to arrest, however, must, like any other search, be strictly circumscribed by the exigencies which justify its initiation. Warden v. Hayden, 387 U.S. 294, 310, 87 S.Ct. 1642, 1651, 1652 (1967) (Mr. Justice Fortas, concurring). Thus it must be limited to that which is necessary for the discovery of weapons which might be used to harm the officer or others nearby, and may realistically be characterized as something less than a "full" search, even though it remains a serious intrusion.

A second, and related, objection to petitioner's argument is that it assumes that the law of arrest has already worked out the balance between the particular interests involved here—the neutralization of danger to the policeman in the investigative circumstance and the sanctity of the individual. But this is not so. An arrest is a wholly different kind of intrusion upon individual freedom from a limited search for weapons, and the interests each is designed to serve are likewise quite different. An arrest is the initial stage of a criminal prosecution. It is intended to vindicate society's interest in having its laws obeyed, and it is inevitably accompanied by future interference with the individual's freedom of movement, whether or not trial or conviction ultimately follows. The protective search for weapons, on the other hand, constitutes a brief, though far from inconsiderable, intrusion upon the sanctity of the person. It does not follow that because an officer may lawfully arrest a person only when he is apprised of facts sufficient to warrant a belief that the person has committed or is committing a crime, the officer is equally unjustified, absent that kind of evidence, in making any intrusions short of an arrest. Moreover, a perfectly reasonable apprehension of danger may arise long before the officer is possessed of adequate information to justify taking a person into custody for the purpose of prosecuting him for a crime. Petitioner's reliance on cases which have worked out standards of reasonableness with regard to "seizures" constituting arrests and searches incident thereto is thus misplaced. It assumes that the interests sought to be vindicated and the invasions of personal security may be equated in the two cases, and thereby ignores a vital aspect of the analysis of the reasonableness of particular types of conduct under the Fourth Amendment. See Camara v. Municipal Court, supra.

Our evaluation of the proper balance that has to be struck in this type of case leads us to conclude that there must be a narrowly drawn authority to permit a reasonable search for weapons for the protection of the police officer, where he has reason to believe that he is dealing with an armed and dangerous individual, regardless of whether he has probable cause to arrest the individual for a crime. The officer need not be absolutely certain that the individual is armed; the issue is whether a reasonably prudent man in the circumstances would be warranted in the belief that his safety or that of others was in danger. And in determining whether the officer acted reasonably in such circumstances, due weight must be given, not to his inchoate and unparticularized suspicion or "hunch," but to the specific reasonable inferences which he is entitled to draw from the facts in light of his experience. Cf. Brinegar v. United States, supra.

IV.

We must now examine the conduct of Officer McFadden in this case to determine whether his search and seizure of petitioner were reasonable, both at their inception and as conducted. He had observed Terry, together with Chilton and another man, acting in a manner he took to be preface to a "stick-up." We think on the facts and circumstances Officer McFadden detailed before the trial judge a reasonably prudent man would have been warranted in believing petitioner was armed and thus presented a threat to the officer's safety while he was investigating his suspicious behavior. The actions of Terry and Chilton were consistent with McFadden's hypothesis that these men were contemplating a daylight robbery—which, it is reasonable to assume, would be likely to involve the use of weapons—and nothing in their conduct from the time he first noticed them until the time he confronted them and identified himself as a police officer gave him sufficient reason to negate that hypothesis. Although the trio had departed the original scene, there was nothing to indicate abandonment of an intent to commit a robbery at some point. Thus, when Officer McFadden approached the three men gathered before the display window at Zucker's store he had observed enough to make it quite reasonable to fear that they were armed; and nothing in their response to his hailing them, identifying himself as a police officer, and asking their names served to dispel that reasonable belief. We cannot say his decision at that point to seize Terry and pat his clothing for weapons was the product of a volatile or inventive imagination, or was undertaken simply as an act of harassment; the record evidences the tempered act of a policeman who in the course of an investigation had to make a quick decision as to how to protect himself and others from possible danger, and took limited steps to do so.

The manner in which the seizure and search were conducted is, of course, as vital a part of the inquiry as whether they were warranted at all. The Fourth Amendment proceeds as much by limitations upon the scope of governmental action as by imposing preconditions upon its initiation. The entire deterrent purpose of the rule excluding evidence seized in violation of the Fourth Amendment rests on the assumption that "limitations upon the fruit to be gathered tend to limit the quest itself." United States v. Poller, 43 F.2d 911, 914 (C.A.2d Cir.1930). Thus, evidence may not be introduced if it was discovered by means of a seizure and search which were not reasonably related in scope to the justification for their initiation.

We need not develop at length in this case, however, the limitations which the Fourth Amendment places upon a protective seizure and search for weapons. These limitations will have to be developed in the concrete factual circumstances of individual cases. See Sibron v. New York, decided today. Suffice it to note that such a search, unlike a search without a warrant incident to a lawful arrest, is not justified by any need to prevent the disappearance or destruction of evidence of crime. The sole justification of the search in the present situation is the protection of the police officer and others nearby, and it must therefore be confined in scope to an intrusion reasonably designed to discover guns, knives, clubs, or other hidden instruments for the assault of the police officer.

The scope of the search in this case presents no serious problem in light of these standards. Officer McFadden patted down the outer clothing of petitioner and his two companions. He did not place his hands in their pockets or under the outer surface of their garments until he had felt weapons, and then he merely reached for and removed the guns. He never did invade Katz's person beyond the outer surfaces of his clothes, since he discovered nothing in his pat down which might have been a weapon. Officer McFadden confined his search strictly to what was minimally necessary to learn whether the men were armed and to disarm them once he discovered the weapons. He did not conduct a general exploratory search for whatever evidence of criminal activity he might find.

V.

We conclude that the revolver seized from Terry was properly admitted in evidence against him. At the time he seized petitioner and searched him for weapons, Officer McFadden had reasonable grounds to believe that petitioner was armed and dangerous, and it was necessary for the protection of himself and others to take swift measures to discover the true facts and neutralize the threat of harm if it materialized. The policeman carefully restricted his search to what was appropriate to the discovery of the particular items which he sought. Each case of this sort will, of course, have to be decided on its own facts. We merely hold today that where a police officer observes unusual conduct which leads him reasonably to conclude in light of his experience that criminal activity may be afoot and that the persons with whom he is dealing may be armed and presently dangerous; where in the course of investigating this behavior he identifies himself as a policeman and makes reasonable inquiries; and where nothing in the initial stages of the encounter serves to dispel his reasonable fear for his own or others' safety, he is entitled for the protection of himself and others in the area to conduct a carefully limited search of the outer clothing of such persons in an attempt to discover weapons which might be used to assault him. Such a search is a reasonable search under the Fourth Amendment, and any weapons seized may properly be introduced in evidence against the person from whom they were taken.

Affirmed.

* * *

MR. JUSTICE HARLAN, concurring.

While I unreservedly agree with the Court's ultimate holding in this case, I am constrained to fill in a few gaps, as I see them, in its opinion. I do this because what is said by this Court today will serve as initial guidelines for law enforcement authorities and courts throughout the land as this important new field of law develops....

If the State of Ohio were to provide that police officers could, on articulable suspicion less than probable cause, forcibly frisk and disarm persons thought to be carrying concealed weapons, I would have little doubt that action taken pursuant to such authority could be constitutionally reasonable. Concealed weapons create an immediate and severe danger to the public, and though that danger might not warrant routine general weapons checks, it could well warrant action on less than a "probability." I mention this line of analysis because I think it vital to point out that it cannot be applied in this case. On the record before us Ohio has not clothed its policemen with routine authority to frisk and disarm on suspicion; in the absence of state authority, policemen have no more right to "pat down" the outer clothing of passers-by, or of persons to whom they address casual questions, than does any other citizen....

The state courts held, instead, that when an officer is lawfully confronting a possibly hostile person in the line of duty he has a right, springing only from the necessity of the situation and not from any broader right to disarm, to frisk for his own protection. This holding, with which I agree and with which I think the Court agrees, offers the only satisfactory basis I can think of for affirming this conviction. The holding has, however, two logical corollaries that I do not think the Court has fully expressed.

In the first place, if the frisk is justified in order to protect the officer during an encounter with a citizen, the officer must first have constitutional grounds to insist on an encounter, to make a *forcible* stop. Any person, including a policeman, is at liberty to avoid a person he considers dangerous. If and when a policeman has a right instead to disarm such a person for his own protection, he must first have a right not to avoid him but to be in his presence. That right must be more than the liberty (again, possessed by every citizen) to address questions to other persons, for ordinarily the person addressed has an equal right to ignore his interrogator and walk away; he certainly need not submit to a frisk for the questioner's protection. I would make it perfectly clear that the right to frisk in this case depends upon the reasonableness of a forcible stop to investigate a suspected crime.

Where such a stop is reasonable, however, the right to frisk must be immediate and automatic if the reason for the stop is, as here, an articulable suspicion of a crime of violence. Just as a full search incident to a lawful arrest requires no additional justification, a limited frisk incident to a lawful stop must often be rapid and routine. There is no reason why an officer, rightfully but forcibly confronting a person suspected of a serious crime, should have to ask one question and take the risk that the answer might be a bullet.

The facts of this case are illustrative of a proper stop and an incident frisk. Officer McFadden had no probable cause to arrest Terry for anything, but he had observed circumstances that would reasonably lead an experienced, prudent policeman to suspect that Terry was about to engage in burglary or robbery. His justifiable suspicion afforded a proper constitutional basis for accosting Terry, restraining his liberty of movement briefly, and addressing questions to him, and Officer McFadden did so. When he did, he had no reason whatever to suppose that Terry might be armed, apart from the fact that he suspected him of planning a violent crime. McFadden asked Terry his name, to which Terry "mumbled something." Whereupon McFadden, without asking Terry to speak louder and without giving him any chance to explain his presence or his actions, forcibly frisked him.

I would affirm this conviction for what I believe to be the same reasons the Court relies on. I would, however, make explicit what I think is implicit in affirmance on the present facts. Officer McFadden's right to interrupt Terry's freedom of movement and invade his privacy arose only because circumstances warranted forcing an encounter with Terry in an effort to prevent or investigate a crime. Once that forced encounter was justified, however, the officer's right to take suitable measures for his own safety followed automatically.

Upon the foregoing premises, I join the opinion of the Court.

MR. JUSTICE WHITE, concurring.

I join the opinion of the Court, reserving judgment, however, on some of the Court's general remarks about the scope and purpose of the exclusionary rule which the Court has fashioned in the process of enforcing the Fourth Amendment.

Also, although the Court puts the matter aside in the context of this case, I think an additional word is in order concerning the matter of interrogation during an investigative stop. There is nothing in the Constitution which prevents a policeman from addressing questions to anyone on the streets. Absent special circumstances, the person approached may not be detained or frisked but may refuse to cooperate and go on his way. However, given the proper circumstances, such as those in this case, it seems to me the person may be briefly detained against his will while pertinent questions are directed to him. Of course, the person stopped is not obliged to answer, answers may not be compelled, and refusal to answer furnishes no basis for an arrest, although it may alert the officer to the need for continued observation. In my view, it is temporary detention, warranted by the circumstances, which chiefly justifies the protective frisk for weapons. Perhaps the frisk itself, where proper, will have beneficial results whether questions are asked or not. If weapons are found, an arrest will follow. If none are found, the frisk may nevertheless serve preventive ends because of its unmistakable message that suspicion has been aroused. But if the investigative stop is sustainable at all, constitutional rights are not necessarily violated if pertinent questions are asked and the person is restrained briefly in the process.

MR. JUSTICE DOUGLAS, dissenting.

I agree that petitioner was "seized" within the meaning of the Fourth Amendment. I also agree that frisking petitioner and his companions for guns was a "search." But it is a mystery how that "search" and that "seizure" can be constitutional by Fourth Amendment standards, unless there was "probable cause" to believe that (1) a crime had been committed or (2) a crime was in the process of being committed or (3) a crime was about to be committed.

The opinion of the Court disclaims the existence of "probable cause." If loitering were an issue and that was the offense charged, there would be "probable cause" shown. But the crime here is carrying concealed weapons; and there is no basis for concluding that the officer had "probable cause" for believing that crime was being committed. Had a warrant been sought, a magistrate would, therefore, have been unauthorized to issue one, for he can act only if there is a showing of "probable cause." We hold today that the police have greater authority to make a "seizure" and conduct a "search" than a judge has to authorize such action. We have said precisely the opposite over and over again.

In other words, police officers, up to today have been permitted to effect arrests or searches without warrants only when the facts within their personal knowledge would satisfy the constitutional standard of *probable cause.* At the time of their "seizure" without a warrant they must possess facts concerning the person arrested that would have satisfied a magistrate that "probable cause" was indeed present. The term "probable cause" rings a bell of certainty that is not sounded by phrases such as "reasonable suspicion." Moreover, the meaning of "probable cause" is deeply imbedded in our constitutional history. As we stated in Henry v. United States, 361 U.S. 98, 100–102, 80 S.Ct. 168, 171.

"The requirement of probable cause has roots that are deep in our history. The general warrant, in which the name of the person to be arrested was left blank, and the writs of assistance, against which James Otis inveighed, both perpetuated the oppressive practice of allowing the police to arrest and search on suspicion. Police control took the place of judicial control, since no showing of 'probable cause' before a magistrate was required.

* * *

"That philosophy [rebelling against these practices] later was reflected in the Fourth Amendment. And as the early American decisions both before and immediately after its adoption show, common rumor or report, suspicion, or even 'strong reason to suspect' was not adequate to support a warrant for arrest. And that principle has survived to this day.

* * *

"It is important, we think, that this requirement [of probable cause] be strictly enforced, for the standard set by the Constitution protects both the officer and the citizen. If the officer acts with probable cause, he is protected even though it turns out that the citizen is innocent.... And while a search without a warrant is, within limits, permissible if incident to a lawful arrest, if an arrest without a warrant is to support an incidental search, it must be made with probable cause.... This immunity of officers cannot fairly be enlarged without jeopardizing the privacy or security of the citizen."

The infringement on personal liberty of any "seizure" of a person can only be "reasonable" under the Fourth Amendment if we require the police to possess "probable cause" before they seize him. Only that line draws a meaningful distinction between an officer's mere inkling and the presence of facts within the officer's personal knowledge which would convince a reasonable man that the person seized has committed, is committing, or is about to commit a particular crime. "In dealing with probable cause, ... as the very name implies, we deal with probabilities. These are not technical; they are the factual and practical considerations of everyday life on which reasonable and prudent men, not legal technicians, act." Brinegar v. United States, 338 U.S. 160, 175, 69 S.Ct. 1302, 1310.

To give the police greater power than a magistrate is to take a long step down the totalitarian path. Perhaps such a step is desirable to cope with modern forms of lawlessness. But if it is taken, it should be the deliberate choice of the people through a constitutional amendment.

SIBRON v. NEW YORK

PETERS v. NEW YORK

Supreme Court of the United States, 1968.
392 U.S. 40, 88 S.Ct. 1889.

MR. CHIEF JUSTICE WARREN delivered the opinion of the Court.

These are companion cases to No. 67, Terry v. Ohio, decided today. They present related questions under the Fourth and Fourteenth Amendments, but the cases arise in the context of New York's "stop-and-frisk" law, N.Y.Code Crim.Proc. § 180–a. This statute provides:

> "1. A police officer may stop any person abroad in a public place whom he reasonably suspects is committing, has committed or is about to commit a felony or any of the crimes specified in section five hundred fifty-two of this chapter, and may demand of him his name, address and an explanation of his actions.
>
> "2. When a police officer has stopped a person for questioning pursuant to this section and reasonably suspects that he is in danger of life or limb, he may search such person for a dangerous weapon. If the police officer finds such a weapon or any other thing the possession of which may constitute a crime, he may take and keep it until the completion of the questioning, at which time he shall either return it, if lawfully possessed, or arrest such person."

The appellants, Sibron and Peters, were both convicted of crimes in New York state courts on the basis of evidence seized from their persons by police officers. The Court of Appeals of New York held that the evidence was properly admitted, on the ground that the searches which uncovered it were authorized by the statute....

The facts in these cases may be stated briefly. Sibron, the appellant in No. 63, was convicted of the unlawful possession of heroin.... At the hearing on the motion to suppress, Officer Martin testified that while he was patrolling his beat in uniform on March 9, 1965, he observed Sibron "continually from the hours of 4:00 P.M. to 12:00, midnight.... in the vicinity of 742 Broadway." He stated that during this period of time he saw Sibron in conversation with six or eight persons whom he (Patrolman Martin) knew from past experience to be narcotics addicts. The officer testified that he did not overhear any of these conversations, and that he did not see anything pass between Sibron and any of the others. Late in the evening Sibron entered a restaurant. Patrolman Martin saw Sibron speak with three more known addicts inside the restaurant. Once again, nothing was overheard and nothing was seen to pass between Sibron and the addicts. Sibron sat down and ordered pie and coffee, and as he was eating, Patrolman Martin approached him and told him to come outside. Once outside, the officer said to Sibron, "You know what I am after." According to the officer, Sibron "mumbled something and reached into his pocket." Simultaneously, Patrolman Martin thrust his hand into the same pocket, discovering several glassine envelopes, which, it turned out, contained heroin.

The State has had some difficulty in settling upon a theory for the admissibility of these envelopes of heroin. In his sworn complaint Patrolman Martin stated:

> "As the officer approached the defendant, the latter being in the direction of the officer and seeing him, he did put his hand in his left jacket pocket and pulled out a tinfoil envelope and did attempt to throw same to the ground. The officer never losing sight of the said envelope seized it from the def[endan]t's left hand, examined it and found it to contain ten glascine [*sic*] envelopes with a white substance alleged to be Heroin."

This version of the encounter, however, bears very little resemblance to Patrolman Martin's testimony at the hearing on the motion to suppress. In fact, he discarded the abandonment theory at the hearing.[1] Nor did the officer ever seriously suggest that he was in fear of bodily harm and that he searched Sibron in self-protection to find weapons.[2]

The prosecutor's theory at the hearing was that Patrolman Martin had probable cause to believe that Sibron was in possession of narcotics because he had seen him conversing with a number of known addicts over an eight-hour period. In the absence of any knowledge on Patrolman Martin's part concerning the nature of the intercourse between Sibron and the addicts, however, the trial court was inclined to grant the motion to suppress. As the judge stated, "All he knows about the unknown men: They are narcotics addicts. They might have been talking about the World Series. They might have been talking about prize fights." The prosecutor, however, reminded the judge that Sibron had admitted on the stand, in Patrolman Martin's absence, that he had been talking to the addicts about narcotics. Thereupon, the trial judge

1. Patrolman Martin stated several times that he put his hand into Sibron's pocket and seized the heroin before Sibron had any opportunity to remove his own hand from the pocket. The trial court questioned him on this point:

> "Q. Would you say at that time that he reached into his pocket and handed the packets to you? Is that what he did or did he drop the packets?
>
> "A. He did not drop them. *I do not know what his intentions were.* He pushed his hand into his pocket.
>
> "Mr. Joseph [Prosecutor]: You intercepted it; didn't you, Officer?
>
> "The Witness: Yes." (Emphasis added.)

It is of course highly unlikely that Sibron, facing the officer at such close quarters, would have tried to remove the heroin from his pocket and throw it to the ground in the hope that he could escape responsibility for it.

2. The possibility that Sibron, who never, so far as appears from the record, offered any resistance, might have posed a danger to Patrolman Martin's safety was never even discussed as a potential justification for the search. The only mention of weapons by the officer in his entire testimony came in response to a leading question by Sibron's counsel, when Martin stated that he "thought he [Sibron] might have been" reaching for a gun. Even so, Patrolman Martin did not accept this suggestion by the opposition regarding the reason for his action; the discussion continued upon the plain premise that he had been looking for narcotics all the time.

changed his mind and ruled that the officer had probable cause for an arrest.

Section 180–a, the "stop-and-frisk" statute, was not mentioned at any point in the trial court. The Appellate Term of the Supreme Court affirmed the conviction without opinion. In the Court of Appeals of New York, Sibron's case was consolidated with the *Peters* case, No. 74. The Court of Appeals held that the search in *Peters* was justified under the statute, but it wrote no opinion in Sibron's case. The dissents of Judges Fuld and Van Voorhis, however, indicate that the court rested its holding on § 180–a. At any rate, in its Brief in Opposition to the Jurisdictional Statement in this Court, the State sought to justify the search on the basis of the statute. After we noted probable jurisdiction, the District Attorney for Kings County confessed error.

Peters, the appellant in No. 74, was convicted of possessing burglary tools under circumstances evincing an intent to employ them in the commission of a crime. Officer Samuel Lasky of the New York City Police Department testified at the hearing on the motion that he was at home in his apartment in Mount Vernon, New York, at about 1 p.m. on July 10, 1964. He had just finished taking a shower and was drying himself when he heard a noise at his door. His attempt to investigate was interrupted by a telephone call, but when he returned and looked through the peephole into the hall, Officer Lasky saw "two men tiptoeing out of the alcove toward the stairway." He immediately called the police, put on some civilian clothes and armed himself with his service revolver. Returning to the peephole, he saw "a tall man tiptoeing away from the alcove and followed by this shorter man, Mr. Peters, toward the stairway." Officer Lasky testified that he had lived in the 120-unit building for 12 years and that he did not recognize either of the men as tenants. Believing that he had happened upon the two men in the course of an attempted burglary,[3] Officer Lasky opened his door, entered the hallway and slammed the door loudly behind him. This precipitated a flight down the stairs on the part of the two men,[4] and Officer Lasky gave chase. His apartment was located on the sixth floor, and he apprehended Peters between the fourth and fifth floors. Grabbing Peters by the collar, he continued down another flight in unsuccessful pursuit of the other man. Peters explained his presence in the building to Officer Lasky by saying that he was visiting a girl friend. However,

3. Officer Lasky testified that when he called the police immediately before leaving his apartment, he "told the Sergeant at the desk that two burglars were on my floor."

4. Officer Lasky testified that when he emerged from his apartment, "I slammed the door, I had my gun and I ran down the stairs after them." A sworn affidavit of the Assistant District Attorney, which was before the trial court when it ruled on the motion to suppress, stated that when apprehended Peters was "fleeing down the steps of the building." The trial court explicitly took note of the flight of Peters and his companion as a factor contributing to Officer Lasky's "reasonable suspicion" of them:

"We think the testimony at the hearing does not require further laboring of this aspect of the matter, unless one is to believe that it is legitimately normal for a man to tip-toe about in the public hall of an apartment house while on a visit to his unidentified girl-friend, and, when observed by another tenant, to rapidly descend by stairway in the presence of elevators."

he declined to reveal the girl friend's name, on the ground that she was a married woman. Officer Lasky patted Peters down for weapons, and discovered a hard object in his pocket. He stated at the hearing that the object did not feel like a gun, but that it might have been a knife. He removed the object from Peters' pocket. It was an opaque plastic envelope, containing burglar's tools.

The trial court explicitly refused to credit Peters' testimony that he was merely in the building to visit his girl friend. It found that Officer Lasky had the requisite "reasonable suspicion" of Peters under § 180–a to stop him and question him. It also found that Peters' response was "clearly unsatisfactory," and that "under the circumstances Lasky's action in frisking Peters for a dangerous weapon was reasonable, even though Lasky was himself armed." It held that the hallway of the apartment building was a "public place" within the meaning of the statute. The Appellate Division of the Supreme Court affirmed without opinion. The Court of Appeals also affirmed, essentially adopting the reasoning of the trial judge, with Judges Fuld and Van Voorhis dissenting separately....

III.

The parties on both sides of these two cases have urged that the principal issue before us is the constitutionality of § 180–a "on its face." We decline, however, to be drawn into what we view as the abstract and unproductive exercise of laying the extraordinarily elastic categories of § 180–a next to the categories of the Fourth Amendment in an effort to determine whether the two are in some sense compatible. The constitutional validity of a warrantless search is pre-eminently the sort of question which can only be decided in the concrete factual context of the individual case....

Section 180–a, deals with the substantive validity of certain types of seizures and searches without warrants. It purports to authorize police officers to "stop" people, "demand" explanations of them and "search [them] for dangerous weapon[s]" in certain circumstances upon "reasonable suspicion" that they are engaged in criminal activity and that they represent a danger to the policeman. The operative categories of § 180–a are not the categories of the Fourth Amendment, and they are susceptible of a wide variety of interpretations. New York is, of course, free to develop its own law of search and seizure to meet the needs of local law enforcement, see Ker v. California, 374 U.S. 23, 34, 83 S.Ct. 1623, 1630 (1963), and in the process it may call the standards it employs by any names it may choose. It may not, however, authorize police conduct which trenches upon Fourth Amendment rights, regardless of the labels which it attaches to such conduct. The question in this Court upon review of a state-approved search or seizure "is not whether the search [or seizure] was authorized by state law. The question is rather whether the search was reasonable under the Fourth Amendment. Just as a search authorized by state law may be an unreasonable one under that amendment, so may a search not expressly authorized by state law be justified as a constitutionally reasonable one." Cooper v. California, 386 U.S. 58, 61, 87 S.Ct. 788, 790 (1967).

Accordingly, we make no pronouncement on the facial constitutionality of § 180–a. The constitutional point with respect to a statute of this peculiar sort, as the Court of Appeals of New York recognized, is "not so much ... the language employed as ... the conduct it authorizes." People v. Peters, 18 N.Y.2d 238, 245, 219 N.E.2d 595, 599, 273 N.Y.S.2d 217, 222 (1966). We have held today in Terry v. Ohio, that police conduct of the sort with which § 180–a deals must be judged under the Reasonable Search and Seizure Clause of the Fourth Amendment. The inquiry under that clause may differ sharply from the inquiry set up by the categories of § 180–a. Our constitutional inquiry would not be furthered here by an attempt to pronounce judgment on the words of the statute. We must confine our review instead to the reasonableness of the searches and seizures which underlie these two convictions.

IV.

Turning to the facts of Sibron's case, it is clear that the heroin was inadmissible in evidence against him. The prosecution has quite properly abandoned the notion that there was probable cause to arrest Sibron for any crime at the time Patrolman Martin accosted him in the restaurant, took him outside and searched him. The officer was not acquainted with Sibron and had no information concerning him. He merely saw Sibron talking to a number of known narcotics addicts over a period of eight hours. It must be emphasized that Patrolman Martin was completely ignorant regarding the content of these conversations, and that he saw nothing pass between Sibron and the addicts. So far as he knew, they might indeed "have been talking about the World Series." The inference that persons who talk to narcotics addicts are engaged in the criminal traffic in narcotics is simply not the sort of reasonable inference required to support an intrusion by the police upon an individual's personal security. Nothing resembling probable cause existed until after the search had turned up the envelopes of heroin. It is axiomatic that an incident search may not precede an arrest and serve as part of its justification. Thus the search cannot be justified as incident to a lawful arrest.

If Patrolman Martin lacked probable cause for an arrest, however, his seizure and search of Sibron might still have been justified at the outset if he had reasonable grounds to believe that Sibron was armed and dangerous. Terry v. Ohio. We are not called upon to decide in this case whether there was a "seizure" of Sibron inside the restaurant antecedent to the physical seizure which accompanied the search. The record is unclear with respect to what transpired between Sibron and the officer inside the restaurant. It is totally barren of any indication whether Sibron accompanied Patrolman Martin outside in submission to a show of force or authority which left him no choice, or whether he went voluntarily in a spirit of apparent cooperation with the officer's investigation. In any event, this deficiency in the record is immaterial, since Patrolman Martin obtained no new information in the interval between his initiation of the encounter in the restaurant and his physical seizure and search of Sibron outside.

Although the Court of Appeals of New York wrote no opinion in this case, it seems to have viewed the search here as a self-protective search for weapons and to have affirmed on the basis of § 180–a, which authorizes such a search when the officer "reasonably suspects that he is in danger of life or limb." The Court of Appeals has, at any rate, justified searches during field interrogation on the ground that "the answer to the question propounded by the policeman may be a bullet; in any case the exposure to danger could be very great." People v. Rivera, 14 N.Y.2d 441, 446, 201 N.E.2d 32, 35, 252 N.Y.S.2d 458, 463 (1964), cert. denied, 379 U.S. 978, 85 S.Ct. 679 (1965). But the application of this reasoning to the facts of this case proves too much. The police officer is not entitled to seize and search every person whom he sees on the street or of whom he makes inquiries. Before he places a hand on the person of a citizen in search of anything, he must have constitutionally adequate reasonable grounds for doing so. In the case of the self-protective search for weapons, he must be able to point to particular facts from which he reasonably inferred that the individual was armed and dangerous. Terry v. Ohio, supra. Patrolman Martin's testimony reveals no such facts. The suspect's mere act of talking with a number of known narcotics addicts over an eight-hour period no more gives rise to reasonable fear of life or limb on the part of the police officer than it justifies an arrest for committing a crime. Nor did Patrolman Martin urge that when Sibron put his hand in his pocket, he feared that he was going for a weapon and acted in self-defense. His opening statement to Sibron—"You know what I am after"—made it abundantly clear that he sought narcotics, and his testimony at the hearing left no doubt that he thought there were narcotics in Sibron's pocket.

Even assuming *arguendo* that there were adequate grounds to search Sibron for weapons, the nature and scope of the search conducted by Patrolman Martin were so clearly unrelated to that justification as to render the heroin inadmissible. The search for weapons approved in *Terry* consisted solely of a limited patting of the outer clothing of the suspect for concealed objects which might be used as instruments of assault. Only when he discovered such objects did the officer in *Terry* place his hands in the pockets of the men he searched. In this case, with no attempt at an initial limited exploration for arms, Patrolman Martin thrust his hand into Sibron's pocket and took from him envelopes of heroin. His testimony shows that he was looking for narcotics, and he found them. The search was not reasonably limited in scope to the accomplishment of the only goal which might conceivably have justified its inception—the protection of the officer by disarming a potentially dangerous man. Such a search violates the guarantee of the Fourth Amendment, which protects the sanctity of the person against unreasonable intrusions on the part of all government agents.

We think it is equally clear that the search in Peters' case was wholly reasonable under the Constitution. The Court of Appeals of New York held that the search was made legal by § 180–a, since Peters was "abroad in a public place," and since Officer Lasky was reasonably suspicious of his activities and, once he had stopped Peters, reasonably suspected that he was in danger of life or limb, even though he held Peters at gun point. This may be the justification for the search under state law. We think, however, that for purposes of the Fourth Amendment the search was properly incident to a lawful arrest. By the time Officer Lasky caught up with Peters on the stairway between the fourth and fifth floors of the apartment building, he had probable cause to arrest him for attempted burglary. The officer heard strange noises at his door which apparently led him to believe that someone sought to force entry. When he investigated these noises he saw two men, whom he had never seen before in his 12 years in the building, tiptoeing furtively about the hallway. They were still engaged in these maneuvers after he called the police and dressed hurriedly. And when Officer Lasky entered the hallway, the men fled down the stairs. It is difficult to conceive of stronger grounds for an arrest, short of actual eyewitness observation of criminal activity. As the trial court explicitly recognized, deliberately furtive actions and flight at the approach of strangers or law officers are strong indicia of *mens rea,* and when coupled with specific knowledge on the part of the officer relating the suspect to the evidence of crime, they are proper factors to be considered in the decision to make an arrest.

As we noted in Sibron's case, a search incident to a lawful arrest, may not precede the arrest and serve as part of its justification. It is a question of fact precisely when, in each case, the arrest took place. Rios v. United States, 364 U.S. 253, 261–262, 80 S.Ct. 1431, 1436, 1437 (1960). And while there was some inconclusive discussion in the trial court concerning when Officer Lasky "arrested" Peters, it is clear that the arrest had for purposes of constitutional justification already taken place before the search commenced. When the policeman grabbed Peters by the collar, he abruptly "seized" him and curtailed his freedom of movement on the basis of probable cause to believe that he was engaged in criminal activity. At that point he had the authority to search Peters, and the incident search was obviously justified "by the need to seize weapons and other things which might be used to assault an officer or effect an escape, as well as by the need to prevent the destruction of evidence of the crime." Preston v. United States, 376 U.S. 364, 367, 84 S.Ct. 881, 883 (1964). Moreover, it was reasonably limited in scope by these purposes. Officer Lasky did not engage in an unrestrained and thorough-going examination of Peters and his personal effects. He seized him to cut short his flight, and he searched him primarily for weapons. While patting down his outer clothing, Officer Lasky discovered an object in his pocket which might have been used as a weapon. He seized it and discovered it to be a potential instrument of the crime of burglary.

We have concluded that Peters' conviction fully comports with the commands of the Fourth and Fourteenth Amendments, and must be affirmed. The conviction in No. 63, however, must be reversed, on the ground that the heroin was unconstitutionally admitted in evidence against the appellant.

It is so ordered.

MR. JUSTICE BLACK, concurring and dissenting.

I concur in the affirmance of the judgment against Peters but dissent from the reversal of No. 63, Sibron v. New York and would affirm this conviction....

* * *

First. I think there was probable cause for the policeman to believe that when Sibron reached his hand to his coat pocket, Sibron had a dangerous weapon which he might use if it were not taken away from him.... It seems to me to be a reasonable inference that when Sibron, who had been approaching and talking to addicts for eight hours, reached his hand quickly to his left coat pocket, he might well be reaching for a gun. And as the Court has emphasized today in its opinions in the other stop and frisk cases, a policeman under such circumstances has to act in a split second; delay may mean death for him. No one can know when an addict may be moved to shoot or stab, and particularly when he moves his hand hurriedly to a pocket where weapons are known to be habitually carried, it behooves an officer who wants to live to act at once as this officer did. It is true that the officer might also have thought Sibron was about to get heroin instead of a weapon. But the law enforcement officers all over the Nation have gained little protection from the courts through opinions here if they are now left helpless to act in self defense when a man associating intimately and continuously with addicts, upon meeting an officer, shifts his hand immediately to a pocket where weapons are constantly carried.

* * *

Second. I think also that there was sufficient evidence here on which to base findings that after recovery of the heroin, in particular, an officer could reasonably believe there was probable cause to charge Sibron with violating New York's narcotics laws. As I have previously argued, there was, I think, ample evidence to give the officer probable cause to believe Sibron had a dangerous weapon and that he might use it. Under such circumstances the officer had a right to search him in the very limited fashion he did here. Since, therefore, this was a reasonable and justified search, the use of the heroin discovered by it was admissible in evidence.

I would affirm.

MR. JUSTICE HARLAN, concurring in the results.

I fully agree with the results the Court has reached in these cases....

* * *

Turning to the individual cases, I agree that the conviction in No. 63, *Sibron,* should be reversed, and would do so upon the premises of *Terry*....

The considerable confusion that has surrounded the "search" or "frisk" of Sibron that led to the actual recovery of the heroin seems to me irrelevant for our purposes. Officer Martin repudiated his first statement, which might conceivably have indicated a theory of "abandonment". No matter which of the other theories is adopted, it is clear that there was at least a forcible frisk, comparable to that which occurred in *Terry,* which requires constitutional justification.

Since carrying heroin is a crime in New York, probable cause to believe Sibron was carrying heroin would also have been probable cause to arrest him. As the Court says, Officer Martin clearly had neither. Although Sibron had had conversations with several known addicts, he had done nothing, during the several hours he was under surveillance, that made it "probable" that he was either carrying heroin himself or engaging in transactions with these acquaintances.

Nor were there here reasonable grounds for a *Terry*-type "stop" short of an arrest....

The forcible encounter between Officer Martin and Sibron did not meet the *Terry* reasonableness standard. In the first place, although association with known criminals may, I think, properly be a factor contributing to the suspiciousness of circumstances, it does not, entirely by itself, create suspicion adequate to support a stop. There must be something at least in the activities of the person being observed or in his surroundings that affirmatively suggests particular criminal activity, completed, current, or intended. That was the case in *Terry,* but it palpably was not the case here. For eight continuous hours, up to the point when he interrupted Sibron eating a piece of pie, Officer Martin apparently observed not a single suspicious action and heard not a single suspicious word on the part of Sibron himself or any person with whom he associated. If anything, that period of surveillance pointed away from suspicion.

Furthermore, in *Terry,* the police officer judged that his suspect was about to commit a violent crime and that he had to assert himself in order to prevent it. Here there was no reason for Officer Martin to think that an incipient crime, or flight, or the destruction of evidence would occur if he stayed his hand; indeed, there was no more reason for him to intrude upon Sibron at the moment when he did than there had been four hours earlier, and no reason to think the situation would have changed four hours hence. While no hard-and-fast rule can be drawn, I would suggest that one important factor, missing here, that should be taken into account in determining whether there are reasonable grounds for a forcible intrusion is whether there is any need for immediate action.

For these reasons I would hold that Officer Martin lacked reasonable grounds to introduce forcibly upon Sibron. In consequence, the essential premise for the right to conduct a self-protective frisk was lacking. See my concurring opinion in *Terry.* I therefore find it unnecessary to reach two further troublesome questions. First, although I think that, as in *Terry,* the right to frisk is automatic when an officer lawfully stops a person suspected of a crime whose nature creates a substantial likelihood that he is armed, it is not clear that suspected possession of narcotics falls into this category. If the nature of the suspected offense creates no reasonable apprehension for the officer's safety, I would not permit him to frisk unless other circumstances did so. Second, I agree with the Court that even where a self-protective frisk is proper, its scope should be limited to what is adequate for its purposes. I see no need here to resolve the question whether this frisk exceeded those bounds.

Turning now to No. 74, *Peters,* I again agree that the conviction should be upheld, but here I would differ strongly and fundamentally with the Court's approach. The Court holds that the burglar's tools were recovered from Peters in a search incident to a lawful arrest. I do not think that Officer Lasky had anything close to probable cause to arrest Peters before he recovered the burglar's tools. Indeed, if probable cause existed here, I find it difficult to see why a different rationale was necessary to support the stop and frisk in *Terry* and why States such as New York have had to devote so much thought to the constitutional problems of field interrogation. This case will be the latest in an exceedingly small number of cases in this Court indicating what suffices for probable cause. While, as the Court noted in *Terry,* the influence of this Court on police tactics "in the field" is necessarily limited, the influence of a decision here on hundreds of courts and magistrates who have to decide whether there is probable cause for a real arrest or a full search will be large.

Officer Lasky testified that at 1 o'clock in the afternoon he heard a noise at the door to his apartment. He did not testify, nor did any state court conclude, that this "led him to believe that someone sought to force entry." He looked out into the public hallway and saw two men whom he did not recognize, surely not a strange occurrence in a large apartment building. One of them appeared to be tip-toeing. Lasky did not testify that the other man was tip-toeing or that either of them was behaving "furtively." Lasky left his apartment and ran to them, gun in hand. He did not testify that there was any "flight," though flight at the approach of gun-carrying strangers (Lasky was apparently not in uniform) is hardly indicative of *mens rea.*

Probable cause to arrest means evidence that would warrant a prudent and reasonable man (such as a magistrate, actual or hypothetical) in believing that a particular person has committed or is committing a crime. Officer Lasky had no extrinsic reason to think that a crime had been or was being committed, so whether it would have been proper to issue a warrant depends entirely on his statements of his observations of the men. Apart from his conclusory statement that he thought the men were burglars, he offered very little specific evidence. I find it hard to believe that if Peters had made good his escape and there were no report of a burglary in the neighborhood, this Court would hold it proper for a prudent neutral magistrate to issue a warrant for his arrest.

* * *

Although the articulable circumstances are somewhat less suspicious here than they were in *Terry,* I would affirm on the *Terry* ground that Officer Lasky had reasonable cause to make a forced stop. Unlike probable cause to arrest, reasonable grounds to stop do not depend on any degree of likelihood that a crime *has* been committed. An officer may forcibly intrude upon an incipient crime even where he could not make an arrest for the simple reason that there is nothing to arrest anyone for. Hence although Officer Lasky had small reason to believe that a crime had been committed, his right to stop Peters can be justified if he had a reasonable suspicion that he was about to attempt burglary.

It was clear that the officer had to act quickly if he was going to act at all, and, as stated above, it seems to me that where immediate action is obviously required, a police officer is justified in acting on rather less objectively articulable evidence than when there is more time for consideration of alternative courses of action. Perhaps more important, the Court's opinion in *Terry* emphasized the special qualifications of an experienced police officer. While "probable cause" to arrest or search has always depended on the existence of hard evidence that would persuade a "reasonable man," in judging on-the-street encounters it seems to me proper to take into account a police officer's trained instinctive judgment operating on a multitude of small gestures and actions impossible to reconstruct. Thus the statement by an officer that "he looked like a burglar to me" adds little to an affidavit filed with a magistrate in an effort to obtain a warrant. When the question is whether it was reasonable to take limited but forcible steps in a situation requiring immediate action, however, such a statement looms larger. A court is of course entitled to disbelieve the officer (who is subject to cross-examination), but when it believes him and when there are some articulable supporting facts, it is entitled to find action taken under fire to be reasonable.

Given Officer Lasky's statement of the circumstances, and crediting his experienced judgment as he watched the two men, the state courts were entitled to conclude, as they did, that Lasky forcibly stopped Peters on "reasonable suspicion." The frisk made incident to that stop was a limited one, which turned up burglar's tools. Although the frisk is constitutionally permitted only in order to protect the officer, if it is lawful the State is of course entitled to the use of any other contraband that appears.

For the foregoing reasons I concur in the results in these cases.

MR. JUSTICE WHITE, concurring.

... With respect to appellant Peters, I join the affirmance of his conviction, not because there was probable cause to arrest, a question I do not reach, but because there was probable cause to stop Peters for questioning and thus to frisk him for dangerous weapons. See my concurring opinion in Terry v. Ohio. While patting down Peters' clothing the officer "discovered an object in his pocket which might have been used as a weapon." That object turned out to be a package of burglar's tools. In my view those tools were properly admitted into evidence.

[The concurring opinions of JUSTICES DOUGLAS and FORTAS are omitted.]

UNITED STATES v. CORTEZ

Supreme Court of the United States, 1981.
449 U.S. 411, 101 S.Ct. 690.

CHIEF JUSTICE BURGER delivered the opinion of the Court.

We granted certiorari, 447 U.S. 904, 100 S.Ct. 2983, to consider whether objective facts and circumstantial evidence suggesting that a particular vehicle is involved in criminal activity may provide a sufficient basis to justify an investigative stop of that vehicle.

I

Late in 1976, Border Patrol officers patrolling a sparsely populated section of southern central Arizona found human footprints in the desert. In time, other sets of similar footprints were discovered in the same area. From these sets of footprints, it was deduced that, on a number of occasions, groups of from 8 to 20 persons had walked north from the Mexican border, across 30 miles of desert and mountains, over a fairly well-defined path, to an isolated point on Highway 86, an east-west road running roughly parallel to the Mexican border.

Officers observed that one recurring shoeprint bore a distinctive and repetitive V-shaped or chevron design. Because the officers knew from recorded experience that the area through which the groups passed was heavily trafficked by aliens illegally entering the country from Mexico, they surmised that a person, to whom they gave the case-name "Chevron," was guiding aliens illegally into the United States over the path marked by the tracks to a point where they could be picked up by a vehicle.

The tracks led into or over obstacles that would have been avoided in daylight. From this, the officers deduced that "Chevron" probably led his groups across the border and to the pickup point at night. Moreover, based upon the times when they had discovered the distinctive sets of tracks, they concluded that "Chevron" generally traveled during or near weekends and on nights when the weather was clear.

Their tracking disclosed that when "Chevron's" groups came within 50 to 75 yards of Highway 86, they turned right and walked eastward, parallel to the road. Then, approximately at highway milepost 122, the tracks would turn north and disappear at the road. From this pattern, the officers concluded that the aliens very likely were picked up by a vehicle—probably one approaching from the east, for after a long overland march the group was most likely to walk parallel to the highway *toward* the approaching vehicle. The officers also concluded that, after the pickup, the vehicle probably returned to the east, because it was unlikely that the group would be walking away from its ultimate destination.

On the Sunday night of January 30–31, 1977, Officers Gray and Evans, two Border Patrolmen who had been pursuing the investigation of "Chevron," were on duty in the Casa Grande area. The latest set of observed "Chevron" tracks had been made on Saturday night, January 15–16. January 30–31 was the first clear night after three days of rain. For these reasons, Gray and Evans decided there was a strong possibility that "Chevron" would lead aliens from the border to the highway that night.

The officers assumed that, if "Chevron" did conduct a group that night, he would not leave Mexico until after dark, that is, about 6 p.m. They knew from their experience that groups of this sort, traveling on foot, cover about two and a half to three miles an hour. Thus, the 30-mile journey would take from 8 to 12 hours. From this, the officers calculated that "Chevron" and his group would arrive at Highway 86 somewhere between 2 a.m. and 6 a.m. on January 31.

About 1 a.m., Gray and Evans parked their patrol car on an elevated location about 100 feet off Highway 86 at milepost 149, a point some 27 miles east of milepost 122. From their vantage point, the officers could observe the Altar Valley, an adjoining territory they had been assigned to watch that night, and they also could see vehicles passing on Highway 86. They estimated that it would take approximately one hour and a half for a vehicle to make a round trip from their vantage point to milepost 122. Working on the hypothesis that the pickup vehicle approached milepost 122 from the east and thereafter returned to its starting point, they focused upon vehicles that passed them from the east and, after about one hour and a half, passed them returning to the east.

Because "Chevron" appeared to lead groups of between 8 and 20 aliens at a time, the officers deduced that the pickup vehicle would be one that was capable of carrying that large a group without arousing suspicion. For this reason, and because they knew that certain types of vehicles were commonly used for smuggling sizable groups of aliens, they decided to limit their attention to vans, pickup trucks, other small trucks, campers, motor homes, and similar vehicles.

Traffic on Highway 86 at milepost 149 was normal on the night of the officers' surveillance. In the 5-hour period between 1 a.m. and 6 a.m., 15 to 20 vehicles passed the officers heading west, toward milepost 122. Only two of them—both pickup trucks with camper shells—were of the kind that the officers had concluded "Chevron" would likely use if he was to carry aliens that night. One, a distinctively colored pickup truck with a camper shell, passed for the first time at 4:30 a.m. Officer Gray was able to see and record only a partial license number, "GN 88—." At 6:12 a.m., almost exactly the estimated one hour and a half later, a vehicle looking like this same pickup passed them again, this time heading east.

The officers followed the pickup and were satisfied from its license plate, "GN 8804," that it was the same vehicle that had passed at 4:30 a.m. At that point, they flashed their police lights and intercepted the vehicle. Respondent Jesus Cortez was the driver and owner of the pickup; respondent Pedro Hernandez-Loera was sitting in the passenger's seat. Hernandez-Loera was wearing shoes with soles matching the distinctive "chevron" shoeprint.

The officers identified themselves and told Cortez they were conducting an immigration check. They asked if he was carrying any passengers in the camper. Cortez told them he had picked up some hitchhikers, and he proceeded to open the back of the camper. In the camper, there were six illegal aliens. The officers then arrested the respondents.

Cortez and Hernandez-Loera were charged with six counts of transporting illegal aliens in violation of 8 U.S.C. § 1324(a). By pretrial motion, they sought to suppress the evidence obtained by Officers Gray and Evans as a result of stopping their vehicle. They argued that the officers did not have adequate cause to make the investigative stop. The District Court denied the motion. A jury found the respondents guilty as charged. They were sentenced to concurrent prison terms of five years on each of six counts. In addition, Hernandez-Loera was fined $12,000.

A divided panel of the Court of Appeals for the Ninth Circuit reversed, holding that the officers lacked a sufficient basis to justify the stop of the pickup. That court recognized that United States v. Brignoni-Ponce, 422 U.S. 873, 95 S.Ct. 2574 (1975), provides a standard governing investigative stops of the kind involved in this case, stating:

> "The quantum of cause necessary in ... cases [like this one] was established ... in United States v. Brignoni-Ponce.... '[O]fficers on roving patrol may stop vehicles only if they are aware of specific articulable facts, together with rational inferences from those facts, that reasonably warrant suspicion that the vehicles contain aliens who may be illegally in the country.' "

The court also recognized that "the ultimate question on appeal is whether the trial judge's finding that founded suspicion was present here was clearly erroneous." Here, because, in the view of the facts of the two judges constituting the majority, "[t]he officers did not have a valid basis for singling out the Cortez vehicle," and because the circumstances admitted "far too many innocent inferences to make the officers' suspicions reasonably warranted," ibid., the panel concluded that the stop of Cortez' vehicle was a violation of the respondents' rights under the Fourth Amendment. In dissent, Judge Chambers was persuaded that *Brignoni-Ponce* recognized the validity of permitting an officer to assess the facts in light of his past experience.

II

A

The Fourth Amendment applies to seizures of the person, including brief investigatory stops such as the stop of the vehicle here. Reid v. Georgia, 448 U.S. 438, 440, 100 S.Ct. 2752, 2753 (1980); United States v. Brignoni-Ponce, supra, at 878; Davis v. Mississippi, 394 U.S. 721, 89 S.Ct. 1394 (1969); Terry v. Ohio, 392 U.S. 1, 16–19, 88 S.Ct. 1868, 1877–1879 (1968). An investigatory stop must be justified by some objective manifestation that the person stopped is, or is about to be, engaged in criminal activity. Brown v. Texas, 443 U.S. 47, 51, 99 S.Ct. 2637, 2640 (1979); Delaware v. Prouse, 440 U.S. 648, 661, 99 S.Ct. 1391, 1400 (1979); United States v. Brignoni-Ponce, supra, at 884; Adams v. Williams, 407 U.S. 143, 146–149, 92 S.Ct. 1921, 1923–1924 (1972); Terry v. Ohio, supra, 392 U.S., at 16–19, 88 S.Ct., at 1877–1879.

Courts have used a variety of terms to capture the elusive concept of what cause is sufficient to authorize police to stop a person. Terms like "articulable reasons" and "founded suspicion" are not self-defining; they fall short of providing clear guidance dispositive of the myriad factual situations that arise. But the essence of all that has been written is that the totality of the circumstances—the whole picture—must be taken into account. Based upon that whole picture the detaining officers must have a particularized and objective basis for suspecting the particular person stopped of criminal activity.

The idea that an assessment of the whole picture must yield a particularized suspicion contains two elements, each of which must be present before a stop is permissible. First, the assessment must be based upon all of the circumstances. The analysis proceeds with various objective observations, information from police reports, if such are available, and consideration of the modes or patterns of operation of certain kinds of lawbreakers. From these data, a trained officer draws inferences and makes deductions—inferences and deductions that might well elude an untrained person.

The process does not deal with hard certainties, but with probabilities. Long before the law of probabilities was articulated as such, practical people formulated certain commonsense conclusions about human behavior; jurors as factfinders are permitted to do the same—and so are law enforcement officers. Finally, the evidence thus collected must be seen and weighed not in terms of library analysis by scholars, but as understood by those versed in the field of law enforcement.

The second element contained in the idea that an assessment of the whole picture must yield a particularized suspicion is the concept that the process just described must raise a suspicion that the particular individual being stopped is engaged in wrongdoing. Chief Justice Warren, speaking for the Court in Terry v. Ohio, supra, said that "[t]his demand for specificity in the information upon which police action is predicated is *the central teaching of this Court's Fourth Amendment jurisprudence.*" (emphasis added).

B

This case portrays at once both the enormous difficulties of patrolling a 2,000-mile open border and the patient skills needed by those charged with halting illegal entry into this country. It implicates all of the principles just discussed—especially the imperative of recognizing that, when used by trained law enforcement officers, objective facts, meaningless to the untrained, can be combined with permissible deductions from such facts to form a legitimate basis for suspicion of a particular person and for action on that suspicion. We see here the kind of police work often suggested by judges and scholars as examples of appropriate and reasonable means of law enforcement. Here, fact on fact and clue on clue afforded a basis for the deductions and inferences that brought the officers to focus on "Chevron."

Of critical importance, the officers knew that the area was a crossing point for illegal aliens. They knew that it was common practice for persons to lead aliens through the desert from the border to Highway 86, where they could—by prearrangement—be picked up by a vehicle. Moreover, based upon clues they had discovered in the 2-month period prior to the events at issue here, they believed that one such guide, whom they designated "Chevron," had a particular pattern of operations.

By piecing together the information at their disposal, the officers tentatively concluded that there was a reasonable likelihood that "Chevron" would attempt to lead a group of aliens on the night of Sunday, January 30–31. Someone with chevron-soled shoes had led several groups of aliens in the previous two months, yet it had been two weeks since the latest crossing. "Chevron," they deduced, was therefore due reasonably soon. "Chevron" tended to travel on clear weekend nights. Because it had rained on the Friday and Saturday nights of the weekend involved here, Sunday was the only clear night of that weekend; the officers surmised it was therefore a likely night for a trip.

Once they had focused on that night, the officers drew upon other objective facts known to them to deduce a time frame within which "Chevron" and the aliens were likely to arrive. From what they knew of the practice of those who smuggle aliens, including what they knew of "Chevron's" previous activities, they deduced that the border crossing and journey through the desert would probably be at night. They knew the time when sunset would occur at the point of the border crossing; they knew about how long the trip would take. They were thus able to deduce that "Chevron" would likely arrive at the pickup point on Highway 86 in the time frame between 2 a.m. and 6 a.m.

From objective facts, the officers also deduced the probable point on the highway—milepost 122—at which "Chevron" would likely rendezvous with a pickup vehicle. They deduced from the direction taken by the sets of "Chevron" footprints they had earlier discovered that the pickup vehicle would approach the aliens from, and return with them to, a point east of milepost 122. They therefore staked out a position east of milepost 122 (at milepost 149) and watched for vehicles that passed them going west and then, approximately one and a half hours later, passed them again, this time going east.

From what they had observed about the previous groups guided by the person with "chevron" shoes, they deduced that "Chevron" would lead a group of 8 to 20 aliens. They therefore focused their attention on enclosed vehicles of that passenger capacity.

The analysis produced by Officers Gray and Evans can be summarized as follows: if, on the night upon which they believed "Chevron" was likely to travel, sometime between 2 a.m. and 6 a.m., a large enclosed vehicle was seen to make an east-west-east round trip to and from a deserted point (milepost 122) on a deserted road (Highway 86), the officers would stop the vehicle on the return trip. In a 4-hour period the officers observed only one vehicle meeting that description. And it is not surprising that when they stopped the vehicle on its return trip it contained "Chevron" and several illegal aliens.

C

The limited purpose of the stop in this case was to question the occupants of the vehicle about their citizenship and immigration status and the reasons for the round trip in a short timespan in a virtually deserted area. No search of the camper or any of its occupants occurred until after respondent Cortez voluntarily opened the back door of the camper; thus, only the stop, not the search is at issue here. The intrusion upon privacy associated with this stop was limited and was "reasonably related in scope to the justification for [its] initiation," Terry v. Ohio, 392 U.S., at 29, 88 S.Ct., at 1883.

We have recently held that stops by the Border Patrol may be justified under circumstances less than those constituting probable cause for arrest or search. United States v. Brignoni-Ponce, 422 U.S., at 880, 95 S.Ct., at 2579. Thus, the test is not whether Officers Gray and Evans had probable cause to conclude that the vehicle they stopped would contain "Chevron" and a group of illegal aliens. Rather the question is whether, based upon the whole picture, they, as experienced Border Patrol officers, could reasonably surmise that the particular vehicle they stopped was engaged in criminal activity. On this record, they could so conclude. Reversed.

[The concurring opinions of Justices Stewart and Marshall are omitted.]

ALABAMA v. WHITE

Supreme Court of the United States, 1990.
496 U.S. 325, 110 S.Ct. 2412.

JUSTICE WHITE delivered the opinion of the Court.

Based on an anonymous telephone tip, police stopped respondent's vehicle. A consensual search of the car revealed drugs. The issue is whether the tip, as corroborated by independent police work, exhibited sufficient indicia of reliability to provide reasonable suspicion to make the investigatory stop. We hold that it did.

On April 22, 1987, at approximately 3 p.m., Corporal B.H. Davis of the Montgomery Police Department received a telephone call from an anonymous person, stating that Vanessa White would be leaving 235–C Lynwood Terrace Apartments at a particular time in a brown Plymouth station wagon with the right taillight lens broken, that she would be going to Dobey's Motel, and that she would be in possession of about an ounce of cocaine inside a brown attaché case. Corporal Davis and his partner, Corporal P.A. Reynolds, proceeded to the Lynwood Terrace Apartments. The officers saw a brown Plymouth station wagon with a broken right taillight in the parking lot in front of the 235 building. The officers observed respondent leave the 235 building, carrying nothing in her hands, and enter the station wagon. They followed the vehicle as it drove the most direct route to Dobey's Motel. When the vehicle reached the Mobile Highway, on which Dobey's Motel is located, Corporal Reynolds requested a patrol unit to stop the vehicle. The vehicle was stopped at approximately 4:18 p.m., just short of Dobey's Motel. Corporal Davis asked respondent to step to the rear of her car, where he informed her that she had been stopped because she was suspected of carrying cocaine in the vehicle. He asked if they could look for cocaine and respondent said they could look. The officers found a locked brown attaché case in the car and, upon request, respondent provided the combination to the lock. The officers found marijuana in the attaché case and placed respondent under arrest. During processing at the station, the officers found three milligrams of cocaine in respondent's purse.

Respondent was charged in Montgomery County court with possession of marijuana and possession of cocaine. The trial court denied respondent's motion to suppress and she pleaded guilty to the charges, reserving the right to appeal the denial of her suppression motion. The Court of Criminal Appeals of Alabama held that the officers did not have the reasonable suspicion necessary under *Terry v. Ohio* (1968), to justify the investigatory stop of respondent's car, and that the marijuana and cocaine were fruits of respondent's unconstitutional detention. The court concluded that respondent's motion to dismiss should have been granted and reversed her conviction. The Supreme Court of Alabama denied the State's petition for writ of certiorari, two justices dissenting.

* * *

Reasonable suspicion is a less demanding standard than probable cause not only in the sense that reasonable suspicion can be established with information that is different in quantity or content than that required to establish probable cause, but also in the sense that reasonable suspicion can arise from information that is less reliable than that required to show probable cause.... Reasonable suspicion, like probable cause, is dependent upon both the content of information possessed by police and its degree of reliability. Both factors—quantity and quality—are considered in the "totality of the circumstances—the whole picture," *United States v. Cortez* (1981), that must be taken into account when evaluating whether there is reasonable suspicion. Thus, if a tip has a relatively low degree of reliability, more information will be required to establish the requisite quantum of suspicion than would be required if the tip were more reliable. The *Gates v. Illinois* (1983) Court applied its totality of the circumstances approach in this manner, taking into account the facts known to the officers from personal observation, and giving the anonymous tip the weight it deserved in light of its indicia of reliability as established through independent police work. The same approach applies in the reasonable suspicion context, the only difference being the level of suspicion that must be established. Contrary to the court below, we conclude that when the officers stopped respondent, the anonymous tip had been sufficiently corroborated to furnish reasonable suspicion that respondent was engaged in criminal activity and that the investigative stop therefore did not violate the Fourth Amendment.

It is true that not every detail mentioned by the tipster was verified, such as the name of the woman leaving the building or the precise apartment from which she left; but the officers did corroborate that a woman left the 235 building and got into the particular vehicle that was described by the caller. With respect to the time of departure predicted by the informant, Corporal Davis testified that the caller gave a particular time when the woman would be leaving, but he did not state what that time was. He did testify that, after the call, he and his partner proceeded to the Lynwood Terrace Apartments to put the 235 building under surveillance. Given the fact that the officers proceeded to the indicated address immediately after the call and that respondent emerged not too long thereafter, it appears from the record before us that respondent's departure from the building was within the time frame predicted by the caller. As for the caller's prediction of respondent's destination, it is true that the officers stopped her just short of Dobey's Motel and did not know whether she would have pulled in or continued on past it. But given that the four-mile route driven by respondent was the most direct route possible to Dobey's Motel, but nevertheless involved several turns, we think respondent's destination was significantly corroborated.

The Court's opinion in *Gates* gave credit to the proposition that because an informant is shown to be right about some things, he is probably right about other facts that he has alleged, including the claim that the object of the tip is engaged in criminal activity. Thus, it is not unreasonable to conclude in this case that the independent corroboration by the police of significant aspects of the informer's predictions imparted some degree of reliability to the other allegations made by the caller.

We think it also important that, as in *Gates,* "the anonymous [tip] contained a range of details relating not just to easily obtained facts and conditions existing at the time of the tip, but to future actions of third parties ordinarily not easily predicted." The fact that the officers found a car precisely matching the caller's description in front of the 235 building is an example of the former. Anyone could have "predicted" that fact because it was a condition presumably existing at the time of the call. What was important was the caller's ability to predict respondent's *future behavior,* because it demonstrated inside information—a special familiarity with respondent's affairs. The general public would have had no way of knowing that respondent would shortly leave the building, get in the described car, and drive the most direct route to Dobey's Motel. Because only a small number of people are generally privy to an individual's itinerary, it is reasonable for police to believe that a person with access to such information is likely to also have access to reliable information about that individual's illegal activities. When significant aspects of the caller's predictions were verified, there was reason to believe not only that the caller was honest but also that he was well informed, at least well enough to justify the stop.

Although it is a close case, we conclude that under the totality of the circumstances the anonymous tip, as corroborated, exhibited sufficient indicia of reliability to justify the investigatory stop of respondent's car. . . .

JUSTICE STEVENS, with whom JUSTICE BRENNAN and JUSTICE MARSHALL join, dissenting.

Millions of people leave their apartments at about the same time every day carrying an attaché case and heading for a destination known to their neighbors. Usually, however, the neighbors do not know what the briefcase contains. An anonymous neighbor's prediction about somebody's time of departure and probable destination is anything but a reliable basis for assuming that the commuter is in possession of an illegal substance—particularly when the person is not even carrying the attaché case described by the tipster.

The record in this case does not tell us how often respondent drove from the Lynwood Terrace Apartments to Dobey's Motel; for all we know, she may have been a room clerk or telephone operator working the evening shift. It does not tell us whether Officer Davis made any effort to ascertain the informer's identity, his reason for calling, or the basis of his prediction about respondent's destination. Indeed, for all that this record tells us, the tipster may well have been another police officer who had a "hunch" that respondent might have cocaine in her attaché case.

Anybody with enough knowledge about a given person to make her the target of a prank, or to harbor a grudge against her, will certainly be able to formulate a tip about her like the one predicting Vanessa White's excursion. In addition, under the Court's holding, every citizen is subject to being seized and questioned by any officer who is prepared to testify that the warrantless stop was based on an anonymous tip predicting whatever conduct the officer just observed. Fortunately, the vast majority of those in our law enforcement community would not adopt such a practice. But the Fourth Amendment was intended to protect the citizen from the overzealous and unscrupulous officer as well as from those who are conscientious and truthful. This decision makes a mockery of that protection.

I respectfully dissent.

NOTE

The stop of a vehicle may seem relatively minor, although less so when the subsequent questioning concerns cocaine. Would the officers have had a right to frisk White on the basis of the information they had? Does reasonable suspicion of carrying an ounce of cocaine create reasonable suspicion that the individual is armed and dangerous?

Presumably if the tip had alleged that White was carrying a gun in her purse, and if the officers observed a purse following the stop, officers could have inspected the purse. Does the possibility of a greater intrusion make it harder to approve *White's* finding of reasonable suspicion based on what seems to be so little data?

FLORIDA v. BOSTICK

United States Supreme Court, 1991.
501 U.S. 429, 111 S.Ct. 2382.

[Two sheriff's department officers boarded a bus bound from Miami to Atlanta during a stopover in Fort Lauderdale. The officers had badges, insignias, and one of them held a "recognizable zipper bag, containing a pistol." Eyeing the passengers, without reasonable suspicion, they picked out passenger Terrance Bostick. They asked to inspect his ticket and his identification. Bostick cooperated. They returned his ticket and identification when nothing remarkable appeared. They then asked Bostick's permission to search his luggage, telling him they were narcotics agents in quest of drugs, and informing Bostick of his right to refuse consent, according to the Florida trial court's finding. Bostick agreed to the search. Officers discovered cocaine in one of his suitcases.

The Florida Supreme Court held that the police conduct constituted a seizure within the meaning of the Fourth Amendment. It held the seizure unlawful for want of reasonable seizure. The illegal detention invalidated the consent to search, according to the Florida Supreme Court.

The procedure used in *Bostick* was a method of drug investigation used with increasing frequency. Upon further review, the United States Supreme Court said that the sole issue was "whether a police encounter on a bus of the type described above necessarily constitutes a 'seizure' within the meaning of the Fourth Amendment."]

JUSTICE O'CONNOR delivered the opinion of the Court:

* * *

There is no doubt that if this same encounter had taken place before Bostick boarded the bus or in the lobby of the bus terminal, it would not rise to the level of a seizure. The Court has dealt with similar encounters in airports and has found them to be "the sort of consensual encounter[s] that implicat[e] no Fourth Amendment interest." *Florida v. Rodriguez* (1984). We have stated that even when officers have no basis for suspecting a particular individual, they may generally ask questions of that individual, see *INS v. Delgado* (1984); *Rodriguez,* ask to examine the individual's identification, see *Delgado, Royer* (plurality opinion); *United States v. Mendenhall* (1980); and request consent to search his or her luggage, see *Royer,* supra (plurality opinion)—as long as the police do not convey a message that compliance with their requests is required.

Bostick insists that this case is different because it took place in the cramped confines of a bus. A police encounter is much more intimidating in this setting, he argues, because police tower over a seated passenger and there is little room to move around.... Bostick was a passenger on a bus that was scheduled to depart. He would not have felt free to leave the bus even if the police had not been present. Bostick's movements were "confined" in a sense, but this was the natural result of his decision to take the bus; it says nothing about whether or not the police conduct at issue was coercive.

In this respect, the Court's decision in *INS v. Delgado,* is dispositive. At issue there was the INS' practice of visiting factories at random and questioning employees to determine whether any were illegal aliens. Several INS agents would stand near the building's exits, while other agents walked through the factory questioning workers. The Court acknowledged that the workers may not have been free to leave their worksite, but explained that this was not the result of police activity: "Ordinarily, when people are at work their freedom to move about has been meaningfully restricted, not by the actions of law enforcement officials, but by the workers' voluntary obligations to their employers." We concluded that there was no seizure because, even though the workers were not free to leave the building without being questioned, the agents' conduct should have given employees "no reason to believe that they would be detained if they gave truthful answers to the questions put to them or if they simply refused to answer."

The present case is analytically indistinguishable from *Delgado*. Like the workers in that case, Bostick's freedom of movement was restricted by a factor independent of police conduct—*i.e.,* by his being a passenger on a bus. Accordingly, the "free to leave" analysis on which Bostick relies is inapplicable. In such a situation, the appropriate inquiry is whether a reasonable person would feel free to decline the officers' requests or otherwise terminate the encounter.

* * *

The facts of this case, as described by the Florida Supreme Court, leave some doubt whether a seizure occurred. Two officers walked up to Bostick on the bus, asked him a few questions, and asked if they could search his bags. As we have explained, no seizure occurs when police ask questions of an individual, ask to examine the individual's identification, and request consent to search his or her luggage—so long as the officers do not convey a message that compliance with their requests is required. Here, the facts recited by the Florida Supreme Court indicate that the officers did not point guns at Bostick or otherwise threaten him and that they specifically advised Bostick that he could refuse consent.

Nevertheless, we refrain from deciding whether or not a seizure occurred in this case. The trial court made no express findings of fact, and the Florida Supreme Court rested its decision on a single fact—that the encounter took place on a bus—rather than on the totality of the circumstances. We remand so that the Florida courts may evaluate the seizure question under the correct legal standard. We do reject, however, Bostick's argument that he must have been seized because no reasonable person would freely consent to a search of luggage that he or she knows contains drugs. This argument cannot prevail because the "reasonable person" test presupposes an *innocent* person. See *Royer* (Blackmun, J., dissenting) ("The fact that [respondent] knew the search was likely to turn up contraband is of course irrelevant; the potential intrusiveness of the officers' conduct must be judged from the viewpoint of an innocent person in [his] position").

* * *

JUSTICE MARSHALL, joined by JUSTICES BLACKMUN and STEVENS, dissenting:

* * *

The question for this Court, then, is whether the suspicionless, dragnet-style sweep of buses in intrastate and interstate travel is consistent with the Fourth Amendment. The majority suggests that this latest tactic in the drug war is perfectly compatible with the Constitution. I disagree.

* * *

These facts exhibit all of the elements of coercion associated with a typical bus sweep. Two officers boarded the Greyhound bus on which respondent was a passenger while the bus, en route from Miami to Atlanta, was on a brief stop to pick up passengers in Fort Lauderdale. The officers made a visible display of their badges and wore bright green "raid" jackets bearing the insignia of the Broward County Sheriff's Department; one held a gun in a recognizable weapons pouch. These facts alone constitute an intimidating "show of authority." Once on board, the officers approached respondent, who was sitting in the back of the bus, identified themselves as narcotics officers and began to question him. One officer stood in front of respondent's seat, partially blocking the narrow aisle through which respondent would have been required to pass to reach the exit of the bus.

As far as is revealed by facts on which the Florida Supreme Court premised its decision, the officers did not advise respondent that he was free to break off this "interview." Inexplicably, the majority repeatedly stresses the trial court's implicit finding that the police officers advised respondent that he was free to refuse permission to search his travel bag. This aspect of the exchange between respondent and the police is completely irrelevant to the issue before us. For as the State concedes, and as the majority purports to "accept," *if* respondent was unlawfully seized when the officers approached him and initiated questioning, the resulting search was likewise unlawful no matter how well advised respondent was of his right to refuse it. Consequently, the issue is not whether a passenger in respondent's position would have felt free to deny consent to the search of his bag, but whether such a passenger—without being apprised of his rights—would have felt free to terminate the antecedent encounter with the police.

Unlike the majority, I have no doubt that the answer to this question is no. Apart from trying to accommodate the officers, respondent had only two options. First, he could have remained seated while obstinately refusing to respond to the officers' questioning. But in light of the intimidating show of authority that the officers made upon boarding the bus, respondent reasonably could have believed that such behavior would only arouse the officers' suspicions and intensify their interrogation. Indeed, officers who carry out bus sweeps like the one at issue here frequently admit that this is the effect of a passenger's refusal to cooperate. The majority's observation that a mere refusal to answer questions, "without more," does not give rise to a reasonable basis for seizing a passenger, is utterly beside the point, because a passenger unadvised of his rights and otherwise unversed in constitutional law *has no reason to know* that the police cannot hold his refusal to cooperate against him.

Second, respondent could have tried to escape the officers' presence by leaving the bus altogether. But because doing so would have required respondent to squeeze past the gun-wielding inquisitor who was blocking the aisle of the bus, this hardly seems like a course that respondent reasonably would have viewed as available to him. The majority lamely protests that nothing in the stipulated facts shows that the questioning officer "*point[ed]* [his] gu[n] at [respondent] or otherwise *threatened* him" with the weapon. Our decisions recognize the obvious point, however, that the choice of the police to "display" their weapons during an encounter exerts significant coercive pressure on the confronted citizen. We have never suggested that the police must go so far as to put a citizen in immediate apprehension of *being shot* before a court can take account of the intimidating effect of being questioned by an officer with weapon in hand.

Even if respondent had perceived that the officers would *let* him leave the bus, moreover, he could not reasonably have been expected to resort to this means of evading their intrusive questioning. For so far as respondent knew, the bus' departure from the terminal was imminent. Unlike a person approached by the police on the street, see *Michigan v. Chesternut,* supra, or at a bus or airport terminal after reaching his destination, see *United States v. Mendenhall,* supra, a passenger approached by the police at an intermediate point in a long bus journey cannot simply leave the scene and repair to a safe haven to avoid unwanted probing by law-enforcement officials. The vulnerability that an intrastate or interstate traveler experiences when confronted by the police outside of his "own familiar territory" surely aggravates the coercive quality of such an encounter.

* * *

Rather than requiring the police to justify the coercive tactics employed here, the majority blames respondent for his own sensation of constraint.... The police would remain free, for example, to approach passengers whom they have a reasonable, articulable basis to suspect of criminal wrongdoing. Alternatively, they could continue to confront passengers without suspicion so long as they took simple steps, like advising the passengers confronted of their right to decline to be questioned, to dispel the aura of coercion and intimidation that pervades such encounters. There is no reason to expect that such requirements would render the Nation's buses law-enforcement-free zones.

The majority attempts to gloss over the violence that today's decision does to the Fourth Amendment with empty admonitions. "If th[e] [war on drugs] is to be fought," the majority intones, "those who fight it must respect the rights of individuals, whether or not those individuals are suspected of having committed a crime." The majority's actions, however, speak louder than its words.

PENNSYLVANIA v. MIMMS

Supreme Court of the United States, 1977.
434 U.S. 106, 98 S.Ct. 330.

PER CURIAM.

. . . While on routine patrol, two Philadelphia police officers observed respondent Harry Mimms driving an automobile with an expired license plate. The officers stopped the vehicle for the purpose of issuing a traffic summons. One of the officers approached and asked respondent to step out of the car and produce his owner's card and operator's license. Respondent alighted, whereupon the officer noticed a large bulge under respondent's sports jacket. Fearing that the bulge might be a weapon, the officer frisked respondent and discovered in his waistband a .38-caliber revolver loaded with five rounds of ammunition. The other occupant of the car was also carrying a .32-caliber revolver. Respondent was immediately arrested and subsequently indicted for carrying a concealed deadly weapon and for unlawfully carrying a firearm without a license. . . .

In this case, unlike Terry v. Ohio, there is no question about the propriety of the initial restrictions on respondent's freedom of movement. Respondent was driving an automobile with expired license tags in violation of the Pennsylvania Motor Vehicle Code. Deferring for a moment the legality of the "frisk" once the bulge had been observed, we need presently deal only with the narrow question of whether the order to get out of the car, issued after the driver was lawfully detained, was reasonable and thus permissible under the Fourth Amendment. This inquiry must therefore focus not on the intrusion resulting from the request to stop the vehicle or from the later "pat-down," but on the incremental intrusion resulting from the request to get out of the car once the vehicle was lawfully stopped.

Placing the question in this narrowed frame, we look first to that side of the balance which bears the officer's interest in taking the action that he did. The State freely concedes the officer had no reason to suspect foul play from the particular driver at the time of the stop, there having been nothing unusual or suspicious about his behavior. It was apparently his practice to order all drivers out of their vehicles as a matter of course whenever they had been stopped for a traffic violation. The State argues that this practice was adopted as a precautionary measure to afford a degree of protection to the officer and that it may be justified on that ground. Establishing a face-to-face confrontation diminishes the possibility, otherwise substantial, that the driver can make unobserved movements; this, in turn, reduces the likelihood that the officer will be the victim of an assault.

We think it too plain for argument that the State's proffered justification—the safety of the officer—is both legitimate and weighty. "Certainly it would be unreasonable to require that police officers take unnecessary risks in the performance of their duties." Terry v. Ohio. And we have specifically recognized the inordinate risk confronting an officer as he approaches a person seated in an automobile. "According to one study, approximately 30% of police shootings occurred when a police officer approached a suspect seated in an automobile." Bristow, "Police Officer Shootings—A Tactical Evaluation." 54 Crim. LC & PS 93 (1963). We are aware that not all these assaults occur when issuing traffic summons, but we have before expressly declined to accept the argument that traffic violations necessarily involve less danger to officers than other types of confrontations. United States v. Robinson. Indeed, it appears "that a significant percentage of murders of police officers occurs when the officers are making traffic stops."

The hazard of accidental injury from passing traffic to an officer standing on the driver's side of the vehicle may also be appreciable in some situations. Rather than conversing while standing exposed to moving traffic, the officer prudently may prefer to ask the driver of the vehicle to step out of the car and off onto the shoulder of the road where the inquiry may be pursued with greater safety to both.

Against this important interest we are asked to weigh the intrusion into the driver's personal liberty occasioned not by the initial stop of the vehicle, which was admittedly justified, but by the order to get out of the car. We think this additional intrusion can only be described as de minimis. The driver is being asked to expose to view very little more of his person than is already exposed. The police have already lawfully decided that the driver shall be briefly detained; the only question is whether he shall spend that period sitting in the driver's seat of his car or standing alongside it. Not only is the insistence of the police on the latter choice not a "serious intrusion upon the sanctity of the person," but it hardly rises to the level of a " 'petty indignity.' " Terry v. Ohio. What is at most a mere inconvenience cannot prevail when balanced against legitimate concerns for the officer's safety.

There remains the second question of the propriety of the search once the bulge in the jacket was observed. We have as little doubt on this point as on the first; the answer is controlled by Terry v. Ohio. In that case we thought the officer justified in conducting a limited search for weapons once he had reasonably concluded that the person whom he had legitimately stopped might be armed and presently dangerous. Under the standard enunciated in that case—whether "the facts available to the officer at the moment of the seizure or the search 'warrant a man of reasonable caution in the belief' that the action taken was appropriate"—there is little question the officer was justified. The bulge in the jacket permitted the officer to conclude that Mimms was armed and thus posed a serious and present danger to the safety of the officer. In these circumstances, any man of "reasonable caution" would likely have conducted the "pat-down."

MR. JUSTICE MARSHALL, dissenting.

* * *

The "stop and frisk" in Terry was ... justified by the probability, not only that a crime was about to be committed, but also that the crime "would be likely to involve the use of weapons." The Court confined its holding to situations in which the officer believes "that the persons with whom he is dealing may be armed and presently dangerous" and "fear[s] for his own or others' safety." Such a situation was held to be present in Adams v. Williams....

In the instant case, the officer did not have even the slightest hint, prior to ordering respondent out of the car, that respondent might have a gun. As the Court notes, "the officer had no reason to suspect foul play." The car was stopped for the most routine of police procedures, the issuance of a summons for an expired license plate. Yet the Court holds that, once the officer had made this routine stop, he was justified in imposing the additional intrusion of ordering respondent out of the car, regardless of whether there was any individualized reason to fear respondent.

Such a result cannot be explained by Terry, which limited the nature of the intrusion by reference to the reason for the stop. The Court held that "the officer's action [must be] reasonably related in scope to the circumstances which justified the interference in the first place." In Terry there was an obvious connection, emphasized by the Court, between the officer's suspicion that an armed robbery was being planned and his frisk for weapons. In the instant case "the circumstance which justified the interference in the first place" was an expired license plate. There is simply no relation at all between that circumstance and the order to step out of the car.

MR. JUSTICE STEVENS, with whom MR. JUSTICE BRENNAN and MR. JUSTICE MARSHALL join, dissenting.

* * *

... the Court has based its legal ruling on a factual assumption about police safety that is dubious at best; second, the Court has created an entirely new legal standard of justification for intrusions on the liberty of the citizen.

Without any attempt to differentiate among the multitude of varying situations in which an officer may approach a person seated in an automobile, the Court characterizes the officer's risk as "inordinate" on the basis of this statement [that]

"According to one study, approximately 30% of police shootings occurred when a police officer approached a suspect seated in an automobile."

That statement does not fairly characterize the study to which it refers. Moreover, the study does not indicate that police officers can minimize the risk of being shot by ordering drivers stopped for routine traffic violations out of their cars. The study reviewed 110 selected police shootings that occurred in 1959, 1960, and 1961. In 35 of those cases, "officers were attempting to investigate, control, or pursue suspects who were in automobiles." Within the group of 35 cases, there were examples of officers who "were shot through the windshield or car body while their vehicle was moving"; examples in which "the officer was shot while dismounting from his vehicle or while approaching the suspect's vehicle"; and, apparently, instances in which the officer was shot by a passenger in the vehicle.

In only 28 of the 35 cases was the location of the suspect who shot the officer verified. In 12 of those cases the suspect was seated behind the wheel of the car, but that figure seems to include cases in which the shooting occurred before the officer had an opportunity to order the suspect to get out. In nine cases the suspect was outside the car talking to the officer when the shooting occurred.

These figures tell us very little about the risk associated with the routine traffic stop; and they lend no support to the Court's assumption that ordering the routine traffic offender out of his car significantly enhances the officer's safety. Arguably, such an order could actually aggravate the officer's danger because the fear of a search might cause a serious offender to take desperate action that would be unnecessary if he remained in the vehicle while being ticketed. Whatever the reason, it is significant that some experts in this area of human behavior strongly recommend that the police officer "never allow the violator to get out of the car. . . ."

Obviously, it is not my purpose to express an opinion on the safest procedure to be followed in making traffic arrests or to imply that the arresting officer faces no significant hazard, even in the apparently routine situation. I do submit, however, that no matter how hard we try we cannot totally eliminate the danger associated with law enforcement, and that before adopting a nationwide rule, we should give further consideration to the infinite variety of situations in which today's holding may be applied.

The Court cannot seriously believe that the risk to the arresting officer is so universal that his safety is *always* a reasonable justification for ordering a driver out of his car. The commuter on his way home to dinner, the parent driving children to school, the tourist circling the Capitol, or the family on a Sunday afternoon outing hardly pose the same threat as a driver curbed after a high speed chase through a high-crime area late at night. Nor is it universally true that the driver's interest in remaining in the car is negligible. A woman stopped at night may fear for her own safety; a person in poor health may object to standing in the cold or rain; another who left home in haste to drive children or spouse to school or to the train may not be fully dressed; an elderly driver who presents no possible threat of violence may regard the police command as nothing more than an arrogant and unnecessary display of authority. Whether viewed from the standpoint of the officer's interest in his own safety, or of the citizen's interest in not being required to obey an arbitrary command, it is perfectly obvious that the millions of traffic stops that occur every year are not fungible.

Until today the law applicable to seizures of a person has required individualized inquiry into the reason for each intrusion, or some comparable guarantee against arbitrary harassment. A factual demonstration of probable cause is required to justify an arrest; an articulable reason to suspect criminal activity and possible violence is needed to justify a stop and frisk. But to eliminate any requirement that an officer be able to explain the reasons for his actions signals an abandonment of effective judicial supervision of this kind of seizure and leaves police discretion utterly without limits. Some citizens will be subjected to this minor indignity while others—perhaps those with more expensive cars or different bumper stickers, or different-colored skin—may escape it entirely.

The Court holds today that "third-class" seizures may be imposed without reason; how large this class of seizures may be or become we cannot yet know. Most narrowly, the Court has simply held that whenever an officer has an occasion to speak with the driver of a vehicle, he may also order the driver out of the car. Because the balance of convenience and danger is no different for passengers in stopped cars, the Court's logic necessarily encompasses the passenger. This is true even though the passenger has committed no traffic offense. If the rule were limited to situations in which individualized inquiry identified a basis for concern in particular cases, then the character of the violation might justify different treatment of the driver and the passenger. But when the justification rests on nothing more than an assumption about the danger associated with every stop—no matter how trivial the offense—the new rule must apply to the passenger as well as to the driver.

If this new rule is truly predicated on a safety rationale—rather than a desire to permit pretextual searches—it should also justify a frisk for weapons, or at least an order directing the driver to lean on the hood of the car with legs and arms spread out. For unless such precautionary measures are also taken, the added safety—if any—in having the driver out of the car is of no value when a truly dangerous offender happens to be caught.

I am not yet persuaded that the interest in police safety requires the adoption of a standard any more lenient than that permitted by Terry v. Ohio. In this case the offense might well have gone undetected if respondent had not been ordered out of his car, but there is no reason to assume that he otherwise would have shot the officer. Indeed, there has been no showing of which I am aware that the Terry standard will not provide the police with a sufficient basis to take appropriate protective measures whenever there is any real basis for concern. When that concern does exist, they should be able to frisk a violator, but I question the need to eliminate the requirement of an articulable justification in each case and to authorize the indiscriminate invasion of the liberty of every citizen stopped for a traffic violation, no matter how petty.

NOTES

1. After Adams v. Williams, but before *Mimms,* several courts began to emphasize factors beyond the specific conduct of the suspect to justify the frisk.

In re H.B., 75 N.J. 243, 381 A.2d 759 (1977), two uniformed Newark officers received a radio dispatch of an anonymous tip that a black youth wearing a black hat, leather coat and checkered pants was at a certain restaurant. The officers entered the place, saw a young black fitting the description and frisked him. The frisk was sustained partly on the basis of the problems of urban violence, uncontrolled handguns, and danger to police. See also People v. McGowan, 69 Ill.2d 73, 12 Ill.Dec. 733, 370 N.E.2d 537 (1977) (relying on recent burglaries in area to justify frisk).

There have been several cases dealing with justification for a stop or other form of police action without a frisk. In United States v. Magda, 547 F.2d 756 (2nd Cir.1976), a police officer stopped and twice asked Magda what had occurred at a conversation, observed by the officer, between Magda and another man. Magda eventually admitted he bought marijuana. The Court sustained the police action in light of the fact that the area was "narcotics prone," which the officer knew. In People v. DeBour, 40 N.Y.2d 210, 386 N.Y.S.2d 375, 352 N.E.2d 562 (1976), a majority of the court upheld a decision by a Brooklyn officer to "approach" and question an individual he encountered while on foot patrol just after midnight in an area with a heavy incidence of narcotics activity. Officer Steck and his partner saw DeBour walking toward them; when DeBour was within thirty to forty feet of the officers he crossed the street. The officers did the same and when DeBour reached them, Officer Steck asked him what he was doing in the neighborhood. DeBour clearly but nervously replied that he had just parked his car and was going to a friend's house. Steck asked him for identification. While DeBour was answering that he had none Steck noticed a slight waist-high bulge in DeBour's waistband. Steck asked DeBour to unzip his coat and DeBour's compliance with the request revealed a gun. The majority agreed that at its inception "this encounter was supported by less than reasonable suspicion and consequently would not justify a stop involving actual or constructive restraint." However, the officers did not make such a stop; they did no more than approach DeBour to question him about his identity. They did not harass him or subject him to any indignity, and their questions were limited to their duties as patrolmen. Moreover, the officers did have specific reasons for stopping him—the time of night, the nature of the area, and DeBour's evident desire to avoid them.

DELAWARE v. PROUSE

Supreme Court of the United States, 1979.
440 U.S. 648, 99 S.Ct. 1391.

MR. JUSTICE WHITE delivered the opinion of the Court.

The question is whether it is an unreasonable seizure under the Fourth and Fourteenth Amendments to stop an automobile, being driven on a public highway, for the purpose of checking the driving license of the operator and the registration of the car, where there is neither probable cause to believe nor reasonable suspicion that the car is being driven contrary to the laws governing the operation of motor vehicles or that either the car or any of its occupants is subject to seizure or detention in connection with the violation of any other applicable law.

I

At 7:20 p.m. on November 30, 1976, a New Castle County, Del., patrolman in a police cruiser stopped the automobile occupied by respondent. The patrolman smelled marihuana smoke as he was walking toward the stopped vehicle, and he seized marihuana in plain view on the car floor. Respondent was subsequently indicted for illegal possession of a controlled substance. At a hearing on respondent's motion to suppress the marihuana seized as a result of the stop, the patrolman testified that prior to stopping the vehicle he had observed neither traffic or equipment violations nor any suspicious activity, and that he made the stop only in order to check the driver's license and registration. The patrolman was not acting pursuant to any standards, guidelines, or procedures pertaining to document spot checks, promulgated by either his department or the State Attorney General. Characterizing the stop as "routine," the patrolman explained, "I saw the car in the area and wasn't answering any complaints, so I decided to pull them off." The trial court granted the motion to suppress, finding the stop and detention to have been wholly capricious and therefore violative of the Fourth Amendment.

The Delaware Supreme Court affirmed, noting first that "[t]he issue of the legal validity of systematic, roadblock-type stops of a number of vehicles for license and vehicle registration check is *not* now before the Court" (1978) (emphasis in original). The court held that "a random stop of a motorist in the absence of specific articulable facts which justify the stop by indicating a reasonable suspicion that a violation of the law has occurred is constitutionally impermissible and violative of the Fourth and Fourteenth Amendments to the United States Constitution." We granted certiorari to resolve the conflict between this decision, which is in accord with decisions in five other jurisdictions, and the contrary determination in six jurisdictions that the Fourth Amendment does not prohibit the kind of automobile stop that occurred here.

* * *

III

The Fourth and Fourteenth Amendments are implicated in this case because stopping an automobile and detaining its occupants constitute a "seizure" within the meaning of those Amendments, even though the purpose of the stop is limited and the resulting detention quite brief. United States v. Martinez-Fuerte, 428 U.S. 543, 96 S.Ct. 3074 (1976); United States v. Brignoni-Ponce, 422 U.S. 873, 95 S.Ct. 2574 (1975). The essential purpose of the proscriptions in the Fourth Amendment is to impose a standard of "reasonableness" upon the exercise of discretion by government officials, including law enforcement agents, in order " 'to safeguard the privacy and security of individuals against arbitrary invasions....' " Thus, the permissibility of a particular law enforcement practice is judged by balancing its intrusion on the individual's Fourth Amendment interests against its promotion of legitimate governmental interests. Implemented in this manner, the reasonableness standard usually requires, at a minimum, that the facts upon which an intrusion is based be capable of measurement against "an objective standard," whether this be probable cause or a less stringent test. In those situations in which the balance of interests precludes insistence upon "some quantum of individualized suspicion." other safeguards are generally relied upon to assure that the individual's reasonable expectation of privacy is not "subject to the discretion of the official in the field."

In this case, however, the State of Delaware urges that patrol officers be subject to no constraints in deciding which automobiles shall be stopped for a license and registration check because the State's interest in discretionary spot checks as a means of ensuring the safety of its roadways outweighs the resulting intrusion on the privacy and security of the persons detained.

IV

We have only recently considered the legality of investigative stops of automobiles where the officers making the stop have neither probable cause to believe nor reasonable suspicion that either the automobile or its occupants are subject to seizure under the applicable criminal laws. In United States v. Brignoni-Ponce, supra, Border Patrol agents conducting roving patrols in areas near the international border asserted statutory authority to stop at random any vehicle in order to determine whether it contained illegal aliens or was involved in smuggling operations. The practice was held to violate the Fourth Amendment, but the Court did not invalidate all warrantless automobile stops upon less than probable cause. Given "the importance of the governmental interest at stake, the minimal intrusion of a brief stop, and the absence of practical alternatives for policing the border," the Court analogized the roving-patrol stop to the on-the-street encounter addressed in Terry v. Ohio and held:

> "Except at the border and its functional equivalents, officers on roving patrol may stop vehicles only if they are aware of specific articulable facts, together with rational inferences from those facts, that reasonably warrant suspicion that the vehicles contain aliens who may be illegally in the country."

Because "the nature of illegal alien traffic and the characteristics of smuggling operations tend to generate articulable grounds for identifying violators," "a requirement of reasonable suspicion for stops allows the Government adequate means of guarding the public interest and also protects residents of the border areas from indiscriminate official interference."

The constitutionality of stops by Border Patrol agents was again before the Court in United States v. Martinez-Fuerte, supra, in which we addressed the permissibility of checkpoint operations. This practice involved slowing all oncoming traffic "to a virtual, if not a complete, halt," at a highway roadblock, and referring vehicles chosen at the discretion of Border Patrol agents to an area for secondary inspection. Recognizing that the governmental interest involved was the same as that furthered by roving-patrol stops, the Court nonetheless sustained the constitutionality of the Border Patrol's checkpoint operations. The crucial distinction was the lesser intrusion upon the motorist's Fourth Amendment interests:

> "[The] objective intrusion—the stop itself, the questioning, and the visual inspection—also existed in roving-patrol stops. But we view checkpoint stops in a different light because the subjective intrusion—the generating of concern or even fright on the part of lawful travelers—is appreciably less in the case of a checkpoint stop."

Although not dispositive, these decisions undoubtedly provide guidance in balancing the public interest against the individual's Fourth Amendment interests implicated by the practice of spot checks such as occurred in this case. We cannot agree that stopping or detaining a vehicle on an ordinary city street is less intrusive than a roving-patrol stop on a major highway and that it bears greater resemblance to a permissible stop and secondary detention at a checkpoint near the border. In this regard, we note that Brignoni-Ponce was not limited to roving-patrol stops on limited access roads, but applied to any roving-patrol stop by Border Patrol agents on any type of roadway on less than reasonable suspicion. We cannot assume that the physical and psychological intrusion visited upon the occupants of a vehicle by a random stop to check documents is of any less moment than that occasioned by a stop by border agents on roving patrol. Both of these stops generally entail law enforcement officers signaling a moving automobile to pull over to the side of the roadway, by means of a possibly unsettling show of authority. Both interfere with freedom of movement, are inconvenient, and consume time. Both may create substantial anxiety. For Fourth Amendment purposes, we also see insufficient resemblance between sporadic and random stops of individual vehicles making their way through city traffic and those stops occasioned by roadblocks where all vehicles are brought to a halt or to a near halt, and all are subjected to a show of the police power of the community. "At traffic checkpoints the motorist can see that other vehicles are being stopped, he can see visible signs of the officers' authority, and he is much less likely to be frightened or annoyed by the intrusion."

V

But the State of Delaware urges that even if discretionary spot checks such as occurred in this case intrude upon motorists as much as or more than do the roving patrols held impermissible in Brignoni-Ponce, these stops are reasonable under the Fourth Amendment because the State's interest in the practice as a means of promoting public safety upon its roads more than outweighs the intrusion entailed. Although the record discloses no statistics concerning the extent of the problem of lack of highway safety, in Delaware or in the Nation as a whole, we are aware of the danger to life and property posed by vehicular traffic and of the difficulties that even a cautious and an experienced driver may encounter. We agree that the States have a vital interest in ensuring that only those qualified to do so are permitted to operate motor vehicles, that these vehicles are fit for safe operation, and hence that licensing, registration, and vehicle inspection requirements are being observed. Automobile licenses are issued periodically to evidence that the drivers holding them are sufficiently familiar with the rules of the road and are physically qualified to operate a motor vehicle. The registration requirement and, more pointedly, the related annual inspection requirement in Delaware are designed to keep dangerous automobiles off the road. Unquestionably, these provisions, properly administered, are essential elements in a highway safety program. Furthermore, we note that the State of Delaware requires a minimum amount of insurance coverage as a condition to automobile registration, implementing its legitimate interest in seeing to it that its citizens have protection when involved in a motor vehicle accident.

The question remains, however, whether in the service of these important ends the discretionary spot check is a sufficiently productive mechanism to justify the intrusion upon Fourth Amendment interests which such stops entail. On the record before us, that question must be answered in the negative. Given the alternative mechanisms available, both those in use and those that might be adopted, we are unconvinced that the incremental contribution to highway safety of the random spot check justifies the practice under the Fourth Amendment.

The foremost method of enforcing traffic and vehicle safety regulations, it must be recalled, is acting upon observed violations. Vehicle stops for traffic violations occur countless times each day; and on these occasions, licenses and registration papers are subject to inspection and drivers without them will be ascertained. Furthermore, drivers without licenses are presumably the less safe drivers whose propensities may well exhibit themselves. Absent some empirical data to the contrary, it must be assumed that finding an unlicensed driver among those who commit traffic violations is a much more likely event than finding an unlicensed driver by choosing randomly from the entire universe of drivers. If this were not so, licensing of drivers would hardly be an effective means of promoting roadway safety. It seems common sense that the percentage of all drivers on the road who are driving without a license is very small and that the number of licensed drivers who will be stopped in order to find one unlicensed operator will be large indeed. The contribution to highway safety made by discretionary stops selected from among drivers generally will therefore be marginal at best. Furthermore, and again absent something more than mere assertion to the contrary, we find it difficult to believe that the unlicensed driver would not be deterred by the possibility of being involved in a traffic violation or having some other experience calling for proof of his entitlement to drive but that he would be deterred by the possibility that he would be one of those chosen for a spot check. In terms of actually discovering unlicensed drivers or deterring them from driving, the spot check does not appear sufficiently productive to qualify as a reasonable law enforcement practice under the Fourth Amendment.

Much the same can be said about the safety aspects of automobiles as distinguished from drivers. Many violations of minimum vehicle-safety requirements are observable, and something can be done about them by the observing officer, directly and immediately. Furthermore, in Delaware, as elsewhere, vehicles must carry and display current license plates, which themselves evidence that the vehicle is properly registered; and, under Delaware law, to qualify for annual registration a vehicle must pass the annual safety inspection and be properly insured. It does not appear, therefore, that a stop of a Delaware-registered vehicle is necessary in order to ascertain compliance with the State's registration requirements; and because there is nothing to show that a significant percentage of automobiles from other States do not also require license plates indicating current registration, there is no basis for concluding that stopping even out-of-state cars for document checks substantially promotes the State's interest.

The marginal contribution to roadway safety possibly resulting from a system of spot checks cannot justify subjecting every occupant of every vehicle on the roads to a seizure—limited in magnitude compared to other intrusions but nonetheless constitutionally cognizable—at the unbridled discretion of law enforcement officials. To insist neither upon an appropriate factual basis for suspicion directed at a particular automobile nor upon some other substantial and objective standard or rule to govern the exercise of discretion "would invite intrusions upon constitutionally guaranteed rights based on nothing more substantial than inarticulate hunches. . . ." By hypothesis, stopping apparently safe drivers is necessary only because the danger presented by some drivers is not observable at the time of the stop. When there is not probable cause to believe that a driver is violating any one of the multitude of applicable traffic and equipment regulations—or other articulable basis amounting to reasonable suspicion that the driver is unlicensed or his vehicle unregistered—we cannot conceive of any legitimate basis upon which a patrolman could decide that stopping a particular driver for a spot check would be more productive than stopping any other driver. This kind of standardless and unconstrained discretion is the evil the Court has discerned when in previous cases it has insisted that the discretion of the official in the field be circumscribed, at least to some extent. Almeida-Sanchez v. United States, 413 U.S. 266, 270, 93 S.Ct. 2535 (1973).

VI

The "grave danger" of abuse of discretion does not disappear simply because the automobile is subject to state regulation resulting in numerous instances of police-citizen contact. Only last Term we pointed out that "if the government intrudes . . . the privacy interest suffers whether the government's motivation is to investigate violations of criminal laws or breaches of other statutory or regulatory standards." There are certain "relatively unique circumstances" in which consent to regulatory restrictions is presumptively concurrent with participation in the regulated enterprise. [Federal regulation of firearms and of liquor]. Otherwise, regulatory inspections unaccompanied by any quantum of individualized, articulable suspicion must be undertaken pursuant to previously specified "neutral criteria."

An individual operating or traveling in an automobile does not lose all reasonable expectation of privacy simply because the automobile and its use are subject to government regulation. Automobile travel is a basic, pervasive, and often necessary mode of transportation to and from one's home, workplace, and leisure activities. Many people spend more hours each day traveling in cars than walking on the streets. Undoubtedly, many find a greater sense of security and privacy in traveling in an automobile than they do in exposing themselves by pedestrian or other modes of travel. Were the individual subject to unfettered governmental intrusion every time he entered an automobile, the security guaranteed by the Fourth Amendment would be seriously circumscribed. As Terry v. Ohio recognized, people are not shorn of all Fourth Amendment protection when they step from their homes onto the public sidewalks. Nor are they shorn of those interests when they step from the sidewalks into their automobiles.

VII

Accordingly, we hold that except in those situations in which there is at least articulable and reasonable suspicion that a motorist is unlicensed or that an automobile is not registered, or that either the vehicle or an occupant is otherwise subject to seizure for violation of law, stopping an automobile and detaining the driver in order to check his driver's license and the registration of the automobile are unreasonable under the Fourth Amendment. This holding does not preclude the State of Delaware or other States from developing methods for spot checks that involve less intrusion or that do not involve the unconstrained exercise of discretion. Questioning of all oncoming traffic at roadblock-type stops is one possible alternative. We hold only that persons in automobiles on public roadways may not for that reason alone have their travel and privacy interfered with at the unbridled discretion of police officers. The judgment below is affirmed.

So ordered.

MR. JUSTICE BLACKMUN, with whom MR. JUSTICE POWELL joins, concurring.

The Court carefully protects from the reach of its decision other less intrusive spot checks "that do not involve the unconstrained exercise of discretion." The roadblock stop for all traffic is given as an example. I necessarily assume that the Court's reservation also includes other not purely random stops (such as every 10th car to pass a given point) that equate with, but are less intrusive than, a 100% roadblock stop. And I would not regard the present case as a precedent that throws any constitutional shadow upon the necessarily somewhat individualized and perhaps largely random examinations by game wardens in the performance of their duties. In a situation of that type, it seems to me, the

Court's balancing process, and the value factors under consideration, would be quite different.

With this understanding, I join the Court's opinion and its judgment.

MR. JUSTICE REHNQUIST, dissenting.

The Court holds, in successive sentences, that absent an articulable, reasonable suspicion of unlawful conduct, a motorist may not be subjected to a random license check, but that the States are free to develop "methods for spot checks that ... do not involve the unconstrained exercise of discretion," such as "[q]uestioning ... all oncoming traffic at roadblock-type stops...." Because motorists, apparently like sheep, are much less likely to be "frightened" or "annoyed" when stopped en masse, a highway patrolman needs neither probable cause nor articulable suspicion to stop *all* motorists on a particular thoroughfare, but he cannot without articulable suspicion stop *less* than all motorists. The Court thus elevates the adage "misery loves company" to a novel role in Fourth Amendment jurisprudence. The rule becomes "curiouser and curiouser" as one attempts to follow the Court's explanation for it.

As the Court correctly points out, people are not shorn of their Fourth Amendment protection when they step from their homes onto the public sidewalks or from the sidewalks into their automobiles. But a random license check on a motorist operating a vehicle on highways owned and maintained by the State is quite different from a random stop designed to uncover violations of laws that have nothing to do with motor vehicles. No one questions that the State may require the licensing of those who drive on its highways and the registration of vehicles which are driven on those highways. If it may insist on these requirements, it obviously may take steps necessary to enforce compliance. The reasonableness of the enforcement measure chosen by the State is tested by weighing its intrusion on the motorists' Fourth Amendment interests against its promotion of the State's legitimate interests.

In executing this balancing process, the Court concludes that given the alternative mechanisms available, discretionary spot checks are not a "sufficiently productive mechanism" to safeguard the State's admittedly "vital interest in ensuring that only those qualified to do so are permitted to operate motor vehicles, that these vehicles are fit for safe operation, and hence that licensing, registration, and vehicle inspection requirements are being observed." Foremost among the alternative methods of enforcing traffic and vehicle safety regulations, according to the Court, is acting upon observed violations, for "drivers without licenses are presumably the less safe drivers whose propensities may well exhibit themselves." Ante, at 659, 59 L.Ed.2d, at 671. Noting that "finding an unlicensed driver among those who commit traffic violations is a much more likely event than finding an unlicensed driver by choosing randomly from the entire universe of drivers," ibid., the Court concludes that the contribution to highway safety made by random stops would be marginal at best. The State's primary interest, however, is in traffic safety, not in apprehending unlicensed motorists for the sake of apprehending unlicensed motorists. The whole point of enforcing motor vehicle safety regulations is to remove from the road the unlicensed driver before he demonstrates why he is unlicensed. The Court would apparently prefer that the State check licenses and vehicle registrations as the wreckage is being towed away.

Nor is the Court impressed with the deterrence rationale, finding it inconceivable that an unlicensed driver who is not deterred by the prospect of being involved in a traffic violation or other incident requiring him to produce a license would be deterred by the possibility of being subjected to a spot check. The Court arrives at its conclusion without the benefit of a shred of empirical data in this record suggesting that a system of random spot checks would fail to deter violators. In the absence of such evidence, the State's determination that random stops would serve a deterrence function should stand.

On the other side of the balance, the Court advances only the most diaphanous of citizen interests. Indeed, the Court does not say that these interests can never be infringed by the State, just that the State must infringe them en masse rather than citizen by citizen. To comply with the Fourth Amendment, the State need only subject *all* citizens to the same "anxiety" and "inconvenien[ce]" to which it now subjects only a few.

For constitutional purposes, the action of an individual law enforcement officer is the action of the State itself, and state acts are accompanied by a presumption of validity until shown otherwise. Although a system of discretionary stops could conceivably be abused, the record before us contains no showing that such abuse is probable or even likely. Nor is there evidence in the record that a system of random license checks would fail adequately to further the State's interest in deterring and apprehending violators. Nevertheless, the Court concludes "[o]n the record before us" that the random spot check is not "a sufficiently productive mechanism to justify the intrusion upon Fourth Amendment interests which such stops entail." I think that the Court's approach reverses the presumption of constitutionality accorded acts of the States. The burden is not upon the State to demonstrate that its procedures are consistent with the Fourth Amendment, but upon respondent to demonstrate that they are not. "On this record" respondent has failed to make such a demonstration.

Neither the Court's opinion, nor the opinion of the Supreme Court of Delaware, suggests that the random stop made in this case was carried out in a manner inconsistent with the Equal Protection Clause of the Fourteenth Amendment. Absent an equal protection violation, the fact that random stops may entail "a possibly unsettling show of authority," and "may create substantial anxiety," seems an insufficient basis to distinguish for Fourth Amendment purposes between a roadblock stopping all cars and the random stop at issue here. Accordingly, I would reverse the judgment of the Supreme Court of Delaware.

NOTES

1. Can a *Terry*-type frisk extend to the interior of a motor vehicle? In Michigan v. Long, 463 U.S. 1032, 103 S.Ct. 3469 (1983), the Court noted that in Terry v. Ohio it had upheld the validity of a protective search for weapons in the absence of probable cause to arrest because it is unreasonable to deny a police officer the right "to neutralize the threat of physical harm," ... when he possesses an articulable suspicion that an individual is armed and dangerous. The *Terry* Court did not, however, expressly address whether such a protective search for weapons could extend to an area beyond the person in the absence of probable cause to arrest. In *Long* the defendant was convicted for possession of marijuana found by police in the passenger compartment and trunk of the automobile that he was driving. The police searched the passenger compartment after what began as an investigation of erratic driving and speeding, because they had reason to believe that the vehicle contained weapons potentially dangerous to the officers. The Court, in a 5–4 decision, held that the protective search of the passenger compartment was reasonable under the principles articulated in *Terry* and other decisions of the Court. Thus, the rule emerges that law enforcement officers who have detained but not arrested the occupant of an automobile may, under *Terry,* conduct a warrantless search of the automobile's passenger compartment, limited to those areas in which a weapon may be placed or hidden, if the officers possess a reasonable belief, based on specific and articulable facts and rational inferences from those facts, that the occupant is dangerous and may gain immediate control of a weapon. Furthermore, it makes no difference that the defendant is physically controlled by the police *at the time of the search.* "The Michigan Supreme Court appeared to believe that it was not reasonable for the officers to fear that Long could injure them, because he was effectively under their control during the investigative stop and could not get access to any weapons that might have been located in the automobile.... This reasoning is mistaken in several respects. During any investigative detention, the suspect is 'in the control' of the officers in the sense that he 'may be briefly detained against his will....' Just as a *Terry* suspect on the street may, despite being under the brief control of a police officer, reach into his clothing and retrieve a weapon, so might a *Terry* suspect in Long's position break away from police control and retrieve a weapon from his automobile.... In addition, if the suspect is not placed under arrest, he will be permitted to reenter his automobile, and he will then have access to any weapons inside.... Or, as here, the suspect may be permitted to reenter the vehicle before the *Terry* investigation is over, and again, may have access to weapons." The Court remanded the case to the state court to consider whether the subsequent search of the defendant's trunk was permissible as an inventory search, or on the basis of probable cause and exigent circumstances arising after the search of the passenger compartment which produced the initial finding of marijuana.

2. For some cases that have applied the general principles set forth in Delaware v. Prouse, see United States v. Prichard, 645 F.2d 854 (10th Cir.1981), cert. denied 454 U.S. 832, 102 S.Ct. 130 (1981), (roadblock proper); United States v. Harper, 617 F.2d 35 (4th Cir.1980), cert. denied 449 U.S. 887, 101 S.Ct. 243 (1980), (proper for Coast Guard to stop ship on the high seas when stopping all ships on known access route to place where marijuana was to be unloaded); State v. Coccomo, 177 N.J.Super. 575, 427 A.2d 131 (1980), (roadblock involving a stop of every fifth vehicle during light traffic hours in an attempt to find drunk

drivers proper); State v. Tourtillott, 289 Or. 845, 618 P.2d 423 (1980), cert. denied 451 U.S. 972, 101 S.Ct. 2051 (1981), (checkpoint set up to investigate compliance with game regulations proper); Lacy v. State, 608 P.2d 19 (Alaska 1980), (where serious crime such as rape, assault with a deadly weapon and kidnapping was committed, proper to set up roadblock for investigation or apprehension immediately after); and State v. Hilleshiem, 291 N.W.2d 314 (Iowa 1980), (haphazard roadblock located in field late at night improper where no system established to systematically stop traffic and maintain roadblock for significant period of time). By 1989 most state courts had considered the constitutionality of roadblocks and most courts had approved them. See, LaFave, Search and Seizure (2nd Ed.West 1987), 1989 Supp., Sections 9.5 and 10.8, and 37 ALR 4th 10, "Validity of Routine Roadblocks by State or Local Police for Purposes of Discovery of Vehicular or Driving Violations." The criteria for a valid roadblock set forth in the *Hilleshiem* case have become a standard. The United States Supreme Court gave full approval to the use of roadblocks in Michigan Dept. of State Police v. Sitz, 496 U.S. 444, 110 S.Ct. 2481 (1990). The Minnesota Supreme Court rejected the U.S. Supreme Court's analysis of roadblocks, holding them unconstitutional under its state constitution. Reasonable suspicion focused on a particular individual is necessary before police may stop a vehicle, the majority held. Ascher v. Commissioner of Public Safety, 519 N.W.2d 183 (Minn.1994).

3. The U.S. Supreme Court has never directly ruled on how long a *Terry*-type investigatory detention can last. In United States v. Sharpe, 470 U.S. 675, 105 S.Ct. 1568 (1985), the Court rejected any attempt to fashion a "hard-and-fast time limit for a permissible *Terry* stop ...", finding that a 20 minute detention of a camper and its driver based on reasonable suspicion that it contained marijuana was reasonable under the circumstances. The Court stated that in determining the reasonableness of the length of a *Terry* stop, three factors should be taken into consideration: (1) the purpose of the stop, (2) the time reasonably needed to carry it out, and (3) whether the police adopted a procedure "likely to confirm or dispel their suspicion quickly...." On this last factor, however, the courts should not second-guess the police on their choice of procedure in a rapidly developing scenario. The Court concluded that the delay in this case was occasioned by the defendants' own evasive maneuvers which forced the law enforcement officers to split up and take separate enforcement actions, but the officers acted reasonably and diligently under the circumstances.

4. In United States v. Sokolow, 490 U.S. 1, 109 S.Ct. 1581 (1989), the U.S. Supreme Court indirectly approved the use of "drug courier profiles" for giving drug agents reasonable suspicion for stopping air travellers. The Ninth Circuit Court of Appeals had constructed a bifurcated approach to such profiles, splitting facts known to such agents into two categories: (1) facts of "ongoing criminal activity" and (2) facts of "personal characteristics."

The Supreme Court, while not expressly approving the use of profiles, rejected such a split approach to finding reasonable suspicion. The effort of the court below, it complained, to "refine and elaborate the requirements of 'reasonable suspicion' in this case creates unnecessary difficulty in dealing with one of the relatively simple concepts embodied in the Fourth Amendment [...] [The focus in such cases should be on ...] the totality of the circumstances." Instead of technical rules of analysis, law enforcement agents using such devices as "profiles" should simply draw "common-sense conclusions about human behavior [...]" The facts in this case involved a round trip traveller from Hawaii to Miami who paid for his ticket and the ticket of a companion with $2,100 in $20 bills, gave a phony name to the ticket agent, stayed in Miami (known in the profile as a "drug source" city) for only 48 hours even though the round trip flight is 20 hours long, checked no luggage, and acted "nervously." When the pair was stopped on their return to Hawaii, cocaine was found in the defendant's carry-on bag. No single fact gave reasonable suspicion, but taken together they did, and "the fact that these factors may be set forth in a 'profile' does not somehow detract from their evidentiary significance as seen by a trained agent."

2. ADMINISTRATIVE SEARCHES

The term "Administrative Searches" encompasses, of course, searches by representatives or governmental agency personnel such as health and safety inspectors. That phase of the subject is covered by a number of cases which we cannot reproduce in the present casebook because of (a) space consideration, and (b) the limited extent to which regular law enforcement personnel will be involved. We are, therefore, restricting our material upon the subject to those types of situations facing usual law enforcement personnel in a reasonable number of circumstances.

NOTES

1. Among the typical administrative search cases falling short of regular law enforcement personnel concern are: Camara v. Municipal Court of San Francisco, 387 U.S. 523, 87 S.Ct. 1727 (1967) (health inspectors on routine housing code compliance—warrant required, absent owner's consent); See v. City of Seattle, 387 U.S. 541, 87 S.Ct. 1737 (1967) (fire department inspectors of a commercial warehouse—warrant required, absent consent); Colonnade Catering Corp. v. United States, 397 U.S. 72, 90 S.Ct. 774 (1970) (improper for federal agents, without warrant, to forcibly enter a locked storeroom on the premises of a federally licensed dealer in alcoholic beverages). However, in United States v. Biswell, 406 U.S. 311, 92 S.Ct. 1593 (1972), in which the Supreme Court approved a federal agent's inspection of a federally licensed gun dealer's storeroom because of a condition in the license permitting inspections during business hours).

2. There are many recognized forms of administrative searches or seizures which are permissible regardless of the absence of probable cause. Some common categories are these:

a. Border searches and customs inspections are exempt from the requirement of probable cause but must be reasonable. Border searches include searches well within the border or at checkpoints. Duprez v. United States, 435 F.2d 1276 (9th Cir.1970), or searches where observation has been continuous since border was crossed. Thomas v. United States, 372 F.2d 252 (5th Cir.1967); United States v. DeLeon, 462 F.2d 170 (5th Cir.1972) (10 miles from border). Searches some distance from the border must be specially justified by circumstances known to the border officers although probable cause is not necessary. In striking down a search made sixty three miles from the border one Court required a special justification saying that "any other doctrine would render travelers who had recently entered this country subject to almost unlimited search and seizure without any cause save the simple request from a border official to one at an interior point." Marsh v. United States, 344 F.2d 317 (5th Cir.1965). Ordinary border searches need not even be based on real suspicion but where the search extends to body cavities, a very real suspicion (although not necessarily amounting to probable cause) must be demonstrated. Henderson v. United States, 390 F.2d 805 (9th Cir.1967). One court applied the real suspicion test to "mere" strip searches, United States v. Johnson, 425 F.2d 630 (9th Cir.1970) (cert. granted but case later dismissed by stipulation of parties). Generally it is said that test should be different since search through underclothing that has been removed is less offensive than search through same clothing still being worn. People v. Eggleston, 15 Cal.App.3d 1026, 93 Cal.Rptr. 776 (1971). Border search theory has been extended to justify the search of a car believed to have been loaded with Mexican marijuana although car itself did not cross border. United States v. Markham, 440 F.2d 1119 (9th Cir.1971).

In United States v. Ramsey, 431 U.S. 606, 97 S.Ct. 1972 (1977), the Supreme Court upheld a statute which allows government inspectors to open (but not to read) mail which is entering the United States from a foreign country. The provision includes a requirement that officials have "reasonable suspicion" to believe that the mail contains merchandise which is being illegally imported through the use of the mails. The Court indicated that it could perceive no rational distinction between the right to inspect objects carried into the country and the right to inspect objects sent across the border via the postal service.

A decision that spells bad news for alimentary canal smugglers is United States v. Montoya de Hernandez, 473 U.S. 531, 105 S.Ct. 3304 (1985), where the Court ruled that the "reasonable suspicion" standard is sufficient to permit customs agents to detain, at the border, a traveler suspected of smuggling contraband in his or her alimentary canal, and a 16-hour period during which the suspect was held incommunicado until federal agents decided to obtain a warrant for an X-ray after the defendant staunchly refused to defecate was not unreasonable. Mr. Justice Stevens concurred in the judgment, arguing that an alimentary canal smuggling suspect can be made to submit to an X-ray as part of a border search.

b. In a related area, immigration authorities had been granted the right to make a random stop of automobiles within 100 miles of an international border and to look anywhere (in the trunk, under the seat) where an illegal alien might be hidden, but the Court overturned this practice in Almeida-Sanchez v. United States, 413 U.S. 266, 93 S.Ct. 2535 (1973). Almeida-Sanchez involved a Mexican alien, with a valid work permit, whose car was stopped and searched at a point 25 miles north of the Mexican border.

In United States v. Martinez-Fuerte, 428 U.S. 543, 96 S.Ct. 3074 (1976), the Supreme Court summarized *Almeida-Sanchez* and two later decisions:

> In Almeida-Sanchez v. United States the question was whether a roving-patrol unit constitutionally could search a vehicle for illegal aliens simply because it was in the general vicinity of the border. We held that searches by roving patrols could be conducted without consent only if there was probable cause to believe that a car contained illegal aliens, at least in the absence of a judicial warrant authorizing random stops by roving patrols in a given area. We held in United States v. Ortiz, 422 U.S. 891, 95 S.Ct. 2585 (1975), that the same limitations applied to vehicle searches conducted at a permanent checkpoint.
>
> In United States v. Brignoni-Ponce, 422 U.S. 873, 95 S.Ct. 2574 (1975), however, we recognized that other traffic-checking practices involve a different balance of public and private interest and appropriately are subject to less stringent constitutional safeguards. The ques-

> tion was under what circumstances a roving patrol could stop motorists in the general area of the border for inquiry into their residence status. We held that a roving-patrol stop need not be justified by probable cause and may be undertaken if the stopping officer is "aware of specific articulable facts, together with rational inferences from those facts, that reasonably warrant suspicion" that a vehicle contains illegal aliens.

The Court in *Martinez-Fuerte* then held that even without reasonable suspicion, vehicles may be stopped at fixed checkpoints in the vicinity of a border and the occupants briefly questioned. It rejected the argument that, at a minimum, such detentions for questioning could be considered reasonable only if done under the authority of an "area warrant" issued upon a judicial determination that it was reasonable to stop cars, in accord with certain guidelines, at that particular checkpoint.

In the context of a search on the Calcasieu River Ship Channel, some 18 miles inland from the Gulf coast of Louisiana (near a designated Customs Port of Entry), the U.S. Supreme Court upheld a customs search and the constitutionality of a statute authorizing customs officials to board any vessel to examine the vessel's manifest and other documents. In this case, the vessel was located in waters providing ready access to the open sea. The Court held that, while random stops without any articulable suspicion of vehicles away from the border are not permissible under the Fourth Amendment, stops at fixed checkpoints are. United States v. Villamonte-Marquez, 462 U.S. 579, 103 S.Ct. 2573 (1983).

For another important immigration case involving stops of pedestrians in Illinois and inspection of migrant workers' residences and places of work, see Illinois Migrant Council v. Pilliod, 398 F.Supp. 882 (N.D.Ill.1975), affirmed 540 F.2d 1062 (7th Cir.1976), *modified* 548 F.2d 715 (7th Cir.1977).

c. Some cases hold that the Fourth Amendment is not violated when probationers or parolees are searched without probable cause. See People v. Chinnici, 51 Misc.2d 570, 273 N.Y.S.2d 538 (1966) (probationer's car by probation officer); People v. Adams, 36 A.D.2d 784, 319 N.Y.S.2d 372 (1971) (parolee's apartment by parole officer); United States ex rel. Santos v. New York State Board of Parole, 441 F.2d 1216 (2d Cir.1971) (parolee's premises by parole officer).

Some courts have held that the status of probationer or parolee does not strip an individual of all Fourth Amendment rights, although it may permit the authorities to act on less than probable cause. Another approach is to permit only such warrantless searches as are authorized under the terms of probation or as are spelled out in the parole agreement. See generally United States v. Consuelo-Gonzalez, 521 F.2d 259 (9th Cir.1975).

One possible limitation of searches of parolees and probationers may occur if the searches are conducted by parole or probation officers at the instance of the police or the prosecutor. If there is no legitimate relationship between the search and the parole or probation supervision of the subject, the search may be considered unjustifiably abusive. There have been warnings against the use of administrative searches solely for law enforcement purposes (Abel v. United States, 362 U.S. 217, 80 S.Ct. 683 (1960)), and one court has considered excluding parole search evidence from criminal cases. People v. Way, 65 Misc.2d 865, 319 N.Y.S.2d 16 (1971). In any event evidence seized during a parole or probation search would be admissible at a hearing to revoke parole or probation. See United States ex rel. Sperling v. Fitzpatrick, 426 F.2d 1161 (2d Cir.1970); Lombardino v. Heyd, 438 F.2d 1027 (5th Cir.1971).

In Griffin v. Wisconsin, 483 U.S. 868, 107 S.Ct. 3164 (1987), the U.S. Supreme Court held that the homes of probationers can be searched on reasonable suspicion and without a warrant. Probationers, the Court ruled, have fewer privacy rights than members of the "public at large." They remain under court supervision, usually with a list of restricted activities, etc. Effective supervision of probationers by the probation authorities ("special needs") justifies dispensing with the warrant and probable cause rules. Requiring a warrant in the probation context is "impractical"; requiring probable cause instead of, in effect, the *Terry* standard of "reasonable suspicion," would be "unduly disrupt[ive]" to the probation system. The Court likened the search of probationers' *homes* to the search of student *lockers* by school officials, which can be searched without a warrant and on the basis of reasonable suspicion.

d. Inspection of automobile identification numbers is valid on less than probable cause. United States v. Powers, 439 F.2d 373 (4th Cir.1971). Some courts do not consider such inspections to be searches. United States v. Ware, 457 F.2d 828 (7th Cir.1972); United States v. Johnson, 431 F.2d 441 (5th Cir.1970). Compare United States v. Bronstein, 521 F.2d 459 (2d Cir.1975) (use of marijuana sniffing dog to walk among suitcases at airport is not a search).

e. In O'Connor v. Ortega, 480 U.S. 709, 107 S.Ct. 1492 (1987), the U.S. Supreme Court ruled that a government employer may search an employee's desks and files on reasonable suspicion, rather than probable cause, if the search is reasonable in scope, and conducted for a non-investigatory work-related purpose or to investigate work-related misconduct. The opinion adopted a case-by-case approach to determine the reasonableness of such searches and remanded the case—which involved the search of a state-employed doctor's desk and files by his superiors—for a determination of reasonableness.

f. In New Jersey v. T.L.O., 469 U.S. 325, 105 S.Ct. 733 (1985), the U.S. Supreme Court ruled that the Fourth Amendment applies to searches of students conducted by public school officials. Such officials, the Court reasoned, act in their capacity as state officials, and not in the place of parents (*loco parentis*). However, the constitutional standard for such searches is "reasonableness," not probable cause.

In Vernonia School District v. Acton, ___ U.S. ___, 115 S.Ct. 2386 (1995), the Court ruled that random, suspicionless drug testing of student athletes did not violate the Fourth Amendment.

g. In New York v. Burger, 482 U.S. 691, 107 S.Ct. 2636 (1987), the U.S. Supreme Court dealt with this issue involving administrative searches: "This case presents the question whether the warrantless search of an automobile junkyard, conducted pursuant to a statute authorizing such a search, falls within the exception to the warrant requirement for administrative inspections of pervasively regulated industries. The case also presents the question whether an otherwise proper administrative inspection is unconstitutional because the ultimate purpose of the regulatory statute pursuant to which the search is done—the deterrence of criminal behavior—is the same as that of penal laws, with the result that the inspection may disclose violations not only of the regulatory statute but also of the penal statutes." The Court answered the first question in the affirmative, and the second in the negative. Such a statute is reasonable under the Fourth Amendment because auto junkyards are a "closely regulated" business. The state has a "substantial interest" in regulating such business because of the pervasiveness of auto theft and the pivotal role played by junkyards in such criminal activity. "Surprise is crucial" to such inspections, making their warrantless nature reasonable. The owners of such junkyards were put on notice by the statute of the possibility of surprise inspections and the inspections were limited to "regular business hours"; this in itself was an adequate substitute for a warrant in the regulatory context. A regulatory scheme is not unreasonable under the Fourth Amendment merely because it has the same ultimate purpose as a criminal statute. Finally, merely because police officers made the inspections under the regulatory statute, rather than "administrative employees" of the State, did not render the regulatory scheme unreasonable. Of course, evidence of crimes uncovered during the warrantless "administrative inspections" was admissible in criminal prosecutions.

3. EMERGENCY SEARCHES

PATRICK v. STATE

Supreme Court of Delaware, 1967.
227 A.2d 486.

The defendant appeals from his conviction of murder in the second degree on the grounds . . . that evidence introduced at trial was illegally obtained.

The pertinent threshold facts are undisputed:

Ernest R. Patrick, the defendant, lived with Joseph Woods and Beverly Goodwyn. Beverly was Woods' mistress but she was also intimate with Patrick on occasion. On the night before the killing, Beverly and Woods had an altercation, over her leaving the house without him, during which Woods struck Beverly, drawing blood, and she attempted to cut him with a razor blade. Beverly and Patrick spent the next day and evening together. After some drinking, they returned to the Woods apartment about 11:00 p.m. En route, Beverly expressed fear of what Woods might do when they arrived. The door of the apartment was open; they entered the living room; and Beverly asked Patrick if Woods was in the bedroom. Patrick went to the bedroom and returned, saying that Woods was there.

Against this background, the jury heard Beverly, called by the State, testify as follows:

That after returning to the living room, Patrick stated that he was going to kill Woods; that Patrick picked up a brick supporting the sofa, entered the hallway, and turned toward the bedroom. Beverly testified that she heard noises which sounded like a brick hitting the bed and like Woods choking; that it did not sound like the brick was hitting Woods. Beverly testified that Patrick returned to the living room with blood on his hands, saying Woods was dead, and then went to the bathroom to wash his hands; that she went into the bedroom and saw Woods' bloody body on the bed; that, in response to her question, Patrick repeated that Woods was dead; that she and Patrick immediately left the apartment and returned to her sister's home where they spent the balance of the night.

Patrick, testifying in his own defense, stated that it was Beverly who took the brick from under the sofa, went to the bedroom, and killed Woods; that it was he in the living room, not Beverly, who heard the thuds of the blows.

Admitted in evidence was the shirt worn by Patrick on the night in question, bearing stains of Group A blood—Woods' blood type but not Patrick's. Also admitted were pieces of brick, stained with Group A blood, found on the bed and headboard, bloodstained bed clothing, and other items taken by the police from the room in which Woods' body was found. The State proved that the cause of Woods' death was depressed fracture of the skull. Patrick was indicted for murder in the second degree and was found guilty. He appeals....

The defendant claims that articles introduced in evidence against him were obtained by the police by unlawful search and seizure. The facts pertinent to this issue are as follows:

Woods' body was discovered by his employer, W.A. Larrimore, on the morning after the killing. Larrimore found Woods in bed, a bloody "mess", with his head "beaten in with a brick." Larrimore, "panicked"; he could not tell whether Woods was dead or alive. He immediately called the police and, upon their arrival, stated that Woods had a head wound and might be dead. The police officers immediately entered the premises. They found Woods dead, with fragments of brick "five to six inches from his left ear"; and on the headboard of the bed they found half a brick bearing apparent blood stains. The police took photographs in the room, had the body removed, and took into custody the brick pieces, the bed clothing, Woods' clothing, and a wire cord. All items taken were open to view in the room in which the body was found. The police had no search warrant when they entered the premises.

The contention is now made that, absent a warrant, the articles were taken in violation of ... the defendant's constitutional guaranties against unreasonable search and seizure; that the admission in evidence of such articles requires reversal of the conviction.

The basic question is whether the police were in the Woods apartment lawfully. That this question must be answered in the affirmative is obvious.

The general rules governing searches and seizures are subject to the exception of emergency situations, sometimes called the "exigency rule." The reasonableness of an entry by the police upon private property is measured by the circumstances then existing. The right of police to enter and investigate in an emergency, without an accompanying intent either to seize or arrest, is inherent in the very nature of their duties as peace officers, and derives from the common law. United States v. Barone (C.A.2) 330 F.2d 543 (1964). The preservation of human life is paramount to the right of privacy protected by search and seizure laws and constitutional guaranties; it is an overriding justification for what otherwise may be an illegal entry. It follows that a search warrant is not required to legalize an entry by police for the purpose of bringing emergency aid to an injured person. Frequently, the report of a death proves inaccurate and a spark of life remains, sufficient to respond to emergency police aid. As a general rule, we think, an emergency may be said to exist, within the meaning of the "exigency" rule, whenever the police have credible information that an unnatural death has, or may have, occurred. And the criterion is the reasonableness of the belief of the police as to the existence of an emergency, not the existence of an emergency in fact. Wayne v. United States, 115 U.S.App.D.C. 234, 318 F.2d 205 (1963); Davis v. State, 236 Md. 389, 204 A.2d 76 (1964); compare Miller v. United States, 357 U.S. 301, 78 S.Ct. 1190, 1200 (1958).

Applying these tenets to the instant case, we have no doubt that the entry of the police was reasonable under the circumstances. The officers were informed by Larrimore that Woods was dead or dying from a head wound. Clearly, the police had good reason to believe that a life was in balance and that emergency aid might be needed. Under the circumstances, it was the duty of the police to act forthwith upon the report of the emergency—not to speculate upon the accuracy of the report or upon legal technicalities regarding search warrants. It follows that the entry by the police was reasonable and lawful.

After the entry, there was no further search by the officers. All articles taken were in open view in the room in which the body was found. The seizure of evidence in open view upon a lawful entry violates no right of privacy. Wayne v. United States, supra. That which is in open view is not the product of a search. United States v. Barone, supra; Ker v. State of California, 374 U.S. 23, 36–37, 83 S.Ct. 1623, 1635 (1963).

Accordingly, we conclude that there was no violation of statute or constitutional guaranty as to the evidence here in question....

4. PROCUREMENT OF PHYSICAL EVIDENCE UPON SUSPECT'S BODY IN ABSENCE OF PROBABLE CAUSE

DAVIS v. MISSISSIPPI

Supreme Court of the United States, 1969.
394 U.S. 721, 89 S.Ct. 1394.

MR. JUSTICE BRENNAN delivered the opinion of the Court.

Petitioner was convicted of rape and sentenced to life imprisonment by a jury in the Circuit Court of Lauderdale County, Mississippi. The only issue before us is whether fingerprints obtained from petitioner should have been excluded from evidence as the product of a detention which was illegal under the Fourth and Fourteenth Amendments.

The rape occurred on the evening of December 2, 1965, at the victim's home in Meridian, Mississippi. The victim could give no better description of her assailant than that he was a Negro youth. Finger and palm prints found on the sill and borders of the window through which the assailant apparently entered the victim's home constituted the only other lead available at the outset of the police investigation. Beginning on December 3, and for a period of about 10 days, the Meridian police, without warrants, took at least 24 Negro youths to police headquarters where they were questioned briefly, fingerprinted, and then released without charge. The police also interrogated 40 or 50 other Negro youths either at police headquarters, at school, or on the street. Petitioner, a 14-year-old youth who had occasionally worked for the victim as a yardboy, was brought in on December 3 and released after being fingerprinted and routinely questioned. Between December 3 and December 7, he was interrogated by the police on several occasions—sometimes in his home or in a car, other times at police headquarters. This questioning apparently related primarily to investigation of other potential suspects. Several times during this same period petitioner was exhibited to the victim in her hospital room. A police officer testified that these confrontations were for the purpose of sharpening the victim's description of her assailant by providing "a gauge to go by on size and color." The victim did not identify petitioner as her assailant at any of these confrontations.

On December 12, the police drove petitioner 90 miles to the city of Jackson and confined him overnight in the Jackson jail. The State conceded on oral argument in this Court that there was neither a warrant nor probable cause for this arrest. The next day, petitioner, who had not yet been afforded counsel, took a lie detector test and signed a statement [which was not used at the trial]. He was then returned to and confined in the Meridian jail. On December 14, while so confined, petitioner was fingerprinted a second time. That same day, these December 14 prints, together with the fingerprints of 23 other Negro youths apparently still under suspicion, were sent to the Federal Bureau of Investigation in Washington, D.C., for comparison with the latent prints taken from the window of the victim's house. The FBI reported that petitioner's prints matched those taken from the window. Petitioner was subsequently indicted and tried for the rape, and the fingerprint evidence was admitted in evidence at trial over petitioner's timely objections that the fingerprints should be excluded as the product of an unlawful detention. The Mississippi Supreme Court sustained the admission of the fingerprint evidence and affirmed the conviction. 204 So.2d 270 (1967). We granted certiorari. 393 U.S. 821, 89 S.Ct. 149 (1968). We reverse.

At the outset, we find no merit in the suggestion in the Mississippi Supreme Court's opinion that fingerprint evidence, because of its trustworthiness, is not subject to the proscriptions of the Fourth and Fourteenth Amendments.[1] Our decisions recognize no exception to the rule

1. Fingerprint evidence would seem no more "trustworthy" than other types of evidence—such as guns, narcotics, gambling equipment—which are routinely excluded if illegally obtained.

that illegally seized evidence is inadmissible at trial, however relevant and trustworthy the seized evidence may be as an item of proof. The exclusionary rule was fashioned as a sanction to redress and deter overreaching governmental conduct prohibited by the Fourth Amendment. To make an exception for illegally seized evidence which is trustworthy would fatally undermine these purposes. Thus, in Mapp v. Ohio, 367 U.S. 643, 655, 81 S.Ct. 1684 (1961), we held that "*all* evidence obtained by searches and seizures in violation of the Constitution is, by that same authority, inadmissible in a state court." (Italics supplied.) Fingerprint evidence is no exception to this comprehensive rule. We agree with and adopt the conclusion of the Court of Appeals for the District of Columbia Circuit in Bynum v. United States, 104 U.S.App. D.C. 368, 370, 262 F.2d 465, 467 (1958):

> "True, fingerprints can be distinguished from statements given during detention. They can also be distinguished from articles taken from a prisoner's possession. Both similarities and differences of each type of evidence to and from the others are apparent. But all three have the decisive common characteristic of being something of evidentiary value which the public authorities have caused an arrested person to yield to them during illegal detention. If one such product of illegal detention is proscribed, by the same token all should be proscribed."

We turn then to the question whether the detention of petitioner during which the fingerprints used at trial were taken constituted an unreasonable seizure of his person in violation of the Fourth Amendment. The opinion of the Mississippi Supreme Court proceeded on the mistaken premise that petitioner's prints introduced at trial were taken during his brief detention on December 3. In fact, as both parties before us agree, the fingerprint evidence used at trial was obtained on December 14, while petitioner was still in detention following his December 12 arrest. The legality of his arrest was not determined by the Mississippi Supreme Court. However, on oral argument here, the State conceded that the arrest on December 12 and the ensuing detention through December 14 were based on neither a warrant nor probable cause and were therefore constitutionally invalid. The State argues, nevertheless, that this invalidity should not prevent us from affirming petitioner's conviction. The December 3 prints were validly obtained, it is argued, and "it should make no difference in the practical or legal sense which [fingerprint] card was sent to the F.B.I. for comparison." It may be that it does make a difference in light of the objectives of the exclusionary rule, see Bynum v. United States, supra, at 371–372, 262 F.2d, at 468–469,[2] but we need not decide the question since we have concluded that the prints of December 3 were not validly obtained.

2. The Government argued in *Bynum* that the controversy over the introduction in evidence of a particular set of fingerprints was "much ado over very little," because another set properly taken was available and might have been used. The

The State makes no claim that petitioner voluntarily accompanied the police officers to headquarters on December 3 and willingly submitted to fingerprinting. The State's brief also candidly admits that "[a]ll that the Meridian Police could possibly have known about petitioner at the time ... would not amount to probable cause for his arrest...." The State argues, however, that the December 3 detention was of a type which does not require probable cause. Two rationales for this position are suggested. First, it is argued that the detention occurred during the investigatory rather than accusatory stage and thus was not a seizure requiring probable cause. The second and related argument is that, at the least, detention for the sole purpose of obtaining fingerprints does not require probable cause.

It is true that at the time of the December 3 detention the police had no intention of charging petitioner with the crime and were far from making him the primary focus of their investigation. But to argue that the Fourth Amendment does not apply to the investigatory stage is fundamentally to misconceive the purposes of the Fourth Amendment. Investigatory seizures would subject unlimited numbers of innocent persons to the harassment and ignominy incident to involuntary detention. Nothing is more clear than that the Fourth Amendment was meant to prevent wholesale intrusions upon the personal security of our citizenry, whether these intrusions be termed "arrests" or "investigatory detentions."[3] We made this explicit only last Term in Terry v. Ohio, 392 U.S. 1, 19, 88 S.Ct. 1868, 1878 (1968), when we rejected "the notions that the Fourth Amendment does not come into play at all as a limitation upon police conduct if the officers stop short of something called a 'technical arrest' or a 'full-blown search.' "

Detentions for the sole purpose of obtaining fingerprints are no less subject to the constraints of the Fourth Amendment. It is arguable, however, that, because of the unique nature of the fingerprinting process, such detentions might, under narrowly defined circumstances, be found to comply with the Fourth Amendment even though there is no probable cause in the traditional sense. See Camara v. Municipal Court,

Court of Appeals rejected this argument: "It bears repeating that the matter of primary judicial concern in all cases of this type is the imposition of effective sanctions implementing the Fourth Amendment guarantee against illegal arrest and detention. Neither the fact that the evidence obtained through such detention is itself trustworthy or the fact that equivalent evidence can conveniently be obtained in a wholly proper way militates against this overriding consideration. It is entirely irrelevant that it may be relatively easy for the government to prove guilt without using the product of illegal detention. The important thing is that those administering the criminal law understand that they must do it that way." 104 U.S.App.D.C., at 371–372, 262 F.2d at 468–469. On Bynum's retrial another set of fingerprints in no way connected with his unlawful arrest was used, and he was again convicted. The Court of Appeals affirmed this conviction. 107 U.S.App.D.C. 109, 274 F.2d 767 (1960).

3. The State relies on various statements in our cases which approve general questioning of citizens in the course of investigating a crime. See Miranda v. Arizona, 384 U.S. 436, 477–478, 86 S.Ct. 1602, 1629–1630 (1966); Culombe v. Connecticut, 367 U.S. 568, 635, 81 S.Ct. 1860, 1896 (concurring opinion) (1961). But these statements merely reiterated the settled principle that while the police have the right to request citizens to answer voluntarily questions concerning unsolved crimes they have no right to compel them to answer.

387 U.S. 523, 87 S.Ct. 1727 (1967). Detention for fingerprinting may constitute a much less serious intrusion upon personal security than other types of police searches and detentions. Fingerprinting involves none of the probing into an individual's private life and thoughts that marks an interrogation or search. Nor can fingerprint detention be employed repeatedly to harass any individual, since the police need only one set of each person's prints. Furthermore, fingerprinting is an inherently more reliable and effective crime-solving tool than eyewitness identifications or confessions and is not subject to such abuses as the improper line-up and the "third degree." Finally, because there is no danger of destruction of fingerprints, the limited detention need not come unexpectedly or at an inconvenient time. For this same reason, the general requirement that the authorization of a judicial officer be obtained in advance of detention would seem not to admit of any exception in the fingerprinting context.

We have no occasion in this case, however, to determine whether the requirements of the Fourth Amendment could be met by narrowly circumscribed procedures for obtaining, during the course of a criminal investigation, the fingerprints of individuals for whom there is no probable cause to arrest. For it is clear that no attempt was made here to employ procedures which might comply with the requirements of the Fourth Amendment: the detention at police headquarters of petitioner and the other young Negroes was not authorized by a judicial officer; petitioner was unnecessarily required to undergo two fingerprinting sessions; and petitioner was not merely fingerprinted during the December 3 detention but also subjected to interrogation. The judgment of the Mississippi Supreme Court is therefore

Reversed.

MR. JUSTICE FORTAS took no part in the consideration or decision of this case.

MR. JUSTICE HARLAN, concurring.

I join the opinion of the Court, with one reservation. The Court states in dictum that, because fingerprinting may be scheduled for a time convenient to the citizen, "the general requirement that the authorization of a judicial officer be obtained in advance of detention would seem not to admit of any exception in the fingerprinting context." Ante, this page. I cannot concur in so sweeping a proposition. There may be circumstances, falling short of the "dragnet" procedures employed in this case, where compelled submission to fingerprinting would not amount to a violation of the Fourth Amendment even in the absence of a warrant, and I would leave that question open.

MR. JUSTICE BLACK, dissenting.

The petitioner here was convicted of a brutal rape of a woman, committed in her own home. Fingerprints of the petitioner, left on the window sill of her home, were the clinching evidence bringing about petitioner's conviction. The Court, by once more expanding the reach of the judicially declared exclusionary rule, ostensibly resting on the Fourth Amendment, holds the fingerprint evidence constitutionally inadmissible and thereby reverses petitioner's conviction. The rape occurred on December 2, 1965, and, as was their duty, the police authorities began to make a searching investigation the morning of December 3. The raped woman was originally able to describe the rapist only as a young Negro male. With this evidence the police proceeded to interrogate a number of young Negroes on the streets, at their homes, or at the police station, and then permitted them to go on their way. The petitioner was among those so interrogated on December 3, at which time his fingerprints were made. The fingerprints were again taken on December 14. The record does not show that petitioner or any other young man who was questioned and fingerprinted ever made the slightest objection. Apparently all of them cooperated with the police in efforts to find out who had committed the rape. This case is but one more in an ever-expanding list of cases in which this Court has been so widely blowing up the Fourth Amendment's scope that its original authors would be hard put to recognize their creation. For this most unnecessary expansion of the Amendment, the Court is compelled to put its chief reliance on a Court of Appeals decision, Bynum v. United States, 104 U.S.App.D.C. 368, 262 F.2d 465. I think it is high time this Court, in the interest of the administration of criminal justice, made a new appraisal of the language and history of the Fourth Amendment and cut it down to its intended size. Such a judicial action would, I believe, make our cities a safer place for men, women, and children to live.

I dissent from this reversal.

MR. JUSTICE STEWART, dissenting.

I do not disagree with the Court's conclusion that the petitioner was arrested and detained without probable cause. But it does not follow that his fingerprints were inadmissible at the trial.

Fingerprints are not "evidence" in the conventional sense that weapons or stolen goods might be. Like the color of a man's eyes, his height, or his very physiognomy, the tips of his fingers are an inherent and unchanging characteristic of the man. And physical impressions of his fingertips can be exactly and endlessly reproduced.

We do not deal here with a confession wrongfully obtained or with property wrongfully seized—so tainted as to be forever inadmissible as evidence against a defendant. We deal, instead, with "evidence" that can be identically reproduced and lawfully used at any subsequent trial.[1]

I cannot believe that the doctrine of Mapp v. Ohio, 367 U.S. 643, 81 S.Ct. 1684, requires so useless a gesture as the reversal of this conviction.

1. At the original trial the victim of the rape, under oath, positively identified the petitioner as her assailant. There now exists, therefore, ample probable cause to detain him and take his fingerprints.

NOTES

1. Though Davis v. Mississippi left room for the development of techniques for securing physical evidence without requiring probable cause, some courts expressed a reluctance to take up the challenge. See e.g. United States v. Jennings, 468 F.2d 111 (9th Cir.1972):

"Appellee points out that the Supreme Court in Davis v. Mississippi, 394 U.S. 721, 727–728, 89 S.Ct. 1394 (1969), intimated that a detention for fingerprinting, which lacked probable cause for arrest, might be found to comply with the Fourth Amendment under certain narrowly defined circumstances, presumably with judicial authorization. It is contended that appellant's detention at the Sheriff's office is constitutionally sufficient within *Davis*. The language in *Davis* was, however, dicta.

"This Court is not inclined to adopt on its own initiative, the suggestion that probable cause to arrest need not exist to impose burdens substantially like those of arrest-transportation to the police station, fingerprinting, photographing and completion of a lengthy arrest form."

In light of these comments, would it be wise for the police to adopt a practice of taking portable fingerprint and camera equipment to where the suspect lives or works and secure the needed physical evidence without taking the suspect to the police station and detaining him there?

In one recent case, a warrant based upon a probable cause affidavit was properly used to arrest, fingerprint, and photograph a rape suspect, who was then immediately released by the police. The warrant specified the procedures to be performed, directed the police to immediately release the defendant upon completion of the photographing and fingerprinting session, and directed the photograph to be placed with others in a photographic array to be displayed to the victim. The reviewing court, in approving the procedure, noted that there was "no evidence of interrogation, duplicate processes or any violation of the arrest warrant." The court noted that in Davis v. Mississippi, the Supreme Court had intimated that judicially authorized procedures for obtaining a suspect's fingerprints would not offend the Fourth Amendment, even in the absence of probable cause to arrest the suspect. Baker v. State, 449 N.E.2d 1085 (Ind.1983). In the case of Hayes v. Florida, which follows, the Court continued to hold out the possibility of a judicially authorized seizure of a person for fingerprinting on less than probable cause, but that case, like *Davis*, was not a proper vehicle for a holding to that effect.

HAYES v. FLORIDA

Supreme Court of the United States, 1985.
470 U.S. 811, 105 S.Ct. 1643.

JUSTICE WHITE delivered the opinion of the Court.

The issue before us in this case is whether the Fourth Amendment to the Constitution of the United States, applicable to the States by virtue of the Fourteenth Amendment, was properly applied by the Court of Appeal of Florida, Second District, to allow police to transport a suspect to the station house for fingerprinting, without his consent and without probable cause or prior judicial authorization.

A series of burglary-rapes occurred in Punta Gorda, Florida, in 1980. Police found latent fingerprints on the door-knob of the bedroom of one of the victims, fingerprints they believed belonged to the assailant. The police also found a herring-bone pattern tennis shoe print near the victim's front porch. Although they had little specific information to tie petitioner Hayes to the crime, after police interviewed him along with 30 to 40 other men who generally fit the description of the assailant, the investigators came to consider petitioner a principal suspect. They decided to visit petitioner's home to obtain his fingerprints or, if he was uncooperative, to arrest him. They did not seek a warrant authorizing this procedure.

Arriving at petitioner's house, the officers spoke to petitioner on his front porch. When he expressed reluctance voluntarily to accompany them to the station for fingerprinting, one of the investigators explained that they would therefore arrest him. Petitioner, in the words of the investigator, then "blurted out" that he would rather go with the officers to the station than be arrested. App. 20. While the officers were on the front porch, they also seized a pair of herringbone pattern tennis shoes in plain view.

Petitioner was then taken to the station house, where he was fingerprinted. When police determined that his prints matched those left at the scene of the crime, petitioner was placed under formal arrest. Before trial, petitioner moved to suppress the fingerprint evidence, claiming it was the fruit of an illegal detention. The trial court denied the motion and admitted the evidence without expressing a reason. Petitioner was convicted of the burglary and sexual battery committed at the scene where the latent fingerprints were found.

The District Court of Appeal of Florida, Second District, affirmed the conviction. 439 So.2d 896 (1983). The court declined to find consent, reasoning that in view of the threatened arrest it was, "at best, highly questionable" that Hayes voluntarily accompanied the officers to the station. Id., at 898. The court also expressly found that the officers did not have probable cause to arrest petitioner until after they obtained his fingerprints. Id., at 899. Nevertheless, although finding neither consent nor probable cause, the court held, analogizing to the stop and frisk rule of Terry v. Ohio, 392 U.S. 1, 88 S.Ct. 1868, 20 L.Ed.2d 889 (1968), that the officers could transport petitioner to the station house and take his fingerprints on the basis of their reasonable suspicion that he was involved in the crime. 439 So.2d, at 899, 904.

The Florida Supreme Court denied review by a four-to-three decision, 447 So.2d 886 (1983). We granted certiorari to review this application of Terry, 469 U.S. ___, 105 S.Ct. 82, 83 L.Ed.2d 30 (1984), and we now reverse.

We agree with petitioner that Davis v. Mississippi, 394 U.S. 721, 89 S.Ct. 1394, 22 L.Ed.2d 676 (1969), requires reversal of the judgment below. In *Davis,* in the course of investigating a rape, police officers brought petitioner Davis to police headquarters on December 3, 1965. He was fingerprinted and briefly questioned before being released. He was later charged and convicted of the rape. An issue there was whether the fingerprints taken on December 3 were the inadmissible fruits of an illegal detention. Concededly, the police at that time were without probable cause for an arrest, there was no warrant, and Davis had not consented to being taken to the station house. The State nevertheless contended that the Fourth Amendment did not forbid an investigative detention for the purpose of a fingerprinting, even in the absence of probable cause or a warrant. We rejected that submission, holding that Davis' detention for the purpose of fingerprinting was subject to the constraints of the Fourth Amendment and exceeded the permissible limits of those temporary seizures authorized by Terry v. Ohio, supra. This was so even though fingerprinting, because it involves neither repeated harassment nor any of the probing into private life and thoughts that often marks interrogation and search, represents a much less serious intrusion upon personal security than other types of searches and detentions. 394 U.S., at 727, 89 S.Ct., at 1397. Nor was it a sufficient answer to the Fourth Amendment issue to recognize that fingerprinting is an inherently more reliable and effective crime-solving mechanism than other types of evidence such as lineups and confessions. Ibid. The Court indicated that perhaps under narrowly confined circumstances, a detention for fingerprinting on less than probable cause might comply with the Fourth Amendment, but found it unnecessary to decide that question since no effort was made to employ the procedures necessary to satisfy the Fourth Amendment. Id., at 728, 89 S.Ct., at 1398. Rather, Davis had been detained at police headquarters without probable cause to arrest and without authorization by a judicial officer.

Here, as in *Davis,* there was no probable cause to arrest, no consent to the journey to the police station, and no judicial authorization for such a detention for fingerprinting purposes. Unless later cases have undermined *Davis* or we now disavow that decision, the judgment below must be reversed.

None of our later cases have undercut the holding in *Davis* that transportation to and investigative detention at the station house without probable cause or judicial authorization together violate the Fourth Amendment. Indeed, some 10 years later, in Dunaway v. New York, 442 U.S. 200, 99 S.Ct. 2248, 60 L.Ed.2d 824 (1979), we refused to extend Terry v. Ohio, supra, to authorize investigative interrogations at police stations on less than probable cause, even though proper warnings under Miranda v. Arizona, 384 U.S. 436, 86 S.Ct. 1602, 16 L.Ed.2d 694 (1966), had been given. We relied on and reaffirmed the holding in *Davis* that in the absence of probable cause or a warrant investigative detentions at the police station for fingerprinting purposes could not be squared with the Fourth Amendment, 442 U.S., at 213–216, 99 S.Ct., at 2257–2258, while at the same time repeating the possibility that the Amendment might permit a narrowly circumscribed procedure for fingerprinting detentions on less than probable cause. Since that time, we have several times revisited and explored the reach of Terry v. Ohio, most recently in United States v. Sharpe, ___ U.S. ___, 105 S.Ct. 1568, 83 L.Ed.2d ___ (1985), and United States v. Hensley, 469 U.S. ___, 105 S.Ct. 675, 83

L.Ed.2d 604 (1985). But none of these cases has sustained against Fourth Amendment challenge the involuntary removal of a suspect from his home to a police station and his detention there for investigative purposes, whether for interrogation or fingerprinting, absent probable cause or judicial authorization.

Nor are we inclined to forswear *Davis*. There is no doubt that at some point in the investigative process, police procedures can qualitatively and quantitatively be so intrusive with respect to a suspect's freedom of movement and privacy interests as to trigger the full protection of the Fourth and Fourteenth Amendments. Dunaway, 442 U.S., at 212, 99 S.Ct., at 2256; Florida v. Royer, 460 U.S. 491, 499, 103 S.Ct. 1319, 1325, 75 L.Ed.2d 229 (1983) (plurality opinion). And our view continues to be that the line is crossed when the police, without probable cause or a warrant, forcibly remove a person from his home or other place in which he is entitled to be and transport him to the police station, where he is detained, although briefly, for investigative purposes. We adhere to the view that such seizures, at least where not under judicial supervision, are sufficiently like arrests to invoke the traditional rule that arrests may constitutionally be made only on probable cause.[1]

None of the foregoing implies that a brief detention in the field for the purpose of fingerprinting, where there is only reasonable suspicion not amounting to probable cause, is necessarily impermissible under the Fourth Amendment. In addressing the reach of a *Terry* stop in Adams v. Williams, 407 U.S. 143, 146, 92 S.Ct. 1921, 1923, 32 L.Ed.2d 612 (1972), we observed that "[a] brief stop of a suspicious individual, in order to determine his identity or to maintain the status quo momentarily while obtaining more information, may be most reasonable in light of the facts known to the officer at the time." Also, just this Term, we concluded that if there are articulable facts supporting a reasonable suspicion that a person has committed a criminal offense, that person may be stopped in order to identify him, to question him briefly, or to detain him briefly while attempting to obtain additional information.... There is thus support in our cases for the view that the Fourth Amendment would permit seizures for the purpose of fingerprinting, if there is reasonable suspicion that the suspect has committed a criminal act, if there is a reasonable basis for believing that fingerprinting will establish or negate the suspect's connection with that crime, and if the procedure is carried out with dispatch.... Of course, neither reasonable suspicion nor probable cause would suffice to permit the officers to make a warrantless entry into a person's house for the purpose of obtaining fingerprint identification....

1. Thus, in United States v. Sharpe, ___ U.S. ___, 105 S.Ct. 1568, 83 L.Ed.2d ___ (1985), where we recently sustained a 20-minute investigatory stop on a highway, we pointed out that the pertinent facts in *Dunaway,* where we invalidated the detention, were "that (1) the defendant was taken from a private dwelling; (2) he was transported unwillingly to the police station; and (3) he there was subjected to custodial interrogation resulting in a confession." ___ U.S. ___, ___, n. 4, 105 S.Ct. 1568, 1574, n. 4.

We also do not abandon the suggestion in *Davis* and *Dunaway* that under circumscribed procedures, the Fourth Amendment might permit the judiciary to authorize the seizure of a person on less than probable cause and his removal to the police station for the purpose of fingerprinting. We do not, of course, have such a case before us. We do note, however, that some States, in reliance on the suggestion in *Davis,* have enacted procedures for judicially authorized seizures for the purpose of fingerprinting. The state courts are not in accord on the validity of these efforts to insulate investigative seizures from Fourth Amendment invalidation....

As we have said, absent probable cause and a warrant, Davis v. Mississippi, 394 U.S. 721, 89 S.Ct. 1394, 22 L.Ed.2d 676 (1969), requires the reversal of the judgment of the Florida Court of Appeal.

It is so ordered.

JUSTICE BLACKMUN concurs in the judgment.

JUSTICE POWELL took no part in the consideration or decision in this case.

JUSTICE BRENNAN, with whom JUSTICE MARSHALL joins, concurring in the judgment.

Chapter 15

THE EXCLUSIONARY RULE AND ITS ALTERNATIVES

A. THE EXCLUSIONARY RULE

The court-established rule whereby various kinds of evidence of guilt are excluded ("suppressed") from consideration in the course of a judicial determination of the issue of guilt or innocence usually involves one or more of the following provisions of the Bill of Rights (the first eight Amendments) of the Constitution of the United States, all of which have their counterparts in almost every state constitution:

The Fourth Amendment—

The right of the people to be secure in their persons, houses, papers, and effects, against unreasonable searches and seizures, shall not be violated, and no warrants shall issue, but upon probable cause, supported by oath or affirmation, and particularly describing the place to be searched, and the persons or things to be seized.

The Fifth Amendment—

No person shall be ... compelled in any criminal case to be a witness against himself....

The Sixth Amendment—

In all criminal prosecutions, the accused shall enjoy the right ... to have the assistance of counsel for his defense.

The Fourteenth Amendment—

No State shall ... deprive any person of life, liberty, or property, without due process of law; ....

A central thesis of the exclusionary rule is that police will be compelled to comply with the substantive commands of the law if the penalty for failure to comply is the exclusion, from a criminal trial, of evidence of guilt which is otherwise relevant and competent. The following cases and note materials present the concept and philosophy of the rule, supplemented by commentaries upon the question of whether its central thesis is actually served in practice and whether there are workable alternatives which may be employed in its stead.

MAPP v. OHIO

Supreme Court of the United States, 1961.
367 U.S. 643, 81 S.Ct. 1684.

MR. JUSTICE CLARK delivered the opinion of the Court.

Appellant stands convicted of knowingly having had in her possession and under her control certain lewd and lascivious books, pictures, and photographs in violation of § 2905.34 of Ohio's Revised Code. As officially stated in the syllabus to its opinion, the Supreme Court of Ohio found that her conviction was valid though "based primarily upon the introduction in evidence of lewd and lascivious books and pictures unlawfully seized during an unlawful search of defendant's home. . . ."

On May 23, 1957, three Cleveland police officers arrived at appellant's residence in that city pursuant to information that "a person [was] hiding out in the home, who was wanted for questioning in connection with a recent bombing, and that there was a large amount of policy paraphernalia being hidden in the home." Miss Mapp and her daughter by a former marriage lived on the top floor of the two-family dwelling. Upon their arrival at that house, the officers knocked on the door and demanded entrance but appellant, after telephoning her attorney, refused to admit them without a search warrant. They advised their headquarters of the situation and undertook a surveillance of the house.

The officers again sought entrance some three hours later when four or more additional officers arrived on the scene. When Miss Mapp did not come to the door immediately, at least one of the several doors to the house was forcibly opened and the policemen gained admittance. Meanwhile Miss Mapp's attorney arrived, but the officers, having secured their own entry, and continuing in their defiance of the law, would permit him neither to see Miss Mapp nor to enter the house. It appears that Miss Mapp was halfway down the stairs from the upper floor to the front door when the officers, in this highhanded manner, broke into the hall. She demanded to see the search warrant. A paper, claimed to be a warrant, was held up by one of the officers. She grabbed the "warrant" and placed it in her bosom. A struggle ensued in which the officers recovered the piece of paper and as a result of which they handcuffed appellant because she had been "belligerent" in resisting their official rescue of the "warrant" from her person. Running roughshod over appellant, a policeman "grabbed" her, "twisted [her] hand," and she "yelled [and] pleaded with him" because "it was hurting." Appellant, in handcuffs, was then forcibly taken upstairs to her bedroom where the officers searched a dresser, a chest of drawers, a closet and some suitcases. They also looked into a photo album and through personal papers belonging to the appellant. The search spread to the rest of the second floor including the child's bedroom, the living room, the kitchen and a dinette. The basement of the building and a trunk found therein were also searched. The obscene materials for possession of which she was ultimately convicted were discovered in the course of that widespread search.

At the trial no search warrant was produced by the prosecution, nor was the failure to produce one explained or accounted for. At best, "There is, in the record, considerable doubt as to whether there ever was any warrant for the search of defendant's home." The Ohio Supreme Court believed a "reasonable argument" could be made that the conviction should be reversed "because the 'methods' employed to obtain the [evidence] were such as to 'offend "a sense of justice," ' " but the court found determinative the fact that the evidence had not been taken "from defendant's person by the use of brutal or offensive physical force against defendant...."

The State says that even if the search were made without authority, or otherwise unreasonably, it is not prevented from using the unconstitutionally seized evidence at trial, citing Wolf v. People of State of Colorado, 1949, 338 U.S. 25, 69 S.Ct. 1359, in which this Court did indeed hold "that in a prosecution in a State court for a State crime the Fourteenth Amendment does not forbid the admission of evidence obtained by an unreasonable search and seizure." On this appeal, of which we have noted probable jurisdiction, it is urged once again that we review that holding.

I.

Seventy-five years ago, in Boyd v. United States, 1886, 116 U.S. 616, 630, 6 S.Ct. 524, 532, considering the Fourth and Fifth Amendments as running "almost into each other" on the facts before it, this Court held that the doctrines of those Amendments

> "apply to all invasions on the part of the government and its employes of the sanctity of a man's home and the privacies of life. It is not the breaking of his doors, and the rummaging of his drawers, that constitutes the essence of the offence; but it is the invasion of his indefeasible right of personal security, personal liberty and private property.... Breaking into a house and opening boxes and drawers are circumstances of aggravation; but any forcible and compulsory extortion of a man's own testimony or of his private papers to be used as evidence to convict him of crime or to forfeit his goods, is within the condemnation ... [of those Amendments]."

The Court noted that

> "constitutional provisions for the security of person and property should be liberally construed.... It is the duty of courts to be watchful for the constitutional rights of the citizen, and against any stealthy encroachments thereon."

Less than 30 years after Boyd, this Court, in Weeks v. United States, 1914, 232 U.S. 383, 34 S.Ct. 341, ... stated that "the 4th Amendment

... put the courts of the United States and Federal officials, in the exercise of their power and authority, under limitations and restraints [and] ... forever secure[d] the people, their persons, houses, papers, and effects, against all unreasonable searches and seizures under the guise of law ... and the duty of giving to it force and effect is obligatory upon all entrusted under our Federal system with the enforcement of the laws."

Specifically dealing with the use of the evidence unconstitutionally seized, the Court concluded:

> "If letters and private documents can thus be seized and held and used in evidence against a citizen accused of an offense, the protection of the Fourth Amendment declaring his right to be secure against such searches and seizures is of no value, and, so far as those thus placed are concerned, might as well be stricken from the Constitution. The efforts of the courts and their officials to bring the guilty to punishment, praiseworthy as they are, are not to be aided by the sacrifice of those great principles established by years of endeavor and suffering which have resulted in their embodiment in the fundamental law of the land."

Finally, the Court in that case clearly stated that use of the seized evidence involved "a denial of the constitutional rights of the accused." Thus, in the year 1914, in the Weeks case, this Court "for the first time" held that "in a federal prosecution the Fourth Amendment barred the use of evidence secured through an illegal search and seizure." Wolf v. People of State of Colorado, supra. This Court has ever since required of federal law officers a strict adherence to that command which this Court has held to be a clear, specific, and constitutionally required—even if judicially implied—deterrent safeguard without insistence upon which the Fourth Amendment would have been reduced to "a form of words." Holmes, J., Silverthorne Lumber Co. v. United States, 1920, 251 U.S. 385, 392, 40 S.Ct. 182, 183. It meant, quite simply, that "conviction by means of unlawful seizures and enforced confessions ... should find no sanction in the judgments of the courts ...," Weeks v. United States, supra, and that such evidence "shall not be used at all." Silverthorne Lumber Co. v. United States, supra.

There are in the cases of this Court some passing references to the Weeks rule as being one of evidence. But the plain and unequivocal language of Weeks—and its later paraphrase in Wolf—to the effect that the Weeks rule is of constitutional origin, remains entirely undisturbed. In Byars v. United States, 1927, a unanimous Court declared that "the doctrine [cannot] ... be tolerated *under our constitutional system,* that evidences of crime discovered by a federal officer in making a search without lawful warrant may be used against the victim of the unlawful search where a timely challenge has been interposed." (Emphasis added.) The Court, in Olmstead v. United States, 1928, 277 U.S. 438, at page 462, 48 S.Ct. 564, 567, 72 L.Ed. 944, in unmistakable language restated the Weeks rule:

"The striking outcome of the Weeks case and those which followed it was the sweeping declaration that the Fourth Amendment, although not referring to or limiting the use of evidence in court, really forbade its introduction if obtained by government officers through a violation of the amendment." . . .

II.

In 1949, 35 years after Weeks was announced, this Court, in Wolf v. People of State of Colorado, supra, again for the first time, discussed the effect of the Fourth Amendment upon the States through the operation of the Due Process Clause of the Fourteenth Amendment. It said:

"[W]e have no hesitation in saying that were a State affirmatively to sanction such police incursion into privacy it would run counter to the guaranty of the Fourteenth Amendment."

Nevertheless, after declaring that the "security of one's privacy against arbitrary intrusion by the police" is "implicit in 'the concept of ordered liberty' and as such enforceable against the States through the Due Process Clause," and announcing that it "stoutly adhere[d]" to the Weeks decision, the Court decided that the Weeks exclusionary rule would not then be imposed upon the States as "an essential ingredient of the right." ... The Court's reasons for not considering essential to the right to privacy, as a curb imposed upon the States by the Due Process Clause, that which decades before had been posited as part and parcel of the Fourth Amendment's limitation upon federal encroachment of individual privacy, were bottomed on factual considerations.

While they are not basically relevant to a decision that the exclusionary rule is an essential ingredient of the Fourth Amendment as the right it embodies is vouchsafed against the States by the Due Process Clause, we will consider the current validity of the factual grounds upon which Wolf was based.

The Court in Wolf first stated that "[t]he contrariety of views of the States" on the adoption of the exclusionary rule of Weeks was "particularly impressive" ...; and, in this connection, that it could not "brush aside the experience of States which deem the incidence of such conduct by the police too slight to call for a deterrent remedy ... by overriding the [States'] relevant rules of evidence." ... While in 1949, prior to the Wolf case, almost two-thirds of the States were opposed to the use of the exclusionary rule, now, despite the Wolf case, more than half of those since passing upon it, by their own legislative or judicial decision, have wholly or partly adopted or adhered to the Weeks rule.... Significantly, among those now following the rule is California, which, according to its highest court, was "compelled to reach that conclusion because other remedies have completely failed to secure compliance with the constitutional provisions...." People v. Cahan, 1955, ... In connection with this California case, we note that the second basis elaborated in Wolf in support of its failure to enforce the exclusionary doctrine against the States was that "other means of protection" have been afforded "the right to privacy." ... The experience of California that such other remedies have been worthless and futile is buttressed by the experience of other States. The obvious futility of relegating the Fourth Amendment to the protection of other remedies has, moreover, been recognized by this Court since Wolf. See Irvine v. People of State of California, 1954,....

Likewise, time has set its face against what Wolf called the "weighty testimony" of People v. Defore, 1926, 242 N.Y. 13, 150 N.E. 585. There Justice (then Judge) Cardozo, rejecting adoption of the Weeks exclusionary rule in New York, had said that "[t]he Federal rule as it stands is either too strict or too lax." However, the force of that reasoning has been largely vitiated by later decisions of this Court. These include the recent discarding of the "silver platter" doctrine which allowed federal judicial use of evidence seized in violation of the Constitution by state agents, Elkins v. United States, [364 U.S. 206, 80 S.Ct. 1437]; the relaxation of the formerly strict requirements as to standing to challenge the use of evidence thus seized, so that now the procedure of exclusion, "ultimately referable to constitutional safeguards," is available to anyone even "legitimately on [the] premises" unlawfully searched, Jones v. United States, 1960; and finally, the formulation of a method to prevent state use of evidence unconstitutionally seized by federal agents, Rea v. United States, 1956. Because there can be no fixed formula, we are admittedly met with "recurring questions of the reasonableness of searches," but less is not to be expected when dealing with a Constitution, and, at any rate, "[r]easonableness is in the first instance for the [trial court] to determine." ...

It, therefore, plainly appears that the factual considerations supporting the failure of the Wolf Court to include the Weeks exclusionary rule when it recognized the enforceability of the right to privacy against the States in 1949, while not basically relevant to the constitutional consideration, could not, in any analysis, now be deemed controlling.

III.

[Omitted]

IV.

Since the Fourth Amendment's right of privacy has been declared enforceable against the States through the Due Process Clause of the Fourteenth, it is enforceable against them by the same sanction of exclusion as is used against the Federal Government. Were it otherwise, then just as without the Weeks rule the assurance against unreasonable federal searches and seizures would be "a form of words", valueless and undeserving of mention in a perpetual charter of inestimable human liberties, so too, without that rule the freedom from state invasions of privacy would be so ephemeral and so neatly severed from its conceptual nexus with the freedom from all brutish means of coercing evidence as not to merit this Court's high regard as a freedom "implicit in 'the concept of ordered liberty.'" At the time that the Court held in Wolf that the Amendment was applicable to the States through the Due Process Clause, the cases of this Court, as we have seen, had steadfastly held that as to federal officers the Fourth Amendment included the exclusion of the evidence seized in violation of its provisions. Even Wolf "stoutly adhered" to that proposition. The right to privacy, when conceded operatively enforceable against the States, was not susceptible of destruction by avulsion of the sanction upon which its protection and enjoyment had always been deemed dependent under the Boyd, Weeks and Silverthorne cases. Therefore, in extending the substantive protections of due process to all constitutionally unreasonable searches—state or federal—it was logically and constitutionally necessary that the exclusion doctrine—an essential part of the right to privacy—be also insisted upon as an essential ingredient of the right newly recognized by the Wolf case. In short, the admission of the new constitutional right by Wolf could not consistently tolerate denial of its most important constitutional privilege, namely, the exclusion of the evidence which an accused had been forced to give by reason of the unlawful seizure. To hold otherwise is to grant the right but in reality to withhold its privilege and enjoyment. Only last year the Court itself recognized that the purpose of the exclusionary rule "is to deter—to compel respect for the constitutional guaranty in the only effectively available way—by removing the incentive to disregard it."

Indeed, we are aware of no restraint, similar to that rejected today, conditioning the enforcement of any other basic constitutional right. The right to privacy, no less important than any other right carefully and particularly reserved to the people, would stand in marked contrast to all other rights declared as "basic to a free society." Wolf v. People of State of Colorado, supra,.... This Court has not hesitated to enforce as strictly against the States as it does against the Federal Government the rights of free speech and of a free press, the rights to notice and to a fair, public trial, including, as it does, the right not to be convicted by use of a coerced confession, however logically relevant it be, and without regard to its reliability. And nothing could be more certain than that when a coerced confession is involved, "the relevant rules of evidence" are overridden without regard to "the incidence of such conduct by the police," slight or frequent. Why should not the same rule apply to what is tantamount to coerced testimony by way of unconstitutional seizure of goods, papers, effects, documents, etc.? We find that, as to the Federal Government, the Fourth and Fifth Amendments and, as to the States, the freedom from unconscionable invasions of privacy and the freedom from convictions based upon coerced confessions do enjoy an "intimate relation" in their perpetuation of "principles of humanity and civil liberty [secured] ... only after years of struggle." Bram v. United States, 1897. They express "supplementing phases of the same constitutional purpose—to maintain inviolate large areas of personal privacy." Feldman v. United States, 1944. The philosophy of each Amendment and of each freedom is complementary to, although not dependent upon, that of the other in its sphere of influence—the very least that together they assure in either sphere is that no man is to be convicted on unconstitutional evidence....

V.

Moreover, our holding that the exclusionary rule is an essential part of both the Fourth and Fourteenth Amendments is not only the logical dictate of prior cases, but it also makes very good sense. There is no war between the Constitution and common sense. Presently, a federal prosecutor may make no use of evidence illegally seized, but a State's attorney across the street may, although he supposedly is operating under the enforceable prohibitions of the same Amendment. Thus the State, by admitting evidence unlawfully seized, serves to encourage disobedience to the Federal Constitution which it is bound to uphold. Moreover, as was said in Elkins, "[t]he very essence of a healthy federalism depends upon the avoidance of needless conflict between state and federal courts." Such a conflict, hereafter needless, arose this very Term, in Wilson v. Schnettler, 1961, in which, and in spite of the promise made by Rea, we gave full recognition to our practice in this regard by refusing to restrain a federal officer from testifying in a state court as to evidence unconstitutionally seized by him in the performance of his duties. Yet the double standard recognized until today hardly put such a thesis into practice. In nonexclusionary States, federal officers, being human, were by it invited to and did, as our cases indicate, step across the street to the State's attorney with their unconstitutionally seized evidence. Prosecution on the basis of that evidence was then had in a state court in utter disregard of the enforceable Fourth Amendment. If the fruits of an unconstitutional search had been inadmissible in both state and federal courts, this inducement to evasion would have been sooner eliminated. There would be no need to reconcile such cases as Rea and Schnettler, each pointing up the hazardous uncertainties of our heretofore ambivalent approach.

Federal-state cooperation in the solution of crime under constitutional standards will be promoted, if only by recognition of their now mutual obligation to respect the same fundamental criteria in their approaches. "However much in a particular case insistence upon such rules may appear as a technicality that inures to the benefit of a guilty person, the history of the criminal law proves that tolerance of shortcut methods in law enforcement impairs its enduring effectiveness." Denying shortcuts to only one of two cooperating law enforcement agencies tends naturally to breed legitimate suspicion of "working arrangements" whose results are equally tainted....

There are those who say, as did Justice (then Judge) Cardozo, that under our constitutional exclusionary doctrine "[t]he criminal is to go free because the constable has blundered." People v. Defore [supra]. In some cases this will undoubtedly be the result. But, as was said in Elkins, "there is another consideration—the imperative of judicial integrity." ... The criminal goes free, if he must, but it is the law that sets him free. Nothing can destroy a government more quickly than its failure to observe its own laws, or worse, its disregard of the charter of its own existence. As Mr. Justice Brandeis, dissenting, said in Olmstead v. United States, 1928, 277 U.S. 438, 485, 48 S.Ct. 564, 575: "Our government is the potent, the omnipresent teacher. For good or for ill, it teaches the whole people by its example.... If the government becomes a lawbreaker, it breeds contempt for law; it invites every man to become a law unto himself; it invites anarchy." Nor can it lightly be assumed that, as a practical matter, adoption of the exclusionary rule fetters law enforcement. Only last year this Court expressly considered that contention and found that "pragmatic evidence of a sort" to the contrary was not wanting. Elkins v. United States, supra. The Court noted that

> "The federal courts themselves have operated under the exclusionary rule of Weeks for almost half a century; yet it has not been suggested either that the Federal Bureau of Investigation has thereby been rendered ineffective, or that the administration of criminal justice in the federal courts has thereby been disrupted. Moreover, the experience of the states is impressive.... The movement towards the rule of exclusion has been halting but seemingly inexorable." ...

The ignoble shortcut to conviction left open to the State tends to destroy the entire system of constitutional restraints on which the liberties of the people rest. Having once recognized that the right to privacy embodied in the Fourth Amendment is enforceable against the States, and that the right to be secure against rude invasions of privacy by state officers is, therefore, constitutional in origin, we can no longer permit that right to remain an empty promise. Because it is enforceable in the same manner and to like effect as other basic rights secured by the Due Process Clause, we can no longer permit it to be revocable at the whim of any police officer who, in the name of law enforcement itself, chooses to suspend its enjoyment. Our decision, founded on reason and truth, gives to the individual no more than that which the Constitution guarantees him, to the police officer no less than that to which honest law enforcement is entitled, and, to the courts, that judicial integrity so necessary in the true administration of justice.

The judgment of the Supreme Court of Ohio is reversed and the cause remanded for further proceedings not inconsistent with this opinion.

Reversed and remanded.

MR. JUSTICE BLACK, concurring.

* * *

I am still not persuaded that the Fourth Amendment, standing alone, would be enough to bar the introduction into evidence against an accused of papers and effects seized from him in violation of its commands. For the Fourth Amendment does not itself contain any provision expressly precluding the use of such evidence, and I am extremely doubtful that such a provision could properly be inferred from nothing more than the basic command against unreasonable searches and seizures. Reflection of the problem, however, in the light of cases coming before the Court since Wolf, has led me to conclude that when the Fourth Amendment's ban against unreasonable searches and seizures is considered together with the Fifth Amendment's ban against compelled self-incrimination, a constitutional basis emerges which not only justifies but actually requires the exclusionary rule.

The close interrelationship between the Fourth and Fifth Amendments, as they apply to this problem, has long been recognized and, indeed, was expressly made the ground for this Court's holding in Boyd v. United States. There the Court fully discussed this relationship and declared itself "unable to perceive that the seizure of a man's private books and papers to be used in evidence against him is substantially different from compelling him to be a witness against himself." ... In the final analysis, it seems to me that the Boyd doctrine, though perhaps not required by the express language of the Constitution strictly construed, is amply justified from an historical standpoint, soundly based in reason, and entirely consistent with what I regard to be the proper approach to interpretation of our Bill of Rights—an approach well set out by Mr. Justice Bradley in the Boyd case:

> "[C]onstitutional provisions for the security of person and property should be liberally construed. A close and literal construction deprives them of half their efficacy, and leads to gradual depreciation of the right, as if it existed more in sound than in substance. It is the duty of [the] courts to be watchful for the constitutional rights of the citizen, and against any stealthy encroachments thereon."

... As I understand the Court's opinion in this case, we ... set aside this state conviction in reliance upon the precise, intelligible and more predictable constitutional doctrine enunciated in the Boyd case. I fully agree with Mr. Justice Bradley's opinion that the two Amendments upon which the Boyd doctrine rests are of vital importance in our constitutional scheme of liberty and that both are entitled to a liberal rather than a niggardly interpretation. The courts of the country are entitled to know with as much certainty as possible what scope they cover. The Court's opinion, in my judgment, dissipates the doubt and uncertainty in this field of constitutional law and I am persuaded, for this and other reasons stated, to depart from my prior views, to accept the Boyd doctrine as controlling in this state case and to join the Court's judgment and opinion which are in accordance with that constitutional doctrine.

MR. JUSTICE DOUGLAS, concurring.

Though I have joined the opinion of the Court, I add a few words. This criminal proceeding started with a lawless search and seizure. The police entered a home forcefully, and seized documents that were later used to convict the occupant of a crime.

She lived alone with her fifteen-year-old daughter in the second-floor flat of a duplex in Cleveland. At about 1:30 in the afternoon of May 23, 1957, three policemen arrived at this house. They rang the bell, and the appellant, appearing at her window, asked them what they wanted. According to their later testimony, the policemen had come to the house on information from "a confidential source that there was a person hiding out in the home, who was wanted for questioning in connection with a recent bombing." To the appellant's question, however, they replied only that they wanted to question her and would not state the subject about which they wanted to talk.

The appellant, who had retained an attorney in connection with a pending civil matter, told the police she would call him to ask if she should let them in. On her attorney's advice, she told them she would let them in only when they produced a valid search warrant. For the next two and a half hours, the police laid siege to the house. At four o'clock, their number was increased to at least seven. Appellant's lawyer appeared on the scene; and one of the policemen told him that they now had a search warrant, but the officer refused to show it. Instead, going to the back door, the officer first tried to kick it in and, when that proved unsuccessful, he broke the glass in the door and opened it from the inside.

The appellant, who was on the steps going up to her flat, demanded to see the search warrant; but the officer refused to let her see it although he waved a paper in front of her face. She grabbed it and thrust it down the front of her dress. The policemen seized her, took the paper from her, and had her handcuffed to another officer. She was taken upstairs, thus bound, and into the larger of the two bedrooms in the apartment; there she was forced to sit on the bed. Meanwhile, the officers entered the house and made a complete search of the four rooms of her flat and of the basement of the house.

The testimony concerning the search is largely nonconflicting. The approach of the officers; their long wait outside the home, watching all its doors; the arrival of reinforcements armed with a paper; breaking into the house; putting their hands on appellant and handcuffing her; numerous officers ransacking through every room and piece of furniture, while the appellant sat, a prisoner in her own bedroom.... One must understand that this case is based on the knowing possession of four little pamphlets, a couple of photographs and a little pencil doodle—all of which are alleged to be pornographic.

* * *

We held in Wolf v. People of State of Colorado, [supra] that the Fourth Amendment was applicable to the States by reason of the Due Process Clause of the Fourteenth Amendment. But a majority held that the exclusionary rule of the Weeks case was not required of the States, that they could apply such sanctions as they chose. That position had the necessary votes to carry the day. But with all respect it was not the voice of reason or principle.

As stated in the Weeks case, if evidence seized in violation of the Fourth Amendment can be used against an accused, "his right to be secure against such searches and seizures, is of no value, and ... might as well be stricken from the Constitution." ...

When we allowed States to give constitutional sanction to the "shabby business" of unlawful entry into a home ... we did indeed rob the Fourth Amendment of much meaningful force. There are, of course, other theoretical remedies. One is disciplinary action within the hierarchy of the police system, including prosecution of the police officer for a crime. Yet as Mr. Justice Murphy said in Wolf v. People of State of Colorado, ... "Self-scrutiny is a lofty ideal, but its exaltation reaches new heights if we expect a District Attorney to prosecute himself or his associates for well-meaning violations of the search and seizure clause during a raid the District Attorney or his associates have ordered."

The only remaining remedy, if exclusion of the evidence is not required, is an action of trespass by the homeowner against the offending officer. Mr. Justice Murphy showed how onerous and difficult it would be for the citizen to maintain that action and how meagre the relief even if the citizen prevails. The truth is that trespass actions against officers who make unlawful searches and seizures are mainly illusory remedies.

Without judicial action making the exclusionary rule applicable to the States, Wolf v. People of State of Colorado in practical effect reduced the guarantee against unreasonable searches and seizures to "a dead letter," as Mr. Justice Rutledge said in his dissent.

Wolf v. People of State of Colorado, supra, was decided in 1949. The immediate result was a storm of constitutional controversy which only today finds its end. I believe that this is an appropriate case in which to put an end to the asymmetry which Wolf imported into the law. It is an appropriate case because the facts it presents show—as would few other cases—the casual arrogance of those who have the untrammelled power to invade one's home and to seize one's person.

* * *

Moreover, continuance of Wolf v. People of State of Colorado in its full vigor breeds the unseemly shopping around of the kind revealed in Wilson v. Schnettler, 365 U.S. 381, 81 S.Ct. 632. Once evidence, inadmissible in a federal court, is admissible in a state court a "double standard" exists which, as the Court points out, leads to "working arrangements" that undercut federal policy and reduce some aspects of law enforcement to shabby business. The rule that supports that practice does not have the force of reason behind it.

[The Memorandum of MR. JUSTICE STEWART is omitted.]

MR. JUSTICE HARLAN, whom MR. JUSTICE FRANKFURTER and MR. JUSTICE WHITTAKER join, dissenting.

In overruling the Wolf case the Court, in my opinion, has forgotten the sense of judicial restraint which, with due regard for *stare decisis,* is one element that should enter into deciding whether a past decision of this Court should be overruled. Apart from that I also believe that the Wolf rule represents sounder Constitutional doctrine than the new rule which now replaces it.

I.

From the Court's statement of the case one would gather that the central, if not controlling, issue on this appeal is whether illegally state-seized evidence is Constitutionally admissible in a state prosecution, an issue which would of course face us with the need for reexamining Wolf. However, such is not the situation. For, although that question was indeed raised here and below among appellant's subordinate points, the new and pivotal issue brought to the Court by this appeal is whether § 2905.34 of the Ohio Revised Code making criminal the *mere* knowing possession or control of obscene material, and under which appellant has been convicted, is consistent with the rights of free thought and expression assured against state action by the Fourteenth Amendment. That was the principal issue which was decided by the Ohio Supreme Court, which was tendered by appellant's Jurisdictional Statement, and which was briefed and argued in this Court.

In this posture of things, I think it fair to say that five members of this Court have simply "reached out" to overrule Wolf. With all respect for the views of the majority, and recognizing that *stare decisis* carries different weight in Constitutional adjudication than it does in nonconstitutional decision, I can perceive no justification for regarding this case as an appropriate occasion for re-examining Wolf.

Since the demands of the case before us do not require us to reach the question of the validity of Wolf, I think this case furnishes a singularly inappropriate occasion for reconsideration of that decision, if reconsideration is indeed warranted. Even the most cursory examination will reveal that the doctrine of the Wolf case has been of continuing importance in the administration of state criminal law. Indeed, certainly as regards its "nonexclusionary" aspect, Wolf did no more than articulate the then existing assumption among the States that the federal cases enforcing the exclusionary rule "do not bind [the States], for they construe provisions of the federal Constitution, the Fourth and Fifth Amendments, not applicable to the states." Though, of course, not reflecting the full measure of this continuing reliance, I find that during the last three Terms, for instance, the issue of the inadmissibility of illegally state-obtained evidence appears on an average of about fifteen times per Term just in the *in forma pauperis* cases summarily disposed of by us. This would indicate both that the issue which is now being decided may well have untoward practical ramifications respecting state cases long since disposed of in reliance on Wolf, and that were we determined to re-examine that doctrine we would not lack future opportunity.

The occasion which the Court has taken here is in the context of a case where the question was briefed not at all and argued only extremely tangentially. The unwisdom of overruling Wolf without full-dress argument is aggravated by the circumstance that that decision is a comparatively recent one (1949) to which three members of the present majority have at one time or other expressly subscribed, one to be sure with explicit misgivings. I would think that our obligation to the States, on whom we impose this new rule, as well as the obligation of orderly adherence to our own processes would demand that we seek that aid which adequate briefing and argument lends to the determination of an important issue. It certainly has never been a postulate of judicial power that mere altered disposition, or subsequent membership on the Court, is sufficient warrant for overturning a deliberately decided rule of Constitutional law....

I am bound to say that what has been done is not likely to promote respect either for the Court's adjudicatory process or for the stability of its decisions. Having been unable, however, to persuade any of the majority to a different procedural course, I now turn to the merits of the present decision.

II.

Essential to the majority's argument against Wolf is the proposition that the rule of Weeks v. United States, [supra] excluding in federal criminal trials the use of evidence obtained in violation of the Fourth Amendment, derives not from the "supervisory power" of this Court over the federal judicial system, but from Constitutional requirement. This is so because no one, I suppose, would suggest that this Court possesses any general supervisory power over the state courts. Although I entertain considerable doubt as to the soundness of this foundational proposition of the majority, ... I shall assume, for present purposes, that the Weeks rule "is of constitutional origin."

At the heart of the majority's opinion in this case is the following syllogism: (1) the rule excluding in federal criminal trials evidence which is the product of an illegal search and seizure is a "part and parcel" of the Fourth Amendment; (2) Wolf held that the "privacy" assured against federal action by the Fourth Amendment is also protected against state action by the Fourteenth Amendment; and (3) it is therefore "logically and constitutionally necessary" that the Weeks exclusionary rule should also be enforced against the States.

This reasoning ultimately rests on the unsound premise that because Wolf carried into the States, as part of "the concept of ordered liberty" embodied in the Fourteenth Amendment, the principle of "privacy" underlying the Fourth Amendment ..., it must follow that whatever configurations of the Fourth Amendment have been developed in the particularizing federal precedents are likewise to be deemed a part of "ordered liberty," and as such are enforceable against the States. For me, this does not follow at all.

It cannot be too much emphasized that what was recognized in Wolf was not that the Fourth Amendment *as such* is enforceable against the States as a facet of due process, a view of the Fourteenth Amendment which, as Wolf itself pointed out . . ., has long since been discredited, but the principle of privacy "which is at the core of the Fourth Amendment." . . . It would not be proper to expect or impose any precise equivalence, either as regards the scope of the right or the means of its implementation, between the requirements of the Fourth and Fourteenth Amendments. For the Fourth, unlike what was said in Wolf of the Fourteenth, does not state a general principle only; it is a particular command, having its setting in a pre-existing legal context on which both interpreting decisions and enabling statutes must at least build.

Thus, even in a case which presented simply the question of whether a particular search and seizure was constitutionally "unreasonable"—say in a tort action against state officers—we would not be true to the Fourteenth Amendment were we merely to stretch the general principle of individual privacy on a Procrustean bed of federal precedents under the Fourth Amendment. But in this instance more than that is involved, for here we are reviewing not a determination that what the state police did was Constitutionally permissible (since the state court quite evidently assumed that it was not), but a determination that appellant was properly found guilty of conduct which, for present purposes, it is to be assumed the State could Constitutionally punish. Since there is not the slightest suggestion that Ohio's policy is "affirmatively to sanction . . . police incursion into privacy," what the Court is now doing is to impose upon the States not only federal substantive standards of "search and seizure" but also the basic federal remedy for violation of those standards. For I think it entirely clear that the Weeks exclusionary rule is but a remedy which, by penalizing past official misconduct, is aimed at deterring such conduct in the future.

I would not impose upon the States this federal exclusionary remedy. The reasons given by the majority for now suddenly turning its back on Wolf seem to me notably unconvincing.

First, it is said that "the factual grounds upon which Wolf was based" have since changed, in that more States now follow the Weeks exclusionary rule than was so at the time Wolf was decided. While that is true, a recent survey indicates that at present one-half of the States still adhere to the common-law non-exclusionary rule, and one, Maryland, retains the rule as to felonies. Berman and Oberst, Admissibility of Evidence Obtained by an Unconstitutional Search and Seizure, 55 N.W.L.Rev. 525, 532–533. But in any case surely all this is beside the point, as the majority itself indeed seems to recognize. Our concern here, as it was in Wolf, is not with the desirability of that rule but only with the question whether the States are Constitutionally free to follow it or not as they may themselves determine, and the relevance of the disparity of views among the States on this point lies simply in the fact that the judgment involved is a debatable one. Moreover, the very fact on which the majority relies, instead of lending support to what is now being done, points away from the need of replacing voluntary state action with federal compulsion.

The preservation of a proper balance between state and federal responsibility in the administration of criminal justice demands patience on the part of those who might like to see things move faster among the States in this respect. Problems of criminal law enforcement vary widely from State to State. One State, in considering the totality of its legal picture, may conclude that the need for embracing the Weeks rule is pressing because other remedies are unavailable or inadequate to secure compliance with the substantive Constitutional principle involved. Another, though equally solicitous of Constitutional rights, may choose to pursue one purpose at a time, allowing all evidence relevant to guilt to be brought into a criminal trial, and dealing with Constitutional infractions by other means. Still another may consider the exclusionary rule too rough-and-ready a remedy, in that it reaches only unconstitutional intrusions which eventuate in criminal prosecution of the victims. Further, a State after experimenting with the Weeks rule for a time may, because of unsatisfactory experience with it, decide to revert to a non-exclusionary rule. And so on. From the standpoint of Constitutional permissibility in pointing a State in one direction or another, I do not see at all why "time has set its face against" the considerations which led Mr. Justice Cardozo, then chief judge of the New York Court of Appeals, to reject for New York in People v. Defore, [supra], the Weeks exclusionary rule. For us the question remains, as it has always been, one of state power, not one of passing judgment on the wisdom of one state course or another. In my view this Court should continue to forbear from fettering the States with an adamant rule which may embarrass them in coping with their own peculiar problems in criminal law enforcement.

Further, we are told that imposition of the Weeks rule on the States makes "very good sense," in that it will promote recognition by state and federal officials of their "mutual obligation to respect the same fundamental criteria" in their approach to law enforcement, and will avoid " 'needless conflict between state and federal courts.' " Indeed the majority now finds an incongruity in Wolf's discriminating perception between the demands of "ordered liberty" as respects the basic right of "privacy" and the means of securing it among the States. That perception, resting both on a sensitive regard for our federal system and a sound recognition of this Court's remoteness from particular state problems, is for me the strength of that decision.

An approach which regards the issue as one of achieving procedural symmetry or of serving administrative convenience surely disfigures the boundaries of this Court's functions in relation to the state and federal courts. Our role in promulgating the Weeks rule and its extensions in such cases as Rea, Elkins, and Rios was quite a different one than it is here. There, in implementing the Fourth Amendment, we occupied the position of a tribunal having the ultimate responsibility for developing the standards and procedures of judicial administration within the judicial system over which it presides. Here we review state procedures whose measure is to be taken not against the specific substantive commands of the Fourth Amendment but under the flexible contours of the Due Process Clause. I do not believe that the Fourteenth Amendment empowers this Court to mould state remedies effectuating the right to freedom from "arbitrary intrusion by the police" to suit its own notions of how things should be done, as, for instance, the California Supreme Court did in People v. Cahan, ... with reference to procedures in the California courts or as this Court did in Weeks for the lower federal courts.

A state conviction comes to us as the complete product of a sovereign judicial system. Typically a case will have been tried in a trial court, tested in some final appellate court, and will go no further. In the comparatively rare instance when a conviction is reviewed by us on due process grounds we deal then with a finished product in the creation of which we are allowed no hand, and our task, far from being one of overall supervision, is, speaking generally, restricted to a determination of whether the prosecution was Constitutionally fair. The specifics of trial procedure, which in every mature legal system will vary greatly in detail, are within the sole competence of the States. I do not see how it can be said that a trial becomes unfair simply because a State determines that evidence may be considered by the trier of fact, regardless of how it was obtained, if it is relevant to the one issue with which the trial is concerned, the guilt or innocence of the accused. Of course, a court may use its procedures as an incidental means of pursuing other ends than the correct resolution of the controversies before it. Such indeed is the Weeks rule, but if a State does not choose to use its courts in this way, I do not believe that this Court is empowered to impose this much-debated procedure on local courts, however efficacious we may consider the Weeks rule to be as a means of securing Constitutional rights.

Finally, it is said that the overruling of Wolf is supported by the established doctrine that the admission in evidence of an involuntary confession renders a state conviction Constitutionally invalid. Since such a confession may often be entirely reliable, and therefore of the greatest relevance to the issue of the trial, the argument continues, this doctrine is ample warrant in precedent that the way evidence was obtained, and not just its relevance, is Constitutionally significant to the fairness of a trial. I believe this analogy is not a true one. The "coerced confession" rule is certainly not a rule that any illegally obtained statements may not be used in evidence. I would suppose that a statement which is procured during a period of illegal detention is, as much as unlawfully seized evidence, illegally obtained, but this Court has consistently refused to reverse state convictions resting on the use of such statements. Indeed it would seem the Court laid at rest the very argument now made by the majority when in Lisenba v. People of State of California, a state-coerced confession case, it said:

> "It may be assumed [that the] treatment of the petitioner [by the police] ... deprived him of his liberty without due process and that the petitioner would have been afforded preventive relief if he could have gained access to a court to seek it.
>
> "But illegal acts, as such, committed in the course of obtaining a confession ... do not furnish an answer to the constitutional question we must decide.... The gravamen of his complaint is the unfairness of the *use* of his confessions, and what occurred in their procurement is relevant only as it bears on that issue." (Emphasis supplied.)

The point, then, must be that in requiring exclusion of an involuntary statement of an accused, we are concerned not with an appropriate remedy for what the police have done, but with something which is regarded as going to the heart of our concepts of fairness in judicial procedure. The operative assumption of our procedural system is that "Ours is the accusatorial as opposed to the inquisitorial system. Such has been the characteristic of Anglo-American criminal justice since it freed itself from practices borrowed by the Star Chamber from the Continent whereby an accused was interrogated in secret for hours on end." ... The pressures brought to bear against an accused leading to a confession, unlike an unconstitutional violation of privacy, do not, apart from the use of the confession at trial, necessarily involve independent Constitutional violations. What is crucial is that the trial defense to which an accused is entitled should not be rendered an empty formality by reason of statements wrung from him, for then "a prisoner ... [has been] made the deluded instrument of his own conviction." 2 Hawkins, Pleas of the Crown (8th ed., 1824), c. 46, § 34. That this is a *procedural right,* and that its violation occurs at the time his improperly obtained statement is admitted at trial, is manifest. For without this right all the careful safeguards erected around the giving of testimony, whether by an accused or any other witness, would become empty formalities in a procedure where the most compelling possible evidence of guilt, a confession, would have already been obtained at the unsupervised pleasure of the police.

This, and not the disciplining of the police, as with illegally seized evidence, is surely the true basis for excluding a statement of the accused which was unconstitutionally obtained. In sum, I think the coerced confession analogy works strongly *against* what the Court does today.

In conclusion, it should be noted that the majority opinion in this case is in fact an opinion only for the *judgment* overruling Wolf, and not for the basic rationale by which four members of the majority have reached that result. For my Brother Black is unwilling to subscribe to their view that the Weeks exclusionary rule derives from the Fourth Amendment itself, but joins the majority opinion on the premise that its end result can be achieved by bringing the Fifth Amendment to the aid of the Fourth. On that score I need only say that whatever the validity of the "Fourth-Fifth Amendment" correlation which the Boyd case [supra] found, we have only very recently again reiterated the long-established doctrine of this Court that the Fifth Amendment privilege against self-incrimination is not applicable to the States....

I regret that I find so unwise in principle and so inexpedient in policy a decision motivated by the high purpose of increasing respect for Constitutional rights. But in the last analysis I think this Court can increase respect for the Constitution only if it rigidly respects the limitations which the Constitution places upon it, and respects as well the principles inherent in its own processes. In the present case I think we exceed both, and that our voice becomes only a voice of power, not of reason.

UNITED STATES v. LEON

Supreme Court of the United States, 1984.
468 U.S. 897, 104 S.Ct. 3405.

JUSTICE WHITE delivered the opinion of the Court.

This case presents the question whether the Fourth Amendment exclusionary rule should be modified so as not to bar the use in the prosecution's case in chief of evidence obtained by officers acting in reasonable reliance on a search warrant issued by a detached and neutral magistrate but ultimately found to be unsupported by probable cause. To resolve this question, we must consider once again the tension between the sometimes competing goals of, on the one hand, deterring official misconduct and removing inducements to unreasonable invasions of privacy and, on the other, establishing procedures under which criminal defendants are "acquitted or convicted on the basis of all the evidence which exposes the truth." Alderman v. United States, 394 U.S. 165, 175, 89 S.Ct. 961, 967 (1969).

I

In August 1981, a confidential informant of unproven reliability informed an officer of the Burbank Police Department that two persons known to him as "Armando" and "Patsy" were selling large quantities of cocaine and methaqualone from their residence at 620 Price Drive in Burbank, Cal. The informant also indicated that he had witnessed a sale of methaqualone by "Patsy" at the residence approximately five months earlier and had observed at that time a shoebox containing a large amount of cash that belonged to "Patsy." He further declared that "Armando" and "Patsy" generally kept only small quantities of drugs at their residence and stored the remainder at another location in Burbank.

On the basis of this information, the Burbank police initiated an extensive investigation focusing first on the Price Drive residence and later on two other residences as well. Cars parked at the Price Drive residence were determined to belong to respondents Armando Sanchez, who had previously been arrested for possession of marihuana, and Patsy Stewart, who had no criminal record. During the course of the investigation, officers observed an automobile belonging to respondent Ricardo Del Castillo, who had previously been arrested for possession of 50 pounds of marihuana, arrive at the Price Drive residence. The driver of that car entered the house, exited shortly thereafter carrying a small paper sack, and drove away. A check of Del Castillo's probation records led the officers to respondent Alberto Leon, whose telephone number Del Castillo had listed as his employer's. Leon had been arrested in 1980 on drug charges, and a companion had informed the police at that time that Leon was heavily involved in the importation of drugs into this country. Before the current investigation began, the Burbank officers had learned that an informant had told a Glendale police officer that Leon stored a large quantity of methaqualone at his residence in Glendale. During the course of this investigation, the Burbank officers learned that Leon was living at 716 South Sunset Canyon in Burbank.

Subsequently, the officers observed several persons, at least one of whom had prior drug involvement, arriving at the Price Drive residence and leaving with small packages; observed a variety of other material activity at the two residences as well as at a condominium at 7902 Via Magdalena; and witnessed a variety of relevant activity involving respondents' automobiles. The officers also observed respondents Sanchez and Stewart board separate flights for Miami. The pair later returned to Los Angeles together, consented to a search of their luggage that revealed only a small amount of marihuana, and left the airport. Based on these and other observations summarized in the affidavit, App. 34, Officer Cyril Rombach of the Burbank Police Department, an experienced and well-trained narcotics investigator, prepared an application for a warrant to search 620 Price Drive, 716 South Sunset Canyon, 7902 Via Magdalena, and automobiles registered to each of the respondents for an extensive list of items believed to be related to respondents' drug-trafficking activities. Officer Rombach's extensive application was reviewed by several Deputy District Attorneys.

A facially valid search warrant was issued in September 1981 by a State Superior Court Judge. The ensuing searches produced large quantities of drugs at the Via Magdalena and Sunset Canyon addresses and a small quantity at the Price Drive residence. Other evidence was discovered at each of the residences and in Stewart's and Del Castillo's automobiles. Respondents were indicted by a grand jury in the District Court for the Central District of California and charged with conspiracy to possess and distribute cocaine and a variety of substantive counts.

The respondents then filed motions to suppress the evidence seized pursuant to the warrant.[1] The District Court held an evidentiary

1. Respondent Leon moved to suppress the evidence found on his person at the time of his arrest and the evidence seized from his residence at 716 South Sunset Canyon. Respondent Stewart's motion covered the fruits of searches of her residence

hearing and, while recognizing that the case was a close one, see id., at 131, granted the motions to suppress in part. It concluded that the affidavit was insufficient to establish probable cause,[2] but did not suppress all of the evidence as to all of the respondents because none of the respondents had standing to challenge all of the searches.[3] In response to a request from the Government, the court made clear that Officer Rombach had acted in good faith, but it rejected the Government's suggestion that the Fourth Amendment exclusionary rule should not apply where evidence is seized in reasonable, good-faith reliance on a search warrant.[4]

The District Court denied the Government's motion for reconsideration, id., at 147, and a divided panel of the Court of Appeals for the Ninth Circuit affirmed, judgt. order reported at 701 F.2d 187 (1983). The Court of Appeals first concluded that Officer Rombach's affidavit could not establish probable cause to search the Price Drive residence. To the extent that the affidavit set forth facts demonstrating the basis of the informant's knowledge of criminal activity, the information included was fatally stale. The affidavit, moreover, failed to establish the informant's credibility. Accordingly, the Court of Appeals concluded that the information provided by the informant was inadequate under both prongs of the two-part test established in Aguilar v. Texas, 378 U.S. 108, 84 S.Ct. 1509 (1964), and Spinelli v. United States, 393 U.S. 410, 89

at 620 Price Drive and the condominium at 7902 Via Magdalena and statements she made during the search of her residence. Respondent Sanchez sought to suppress the evidence discovered during the search of his residence at 620 Price Drive and statements he made shortly thereafter. He also joined Stewart's motion to suppress evidence seized from the condominium. Respondent Del Castillo apparently sought to suppress all of the evidence seized in the searches. App. 78–80. The respondents also moved to suppress evidence seized in the searches of their automobiles.

2. "I just cannot find this warrant sufficient for a showing of probable cause.

* * *

"There is no question of the reliability and credibility of the informant as not being established.

"Some details given tended to corroborate, maybe, the reliability of [the informant's] information about the previous transaction, but if it is not a stale transaction, it comes awfully close to it; and all the other material I think is as consistent with innocence as it is with guilt.

* * *

"So I just do not think this affidavit can withstand the test. I find, then, that there is no probable cause in this case for the issuance of the search warrant. . . ." Id., at 127.

3. The District Court concluded that Sanchez and Stewart had standing to challenge the search of 620 Price Drive; that Leon had standing to contest the legality of the search of 716 South Sunset Canyon; that none of the respondents had established a legitimate expectation of privacy in the condominium at 7902 Via Magdalena; and that Stewart and Del Castillo each had standing to challenge the searches of their automobiles. The Government indicated that it did not intend to introduce evidence seized from the other respondents' vehicles. Id., at 127–129. Finally, the court suppressed statements given by Sanchez and Stewart. Id., at 129–130.

4. "On the issue of good faith, obviously that is not the law of the Circuit, and I am not going to apply that law.

"I will say certainly in my view, there is not any question about good faith. [Officer Rombach] went to a Superior Court judge and got a warrant; obviously laid a meticulous trail. Had surveilled for a long period of time, and I believe his testimony—and I think he said he consulted with three Deputy District Attorneys before proceeding himself, and I certainly have no doubt about the fact that that is true." Id., at 140.

S.Ct. 584 (1969).[5] The officers' independent investigation neither cured the staleness nor corroborated the details of the informant's declarations. The Court of Appeals then considered whether the affidavit formed a proper basis for the search of the Sunset Canyon residence. In its view, the affidavit included no facts indicating the basis for the informants' statements concerning respondent Leon's criminal activities and was devoid of information establishing the informants' reliability. Because these deficiencies had not been cured by the police investigation, the District Court properly suppressed the fruits of the search. The Court of Appeals refused the Government's invitation to recognize a good-faith exception to the Fourth Amendment exclusionary rule. App. to Pet. for Cert. 4a.

The Government's petition for certiorari expressly declined to seek review of the lower courts' determinations that the search warrant was unsupported by probable cause and presented only the question "[w]hether the Fourth Amendment exclusionary rule should be modified so as not to bar the admission of evidence seized in reasonable, good-faith reliance on a search warrant that is subsequently held to be defective." We granted certiorari to consider the propriety of such a modification. 463 U.S. 1206, 103 S.Ct. 3535 (1983). Although it undoubtedly is within our power to consider the question whether probable cause existed under the "totality of the circumstances" test announced last Term in Illinois v. Gates, 462 U.S. 213, 103 S.Ct. 2317 (1983), that question has not been briefed or argued; and it is also within our authority, which we choose to exercise, to take the case as it comes to us, accepting the Court of Appeals' conclusion that probable cause was lacking under the prevailing legal standards. See this Court's Rule 21.1(a).

We have concluded that, in the Fourth Amendment context, the exclusionary rule can be modified somewhat without jeopardizing its ability to perform its intended functions. Accordingly, we reverse the judgment of the Court of Appeals.

II

Language in opinions of this Court and of individual Justices has sometimes implied that the exclusionary rule is a necessary corollary of the Fourth Amendment, Mapp v. Ohio, 367 U.S. 643, 651, 655–657, 81 S.Ct. 1684, 1689, 1691–1692 (1961); Olmstead v. United States, 277 U.S. 438, 462–463, 48 S.Ct. 564, 567 (1928), or that the rule is required by the conjunction of the Fourth and Fifth Amendments. Mapp v. Ohio, supra, 367 U.S., at 661–662, 81 S.Ct., at 1694–1695 (Black, J., concurring); Agnello v. United States, 269 U.S. 20, 33–34, 46 S.Ct. 4, 6–7 (1925). These implications need not detain us long. The Fifth Amendment theory has not withstood critical analysis or the test of time, see

5. In Illinois v. Gates, 462 U.S. 213, 103 S.Ct. 2317 (1983), decided last Term, the Court abandoned the two-pronged *Aguilar–Spinelli* test for determining whether an informant's tip suffices to establish probable cause for the issuance of a warrant and substituted in its place a "totality of the circumstances" approach.

Andresen v. Maryland, 427 U.S. 463, 96 S.Ct. 2737 (1976), and the Fourth Amendment "has never been interpreted to proscribe the introduction of illegally seized evidence in all proceedings or against all persons." Stone v. Powell, 428 U.S. 465, 486, 96 S.Ct. 3037, 3048 (1976).

A

The Fourth Amendment contains no provision expressly precluding the use of evidence obtained in violation of its commands, and an examination of its origin and purposes makes clear that the use of fruits of a past unlawful search or seizure "work[s] no new Fourth Amendment wrong." United States v. Calandra, 414 U.S. 338, 354, 94 S.Ct. 613, 623 (1974). The wrong condemned by the Amendment is "fully accomplished" by the unlawful search or seizure itself, ibid., and the exclusionary rule is neither intended nor able to "cure the invasion of the defendant's rights which he has already suffered." Stone v. Powell, supra, 428 U.S., at 540, 96 S.Ct., at 3073 (White, J., dissenting). The rule thus operates as "a judicially created remedy designed to safeguard Fourth Amendment rights generally through its deterrent effect, rather than a personal constitutional right of the party aggrieved." United States v. Calandra, supra, 414 U.S., at 348, 94 S.Ct., at 620.

Whether the exclusionary sanction is appropriately imposed in a particular case, our decisions make clear, is "an issue separate from the question whether the Fourth Amendment rights of the party seeking to invoke the rule were violated by police conduct." Illinois v. Gates, supra, 426 U.S. at 223, 103 S.Ct., at 2324. Only the former question is currently before us, and it must be resolved by weighing the costs and benefits of preventing the use in the prosecution's case in chief of inherently trustworthy tangible evidence obtained in reliance on a search warrant issued by a detached and neutral magistrate that ultimately is found to be defective.

The substantial social costs exacted by the exclusionary rule for the vindication of Fourth Amendment rights have long been a source of concern. "Our cases have consistently recognized that unbending application of the exclusionary sanction to enforce ideals of governmental rectitude would impede unacceptably the truth-finding functions of judge and jury." United States v. Payner, 447 U.S. 727, 734, 100 S.Ct. 2439, 2445 (1980). An objectionable collateral consequence of this interference with the criminal justice system's truth-finding function is that some guilty defendants may go free or receive reduced sentences as a result of favorable plea bargains.[6] Particularly when law enforcement

6. Researchers have only recently begun to study extensively the effects of the exclusionary rule on the disposition of felony arrests. One study suggests that the rule results in the nonprosecution or nonconviction of between 0.6% and 2.35% of individuals arrested for felonies. Davies, A Hard Look at What We Know (and Still Need to Learn) About the "Costs" of the Exclusionary Rule: The NIJ Study and Other Studies of "Lost" Arrests, 1983 A.B.F.Res.J. 611, 621. The estimates are higher for particular crimes the prosecution of which depends heavily on physical evidence. Thus, the cumulative loss due to nonprosecution or nonconviction of individuals arrested on fel-

officers have acted in objective good faith or their transgressions have been minor, the magnitude of the benefit conferred on such guilty defendants offends basic concepts of the criminal justice system. Stone v. Powell, 428 U.S., at 490, 96 S.Ct., at 3050. Indiscriminate application of the exclusionary rule, therefore, may well "generat[e] disrespect for the law and administration of justice." Id., at 491, 96 S.Ct., at 3051. Accordingly, "[a]s with any remedial device, the application of the rule has been restricted to those areas where its remedial objectives are thought most efficaciously served." United States v. Calandra, supra, 414 U.S., at 348, 94 S.Ct., at 670; see Stone v. Powell, supra, 428 U.S., at 486–487, 96 S.Ct., at 3048–3049; United States v. Janis, 428 U.S. 433, 447, 96 S.Ct. 3021, 3028 (1976).

B

Close attention to those remedial objectives has characterized our recent decisions concerning the scope of the Fourth Amendment exclusionary rule. The Court has, to be sure, not seriously questioned, "in the absence of a more efficacious sanction, the continued application of the rule to suppress evidence from the [prosecution's] case where a Fourth Amendment violation has been substantial and deliberate...." Franks v. Delaware, 438 U.S. 154, 171, 98 S.Ct. 2674, 2684 (1978); Stone v. Powell, supra, 428 U.S., at 492, 96 S.Ct., at 3051. Nevertheless, the balancing approach that has evolved in various contexts—including criminal trials—"forcefully suggest[s] that the exclusionary rule be more generally modified to permit the introduction of evidence obtained in the reasonable good-faith belief that a search or seizure was in accord with

ony drug charges is probably in the range of 2.8% to 7.1%. Id., at 680. Davies' analysis of California data suggests that screening by police and prosecutors results in the release because of illegal searches or seizures of as many as 1.4% of all felony arrestees, id., at 650, that 0.9% of felony arrestees are released, because of illegal searches or seizures, at the preliminary hearing or after trial, id., at 653, and that roughly 0.5% of all felony arrestees benefit from reversals on appeal because of illegal searches. Id., at 654. See also K. Brosi, A Cross–City Comparison of Felony Case Processing 16, 18–19 (1979); U.S. General Accounting Office, Report of the Comptroller General of the United States, Impact of the Exclusionary Rule on Federal Criminal Prosecutions 10–11, 14 (1979); F. Feeney, F. Dill, & A. Weir, Arrests Without Convictions: How Often They Occur and Why 203–206 (National Institute of Justice 1983); National Institute of Justice, The Effects of the Exclusionary Rule: A Study in California 1–2 (1982); Nardulli, The Societal Cost of the Exclusionary Rule: An Empirical Assessment, 1983 A.B.F.Res.J. 585, 600. The exclusionary rule also has been found to affect the plea-bargaining process. S. Schlesinger, Exclusionary Injustice: The Problem of Illegally Obtained Evidence 63 (1977). But see Davies, supra, at 668–669; Nardulli, supra, at 604–606.

Many of these researchers have concluded that the impact of the exclusionary rule is insubstantial, but the small percentages with which they deal mask a large absolute number of felons who are released because the cases against them were based in part on illegal searches or seizures. "[A]ny rule of evidence that denies the jury access to clearly probative and reliable evidence must bear a heavy burden of justification, and must be carefully limited to the circumstances in which it will pay its way by deterring official unlawlessness." Illinois v. Gates, 462 U.S., at 257–258, 103 S.Ct., at 2342 (White, J., concurring in judgment). Because we find that the rule can have no substantial deterrent effect in the sorts of situations under consideration in this case, see infra, at 3417–3419, we conclude that it cannot pay its way in those situations.

the Fourth Amendment." Illinois v. Gates, 462 U.S., at 255, 103 S.Ct., at 2340 (White, J., concurring in judgment).

In *Stone v. Powell,* supra, the Court emphasized the costs of the exclusionary rule, expressed its view that limiting the circumstances under which Fourth Amendment claims could be raised in federal habeas corpus proceedings would not reduce the rule's deterrent effect, id., 428 U.S., at 489–495, 96 S.Ct., at 3050–3052, and held that a state prisoner who has been afforded a full and fair opportunity to litigate a Fourth Amendment claim may not obtain federal habeas relief on the ground that unlawfully obtained evidence had been introduced at his trial. Cf. Rose v. Mitchell, 443 U.S. 545, 560–563, 99 S.Ct. 2993, 3002–3004 (1979). Proposed extensions of the exclusionary rule to proceedings other than the criminal trial itself have been evaluated and rejected under the same analytic approach. In *United States v. Calandra,* for example, we declined to allow grand jury witnesses to refuse to answer questions based on evidence obtained from an unlawful search or seizure since "[a]ny incremental deterrent effect which might be achieved by extending the rule to grand jury proceedings is uncertain at best." 414 U.S., at 348, 94 S.Ct., at 620. Similarly, in *United States v. Janis,* supra, we permitted the use in federal civil proceedings of evidence illegally seized by state officials since the likelihood of deterring police misconduct through such an extension of the exclusionary rule was insufficient to outweigh its substantial social costs. In so doing, we declared that, "[i]f . . . the exclusionary rule does not result in appreciable deterrence, then, clearly, its use in the instant situation is unwarranted." Id., 428 U.S., at 454, 96 S.Ct., at 3032.

As cases considering the use of unlawfully obtained evidence in criminal trials themselves make clear, it does not follow from the emphasis on the exclusionary rule's deterrent value that "anything which deters illegal searches is thereby commanded by the Fourth Amendment." Alderman v. United States, 394 U.S., at 174, 89 S.Ct., at 967. In determining whether persons aggrieved solely by the introduction of damaging evidence unlawfully obtained from their co-conspirators or co-defendants could seek suppression, for example, we found that the additional benefits of such an extension of the exclusionary rule would not outweigh its costs. Id., at 174–175, 89 S.Ct., at 967. Standing to invoke the rule has thus been limited to cases in which the prosecution seeks to use the fruits of an illegal search or seizure against the victim of police misconduct. Rakas v. Illinois, 439 U.S. 128, 99 S.Ct. 421 (1978); Brown v. United States, 411 U.S. 223, 93 S.Ct. 1565 (1973); Wong Sun v. United States, 371 U.S. 471, 491–492, 83 S.Ct. 407, 419–420 (1963). Cf. United States v. Payner, 447 U.S. 727, 100 S.Ct. 2439 (1980).

Even defendants with standing to challenge the introduction in their criminal trials of unlawfully obtained evidence cannot prevent every conceivable use of such evidence. Evidence obtained in violation of the Fourth Amendment and inadmissible in the prosecution's case in chief may be used to impeach a defendant's direct testimony. Walder v. United States, 347 U.S. 62, 74 S.Ct. 354 (1954). See also Oregon v.

Hass, 420 U.S. 714, 95 S.Ct. 1215 (1975); Harris v. New York, 401 U.S. 222, 91 S.Ct. 643 (1971). A similar assessment of the "incremental furthering" of the ends of the exclusionary rule led us to conclude in United States v. Havens, 446 U.S. 620, 627, 100 S.Ct. 1912, 1916 (1980), that evidence inadmissible in the prosecution's case in chief or otherwise as substantive evidence of guilt may be used to impeach statements made by a defendant in response to "proper cross-examination reasonably suggested by the defendant's direct examination." Id., at 627–628, 100 S.Ct. at 1916–1917.

When considering the use of evidence obtained in violation of the Fourth Amendment in the prosecution's case in chief, moreover, we have declined to adopt a per se or "but for" rule that would render inadmissible any evidence that came to light through a chain of causation that began with an illegal arrest. Brown v. Illinois, 422 U.S. 590, 95 S.Ct. 2254 (1975); Wong Sun v. United States, supra, 371 U.S., at 487–488, 83 S.Ct., at 417. We also have held that a witness' testimony may be admitted even when his identity was discovered in an unconstitutional search. United States v. Ceccolini, 435 U.S. 268, 98 S.Ct. 1054 (1978). The perception underlying these decisions—that the connection between police misconduct and evidence of crime may be sufficiently attenuated to permit the use of that evidence at trial—is a product of considerations relating to the exclusionary rule and the constitutional principles it is designed to protect. Dunaway v. New York, 442 U.S. 200, 217–218, 99 S.Ct. 2248, 2259–2260 (1979); United States v. Ceccolini, supra, 435 U.S., at 279, 98 S.Ct., at 1061.[7] In short, the "dissipation of the taint" concept that the Court has applied in deciding whether exclusion is appropriate in a particular case "attempts to mark the point at which the detrimental consequences of illegal police action become so attenuated that the deterrent effect of the exclusionary rule no longer justifies its cost." Brown v. Illinois, supra, 422 U.S., at 609, 95 S.Ct., at 2264 (Powell, J., concurring in part). Not surprisingly in view of this purpose, an assessment of the flagrancy of the police misconduct constitutes an important step in the calculus. Dunaway v. New York, supra, 442 U.S., at 218, 99 S.Ct., at 2259; Brown v. Illinois, supra, 422 U.S., at 603–604, 95 S.Ct., 2261–2262.

The same attention to the purposes underlying the exclusionary rule also has characterized decisions not involving the scope of the rule itself. We have not required suppression of the fruits of a search incident to an arrest made in good-faith reliance on a substantive criminal statute that subsequently is declared unconstitutional. Michigan v. DeFillippo, 443 U.S. 31, 99 S.Ct. 2627 (1979).[8] Similarly, although the Court has been unwilling to conclude that new Fourth Amendment principles are always

7. "*Brown*'s focus on 'the causal connection between the illegality and the confession' reflected the two policies behind the use of the exclusionary rule to effectuate the Fourth Amendment. Where there is a close causal connection between the illegal seizure and the confession, not only is exclusion of the evidence more likely to deter similar police misconduct in the future, but use of the evidence is more likely to compromise the integrity of the courts." Dunaway v. New York, 442 U.S., at 217–218, 99 S.Ct. 2248, 2259–2260 (citation omitted).

8. We have held, however, that the exclusionary rule requires suppression of evito have only prospective effect, United States v. Johnson, 457 U.S. 537, 560, 102 S.Ct. 2579, 2593 (1982),[9] no Fourth Amendment decision marking a "clear break with the past" has been applied retroactively. See United States v. Peltier, 422 U.S. 531, 95 S.Ct. 2313 (1975); Desist v. United States, 394 U.S. 244, 89 S.Ct. 1030 (1969); Linkletter v. Walker, 381 U.S. 618, 85 S.Ct. 1731 (1965).[10] The propriety of retroactive application of a newly announced Fourth Amendment principle, moreover, has been assessed largely in terms of the contribution retroactivity might make to the deterrence of police misconduct. United States v. Johnson, supra, 457 U.S., at 560–561, 102 S.Ct., at 2593–2594; United States v. Peltier, supra, 422 U.S., at 536–539, 542, 95 S.Ct., at 2317–2318, 2320.

As yet, we have not recognized any form of good-faith exception to the Fourth Amendment exclusionary rule.[11] But the balancing approach that has evolved during the years of experience with the rule provides

dence obtained in searches carried out pursuant to statutes, not yet declared unconstitutional, purporting to authorize searches and seizures without probable cause or search warrants. See, e.g., Ybarra v. Illinois, 444 U.S. 85, 100 S.Ct. 338 (1979); Torres v. Puerto Rico, 442 U.S. 465, 99 S.Ct. 2425 (1979); Almeida–Sanchez v. United States, 413 U.S. 266, 93 S.Ct. 2535 (1973); Sibron v. New York, 392 U.S. 40, 88 S.Ct. 1889 (1968); Berger v. New York, 388 U.S. 41, 87 S.Ct. 1873 (1967). "Those decisions involved statutes which, by their own terms, authorized searches under circumstances which did not satisfy the traditional warrant and probable-cause requirements of the Fourth Amendment." Michigan v. DeFillippo, 443 U.S., at 39, 99 S.Ct., at 2633. The substantive Fourth Amendment principles announced in those cases are fully consistent with our holding here.

9. The Court held in United States v. Johnson that a construction of the Fourth Amendment that did not constitute a "clear break with the past" is to be applied to all convictions not yet final when the decision was handed down. The limited holding, see 457 U.S., at 562, 102 S.Ct., at 2594, turned in part on the Court's judgment that "[f]ailure to accord any retroactive effect to Fourth Amendment rulings would 'encourage police or other courts to disregard the plain purport of our decisions and to adopt a let's-wait-until-it's-decided approach.' " Id., at 561, 102 S.Ct., at 2593 (emphasis in original) (quoting Desist v. United States, 394 U.S. 244, 277, 89 S.Ct. 1030, 1052 (1969) (Fortas, J., dissenting)). Contrary to respondents' assertions, nothing in *Johnson* precludes adoption of a good-faith exception tailored to situations in which the police have reasonably relied on a warrant issued by a detached and neutral magistrate but later found to be defective.

10. Our retroactivity decisions have, for the most part, turned on our assessments of "(a) the purpose to be served by the new standards, (b) the extent of the reliance by law enforcement authorities on the old standards, and (c) the effect on the administration of justice of a retroactive application of the new standards." Stovall v. Denno, 388 U.S. 293, 297, 87 S.Ct. 1967, 1970 (1967). As we observed earlier this Term:

> "In considering the reliance factor, this Court's cases have looked primarily to whether law enforcement authorities and state courts have justifiably relied on a prior rule of law said to be different from that announced by the decision whose retroactivity is at issue. Unjustified 'reliance' is no bar to retroactivity. This inquiry is often phrased in terms of whether the new decision was foreshadowed by earlier cases or was a 'clear break with the past.' " Solem v. Stumes, 465 U.S. 638, 645–647, 104 S.Ct. 1338, 1343 (1984).

11. Members of the Court have, however, urged reconsideration of the scope of the exclusionary rule. See, e.g., Stone v. Powell, 428 U.S. 465, 496, 96 S.Ct. 3037, 3053 (1976) (Burger, C.J., concurring); id., at 536, 96 S.Ct., at 3072 (White, J., dissenting); Illinois v. Gates, 462 U.S., at 254–267, 103 S.Ct., at 2340–2347 (White, J., concurring in judgment); Brown v. Illinois, 422 U.S. 590, 609–612, 95 S.Ct. 2254, 2264–2266 (1975) (Powell, J., concurring in part); Schneckloth v. Bustamonte, 412 U.S. 218, 261–271, 93 S.Ct. 2041, 2065–2070 (1973) (Powell, J., concurring); California v. Minjares, 443 U.S. 916, 100 S.Ct. 9 (1979)

strong support for the modification currently urged upon us. As we discuss below, our evaluation of the costs and benefits of suppressing reliable physical evidence seized by officers reasonably relying on a warrant issued by a detached and neutral magistrate leads to the conclusion that such evidence should be admissible in the prosecution's case in chief.

III

A

Because a search warrant "provides the detached scrutiny of a neutral magistrate, which is a more reliable safeguard against improper searches than the hurried judgment of a law enforcement officer 'engaged in the often competitive enterprise of ferreting out crime,'" United States v. Chadwick, 433 U.S. 1, 9, 97 S.Ct. 2476, 2482 (1977) (quoting Johnson v. United States, 333 U.S. 10, 14, 68 S.Ct. 367, 369 (1948)), we have expressed a strong preference for warrants and declared that "in a doubtful or marginal case a search under a warrant may be sustainable where without one it would fall." United States v. Ventresca, 380 U.S. 102, 106, 85 S.Ct. 741, 744 (1965). See Aguilar v. Texas, 378 U.S., at 111, 84 S.Ct., at 1512. Reasonable minds frequently may differ on the question whether a particular affidavit establishes probable cause, and we have thus concluded that the preference for warrants is most appropriately effectuated by according "great deference" to a magistrate's determination. Spinelli v. United States, 393 U.S., at 419, 89 S.Ct., at 590. See Illinois v. Gates, 462 U.S., at 236, 103 S.Ct., at 2331; United States v. Ventresca, supra, 380 U.S., at 108–109, 85 S.Ct., at 745–746.

Deference to the magistrate, however, is not boundless. It is clear, first, that the deference accorded to a magistrate's finding of probable cause does not preclude inquiry into the knowing or reckless falsity of the affidavit on which that determination was based. Franks v. Delaware, 438 U.S. 154, 98 S.Ct. 2674 (1978).[12] Second, the courts must also insist that the magistrate purport to "perform his 'neutral and detached' function and not serve merely as a rubber stamp for the police." Aguilar v. Texas, supra, 378 U.S., at 111, 84 S.Ct., at 1512. See Illinois v. Gates, supra, 462 U.S., at 239, 103 S.Ct., at 2332. A magistrate failing to "manifest that neutrality and detachment demanded of a judicial officer when presented with a warrant application" and who acts instead as "an adjunct law enforcement officer" cannot provide valid authorization for an otherwise unconstitutional search. Lo–Ji Sales, Inc. v. New York, 442 U.S. 319, 326–327, 99 S.Ct. 2319, 2324–2325 (1979).

(Rehnquist, J., dissenting from denial of stay). One Court of Appeals, no doubt influenced by these individual urgings, has adopted a form of good-faith exception to the exclusionary rule. United States v. Williams, 622 F.2d 830 (CA5 1980) (en banc), cert. denied, 449 U.S. 1127, 101 S.Ct. 946 (1981).

12. Indeed, "it would be an unthinkable imposition upon [the magistrate's] authority if a warrant affidavit, revealed after the fact to contain a deliberately or recklessly false statement, were to stand beyond impeachment." 438 U.S., at 165, 98 S.Ct., at 2681.

Third, reviewing courts will not defer to a warrant based on an affidavit that does not "provide the magistrate with a substantial basis for determining the existence of probable cause." Illinois v. Gates, 462 U.S., at 239, 103 S.Ct., at 2332. "Sufficient information must be presented to the magistrate to allow that official to determine probable cause; his action cannot be a mere ratification of the bare conclusions of others." Ibid. See Aguilar v. Texas, supra, 378 U.S., at 114–115, 84 S.Ct., at 1513–1514; Giordenello v. United States, 357 U.S. 480, 78 S.Ct. 1245 (1958); Nathanson v. United States, 290 U.S. 41, 54 S.Ct. 11 (1933).[13] Even if the warrant application was supported by more than a "bare bones" affidavit, a reviewing court may properly conclude that, notwithstanding the deference that magistrates deserve, the warrant was invalid because the magistrate's probable-cause determination reflected an improper analysis of the totality of the circumstances, Illinois v. Gates, supra, 462 U.S., at 238–239, 103 S.Ct., at 2332–2333, or because the form of the warrant was improper in some respect.

Only in the first of these three situations, however, has the Court set forth a rationale for suppressing evidence obtained pursuant to a search warrant; in the other areas, it has simply excluded such evidence without considering whether Fourth Amendment interests will be advanced. To the extent that proponents of exclusion rely on its behavioral effects on judges and magistrates in these areas, their reliance is misplaced. First, the exclusionary rule is designed to deter police misconduct rather than to punish the errors of judges and magistrates. Second, there exists no evidence suggesting that judges and magistrates are inclined to ignore or subvert the Fourth Amendment or that lawlessness among these actors requires application of the extreme sanction of exclusion.[14]

Third, and most important, we discern no basis, and are offered none, for believing that exclusion of evidence seized pursuant to a

13. See also Beck v. Ohio, 379 U.S. 89, 85 S.Ct. 223 (1964), in which the Court concluded that "the record ... does not contain a single objective fact to support a belief by the officers that the petitioner was engaged in criminal activity at the time they arrested him." Id., at 95, 85 S.Ct., at 227. Although the Court was willing to assume that the arresting officers acted in good faith, it concluded that:

> " '[G]ood faith on the part of the arresting officers is not enough.' Henry v. United States, 361 U.S. 98, 102, 80 S.Ct. 168, 171. If subjective good faith alone were the test, the protections of the Fourth Amendment would evaporate, and the people would be 'secure in their persons, houses, papers, and effects,' only in the discretion of the police." Id., at 97, 85 S.Ct., at 228.

We adhere to this view and emphasize that nothing in this opinion is intended to suggest a lowering of the probable-cause standard. On the contrary, we deal here only with the remedy to be applied to a concededly unconstitutional search.

14. Although there are assertions that some magistrates become rubber stamps for the police and others may be unable effectively to screen police conduct, see, e.g., 2 W. LaFave, Search and Seizure § 4.1 (1978); Kamisar, Does (Did) (Should) The Exclusionary Rule Rest on a "Principled Basis" Rather than an "Empirical Proposition"?, 16 Creighton L.Rev. 565, 569–571 (1983); Schroeder, Deterring Fourth Amendment Violations: Alternatives to the Exclusionary Rule, 69 Geo.L.J. 1361, 1412 (1981), we are not convinced that this is a problem of major proportions. See L. Tiffany, D. McIntyre, & D. Rotenberg, Detection of Crime 119 (1967); Israel, Criminal Procedure, the Burger Court, and the Legacy of the Warren Court, 75 Mich.L.Rev. 1319,

warrant will have a significant deterrent effect on the issuing judge or magistrate.[15] Many of the factors that indicate that the exclusionary rule cannot provide an effective "special" or "general" deterrent for individual offending law enforcement officers [16] apply as well to judges or magistrates. And, to the extent that the rule is thought to operate as a "systemic" deterrent on a wider audience,[17] it clearly can have no such effect on individuals empowered to issue search warrants. Judges and magistrates are not adjuncts to the law enforcement team; as neutral judicial officers, they have no stake in the outcome of particular criminal prosecutions. The threat of exclusion thus cannot be expected significantly to deter them. Imposition of the exclusionary sanction is not necessary meaningfully to inform judicial officers of their errors, and we cannot conclude that admitting evidence obtained pursuant to a warrant while at the same time declaring that the warrant was somehow defective will in any way reduce judicial officers' professional incentives to comply with the Fourth Amendment, encourage them to repeat their mistakes, or lead to the granting of all colorable warrant requests.[18]

B

If exclusion of evidence obtained pursuant to a subsequently invalidated warrant is to have any deterrent effect, therefore, it must alter the

1414, n. 396 (1977); P. Johnson, New Approaches to Enforcing the Fourth Amendment 8–10 (Working Paper, Sept. 1978), quoted in Y. Kamisar, W. LaFave, & J. Israel, Modern Criminal Procedure 229–230 (5th ed. 1980); R. Van Duizend, L. Sutton, & C. Carter, The Search Warrant Process, ch. 7 (Review Draft, National Center for State Courts, 1983).

15. As the Supreme Judicial Court of Massachusetts recognized in Commonwealth v. Sheppard, 387 Mass. 488, 506, 441 N.E.2d 725, 735 (1982):

> "The exclusionary rule may not be well tailored to deterring judicial misconduct. If applied to judicial misconduct, the rule would be just as costly as it is when it is applied to police misconduct, but it may be ill-fitted to the job-created motivations of judges.... [I]deally a judge is impartial as to whether a particular piece of evidence is admitted or a particular defendant convicted. Hence, in the abstract, suppression of a particular piece of evidence may not be as effective a disincentive to a neutral judge as it would be to the police. It may be that a ruling by an appellate court that a search warrant was unconstitutional would be sufficient to deter similar conduct in the future by magistrates."

But see United States v. Karathanos, 531 F.2d 26, 33–34 (CA2), cert. denied, 428 U.S. 910, 96 S.Ct. 3221 (1976).

16. See, e.g., Stone v. Powell, 428 U.S., at 498, 96 S.Ct., at 3054 (Burger, C.J., concurring); Oaks, Studying the Exclusionary Rule in Search and Seizure, 37 U.Chi. L.Rev. 665, 709–710 (1970).

17. See, e.g., Dunaway v. New York, 442 U.S. 200, 221, 99 S.Ct. 2248, 2261 (1979) (Stevens, J., concurring); Mertens & Wasserstrom, The Good Faith Exception to the Exclusionary Rule: Deregulating the Police and Derailing the Law, 70 Geo.L.J. 365, 399–401 (1981).

18. Limiting the application of the exclusionary sanction may well increase the care with which magistrates scrutinize warrant applications. We doubt that magistrates are more desirous of avoiding the exclusion of evidence obtained pursuant to warrants they have issued than of avoiding invasions of privacy.

Federal magistrates, moreover, are subject to the direct supervision of district courts. They may be removed for "incompetency, misconduct, neglect of duty, or physical or mental disability." 28 U.S.C. § 631(i). If a magistrate serves merely as a "rubber stamp" for the police or is unable to exercise mature judgment, closer supervision or removal provides a more effective remedy than the exclusionary rule.

behavior of individual law enforcement officers or the policies of their departments. One could argue that applying the exclusionary rule in cases where the police failed to demonstrate probable cause in the warrant application deters future inadequate presentations or "magistrate shopping" and thus promotes the ends of the Fourth Amendment. Suppressing evidence obtained pursuant to a technically defective warrant supported by probable cause also might encourage officers to scrutinize more closely the form of the warrant and to point out suspected judicial errors. We find such arguments speculative and conclude that suppression of evidence obtained pursuant to a warrant should be ordered only on a case-by-case basis and only in those unusual cases in which exclusion will further the purposes of the exclusionary rule.[19]

We have frequently questioned whether the exclusionary rule can have any deterrent effect when the offending officers acted in the objectively reasonable belief that their conduct did not violate the Fourth Amendment. "No empirical researcher, proponent or opponent of the rule, has yet been able to establish with any assurance whether the rule has a deterrent effect...." United States v. Janis, 428 U.S., at 452, n. 22, 96 S.Ct., at 3031, n. 22. But even assuming that the rule effectively deters some police misconduct and provides incentives for the law enforcement profession as a whole to conduct itself in accord with the Fourth Amendment, it cannot be expected, and should not be applied, to deter objectively reasonable law enforcement activity.

As we observed in Michigan v. Tucker, 417 U.S. 433, 447, 94 S.Ct. 2357, 2365 (1974), and reiterated in United States v. Peltier, 422 U.S., at 539, 95 S.Ct., at 2318:

> "The deterrent purpose of the exclusionary rule necessarily assumes that the police have engaged in willful, or at the very least negligent, conduct which has deprived the defendant of some right. By refusing to admit evidence gained as a result of such conduct, the courts hope to instill in those particular investigating officers, or in their future counterparts, a greater degree of care toward the rights of an accused. Where the official action was pursued in complete good faith, however, the deterrence rationale loses much of its force."

The Peltier Court continued, id., at 542, 95 S.Ct., at 2320:

> "If the purpose of the exclusionary rule is to deter unlawful police conduct, then evidence obtained from a search should be suppressed only if it can be said that the law enforcement officer had knowledge, or may properly be charged with knowl-

19. Our discussion of the deterrent effect of excluding evidence obtained in reasonable reliance on a subsequently invalidated warrant assumes, of course, that the officers properly executed the warrant and searched only those places and for those objects that it was reasonable to believe were covered by the warrant. Cf. Massachusetts v. Sheppard, 468 U.S. 981, 989, n. 6, 104 S.Ct. 3424, 3429, n. 6 ("[I]t was not unreasonable for the police in this case to rely on the judge's assurances that the warrant authorized the search they had requested").

edge, that the search was unconstitutional under the Fourth Amendment."

See also Illinois v. Gates, 462 U.S., at 260–261, 103 S.Ct., at 2344 (White, J., concurring in judgment); United States v. Janis, supra, 428 U.S., at 459, 96 S.Ct., at 3034; Brown v. Illinois, 422 U.S., at 610–611, 95 S.Ct., at 2265–2266 (Powell, J., concurring in part).[20] In short, where the officer's conduct is objectively reasonable,

> "excluding the evidence will not further the ends of the exclusionary rule in any appreciable way; for it is painfully apparent that ... the officer is acting as a reasonable officer would and should act in similar circumstances. Excluding the evidence can in no way affect his future conduct unless it is to make him less willing to do his duty." Stone v. Powell, 428 U.S., at 539–540, 96 S.Ct., at 3073–3074 (White, J., dissenting).

This is particularly true, we believe, when an officer acting with objective good faith has obtained a search warrant from a judge or magistrate and acted within its scope.[21] In most such cases, there is no police illegality and thus nothing to deter. It is the magistrate's responsibility to determine whether the officer's allegations establish probable cause and, if so, to issue a warrant comporting in form with the requirements of the Fourth Amendment. In the ordinary case, an officer cannot be expected to question the magistrate's probable-cause determination or his judgment that the form of the warrant is technically sufficient. "[O]nce the warrant issues, there is literally nothing more

20. We emphasize that the standard of reasonableness we adopt is an objective one. Many objections to a good-faith exception assume that the exception will turn on the subjective good faith of individual officers. "Grounding the modification in objective reasonableness, however, retains the value of the exclusionary rule as an incentive for the law enforcement profession as a whole to conduct themselves in accord with the Fourth Amendment." Illinois v. Gates, 462 U.S., at 261, n. 15, 103 S.Ct., at 2344, n. 15 (White, J., concurring in judgment); see Dunaway v. New York, 442 U.S., at 221, 99 S.Ct., at 2261 (Stevens, J., concurring). The objective standard we adopt, moreover, requires officers to have a reasonable knowledge of what the law prohibits. United States v. Peltier, 422 U.S. 531, 542, 95 S.Ct. 2313, 2320 (1975). As Professor Jerold Israel has observed:

> "The key to the [exclusionary] rule's effectiveness as a deterrent lies, I believe, in the impetus it has provided to police training programs that make officers aware of the limits imposed by the fourth amendment and emphasize the need to operate within those limits. [An objective good-faith exception] is not likely to result in the elimination of such programs, which are now viewed as an important aspect of police professionalism. Neither is it likely to alter the tenor of those programs; the possibility that illegally obtained evidence may be admitted in borderline cases is unlikely to encourage police instructors to pay less attention to fourth amendment limitations. Finally, [it] should not encourage officers to pay less attention to what they are taught, as the requirement that the officer act in 'good faith' is inconsistent with closing one's mind to the possibility of illegality." Israel, supra n. 14, at 1412–1413 (footnotes omitted).

21. According to the Attorney General's Task Force on Violent Crime, Final Report (1981), the situation in which an officer relies on a duly authorized warrant

> "is a particularly compelling example of good faith. A warrant is a judicial mandate to an officer to conduct a search or make an arrest, and the officer has a sworn duty to carry out its provisions. Accordingly, we believe that there should be a rule which states that evidence obtained pursuant to and within the scope of a warrant is prima facie the result of good faith on the part of the officer seizing the evidence." Id., at 55.

the policeman can do in seeking to comply with the law." Id., 428 U.S., at 498, 96 S.Ct., at 3054 (Burger, C.J., concurring). Penalizing the officer for the magistrate's error, rather than his own, cannot logically contribute to the deterrence of Fourth Amendment violations.[22]

C

We conclude that the marginal or nonexistent benefits produced by suppressing evidence obtained in objectively reasonable reliance on a subsequently invalidated search warrant cannot justify the substantial costs of exclusion. We do not suggest, however, that exclusion is always inappropriate in cases where an officer has obtained a warrant and abided by its terms. "[S]earches pursuant to a warrant will rarely require any deep inquiry into reasonableness," Illinois v. Gates, 462 U.S., at 267, 103 S.Ct., at 2347 (White, J., concurring in judgment), for "a warrant issued by a magistrate normally suffices to establish" that a law enforcement officer has "acted in good faith in conducting the search." United States v. Ross, 456 U.S. 798, 823, n. 32, 102 S.Ct. 2157, 2172, n. 32 (1982). Nevertheless, the officer's reliance on the magistrate's probable-cause determination and on the technical sufficiency of the warrant he issues must be objectively reasonable, cf. Harlow v. Fitzgerald, 457 U.S. 800, 815–819, 102 S.Ct. 2727, 2737–2739 (1982),[23]

22. To the extent that Justice Stevens' conclusions concerning the integrity of the courts, post, at 3454–3455, rest on a foundation other than his judgment, which we reject, concerning the effects of our decision on the deterrence of police illegality, we find his argument unpersuasive. "Judicial integrity clearly does not mean that the courts must never admit evidence obtained in violation of the Fourth Amendment." United States v. Janis, 428 U.S. 433, 458, n. 35, 96 S.Ct. 3021, 3034, n. 35 (1976). "While courts, of course, must ever be concerned with preserving the integrity of the judicial process, this concern has limited force as a justification for the exclusion of highly probative evidence." Stone v. Powell, 428 U.S., at 485, 96 S.Ct., at 3048. Our cases establish that the question whether the use of illegally obtained evidence in judicial proceedings represents judicial participation in a Fourth Amendment violation and offends the integrity of the courts

> "is essentially the same as the inquiry into whether exclusion would serve a deterrent purpose.... The analysis showing that exclusion in this case has no demonstrated deterrent effect and is unlikely to have any significant such effect shows, by the same reasoning, that the admission of the evidence is unlikely to encourage violations of the Fourth Amendment." United States v. Janis, supra, 428 U.S., at 459, n. 35, 96 S.Ct., at 3034, n. 35.

Absent unusual circumstances, when a Fourth Amendment violation has occurred because the police have reasonably relied on a warrant issued by a detached and neutral magistrate but ultimately found to be defective, "the integrity of the courts is not implicated." Illinois v. Gates, supra, 462 U.S., at 259, n. 14, 103 S.Ct., at 2343, n. 14 (White, J., concurring in judgment). See Stone v. Powell, 428 U.S., at 485, n. 23, 96 S.Ct., at 3048, n. 23; id., at 540, 96 S.Ct., at 3073 (White, J., dissenting); United States v. Peltier, 422 U.S. 531, 536–539, 95 S.Ct. 2313, 2317–2318 (1975).

23. In *Harlow,* we eliminated the subjective component of the qualified immunity public officials enjoy in suits seeking damages for alleged deprivations of constitutional rights. The situations are not perfectly analogous, but we also eschew inquiries into the subjective beliefs of law enforcement officers who seize evidence pursuant to a subsequently invalidated warrant. Although we have suggested that, "[o]n occasion, the motive with which the officer conducts an illegal search may have some relevance in determining the propriety of applying the exclusionary rule," Scott v. United States, 436 U.S. 128, 139, n. 13, 98 S.Ct. 1717, 1724, n. 13 (1978), we believe that "sending state and federal courts on an expedition into the minds of police officers would produce a grave and fruitless misallocation of judicial

and it is clear that in some circumstances the officer[24] will have no reasonable grounds for believing that the warrant was properly issued.

Suppression therefore remains an appropriate remedy if the magistrate or judge in issuing a warrant was misled by information in an affidavit that the affiant knew was false or would have known was false except for his reckless disregard of the truth. Franks v. Delaware, 438 U.S. 154, 98 S.Ct. 2674 (1978). The exception we recognize today will also not apply in cases where the issuing magistrate wholly abandoned his judicial role in the manner condemned in Lo–Ji Sales, Inc. v. New York, 442 U.S. 319, 99 S.Ct. 2319 (1979); in such circumstances, no reasonably well trained officer should rely on the warrant. Nor would an officer manifest objective good faith in relying on a warrant based on an affidavit "so lacking in indicia of probable cause as to render official belief in its existence entirely unreasonable." Brown v. Illinois, 422 U.S., at 610–611, 95 S.Ct., at 2265–2266 (Powell, J., concurring in part); see Illinois v. Gates, supra, 462 U.S., at 263–264, 103 S.Ct., at 2345–2346 (White, J., concurring in the judgment). Finally, depending on the circumstances of the particular case, a warrant may be so facially deficient—i.e., in failing to particularize the place to be searched or the things to be seized—that the executing officers cannot reasonably presume it to be valid. Cf. Massachusetts v. Sheppard, 468 U.S., at 988–991, 104 S.Ct., at 3428–3430.

In so limiting the suppression remedy, we leave untouched the probable-cause standard and the various requirements for a valid warrant. Other objections to the modification of the Fourth Amendment exclusionary rule we consider to be insubstantial. The good-faith exception for searches conducted pursuant to warrants is not intended to signal our unwillingness strictly to enforce the requirements of the Fourth Amendment, and we do not believe that it will have this effect. As we have already suggested, the good-faith exception, turning as it does on objective reasonableness, should not be difficult to apply in practice. When officers have acted pursuant to a warrant, the prosecution should ordinarily be able to establish objective good faith without a substantial expenditure of judicial time.

Nor are we persuaded that application of a good-faith exception to searches conducted pursuant to warrants will preclude review of the

resources." Massachusetts v. Painten, 389 U.S. 560, 565, 88 S.Ct. 660, 663 (1968) (White, J., dissenting). Accordingly, our good-faith inquiry is confined to the objectively ascertainable question whether a reasonably well trained officer would have known that the search was illegal despite the magistrate's authorization. In making this determination, all of the circumstances—including whether the warrant application had previously been rejected by a different magistrate—may be considered.

24. References to "officer" throughout this opinion should not be read too narrowly. It is necessary to consider the objective reasonableness, not only of the officers who eventually executed a warrant, but also of the officers who originally obtained it or who provided information material to the probable-cause determination. Nothing in our opinion suggests, for example, that an officer could obtain a warrant on the basis of a "bare bones" affidavit and then rely on colleagues who are ignorant of the circumstances under which the warrant was obtained to conduct the search. See Whiteley v. Warden, 401 U.S. 560, 568, 91 S.Ct. 1031, 1037 (1971).

constitutionality of the search or seizure, deny needed guidance from the courts, or freeze Fourth Amendment law in its present state.[25] There is no need for courts to adopt the inflexible practice of always deciding whether the officers' conduct manifested objective good faith before turning to the question whether the Fourth Amendment has been violated. Defendants seeking suppression of the fruits of allegedly unconstitutional searches or seizures undoubtedly raise live controversies which Art. III empowers federal courts to adjudicate. As cases addressing questions of good-faith immunity under 42 U.S.C. § 1983, compare O'Connor v. Donaldson, 422 U.S. 563, 95 S.Ct. 2486 (1975), with Procunier v. Navarette, 434 U.S. 555, 566, n. 14, 98 S.Ct. 855, 862, n. 14 (1978), and cases involving the harmless-error doctrine, compare Milton v. Wainwright, 407 U.S. 371, 372, 92 S.Ct. 2174, 2175 (1972), with Coleman v. Alabama, 399 U.S. 1, 90 S.Ct. 1999 (1970), make clear, courts have considerable discretion in conforming their decisionmaking processes to the exigencies of particular cases.

If the resolution of a particular Fourth Amendment question is necessary to guide future action by law enforcement officers and magistrates, nothing will prevent reviewing courts from deciding that question before turning to the good-faith issue.[26] Indeed, it frequently will be difficult to determine whether the officers acted reasonably without resolving the Fourth Amendment issue. Even if the Fourth Amendment question is not one of broad import, reviewing courts could decide in particular cases that magistrates under their supervision need to be informed of their errors and so evaluate the officers' good faith only after finding a violation. In other circumstances, those courts could reject suppression motions posing no important Fourth Amendment questions by turning immediately to a consideration of the officers' good faith. We have no reason to believe that our Fourth Amendment jurisprudence would suffer by allowing reviewing courts to exercise an informed discretion in making this choice.

IV

When the principles we have enunciated today are applied to the facts of this case, it is apparent that the judgment of the Court of Appeals cannot stand. The Court of Appeals applied the prevailing legal standards to Officer Rombach's warrant application and concluded that the application could not support the magistrate's probable-cause deter-

25. The argument that defendants will lose their incentive to litigate meritorious Fourth Amendment claims as a result of the good-faith exception we adopt today is unpersuasive. Although the exception might discourage presentation of insubstantial suppression motions, the magnitude of the benefit conferred on defendants by a successful motion makes it unlikely that litigation of colorable claims will be substantially diminished.

26. It has been suggested, in fact, that "the recognition of a 'penumbral zone,' within which an inadvertent mistake would not call for exclusion, ... will make it less tempting for judges to bend fourth amendment standards to avoid releasing a possibly dangerous criminal because of a minor and unintentional miscalculation by the police." Schroeder, supra n. 14, at 1420–1421 (footnote omitted); see Ashdown, Good Faith, the Exclusionary Remedy, and Rule–Oriented Adjudication in the Criminal Process, 24 Wm. & Mary L.Rev. 335, 383–384 (1983).

mination. In so doing, the court clearly informed the magistrate that he had erred in issuing the challenged warrant. This aspect of the court's judgment is not under attack in this proceeding.

Having determined that the warrant should not have issued, the Court of Appeals understandably declined to adopt a modification of the Fourth Amendment exclusionary rule that this Court had not previously sanctioned. Although the modification finds strong support in our previous cases, the Court of Appeals' commendable self-restraint is not to be criticized. We have now reexamined the purposes of the exclusionary rule and the propriety of its application in cases where officers have relied on a subsequently invalidated search warrant. Our conclusion is that the rule's purposes will only rarely be served by applying it in such circumstances.

In the absence of an allegation that the magistrate abandoned his detached and neutral role, suppression is appropriate only if the officers were dishonest or reckless in preparing their affidavit or could not have harbored an objectively reasonable belief in the existence of probable cause. Only respondent Leon has contended that no reasonably well trained police officer could have believed that there existed probable cause to search his house; significantly, the other respondents advance no comparable argument. Officer Rombach's application for a warrant clearly was supported by much more than a "bare bones" affidavit. The affidavit related the results of an extensive investigation and, as the opinions of the divided panel of the Court of Appeals make clear, provided evidence sufficient to create disagreement among thoughtful and competent judges as to the existence of probable cause. Under these circumstances, the officers' reliance on the magistrate's determination of probable cause was objectively reasonable, and application of the extreme sanction of exclusion is inappropriate.

Accordingly, the judgment of the Court of Appeals is

Reversed.

JUSTICE BLACKMUN, concurring.

The Court today holds that evidence obtained in violation of the Fourth Amendment by officers acting in objectively reasonable reliance on a search warrant issued by a neutral and detached magistrate need not be excluded, as a matter of federal law, from the case in chief of federal and state criminal prosecutions. In so doing, the Court writes another chapter in the volume of Fourth Amendment law opened by Weeks v. United States, 232 U.S. 383, 34 S.Ct. 341 (1914). I join the Court's opinion in this case and the one in Massachusetts v. Sheppard, 468 U.S. 981, 104 S.Ct. 3424 (1984), because I believe that the rule announced today advances the legitimate interests of the criminal justice system without sacrificing the individual rights protected by the Fourth Amendment. I write separately, however, to underscore what I regard as the unavoidably provisional nature of today's decisions.

As the Court's opinion in this case makes clear, the Court has narrowed the scope of the exclusionary rule because of an empirical judgment that the rule has little appreciable effect in cases where officers act in objectively reasonable reliance on search warrants. See ante, at 3419–3420. Because I share the view that the exclusionary rule is not a constitutionally compelled corollary of the Fourth Amendment itself, see ante, at 3412, I see no way to avoid making an empirical judgment of this sort, and I am satisfied that the Court has made the correct one on the information before it. Like all courts, we face institutional limitations on our ability to gather information about "legislative facts," and the exclusionary rule itself has exacerbated the shortage of hard data concerning the behavior of police officers in the absence of such a rule. See United States v. Janis, 428 U.S. 433, 448–453, 96 S.Ct. 3021, 3029–3031 (1976). Nonetheless, we cannot escape the responsibility to decide the question before us, however imperfect our information may be, and I am prepared to join the Court on the information now at hand.

What must be stressed, however, is that any empirical judgment about the effect of the exclusionary rule in a particular class of cases necessarily is a provisional one. By their very nature, the assumptions on which we proceed today cannot be cast in stone. To the contrary, they now will be tested in the real world of state and federal law enforcement, and this Court will attend to the results. If it should emerge from experience that, contrary to our expectations, the good-faith exception to the exclusionary rule results in a material change in police compliance with the Fourth Amendment, we shall have to reconsider what we have undertaken here. The logic of a decision that rests on untested predictions about police conduct demands no less.

If a single principle may be drawn from this Court's exclusionary rule decisions, from *Weeks* through Mapp v. Ohio, 367 U.S. 643, 81 S.Ct. 1684 (1961), to the decisions handed down today, it is that the scope of the exclusionary rule is subject to change in light of changing judicial understanding about the effects of the rule outside the confines of the courtroom. It is incumbent on the Nation's law enforcement officers, who must continue to observe the Fourth Amendment in the wake of today's decisions, to recognize the double-edged nature of that principle.

MASSACHUSETTS v. SHEPPARD

Supreme Court of the United States, 1984.
468 U.S. 981, 104 S.Ct. 3424.

JUSTICE WHITE delivered the opinion of the Court.

This case involves the application of the rules articulated today in United States v. Leon, 468 U.S. 897, 104 S.Ct. 3405, to a situation in which police officers seize items pursuant to a warrant subsequently invalidated because of a technical error on the part of the issuing judge.

I

The badly burned body of Sandra Boulware was discovered in a vacant lot in the Roxbury section of Boston at approximately 5 a.m., Saturday, May 5, 1979. An autopsy revealed that Boulware had died of multiple compound skull fractures caused by blows to the head. After a brief investigation, the police decided to question one of the victim's boyfriends, Osborne Sheppard. Sheppard told the police that he had last seen the victim on Tuesday night and that he had been at a local gaming house (where card games were played) from 9 p.m. Friday until 5 a.m. Saturday. He identified several people who would be willing to substantiate the latter claim.

By interviewing the people Sheppard had said were at the gaming house on Friday night, the police learned that although Sheppard was at the gaming house that night, he had borrowed an automobile at about 3 o'clock Saturday morning in order to give two men a ride home. Even though the trip normally took only 15 minutes, Sheppard did not return with the car until nearly 5 a.m.

On Sunday morning, police officers visited the owner of the car Sheppard had borrowed. He consented to an inspection of the vehicle. Bloodstains and pieces of hair were found on the rear bumper and within the trunk compartment. In addition, the officers noticed strands of wire in the trunk similar to wire strands found on and near the body of the victim. The owner of the car told the officers that when he last used the car on Friday night, shortly before Sheppard borrowed it, he had placed articles in the trunk and had not noticed any stains on the bumper or in the trunk.

On the basis of the evidence gathered thus far in the investigation, Detective Peter O'Malley drafted an affidavit designed to support an application for an arrest warrant and a search warrant authorizing a search of Sheppard's residence. The affidavit set forth the results of the investigation and stated that the police wished to search for

> "[a] fifth bottle of amaretto liquor, 2 nickel bags of marijuana, a woman's jacket that has been described as black-grey (charcoal), possessions of Sandra D. Boulware, similar type wire and rope that match those on the body of Sandra D. Boulware, or in the above [T]hunderbird. Blunt instrument that might have been used on the victim. Men's or women's clothing that may have blood, gasoline, burns on them. Items that may have fingerprints of the victim." [1]

Detective O'Malley showed the affidavit to the District Attorney, the District Attorney's first assistant, and a sergeant, who all concluded that it set forth probable cause for the search and the arrest. 387 Mass. 488, 492, 441 N.E.2d 725, 727 (1982).

1. The liquor and marihuana were included in the request because Sheppard had told the officers that when he was last with the victim, the two had purchased two bags of marihuana and a fifth of amaretto before going to his residence.

Because it was Sunday, the local court was closed, and the police had a difficult time finding a warrant application form. Detective O'Malley finally found a warrant form previously in use in the Dorchester District. The form was entitled "Search Warrant—Controlled Substance G.L. c. 276 §§ 1 through 3A." Realizing that some changes had to be made before the form could be used to authorize the search requested in the affidavit, Detective O'Malley deleted the subtitle "controlled substance" with a typewriter. He also substituted "Roxbury" for the printed "Dorchester" and typed Sheppard's name and address into blank spaces provided for that information. However, the reference to "controlled substance" was not deleted in the portion of the form that constituted the warrant application and that, when signed, would constitute the warrant itself.

Detective O'Malley then took the affidavit and the warrant form to the residence of a judge who had consented to consider the warrant application. The judge examined the affidavit and stated that he would authorize the search as requested. Detective O'Malley offered the warrant form and stated that he knew the form as presented dealt with controlled substances. He showed the judge where he had crossed out the subtitles. After unsuccessfully searching for a more suitable form, the judge informed O'Malley that he would make the necessary changes so as to provide a proper search warrant. The judge then took the form, made some changes on it, and dated and signed the warrant. However, he did not change the substantive portion of the warrant, which continued to authorize a search for controlled substances;[2] nor did he alter the form so as to incorporate the affidavit. The judge returned the affidavit and the warrant to O'Malley, informing him that the warrant was sufficient authority in form and content to carry out the search as requested.[3] O'Malley took the two documents and, accompanied by other officers, proceeded to Sheppard's residence. The scope of the ensuing search was limited to the items listed in the affidavit, and several incriminating pieces of evidence were discovered.[4] Sheppard was then charged with first-degree murder.

2. The warrant directed the officers to "search for any controlled substance, article, implement or other paraphernalia used in, for, or in connection with the unlawful possession or use of any controlled substance, and to seize and securely keep the same until final action...."

3. Sheppard contends that there is no evidence in the record that the judge spoke to O'Malley after he made the changes. Brief for Respondent 11, n. 4. However, the trial judge expressly found that the judge "informed Detective O'Malley that the warrant as delivered over was sufficient authority in form and content to carry out the search as requested," App. 27a, and a plurality of the Supreme Judicial Court noted that finding without any apparent disapproval. 387 Mass. 488, 497, 441 N.E.2d 725, 730 (1982). Since it would have been reasonable for O'Malley to infer that the warrant was valid when the judge made some changes after assuring him that the form would be corrected, an express assurance that the warrant was adequate would add little to the reasonableness of O'Malley's belief that the necessary changes had been made. Therefore, nothing would be served by combing the record to determine whether there is sufficient evidence to support the trial court's finding that the judge spoke to O'Malley after signing the warrant.

4. The police found a pair of bloodstained boots, bloodstains on the concrete floor, a woman's earring with bloodstains on it, a bloodstained envelope, a pair of men's jockey shorts and women's leotards

At a pretrial suppression hearing, the trial judge concluded that the warrant failed to conform to the commands of the Fourth Amendment because it did not particularly describe the items to be seized. The judge ruled, however, that the evidence could be admitted notwithstanding the defect in the warrant because the police had acted in good faith in executing what they reasonably thought was a valid warrant. App. 35a. At the subsequent trial, Sheppard was convicted.

On appeal, Sheppard argued that the evidence obtained pursuant to the defective warrant should have been suppressed. The Supreme Judicial Court of Massachusetts agreed. A plurality of the justices concluded that although "the police conducted the search in a good faith belief, reasonably held, that the search was lawful and authorized by the warrant issued by the judge," 387 Mass., at 503, 441 N.E.2d, at 733, the evidence had to be excluded because this Court had not recognized a good-faith exception to the exclusionary rule. Two justices combined in a separate concurrence to stress their rejection of the good-faith exception, and one justice dissented, contending that since exclusion of the evidence in this case would not serve to deter any police misconduct, the evidence should be admitted. We granted certiorari and set the case for argument in conjunction with United States v. Leon, 468 U.S. 897, 104 S.Ct. 3405, 463 U.S. 1205, 103 S.Ct. 3534 (1983).

II

Having already decided that the exclusionary rule should not be applied when the officer conducting the search acted in objectively reasonable reliance on a warrant issued by a detached and neutral magistrate that subsequently is determined to be invalid, at 922–923, 104 S.Ct., at 3421, the sole issue before us in this case is whether the officers reasonably believed that the search they conducted was authorized by a valid warrant.[5] There is no dispute that the officers believed

with blood on them, three types of wire, and a woman's hairpiece, subsequently identified as the victim's.

5. Both the trial court, App. 32a, and a majority of the Supreme Judicial Court, 387 Mass., at 500–501, 441 N.E.2d, at 731–732; id., at 510, 441 N.E.2d, at 737 (Liacos, J., joined by Abrams, J., concurring), concluded that the warrant was constitutionally defective because the description in the warrant was completely inaccurate and the warrant did not incorporate the description contained in the affidavit. Petitioner does not dispute this conclusion.

Petitioner does argue, however, that even though the warrant was invalid, the search was constitutional because it was reasonable within the meaning of the Fourth Amendment. Brief for Petitioner 28–32. The uniformly applied rule is that a search conducted pursuant to a warrant that fails to conform to the particularity requirement of the Fourth Amendment is unconstitutional. Stanford v. Texas, 379 U.S. 476, 85 S.Ct. 506 (1965); United States v. Cardwell, 680 F.2d 75, 77–78 (CA9 1982); United States v. Crozier, 674 F.2d 1293, 1299 (CA9 1982); United States v. Klein, 565 F.2d 183, 185 (CA1 1977); United States v. Gardner, 537 F.2d 861, 862 (CA6 1976); United States v. Marti, 421 F.2d 1263, 1268–1269 (CA2 1970). That rule is in keeping with the well-established principle that "except in certain carefully defined classes of cases, a search of private property without proper consent is 'unreasonable' unless it has been authorized by a valid search warrant." Camara v. Municipal Court, 387 U.S. 523, 528–529, 87 S.Ct. 1727, 1730–1731 (1967). See Steagald v. United States, 451 U.S. 204, 211–212, 101 S.Ct. 1642, 1647 (1981); Jones v. United States, 357 U.S. 493, 499, 78 S.Ct. 1253, 1257 (1958). Whether the present case fits into one of those carefully defined classes is a fact-bound issue of little importance since

that the warrant authorized the search that they conducted. Thus, the only question is whether there was an objectively reasonable basis for the officers' mistaken belief. Both the trial court, App. 35a, and a majority of the Supreme Judicial Court, 387 Mass., at 503, 441 N.E.2d, at 733; id., at 524–525, 441 N.E.2d, at 745 (Lynch, J., dissenting), concluded that there was. We agree.

The officers in this case took every step that could reasonably be expected of them. Detective O'Malley prepared an affidavit which was reviewed and approved by the District Attorney. He presented that affidavit to a neutral judge. The judge concluded that the affidavit established probable cause to search Sheppard's residence, App. 26a, and informed O'Malley that he would authorize the search as requested. O'Malley then produced the warrant form and informed the judge that it might need to be changed. He was told by the judge that the necessary changes would be made. He then observed the judge make some changes and received the warrant and the affidavit. At this point, a reasonable police officer would have concluded, as O'Malley did, that the warrant authorized a search for the materials outlined in the affidavit.

Sheppard contends that since O'Malley knew the warrant form was defective, he should have examined it to make sure that the necessary changes had been made. However, that argument is based on the premise that O'Malley had a duty to disregard the judge's assurances that the requested search would be authorized and the necessary changes would be made. Whatever an officer may be required to do when he executes a warrant without knowing beforehand what items are to be seized,[6] we refuse to rule that an officer is required to disbelieve a judge who has just advised him, by word and by action, that the warrant he possesses authorizes him to conduct the search he has requested. In Massachusetts, as in most jurisdictions, the determinations of a judge acting within his jurisdiction, even if erroneous, are valid and binding until they are set aside under some recognized procedure. Streeter v. City of Worcester, 336 Mass. 469, 472, 146 N.E.2d 514, 517 (1957); Moll v. Township of Wakefield, 274 Mass. 505, 507, 175 N.E. 81, 82 (1931). If an officer is required to accept at face value the judge's conclusion that a warrant form is invalid, there is little reason why he should be expected to disregard assurances that everything is all right, especially when he has alerted the judge to the potential problems.

similar situations are unlikely to arise with any regularity.

6. Normally, when an officer who has not been involved in the application stage receives a warrant, he will read it in order to determine the object of the search. In this case, Detective O'Malley, the officer who directed the search, knew what items were listed in the affidavit presented to the judge, and he had good reason to believe that the warrant authorized the seizure of those items. Whether an officer who is less familiar with the warrant application or who has unalleviated concerns about the proper scope of the search would be justified in failing to notice a defect like the one in the warrant in this case is an issue we need not decide. We hold only that it was not unreasonable for the police in this case to rely on the judge's assurances that the warrant authorized the search they had requested.

In sum, the police conduct in this case clearly was objectively reasonable and largely error-free. An error of constitutional dimensions may have been committed with respect to the issuance of the warrant, but it was the judge, not the police officers, who made the critical mistake. "[T]he exclusionary rule was adopted to deter unlawful searches by police, not to punish the errors of magistrates and judges." Illinois v. Gates, 462 U.S. 213, 263, 103 S.Ct. 2317, 2346 (1983) (White, J., concurring in judgment).[7] Suppressing evidence because the judge failed to make all the necessary clerical corrections despite his assurances that such changes would be made will not serve the deterrent function that the exclusionary rule was designed to achieve. Accordingly, federal law does not require the exclusion of the disputed evidence in this case. The judgment of the Supreme Judicial Court is therefore reversed, and the case is remanded for further proceedings not inconsistent with this opinion.

It is so ordered.

UNITED STATES v. LEON, 1984
and
MASSACHUSETTS v. SHEPPARD, 1984

468 U.S. 897, 104 S.Ct. 3430.

Dissenting Opinions

JUSTICE BRENNAN, with whom JUSTICE MARSHALL joins, dissenting.*

Ten years ago in United States v. Calandra, 414 U.S. 338, 94 S.Ct. 613 (1974), I expressed the fear that the Court's decision "may signal that a majority of my colleagues have positioned themselves to reopen the door [to evidence secured by official lawlessness] still further and abandon altogether the exclusionary rule in search-and-seizure cases." Id., at 365, 94 S.Ct., at 628 (dissenting opinion). Since then, in case after case, I have witnessed the Court's gradual but determined strangulation of the rule.[1] It now appears that the Court's victory over the

7. This is not an instance in which "it is plainly evident that a magistrate or judge had no business issuing a warrant." Illinois v. Gates, 462 U.S., at 264, 103 S.Ct. 2346 (White J., concurring in the judgment). The judge's error was not in concluding that a warrant should issue but in failing to make the necessary changes on the form. Indeed, Sheppard admits that if the judge had crossed out the reference to controlled substances, written "see attached affidavit" on the form, and attached the affidavit to the warrant, the warrant would have been valid. Tr. of Oral Arg. 27, 50. See United States v. Johnson, 690 F.2d 60, 64–65 (CA3 1982), cert. denied, 459 U.S. 1214, 103 S.Ct. 1212 (1983); In re Property Belonging to Talk of the Town Bookstore, Inc., 644 F.2d 1317, 1318–1319 (CA9 1981); United States v. Johnson, 541 F.2d 1311, 1315–1316 (CA8 1976); United States v. Womack, 509 F.2d 368, 382 (CADC 1974); Commonwealth v. Todisco, 363 Mass. 445, 450, 294 N.E.2d 860, 864 (1973).

* [This opinion applies also to No. 82–963, Massachusetts v. Sheppard, 468 U.S. 981, 104 S.Ct. 3424 (1984).]

1. See, e.g., United States v. Peltier, 422 U.S. 531, 544, 95 S.Ct. 2313, 2321 (1975) (Brennan, J., dissenting); United States v. Janis, 428 U.S. 433, 460, 96 S.Ct. 3021, 3035 (1976) (Brennan, J., dissenting); Stone v. Powell, 428 U.S. 465, 502, 96 S.Ct. 3037, 3056 (1976) (Brennan, J., dissenting); Michigan v. DeFillippo, 443 U.S. 31, 41, 99 S.Ct. 2627, 2634 (1979) (Brennan, J., dissenting); United States v. Havens, 446 U.S.

Fourth Amendment is complete. That today's decisions represent the *pièce de résistance* of the Court's past efforts cannot be doubted, for today the Court sanctions the use in the prosecution's case in chief of illegally obtained evidence against the individual whose rights have been violated—a result that had previously been thought to be foreclosed.

The Court seeks to justify this result on the ground that the "costs" of adhering to the exclusionary rule in cases like those before us exceed the "benefits." But the language of deterrence and of cost/benefit analysis, if used indiscriminately, can have a narcotic effect. It creates an illusion of technical precision and ineluctability. It suggests that not only constitutional principle but also empirical data support the majority's result. When the Court's analysis is examined carefully, however, it is clear that we have not been treated to an honest assessment of the merits of the exclusionary rule, but have instead been drawn into a curious world where the "costs" of excluding illegally obtained evidence loom to exaggerated heights and where the "benefits" of such exclusion are made to disappear with a mere wave of the hand.

The majority ignores the fundamental constitutional importance of what is at stake here. While the machinery of law enforcement and indeed the nature of crime itself have changed dramatically since the Fourth Amendment became part of the Nation's fundamental law in 1791, what the Framers understood then remains true today—that the task of combating crime and convicting the guilty will in every era seem of such critical and pressing concern that we may be lured by the temptations of expediency into forsaking our commitment to protecting individual liberty and privacy. It was for that very reason that the Framers of the Bill of Rights insisted that law enforcement efforts be permanently and unambiguously restricted in order to preserve personal freedoms. In the constitutional scheme they ordained, the sometimes unpopular task of ensuring that the government's enforcement efforts remain within the strict boundaries fixed by the Fourth Amendment was entrusted to the courts. As James Madison predicted in his address to the First Congress on June 8, 1789:

> "If [these rights] are incorporated into the Constitution, independent tribunals of justice will consider themselves in a peculiar manner the guardians of those rights; they will be an impenetrable bulwark against every assumption of power in the Legislative or Executive; they will be naturally led to resist every encroachment upon rights expressly stipulated for in the Constitution by the declaration of rights." 1 Annals of Cong. 439.

If those independent tribunals lose their resolve, however, as the Court has done today, and give way to the seductive call of expediency, the vital guarantees of the Fourth Amendment are reduced to nothing more than a "form of words." Silverthorne Lumber Co. v. United States, 251 U.S. 385, 392, 40 S.Ct. 182, 183 (1920).

620, 629, 100 S.Ct. 1912, 1917 (1980) (Brennan, J., dissenting).

A proper understanding of the broad purposes sought to be served by the Fourth Amendment demonstrates that the principles embodied in the exclusionary rule rest upon a far firmer constitutional foundation than the shifting sands of the Court's deterrence rationale. But even if I were to accept the Court's chosen method of analyzing the question posed by these cases, I would still conclude that the Court's decision cannot be justified.

I

The Court holds that physical evidence seized by police officers reasonably relying upon a warrant issued by a detached and neutral magistrate is admissible in the prosecution's case in chief, even though a reviewing court has subsequently determined either that the warrant was defective, No. 82–963, or that those officers failed to demonstrate when applying for the warrant that there was probable cause to conduct the search, No. 82–1771. I have no doubt that these decisions will prove in time to have been a grave mistake. But, as troubling and important as today's new doctrine may be for the administration of criminal justice in this country, the mode of analysis used to generate that doctrine also requires critical examination, for it may prove in the long run to pose the greater threat to our civil liberties.

A

At bottom, the Court's decision turns on the proposition that the exclusionary rule is merely a " 'judicially created remedy designed to safeguard Fourth Amendment rights generally through its deterrent effect, rather than a personal constitutional right.' " Ante, at 3412, quoting United States v. Calandra, 414 U.S., at 348, 94 S.Ct., at 620. The germ of that idea is found in Wolf v. Colorado, 338 U.S. 25, 69 S.Ct. 1359 (1949), and although I had thought that such a narrow conception of the rule had been forever put to rest by our decision in Mapp v. Ohio, 367 U.S. 643, 81 S.Ct. 1684 (1961), it has been revived by the present Court and reaches full flower with today's decision. The essence of this view, as expressed initially in the *Calandra* opinion and as reiterated today, is that the sole "purpose of the Fourth Amendment is to prevent unreasonable governmental intrusions into the privacy of one's person, house, papers, or effects. The wrong condemned is the unjustified governmental invasion of these areas of an individual's life. That wrong . . . is *fully accomplished* by the original search without probable cause." 414 U.S., at 354, 94 S.Ct., at 623 (emphasis added); see also ante, at 3411. This reading of the Amendment implies that its proscriptions are directed solely at those government agents who may actually invade an individual's constitutionally protected privacy. The courts are not subject to any direct constitutional duty to exclude illegally obtained evidence, because the question of the admissibility of such evidence is not addressed by the Amendment. This view of the scope of the Amendment relegates the judiciary to the periphery. Because the only constitutionally cognizable injury has already been "fully accomplished" by the police by the time a case comes before the courts, the Constitution is not itself violated if the judge decides to admit the tainted evidence. Indeed, the most the judge *can* do is wring his hands and hope that perhaps by excluding such evidence he can deter future transgressions by the police.

Such a reading appears plausible, because, as critics of the exclusionary rule never tire of repeating,[2] the Fourth Amendment makes no express provision for the exclusion of evidence secured in violation of its commands. A short answer to this claim, of course, is that many of the Constitution's most vital imperatives are stated in general terms and the task of giving meaning to these precepts is therefore left to subsequent judicial decisionmaking in the context of concrete cases. The nature of our Constitution, as Chief Justice Marshall long ago explained, "requires that only its great outlines should be marked, its important objects designated, and the minor ingredients which compose those objects be deduced from the nature of the objects themselves." McCulloch v. Maryland, 4 Wheat. 316, 407 (1819).

A more direct answer may be supplied by recognizing that the Amendment, like other provisions of the Bill of Rights, restrains the power of the government as a whole; it does not specify only a particular agency and exempt all others. The judiciary is responsible, no less than the executive, for ensuring that constitutional rights are respected.

When that fact is kept in mind, the role of the courts and their possible involvement in the concerns of the Fourth Amendment comes into sharper focus. Because seizures are executed principally to secure evidence, and because such evidence generally has utility in our legal system only in the context of a trial supervised by a judge, it is apparent that the admission of illegally obtained evidence implicates the same constitutional concerns as the initial seizure of that evidence. Indeed, by admitting unlawfully seized evidence, the judiciary becomes a part of what is in fact a single governmental action prohibited by the terms of the Amendment.[3] Once that connection between the evidence-gathering role of the police and the evidence-admitting function of the courts is acknowledged, the plausibility of the Court's interpretation becomes more suspect. Certainly nothing in the language or history of the Fourth Amendment suggests that a recognition of this evidentiary link

2. See, e.g., Wilkey, The Exclusionary Rule: Why Suppress Valid Evidence?, 62 Judicature 215 (1978); S. Schlesinger, Exclusionary Injustice (1977).

3. In deciding to enforce the exclusionary rule as a matter of state law, the California Supreme Court clearly recognized this point:

"When, as in the present case, the very purpose of an illegal search and seizure is to get evidence to introduce at a trial, the success of the lawless venture depends entirely on the court's lending its aid by allowing the evidence to be introduced. It is no answer to say that a distinction should be drawn between the government acting as law enforcer and the gatherer of evidence and the government acting as judge." People v. Cahan, 44 Cal.2d 434, 445, 282 P.2d 905, 912 (1955).

For a thoughtful examination of this point, see Schrock & Welsh, Up from Calandra: The Exclusionary Rule as a Constitutional Requirement, 59 Minn.L.Rev. 251, 289–307 (1974).

between the police and the courts was meant to be foreclosed.[4] It is difficult to give any meaning at all to the limitations imposed by the Amendment if they are read to proscribe only certain conduct by the police but to allow other agents of the same government to take advantage of evidence secured by the police in violation of its requirements.[5] The Amendment therefore must be read to condemn not only the initial unconstitutional invasion of privacy—which is done, after all, for the purpose of securing evidence—but also the subsequent use of any evidence so obtained.

The Court evades this principle by drawing an artificial line between the constitutional rights and responsibilities that are engaged by actions of the police and those that are engaged when a defendant appears before the courts. According to the Court, the substantive protections of the Fourth Amendment are wholly exhausted at the moment when police unlawfully invade an individual's privacy and thus no substantive force remains to those protections at the time of trial when the government seeks to use evidence obtained by the police.

I submit that such a crabbed reading of the Fourth Amendment casts aside the teaching of those Justices who first formulated the exclusionary rule, and rests ultimately on an impoverished understanding of judicial responsibility in our constitutional scheme. For my part,

4. Examination of the early state declarations of rights which formed the models for the Fourth Amendment reveals that they were aimed as much at explicitly limiting the manner in which government could gather evidence as at protecting individual privacy. For example, the Massachusetts Constitution of 1780 provided:

> "Every subject has a right to be secure from all unreasonable searches, and seizures, of his person, his houses, his papers, and his possessions. All warrants, therefore, are contrary to this right, if the cause or foundation of them be not previously supported by oath or affirmation; and if the order in the warrant to a civil Officer, to make search in suspected places, or to arrest one or more suspected persons, or to seize their property, be not accompanied with a special designation of the persons or objects of search, arrest, or seizure: and no warrant ought to be issued, but in cases, and with the formalities prescribed by the laws." Art. XIV of the Declaration of Rights of 1780.

See generally T. Taylor, Two Studies in Constitutional Interpretation 41–43 (1969); N. Lasson, The History and Development of the Fourth Amendment to the United States Constitution 51–105 (1970); J. Lanynski, Search and Seizure and the Supreme Court: A Study in Constitutional Interpretation 30–48 (1966); Stewart, The Road to *Mapp v. Ohio* and Beyond: The Origins, Development, and Future of the Exclusionary Rule in Search-and-Seizure Cases, 83 Colum.L.Rev. 1365, 1369 (1983).

5. In Silverthorne Lumber Co. v. United States, 251 U.S. 385, 40 S.Ct. 182 (1920), the Court expressly recognized this point in rejecting the Government's contention that it should be permitted to make use of knowledge obtained in violation of the Fourth Amendment:

> "The Government now while in form repudiating and condemning the illegal seizure, seeks to maintain its right to avail itself of the knowledge obtained by that means which otherwise it would not have had.
>
> "The proposition could not be presented more nakedly. It is that although of course its seizure was an outrage which the Government now regrets, it may study the papers before it returns them, copy them, and then may use the knowledge that it has gained to call upon the owners in a more regular form to produce them.... In our opinion such is not the law. It reduces the Fourth Amendment to a form a words. *The essence of a provision forbidding the acquisition of evidence in a certain way is that not merely evidence so acquired shall not be used before the Court but that it shall not be used at all.*" Id., at 391–392, 40 S.Ct., at 182–183 (citations omitted) (emphasis added).

"[t]he right of the people to be secure in their persons, houses, papers, and effects, against unreasonable searches and seizures" comprises a personal right to exclude all evidence secured by means of unreasonable searches and seizures. The right to be free from the initial invasion of privacy and the right of exclusion are coordinate components of the central embracing right to be free from unreasonable searches and seizures.

Such a conception of the rights secured by the Fourth Amendment was unquestionably the original basis of what has come to be called the exclusionary rule when it was first formulated in Weeks v. United States, 232 U.S. 383, 34 S.Ct. 341 (1914). There the Court considered whether evidence seized in violation of the Fourth Amendment by a United States Marshal could be admitted at trial after the defendant had moved that the evidence be returned. Significantly, although the Court considered the Marshal's initial invasion of the defendant's home to be unlawful, it went on to consider a question that "involves the right of the court in a criminal prosecution to retain for the purposes of evidence the letters and correspondence of the accused, seized in his house in his absence without his authority, by a United States Marshal holding no warrant for ... the search of his premises." Id., at 393, 34 S.Ct., at 344. In answering that question, Justice Day, speaking for a unanimous Court, expressly recognized that the commands of the Fourth Amendment were addressed to both the courts and the Executive Branch:

> "The effect of the Fourth Amendment is to put the courts of the United States and Federal officials, in the exercise of their power and authority, under limitations and restraints as to the exercise of such power and authority, and to forever secure the people, their persons, houses, papers and effects against all unreasonable searches and seizures under the guise of law. This protection reaches all alike, whether accused of crime or not, and *the duty of giving to it force and effect is obligatory upon all entrusted under our Federal system with the enforcement of the laws.* The tendency of those who execute the criminal laws of the country to obtain conviction by means of unlawful seizures ... should find no sanction in the judgments of the courts which are charged at all times with the support of the Constitution and to which people of all conditions have a right to appeal for the maintenance of such fundamental rights." Id., at 391–392, 34 S.Ct., at 344.

The heart of the *Weeks* opinion, and for me the beginning of wisdom about the Fourth Amendment's proper meaning, is found in the following passage:

> "If letters and private documents can ... be seized and held and used in evidence against a citizen accused of an offense, the protection of the Fourth Amendment declaring his right to be secure against such searches and seizures is of no value, and, so far as those thus placed are concerned, might as well be stricken

> from the Constitution. The efforts of the courts and [federal] officials to bring the guilty to punishment, praiseworthy as they are, are not to be aided by the sacrifice of those great principles established by years of endeavor and suffering which have resulted in their embodiment in the fundamental law of the land. The United States Marshal could only have invaded the house of the accused when armed with a warrant issued as required by the Constitution.... Instead, he acted without sanction of law, doubtless prompted by the desire to bring further proof to the aid of the Government, and under color of his office undertook to make a seizure of private papers in direct violation of the constitutional prohibition against such action.... To sanction such proceedings would be to affirm by judicial decision a manifest neglect if not an open defiance of the prohibitions of the Constitution, intended for the protection of the people against such unauthorized action." Id., at 393–394, 34 S.Ct., at 344–345.

What this passage succinctly captures is the essential recognition, ignored by the present Court, that seizures are generally executed for the purpose of bringing "proof to the aid of the Government," *id.,* at 393, 34 S.Ct., at 344 that the utility of such evidence in a criminal prosecution arises ultimately in the context of the courts, and that the courts therefore cannot be absolved of responsibility for the means by which evidence is obtained. As the Court in *Weeks* clearly recognized, the obligations cast upon government by the Fourth Amendment are not confined merely to the police. In the words of Justice Holmes: "If the search and seizure are unlawful as invading personal rights secured by the Constitution those rights would be infringed yet further if the evidence were allowed to be used." Dodge v. United States, 272 U.S. 530, 532, 47 S.Ct. 191, 192 (1926). As the Court further explained in Olmstead v. United States, 277 U.S. 438, 48 S.Ct. 564 (1928):

> "The striking outcome of the *Weeks* case and those which followed it was the sweeping declaration that the Fourth Amendment, although not referring to or limiting the use of evidence in courts, really forbade its introduction if obtained by government officers through a violation of the Amendment. Theretofore many had supposed under the ordinary common law rules, if the tendered evidence was pertinent, the method of obtaining it was unimportant.... But in the *Weeks* case, and those which followed, this Court decided with great emphasis, and established as the law for the federal courts, that the protection of the Fourth Amendment would be much impaired unless it was held that not only was the official violator of the rights under the Amendment subject to an action at the suit of the injured defendant, but also that the evidence thereby obtained could not be received." Id., at 462–463, 48 S.Ct., at 567.

That conception of the rule, in my view, is more faithful to the meaning and purpose of the Fourth Amendment and to the judiciary's role as the guardian of the people's constitutional liberties. In contrast to the present Court's restrictive reading, the Court in *Weeks* recognized that, if the Amendment is to have any meaning, police and the courts cannot be regarded as constitutional strangers to each other; because the evidence-gathering role of the police is directly linked to the evidence-admitting function of the courts, an individual's Fourth Amendment rights may be undermined as completely by one as by the other.

B

From the foregoing, it is clear why the question whether the exclusion of evidence would deter future police misconduct was never considered a relevant concern in the early cases from *Weeks* to *Olmstead.*[6] In those formative decisions, the Court plainly understood that the exclusion of illegally obtained evidence was compelled not by judicially fashioned remedial purposes, but rather by a direct constitutional command. A new phase in the history of the rule, however, opened with the Court's decision in Wolf v. Colorado, 338 U.S. 25, 69 S.Ct. 1359 (1949). Although that decision held that the security of one's person and privacy protected by the Fourth Amendment was "implicit in 'the concept of ordered liberty' and as such enforceable against the States through the Due Process Clause" of the Fourteenth Amendment, id., at 27–28, 69 S.Ct., at 1361, quoting Palko v. Connecticut, 302 U.S. 319, 325, 58 S.Ct. 149, 152 (1937), the Court went on, in what can only be regarded as a *tour de force* of constitutional obfuscation, to say that the "ways of enforcing such a basic right raise questions of a different order," 338 U.S., at 28, 69 S.Ct., at 1361. Notwithstanding the force of the *Weeks* doctrine that the Fourth Amendment required exclusion, a state court was free to admit illegally seized evidence, according to the Court in *Wolf,* so long as the State had devised some other "effective" means of vindicating a defendant's Fourth Amendment rights. 338 U.S., at 31, 69 S.Ct., at 1362.

Twelve years later, in Mapp v. Ohio, 367 U.S. 643, 81 S.Ct. 1684 (1961), however, the Court restored the original understanding of the *Weeks* case by overruling the holding of *Wolf* and repudiating its rationale. Although in the course of reaching this conclusion the Court in *Mapp* responded at certain points to the question, first raised in *Wolf,* of whether the exclusionary rule was an "effective" remedy compared to alternative means of enforcing the right, see 367 U.S., at 651–653, 81 S.Ct., at 1689–1690, it nevertheless expressly held that "all evidence obtained by searches and seizures in violation of the Constitution is, *by that same authority,* inadmissible in a state court." Id., at 655, 81 S.Ct., at 1691 (emphasis added). In the Court's view, the exclusionary rule

6. See generally Kamisar, Does (Did) (Should) The Exclusionary Rule Rest on a "Principled Basis" Rather than an "Empirical Proposition"?, 16 Creighton L.Rev. 565, 598–599 (1983); Mertens & Wasserstrom, The Good Faith Exception to the Exclusionary Rule: Deregulating the Police and Derailing the Law, 70 Geo.L.J. 365, 379–380 (1981).

was not one among a range of options to be selected at the discretion of judges; it was "an essential part of both the Fourth and Fourteenth Amendments." Id., at 657, 81 S.Ct., at 1693. Rejection of the *Wolf* approach was constitutionally required, the Court explained, because "the admission of the new constitutional right by *Wolf* could not consistently tolerate denial of its most important constitutional privilege, namely, the exclusion of the evidence which an accused had been forced to give by reason of the unlawful seizure. To hold otherwise is to grant the right but in reality to withhold its privilege and enjoyment." 367 U.S., at 656, 81 S.Ct., at 1692. Indeed, no other explanation suffices to account for the Court's holding in *Mapp,* since the only possible predicate for the Court's conclusion that the States were bound by the Fourteenth Amendment to honor the *Weeks* doctrine is that the exclusionary rule was "part and parcel of the Fourth Amendment's limitation upon [governmental] encroachment of individual privacy." 367 U.S., at 651, 81 S.Ct., at 1689.[7]

Despite this clear pronouncement, however, the Court since *Calandra* has gradually pressed the deterrence rationale for the rule back to center stage. See, e.g., United States v. Peltier, 422 U.S. 531, 95 S.Ct. 2313 (1975); United States v. Janis, 428 U.S. 433, 96 S.Ct. 3021 (1976); Stone v. Powell, 428 U.S. 465, 96 S.Ct. 3037 (1976). The various arguments advanced by the Court in this campaign have only strengthened my conviction that the deterrence theory is both misguided and unworkable. First, the Court has frequently bewailed the "cost" of excluding reliable evidence. In large part, this criticism rests upon a refusal to acknowledge the function of the Fourth Amendment itself. If nothing else, the Amendment plainly operates to disable the government from gathering information and securing evidence in certain ways. In practical terms, of course, this restriction of official power means that some incriminating evidence inevitably will go undetected if the government obeys these constitutional restraints. It is the loss of that evidence that is the "price" our society pays for enjoying the freedom and privacy safeguarded by the Fourth Amendment. Thus, some criminals will go free *not,* in Justice (then Judge) Cardozo's misleading epigram, "because the constable has blundered," People v. Defore, 242 N.Y. 13, 21, 150

7. Indeed, the Court in *Mapp* expressly noted that the "factual considerations" raised in *Wolf* concerning the effectiveness of alternative remedies "are not basically relevant to a decision that the exclusionary rule is an essential ingredient of the Fourth Amendment." 367 U.S., at 651, 81 S.Ct., at 1689. It is true that in Linkletter v. Walker, 381 U.S. 618, 85 S.Ct. 1731 (1965), in holding that *Mapp* was not to be applied retroactively, the Court described the exclusionary rule as the "only effective deterrent to lawless police action," 381 U.S., at 636, 85 S.Ct., at 1742, thereby suggesting that the rule rested on a deterrence rationale. But, as I have explained on another occasion, "[t]he emphasis upon deterrence in *Linkletter* must be understood in the light of the crucial fact that the States had justifiably relied from 1949 to 1961 upon *Wolf* . . ., and consequently, that application of *Mapp* would have required the wholesale release of innumerable convicted prisoners, few of whom could have been successfully retried. In that circumstance, *Linkletter* held not only that retrospective application of *Mapp* would not further the goal of deterrence but also that it would not further 'the administration of justice and the integrity of the judicial process.' 381 U.S., at 637 [85 S.Ct., at 1742]." United States v. Calandra, 414 U.S. 338, 359–360, 94 S.Ct. 613, 625 (1974) (dissenting opinion).

N.E. 585, 587 (1926), but rather because official compliance with Fourth Amendment requirements makes it more difficult to catch criminals. Understood in this way, the Amendment directly contemplates that some reliable and incriminating evidence will be lost to the government; therefore, it is not the exclusionary rule, but the Amendment itself that has imposed this cost.[8]

In addition, the Court's decisions over the past decade have made plain that the entire enterprise of attempting to assess the benefits and costs of the exclusionary rule in various contexts is a virtually impossible task for the judiciary to perform honestly or accurately. Although the Court's language in those cases suggests that some specific empirical basis may support its analyses, the reality is that the Court's opinions represent inherently unstable compounds of intuition, hunches, and occasional pieces of partial and often inconclusive data. In *Calandra,* for example, the Court, in considering whether the exclusionary rule should apply in grand jury proceedings, had before it no concrete evidence whatever concerning the impact that application of the rule in such proceedings would have either in terms of the long-term costs or the expected benefits. To the extent empirical data are available regarding the general costs and benefits of the exclusionary rule, such data have shown, on the one hand, as the Court acknowledges today, that the costs are not as substantial as critics have asserted in the past, see ante, at 3435, n. 6, and, on the other hand, that while the exclusionary rule may well have certain deterrent effects, it is extremely difficult to determine with any degree of precision whether the incidence of unlawful conduct by police is now lower than it was prior to *Mapp.* See United States v. Janis, 428 U.S., at 449–453, and n. 22, 96 S.Ct., at 3029–3031 and n. 22; Stone v. Powell, 428 U.S., at 492, n. 32, 96 S.Ct., at 3051, n. 32.[9] The

8. Justice Stewart has explained this point in detail in a recent article:

> "Much of the criticism leveled at the exclusionary rule is misdirected; it is more properly directed at the Fourth Amendment itself. It is true that, as many observers have charged, the effect of the rule is to deprive the courts of extremely relevant, often direct evidence of the guilt of the defendant. But these same critics fail to acknowledge that, in many instances, the same extremely relevant evidence would not have been obtained had the police officer complied with the commands of the fourth amendment in the first place....
>
> "... The exclusionary rule places no limitations on the actions of the police. The fourth amendment does. The inevitable result of the Constitution's prohibition against unreasonable searches and seizures and its requirement that no warrant shall issue but upon probable cause is that police officers who obey its strictures will catch fewer criminals.... [T]hat is the price the framers anticipated and were willing to pay to ensure the sanctity of the person, the home, and property against unrestrained governmental power." Stewart, 83 Colum.L.Rev., at 1392–1393.

See also Dellinger, Of Rights and Remedies: The Constitution as a Sword, 85 Harv. L.Rev. 1532, 1563 (1972) ("Under the exclusionary rule a court attempts to maintain the status quo that would have prevailed if the constitutional requirement had been obeyed").

9. See generally on this point, Davies, A Hard Look at What We Know (and Still Need to Learn) About the "Costs" of the Exclusionary Rule: The NIJ Study and Other Studies of "Lost" Arrests, 1983 A.B.F.Res.J. 611, 627–629; Canon, Ideology and Reality in the Debate over the Exclusionary Rule: A Conservative Argument for its Retention, 23 S.Tex.L.J. 559, 561–563 (1982); Critique, On the Limitations of Empirical Evaluations of the Exclusionary Rule: A Critique of the Spiotto Research and United States v. Calandra, 69 Nw. U.L.Rev. 740 (1974).

Court has sought to turn this uncertainty to its advantage by casting the burden of proof upon proponents of the rule, see, e.g., United States v. Janis, supra, 428 U.S., at 453–454, 96 S.Ct., at 3031–3032. "Obviously," however, "the assignment of the burden of proof on an issue where evidence does not exist and cannot be obtained is outcome determinative. [The] assignment of the burden is merely a way of announcing a predetermined conclusion." [10]

By remaining within its redoubt of empiricism and by basing the rule solely on the deterrence rationale, the Court has robbed the rule of legitimacy. A doctrine that is explained as if it were an empirical proposition but for which there is only limited empirical support is both inherently unstable and an easy mark for critics. The extent of this Court's fidelity to Fourth Amendment requirements, however, should not turn on such statistical uncertainties. I share the view, expressed by Justice Stewart for the Court in Faretta v. California, 422 U.S. 806, 95 S.Ct. 2525 (1975), that "[p]ersonal liberties are not rooted in the law of averages." Id., at 834, 95 S.Ct., at 2540. Rather than seeking to give effect to the liberties secured by the Fourth Amendment through guesswork about deterrence, the Court should restore to its proper place the principle framed 70 years ago in *Weeks* that an individual whose privacy has been invaded in violation of the Fourth Amendment has a right grounded in that Amendment to prevent the government from subsequently making use of any evidence so obtained.

II

Application of that principle clearly requires affirmance in the two cases decided today. In the first, United States v. Leon, 468 U.S. 897, 104 S.Ct. 3405, it is conceded by the Government and accepted by the Court that the affidavit filed by the police officers in support of their application for a search warrant failed to provide a sufficient basis on which a neutral and detached magistrate could conclude that there was probable cause to issue the warrant. Specifically, it is conceded that the officers' application for a warrant was based in part on information supplied by a confidential informant of unproven reliability that was over five months old by the time it was relayed to the police. Although the police conducted an independent investigation on the basis of this tip, both the District Court and the Court of Appeals concluded that the additional information gathered by the officers failed to corroborate the details of the informant's tip and was "as consistent with innocence as ... with guilt." App. to Pet. for Cert. 10a. The warrant, therefore, should never have issued. Stripped of the authority of the warrant, the conduct of these officers was plainly unconstitutional—it amounted to

10. Dworkin, Fact Style Adjudication and the Fourth Amendment: The Limits of Lawyering, 48 Ind.L.J. 329, 332–333 (1973). See also White, Forgotten Points in the "Exclusionary Rule" Debate, 81 Mich. L.Rev. 1273, 1281–1282 (1983) (balancing of deterrent benefits and costs is an "inquiry [that] can never be performed in an adequate way and the reality is thus that the decision must rest not upon those grounds, but upon prior dispositions or unarticulated intuitions that are never justified"); Canon, supra, at 564; Kamisar, 16 Creighton L.Rev., at 646.

nothing less than a naked invasion of the privacy of respondents' homes without the requisite justification demanded by the Fourth Amendment. In order to restore the Government to the position it would have occupied had this unconstitutional search not occurred, therefore, it was necessary that the evidence be suppressed. As we said in Coolidge v. New Hampshire, 403 U.S. 443, 91 S.Ct. 2022 (1971), the Warrant Clause is not "an inconvenience to be somehow 'weighed' against the claims of police efficiency. It is, or should be, an important working part of our machinery of government, operating as a matter of course to check the 'well-intentioned but mistakenly overzealous executive officers' who are part of any system of law enforcement." Id., at 481, 91 S.Ct., at 2046 (footnote omitted).

A close examination of the facts of this case reveals that this is neither an extraordinary nor indeed a very costly step. The warrant had authorized a search for cocaine, methaqualone tablets, and miscellaneous narcotics paraphernalia at several locations: a condominium at 7902 Via Magdalena in Los Angeles; a residence at 620 Price Drive in Burbank; a residence at 716 South Sunset Canyon in Burbank; and four automobiles owned respectively by respondents Leon, Sanchez, Stewart, and Del Castillo. App. 31–33. Pursuant to this warrant, the officers seized approximately four pounds of cocaine and over 1,000 methaqualone tablets from the Via Magdalena condominium, nearly one pound of cocaine from the Sunset Canyon residence, about an ounce of cocaine from the Price Drive residence, and certain paraphernalia from Del Castillo's and Stewart's automobiles. On the basis of this and other evidence, the four respondents were charged with violating 21 U.S.C. § 846 for conspiring to possess and distribute cocaine, and § 841(a)(1) for possessing methaqualone and cocaine with intent to distribute. The indictment specifically alleged that respondents had maintained the Via Magdalena condominium as a storage area for controlled substances which they distributed to prospective purchasers. App. 27–28.

At the suppression hearing, the District Court determined that none of the respondents had a sufficient expectation of privacy to contest the search of the Via Magdalena condominium, that respondents Stewart and Sanchez could challenge the search of their home at Price Drive, that respondent Leon was entitled to challenge the search of his home at Sunset Canyon, and that respondents Del Castillo and Stewart could contest the search of their cars. Given its finding that probable cause to issue the warrant was lacking, the District Court ruled that the evidence from the Price Drive residence could not be used against respondents Stewart and Sanchez, that evidence from the Sunset Canyon residence could not be used against Leon, and that evidence obtained from both Del Castillo's and Stewart's automobiles could not be used against them. App. to Pet. for Cert. 10a–13a.

The tenor of the Court's opinion suggests that this order somehow imposed a grave and presumably unjustifiable cost on society. Such a suggestion, however, is a gross exaggeration. Since the indictment focused upon a conspiracy among all respondents to use the Via Magdalena condominium as a storage area for controlled substances, and since the bulk of the evidence seized was from that condominium and was plainly admissible under the District Court's order, the Government would clearly still be able to present a strong case to the jury following the court's suppression order. I emphasize these details not to suggest how the Government's case would fare before the jury but rather to clarify a point that is lost in the Court's rhetorical excesses over the costs of the exclusionary rule—namely, that the suppression of evidence will certainly tend to weaken the Government's position but it will rarely force the Government to abandon a prosecution. Cf. infra, at 3441–3442, and n. 11. In my view, a doctrine that preserves intact the constitutional rights of the accused, and, at the same time, is sufficiently limited to permit society's legitimate and pressing interest in criminal law enforcement to be served should not be so recklessly discarded. It is a doctrine that gives life to the "very heart of the Fourth Amendment directive: that ... a governmental search and seizure should represent both the efforts of the officer to gather evidence of wrongful acts and the judgment of the magistrate that the collected evidence is sufficient to justify invasion of a citizen's private premises." United States v. United States District Court, 407 U.S. 297, 316, 92 S.Ct. 2125, 2136 (1972).

In the second case before the Court, Massachusetts v. Sheppard, 468 U.S. 981, 104 S.Ct. 3424, the State concedes and the Court accepts that the warrant issued to search respondent's home completely failed to state with particularity the things to be seized. Indeed, the warrant expressly and particularly described things such as "controlled substance[s]" and "other paraphernalia used in, for, or in connection with the unlawful possession or use of any controlled substance[s]" that the police had no reason whatsoever to believe were to be found in respondent's home. App. 17a. Given the Fourth Amendment's requirement that "no Warrants shall issue, but upon probable cause ... and particularly describing the ... things to be seized," this warrant should never have been issued. The police who entered respondent's home, therefore, were without constitutional authority to do so.

Although the Court's opinion tends to overlook this fact, the requirement of particularity is not a mere "technicality," it is an express constitutional command. Ybarra v. Illinois, 444 U.S. 85, 92, 100 S.Ct. 338, 342 (1979); Lo–Ji Sales, Inc. v. New York, 442 U.S. 319, 99 S.Ct. 2319 (1979); Stanford v. Texas, 379 U.S. 476, 85 S.Ct. 506 (1965); Marron v. United States, 275 U.S. 192, 196, 48 S.Ct. 74, 76 (1927). The purpose of that requirement is to prevent precisely the kind of governmental conduct that the faulty warrant at issue here created a grave risk of permitting—namely, a search that was not narrowly and particularly limited to the things that a neutral and detached magistrate had reason to believe might be found at respondent's home. Although it is true, as Justice Stevens observes, see post, at 3448, that the affidavit submitted by the police set forth with particularity those items that they sought authority to search for, it is nevertheless clear that the warrant itself—the document which actually gave the officers legal authority to invade respondent's privacy—made no mention of these items. And, although it is true that the particular officers who applied for the warrant also happened to execute it and did so in accordance with the limits proposed in their affidavit, this happenstance should have no bearing on the central question whether these officers secured that prior judicial authority to conduct their search required by the Fourth Amendment. As we made clear in United States v. United States District Court, supra, 407 U.S., at 317, 92 S.Ct., at 2137 (footnote omitted), "[t]he Fourth Amendment contemplates a prior judicial judgment, not the risk that exective discretion may be reasonably exercised." See also Katz v. United States, 389 U.S. 347, 356–357, 88 S.Ct. 507, 514 (1967) ("this Court has never sustained a search upon the sole ground that officers reasonably expected to find evidence of a particular crime and voluntarily confined their activities to the least intrusive means consistent with that end"). Had the warrant actually been enforced by officers other than those who prepared the affidavit, the same result might not have occurred; indeed, the wholly erroneous nature of the warrant might have led such officers to feel at liberty to roam throughout respondent's home in search of drugs. Cf. Whiteley v. Warden, 401 U.S. 560, 91 S.Ct. 1031 (1971). I therefore fail to see how a search pursuant to such a fundamentally defective warrant can be characterized as "reasonable."

What the Framers of the Bill of Rights sought to accomplish through the express requirements of the Fourth Amendment was to define precisely the conditions under which government agents could search private property so that citizens would not have to depend solely upon the discretion and restraint of those agents for the protection of their privacy. Although the self-restraint and care exhibited by the officers in this case is commendable, that alone can never be a sufficient protection for constitutional liberties. I am convinced that it is not too much to ask that an attentive magistrate take those minimum steps necessary to ensure that every warrant he issues describes with particularity the things that his independent review of the warrant application convinces him are likely to be found in the premises. And I am equally convinced that it is not too much to ask that well-trained and experienced police officers take a moment to check that the warrant they have been issued at least describes those things for which they have sought leave to search. These convictions spring not from my own view of sound criminal law enforcement policy, but are instead compelled by the language of the Fourth Amendment and the history that led to its adoption.

III

Even if I were to accept the Court's general approach to the exclusionary rule, I could not agree with today's result. There is no question that in the hands of the present Court the deterrence rationale has proved to be a powerful tool for confining the scope of the rule. In *Calandra*, for example, the Court concluded that the "speculative and undoubtedly minimal advance in the deterrence of police misconduct,"

was insufficient to outweigh the "expense of substantially impeding the role of the grand jury." 414 U.S., at 351–352, 94 S.Ct., at 621–622. In Stone v. Powell, the Court found that "the additional contribution, if any, of the consideration of search-and-seizure claims of state prisoners on collateral review is small in relation to the costs." 428 U.S., at 493, 96 S.Ct., at 3052. In United States v. Janis, 428 U.S. 433, 96 S.Ct. 3021 (1976), the Court concluded that "exclusion from federal civil proceedings of evidence unlawfully seized by a state criminal enforcement officer has not been shown to have a sufficient likelihood of deterring the conduct of the state police so that it outweighs the societal costs imposed by the exclusion." Id., at 454, 96 S.Ct., at 3032. And in an opinion handed down today, the Court finds that the "balance between costs and benefits comes out against applying the exclusionary rule in civil deportation hearings held by the [Immigration and Naturalization Service]." INS v. Lopez–Mendoza, 468 U.S. 1032, 1050, 104 S.Ct. 3479, 3490.

Thus, in this bit of judicial stagecraft, while the sets sometimes change, the actors always have the same lines. Given this well-rehearsed pattern, one might have predicted with some assurance how the present case would unfold. First there is the ritual incantation of the "substantial social costs" exacted by the exclusionary rule, followed by the virtually foreordained conclusion that, given the marginal benefits, application of the rule in the circumstances of these cases is not warranted. Upon analysis, however, such a result cannot be justified even on the Court's own terms.

At the outset, the Court suggests that society has been asked to pay a high price—in terms either of setting guilty persons free or of impeding the proper functioning of trials—as a result of excluding relevant physical evidence in cases where the police, in conducting searches and seizing evidence, have made only an "objectively reasonable" mistake concerning the constitutionality of their actions. See ante, at 3412–3413. But what evidence is there to support such a claim?

Significantly, the Court points to none, and, indeed, as the Court acknowledges, see ante, at 3412, n. 6, recent studies have demonstrated that the "costs" of the exclusionary rule—calculated in terms of dropped prosecutions and lost convictions—are quite low. Contrary to the claims of the rule's critics that exclusion leads to "the release of countless guilty criminals," Bivens v. Six Unknown Federal Narcotics Agents, 403 U.S. 388, 416, 91 S.Ct. 1999, 2014 (1971) (Burger, C.J., dissenting), these studies have demonstrated that federal and state prosecutors very rarely drop cases because of potential search and seizure problems. For example, a 1979 study prepared at the request of Congress by the General Accounting Office reported that only 0.4% of all cases actually declined for prosecution by federal prosecutors were declined primarily because of illegal search problems. Report of the Comptroller General of the United States, Impact of the Exclusionary Rule on Federal Criminal Prosecutions 14 (1979). If the GAO data are restated as a percentage of all arrests, the study shows that only 0.2% of all felony arrests are declined for prosecution because of potential exclusionary rule problems.

See Davies, A Hard Look at What We Know (and Still Need to Learn) About the "Costs" of the Exclusionary Rule: The NIJ Study and Other Studies of "Lost" Arrests, 1983 A.B.F.Res.J. 611, 635.[11] Of course, these data describe only the costs attributable to the exclusion of evidence in all cases; the costs due to the exclusion of evidence in the narrower category of cases where police have made objectively reasonable mistakes must necessarily be even smaller. The Court, however, ignores this distinction and mistakenly weighs the aggregated costs of exclusion in *all* cases, irrespective of the circumstances that led to exclusion, see ante, at 3412, against the potential benefits associated with only those cases in which evidence is excluded because police reasonably but mistakenly believe that their conduct does not violate the Fourth Amendment, see ante, at 3417–3419. When such faulty scales are used, it is little wonder that the balance tips in favor of restricting the application of the rule.

What then supports the Court's insistence that this evidence be admitted? Apparently, the Court's only answer is that even though the costs of exclusion are not very substantial, the potential deterrent effect in these circumstances is so marginal that exclusion cannot be justified. The key to the Court's conclusion in this respect is its belief that the prospective deterrent effect of the exclusionary rule operates only in those situations in which police officers, when deciding whether to go forward with some particular search, have reason to know that their planned conduct will violate the requirements of the Fourth Amendment. See ante, at 3418–3419. If these officers in fact understand (or reasonably should understand because the law is well settled) that their

11. In a series of recent studies, researchers have attempted to quantify the actual costs of the rule. A recent National Institute of Justice study based on data for the 4-year period 1976–1979 gathered by the California Bureau of Criminal Statistics showed that 4.8% of all cases that were declined for prosecution by California prosecutors were rejected because of illegally seized evidence. National Institute of Justice, Criminal Justice Research Report—The Effects of the Exclusionary Rule: A Study in California 1 (1982). However, if these data are calculated as a percentage of all arrests, they show that only 0.8% of all arrests were rejected for prosecution because of illegally seized evidence. See Davies, 1983 A.B.F.Res.J., at 619.

In another measure of the rule's impact—the number of prosecutions that are dismissed or result in acquittals in cases where evidence has been excluded—the available data again show that the Court's past assessment of the rule's costs has generally been exaggerated. For example, a study based on data from nine midsized counties in Illinois, Michigan, and Pennsylvania reveals that motions to suppress physical evidence were filed in approximately 5% of the 7,500 cases studied, but that such motions were successful in only 0.7% of all these cases. Nardulli, The Societal Cost of the Exclusionary Rule: An Empirical Assessment, 1983 A.B.F.Res.J. 585, 596. The study also shows that only 0.6% of all cases resulted in acquittals because evidence had been excluded. Id., at 600. In the GAO study, suppression motions were filed in 10.5% of all federal criminal cases surveyed, but of the motions filed, approximately 80–90% were denied. GAO Report, at 8, 10. Evidence was actually excluded in only 1.3% of the cases studied, and only 0.7% of all cases resulted in acquittals or dismissals after evidence was excluded. Id., at 9–11. See Davies, supra, at 660. And in another study based on data from cases during 1978 and 1979 in San Diego and Jacksonville, it was shown that only 1% of all cases resulting in nonconviction were caused by illegal searches. F. Feeney, F. Dill, & A. Weir, Arrests Without Conviction: How Often They Occur and Why (National Institute of Justice 1983). See generally Davies, supra, at 663.

proposed conduct will offend the Fourth Amendment and that, consequently, any evidence they seize will be suppressed in court, they will refrain from conducting the planned search. In those circumstances, the incentive system created by the exclusionary rule will have the hoped-for deterrent effect. But in situations where police officers reasonably (but mistakenly) believe that their planned conduct satisfies Fourth Amendment requirements—presumably either (a) because they are acting on the basis of an apparently valid warrant, or (b) because their conduct is only later determined to be invalid as a result of a subsequent change in the law or the resolution of an unsettled question of law—then such officers will have no reason to refrain from conducting the search and the exclusionary rule will have no effect.

At first blush, there is some logic to this position. Undoubtedly, in the situation hypothesized by the Court, the existence of the exclusionary rule cannot be expected to have any deterrent effect on the particular officers at the moment they are deciding whether to go forward with the search. Indeed, the subsequent exclusion of any evidence seized under such circumstances appears somehow "unfair" to the particular officers involved. As the Court suggests, these officers have acted in what they thought was an appropriate and constitutionally authorized manner, but then the fruit of their efforts is nullified by the application of the exclusionary rule. Ante, at 3420.

The flaw in the Court's argument, however, is that its logic captures only one comparatively minor element of the generally acknowledged deterrent purposes of the exclusionary rule. To be sure, the rule operates to some extent to deter future misconduct by individual officers who have had evidence suppressed in their own cases. But what the Court overlooks is that the deterrence rationale for the rule is not designed to be, nor should it be thought of as, a form of "punishment" of individual police officers for their failures to obey the restraints imposed by the Fourth Amendment. See United States v. Peltier, 422 U.S., at 556–557, 95 S.Ct., at 2327 (Brennan, J., dissenting). Instead, the chief deterrent function of the rule is its tendency to promote institutional compliance with Fourth Amendment requirements on the part of law enforcement agencies generally.[12] Thus, as the Court has previously

12. As Justice Stewart has observed:

"[T]he exclusionary rule is not designed to serve a specific deterrence function; that is, it is not designed to punish the particular police officer for violating a person's fourth amendment rights. Instead, the rule is designed to produce a 'systematic deterrence': the exclusionary rule is intended to create an incentive for law enforcement officials to establish procedures by which police officers are trained to comply with the fourth amendment because the purpose of the criminal justice system—bringing criminals to justice—can be achieved only when evidence of guilt may be used against defendants." Stewart, 83 Colum.L.Rev., at 1400. See also Oaks, Studying the Exclusionary Rule in Search and Seizure, 37 U.Chi. L.Rev. 665, 709–710 (1970) ("The exclusionary rule is not aimed at special deterrence since it does not impose any direct punishment on a law enforcement official who has broken the rule.... The exclusionary rule is aimed at affecting the wider audience of all law enforcement officials and society at large. It is meant to discourage violations by individuals who have never experienced any sanction for them"); Mertens & Wasserstrom, 70 Geo.L.J., at 399–401; Kamisar, 16 Creighton L.Rev., at 597, n. 204.

recognized, "over the long term, [the] demonstration [provided by the exclusionary rule] that our society attaches serious consequences to violation of constitutional rights is thought to encourage those who formulate law enforcement policies, and the officers who implement them, to incorporate Fourth Amendment ideals into their value system." Stone v. Powell, 428 U.S., at 492, 96 S.Ct., at 3051. It is only through such an institutionwide mechanism that information concerning Fourth Amendment standards can be effectively communicated to rank-and-file officers.[13]

If the overall educational effect of the exclusionary rule is considered, application of the rule to even those situations in which individual police officers have acted on the basis of a reasonable but mistaken belief that their conduct was authorized can still be expected to have a considerable long-term deterrent effect. If evidence is consistently excluded in these circumstances, police departments will surely be prompted to instruct their officers to devote greater care and attention to providing sufficient information to establish probable cause when applying for a warrant, and to review with some attention the form of the warrant that they have been issued, rather than automatically assuming that whatever document the magistrate has signed will necessarily comport with Fourth Amendment requirements.

After today's decisions, however, that institutional incentive will be lost. Indeed, the Court's "reasonable mistake" exception to the exclu-

13. Although specific empirical data on the systemic deterrent effect of the rule are not conclusive, the testimony of those actually involved in law enforcement suggests that, at the very least, the *Mapp* decision had the effect of increasing police awareness of Fourth Amendment requirements and of prompting prosecutors and police commanders to work towards educating rank-and-file officers. For example, as former New York Police Commissioner Murphy explained the impact of the *Mapp* decision: "I can think of no decision in recent times in the field of law enforcement which had such a dramatic and traumatic effect.... I was immediately caught up in the entire program of reevaluating our procedures, which had followed the *Defore* rule, and modifying, amending, and creating new policies and new instructions for the implementation of *Mapp*.... Retraining sessions had to be held from the very top administrators down to each of the thousands of foot patrolmen." Murphy, Judicial Review of Police Methods in Law Enforcement: The Problem of Compliance by Police Departments, 44 Texas L.Rev. 939, 941 (1966).

Further testimony about the impact of the *Mapp* decision can be found in the statement of Deputy Commissioner Reisman: "The *Mapp* case was a shock to us. We had to reorganize our thinking, frankly. Before this, nobody bothered to take out search warrants. Although the U.S. Constitution requires warrants in most cases, the U.S. Supreme Court had ruled that evidence obtained without a warrant—illegally, if you will—was admissible in state courts. So the feeling was, why bother? Well, once that rule was changed we knew we had better start teaching our men about it." N.Y. Times, Apr. 28, 1965, p. 50, col. 1. A former United States Attorney and now Attorney General of Maryland, Stephen Sachs, has described the impact of the rule on police practices in similar terms: "I have watched the rule deter, routinely, throughout my years as a prosecutor.... [P]olice-prosecutor consultation is customary in all our cases when Fourth Amendment concerns arise.... In at least three Maryland jurisdictions, for example, prosecutors are on twenty-four hour call to field search and seizure questions presented by police officers." Sachs, The Exclusionary Rule: A Prosecutor's Defense, 1 Crim.Justice Ethics 28, 30 (Summer/Fall 1982). See also LaFave, The Fourth Amendment in an Imperfect World: On Drawing "Bright Lines" and "Good Faith," 43 U.Pitt.L.Rev. 307, 319 (1982); Mertens & Wasserstrom, supra, at 394–401.

sionary rule will tend to put a premium on police ignorance of the law. Armed with the assurance provided by today's decisions that evidence will always be admissible whenever an officer has "reasonably" relied upon a warrant, police departments will be encouraged to train officers that if a warrant has simply been signed, it is reasonable, without more, to rely on it. Since in close cases there will no longer be any incentive to err on the side of constitutional behavior, police would have every reason to adopt a "let's-wait-until-it's-decided" approach in situations in which there is a question about a warrant's validity or the basis for its issuance. Cf. United States v. Johnson, 457 U.S. 537, 561, 102 S.Ct. 2579, 2593 (1982).[14]

Although the Court brushes these concerns aside, a host of grave consequences can be expected to result from its decision to carve this new exception out of the exclusionary rule. A chief consequence of today's decisions will be to convey a clear and unambiguous message to magistrates that their decisions to issue warrants are now insulated from subsequent judicial review. Creation of this new exception for good-faith reliance upon a warrant implicitly tells magistrates that they need not take much care in reviewing warrant applications, since their mistakes will from now on have virtually no consequence: If their decision to issue a warrant was correct, the evidence will be admitted; if their decision was incorrect but the police relied in good faith on the warrant, the evidence will also be admitted. Inevitably, the care and attention devoted to such an inconsequential chore will dwindle. Although the Court is correct to note that magistrates do not share the same stake in the outcome of a criminal case as the police, they nevertheless need to appreciate that their role is of some moment in order to continue performing the important task of carefully reviewing warrant applications. Today's decisions effectively remove that incentive.[15]

14. The authors of a recent study of the warrant process in seven cities concluded that application of a good-faith exception where an officer relies upon a warrant "would further encourage police officers to seek out the less inquisitive magistrates and to rely on boilerplate formulae, thereby lessening the value of search warrants overall. Consequently, the benefits of adoption of a broad good faith exception in terms of a few additional prosecutions appears to be outweighed by the harm to the quality of the entire search warrant process and the criminal justice system in general." R. Van Duizend, L. Sutton, & C. Carter, The Search Warrant Process: Preconceptions, Perceptions, and Practices 8–12 (Review Draft, National Center for State Courts, 1983). See also Stewart, 83 Colum.L.Rev., at 1403.

15. Just last Term in Illinois v. Gates, 462 U.S. 213, 103 S.Ct. 2317 (1983), the Court noted:

"Sufficient information must be presented to the magistrate to allow that official to determine probable cause; his action cannot be a mere ratification of the bare conclusions of others. In order to ensure that such an abdication of the magistrate's duty does not occur, courts must continue to conscientiously review the sufficiency of affidavits on which warrants are issued." Id., at 239, 103 S.Ct., at 2332.

After today's decisions, there will little reason for reviewing courts to conduct such a conscientious review; rather, these courts will be more likely to focus simply on the question of police good faith. Despite the Court's confident prediction that such review will continue to be conducted, see ante, at 3421–3422, it is difficult to believe that busy courts faced with heavy dockets will take the time to render essentially advisory opinions concerning the constitutional-

Moreover, the good-faith exception will encourage police to provide only the bare minimum of information in future warrant applications. The police will now know that if they can secure a warrant, so long as the circumstances of its issuance are not "entirely unreasonable," ante, at 3422, all police conduct pursuant to that warrant will be protected from further judicial review.[16] The clear incentive that operated in the past to establish probable cause adequately because reviewing courts would examine the magistrate's judgment carefully, see, e.g., Franks v. Delaware, 438 U.S. 154, 169–170, 98 S.Ct. 2674, 2683 (1978); Jones v. United States, 362 U.S. 257, 271–272, 80 S.Ct. 725, 736 (1960); Giordenello v. United States, 357 U.S. 480, 483, 78 S.Ct. 1245, 1248 (1958), has now been so completely vitiated that the police need only show that it was not "entirely unreasonable" under the circumstances of a particular case for them to believe that the warrant they were issued was valid. See ante, at 3421. The long-run effect unquestionably will be to undermine the integrity of the warrant process.

Finally, even if one were to believe, as the Court apparently does, that police are hobbled by inflexible and hypertechnical warrant procedures, today's decisions cannot be justified. This is because, given the relaxed standard for assessing probable cause established just last Term in Illinois v. Gates, 462 U.S. 213, 103 S.Ct. 2317 (1983), the Court's newly fashioned good-faith exception, when applied in the warrant context, will rarely, if ever, offer any greater flexibility for police than the *Gates* standard already supplies. In *Gates,* the Court held that "[t]he task of the issuing magistrate is simply to make a practical, common-sense decision whether, given all the circumstances set forth in the affidavit before him, . . . there is a fair probability that contraband or evidence of a crime will be found in a particular place." Id., at 238, 103 S.Ct., at 2332. The task of a reviewing court is confined to determining whether "the magistrate had a 'substantial basis' for . . . conclud[ing] that probable cause existed." Ibid. Given such a relaxed standard, it is virtually inconceivable that a reviewing court, when faced with a defendant's motion to suppress, could first find that a warrant was invalid under the new *Gates* standard, but then, at the same time, find that a police officer's reliance on such an invalid warrant was nevertheless "objectively reasonable" under the test announced today.[17] Because the

ity of the magistrate's decision before considering the officer's good faith.

16. As the Court of Appeals for the Second Circuit has observed in this regard:

"If a magistrate's issuance of a warrant were to be, as the government would have it, an all but conclusive determination of the validity of the search and of the admissibility of the evidence seized thereby, police officers might have a substantial incentive to submit their warrant applications to the least demanding magistrates, since once the warrant was issued, it would be exceedingly difficult later to exclude any evidence seized in the resulting search even if the warrant was issued without probable cause.... For practical purposes, therefore, the standard of probable cause might be diluted to that required by the least demanding official authorized to issue warrants, even if this fell well below what the Fourth Amendment required." United States v. Karathanos, 531 F.2d 26, 34 (1976).

17. See Kamisar, Gates, "Probable Cause," "Good Faith," and Beyond, 69 Iowa L.Rev. 551, 588–589 (1984); Wasserstrom, The Incredible Shrinking Fourth

two standards overlap so completely, it is unlikely that a warrant could be found invalid under *Gates* and yet the police reliance upon it could be seen as objectively reasonable; otherwise, we would have to entertain the mind-boggling concept of objectively reasonable reliance upon an objectively unreasonable warrant.

This paradox, as Justice Stevens suggests, see post, at 3446–3447, perhaps explains the Court's unwillingness to remand No. 82–1771 for reconsideration in light of *Gates*, for it is quite likely that on remand the Court of Appeals would find no violation of the Fourth Amendment, thereby demonstrating that the supposed need for the good-faith exception in this context is more apparent than real. Therefore, although the Court's decisions are clearly limited to the situation in which police officers reasonably rely upon an apparently valid warrant in conducting a search, I am not at all confident that the exception unleashed today will remain so confined. Indeed, the full impact of the Court's regrettable decisions will not be felt until the Court attempts to extend this rule to situations in which the police have conducted a warrantless search solely on the basis of their own judgment about the existence of probable cause and exigent circumstances. When that question is finally posed, I for one will not be surprised if my colleagues decide once again that we simply cannot afford to protect Fourth Amendment rights.

IV

When the public, as it quite properly has done in the past as well as in the present, demands that those in government increase their efforts to combat crime, it is all too easy for those government officials to seek expedient solutions. In contrast to such costly and difficult measures as building more prisons, improving law enforcement methods, or hiring more prosecutors and judges to relieve the overburdened court systems in the country's metropolitan areas, the relaxation of Fourth Amendment standards seems a tempting, costless means of meeting the public's demand for better law enforcement. In the long run, however, we as a society pay a heavy price for such expediency, because as Justice Jackson observed, the rights guaranteed in the Fourth Amendment "are not mere second-class rights but belong in the catalog of indispensable freedoms." Brinegar v. United States, 338 U.S. 160, 180, 69 S.Ct. 1302, 1313 (1949) (dissenting opinion). Once lost, such rights are difficult to recover. There is hope, however, that in time this or some later Court will restore these precious freedoms to their rightful place as a primary protection for our citizens against overreaching officialdom.

I dissent.

JUSTICE STEVENS, concurring in the judgment in *Sheppard,* and dissenting in *Leon.*

It is appropriate to begin with the plain language of the Fourth Amendment:

Amendment, 21 Am.Crim.L.Rev. 257 (1984); LaFave, 43 U.Pitt.L.Rev., at 307.

> "The right of the people to be secure in their persons, houses, papers, and effects, against unreasonable searches and seizures, shall not be violated; and no Warrants shall issue but upon probable cause, supported by Oath or affirmation, and particularly describing the place to be searched, and the persons or things to be seized."

The Court assumes that the searches in these cases violated the Fourth Amendment, yet refuses to apply the exclusionary rule because the Court concludes that it was "reasonable" for the police to conduct them. In my opinion an official search and seizure cannot be both "unreasonable" and "reasonable" at the same time. The doctrinal vice in the Court's holding is its failure to consider the separate purposes of the two prohibitory Clauses in the Fourth Amendment.

The first Clause prohibits unreasonable searches and seizures and the second prohibits the issuance of warrants that are not supported by probable cause or that do not particularly describe the place to be searched and the persons or things to be seized. We have, of course, repeatedly held that warrantless searches are presumptively unreasonable,[1] and that there are only a few carefully delineated exceptions to that basic presumption.[2] But when such an exception has been recognized, analytically we have necessarily concluded that the warrantless activity was not "unreasonable" within the meaning of the first Clause. Thus, any Fourth Amendment case may present two separate questions: whether the search was conducted pursuant to a warrant issued in accordance with the second Clause, and, if not, whether it was nevertheless "reasonable" within the meaning of the first. On these questions, the constitutional text requires that we speak with one voice. We cannot intelligibly assume, *arguendo,* that a search was constitutionally unreasonable but that the seized evidence is admissible because the same search was reasonable.

I

In No. 82–963 [*Sheppard*], the Supreme Judicial Court of Massachusetts determined that a warrant which purported to authorize a search of respondent's home had been issued in violation of the Warrant Clause. In its haste to make new law, this Court does not tarry to consider this holding. Yet, as I will demonstrate, this holding is clearly wrong; I would reverse the judgment on that ground alone.

In No. 82–1771 [*Leon*], there is also a substantial question whether the warrant complied with the Fourth Amendment. There was a strong dissent on the probable-cause issue when *Leon* was before the Court of Appeals, and that dissent has been given added force by this Court's intervening decision in Illinois v. Gates, 462 U.S. 213, 103 S.Ct. 2317 (1983), which constituted a significant development in the law. It is

1. See, e.g., Payton v. New York, 445 U.S. 573, 586, 100 S.Ct. 1371, 1380 (1980); Chimel v. California, 395 U.S. 752, 762–763, 89 S.Ct. 2034, 2039–2040 (1969).

2. See, e.g., Coolidge v. New Hampshire, 403 U.S. 443, 474–475, 91 S.Ct. 2022, 2042–2043 (1971); Vale v. Louisiana, 399 U.S. 30, 90 S.Ct. 1969 (1970).

probable, though admittedly not certain, that the Court of Appeals would now conclude that the warrant in *Leon* satisfied the Fourth Amendment if it were given the opportunity to reconsider the issue in the light of *Gates*. Adherence to our normal practice following the announcement of a new rule would therefore postpone, and probably obviate, the need for the promulgation of the broad new rule the Court announces today.[3]

It is, of course, disturbing that the Court chooses one case in which there was no violation of the Fourth Amendment, and another in which there is grave doubt on the question, in order to promulgate a "good faith" exception to the Fourth Amendment's exclusionary rule. The Court's explanation for its failure to decide the merits of the Fourth Amendment question in No. 82–963 is that it "is a factbound issue of little importance," Massachusetts v. Sheppard, 468 U.S. 981, 988, n. 5, 104 S.Ct. 3424, 3428, n. 5. In No. 82–1771, the Court acknowledges that the case could be remanded to the Court of Appeals for reconsideration in light of Gates, yet does not bother to explain why it fails to do so except to note that it is "within our power" to decide the broader question in the case. United States v. Leon, 468 U.S. 897, 905, 104 S.Ct. 3405, 3411. The Court seems determined to decide these cases on the broadest possible grounds; such determination is utterly at odds with the Court's traditional practice as well as any principled notion of judicial restraint. Decisions made in this manner are unlikely to withstand the test of time.

Judges, more than most, should understand the value of adherence to settled procedures. By adopting a set of fair procedures, and then adhering to them, courts of law ensure that justice is administered with an even hand. "These are subtle matters, for they concern the ingredients of what constitutes justice. Therefore, justice must satisfy the appearance of justice." Offutt v. United States, 348 U.S. 11, 14, 75 S.Ct. 11, 13 (1954). Of course, this Court has a duty to face questions of constitutional law when necessary to the disposition of an actual case or controversy. Marbury v. Madison, 1 Cranch 137, 177 (1803). But when the Court goes beyond what is necessary to decide the case before it, it can only encourage the perception that it is pursuing its own notions of wise social policy, rather than adhering to its judicial role. I do not believe the Court should reach out to decide what is undoubtedly a profound question concerning the administration of criminal justice before assuring itself that this question is actually and of necessity presented by the concrete facts before the Court. Although it may appear that the Court's broad holding will serve the public interest in enforcing obedience to the rule of law, for my part, I remain firmly convinced that "the preservation of order in our communities will be best ensured by adherence to established and respected procedures."

3. In his petition for certiorari in *Leon*, the Solicitor General did not seek plenary review, but only that the petition "be disposed of as appropriate in light of the Court's decision in Illinois v. Gates," Pet. for Cert. in United States v. Leon, No. 82–1771, p. 10.

Groppi v. Leslie, 436 F.2d 331, 336 (CA7 1971) (en banc) (Stevens, J., dissenting), rev'd, 404 U.S. 496, 92 S.Ct. 582 (1972).

II

In No. 82–963, there is no contention that the police officers did not receive appropriate judicial authorization for their search of respondent's residence. A neutral and detached judicial officer had correctly determined that there was probable cause to conduct a search. Nevertheless, the Supreme Judicial Court suppressed the fruits of the search because the warrant did not particularly describe the place to be searched and the things to be seized.

The particularity requirement of the Fourth Amendment has a manifest purpose—to prevent general searches. By limiting the authorization to search to the specific areas and things for which there is probable cause to search, the requirement ensures that the search is carefully tailored to its justification, and does not resemble the wide-ranging general searches that the Framers intended to prohibit.[4] In this case the warrant did not come close to authorizing a general search.[5]

The affidavit supporting the application for the warrant correctly identified the things to be seized, and on its face the affidavit indicated that it had been presented to the judge who had issued the warrant.[6] Both the police officers and the judge were fully aware of the contents of the affidavit, and therefore knew precisely what the officers were authorized to search for. Since the affidavit was available for after-the-fact review, the Massachusetts courts could readily ascertain the limits of the officers' authority under the warrant. In short, the judge who issued the warrant, the police officers who executed it, and the reviewing courts all were able easily to ascertain the precise scope of the authorization provided by the warrant.

All that our cases require is that a warrant contain a description sufficient to enable the officers who execute it to ascertain with reasonable effort where they are to search and what they are to seize.[7] The

4. See Andresen v. Maryland, 427 U.S. 463, 480, 96 S.Ct. 2737, 2748 (1976); Stanley v. Georgia, 394 U.S. 557, 569–572, 89 S.Ct. 1243, 1250–1252 (1969) (Stewart, J., concurring in result); Stanford v. Texas, 379 U.S. 476, 481–482, 485, 85 S.Ct. 506, 509–510, 511 (1965); Go–Bart Importing Co. v. United States, 282 U.S. 344, 357, 51 S.Ct. 153, 158 (1931); Marron v. United States, 275 U.S. 192, 195–196, 48 S.Ct. 74, 75–76 (1927).

5. Indeed, the "defect" in the warrant was that it authorized—albeit mistakenly—a search for quite particular "things to be seized," controlled substances, rather than the evidence described in the affidavit supporting the warrant application. This "defect" posed no risk of a general search. On its face, the warrant correctly identified the place to be searched. Thus, the threshold invasion of privacy—entry into respondent's home—was properly and specifically authorized. Moreover, the four corners of the warrant plainly indicate that it was not intended to authorize a search for controlled substances. On the cover of the warrant the caption "Controlled Substances" had been crossed out, and an "addendum" to the warrant authorized a search for and seizure of a rifle and ammunition, indicating that the warrant was not limited to controlled substances.

6. The issuing judge attested to the affiant's signature on the affidavit.

7. See Steele v. United States, 267 U.S. 498, 503, 45 S.Ct. 414, 416 (1925).

test is whether the executing officers' discretion has been limited in a way that forbids a general search.[8] Here there was no question that the executing officers' discretion had been limited—they, as well as the reviewing courts, knew the precise limits of their authorization. There was simply no "occasion or opportunity for officers to rummage at large," Zurcher v. Stanford Daily, 436 U.S. 547, 566, 98 S.Ct. 1970, 1982 (1978).[9]

The only Fourth Amendment interest that is arguably implicated by the "defect" in the warrant is the citizen's interest in being able to ascertain the limits of the officers' authorization by examining the warrant.[10] Respondent, however, was not home at the time the warrant was executed, and therefore had no occasion to see the warrant. The two persons who were present when the warrant was executed, respondent's mother and sister, did not read the warrant or ask to have it read. "[T]he general rule [is] that Fourth Amendment rights are personal rights which, like some other constitutional rights, may not be vicariously asserted." Alderman v. United States, 394 U.S. 165, 174, 89 S.Ct. 961, 966 (1969). Thus, respondent, who has standing to assert only his own Fourth Amendment interests,[11] cannot complain that his interest in ascertaining the limits of the officers' authority under the search warrant was infringed.[12] In short, our precedents construing the particularity requirement of the Warrant Clause unambiguously demonstrate that this warrant did not violate the Fourth Amendment.

III

Even if it be assumed that there was a technical violation of the particularity requirement in No. 82–963, it by no means follows that the "warrantless" search in that case was "unreasonable" within the meaning of the Fourth Amendment. For this search posed none of the dangers to which the Fourth Amendment is addressed. It was justified by a neutral magistrate's determination of probable cause and created no risk of a general search. It was eminently "reasonable."

8. See Lo–Ji Sales, Inc. v. New York, 442 U.S. 319, 325, 99 S.Ct. 2319, 2323 (1979); Andresen v. Maryland, 427 U.S., at 480–482, 96 S.Ct., at 2748–2749; Marcus v. Search Warrant, 367 U.S. 717, 732–733, 81 S.Ct. 1708, 1716–1717 (1961).

9. See also Coolidge v. New Hampshire, 403 U.S., at 467, 91 S.Ct., at 2038.

10. See Illinois v. Gates, 462 U.S. 213, 236, 103 S.Ct. 2317, 2331 (1983); United States v. Chadwick, 433 U.S. 1, 9, 97 S.Ct. 2476, 2482 (1977); Camara v. Municipal Court, 387 U.S. 523, 532, 87 S.Ct. 1727, 1732 (1967).

11. See, e.g., Rawlings v. Kentucky, 448 U.S. 98, 104–106, 100 S.Ct. 2556, 2561–2562 (1980); Rakas v. Illinois, 439 U.S. 128, 99 S.Ct. 421 (1978).

12. Even if respondent had standing to assert his right to be able to ascertain the officers' authority from the four corners of the warrant, it is doubtful that he could succeed. On its face the warrant authorized a search of respondent's residence, "42 Deckard Street." Had respondent read the warrant he would have had no reason to question the officers' right to enter the premises. Moreover, the face of the warrant indicated that the caption "Controlled Substances" had been stricken, and at the bottom of the warrant an addendum authorized the search for and seizure of a rifle and ammunition. The supporting affidavit, which the police had with them when they executed the warrant, and which was attested by the same judge who had issued the warrant, described in detail the items which the police were authorized to search for and to seize.

In No. 82–1771, however, the Government now admits—at least for the tactical purpose of achieving what it regards as a greater benefit—that the substance, as well as the letter, of the Fourth Amendment was violated. The Court therefore assumes that the warrant in that case was not supported by probable cause, but refuses to suppress the evidence obtained thereby because it considers the police conduct to satisfy a "newfangled" nonconstitutional standard of reasonableness.[13] Yet if the Court's assumption is correct—if there was no probable cause—it must follow that it was "unreasonable" for the authorities to make unheralded entries into and searches of private dwellings and automobiles. The Court's conclusion that such searches undertaken without probable cause can nevertheless be "reasonable" is totally without support in our Fourth Amendment jurisprudence.

Just last Term, the Court explained what probable cause to issue a warrant means:

> "The task of the issuing magistrate is simply to make a practical, common-sense decision whether, given all the circumstances set forth in the affidavit before him, including the 'veracity' and the 'basis of knowledge' of persons supplying hearsay information, there is a fair probability that contraband or evidence of a crime will be found in a particular place." Illinois v. Gates, 462 U.S., at 238, 103 S.Ct., at 2332.

Moreover, in evaluating the existence of probable cause, reviewing courts must give substantial deference to the magistrate's determination.[14] In

13. I borrow the adjective from Justice Clark, who so characterized the warrants authorized by the Court in Camara v. Municipal Court, 387 U.S. 523, 87 S.Ct. 1727 (1967), but not authorized by the Constitution itself. In an opinion joined by Justice Harlan and Justice Stewart, he wrote:

> "Today the Court renders this municipal experience, which dates back to Colonial days, for naught by overruling Frank v. Maryland [359 U.S. 360, 79 S.Ct. 804 (1959)] and by striking down hundreds of city ordinances throughout the country and jeopardizing thereby the health, welfare, and safety of literally millions of people.
>
> "But this is not all. It prostitutes the command of the Fourth Amendment that 'no Warrants shall issue, but upon probable cause' and sets up in the health and safety codes area inspection a newfangled 'warrant' system that is entirely foreign to Fourth Amendment standards. It is regrettable that the Court wipes out such a long and widely accepted practice and creates in its place such enormous confusion in all of our towns and metropolitan cities in one fell swoop." See v. City of Seattle, 387 U.S. 541, 547, 87 S.Ct. 1737, 1741 (1967) (dissenting in both *Camara* and *See*).

The kind of doctrinal difficulties in the two lines of cases engendered by the Court's creation of a newfangled warrant, compare Marshall v. Barlow's, Inc., 436 U.S. 307, 98 S.Ct. 1816 (1978), with Donovan v. Dewey, 452 U.S. 594, 101 S.Ct. 2534 (1981), can be expected to grow out of the Court's creation of a new double standard of reasonableness today. Ironically, as I have previously suggested, the failure to consider both Clauses of the Amendment infects both lines of decision. See Michigan v. Clifford, 464 U.S. 287, 301–303, 104 S.Ct. 641, 651–652 (1984) (Stevens, J., concurring in judgment); Dewey, 452 U.S., at 606–608, 101 S.Ct., at 2542–2543 (Stevens, J., concurring); Michigan v. Tyler, 436 U.S. 499, 513, 98 S.Ct. 1942, 1951 (1978) (Stevens, J., concurring in part and concurring in judgment); Barlow's, 436 U.S., at 325–339, 98 S.Ct., at 1827–1834 (Stevens, J., dissenting).

14. See Massachusetts v. Upton, 466 U.S. 727, 732–733, 104 S.Ct. 2085, 2087–2088 (1984) (per curiam); Illinois v. Gates, 462 U.S., at 236, 103 S.Ct., at 2331; United States v. Harris, 403 U.S. 573, 577–583, 91

doubtful cases the warrant should be sustained.[15] The judgment as to whether there is probable cause must be made in a practical and nontechnical manner.[16] The probable-cause standard therefore gives law enforcement officers ample room to engage in any reasonable law enforcement activity. What is more, the standard has been familiar to the law enforcement profession for centuries.[17] In an opinion written in 1949, and endorsed by the Court last Term in *Gates,* we explained:

> "These long-prevailing standards seek to safeguard citizens from rash and unreasonable interferences with privacy and from unfounded charges of crime. They also seek to give fair leeway for enforcing the law in the community's protection. Because many situations which confront officers in the course of executing their duties are more or less ambiguous, room must be allowed for some mistakes on their part. But the mistakes must be those of reasonable men, acting on facts leading sensibly to their conclusions of probability. The rule of probable cause is a practical, nontechnical conception affording the best compromise that has been found for accommodating these often opposing interests. Requiring more would unduly hamper law enforcement. To allow less would be to leave law-abiding citizens at the mercy of the officers' whim or caprice." Brinegar v. United States, 338 U.S. 160, 176, 69 S.Ct. 1302, 1311.

Thus, if the majority's assumption is correct, that even after paying heavy deference to the magistrate's finding and resolving all doubt in its favor, there is no probable cause here, then by definition—as a matter of constitutional law—the officers' conduct was unreasonable.[18] The Court's own hypothesis is that there was no fair likelihood that the officers would find evidence of a crime, and hence there was no reasonable law enforcement justification for their conduct.[19]

The majority's contrary conclusion rests on the notion that it must be reasonable for a police officer to rely on a magistrate's finding. Until today that has plainly not been the law; it has been well settled that

S.Ct. 2075, 2078–2082 (1971) (plurality opinion); Spinelli v. United States, 393 U.S. 410, 419, 89 S.Ct. 584, 590 (1969); Aguilar v. Texas, 378 U.S. 108, 111, 84 S.Ct. 1509, 1512 (1964); Jones v. United States, 362 U.S. 257, 271, 80 S.Ct. 725, 736 (1960).

15. See Illinois v. Gates, 462 U.S., at 237, n. 10, 103 S.Ct., at 2331, n. 10; United States v. Ventresca, 380 U.S. 102, 109, 85 S.Ct. 741, 746 (1965).

16. See Massachusetts v. Upton, 466 U.S., at 732, 104 S.Ct., at 2087, (per curiam); Illinois v. Gates, 462 U.S., at 231, 103 S.Ct., at 2328; United States v. Ventresca, 380 U.S., at 108, 85 S.Ct., at 745.

17. See, e.g., 2 M. Hale, Pleas of the Crown 150 (1st Am. ed. 1847).

18. "[I]f nothing said under oath in the warrant application demonstrates the need for an unannounced search by force, the probable-cause requirement is not satisfied. In the absence of some other showing of reasonableness, the ensuing search violates the Fourth Amendment." Zurcher v. Stanford Daily, 436 U.S. 547, 583, 98 S.Ct. 1970, 1990 (1978) (Stevens, J., dissenting).

19. As the majority recognizes, United States v. Leon, ante, ___ S.Ct., at ___, n. 13, an officer's good faith cannot make otherwise "unreasonable" conduct reasonable. See Terry v. Ohio, 392 U.S. 1, 22, 88 S.Ct. 1868, 1880 (1968); Beck v. Ohio, 379 U.S. 89, 97, 85 S.Ct. 223, 228 (1964); Henry v. United States, 361 U.S. 98, 102, 80 S.Ct. 168, 171 (1959). The majority's failure to appreciate the significance of that recognition is inexplicable.

even when a magistrate issues a warrant there is no guarantee that the ensuing search and seizure is constitutionally reasonable. Law enforcement officers have long been on notice that despite the magistrate's decision a warrant will be invalidated if the officers did not provide sufficient facts to enable the magistrate to evaluate the existence of probable cause responsibly and independently.[20] Reviewing courts have always inquired into whether the magistrate acted properly in issuing the warrant—not merely whether the officers acted properly in executing it. See Jones v. United States, 362 U.S. 257, 271–272, 80 S.Ct. 725, 736–737 (1960).[21] Indeed, just last Term, in *Gates,* after noting that " 'the duty of a reviewing court is simply to ensure that the magistrate had a "substantial basis for conclud[ing]" that probable cause existed,' " 462 U.S., at 238–239, 103 S.Ct., at 2332 (quoting *Jones,* 362 U.S., at 271, 80 S.Ct., at 736), the Court added:

> "Sufficient information must be presented to the magistrate to allow that official to determine probable cause; his action cannot be a mere ratification of the bare conclusions of others. In order to ensure that such an abdication of the magistrate's duty does not occur, courts must continue to conscientiously review the sufficiency of affidavits on which warrants are issued." 462 U.S., at 239, 103 S.Ct., at 2332.[22]

Thus, under our cases it has never been "reasonable" for the police to rely on the mere fact that a warrant has issued; the police have always known that if they fail to supply the magistrate with sufficient information, the warrant will be held invalid and its fruits excluded.[23]

The notion that a police officer's reliance on a magistrate's warrant is automatically appropriate is one the Framers of the Fourth Amend-

20. See Franks v. Delaware, 438 U.S. 154, 165, 169–170, 98 S.Ct. 2674, 2683–2684 (1978); Whiteley v. Warden, 401 U.S. 560, 564, 91 S.Ct. 1031, 1034 (1971); Spinelli v. United States, 393 U.S., at 415–416, 89 S.Ct., at 588–589; United States v. Ventresca, 380 U.S., at 108–109, 85 S.Ct., at 745–746; Aguilar v. Texas, 378 U.S., at 113–115, 84 S.Ct., at 1513–1514; Nathanson v. United States, 290 U.S. 41, 54 S.Ct. 11 (1933); Byars v. United States, 273 U.S. 28, 47 S.Ct. 248 (1927).

21. In making this point in Franks v. Delaware, 438 U.S. 154, 98 S.Ct. 2674 (1978), Justice Blackmun wrote for the Court: "We see no principled basis for distinguishing between the question of the sufficiency of an affidavit, which is also subject to a post-search examination, and the question of its integrity." Id., at 171, 98 S.Ct., at 2684. Yet today the Court justifies its holding in part by distinguishing veracity claims, United States v. Leon, 468 U.S., at 922–923, 104 S.Ct., at 3421–3422, thereby distinguishing what we previously held could not be distinguished on a principled basis. Just why it should be less reasonable for an innocent officer to rely on a warrant obtained by another officer's fraud than for him to rely on a warrant that is not supported by probable cause is entirely unclear to me.

22. Judicial review of magisterial determinations is all the more necessary since the magistrate acts without benefit of adversarial presentation; his determination partakes of the unreliability inherent in any *ex parte* proceeding. See Franks v. Delaware, 438 U.S., at 169, 98 S.Ct. 2674, 2683.

23. The majority seems to be captivated by a vision of courts invalidating perfectly reasonable police conduct because of "technical" violations of the Fourth Amendment. In my view there is no such thing as a "technical" violation of the Fourth Amendment. No search or seizure can be unconstitutional unless it is "unreasonable." By definition a Fourth Amendment violation cannot be reasonable. My analysis of No. 82–963 illustrates this point.

ment would have vehemently rejected. The precise problem that the Amendment was intended to address was *the unreasonable issuance of warrants.* As we have often observed, the Amendment was actually motivated by the practice of issuing general warrants—warrants which did not satisfy the particularity and probable-cause requirements.[24] The resentments which led to the Amendment were directed at the issuance of warrants unjustified by particularized evidence of wrongdoing.[25] Those who sought to amend the Constitution to include a Bill of Rights repeatedly voiced the view that the evil which had to be addressed was the issuance of warrants on insufficient evidence.[26] As Professor Taylor has written:

> "[O]ur constitutional fathers were not concerned about warrantless searches, but about overreaching warrants. It is perhaps too much to say that they feared the warrant more than the search, but it is plain enough that the warrant was the prime object of their concern. Far from looking at the warrant as a protection against unreasonable searches, they saw it as an authority for unreasonable and oppressive searches. . . ." T. Taylor, Two Studies in Constitutional Interpretation 41 (1969).

In short, the Framers of the Fourth Amendment were deeply suspicious of warrants; in their minds the paradigm of an abusive search was the execution of a warrant not based on probable cause. The fact that colonial officers had magisterial authorization for their conduct when they engaged in general searches surely did not make their conduct "reasonable." The Court's view that it is consistent with our Constitution to adopt a rule that it is presumptively reasonable to rely

24. See, e.g., Steagald v. United States, 451 U.S. 204, 220, 101 S.Ct. 1642, 1651 (1981); Payton v. New York, 445 U.S., at 583–584, 100 S.Ct., at 1378–1379; Lo–Ji Sales, Inc. v. New York, 442 U.S., at 325, 99 S.Ct., at 2323; Marshall v. Barlow's, Inc., 436 U.S., at 327–328, 98 S.Ct., at 1828–1829 (Stevens, J., dissenting); United States v. Chadwick, 433 U.S., at 7–8, 97 S.Ct., at 2481–2482; Chimel v. California, 395 U.S., at 760–762, 89 S.Ct., at 2038–2040; Stanford v. Texas, 379 U.S., at 480–485, 85 S.Ct., at 509–511; Marcus v. Search Warrant, 367 U.S., at 727–729, 81 S.Ct., at 1713–1715; Henry v. United States, 361 U.S., at 100–101, 80 S.Ct., at 169–171; Frank v. Maryland, 359 U.S. 360, 363–365, 79 S.Ct. 804, 807–808 (1959); United States v. Rabinowitz, 339 U.S. 56, 69–70, 70 S.Ct. 430, 436–437 (1950) (Frankfurter, J., dissenting); Marron v. United States, 275 U.S., at 195–196, 48 S.Ct., at 75–76; Weeks v. United States, 232 U.S. 383, 390–391, 34 S.Ct. 341, 343–344 (1914); Boyd v. United States, 116 U.S. 616, 624–630, 6 S.Ct. 524, 528–532 (1886).

25. See J. Landynski, Search and Seizure and the Supreme Court 19–47 (1966); N. Lasson, The History and Development of the Fourth Amendment to the United States Constitution 53–98 (1937); R. Rutland, The Birth of the Bill of Rights 11 (rev. ed. 1983); Marke, The Writs of Assistance Case and the Fourth Amendment, in Essays in Legal History in Honor of Felix Frankfurter 351 (M. Forkosch ed. 1966).

26. See 1 The Bill of Rights: A Documentary History 473, 488–489, 508 (B. Schwartz ed. 1971); 2 id., at 658, 665, 730, 733–734, 805–806, 815, 841–842, 913, 968. In fact, the original version of the Fourth Amendment contained only one clause providing that the right to be protected against unreasonable searches and seizures "shall not be violated by warrants issuing. . . ." The change to its present form broadened the coverage of the Amendment but did not qualify the unequivocal prohibition against the issuance of warrants without probable cause. See 2 id., at 1112; N. Lasson, supra n. 25, at 101–103.

on a defective warrant is the product of constitutional amnesia.[27]

IV

In *Brinegar,* Justice Jackson, after observing that "[i]ndications are not wanting that Fourth Amendment freedoms are tacitly marked as secondary rights, to be relegated to a deferred position," 338 U.S., at 180, 69 S.Ct., at 1313 (dissenting opinion), continued:

> "These, I protest, are not mere second-class rights but belong in the catalog of indispensable freedoms. Among deprivations of rights, none is so effective in cowing a population, crushing the spirit of the individual and putting terror in every heart. Uncontrolled search and seizure is one of the first and most effective weapons in the arsenal of every arbitrary government. And one need only briefly to have dwelt and worked among a people possessed of many admirable qualities but deprived of these rights to know that the human personality deteriorates and dignity and self-reliance disappear where homes, persons and possessions are subject at any hour to unheralded search and seizure by the police.
>
> * * * * * * * * *
>
> "Only occasional and more flagrant abuses come to the attention of the courts, and then only those where the search and seizure yields incriminating evidence and the defendant is at least sufficiently compromised to be indicted. If the officers raid a home, an office, or stop and search an automobile but find nothing incriminating, this invasion of the personal liberty of the innocent too often finds no practical redress. There may be, and I am convinced that there are, many unlawful searches of homes and automobiles of innocent people which turn up nothing incriminating, in which no arrest is made, about which courts do nothing, and about which we never hear.
>
> "Courts can protect the innocent against such invasions only indirectly and through the medium of excluding evidence obtained against those who frequently are guilty.... So a search against Brinegar's car must be regarded as a search of the car of Everyman." Id., at 180–181, 69 S.Ct., at 1313–1314.

Justice Jackson's reference to his experience at Nuremberg should remind us of the importance of considering the consequences of today's decision for "Everyman."

27. "It makes all the difference in the world whether one recognizes the central fact about the Fourth Amendment, namely, that it was a safeguard against recurrence of abuses so deeply felt by the Colonies as to be one of the potent causes of the Revolution, or one thinks of it as merely a requirement for a piece of paper." United States v. Rabinowitz, 339 U.S., at 69, 70 S.Ct., at 436 (Frankfurter, J., dissenting).

The exclusionary rule is designed to prevent violations of the Fourth Amendment.[28] "Its purpose is to deter—to compel respect for the constitutional guaranty in the only effectively available way, by removing the incentive to disregard it." Elkins v. United States, 364 U.S. 206, 217, 80 S.Ct. 1437, 1444 (1960).[29] If the police cannot use evidence obtained through warrants issued on less than probable cause, they have less incentive to seek those warrants, and magistrates have less incentive to issue them.

Today's decisions do grave damage to that deterrent function. Under the majority's new rule, even when the police know their warrant application is probably insufficient, they retain an incentive to submit it to a magistrate, on the chance that he may take the bait. No longer must they hesitate and seek additional evidence in doubtful cases. Thus, what we said two Terms ago about a rule that would prevent exclusion except in cases in which the authorities violate well-settled law applies fully to the rule the Court adopts today:

> "If, as the Government argues, all rulings resolving unsettled Fourth Amendment questions should be nonretroactive, then, in close cases law enforcement officials would have little incentive to err on the side of constitutional behavior. Official awareness of the dubious constitutionality of a practice would be counter-balanced by official certainty that, so long as the Fourth Amendment law in the area remained unsettled, evidence obtained through the questionable practice would be excluded only in the one case definitively resolving the unsettled

28. For at least two reasons, the exclusionary rule is a better remedy than a civil action against an offending officer. Unlike the fear of personal liability, it should not create excessive deterrence; moreover, it avoids the obvious unfairness of subjecting the dedicated officer to the risk of monetary liability for a misstep while endeavoring to enforce the law. Society, rather than the individual officer, should accept the responsibility for inadequate training or supervision of officers engaged in hazardous police work. What The Chief Justice wrote, some two decades ago, remains true today:

> "It is the proud claim of a democratic society that the people are masters and all officials of the state are servants of the people. That being so, the ancient rule of respondeat superior furnishes us with a simple, direct and reasonable basis for refusing to admit evidence secured in violation of constitutional or statutory provisions. Since the policeman is society's servant, his acts in the execution of his duty are attributable to the master or employer. Society as a whole is thus responsible and society is 'penalized' by refusing it the benefit of evidence secured by the illegal action. This satisfies me more than the other explanations because it seems to me that society—in a country like ours—*is* involved in and *is* responsible for what is done in its name and by its agents. Unlike the Germans of the 1930s and early '40s, we cannot say 'it is all The Leader's doing. I am not responsible.' In a representative democracy we are responsible, whether we like it or not. And so each of us is involved and each is in this sense responsible when a police officer breaks rules of law established for our common protection." Burger, Who Will Watch the Watchman?, 14 Am. U.L.Rev. 1, 14 (1964) (emphasis in original) (footnote omitted).

29. See Stone v. Powell, 428 U.S. 465, 484, 96 S.Ct. 3037, 3047 (1976); United States v. Janis, 428 U.S. 433, 443, n. 12, 96 S.Ct. 3021, 3027, n. 12 (1976); United States v. Calandra, 414 U.S. 338, 347–348, 94 S.Ct. 613, 619–620 (1974); Terry v. Ohio, 392 U.S., at 29, 88 S.Ct., at 1883; Tehan v. United States ex rel. Shott, 382 U.S. 406, 413, 86 S.Ct. 459, 463 (1966); Mapp v. Ohio, 367 U.S. 643, 656, 81 S.Ct. 1684, 1692 (1961).

question. Failure to accord *any* retroactive effect to Fourth Amendment rulings would 'encourage police or other courts to disregard the plain purport of our decisions and to adopt a let's-wait-until-it's-decided approach.'" United States v. Johnson, 457 U.S. 537, 561, 102 S.Ct. 2579, 2593 (1982) (emphasis in original) (footnote omitted) (quoting Desist v. United States, 394 U.S. 244, 277, 89 S.Ct. 1030, 1052 (1969) (Fortas, J., dissenting)).[30]

The Court is of course correct that the exclusionary rule cannot deter when the authorities have no reason to know that their conduct is unconstitutional. But when probable cause is lacking, then by definition a reasonable person under the circumstances would not believe there is a fair likelihood that a search will produce evidence of a crime. Under such circumstances well-trained professionals must know that they are violating the Constitution. The Court's approach—which, in effect, encourages the police to seek a warrant even if they know the existence of probable cause is doubtful—can only lead to an increased number of constitutional violations.

Thus, the Court's creation of a double standard of reasonableness inevitably must erode the deterrence rationale that still supports the exclusionary rule. But we should not ignore the way it tarnishes the role of the judiciary in enforcing the Constitution. For the original rationale for the exclusionary rule retains its force as well as its relevance:

> "The tendency of those who execute the criminal laws of the country to obtain conviction by means of unlawful seizures ... should find no sanction in the judgments of the courts which are charged at all times with the support of the Constitution and to which people of all conditions have a right to appeal for the maintenance of such fundamental rights." Weeks v. United States, 232 U.S. 383, 392, 34 S.Ct. 341, 344 (1914).[31]

30. See also LaFave, The Fourth Amendment in an Imperfect World: On Drawing "Bright Lines" and "Good Faith," 43 U.Pitt.L.Rev. 307, 358 (1982); Stewart, The Road to *Mapp v. Ohio* and Beyond: The Origins, Development and Future of the Exclusionary Rule in Search-and-Seizure Cases, 83 Colum.L.Rev. 1365, 1401–1403 (1983); Wasserstrom, The Incredible Shrinking Fourth Amendment, 21 Am. Crim.L.Rev. 257, 395–397 (1984).

31. The Court continued:

"The efforts of the courts and their officials to bring the guilty to punishment, praiseworthy as they are, are not to be aided by the sacrifice of those great principles established by years of endeavor and suffering which have resulted in their embodiment in the fundamental law of the land. The United States Marshal could only have invaded the house of the accused when armed with a warrant issued as required by the Constitution, upon sworn information and describing with reasonable particularity the things for which the search was to be made. Instead, he acted without sanction of law, doubtless prompted by the desire to bring further proof to the aid of the Government, and under color of his office undertook to make a seizure of private papers in direct violation of the constitutional prohibition against such action. Under such circumstances, without sworn information and particular description, not even an order of court would have justified such procedure.... To sanction such proceedings would be to affirm by judicial decision a manifest neglect if not an open defiance of the prohibitions of the Constitution, intended for the protection of the people against such unautho-

Thus, "Courts which sit under our Constitution cannot and will not be made party to lawless invasions of the constitutional rights of citizens by permitting unhindered governmental use of the fruits of such invasions. . . ." Terry v. Ohio, 392 U.S. 1, 13, 88 S.Ct. 1868, 1875 (1968).[32] As the Court correctly notes,[33] we have refused to apply the exclusionary rule to collateral contexts in which its marginal efficacy is questionable; until today, however, every time the police have violated the applicable commands of the Fourth Amendment a court has been prepared to vindicate that Amendment by preventing the use of evidence so obtained in the prosecution's case in chief against those whose rights have been violated.[34] Today, for the first time, this Court holds that although the Constitution has been violated, no court should do anything about it at any time and in any proceeding.[35] In my judgment, the Constitution requires more. Courts simply cannot escape their responsibility for redressing constitutional violations if they admit evidence obtained through unreasonable searches and seizures, since the entire point of police conduct that violates the Fourth Amendment is to obtain evidence for use at trial. If such evidence is admitted, then the courts become not merely the final and necessary link in an unconstitutional chain of events, but its actual motivating force. "If the existing code does not permit district attorneys to have a hand in such dirty business it does not permit the judge to allow such iniquities to succeed." Olmstead v. United States, 277 U.S. 438, 470, 48 S.Ct. 564, 575, 72 L.Ed. 944 (1928) (Holmes, J., dissenting). Nor should we so easily concede the existence

rized action." 232 U.S., at 393–394, 34 S.Ct., at 344–345.

32. See United States v. Peltier, 422 U.S. 531, 536, 95 S.Ct. 2313, 2316 (1975); Lee v. Florida, 392 U.S. 378, 385–386, 88 S.Ct. 2096, 2100–2101 (1968); Berger v. New York, 388 U.S. 41, 50, 87 S.Ct. 1873, 1879 (1967); Mapp v. Ohio, 367 U.S., at 647–650, 81 S.Ct., at 1687–1688; Byars v. United States, 273 U.S., at 33–34, 47 S.Ct., at 250.

33. United States v. Leon, 468 U.S., at 908–913, 104 S.Ct. at 3412–3415.

34. Indeed, we have concluded that judicial integrity is not compromised by the refusal to apply the exclusionary rule to collateral contexts precisely because the defendant is able to vindicate his rights in the primary context—his trial and direct appeal therefrom. See Stone v. Powell, 428 U.S., at 485–486, 96 S.Ct., at 3048–3049.

35. As the majority recognizes, United States v. Leon, 468 U.S., at 922–923, n. 23, at 3420, and n. 23, in all cases in which its "good faith" exception to the exclusionary rule would operate, there will also be immunity from civil damages. See also United States v. Ross, 456 U.S. 798, 823, n. 32, 102 S.Ct. 2157, 2172, n. 32 (1982); Stadium Films, Inc. v. Baillargeon, 542 F.2d 577, 578 (CA1 1976); Madison v. Manter, 441 F.2d 537 (CA1 1971). See generally Pierson v. Ray, 386 U.S. 547, 87 S.Ct. 1213 (1967). The Court amazingly suggests that in some cases in which suppression would not be appropriate courts should nevertheless adjudicate the merits of Fourth Amendment claims to provide guidance to police and magistrates but not a remedy. United States v. Leon, 468 U.S., at 925, 104 S.Ct. at 3421–3422. Not only is the propriety of deciding constitutional questions in the absence of the strict necessity to do so open to serious question, see Bowen v. United States, 422 U.S. 916, 920, 95 S.Ct. 2569, 2572 (1975), but such a proceeding, in which a court would declare that the Constitution had been violated but that it was unwilling to do anything about it, seems almost a mockery: "[T]he assurance against unreasonable federal searches and seizures would be 'a form of words,' valueless and undeserving of mention in a perpetual charter of inestimable human liberties." Mapp v. Ohio, 367 U.S., at 655, 81 S.Ct., at 1691. See also Segura v. United States, 468 U.S. 796 at 838–840, 104 S.Ct. 3380 at 3403–3405 (Stevens, J., dissenting).

of a constitutional violation for which there is no remedy.[36] To do so is to convert a bill of *Rights* into an unenforced honor code that the police may follow in their discretion. The Constitution requires more; it requires a *remedy*.[37] If the Court's new rule is to be followed, the Bill of Rights should be renamed.

It is of course true that the exclusionary rule exerts a high price—the loss of probative evidence of guilt. But that price is one courts have often been required to pay to serve important social goals.[38] That price is also one the Fourth Amendment requires us to pay, assuming as we must that the Framers intended that its strictures "shall not be violated." For in all such cases, as Justice Stewart has observed, "the same extremely relevant evidence would not have been obtained had the police officer complied with the commands of the fourth amendment in the first place."[39]

> "[T]he forefathers thought this was not too great a price to pay for that decent privacy of home, papers and effects which is indispensable to individual dignity and self-respect. They may have overvalued privacy, but I am not disposed to set their command at naught." Harris v. United States, 331 U.S. 145, 198, 67 S.Ct. 1098, 1120 (1947) (Jackson, J., dissenting).[40]

We could, of course, facilitate the process of administering justice to those who violate the criminal laws by ignoring the commands of the Fourth Amendment—indeed, by ignoring the entire Bill of Rights—but it

36. "The very essence of civil liberty certainly consists in the right of every individual to claim the protection of the laws, whenever he receives an injury." Marbury v. Madison, 1 Cranch 137, 163 (1803). See generally Schrock & Welsh, Up From Calandra: The Exclusionary Rule as a Constitutional Requirement, 59 Minn.L.Rev. 251, 350–372 (1974).

37. See Stewart, 83 Colum.L.Rev., at 1383–1384 (footnotes omitted) ("In my opinion, however, the framers did not intend the Bill of Rights to be no more than unenforceable guiding principles—no more than a code of ethics under an honor system. The proscriptions and guarantees in the amendments were intended to create legal rights and duties"). See also Ervin, The Exclusionary Rule: An Essential Ingredient of the Fourth Amendment, 1983 S.Ct. Rev. 283. In fact, if the Constitution of the United States does not compel use of the exclusionary rule, Mapp v. Ohio, 367 U.S. 643, 81 S.Ct. 1684 (1961), which the majority does not purport to question, could not have been decided as it was. See id., at 655, 81 S.Ct., at 1691 ("We hold that all evidence obtained by searches and seizures in violation of the Constitution is, by that same authority, inadmissible in a state court").

38. The exclusion of probative evidence in order to serve some other policy is by no means unique to the Fourth Amendment. In his famous treatise on evidence, Dean Wigmore devoted an entire volume to such exclusionary rules, which are common in the law of evidence. See 8 J. Wigmore, Evidence (J. McNaughton rev. 1961) (discussing, *inter alia,* marital privilege, attorney-client privilege, communications among jurors, state secrets privilege, physician-patient privilege, priest-penitent privilege).

39. Stewart, 83 Colum.L.Rev., at 1392 (footnote omitted). See also Traynor, Mapp v. Ohio at Large in the Fifty States, 1962 Duke L.J. 319, 322 ("Ah, but surely the guilty should not go free? However grave the question, it seemed improperly directed at the exclusionary rule. The hard answer is in the United States Constitution as well as in state constitutions. They make it clear that the guilty would go free if the evidence necessary to convict could only have been obtained illegally, just as they would go free if such evidence were lacking because the police had observed the constitutional restraints upon them").

40. See also United States v. Di Re, 332 U.S. 581, 595, 68 S.Ct. 222, 228 (1948).

is the very purpose of a Bill of Rights to identify values that may not be sacrificed to expediency. In a just society those who govern, as well as those who are governed, must obey the law.

While I concur in the Court's judgment in No. 82–963, I would vacate the judgment in No. 82–1771 and remand the case to the Court of Appeals for reconsideration in the light of *Gates*. Accordingly, I respectfully dissent from the disposition in No. 82–1771.

NOTE

Reliance on incorrect computer data as a basis for good faith was addressed in Arizona v. Evans, ___ U.S. ___, 115 S.Ct. 1185 (1995).

"Chief Justice Rehnquist delivered the opinion of the Court.

In January 1991, Phoenix police officer Bryan Sargent observed respondent Evans driving the wrong way on a one-way street in front of the police station. The officer stopped respondent and asked to see his driver's license. After respondent told him that his license had been suspended, the officer entered respondent's name into a computer data terminal located in his patrol car. The computer inquiry confirmed that respondent's license had been suspended and also indicated that there was an outstanding misdemeanor warrant for his arrest. Based upon the outstanding warrant, Officer Sargent placed respondent under arrest. While being handcuffed, respondent dropped a hand-rolled cigarette that the officers determined smelled of marijuana. Officers proceeded to search his car and discovered a bag of marijuana under the passenger's seat.

The State charged respondent with possession of marijuana. When the police notified the Justice Court that they had arrested him, the Justice Court discovered that the arrest warrant previously had been quashed and so advised the police. Respondent argued that because his arrest was based on a warrant that had been quashed 17 days prior to his arrest, the marijuana seized incident to the arrest should be suppressed as the fruit of an unlawful arrest. Respondent also argued that "[t]he 'good faith' exception to the exclusionary rule [was] inapplicable ... because it was police error, not judicial error, which caused the invalid arrest."

At the suppression hearing, the Chief Clerk of the Justice Court testified that a Justice of the Peace had issued the arrest warrant on December 13, 1990, because respondent had failed to appear to answer for several traffic violations. On December 19, 1990, respondent appeared before a *pro tem* Justice of the Peace who entered a notation in respondent's file to "quash warrant."

The Chief Clerk also testified regarding the standard court procedure for quashing a warrant. Under that procedure a justice court clerk calls and informs the warrant section of the Sheriff's Office when a warrant has been quashed. The Sheriff's Office then removes the warrant from its computer records. After calling the Sheriff's Office, the clerk makes a note in the individual's file indicating the clerk who made the phone call and the person at the Sheriff's Office to whom the clerk spoke. The Chief Clerk testified that there was no indication in respondent's file that a clerk had called and notified the Sheriff's Office that his arrest warrant had been quashed. A records clerk from the Sheriff's Office also testified that the Sheriff's Office had no record of a telephone call informing it that respondent's arrest warrant had been quashed.

At the close of testimony, respondent argued that the evidence obtained as a result of the arrest should be suppressed because "the purposes of the exclusionary rule would be served here by making the clerks for the court, or the clerk for the Sheriff's Office, whoever is responsible for this mistake, to be more careful about making sure that warrants are removed from the records." The trial court granted the motion to suppress because it concluded that the State had been at fault for failing to quash the warrant. Presumably because it could find no "distinction between State action, whether it happens to be the police department or not," the trial court made no factual finding as to whether the Justice Court or Sheriff's Office was responsible for the continued presence of the quashed warrant in the police records.

* * *

Applying the reasoning of *Leon* to the facts of this case, we conclude that the decision must be reversed. The Court determined that it could not "support the distinction drawn ... between clerical errors committed by law enforcement personnel and similar mistakes by court employees," and that "even assuming ... that responsibility for the error rested with the justice court, it does not follow that the exclusionary rule should be inapplicable to these facts,".

This holding is contrary to the reasoning of *Leon,* Massachusetts v. Sheppard, and, *Krull.* If court employees were responsible for the erroneous computer record, the exclusion of evidence at trial would not sufficiently deter future errors so as to warrant such a severe sanction. First, as we noted in *Leon,* the exclusionary rule was historically designed as a means of deterring police misconduct, not mistakes by court employees. Second, respondent offers no evidence that court employees are inclined to ignore or subvert the Fourth Amendment or that lawlessness among these actors requires application of the extreme sanction of exclusion. To the contrary, the Chief Clerk of the Justice Court testified at the suppression hearing that this type of error occurred once every three or four years.

Finally, and most important, there is no basis for believing that application of the exclusionary rule in these circumstances will have a significant effect on court employees responsible for informing the police that a warrant has been quashed. Because court clerks are not adjuncts to the law enforcement team engaged in the often competitive enterprise of ferreting out crime, see Johnson v. United States, 333 U.S. 10, 14, 68 S.Ct. 367, 369, 92 L.Ed. 436 (1948), they have no stake in the outcome of particular criminal prosecutions. The threat of exclusion of evidence could not be expected to deter such individuals from failing to inform police officials that a warrant had been quashed.

If it were indeed a court clerk who was responsible for the erroneous entry on the police computer, application of the exclusionary rule also could not be expected to alter the behavior of the arresting officer. As the trial court in this case stated: "I think the police officer [was] bound to arrest. I think he would [have been] derelict in his duty if he failed to arrest." The Chief Clerk of the Justice Court testified that this type of error occurred "on[c]e every three or four years." In fact, once the court clerks discovered the error, they immediately corrected it, and then proceeded to search their files to make sure that no similar mistakes had occurred. There is no indication that the arresting officer was not acting objectively reasonably when he relied upon the police computer record. Application of the *Leon* framework supports a categorical exception to the exclusionary rule for clerical errors of court employees.*

The judgment of the Supreme Court of Arizona is therefore reversed, and the case is remanded to that court for proceedings not inconsistent with this opinion.

It is so ordered.

JUSTICE O'CONNOR, with whom JUSTICE SOUTER and JUSTICE BREYER join, concurring.

The evidence in this case strongly suggests that it was a court employee's departure from established record-keeping procedures that caused the record of respondent's arrest warrant to remain in the computer system after the warrant had been quashed. Prudently, then, the Court limits itself to the question whether a court employee's departure from such established procedures is the kind of error to which the exclusionary rule should apply. The Court holds that it is not such an error, and I agree with that conclusion and join the Court's opinion. The Court's holding reaffirms that the exclusionary rule imposes significant costs on society's law enforcement interests and thus should apply only where its deterrence purposes are "most efficaciously served," *ante*, at 1191.

In limiting itself to that single question, however, the Court does not hold that the court employee's mistake in this case was necessarily the *only* error that may have occurred and to which the exclusionary rule might apply. While the police were innocent of the court employee's mistake, they may or may not have acted reasonably in their reliance *on the recordkeeping system itself.* Surely it would *not* be reasonable for the police to rely, say, on a recordkeeping system, their own or some other agency's, that has no mechanism to ensure its accuracy over time and that routinely leads to false arrests, even years after the probable cause for any such arrest has ceased to exist (if it ever existed).

* * *

In recent years, we have witnessed the advent of powerful, computer-based record-keeping systems that facilitate arrests in ways that have never before been possible. The police, of course, are entitled to enjoy the substantial advantages this technology confers. They may not, however, rely on it blindly. With the benefits of more efficient law

* The Solicitor General, as *amicus curiae*, argues that an analysis similar to that we apply here to court personnel also would apply in order to determine whether the evidence should be suppressed if police personnel were responsible for the error. As the State has not made any such argument here, we agree that "[t]he record in this case ... does not adequately present that issue for the Court's consideration." Brief for United States as *Amicus Curiae* 13. Accordingly, we decline to address that question.

enforcement mechanisms comes the burden of corresponding constitutional responsibilities.

JUSTICE SOUTER, with whom JUSTICE BREYER joins, concurring.

In joining the Court's opinion, I share Justice O'Connor's understanding of the narrow scope of what we hold today. To her concurrence, which I join as well, I add only that we do not answer another question that may reach us in due course, that is, how far, in dealing with fruits of computerized error, our very concept of deterrence by exclusion of evidence should extend to the government as a whole, not merely the police, on the ground that there would otherwise be no reasonable expectation of keeping the number of resulting false arrests within an acceptable minimum limit.

JUSTICE STEVENS, dissenting.

* * *

Leon stands for the dubious but limited proposition that courts should not look behind the face of a warrant on which police have relied in good faith. The *Leon* Court's exemption of judges and magistrates from the deterrent ambit of the exclusionary rule rested, consistently with the emphasis on the warrant requirement, on those officials' constitutionally determined role in issuing warrants. Taken on its own terms, *Leon* 's logic does not extend to the time after the warrant has issued; nor does it extend to court clerks and functionaries, some of whom work in the same building with police officers and may have more regular and direct contact with police than with judges or magistrates.

The Phoenix Police Department was part of the chain of information that resulted in petitioner's unlawful, warrantless arrest. We should reasonably presume that law enforcement officials, who stand in the best position to monitor such errors as occurred here, can influence mundane communication procedures in order to prevent those errors. That presumption comports with the notion that the exclusionary rule exists to deter future police misconduct systemically.

* * *

The deterrent purpose extends to law enforcement as a whole, not merely to "the arresting officer." Consequently, the Phoenix officers' good faith does not diminish the deterrent value of invalidating their arrest of petitioner.

The Court seeks to minimize the impact of its holding on the security of the citizen by referring to the testimony of the chief clerk of the East Phoenix Number One Justice Court that in her "particular court" this type of error occurred " 'maybe [once] every three or four years.' " Apart from the fact that the clerk promptly contradicted herself, this is slim evidence on which to base a conclusion that computer error poses no appreciable threat to Fourth Amendment interests. The Court overlooks the reality that computer technology has changed the nature of threats to citizens' privacy over the past half century. What has not changed is the reality that only that fraction of Fourth Amendment violations held to have resulted in unlawful arrests is ever noted and redressed. As Justice Jackson observed:

"There may be, and I am convinced that there are, many unlawful searches . . . of innocent people which turn up nothing incriminating, in which no arrest is made, about which courts do nothing, and about which we never hear." Moreover, even if errors in computer records of warrants were rare, that would merely minimize the cost of enforcing the exclusionary rule in cases like this.

While I agree with Justice Ginsburg that premature adjudication of this issue is particularly unwise because we have much to learn about the consequences of computer error as well as the efficacy of other preventive measures, one consequence of the Court's holding seems immediately obvious. Its most serious impact will be on the otherwise innocent citizen who is stopped for a minor traffic infraction and is wrongfully arrested based on erroneous information in a computer data base. I assume the police officer who reasonably relies on the computer information would be immune from liability in a § 1983 action. Of course, the Court has held that *respondeat superior* is unavailable as a basis for imposing liability on her municipality.

The dissent of Justice Ginsburg is omitted.

B. THE SCOPE OF EXCLUSION REGARDING EVIDENCE DERIVED FROM INITIAL ILLEGAL POLICE ACTIVITY

DUNAWAY v. NEW YORK

Supreme Court of the United States, 1979.
442 U.S. 200, 99 S.Ct. 2248.

MR. JUSTICE BRENNAN delivered the opinion of the Court.

We decide in this case the question reserved 10 years ago in Morales v. New York, 396 U.S. 102, 90 S.Ct. 291 (1969), namely, "the question of the legality of custodial questioning on less than probable cause for a full-fledged arrest."

I

On March 26, 1971, the proprietor of a pizza parlor in Rochester, N.Y. was killed during an attempted robbery. On August 10, 1971, Detective Anthony Fantigrossi of the Rochester Police was told by another officer that an informant had supplied a possible lead implicating petitioner in the crime. Fantigrossi questioned the supposed source of the lead—a jail inmate awaiting trial for burglary—but learned nothing that supplied "enough information to get a warrant" for petitioner's arrest. Nevertheless, Fantigrossi ordered other detectives to "pick up" petitioner and "bring him in." Three detectives located petitioner at a neighbor's house on the morning of August 11. Petitioner was taken into custody; although he was not told he was under arrest, he would have been physically restrained if he had attempted to leave. He was driven to police headquarters in a police car and placed in an interrogation room, where he was questioned by officers after being given the warnings required by Miranda v. Arizona [Ch. 12–B(1) of casebook]. Petitioner waived counsel and eventually made statements and drew sketches that incriminated him in the crime.

At petitioner's jury trial for attempted robbery and felony murder, his motions to suppress the statements and sketches were denied, and he was convicted. On appeal, both the Appellate Division of the Fourth Department and the New York Court of Appeals initially affirmed the conviction without opinion. However, this Court granted certiorari, vacated the judgment, and remanded the case for further consideration in light of the Court's supervening decision in Brown v. Illinois, 422 U.S. 590, 95 S.Ct. 2254 (1975). The petitioner in *Brown,* like petitioner Dunaway, made inculpatory statements after receiving *Miranda* warnings during custodial interrogation following his seizure—in that case a formal arrest—on less than probable cause. Brown's motion to suppress the statements was also denied and the statements were used to convict him. Although the Illinois Supreme Court recognized that Brown's arrest was unlawful, it affirmed the admission of the statements on the ground that the giving of *Miranda* warnings served to break the causal connection between the illegal arrest and the giving of the statements. This Court reversed, holding that the Illinois courts erred in adopting a *per se* rule that *Miranda* warnings in and of themselves sufficed to cure the Fourth Amendment violation; rather the Court held that in order to use such statements, the prosecution must show not only that the statements meet the Fifth Amendment voluntariness standard, but also that the causal connection between the statements and the illegal arrest is broken sufficiently to purge the primary taint of the illegal arrest in light of the distinct policies and interests of the Fourth Amendment.

In compliance with the remand, the New York Court of Appeals directed the Monroe County Court to make further factual findings as to whether there was a detention of petitioner, whether the police had probable cause, "and, in the event there was a detention and probable cause is not found for such detention, to determine the further question as to whether the making of the confessions was rendered infirm by the illegal arrest."

The County Court determined after a supplementary suppression hearing that Dunaway's motion to suppress should have been granted. Although reaffirming that there had been "full compliance with the mandate of Miranda v. Arizona," the County Court found that "this case does not involve a situation where the defendant voluntarily appeared at police headquarters in response to a request of the police...." The State's attempt to justify petitioner's involuntary investigatory detention on the authority of People v. Morales, which upheld a similar detention on the basis of information amounting to less than probable cause for arrest—was rejected on the grounds that the precedential value of *Morales* was questionable, and that the controlling authority was the "strong language" in Brown v. Illinois indicating "disdain for custodial questioning without probable cause to arrest." The County Court further held that "the factual predicate in this case did not amount to probable cause sufficient to support the arrest of defendant," that "the *Miranda* warnings by themselves did not purge the taint of the defendant's illegal seizure Brown v. Illinois, supra ... and [that] there was no claim or showing by the People of any attenuation of the defendant's illegal detention,". Accordingly petitioner's motion to suppress was granted.

A divided Appellate Division reversed. Although agreeing that the police lacked probable cause to arrest petitioner, the majority relied on the Court of Appeals' reaffirmation, subsequent to the County Court's decision, that "[l]aw enforcement officials may detain an individual upon reasonable suspicion for questioning for a reasonable and brief period of time under carefully controlled conditions which are ample to protect the individual's Fifth and Sixth Amendment Rights." The Appellate Division also held that even if petitioner's detention were illegal, the taint of his illegal detention was sufficiently attenuated to allow the admission of his statements and sketches. The Appellate Division emphasized that petitioner was never threatened or abused by the police and purported to distinguish Brown v. Illinois. The Court of Appeals dismissed petitioner's application for leave to appeal.

We granted certiorari to clarify the Fourth Amendment's requirements as to the permissible grounds for custodial interrogation and to review the New York court's application of Brown v. Illinois. We reverse.

II

We first consider whether the Rochester police violated the Fourth and Fourteenth Amendments when, without probable cause to arrest, they took petitioner into custody, transported him to the police station, and detained him there for interrogation.

The Fourth Amendment, applicable to the States through the Fourteenth Amendment, provides: "The right of the people to be secure in their persons ... against unreasonable searches and seizures, shall not be violated, and no Warrants shall issue, but upon probable cause...." There can be little doubt that petitioner was "seized" in the Fourth Amendment sense when he was taken involuntarily to the police station.[1] And respondent State concedes that the police lacked probable cause to arrest petitioner before his incriminating statement during interrogation. Nevertheless respondent contends that the seizure of petitioner did not amount to an arrest and was therefore permissible under the Fourth Amendment because the police had a "reasonable suspicion" that petitioner possessed "intimate knowledge about a serious and unsolved crime." We disagree.

1. "It must be recognized that whenever a police officer accosts an individual and restrains his freedom to walk away, he has 'seized' that person." Respondent contends that petitioner accompanied the police voluntarily and therefore was not "seized." The County Court found otherwise, and the Appellate Division treated the case as an involuntary detention justified by reasonable suspicion....

Before Terry v. Ohio [which was reproduced in Chapter 14–G of this casebook], the Fourth Amendment's guarantee against unreasonable seizures of persons was analyzed in terms of arrest, probable cause for arrest, and warrants based on such probable cause. The basic principles were relatively simple and straightforward: The term "arrest" was synonymous with those seizures governed by the Fourth Amendment. While warrants were not required in all circumstances, the requirement of probable cause, as elaborated in numerous precedents, was treated as absolute. The "long prevailing standards" of probable cause embodied "the best compromise that has been found for accommodating the[ ] often opposing interests" in "safeguard[ing] citizens from rash and unreasonable interferences with privacy" and in "seek[ing] to give fair leeway for enforcing the law in the community's protection." Brinegar v. United States, 338 U.S. 160, 69 S.Ct. 1302 (1949). The standard of probable cause thus represented the accumulated wisdom of precedent and experience as to the minimum justification necessary to make the kind of intrusion involved in an arrest "reasonable" under the Fourth Amendment. The standard applied to all arrests, without the need to "balance" the interests and circumstances involved in particular situations.

Terry for the first time recognized an exception to the requirement that Fourth Amendment seizures of persons must be based on probable cause. That case involved a brief, on-the-spot stop on the street and a frisk for weapons, a situation that did not fit comfortably within the traditional concept of an "arrest." Nevertheless, the Court held that even this type of "necessarily swift action predicated upon the on-the-spot observations of the officer on the beat" constituted a "serious intrusion upon the sanctity of the person, which may inflict great indignity and arouse strong resentment," and therefore "must be tested by the Fourth Amendment's general proscription against unreasonable searches and seizures." However, since the intrusion involved in a "stop and frisk" was so much less severe than that involved in traditional "arrests," the Court declined to stretch the concept of "arrest"—and the general rule requiring probable cause to make arrests "reasonable" under the Fourth Amendment—to cover such intrusions. Instead, the Court treated the stop and frisk intrusion as a *sui generis* "rubric of police conduct." And to determine the justification necessary to make this specially limited intrusion "reasonable" under the Fourth Amendment, the Court balanced the limited violation of individual privacy involved against the opposing interests in crime prevention and detection and in the police officer's safety. As a consequence, the Court established "a narrowly drawn authority to permit a reasonable search for weapons for the protection of the police officer, where he has reason to believe that he is dealing with an armed and dangerous individual, regardless of whether he has probable cause to arrest the individual for a crime." Thus, *Terry* departed from traditional Fourth Amendment analysis in two respects. First, it defined a special category of Fourth Amendment "seizures" so substantially less intrusive than arrests that the general rule requiring probable cause to make Fourth Amendment "seizures" reasonable could be replaced by a balancing test. Second, the application of this balancing test led the Court to approve this narrowly defined less intrusive seizure on grounds less rigorous than probable cause, but only for the purpose of a pat-down for weapons.

Because *Terry* involved an exception to the general rule requiring probable cause, this Court has been careful to maintain its narrow scope. *Terry* itself involved a limited, on-the-street frisk for weapons. Two subsequent cases which applied *Terry* also involved limited weapons frisks. See Adams v. Williams [reproduced in Ch. 14–G of this casebook] (frisk for weapons on basis of reasonable suspicion); Pennsylvania v. Mimms [Ch. 14–G of casebook] (order to get out of car is permissible "de minimis" intrusion after car is lawfully detained for traffic violations; frisk for weapons justified after "bulge" observed in jacket). United States v. Brignoni-Ponce, 422 U.S. 873, 95 S.Ct. 2574 (1975), applied *Terry* in the special context of roving border patrols stopping automobiles to check for illegal immigrants. The investigative stops usually consumed less than a minute and involved "a brief question or two." The Court stated that "[b]ecause of the limited nature of the intrusion, stops of this sort may be justified on facts that do not amount to the probable cause required for an arrest." See also United States v. Martinez-Fuerte, 428 U.S. 543 (1976) (fixed checkpoint to stop and check vehicles for aliens); Delaware v. Prouse, (random checks for drivers' licenses and proper vehicle registration not permitted on less than articulable reasonable suspicion).

Respondent State now urges the Court to apply a balancing test, rather than the general rule, to custodial interrogations, and to hold that "seizures" such as that in this case may be justified by mere "reasonable suspicion." *Terry* and its progeny clearly do not support such a result. The narrow intrusions involved in those cases were judged by a balancing test rather than by the general principle that Fourth Amendment seizures must be supported by the "long prevailing standards" of probable cause, Brinegar v. United States, supra, only because these intrusions fell far short of the kind of intrusion associated with an arrest. Indeed, *Brignoni-Ponce* expressly refused to extend *Terry* in the manner respondent now urges. The Court there stated: "The officer may question the driver and passengers about their citizenship and immigration status, and he may ask them to explain suspicious circumstances, *but any further detention or search must be based on consent or probable cause.*" (emphasis added).

In contrast to the brief and narrowly circumscribed intrusions involved in those cases, the detention of petitioner was in important respects indistinguishable from a traditional arrest. Petitioner was not questioned briefly where he was found. Instead, he was taken from a neighbor's home to a police car, transported to a police station, and placed in an interrogation room. He was never informed that he was "free to go"; indeed, he would have been physically restrained if he had refused to accompany the officers or had tried to escape their custody.

The application of the Fourth Amendment's requirement of probable cause does not depend on whether an intrusion of this magnitude is termed an "arrest" under state law. The mere facts that petitioner was not told he was under arrest, was not "booked," and would not have had an arrest record if the interrogation had proved fruitless, while not insignificant for all purposes, obviously do not make petitioner's seizure even roughly analogous to the narrowly defined intrusions involved in *Terry* and its progeny. Indeed, any "exception" that could cover a seizure as intrusive as that in this case would threaten to swallow the general rule that Fourth Amendment seizures are "reasonable" only if based on probable cause.

The central importance of the probable cause requirement to the protection of a citizen's privacy afforded by the Fourth Amendment's guarantees cannot be compromised in this fashion. "The requirement of probable cause has roots that are deep in our history." Hostility to seizures based on mere suspicion was a prime motivation for the adoption of the Fourth Amendment, and decisions immediately after its adoption affirmed that "common rumor or report, suspicion, or even 'strong reason to suspect' was not adequate to support a warrant for arrest". The familiar threshold standard of probable cause for Fourth Amendment seizures reflects the benefit of extensive experience accommodating the factors relevant to the "reasonableness" requirement of the Fourth Amendment, and provides the relative simplicity and clarity necessary to the implementation of a workable rule.

In effect, respondents urge us to adopt a multifactor balancing test of "reasonable police conduct under the circumstances" to cover all seizures that do not amount to technical arrests. But the protections intended by the Framers could all too easily disappear in the consideration and balancing of the multifarious circumstances presented by different cases, especially when that balancing may be done in the first instance by police officers engaged in the "often competitive enterprise of ferreting out crime." A single, familiar standard is essential to guide police officers, who have only limited time and expertise to reflect on and balance the social and individual interests involved in the specific circumstances they confront. Indeed, our recognition of these dangers, and our consequent reluctance to depart from the proven protections afforded by the general rule, is reflected in the narrow limitations emphasized in the cases employing the balancing test. For all but those narrowly defined intrusions, the requisite "balancing" has been performed in centuries of precedent and is embodied in the principle that seizures are "reasonable" only if supported by probable cause.

Moreover, two important decisions since *Terry* confirm the conclusion that the treatment of petitioner, whether or not it is technically characterized as an arrest, must be supported by probable cause. Davis v. Mississippi [Ch. 14–G(4) of casebook] decided the term after *Terry*, considered whether fingerprints taken from a suspect detained without probable cause must be excluded from evidence. The State argued that the detention "was of a type which does not require probable cause," because it occurred during an investigative, rather than accusatory stage, and because it was for the sole purpose of taking fingerprints. Rejecting the State's first argument, the Court warned:

> "[T]o argue that the Fourth Amendment does not apply to the investigatory stage is fundamentally to misconceive the purposes of the Fourth Amendment. Investigatory seizures would subject unlimited numbers of innocent persons to the harassment and ignominy incident to involuntary detention. Nothing is more clear than that the Fourth Amendment was meant to prevent wholesale intrusions upon the personal security of our citizenry, whether these intrusions be termed 'arrests' or 'investigatory detentions.' "

The State's second argument in *Davis* was more substantial, largely because of the *distinctions* between taking fingerprints and interrogation:

> "Fingerprinting involves none of the probing into an individual's private life and thoughts that marks an interrogation or search. Nor can fingerprint detention be employed repeatedly to harass any individual, since the police need only one set of each person's prints. Furthermore, fingerprinting is an inherently more reliable and effective crime-solving tool than eyewitness identifications or confessions and is not subject to such abuses as the improper line-up and the 'third degree.' Finally, because there is no danger of destruction of fingerprints, the limited detention need not come unexpectedly or at an inconvenient time."

In *Davis,* however, the Court found it unnecessary to decide the validity of a "narrowly circumscribed procedure for obtaining" the fingerprints of suspects without probable cause—in part because, as the Court emphasized, "petitioner was not merely fingerprinted during the ... detention but *also subjected to interrogation*." (emphasis added). The detention therefore violated the Fourth Amendment.

Brown v. Illinois, similarly disapproved arrests made for "investigatory" purposes on less than probable cause. Although Brown's arrest had more of the trappings of a technical formal arrest than petitioner's, such differences in form must not be exalted over substance. Once in the police station, Brown was taken to an interrogation room, and his experience was indistinguishable from petitioner's. Our condemnation of the police conduct in *Brown* fits equally the police conduct in this case:

> "The impropriety of the arrest was obvious; awareness of the fact was virtually conceded by the two detectives when they repeatedly acknowledged, in their testimony, that the purpose of their action was 'for investigation' or for 'questioning.' ... The arrest, both in design and in execution, was investigatory. The detectives embarked upon this expedition for evidence in the hope that something might turn up."

These passages from *Davis* and *Brown* reflect the conclusion that detention for custodial interrogation—regardless of its label—intrudes so severely on interests protected by the Fourth Amendment as necessarily to trigger the traditional safeguards against illegal arrest. We accordingly hold that the Rochester police violated the Fourth and Fourteenth Amendments when, without probable cause, they seized petitioner and transported him to the police station for interrogation.

III

There remains the question whether the connection between this unconstitutional police conduct and the incriminating statements and sketches obtained during petitioner's illegal detention was nevertheless sufficiently attenuated to permit the use at trial of the statements and sketches.

The New York courts have consistently held, and petitioner does not contest, that proper *Miranda* warnings were given and that his statements were "voluntary" for purposes of the Fifth Amendment. But Brown v. Illinois settled that "[t]he exclusionary rule, . . . when utilized to effectuate the Fourth Amendment, serves interests and policies that are distinct from those it serves under the Fifth," 422 U.S., at 601, 95 S.Ct., at 2260, and held therefore that "*Miranda* warnings, and the exclusion of a confession made without them, do not alone sufficiently deter a Fourth Amendment violation."

> "If *Miranda* warnings, by themselves, were held to attenuate the taint of an unconstitutional arrest, regardless of how wanton and purposeful the Fourth Amendment violation, the effect of the exclusionary rule would be substantially diluted. . . . Arrests made without warrant or without probable cause, for questioning or 'investigation,' would be encouraged by the knowledge that evidence derived therefrom could well be made admissible at trial by the simple expedient of giving *Miranda* warnings."

Consequently, although a confession after proper *Miranda* warnings may be found "voluntary" for purposes of the Fifth Amendment, this type of "voluntariness" is merely a "threshold requirement" for Fourth Amendment analysis. Indeed, if the Fifth Amendment has been violated, the Fourth Amendment issue would not have to be reached.

Beyond this threshold requirement, *Brown* articulated a test designed to vindicate the "distinct policies and interests of the Fourth Amendment." Following *Wong Sun*, the Court eschewed any *per se* or "but for" rule, and identified the relevant inquiry as "whether Brown's statements were obtained by exploitation of the illegality of his arrest." *Brown*'s focus on "the causal connection between the illegality and the confession" reflected the two policies behind the use of the exclusionary rule to effectuate the Fourth Amendment. When there is a close causal connection between the illegal seizure and the confession, not only is exclusion of the evidence more likely to deter similar police misconduct in the future, but use of the evidence is more likely to compromise the integrity of the courts.

Brown identified several factors to be considered "in determining whether the confession is obtained by exploitation of an illegal arrest[:] [t]he temporal proximity of the arrest and the confession, the presence of intervening circumstances, ... and, particularly, the purpose and flagrancy of the official misconduct.... And the burden of showing admissibility rests, of course, on the prosecution." Examining the case before it, the Court readily concluded that the State had failed to sustain its burden of showing the confession was admissible. In the "less than two hours" that elapsed between the arrest and the confession "there was no intervening event of significance whatsoever." Ibid. Furthermore, the arrest without probable cause had a "quality of purposefulness" in that it was an "expedition for evidence" admittedly undertaken "in the hope that something might turn up."

The situation in this case is virtually a replica of the situation in *Brown*. Petitioner was also admittedly seized without probable cause in the hope that something might turn up, and confessed without any intervening event of significance. Nevertheless, three members of the Appellate Division purported to distinguish *Brown* on the ground that the police did not threaten or abuse petitioner (presumably putting aside his illegal seizure and detention) and that the police conduct was "highly protective of defendant's Fifth and Sixth Amendment rights." This betrays a lingering confusion between "voluntariness" for purposes of the Fifth Amendment and the "causal connection" test established in *Brown*. Satisfying the Fifth Amendment is only the "threshold" condition of the Fourth Amendment analysis required by *Brown*. No intervening events broke the connection between petitioner's illegal detention and his confession. To admit petitioner's confession in such a case would allow "law enforcement officers to violate the Fourth Amendment with impunity, safe in the knowledge that they could wash their hands in the 'procedural safeguards' of the Fifth."

Reversed.

Mr. Justice Powell took no part in the consideration or decision of this case.

MR. JUSTICE WHITE, concurring in the judgment and opinion.

The opinion of the Court might be read to indicate that Terry v. Ohio is an almost unique exception to a hard-and-fast standard of probable cause. As our prior cases hold, however, the key principle of the Fourth Amendment is reasonableness—the balancing of competing interests. But if courts and law-enforcement officials are to have workable rules, this balancing must in large part be done on a categorical basis—not in an ad hoc, case-by-case fashion by individual police officers. On the other hand, the need for rules of general applicability precludes neither the recognition in particular cases of extraordinary private or public interests, nor the generic recognition of certain exceptions to the normal rule of probable cause where more flexibility is essential. It is enough, for me, that the police conduct here is similar enough to an arrest that the normal level of probable cause is necessary before the interests of privacy and personal security must give way.

MR. JUSTICE STEVENS, concurring.

Although I join the Court's opinion, I add this comment on the significance of two factors that may be considered when determining whether a confession has been obtained by exploitation of an illegal arrest.

The temporal relationship between the arrest and the confession may be an ambiguous factor. If there are no relevant intervening circumstances, a prolonged detention may well be a more serious exploitation of an illegal arrest than a short one. Conversely, even an immediate confession may have been motivated by a prearrest event such as a visit with a minister.

The flagrancy of the official misconduct is relevant, in my judgment, only insofar as it has a tendency to motivate the defendant. A midnight arrest with drawn guns will be equally frightening whether the police acted recklessly or in good faith. Conversely, a courteous command has the same effect on the arrestee whether the officer thinks he has probable cause or knows that he does not. In either event, if the Fourth Amendment is violated, the admissibility question will turn on the causal relationship between that violation and the defendant's subsequent confession.

I recognize that the deterrence rationale for the exclusionary rule is sometimes interpreted quite differently. Under that interpretation exclusion is applied as a substitute for punishment of the offending officer; if he acted recklessly or flagrantly, punishment is appropriate, but if he acted in good faith, it is not. But when evidence is excluded at a criminal trial, it is the broad societal interest in effective law enforcement that suffers. The justification for the exclusion of evidence obtained by improper methods is to motivate the law enforcement profession as a whole—not the aberrant individual officer—to adopt and enforce regular procedures that will avoid the future invasion of the citizen's constitutional rights. For that reason, exclusionary rules should embody objective criteria rather than subjective considerations.

MR. JUSTICE REHNQUIST, with whom THE CHIEF JUSTICE joins, dissenting.

If the Court did no more in this case than it announced in the opening sentence of its opinion—"decide . . . the question reserved 10 years ago in Morales v. New York, namely 'the question of the legality of custodial questioning on less than probable cause for a full fledged arrest' "—I would have little difficulty joining its opinion. The decision of this question, however, does not, contrary to the implication in the Court's opening sentence, decide this case. For the Court goes on to conclude that petitioner Dunaway was in fact "seized" within the meaning of the Fourth Amendment, and that the connection between

Dunaway's purported detention and the evidence obtained therefrom was not sufficiently attenuated as to dissipate the taint of the alleged unlawful police conduct. I cannot agree with either conclusion, and accordingly, I dissent.

I

There is obviously nothing in the Fourth Amendment that prohibits police from calling from their vehicle to a particular individual on the street and asking him to come over and talk with them; nor is there anything in the Fourth Amendment that prevents the police from knocking on the door of a person's house and when the person answers the door, inquiring whether he is willing to answer questions that they wish to put to him. "Obviously, not all personal intercourse between policemen and citizens involves 'seizures' of persons." Voluntary questioning not involving any "seizure" for Fourth Amendment purposes may take place under any number of varying circumstances. And the occasions will not be few when a particular individual agrees voluntarily to answer questions that the police wish to put to him either on the street, at the station, or in his house, and later regrets his willingness to answer those questions. However, such morning-after regrets do not render involuntary responses that were voluntary at the time they were made. In my view, this is a case where the defendant voluntarily accompanied the police to the station to answer their questions.

In Terry v. Ohio, the Court set out the test for determining whether a person has been "seized" for Fourth Amendment purposes. "Only when the officer, by means of physical force or show of authority, has in some way restrained the liberty of a citizen may we conclude that a 'seizure' has occurred." In this case, three police officers were dispatched to petitioner's house to question him about his participation in a robbery. According to the testimony of the police officers, one officer approached a house where petitioner was thought to be located and knocked on the door. When a person answered the door, the officer identified himself and asked the individual his name. After learning that the person who answered the door was petitioner, the officer asked him if he would accompany the officers to police headquarters for questioning, and petitioner responded that he would. Petitioner was not told that he was under arrest or in custody and was not warned not to resist or flee. No weapons were displayed and petitioner was not handcuffed. Each officer testified that petitioner was not touched or held during the trip downtown; his freedom of action was not in any way restrained by the police. In short, the police behavior in this case was entirely free of "physical force or show of authority."

The Court, however, categorically states in text that "there can be little doubt that petitioner was 'seized' in the Fourth Amendment sense when he was taken involuntarily to the police station." In an accompanying footnote, the Court states that "respondent contends that petitioner accompanied the police voluntarily and therefore was not 'seized.' ... The County Court found otherwise ... and the Appellate Division treated the case as an involuntary detention justified by reasonable suspicion." The Court goes on to cite a commentary from the Tentative Draft of the A.L.I. Model Code of Pre-Arraignment Procedure to the effect that a "request to come to [the] police station 'may easily carry an implication of obligation, while the appearance itself, unless clearly stated to be voluntary, may be an awesome experience for the ordinary citizen.' "

The Court's heavy reliance on the conclusions of the Monroe County Court on this issue is misplaced, however. That court clearly did not apply the *Terry* standard in determining whether there had been a seizure. Instead, that court's conclusions were based solely on the facts that petitioner was in the physical custody of detectives until he reached police headquarters and that "had he attempted to leave the company of the said detectives, they would have physically restrained him (per stipulation of People at conclusion of hearing)." But the fact that the officers accompanied petitioner from his house to the station in no way vitiates the State's claim that petitioner acted voluntarily. Similarly, the unexpressed intentions of police officers as to hypothetical situations have little bearing on the question whether the police conduct, objectively viewed, restrained petitioner's liberty by show of force or authority.

The Appellate Division's opinion also can be of no assistance to the Court. The Court's opinion characterizes the Appellate Division's treatment of the case "as an involuntary detention justified by reasonable suspicion." But the Appellate Division did not accept the County Court's conclusion that petitioner did not voluntarily accompany the police to the station. To the contrary, in its recitation of the facts, the Appellate Division recites the officers' testimony that petitioner voluntarily agreed to come downtown to talk with them. That the Appellate Division found that it was able to resolve the case on the basis of the Court of Appeals' decision in People v. Morales, supra, does not mean that the Appellate Division decided that petitioner had been "seized" within the meaning of the Fourth Amendment.

Finally, the Court quotes the Model Code for Pre-Arraignment Procedure to support its assertion. I do not dispute the fact that a police request to come to the station may indeed be an "awesome experience." But I do not think that that fact alone means that in every instance where a person assents to a police request to come to headquarters, there has been a "seizure" within the meaning of the Fourth Amendment. The question turns on whether the officer's conduct is objectively coercive or physically threatening, not on the mere fact that a person might in some measure feel cowed by the fact that a request is made by a police officer. Cf. Oregon v. Mathiason, 429 U.S. 492, 495, 97 S.Ct. 711, 713 (1977).[1]

1. Neither Davis v. Mississippi, nor Brown v. Illinois, which the Court treats as points of departure for today's opinion, support the Court's conclusion that petitioner was "seized" within the meaning of the Fourth Amendment. In *Davis*, the State made no claim that Davis had voluntarily accompanied the police officers to headquarters. Similarly, in *Brown* there could be no reasonable disagreement that the de-

Therefore, although I agree that the police officers in this case did not have that degree of suspicion or probable cause that would have justified them in physically compelling petitioner to accompany them to the police station for questioning, I do not believe that the record demonstrates as a fact that this is what happened. No involuntary detention for questioning was shown to have taken place. The Fourth Amendment, accordingly, does not require suppression of petitioner's statements.

II

Assuming *arguendo* that there was a "seizure" in this case, I still cannot agree with the Court that the Fourth Amendment requires suppression of petitioner's statements and sketches. Relying on Brown v. Illinois, 422 U.S. 590, 95 S.Ct. 2254 (1975), the Court concludes that this evidence must be suppressed primarily, it seems, because no intervening events broke the connection between petitioner's detention and his confession. *Ante*, at 17. In my view, the connection between petitioner's allegedly unlawful detention and the incriminating statements and sketches is sufficiently attenuated to permit their use at trial. See Wong Sun v. United States, 371 U.S. 471, 83 S.Ct. 407 (1963).

In Brown v. Illinois, supra, we identified several factors to be considered in determining whether inculpatory statements were sufficiently a product of free will to be admissible under the Fourth Amendment. The voluntariness of the statements is a threshold requirement. That *Miranda* warnings are given is "an important factor." Also relevant are "[t]he temporal proximity of the arrest and the confession, the presence of intervening circumstances, ... and, particularly, the purpose and flagrancy of the official misconduct." But the Court did not assign equal weight to each of these factors. Given the deterrent purposes of the exclusionary rule, the "purpose and flagrancy" of the police conduct is, in my view, the most important factor. Where police have acted in good faith and not in a flagrant manner, I would require no more than that proper *Miranda* warnings be given and that the statement be voluntary within the meaning of the Fifth Amendment. "Absent aggravating circumstances, I would consider a statement given at the station house after one has been advised of *Miranda* rights to be sufficiently removed from the immediate circumstances of the illegal arrest to justify its admission at trial."

The Court concedes that petitioner received proper *Miranda* warnings and that his statements were "voluntary" for purposes of the Fifth

fendant had been "seized" for Fourth Amendment purposes. In *Brown*, two detectives of the Chicago police force broke into Brown's apartment and searched it. When Brown entered the apartment, he was told that he was under arrest, was held at gunpoint and was searched. He then was handcuffed and escorted to the squad car that eventually took him to the police station. No doubt this police activity was the cause of the Court's observation that "[t]he illegality here, moreover, had a quality of purposefulness.... The manner in which Brown's arrest was effected gives the appearance of having been calculated to cause surprise, fright, and confusion." No such circumstances occurred here.

Amendment. And the police acted in good faith. At the time of petitioner's detention, the New York Court of Appeals had held that custodial questioning on less than probable cause for an arrest was permissible under the Fourth Amendment. Petitioner testified that the police never threatened or abused him. Petitioner voluntarily gave his first statement to police about an hour after he reached the police station and then gave another statement to police the following day. Contrary to the Court's suggestion, the police conduct in this case was in no manner as flagrant as that of the police in Brown v. Illinois. Thus, in my view, the record convincingly demonstrates that the statements and sketches given police by petitioner were of sufficient free will as to purge the primary taint of his alleged illegal detention. I would, therefore, affirm the judgment of the Appellate Division of the Supreme Court of New York.

UNITED STATES v. CECCOLINI

Supreme Court of the United States, 1978.
435 U.S. 268, 98 S.Ct. 1054.

MR. JUSTICE REHNQUIST delivered the opinion of the Court.

In December 1974, Ronald Biro, a uniformed police officer on assignment to patrol school crossings, entered respondent's place of business, The Sleepy Hollow Flower Shop, in North Tarrytown, N.Y. He went behind the customer counter and, in the words of Ichabod Crane, one of Tarrytown's more illustrious inhabitants of days gone past, "tarried," spending his short break engaged in conversation with his friend Lois Hennessey, an employee of the shop. During the course of the conversation he noticed an envelope with money sticking out of it lying on the drawer of the cash register behind the counter. Biro picked up the envelope and, upon examining its contents, discovered that it contained not only money but policy slips. He placed the envelope back on the register and, without telling Hennessey of what he had seen, asked her to whom the envelope belonged. She replied that the envelope belong[ed] to respondent Ceccolini, and that he had instructed her to give it to someone.

The next day, Officer Biro mentioned his discovery to North Tarrytown detectives who in turn told Lance Emory, an FBI agent. This very ordinary incident in the lives of Biro and Hennessey requires us, four years later, to decide whether Hennessey's testimony against respondent Ceccolini should have been suppressed in his trial for perjury. Respondent was charged with that offense because he denied that he knew anything of, or was in any way involved with, gambling operations....

* * *

I

During the latter part of 1973, the Federal Bureau of Investigation was exploring suspected gambling operations in North Tarrytown.

Among the establishments under surveillance was respondent's place of business, which was a frequent and regular stop of one Francis Millow, himself a suspect in the investigation. While the investigation continued on a reduced scale after December 1973, surveillance of the flower shop was curtailed at that time. It was thus a full year after this discontinuance of FBI surveillance that Biro spent his patrol break behind the counter with Hennessey. When Biro's discovery of the policy slips was reported the following day to Emory, Emory was not fully informed of the manner in which Biro had obtained the information. Four months later, Emory interviewed Hennessey at her home for about half an hour in the presence of her mother and two sisters. He identified himself, indicated that he had learned through the local police department that she worked for respondent, and told her that the Government would appreciate any information regarding respondent's activities that she had acquired in the shop. Emory did not specifically refer to the incident involving Officer Biro. Hennessey told Emory that she was studying police science in college and would be willing to help. She then related the events which had occurred during her visit with Officer Biro.

In May of 1975, respondent was summoned before a federal grand jury and testified that he had never taken policy bets for Francis Millow at the flower shop. The next week Hennessey testified to the contrary, and shortly thereafter respondent was indicted for perjury. Respondent waived a jury, and with the consent of all parties the District Court considered simultaneously with the trial on the merits respondent's motion to suppress both the policy slips and the testimony of Hennessey. At the conclusion of the evidence, the District Court excluded from its consideration "the envelope and the contents of the envelope," but nonetheless found respondent guilty of the offense charged. The court then granted respondent's motion to suppress the testimony of Hennessey, because she "first came directly to the attention of the government as the result of an illegal search" and the Government had not "sustained its burden of showing that Lois Hennessy's [sic] testimony definitely would not have been obtained without the illegal search."

The Court of Appeals affirmed this ruling on the Government's appeal, reasoning that "the road to Miss Hennessy's [sic] testimony from Officer Biro's concededly unconstitutional search is both straight and uninterrupted." The Court of Appeals also concluded that there was support in the record for the District Court's finding that the ongoing investigation would not have inevitably led to the evidence in question even without Biro's discovery of the two policy slips....

II

The "road" to which the Court of Appeals analogized the train of events from Biro's discovery of the policy slips to Hennessey's testimony at respondent's trial for perjury is one of literally thousands of such roads traveled periodically between an original investigative discovery and the ultimate trial of the accused. The constitutional question under the Fourth Amendment was phrased in Wong Sun v. United States, 371

U.S. 471, 83 S.Ct. 407 (1963), as whether "the connection between the lawless conduct of the police and the discovery of the challenged evidence has become 'so attenuated as to dissipate the taint.'" The question was in turn derived from the Court's earlier decision in Nardone v. United States, 308 U.S. 338, 341, 60 S.Ct. 266, 268 (1939), where Mr. Justice Frankfurter stated for the Court:

> "Here, as in the Silverthorne case, the facts improperly obtained do not 'become sacred and inaccessible. If knowledge of them is gained from an independent source they may be proved like any others, but the knowledge gained by the Government's own wrong cannot be used by it' simply because it is used derivatively.
>
> "In practice this generalized statement may conceal concrete complexities. Sophisticated argument may prove a causal connection between information obtained through illicit wiretapping and the Government's proof. As a matter of good sense, however, such connection may have become so attenuated as to dissipate the taint."

This, of course, makes it perfectly clear, if indeed ever there was any doubt about the matter, that the question of causal connection in this setting, as in so many other questions with which the law concerns itself, is not to be determined solely through the sort of analysis which would be applicable in the physical sciences. The issue cannot be decided on the basis of causation in the logical sense alone, but necessarily includes other elements as well. And our cases subsequent to Nardone, supra, have laid out the fundamental tenets of the exclusionary rule, from which the elements that are relevant to the causal inquiry can be divined.

An examination of these cases leads us to reject the Government's suggestion that we adopt what would in practice amount to a per se rule that the testimony of a live witness should not be excluded at trial no matter how close and proximate the connection between it and a violation of the Fourth Amendment. We also reaffirm the holding of Wong Sun that "verbal evidence which derives so immediately from unlawful entry and an unauthorized arrest as the officer's action in the present case is no less the 'fruit' of official illegality than the more commonplace tangible fruits of the unwarranted intrusion." We are of the view, however, that cases decided since Wong Sun significantly qualify its further observation that "the policies underlying the exclusionary rule [do not] invite any logical distinction between physical and verbal evidence." . . .

. . . Recognizing not only the benefits but the costs, which are often substantial, of the exclusionary rule, we have said that "application of the rule has been restricted to those areas where its remedial objectives are thought most efficaciously served," United States v. Calandra, 414 U.S. 338, 348, 94 S.Ct. 613, 620 (1974). . . . We have likewise declined to prohibit the use of such evidence for the purpose of impeaching a defendant who testifies in his own behalf.

... Even in situations where the exclusionary rule is plainly applicable, we have declined to adopt a "per se or 'but for' rule" that would make inadmissible any evidence, whether tangible or live-witness testimony, which somehow came to light through a chain of causation that began with an illegal arrest.

Evaluating the standards for application of the exclusionary rule to live-witness testimony in light of this balance, we are first impelled to conclude that the degree of free will exercised by the witness is not irrelevant in determining the extent to which the basic purpose of the exclusionary rule will be advanced by its application. This is certainly true when the challenged statements are made by a putative defendant after arrest, and a fortiori is true of testimony given by nondefendants.

The greater the willingness of the witness to freely testify, the greater the likelihood that he or she will be discovered by legal means and, concomitantly, the smaller the incentive to conduct an illegal search to discover the witness. Witnesses are not like guns or documents which remain hidden from view until one turns over a sofa or opens a filing cabinet. Witnesses can, and often do, come forward and offer evidence entirely of their own volition. And evaluated properly, the degree of free will necessary to dissipate the taint will very likely be found more often in the case of live-witness testimony than other kinds of evidence. The time, place and manner of the initial questioning of the witness may be such that any statements are truly the product of detached reflection and a desire to be cooperative on the part of the witness. And the illegality which led to the discovery of the witness very often will not play any meaningful part in the witness's willingness to testify.

> "The proffer of a living witness is not to be mechanically equated with the proffer of inanimate evidentiary objects illegally seized. The fact that the name of a potential witness is disclosed to police is of no evidentiary significance, per se, since the living witness is an individual human personality whose attributes of will, perception, memory and volition interact to determine what testimony he will give. The uniqueness of this human process distinguishes the evidentiary character of a witness from the relative immutability of inanimate evidence." Smith v. United States, 324 F.2d 879, 881 (D.C.Cir.1963). Per Burger, J.

Another factor which is not only relevant in determining the usefulness of the exclusionary rule in a particular context, but also seems to us to differentiate the testimony of all live witnesses—even putative defendants—from the exclusion of the typical documentary evidence, is that such exclusion would perpetually disable a witness from testifying about relevant and material facts, regardless of how unrelated such testimony might be to the purpose of the originally illegal search or the evidence discovered thereby. Rules which disqualify knowledgeable witnesses from testifying at trial are, in the words of Professor McCormick, "serious obstructions to the ascertainment of truth"; accordingly, "[f]or a century the course of legal evolution has been in the direction of sweeping away these obstructions." McCormick on Evidence § 71, p. 150 (1954). Alluding to the enormous cost engendered by such a permanent disability in an analogous context, we have specifically refused to hold that "making a confession under circumstances which preclude its use perpetually disables the confessor from making a usable one after those conditions have been removed." United States v. Bayer, 331 U.S. 532, 540, 67 S.Ct. 1394, 1398 (1947). For many of these same reasons, the Court has also held admissible at trial testimony of a witness whose identity was disclosed by the defendant's statement given after inadequate Miranda warnings. Michigan v. Tucker, 417 U.S. 433, 450–451, 94 S.Ct. 2357, 2367 (1974).

> "For, when balancing the interests involved, we must weigh the strong interest under any system of justice of making available to the trier of fact all concededly relevant and trustworthy evidence which either party seeks to adduce.... Here respondent's own statement, which might have helped the prosecutor show respondent's guilty conscience at trial, had already been excused from the prosecutor's case.... To extend the excision further under the circumstances of this case and exclude relevant testimony of a third-party witness would require far more persuasive arguments than those advanced by respondent."

In short, since the cost of excluding live-witness testimony often will be greater, a closer, more direct link between the illegality and that kind of testimony is required.

This is not to say, of course, that live-witness testimony is always or even usually more reliable or dependable than inanimate evidence. Indeed, just the opposite may be true. But a determination that the discovery of certain evidence is sufficiently unrelated to or independent of the constitutional violation to permit its introduction at trial is not a determination which rests on the comparative reliability of that evidence. Attenuation analysis, appropriately concerned with the differences between live-witness testimony and inanimate evidence, can consistently focus on the factors enumerated above with respect to the former, but on different factors with respect to the latter.

In holding that considerations relating to the exclusionary rule and the constitutional principles which it is designed to protect must play a factor in the attenuation analysis, we do no more than reaffirm an observation made by this Court half a century ago:

> "A criminal prosecution is more than a game in which the Government may be checkmated and the game lost merely because its officers have not played according to rule."

McGuire v. United States, 273 U.S. 95, 99, 47 S.Ct. 259, 260 (1927).

The penalties visited upon the Government, and in turn upon the public, because its officers have violated the law must bear some relation to the purposes which the law is to serve.

III

Viewing this case in the light of the principles just discussed, we hold that the Court of Appeals erred in holding that the degree of attenuation was not sufficient to dissipate the connection between the illegality and the testimony. The evidence indicates overwhelmingly that the testimony given by the witness was an act of her own free will in no way coerced or even induced by official authority as a result of Biro's discovery of the policy slips. Nor were the slips themselves used in questioning Hennessey. Substantial periods of time elapsed between the time of the illegal search and the initial contact with the witness, on the one hand, and between the latter and the testimony at trial on the other. While the particular knowledge to which Hennessey testified at trial can be logically traced back to Biro's discovery of the policy slips, both the identity of Hennessey and her relationship with the respondent was well known to those investigating the case. There is, in addition, not the slightest evidence to suggest that Biro entered the shop or picked up the envelope with the intent of finding tangible evidence bearing on an illicit gambling operation, much less any suggestion that he entered the shop and searched with the intent of finding a willing and knowledgeable witness to testify against respondent. Application of the exclusionary rule in this situation could not have the slightest deterrent effect on the behavior of an officer such as Biro. The cost of permanently silencing Hennessey is too great for an even-handed system of law enforcement to bear in order to secure such a speculative and very likely negligible deterrent effect.

Obviously no mathematical weight can be assigned to any of the factors which we have discussed, but just as obviously they all point to the conclusion that the exclusionary rule should be invoked with much greater reluctance where the claim is based on a causal relationship between a constitutional violation and the discovery of a live witness than when a similar claim is advanced to support suppression of an inanimate object. The judgment of the Court of Appeals is accordingly reversed.

Mr. Justice Blackmun took no part in the consideration or decision of this case.

MR. CHIEF JUSTICE BURGER, concurring in the judgment.

I agree with the Court's ultimate conclusion that there is a fundamental difference, for purposes of the exclusionary rule, between live-witness testimony and other types of evidence. I perceive this distinction to be so fundamental, however, that I would not prevent a factfinder from hearing and considering the relevant statements of any witness, except perhaps under the most remarkable of circumstances—although none such have ever been postulated that would lead me to exclude the testimony of a live witness.

* * *

It can, of course, be argued that the prospect of finding a helpful witness may play *some* role in a policeman's decision to be indifferent about Fourth Amendment procedures. The answer to this point, however, is that we have never insisted on employing the exclusionary rule whenever there is some possibility, no matter how remote, of deterring police misconduct. Rather, we balance the cost to society of losing perfectly competent evidence against the prospect of incrementally enhancing Fourth Amendment values.

Using this approach it strikes me as evident that the permanent silencing of a witness—who, after all, is appearing under oath—is not worth the high price the exclusionary rule exacts. Any rule of law which operates to keep an eye witness to a crime—a murder, for example—from telling the jury what that person saw has a rational basis roughly comparable to the primitive rituals of human sacrifice.

I would, therefore, resolve the case of a living witness on a per se basis, holding that such testimony is always admissible, provided it meets all other traditional evidentiary requirements. At very least this solution would alleviate the burden—now squarely thrust upon courts—of determining in each instance whether the witness possessed that elusive quality characterized by the term "free will."

MR. JUSTICE MARSHALL, with whom MR. JUSTICE BRENNAN joins, dissenting.

While "reaffirm[ing]" the holding of Wong Sun v. United States, that verbal evidence, like physical evidence, may be "fruit of the poisonous tree," the Court today "significantly qualif[ies]" Wong Sun's further conclusion, that no "logical distinction" can be drawn between verbal and physical evidence for purposes of the exclusionary rule. In my view, the distinction that the Court attempts to draw cannot withstand close analysis. To extend "a time-worn metaphor," Harrison v. United States, I do not believe that the same tree, having its roots in an unconstitutional search or seizure, can bear two different kinds of fruit, with one kind less susceptible than the other to exclusion on Fourth Amendment grounds. I therefore dissent.

... The Court ... states that "[a]ttenuation analysis" should be "concerned with the difference between live-witness testimony and inanimate evidence." The differences noted by the Court, however, have to a large extent already been accommodated by current doctrine. Where they have not been so accommodated, it is because the differences asserted are either illusory or of no relevance to the issue of attenuation.

One difference mentioned by the Court is that witnesses, unlike inanimate objects, "can, and often do, come forward and offer evidence entirely of their own volition." Recognition of this obvious fact does nothing to advance the attenuation inquiry. We long ago held that, if knowledge of evidence is gained from a source independent of police illegality, the evidence should be admitted. This "independent source" rule would plainly apply to a witness whose identity is discovered in an illegal search but who later comes to the police for reasons unrelated to the official misconduct. In the instant case, however, as the Court recognizes, there is a " 'straight and uninterrupted' " road between the illegal search and the disputed testimony.

Even where the road is uninterrupted, in some cases the Government may be able to show that the illegally discovered evidence would inevitably have come to light in the normal course of a legal police investigation. Assuming such evidence is admissible—a proposition that has been questioned, this "inevitable discovery" rule would apply to admit the testimony of a witness who, in the absence of police misconduct, would have come forward "entirely of [his or her] own volition." Again, however, no such situation is presented by this case, since the Court accepts the findings of the two lower courts that Hennessey's testimony would not inevitably have been discovered.

Both the independent source and inevitable discovery rules, moreover, can apply to physical evidence as well as to verbal evidence. The police may show, for example, that they learned from an independent source, or would inevitably have discovered through legal means, the location of an object that they also knew about as a result of illegal police activity. It may be that verbal evidence is more likely to have an independent source, because live witnesses can indeed come forward of their own volition, but this simply underscores the degree to which the Court's approach involves a form of judicial "double counting." The Court would apparently first determine whether the evidence stemmed from an independent source or would inevitably have been discovered; if neither of these rules were found to apply, as here, the Court would still somehow take into account the fact that, as a general proposition (but not in the particular case), witnesses sometimes do come forward of their own volition.

The Court makes a related point that "[t]he greater the willingness of the witness to freely testify, . . . the smaller the incentive to conduct an illegal search to discover the witness." The somewhat incredible premise of this statement is that the police in fact refrain from illegal behavior in which they would otherwise engage because they know in advance both that a witness will be willing to testify and that he or she "will be discovered by legal means." This reasoning surely reverses the normal sequence of events; the instances must be very few in which a witness' willingness to testify is known before he or she is discovered. In this case, for example, the police did not even know that Hennessey was a potentially valuable witness, much less whether she would be willing to testify, prior to conducting the illegal search. When the police are certain that a witness "will be discovered by legal means," if they ever can be certain about such a fact—they of course have no incentive to find him or her by illegal means, but the same can be said about physical objects that the police know will be discovered legally.

The only other point made by the Court is that exclusion of testimony "perpetually disable[s] a witness from testifying about relevant and material facts." The "perpetual ... disable[ment]" of which the Court speaks, however, applies as much to physical as to verbal evidence. When excluded, both types of evidence are lost for the duration of the particular trial, despite their being "relevant and material ... [and] unrelated ... to the purpose of the originally illegal search." Moreover, while it is true that "often" the exclusion of testimony will be very costly to society, at least as often the exclusion of physical evidence—such as heroin in a narcotics possession case or business records in a tax case—will be as costly to the same societal interests. But other, more important societal interests have led to the rule, which the Court today reaffirms, that "fruits of the poisonous tree" must be excluded despite their probative value, unless the facts of the case justify a finding of sufficient attenuation.

The facts of this case do not justify such a finding. Although, as the Court notes, four months elapsed between the illegal search and the FBI's first contact with Hennessey, the critical evidence was provided at the time and place of the search, when the police officer questioned Hennessey and she identified respondent. The time that elapsed thereafter is of no more relevance than would be a similar time period between the discovery of an object during an illegal search and its later introduction into evidence at trial. In this case, moreover, there were no intervening circumstances between Hennessey's statement at the time of the search and her later testimony. She did not come to the authorities and ask to testify, despite being a student of police science; an FBI agent had to go to her home and interrogate her.

Finally, whatever the police officer's purpose in the flower shop on the day of the search, the search itself was not even of arguable legality, as was conceded by the Government below. It is also undisputed that the shop had been under surveillance as part of an ongoing gambling investigation in which the local police force had actively participated; its participation included interception of at least one of respondent's telephone conversations in the very month of the search. Under all of the circumstances, the connection here between the official illegality and the disputed testimony cannot be deemed "so attenuated as to dissipate the taint." The District Court therefore properly excluded the testimony.

I would affirm the judgment of the Court of Appeals.

OREGON v. ELSTAD

Supreme Court of the United States, 1985.
470 U.S. 298, 105 S.Ct. 1285.

[Editor's note: Although this case involves a *Miranda* violation, not a Fourth Amendment violation, it is presented here at length, rather than in Chapter 12, as an example of an application—or non-application—of the fruit of the poisonous tree doctrine.]

JUSTICE O'CONNOR delivered the opinion of the Court.

This case requires us to decide whether an initial failure of law enforcement officers to administer the warnings required by Miranda v. Arizona, 384 U.S. 436, 86 S.Ct. 1602, 16 L.Ed.2d 694 (1966), without more, "taints" subsequent admissions made after a suspect has been fully advised of and has waived his *Miranda* rights. Respondent, Michael James Elstad, was convicted of burglary by an Oregon trial court. The Oregon Court of Appeals reversed, holding that respondent's signed confession, although voluntary, was rendered inadmissible by a prior remark made in response to questioning without benefit of *Miranda* warnings. We granted certiorari, 465 U.S. 1078, 104 S.Ct. 1437, 79 L.Ed.2d 759 (1984), and we now reverse.

I

In December, 1981, the home of Mr. and Mrs. Gilbert Gross, in the town of Salem, Polk County, Ore., was burglarized. Missing were art objects and furnishings valued at $150,000. A witness to the burglary contacted the Polk County Sheriff's office, implicating respondent Michael Elstad, an 18-year-old neighbor and friend of the Grosses' teenage son. Thereupon, Officers Burke and McAllister went to the home of respondent Elstad, with a warrant for his arrest. Elstad's mother answered the door. She led the officers to her son's room where he lay on his bed, clad in shorts and listening to his stereo. The officers asked him to get dressed and to accompany them into the living room. Officer McAllister asked respondent's mother to step into the kitchen, where he explained that they had a warrant for her son's arrest for the burglary of a neighbor's residence. Officer Burke remained with Elstad in the living room. He later testified:

> "I sat down with Mr. Elstad and I asked him if he was aware of why Detective McAllister and myself were there to talk with him. He stated no, he had no idea why we were there. I then asked him if he knew a person by the name of Gross, and he said yes, he did, and also added that he heard that there was a robbery at the Gross house. And at that point I told Mr. Elstad that I felt he was involved in that, and he looked at me and stated, 'Yes, I was there.'" App. 19–20.

The officers then escorted Elstad to the back of the patrol car. As they were about to leave for the Polk County Sheriff's office, Elstad's father arrived home and came to the rear of the patrol car. The officers advised him that his son was a suspect in the burglary. Officer Burke testified that Mr. Elstad became quite agitated, opened the rear door of the car and admonished his son: "I told you that you were going to get into trouble. You wouldn't listen to me. You never learn." Id., at 21.

Elstad was transported to the Sheriff's headquarters and approximately one hour later, Officers Burke and McAllister joined him in McAllister's office. McAllister then advised respondent for the first time of his *Miranda* rights, reading from a standard card. Respondent indicated he understood his rights, and, having these rights in mind, wished to speak with the officers. Elstad gave a full statement, explaining that he had known that the Gross family was out of town and had been paid to lead several acquaintances to the Gross residence and show them how to gain entry through a defective sliding glass door. The statement was typed, reviewed by respondent, read back to him for correction, initialed and signed by Elstad and both officers. As an afterthought, Elstad added and initialed the sentence, "After leaving the house Robby & I went back to [the] van & Robby handed me a small bag of grass." App. 42. Respondent concedes that the officers made no threats or promises either at his residence or at the Sheriff's office.

Respondent was charged with first-degree burglary. He was represented at trial by retained counsel. Elstad waived his right to a jury and his case was tried by a Circuit Court Judge. Respondent moved at once to suppress his oral statement and signed confession. He contended that the statement he made in response to questioning at his house "let the cat out of the bag," citing United States v. Bayer, 331 U.S. 532, 67 S.Ct. 1394, 91 L.Ed. 1654 (1947), and tainted the subsequent confession as "fruit of the poisonous tree," citing Wong Sun v. United States, 371 U.S. 471, 83 S.Ct. 407, 9 L.Ed.2d 441 (1963). The judge ruled that the statement, "I was there," had to be excluded because the defendant had not been advised of his *Miranda* rights. The written confession taken after Elstad's arrival at the Sheriff's office, however, was admitted in evidence. The court found:

> "[H]is written statement was given freely, voluntarily and knowingly by the defendant after he had waived his right to remain silent and have counsel present which waiver was evidenced by the card which the defendant had signed. [It] was not tainted in any way by the previous brief statement between the defendant and the Sheriff's Deputies that had arrested him." App. 45.

Elstad was found guilty of burglary in the first degree. He received a 5-year sentence and was ordered to pay $18,000 in restitution.

Following his conviction, respondent appealed to the Oregon Court of Appeals, relying on *Wong Sun* and *Bayer*. The State conceded that Elstad had been in custody when he made his statement, "I was there," and accordingly agreed that this statement was inadmissible as having been given without the prescribed *Miranda* warning. But the State maintained that any conceivable "taint" had been dissipated prior to the respondent's written confession by McAllister's careful administration of the requisite warnings. The Court of Appeals reversed respondent's conviction, identifying the crucial constitutional inquiry as "whether there was a sufficient break in the stream of events between [the]

inadmissible statement and the written confession to insulate the latter statement from the effect of what went before." 61 Ore.App. 673, 676, 658 P.2d 552, 554 (1983). The Oregon court concluded:

> "Regardless of the absence of actual compulsion, the coercive impact of the unconstitutionally obtained statement remains, because in a defendant's mind it has sealed his fate. It is this impact that must be dissipated in order to make a subsequent confession admissible. In determining whether it has been dissipated, lapse of time, and change of place from the original surroundings are the most important considerations." Id., at 677, 658 P.2d, at 554.

Because of the brief period separating the two incidents, the "cat was sufficiently out of the bag to exert a coercive impact on [respondent's] later admissions." Id., at 678, 658 P.2d, at 555.

The State of Oregon petitioned the Oregon Supreme Court for review, and review was declined. This Court granted certiorari to consider the question whether the Self-Incrimination Clause of the Fifth Amendment requires the suppression of a confession, made after proper *Miranda* warnings and a valid waiver of rights, solely because the police had obtained an earlier voluntary but unwarned admission from the defendant.

II

The arguments advanced in favor of suppression of respondent's written confession rely heavily on metaphor. One metaphor, familiar from the Fourth Amendment context, would require that respondent's confession, regardless of its integrity, voluntariness, and probative value, be suppressed as the "tainted fruit of the poisonous tree" of the *Miranda* violation. A second metaphor questions whether a confession can be truly voluntary once the "cat is out of the bag." Taken out of context, each of these metaphors can be misleading. They should not be used to obscure fundamental differences between the role of the Fourth Amendment exclusionary rule and the function of *Miranda* in guarding against the prosecutorial use of compelled statements as prohibited by the Fifth Amendment. The Oregon court assumed and respondent here contends that a failure to administer *Miranda* warnings necessarily breeds the same consequences as police infringement of a constitutional right, so that evidence uncovered following an unwarned statement must be suppressed as "fruit of the poisonous tree." We believe this view misconstrues the nature of the protections afforded by *Miranda* warnings and therefore misreads the consequences of police failure to supply them.

A

Prior to *Miranda,* the admissibility of an accused's in custody statements was judged solely by whether they were "voluntary" within the meaning of the Due Process Clause.... If a suspect's statements had been obtained by "techniques and methods offensive to due process," ... or under circumstances in which the suspect clearly had no opportunity to exercise "a free and unconstrained will," ... the statements would not be admitted. The Court in *Miranda* required suppression of many statements that would have been admissible under traditional due process analysis by presuming that statements made while in custody and without adequate warnings were protected by the Fifth Amendment. The Fifth Amendment, of course, is not concerned with nontestimonial evidence.... Nor is it concerned with moral and psychological pressures to confess emanating from sources other than official coercion.... Voluntary statements "remain a proper element in law enforcement." Miranda v. Arizona, 384 U.S., at 478, 86 S.Ct., at 1630. "Indeed, far from being prohibited by the Constitution, admissions of guilt by wrongdoers, if not coerced, are inherently desirable.... Absent some officially coerced self-accusation, the Fifth Amendment privilege is not violated by even the most damning admissions." United States v. Washington, 431 U.S. 181, 187, 97 S.Ct. 1814, 1818, 52 L.Ed.2d 238 (1977)....

Respondent's contention that his confession was tainted by the earlier failure of the police to provide *Miranda* warnings and must be excluded as "fruit of the poisonous tree" assumes the existence of a constitutional violation. This figure of speech is drawn from Wong Sun v. United States, 371 U.S. 471, 83 S.Ct. 407, 9 L.Ed.2d 441 (1963), in which the Court held that evidence and witnesses discovered as a result of a search in violation of the Fourth Amendment must be excluded from evidence. The *Wong Sun* doctrine applies as well when the fruit of the Fourth Amendment violation is a confession. It is settled law that "a confession obtained through custodial interrogation after an illegal arrest should be excluded unless intervening events break the causal connection between the illegal arrest and the confession so that the confession is 'sufficiently an act of free will to purge the primary taint.' " ...

But ... a procedural *Miranda* violation differs in significant respects from violations of the Fourth Amendment, which have traditionally mandated a broad application of the "fruits" doctrine. The purpose of the Fourth Amendment exclusionary rule is to deter unreasonable searches, no matter how probative their fruits.... "The exclusionary rule, ... when utilized to effectuate the Fourth Amendment, serves interests and policies that are distinct from those it serves under the Fifth." ... Where a Fourth Amendment violation "taints" the confession, a finding of voluntariness for the purposes of the Fifth Amendment is merely a threshold requirement in determining whether the confession may be admitted in evidence.... Beyond this, the prosecution must show a sufficient break in events to undermine the inference that the confession was caused by the Fourth Amendment violation.

The *Miranda* exclusionary rule, however, serves the Fifth Amendment and sweeps more broadly than the Fifth Amendment itself. It may be triggered even in the absence of a Fifth Amendment violation. The

Fifth Amendment prohibits use by the prosecution in its case in chief only of *compelled* testimony. Failure to administer *Miranda* warnings creates a presumption of compulsion. Consequently, unwarned statements that are otherwise voluntary within the meaning of the Fifth Amendment must nevertheless be excluded from evidence under *Miranda.* Thus, in the individual case, *Miranda's* preventive medicine provides a remedy even to the defendant who has suffered no identifiable constitutional harm....

But the *Miranda* presumption, though irrebuttable for purposes of the prosecution's case in chief, does not require that the statements and their fruits be discarded as inherently tainted. Despite the fact that patently *voluntary* statements taken in violation of *Miranda* must be excluded from the prosecution's case, the presumption of coercion does not bar their use for impeachment purposes on cross-examination. Harris v. New York, 401 U.S. 222, 91 S.Ct. 643, 28 L.Ed.2d 1 (1971). The Court in *Harris* rejected as an "extravagant extension of the Constitution," the theory that a defendant who had confessed under circumstances that made the confession inadmissible, could thereby enjoy the freedom to "deny every fact disclosed or discovered as a 'fruit' of his confession, free from confrontation with his prior statements" and that the voluntariness of his confession would be totally irrelevant. Id., at 225, and n. 2, 91 S.Ct., at 645, and n. 2. Where an unwarned statement is preserved for use in situations that fall outside the sweep of the *Miranda* presumption, "the primary criterion of admissibility [remains] the 'old' due process voluntariness test." Schulhofer, Confessions and the Court, 79 Mich.L.Rev. 865, 877 (1981).

In Michigan v. Tucker, 417 U.S. 433, 94 S.Ct. 2357, 41 L.Ed.2d 182 (1974), the Court was asked to extend the *Wong Sun* fruits doctrine to suppress the testimony of a witness for the prosecution whose identity was discovered as the result of a statement taken from the accused without benefit of full *Miranda* warnings. As in respondent's case, the breach of the *Miranda* procedures in *Tucker* involved no actual compulsion. The Court concluded that the unwarned questioning "did not abridge respondent's constitutional privilege ... but departed only from the prophylactic standards later laid down by this Court in *Miranda* to safeguard that privilege." 417 U.S., at 446, 94 S.Ct., at 2364. Since there was no actual infringement of the suspect's constitutional rights, the case was not controlled by the doctrine expressed in *Wong Sun* that fruits of a constitutional violation must be suppressed. In deciding "how sweeping the judicially imposed consequences" of a failure to administer *Miranda* warnings should be, 417 U.S., at 445, 94 S.Ct., at 2364, the *Tucker* Court noted that neither the general goal of deterring improper police conduct nor the Fifth Amendment goal of assuring trustworthy evidence would be served by suppression of the witness' testimony. The unwarned confession must, of course, be suppressed, but the Court ruled that introduction of the third-party witness' testimony did not violate Tucker's Fifth Amendment rights.

We believe that this reasoning applies with equal force when the alleged "fruit" of a noncoercive *Miranda* violation is neither a witness nor an article of evidence but the accused's own voluntary testimony. As in *Tucker,* the absence of any coercion or improper tactics undercuts the twin rationales—trustworthiness and deterrence—for a broader rule. Once warned, the suspect is free to exercise his own volition in deciding whether or not to make a statement to the authorities. The Court has often noted that " 'a living witness is not to be mechanically equated with the proffer of inanimate evidentiary objects illegally seized.... [T]he living witness is an individual human personality whose attributes of will, perception, memory and *volition* interact to determine what testimony he will give.' " United States v. Ceccolini, 435 U.S. 268, 277, 98 S.Ct. 1054, 1060, 55 L.Ed.2d 268 (1978) (emphasis added) (quoting from Smith v. United States, 117 U.S.App.D.C. 1, 3–4, 324 F.2d 879, 881–882 (1963) (Burger, J.) (footnotes omitted), cert. denied, 377 U.S. 954, 84 S.Ct. 1632, 12 L.Ed.2d 498 (1964)).

Because *Miranda* warnings may inhibit persons from giving information, this Court has determined that they need be administered only after the person is taken into "custody" or his freedom has otherwise been significantly restrained. Miranda v. Arizona, 384 U.S., at 478, 86 S.Ct., at 1629. Unfortunately, the task of defining "custody" is a slippery one, and "policemen investigating serious crimes [cannot realistically be expected to] make no errors whatsoever." Michigan v. Tucker, supra, 417 U.S., at 446, 94 S.Ct., at 2365. If errors are made by law enforcement officers in administering the prophylactic *Miranda* procedures, they should not breed the same irremediable consequences as police infringement of the Fifth Amendment itself. It is an unwarranted extension of *Miranda* to hold that a simple failure to administer the warnings, unaccompanied by any actual coercion or other circumstances calculated to undermine the suspect's ability to exercise his free will so taints the investigatory process that a subsequent voluntary and informed waiver is ineffective for some indeterminate period. Though *Miranda* requires that the unwarned admission must be suppressed, the admissibility of any subsequent statement should turn in these circumstances solely on whether it is knowingly and voluntarily made.

B

The Oregon court, however, believed that the unwarned remark compromised the voluntariness of respondent's later confession. It was the court's view that the prior *answer* and not the unwarned questioning impaired respondent's ability to give a valid waiver and that only lapse of time and change of place could dissipate what it termed the "coercive impact" of the inadmissible statement. When a prior statement is actually coerced, the time that passes between confessions, the change in place of interrogations, and the change in identity of the interrogators all bear on whether that coercion has carried over into the second confession. See Westover v. United States, decided together with Miranda v. Arizona, 384 U.S., at 494, 86 S.Ct., at 1638; Clewis v. Texas, 386 U.S.

707, 87 S.Ct. 1338, 18 L.Ed.2d 423 (1967). The failure of police to administer *Miranda* warnings does not mean that the statements received have actually been coerced, but only that courts will presume the privilege against compulsory self-incrimination has not been intelligently exercised.... Of the courts that have considered whether a properly warned confession must be suppressed because it was preceded by an unwarned but clearly voluntary admission, the majority have explicitly or implicitly recognized that *Westover's* requirement of a break in the stream of events is inapposite. In these circumstances, a careful and thorough administration of *Miranda* warnings serves to cure the condition that rendered the unwarned statement inadmissible. The warning conveys the relevant information and thereafter the suspect's choice whether to exercise his privilege to remain silent should ordinarily be viewed as an "act of free will." Wong Sun v. United States, 371 U.S., at 486, 83 S.Ct., at 416.

The Oregon court nevertheless identified a subtle form of lingering compulsion, the psychological impact of the suspect's conviction that he has let the cat of the bag and, in so doing, has sealed his own fate. But endowing the psychological effects of *voluntary* unwarned admissions with constitutional implications would, practically speaking, disable the police from obtaining the suspect's informed co-operation even when the official coercion proscribed by the Fifth Amendment played no part in either his warned or unwarned confessions. As the Court remarked in *Bayer:*

> "[A]fter an accused has once let the cat out of the bag by confessing, no matter what the inducement, he is never thereafter free of the psychological and practical disadvantages of having confessed. He can never get the cat back in the bag. The secret is out for good. In such a sense, a later confession may always be looked upon as fruit of the first. But this Court has never gone so far as to hold that making a confession under circumstances which preclude its use, perpetually disables the confessor from making a usable one after those conditions have been removed." 331 U.S., at 540–541, 67 S.Ct., at 1398.

Even in such extreme cases as Lyons v. Oklahoma, 322 U.S. 596, 64 S.Ct. 1208, 88 L.Ed. 1481 (1944), in which police forced a full confession from the accused through unconscionable methods of interrogation, the Court has assumed that the coercive effect of the confession could, with time, be dissipated. See also Westover v. United States, supra, 384 U.S., at 496, 86 S.Ct., at 1639.

This Court has never held that the psychological impact of voluntary disclosure of a guilty secret qualifies as state compulsion or compromises the voluntariness of a subsequent informed waiver. The Oregon court, by adopting this expansive view of Fifth Amendment compulsion, effectively immunizes a suspect who responds to pre-*Miranda* warning questions from the consequences of his subsequent informed waiver of the privilege of remaining silent. See 61 Ore.App., at 679, 658 P.2d, at 555

(Gillette, P.J., concurring). This immunity comes at a high cost to legitimate law enforcement activity, while adding little desirable protection to the individual's interest in not being *compelled* to testify against himself.... When neither the initial nor the subsequent admission is coerced, little justification exists for permitting the highly probative evidence of a voluntary confession to be irretrievably lost to the factfinder.

There is a vast difference between the direct consequences flowing from coercion of a confession by physical violence or other deliberate means calculated to break the suspect's will and the uncertain consequences of disclosure of a "guilty secret" freely given in response to an unwarned but noncoercive question, as in this case.... Certainly, in respondent's case, the causal connection between any psychological disadvantage created by his admission and his ultimate decision to cooperate is speculative and attenuated at best. It is difficult to tell with certainty what motivates a suspect to speak. A suspect's confession may be traced to factors as disparate as "a prearrest event such as a visit with a minister," ... or an intervening event such as the exchange of words respondent had with his father. We must conclude that, absent deliberately coercive or improper tactics in obtaining the initial statement, the mere fact that a suspect has made an unwarned admission does not warrant a presumption of compulsion. A subsequent administration of *Miranda* warnings to a suspect who has given a voluntary but unwarned statement ordinarily should suffice to remove the conditions that precluded admission of the earlier statement. In such circumstances, the finder of fact may reasonably conclude that the suspect made a rational and intelligent choice whether to waive or invoke his rights.

III

Though belated, the reading of respondent's rights was undeniably complete. McAllister testified that he read the *Miranda* warnings aloud from a printed card and recorded Elstad's responses.[1] There is no question that respondent knowingly and voluntarily waived his right to remain silent before he described his participation in the burglary. It is also beyond dispute that respondent's earlier remark was voluntary, within the meaning of the Fifth Amendment. Neither the environment

1. The *Miranda* advice on the card was clear and comprehensive, incorporating the warning that any statements could be used in a court of law; the rights to remain silent, consult an attorney at state expense, and interrupt the conversation at any time; and the reminder that any statements must be voluntary. The reverse side of the card carried three questions in boldface and recorded Elstad's responses:

"DO YOU UNDERSTAND THESE RIGHTS?

'Yeh'

"DO YOU HAVE ANY QUESTIONS ABOUT YOUR RIGHTS?

'No'

"HAVING THESE RIGHTS IN MIND, DO YOU WISH TO TALK TO US NOW?

'Yeh I do!' "

The card is dated and signed by respondent and by Deputy McAllister. A recent high school graduate, Elstad was fully capable of understanding this careful administration of *Miranda* warnings.

nor the manner of either "interrogation" was coercive. The initial conversation took place at midday, in the living room area of respondent's own home, with his mother in the kitchen area, a few steps away. Although in retrospect the officers testified that respondent was then in custody, at the time he made his statement he had not been informed that he was under arrest. The arresting officers' testimony indicates that the brief stop in the living room before proceeding to the station house was not to interrogate the suspect but to notify his mother of the reason for his arrest.

The state has conceded the issue of custody and thus we must assume that Burke breached *Miranda* procedures in failing to administer *Miranda* warnings before initiating the discussion in the living room. This breach may have been the result of confusion as to whether the brief exchange qualified as "custodial interrogation" or it may simply have reflected Burke's reluctance to initiate an alarming police procedure before McAllister had spoken with respondent's mother. Whatever the reason for Burke's oversight, the incident had none of the earmarks of coercion.... Nor did the officers exploit the unwarned admission to pressure respondent into waiving his right to remain silent.

Respondent, however, has argued that he was unable to give a fully *informed* waiver of his rights because he was unaware that his prior statement could not be used against him. Respondent suggests that Deputy McAllister, to cure this deficiency, should have added an additional warning to those given him at the Sheriff's office. Such a requirement is neither practicable nor constitutionally necessary. In many cases, a breach of *Miranda* procedures may not be identified as such until long after full *Miranda* warnings are administered and a valid confession obtained.... The standard *Miranda* warnings explicitly inform the suspect of his right to consult a lawyer before speaking. Police officers are ill equipped to pinch-hit for counsel, construing the murky and difficult questions of when "custody" begins or whether a given unwarned statement will ultimately be held admissible....

This Court has never embraced the theory that a defendant's ignorance of the full consequences of his decisions vitiates their voluntariness.... If the prosecution has actually violated the defendant's Fifth Amendment rights by introducing an inadmissible confession at trial, compelling the defendant to testify in rebuttal, the rule announced in Harrison v. United States precludes use of that testimony on retrial. 392 U.S. 219, 88 S.Ct. 2008, 20 L.Ed.2d 1047 (1968). "Having 'released the spring' by using the petitioner's unlawfully obtained confessions against him, the Government must show that its illegal action did not induce his testimony." Id., at 224–225, 88 S.Ct., at 2011. But the Court has refused to find that a defendant who confesses, after being falsely told that his codefendant has turned state's evidence, does so involuntarily.... The Court has also rejected the argument that a defendant's ignorance that a prior coerced confession could not be admitted in evidence compromised the voluntariness of his guilty plea.... Likewise, ... the Court [has] declined to accept defendant's contention that, because he was unaware of the potential adverse consequences of statements he made to the police, his participation in the interview was involuntary. Thus we have not held that the *sine qua non* for a knowing and voluntary waiver of the right to remain silent is a full and complete appreciation of all of the consequences flowing from the nature and the quality of the evidence in the case.

IV

When police ask questions of a suspect in custody without administering the required warnings, *Miranda* dictates that the answers received be presumed compelled and that they be excluded from evidence at trial in the State's case in chief. The Court has carefully adhered to this principle, permitting a narrow exception only where pressing public safety concerns demanded. See New York v. Quarles, 467 U.S., at ___, 104 S.Ct., at ___. The Court today in no way retreats from the bright line rule of *Miranda*. We do not imply that good faith excuses a failure to administer *Miranda* warnings; nor do we condone inherently coercive police tactics or methods offensive to due process that render the initial admission involuntary and undermine the suspect's will to invoke his rights once they are read to him. A handful of courts has, however, applied our precedents relating to confessions obtained under coercive circumstances to situations involving wholly voluntary admissions, requiring a passage of time or break in events before a second, fully warned statement can be deemed voluntary. Far from establishing a rigid rule, we direct courts to avoid one; there is no warrant for presuming coercive effect where the suspect's initial inculpatory statement, though technically in violation of *Miranda,* was voluntary. The relevant inquiry is whether, in fact, the second statement was also voluntarily made. As in any such inquiry, the finder of fact must examine the surrounding circumstances and the entire course of police conduct with respect to the suspect in evaluating the voluntariness of his statements. The fact that a suspect chooses to speak after being informed of his rights is, of course, highly probative. We find that the dictates of *Miranda* and the goals of the Fifth Amendment proscription against use of compelled testimony are fully satisfied in the circumstances of this case by barring use of the unwarned statement in the case in chief. No further purpose is served by imputing "taint" to subsequent statements obtained pursuant to a voluntary and knowing waiver. We hold today that a suspect who has once responded to unwarned yet uncoercive questioning is not thereby disabled from waiving his rights and confessing after he has been given the requisite *Miranda* warnings.

The judgment of the Court of Appeals of Oregon is reversed, and the case is remanded for further proceedings not inconsistent with this opinion.

It is so ordered.

MR. JUSTICE BRENNAN, joined by JUSTICE MARSHALL, dissented, calling the majority opinion "a crippling blow to *Miranda*."

MR. JUSTICE STEVENS dissented in a separate opinion "because even such a narrowly confined exception is inconsistent with the Court's prior cases, because the attempt to identify its boundaries in future cases will breed confusion and uncertainty in the administration of criminal justice, and because it denigrates the importance of one of the core constitutional rights that protects every American citizen from the kind of tyranny that has flourished in other societies."

NIX v. WILLIAMS

Supreme Court of the United States, 1984.
467 U.S. 431, 104 S.Ct. 2501.

CHIEF JUSTICE BURGER delivered the opinion of the Court.

We granted certiorari to consider whether, at respondent Williams' second murder trial in state court, evidence pertaining to the discovery and condition of the victim's body was properly admitted on the ground that it would ultimately or inevitably have been discovered even if no violation of any constitutional or statutory provision had taken place.

I

A

On December 24, 1968, 10-year-old Pamela Powers disappeared from a YMCA building in Des Moines, Iowa, where she had accompanied her parents to watch an athletic contest. Shortly after she disappeared, Williams was seen leaving the YMCA carrying a large bundle wrapped in a blanket; a 14-year-old boy who had helped Williams open his car door reported that he had seen "two legs in it and they were skinny and white."

Williams' car was found the next day 160 miles east of Des Moines in Davenport, Iowa. Later several items of clothing belonging to the child, some of Williams' clothing, and an army blanket like the one used to wrap the bundle that Williams carried out of the YMCA were found at a rest stop on Interstate 80 near Grinnell, between Des Moines and Davenport. A warrant was issued for Williams' arrest.

Police surmised that Williams had left Pamela Powers or her body somewhere between Des Moines and the Grinnell rest stop where some of the young girl's clothing had been found. On December 26, the Iowa Bureau of Criminal Investigation initiated a large-scale search. Two hundred volunteers divided into teams began the search 21 miles east of Grinnell, covering an area several miles to the north and south of Interstate 80. They moved westward from Poweshiek County, in which Grinnell was located, into Jasper County. Searchers were instructed to check all roads, abandoned farm buildings, ditches, culverts, and any other place in which the body of a small child could be hidden.

Meanwhile, Williams surrendered to local police in Davenport, where he was promptly arraigned. Williams contacted a Des Moines attorney who arranged for an attorney in Davenport to meet Williams at the Davenport police station. Des Moines police informed counsel they would pick Williams up in Davenport and return him to Des Moines without questioning him. Two Des Moines detectives then drove to Davenport, took Williams into custody, and proceeded to drive him back to Des Moines.

During the return trip, one of the policemen, Detective Leaming, began a conversation with Williams, saying:

> "I want to give you something to think about while we're traveling down the road.... They are predicting several inches of snow for tonight, and I feel that you yourself are the only person that knows where this little girl's body is ... and if you get a snow on top of it you yourself may be unable to find it. And since we will be going right past the area [where the body is] on the way into Des Moines, I feel that we could stop and locate the body, that the parents of this little girl should be entitled to a Christian burial for the little girl who was snatched away from them on Christmas [E]ve and murdered.... [A]fter a snow storm [we may not be] able to find it at all."

Leaming told Williams he knew the body was in the area of Mitchellville—a town they would be passing on the way to Des Moines. He concluded the conversation by saying, "I do not want you to answer me.... Just think about it...."

Later, as the police car approached Grinnell, Williams asked Leaming whether the police had found the young girl's shoes. After Leaming replied that he was unsure, Williams directed the police to a point near a service station where he said he had left the shoes; they were not found. As they continued to drive to Des Moines, Williams asked whether the blanket had been found and then directed the officers to a rest area in Grinnell where he said he had disposed of the blanket; they did not find the blanket. At this point Leaming and his party were joined by the officers in charge of the search. As they approached Mitchellville, Williams, without any further conversation, agreed to direct the officers to the child's body.

The officers directing the search had called off the search at 3 p.m., when they left the Grinnell Police Department to join Leaming at the rest area. At that time, one search team near the Jasper County-Polk County line was only two and one-half miles from where Williams soon guided Leaming and his party to the body. The child's body was found next to a culvert in a ditch beside a gravel road in Polk County, about two miles south of Interstate 80, and essentially within the area to be searched.

B

First Trial

In February 1969 Williams was indicted for first-degree murder. Before trial in the Iowa court, his counsel moved to suppress evidence of the body and all related evidence including the condition of the body as shown by the autopsy. The ground for the motion was that such evidence was the "fruit" or product of Williams' statements made during the automobile ride from Davenport to Des Moines and prompted by Leaming's statements. The motion to suppress was denied.

The jury found Williams guilty of first-degree murder; the judgment of conviction was affirmed by the Iowa Supreme Court. State v. Williams, 182 N.W.2d 396 (1970). Williams then sought release on habeas corpus in the United States District Court for the Southern District of Iowa. That court concluded that the evidence in question had been wrongly admitted at Williams' trial, Williams v. Brewer, 375 F.Supp. 170 (1974); a divided panel of the Court of Appeals for the Eighth Circuit agreed. 509 F.2d 227 (1974).

We granted certiorari, 423 U.S. 1031, 96 S.Ct. 561, 46 L.Ed.2d 404 (1975), and a divided Court affirmed, holding that Detective Leaming had obtained incriminating statements from Williams by what was viewed as interrogation in violation of his right to counsel. Brewer v. Williams, 430 U.S. 387, 97 S.Ct. 1232, 51 L.Ed.2d 424 (1977). This Court's opinion noted, however, that although Williams' incriminating statements could not be introduced into evidence at a second trial, evidence of the body's location and condition "might well be admissible on the theory that the body would have been discovered in any event, even had incriminating statements not been elicited from Williams." Id., at 407, n. 12, 97 S.Ct., at 1243, n. 12.

C

Second Trial

At Williams' second trial in 1977 in the Iowa court, the prosecution did not offer Williams' statements into evidence, nor did it seek to show that Williams had directed the police to the child's body. However, evidence of the condition of her body as it was found, articles and photographs of her clothing, and the results of post mortem medical and chemical tests on the body were admitted. The trial court concluded that the State had proved by a preponderance of the evidence that, if the search had not been suspended and Williams had not led the police to the victim, her body would have been discovered "*within a short time*" in essentially the same condition as it was actually found. The trial court also ruled that if the police had not located the body, "the search would clearly have been taken up again where it left off, given the extreme circumstances of this case and the body would [have] been found *in short order.*" App. 86 (emphasis added).

In finding that the body would have been discovered in essentially the same condition as it was actually found, the court noted that freezing temperatures had prevailed and tissue deterioration would have been suspended. Id., at 87. The challenged evidence was admitted and the jury again found Williams guilty of first-degree murder; he was sentenced to life in prison.

On appeal, the Supreme Court of Iowa again affirmed. 285 N.W.2d 248 (1979). That court held that there was in fact a "hypothetical independent source" exception to the Exclusionary Rule:

> "After the defendant has shown unlawful conduct on the part of the police, the State has the burden to show by a preponderance of the evidence that (1) the police did not act in bad faith for the purpose of hastening discovery of the evidence in question, and (2) that the evidence in question would have been discovered by lawful means." Id., at 260.

As to the first element, the Iowa Supreme Court, having reviewed the relevant cases, stated:

> "The issue of the propriety of the police conduct in this case, as noted earlier in this opinion, has caused the closest possible division of views in every appellate court which has considered the question. In light of the legitimate disagreement among individuals well versed in the law of criminal procedure who were given the opportunity for calm deliberation, it cannot be said that the actions of the police were taken in bad faith." Id., at 260–261.

The Iowa court then reviewed the evidence *de novo* and concluded that the State had shown by a preponderance of the evidence that, even if Williams had not guided police to the child's body, it would inevitably have been found by lawful activity of the search party before its condition had materially changed.

In 1980 Williams renewed his attack on the state-court conviction by seeking a writ of habeas corpus in the United States District Court for the Southern District of Iowa. The District Court conducted its own independent review of the evidence and concluded, as had the state courts, that the body would inevitably have been found by the searchers in essentially the same condition it was in when Williams led police to its discovery. The District Court denied Williams' petition. 528 F.Supp. 664 (1981).

The Court of Appeals for the Eighth Circuit reversed. 700 F.2d 1164 (1983); an equally divided court denied rehearing en banc. Id., at 1175. That court assumed, without deciding, that there is an inevitable discovery exception to the Exclusionary Rule and that the Iowa Supreme Court correctly stated that exception to require proof that the police did not act in bad faith and that the evidence would have been discovered absent any constitutional violation. In reversing the District Court's denial of habeas relief, the Court of Appeals stated:

> "We hold that the State has not met the first requirement. It is therefore unnecessary to decide whether the state courts' finding that the body would have been discovered anyway is fairly supported by the record. It is also unnecessary to decide whether the State must prove the two elements of the exception

by clear and convincing evidence, as defendant argues, or by a preponderance of the evidence, as the state courts held.

"The state trial court, in denying the motion to suppress, made no finding one way or the other on the question of bad faith. Its opinion does not even mention the issue and seems to proceed on the assumption—contrary to the rule of law later laid down by the Supreme Court of Iowa—that the State needed to show only that the body would have been discovered in any event. The Iowa Supreme Court did expressly address the issue ... and a finding by an appellate court of a state is entitled to the same presumption of correctness that attaches to trial-court findings under 28 U.S.C. § 2254(d).... We conclude, however, that the state Supreme Court's finding that the police did not act in bad faith is not entitled to the shield of § 2254(d)...." 700 F.2d, at 1169–1170 (footnotes omitted).

We granted the State's petition for certiorari, 461 U.S. ___, 103 S.Ct. 2427, 77 L.Ed.2d 1315 (1983), and we reverse.

II

A

The Iowa Supreme Court correctly stated that the "vast majority" of all courts, both state and federal, recognize an inevitable discovery exception to the Exclusionary Rule. We are now urged to adopt and apply the so-called ultimate or inevitable discovery exception to the Exclusionary Rule.

Williams contends that evidence of the body's location and condition is "fruit of the poisonous tree," i.e., the "fruit" or product of Detective Leaming's plea to help the child's parents give her "a Christian burial," which this Court had already held equated to interrogation. He contends that admitting the challenged evidence violated the Sixth Amendment whether it would have been inevitably discovered or not. Williams also contends that, if the inevitable discovery doctrine is constitutionally permissible, it must include a threshold showing of police good faith.

B

The doctrine requiring courts to suppress evidence as the tainted "fruit" of unlawful governmental conduct had its genesis in Silverthorne Lumber Co. v. United States, 251 U.S. 385, 40 S.Ct. 182, 64 L.Ed. 319 (1920); there, the Court held that the Exclusionary Rule applies not only to the illegally obtained evidence itself, but also to other incriminating evidence derived from the primary evidence. The holding of Silverthorne was carefully limited, however, for the Court emphasized that such information does not automatically become "sacred and inaccessible." Id., at 392, 40 S.Ct., at 183.

"If knowledge of [such facts] is gained from an *independent source,* they may be proved like any others...." Ibid. (emphasis added).

Wong Sun v. United States, 371 U.S. 471, 83 S.Ct. 407, 9 L.Ed.2d 441 (1963), extended the Exclusionary Rule to evidence that was the indirect product or "fruit" of unlawful police conduct, but there again the Court emphasized that evidence that has been illegally obtained need not always be suppressed, stating:

> "We need not hold that all evidence is 'fruit of the poisonous tree' simply because it would not have come to light *but for the illegal actions* of the police. Rather, the more apt question in such a case is 'whether, granting establishment of the primary illegality, the evidence to which instant objection is made has been come at by exploitation of that illegality or instead by means sufficiently distinguishable to be purged of the primary taint.'" Id., at 487–488, 83 S.Ct., at 417 (emphasis added) (quoting J. Maguire, Evidence of Guilt 221 (1959)).

The Court thus pointedly negated the kind of good-faith requirement advanced by the Court of Appeals in reversing the District Court.

Although *Silverthorne* and *Wong Sun* involved violations of the Fourth Amendment, the "fruit of the poisonous tree" doctrine has not been limited to cases in which there has been a Fourth Amendment violation. The Court has applied the doctrine where the violations were of the Sixth Amendment, see United States v. Wade, 388 U.S. 218, 87 S.Ct. 1926, 18 L.Ed.2d 1149 (1967), as well as of the Fifth Amendment.

The core rationale consistently advanced by this Court for extending the Exclusionary Rule to evidence that is the fruit of unlawful police conduct has been that this admittedly drastic and socially costly course is needed to deter police from violations of constitutional and statutory protections. This Court has accepted the argument that the way to ensure such protections is to exclude evidence seized as a result of such violations notwithstanding the high social cost of letting persons obviously guilty go unpunished for their crimes. On this rationale, the prosecution is not to be put in a better position than it would have been in if no illegality had transpired.

By contrast, the derivative evidence analysis ensures that the prosecution is not put in a *worse* position simply because of some earlier police error or misconduct. The independent source doctrine allows admission of evidence that has been discovered by means wholly independent of any constitutional violation. That doctrine, although closely related to the inevitable discovery doctrine, does not apply here; Williams' statements to Leaming indeed led police to the child's body, but that is not the whole story. The independent source doctrine teaches us that the interest of society in deterring unlawful police conduct and the public interest in having juries receive all probative evidence of a crime are properly balanced by putting the police in the same, not a *worse*, position than they would have been in if no police error or misconduct had occurred.[1] ... When the challenged evidence has an independent

1. The ultimate or inevitable discovery exception to the Exclusionary Rule is closely related in purpose to the harmless-error rule of Chapman v. California, 386 U.S. 18,

source, exclusion of such evidence would put the police in a worse position than they would have been in absent any error or violation. There is a functional similarity between these two doctrines in that exclusion of evidence that would inevitably have been discovered would also put the government in a worse position, because the police would have obtained that evidence if no misconduct had taken place. Thus, while the independent source exception would not justify admission of evidence in this case, its rationale is wholly consistent with and justifies our adoption of the ultimate or inevitable discovery exception to the Exclusionary Rule.

It is clear that the cases implementing the Exclusionary Rule "begin with the premise that the challenged evidence is *in some sense* the product of illegal governmental activity." United States v. Crews, 445 U.S. 463, 471, 100 S.Ct. 1244, 1250, 63 L.Ed.2d 537 (1980) (emphasis added). Of course, this does not end the inquiry. If the prosecution can establish by a preponderance of the evidence that the information ultimately or inevitably would have been discovered by lawful means—here the volunteers' search—then the deterrence rationale has so little basis that the evidence should be received.[2] Anything less would reject logic, experience, and common sense.

The requirement that the prosecution must prove the absence of bad faith, imposed here by the Court of Appeals, would place courts in the position of withholding from juries relevant and undoubted truth that would have been available to police absent any unlawful police activity.

22, 87 S.Ct. 824, 827, 17 L.Ed.2d 705 (1967). The harmless-constitutional-error rule "serve[s] a very useful purpose insofar as [it] block[s] setting aside convictions for small errors or defects that have little, if any, likelihood of having changed the result of the trial." The purpose of the inevitable discovery rule is to block setting aside convictions that would have been obtained without police misconduct.

2. As to the quantum of proof, we have already established some relevant guidelines. In United States v. Matlock, 415 U.S. 164, 178, n. 14, 94 S.Ct. 988, 996, n. 14, 39 L.Ed.2d 242 (1974) (emphasis added), we stated that "the controlling burden of proof at suppression hearings should impose *no greater burden* than proof by a preponderance of the evidence." In Lego v. Twomey, 404 U.S. 477, 488, 92 S.Ct. 619, 626, 30 L.Ed.2d 618 (1972), we observed "from our experience [that] no substantial evidence has accumulated that federal rights have suffered from determining admissibility by a preponderance of the evidence" and held that the prosecution must prove by a preponderance of the evidence that a confession sought to be used at trial was voluntary. We are unwilling to impose added burdens on the already difficult task of proving guilt in criminal cases by enlarging the barrier to placing evidence of unquestioned truth before juries.

Williams argues that the preponderance of the evidence standard used by the Iowa courts is inconsistent with United States v. Wade, 388 U.S. 218, 87 S.Ct. 1926, 18 L.Ed.2d 1149 (1967). In requiring clear and convincing evidence of an independent source for an in-court identification, the Court gave weight to the effect an uncounseled pre-trial identification has in "crystalliz[ing] the witnesses' identification of the defendant for the future reference." Id., at 240, 87 S.Ct., at 1939. The Court noted as well that possible unfairness at the lineup "may be the sole means of attack upon the unequivocal courtroom identification," ibid., and recognized the difficulty of determining whether an in-court identification was based on independent recollection unaided by the lineup identification, id., at 240–241, 87 S.Ct., at 1939–1940. By contrast, inevitable discovery involves no speculative elements but focuses on demonstrated historical facts capable of ready verification or impeachment and does not require a departure from the usual burden of proof at suppression hearings.

Of course, that view would put the police in a *worse* position than they would have been in if no unlawful conduct had transpired. And, of equal importance, it wholly fails to take into account the enormous societal cost of excluding truth in the search for truth in the administration of justice. Nothing in this Court's prior holdings supports any such formalistic, pointless, and punitive approach.

The Court of Appeals concluded, without analysis, that if an absence of bad faith requirement were not imposed, "the temptation to risk deliberate violations of the Sixth Amendment would be too great, and the deterrent effect of the Exclusionary Rule reduced too far." 700 F.2d, at 1169, n. 5. We reject that view. A police officer who is faced with the opportunity to obtain evidence illegally will rarely, if ever, be in a position to calculate whether the evidence sought would inevitably be discovered.... On the other hand, when an officer is aware that the evidence will inevitably be discovered, he will try to avoid engaging in any questionable practice. In that situation, there will be little to gain from taking any dubious "shortcuts" to obtain the evidence. Significant disincentives to obtaining evidence illegally—including the possibility of departmental discipline and civil liability—also lessen the likelihood that the ultimate or inevitable discovery exception will promote police misconduct.... In these circumstances, the societal costs of the Exclusionary Rule far outweigh any possible benefits to deterrence that a good-faith requirement might produce.

Williams contends that because he did not waive his right to the assistance of counsel, the Court may not balance competing values in deciding whether the challenged evidence was properly admitted. He argues that, unlike the Exclusionary Rule in the Fourth Amendment context, the essential purpose of which is to deter police misconduct, the Sixth Amendment Exclusionary Rule is designed to protect the right to a fair trial and the integrity of the factfinding process. Williams contends that, when those interests are at stake, the societal costs of excluding evidence obtained from responses presumed involuntary are irrelevant in determining whether such evidence should be excluded. We disagree.

Exclusion of physical evidence that would inevitably have been discovered adds nothing to either the integrity or fairness of a criminal trial. The Sixth Amendment right to counsel protects against unfairness by preserving the adversary process in which the reliability of proffered evidence may be tested in cross-examination.... Here, however, Detective Leaming's conduct did nothing to impugn the reliability of the evidence in question—the body of the child and its condition as it was found, articles of clothing found on the body, and the autopsy. No one would seriously contend that the presence of counsel in the police car when Leaming appealed to Williams' decent human instincts would have had any bearing on the reliability of the body as evidence. Suppression, in these circumstances, would do nothing whatever to promote the integrity of the trial process, but would inflict a wholly unacceptable burden on the administration of criminal justice.

Nor would suppression ensure fairness on the theory that it tends to safeguard the adversary system of justice. To assure the fairness of trial proceedings, this Court has held that assistance of counsel must be available at pretrial confrontations where "the subsequent trial [cannot] cure a[n otherwise] one-sided confrontation between prosecuting authorities and the uncounseled defendant." United States v. Ash, supra, at 315, 93 S.Ct., at 2576. Fairness can be assured by placing the State and the accused in the same positions they would have been in had the impermissible conduct not taken place. However, if the government can prove that the evidence would have been obtained inevitably and, therefore, would have been admitted regardless of any overreaching by the police, there is no rational basis to keep that evidence from the jury in order to ensure the fairness of the trial proceedings. In that situation, the State has gained no advantage at trial and the defendant has suffered no prejudice. Indeed, suppression of the evidence would operate to undermine the adversary system by putting the State in a *worse* position than it would have occupied without any police misconduct. Williams' argument that inevitable discovery constitutes impermissible balancing of values is without merit.

More than a half century ago, Judge, later Justice, Cardozo made his seminal observation that under the Exclusionary Rule "[t]he criminal is to go free because the constable has blundered." People v. Defore, 242 N.Y. 13, 21, 150 N.E. 585, 587 (1926). Prophetically, he went on to consider "how far-reaching in its effect upon society" the Exclusionary Rule would be when

> "[t]he pettiest peace officer would have it in his power through overzeal or indiscretion to confer immunity upon an offender for crimes the most flagitious." Id., at 23, 150 N.E., at 588.

Some day, Cardozo speculated, some court might press the Exclusionary Rule to the outer limits of its logic—or beyond—and suppress evidence relating to the "body of a murdered" victim because of the means by which it was found. *Id.*, at 23–24, 150 N.E., at 588. Cardozo's prophecy was fulfilled in Killough v. United States, 114 U.S.App.D.C. 305, 309, 315 F.2d 241, 245 (1962) (en banc). But when, as here, the evidence in question would inevitably have been discovered without reference to the police error or misconduct, there is no nexus sufficient to provide a taint and the evidence is admissible.

C

The Court of Appeals did not find it necessary to consider whether the record fairly supported the finding that the volunteer search party would ultimately or inevitably have discovered the victim's body. However, three courts independently reviewing the evidence have found that the body of the child inevitably would have been found by the searchers. Williams challenges these findings, asserting that the record contains only the "*post hoc* rationalization" that the search efforts would have proceeded two and one-half miles into Polk County where Williams had led police to the body.

When that challenge was made at the suppression hearing preceding Williams' second trial, the prosecution offered the testimony of Agent Ruxlow of the Iowa Bureau of Criminal Investigation. Ruxlow had organized and directed some 200 volunteers who were searching for the child's body.... The searchers were instructed "to check all the roads, the ditches, any culverts.... If they came upon any abandoned farm buildings, they were instructed to go onto the property and search those abandoned farm buildings or any other places where a small child could be secreted."... Ruxlow testified that he marked off highway maps of Poweshiek and Jasper Counties in grid fashion, divided the volunteers into teams of four to six persons, and assigned each team to search specific grid areas.... Ruxlow also testified that, if the search had not been suspended because of Williams' promised cooperation, it would have continued into Polk County, using the same grid system.... Although he had previously marked off into grids only the highway maps of Poweshiek and Jasper Counties, Ruxlow had obtained a map of Polk County, which he said he would have marked off in the same manner had it been necessary for the search to continue....

The search had commenced at approximately 10 a.m. and moved westward through Poweshiek County into Jasper County. At approximately 3 p.m., after Williams had volunteered to cooperate with the police, Officer Leaming, who was in the police car with Williams, sent word to Ruxlow and the other Special Agent directing the search to meet him at the Grinnell truck stop and the search was suspended at that time.... Ruxlow also stated that he was "under the impression that there was a possibility" that Williams would lead them to the child's body at that time.... The search was not resumed once it was learned that Williams had led the police to the body, ... which was found two and one-half miles from where the search had stopped in what would have been the easternmost grid to be searched in Polk County,.... There was testimony that it would have taken an additional three to five hours to discover the body if the search had continued, ... the body was found near a culvert, one of the kinds of places the teams had been specifically directed to search.

On this record it is clear that the search parties were approaching the actual location of the body and we are satisfied, along with three courts earlier, that the volunteer search teams would have resumed the search had Williams not earlier led the police to the body and the body inevitably would have been found. The evidence asserted by Williams as newly discovered, i.e., certain photographs of the body and deposition testimony of Agent Ruxlow made in connection with the federal habeas proceeding, does not demonstrate that the material facts were inadequately developed in the suppression hearing in state court or that Williams was denied a full, fair, and adequate opportunity to present all relevant facts at the suppression hearing.

The judgment of the Court of Appeals is reversed, and the case is remanded for further proceedings consistent with this opinion.

It is so ordered.

MR. JUSTICE WHITE concurred, and MR. JUSTICE STEVENS concurred in the judgment [opinions omitted].

Mr. Justice Brennan dissented, joined by Mr. Justice Marshall.

* * *

To the extent that today's decision adopts this "inevitable discovery" exception to the exclusionary rule, it simply acknowledges a doctrine that is akin to the "independent source" exception first recognized by the Court in Silverthorne Lumber Co. v. United States, 251 U.S. 385, 392, 40 S.Ct. 182, 183, 64 L.Ed. 319 (1920). See United States v. Wade, 388 U.S. 218, 242, 87 S.Ct. 1926, 1940, 18 L.Ed.2d 1149 (1967); Wong Sun v. United States, 371 U.S. 471, 487, 83 S.Ct. 407, 417, 9 L.Ed.2d 441 (1963). In particular, the Court concludes that unconstitutionally obtained evidence may be admitted at trial if it inevitably would have been discovered in the same condition by an independent line of investigation that was already being pursued when the constitutional violation occurred. As has every federal Court of Appeals previously addressing this issue, I agree that in these circumstances the "inevitable discovery" exception to the exclusionary rule is consistent with the requirements of the Constitution.

In its zealous efforts to emasculate the exclusionary rule, however, the Court loses sight of the crucial difference between the "inevitable discovery" doctrine and the "independent source" exception from which it is derived. When properly applied, the "independent source" exception allows the prosecution to use evidence only if it was, in fact, obtained by fully lawful means. It therefore does no violence to the constitutional protections that the exclusionary rule is meant to enforce. The "inevitable discovery" exception is likewise compatible with the Constitution, though it differs in one key respect from its next of kin: specifically, the evidence sought to be introduced at trial has not actually been obtained from an independent source, but rather would have been discovered as a matter of course if independent investigations were allowed to proceed.

In my view, this distinction should require that the government satisfy a heightened burden of proof before it is allowed to use such evidence. The inevitable discovery exception necessarily implicates a hypothetical finding that differs in kind from the factual finding that precedes application of the independent source rule. To ensure that this hypothetical finding is narrowly confined to circumstances that are functionally equivalent to an independent source, and to protect fully the fundamental rights served by the exclusionary rule, I would require clear and convincing evidence before concluding that the government had met its burden of proof on this issue.... Increasing the burden of proof serves to impress the factfinder with the importance of the decision and thereby reduces the risk that illegally obtained evidence will be admitted.... Because the lower courts did not impose such a requirement, I would remand this case for application of this heightened burden of proof by the lower courts in the first instance. I am therefore unable to join either the Court's opinion or its judgment.

NOTES

1. In Segura v. United States, 468 U.S. 796, 104 S.Ct. 3380 (1984), the Court held that police officers' illegal entry upon private premises did not require suppression of evidence subsequently discovered at those premises when executing a search warrant obtained on the basis of information wholly unconnected with the initial entry. In Murray v. United States, 487 U.S. 533, 108 S.Ct. 2529 (1988), the Court was faced with the question whether again assuming evidence obtained pursuant to an independently obtained search warrant, the portion of such evidence that had been observed in plain view at the time of a prior illegal entry must be suppressed. While surveilling defendants and others suspected of illegal drug activities, federal agents observed them driving vehicles into, and later out of, a warehouse, and, upon their exit, saw that the warehouse contained a tractor-trailer rig bearing a long container. Defendants later turned over their vehicles to other drivers, who were in turn followed and ultimately arrested, and the vehicles were lawfully seized and found to contain marijuana. After receiving this information, several agents forced their way into the warehouse and observed in plain view numerous burlap-wrapped bales. The agents left without disturbing the bales and did not return until they had obtained a warrant to search the warehouse. In applying for the warrant, they did not mention the prior entry or include any recitation of their observations made during that entry. Upon issuance of the warrant, they reentered the warehouse and seized the bales of marijuana and other evidence of crime. The court below refused to suppress the evidence, assuming for purposes of its decision that the first entry into the warehouse was unlawful.

The Court found no error. The opinion stated:

"The exclusionary rule prohibits introduction into evidence of tangible materials seized during an unlawful search, [. . .] and of testimony concerning knowledge acquired during an unlawful search, [. . .] Beyond that, the exclusionary rule also prohibits the introduction of derivative evidence, both tangible and testimonial, that is the product of the primary evidence, or that is otherwise acquired as an indirect result of the unlawful search, up to the point at which the connection with the unlawful search becomes 'so attenuated as to dissipate the taint.' [. . .] [par.] Almost simultaneously with our development of the exclusionary rule, [. . .] we also announced what has come to be known as the 'independent source' doctrine. * * * The dispute here is over the scope of this doctrine. Defendants contend that it applies only to evidence obtained for the first time during an independent lawful search. The Government argues that it applies also to evidence initially discovered during, or as a consequence of, an unlawful search, but later obtained independently from activities untainted by the initial illegality. We think the Government's view has better support in both precedent and policy. [. . .] [par.] To apply what we have said to the present case: Knowledge that the marijuana was in the warehouse was assuredly acquired at the time of the unlawful entry. But it was also acquired at the time of entry pursuant to the warrant, and if that later acquisition was not the result of the earlier entry there is no reason why the independent source doctrine should not apply. Invoking the exclusionary rule would put the police (and society) not in the *same* position they would have occupied if no violation occurred, but in a *worse* one. [par.] We think this is also true with respect to the tangible evidence, the bales of marijuana. [. . .] So long as a later, lawful seizure is genuinely independent of an earlier, tainted one (which may well be difficult to establish where the seized goods are kept in the police's possession) there is no reason why the independent source doctrine should not apply. [par.] The ultimate question, therefore, is whether the search pursuant to warrant was in fact a genuinely independent source of the information and tangible evidence at issue here. This would not have been the case if the agents' decision to seek the warrant was prompted by what they had seen during the initial entry, or if information obtained during that entry was presented to the Magistrate and affected his decision to issue the warrant."

Because the lower court did not explicitly find that the agents would have sought a warrant if they had not earlier entered the warehouse, the Court remanded the case for a determination whether the warrant-authorized search of the warehouse was an independent source in the sense described in the Court's opinion.

In a post-*Murray* case, police officers arrested the defendant as he was leaving his house, after the sale of narcotics to an informer. The defendant was with another man and a child at the time. On the basis that it was "cold" outside, the police took the group back into the house (living room), where they saw drug paraphernalia in plain view. They did not seize the paraphernalia but instead proceeded to obtain a search warrant for the house based on allegations involving the drug sale to the informer. When the warrant was executed, the paraphernalia was seized. On the basis of the "independent source" rule enunciated in *Murray,* the Colorado Supreme Court held that the search would be proper *if* the officers would have sought the search warrant *in spite of* the observations made during the illegal entry. The case was remanded to the trial court for a hearing to determine what was the motivation for the police in seeking the search warrant. People v. Schoondermark, 759 P.2d 715 (Colo. 1988).

* * *

2. In Taylor v. Alabama, 457 U.S. 687, 102 S.Ct. 2664 (1982), the Court, with four justices dissenting, applied *Brown* and *Dunaway* to exclude a statement made following an unlawful arrest. In *Taylor* six hours elapsed between the arrest and the incriminating statement. The suspect was unrepresented by counsel, was given *Miranda* warnings three times, and, after waiver of *Miranda* rights, was questioned several times. He also had been allowed to visit with his emotionally upset girl friend and with a male companion. He was confronted with the result of a fingerprint comparison, which itself was the product of evidence derived from the unlawful arrest. Based upon this same fingerprint comparison, which had made use of rolled fingerprint impressions taken following the accused's unlawful arrest, a court had issued an arrest warrant before the defendant had made his incriminating statement. Stating that this was a "virtual replica of both *Brown* and *Dunaway,*" the Court held that because the warrant was based upon illegally obtained evidence, it did not constitute a legally cognizable "attenuation." In suppressing the statement the Court also emphasized that the data upon which the original arrest was made fell far short of probable cause, as it had in *Brown* and *Dunaway.*

C. TORT LIABILITY OF THE POLICE—THE FEDERAL CIVIL RIGHTS ALTERNATIVE

MONROE v. PAPE

Supreme Court of the United States, 1961.
365 U.S. 167, 81 S.Ct. 473.

MR. JUSTICE DOUGLAS delivered the opinion of the Court.

This case presents important questions concerning the construction of R.S. § 1979, 42 U.S.C.A. § 1983, which reads as follows:

> "Every person who, under color of any statute, ordinance, regulation, custom, or usage, of any State or Territory, subjects, or causes to be subjected, any citizen of the United States or other person within the jurisdiction thereof to the deprivation of any rights, privileges, or immunities secured by the Constitution and laws, shall be liable to the party injured in an action at law, suit in equity, or other proper proceeding for redress."

The complaint alleges that 13 Chicago police officers broke into petitioners' home in the early morning, routed them from bed, made them stand naked in the living room, and ransacked every room, emptying drawers and ripping mattress covers. It further alleges that Mr. Monroe was then taken to the police station and detained on "open" charges for 10 hours, while he was interrogated about a two-day-old murder, that he was not taken before a magistrate, though one was accessible, that he was not permitted to call his family or attorney, that he was subsequently released without criminal charges being preferred against him. It is alleged that the officers had no search warrant and no arrest warrant and that they acted "under color of the statutes, ordinances, regulations, customs and usages" of Illinois and of the City of Chicago....

The City of Chicago moved to dismiss the complaint on the ground that it is not liable under the Civil Rights Acts nor for acts committed in performance of its governmental functions. All defendants moved to dismiss, alleging that the complaint alleged no cause of action under those Acts or under the Federal Constitution. The District Court dismissed the complaint. The Court of Appeals affirmed....

I.

Petitioners claim that the invasion of their home and the subsequent search without a warrant and the arrest and detention of Mr. Monroe without a warrant and without arraignment constituted a deprivation of their "rights, privileges, or immunities secured by the Constitution" within the meaning of R.S. § 1979. It has been said that when

18 U.S.C.A. § 241 made criminal a conspiracy "to injure, oppress, threaten, or intimidate any citizen in the free exercise or enjoyment of any right or privilege secured to him by the Constitution," it embraced only rights that an individual has by reason of his relation to the central government, not to state governments. United States v. Williams, 341 U.S. 70, 71 S.Ct. 581. But the history of the section of the Civil Rights Act presently involved does not permit such a narrow interpretation.

Section 1979 came onto the books as § 1 of the Ku Klux Act of April 20, 1871. It was one of the means whereby Congress exercised the power vested in it by § 5 of the Fourteenth Amendment to enforce the provisions of that Amendment.... Allegation of facts constituting a deprivation under color of state authority of a right guaranteed by the Fourteenth Amendment satisfies to that extent the requirement of R.S. § 1979. See Douglas v. Jeannette, 319 U.S. 157, 161–162, 63 S.Ct. 877, 880. So far petitioners are on solid ground. For the guarantee against unreasonable searches and seizures contained in the Fourth Amendment has been made applicable to the States by reason of the Due Process Clause of the Fourteenth Amendment....

II.

There can be no doubt at least since Ex parte Virginia, 100 U.S. 339, 346–347, that Congress has the power to enforce provisions of the Fourteenth Amendment against those who carry a badge of authority of a State and represent it in some capacity, whether they act in accordance with their authority or misuse it. See Home Tel. & Tel. Co. v. Los Angeles, 227 U.S. 278, 287–296, 33 S.Ct. 312, 314, 318. The question with which we now deal is the narrower one of whether Congress, in enacting § 1979, meant to give a remedy to parties deprived of constitutional rights, privileges and immunities by an official's abuse of his position.

We conclude that it did so intend.

It is argued that "under color of" enumerated state authority excludes acts of an official or policeman who can show no authority under state law, state custom, or state usage to do what he did. In this case it is said that these policemen, in breaking into petitioners' apartment, violated the Constitution and laws of Illinois. It is pointed out that under Illinois law a simple remedy is offered for that violation and that, so far as it appears, the courts of Illinois are available to give petitioners that full redress which the common law affords for violence done to a person; and it is earnestly argued that no "statute, ordinance, regulation, custom or usage" of Illinois bars that redress.

The Ku Klux Act grew out of a message sent to Congress by President Grant on March 23, 1871, reading:

> "A condition of affairs now exists in some States of the Union rendering life and property insecure and the carrying of the mails and the collection of the revenue dangerous. The proof that such a condition of affairs exists in some localities is

now before the Senate. That the power to correct these evils is beyond the control of State authorities I do not doubt; that the power of the Executive of the United States, acting within the limits of existing laws, is sufficient for present emergencies is not clear. Therefore, I urgently recommend such legislation as in the judgment of Congress shall effectually secure life, liberty, and property, and the enforcement of law in all parts of the United States. . . ."

The legislation—in particular the section with which we are now concerned—had several purposes. There are threads of many thoughts running through the debates. One who reads them in their entirety sees that the present section had three main aims.

First, it might, of course, override certain kinds of state laws. . . .

Second, it provided a remedy where state law was inadequate. . . .

But the purposes were much broader. The *third* aim was to provide a federal remedy where the state remedy, though adequate in theory, was not available in practice. The opposition to the measure complained that "It overrides the reserved powers of the States," just as they argued that the second section of the bill "absorb[ed] the entire jurisdiction of the States over their local and domestic affairs."

This Act of April 20, 1871, sometimes called "the third 'force bill,' " was passed by a Congress that had the Klan "particularly in mind." The debates are replete with references to the lawless conditions existing in the South in 1871. . . . It was not the unavailability of state remedies but the failure of certain States to enforce the laws with an equal hand that furnished the powerful momentum behind this "force bill." . . .

While one main scourge of the evil—perhaps the leading one—was the Ku Klux Klan, the remedy created was not a remedy against it or its members but against those who representing a State in some capacity were *unable* or *unwilling* to enforce a state law. . . .

There was, it was said, no quarrel with the state laws on the books. It was their lack of enforcement that was the nub of the difficulty. . . .

It was precisely that breadth of the remedy which the opposition emphasized. . . .

The debates were long and extensive. It is abundantly clear that one reason the legislation was passed was to afford a federal right in federal courts because, by reason of prejudice, passion, neglect, intolerance or otherwise, state laws might not be enforced and the claims of citizens to the enjoyment of rights, privileges, and immunities guaranteed by the Fourteenth Amendment might be denied by the state agencies. . . .

Although the legislation was enacted because of the conditions that existed in the South at that time, it is cast in general language and is as applicable to Illinois as it is to the States whose names were mentioned over and again in the debates. It is no answer that the State has a law which if enforced would give relief. The federal remedy is supplementary to the state remedy, and the latter need not be first sought and refused before the federal one is invoked. Hence the fact that Illinois by its constitution and laws outlaws unreasonable searches and seizures is no barrier to the present suit in the federal court.

We had before us in United States v. Classic, supra, § 20 of the Criminal Code, 18 U.S.C.A. § 242, which provides a criminal punishment for anyone who "under color of any law, statute, ordinance, regulation, or custom" subjects any inhabitant of a State to the deprivation of "any rights, privileges, or immunities secured or protected by the Constitution or laws of the United States." ... The right involved in the *Classic* case was the right of voters in a primary to have their votes counted. The laws of Louisiana required the defendants "to count the ballots, to record the result of the count, and to certify the result of the election." United States v. Classic, supra, 313 U.S. 325–326, 61 S.Ct. 1043. But according to the indictment they did not perform their duty. In an opinion written by Mr. Justice (later Chief Justice) Stone, in which Mr. Justice Roberts, Mr. Justice Reed, and Mr. Justice Frankfurter joined, the Court ruled, "Misuse of power, possessed by virtue of state law and made possible only because the wrongdoer is clothed with the authority of state law, is action taken 'under color of' state law." There was a dissenting opinion; but the ruling as to the meaning of "under color of" state law was not questioned.

That view of the meaning of the words "under color of" state law, 18 U.S.C.A. § 242, was reaffirmed in Screws v. United States. The acts there complained of were committed by state officers in performance of their duties, *viz.*, making an arrest effective. It was urged there, as it is here, that "under color of" state law should not be construed to duplicate in federal law what was an offense under state law (dissenting opinion). It was said there, as it is here, that the ruling in the *Classic* case as to the meaning of "under color of" state law was not in focus and was ill-advised (dissenting opinion). It was argued there, as it is here, that "under color of" state law included only action taken by officials pursuant to state law (dissenting opinion). We rejected that view.... it is beyond doubt that this phrase should be accorded the same construction in both statutes—in § 1979 and in 18 U.S.C.A. § 242.

Since the *Screws* and *Williams* decisions, Congress has had several pieces of civil rights legislation before it.

If the results of our construction of "under color of" law were as horrendous as now claimed, if they were as disruptive of our federal scheme as now urged, if they were such an unwarranted invasion of States' rights as pretended, surely the voice of the opposition would have been heard in Committee reports. Their silence and the new uses to which "under color of" law have recently been given reinforce our conclusion that our prior decisions were correct on this matter of construction.

We conclude that the meaning given "under color of" law in the *Classic* case and in the *Screws* and *Williams* cases was the correct one; and we adhere to it.

In the *Screws* case we dealt with a statute that imposed criminal penalties for acts "wilfully" done. We construed that word in its setting to mean the doing of an act with "a specific intent to deprive a person of a federal right." We do not think that gloss should be placed on § 1979 which we have here. The word "wilfully" does not appear in § 1979. Moreover, § 1979 provides a civil remedy, while in the *Screws* case we dealt with a criminal law challenged on the ground of vagueness. Section 1979 should be read against the background of tort liability that makes a man responsible for the natural consequences of his actions.

So far, then, the complaint states a cause of action. There remains to consider only a defense peculiar to the City of Chicago.

III.

The City of Chicago asserts that it is not liable under § 1979. We do not stop to explore the whole range of questions tendered us on this issue at oral argument and in the briefs. For we are of the opinion that Congress did not undertake to bring municipal corporations within the ambit of § 1979.

When the bill that became the Act of April 20, 1871, was being debated in the Senate, Senator Sherman of Ohio proposed an amendment which would have made "the inhabitants of the county, city, or parish" in which certain acts of violence occurred liable "to pay full compensation" to the person damaged or his widow or legal representative. The amendment was adopted by the Senate. The House, however, rejected it.... In a second conference the Sherman amendment was dropped.... Mr. Poland, speaking for the House Conferees about the Sherman proposal to make municipalities liable, said:

> "We informed the conferees on the part of the Senate that the House had taken a stand on that subject and would not recede from it; that that section imposing liability upon towns and counties must go out or we should fail to agree."

It is said that doubts should be resolved in favor of municipal liability because private remedies against officers for illegal searches and seizures are conspicuously ineffective, and because municipal liability will not only afford plaintiffs responsible defendants but cause those defendants to eradicate abuses that exist at the police level. We do not reach those policy considerations. Nor do we reach the constitutional question whether Congress has the power to make municipalities liable for acts of its officers that violate the civil rights of individuals.

The response of the Congress to the proposal to make municipalities liable ... was so antagonistic that we cannot believe that the word "person" was used in this particular Act to include them....

[The concurring opinion of Mr. Justice Harlan is omitted.]

MR. JUSTICE FRANKFURTER, dissenting....

[All] the evidence converges to the conclusion that Congress by § 1979 created a civil liability enforceable in the federal courts only in instances of injury for which redress was barred in the state courts because some "statute, ordinance, regulation, custom, or usage" sanctioned the grievance complained of.... The jurisdiction which Article III of the Constitution conferred on the national judiciary reflected the assumption that the state courts, not the federal courts, would remain the primary guardians of that fundamental security of person and property which the long evolution of the common law had secured to one individual as against other individuals. The Fourteenth Amendment did not alter this basic aspect of our federalism.

Its commands were addressed to the States. Only when the States, through their responsible organs for the formulation and administration of local policy, sought to deny or impede access by the individual to the central government in connection with those enumerated functions assigned to it, or to deprive the individual of a certain minimal fairness in the exercise of the coercive forces of the State, or without reasonable justification to treat him differently than other persons subject to their jurisdiction, was an overriding federal sanction imposed.... This conception begot the "State action" principle on which, from the time of the Civil Rights Cases, 109 U.S. 3, 3 S.Ct. 18, this Court has relied in its application of Fourteenth Amendment guarantees. As between individuals, that body of mutual rights and duties which constitute the civil personality of a man remains essentially the creature of the legal institutions of the States.

But, of course, in the present case petitioners argue that the wrongs done them were committed not by individuals but by the police as state officials. There are two senses in which this might be true. It might be true if petitioners alleged that the redress which state courts offer them against the respondents is different than that which those courts would offer against other individuals, guilty of the same conduct, who were not the police. This is not alleged. It might also be true merely because the respondents *are* the police—because they are clothed with an appearance of official authority which is in itself a factor of significance in dealings between individuals. Certainly the night-time intrusion of the man with a star and a police revolver is a different phenomenon than the night-time intrusion of a burglar. The aura of power which a show of authority carries with it has been created by state government. The pretense of authority alone might seem to Congress sufficient basis for creating an exception to the ordinary rule that it is to the state tribunals that individuals within a State must look for redress against other individuals within that State. The same pretense of authority might suffice to sustain congressional legislation creating the exception. See Ex parte Virginia, 100 U.S. 339. Congress has not in § 1979 manifested that intention.

[E]xtending federal civil jurisdiction into the traditional realm of state tort law presents problems of policy appropriately left to Congress. Suppose that a state legislature or the highest court of a State should determine that within its territorial limits no damages should be recovered in tort for pain and suffering, or for mental anguish, or that no punitive damages should be recoverable. Since the federal courts went out of the business of making "general law," Erie R. Co. v. Tompkins, 304 U.S. 64, 58 S.Ct. 817, such decisions of local policy have admittedly been the exclusive province of state lawmakers. Should the civil liability for police conduct which can claim no authority under local law, which is actionable as common-law assault or trespass in the local courts, comport different rules? Should an unlawful intrusion by a policeman in Chicago entail different consequences than an unlawful intrusion by a hoodlum? These are matters of policy in its strictly legislative sense, not for determination by this Court.... If § 1979 is made a vehicle of constitutional litigation in cases where state officers have acted lawlessly at state law, difficult questions of the federal constitutionality of certain official practices—lawful perhaps in some States, unlawful in others—may be litigated between private parties without the participation of responsible state authorities which is obviously desirable to protect legitimate state interests, but also to better guide adjudication by competent record-making and argument.

Of course, these last considerations would be irrelevant to our duty if Congress had demonstrably meant to reach by § 1979 activities like those of respondents in this case. But where it appears that Congress plainly did not have that understanding, respect for principles ... of our federalism should avoid extension of a statute beyond its manifest area of operation into applications which invite conflict with the administration of local policies. Such an extension makes the extreme limits of federal constitutional power a law to regulate the quotidian business of every traffic policeman, every registrar of elections, every city inspector or investigator, every clerk in every municipal licensing bureau in this country. The text of the statute, reinforced by its history, precludes such a reading.

In concluding that police intrusion in violation of state law is not a wrong remediable under R.S. § 1979, the pressures which urge an opposite result are duly felt. The difficulties which confront private citizens who seek to vindicate in traditional common-law actions their state-created rights against lawless invasion of their privacy by local policemen are obvious, and obvious is the need for more effective modes of redress. The answer to these urgings must be regard for our federal system which presupposes a wide range of regional autonomy in the kinds of protection local residents receive. If various common-law concepts make it possible for a policeman—but no more possible for a policeman than for any individual hoodlum intruder—to escape without liability when he has vandalized a home, that is an evil. But, surely, its remedy devolves, in the first instance, on the States. Of course, if the States afford less protection against the police, as police, than against the hoodlum—if under authority of state "statute, ordinance, regulation, custom, or usage" the police are specially shielded—§ 1979 provides a remedy which dismissal of petitioners' complaint in the present case does not impair.... Federal intervention may in the long run do the individual a disservice by deflecting responsibility from the state lawmakers, who hold the power of providing a far more comprehensive scope of protection. Local society, also, may well be the loser, by relaxing its sense of responsibility and, indeed, perhaps resenting what may appear to it to be outside interference where local authority is ample and more appropriate to supply needed remedies.

This is not to say that there may not exist today, as in 1871, needs which call for congressional legislation to protect the civil rights of individuals in the States. Strong contemporary assertions of these needs have been expressed. Report of the President's Committee on Civil Rights, To Secure These Rights (1947); Chafee, Safeguarding Fundamental Human Rights: The Tasks of States and Nation, 27 Geo. Wash.L.Rev. 519 (1959). But both the insistence of the needs and the delicacy of the issues involved in finding appropriate means for their satisfaction demonstrate that their demand is for legislative, not judicial, response. We cannot expect to create an effective means of protection for human liberties by torturing an 1871 statute to meet the problems of 1960.

* * *

It is not a work for courts to melt and recast this statute. "Under color" of law meant by authority of law in the nineteenth century. No judicial sympathy, however strong, for needs now felt can give the phrase—a phrase which occurs in a statute, not in a constitution—any different meaning in the twentieth.

* * *

This meaning, no doubt, poses difficulties for the case-by-case application of § 1979. Manifestly the applicability of the section in an action for damages cannot be made to turn upon the actual availability or unavailability of a state-law remedy for each individual plaintiff's situation. Prosecution to adverse judgment of a state-court damage claim cannot be made prerequisite to § 1979 relief. In the first place, such a requirement would effectively nullify § 1979 as a vehicle for recovering damages. In the second place, the conclusion that police activity which violates state law is not "under color" of state law does not turn upon the existence of a state tort remedy. Rather, it recognizes the freedom of the States to fashion their own laws of torts in their own way under no threat of federal intervention save where state law makes determinative of a plaintiff's rights the particular circumstance that defendants are acting by state authority. Section 1979 was not designed to cure and level all the possible imperfections of local common-law doctrines, but to provide for the case of the defendant who can claim that some particular dispensation of state authority immunizes him from the ordinary processes of the law.

It follows that federal courts in actions at law under § 1979 would have to determine whether defendants' conduct is in violation of, or under color of, state law often with little guidance from earlier state decisions. Such a determination will sometimes be difficult, of course. But Federal District Courts sitting in diversity cases are often called upon to determine as intricate and uncertain questions of local law as whether official authority would cloak a given practice of the police from liability in a state-court suit. Certain fixed points of reference will be available. If a plaintiff can show that defendant is acting pursuant to the specific terms of a state statute or of a municipal ordinance, § 1979 will apply. See Lane v. Wilson, 307 U.S. 268, 59 S.Ct. 872. If he can show that defendant's conduct is within the range of executive discretion in the enforcement of a state statute, or municipal ordinance, § 1979 will apply. See Hague v. C.I.O., 307 U.S. 496, 59 S.Ct. 954. Beyond these cases will lie the admittedly more difficult ones in which he seeks to show some " 'custom or usage' which has become common law." ...

The present case comes here from a judgment sustaining a motion to dismiss petitioners' complaint. That complaint, insofar as it describes the police intrusion, makes no allegation that that intrusion was authorized by state law other than the conclusory and unspecific claim that "During all times herein mentioned the individual defendants and each of them were acting under color of the statutes, ordinances, regulations, customs and usages of the State of Illinois, of the County of Cook and of the defendant City of Chicago." In the face of Illinois decisions holding such intrusions unlawful and in the absence of more precise factual averments to support its conclusion, such a complaint fails to state a claim under § 1979.

However, the complaint does allege, as to the ten-hour detention of Mr. Monroe, that "it was, and it is now, the custom or usage of the Police Department of the City of Chicago to arrest and confine individuals in the police stations and jail cells of the said department for long periods of time on 'open' charges." These confinements, it is alleged, are for the purpose of interrogating and investigating the individuals arrested, in the aim of inducing incriminating statements, permitting possible identification of suspects in lineups, holding suspects *incommunicado* while police conduct field investigations of their associates and background, and punishing the arrested persons without trial. Such averments do present facts which, admitted as true for purposes of a motion to dismiss, seem to sustain petitioners' claim that Mr. Monroe's detention—as contrasted with the night-time intrusion into the Monroe apartment—was "under color" of state authority. Under the few relevant Illinois decisions it is impossible to say with certainty that a detention *incommunicado* for ten hours is unlawful *per se*, or that the courts of that State would hold that the lawless circumstances surrounding Mr. Monroe's arrest made his subsequent confinement illegal. On this record, then, petitioners' complaint suffices to raise the narrow issue of whether the detention *incommunicado*, considered alone, violates due process.

Since the majority's disposition of the case causes the Court not to reach that constitutional issue, it is neither necessary nor appropriate to discuss it here.

NOTES

1. In *Monroe* the Court held that the employer of the offending police officers was not liable under 42 U.S.C.A. § 1983 because a city was not a "person" within the meaning of that statute. However, in Monell v. Department of Social Services, 436 U.S. 658, 98 S.Ct. 2018 (1978), the Court overturned that aspect of *Monroe* and held that a municipality was a person within the meaning of the act. The Court indicated that a city would not be automatically liable for the constitutional violations of its officers under the principle of respondeat superior. Rather some additional conduct on the part of the employer—not yet well defined—is required. In Will v. Michigan Dept. of State Police, 491 U.S. 58, 109 S.Ct. 2304 (1989), the Court held that neither states nor state officials are "persons" within the meaning of § 1983. Thus, the statute does not apply to them.

2. After *Monell*, note 1, supra, the Court held that if a municipality is responsible under the *Monell* principle for the violation of civil rights by a municipal agent, unlike the agent himself, the city cannot use the defense that it acted in good faith. For example, if by policy the city provides for highly intrusive searches of persons arrested on very minor charges, and if such searches are later declared to be violative of the Fourth Amendment, the city has no good faith defense even if the policy-makers had relied upon the apparently reasonable advice of legal counsel that such searches were lawful. See Owen v. City of Independence, Missouri, 445 U.S. 622, 100 S.Ct. 1398 (1980). Suppose that a new decision expanding Fourth Amendment rights is declared non-retroactive. In light of *Owen*, if good faith is irrelevant, should the non-retroactivity extend to civil rights actions against the municipality?

D. ADMINISTRATIVE REVIEW

1. DAMAGE CLAIMS

BIVENS v. SIX UNKNOWN NAMED AGENTS OF FEDERAL BUREAU OF NARCOTICS

Supreme Court of the United States, 1971.
403 U.S. 388, 91 S.Ct. 1999.

* * *

MR. CHIEF JUSTICE BURGER, dissenting.

* * *

This case has significance far beyond its facts and its holding. For more than 55 years this Court has enforced a rule under which evidence of undoubted reliability and probative value has been suppressed and excluded from criminal cases whenever it was obtained in violation of the Fourth Amendment. The rule has rested on a theory that suppression of evidence in these circumstances was imperative to deter law enforcement authorities from using improper methods to obtain evidence.

The deterrence theory underlying the suppression doctrine, or exclusionary rule, has a certain appeal in spite of the high price society pays for such a drastic remedy. . . .

The plurality opinion in Irvine v. California, 347 U.S. 128, 136, 74 S.Ct. 381, 385 (1954), catalogued the doctrine's defects:

> "Rejection of the evidence does nothing to punish the wrong-doing official, while it may, and likely will, release the wrong-doing defendant. It deprives society of its remedy against one lawbreaker because he has been pursued by another. It protects one against whom incriminating evidence is discovered, but does nothing to protect innocent persons who are the victims of illegal but fruitless searches."

From time to time members of the Court, recognizing the validity of these protests, have articulated varying alternative justifications for the suppression of important evidence in a criminal trial. Under one of these alternative theories the rule's foundation is shifted to the "sporting contest" thesis that the government must "play the game fairly" and cannot be allowed to profit from its own illegal acts. But the exclusionary rule does not ineluctably flow from a desire to ensure that government plays the "game" according to the rules. If an effective alternative remedy is available, concern for official observance of the law does not require adherence to the exclusionary rule. Nor is it easy to understand how a court can be thought to endorse a violation of the Fourth Amendment by allowing illegally seized evidence to be introduced against a defendant if an effective remedy is provided against the government.

The exclusionary rule has also been justified on the theory that the relationship between the Self-Incrimination Clause of the Fifth Amendment and the Fourth Amendment requires the suppression of evidence seized in violation of the latter.

Even ignoring, however, the decisions of this Court that have held that the Fifth Amendment applies only to "testimonial" disclosures, it seems clear that the Self-Incrimination Clause does not protect a person from the seizure of evidence that is incriminating. It protects a person only from being the conduit by which the police acquire evidence. Mr. Justice Holmes once put it succinctly, "A party is privileged from producing the evidence, but not from its production." Johnson v. United States, 228 U.S. 457, 458, 33 S.Ct. 572 (1913).

It is clear, however, that neither of these theories undergirds the decided cases in this Court. Rather the exclusionary rule has rested on

Once the constitutional validity of such a statute is established, it can reasonably be assumed that the States would develop their own remedial systems on the federal model. Indeed there is nothing to prevent a State from enacting a comparable statutory scheme without waiting for the Congress. Steps along these lines would move our system toward more responsible law enforcement on the one hand and away from the irrational and drastic results of the suppression doctrine on the other. Independent of the alternative embraced in this dissenting opinion, I believe the time has come to re-examine the scope of the exclusionary rule and consider at least some narrowing of its thrust so as to eliminate the anomalies it has produced.

In a country that prides itself on innovation, inventive genius, and willingness to experiment, it is a paradox that we should cling for more than a half century to a legal mechanism that was poorly designed and never really worked. I can only hope now that the Congress will manifest a willingness to view realistically the hard evidence of the half-century history of the suppression doctrine revealing thousands of cases in which the criminal was set free because the constable blundered and virtually no evidence that innocent victims of police error—such as petitioner claims to be—have been afforded meaningful redress.

2. DISCIPLINARY ACTION—CIVILIAN REVIEW BOARDS

WHO WILL WATCH THE WATCHMAN?

Warren E. Burger*

* * *

"I will anticipate the suggestion that what I am about to propose is theoretical, visionary or impractical, by pointing to procedures long used in industry to prevent industrial accidents. In every modern factory accidents cause injury to persons and damage to equipment or to products. More often than not the resulting losses are covered by insurance, but invariably the owner and the insurer working together conduct an inquiry into the causes of every accident. The purpose is to determine what happened, why it happened, to fix responsibility, to make monetary reparation in some cases and always to take preventive steps to avoid repetition of the accident.

"Industry does not like to have expensive machinery damaged; neither industry nor its workers want human beings injured. This combination of sound frugality and decent humanitarian considerations leads industry and its insurance companies to study and teach safety

* The quoted material is from an article by Chief Justice Burger under the title "Who Will Watch the Watchman?", in 14 Am.U.L.Rev. 1–2; 9–23 (1964). It was written when the author was a Judge of the United States Court of Appeals for the District of Columbia Circuit.

measures constantly. Chronic accident makers are removed from their jobs.

"Another example is found in the airline industry and the operation of aircraft generally. Every accident is made the subject of careful inquiry by a board of independent people who are qualified by training and experience to understand aircraft operations. When the cause of a failure or accident is determined, whether pilot error, mechanical failure, or other cause, a report is made and circulated in the industry. In order to prevent loss of life and property, all those who fly or maintain airplanes learn from the experience of others. The question at once suggests itself whether we can afford to be less concerned about protecting the functioning of the machinery of justice than the functioning of the machinery of industry. I think not.

"Training and education of police and the limitations which the law places upon them are not the central subject of discussion. Nevertheless, the years of judicial frustration at failure of police to observe the commands of the courts and the rising frequency of suppression of evidence cry out for better training of police officers and elevation of police standards. That improvements are possible, and that preventive measures are feasible, is suggested by the performance of some of the federal agencies, notably the Federal Bureau of Investigation, which has a remarkable record as to the incidence of suppression of evidence secured by its agents.

"Over the years most metropolitan police departments in the United States have developed some form of organization to receive and process complaints from civilians relating to alleged police misconduct. There is a wide variety of procedures and methods in use in one hundred or more cities and I would accept as true that these mechanisms have been established in a sincere desire to afford citizens the means by which a complaint may be registered with responsible administrators. I also believe that police administrators want this information in order to maintain fairness and improve police work. However, where these review bodies have been established they are almost invariably part of the police organization, often with a minority of civilian members. It is with no thought to disparage what has been done in this field that I suggest that none of the systems which are now in operation fully meets the need which exists.

"To accomplish the objective of maintaining lawful law enforcement calls for a commission or board which is predominantly *civilian* and external rather than an internal *police* agency. The civilian members should be persons well versed by experience in the legal subtleties of arrest, search, seizure, interrogations and related matters. Although such a review body would of necessity cooperate with a police department, it must be *independent* of police administration in the same sense—and for some of the same reasons—that courts must be independent of prosecutors.

"To provoke much-needed discussion, debate, and exploration, I will outline one suggested program to meet this need. I will be specific to some degree for the express purpose of engaging others to challenge and to offer alternatives. I believe debate among those who are interested in the improvement of the administration of justice may well develop a mechanism that would prevent a large proportion of the police errors causing the suppression of evidence. Over a period of time an independent Review Board would serve the much needed function of making clear to police officers generally, as well as to those called before the board, precisely where they had erred.

"There are certain features which seem to me fundamental and crucial in the structure of such a board as this. To make my points concrete I will direct them within the existing framework of the District of Columbia Government.

"(1) *Independence.* The Board should be independent of police administration and responsible directly to the Executive Branch of Government.

"(2) *Composition.* The Board should consist of five to seven members; two should be senior police officers of wide law enforcement experience, and the balance should be drawn from leaders of the legal profession, although one non-lawyer might well serve a useful purpose. The presence of a majority of lawyers on such a Board is indispensable, for they are trained in sorting out facts, getting at truth and then applying rules of law to known facts. To preserve continuity and allow for the accumulation of the special experience needed, members should have staggered terms so that not more than one-third of the membership would change each year.

"(3) *Subpoena Power.* Although the cooperation of most policemen and citizens can be assumed, the Board should be empowered to compel testimony and have access to police files. The matter of access to police files needs careful study in order to impose proper limits on using contents of such files; disclosure should not be permitted at any stage where it would prejudice or impede other pending criminal investigations.

"(4) *Pending Litigation.* Careful study would determine what provisions are needed to avoid conflict between Board review proceedings and other cases then pending in court or under study by the prosecution.

"(5) *Board Immunity.* Members of the Board acting in the performance of their duties and especially in making findings and recommendations should be covered by the same general immunity as that protecting members of a grand jury.

"(6) *Initiation of Complaints.* The mechanics and procedures for initiating complaints cannot be fully set forth without a joint study by police administrators and lawyers experienced in such matters. However, as a minimum, the Board's jurisdiction would include the following:

(a) The Board would consider complaints made directly to it by individuals.

(b) The Board would secure and review the transcript of every case in the District Court and the Court of General Sessions in which a motion to suppress evidence was granted.

(c) The Board would secure and review the appellate opinion and the basic transcript in every case in which an appellate court directs the suppression of evidence by the trial court.

"(7) *Nature of Hearing.* The Board should probably be empowered to conduct executive hearings within limits, provided that transcripts of hearings become public when findings are made public. Any officer appearing before the Board should be allowed counsel if desired. The details of how examination of witnesses should be conducted and to what extent rules of evidence would control require study in depth and to some extent would evolve from experience and practice.

"(8) *Counsel and Investigation.* A necessary incident of the independent status of the Board would be an independent investigator and counsel selected by the Board and responsible directly to the Board.

"(9) *Board Powers.* Careful study is needed to determine the scope of the Board's powers; the following areas of specific power should be considered:

(a) Power to direct or recommend suspension or dismissal of an officer; power to direct a hearing by a tribunal having disciplinary authority;

(b) Power to direct or recommend inquiry by the Police Department as to general police procedures;

(c) Power to direct or recommend reprimands short of dismissal or suspension;

(d) Power to direct or recommend specific in-job training for a particular officer;

(e) Power to direct or recommend that records be expunged, as for illegal arrest or illegal warrants.

I do not suggest this Review Board should have all these broad powers but only that these are some of the difficult problems which must be studied carefully before this machinery is set in motion. Our experience in other areas may indicate that direct action against an individual officer should not be within the jurisdiction of such a Review Board as this. The power to *recommend* such departmental action may be sufficient; when the officer's individual job rights or other related rights are in jeopardy, he is entitled to the protection of a separate proceeding with all the safeguards now afforded to an officer charged with a breach of duty.

"(10) *Board Action.* After hearing or inquiry the Review Board would render a report or make findings, depending upon the nature of the complaint and the facts disclosed. Its conclusions could take any one of several forms, for example:

(a) It might conclude that in all the circumstances the police action was justified or if not justified that it was due to an honest error of judgment.

Findings in this category could lead to recommendations that the officer be required to remedy defects in his basic training at a police training school.

(b) It might conclude that the officer had violated a statute or a constitutional provision without culpable intent and simply because he did not fully know the rules which limited his power to act or because he acted under the excitement of some emergency.

Findings in this second category might lead to recommendations for official reprimand, discipline, or limited suspension.

(c) It might conclude that the police acted in reckless or careless or conscious disregard of known rules, statutes or rights.

Such a flagrant case might well be one involving recommendation for departmental trial on charges leading to dismissal; this third category would, I hope, be the unusual case, but when found, firm action would be required.

"It is fair to anticipate that police administrators will look with skepticism on a Review Board which is independent and predominantly civilian in composition. Over the years judicial decisions have gradually taken from police many tools which were deeply imbedded in police practice and few substitute tools have been developed. Where the fault lies for failure to develop new tools, or whether new tools can be found, is beside the point at this stage. As I see it, the work of the Review Board would shed light on every aspect of the problem.

"One objection to a civilian Review Board is that non-experts are not competent to review the work of trained police. Certainly if the reviewers approach the problem in a spirit of hostility toward police or if the police respond in that spirit, progress would be difficult. But we must remember that suppression of evidence arises out of the application of provisions of the Constitution and statutes to concrete fact situations, and in this area it is the lawyer, not the policeman, who is the expert.

"It may be said that police administrators can put their own houses in order. I believe they can do so with the aid of such a Board, but the record up to this date is against the effectiveness of internal police controls. If police administrators find that they can establish effective internal controls, the need for external control would then have been eliminated.

"It may be said that the very existence of such an external Review Board would reflect on the integrity and competence of police administrators who are directly responsible, and would undermine police morale.

This argument overlooks the fact that in a complex society virtually everyone at every level of government, and many outside government, is subject to external controls. Judges are in the forefront of those subject to this external influence. In Washington the Court of General Sessions is reviewed by the District of Columbia Court of Appeals; the United States Court of Appeals can in turn review the latter and the Supreme Court can review us. Even the Supreme Court is not fully immune, for in common with all judges they are at the mercy of the most cold-blooded external review ever devised by Man. I refer to the law professors who spend six months doing an autopsy on an appellate opinion often written under pressure in four or five days. Judges are indeed subject to deterrence by this unofficial 'external control' exercised by the academic community. When a law review article has laid bare the fact that a judge has written an opinion too broadly for the needs of a case, or that he has overlooked some important legislative history, or cited cases which do not support his thesis, there is no doubt the judge takes note. All rational human beings are subject to deterrence if there is prompt, direct, intelligent and affirmative purpose to the deterrence procedure. When the protest against external control is raised, we must also remember that law enforcement officers, like judges, congressmen, and presidents, work for the people and are accountable to them.

"It may be said that the very existence of such a Review Board will hamper police action, impede law enforcement by making officers timid and ineffective. Grave problems would arise if the members of such a Board approached their task in a spirit of hostility toward police or an attitude that they were the Commissars of the Police Force. No doubt there would be an interim period of adjustment during which some uncertainty would prevail, but I think a timid or immobilized police force can be avoided and is a spectre I have difficulty imagining. I point again to the example of the rigid control of every aircraft in this country, and particularly the regular airlines. I see no evidence that airlines have suffered. On the contrary they have benefited and the public has had the protection of safer and more efficient transportation because of the system of independent and external control. Moreover the surveillance of airlines is far more detailed and stringent on an hour-to-hour basis than anything needed for or appropriate to police operations.

"In this strong dissent in the *Olmstead* case, Justice Brandeis made a stirring plea for keeping law enforcement on a high plane:

> Decency, security and liberty alike demand that government officials shall be subjected to the same rules of conduct that are commands to the citizen. In a government of laws, existence of the government will be imperilled if it fails to observe the law scrupulously. Our Government is the potent, the omnipresent teacher. For good or for ill, it teaches the whole people by its example. Crime is contagious. If the Government becomes a lawbreaker, it breeds contempt for law; it invites every man to become a law unto himself; it invites

> anarchy. To declare that in the administration of the criminal law the end justifies the means—to declare that the Government may commit crimes in order to secure the conviction of a private criminal—would bring terrible retribution. Against that pernicious doctrine this Court should resolutely set its face.

No one can take issue with the Brandeis thesis, but there is another side to the coin.

"If a majority—or even a substantial minority—of the people in any given community, whether it be Washington, D.C., or Charlottesville, Virginia, come to believe that law enforcement is being frustrated by what laymen call 'technicalities,' there develops a sour and bitter feeling that is psychologically and sociologically unhealthy. Let me illustrate this. In recent years in Washington a series of cases involving the Suppression Doctrine has led to extended public debates, mass meetings, and bar association and congressional committees, all arousing bitter controversy. I refrain from naming the particular cases, for the very names have taken on the quality of slogans which tend to stifle thought and arouse emotions. National magazines have added to this unhealthy situation, describing Washington as a crime-ridden city; and genuinely thoughtful consideration has reached an impasse.

"I do not challenge these rules of law. But I do suggest that we may have come the full circle from the place where Brandeis stood, and that a vast number of people are losing respect for law and the administration of justice because they think that the Suppression Doctrine is *defeating* justice. That much of this reaction is due to lack of understanding does not mean we can ignore it. To a lesser degree this feeling can be found in many other cities in America. I suggest that this controversy, like both the rationale and the effect of the Suppression Doctrine itself, is sterile and futile. Apart from the imperative need to end this unwholesome controversy over some manifestations of the Suppression Doctrine and the need to improve law enforcement, we in the Nation's Capital have an added incentive to take some positive steps to change the unhappy image of Washington as a 'cesspool' of crime.

"The judges who shaped the Suppression Doctrine over the years may have been mistaken in particular cases, but we must remember that the rule was made to protect the integrity of law enforcement, not to cripple it. I suggest judges had a right to assume that other branches of government, and police in particular, would recognize that this mechanism of suppression was not an end in itself but a means, which needed implementation from the legislative and the executive branches. Those branches of government, not the courts, have the jurisdiction and power to make the doctrine a positive force. Courts cannot conduct postmortem examinations of police action or conduct training courses for the police. That is the responsibility of others. Judges construe the Constitution and laws and define standards; beyond that all they can do is suggest, as I do tonight, the need for more.

"As you can readily observe the very statement, in barest outline, of the scope and function of such a Review Board demonstrates the complexity of the problems presented. The dimensions of these problems call for the most thoughtful study and consideration by leaders of the legal profession and police administrators. This is a study for which there are few guidelines and those who approach it must realize that they will be plowing in hard-packed soil filled with many rocks.

"It would be naive to suggest that Congress consider this problem at this stage, even though congressional action would ultimately be required. First, the entire subject should run the gauntlet of study and criticism by the legal profession and law enforcement agencies, and the results of such studies should be presented to Congress.

"The public has accepted—largely on faith in the Judiciary—the distasteful results of the Suppression Doctrine; but the wrath of public opinion may descend alike on police and judges if we persist in the view that suppression is a solution. At best it is a necessary evil and hardly more than a manifestation of sterile judicial indignation even in the view of well motivated and well informed laymen. We can well ponder whether any community is entitled to call itself an 'organized society' if it can find no way to solve this problem except by suppression of truth in the search for truth."

NOTES

1. In 1982 the citizens' law enforcement group, Americans for Effective Law Enforcement, Inc. (AELE), published a research paper entitled "Police Civilian Review Boards: Pros and Cons and a Current Status Report," (82–3) Defense Manual. The paper deals with the nature and purpose of civilian review boards, their composition, powers and operational procedures. It also presents arguments in opposition to the establishment of these boards and cites and discusses precedents relating to the legality of such boards and alternative legal remedies available to aggrieved citizens under the Civil Rights Act. It also describes the results of a recent AELE study regarding the effectiveness of review boards' complaint procedures, and includes complaint statistics and a summary of statements made by those associated with the review board process in various cities. The arguments presented in the paper are designed to assist the law enforcement community in drafting an articulate defense in favor of internal departmental administration of police misconduct complaints. It also marshals arguments challenging the efficacy of such boards. The paper concludes as follows:

> "Civilian review boards are panels of appointed citizens formed to investigate complaints regarding alleged police misconduct, and to hold hearings on such complaints. Their purpose is to provide impartial review of complaints against officers, free of any influence by the police department or other municipal officials. The concept is based upon the belief that police officers will not properly investigate complaints against other officers, and thus, such complaints should be investigated by non-police personnel.
>
> "Police departments have several strong arguments against the establishment of a review board.

- Most of the early boards are no longer in existence, and it is too early to tell whether the later ones have been successful.

- Strong internal administrative procedures for review of police misconduct are more effective than review by nondepartmental civilian boards. The President's Commission on Law Enforcement and the American Bar Association have backed this position.

- Creation of a separate board to investigate complaints against police officers is a costly and unnecessary burden on the taxpayers. Most cities already have several agencies that have the power to examine allegations of misconduct.

- Implementation of a civilian review board has a disastrous impact upon police officers' morale. Officers feel they are being second guessed by those who know little of their work. They also feel that they are being subjected to double jeopardy; having to be investigated and cleared by both Internal Affairs and by a group of civilians.

- Officers feel intimidated in making arrests. They become fearful that an arrestee will automatically bring a complaint before a review board.

- Removing the investigation of complaints from police administrators undermines the officials' control within the department. Officers begin to feel that they are answerable to outside persons rather than to their direct superiors.

- Investigations by persons outside the department create problems of credibility. Citizens can make unsubstantiated complaints, officers cannot be compelled to answer questions, or even attend, and boards usually have no power to discipline. These factors may result in heightened negative feelings when complaints are denied or when discipline is not meted out.

"A recent survey by AELE indicated that the most positive benefit of civilian review boards was that they provided a forum for expression of grievances. It was also felt that the boards being open to public scrutiny and criticism independent of the police, gave it credibility as being unbiased. The survey revealed, however, that these boards created feelings of frustration on the part of police officers, who believed they were being subject to double jeopardy in terms of their actions."

2. As to possible use of contempt of court, see McNear v. Rhay, 65 Wash.2d 530, 398 P.2d 732 (1965); Comment, 72 J.Crim.L. & E. 993 (1981). Concerning "self-help," that is, resisting unlawful police conduct, see W. LaFave, Search and Seizure (2d Ed.1987), § 1.11, and also see § 1.10 of the same volume concerning injunctions against unlawful police conduct.

*

APPENDIX

Provisions of the Constitution of the United States, and certain Amendments thereto, of particular significance in the administration of criminal justice:

Preamble

We the People of the United States, in Order to form a more perfect Union, establish Justice, insure domestic Tranquility, provide for the common defense, promote the general Welfare, and secure the Blessings of Liberty to ourselves and our Posterity, do ordain and establish this Constitution for the United States of America.

Article I.

* * *

Section 8. The Congress shall have Power To lay and collect Taxes, Duties, Imposts and Excises, to pay the Debts and provide for the common Defence and general Welfare of the United States; but all Duties, Imposts and Excises shall be uniform throughout the United States; ....

To regulate Commerce with foreign Nations, and among the several States and with the Indian Tribes; ....

To provide for the Punishment of counterfeiting the Securities and current Coin of the United States; ....

To constitute Tribunals inferior to the supreme Court;

To define and punish Piracies and Felonies committed on the high Seas, and Offences against the Law of Nations;

To declare War, grant Letters of Marque and Reprisal, and make Rules concerning Captures on Land and Water; ....

To make Rules for the Government and Regulation of the land and naval forces;

To provide for calling forth the Militia to execute the Laws of the Union, suppress Insurrections and repel Invasions;

To provide for organizing, arming, and disciplining, the Militia, and for governing such Part of them as may be employed in the Service of the United States, reserving to the States respectively, the Appointment of the Officers, and the Authority of training the Militia according to the discipline prescribed by Congress;

To exercise exclusive Legislation in all Cases whatsoever, over such District (not exceeding ten Miles square) as may, by Cession of particular States, and the Acceptance of Congress, become the Seat of the Government of the United States, and to exercise like Authority over all Places purchased by the Consent of the Legislature of the State in which the Same shall be, for the Erection of Forts, Magazines, Arsenals, dock-Yards, and other needful Buildings;—And

To make all Laws which shall be necessary and proper for carrying into Execution the foregoing Powers, and all other Powers vested by this Constitution in the Government of the United States, or in any Department or Officer thereof.

Section 9.

* * *

No Bill of Attainder or ex post facto Law shall be passed.

Article III.

Section 1. The judicial Power of the United States, shall be vested in one supreme Court, and in such inferior Courts as the Congress may from time to time ordain and establish. The Judges, both of the supreme and inferior Courts, shall hold their Offices during good Behaviour, and shall, at stated Times, receive for their Services, a Compensation, which shall not be diminished during their Continuance in Office.

Section 2.

... the supreme Court shall have appellate Jurisdiction, both as to Law and Fact, with such Exceptions, and under such Regulations as the Congress shall make.

The Trial of all Crimes, except in Cases of Impeachment, shall be by Jury; and such Trial shall be held in the State where the said Crimes shall have been committed; but when not committed within any State, the Trial shall be at such Place or Places as the Congress may by Law have directed.

Section 3. Treason against the United States, shall consist only in levying War against them, or in adhering to their Enemies, giving them Aid and Comfort. No Person shall be convicted of Treason unless on the Testimony of two Witnesses to the same overt Act, or on Confession in open Court.

The Congress shall have Power to declare the Punishment of Treason, but no Attainder of Treason shall work Corruption of Blood, or Forfeiture except during the Life of the Person attainted.

Article VI.

* * *

This Constitution, and the Laws of the United States which shall be made in Pursuance thereof; and all Treaties made, or which shall be made, under the Authority of the United States, shall be the supreme Law of the Land; and the Judges in every State shall be bound thereby, any Thing in the Constitution or Laws of any State to the Contrary notwithstanding.

* * *

AMENDMENTS

Amendment I.

Congress shall make no law respecting an establishment of religion, or prohibiting the free exercise thereof; or abridging the freedom of speech, or of the press; or the right of the people peaceably to assemble, and to petition the Government for a redress of grievances.

Amendment II.

A well regulated militia, being necessary to the security of a free State, the right of the people to keep and bear arms, shall not be infringed.

Amendment III.

No Soldier shall, in time of peace be quartered in any house, without the consent of the owner, nor in time of war, but in a manner to be prescribed by law.

Amendment IV.

The right of the people to be secure in their persons, houses, papers, and effects, against unreasonable searches and seizures, shall not be violated, and no warrants shall issue, but upon probable cause, supported by oath or affirmation, and particularly describing the place to be searched, and the persons or things to be seized.

Amendment V.

No person shall be held to answer for a capital, or otherwise infamous crime, unless on a presentment or indictment of a Grand Jury, except in cases arising in the land or naval forces, or in the militia, when in actual service in time of war or public danger; nor shall any person be subject for the same offence to be twice put in jeopardy of life or limb; nor shall be compelled in any criminal case to be a witness against himself, nor be deprived of life, liberty, or property, without due process of law; nor shall private property be taken for public use, without just compensation.

Amendment VI.

In all criminal prosecutions, the accused shall enjoy the right to a speedy and public trial, by an impartial jury of the State and district wherein the crime shall have been committed, which district shall have been previously ascertained by law, and to be informed of the nature and cause of the accusation; to be confronted with the witnesses against him; to have compulsory process for obtaining witnesses in his favor, and to have the assistance of Counsel for his defence.

Amendment VII.

In Suits at common law, where the value in controversy shall exceed twenty dollars, the right of trial by jury shall be preserved, and no fact tried by a jury, shall be otherwise re-examined in any Court of the United States, than according to the rules of the common law.

Amendment VIII.

Excessive bail shall not be required, nor excessive fines imposed, nor cruel and unusual punishments inflicted.

Amendment IX.

The enumeration in the Constitution, of certain rights, shall not be construed to deny or disparage others retained by the people.

Amendment X.

The powers not delegated to the United States by the Constitution, nor prohibited by it to the States, are reserved to the States respectively, or to the people.

* * *

Amendment XIII.

SECTION 1. Neither slavery nor involuntary servitude, except as a punishment for crime whereof the party shall have been duly convicted, shall exist within the United States, or any place subject to their jurisdiction.

SECTION 2. Congress shall have power to enforce this article by appropriate legislation.

Amendment XIV.

SECTION 1. All persons born or naturalized in the United States, and subject to the jurisdiction thereof, are citizens of the United States and of the State wherein they reside. No State shall make or enforce any law which shall abridge the privileges or immunities of citizens of the United States; nor shall any State deprive any person of life, liberty, or property, without due process of law; nor deny to any person within its jurisdiction the equal protection of laws....

SECTION 5. The Congress shall have power to enforce, by appropriate legislation, the provisions of this article.

Amendment XV.

SECTION 1. The right of citizens of the United States to vote shall not be denied or abridged by the United States or by any State on account of race, color, or previous condition of servitude.

SECTION 2. The Congress shall have power to enforce this article by appropriate legislation.

Amendment XVI.

The Congress shall have power to lay and collect taxes on incomes, from whatever source derived, without apportionment among the several States, and without regard to any census or enumeration....

INDEX

References are to Pages